Retail Crime, Security, and Loss Prevention

Retail Crime, Security, and Loss Prevention:
An Encyclopedic Reference

Edited by

Charles A. Sennewald, CPP, CSC, CPO and
John H. Christman, CPP

AMSTERDAM • BOSTON • HEIDELBERG • LONDON
NEW YORK • OXFORD • PARIS • SAN DIEGO
SAN FRANCISCO • SINGAPORE • SYDNEY • TOKYO

Butterworth-Heinemann is an imprint of Elsevier

Acquisitions Editor: Pamela Chester
Marketing Manager: Marissa Hederson
Project Manager: Jay Donahue
Design Direction: Joanne Blank
Cover Design: Gary Ragaglia
Cover Images © iStockphoto and Maxsell Corporation
Compositor: SPI/Kolam
Printer/Binder: Sheridan Books, Inc.

Butterworth-Heinemann is an imprint of Elsevier
30 Corporate Drive, Suite 400, Burlington, MA 01803, USA
Linacre House, Jordan Hill, Oxford OX2 8DP, UK

Recognizing the importance of preserving what has been written, Elsevier prints its books on acid-free
paper whenever possible.

Library of Congress Cataloging-in-Publication Data
Application submitted

British Library Cataloguing-in-Publication Data
A catalogue record for this book is available from the British Library.

ISBN: 978-0-12-370529-7

For information on all Butterworth–Heinemann publications
visit our Web site at www.books.elsevier.com

Printed in United States of America
08 09 10 11 12 13   10 9 8 7 6 5 4 3 2 1

Working together to grow
libraries in developing countries

www.elsevier.com | www.bookaid.org | www.sabre.org

ELSEVIER   BOOK AID International   Sabre Foundation

Dedication

This book is dedicated to the memory of Jerry O'Rourke, CPP, a founding member of the International Association of Professional Security Consultants (IAPSC) and a respected security consultant.

About the Authors

Charles A. "Chuck" Sennewald, CPP, CSC, CPO, the author of numerous Butterworth-Heinemann security titles, is a Certified Security Consultant (CSC) and a former Certified Management Consultant (CMC). Chuck commenced his long career upon graduating from the Army's Military Police School in Georgia in 1949. He served as a military policeman in the Korean War. He was a deputy sheriff with the Los Angeles Country Sheriff's Department, Chief of Campus Security with the Claremont Colleges, and was with the Broadway Department Stores for 18 years, concluding his service there as Director of Security. He subsequently started his own consulting practice in 1979. In the 1980s he was appointed as the Security Industry Representative of the U.S. Department of Commerce, serving in Sweden, Denmark, Taiwan, Hong Kong, and Japan. Chuck has published 14 books including *Effective Security Management*, now in its fourth edition, *The Process of Investigation*, now in its third edition, *Shoplifting* and *Shoplifting: Managing the Problem*, co-authored with John Christman, *Security Consulting* (also in its third edition) and *Shoplifters vs. Retailers, The Rights of Both*. He founded, and was the first president of, the International Association of Professional Security Consultants (IAPSC). Chuck holds a BS Degree in Police Science and Administration from California State University at Los Angeles, where he subsequently taught on a part-time basis for 13 years. In 2006 *Security Magazine* identified him as one of the country's "25 Most Influential Security Executives."

John H. Christman, CPP, retired in 1994 after 22 years as Vice President and Director of Security for Macy's West, where he directed a staff of over 500 security personnel in some 60 stores and facilities in various states west of the Mississippi. After retiring, he began his practice as a security management consultant specializing in expert witness assignments in the retail venue, serving clients from coast to coast. He has over 40 years' work experience in security, law enforcement and intelligence.

John graduated from Muhlenberg College and attended the University of Pennsylvania Law School. During and after the Korean War he served as a special agent of two federal intelligence/investigative agencies, and is a retired Commander (Intelligence), U.S. Naval Reserve.

Prior to joining Macy's, Mr. Christman worked as a security executive in regional supermarket and drug store companies. He is an honor graduate of the Los Angeles County Sheriff's Academy, and member of the International Association of Professional Security Consultants and ASIS, having been granted lifetime status as a Certified Protection Professional. John has co-authored two books with Chuck Sennewald—*Shoplifting* (1992) and *Shoplifting: Managing the Problem* (2006), as well as contributing articles to numerous security-related publications. He served for twelve years on the Board of Directors of the National Retail Federation's Loss Prevention Group, and has taught security courses at the college level. In 2007 he was inducted into the NRF's Loss Prevention Ring of Excellence.

Currently, John is semi-retired, accepting only assignments which involve unique and/or high profile/value cases.

□ □ □
□ □ □
□ □ □

Contributors

Contributing Authors:

Sally A. Bacchetta is an award-winning freelance writer and sales trainer. She publishes articles on a variety of topics, including emerging technologies, parenting, and sales training and motivation. Her work has been featured in *Computer Link, Country Business, FOCUS* (journal of the Society of Pharmaceutical and Biotech Trainers), *Pharmaceutical Executive, Pharmaceutical Representative,* and *Phenomena* magazines. Bacchetta authors *Onwords*™, a monthly online column about the power of the written word, as well as RFID Today, a blog exploring the impact of RFID on daily life (www.rfidtoday.blogspot.com). Visit her website at www.sallybacchetta.com or contact her at info@sallybacchetta.com.

Curtis Baillie is the President of Security Consulting Strategies, LLC, an independent security management consulting firm based in West Chester, Pennsylvania. Baillie's professional background, which spans over 30 years, includes service with federal, state, and local law enforcement agencies, along with some of the largest retailers headquartered in the United States and Canada. Baillie's retail security experience includes directing the Loss Prevention Services Department for one of the "top 50" grocery chains in the United States, along with other senior security management positions for Fortune 500 "big box" and "specialty" retailers. His background encompasses all phases of security and loss prevention management operations.

Norman D. Bates, Esq., President and Founder of Liability Consultants, Inc., is a nationally recognized expert in security and the law. For over 20 years, he has provided security management consulting services to private industry as well as court-certified expert witness services nationwide to both plaintiff and defense firms in civil cases regarding inadequate security, negligent hiring or training, and workplace violence. Formerly, Bates was an Assistant Professor of Criminal Justice at Northeastern University in Boston and Director of Security and Legal Counsel to the Saunders Hotel Corporation. He received his Juris Doctor degree from Suffolk University and a Bachelor of Science degree in Criminal Justice from Northeastern University. He is a member of the Massachusetts Bar, the International Association of Professional Security Consultants, the American Justice Association (formerly ATLA), the Defense Research Institute (DRI), the National Crime Victim Bar Association, and ASIS International.

Peter Berlin, an international consultant on retail theft, was called by *The New York Times* the nation's best known and most active consultant on inventory shrinkage. He is President of The Peter Berlin Consulting Group, Inc.; publisher of two leading retail industry newsletters on inventory shrinkage (named *The Peter Berlin Report on Shrinkage Control – Executive Edition* and *Store Managers' Edition*); and founder of the national Association for Shoplifting Prevention, Inc., a nonprofit organization directed toward shoplifting prevention and the rehabilitation of offenders. Berlin started his career in retailing in 1966, holding positions during his first 10 years as Director of Loss Prevention for a department store chain and Corporate Director of Security and Internal Audit for a specialty store chain. He later spent 5 years as the National Director of the Retail Loss Prevention Consulting Group for Price Waterhouse, traveling worldwide and consulting with more than 100 retail firms about how to prevent shoplifting and employee theft. Berlin has conducted advanced educational seminars for retail executives; works with the criminal justice system to provide effective treatment for offenders; and is frequently quoted on radio, TV, and in the media. He received his degree in Psychology in 1963 from Long Island University in New York.

Van Carlisle is the President and CEO of FireKing Security Group, a broad-based security and asset protection company with a multitude of product and service offerings. Since he became CEO in 1976, under Carlisle's direction, FireKing Security Group has achieved a position of market leadership in the asset protection industry. Carlisle studied Criminal Justice at the University of Louisville and served in the Kentucky Air National Guard Security Police Force. A prolific writer, he typically authors several dozen guest columns and white papers annually for various trade and business publications.

Paul B. Cogswell, CPP, CFE, is the Vice President of Loss Prevention and Risk Services for Comdata Network, Inc. Comdata Payment Innovations is an issuer and processor of payment solutions for corporations. Comdata has been a pioneer in the concept of stored value, serving approximately half of the retail industry. Prior to that posting, Cogswell was the Director of Corporate Security and Chief Security Officer (CSO) for USF Corporation, a transportation holding company. Cogswell has held senior positions at Kmart Holding Corporation as the Director of Asset Protection, Compliance, and Financial Recovery; and Sears, Roebuck and Co., where he was the Director of Corporate Investigations. Cogswell has served both the government and private sector in senior management positions for the past 20 years. Cogswell has been a Certified Protection Professional (CPP) since 1979 and a Certified Fraud Examiner since 1989. He is a graduate of St. John's University, where he also attended law school.

Timothy D. Crowe has over 35 years of experience providing consulting and training services in law enforcement and crime prevention areas, including directed patrol, school security, youth-focused community policing, serious habitual offender programs, and Crime Prevention Through Environmental Design (CPTED). His experience in planning of security and safety includes the 1972 Republican and Democratic Conventions, the 1979 Pan American Games, and the 1982 World's Fair. He is the author of a number of books, manuals, and guidelines in his areas of expertise. The second edition of his 1991 textbook, *Crime Prevention Through Environmental Design: Applications of Architectural Design and Space Management Concepts,* was released in March 2000. Crowe has a BS degree in Criminology and Humanities and an MS degree in Criminology and Higher Education. Crowe has worked in CPTED programs in housing, school security, transportation, and major events in Japan, New Zealand, Australia, Canada, the Virgin Islands, Puerto Rico, and Singapore.

John Dahlberg, Esq., a California attorney since 1979, is a partner with Dillingham & Murphy LLP in its San Francisco office since 1984, a reserve police officer, Oakland (CA) Police Department, 1988–1996.

Sandi J. Davies began her career in contract security in 1980 with a primary focus on personnel administration. She became involved in training and was instrumental in developing security officer training programs for a major national guard company. Her interest in security training grew, and in 1988 she joined the newly formed International Foundation for Protection Officers (IFPO), as a program administrative assistant. In 1991 she was elected Executive Director of the International Foundation for Protection Officers and has been a driving force in foundation programs, development, and administration. Davies has had numerous articles published in security publications such as *Security Management,* relating to certifications and training of security personnel. In the early 1990s, Davies, in a cooperative effort with the IFPO Founding Director, Ronald R. Minion, coedited the *Protection Officer Training Manual,* with an eighth edition in preparation. In 1999 Davies's and Minion's *Security Supervision: Theory and Practices of Asset Protection* was published.

Robert M. Denny, CSC, CHS, is an independent security management consultant. Denny is a board-certified Security Consultant (CSC) by the International Association of Professional Security Consultants and is certified in Homeland Security (CHS) by the American College of Forensic Examiners. He is a life member of the American Society for Industrial Security–International. Denny has extensive loss prevention experience with Macy's, California; and with Mervyn's Department Stores in five western states. He taught Retail Security and Loss Prevention at Chabot College in Hayward, California. Denny holds a bachelor's degree in Business Management from Saint Mary's College in Moraga, California. He is a contributing author of the *Security Management and Accident Prevention Manual,* published by the National Safety Council.

Robert L. DiLonardo is Principal of Retail Consulting, engaging in strategic planning and financial analysis for retailers, consumer products manufacturers, and security equipment providers. He is an authority on security technology and the cost justification of security products and services. DiLonardo has contributed chapters in security industry textbooks, including *Shoplifting: Managing the Problem* (Christman, J. & Sennewald, C., ASIS International) and *Business and Crime Prevention* (Felson, M. & Clarke, R.V., Criminal Justice Press). He has published articles and academic research in *Security Technology & Design Magazine, Retail Business Review, Stores Magazine, International Journal of Risk, Loss Prevention Magazine, Security and Crime Prevention,* and *Security Journal.* He earned an MBA (Finance and Investments) from George Washington University and a BA (Economics) from Georgetown University, both in Washington, D.C. In addition, he is a member of ASIS International.

David Donnan, Former President, Checkpoint Systems, Inc.

Jeffrey A. Dussich is the President and Cofounder of JAD Communications & Security (JAD CS), located in New York City. JAD CS specializes in advanced biometric identification solutions, designed specifically for the retail and financial services industry. JAD CS is an affiliate of JAD Corporation of America, one of New York's largest building maintenance supply distributors. Upon graduating from Colgate University in Hamilton, New York, Dussich joined JAD Corporation. Shortly thereafter, JAD CS continued its expansion by evaluating alternative physical security technologies to improve access control and visitor management. JAD CS became heavily entrenched in the biometrics industry and is currently one of only a few systems integrators focused exclusively in biometric technology. JAD CS's current focus on improved loss prevention and operational measures places the company in a niche category of security companies. Under Dussich, JAD CS is staffed by established biometric and security industry professionals.

Jason Elwell is the Director of Client Services at LP Software, Inc., a software company that specializes in incident management and compliance auditing solutions. Elwell has 12 years of combined experience in loss prevention and information technology, which gives him a unique perspective on using technology to help retail organizations.

Gary M. Farkas, PhD, received his master's and doctoral degrees in Clinical Psychology from the University of Hawaii, his AB degree from Rutgers College, and trained at the University of Virginia's Institute of Law, Psychiatry, and Public Policy. Farkas developed the first psychological services program for the Honolulu Police Department in 1981. While at HPD, he graduated recruit school and became a sworn reserve police officer. Farkas has consulted with private businesses and public agencies on the topics of threat assessment and violence in the workplace. He testifies in criminal court on issues related to violence prediction and dangerousness. Farkas is a licensed clinical psychologist and certified substance abuse counselor, with more than 20 publications in professional journals and books, and many presentations to professional and trade groups on threat assessment.

John J. Fay is the Owner/Operator of Security Management Online and The Learning Shop, providers of online courses and tests for security professionals and private investigators. Degrees include a Bachelor of General Education, University of Nebraska at Omaha, and Master of Business Administration, University of Hawaii. Fay is the author of numerous books on security and security management. He is an Adjunct Instructor, Texas A&M University. His prior employment included Adjunct Instructor, DeKalb Institute; Security Manager, British Petroleum Exploration; Adjunct Professor, University of Houston; Director of Corporate Security, The Charter Company; Director; National Crime Prevention Institute; Chief of Plans and Training, Georgia Bureau of Investigation; Chief of Training Standards, Georgia Peace Officer Standards and Training Council; Special Agent, U.S. Army Criminal Investigation Division; Lecturer, Police Science Division, University of Georgia; and Adjunct Professor, University of North Florida. Accomplishments and memberships include being a former Certified Protection Professional (CPP), Regional Vice President, Chapter Chairman, and member of the CPP Board, American Society for Industrial Security–International; Association of Chiefs of Police; Peace Officers Association of Georgia; and Texas Police Association.

Eugene F. Ferraro, CPP, CFE, PCI is the President and CEO of Business Controls, Inc., a risk-mitigation and consulting firm. Ferraro has been a corporate investigator for over 24 years and specializes in the investigation of employee dishonesty, substance abuse, and criminal activity in the workplace. He is board certified in Security Management (CPP designation) by ASIS International. He is also a member of the Association of Certified Fraud Examiners and is a Certified Fraud Examiner (CFE) and faculty member. He is also a Professional Certified Investigator (PCI designation). Ferraro is a former military pilot, intelligence officer, and a graduate of the Naval Justice School. He is a frequent book critic for *Security Management* and wrote *Undercover Investigations in the Workplace*, which is currently used as a textbook by universities and law enforcement agencies across the country. He is also the author of *Investigations in the Workplace*, published in 2006.

Richard H. Frank, CPP, is the Group Manager of Loss Prevention and Safety Services for Eddie Bauer Fulfillment Services, Inc., in Columbus, Ohio. EBFS, as the company is known, is a subsidiary of Eddie Bauer Holdings, Inc. It provides retail and direct-to-customer distribution services and operates customer contact centers in the United States and Canada. Frank has been at EBFS since 1993 when the company was formed. Prior to moving to Ohio, Frank held several positions at Spiegel, Inc., in Chicago, including Corporate Loss Prevention Manager and Corporate Retail Security Manager. His security career began in 1972, holding positions with several retail firms. Frank is a graduate of the University of Illinois with a degree in Administration of Criminal Justice. He is board certified in security management, which is the Certified Protection Professional or CPP designation of the American Society for Industrial Security. Frank has been a member of the Retail Loss Prevention Council since 1985.

Michael Gach is the Owner and Chief Investigator for Gach & Associates, a licensed investigative company in Nevada and California. Gach is a former police officer and has held executive positions in the security departments of two Fortune 500 retail corporations. He has extensive work experience in both retail and logistics security. Gach is a former director and a security consultant to the Nevada Retail Association. He has written, coauthored, and lobbied for several bills that support the retail industry and are currently state laws in Nevada. Gach is a past president of the Nevada Check and Credit Card Investigators Association and the Northern Nevada Security Association. Also, he is an active member of the American Society for Industrial Security, California Association of Licensed Investigators, and Professional Investigators of California.

Robert A. Gardner, CPP, is a board-certified security management professional and former police crime prevention specialist with more than 36 years of experience in evaluating, developing, and managing security and crime prevention programs. He provides security and crime prevention consulting and forensic expert witness services from offices in Camarillo, California, and Las Vegas, Nevada. Website: www.crimewise.com.

David Gorman is the President and CEO of David Gorman & Associates (www.davidgorman. org), a retail loss prevention consulting firm. Gorman is an internationally recognized loss prevention expert, having spent over 21 years with Wal-Mart stores, where he served as Vice President of Loss Prevention, Risk Control, & Quality Assurance before retiring in January 2002. He has a BS/BA from Southern Illinois University in Edwardsville, IL. He is a member of the National Retail Federation, the National Speakers Association, and ASIS International, for which he currently serves as Chair of the Retail Loss Prevention Council. He also served for 18 years on the Retail Industry Leaders Association (RILA) Loss Prevention Conference Steering Committee and was chair of that committee for two separate terms.

Michael Hoeflich is currently a Loss Prevention Manager with a nationally known department store and has 10 years' experience in retail loss prevention. He started his career as a store detective in a combination grocery/department store in the Midwest. Hoeflich holds a Bachelor of Science degree in Criminal Justice from the University of Cincinnati.

Richard Hollinger, PhD, is a Professor in the Department of Criminology, Law, and Society at the University of Florida in Gainesville. He is also the Director of the Security Research Project, an academic research institute that focuses exclusively on retail loss prevention and security issues. The Security Research Project annually conducts the *National Retail Security Survey,* along with a number of other empirical research activities. Throughout Hollinger's career, his research has been principally focused on the topic of white collar crime—more specifically, deviant and criminal behavior committed in the course of one's occupation. Hollinger currently serves on the editorial advisory board of the *Security Journal* and is a regular columnist for *Loss Prevention Magazine.* He also sits on the Loss Prevention Advisory Committee of the National Retail Federation. Hollinger is the author of three books: *Theft by Employees* (with John P. Clark; Lexington Books, 1983), *Dishonesty in the Workplace: A Manager's Guide to Preventing Employee Theft* (London House Press, 1989), and *Crime, Deviance and the Computer* (Dartmouth Press, 1997).

Donald J. Horan, CPP, is the President of Loss Control Concepts, Inc., an independent resource for loss prevention and security programs specializing in the retail sector. Horan is an active member of the ASIS Retail Loss Prevention Council, the Retail Industry Leaders Association's (RILA) LP Steering Committee, and the International Association of Professional Security Consultants (IAPSC). Horan's earlier career comprised senior LP positions in department store and specialty retail companies that led to a private practice for the past 10 years, providing specialized LP consulting services for retail clientele. In 1996, he developed the security and logistics programs for retail venues at the Summer Olympic Games in Atlanta and in 1998 published *The Retailer's Guide to Loss Prevention and Security* from CRC Press.

David A. Jones is the President and CEO of Cost Benefit Consultants, Inc., a New York–based loss prevention consulting firm. Jones is board certified as a Protection Professional (CPP) by the American Society for Industrial Security. He has 30 years of experience in the retail loss prevention/security arena, including Regional Security Director for Macy's East; Director of Loss Prevention for world renowned jeweler Tiffany & Co. in New York, where he was responsible for worldwide security operations; Director of Loss Prevention for The Home Shopping Network in St. Petersburg, Florida; and Vice President, Corporate Loss Prevention and Security for Tommy Hilfiger USA, Inc. Jones served as the 2004 chairman of the 1,200 member International Cargo Security Council. He has been a member of this organization since 1999 and currently sits on the board of directors. Jones has written several trade publication articles on the topic of cargo and warehouse security.

Mike Keenan, CPP, CFI, is currently the Director of Loss Prevention for Mervyns, LLC, an apparel retailer based in Hayward, California. His prior experience includes 16 years with Macy's West, where he started as a Loss Prevention Manager and worked his way to Director of Loss Prevention. He then held Director of LP positions with Ross Stores and Longs Drugs. He started his career with the Federal Bureau of Investigation. Keenan has a degree in Criminal

Justice from California State University, Sacramento. He has served on the NRF LP Advisory Council and was the Chairperson in 2001 and 2002. He is a licensed private investigator in the state of California and a Certified Forensic Interviewer (CFI). In addition, he taught Retail and Corporate Loss Prevention classes at Golden Gate University in San Francisco, California.

Stanley Kirsch is the Director of National Accounts for Civil Demand Associates located in Van Nuys, California. His background includes Manager of Investigation for Wackenhut, New York; VP Holmes Security CP; Licensed Private Investigator, New York state; Director Administrative Practices, Macy's East; Regional Sales Manager, Se-Kure Controls; and Vice President for his own company. Stanley was an Adjunct Professor at New York University's School of Continuing Adult Education, teaching a course titled "The Start Up and Administration of a Private Security Company."

Karl F. Langhorst, CPP, Director, Loss Prevention Randalls & Tom Thumb Food and Pharmacy, has over 25 years' law enforcement and retail loss prevention experience and is a member of the American Society for Industrial Security–International, chairman of the Loss Prevention subcommittee for Texas Retailers Association (TRA), board member for Crime Stoppers of Houston, and former member of the Food Marketing Institute (FMI) Loss Prevention Committee. He received his Bachelor of Political Science degree from the University of Texas at Arlington. An author and frequent speaker on various loss prevention topics, including physical security and organized retail crime, he is board certified in security management by ASIS; licensed as a master peace officer, instructor, and investigative hypnotist by the Texas Commission on Law Enforcement Officer Standards and Education (TCLOSE). As a guest lecturer at the University of Houston-Downtown, Langhorst instructed graduate-level security courses for the College of Criminal Justice's Security Management Program.

Jim Lansberry, PCI, has been the Loss Prevention Manager at LEGOLAND California since it opened in 1999. He is an ASIS board-certified professional investigator (PCI). He has over 25 years' experience in both retail and grocery loss prevention.

Joseph LaRocca, Vice President, Loss Prevention, National Retail Federation, has 20 years of retail loss prevention, security, and operations experience. LaRocca serves on the U.S. Department of Homeland Security, Commercial Facilities and Food–Agriculture Sector Coordinating Councils, the Homeland Security Information Network Critical Infrastructure National Governance Board, and the national board for the International Association of Financial Crimes Investigators (IAFCI) and works with federal, state, and local law enforcement agencies. In 1997, LaRocca founded www.LPInformation.com, an online portal specializing in information, tools, and networking for loss prevention and related professions. LPInformation.com now serves as the NRF's online headquarters for loss prevention services. Prior to joining the National Retail Federation, LaRocca served in various executive LP positions, most recently as the Director of Loss Prevention for The Disney Stores, a worldwide division of The Walt Disney Company, where he spent over 9 years directing strategic and tactical loss prevention, crisis management, and business continuity programs.

Lindsey M. Lee, B.S., M.A. is an Investigative Consultant for the Investigations Department, and a forensic clinician on the Behavioral Sciences Team at Business Controls, Inc., Littleton, CO. She is responsible for consulting and supporting special investigations and assisting in the development and expansion of the Behavioral Sciences Department, to include forensically related evaluations, trainings, and other activities. She furthermore manages and supervises the call center representatives responsible for the intake of highly sensitive reports on the MySafeWorkplace and MySafeCampus systems. Ms. Lee is a contributing editor for *Security Newsletters*, published by Business Controls, Inc. In 2002, Ms. Lee obtained her Bachelor of Sciences degree in Experimental Psychology from Millikin University in Decatur, Illinois and her Master of Arts degree in Forensic Psychology from the University of Denver, Denver, Colorado, in 2005. Prior to her arrival in Denver, Ms. Lee worked in the Division of Women and Family Services for the Illinois Department of Corrections at Lincoln Correctional Center (LCC), a medium security women's prison. She is a member of The Association of Threat Assessment Professionals (ATAP).

Frank Luciano joined Civil Demand Associates, Inc., in 1987 as the Director of Marketing, when only 15 states and about 25% of retailers collected civil recovery. Over the following 10 years, civil recovery laws were passed in all 50 states. Luciano has worked with retail merchants associations nationwide and the National Association of Independent Businesses to help passage of these laws. Today, Luciano is an equity partner and Executive Vice President of Civil Demand Associates, one of the industry leaders. His foresight has brought about the out-sourcing of the collection of promissory notes and 1099 filings on former employees, with the over 100 clients CDA currently services. His vision of connecting retail loss prevention, food service, and the petroleum industry with collection attorneys by using technology has resulted in the business logic used by many companies today. His hobbies include outdoor recreation, college football, and Texas Hold 'Em—not necessarily in that order.

Michael S. Magill, CFE, is the Owner and President of Magill & Associates, a private inves-tigation, loss prevention consulting, and litigation support firm. He is a former Certified Protection Professional, a Certified Fraud Examiner, and a Licensed Private Investigator in the state of California. He is a life member of ASIS International and serves on its Retail Loss Prevention Council. Magill has been in the loss prevention, security, and investigative fields for almost 40 years and has dealt with credit frauds, embezzlements, white collar crime, refund fraud, general theft, computer crime and fraud, prescription fraud and theft, CPTED, and other retail-related issues. Magill began his LP career as the California/Nevada District Security and Safety Manager for Montgomery Ward, and was the first Loss Prevention Direc-tor for Longs Drug Stores, a Fortune 500 company, where he worked for 16 years until his retirement in 1997.

Paul Mains is the President of West Bay Security Training, Inc., a policy development and consulting firm. He has been a board-certified Protection Professional (CPP) since 1988. He is a Certified Security Consultant (CSC) and a member of the International Association of Pro-fessional Security Consultants. He has degrees from the University of Florida and University of South Florida. Mains specializes in the training and policy development of the use of force application in the private sector. He can be reached at pmains@tampabay.rr.com.

Joan Manson is the Director of Loss Prevention for The Container Store, the nation's origina-tor and leading retailer of storage and organization products. Her responsibilities include loss prevention, risk management, brand protection, legal compliance, benefits, and payroll for this flourishing retail chain. The Container Store is nationally recognized as one of the best places to work in America. In the loss prevention profession, the retailer is also recognized as a true case study, proving that an embraced culture, valuing employees with great pay, benefits, training, communication, and recognition will result in a sustained commitment by employees and lower turnover, ultimately resulting in lower shrink and higher profitability. Manson has more than 25 years of experience in loss prevention and human resources. Prior to joining The Container Stores, she held various leadership positions with Pearle Vision, Neiman Marcus, and Montgomery Ward. Manson is a member of the National Retail Federation Advisory Council and serves as the Chairperson for the Women in Loss Prevention Caucus.

Liz Martínez is an Adjunct Professor at Katharine Gibbs School, where she teaches Security Management and Criminal Justice. She is a certified NY DCJS and Office of Homeland Security trainer and an international retail security consultant. She is the author of the book *The Retail Manager's Guide to Crime and Loss Prevention: Protecting Your Business from Theft, Fraud and Violence* (Looseleaf Law Publications, 2004) and a contributor to *The Encyclopedia of Security Management*, 2nd Edition (ASIS International, 2007). She writes extensively for secu-rity and police publications, including SecurityInfoWatch.com, *Law Enforcement Technology, Loss Prevention Magazine*, and *Security Technology & Design*. She holds a BA in Criminal Justice from John Jay College of Criminal Justice, an MA from Seton Hill University, and is completing an MS in Loss Prevention and Safety from Eastern Kentucky University. In addition, she is a member of the Retail Loss Prevention Council of ASIS International.

Carol A. Martinson is Vice President, Asset Protection, at Supervalu, Inc., a wholesale and retail grocery company. She has security and asset protection management experience in the financial, big box retail, and food industry. Martinson is a Certified Security Services Financial Professional, active in ASIS International, ISMA, IACFI, and has served on the planning commission and boards of Bank Administration Institute, Food Marketing Institute, and Crime Stoppers, Inc.

Chris E. McGoey is President of McGoey Security Consulting. He is an internationally known author, trainer, and frequent speaker on the subjects of crime prevention, retail security, and premises liability. He has conducted over 6,000 security surveys of commercial properties where crime has been a problem and has provided advice on how to reduce the risk. He has earned 11 professional designations and certifications as a professional security consultant and licensed private investigator. McGoey has an AA degree in Police Science and a BS degree in Criminal Justice Administration. He is currently writing two books, *Nightclub Security* and *Apartment Security.* He has published one book, *Security Adequate or Not,* six book chapters, and over 90 articles for industry trade journals and for the CrimeDoctor.com website.

J. Patrick Murphy is a respected Loss Prevention and Security Consultant based in Houston, Texas. Mr. Murphy's career has spanned over 32 years in the security, law enforcement, and loss prevention arenas. He is one of the few retail loss prevention consultants with experience in the retail drug store sector. His expertise in pharmacy operations, DEA compliance, and drug diversion investigations is widely recognized. Murphy has served as an adjunct instructor at the Houston Police Academy, member of the Board of Directors Houston Retail Merchants Association, and guest lecturer at Sam Houston State University and the University of Florida for Richard Hollinger, PhD. He has also written articles for *Loss Prevention and Security Journal, The CEO Refresher*, and the Warehousing Education and Research Council. He is currently President of LPT Security Consulting, where he provides services as an expert witness, providing testimony on security and loss prevention–related litigation, physical security analysis, school security, loss prevention assessments, and training seminars.

D. Anthony Nichter, ARM, CHE, CPP, CPS, CDTI, is a veteran in the security tradecrafts with over 25 years of active service. He has conducted senior management-level seminars throughout the United States, Puerto Rico, and Australia on behalf of private organizations and governmental tourism ministries. He has provided consultative and protective services to private companies, corporate executives, high-profile celebrities, and public agencies. Nichter is board certified in Security Management (CPP). He is also certified as a Hospitality Educator, a Defensive Tactics Instructor, a Handcuff Instructor, a Protection Specialist, and an Associate in Risk Management. Nichter is currently a faculty member at the Community College of Southern Nevada. As a state of Nevada approved instructor for the Las Vegas Metropolitan Police Department, Nichter conducts the popular program "Trial Testimony Preparation for Law Enforcement." Also, he has authored over 25 articles that have been published in security newsletters and leading industry trade publications.

Dave Niemeyer is a Loss Prevention Supervisor for a major national retailer in the Midwest. Niemeyer started in the security field after 6 years of service in the U.S. Air Force. He specialized in hospital security from 1988 to 1997 and holds a certification from the International Association of Hospital Safety and Security (IAHSS). He also holds certifications from the St. Louis, Missouri City Police Academy and St. Louis County, Missouri Fire Departments for Security Officer Specific training programs. Discovering the field of loss prevention in 1997, Niemeyer quickly advanced and excelled in the field and has been a supervisor since 2004. Since early 2003 he has focused on retail fraud and has more than 80 fraud apprehensions to his credit, with a 100% conviction rate and a combined case value of over $1.5 million. In 2004 Niemeyer was invited to join the St. Louis Area Identity Theft Task Force and remains the force's only retail member.

W. Barry Nixon, SPHR, President, National Institute for Prevention of Workplace Violence, Inc., is a recognized expert who frequently speaks at conferences such as ASIS International

(United States/Europe), Staffing Management, and SHRM. He has been published in *Security Management, Security magazine, Loss Prevention, Campus Security Journal, Staffing,* and *Security Products,* among others; has appeared on MSNBC, ABC, and CBS; and has hosted the popular talk radio show *Workplace Violence Today.* He is also the creator of a site for comprehensive workplace violence information on the Internet: www.workplaceviolence911.com. He is a graduate of the Executive Management Program, University of Hawaii, and earned his MA from the New School University and his BS from Northeastern University. He is certified in Workplace Security, Trauma Response, Anger Management Facilitation, Organization Development, Systems Thinking, Mediation, and is a Senior Human Resource Professional (SPHR). He is also an active member of the ASIS International's Crime Loss Prevention Council and Society for Human Resource Management.

Patrick M. Patton works in a Loss Prevention supervisory capacity for Mervyns, LLC. He handles store-level investigations as well as serves as the coordinator for Organized Retail Crime information within his district. Somewhat new to the retail loss prevention community, Patton served in management in a theme park security environment, specializing in medical response. He is also involved with Search and Rescue for the county in which he resides. Patton received schooling in the areas of Criminal Justice and Emergency Medical Technology from Scottsdale Community College and Paradise Valley Community College. He has been published in several literary magazines; this, however, will be his first work in regards to retail crime, security, and loss prevention.

Angélica Rodríguez was named as NRF's Director, Loss Prevention, in March 2007. Prior to her appointment, Rodríguez worked in the NRF membership department as a Manager, Member Relations. Rodríguez will join Vice President of Loss Prevention Joseph LaRocca in serving as a liaison for loss prevention committees, members, and governing boards. She will also act as an NRF spokesperson on loss prevention topics. Previously, Rodríguez worked with an international management company based in Washington, D.C., and a security design and installation company in Austin, Texas, as its Manager of Business Development and Communications. Rodríguez holds a Bachelor of Arts degree from Rice University in Political Science with a focus on International Relations.

King Rogers retired in early 2001 after almost 17 years as Vice President, Assets Protection for the Target Corporation. Prior to joining Target, he was Director of Assets Protection for Strawbridge and Clothier in Philadelphia for over 14 years. He started his career as an intelligence officer in the military and with the federal government. During his 31 years in retail loss prevention/security, Rogers was an early discoverer of the organized retail crime phenomena and developed one of the first national investigation teams to combat the problem. After retiring from Target Corporation, Rogers started the consulting firm King Rogers International, which was subsequently acquired by SC-integrity, Inc. Rogers now serves as Executive Vice President of that supply chain security and intelligence services company.

Tom Rood is the Sales Manager for Protection Service Industries, a commercial alarm company located in California. Rood is currently President of the East Bay Alarm Association. He has worked in the retail security industry for 30 years as a security manager and commercial security consultant.

Lester S. Rosen, Esq., is an attorney at law and President of Employment Screening Resources (www.ESRcheck.com), a national background screening company located in California. He is the author of *The Safe Hiring Manual—Complete Guide to Keeping Criminals, Imposters and Terrorists Out of Your Workplace* (Facts on Demand Press), the first comprehensive book on employment screening. He is also a consultant, writer, and frequent presenter nationwide on pre-employment screening and safe hiring issues and has testified as an expert witness. His speaking appearances have included numerous national and statewide conferences. Mr. Rosen was the chairperson of the steering committee that founded the National Association of

Professional Background Screeners (NAPBS), a professional trade organization for the screening industry, which has over 500 members, and served as its first cochairman. He is a former deputy district attorney and criminal defense attorney. He graduated UCLA with Phi Beta Kappa honors and received a JD degree from the University of California at Davis, serving on the Law Review.

James H. Ryan, PhD, CPP, retired from the U.S. Army as a Lt. Col., where his duties involved emergency planning while on the Army General Staff.. In his civilian career of 25 years, Ryan was vice president and country president of an international retail chain. He then started his own company and served as security consultant to several retail chains, including one with over 5,000 retail outlets in 29 countries. During his civilian career, he was admitted in both state and federal courts as an expert in retail security issues. Ryan is a Past President, International Association of Professional Security Consultants, and a Meritorious Life Member of that organization. He had the opportunity during a long career in the military and in business to read, write, and put into operation many different types of emergency plans. The material in the work at hand is distilled from his variety of experiences in emergency planning.

Lawrence Schuck, CPP, CSC, is Founder and Manager of AAA Risk Management, a Loss Prevention and Security Consulting firm located on Wellington, Ohio. He has spent over 32 years in public and private law enforcement, the last 10 years as Special Agent in Charge of the Norfolk Southern Railway Police Department. He received a Bachelor's of Science degree in Security Management, an Associates of Applied Science degree in Police Science, and an Associates of Applied Business degree in Business Administration. Schuck is a member of the International Association of Chiefs of Police, the Pennsylvania Association of Chiefs of Police, and the Ohio Association of Chiefs of Police. He holds board certification as a Certified Protection Professional (CPP) through the American Association for Industrial Security (ASIS International) and is also board certified as a Certified Security Consultant (CSC) by the International Association of Professional Security Consultants (IAPSC).

Sanford Sherizen, PhD, CISSP, consults with senior management, emphasizing ways to maximize information protection strategies and minimize legal and public relations liabilities. He has extensive seminar and conference presentation experience and has authored or coauthored four books and over 50 articles on computer crimes and criminals, making cyber security work, and the insider threat. Sherizen is an adjunct professor in Norwich University's online Master of Science in Information Assurance program. He was inducted into the Information System Security Association's Hall of Fame for his contributions to the field. Sherizen holds the CISSP designation from the International Information Systems Security Certification Consortium (ISC^2) and was a seminar instructor for those preparing to take the certification exam. He is a member of the International Association of Professional Security Consultants and can be contacted at sherizen@verizon.net.

Daniel Adam Smith holds a bachelor's degree in Business Administration & Corporate Accounting from Auburn University. He began his loss prevention career with Saks, Inc., as a Loss Prevention Associate. During the next 8 years, he progressed through the LPM position, Area LPM, and ultimately served as Corporate Investigative Systems Manager. He is currently an serving as a District Asset Protection Manager with Winn-Dixie Stores in the southeastern United States.

Kathleen Smith, CFI, is Vice President of Loss Prevention for Safeway, where she is responsible for security and loss prevention for over 1,800 stores in the United States and Canada, 33 manufacturing facilities, 20 warehouse facilities, and buying offices worldwide. With over 30 years of security management and law enforcement experience, Smith is chairperson of the Food Marketing Institute's loss prevention committee. She is also on the advisory committee for the Center for Interviewer Standards and Assessment, the loss prevention committees for the California Grocers Association and California Retailers Association, and the board of directors for California Shopping Cart Retrieval Corporation. Smith earned a master's degree in communications from Pepperdine University, Advanced Police Officer Standards and Training certificate from the State of California, and was elected to the "Who's Who of American Women" in 1999.

Shannen Stenerson, who currently calls Northern California her home, is a Regional Loss Prevention Manager for a major grocery store chain where she is responsible for training and hiring of the loss prevention team, awareness training for employees, and internal investigations. Stenerson has spent the past 15 years involved in loss prevention with experience including operations and human resources.

Randy Tennison, CPP, CFE, CFI, is a corporate fraud investigator with Ferrellgas Partners LP. Tennison is board certified as a Protection Professional (CPP) by the American Society for Industrial Security, a Certified Fraud Examiner (CFE) by the Association of Certified Fraud Examiners, and Certified Forensic Interviewer (CFI) by the Center for Interviewer Standards and Assessment. He holds a master's degree in Security Management from the University of Central Missouri in Warrensburg, Missouri. He has previously worked as a police officer, director of security, and special agent.

Roger Thompson, author, writes for the Harvard Business School *Alumni Bulletin*.

John K. Tsukayama, CPP, CFE, PCI, has been a professional investigator since 1982, specializing in financial fraud, workplace misconduct, and workplace violence. He is the coauthor of *The Process of Investigation*, a leading text on professional investigations in the private sector, and a contributor to *Workplace Violence Prevention, Intervention, and Recovery*, a Hawaii State Attorney General guide for employers. Tsukayama has led task forces on investigations as a private consultant into official misfeasance and malfeasance in the state of Hawaii on behalf of state and county government clients. He has been a Certified Protection Professional, Certified Fraud Examiner, and Professional Certified Investigator.

Karim H. Vellani, CPP, CSC, is the President of Threat Analysis Group, LLC, an independent security consulting firm. Vellani is board certified as a Protection Professional (CPP) by the American Society for Industrial Security–International and board certified as a Security Consultant (CSC) by the International Association of Professional Security Consultants. He holds a master's degree in Criminal Justice Management from Sam Houston State University in Huntsville, Texas. Karim has written two books, *Applied Crime Analysis* and *Strategic Security Management*, both available from Elsevier Butterworth-Heinemann. As an Adjunct Professor at the University of Houston—Downtown, Vellani taught graduate courses in Security Management and Risk Analysis for the College of Criminal Justice's Security Management Program.

John A. Velke III is a 30-year veteran of retail loss prevention. He served in a vice president capacity at Lord & Taylor after it was purchased by The May Company; at Fred Meyer before that company was sold to Kroger; and at Saks, Inc., until the department store group was broken up and sold to Bon-Ton and Belk. His loss prevention credentials include appointment by the governor of Oregon to The Board of Public Standards and Training, service on the National Retail Federation's Loss Prevention Advisory Committee, the Food Marketing Institute's Loss Prevention Committee, the Illinois Attorney General's task force on computer crime, the Citizen's Crime Commission in Portland, Oregon, and other industry and legislative groups. He has written numerous magazine articles and is the author of *The True Story of the Baldwin-Felts Detective Agency*, a historical nonfiction book about a turn-of-the-century private detective agency.

Douglas E. Wicklander, CFI, CFE, has personally conducted over 10,000 investigative interviews in the public and private sectors. He has investigated thousands of employee theft and dishonesty cases over the past 24 years and has personally directed hundreds of investigations. He has testified as an expert in interview and interrogation. He is a member of the Advisory Board for the Center for Interviewer Standards and Assessment. He is also an active member of the Item Writing Committee, which develops test questions for the Certified Forensic Interviewer examination. Wicklander coauthored, with David E. Zulawski, *Practical Aspects of Interview and Interrogation*, now in its second edition. This text has been used in college and university classes and has been selected as source material for the Certified Forensic Interviewer examination.

Ralph Witherspoon, CPP, CSC, has worked in the security field for almost 40 years, first with the Corporate Security department of a highly diversified Fortune 100 company. There he worked with thousands of the company's varied retail facilities for over a dozen years. Since 1991 Witherspoon has been an independent, nonproduct-affiliated security consultant advising businesses, government agencies, and litigating attorneys, both plaintiff and defense. Witherspoon has served on the adjunct faculty of a local college. He also serves on the Board of Directors of the International Association of Professional Security Consultants.

Thomas Yuhas is the National Sales Manager of the VIP and Security Sales Group, responsible for sales of the company's Visual Imaging and Security products, specifically the IPELA IP Surveillance products, analog CCTV products, and Machine vision products. Prior to his present position, Yuhas represented Sony in the role of Director of the Data and Transmission Systems Division and National Account Director of Sales for Walt Disney Inc./ABC Television. Yuhas joined Sony in 1981 and since then has held a variety of management positions. In 1990, he received a Sony Samurai Award for excellence in sales; in 1999, he became a Six Sigma Champion, and the company honored him with the President's Excellent Activity Award. Yuhas earned a BA in Economics from East Stroudsburg University. He resides in Montvale, New Jersey, with his wife Renee, daughter Lauren, and son Drew.

David E. Zulawski, CFI, CFE, is a 1973 graduate of Knox College, where he received a Bachelor of Arts degree. After college he spent 2 years with the Chicago & Northwestern Railroad as a special agent. He then accepted a position with the Barrington, Illinois, Police Department. Zulawski is a licensed polygraph examiner and has personally conducted over 9,000 interviews and polygraph examinations. He is an expert witness on interviews and interrogations and was a consulting expert during the development of the interactive training program *The Art of Interviewing.* Zulawski has coauthored the text *Practical Aspects of Interview and Interrogation,* 2nd edition, with Douglas E. Wicklander. He is the Chairman of the Advisory Board for the Center for Interviewer Standards and Assessment. He is also a member of the Item Writing Committee that develops questions for the Certified Forensic Interviewer examination.

Preface

After coauthoring our first book in 1992 (now out of print) and collaborating on our second book *Shoplifting: Managing the Problem,* published in 2006, we were approached about writing a book covering the entire gamut of retail crime and loss prevention issues. After some discussion of how to approach a project of such scope, we agreed to undertake the project.

Since many of the procedures and methods of dealing with the myriad of retail security/loss prevention issues have changed over the past four decades from those outlined in Bob Curtis's seminal work *Retail Security,* and many of these changes were the result of advances in both technology and the law, we determined to solicit the advice and help of experts in certain areas to assist us to assure that this book will present both the tried and true as well as the cutting edge of retail loss prevention techniques, procedures, and practices. With this as our goal, the reader will find some portions of this work to be authored by those contributing experts; their help will be appropriately identified and is herewith gratefully acknowledged. The views expressed by these contributors are exclusively theirs and may, or may not, be shared by your authors.

Similarly, when we mention a specific company or product by name, such mention is not meant as an endorsement but is done solely as a convenience to the reader should you wish to pursue more information.

Finally, it is our hope that this book will serve as a practical guide to solving those security/loss prevention issues encountered by the mom-and-pop store owner, the specialty retailer, and the big box regional and national chain stores. We have written it with the thought that readers will cover the spectrum of retailers, including drug, grocery, RTW, book, and convenience stores ranging from those with no loss prevention staff or training to sophisticated loss prevention departments with a vice president or CSO-level loss prevention executive. The book is also written with the thought it will assist attorneys involved with security/loss prevention litigation, providing them with generally accepted loss prevention practices and procedures.

In some cases a topic is covered by more than one author; this was not an oversight. Occasionally, we found different perspectives, nuances, or additional information which we felt both meritorious and deserving of consideration. In those instances, they are included.

Note: This book is not intended to provide legal advice or be a substitute for competent legal services. This book contains the opinions and ideas of its authors and contributors, and is intended to provide helpful and informative material on the topics covered. The authors specifically disclaim any responsibility for any liability, loss, or risk incurred as a consequence by the use or application of any of the contents of this book. Whenever legal issues come into question, we urge that the services of a competent attorney be sought.

□ □ □
□ □ □
□ □ □

Introduction

Irrespective of the size of the company, from a single retail outlet to a multiunit chain of stores, and irrespective of the goods offered for sale to the public, be it high-end jewelry or a thrift shop, a wide variety of risks inherent to retail face management and must be addressed. At the risk of oversimplification, let's briefly examine a single store which sells auto parts and review but a handful of the risks that must be considered:

- The receiving of incoming cartons of oil from a vendor can be less than the number reflected on the manifest. The missing oil creates a shortage which may result from a simple error or intentional theft by the shipper, or stolen from the shipper's truck or trailer during its initial loading, an earlier delivery, or even during the current delivery.
- The store can be forcibly entered during the hours it's closed, and goods can be carried out.
- The store's daily receipts can be taken during a forcible entry, unless secured in a safe.
- The safe itself may be vulnerable to being carried out during a forcible entry.
- The store can be surreptitiously entered when it's closed, without leaving evidence of a forcible entry by unknown means during which items are stolen.
- The many items of goods offered for sale can be stealthily stolen by customers (shoplifted).
- Goods can be pocketed by one or more employees and never paid for.
- Employees can sell items to friends or family members at discounted prices.
- Employees can sell items and not record the sale but rather pocket part or all of the sale proceeds.
- Employees can give away items to what appears to be legitimate customers but are in reality friends or associates.

The situations described here represent only a small sampling of the types of incidents which can easily drain profits and, in the extreme, threaten the continued life of a business.

Not included in these scenarios are criminal threats involving robbery, arson, credit card fraud, fraudulent and NSF checks, bomb threats, gift cards, returned merchandise fraud, as well as the potential for civil suits (with their concomitant damage awards) should merchants mishandle their response to such situations.

Two questions immediately come to mind: **Who** is going to deal with these problems? and **How** are they going to be dealt with? This book will provide suggested answers to both questions.

Who's going to deal with these risks? Clearly, in a single store, the owner will need to address these issues, or in the absence of the owner, his or her "manager." But what about the manager? We know of a manager in a ladies' apparel store who "ran" the store, along with two part-time employees on Saturdays. The manager always arrived early in her station wagon and brought her own cash register. Half the sales were duly recorded on the store's register, and the other sales she captured on her own. Needless to say, Saturday sales were never remarkable. One Saturday the owner happened to drop in and discovered what was happening.

How will the problem be dealt with? The answer to this question is equally if not more important, since errors may not only place the owner or manager in physical jeopardy but also subject him or her to potential civil liability.

We know of another situation, an auto parts store, wherein the owner admitted he was aware of the fact his long-time employees were stealing, but he allowed the thefts because the employees were judicious in the amount they took each week (the loss was "tolerable," i.e., affordable). The employees were most diligent about protecting the assets of the store from outside pilferage. To terminate the current employees for dishonesty and replace them with "unknowns" was not an acceptable option for this owner. It was a business decision to stay with the status quo. While the authors would not opt for this option, it remains a business decision for the owner.

Single or even two-store operations can tolerate or survive criminal events if they're not catastrophic; owners may survive a marginal level of theft which they consider "acceptable." After all, hundreds of thousands of sole proprietor or family-owned stores have survived throughout the world with only a rudimentary knowledge of and/or without any particularly sophisticated security or loss prevention program in place. But how many didn't survive? There's no answer, except, perhaps, too many!

Clearly, though, big box single unit retailers and multiunit operations can't achieve financial success unless the assets are protected in a systematic, professional fashion.

Before a retailer, large or small, can implement security and loss prevention strategies and the programs to achieve them, some fundamental questions must be asked and answered. These questions fall under two categories: (1) The impact of retail inventory shrinkage or cash losses not related to a criminal act, and (2) inventory shrinkage or cash losses suspected or known to have resulted from criminal victimization.

For clarification purposes, let's define "inventory shrinkage." This is the perfect time to ensure this most important retail term is fully understood and thereafter all security and loss prevention *losses* can be held up to and measured against the term. An "inventory shrinkage" or "inventory shrink" or "inventory shortage" is the difference between book inventory (what the records reflect we have) and actual physical inventory as determined by the process of taking one's inventory of goods on hand (what we count and know we actually have). So, if our records reflect we purchased 100 bottles of wine, our sales records reflect we sold 60 bottles, and our inventory of actual bottles on the shelf reflects we have 35 bottles, we have 5 bottles unaccounted for, amounting to an inventory shortage of 5 bottles, or 5% shrinkage. We don't know what happened to those missing 5 bottles.

Now, if during the night someone breaks through the skylight in the ceiling and steals our 40 bottles, we know they were taken. Hence, their absence is not a mysterious or otherwise unexplained disappearance but is considered a known loss but, nevertheless, shrinkage unless and until it is accounted for financially as something other than shrink.

When the Crime Doesn't Affect Inventory Shrinkage

Our example of the nighttime burglary clearly is one crime which, while initially affecting inventory shrinkage, may eventually be financially accounted for in another category (e.g., known losses replaced by insurance or carried on the books as separate from shrinkage). The store suffers, by virtue of being victimized by a burglar, exactly the same loss as shrink from unknown causes, but the loss caused by the burglar is really more easily managed because we know how that loss occurred. Depending on how known losses are carried on the books determines whether or not they are included as shrinkage.

Say the sale of the 60 bottles was recorded on a POS terminal or cash register, and at the end of the night the cash, checks, and credit card receipts were placed in a bag in anticipation of making a bank deposit the next morning. During closing, a man enters, produces a gun, and demands the bag. In this case, the loss is certainly real, but such loss would never be reflected in the year's inventory shortage, since the merchandise can be accounted for, and the theft of cash would be reflected in another financial account, but not as inventory shrink.

If the sale of the 60 bottles was handled by an employee who rang the sale but failed to put the money in the register and pocketed the money, the store again has no inventory shortage, only a shortage of cash. Cash shortages have nothing to do with inventory shortages. But if the same sales associate did not record the sale, but just pretended he handled the transaction correctly and pocketed the cash, we would have no cash shortage but would have an inventory shortage!

The bottom line is that the retailer is harmed and suffers a reduction of profitability whether the losses are in the form of cash receipts or pure product; the form of the loss, however, dictates that differing strategies of prevention are required.

Other forms of retail crime victimization which need attention include injuries to customers or employees as a consequence of crime, loss of goodwill or customers, business continuity issues if the store is a victim of an arson attack, and so on.

When Losses Affect Inventory Shrink

What is the shrink or shortage, in terms of a percentage of sales? 1%? 1.4%? 3%? Is it high or low compared to industry averages? Do we know what is causing an above average shrink? What can we do without further assistance to reduce these losses? Do we need professional help?

Before a retailer, large or small, can implement security and loss prevention strategies and the programs to achieve them, some fundamental questions must be asked and answered.

These questions include

> How much can the business afford to obtain professional loss prevention assistance?
> Where is such help available?
> What form need such help take?
> How are the alternatives determined?
> How is such help selected?
> Does the local "merchant's association" offer any solutions?

Assuming the retailer's shrink is average or below, and the owner is comfortable with the level of shrink, perhaps nothing more need be done except to maintain vigilance and monitor the shrink for signs of emerging problems.

If, however, the shrink is excessive and above tolerable levels, action is indicated to both prevent further deterioration and reduce current losses.

For the average single-store operation and smaller multiunit businesses, often the most cost-effective approach is to bring in a security consultant for a one-shot review of the business and shrink reduction suggestions. Such an approach may be, depending on budget and business type, nothing more than a half-day walkthrough and discussion with the owner. Larger operations may require a more extensive review, beginning with the owner/manager (and perhaps others) answering a detailed questionnaire about various aspects of the business, followed by an extensive onsite inspection and interviews with both key executives and staff, and ending with a detailed written report by the consultant detailing his or her observations and recommendations.

For those large regional and national chains with existing security/loss prevention staffs, whose efforts senior management feels are less than effective or produce other unintended adverse consequences (e.g., civil damage suits or unfavorable employee reactions), the use of a security consultant is perhaps the only viable alternative.

In any event, narrowing down the causes of excessive shrink (and there are usually more than one) is the first step toward reducing it. This process will often also dictate the type and degree of response required: Will changes in internal policies be sufficient? Or will full- or part-time loss prevention personnel be required? Or does the solution lie somewhere in between?

Losses of cash or product from known criminal attack will probably require a totally different set of potential prophylactic treatment, generally requiring less investigative effort to determine the source and means of the loss and more directed toward hardening those weaknesses (whether physical or procedural) which permitted the attack. For example, consider a burglary which went unreported during its commission because of a failure of the alarm system to signal an intrusion. This situation is normally easily fixed. Once the system itself is determined to be functioning properly, a formalized and systematic procedure for daily testing can be initiated. This system should prevent future intrusions that go unreported to the central monitoring station, who in turn will request police to be dispatched.

How are the causes of loss identified? Aside from those which are obvious (e.g., robbery or burglary), most causes of shrinkage are more subtle and less obvious. Frequently, they require someone with some expertise in loss prevention to discover them and suggest appropriate means to correct the root causes of the problems identified. Aside from paperwork errors or other procedural aspects of handling the business's financial accounting, more than likely, the causes involve some element of criminality.

Seeking Appropriate Assistance

At this point, the retailer has various options as to how and where to seek help:

1. He may approach a fellow retailer or members of any local retail group of which he is a member and make inquiry of them. However, he may be reluctant to do this, since he may not want to either disclose his problem and/or any shortage numbers. He might also simply make an inquiry as to whether any fellow members know someone who can help him with a problem described by him only in general terms. How quickly he will find a qualified person to help him using this approach is problematic.
2. He can consult the local yellow pages for a security consultant.
3. He can consult the local yellow pages for a private detective.
4. He can consult with any local police department crime prevention officer.
5. He can search the Web.
6. He can do nothing and hope the problem solves itself, an alternative not recommended since shrinkage from criminality normally increases over time rather than decreases.

Once a decision as to the approach to be taken is made, we suggest that the owner conduct interviews with at least two of the potential sources of help so that the best "match" is made and all the specifics of the owner's expectations are understood and the costs connected with the help are fully disclosed and agreed to. Only after this procedure can an owner best select the person or organization to which he will turn for help.

Your authors wrote this book to provide a ready and complete reference to assist retailers of all dimensions in answering the two questions fundamental to security and loss prevention: **Who** should handle the problem? And **How** should it be handled? If we can, through this book, help retailers (and professional loss prevention practitioners) answer these questions and provide them with solutions to address their crime and loss prevention–related issues, while simultaneously warning of actions which lead to legal or liability problems, then we've achieved our mission.

Academic Programs

Information provided by *Loss Prevention* magazine and published with permission:

Eastern Kentucky University, Department of Loss Prevention and Safety, Richmond, KY
Online MS degree in loss prevention and safety
BS degree in assets protection with multiple options
Info: 859-622-1051 or www.eku.edu

Farmingdale State University of New York, Department of Security Systems, Farmingdale, NY
BS degree in security systems, managing security technology
Info: 631-420-2538

Fox Valley Technical College, Department of Security and Crime Prevention, Appleton, WI
Online associate degree in security and loss prevention
Online certificate for 17 hours in private investigation
Info: 920-735-2410 or www.fvtc.edu/security-crimeprevention

Michigan State University, School of Criminal Justice, East Lansing, MI
Online MS degree in criminal justice with security management specialization
Online graduate level certificate program in security management
BA degree in criminal justice
Info: 517-355-2228 or www.cj.msu.edu

Northern Michigan University, Department of Criminal Justice, Marquette, MI
Online certificate for 12 hours of loss prevention coursework
Info: 906-227-2660 or www.nmu.edu/cj

St. Cloud State University, Department of Criminal Justice, St. Cloud, MN
BA degree in criminal justice with private security minor
Info: 320-308-5541 or www.stcloudstate.edu

Tri-State University, Department of Criminal Justice, Psychology and Social Sciences, Angola, IN
BS degree in criminal justice
Associate degree in criminal justice
Satellite locations: Fort Wayne and South Bend, IN
Info: 260-665-4862 or www.tristate.edu

University of California, Department of Criminology, Law and Society, Irvine, CA
Online master of advanced study degree in criminology, law, and society
Info: 949-824-1442 or www.seweb.uci.edu/distance/mas-cls/

University of Detroit Mercy, Department of Criminal Justice and Security Administration, Detroit, MI
MS degree in security administration
Info: 313-993-1051 or www.udmercy.edu

University of Florida, Department of Criminology, Gainesville, FL
MA degree in criminology with loss prevention coursework
BA degree in criminology with loss prevention coursework
Info: 352-392-1025 or www.crim.ufl.edu

Vincennes University, Department of Loss Prevention and Safety, Vincennes, IN
Associate degree in loss prevention and safety
Info: 812-888-6839 or www.vinu.edu

Western Illinois University, Department of Law Enforcement and Justice Administration, Macomb, IL
MA degree in law enforcement and justice administration
BS degree in law enforcement and justice administration
Minors available in security administration and fire administration
Satellite location: Moline, IL
Info: 309-298-1038 or www.wiu.edu

York College of Pennsylvania, Department of Behavioral Sciences, York, PA
BS degree in criminal justice administration with asset protection minor, internship required
Info: 717-849-1600 or www.ycp.edu

Youngstown State University, Department of Criminal Justice, Youngstown, OH
BS degree in criminal justice with loss prevention emphasis
Associate degree in applied science with loss prevention track
Info: 330-941-3279 or http://bchhs.ysu.edu/dcj/dcj.html

Alarm Systems

Tom Rood

A burglar alarm system must be a part of any retail security program. A burglar alarm system is not just a tool used to protect the assets of your business, but it is a valuable management tool. An alarm system should not just be used to "catch" a burglar. It should be a system that protects the assets of your facility, which includes the building itself, the property inside, and most importantly your employees. Alarm system technology is designed to report events that are deemed "abnormal" conditions.

A burglar alarm system is a major investment for any business. Therefore, the design, management, and supervision of the system should be a top priority. A burglar alarm system must be under the direct control of a security manager or owner. This will ensure that the system is under the supervision of one or two people who have the responsibility for the records of the alarm system. Documents such as the alarm contract, schedule of protection, passcodes, alarm condition reports, emergency call lists, user's identification, testing, billing records, and maintenance records should be organized and kept in a secure location.

A. Designing a Burglar Alarm System

The design of a burglar alarm system can be complex, depending on the type of retail business. A small retail business may require only a basic system, while a large department store will require a more complex one. When designing your alarm system, use an alarm company that will assist you with the design of the system as well as provide you with the monitoring, maintenance, and other services that enhance the security features of the system. Alarm company sales representatives must have the knowledge to help you with your system needs. This is particularly important if you are unsure about what products and services are needed. Before choosing an alarm company, obtain multiple proposals and compare them. Do not choose your provider based on the lowest price. Remember, service and reputation of the alarm company are very important considerations. Specify a system with individual addressable alarm "zones" or "points." This type of system allows for the easy identification of alarms, trouble signals, and maintenance issues that may occur.

There are two types of alarm field transmitting devices: hard-wired and wireless. A hard-wired system uses data cable that is run from the field devices, i.e., contacts and motion detectors to the alarm control panel. A "wireless" system utilizes field devices that transmit signals to a wireless receiver that is located near or at the control panel. Wireless devices are often used in place of hard-wired ones due to physical issues that would prevent hardwiring the devices. Wireless and hard-wired devices can be used in conjunction with each other. Wireless devices can be reliable; however, the size and physical layout of a building may restrict or prohibit signal integrity, and the wireless device may not work. Hard-wired systems should be used so that signal integrity is not compromised.

An alarm system design begins with the protection of the footprint of the building. A review of the perimeter of the building should be done to determine its vulnerability to unlawful or unauthorized access. Parking lot security protection may be your first consideration. If so, exterior beams and motion detectors can be used to protect the perimeter of the building. However, if the parking lot area is open or must be accessed, such as in a shopping center, protection of the parking lot may be impractical. The objective of alarm system protection is to install devices that will provide the earliest possible detection of a burglar or intruder. This is particularly important because even if the intruder is detected and the police are notified, the response time of the police may be limited depending on their proximity to the site. Therefore, when designing the system, you should keep in mind that the loss sustained in a burglary may be reduced if the proper detection and sounding equipment is used.

All perimeter doors should have a magnetic door contact. All windows should have either an infrared motion detector and/or a glassbreak sensor installed. Redundant protection of doors should be considered by using infrared motion detectors to cover the door entrances in addition to door contacts. Multistory buildings present additional security issues. Typically, the second or third floor of a building would not need protection unless the doors and windows are accessible from the outside. If they are, then each door and window area should likewise be protected using door contacts and infrared motion detectors and/or glassbreak sensors. The top floor of a building may have a roof hatch installed. If so, a roof hatch contact should be installed. Buildings that are connected to each other, such as a mall configuration, may require additional roof protection using photoelectric beams.

A warehouse or receiving dock should be treated as a high security area. These areas are used to receive merchandise and to store it after receipt. Infrared motion detectors should be used to protect overhead roll-up doors. Many burglaries are committed by offenders who back up a van to the overhead door and, using the van as a shield, cut holes into the roll-up door and gain entry into the warehouse. Without interior protection, these offenders then load the merchandise into the van and are undetected. Additional infrared motion detectors should be installed at all entry locations within the warehouse.

Cashier offices are also high security areas. Businesses that store large amounts of cash or handle cash in a remote location must utilize an alarm system for protection of money and employees. Safes should have contacts on each door. In addition, a vibration alarm should be used to detect any vibration to the safe. Infrared motion detectors should also be used to cover the safe area for protection after hours. Electronic lock door release controls may be useful in protecting the cash room from unauthorized entry. These systems can be used in conjunction with a doorbell that alerts personnel that entry is requested. Hold-up buttons should be installed in the event of a robbery or duress incident. The installation and use of hold-up buttons must be carefully considered when designing the cashier alarm system. Some security professionals prefer hidden buttons, whereas others prefer exposed ones. In either case, training on the use of these devices is critical. If your cash room is compromised by an intruder while your employee is present, the use of the hold-up button may not be practical or safe to activate. In fact, safety of the employee is a priority, and these devices should not be used until the perpetrator leaves the area.

Computer server rooms are also high security areas. The loss of information to any business can be catastrophic. Protection of these areas must be a priority for any security professional. Server rooms should have a door contact and an infrared motion detector installed. In addition, a high temperature sensor should be installed so that in the event of a room cooling failure, alternative cooling can be provided to keep equipment from overheating.

High value merchandise areas, such as fine jewelry departments, should have additional protection. Safes should be contacted, and additional infrared motion detection should be installed. Hold-up buttons are also an option; however, the use of these devices must be carefully considered.

Other interior areas should be reviewed for vulnerability. If the building is susceptible to a "hide-in" offender, additional motion detection should be installed, particularly if the building has elevators, escalators, or stairwells.

B. Control Panels

The alarm control panel is the "brain" of the system. The control panel houses the electronic components that make the system function. Among those components are the wiring, circuit boards, modules, keypad, telephone dialer, and batteries. The control panel should be placed in a secure area away from the general public. Small businesses often use a telephone or electrical room while larger businesses may use a security office to house the control panel. The control panel acts as a communicator to the Alarm Monitoring Station. Each control panel must have 110 volt electrical power and a dedicated telephone line available for it to function.

Alarm control panels vary in size and features. Alarm control panels are measured by the number of "zones" or "points" that it can accommodate. A "zone" or "point" is defined as one protection device in the system. For example, a door contact is one "zone" or "point" in the system. A basic alarm control panel may consist of six or eight standard zones which can be expanded using zone expansion modules up to a maximum number of zones. Expansion modules are usually in multiples of eight zones. Larger control panels may have eight standard zones and be expandable to 128 or more zones. In addition, the number of available user codes will depend on the size of the control panel. Some control panels can be "partitioned." A "partition" is a group of zones or points that are "divided" or "partitioned" so that the control panel can have two or more systems within one control panel. For example, the owner of a small business has a warehouse and an office within one building. The office area is staffed from 0800 hours until 1700 hours Monday through Friday. The warehouse is staffed from 0700 hours until 1800 hours Monday through Saturday. The warehouse personnel are not allowed access to the office during nonoffice hours. The office area can be "partitioned" from the warehouse so that the office has its own system, restricting access. Larger control panels have up to eight partitions. Each partition must have its own keypad. The selection of the control panel will depend on the number of zones needed, number of users, and number of partitions. When selecting a control panel, keep in mind any future expansion of your system. If you are contemplating a large system, it is best to purchase a control panel that will accommodate your expansion plans ahead of time.

C. Keypads

Several types of keypads are available. The basic keypad is a numeric keypad, which displays the zone number on the keypad. If you have a small system and can remember the zoning information, this may be the appropriate keypad. However, the alphanumeric keypad provides the zone number and the name of the zone on the face of the keypad display. For example, if the front door is open, the keypad will display "Zone 1 Front Door." Alphanumeric keypads are recommended because they provide more detailed information. Other keypads have features that include voice response, two-way voice communications from the Alarm Monitoring Station, and web-based information. Keypads are used to arm and disarm the system, program user codes, retrieve alarm information, and program the system (this task is performed by the alarm installer). A keypad should be located as close to the entry point of the building as possible so that arming and disarming of the system is convenient. Each alarm system must have a delay door so that the keypad user can set the system and exit within a certain period of time, usually one minute or less. Similarly, when someone enters the building to disarm the system, the keypad should be located so that the alarm can be disarmed within a certain period of time. Failure to disarm the system within that period can cause an alarm condition and possible police response. Some systems may have up to a 4-minute delay depending on the user's requirements.

D. Sounders

The use of sounders is recommended for most system applications. Most small businesses utilize an interior siren that activates during an alarm condition. This device can discourage intruders to leave the scene, reducing loss and/or further damage to the premises. One or more of these devices may be needed to adequately cover the size of your facility. Exterior sirens, bells, and strobe lights are also utilized as notification devices.

E. Telephone Line Security

All alarm signals are transmitted over telephone lines. The security of the telephone lines inside a building is very important. If your telephone lines are exposed and can be cut or vandalized, then a secondary transmission system should be installed for your alarm system. Cellular radio transmitters are used for this purpose. These devices take over the transmission of alarm signals if telephone lines are cut or the line fails. An additional monthly charge is assessed for this service. Cellular signal strength is important in this type of application. Your alarm company representative can determine if there is sufficient cellular coverage to accommodate this feature.

F. Alarm Company Services

Alarm companies provide services associated with any alarm system. Monitoring of the system is a basic service, and is either provided at the company's own central monitoring station or is serviced by a major alarm monitoring company. Those companies that do not have their own central monitoring station are "dealers" for the monitoring company and therefore contract the service to the company that has a central monitoring station. Large alarm companies may have one or more central monitoring stations. It is not uncommon for the central monitoring station to be thousands of miles away from the site that is being monitored.

Monitoring of the alarm system means that in the event of an "abnormal" condition, such as alarm activation, the alarm company will then act upon the condition based on your instructions. This may mean that the police are called immediately upon receipt of the alarm, or the subscriber is called first before the police are notified. In any event, alarm companies will relinquish their responsibility of notification once the subscriber is contacted. It is important to remember that anyone who is designated to receive alarm notification from the alarm company be properly trained on how to handle such calls. Many times these calls are made in the middle of the night, and when a call is received, the recipient is not prepared to deal with the alarm incident. Therefore, upon receipt of the call from the alarm company, the recipient should ask the alarm operator several questions:

- What zone(s) or point(s) were activated?
- How many alarm signals were received, and are they the same zone or point?
- Have the police been notified, and if so, when will they arrive at the premises?

Asking these questions will give the subscriber, the alarm company, and the police a clearer understanding of what may have or is occurring at the time of the alarm. The recipient should advise the alarm operator whether he or she intends to respond to the premises. It should be a standard procedure that each alarm be responded to and investigated no matter what time of day or night. The operator should then advise the police accordingly. At no time should a subscriber who responds to an alarm enter the premises with the presence of the police.

In addition to monitoring services, there are system supervision services that are offered by alarm companies. These services enhance the security features of the system and should be included in the monitoring services. Opening and closing reports by user number are tools the alarm system administrator can review to determine the exact times that the system is turned on and off and who operates the system. Supervised openings and closings are used to notify the subscriber in the event that the premises are not opened or closed within a specified period of the scheduled time. Supervised openings and closings are highly recommended in order to adequately ensure that the premise alarm system is turned on and off daily. These services may also be available "online," along with administrative features which allow subscribers to change their emergency list electronically.

Maintenance, or an extended warranty, is another service that can be provided by the alarm company. Most alarm companies guarantee the installation of a new system for a 1-year period. At the end of 1 year, in the event of a part failure, the subscriber can either pay for a service call or, if he or she has a maintenance warranty, the service call and parts replacement are provided free of charge. Alarm companies charge a percentage of the installation of the system as an extended warranty fee and calculate the charge at a monthly rate. The decision whether to purchase a maintenance agreement is purely financial and should be discussed in detail with your alarm company representative.

G. The Proposal

Once you have designed your system with the alarm company representative, a proposal is then prepared and presented to the decision maker. A proposal from the alarm company should include a brief history of the alarm company, the location of the closest field office and its corporate headquarters, the location of its central monitoring station(s), a schedule of protection or list of components for the system, the services provided, any system exclusions or items that you must provide, a complete scope of work to be done, total cost of the system (parts and labor), and the cost of the monthly services provided. Some alarm companies provide rental or lease terms in addition to the outright purchase of the system. Third-party leasing companies also provide an alternative financing choice.

H. The Contract

One of the most misunderstood aspects of any alarm transaction is the monitoring contract, or commercial service agreement. Every alarm company requires that a contract for the installation and the services be signed by the subscriber. Alarm companies do this for a very good reason: to limit their liability. Most alarm companies use the same format for their contracts. Variations in contract terms may be the length of the contract, direct sale or rental/leasing of the system, and the services that are provided. The most important point to remember is that a contract is binding between the parties and it is a legal document. Before a contract is signed, it should be carefully reviewed for its content. Some companies have their legal department review the contract and may add or strike clauses to it. Contracts have a beginning and ending date with a specific procedure on how the services are canceled. Companies that cancel agreements prior to their expiration dates may be subject to paying the balance of the contract's term. Companies that are dissatisfied with their alarm provider will often cancel the agreement without considering the financial impact of such a decision. It also may mean that the equipment can be removed from the premises (if owned by the alarm company), creating an additional expense. The importance of knowing the contract terms and conditions cannot be overstated. Make sure that you understand each and every clause in the contract before signing it.

I. It Is Now Your System

After all the decisions concerning the design of your burglar alarm system have been made, you have signed the contract, and the system is installed, what happens next? The most challenging part of your job will be managing the alarm system. As previously stated, the alarm system must be supervised and managed by one or two responsible people. This may be a security manager and his or her staff, or the business owner. The most important parts of managing the alarm system are good record keeping and regular testing of the system. Record keeping can be very simple. A very good method of record keeping is the use of a binder. Sections should be divided to include the following:

- The name, address, and telephone number of your alarm company.
- The name of your account manager or sales representative.
- Your account number and system number.
- An inventory list of each alarm component including the type of alarm control panel, keypad, "zone" or "point" number, and location of each component.
- A list of each alarm user number, name of user, and passcode. The master code and password should also be listed.
- A current emergency notification list.
- A record of each time that the alarm was tested.
- A record of each alarm condition or abnormal alarm activation.
- All service records provided by the alarm company.
- Any billing records.

The second most important component of managing your alarm system is testing. Testing of the alarm system is absolutely necessary and is your responsibility. Many times subscribers have a break-in and complain that the system did not activate. In most situations, the system components fail because regular testing of the system never occurred, and therefore, the component that failed did so because no one knew that it did not function. Testing should be done on a monthly basis. The best method for testing the system is to call your monitoring station and advise it that you are going to arm the system and test each component. The test begins by turning on the alarm system. Using your alarm inventory list as a guide, open every door, walk-test every motion detector, and activate each hold-up button. Each device should activate and send a signal to the monitoring station. At the conclusion of your test, turn off the alarm system and call the monitoring station to notify the end of the test. Ask the monitoring station to fax you a list of those signals that it received and compare it with those on your alarm inventory. Any discrepancies should be noted and, if necessary, a service call to the alarm company should be initiated.

J. False Alarms

The term "false alarm" is used to describe the activation of an alarm system in which the cause of the alarm cannot be determined or a user error has occurred. An alarm system will activate whenever there is an actual intrusion, the system malfunctions due to a device failure or other catastrophic event, or the user of the system activates the alarm in error. In any case, law enforcement agencies are dispatched to the site and, in the majority of cases, discover that the cause of the alarm cannot be determined. Thus the term "false alarm" is used. False or unfounded alarms are so commonplace that many cities throughout the United States are enacting "Alarm Ordinances" which outline how cities will govern the use of alarm systems. These ordinances may require the payment of fees for an alarm use permit, require a copy of the emergency call list, and list the number of times that the police will respond to a "false" alarm before a fine is assessed to the subscriber. The more false alarms that occur, the higher the fines become. In some cities, the police will not respond to alarms after a certain number of false alarms have occurred. The city may cite the subscriber and require that they appear at a hearing to explain the reasons why the alarms occurred and what steps are being taken to reduce or eliminate the problem. Your alarm company representative should be familiar with which cities have alarm ordinances. You should ensure that you check with your city to verify the requirements that they have before the alarm system is installed.

Some law enforcement agencies have enacted a policy that the police will not respond to any alarm unless actual verification can be made. This can be done by the subscriber responding to the site, which is risky, having a security patrol service respond to the site, which can cause delays and is often a very expensive service, or utilize a closed circuit television system that is integrated with the burglar alarm system so that in the event of an alarm, the monitoring station can "look in" to the site using the camera system and verify whether a burglary has occurred. This service is commonly referred to as "remotely monitored video," and alarm companies charge an additional monitoring fee for this service. Adding a closed circuit television camera system to work in conjunction with the alarm system can add several thousand dollars to the security investment; however, the decision to make this investment may prove valuable in terms of reducing losses to the assets of the business.

As we have previously stated, an alarm system consists of electronic devices that are activated by people. This means that you are responsible for the training, testing, and maintenance of your system. You must ensure that all persons who will operate the system have a complete understanding of the system and its functions, not just how to turn the system on and off. All alarms must be investigated as to the cause of the alarm. Any alarm that is determined to be caused by equipment failure must be corrected. Remember, there is a dual responsibility for the proper operation of your alarm system. The first responsibility is yours, and second is the alarm company's. Your diligence and supervision will make your investment in an alarm system a positive one.

Amateur Shoplifters

CAS, JHC

"Amateur shoplifters" represent one of the two major classifications of persons who engage in shoplifting. Professionals represent the other classification. So-called amateurs by far constitute the greater number of individuals who steal goods from retailers because they comprise the whole range or mix of our society in terms of age, occupation, education, social status, and character. Although these "amateurs" engage in criminal conduct, i.e., larceny, they are not "criminals." They more often than not represent a true and abiding dilemma for our American judicial system.

As *Shoplifters Alternative* reports, amateur shoplifters fall into two categories: casual and habitual. The casual shoplifter constitutes a large percentage of people who steal a little, while the habitual offender represents a small percentage of people who steal a lot. Their calculations indicate the habitual offenders are responsible for over 90% of the nonprofessional shoplifting losses and approximately 85% of total shoplifting losses.(1)

If those calculations are anywhere near accurate, it tells us the vast bulk of the problem of shoplifting is theft committed by the average, ordinary, otherwise law-abiding citizen. Who are these citizens? These amateurs may be subclassified into four groups, as follows:

1. Preteenagers
2. Teenagers
3. Adults
4. Mentally disturbed persons

Rather than stealing for profit (income), they are more compulsive and seize on what they see as the opportune moment to take without being seen or caught. They don't operate with a specific plan or goal. They typically rationalize their behavior to justify their actions, and such rationalization includes

- The store makes too much profit.
- The store will never miss it.

---

(1) *Shoplifting. Managing the Problem.* (2006). ASIS International.

- Prices are too high.
- The store has no identity; hence, no one is hurt by the little loss.
- The store deserves it because of poor service or past bad experiences with the store.

The primary difference between the amateur and professional, other than the activity is not a source of income, is motivation. Amateurs steal for a variety of reasons, but the four most common reasons include

1. To give the item as a gift
2. To keep and use/wear the item
3. To bow to peer pressure, seeking acceptance
4. And perhaps most importantly, to reward oneself and make oneself "feel good" (to compensate oneself when surrounded by circumstances which have negative influence on one's life which makes the person feel depressed or unhappy).

The earlier referred-to "dilemma" faced by the courts when confronted by one of these amateurs? What is the court to do with the lady whose son is the local high school football coach and her husband is the president of the Rotary Club? Or a lady who has no criminal record, who's known in the community as a leader in charitable fund-raising drives, and is a hospital volunteer. And such persons as this lady represent not only the bulk of shoplifters, but they are the ones easiest to catch in the act of shoplifting and hence they are the "face" of shoplifting. The habitual thief and the professional are less likely to be detected, and their true character is obscured behind the image represented by the casual amateur. So the crime of larceny, shoplifting, tends to be viewed as more of a tort, a civil wrong, than a criminal act.

Two relatively effective programs are available today to deal with these amateurs. One is commonly referred to as Civil Recovery or Civil Demand, a legal process whereby the shoplifter is "fined" by the store for his or her theft conduct. The store sends a demand for a given sum, such as $200 to offset store expenses to deal with shoplifters, and the customer can satisfy such demand and the matter is closed. Failure to satisfy the demand may result in civil filing in lower courts, such as Small Claims courts.

The other viable program for amateurs is a diversion program in which the shoplifter must attend state controlled "classes," similar to driver's schools for those who are cited by the police for vehicle code violations.

Asphyxia

CAS, JHC

The dictionary defines "asphyxia" as unconsciousness or death caused by lack of oxygen. You might reasonably ask, "What has asphyxia got to do with retail crime?" The answer is the increasing number of civil suits filed against retailers alleging that a customer's death was caused by asphyxia at the hands of loss prevention (LP) personnel. Such cases usually narrow the cause of action to wrongful death by "positional asphyxia."

The subject of positional asphyxia (originally called "hogtying" or "hobbling") first gained prominence in the late 1990s when suits against police departments for wrongful death from hogtying led to restraints or prohibitions against the practice.

Investigations into positional asphyxia incidents disclosed the typical scenario:

- The suspect is restrained in a face down position, and breathing may become labored.
- Weight is applied to the suspect's back; the more weight, the more the degree of compression and difficulty breathing.
- The suspect's natural reaction to difficulty in breathing is to struggle more violently in an effort to breathe.
- In reaction to the increased violence, the officer applies more weight, and the potentially deadly cycle is repeated.

Investigation also found certain factors exacerbated the deadly potential for positional asphyxia:

- Obesity
- Alcohol use or intoxication
- Drug use or being under the influence of drugs
- Prior history of cardiac problems

Under what circumstances do retail customers succumb to positional asphyxia? When they are detained for shoplifting and either attempt to escape or struggle to prevent apprehension. In the ensuing attempt by loss prevention to bring them under control, they are forced to the ground and sat upon in an attempt to fully restrain them until the police arrive.

In the typical scenario once the suspect is forced to the ground, loss prevention personnel and perhaps store nonloss prevention personnel, including at times customers whose help is either sought or volunteered, all "pile on" the suspect who is face down while, if handcuffs are available, there are attempts to apply them to the suspect. Your authors support the use of handcuffs, but formal training is required and must be documented in the agent's file. If handcuffs are not available (in some cases by company policy), the suspect is spread-eagled on the ground, and one or more persons sit on him or her until the police arrive. As noted previously, these actions can lead to a vicious cycle and produce deadly results!

Loss prevention personnel (whether proprietary or contract) should be trained in proper apprehension techniques and the proper use of force. They should be aware of the potentially deadly effects of using techniques such as hogtying or sitting on a suspect who is face down on the ground as a control technique and avoid using them. If the use of handcuffs is not permitted by company policy and if the suspect cannot be controlled without risking positional asphyxia, he or she should be permitted to escape.

The following factors should be kept in mind when dealing with restrained suspects to will minimize the potential for positional asphyxia:

- Refrain from exerting pressure on the back, especially for extended periods. Exert or leverage pressure on the arms, legs, and shoulders as much as possible to control subjects while they are in the prone position.
- Move restrained individuals from the prone position or face-down position as quickly as possible. This is especially true for obese and overweight individuals. Place the subjects on their side or sit them up to allow for easier breathing.
- The LP agent has a serious responsibility to ensure suspects on the ground are breathing without interruption. One way to do that is to keep talking to them, thus evoking a verbal response. Continuously observe the subjects and be certain they appear coherent and able to communicate adequately.
- If suspects claims they cannot breathe, take immediate remedial action by changing their position to an upright one and remove any pressure from their rib cage.

We are aware of a number of concluded cases and at least two current (2006) cases wherein retailers are being sued for wrongful death caused by positional asphyxia. Needless to say, no act of shoplifting should result in the death of the shoplifter at the hands of loss prevention personnel.

Company policy regarding shoplifting apprehensions should be carefully thought out and crafted in a manner which avoids the possibility of either permitting or not affirmatively prohibiting actions which may lead to deadly results.

Auras (Guilt Auras)

CAS, JHC

There is a belief, especially amongst long-time loss prevention professionals that some agent practitioners can "see" or "sense" a guilt "aura" radiating around someone in the store who is in the process of shoplifting (or employee about to or is engaged in theft). It's that aura which attracts the attention of the LP agent. Consider this: How does a floor agent pick through hundreds or thousands of customers who shop or appear to shop in the store each day and pick out that one person who ends up stealing? One answer: auras. And consider this: Why do some agents excel in detecting shoplifters while coworkers struggle to make a detention? One answer: The former can sense auras and the latter can't.

Persons engaged in the crime (or for that matter, any evil deed) often fear their state of guilt is detectable and that makes them uneasy. That uneasiness is what makes them so "goosey" or hyper, and they dump so quickly, hence the "Oh Shit Syndrome."

It was commonly understood by experienced loss prevention practitioners in retailing that the biggest problem on the floor in catching shoplifters was some innocent customer or sales associate coming on the scene and inadvertently "burning" what surely was going to be, if uninterrupted, a theft followed by an arrest. Eye contact was all that was necessary to spoil a shoplifting act in progress. This was the nemesis of the store detective—good work shattered by innocent eye contact from someone who had no clue the customer was in the process of stealing.

In the 1970s we labeled this the "Oh Shit Syndrome," i.e., the emotional and personal reaction on the part of a person engaged in an evil deed because of the inevitable sense of guilt (guilt aura) and belief he or she has been detected by virtue of seeing someone looking at him o her. It wasn't a "scientifically" proven phenomenon, but rather recognition of a predictable reality.

Award Programs

CAS, JHC

Award programs which reward sales associates with cash rewards for alertness to both external and internal theft can be an effective antitheft tool.

Rewards are normally paid to employees who report customers they believe are attempting to shoplift, provided the customer is subsequently apprehended and stolen merchandise is recovered.

Most such programs provide for minimum and maximum reward dollars, with some programs tying the amount of the reward to the value of the merchandise recovered.

These same programs can reward employees for reporting employee theft and frauds against the company.

Figure A-1 shows a typical incentive award program.

We also suggest that the award be presented in person by the corporate head of loss prevention (LP) or the highest level LP executive available.

loss prevention incentive award program	The Loss Prevention Incentive Award Program provides employees of with an opportunity to share in substantial awards (see Award Formula on reverse side) and at the same time help reduce our inventory shortages.
	awards 50.00 to 1000.00

award formula	**Shoplifters**	**Credit Cards**	**Internal Dishonesty**
	10% of the retail value of merchandise recovered with a minimum award of 50.00 and a maximun award of 1000.00.	10% of the retail value of merchandise recovered with a minimum award of 50.00 and a maximum award of 1000.00.	10% of recovered merchandise value, or 10% of money recovered, with a minimum award of 200.00 and a maximum award of 1000.00

FIGURE A-1 Award program.

In addition to the award itself, we also encourage that a letter along the lines of that shown here be given to the reward recipient.

Company Letterhead
Loss Prevention Department

TO: Recipient's name

Thank you very much for your alertness and assistance to this department.

Losses to our company are of continuous concern, and it is gratifying that employees such as you are dedicated to protecting the best interests of (*Company name*).

I am pleased to have you receive this award for your alertness, and a copy of this letter will be forwarded to the Human Resources department for inclusion in your personnel record.

Thank you again. Your cooperation is greatly appreciated.

Sincerely,

Signed by Senior LP Executive

Cc: HR VP

 B

Badges and Identification Cards

CAS, JHC

A metallic badge is universally recognized as a symbol of lawful authority. In the classic film "*The Treasure of the Sierra Madre,*" the Mexican outlaw identified himself and his gang to the prospector (Humphrey Bogart) as a "federales." The prospector then asked, "If you're the police, where are your badges?" The bad guy responded, "Badges!? We ain't got no badges. We don't need no badges! I don't have to show you any stinking badges!" That line, often quoted, has proven over time to be a classic touch of humor, but failure to display credentials doesn't bode well in the retail industry.

Perhaps one of the most common reasons given by a detainee for his or her refusal to comply with the request or instructions to return to the store is, "I didn't know who this person (loss prevention, or LP, agent) was; he didn't identify himself". "I thought maybe I was going to be mugged." In reality, customers who are challenged outside the store are entitled to know the individual confronting them is a *bona fide* representative of the company and is authorized by state law to stop and question persons involved in what appears to be suspicious conduct. The display of credentials such as a badge and identification card speaks volumes about that authority. A badge is universally instantly recognized as a symbol of authority. Its display immediately upon a detention should remove any doubts as to the holder's authority and remove any fears the detainees may have that their safety is at risk.

Typical examples of LP badges are shown in Figures B-1 and B-2.

Hence, we encourage every retailer to provide such credentials for their LP/security employees. These company badges should bear a number and be controlled and signed for in a department badge control ledger. When an employee leaves the company, termination procedures must require the turning in of the badge. Promotions within the department should allow for the exchange of badges to the next rank. If a badge is reported lost or stolen, the ledger is so noted, and the employee should be required to pay the costs for replacement. The badges, while shaped like those of law enforcement, should clearly indicate that the holder is not a law enforcement officer but represents private security/loss prevention.

Coincidentally, while we were consulting with a large and prestigious department store chain in Mexico, the LP employees complained they were denied the use of badges, and that posed a problem for them when making detentions. Further investigation revealed there was a cultural objection to private sector personnel possessing "police-type" badges, and the company was guided by that sentiment. But the agents needed identification; their complaint was valid. What to do? We designed a gold metallic card, the size of a regular ID card, inscribed with the word "SECURIDAD" and the name of the company and encased the card behind a plastic window in a two-window folded leather case. When the case was opened and presented to a shoplifter, the suspect saw the gold card and a colored identification card with photo and description of the agent. The issue was therefore resolved to everyone's satisfaction.

There's no one right or wrong way for agents to carry and exhibit their badge. We've noted some agents carry the badge on their waist belt, whereas others wear the badge like a necklace and pull it out from their shirt, blouse, or jacket when needed. Others, more commonly, carry the badge along with their ID card in a leather case designed for that purpose

FIGURE B-1 Shield badge

FIGURE B-2 Star badge

and produce the opened case when needed. *A note of warning:* Badges worn like a necklace must have a "break-away" chain or cord in the event that necklace is seized by a combative subject.

Over the years some retailers have established rules that prohibit LP employees from taking the badge home, but the majority have no such restriction. However, written policy should spell out the restrictions on the badge's use; e.g., it must never be displayed, except while "on the clock" and in the line of duty when confronting a detainee.

Loss prevention identification cards are separate from any company ID cards, and are designed specifically for the LP department. The name of the department—Loss Prevention, Loss Control, Security, Security and Safety, or Assets Protection—should be in color and the dominant feature of the card. The secondary feature should be a colored "driver's license" type photo. The balance of information on the card would be boilerplate, name, age, description, etc., and issuer's signature (vice president of LP).

Balancing a Cash Register

CAS, JHC

It is important that cash registers be balanced daily. Following is one example of how that is achieved. The store owner or manager should begin with the amount of cash in the till at the start of the day and end with the amount of cash at the end of the day (accounting for any funds removed during the day, "drops"). The amount of sales, "returns" (or cash paid out to vendors etc.), is then calculated, and when all data is factored in, the register condition (over, short, or balanced) is arrived at.

End Reading (Detail tape)	13249.00
Start Reading	12345.00
[Register records both sales and credits]	
	- - - - - - - - - - -
TOTAL Sales:	$ 904.00
Cash Sales $ 829.00	
Credit Sales $ 75.00	
SALES CASH TO ACCOUNT FOR	$ 829.00
PLUS SETUP	$ 100.00
TOTAL GROSS CASH TO ACCOUNT FOR	**$ 929.00**
TOTAL PAYOUTS	120.00
Bottle Refunds $ 20	
(Documented by paper records*)	
Refunds* $ 50	
Pay Vendor* $ 50	
(Documented by bottles)	
Bottle Refunds $ 20	
TOTAL DEDUCTIONS FROM CASH SALES	$ 120.00
TOTAL CASH TO ACCOUNT FOR	**$ 809.00**
Less Drops	500.00
NET CASH TO ACCOUNT FOR	**$ 309.00**
Cash turned in end of shift	$ 209.00
Cash left for Set-up	$ 100.00
Total	$ 309.00
NET CASH ACCOUNTED FOR	**$ 309.00**
REGISTER IN BALANCE	

Bank Deposits

Curtis Baillie

Making the Deposit

My first experience in making bank deposits was working part time for the security department of an amusement park. Every day, except Sundays, we would drive the cash receipts, at times totaling several million dollars, to the bank and return with the change order.

The responsibility for making the deposits rested with the security department and was a major event. We were escorted to the bank by no fewer than eight municipal police officers in four marked cars, and all officers were armed with either shotguns or Smith and Wesson 9mm submachine guns. Why the amusement park never used an armored service was beyond me.

Making bank deposits in the retail environment can be a stressful event. Many companies choose to have their management teams make them. This decision is usually made as a cost-saving factor, as armored car services are expensive. The newspapers are full of crime stories where employees have been robbed, injured, or killed while making bank deposits. Employees even stage fake robberies at deposit boxes to cover up an employee theft. One such incident occurred when a management employee making a bank deposit on a Sunday morning reported being stabbed, with a knife, in the back by a robber who took the bank bag containing $15,000. Several things were wrong with this robbery, as he had his mother drive him to the bank, parking on the opposite corner from the drop box. It just didn't sound right. There was even a "witness" standing across the street who observed the entire robbery. As it turned out, he staged the robbery, having his "witness" friend, a well-known local criminal, stab him in the back. It did not take long for the manager's girlfriend, who worked in another store, to start bragging about the robbery and how much money her boyfriend received.

Safety in Numbers

If a company chooses to make its own bank deposits, there should always be two members of management making the deposit. Deposits should be made during the daytime, as it is safer to do so. If deposits must be made during the nighttime hours, after closing, the following safety suggestions must be considered:

- Always make deposits after the store is closed. You do not want customers in the store.
- Remove your name badge or cover your company uniform. You do not need to advertise your company while going to the bank.
- Always drive your deposit to the bank, even if your bank is close by in the same shopping center. Always have two people making the deposit.
- One person should exit the store with the second person remaining inside with the doors locked.
- Drive around the parking lot checking for suspicious cars or people. The person conducting the parking lot check should have a cell phone. If you see anything suspicious, drive to a safe location and call the police department.
- If all is clear, drive to main entrance; shine the headlights on the door. The other employee, with the cash, should now exit and immediately enter the vehicle. This is not the time to have a casual smoke before going to the bank.
- Proceed directly to the bank. Drive around the bank, again looking for anything suspicious. If all is clear, proceed to the drop box.
- Quickly make the deposit and leave the bank.

Your Deposit Is Missing

Many thoughts come to mind when you get the phone call from your company's Treasury or Finance department advising you of a missing bank deposit. The first questions you ask yourself are, "Is it cash and checks or just missing cash, and were the checks deposited?" Was it an internal theft, or was the money taken by a bank employee? In the case of robbery at the deposit drop box, was it really a robbery? After you have interviewed the employees responsible for making the deposit and are reasonably comfortable that the deposit was made, it's now time to call the bank.

Where's My Money?

When you are investigating missing bank deposits, it's key to remember that the money may be at the bank. One of the first steps is to call the bank and ask if it has any "unclaimed" funds for the date of your missing deposit. Banks keep unaccounted for funds for one year. At the end of their accounting year, banks will claim the money as assets of the bank. It never hurts to ask if the bank has unaccounted for or unclaimed cash on the date of your deposit; if so, the bank will give you the money.

When contacting the bank, ask for the branch manager. The bank representative should be willing to fully cooperate with you; you're the customer. Ask questions regarding the processing of night deposits. Make careful notes of the answers to your questions, as during your investigation you may find that the bank is not following its own internal policies. Following are some questions to ask.

What Are Your Policies for Checking in Deposits?

Most banks require two people to check in deposits from the drop box. Both employees are required to sign the check in-log. Banks use a log sheet, recording the date and time your deposit was removed from the box and if the integrity of the deposit bag was intact. In one "missing deposit" case, the bank manager boldly stated, "My bank did not receive the deposit." Two weeks later the same manager called stating the bank was crediting the missing funds. When asked why, he replied, "One of my tellers went on vacation, and when they returned, our deposit was located in one of their unlocked desk drawers."

Where Are Deposit Bags Held While Waiting to Be Checked In?

Surprisingly, some banks keep your deposit on a counter or cart in the teller area of the bank while waiting to be counted. In one such investigation, when we were visiting the bank, the "checked-in" deposits were sitting on a counter within easy reach of bank customers. When this discrepancy was brought to the attention of the bank officials, our account was quickly credited, as they were in violation of their own internal cash-handling policies.

When Is My Deposit Verified?

Normally, banks verify deposits later in the afternoon and have a difficult time detailing what happened to your bag. In one such case, the bank received the deposit at 9:00 a.m., as verified by its check-in log. At 3:00 p.m. when the teller conducted the bag examination, prior to counting the funds, he found the cash portion of the bag ripped open and the cash was missing. The bank launched an investigation and discovered who took the cash.

Where Is the Deposit Verified?

If your deposit is not processed at the depositing bank, it is transported to an offsite location or "cash vault" to be counted. Take the time to make an appointment to visit and tour this location. If you can, visit the vault with your finance or operations executives. You may find discrepancies such a poor video quality of the cash count cages. On one tour, it was found that individual cash count booths were only on camera for a 3-second period, every 27 seconds, and cash counters were allowed to keep their coats and purses in their booths. When asked about the coats and purses, the vault manager stated that the union had fought to let the counters keep their personal articles in the counting booths, and the bank was unable to change its policies. Other security discrepancies were discovered, and our company quickly moved the account to another banking operation. Amazingly, our missing cash problems stopped.

How Long Do You Keep Your Trash?

Most bank policies require branches to bag and keep their deposit verification trash for 7–10 days. If you find the bank has not followed its own internal policy, you have an excellent chance of getting your credit.

When Was the Last Time a Physical Inspection of Your Drop Box Was Made?

Many times the deposit is still in the drop box. A bank in the Boston area advised that it would cost $1,000 to have the drop box dismantled to see if our six missing deposits were still in the box. (The actual cost to the bank to dismantle and inspect the box was $70.) They stated that if the deposits were found they would pay the costs, and if not, my company would be charged. After the drop box was opened, all six deposits were found. The practice of charging customers to dismantle the deposit drop box is becoming more popular with banks. The charge of $1,000 is the highest I have encountered. Usually, the cost, if any, is around $65. If a bank wants to charge for a deposit box inspection, it's to discourage you from having the bank do it. If you have developed a solid business relationship with the bank manager, there should be no charge.

Involving the Police

A police report should be made regarding every missing deposit case. Managers have called and confessed to taking deposits after the police have left the store. Just the police showing up and taking an initial report has an effect and tells store staff that you take the matter seriously. Often, when talking by telephone to the person responsible for making the deposit, they ask, "Is it really necessary to involve the police?" This type of response may indicate the problem is at the store. After having this discussion, managers have called back within 15 minutes to say, "I made a mistake."

When the police visit the bank, in response to your complaint to a missing deposit, they ask many of the same questions you do. Often, you will get a call from the bank after the police leave, telling you, "Your company is such a good customer; we don't know if the deposit was made or not, but we're going to credit your account." From a law enforcement point of view, the last thing a bank wants is the police asking questions about its internal operations. It's not that the bank has anything to hide; it is just uncomfortable with the whole process.

In Summary

It is important to remember banks have operational issues, just as your stores have. Make the effort to contact and introduce yourself to your bank security officials; they are there to help you solve your issues. In the rare instance when a bank branch is unwilling to cooperate, contact the bank's security department. You will receive immediate attention to your problem. In one case, a bank's deposit box had a loose screw on the inside. The screw, protruding about one-half inch, was in danger of snaring the plastic deposit bags as they traveled down the chute. The store manager stated he contacted the bank manager several times about the screw, and his efforts were ignored. After the store manager contacted the bank's security department, the deposit box was repaired on the day of his telephone call. Remember, you're the customer.

Best Practice: Shoplifting

IAPSC

Best Practice #1: Detaining Shoplifting Suspects

May 1999

The only known "best practice" that applies to or in any way has been accepted in the Loss Prevention industry is the 1999 "best practice #1" propounded by the IAPSC, and its committee members who developed this "practice" include your authors."

The International Association of Professional Security Consultants is issuing this consensus-based best practice for the guidance of and voluntary use by businesses and individuals who deal or may deal with the issues addressed herein.

A. Background

Definition: As used in this bulletin, the term "security person(s)" is intended to include only store proprietors and managers, store plainclothes security agents sometimes called "detectives," and uniformed security officers also called "security guards" (either proprietary or contract). The term does not include sales clerks, maintenance persons, or stockers, for example. The term "security person(s)" is not intended to apply to off-duty public law enforcement or special police personnel unless they have been instructed by store management to follow the same procedures required of ordinary citizens, which procedures do not include police powers of arrest.

1. Shoplifting is a serious threat to the profitability of retail stores. Losses in stores from shoplifting amount to billions of dollars a year. The public is affected by the increases in prices resulting from shoplifting losses.

2. The ultimate purpose of security precautions in stores is to keep merchandise items in the stores unless they have been paid for by customers. Loss prevention practices and procedures both deter and detect the theft of merchandise. Detention for further arrest and prosecution is a last resort to be used only when other security precautions have failed to keep unpaid-for-merchandise in the store.

3. In almost all jurisdictions in the United States, merchants are legally empowered to detain shoplifting suspects for investigation and possible arrest and prosecution in the criminal justice system. This power is called "merchant's privilege."

    a. The merchant's privilege provides for detention of persons suspected of shoplifting only when probable cause or reasonable cause exists to believe a person has committed theft. The best practice for establishing this probable cause (as compared to any legal standard) is the security person's having met all the following six steps: (1) observe the customer approach the merchandise, (2) observe the customer select the merchandise, (3) observe the customer conceal (or otherwise carry away) the merchandise, (4) keep the customer under constant and uninterrupted observation, (5) see the customer fail to pay for the merchandise, and (6) detain the customer outside the store.

    b. The merchant's privilege permits detention for limited purposes which vary by state. Common among these limited purposes are (1) ascertaining that stolen merchandise is possessed by the suspect, (2) identifying the suspect, (3) investigating the alleged theft, (4) recovering stolen merchandise, and (5) notifying the police of the offense. Some states permit limited searches of the suspect, and some states limit the extent to which identity may be established; the use of force which can legally be used is, if mentioned, always nondeadly. Many company or store policies further restrict permissible actions in dealing with shoplifting suspects, e.g., prohibiting pursuing suspects beyond company property.

4. In some circumstances shoplifting suspects are treated incorrectly by store management and security persons. Such treatment may cause results varying from simple mistakes to the violation of civil rights of suspects. If a best practice is not used, it is better not to detain a suspect than to risk the high cost of a civil liability suit. Two kinds of questionable detentions will illustrate this point. One kind applies to the customer who is truly an innocent party but whose conduct, for any number of reasons, led the security person to believe that a theft had occurred. People in this kind of detention are innocent victims of circumstance. The other kind applies to the customer who is not truly an innocent party, but for any number of reasons is not in possession of stolen merchandise when stopped by a security person.

5. Security persons usually do not actually "arrest" shoplifters but simply detain them for police authorities. Exceptions arise to this practice in those states where private persons' arrest powers exist concurrent with but separate from the "privilege" statutes discussed previously. In these exceptional cases, security persons arrest after proof of the offense of theft.

6. Security persons cannot look into the minds of suspects. Security persons can only observe actions of suspects and completely and accurately report such actions. It is up to a judge or trier of fact to determine intent to deprive a merchant permanently of a taken item. See the discussion in 3.a. Step 6 exists to help the judge or trier of fact determine the intent of the customer because the cash registers inside a store are normally the last place a person would have to pay for an item before departing a store. Reports by security persons are normally detailed enough to include other observations which would tend to establish intent.

The International Association of Professional Security Consultants, Inc. (IAPSC) has examined the methods of detaining suspects recommended by security professionals and practiced by merchants throughout the United States. IAPSC sets forth in the following section what it believes to be the best practices.

B. Best Practices

1. *Practice.* Security persons using best practices detain a suspect only if they have personally seen the suspect approach the merchandise.
   Rationale. The suspect may have entered the store with the merchandise already in hand or otherwise on or about his or her person (say, in a shopping bag or purse).
2. *Practice.* Security persons using best practices detain a suspect only if they have personally observed the suspect select or take possession of or conceal the merchandise.
   Rationale. Security persons trust their own eyes and do not rely on reports by others.
3. *Practice.* Security persons using best practices detain a suspect only if they have observed the suspect with the merchandise continually from the point of selection to the point where the suspect has gone beyond the last checkout station without paying for the item. If the surveillance has been broken, or if the person has gotten rid of the merchandise, the security person breaks off following for that offense but may continue surveillance if it appears the suspect may commit theft again.
   Rationale. The suspect may have "ditched" the merchandise or concealed it. By continually observing the suspect, the security person can observe whether or not the suspect still has the merchandise even if it has been concealed on the suspect's person.
4. *Practice.* Security persons using best practices detain a suspect outside the store after the suspect has passed the last checkout station and has failed to pay for an item of merchandise. At this point security persons using this best practice immediately investigate to verify or refute a suspect's claim of innocence. Special care and consideration are exercised when merchandise is displayed for sale outside the store, such as garden supplies, sidewalk sales, etc., or which is displayed for sale inside the store, but beyond the last sales point.
   Rationale. The security person does not do only what is required to meet the minimum requirements of theft laws. The actions of a suspect make it easier to prove intent to deprive the merchant of an item of merchandise. The farther from the actual taking a suspect is detained, the clearer the offense will appear to a judge or trier of fact. The security person is aware of suspects who might claim they were looking for a matching item or looking for someone to give an opinion on the merchandise before it is purchased. A suspect may, however, offer a logical explanation for actions that initially appeared to the security person to be acts of shoplifting, but which may require only a limited investigation to verify the suspect's explanation.
5. *Practice.* Security persons using best practices normally do not "chase" suspects by running inside a store or in shopping centers that are occupied by customers. Exceptions occur when necessary, but only in such areas as parking lots, and then only when few people are in the area and it is unlikely a bystander could get hurt. Such foot pursuits never leave the property on which the store is located.
   If a suspect runs, the best practice is for the security person to make a mental note of the appearance of the suspect and the merchandise that appears to have been taken and then to make a written report for the store's files.

Rationale. Running may create more problems than it solves. When a suspect runs and a security person chases that person by also running, clients and employees of the store and store employees are endangered more by the combination of two persons running than by the suspect's running alone. Handicapped clients may be knocked off their feet. Wheelchairs may be overturned. Store employees who may intervene to help may be injured by security persons in pursuit, or by running into counters or display devices, or by slipping on polished floors. When clerks leave their posts, they leave their own merchandise exposed to theft. An exception to this best practice may exist when it is necessary to chase down a suspect to protect customers and store employees from ongoing violence by the suspect.

6. *Practice.* Security persons using best practices treat suspects equally and fairly regardless of a suspect's race, color, creed, gender, or national origin.
Rationale. Anecdotal information suggests certain groups have been marked by some store management and security persons for more surveillance and/or more aggressive antishoplifting measures. Color, religious or national dress, gender, and "race" are alleged to have been used to identify persons in such groups. However, there is no scientific evidence regarding the validity of such "profiling," and this practice is avoided by security persons using best practices. Suspicion of shoplifting depends on observed actions, not appearance. All law-abiding persons have the right to be treated the same as any other person in the marketplace.

7. *Practice.* Security persons using best practices do not use weapons such as firearms, batons ("nightsticks"), or restraining devices such as thumb cuffs, "come-alongs," mace, or pepper spray in order to apprehend or detain a shoplifting suspect. Stores using best practices occasionally permit the use of handcuffs by security persons whose training has included instruction in the proper use of handcuffs when necessary to prevent injury to customers or store personnel. Security persons using best practices use handcuffs only when a suspected shoplifter is physically threatening violence or otherwise resisting detention; or there is, in the good judgment of the security person, the risk of imminent serious harm absent their use.
Rationale. There is no merchandise of such value that it warrants a security person's injuring a suspect or an innocent customer. Use of weapons and restraining devices except handcuffs should be left to on-duty public law enforcement officers. If it is not possible to get the suspect's willing cooperation, it is better to let the suspect go free than to risk injuring a suspect or other customer. Risk avoidance is a factor considered in apprehending and detaining suspects. Because handcuffs are restraining devices, they can be painful if improperly applied and can cause injury. Not all persons caught need restraining. Many people caught shoplifting are humiliated by the incident and are cooperative; hence, in such cases restraint is not necessary.

8. *Practice.* Security persons using best practices limit the use of force to "holding" or "restraining" to effect a detention. Security persons using best practices do not use actions such as striking, tackling, sitting on a suspect's body, or any other action that might cause physical injury to the suspect.
Rationale. Use of force is subject to criticism, and assaultive use of force is typically unnecessary and unacceptable in the private sector. However, some holding or restraining may be necessary lest potential thieves learn that by simply resisting they may come and steal with impunity. Use of limited holding or restraining force is sometimes necessary to detain a suspect until police arrive, or to prevent a suspect from injuring security persons. Under no circumstances should the force applied be that which may result in injury or death to a suspect. No merchandise is of such value as to justify physical injury to a suspect. The better practice is to allow the suspect to depart the premises rather than to cause any injury by the use of force in detaining the suspect. Assuming the suspect can be identified, the merchant can file a complaint; then the public police have the option of apprehending the suspect at a later time.

and educational purposes only, and which are not to be considered as legal advice. The IAPSC specifically disclaims all liability for any damages alleged to result from or arise out of any use or misuse of these guidelines.

Bomb Threats

CAS, JHC

Bomb threats are generally received by larger big box stores rather than the "Mom and Pop" stores. The reason is that the larger stores not only provide more opportunity and locations for hiding bombs but also because they have the potential for paying larger amounts of money when bombs are planted for extortion purposes. Why are bombs planted within retail establishments? There are several possible reasons:

- To create a situation which demands a store evacuation, sometimes done to provide an employee legitimate time off or by an outsider who gets satisfaction from the excitement such situations create.
- To create confusion or uncertainty within a store, which, if it receives publicity, may lead to reduced sales; this situation has been known to be a technique used by disgruntled employees or those who are in the midst of divisive labor negotiations.
- To create confusion and disruption to achieve some sought-after objective by an advocacy group, such as the animal rights organizations, who seek an objective of the discontinuance of fur sales.
- As a means of creating fear for extortion purposes.
- Security personnel have also been known to have been responsible for bomb threats (and fires) and then become "heroes" when they "discover" the threat.

How should bomb threats be dealt with? The answer depends on a variety of factors. You must attempt to verify the reliability of the source of the threat. Was it by phone or letter? Was there specific information regarding the nature of the device or the reason it was allegedly planted? Any written letter, envelope, or note should be handled with care to preserve any evidentiary value it may have.

The level of the threat must be assessed. If the threat is carried out, who would be harmed and how badly? Is the threat against people or property? How easy would it be to get access to the threatened target? What is known (or can be learned) about the person making the threat and his or her motivation for doing so?

Let me describe some actual cases and how they were handled.

In the first case, an individual who was a member of a bargaining unit and was, unfortunately, one of the last persons hired for Christmas help was also one of the first persons laid off after the holidays. Shortly after being laid off, this person lost his girl friend, was thrown out of his apartment for failure to pay his rent, and had his car stolen, which contained most of his personal belongings. He was then rehired again but, after a very short period of employment, was laid off again. He blamed the company for his misfortunes and was heard to say when being laid off the second time that he was going to get a gun and shoot up the Human Resources department.

When this information came to light, we had some decisions to make. We obviously had a responsibility to keep the members of the HR department from harm. We decided to do several things to help us assess the level of the threat and its likelihood of performance. We immediately initiated a thorough background investigation of the subject and learned the subject had previously been successfully prosecuted for a weapons violation and was a likely narcotics user. This investigation was completed within 4 hours; we determined the subject had the ability to perform and the level of threat was quite high.

Our next step was to locate the subject, who was now living on the street. We established surveillances (we obtained extra manpower from outside agencies) on places where the subject was likely to show up. We utilized a recent photo taken for his employee ID badge. We also hired armed off-duty police officers to maintain a stakeout of his former work area in the store and the HR area.

Out subject was located within 24 hours, and we maintained a round-the-clock surveillance of him for the next 2 weeks. With the first few days, we discontinued the surveillances within the store, but we were in radio contact with the surveillance teams working the subject. We arranged for armed response if the subject got within one block of the store.

The entire effort was terminated after 2 weeks because the subject showed absolutely no indication he intended to do us any harm and, in fact, had obtained employment some distance from our store. An agent who was able to converse with the subject at a bar was convinced the subject had no intention of carrying out his threat.

Our efforts in this case cost the company about $40,000. However, in such cases cost should not be an issue; the company's legal liability was tremendous, particularly with the foreseeability which existed.

The second case involved an employee who literally jumped over the personnel manager's desk during his termination interview and began beating the female manager with his fists. Her cries drew help, and the employee was arrested, charged with battery, and imprisoned. The personnel manager was sent to the hospital for treatment and released.

We ascertained the suspect would be released from the city jail with a day; we then established a surveillance at his residence. We also posted armed off-duty police in the HR area of the store.

We then learned that the subject intended to leave the state as soon as he was legally permitted to do so. We worked with the district attorney and our subject's attorney to facilitate his move and were able to conclude our protective services at the end of a week. It was also important in this case to spend a considerable amount of time with our personnel manager reassuring her that she was safe and her home was also secure. Again, we had arrangements made to respond to her home if the subject moved in that direction, but we also had every reason to believe he did not know where she lived and that he would not be able to easily obtain that information.

The final case was not really a threat but rather an "incident."

At a major company function, an employee, about to retire, ran up to the stage, grabbed the podium microphone, and began exhorting the audience to listen to some imagined wrong he had suffered. The master of ceremonies was able to get the mic back, and since the event was just about over, our subject proceeded to corner our chairman and tell him his story. Security responded and removed the chairman from the area. No threats were made, but the incident did shake up several people, and the question arose as to what further action might be expected from our retiring (or not so retiring) employee.

Our objective in this case was to protect our chairman from any untoward incidents. We again conducted a background investigation of our subject; he had no criminal record. We determined that, while he was quite vocal, he was not a violent person. We did alert the local police in the town where the chairman lived and arranged for extra police patrols of his residence. In this case, that was the extent of our efforts.

In most cases, threats from outsiders or nonemployees are harder to deal with because it is more difficult to obtain detailed information about the subject.

Whenever these types of incidents arise, they should be handled in such a manner as to protect the individuals involved with as little disruption to their normal routine as possible. We must also, while protecting the company and its personnel, protect the privacy of the subjects, since, in many cases, they have committed no crime. True, they have made threatening statements (which do not rise to the level of an assault) or taken some legal but disquieting action which gives rise to potential harm. Through the use of normal investigative tools and resources, most such threats can be neutralized, people and property protected, liability limited, and one hopes, the subjects will never know how much attention they have attracted.

In the case of bomb threats, which arrive either by letter or by phone, we must attempt to ascertain as much information about the threat as quickly as possible.

If the threat specifies a location where the bomb is planted, that area should be discreetly cordoned off (a water leak can be used as a nonthreatening reason for the area's evacuation), and a search for any suspicious packages should be made. Persons doing the searching should be cautioned that, if anything suspicious is found, not to touch it or attempt to move it, both for safety and evidentiary reasons.

The police should always be alerted to any bomb threats received, and if a suspicious package or device is found, they should be the ones to deal with it.

The question always arises as to whether to evacuate the store. Generally, stores are not evacuated based on a threat only unless, of course, there is other information which makes the threat more creditable. This decision is a management decision, one hopes, made after consultation with security personnel or the police. Experience has shown the police will not recommend evacuation if a search is underway. If a device or suspicious package is found, an area within a radius of 300 feet should be cleared. If the police recommend evacuation, their advice is normally followed, recognizing that store management must make this decision.

We suggest that, for larger stores, a "bomb board" be created. This board, located in a management office, consists of a series of 3 × 5 search cards, each defining a specific area and/or objects (e.g., trash receptacles) to be searched. These cards should be distributed to those conducting the search to assure that no search area will be missed. Every effort should be made to use volunteers for the search who are familiar with the search area and can recognize which "do not belong." The bomb board also contains the procedures to be followed when bomb threats are received.

Recommended procedures are as follows:

1. Complete the Bomb Threat Checklist (see Figure B-3). Record all descriptive data about the caller, such as age, sex, mannerisms, accents, exact words used, etc.
2. Person receiving the phoned bomb treat should be attentive for any identifiable background noises.
3. Person taking the call should press the caller for a specific location of the bomb and/or the general area of its location. Attempt to keep caller on the line as long as possible.
4. If a device is found, and it has been determined to evacuate the store, such evacuation should be done in a manner that does not create a panic. We suggest the following language:

    "May I have your attention please. In cooperation with civil defense authorities, we are conducting a test evacuation of this store. Please leave the store immediately by walking to the nearest exit. We will return to normal business shortly. Thank you."

This message should be repeated twice. If the building is evacuated, the building must be properly secured and all cash registers must be closed and locked. In addition, any cash rooms, vaults, safes, etc., should be secured.

It must be kept in mind that bombs may also include incendiary devices.

One of your authors had the experience of dealing with five incendiary devices planted in three stores in the greater Bay Area between Thanksgiving 1989 and January 1990. The devices were designed to start a fire, not explode. An investigation by store security, local police, and federal agencies never produced positive identification of the person(s) responsible. It was established, however, that the devices were constructed identical to devices described in a United Kingdom publication promulgated by an activist group; it was only because our devices were made with a minor flaw that none ever reached their intended potential.

In this situation, we notified all store personnel at all nearby locations of the problem and sought their assistance in being alert to and reporting any strange or seemingly out-of-place objects to store security. We also prepared and had a senior security executive give a TV news interview in which he stated: "A nonexplosive, fire-starting device was found in (*store named*) today. It was discovered in the furniture department by our security personnel,

BOMB THREAT CHECKLIST

Instructions:

1) When a bomb threat is received, interrupt the caller immediately and ask him to repeat the message After he has done so, ask him the following questions:

When will it go off? _____

Where is it located? _____

What does it look like? _____

What floor is it on? _____

What is your name and address? _____

How do you know so much about the bomb? _____

Do you know this buliding is occupied and people could be injured? _____

The above questions should be asked spontaneously, giving the caller very little time to think about his answers.

When the call is completed – fill in the following checklist.

Time call received _____

Caller's identity –   Male _____   Female _____   Adult _____   Juvenile _____

Approximate Age _____

Origin of call – Local _____   Long Distance _____   Internal _____

Voice Characteristics		*Speech*	
_____ Loud	_____ Soft	_____ Fast	_____ Slow
_____ High Pitch	_____ Deep	_____ Distinct	_____ Distorted
_____ Raspy	_____ Pleasant	_____ Stutter	_____ Nasal
_____ Intoxicated	_____ Other	_____ Slurred	_____ Lisp
			_____ Other

Language		*Accent*	
_____ Excellent	_____ Good	_____ Local	_____ Not Local
_____ Fair	_____ Poor	_____ Foreign	
_____ Foul	_____ Other	_____ Race	

Manner		*Background Noises*	
_____ Calm	_____ Angry	_____ Mechanical	_____ Trains
_____ Rational	_____ Irrational	_____ Bedlam	_____ Animals
_____ Coherent	_____ Emotional	_____ Music	_____ Quiet
_____ Deliberate	_____ Incoherent	_____ Office Machines	_____ Airplanes
_____ Righteous	_____ Laughing	_____ Mixed	_____ Party Atmosphere
		_____ Street Traffic	

Call Security and Senior Executive on duty immediately.

Name of Operator _____

FIGURE B-3: Bomb threat checklist

who are familiar with this type of incendiary device. As a purely precautionary measure to ensure the safety of our customers and employees, who were not in any immediate danger, we evacuated the floor. The device was then removed by ATF [Bureau of Alcohol, Tobacco and Firearms], a federal agency.

BURGLARY (24-hour stores, e.g., Convenience Stores, Gas Stations, Drug, Grocery, and Liquor Stores)

Ralph Witherspoon

"Commercial burglary" is generally defined as the unauthorized entry by force or stealth into any portion of a business for the purpose of stealing anything of value or, in some states, committing any felony.

Today, the majority of convenience stores and gas stations operate 24 hours a day, 7 days a week. Some drug, grocery, and liquor stores also remain open around the clock. As such, except for stealthy trespass into stock areas or break-ins of isolated storage areas or sheds, they are not subject to commercial burglary risks. Even when planned to operate 24/7, however, they may be at risk if they close on a holiday, or in the event of a weather or other emergency. And some stores do, of course, have non-24-hour operations or regular closings.

There are two primary defenses against a burglary: physical barriers to deter or slow entry and measures to detect a break-in if it does occur and summon appropriate response.

Most burglars enter through an existing door or window.

While most owners can't do much about the plate glass windows and glass doors common on the front of stores, side and rear doors and windows are another matter. Such doors should

- Be of hollow metal securely attached to a metal doorframe, which should be firmly attached to the building walls (the door "system" is only as strong as its weakest part).
- Use a spring latch, *plus* a key-operated deadbolt with at least a 1-inch bolt throw. A latch-guard should cover the locking area.
- If possible, use one or two hand-operated bolts or bars attached to the inside of the door to increase its resistance to forceful entry.

Check for other "easy" openings into back areas, such as windows, which can be broken, and wall-mounted air conditioners, which can be pushed in. Both should be replaced with cinder block or other solid building materials. Check for exterior entry restrooms that may have drop-ceilings, permitting entry into the store, or roof entry points.

Safes, including time-delay safes, should be bolted or cemented to the floor to prevent their being simply taken away for later break-in.

High-value stock such as cigarette cartons should be stored in interior "safe rooms" equipped with locked doors.

Slowing down a burglar doesn't do any good if he or she still has hours in which to commit the crime. Detection of entry is essential. Magnetic alarm contacts on the doors, including interior "safe rooms," is a basic requirement. Front doors should also be equipped with glass-break tape or sensors. They should be supplemented with interior motion detectors in the front sales area and the rear stockroom area. Do not rely on an alarm signal being transmitted only over the store's telephone line. Backup signals can be sent using either a radio signal or by cell phone signal. Consult with your alarm company to ensure that, when you need it, your alarm signal will be transmitted under any circumstance. All except the most amateur burglars know to cut the phone lines before trying to enter.

In some situations, stores routinely close using roll-down type metal covers to protect their front doors and windows. These are good, but still need backup at other possible entry points, plus alarms to detect and report any actual intrusion.

Because they are usually not present, the risk of injury or death to employees or customers usually doesn't exist in a commercial burglary. Damages to the building and loss of stock can, however, severely cripple or even bankrupt the business. If a burglar can't be deterred by a business's security measures, detection devices can often summon police or contact security response in time to reduce losses, or even apprehend the burglar before he or she escapes.

Cables

CAS, JHC

The use of clear plastic-coated 1/8- or 3/16-inch steel airplane cable to secure expensive ready-to-wear (RTW) merchandise to fixtures is an effective antitheft technique. The cables are placed through a sleeve, passed over the fixture hanging rod, and have loops at each end which can then be secured together with a small padlock. This arrangement prevents the merchandise from being removed and carried away from the fixture. Merchandise typically secured by this physical control strategy means includes leather jackets and men's suits.

An alternative to the preceding technique is using cables with one end with a ball-like fitting, which in turn fits into a slot in a lockable box-like receptacle. When this arrangement is used, the ball end of the cable is inserted through the loop and then secured in the lockable receptacle.

A third variation of cable-securing devices is the use of small diameter (1/16 or 3/16 inch) electrical two-conductor cable, which connects into a fixture that completes an electrical circuit when the cable is in place. The cable is affixed to the merchandise in the same manner as the nonelectrical cable. If, however, the cable is cut or otherwise removed from its retaining receptacle, an audible alarm sounds, alerting sales associates to the fact that some merchandise is no longer secured.

Modified forms of both the electrical and nonelectrical cables are frequently used to secure electronic equipment such as laptops, digital cameras, and other expensive electronics.

Case Management and Electronic Incident Reporting

Jason Elwell

In recent years, we have seen an explosive growth in the area of loss prevention (LP) technology. Retailers are choosing to implement expensive solutions like digital video systems and exception-based reporting software in hopes that these solutions will help investigators to control shrink more effectively.

Recently, loss prevention departments have begun to invest in centralized incident reporting systems. Incident reporting tools can help an organization to collect, process, and analyze incident data in a way that traditional methods cannot offer.

Elements of an Incident Report

Regardless of whether an incident report is completed on paper or electronically in an incident reporting system, it includes several universal elements:

- Who: The report contains information about the principal subject and witnesses. This typically includes contact information and a review of that person's involvement in the incident.
- What: Details about what happened. Generally, this is in narrative form and is written by the report taker. Often witness statements are included in the incident report.

- When: What date and time the initial incident occurred as well as other major milestones (i.e., interview and court dates).
- Where: Information about where an incident occurred. This would include street address, physical location within a store, etc.
- Why: Information about what caused the incident.

Loss prevention professionals are probably very familiar with writing incident reports for the typical shoplifting and internal theft cases. Almost all reports contain who stole it, what they stole, when they stole it, where they stole it from, and why they stole it.

Interestingly, this same methodology is used by many other departments in the retail organization. For example, the human resources department typically handles reports of violation of company policy. The human resource representative's report will include who violated the policy, what policy they violated, when they violated the policy, where they violated the policy, and why they violated the policy.

Another example is the risk management department. This department is typically tasked with providing a safe work environment but is also responsible for processing customer and employee accident reports when things go wrong. Who had the accident, what kind of accident occurred, when did the accident occur, where did the accident occur, and why did the accident occur?

Get the idea? Incident reporting systems are not just for loss prevention. The flexibility provided by many solutions allows for the system to be utilized by other parts of the retail organization. Incident reporting systems can help the risk management team to manage accident reports just as easily as it can help the loss prevention group to manage theft investigations.

Benefits of Electronic Incident Reporting

Besides the ability to store incident data for many different groups within the retail organization, an incident reporting system has several other benefits. Most importantly, an incident reporting system has the ability to store the incident data in an electronic format at a central location. This seems obvious, but it actually represents the fundamental difference between centralized incident management and traditional methods of collecting and storing incident data. The data collected by an incident reporting system (database) can be a very powerful tool.

Incident reporting systems can be configured to interact with other business systems, such as

- *Internal employee databases:* Link to the HR department's employee master file for enhanced statistical reports.
- *Civil collection providers:* Transmit theft incidents electronically to the collection agency.
- *Background screening providers:* Transmit a prospective employee's (or suspect's) information to the vendor and order a background check.
- *POS exception-based reporting tools:* Start an incident from within an exception-based reporting tool.
- *Digital CCTV systems:* Easily attach video clips to an incident report.

The database can be used to generate statistical reports that can help an organization to gauge various metrics. When combined with other data sources, the data in the incident reporting system can be used to identify trends that otherwise would not be visible.

For example, when linked with data from an HR system, it would be possible to pull a report to analyze the relationship between store shrink, employee turnover, and theft incidents. Another possibility would be to analyze the department in which a suspect was first observed compared to the time of day in shoplifting cases. These types of reports would require significant resources if compiled by hand, but with the use of an electronic incident reporting system, the data are easily accessible.

Pitfalls of Incident Reporting

The benefits of using a centralized incident reporting system can be numerous but require more than just a financial investment in order to be achieved.

The successful implementation of an incident reporting system requires planning, communication, and follow-through. During the implementation process, it is important to maintain partnerships with the departments that will be utilizing the system, the IT department, and the vendor's technical staff. With communication, the vendor can provide a solution that is tailored to the needs of everyone involved.

After a solution is implemented, it is critical that management support the system. It is important that managers train end users on system operations. No matter how easy the system is to use, end users should be taught the proper way to input, retrieve, and report on incident data.

Finally, it is important that the system be kept up-to-date with changes in corporate policies. Invariably, with time, things change. Make sure that the system is reconfigured as needed to accommodate these changes.

Conclusion

Before any system is purchased, research and planning are needed. With a strong commitment from all involved, an electronic incident reporting system can provide a significant contribution to a retail organization.

Cash Control: Automated

Van Carlisle and Dave Hochman

One much-repeated maxim in the loss prevention community goes something like this: "The more rapidly cash tender is recycled or deposited, the lesser the risk of cashier error and internal shrink." At the same time, especially with retailers who see a high volume of cash transactions, the labor expenses and bank fees associated with handling cash are consistently on the rise. So how can retailers impose measures to control cashier errors and reduce theft, while stemming the increase of labor expenses and bank fees?

The issue becomes how to build the infrastructure to return the highest efficiency possible for cash management while striking a balance between the use of manpower and affordable technology. Finding the right formula will positively impact any end user retailer's return on investment (ROI). This business problem led New Albany, Indiana-based FireKing Security Group to develop and bring to market the "PerfectCash" comprehensive cash handling solution suite with both hardware (safe with cash recycler) and software elements, all tied together with IP/LAN-based reporting capabilities (see Figure C-1).

PerfectCash takes cash handling and revenue room activities to the next level of security, efficiency, and automation. According to the company, the PerfectCash solution is "ideal for large retailers, department stores, and mass merchandisers who routinely process tens of thousands of dollars in cash each day."

The vision behind PerfectCash is to move cash collection and processing functions closer to the point-of-sale, which serves to reduce double handling, errors, and opportunities for employee theft. PerfectCash is an enclosed system (similar but smaller scale than that of a bank or back office casino process), combining the preparation of opening tills, verification/preparation of end-of-day deposits, and general ledger reporting.

Via the automation of these processes that PerfectCash enables, end users of the solution, including one of the nation's largest operators of department stores, have realized cost-labor savings that equal many times the purchase price during the first year of installment. With PerfectCash, there is also the added issue of the Sarbanes-Oxley (SOX) Act of 2002. PerfectCash give retailers added control over accounting and treasury functions, which leads to smoother compliance with SOX financial audit and reporting requirements.

FIGURE C-1 The PerfectCash machine.

Benefits to retailers who implement Perfect Cash are as follows:

- Reduced labor for deposit preparation
- Check truncation (Check 21 compliant)
- Reduced bank fees
- Reduced cash on hand
- Reduced change order size and frequency
- Accurate and quicker deposits
- Automated and accurate "make ready" for registers
- Interface to back room settlement software providing real-time information about cash/check activity

By way of example, FireKing recently provided Macy's West a customized PerfectCash solution for automating the deposit process and creating register replenishments, reducing processing time by 50%. PerfectCash can combine all the functions, and it works in a similar (but smaller) scale than that of a bank or back office casino process. Savings are realized through reducing the time to process and increasing accuracy.

For more information about PerfectCash, contact scottm@fireking.com

Cash Office Security

CAS, JHC

Nearly all retailers, large and small, have what serves as a cash office—a place where not only cash is kept, but in many cases accounting records, invoices, employees' schedules, and other miscellaneous business records as well.

All cash offices have some sort of cash storage container, ranging from massive and alarmed safes to simple locking file cabinets, which many or may not have a "lockable strong box" for the cash itself.

Cash offices are as varied in their design and construction as the type of merchandise sold by a big box retailer. Small "Mom and Pop" retailers often use a walled or curtained-off area of the "back room" for a cash office. A major national department store may utilize a room built almost to the standards of a bank vault, complete with bulletproof glass, bulletproof walls, and a "bandit barrier" entrance. We should point out that, while there is normally only one way of ingress and egress into a cash vault, there should exist a breakout panel somewhere within the cash office so that in the case of a fire or other emergency, there is a means of escape.

A "bandit barrier" is a double door (inner and outer door) entrance with a small space between the doors. This is also known as or is called a "man trap" configuration. The doors are electrically controlled from inside the cash office (vault). Each door has a small window so the person seeking entrance (after pressing the "doorbell" to announce his or her presence and desire to enter the vault) can be visually identified. The outer door is electrically unlocked, and the visitor enters the interior space between the doors, closing the outer door behind him or her, since the inner door cannot open if the outer door is also open. Once inside the "barrier," the inner door is then "buzzed" (unlocked electronically) open. More sophisticated vaults also have a phone by the outer door to the bandit barrier (with a corresponding phone just inside the vault by the inner door). This arrangement permits the person seeking entry to announce the purpose of his or her need for entry, which is a step beyond mere visual identification.

Grocery stores and some drug stores (and some other specialty stores) place their "office" on a raised platform above the store floor level; this office is enclosed on at least two (generally three) sides with windows at a height at which someone seated at a desk within the office can see through to the selling floor. This office generally serves as both a cash and paperwork space, as well as the store manager's office. The fact that it is raised above the selling floor level permits anyone working in the office to observe the activities on the selling floor. In this scenario, the bulk of the store's cash is kept in a floor safe and/or a heavy standard safe located near the front windows of the store. The floor safe is buried in the concrete of the selling floor and is extremely difficult to break into. The standard safe, which is on the floor generally, has a time lock and requires two keys to open in addition to the combination lock. One key is held by the store and one by the armored car pickup driver. The time lock prevents the safe from being opened except at specific times during the day, even if the proper combination is used. Many of these safes also have an electronic alarm, which is activated if the dialed combination is dialed incorrectly. For example, if the last number of the correct combination is 30 and the number 40 is intentionally dialed instead, this will automatically send a hold-up signal to the alarm monitoring company.

In large stores, where a vault-like cash office exists, we find no objection to leaving the main safe door closed, but with the combination in an unlocked position. In smaller stores, which do not have a vault-type cash office, we suggest that the safe be kept locked at all times. We must mention one caution here: The combination to any safe in the vault needs to be memorized. If the combination to the safe must be written down, it should be kept in a sealed envelope in an office away from the cash office, for example.

If any portion of the cash office serves an area where customers can obtain refunds, cash checks, and/or pay bills, we then suggest that drawers be built under the counter of the service window and utilized for the receipt and disbursement of cash. Such drawers should be equipped with a "hold-up" alarm triggering device. This device may take the form of a "finger pull" switch or a "bill trap," a device which holds a piece of currency that, if removed, triggers the silent alarm. At one time "kick-bars" located on the floor, which could be activated by a cashier's foot, were popular, but they have fallen out of favor because of the high rate if accidental false alarms. Cashiers and other vault personnel must be trained, however, as to conditions and circumstances under which these alarms should be triggered. They should be taught never to do anything which may provoke the robber. Their best course of action is to carefully observe the robber and get a good physical description, which can later be given to the police, utilizing the Robbery form (which is found in the "Forms" section of this book). Training on the proper actions to take when being held up should be periodically reviewed with all personnel, particularly new cash office employees.

Periodic audits of all with funds and a cash office should be made. We do not suggest the frequency for these audits; that should be determined by the chief of finance or head of the internal audit department. We do suggest, however, that when an audit of the funds in the safe is done, each bill in a bundled (banded) stack be counted. It is not unheard of for an employee in the cash office to steal funds by removing one or two bills from each bundled stack. If the bills in a bundled stack are not individually counted, such thefts could go undetected for extended periods of time.

Cash offices should be adequately alarmed. It is beyond the scope of this book to provide specific details with respect to such alarms, but suffice it to say, a qualified expert should be consulted to determine the most effective way to accomplish alarming the cash office.

It should also go without saying (but we will anyway) that all employees who will have access to the cash office be fully vetted.

A final word about cash deposits: We discuss in the section "Escort Policy and Procedure" (elsewhere in this book) their use when making bank deposits. However, we strongly suggest that if any significant amounts of money are involved, the use of an armored car service be considered. We have seen too many cases where, in the interest of saving the few dollars involved in the cost of an armored car service, the store owner or an employee personally made bank deposits only to be robbed going to or coming from the bank, and in many cases, was injured as well. We do not suggest being penny wise and pound foolish.

Cash Register Manipulations

CAS, JHC

Table C-1 demonstrates the results of various types of cash register manipulations by dishonest employees acting alone or in concert with others.

To use this chart to understand cash register manipulations, you must use the left column in combination with the various situations along the top row of comments. For example, for the Correct Procedure, read down the column noted as "Correct Procedure," while noting the actions of the customer and clerk on the left column. If the correct procedure is followed, the customer will pay $100 for $100 of merchandise, which results in a balanced register.

Table C-1 Assume Merchandise Purchased/ Taken by Customer Is $100 Retail Price

	Correct Procedure	Overring	Underring	Sweetheart Deal	Fraud Voids	FTR
Customer Pays	$100	$100	$100	$10	$100	$100
Clerk Rings up	$100	$200		$10	$100	$ 0
Result	Register Balance	Register short $100	Register over $90	Register Balance $90 Inventory Shortage	Register Balance	Register Over $100
Salesclerk			Steals $90		Keeps Customer Receipt Voids sale Steals $100	Take $100
Result			Register Balance Inventory Shortage of $90		Register Balance Inventory Shortage of $100	Reg Bal Inventory Short $100

Consider, however, the results when a "Sweetheart Deal" (one in which the clerk sells a friend merchandise below the actual value of the goods). Here, the clerk sells $100 of goods for $10, which results in the clerk ringing up $10, causing the register to now balance. However, since $100 in merchandise left the store for a payment of only $10, the store now has a $90 inventory shortage. The other manipulations shown can be followed in the same manner.

CCTV: An Historical Perspective in Retailing

CAS, JHC

The use of visual surveillance by closed-circuit television (CCTV) in business began in the 1960s. Initially, the cameras were large and quite expensive. In large department stores, the initial use of a camera was for internal investigations. Even large chains had only one or two cameras. Smaller retail establishments (such as grocery and drug stores) also used CCTV as an antishoplifting device. Usually, the retailer would install one or two working CCTVs in a manner so that customers could view themselves on a nearby monitor. "Smile, you're on candid camera" signs often hung beneath the monitors; other decals announced "This store utilizes closed-circuit television." This arrangement sought to achieve two objectives: (a) Notify customers about the CCTV to minimize invasion of privacy complaints and (b) imply to the customer that other, less obvious cameras were monitoring and detecting illicit activity throughout the store. In actuality, most if not all other cameras were "dummies," i.e., simply plastic camera body shells with ersatz lenses, blinking red lights, and wires simulating a working camera. The high cost of live CCTV necessitated this approach.

During the intervening 40 plus years, the development of CCTV paralleled the sophistication, miniaturization, and cost reductions reflected in the electronics and computer worlds. Today, color CCTV cameras are as small as a box of matches or the cap of a fountain pen. Their pictures can be transmitted to monitors over almost limitless distances via coax cable, telephone lines, microwave, optic fiber, and just plain wire. Monitors can display images from a dozen cameras simultaneously. Video tape recorders (VTRs) can now record the cameras' images for periods up to 24 hours on one tape; the newest equipment is computerized digital VTRs, which can record on floppy disks and CDs over long periods of time. Modern cameras are capable of panning, tilting, and zooming in on a target, either by manual control or computerized response to predetermined events, such as motion or alarm signals.

Together with the technical developments of CCTV equipment and the significant reduction in its costs, new and effective uses of CCTV are constantly being found. CCTV is used by the Golden Gate Bridge to monitor traffic; by hotel lobbies, museums, and Amtrak stations to monitor patrons; by parking lots and garages to detect criminal activity; by bank ATMs as both a robbery deterrent and to identify those using the machines. Hundreds of businesses, from casinos to convenience stores, utilize CCTV for surveillance and security purposes.

Retailers have found CCTV valuable in not only deterring and detecting shoplifting, but also in investigating and documenting internal theft. They found that stores which installed CCTV had a perceptible drop in theft from shoplifting. One security agent, by monitoring an adequate number of properly placed cameras, could observe virtually the entire store, thus saving manpower costs.

Over 83% of retail establishments of all types utilize live CCTV. Today, retailers plan for CCTV installation in the same fashion as they do for cashiering facilities, merchandise displays, service areas, etc. Computer-controlled cameras are contained in opaque domes in ceilings; it is common to find major stores with dozens of cameras and CCTV monitoring rooms containing banks of dozens of TV screens, any one of which can be switched to a large viewing screen whose picture is simultaneously recorded. I have personally planned numerous such installations, recently having done so for the campus bookstores at major universities such as Stanford, Duke, and the University of California at San Diego. Retailing establishments found that CCTV perceptibly reduced shoplifting. More importantly, when shoplifting, robbery, burglary, or internal theft did occur, what better evidence to help convict the thief than videotape of the person actually committing the crime.

In retailing, CCTV performs many functions:

1. As a theft deterrent
2. As a means of detecting theft
3. As an investigative tool, especially with regard to internal theft and fraud
4. As a management tool
5. As a means of preserving evidence of events which may later become the subject of litigation

The question is often asked what triggers a shopper becoming a subject of CCTV observation and monitoring. The answer is that many things can legitimately result in observation by a loss prevention agent monitoring the store's CCTV system. Among these "triggers" are

- Random monitoring which results in loss prevention recognizing a person as a previously suspected or known shoplifter
- Random monitoring which results in the observation of suspicious behavior by a shopper, which may include:
  1. The shopper paying more attention to his or her surroundings than the merchandise.
  2. The shopper obviously looking around with the purpose to see if a sales associate is nearby.
  3. The shopper wearing inappropriate clothing; e.g., a raincoat on a sunny day or baggy warm clothing during summer months.
  4. The shopper carrying shopping bags, either from other stores, empty, or puffed up but appearing full of air only. There are numerous techniques by which shopping bags can be utilized to facilitate shoplifting.(1)
  5. The shopper who appears to randomly select merchandise which, because of its nature, should be selected by size.
  6. The shopper who appears to be in a group but subsequently splits up and seems to go "helter skelter" through the store.
  7. The "gut feeling" experienced agents get as the result of observing the behavior of shoppers.
  8. The experienced agent's ability to sense or "see" the guilt aura.

While the retail industry was the first major user of CCTV for security purposes, its value as a crime deterrent was quickly recognized by others, and its use began pervading all aspects of society, as was alluded to earlier. It has been reported that the UK has found street surveillance by CCTV to be an effective crime deterrent, and such use is being proliferated throughout England. American businesses are also finding value in utilizing CCTV to surveil parking lots and building exteriors; CCTV is being used and can be seen (and in some cases not seen) in venues ranging from sports stadiums to casinos.

The continuing drop in CCTV prices has also contributed to the increased utilization of this technology. The use of miniaturized and disguised CCTV cameras connected to home VCRs (or the use of self-contained "camcorders") has popularized the use of this technology by parents to monitor the activities of baby-sitters left in charge of their children in the parents' absence.

We cannot discuss the widespread use of CCTV without concomitantly discussing the legal aspects of its use. The emphasis, increasing exponentially, on privacy rights has brought the increasing widespread use of CCTV into question from a privacy standpoint.

The consensus is, at least at the present time, no right to privacy exists when the subject of visual surveillance is in a public place. Obviously, covert surveillance in private areas of public buildings, such as restrooms and fitting rooms, is illegal. Even private office spaces, if occupants have a key and can lock the door, or otherwise make the case that they had a

---

(1) Sennewald, C. A., and Christman, J. H. (1992) Shoplifting. Butterworth-Heinemann.

reasonable expectation of privacy, are more than likely off-limits to covert CCTV surveillance. Any time covert CCTV surveillance is planned, care should be taken to ascertain its proposed use is legal, and the opinion of knowledgeable legal counsel should be obtained. We must also emphasize that our discussion involves only visual surveillance; audio surveillance is an entirely different matter and brings into play a whole new set of rules, laws, and restrictions.

So what does the future hold with regard to visual public surveillance in general and the use of CCTV in particular? In our view, the foreseeable future will see increased visual surveillance. Technical developments, coupled with the increase in security needs of all sorts after September 11, 2001, foretell the ever-increasing use of CCTV by both the civilian, law enforcement, and military communities. We read of surveillance drones replacing manned surveillance aircraft in Afghanistan; we've seen TV shots of the wall-to-wall coverage by CCTV at the Winter Olympics and Super Bowl XLI; we see more advanced uses of technical surveillance such as facial recognition in use at public events and suggested for widespread use at airports to detect and deny access to aircraft for persons on official watch lists. If September 11, as horrendous as it was, had one good result, it was that "security" is no longer a dirty four-letter (times 2) word. This increased emphasis on security throughout the world can only harbinger the ever-increasing use of reasonable surveillance in all aspects of our lives, and in my view, a willingness of a vast majority of the public to forgo some privacy for increased safety.

Celebrity Appearances and Special Events

CAS, JHC

One aspect of loss prevention, although not common, is the need to address protection considerations when "celebrities" either visit stores or the retailer plays a significant role in such appearances.

Your authors have been responsible for the security at large "special events" (many for a local charity) and/or smaller personal appearances, both of which involved the presence of celebrities. In some cases these events involved multiday activities including fashion shows at local venues outside the store. This complicated the security aspects because large quantities of expensive merchandise (RTW, furs, fine jewelry) would have to be moved and stored (sometimes for several days) at a remote location, where it would be exposed to perhaps dozens of models, make-up artists, and other nonstore personnel. In other cases, the simple appearance of a celebrity (e.g., Elizabeth Taylor, Cher, Christie Brinkley, Catherine Deneuve) in the store created security problems ranging from crowd control to the physical protection of the celebrity, who, in some cases, was a vocal advocate for very controversial causes. Often, a private reception followed the celebrity's public appearance, which added unique considerations.

Some celebrities have their own security personnel with whom a working relationship must be established. It is essential that "who will call the shots" must be sorted out in advance to prevent disagreements and confusion in the midst of the event. In other cases, public figures (e.g., Corazon Aquino, Rosalynn Carter) required coordination with the Secret Service (USSS) and/or department of state security (DSS).

The State department played a big role in Prince Charles's visit to the Broadway Department Stores' flagship store and worked closely and coordinated with that store's security staff as well as the Los Angeles Police Department. The rules of the game included that the store was responsible for such in-store functional considerations as control over which elevators would and could operate and/or be used by the prince while inside the store. There was concern an elevator might stop and open on a floor that could compromise security. Such kinds of "proprietary knowledge" makes the private sector an invaluable partner with governmental agents as well as the celebrity's own protection staff.

Additionally, security plans had to be coordinated with the stores' publicity and merchandising departments. Security had to be not only effective, but also as invisible as possible so as not to detract from the visual/promotional aspects of the event. While all these challenges were interesting, they also consumed lots of time with the knowledge that any untoward event would receive national publicity and damage to the company's reputation. Fortunately, my associates were both imaginative and practical in their planning and implementation of the security aspects of these events.

Let me cite just two examples of how celebrity events were dealt with from the security point of view.

Elizabeth Taylor appeared at Macy's San Francisco promoting her "White Diamonds" fragrance. This event was overseen by Ms. Taylor's publicist and the store's public relations and special events departments; security aspects were determined by consultations between Ms. Taylor's own security detail and the store's security department. Based on Ms. Taylor's request, all mail received at the store for her prior to the event and gifts for her during the event were given to store security and examined prior to delivery to Ms. Taylor. At all times during the public appearance, an ambulance (with paramedic crew) was available at the closet exit to the event. Credentials were issued to the press, store nonsecurity personnel, and security personnel. These credentials were color-coded to facilitate the wearer gaining or being denied access to specific areas.

Without my detailing all the specific security precautions, suffice it to say every contingency was planned for, and all security personnel had specific assignments should an untoward event occur. Every aspect of Ms. Taylor's visit—from the arrival of her plane at the airport, her arrival at the store, the event itself, until she reboarded the plane at the conclusion of her visit—was preplanned. This planning included a suitable place for her to relax in the store, backup vehicles, radio communications, hotel security, travel routes, decoy limo, and prescreening of those receiving credentials. All planning was reduced to writing: floor plans for the event venue showing the location of stanchions, travel routes, press areas, holding areas, and security guard locations. A minute-by-minute time table was prepared to assure a smooth-running event.

In previsit correspondence from Ms. Taylor's publicist, the following was noted: "Security control is the most important consideration for Miss Taylor's personal appearance in your store."

While the bulk of the security was performed by the store's security staff (with added personnel from nearby stores), it was prudent to contract with a local guard service to provide approximately 30 uniformed (blazers) personnel, who were stationed at exits and throughout the crowd area. Each of these contracted personnel was prescreened and issued very precise post orders as to exact duties and responsibilities. The aspect of crowd control cannot be overstated: Always allow for more crowd control officers than you think will be needed. It's better to be safe than have an untoward incident.

The second event I'd like to describe was the personal appearance of Luke Perry of the TV show *Beverly Hills 90210*. Figure C-02 shows the letter to the San Francisco Chief of Police that sets the stage for the extensive security arrangements for this event. As background for the letter, you should be aware that over 106,000 phone calls requesting tickets for this event were received; the volume of calls in a 2 ½ hour period actually "blew up" the switchboard and disrupted phone calls to the store until the switchboard could be replaced.

Security planning for this event was extensive. As the *San Francisco Examiner* reported: "Moscone Center hasn't seen such security measures since the 1984 Democratic National Convention."

The letter resulted in the use of 18 officers from the SFPD being assigned and paid for by Macy's. (Note that 10B officers are those assigned by the police department but paid for by private [other than city] funds.) It also produced a four-page memorandum from the commanding officer of the detail with assignments, equipment required, and instructions for executing appropriate police action (e.g., arrests) if necessary.

For the event (two shows of about 1 hour each) itself within Moscone Center, we hired 120 uniformed security personnel from area security providers with experience dealing with large crowds (such as at the San Francisco 49ers football games). We assigned 30 of our own security personnel to the event.

macy's california, inc.

P.O. BOX 7888 • SAN FRANCISCO, CA 94120
(415) 954-6000

August 14, 1991

Chief Willis A. Casey
San Francisco Police Dept.
850 Bryant Street, Hall of Justice
San Francisco, Ca.   94103

Will

Dear Chief Casey:

RE: Request for 10B Officers

What began four months ago as a relatively minor in-store personal appearance by Luke Perry of the TV Show "Beverly Hills, 90210" has escalated into the largest event ever sponsored by Macy's and of such magnitude we had to move it, as of Friday, to Moscone Center.

On Saturday, August 17th, Mr. Perry and other cast members will appear at two fashion show personal appearances sponsored by Macy's at Moscone Center. The shows are at 11AM and 1PM; we have over 12,000 reservations, mainly from pre-teen and teenage girls. The TV show is now a nationally ranked show and Mr. Perry has become a teen idol.

We are hereby requesting the assignments of from 8-14 (the final number to be determined by Lt. Schardt, who has reviewed our security plans) 10B officers for traffic control and pedestrian safety in the Moscone Center area from 8AM to 3PM on Saturday, August 17th.

As noted, we have coordinated and reviewed our crowd control and security plans with Lt. Schardt and Lt. Johnson of Southern Station and they concur in our proposed arrangements.

I should note that at an appearance in Florida by Mr. Perry last week, there was a minor riot and over 20 people injured which received national TV network news coverage last Saturday. We obviously want to avert such an occurrence here and will be doing everything possible to have an incident free event.

The assistance and cooperation of your Department will go a long way to achieving our goals.

Thanks, Will, for your attention to this matter on such short notice; we look forward to another occasion of close cooperation and working with your Department.

With best personal regards,

John H. Christman
Vice President and
Director of Security

JHC:DC

FIGURE C-2

Again, we had to plan for decoy units, communications, issuance of post orders, crowd control, barricades for the stage area, travel routes, medical emergencies, portable restroom facilities, security jackets, bullhorns, observation areas, fire lanes and zones, and credentials for personnel authorized in backstage areas.

The security budget for this event was $36,600, not including the cost of our own personnel.

Lessons Learned

Special events and celebrity appearances present challenging security problems, but the application of basic techniques and procedures, adjusted to meet the peculiar circumstances involved, with some imagination thrown in, will provide solutions.

What are some of the more important considerations in planning for a special event or celebrity appearance? We suggest the following:

Pre-planning: Who knows all the event details?

- Can drawings of the venue be obtained?
- Always overestimate number of security personnel needed.
- Establish an emergency evacuation route.
- Plan on how to detain/confine drunks and disorderlies.
- How will security personnel be fed if needed?
- Consult with and obtain OK from fire marshall.
- Will it be necessary to screen for weapons/explosives
- Need for undercover personnel in crowd?
- Arrange for adequate communications.
- Solidify transportation requirements.
- What communications are needed, frequencies, etc.?
- Adequate relaxation and hold areas for celebrity?
- How to deal with inebriated celebrities? (This does happen.)

The venue: public area or within private property?

- Can access be readily controlled?
- Is admittance by ticket or first-come first-in basis?
- Can the area be adequately secured?
- Other security forces involved?

The celebrity: well-liked or controversial person?

- Does the celebrity have any input into security needs?
- Can the celebrity veto security plans?
- Are any governmental agencies involved?
- Does the celebrity have any of his or her own security personnel?
- Any specials needs, e.g., medical, dietary, etc.?

The event: Length of event

- Must valuables (merchandise, furs, fine jewelry) be left overnight?
- Anticipated crowd dynamics?
- Charity event: Coordinator?
- Black tie? Arrange for proper attire for security.
- How to authenticate legitimate attendees?
- Will food be served? If so, hors d'oeuvres or sitdown dinner?
- Will liquor be served/available?
- If animals involved, who handles?

Post event: Review event and conduct after-action review for lessons learned.

Celebrity and other "Sensitive" Arrest

CAS, JHC

There's an inherent risk that a retailer may find himself or herself with a celebrity in custody for shoplifting. We define a "celebrity" as a person who is a public official, athlete, film personality, musician, or other type of figure with high public visibility. The question is: Now what to do? Should a celebrity be treated any differently than Jane or John Q. Public?

Celebrities may either attempt to hide their identity or use it to overpower employees with their importance and influence.

As soon as it is discovered that a celebrity has been apprehended, it is important to minimize the confusion which will naturally occur and to secure the area and the suspect to prevent any loss of evidence. Senior loss prevention and store management must be promptly informed of the situation for their information and counsel. If the celebrity has not at this point relinquished the item(s) stolen, he or she should now be requested to do so. Be sure that this surrender of merchandise is done in the presence of a witness. At this point, company policy for dealing with celebrities should be followed.

What should that policy be? That is a decision only senior management of the company can make. Management must realize that if an arrest is made, it will become a matter of public record and, most likely, extensive publicity, as best exemplified by Winona Ryder's arrest in 2001, which is a classic and showcase example of the public interest and frenzy over this kind of incident. You can count on publicity if a celebrity is booked for shoplifting. The other side of the coin is why should a celebrity be treated differently than any other shoplifter? Written policy on how to deal with these rare events will dictate the course of action to be followed. And that action must be consistent to avoid subsequent claims of discrimination.

The range of options reflected in the policy could include, but is not limited to the following:

- If the celebrity offers to pay for the merchandise, after receiving an admission of guilt and release, accept payment by having the sale rung up on the selling floor in the normal manner.
- Decline the celebrity's offer to pay, recover the goods, and obtain a written admission of guilt and release.
- Process the celebrity just as any other citizen who has been taken into custody for shoplifting and exercise one of the three normal dispositions; i.e., call the police, arrange for a conditional release, or release.

The other question which often arises is how to deal with law enforcement officers, senior public officials, and members of the celebrity's immediate family. Local customs and the political realities must be taken into account. We suggest that if LEOs are apprehended, the head of the department be contacted and his or her advice followed. If spouses or children of LEOs are apprehended, contact the LEO and advise him or her of the situation and asked for a recommendation.

In the final analysis, however, the owner or senior management of the store must make the final decisions, and such decisions should be reflected in written policy.

Chase/Chasing Policy

CAS, JHC

Every retailer who has a policy authorizing employees to engage in the legal "merchant's privilege" of detaining suspected shoplifters must have a clear written policy specifically addressing the issue of chasing or pursuing those who refuse to cooperate or otherwise attempt to escape. Injuries drive civil lawsuits, and the two most common causes of injuries evolve around (a) use of force and (b) pursuits. Indeed, out of concern over these two integral aspects of a detention process, some retailers have adopted policies which prohibit the use of force and "no touch no chase," which we view as a virtual oxymoron. It simply makes no sense to charge employees with catching shoplifters but to deny them the necessary tools to do the job. This issue is addressed more fully in the " 'No Touch' Policy" section of this book.

Suffice it to say the majority of detentions for shoplifting are made with the understanding that legal, nondeadly force may be used, and if a person pushes or attempts to strike a loss prevention agent or otherwise bolts to escape, a reasonable and measured effort will be made to take that fleeing thief into custody. We subscribe to this strategy.

The chase/pursuit policy then must spell out what is "reasonable" and what is a "measured effort," and that policy, because of the nature and dynamics of the process, must include aspects of the use of force.

The drafting or redrafting of the policy should include the following:

1. Agents charged with the task of detaining customers must undergo structured and professional training in how to approach a person about to be detained so as to minimize the risk of violence and effort to escape. Agents who have not been so trained or "certified" to make detentions should be prohibited from making detentions under any circumstances.
2. Ideally, no touching of the customer will be made while escorting the subject back into the store.
3. Minimal touching, such as guiding the subject with one hand on the subject's upper arm or elbow, is the next level up from no physical contact.
4. Should the subject stop and simply refuse to move or continue, the agent should be authorized to use just that amount of force to overcome the resistance.
5. Should the subject bolt, the agent must make an immediate on-the-spot determination whether a pursuit can safely be made without running into or striking some innocent bystander.
6. If, at the outset of the escape, the subject drops the merchandise, policy must dictate if such action precludes further involvement, i.e., a pursuit, or not. If further pursuit is permitted, it must be kept in mind that any subsequent injuries to the suspect, a bystander, or the agent, the store will have a more difficult time defending a lawsuit, since the merchandise has been recovered and the store has now suffered no loss.
7. No running inside the store.
8. No running in a crowded mall or shopping center.
9. No running in a parking lot if the lot is crowded with pedestrian customers.
10. No pursuit across streets. We note that deaths from shoplifting suspects running into the street and being hit by cars occurs with regrettable frequency. Both of the authors have consulted in such cases and can attest to the utter heartbreak such incidents produce for all concerned parties.
11. Pursuit should not extend beyond the boundaries of the store's property or shopping center limits.
12. If the fleeing subject is seized and goes to the ground, only holding force may be used until assistance arrives, i.e., no striking, kicking, punching, or choking.
13. No "piling on" a prone subject to avoid possible asphyxiation.
14. Handcuffs should quickly be applied and the subject helped to his or her feet and escorted back to the store.

The policy is necessary for several reasons:

- The agent must understand what his or her company expects in terms of performance and has taken reasonable steps to prepare that agent for this important responsibility.
- The safety and welfare of the general public are important to the company.
- The safety and welfare of the agent are important to the company.
- The safety and welfare of the shoplifting suspect are important.

In the event of civil litigation, the policies in place and the actions taken by the agents in making the apprehension must be demonstrably reasonable under the totality of the circumstances.

Check Fraud

Shannen Stenerson

Historically, suspects of check fraud have focused on stealing blank checks, mailed by banks, from unsuspecting customers' unlocked mailboxes. This once-popular type of check fraud is making a comeback, aided by the fact that most bank customers do not include any preprinted information on their checks, such as Social Security numbers, addresses, or phone numbers. This type of information is added at the point of sale, verified by the merchant who is relying on the fraudulent identification manufactured by the criminals. This bogus identification often includes drivers' licenses or state-issued identification cards that, with today's technology, can be easily created.

The thieves continue to cash checks until one is rejected for insufficient funds—that is, if a clerk actually contacts the bank to verify funds. The culprits simply say they don't know why the check was rejected, "I have plenty of money in the bank; I'll get the cash and come back later to pay for it." They never do. The thief just moves on to the next victim.

Although retailers have become more advanced in antifraud techniques, so have the criminals. Most check scams today involve a more detailed execution. Today's fraud has evolved along with the technology, often using colored copiers, high-tech scanners, and over-the-counter solvents. Some of these new fraud techniques are described next.

Check Washing

Using a process known as "check washing," suspects erase the ink on checks using chemicals that can be found on the shelves of a local supermarket:

- Acetone, most commonly used in check washing because it can be found in hand-wipe application
- Bleach
- Clear correction fluids
- High-performance eraser
- Benzene

It is estimated that check washing accounts for over $815 million of fraud losses every year in the United States.

Here's the way the scam works: A suspect removes checks that are often left in an unattended mailbox that the consumer has used to pay personal bills. The suspect then washes the ink from the check, leaving the original signature, but altering the payee and the dollar amount. The suspect often cashes the check at supermarket chains, small gas stations, check cashing outlets, and credit unions using a fraudulent identification.

Despite the fact that check manufactures have tried to prevent check washing and fraud by making checks difficult to wash or copy, many suspects have become so good at check washing that retailers and consumers are unaware until they are given notice from the bank that they were victims.

As a consumer, you can protect yourself by not leaving your mail unattended, using a postal drop box when possible, and using a "gel" pen when writing a check.

As a retailer, you can look for the security features that check manufacturers have used when ordering company checks. Security features may include the following:

- *Watermarks:* Watermarks are made by applying different degrees of pressure during the manufacturing process. Watermarks are subtle and can be seen when a check is held up to the light. This feature is helpful when detecting a counterfeit check because most copiers and scanners that are used to make the counterfeit checks cannot accurately copy the watermark feature.
- *Security inks:* Security inks react with common chemicals that are often used to wash checks, making the check unusable.
- *Chemical voids:* The paper used to make checks is treated with a chemical that is not detectable until mixed with a solvent used to wash the check, producing the word "void" across the check.
- *High-resolution micro printing:* This is small printing that cannot be seen with the naked eye and is most often used in the signature line of the check. When magnified, the series of words becomes visible; if altered, the series of words becomes illegible.

- *Gel-based pens:* When writing a check, consumers should use a gel-based pen. Most gel-based pens have been found extremely difficult to wash from the original check. Ballpoint pens and markers are produced with dye-based ink that is easily washed with the average household product.
- *Holostripe:* Similar to the hologram on a credit card, this feature is inserted into the check and is difficult to duplicate using a color copier or scanner.

Counterfeit Checks

Retailers often fall victim to counterfeit checks and again are not aware the check was counterfeit until they are given notice by their financial institution. Due to the advancement in color copying and desktop publishing, this is also become a fast-growing scam.

Suspects often get their check printing material at a local office supply store where the check writing paper is readily available. (Most over-the-counter paper does not contain the security features mentioned previously.) The suspect then uses an active checking account number and makes several blank checks using a color copier or scanner that is located at his or her home or local printing warehouse. The suspect is then able to use the home-made checks at any retailer that accepts checks. The suspect will frequently write the check for an amount over the purchase price to obtain cash as well as the merchandise.

Suspects also make up checks which appear to be payroll checks from known companies, since major supermarket chains cash payroll checks.

Many retailers combat the check fraud issue by, for a fee, using outside companies that guarantee their checks if the retailer follows certain steps when accepting a check. The benefit of using an outside company is that it guarantees the checks will be paid, regardless whether they are subsequently found to be a fraud. The outside company compares the check data against its database to determine if the company should accept the check from the consumer.

The retailer's responsibility is to download the program, train its employees to take accurate information, and leave the rest to the outside company. Most large retailers are not equipped to investigate and attempt to collect bad checks. By using an outside agency that guarantees the check, that agency then becomes responsible for investigating, collecting, and perhaps prosecuting the perpetrator.

Citizen's Arrest (Private Person's Arrest)

Robert A. Gardner

Citizen's arrest is a concept that dates back to English Common Law. Prior to the development of modern police agencies, responsibility for law enforcement rested with the members of the community. When a crime occurred, every citizen had the right and the responsibility to arrest the criminal and deliver him or her to the local sheriff or other authority.

With the establishment of organized police departments, the need for individual citizens to make arrests has diminished. Still, the right of private citizens to make arrests remains.

Where and When Permitted

Black's Law Dictionary defines an arrest as "The apprehending or detaining of a person in order to be forthcoming to answer an alleged or suspected crime."(1) Ex parte Sherwood, (29 Tex. App. 334, 15 S.W. 812).

Usually, arrests are made by police officers acting as agents of the government. The law gives these officers broad authority and a high degree of immunity while carrying out their duties. There are, however, times when ordinary citizens are confronted by criminal activity and no police officer is available to intervene. Because of this possibility, the laws of every state define certain circumstances under which private citizens are authorized to arrest or detain another person.

---

(1) Black, H.C. (1951). *Black's law dictionary.* St. Paul, Minnesota: West Publishing Company.

Some states permit arrest for a wide range of crimes. Others place strict limits on the type of offenses subject to citizen arrest and on the conditions under which the arrest can be made.

The exact circumstance under which an arrest is authorized varies with each state. Some authorize private citizens to make arrests for felony crimes committed in their presence. Others also allow for the arrest of felons even when the crime was not committed in the presence of the arresting person, as long as there is reasonable cause to believe that the person arrested committed the crime. Many states also permit private citizens to make arrests for other less serious public offenses committed in their presence.

A sampling of citizen's arrest laws shows the following:

- In California: A private person may arrest another:
  1. For a public offense committed or attempted in his presence.
  2. When the person arrested has committed a felony, although not in his presence.
  3. When a felony has been in fact committed, and he has reasonable cause for believing the person arrested to have committed it. (C.P.C 837)
- In New York State: Arrest without a warrant; by any person:
  1. Subject to the provisions of subdivision two, any person may arrest another person (a) for a felony when the latter has in fact committed such felony, and (b) for any offense when the latter has in fact committed such offense in his presence.
  2. Such an arrest, if for a felony, may be made anywhere in the state. If the arrest is for an offense other than a felony, it may be made only in the county in which such offense was committed. (N.Y.C.L. 140.30)
- In North Carolina: G.S. 15A-404 Detention of offenders by private persons.
  (a) No Arrest; Detention Permitted. No private person may arrest another person except as provided in G.S. 15A-405 [assisting law enforcement officers in making an arrest]. A private person may detain another person as provided in this section.
  (b) When Detention Permitted. A private person may detain another person when he has probable cause to believe that the person detained has committed in his presence:
  (1) A felony,
  (2) A breach of the peace,
  (3) A crime involving physical injury to another person, or
  (4) A crime involving theft or destruction of property.

In most cases the person making a citizen's arrest must actually witness the crime. However, many states have enacted so-called Merchant Privilege Statutes. These laws expand the authority of merchants to detain persons for shoplifting and certain other crimes based on a reasonable belief that a crime occurred.

Who Can Make an Arrest?

Although usually referred to as a "citizen's arrest," a more accurate description is "private person arrest." In most jurisdictions where these arrests are permitted, the language of the law extends the authority to any "private person." This may include noncitizens and even those in the country illegally.

Liability

Under the laws of most states, police officers acting lawfully in their official capacity enjoy considerable immunity from lawsuits arising from their actions during arrests. The same is generally not true for private citizens. Performing a citizen's arrest exposes the arresting party to both civil liability and criminal penalties if their actions are later found to be in error or in violation of the law. Where they apply, "Merchant Privilege" laws often provide for limited immunity from civil liability if there is reasonable cause to believe that a crime was committed and the arrest was made in a legal manner.

Before someone makes a citizen's arrest, it is important to fully understand what the law permits in the state where the arrest is to be made.

Civil Disturbances

CAS, JHC

September 11, 2001, placed a whole new perspective to "civil disturbances"; it now includes terrorism attacks. Since the nature and extent of any such attacks, civil or terror, cannot be predicted and may take a variety of forms, we limit or discussion to some general precautions.

Do's and Don'ts

Do's

- All executives and loss prevention/security personnel have keys to lock doors as necessary.
- All executives and loss prevention/security personnel are in possession of the following telephone numbers:
  - Regional Command Post
  - Mall Management General Offices
  - Mall Security
  - Local Law Enforcement
  - Fire Department
  - Store Personnel Emergency Telephone numbers
- Assure trash is removed from the dumpsters on a daily basis, if possible.
- Assure that only "necessary" terminals are opened once threat of civil disturbance is known.
- Both store manager and operations manager should carry one of the security radios at the first sign of any disturbance, if possible.
- Make sure your store command center telephone is staffed at all times by security, senior management, or some other responsible individual at the first sign of any disturbance, if available.
- Have a portable radio available so that local news broadcasts can me monitored.
- Assign a team of store volunteers that would include members from security, stock, dock, etc., to be available to board up windows with premeasured and cut ¾-inch plywood sheets. Assure an ample supply of nails, hammers, gloves, and eye protection is available to handle this task safely.
- Predetermine whether the store will be evacuated upon reasonable belief that it may be in the immediate area of any riot or civil disturbance. This determination should also factor in whether any personnel will remain, to protect the store and its contents, after the general evacuation order is given. If some personnel are to remain, assure they have adequate means to communicate with designated senior management and whether any other special equipment, in the use of which they have been trained, will be issued.
- Determine, in advance, what the pay policy will be for evacuated employees for the period(s) of time off normal work schedules due to an evacuation of the store and/or inability to obtain transportation to work.
- In the extreme event that your store is over run with demonstrators while customers and employees are still present, establish a safe haven such as your office, dock, etc., to shelter these individuals until order is restored. As soon as possible, notify mall security, law enforcement, and regional command for assistance.
- If you are ordered to evacuate the building, obtain the name of the person and the agency he or she represents for insurance purposes.
- Assure all flashlights are in good working order; keep a spare set of batteries.
- Conduct an emergency generator test (if applicable) and assure there is an adequate supply of fuel available.
- Determine, in advance, whether to leave the lights on or off if the store is totally evacuated.

Don't's

- Do not chain or lock fire doors or emergency exits for any reason while employees and customers are in the building.
- Do not allow firearms on the property, unless armed contract guards have been hired (or previously trained armed proprietary personnel) will be on premises to protect company assets.
- Do not attempt to engage in physical altercations with any demonstrators who may enter or attempt to enter the store, unless those on the property have been given specific directions to the contrary detailing the amount and type of force they are permitted to use.
- Do not disobey the orders of any police or government official, i.e., National Guard.
- Stores should not directly communicate with other stores; this will only tie up the phone lines. All communication outward from stores should be restricted to their regional command center or local emergency services.

Figures C-3 and C-4 are forms which may prove beneficial.

CIVIL DISTURBANCE/TERRORISM INCIDENT REPORT

Type of Incident: _____ Store Number: _____

Date and Time Closed: _____

Closure recommended by: _____

Telephone Number: _____

Describe any property damage to location: (Use reverse side if needed)
_____
_____
_____
_____

Describe any injury to associates or customers due to civil disturbance. For any injuries, include complete name and telephone number: (Use reverse side if needed)
_____
_____
_____
_____

Date and Time Location Re-Opened: _____

Authorized by: _____

Report taken by: _____

Date and time: _____

Telephone Number: _____

FIGURE C-3 Civil disturbance/terrorism incident report.

INFORMATION LOG

CONTROL CENTER FOR REGION:

_____

(or other location/function)

              INCOMING   OUTGOING

            INFORMATION   MESSAGE

                      (Circle one)

DATE: _____   TIME: _____

FROM: _____

              Location   Person Calling

CALL BACK NUMBER:_____

TO: _____

              Location   Person Receiving

DETAILS OF INFORMATION:

CALL TAKEN OR PLACED BY: _____

FIGURE C-4 Information log.

Civil Recovery

Frank Luciano

Background

Since the early 1970s states have been passing civil legislation designed to penalize anyone who removes merchandise offered for sale from a store or distribution center without payment. Each state law varies with regard to the penalty amount, damages, and if there is a criminal matter pending.

These laws have proven themselves to be very effective in helping to reduce shrinkage by generating resources for retail loss prevention departments as well as providing a financial deterrent. This income stream helps defray the costs of preventing theft to those who incur it or, in the case of a minor, to the parents.

The language of a few of these laws seems to indicate their intent is to be an alternative to criminal prosecution. Most of the civil recovery laws are not used as an alternative but rather as a consequence to a criminal act. Each of these crimes has a victim. The victims in these cases are retailers, but mainly their good customers who in the past have paid in the form of higher prices.

These laws are currently being used by retailers as an add-on to their loss prevention toolbox. These tools, when added to the entire picture, complement controls and procedures to help bring down shrink.

Generally, theft is a crime of opportunity, and nobody has more of that than employees. Those who are terminated for theft are liable civilly in all states. The major difference between internal and external cases has to do with the condition of the merchandise. Customers are usually caught "red-handed" still in possession of stolen merchandise, which is returned to the retailer once the matter has been dispositioned, either in-house or by the courts. In most employee situations, the case is often built from investigation of past theft, and merchandise is often unrecovered. In this situation the retail value of the loss is added to the penalty. The maximum amount is determined by the small claims maximum in the state where the incident occurred.

For best results, case work should contain a narrative, but the crucial element is the theft admission statement signed by the former employee. This process allows the person to pay back the losses incurred through restitution as well as a portion of the investigative cost involved through the civil penalty.

Recovered *expense dollars* bring 100% to the bottom line, income previously unattainable, and losses which had been previously written off are now being regenerated.

Procedure

Each case must be reviewed by someone who has been properly trained in the area of case review. The condition of the recovered merchandise should be noted, specifically if it was recovered in unsaleable condition or unrecovered. A complete narrative should exist, keeping in compliance with shopkeeper's privilege and private person's arrest procedures. Responsible parent information on minor cases should also indicate to whom the child was released. In all cases, the subject disposition should be indicated. The preceding conditions, together with state law, will determine whether a demand should be issued and for which amount.

A series of letters is then sent to the individual demanding payment, which is either preset by the law or based on loss prevention costs. This process is known as "civil demand." It is an attempt to resolve a financial matter prior to a court action. Once the matter moves to civil court, copies of the demand letters are provided as proof of an attempt to settle this between the parties.

Since there has been no judgment made prior to the civil demand process, care must be taken to limit exposure to liability when engaging a nonadjudicated individual by making outbound calls. In other words, this situation should not be treated as a debt-collection exercise. Once an arrangement has been made between the parties, calls to the individuals are best cast as follow-up to those arrangements.

Recommendations

Upon release of the individual, a notice should be given. The notice should contain language which indicates the state law, the incident, the fact that the store may seek a penalty, and a phone number to call with any questions. Store personnel should not try to explain the notice. They should refer all calls to the recovery agency or suggest the person seek legal counseling.

Store personnel should separate themselves from the collection process. Penalties assessed should be done after the entire case has been reviewed.

A central point for collections and case review should be established so payments, calls, and correspondence can be controlled. A company attorney should be designated to handle inquiries and research.

It is wise to find out what limitations are contained in the individual state statutes. For instance, there are a few states in which a civil demand cannot be issued if there is a criminal matter pending. Understanding the specific criteria to be met on a state-by-state basis is essential.

Effectiveness

The most effective use of civil recovery laws comes in the way of dealing with recidivism. Especially among minors, although most states hold parents responsible, a good way of handling minor cases is by helping parents to exercise control. By allowing the son or daughter to make payments, the consequence for his or her action is realized. Also, this process will not alienate the parents, who are, many times, good customers.

Our internal studies show a rate of recidivism of less than 1% in cases in which the people paid the civil demand. More importantly, in a case study of a major retailer, the overall shrinkage was significantly reduced upon the introduction of a civil demand program.

Outsourcing Collection Services

When a decision is made to create a partnership with a firm to handle any portion of civil collections, several factors should be considered. The first element in this choice should be the services offered by the firm. Many firms today will offer to collect civil recoveries as a return on the services offered by their firm, such as investigation, sale data analysis, and interview costs. Others are law firms, which will add attorney fees to the amount collected and at some point will be retaining more funds than the retailer. Still other firms have the best interest of the industry in mind. They will bring experience in law, loss prevention, and retail. They make the connection between software manufacturers, loss prevention departments, and collection attorneys.

When doing diligence on potential partners, ask for references and also include a request for names of clients lost and why. These requests should also be included in any request for proposal (RFP). Also, some firms will advertise, showing the names of retailers which are only servicing a portion of the cases. Investigate the ownership of the firm, the length of time in the industry, and the amount of litigation encountered along the way.

Currently, there are a few companies active in this arena. My apologies if I have left out any:

1. Civil Demand Associates
   Van Nuys, CA
2. Retail Enterprises
   Winthrop, MA
3. The Zellman Group
   Port Washington, NY
4. Palmer, Reifler & Associates
   Orlando, FL

Civil Restitution

Michael S. Magill

> *Civil restitution is a remedy that operates by state statute and is available to the injured party in addition to sums due by way of other restitution remedies.*

One of the many challenges retail loss prevention professionals have faced over the years is balancing their efforts to reduce shrinkage against the organization's need to reduce costs. Civil restitution initially came about as a bright idea to balance the expenses of store detective payroll by passing those costs along to the people who caused the expenditures in the first place—the shoplifters.

Some History of Civil Restitution

In the early 1970s, the state of Nevada enacted a statute involving the theft of library books and civil remedies available to the victims of these thefts. Later, 10 Western states enacted similar statutes, but specific to the act of shoplifting. At the forefront of this legislation was Ron Clark, then Loss Prevention Director of Payless Drugs in Oregon. Ron recognized the opportunities such legislation offered to loss prevention departments and their retail organizations. It was definitely a useful tool to "manage" shoplifting expenses by passing such costs along to those who caused the losses. Additionally, many loss prevention professionals observed that criminal prosecution of shoplifters was being sidelined by reduced budgets in law enforcement, prosecutors, and what appeared to be an apathetic attitude by some jurisdictions.

In the early 1980s, more and more companies jumped on the bandwagon, after initial court challenges were overturned and the path smoothed by the early pioneers. Many members of ASIS International (then the American Society for Industrial Security) Retail Loss Prevention Council proselytized these laws nationally, and we saw additional states enacting such legislation.

Additionally, many states amended their laws to include parents of juvenile shoplifters.

However, these statutes *did* vary in language and recovery amounts. This occurred because they were enacted by legislators who had to be sensitive to the individual needs, concerns, and the laws of their various jurisdictions.

Most professionals regarded civil restitution as a business tool, rather than punishment.

To Utilize Civil Restitution or Not

Whether a company decides to process civil restitution paperwork internally or opts to use one of the many qualified outside services, several decisions should be considered prior to the adoption of such a program.

First and foremost, upper management *must* buy into the process. To facilitate this, educate them on the laws appropriate in the area in which you do business and what remedies you have under these laws. Besides running a cost-benefit analysis of using such remedies, it would behoove the loss prevention professional to cover such issues as possible loss of business from irate parents who have received demand letters for their miscreant children's illegal acts.

If upper management is adverse to such exposure, one alternative is to send demand letters only to adult shoplifters.

Either way, though, you need to make a decision on just *to whom* you will send demand letters. Will it be *all* shoplifters? Just those you prosecute? Just those you convict? Just those shoplifters stealing more than a specific dollar amount? Once you have made these decisions, you are ready to proceed further.

Once you have the buy-in and decided to whom you will send these demand letters, you need to decide what amount you should demand. Working closely with your attorneys and financial staff, develop what your average cost of handling a shoplifter may entail and document this information.

Costs relevant to shoplifting prevention in your stores may include such items as electronic article surveillance (EAS) systems, electronic and mechanical shoplift prevention devices (such as cables and the like), and labor costs of plainclothes or uniformed shoplift prevention/detention personnel.

Also, in some jurisdictions, you are allowed to ask for a civil penalty and add on the actual cost of the item stolen. In these jurisdictions, the more the shoplifter steals, the more he or she will have to pay for civil restitution!

Prosecute Versus Catch and Release and the Issue of Extortion

Some jurisdictions require you to prosecute the individuals before requesting a demand amount. Most do not. You have the option of catching the shoplifter and releasing him or her, and still making a civil demand for your costs.

Upon review with upper management and your legal department, it will become obvious what tack your company wishes to pursue regarding the issue of prosecution. Every company must make this decision based on what it feel is best for the company, in each individual state's jurisdiction.

Additionally, the issue of catch and release may cause some concern regarding juvenile shoplifters. Most companies will require either law enforcement contact or, in the case of release, parental/guardian response to the location prior to release of a juvenile. Again, this is a matter for each individual company to address.

It is recommended that you *never* present the demand for civil restitution at the time of detention. Any monies gathered at that time could be the basis for allegations of extortion from hungry attorneys who are always on the prowl for a lawsuit against "deep pocket" companies.

However, it is advisable that you give the shoplifter some written document or oral statement backed up in the report that will inform him or her of the possibility of civil demands to be made at a later date. This avoids "surprises" when your demand letter arrives.

Who Decides Who Gets the Demand?

Deciding who gets the demand is an option many companies have agonized about. Many will train their line shoplift detention personnel as to the company's guidelines on sending a civil demand and leave it up to the agent to recommend or not recommend the issuance of such a letter. This approach seems to work best that way, as the person most knowledgeable of the case, with all the facts in hand and with good education of the company's civil demand letter guideline template in hand, calls the shots.

Whoever makes this decision, however, must be cognizant of the company's policy or guideline on the parameters of what qualifies a situation for a civil demand letter and must approve the release of such a letter. This would apply whether the letters are created in-house or outside the company.

Setting Up Your Demand and Collection System

If you decide to create demand letters in-house, you will need to staff up. Consider that you will have to develop a system that will identify which shoplift detentions will merit a demand letter, send a letter on these detentions, track collection or nonpayment, and take further action.

Depending on your jurisdiction and laws, you may wish to pursue nonpayers in civil court. If you decide to follow this course of action, you certainly must first make a decision as to whether it is cost effective to do so. As with decisions to send letters, it is important to be consistent in the application of your decisions. All of this will require time, labor, and systems.

Should you decide to use an outside agency to send your demand letters, your major chore will be to select which detentions merit a demand letter and forward that information to your outside civil restitution agency. In most cases, these agencies will require either a set rate per letter or a percentage of the monies collected. They will follow up on nonpayers, and, in many cases, will function like a collection agency in this matter, sending several letters and even, possibly, making telephone contact with the nonpayers to elicit a payment of the monies due.

It is up to you to determine which will be the most cost-effective method for your company.

In any event, it is always wise to ensure that you are consistent in to whom you send demand letters, and to adhere to your program. This may avoid some legal problems in the future.

Once It Is Up and Running, What Other Issues May Arise?

One major issue is to set up a mechanism that will raise a red flag if a shoplifter is prosecuted and found not guilty. In those cases, it may be advisable to rescind your demand letter. However, you may wish to consult with your company attorney for his or her advice.

Also, it is always advisable to regularly review your cost-benefit analysis regarding costs per shoplifter and, if necessary, change your demand amounts to reflect this cost.

Don't forget to ensure your upper management, who supported your program, receives regular reports on the income generated from your civil restitution program.

In some cases, loss prevention departments will credit part of the costs, or all, back to the retail location which incurred the expenses. Or, it is used to reduce the costs of the loss prevention department. Either way, the company's bottom line is enhanced, and everyone likes that!

Collusion

CAS, JHC

Collusion is best defined as a secretive agreement between two or more people to commit an illegal or deceitful act. In the retail setting, collusion could be an agreement between

- Two or more "customers" to shoplift (as one example),
- A customer and an employee to transact a bogus or otherwise dishonest sales transaction (as a second example), or
- An executive, buyer, or purchasing agent and a second party to bill and pay for goods or services not delivered (as a third example).

We reference "examples" here because the wide range of types of "collusion" is worthy of and is the stuff mystery and crime books are written about. Suffice it then to focus on three examples which should set the stage of understanding for the loss prevention practitioner and/or manager's role in dealing with collusion.

Collusion Between Two Customers to Successfully Shoplift

Customer A attracts some attention to himself in the selection of a relatively small but expensive item of merchandise and "palms" it in his hand. He walks away from the display still carrying the item. Loss prevention takes up the pursuit, following discreetly in anticipation of his leaving the store with the goods in his hand, unpaid for. As this Customer A turns the corner heading toward the door, Customer B, in a group of other customers, passes Customer A. Customer B is carrying a shopping bag. As the two pass, Customer A surreptitiously drops the merchandise into the shopping bag. Both, without acknowledging each other, proceed in different directions. Customer A is stopped outside the store by LP, and he has no merchandise in his possession. Customer B exits by another door with the stolen goods in her shopping bag, unbeknownst to Loss Prevention. The stage is now set for a "false arrest" lawsuit.

Another scenario could be that Customer A intentionally creates a distraction in the middle of the store causing customers and employees to draw toward that area, while a colleague (Customer B) in the corner hides merchandise and subsequently carries it out of the store.

Ad infinitum.

Collusion Between a Customer and an Employee to Commit Theft

Customer A is the roommate of Employee A. Customer A fills her shopping cart with various items of merchandise and enters the checkout lane leading to the checkout cashier, Employee A. Employee A intentionally fails to record the prices of various items. The total sale may reflect the correct price of 20 items of merchandise, but 9 items of merchandise were never rung up or paid for, as intended in this collusive plan.

A second example: Customer B is Employee D's sister-in-law. Customer B brings into the store a store bag and a receipt for $60 worth of merchandise charged to her account, but no merchandise. Employee D writes a fraudulent charge credit for the amount reflected on the charge receipt, which amounts to a theft of $60. The prior agreement between B and D to this scheme for committing this theft is also the crime of collusion.

Collusion Between a Second Party and an Executive, Buyer, or Purchasing Agent for Payment of Goods, Supplies, Materials, or Services Not Received and/or Rendered

The chief engineer of the warehouse and distribution center receives an invoice from a "painting contractor" for painting jobs around the facility. In reality, the painter painted the engineer's mountain cabin and prepared the invoice reflecting work completed on company property, which was never done. The chief engineer approves the invoice and the painter is paid.

The buyer for hardware makes a deal with the stepladder supplier to inflate the invoice by $6 for each ladder purchased by the retailer, with the agreement they will subsequently split the $6 difference between the correct price and the inflated price paid by the company.

The store manager approves an in-store purchase of Christmas decorations, and the invoice is prepared by his brother-in-law. No decorations were received. His brother-in-law isn't in the business of selling decorations. This arrangement represents collusion between the two to cheat the store and illegitimately receive money to which they were not entitled.

Two actual collusion cases are reviewed in the "Fraudulent Outsourcing and Invoicing" section in this book.

In the retail environment, there are endless possibilities for collusion between employees themselves, employees and customers, and between employees and vendors. The possibilities are limited only by imagination and creativeness. This potential for losses, which can easily reach into the thousands of dollars, is but one, albeit an important one, of the reasons for instituting a system of checks and balances and frequent audits, including the vetting of vendors, particularly those of the small independent contractor variety.

Company Property

CAS, JHC

The chief maintenance engineer of a major distribution center was detected stealing paint from the facility, and upon inspection of his garage at home, many items of merchandise and a sizeable collection of equipment and tools were discovered and believed to be the property of the company. The employee refused to admit to any theft other than the paint. A small percentage of merchandise bearing company price tickets was seized, but goods without any form of company identification and all the tools and hardware—from compressors to dollies and power tools—bore no company identification. Despite efforts to seek recovery through the criminal justice system, the then ex-employee was allowed to keep most of what was stolen property. Why? Because the company could not prove the items belonged to it.

This issue of establishing and proving ownership has long been a problem in the retail industry. How many fashion stores have had shipments of high price-point goods stolen, even in mass, like furs, and weeks later the police seize a large quantity of furs during one of their arrests and seek the owners/victims. And at store after store, despite evidence that furs were stolen and with copies of crime reports in hand, no one from any store could actually identify specific fur coats or shawls as theirs. The furs then ended up in police auctions. And so it has been with other kinds of merchandise as well as company property such as POS devices, copiers, computers, and a wide variety of expensive pieces of equipment.

Interestingly, many items of office equipment have serial numbers, but when one disappears, no one knows or has a record of that serial number. The question is: Who is or should be responsible for the inventory control of equipment? The loss prevention/security or operations department? Should the control (and records) be companywide or by individual facility? Who should audit this program and do spot checks to reconcile the books versus the actual inventory? The audit or loss prevention department?

Our recommendation is this: Control and audit of company property and equipment should be the responsibility of the loss prevention department, by individual unit. That said, then the challenge is to develop a program in which all company property is recorded by type and by serial number, if available, and to inscribe a number if no factory number is in place. Many police departments offer a property identification program in which a crime prevention officer comes to a small business or residence and inscribes with an etching tool the owner's Social Security number or other number for future identification purposes in the event of a loss due to criminal activity.

One of your authors was the Chief of Campus Police (later renamed to Chief of Campus Security) of the Claremont Colleges in Southern California. Early in his tenure, he discovered bicycle theft was a serious and ongoing problem. The group of contiguous colleges with its thousands of student bicycles was a target for bicycle thieves. Although every bike had its own manufacturer's identification number, students invariably did not record that number. Even if the student/owner was interested in the number, it was long, small, and hard to read; plus, the bike had to be turned upside-down to see it. An inspection of the various local police departments' evidence rooms disclosed hundreds of recovered bicycles, all of course bearing ID numbers but unclaimed. Indeed, if a student went to a police department and claimed "that bike over there, the red one, is mine," unless he or she had some evidence of ownership, that student walked home.

A workable solution: The campus police purchased a set of 10 numbered dies, a ball-peen hammer, and a ledger book. The various student newspapers of each college announced a new bicycle registration program in which the campus police would at no charge stamp a four-digit number on the upper side of the pedal sprocket and record that number.

Thereafter, when a student reported a missing or stolen bicycle, that loss was duly noted by the campus police, who subsequently would either visit the police station and look for the conspicuous college registration numbers because of the size and location and recover the bikes or delay visits until a few days before public auctions. Students were also encouraged to go to the police, but most opted not to.

The bottom line of this program is that many bicycles were recovered, in sharp contrast to earlier times without the program.

Does this strategy or something similar have application with company property in the retail industry?

Concessionaires and Tenants

CAS, JHC

Concessionaire departments, which comprise retail entities within the confines of a given store, do require special and unique attention. Examples of concessionaires and tenants could include fur salons, beauty salons, optometrists, watch repair, fine jewelry departments, wigs, fast-food entities, etc. These "special and unique" workers, who typically have access to the interior of the store during closed hours, appear to be but are not store employees. Yet they must comply to most store policies and procedures; e.g., if employees are required to enter and exit the store only through a designated "employee door," concessionaire and tenant employees must be instructed to comply with that requirement. These "extraordinary" employees should be badged while in the store yet restricted from "back of the house" areas in which they have no business.

And concessionaires and tenants can pose unusual problems if their owner, operator, or employees are detected in any form of dishonesty. In the event such persons are detected in acts of dishonesty, they are to be processed not as employees but rather in keeping with the store's procedures dealing with any nonemployees, i.e., shoplifters.

Conditional (Controlled) Release

CAS, JHC

Most retailers, when a shoplifter is apprehended, think they have only two courses of action: (a) release the shoplifter after a warning or (b) call the police and start the criminal prosecution procedure. What they do not realize is that they have a third option: the conditional (controlled) release.

What is a conditional release? It is an arrangement and written agreement between the person detained and the store whereby the first time a person is caught shoplifting, the disposition regarding that arrest is stayed with the understanding if not detected again within 1 year the matter will be dropped. If caught again, however, in that period of time in any of the company's stores, the person will be prosecuted on *both* the original as well as the latest theft.

One aspect of the controlled release is that the suspect is aware that the company may file charges at a later date; this knowledge may cause the suspect a sleepless night or two worrying about this possibility. One hopes such worry may dissuade him or her from further acts of shoplifting.

Merchant may use the conditional release under any circumstance in which they feel it is appropriate.

For a suggested form to be given the person being released under this procedure, see the "Forms" section of this book.

Conscience Letters

CAS, JHC

Occasionally, a store will receive a letter, either anonymously or signed, from a person who has stolen from the store in the past and is confessing to that theft. These letters, known as "conscience letters," are usually accompanied by a check or money order (and sometimes cash) to compensate the store for the amount of merchandise taken. These letters are from either shoplifters or former employees.

Such a letter is reproduced in Figures C-5A and C-5B; the name and address have been redacted.

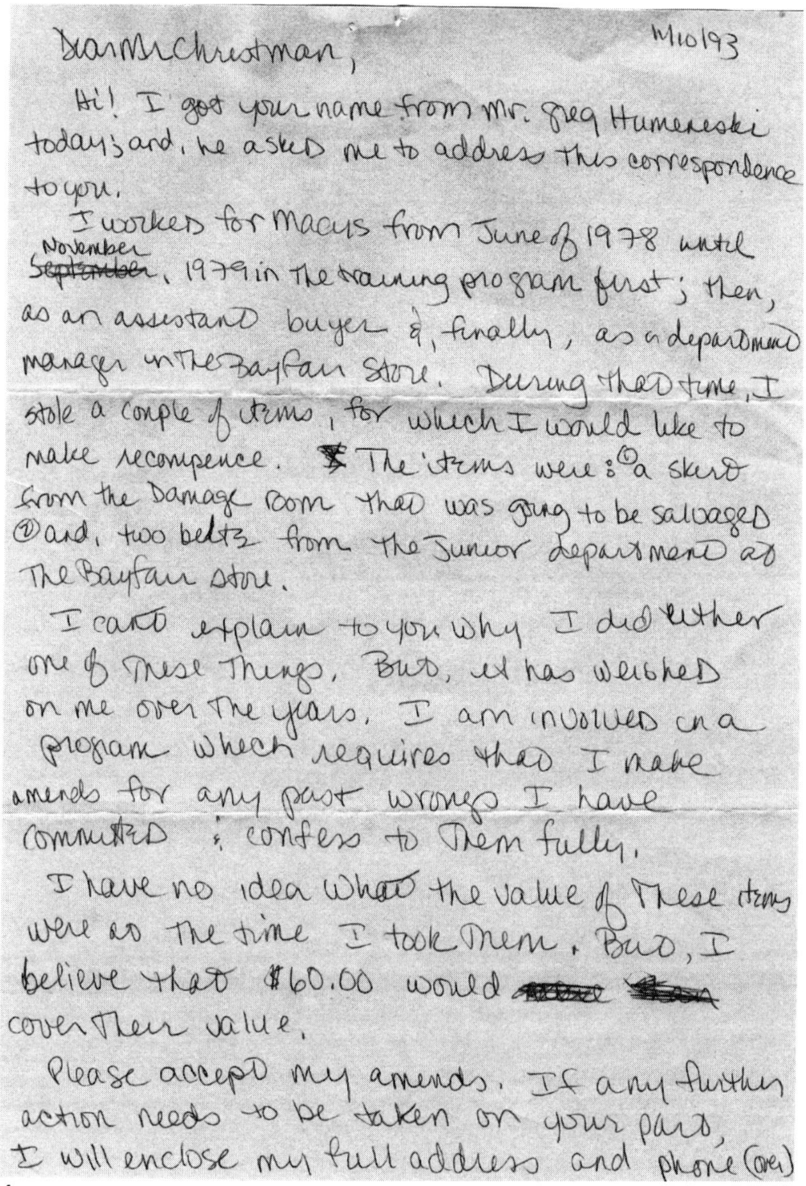

A

FIGURE C-5 Partially redacted conscience letters

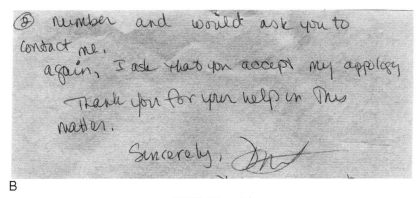

B

FIGURE C-5 cont'd

When a conscience letter contains the name and address of the sender, it is appropriate to write a letter of thanks and acknowledge receipt of the funds, which should be deposited in a "restitution account." If the store doesn't have a restitution account, record the amount in the department from which the goods were taken and attach the cash register throw receipt to the letter and file in loss prevention department's conscience letter file. If the store/company maintains an alpha negative file on all persons detained, add the sender's name to the file and reference it to the conscience letter file.

Consent to Search

CAS, JHC

Occasionally, in connection with a theft investigation, it may prove useful to retrieve evidence by searching an automobile or a house. There are severe restrictions and legalities in pursuing such a search, and our advice is to consult with company or other competent legal counsel before conducting such a search. We set forth a form for obtaining consent for such a search in Figure C-6, but again advise consulting counsel before doing so.

Contract Security in Retail Environments

Don Horan

Ever since the first Pinkertons rode the rails protecting commerce in the Old West, private industry has utilized professional security services to safeguard their assets. The modern retailer is no different; uniformed security officers, often contracted from service providers, still dot the landscape of retail stores, both on the selling floor and behind the scenes. The prevailing reasoning is self-evident: A visible presence of store security deters theft and promotes awareness, and the security officer remains the essence of presence.

Over time, however, retail loss prevention directors have had to modify, reevaluate, and ultimately reinvent the role of contract security in a modern retail loss prevention program. Service providers, ever mindful of changing conditions, strive to meet the evolving needs as well.

Retailers today can choose from variable offerings of contract security services: the well-established uniformed guard; the emerging product offering that is contract store detectives, or "floor walkers"; and the more recent notion of engaging independent contractors, sometimes called "consultants," for specialized LP functions relating to IT, internal audit, and shrink control program development.

Contract Security Guards

Since uniformed guards remain the most prevalent use of contract security in retail, it is appropriate to quickly review the key advantages most often cited in deploying "outside" guards.

CONSENT TO SEARCH

Date:_____

I,_____ employed by _____ and residing at

_____ do willfully and voluntarily, and without fear of threat

or promise of reward, hereby consent to and authorize _____,

of _____ Security Department to search my _____

located at _____ and to seize and take possession of any items

belonging to _____ and in my possession either illegally or without

proper authority. Items specifically to be searched for include:

(1) _____

(2) _____

(3) _____ - but this consent to
search is not in any way limited to the above listed items.

I have also been advised that any items seized may be used as evidence against me in any subsequent

prosecution or other legal proceeding.

With all the above in mind, I again affirm my consent to the above described search.

Signed _____

Witnessed: Time:

------------------------------.

Search commenced at: _____

Search concluded at: _____

Search conducted by: _____

Search witnessed by: _____

Items   seized:

_____

_____

____

Witnessed: Signed:

FIGURE C-6 Consent to search

Flexibility: The better guard companies can fill an immediate need almost instantly. Whether the need is temporary or permanent, night or day, fixed post or patrol, one officer or 10, LP directors using established providers can reliably summon the help they need with one call.

Few LP programs rely solely on contract guards for shrink control. However, the role of contract security officers has expanded well beyond the traditional "door guard": Companies now employ contract security for lobby reception positions at the home office, permanent shift work at warehouses and distribution centers, augmented store presence for special events and the holiday sales season, overnight security on construction and renovation details, and response to adverse incidents such as robbery and other workplace-related violence.

Economy: The flat-rate, hourly billing formula indigenous to contract security provides cost control and accurate expense forecasting more reliably than the vagaries of payroll rates of proprietary staff. Fixed costs, with pay-as-you-go scheduling, allows for planned budgetary allocations by location and shift that eliminates expense "surprises" and provides an unambiguous cost/benefit analysis. Compared to technology and systems-reliant LP resources where ROI justification is sometimes elusive, guards are a tangible commodity, easily quantified: "this many dollars buys this many hours." Further, it has been long held that for some security positions, contract security is more cost effective than proprietary, or in-house, security employees. Contract security advocates point to the corporate pay scales that often result in higher wages for security employees, coupled with overtime opportunity and a benefit package that includes medical insurance, worker's compensation, vacation, sick days, and more to argue that the hourly rate charged by a security service provider can be significantly less costly in the long run than an in-house counterpart. These advocates do not contend you get a better guard—just a cheaper one.

New realities to the marketplace, however, should prompt the prudent LP director to periodically revisit the cost ratios between contract and proprietary security. Liability insurance, worker's compensation, licensing and certifications, unemployment insurance, and payroll taxes continue to encroach on security companies' profit margins, and escalating costs are passed along accordingly. In some states, sales tax can add another 5–8% to the bill in addition to the quoted hourly rate. The contract security industry is also keeping a close eye on the efforts of the Service Employees International Union (SEIU) and others in their drive to organize contract security officers. Such an event, security companies contend, would further elevate their cost of service.

Having quantified the advantages of contract security from the business side, its effectiveness as a loss prevention tool can be examined. It would be appropriate here to first outline the expectations a retail LP executive would have when engaging a contract guard service:

- A visible, competent presence of security that may deter customers from shoplifting.
- Guards who arrive on time, groomed and outfitted in a manner that projects a professional security image.
- Guards who represent the corporate LP program favorably to store management and staff.
- Guards who have minimum training in the basics of retail security, e.g., alert enough to deter a hit-and-run at the door; able to manage an EAS alarm without incident; detect and communicate suspicious customer activity to management.

Welcomed, but not necessarily expected, value-added services may include the following:

- An ability to identify suspicious employee activity and report it to the company supervisor for communication back to you.
- An ability to intercede, within reasonable bounds, to prevent a loss of merchandise to a shoplifter.

- Perhaps, in the right circumstances, escort a manager to and from a bank deposit that involves a short walk to an after-hours bank drop.
- Witness that the building is properly secured and alarmed at closing, and where prudent, see the closing employees safely to their cars.

Reasonable expectations of the service provider include the following:

- That the guard will have undergone and passed a criminal background check with the state prior to being posted to your location.
- That the guard is properly licensed and the guard company is in compliance with state regulatory requirements.
- That the client company has a modicum of protection from liability by virtue of clear indemnification language in your service contract.
- That the guard company will handle schedule rotations in such a way as to provide, if preferred, no more than three different officers to staff a 7-day post.
- Billing integrity, with auditable invoicing accountability.

The ability of service providers to meet or exceed expectations rests chiefly in the relationship cultivated between subscriber and the provider.

Vendor loyalty plays a significant part as providers often "go the extra mile" in both guard quality and cost accommodation for clients offering the prospect of steady work and consistent deployment requirements. LP directors can enhance the guard's effectiveness with detailed post orders and site-specific training, a reasonable and self-serving accommodation the client can make, provided the company assigns a security officer who is educable and committed to making the investment in time worthwhile. For a contract security officer to make a contribution to a store's performance, the cost is both money and time.

Many retail LP practitioners cite a "disconnect" between their expectations and the deliverables from guard companies. Grooming and professional appearance are issues; demeanor and conduct on post are increasingly casual; relevant training vis-à-vis shrink control is virtually absent. There is a perception—some would say a reality—that standards among service industry workers across-the-board have declined and that the contract security officer has followed this trend. As a result, the user's expectations of the service provider may require reconsideration, even on something as basic as credible background checks.

Security jobs are often temporary positions, and the applicants are often transient workers; a criminal background check in one state may not always reveal misdeeds in another. Reference checking can be suspect as well. In some instances a security officer is hired one day and dispatched to your store that same night.

Security companies reflect the changes to the American workforce, and as the workforce continues to absorb workers from outside the country, a state criminal check for a security guard applicant recently immigrated is unlikely to yield any adverse information; fingerprint checks are not run through Interpol. An applicant's criminal past in another country would likely go undetected.

Expectations for relevant training may also have to be curtailed. State and local licensing regulations require costly certifications and training, little of which is relevant to preventing inventory shrink. As a result, any orientation an entry-level security officer receives is that of a "generalist," and the contract provider has little opportunity for additional training specific to the retailer's needs. The days of a guard "in training" standing post with a seasoned officer at the security company's expense are long gone. Moreover, as security companies attract and hire more foreign workers, it becomes questionable how well traditional training curricula allow for cultural differences and language limitations, and enables newly immigrated security officers to interact with retail customers and employees in a manner that reflects positively on the client company.

Another contributing factor for expectations falling short is the reality of litigation-avoidance that guard companies must address aggressively if they are to survive. Costly litigation, punitive awards, and rising premiums have had a numbing effect on the industry, and "marching orders" issued to guards by their employer to prevent confrontation and litigation can be so restrictive as to boil down to a mantra of "see nothing, say nothing, do nothing." The long-held security officer's credo of "observe and report" may now include the caveat: "and take no action." Understandable? Certainly. Does it endear the guard to the store manager who is told a man just ran out with an armful of dresses as the guard looked on? Certainly not.

As with all resources, contract security guards have their benefits and their limitations. The savvy LP professional will understand that background checks are limited, training is questionable, and the security companies must look out for their own bottom line before that of their client. These factors will be weighed in the context of security needs and the economic realities of budget. If a provider cannot balance the mutual interests of the client as well as his or her own, other options will emerge.

Contract Store LP Agents

Store detectives (now called LP agents) had once been the core component of retail LP programs. Over time, as shrink control became the purview of both store operations and finance, these one-dimensional assets dwindled in import and number. Some were redirected to audit functions, others became employee investigation specialists, but many became the payroll trade-off for capital expenditures in systems and technology that have collectively and consistently reduced inventory shrink industrywide.

Yet, occasionally, certain situations arise in which only the apprehension of a shoplifter or dishonest employee is going to protect the assets. There is a hard-core element that will not be deterred by uniformed guards at the door, signs in the fitting room, or cameras behind smoked domes, whether they be daredevils, opportunists, or foot soldiers in an organized retail theft syndicate.

In the days before imbedded EAS, covert CCTV, automated POS exception analysis, RFID inventory control, and extensive security fixturing, it was the store detective who protected merchandise from theft. Some were nondescript floor walkers who blended in; others were eccentric characters who raised the game to an art level. Each, however, possessed a vanishing skill set to exploit the selling floor terrain and observe, react, and close on shoplifters and employees alike, with an impressive record for clean, substantial cases. But their payroll burden on downsizing companies, coupled with the exposure to litigation, augured the winnowing of this profession and ushered in the era of technology and audit, with undeniably favorable results.

Many LP directors understand program effectiveness is cyclical, and although store detectives will never again be the catchall LP solution, some still prefer to have a deployable asset on call that can enter a market and mitigate a debilitating external theft condition. Enter the entrepreneurial contract security provider, eager to either create or diversify product offerings to meet a need in the marketplace.

Since the mid-1990s, contract store detectives have been an innovation touted in discussion but embraced only at arm's length in practice. Variations on the theme have included a "shared pool" of LP personnel provided to multiple users on a mall-by-mall basis; to uniformed guard companies offering "plain-clothes" personnel for patrol and added deterrence; to specialists who monitor CCTV stations remotely or onsite and communicate live-time to store personnel.

Economically, the program suffers from being an "add-on" expense rather than a "trade-off" cost, as would be the case where a contract guard replaces an in-house security employee. The contract security company providing personnel incurs real setup costs in training, travel expense, and exposure to litigation that drives up the hourly rate to the point at which the program becomes an indulgence rather than a necessity. Even success can be damaging to the program: The plaudits earned from sensational cases heralded at the time as legitimate justification wane over time as the case winds its way through the criminal justice system, generating costly invoices for time spent in courts, not in stores.

Still, the concept continues to garner interest. For companies unable to fund advances in systems and technology and unwilling to bear the payroll cost of full-time, in-house store detectives, a contract store detective program can be properly honed to deliver presence, deterrence, and perhaps a quantifiable return on investment through the recovery of merchandise.

Independent Contractors and Consultants

Many retail companies operate with nominal LP staffing; some with only a single LP executive at corporate; others with a small field staff reporting into store operations; still others with none at all. These are generally smaller, regional retailers or growth companies poised to expand through acquisition, or distressed companies that have significantly downsized. As LP needs become realized, management often turns to independent contractors and consultants to provide expertise, guidance, and procedural development to fledgling LP programs.

The ranks of independent LP professionals marketing their services today include some of the best known and highly accomplished practitioners in the industry. They are often called upon to invigorate a company's LP efforts, tasked with creating awareness and training programs, developing policy and procedural guidelines, and negotiating vendor contracts.

It is not unheard of for companies to have an LP professional on retainer, involved in internal audit and inventory control, store planning and construction recommendations, logistics at distribution centers, security planning for special events, and incident management. These are executive functions normally carried out by LP directors, but where that position does not exist, LP consultants have sought to fill the void.

The trend and the resource has by no means been lost on larger companies with fully developed LP structures. In many cases, LP contractors are engaged on a temporary basis to nurture special projects through the developmental stage, provide or augment specialized functions within IT or finance, or fill a crucial job position during an executive search process.

Consulting engagements tend to be costly, and as such, companies prefer a finite timetable for contract security projects. Seldom do consultants remain for extended periods in positions better suited to an executive employee.

As the business of loss prevention continues to evolve and expand, expertise becomes more compartmentalized. Outsourcing to independent contractors proficient in specialized areas of the retail business, loss prevention included, should remain a viable option for companies determined to improve shrink performance.

Counterfeit Currency

Jim Lansberry

We all handle money everyday. The most tested way to tell if you have a counterfeit U.S. bill in your hand is to feel it. When you receive a bill in your hand and that bill feels "funny," it's time to look at a few other security features that are easily identifiable within the new U.S. bills. The following examples will utilize the $20 bill. The new $5, $10, $50, and $100 bills all have similar security features within them.

The most common "test" that we all tend to fall back on is counterfeit marking pens. They leave a nice golden mark on a "good" bill and ugly black mark on a "bad" bill. The problem with the pens is that they will fool with you. If I take a US $1 bill, bleach it out, and then print a new denomination, say $20 on the $1 bill I just bleached out, is the pen going to detect what I did to change that $1 bill to a $20 bill? No, it will not. So, your company just lost $19 because of a $2 pen doing the job it's supposed to do.

Watermark portrait. If you look at the new color $20 bill, you will notice that there is a watermark portrait to the right of the seal. This portrait is of Andrew Jackson. Each denomination has a different portrait with corresponding watermark. Sometimes counterfeiters will bleach out $5 bills and print $20, $50, or $100 denominations on the bleached $5 bill. If a cashier uses the counterfeit pen and holds the bill up to a light and sees the portrait of Abe Lincoln, he or she assumes it's a good bill. It is not. The presidential portraits are not interchangeable:

- Abe Lincoln's portrait belongs on a $5 bill.
- Alexander Hamilton's portrait belongs on a $10 bill.
- Andrew Jackson's portrait belongs on a $20 bill.

- Ulysses S. Grant's portrait belongs on a $50 bill.
- Benjamin Franklin's portrait belongs on a $100 bill.

The $1 and $2 bills do not have watermark portraits.

So far, we have used two security tests to test our bills, and we have still taken in counterfeit money. So now let's move on to some really cool security features that are built right into the bills.

The color shifting ink test. In the lower right corner of the new bills there is a denomination (10, 20, 50, or 100) number. This number, when the bill is tilted up and down, will change the color shifting ink in that number from copper to green.

Security thread or plastic strip There is a security thread that is embedded in the bill and runs vertically up one side of the note. Using a unique thread position for each denomination guards against certain counterfeit techniques, such as bleaching ink off a lower denomination and using the paper to "reprint" the bill as a higher value note. The strip is easily seen when the bill is held up to a light. You should be able to see the words "USA TWENTY" or whatever denomination of bill it is and a small U.S. flag. The security threads glow different colors for different denominations under an ultraviolet light. There are several types of ultraviolet lights available to the general public. These ultraviolet lights are cool in that, when you put real money under the light, the security thread glows:

- The $5 bill security thread glows blue.
- The $10 bill security thread glows orange.
- The $20 bill security thread glows green.
- The $50 bill security thread glows yellow.
- The $100 bill security thread glows red.

In addition, credit cards also have their own ultraviolet glow under these lights. State ID cards and state licenses all glow under an ultraviolet light as well. For instance, when you hold a California driver's license under an ultraviolet light, the California state seal glows. In addition, MasterCard, Visa, and American Express glow under ultraviolet light. These are security features that many people who handle cash don't know about.

The symbols of freedom. Each denomination has a different symbol of freedom on the bill:

- The new $10 bill has two images of the torch carried by the Statue of Liberty printed in red on the face of the note. A large image of the torch is printed in the background to the left of the portrait of Secretary Hamilton, while a second, smaller metallic red image of the torch is found on the lower right side of the portrait.
- The new $20 bill has a large blue eagle in the background of President Andrew Jackson. There is a smaller metallic green eagle with a shield just to the lower right of his portrait.
- The new $50 bill has images that represent the American flag. The traditional stars and stripes of the United States flag are printed in blue and red behind the portrait of President Grant. A field of blue stars is located to the left of the portrait, while three red stripes are located to the right of the portrait. A small metallic silver-blue star is located on the lower right side of the portrait.
- The newest $5 and $100 bills currently in circulation do not have the Symbols of Freedom security features.

Micro printing. Micro-printed words are hard to replicate because they are so small. The new color bills have a lot of newly designed micro printing within the bills:

- The new $5 bill has this feature in two areas. The words "FIVE DOLLARS" can be found in the side borders on the front, and "The United States of America" appears along the lower edge of the portrait's oval frame.
- The new $10 bill has this feature in two areas. The word "USA" and the numeral "10" can be found repeated beneath the large printed torch, and the words "THE UNITED STATES OF AMERICA" and "TEN DOLLARS" can be found below the portrait, as well as vertically inside the left and right borders of the note.

- The new $20 bill has this feature in two areas. Bordering the first three letters of the "TWENTY USA" ribbon to the right of the portrait, the inscription "USA20" is printed in blue. "THE UNITED STATES OF AMERICA 20 USA 20" appears in black on the border below the Treasurer's signature.
- The $50 bill has this feature in three areas. The words "FIFTY," "USA," and the numeral "50" can be found in two of the blue stars to the left of the portrait; the word "FIFTY" can be found repeated within both side borders of the note; and the words "THE UNITED STATES OF AMERICA" appear on President Ulysses S. Grant's collar, under his beard.
- The $100 bill has this feature in two areas. On the face of the note "USA 100" is repeated within the number 100 in the lower left corner. "The United States of America" appears as a line in the left lapel of Franklin's coat.

Acceptance Policies. Acceptance policies will differ from retailer to retailer. Make sure you are within your policies and procedures on what to do if a bad bill is passed.

Following are some general guidelines:

- If a bill is determined to be counterfeit, without putting *anyone* in harm's way, you need to delay the passer of the bill in order to obtain as much information about the passer as you can. In other words, you need to become a very good witness.
- "I'm sorry, sir[ma'am]. I don't have the correct change for this bill." This is an example of a statement that you can make to the passer. Then secure your till and walk directly to your back room. Contact your LP department, manager, or supervisor, whomever your store policies dictate.
- If the passer insists on getting his or her bill back, without getting into any altercation, whether it be verbal or physical, state to the passer, "I'm sorry, sir[ma'am]; by law I cannot give this bill back until a determination has been made regarding the bill." Say this once. If the passer insists or appears as though he or she will become combative or you feel threatened, give the bill back and turn into the best witness you can.
- If you can safely follow the passer to the parking lot and observe what type of vehicle he or she is driving or which direction of travel is used, do so.
- Immediately notify authorities (this is if the situation has become combative) and tell them what happened.
- If the passer stays in the store when you are in the back room and LP or supervisors are checking on the bill, call your local authorities and inform them of the situation if it is determined to be a bad bill.
- *Do not* call the Secret Service directly. They will be notified directly from local law enforcement depending the outcome of their investigation of the counterfeit bill.
- At no time should any retail employee, security, loss prevention, manager, or *any* employee get confrontational with a counterfeit passer. Some of these people are very nasty and are armed or otherwise very, very dangerous.
- No life is worth a passed counterfeit bill.

It has been my experience that a majority of counterfeit bills are passed by people who are ignorant to the fact that they have counterfeit bills. So as not to wrongfully accuse an innocent person of a crime, approach each incident with caution but respect to the person who passed the bill. With a couple of key questions to the passer, you will be able to tell by attitude and body language if this person actually knows why his or her bill has been confiscated. An innocent person will want to know why he or she can't get any money for the bad money just passed. A bad person will run or will insist on getting the money back or will escalate the situation verbally (become loud) or physically (display weapon or become combative). Remember, this a worthless piece of paper. It's not worth your life or the bad press your company could get.

Training posters, DVDs, VHS tapes, flyers, and pamphlets are all free for the asking and are great new hire orientation tools for cash handlers, LP , security, and anybody else who needs or wants to learn about our money. All of this material can be obtained from The U.S. Bureau of Engraving and Printing website (www.moneyfactory.gov/).

Courtroom Appearance and Testimony

CAS, JHC

Loss prevention agents engaged in detection and detention of shoplifters will invariably be summoned to court for the purpose of testifying against a shoplifter or dishonest employee. That past person stands as a defendant in a criminal prosecution and has pled "Not Guilty" to the charge upon which he or she was arrested and is now being prosecuted. The prosecutor represents the people of the state against the defendant and is the LP agent's "attorney." The defendant, with rare exception, is represented by a either a public defender or a privately retained defense attorney.

The trial will be either a "court" trial, i.e., will be heard by a judge only, or a jury trial, wherein the matter will be heard and decided upon by members of the community who serve as jurors, usually 12 in number, but there could be fewer than that number. The summonsing process is typically by way of the issuance of a subpoena.

In preparation for this appearance, the agent is encouraged to review the report of the incident the night before trial and again on the morning of the trial to ensure the details are refreshed and can be recalled while on the stand.

The agent should arrive at the court at least one-half hour prior to the court going into session and upon arrival enter the courtroom and seek out the prosecutor and introduce himself or herself. Commonly, the prosecutor will want to meet and talk to the agent who indeed will be the key witness in the trial. That prosecutor (e.g., deputy district attorney, deputy state attorney) will have a copy of the agent's original report as well as the police department's crime or arrest report. That meeting and brief discussion are most important because it will bring the prosecutor "up to speed" on the matter. This is but one of many cases each prosecutor must handle each week, so he or she needs this quick orientation. At some point the prosecutor will invite the agent to sit at the counsel table with him or her for assistance during the trial.

The agent should be dressed in business attire, preferably a suit and tie or, if a female agent, in a conservative skirt and blouse with a jacket. If evidence was retained by the store, the agent should bring such evidence to court and give it to the prosecutor for his or her use in the trial.

When the judge enters the courtroom, all stand until the judge is seated. When the judge calls the case, the prosecutor will answer "Ready," as does the defense, and the trial is underway. If the agent is seated at the counsel table, he or she should sit with folded hands and exhibit focused interest on the proceedings without any animated expressions or body language.

The prosecutor will make opening remarks to the court and jury, outlining the case and inform them how he or she will prove the guilt of the defendant. The defense then makes opening remarks emphasizing the innocence of the defendant. The agent must refrain from smiling, winking, or rolling his or her eyes during this process, despite the compulsion to do so. This is dead-serious business.

In a criminal trial the "people" (prosecutor) put forth their case first, i.e., call all witnesses and present evidence until their case is completed. It is during the people's case that the LP agent will be called to the stand.

When the prosecutor is ready for the testimony of the agent, he or she will announce, "The people call *Robert Miller* (*the agent*) as our next witness." The agent gets up and approaches the witness stand, which is located next to bench (behind which sits the judge), and before taking the seat in the witness box, will be asked to raise his or her right hand a swear or affirm the testimony about to be given will be the truth. Once the oath is taken, the agent takes the seat.

The agent will be asked, typically by the court clerk, to state his or her full name and address. The prosecutor, who is now standing, will commence with direct examination. For the sake of this writing, there are four examinations, normally: (1) Direct, by the people; (2) Cross-examination, by the defense; (3) Redirect, by the people; and (4) Recross, by the defense. The witness may be subjected to more than one redirect and recross, depending on the complexity of the case and the testimony offered.

Once seated, the agent should look at the jury, recognizing their presence, settle back with clasped hands, not cross one leg over the other, and relax in anticipation of the process of questioning which is about to unfold.

Invariably, in a typical shoplifting prosecution, the prosecutor will commence by re-asking the witness's name and then ask:

> *"What is your occupation, sir?"*
> *"I'm a Loss Prevention Officer with Big Home Stores."*
> *"How long have you been employed with Big Home?"*
> *"Twenty-two months, sir."*
> *"And were you so employed on January 7 of this year?"*
> *"Yes, sir."*
> *"Do you recognize the defendant in this case, seated at the counsel*
>   *table with his attorney?"*
> *"Yes, sir."*
> *"When and where did you first see him?"*
> *"I first observed him in the tool crib area of Big Home on Broadway*
>   *Blvd. about 11:30 in the morning."*
> *"That was on January 7?"*
> *"Yes, sir, January 7. I'm sorry."*
> *"Was he alone in the tool crib?"*
> *"No, sir. There were several customers in the same area."*
> *"What attracted your attention to him?"*
> *"I noticed he was continually looking all around, not paying any*
>   *attention to the merchandise in his hand."*
> *"What kind of merchandise did he have in his hand?"*
> *"A cordless drill."*
> *"Why would looking all around catch your attention?"*

Note the relatively short responsive answers. The agent should only answer the questions and not volunteer any information except to answer questions as succinctly as possible.

The answers are directed to the questioner, but from time to time, part of an answer can be made while looking toward a juror, just to keep them in the loop. There are schools of thought that all answers should be directed to the jury, but we believe there's an artificiality to that strategy, so we encourage most answers be directed back to the person who propounds the question. Indeed, testimony is an exchange between counsel and the witness, and the jurors are like an audience who continually weigh, measure, and assess the exchange. The witness and counsel are as if on stage.

The agent must be aware he or she is in a glass fishbowl while in the witness box, and every move and every word are noted. Jurors are critical in their evaluation of each witness, and they, like most humans, tend not to like some people because of how they look or speak and, on the opposite side of the coin, tend to like others. And those they tend to like, they tend to believe more than those they don't like. It's a weakness of human nature. If you're in this position, the message here is: Don't do or say anything that could alienate yourself from a juror, including using slang or industry jargon, like I went out and "busted" him, or indicating in any way a bias or prejudice. Loss prevention agents testifying in the court system are expected to conduct themselves as professionals.

After the prosecutor completes questions about the involvement in the event, he or she "passes" the witness to the defendant's attorney for "cross-examination."

The cross-examination is a process whereby the witness's credibility is challenged.

Here's an example:

"Now, Mr. Miller. You've told us you've been employed with Big Home for 22 months. Is that correct?"
"Yes, sir."
"And you're a loss prevention officer. Is that correct?"
"Yes, sir."
"Now, you arrested my client in January, which is 7 months ago, correct?"
"Yes, sir."
"So, at the time of this incident, you'd been an employee of Big Home for 15 months, is that so?"
"Yes."
"Now, when you were originally hired by Big Home, was your first assignment with Loss Prevention?"
"No, sir, I was hired as a sales associate in the garden shop."
"In the garden shop as a sales associate! That's interesting. So how long did you work in the garden shop before you went to Loss Prevention?"
"Almost a year."
"A year! So let's see. You were a Loss Prevention Agent for only 3 months at the time you arrested my client. Is that correct?"
"Yes."
"When you were transferred into Loss Prevention, did the store send you to any outside training classes or school to be a Loss Prevention Agent?"
"No, sir. They gave me OJT."
"What does OJT stand for?"
"On the job training. It means I worked alongside an experienced agent, on the job."
"Who was that agent? What was his name?"
"John Mann."
"How long had John Mann worked at Big Store?"
"Over a year, I think."
"Did he train you in understanding the laws of arrest in this state?"
"He and I focused on the rule of when I can stop someone and when I can't."
"But you don't know the statute detailing the laws pertaining to citizen's arrests, do you?"
"No, sir, not by the legal code section or whatever."
"Ever taken any college courses in criminal justice or criminology?"
"No, sir."

Attorneys who engage in cross-examinations employ tactics which tend to unnerve and fluster witnesses in hopes they'll get angry or otherwise do or say things which undermine their credibility in hopes of persuading the jury the witness isn't telling the whole truth. Clearly, in the preceding exchange, the defense counsel is attempting to paint the agent as new, inexperienced, untrained, and unqualified to engage in this very complicated business of arresting customers. Bottom line: The attorney's goal is to discredit the witness's qualifications and his or her version of what transpired, leading, the attorney hopes, to an acquittal.

Hence, the agent undergoing cross-examination must remain calm, must not become argumentative, and must not glare at the attorney.

Two fundamental rules in testifying are as follows:

1. Always tell the truth, the absolute truth.
2. Don't get sassy or argumentative with the opposing attorney. The defendant will win and you will lose.

Once the cross-examination is completed, the prosecutor may choose to exercise the right to engage in a redirect examination. Redirect examination is exercised when the prosecutor wants to clarify a point and expand on what was testified to on cross-examination, or to rehabilitate the witness.

"Rehabilitation" means to "rescue" or "patch up" something the witness said or failed to say which could prove pivotal in the jurors' assessment of his or her qualifications or conduct. With respect to the apparent "success" of the defense attorney, as noted previously, the prosecutor could "rehabilitate" the witness, as follows:

> *"Mr. Miller, you've told the jury you underwent OJT training and*
> *explained it was working along with an experienced agent. Correct?"*
> *"Yes, sir."*
> *"It lasted 90 days?"*
> *"Yes."*
> *"During that period of time, did your OJT training include any classroom*
> *sessions in the store about shoplifting matters and what the company*
> *required?"*
> *"Yes, sir"*
> *"Did the classroom sessions include interactive video scenarios which*
> *tested your understanding of the company's rules about detaining*
> *people for shoplifting?"*
> *"Yes, sir."*
> *"And was it your understanding the rules of the company are based on*
> *state laws?"*
> *"Yes, sir."*
> *"And how many classroom instructional hours did you undergo,*
> *during this OJT period?"*
> *"Forty hours, one full week."*
> *"Was your OJT, aside from the classroom instruction, structured in*
> *various experiences and exposure to policy and procedure?"*
> *"Yes."*
> *"Did that structured training experience lead to some form of*
> *certificate or recognition?"*
> *"Yes, sir."*
> *"What did it lead to? I mean what was the end result of all this?"*
> *"I earned company certification, and that certification qualifies a loss*
> *prevention agent to detain customers for theft if the elements of*
> *theft are present."*
> *"And you had that certification on January 7?"*
> *"Yes, sir."*
> *"Thank you. I have nothing more."*

When both sides have exhausted their examination of the agent, the court (judge) will excuse him or her and ask the witness to step down. The agent may say, "Thank you, your honor" and leave the witness stand and return to his or her seat at the counsel table.

It is the responsibility of the prosecution to prove their case beyond a reasonable doubt. Although the defense is not required to put on a case (call witnesses), more often than not they do. The key witness, aside from the LP agent, in a shoplifting trial is the defendant, who will deny any intention to steal, offering a fabricated version from a wide variety of spins and explanations to overcome the prosecutor's accusation of theft. It is during this testimony when the agent can damage his or her own case, by reacting inappropriately to the defendant's version of what transpired in the store. The damage is done by body language, i.e., raising eyebrows, smiling, sneering, raising the eyes to look upwards, rolling the eyes, shaking the head, or otherwise using his or her facial flexibility to silently express himself or herself. Someone on the jury, if not most jurors, will see this and usually take exception with it, considering such reaction unprofessional.

When both sides in this judicial confrontation rest, the jury will retire and deliberate. So-called facts are considered, but other factors come to bear on the final collective decision, including the appearance and presentation made by the loss prevention agent.

There's much more than a win-or-lose battle between a shoplifter and LP agent here: A verdict of "Not Guilty" often opens the door for a civil suit against the store for arresting a person "not guilty" of any crime. Damage awards from such cases can be substantial.

Crime Prevention through Environmental Design (CPTED)

Timothy D. Crowe

Introduction

Crime Prevention Through Environmental Design (CPTED) is a practical concept that has received considerable interest during the past four decades. It is based on the theory that the proper design and effective use of the built environment can lead to a reduction in the incidence and fear of crime, and to an improvement in the quality of life. This concept is supported by the fields of geography, psychology, and criminology, where it has long been known that

1. The design and use of the physical environment
2. Affects the behavior of people
3. Which influences the productive use of space
4. Leading to an increase or decrease in exposure to crime and loss

CPTED has been used to reduce crime, premise's liability, and fear in a variety of settings. They include schools, neighborhoods, convenience stores, malls and shopping centers, parking structures, transit sites, hotels, hospitals, office buildings, and parks. There are state statutes, regulations, and safety standards that have been developed to promote the use of CPTED concepts. It is important to note that CPTED does not replace traditional approaches to crime and loss prevention. Moreover, it is a tool that helps to remove many barriers to social and management control.

The use of CPTED concepts requires that human activities and spaces be designed or used to incorporate natural strategies. Crime prevention has previously relied nearly exclusively on labor-intensive or mechanical approaches. Guards, hall monitors, and police patrols are examples of labor-intensive strategies. Security cameras, locks alarms, and fences are examples of mechanical approaches. These methods incur costs that are additional to the normal requirements for personnel, equipment, and buildings that are needed to carry out human activities. The four most common CPTED strategies are

- Natural surveillance
- Natural access control
- Territorial reinforcement
- Management and maintenance

Natural surveillance and access control strategies help to limit opportunity for crime. Examples include the placement of windows to overlook sidewalks and parking lots, the use of transparent weather vestibules at building entrances to divert persons to reception areas, the placement of employee work stations in open areas to increase the perception that these locations are being monitored, and the use of maze entrances in public restrooms to decrease the isolation that is produced by an anteroom or double-door system for entry. These concepts increase the perception that people can be seen by others and that there is a clear difference between public and private space. Potential offenders are made to feel at greater risk of scrutiny and that their means of escape are limited.

Territorial reinforcement promotes social control through a variety of means. They include an increased definition of space, improved proprietary concern, expanded sense of ownership, and enhanced activity support and motivation reinforcement. These objectives may be achieved by increasing the assignment of space to the normal users and reducing public or unassigned locations. Residents or desired users of space who participate in the routine maintenance of space increase their proprietary concern through "sweat equity." Placing amenities such as seating or vending machines in common areas helps to attract larger numbers of normal or desired users of these areas. Scheduling activities in common areas increases the proper use, attracts more people, and increases the perception that these areas are under control. This makes the normal user feel safe, and the potential improper or undesired user feel at greater risk of apprehension or scrutiny.

Effective management and maintenance of activities and locations are crucial. Well-managed and maintained spaces have greater return on investment. A well-planned activity will result in fewer unanticipated problems. A well-maintained site will have fewer repairs and interruptions to scheduled activities. Accordingly, there will be fewer exposures to crimes and losses.

CPTED Historical Precedence

CPTED has its origins in the early history of the development of communities. The conscious planning of human habitats to include identity and protection goes back as far as our knowledge of human existence. Eighth century Chinese practitioners of Feng Shui promoted the design of harmony in space, from the size of the smallest rooms up to the planning of cities. Eighth through eleventh century plains dwellers in North America developed hierarchies of family places, community identity, and protection through the design of living space. The cliff dwellers (U.S. Mesa Verde National Park) developed impregnable living areas on the faces of cliffs that were accessible only by ladders and entrances that could be sealed. The cliff dwellers are also important examples of early attempts to use passive environmental engineering for climate control.

Modern warfare demonstrated how design can obviate technological and numerical superiority in the City of Hue, Viet Nam, and in Kuwait City, Kuwait. Both cities were of traditional French design with twisting, narrow streets that allowed for a small number of defenders to block the movements of large numbers of opposing troops. Post WWII residential development replaced grid pattern streets with curvilinear streets, which (in some settings) has improved safety, security, and neighborhood identity and property value.

CPTED Strategies

Many CPTED practitioners use the following strategies to guide their assessments of space and conceptual approaches to design:

- Provide clear border definition of controlled space
- Provide clearly marked transitions from public to private space
- Place gathering areas in locations with natural surveillance and access control
- Place safe activities in unsafe locations
- Place unsafe activities in safe locations
- Provide natural barriers to conflicting activities
- Improve scheduling of space to allow for "critical intensity"
- Increase the perception of natural surveillance
- Overcome distance and isolation through improved communication and design efficiencies

Related Topics

A number of related concepts have often become confused with the CPTED operating theories and applications. Some of these concepts overlap with CPTED, whereas others are very different. Following is an explanation of the unique elements of the related concepts:

- *CPTED (Mechanical vs. natural approaches):* There is some confusion and competition within the CPTED movement. It mostly boils down to one group that casually blends the three strategy areas (organized, mechanical, and natural approaches) versus another group of specialists whose principal emphasis is on natural approaches. The former is more of a crime control model, whereas the latter may be conceived as a planning model.

- *Defensible Space:* This concept was developed in the public housing environment. It is similar to CPTED in that it shares the basic requirements of natural surveillance, natural access control, and territorial concern. CPTED in its modern form was developed as an extension of Defensible Space concepts to commercial, retail, industrial, institutional, and low-density residential environments.
- *Environmental Security:* This concept was developed on a parallel basis to CPTED. It was initially used in residential settings. Environmental Security differs from CPTED in that it contemplates the use of a broad range of crime control strategies, including social, management, target hardening, activity support, and law enforcement.
- *Security by Design:* This concept is most aligned with a repackaging of solid security engineering, physical security, and procedural security measures to provide improved emphasis in the design process.
- *Natural Crime Prevention:* This concept grew out of the CPTED emphasis on natural strategies, those that factor behavior management and control into the design and use of the built environment.
- *Safer Cities:* This is another spin-off of CPTED that attempts to define an approach to crime prevention that incorporates traditional crime prevention and law enforcement strategies with CPTED. Of course, CPTED planners know that CPTED does not replace other crime prevention strategies, but that a high priority should be placed on natural strategies that take advantage of how human and physical resources are being expended.
- *Situational Crime Prevention:* This concept is much more comprehensive than CPTED because it incorporates other crime prevention and law enforcement strategies in an effort that focuses on place-specific crime problems.
- *Place-Specific Crime Prevention:* This is just another name for situational crime prevention and environmental security.
- *2nd Generation CPTED:* This is a program title that was popularized in the mid-1990s by a new group of CPTED enthusiasts. The supporters seek to combine community involvement, a youth component, and other crime prevention strategies with CPTED concepts. This approach is essentially the same as the Environmental Security and Safer Cities programs.

It is clear from a review of these apparently competing concepts that they overlap and are extremely compatible. Many were developed to provide a vehicle for incorporating organized and mechanical strategies into a free-standing model. However, most long-time CPTED planners view CPTED as a small subset of the total set of things that have to be done in crime prevention and control. Criminologists know that a comprehensive system must include strategies on a continuum that ranges from prenatal care to dementia among elderly persons. It would be unconscionable for anyone to think otherwise.

Following are some of the many examples of CPTED applications:

- Weaving pathways or roads are preferred; they promote a wider field of vision for observation because of the need to maneuver.
- Offset-glass-lined store entrances in malls and shopping centers deflect SHA and increase visual access to identify the store and observe activities.
- Bay-type windows increase visual access to and from sidewalks and streets, promoting visual ease and harmony and increasing the perception of natural surveillance.
- Theater, meeting room, or classroom doors that open outward allow easier egress for life safety reasons.
- Eliminating sharp edges on buildings and corners in hallways is helpful. Round or curving edges result in increased comfort, wider fields of vision, and increased perception of surveillance.

- Landscaping which obscures windows and the pedestrian approaches to buildings reduces natural surveillance.
- Enclosed elevators may create anxiety; a glass-back elevator or one with mirrors on the back wall improves comfort; it also allows the potential user to see if anyone is inside and increases natural surveillance.

Visual Bubbles, Landscape, Art, and CPTED

Human beings are born with natural responses to certain environmental stimuli. Others are learned within the context of culture, education, training, and experience. Tests with newborn humans and animals reveal that they inherit natural responses to visual stimuli. For instance, when newborns are shown a film wherein they are approaching the edge of a cliff, the subjects will automatically react when they think they are going over the side. Visual stimuli are some of the most important to humans, but by no means are they mutually exclusive of other forms of perception.

Humans establish "visual bubbles," which vary in depth, height, and width according to territorial definition and geography. A visual bubble may be defined as that space in which a person consciously recognizes things within the environment. Most environmental cues are dealt with subconsciously outside the visual bubble, unless something unusual happens to bring one of these elements to a conscious state.

Why is this important to a study of CPTED? The answer is that the visual sense scans the middle and far environment to collect information for immediate survival and protection. Environmental cues are assessed by all of human perceptual systems. But, the visual sense provides information about hazards, way finding, identity, and attractions For instance, highway safety is almost totally linked to visual perception. Traffic engineers know that certain locations have a high volume of accidents. Other locations seem to induce excessive speeds.

Following are some examples of the importance of planning for visual space in CPTED:

- Downtown pedestrian malls and regional retail malls quite often use landscape elements and sitting areas to push customers closer to businesses in the theory that they will be more likely to make a purchase if they are within the zone of influence of the business.
- The height of ceilings in hallways and meeting rooms has a direct relationship to attentiveness and movement; low ceilings suppress behavior, and high ceilings tend to stimulate activity and attention, which may be important to managing behavior.
- Transitional landscaping on curving portions of walking and bike trails increase the depth of vision and provide the user of this space with more information and choices regarding safety hazards or criminal threats.
- Wider porches in front of convenient stores help to give the customer more choices to avoid potential contact with nuisance persons, thus increasing sales to adult customers who would avoid the store if they had to encountered juveniles or day laborers.
- Towers and spires on buildings located on corners or intersections help in a way of finding and relieving anxiety about distances and identification of places.
- Opaque enclosures of trash receptacles and loading docks will dominate the field of vision of a passerby; conversely, transparent fencing material used in screening of trash receptacles and loading docks will cause these areas to fall into the background, which is precisely what the designer intended.
- Hostile landscaping can reduce maintenance costs and prevent graffiti and unwanted entry to properties.
- Landscaping helps to identify borders between public and private spaces; it also helps to reinforce the definition of desired behaviors by defining movement areas.

CPTED in the United States

Early interest in CPTED began with the research of Jane Jacobs in her book *The Death and Life of Great American Cities*, published in 1961. Jacobs described many observations of the relationships between urban design and crime. Her work stressed the importance of increasing territorial identity and natural surveillance.

Oscar Newman demonstrated the importance of natural surveillance, access control, and territorial concern in his 1972 book, *Defensible Space*. Newman proved that a relationship exists between space management and design and crime in public housing environments.

Dr. C. Ray Jeffery coined the phrase "Crime Prevention Through Environmental Design" in his 1971 book by that title. Jeffery described the relationship between urban design and crime. His book provided quotations from a 1968 report from the National Commission on the Causes and Prevention of Violence (USA) that warned the American public of the direct relationships between urban design and crime. This commission studied the massive urban violence and racial unrest that had occurred in U.S. cities between 1964 and 1968.

Richard Gardiner, a landscape architect and developer, successfully demonstrated the use of CPTED concepts in residential areas. His 1978 manual, *Design for Safe Neighborhoods*, presented the results of a successful project in a Hartford, Connecticut, neighborhood, which significantly reduced crime and improved the quality of life.

The most significant CPTED developmental effort in the United States was conducted from 1972–1980 by the Westinghouse Electric Corporation through a massive contractual effort that was funded by the U.S. Department of Justice. Westinghouse managed a large group of consultants and subcontractors who were responsible for adapting CPTED concepts that had been proven in public housing environments to retail, transportation, and school environments. Much was learned from these efforts, which provides the basis for current CPTED uses in the United States.

Interest in CPTED at the U.S. government level waned during the decade of the 1980s. However, state and local units of government took over the lead and produced a large number of successful projects. These led to the incorporation of CPTED into local building codes. Design review ordinances have been modified to require the use of CPTED in building design. Several state governments have passed legislation and developed new regulations governing the design and management of schools and the convenient food store industry. The states of Florida, Virginia, and Kentucky have taken the most steps by passing legislation and actively conducting training for the public and private sectors.

The National Crime Prevention Institute at the University of Louisville created the first CPTED training program in 1985. A design studio was created to assist in the teaching of CPTED concepts. This program has been attended by thousands of participants who have spread the use of CPTED concepts in their communities around the world. The content of this training program formed the basis for the 1991 book, *Crime Prevention Through Environmental Design: Applications of Architectural Design and Space Management Concepts*, by Timothy D. Crowe. This book—and its second edition (March 2000)—is the most widely used manual for CPTED at the present time in the United States.

The American Institute of Architects conducted the first national CPTED conference in December 1993. The U.S. Conference of Mayors conducted a National CPTED conference in June 1995 to report on the results of their nationwide survey of mayors. This survey documents the extent to which local governments have implemented CPTED concepts.

Results of CPTED

There are many case studies, which demonstrate reductions in crime and fear of crime. Significant results have been produced in many settings, including residential areas, convenience food stores, malls and shopping centers, transit stations, and parking structures. Journal and newspaper articles have reported on these successes.

Descriptive studies have reported on historical relationships between crime and the environment. The U.S. Department of Justice has published a number of bibliographies and documents about these observational studies. Small to medium-size cities have also reported on considerable crime and fear reductions directly attributable to CPTED traffic management strategies.

Statistical results are too numerous to list here, but it is clear that much documentation exists. Moreover, the historical basis of CPTED makes the success of these concepts self-evident. Following is a sample of the many success stories that have resulted from contemporary uses of CPTED concepts:

- *Convenience Stores:* Such stores have used CPTED to increase sales and reduce losses of up to 50% of thefts and 65% in armed robberies.
- *Malls:* Malls in Sacramento, California, and Knoxville, Tennessee, have reduced incidents by 24% and noncrime calls to police by another 14% using CPTED parking management concepts. Many others have achieved the same or better results. The Mall of America in Bloomington, Minnesota, used CPTED from the initial conceptual stage of design; the same or better results have been obtained by many other malls.

Author's Comment: One of the authors was involved in the opening of a major retail store in the Mall of America. During the building of the store, the author had to meet with the Bloomington Police Department CPTED specialist to assure that the store design and security features were in compliance with the police department's CPTED standards. Some of their concerns were the location of the cashiers' (cash) office, emergency egress from the cash vault area, and assuring easy access for police officers from access roads to the security office when responding to requests for service.

- *Corporations:* Westinghouse, IBM, Mobil, TRINOVA, Macy's, Disney World, Sam's Club, and Pace Wholesale Warehouses have reduced losses and improved productivity using CPTED strategies.
- *Office environments:* Interior design research has determined that the lack of territorial identity in the office space contributes to lower morale, less productivity, and greater tolerance of dishonesty among fellow workers.

The Need for CPTED

Profit, productivity, and quality of life are compelling reasons for the use of CPTED concepts. A key element in the CPTED planning process is to develop clear behavioral objectives for spaces. This leads to improved decisions regarding design and use techniques. Civil liability provides a legitimate excuse to use CPTED concepts, that is, if improved profit, productivity, and quality of life are not enough. The U.S. Department of Justice has issued guidelines for the use of CPTED concepts to protect businesses from wrongful death or injury litigation.

The recent case law in general and premises liability has increased the responsibilities of property and business owners. Liability has been extended to architects, engineers, lending companies, and security contractors, when a wrongful injury or death suit is filed. Parking lots have been found by courts to be inherently dangerous, which means that an owner or operator is liable even when there have been no prior incidents. Likewise, the isolation of restrooms by location and by design has been determined to be inherently dangerous. The standard by which a property owner or operator is judged is based on proof of due diligence or having done all things reasonable to prevent injury. Employee, owner, and customer convenience is perhaps the greatest obstacle to maintaining safety and security in retail environments. More accidents and victimization are caused by the defeat of good security practices due to inconvenience than any other hazard. It is worse to have procedures that are not followed than to have none at all.

New properties and operations are held to a different standard than existing ones. The designer, planner, and owner of a new property or operation will be held accountable for conscious decisions that affect the propensity for subsequent injury. Accordingly, a final decision about the design and use plan for a property must be defensible. The opinions of a recognized expert in the substantive area of the loss, peril, and hazard establish proximate cause, which then makes injury foreseeable.

The so-called test of reasonableness that is the backbone of civil liability allows for the support of many factors in making conscious decisions. Aesthetics, mission, life safety, accessibility, feasibility, and environmental factors are weighed in the final determination of the adequacy of a property owner's or manager's duty and responsibility in the care and protection of the users of space. This is why CPTED has become so important to the civil law, because it allows for the blending of good aesthetics, profitability, and safety.

The Future of CPTED

CPTED in the 21st century will emulate the lessons from the past. The first decade has already been a transition period heralding an explosion of technological and space management advances in the use of the environment to promote behavior that is desired and conducive to human existence.

CPTED is a self-evident concept, which has been used successfully for the past 40 years. It has confirmed what many people think—that it is just good, common sense. The greatest impediment to the widespread use of CPTED is ignorance. Many people have never heard of CPTED. Some of the few who have heard of CPTED have attempted to exploit it, without developing an understanding of the concept. Others have attempted to pass off CPTED as another fad that will go away with time.

Note: For additional information on the role of CPTED, see the April 1996 issue of *National Institute of Justice,* published by the U.S. Department of Justice, Office of Justice Programs, discussing CPTED as applied to parking facilities and to premises liability.

Crisis Management

CAS, JHC

The time that crisis management will be required cannot be predicted; hence, the key to successful crisis management is preparation and planning for that eventuality.

Since retailers operate businesses which have members of the public on their premises during business hours, as well as employees during both business and nonbusiness hours, it becomes vital that plans exist to minimize injury to both customers and employees, as well as to protect the other assets of the business during emergency situations.

The start of the preparation process is the formation of a crisis management team and the formulation of their mission and responsibilities.

The purpose of a crisis management team (CMT) is to have a designated group of individuals who, in the event of a major emergency or crisis, are empowered to make decisions and authorize extraordinary action on behalf of the corporation. In general, a crisis exists whenever there is a business-related clear risk of life or grave personal injury to a company employee, a member of his or her family, or a customer or other person, or when some disastrous or calamitous event occurs which disrupts the essential processes of the corporation and threatens its ability to function.

In the event of a crisis, the CMT may be activated by any member; those immediately available from the total membership will then form the CMT.

Because of the extraordinary authority to act independently in the event of a crisis, and the potential for civil liability and/or just plain "finger pointing" based on any actions taken by the CMT, it is essential that the individuals comprising this group be of very senior rank, including the Chief Executive Officer (CEO), Chief Operating Officer (COO), Chief Financial Officer (CFO), Chief Security Officer (CSO), Executive Vice President (EVP), and other senior vice presidents. Both the senior HR person as well as the senior civic affairs or publicity person should be included, since many anticipated actions will involve personnel decisions and/or the need for press releases. Corporate counsel should be included on an ad hoc basis.

A final key component of the CMT (although not a decision-making member) is a recording secretary. From the moment the CMT is activated, the secretary (or someone else in his or her absence) should begin making minute-by-minute notes of the various decisions and actions of the CMT and any factors (such as recommendations by an expert) prompting such actions. A portable battery-operated audio recorder is a valuable aid in keeping such a record.

The CMT should be unfettered to the maximum possible extent in the exercise of their extraordinary responsibilities. However, because reliance upon expert advice is a defense to charges of unlawful or negligent conduct in such matters, early and continuing cooperation with appropriate law enforcement or other public safety agencies should be part of the CMT's operating procedure, recognizing, however, that normally the CMT will be responsible for the ultimate decisions made.

In any crisis, communications assumes paramount importance. With this in mind, the establishment of a predesignated message center is mandated. Such a message center should also have an alternate location should the primary location be within the area of the emergency and unavailable for occupancy. Whenever the CMT declares a geographically large area as within the emergency zone, a pre-established toll-free (800) number should be activated for emergency use.

The CMT should have primary responsibility for

- Assisting stores in management and decision making during an emergency
- Assuring that individual stores are prepared for emergencies by reviewing individual store emergency plans for currency
- Making policy decisions on a companywide basis prior to an emergency
- If time and circumstances permit, reviewing decisions to close/evacuate a store
- Handling public relations following an emergency
- Determining the degree of aid to victims of an emergency
- Coordinating emergency transportation and storage for the protection of cash and target merchandise
- Performing other duties as deemed appropriate

Finally, the CMT should be responsible for a post-event review to determine any weaknesses in pre-emergency planning and making recommendations for corrections to and/or modification of existing plans.

Customer Accident Investigations

Michael Hoeflich

Why care so much about retail accidents? Slips and falls and other forms of injury cost retailers millions of dollars each year. So, it's only logical to know how to respond properly to such incidents.

Types of Accidents/Injuries

When the topic of customer accidents is brought up, slips and falls come to mind. These may be the most common types of accidents, but retailers need to be mindful of other causes, such as

- Items falling from their displays
- Leakage from batteries, bleach, and other hazardous items
- Contaminated/spoiled foods
- Product displays that can cause injury (i.e., shelves with sharp edges)

Purpose of Investigating

Why did the accident occur? What was the cause? The more detailed, the better. Any and all information can be used to help prevent future injuries. A thorough investigation can often limit the company's liability and can expose fraudulent claims. But what I've found to be common is to find the truth in a claim that has been overly exaggerated from what actually happened. Detailed accident investigations will help lower a company's annual loss.

Investigative Steps

So, you've been notified that an accident or injury has occurred. What now?

Step One: Speak with the injured person. I've always encouraged my loss prevention agents to always carry a pen and notepad while on the sales floor. That way, they can respond immediately without having to search for a notepad. Besides, showing up at the scene with a legal pad and clipboard could signal to the customer that this is a more serious situation than he or she thought. Your first duty is to make sure that the customer doesn't need any medical attention. Listen carefully to his or her entire side of the story; then ask any open-ended questions that will help fill in any gaps. Next, ask the customer if he or she would like to make a report. If so, pull out your pen and notepad and jot down the customer's name, phone number, address, age, date, time the accident occurred, exact location, and note the type and condition of shoes. The type or condition of shoes could be an important cause of the fall.

Step Two: After you've spoken with the customer, locate any possible witnesses. The witness could be an employee or customer who happened to be in the area of the accident. If the witness is a customer, get his or her side of the story, obtain his or her phone number, and ask if he or she may be contacted if any further information is required. If the witness is an employee, have him or her write a statement on a legal pad and sign it.

Step Three: Secure the scene. This will ensure that no other customers will be injured and will also protect any evidence of the accident. Immediately take pictures of the area using multiple angles. Every loss prevention or safety department should have a digital camera of at least 3 megapixels. This is enough to allow you to enlarge an image without degrading the clarity. A standard 35 mm camera will work as well; however, development and enlargements will have to take place offsite and could take up valuable time. Most of the time you will not have to bother with a tape measure at the scene. Most stores use tile flooring that is 1×1 foot in size and will allow the investigator to make approximate measurements.

Step Four: Compile your data. Now that you've collected the necessary information, write a narrative of your investigation starting with your interview with the customer. Do not quote the customer within your narrative. You should use another part of your report for the customer's statement. On the report form, include your narrative, customer statement, accident scene observations, and the customer's biographical information that you obtained during your interview. Print and attach photographs of the scene and save the photos to a disk to be included in your accident file or separate storage area. During this process, you should also search your store's camera system to see if it captured the accident. If any video is captured, immediately copy this to disk or tape. Finally, contact your company's insurance company or risk management department. Let them know at that time if you've captured the accident on tape or if you suspect that the accident claim is fraudulent or has been exaggerated. Also, if the accident was caused by a product or display fixture, hold it as evidence until risk management or the insurance company has given you permission to dispose of it.

The work you put into each investigation will serve you for some time to come. Accidents should be reviewed monthly with management. Discuss how these situations could have been prevented and implement these ideas to prevent further accidents.

Cybersecurity Rules for the Retail Industry

Sanford Sherizen

A history of the retail industry shows a clear relationship between the creation of a new technique to help customers make a purchase and criminals using that technique in order to steal. Whether it was the introduction of electricity in stores, locating shopping centers so they would be convenient for car drivers, or creating phone catalog sales for shopping at home, customers and criminals were both attracted.

Today, retail computer and communication advances are making shopping for customers easier, faster, and readily available around the clock. In a similar fashion, computer criminals have learned to take advantage of these advances in ways that threaten our central commercial arrangements, such as using credit cards, and even the identity and privacy of the public. It should also be noted that cyber crimes committed by companies, such as stock manipulations and scamming efforts, have also used technology for illegal purposes.

While earlier retail crimes were responded to with a combination of physical security and monitoring actions, loss absorption, industry cooperation, and legal sanctions, those options may not be sufficient for meeting computer-related crimes. These crimes are more complex than earlier crimes and require retailers to increase security efforts to a much larger and a much different level.

This section will review the nature of these cyber crimes in general and then discuss those cyber crimes specifically related to the retail industry. After that discussion, cybersecurity issues will be analyzed, followed by a presentation of the cybersecurity program elements that need to be found in retail settings.

Introduction

Let's start with general cyber crime statistics. The following are some indications of the seriousness of the problem.

> *In 2006, at least 303 incidents of data disclosures in the United States were reported, potentially affecting 18.8+ individuals. Approximately 30%, governmental or military agencies; 27% of disclosures involve educational institutions; 23%, general business; 12%, healthcare facilities or companies; and 8%, banking, credit, or financial services entities.* (1)

Identity theft has become of major concern to people. And they are right to worry, as indicated by the following statistics. A survey conducted by the Federal Trade Commission (FTC) in 2006 estimated that 8.3 million American consumers, or 3.7% of the adult population, became victims of identity theft in 2005. Most of the financial losses are suffered by credit issuers and banks, as victims are rarely held responsible for fraudulent debts incurred in their name; however, victims often bear the responsibility of contacting their banks and credit issuers after an identity theft has occurred. The same FTC survey determined that victim consumers spent over 200 million hours in 2005 attempting to recover from identity theft. (2)

- "New account" identity theft costs over $25 billion in losses to the victims each year.
- Of the new accounts that are opened by identity thieves, approximately half are credit card accounts, but cell phone accounts, utility accounts, bank accounts, and apartment rentals are also important targets for identity thieves.
- Between February 2005 and March 2006, more than 55 million Americans were put at risk by security breaches, leaving them vulnerable to identity theft. (3)

Even the period of time between when a computer comes online and when it is probed for vulnerabilities has shrunk. An example is found in a study from a major cybersecurity research center. Researchers took an out-of-the-box Linux PC without any special features, connected it to the Internet, and did nothing to announce its existence. The attacks started almost immediately.

Within the first 30 seconds:	First service probes/scans detected.
Within the first hour:	First compromise attempts detected.
Within the first 12 hours:	The PC was fully compromised:
	Administrative access was obtained.
	Event logging was selectively disabled.
	System software was modified to suit the intruder.
	Attack software was installed.
	The PC was actively probing for new hosts to intrude. (4)

Cyber crime has evolved over a relatively short period of time. Starting in the 1980s, some of the early crimes were often unsophisticated, involving methods of guessing, stealing or "social engineering" passwords, gaining physical access to machines, or relatively easily bypassing security controls. As this form of crime advanced, criminals learned how to misuse the technology in order to gain access to computer resources, services, and information. That stage of evolution involved hackers and others who were familiar with vulnerabilities of systems and the use of social engineering to manipulate authorized users. When increased protections were implemented by information security professionals, intruders expanded their illegal activities to cover a larger range of damages, such as distributed denial of service, virus destruction, and scanning of a user's remote access to their organizations.

Currently, there are widespread malware intrusions, including spyware and spamming, while others seek to take advantage of users by means of phishing and identity theft. As wireless communication has grown, attacks on wireless devices have become more frequent. Some of the newer attacks are automated, attention is being directed toward drivers, and thumb drives have become useful crime tools. (5) (6)

There have also been increases in the impact of cyber crimes, creating damage to companies, customers, and the larger society. These damages are like pebbles thrown into water, expanding out from the initial point of contact. There are direct and indirect costs involved with a publicized unauthorized incursion into a company's system. Research findings on these costs indicate that retail firms which have been attacked are penalized financially as well as in terms of customers' willingness to continue to shop with them.

- According to a recent study, companies experiencing a data breach spent
  1. *Total costs:* Averaged $182 per lost customer record, an increase of 30% over 2005 results. The average total cost per reporting company was $4.8 million per breach and ranged from $226,000 to $22 million.
  2. *Direct incremental costs:* Averaged $54 per lost record, an 8% increase over 2005 results for unbudgeted, out-of-pocket spending. Includes free or discounted services offered; notification letters, phone calls, and emails; legal, audit, and accounting fees; call center expenses; public and investor relations; and other costs.
  3. *Lost productivity costs:* Averaged $30 per lost record, an increase of 100% over 2005 results, for lost employee or contractor time and productivity diverted from other tasks.
  4. *Customer opportunity costs:* Averaged $98 per lost record, an increase of 31% over 2005 results, covering turnover of existing customers and increased difficulty in acquiring new customers. Customer turnover averaged 2% and ranged as high as 7%. (7)
- Another study found that customers view trustworthiness in safeguarding information as an important factor in their decision where to shop. While less than half of their consumer respondents rated organizations as particularly trustworthy in safeguarding private information, there were large differences between sectors. Financial institutions, healthcare providers, and law enforcement agencies were seen as the most trusted (60%, 56%, and 53%, respectively), while online Internet retailers (32%) and brick-and-mortar shops (28%) were considered the least trustworthy. (8)
- Related to the trustworthiness, firms which have been publicly exposed for having lost personal information lose an average of 2.6% of their total customer base. Note that under the California Database Protection Act (CA SB 1386) and similar laws being proposed in over 30 other states, organizations must report to affected persons when their information may have been stolen. Of great significance is the effect of a loss on the financial markets. On average, a firm loses around 0.63% to 2.10% value in stock price when a security breach is reported. (9)

The lessons are quite clear. Technology has become a major tool for criminals. They can attack retail companies, targeting them for money, stock manipulation, ransom, trade secrets, customer lists, competitor espionage, or entrance to the larger financial complex within which the company operates. The damages can be severe and may lead to such drastic events as the bankruptcy of companies.

Cyber Crimes in the Retail Industry

Whether it is called "computer crime," "data crime," "information protection," "cyber crime," or countless other terms, the issue discussed is how computers and other high-tech devices are used to gain unauthorized use of information and other assets. The term used here will be "cyber crimes."

These crimes are unique from earlier retail security problems. There are three major new aspects to these crimes that make them so distinctive:

- *New crimes:* Traditional retail crimes, such as inventory shrinkage and fraud, have become computerized. This has created new threats, risks, and vulnerabilities for the use of criminals. Cyber crimes are growing, while responses to them continue to lag. Technical security continues to be difficult to achieve and expensive to implement. In addition, these crimes have produced difficulties for the law and law enforcement. Legal approaches to these crime problems result in legislators creating laws regarding rapidly changing technical factors. Law enforcement and prosecutors are faced with the need to adapt their approaches in order to develop legally acceptable cases.
- *New criminals:* The cyber criminal includes teenagers, organized criminal gangs, competitors, political activists, managers, IT professionals, and others. Some are technically skilled, whereas others may not be so expert but have knowledge, access, and opportunity. The criminal has the advantage in when to strike, what to attempt to strike, how to attack, what system vulnerabilities to take advantage of, how to cover electronic fingerprints, and the difficulties of detecting and prosecuting these acts. Internal crimes are made easier by employee knowledge of financial transactions, security measures, employee inexperience, and the wish of companies to minimize security costs.
- *New dangers:* Beyond the tempting financial targets, there is also a multitude of potential dangers for a company. These dangers have increased as companies have become dependent on technology in order to function. For retail organizations, outsiders could aim to close down a major computer service; make subtle changes to profit and loss data; exert control over certain key applications; or manipulate the computer functions that run a building's air conditioning, water, heat, and electricity. With the Internet, a globalization of specialized criminals has also developed, leading to an international division of labor and crime easily crossing national borders.

Retailers face increased competition and difficulties in making profits. Cyber crimes are causing the industry to have to decide on how best to survive this additional problem. The cybersecurity discussion to follow will indicate the fundamental choices that will have to be met.

Cybersecurity in the Retail Industry

Some recent retail computer crimes provide us with important lessons about the need for cybersecurity. TJX, BJ's Wholesale Club, and DSW are not the only retailers that have had security difficulties, but their very public problems appear to be leading to the creation of additional laws and regulations over how a company processes and protect data. As indicated in the Sarbanes-Oxley Act and Gramm-Leach-Bliley Act, business violations are leading to cybersecurity becoming a requirement that has to be met in order to be in compliance. Similarly, since retailing is a global activity, cyber crime and cybersecurity-related laws in other nations also have to be met.

Retail cybersecurity must develop an approach that is most appropriate for its environment. A major complication, however, is that changes in cybersecurity may run counter to the ways that security has been treated in the industry to date. IT and cybersecurity professionals and a growing number of C-level executives have accepted the view that security is no longer a technical problem but is an enterprisewide approach to business issues.

The result of this important transformation is that basic security concepts have shifted. The network of concern is no longer simply the hardware, software, and infrastructure. It is now viewed as the people, processes, and business units. Rather than viewing a major technical requirement as protecting the perimeter boundaries of the organization, the enterprise requirement focuses on matters of privacy and asset protection. The assets that a firm must protect are more than the desktops, laptops, servers, and databases. Now, in the enterprise view, the most important assets are customer data, employee data, and communication of information. Finally, technical matters are no longer the responsibility of IT and system administrators. Rather, technology and security are enterprise core competencies. (10)

These changes in retail cybersecurity affect how technology must be treated. Many of the newer retail services that are profitable are the result of technological innovations. Technical products and processes offer large opportunities and retailers must use their technology to its fullest. And, under-protected technology may indeed have an impact on that survival.

Technology has a dual use: providing new approaches to store profits as well as opening up opportunities for criminals to drain profits from these companies. If we examine several of the major advantages of technology for creating profitable environments, a parallel list can be drawn of how cybersecurity enhances those same technical features. Given that customers are central to the retail experience, we will emphasize the customer-oriented nature of technology. Certainly, cybersecurity has to be carefully applied so that it will not become counterproductive to the friendly shopper message of retail today.

Table C-7 indicates the contributions that a secure technology can provide to retailers. The technology itself can assist with attracting and gaining customers, but a secured technology will contribute significantly more to improving those efforts.

Table C-2 Security as Value Added to Customer Centered Technology

Customer Emphasis	Technical Approach	Cyber Security Enhances Emphasis
Competitive Price	RFID, inventory management, forecasting, promotion management, supply chain, service level agreements, redundancies	Secure communications, multi-factor identification and authentication, role-based and rule-based authorization, VPN, firewall
Service & Performance	ERP, customer intelligence analysis, data collection, data mining, POS, personalized web sites	Data integrity, data confidentiality, service availability, encryption
Buy & Return Incentives	CRM, customer tracking, web site product appeal, rewards, purchase incentives, cross-linked web sites	Secure web browsing, extending security perimeter, wireless security, remote access protections

These points apply to all aspects of the retail process. The process can be highly effective in anticipating and creating customer interest in particular products and services. International order fulfillment can be established, and monitoring of inventory can change the ways that prices are set. Stores can be opened online, and product presentations can be individualized to be based on a customer's prior purchase patterns. Instantaneous payment is possible, and new profit centers can be established. Updates can be sent to customers with frequent purchase plans creating buyer loyalty.

At the same time, the process can expand the risks. For example, when a company connects to its partners and suppliers in the supply chain, the company potentially opens itself up to the security weaknesses of those involved in these relationships. It is the weak link theory applied on the global level.

Core Features of a Retail Cybersecurity Program

As mentioned earlier, a number of laws and regulations require security in organizations. In essence, those requirements point to elements of a cybersecurity program that companies should initiate. An additional feature of these requirements is that senior executives must sign off on reports that indicate the presence and the adequacy of those requirements in their organization.

Due to the centrality of credit card transactions, retailers have been encouraged and even pushed into accepting the Payment Card Industry Data Security Standard. The PCI DSS spells out the details of security that must be in place and can serve here as one model of the needed elements of a cybersecurity program.

As Dubin points out, "PCI DSS is not groundbreaking; it is simply a set of information security standards no different than those at any large bank or publicly held corporation. But it has molded security throughout the credit card industry lifecycle, from how banks issue cards to how retailers accept them." (11)

In total, there are 12 PCI DSS-required controls. They cover access management, network security, incident response, network monitoring and testing, and information security policies.

Additionally, these 12 controls are grouped together under 6 PCI DSS "control objectives." They include:

- *Build and maintain a secure network.* Ensure firewalls are installed and that changes to rules are adequately logged. Web servers that must access the Internet should be in a DMZ. Database servers holding customer account information should be inside the company's network, protected by a firewall. Note: For the most part, these requirements are already part of the networking staff's routine job responsibilities.
- *Protect cardholder data.* Stored account numbers must be encrypted or truncated, and customer data must be disposed of when no longer needed. This was the fatal mistake in the TJX case. Encryption over public networks for data in motion should be done using SSL.
- *Maintain a vulnerability management program.* This control covers a wide range of requirements. It requires antivirus software on all servers and workstations, and recommends everyone follow guidelines from the Open Web Application Security Project (OWASP) for developing Web applications.
- *Implement strong access control measures.* Restrict access to systems with account numbers and ensure user accounts are audited to remove outdated or malicious accounts. Stored passwords should also be encrypted.
- *Regularly monitor and test networks.* Require regular vulnerability scans, reviews of server logs, and the installation of intrusion detection or prevention systems (IDS and IPS).
- *Maintain an information security policy.* Draft an information security policy that covers access control, network and physical security, and application and system development. It's important to keep the policy updated as systems and needs change, and to make sure it's distributed to system users. (12)

These are the essential elements of a cybersecurity program. The elements are basic features that are found in many other industries but found less often in the retail world. As has been indicated here, there is a large price to be paid by businesses that do not follow these fundamentals.

TJX is the poster child of the price to pay. That company had stored old account information instead of deleting it. The company thus violated a PCI requirement, which mandates that a company remove data it no longer needs. During the breach, hackers stole an undetermined number of credit card accounts, some of which dated back to 2003. As a result, dozens of banks reported incidents of fraud from the compromised cards. There seems to be little doubt that TJX will be punished financially, it will lose customers, and its public reputation is in shambles. Unfortunately, TJX will not be the last retail company to discover that it is less expensive to prevent cyber crimes than to detect them.

Conclusion

The retail industry is struggling through a period of uncertainty. New forms of meeting customer demands and competition from a variety of sources have led to a complex playing field. Technology has added its own complexities, creating new possibilities for profit making as well as new opportunities for criminals. Today's retailers have little choice in deciding whether to have adequate cybersecurity. That question has been resolved by legal and customer pronouncements. How cybersecurity programs will be integrated with business needs will turn out to be a major determinant of which companies will succeed and which will fail.

References

1. Identity Theft Resource Center, http://www.idtheftcenter.org/breaches.pdf.
2. Federal Trade Commission, *The FTC in 2006: Committed to Consumers and Competition.* April 2006.
3. Ibid.
4. Tim Shimeall, *Cyberterrorism*, PowerPoint Presentation, CERT Center, Software Engineering Institute, Carnegie Mellon University, Pittsburgh, PA.
5. Ibid.
6. Dennis Fisher, "Savvy hackers take the hardware approach," March 7, 2007, SearchSecurity.com.
7. Ponemon Institute, *2006 Annual Study: Cost of a Data Breach: Understanding Financial Impact, Customer Turnover, and Preventative Solutions.*
8. *Secure the Trust of Your Brand: How Security and IT Integrity Influence Corporate Reputation.* A CMO Council Report, September 2006.
9. Ibid.
10. Julia Allen, *Governing for Enterprise Security, Networked Systems Survivability Program,* CERT, Technical Note, CMU/SEI-2005-TN-023, June 2005, p. 30.
11. Joel Dubin, "PCI compliance after the TJX data breach." *Security Wire Perspectives.* March 8, 2007.
12. Ibid.

 D

Discount Violations

CAS, JHC

A longstanding and traditional benefit in the retail industry is the employee privilege of purchasing the store's merchandise at a pre-established discounted price. Commonly, discounts range from 10% to 25% or even higher, depending on the store and its goods.

It's a known fact some employees, particularly women who are actively socially, work not so much for the salary, but rather for the benefit of being current in fashion trends and the opportunity to purchase fashion goods at the employee discount price.

Operationally, the discount must be captured in either a POS program electronically, or manually, if the inventory and sales aren't computerized, so as to balance the book inventory with merchandised on hand. For example, if a dress is on the inventory books at $100 but is sold to an employee for $75, failure to capture that discount will result in an inventory shortage, since the dress is still on the books valued at $100 and the reduced sale price is not captured for inventory reconciliation purposes.

Interestingly, this "inventory control" facilitates the loss prevention department's oversight of abuses that do tend to arise in employee discounts. The "abuse" occurs when an employee or associate makes purchases for friends or relatives—people not entitled to the store's benefits. Some retailers may not prohibit the passing on of this benefit to others as long as the book inventory is properly adjusted. But by far, throughout the industry, this benefit is exclusively for employees and their immediate family members residing in the same household or when given as a legitimate gift for which the employee receives no reimbursement or consideration. Employees detected in violating this rule are typically subject to termination.

There are two reasons employees abuse their discount privilege. One is to purchase items which are eventually sold to friends at the discount price. The other reason is to purchase gifts for a variety of persons who are not immediate family members and who the corporate policy defines as unauthorized recipients of merchandise purchased at the employee discount price.

One reason for disallowing the discount privilege to others is the risk nonemployees may return the merchandise at its full price; hence, the store could end up buying back at full retail what it sold for less than that amount. Indeed, some employees have been known to return such purchases to their own company's stores for full retail and have failed to identify themselves as employees. If this activity is detected, it typically results in the employee's termination.

More often than not, violations are handled by store management or the store's human resource department, and the loss prevention department's role, if any, is to provide investigative support, if necessary. For example, if there is suspicion or information that an employee purchase of a side-by-side refrigerator/freezer has been delivered to a given address, LP could be called upon to determine who lives at that location and his or her connection with the employee. It is not unusual, however, for loss prevention to conduct the interview with the offending employee, obtain an admission, and then turn the results over to management or HR for final adjudication.

Displays

CAS, JHC

The display of merchandise to attract buyers and enhance sales may be divided into two separate categories:

1. A display or presentation of goods which the customer and potential purchaser may touch, pick up, select, and make a decision to purchase.
2. A display or presentation of goods which discourages or denies customer access to those goods. The purpose of this display is to promote interest in the merchandise while simultaneously securing the goods, making their theft difficult or impossible. For the sake of this discussion, we'll hereafter refer to the former as "open display" and the latter as "secured display."

Some merchandise is displayed solely to alert the customer to a specific portion of the store where this type of merchandise is located. An example of this form of display would be an elevated mannequin of a child, which, seen from a distance, silently tells customers this is where children's clothing is offered for sale.

Open Displays

The bulk of all goods offered by a merchant would be "open displays," and the focus of most of loss prevention's attention. Common and typical displays include table-top, counter-top, racks (T-stands, costumers, rounders, wall racks, etc.), bins, shelves, end caps, and goods stacked on the selling floor. In some stores, loss prevention has no voice in where or how much merchandise can be on "open displays." Such stores risk display practices which encourage or even promote theft, as well as fail to take advantage of easy cost-free and equally effective strategies which tend to discourage theft.

Various ways displays can encourage theft include but are not limited to

- Elevated displays which block the view from aisle to aisle.
- Crowding rounders and other floor stands so customers have only narrow aisles to move through, and their hands and what they carry in and what they do with their hands can't be seen.
- Rounders or displays with hanging goods which are solidly packed with merchandise whose density creates a hidden center space that can be used to stage bagged stolen merchandise for later pickup.
- Counter tops with heaped goods such that the surreptitious removal can't be noticed.
- Displays of small, expensive, and sought-after goods in obscure or hard-to-observe areas of the store, which tends to invite theft.

The nub of the problem is trying to display too much merchandise in too little space. Display of goods is in the merchant's realm, and the task is to sell the maximum number of goods in the shortest amount of time. Fortunate indeed is the LP executive who can convince the merchant, especially during major sales events and holidays, to place fewer racks on the floor and place fewer goods on counter tops and in bins. Effective indeed is the LP executive who can convince the merchant, during hectic times, to be more conservative in the display of high price-point goods and showcase them in a secure location, such as in locked showcases.

Examples of easy and cost-free strategies to display goods which tend to discourage theft include but are not limited to

- On "T-stands" for hanging merchandise, maintaining a balance of the number of hangers on each side of the stand—e.g., four leather jackets on each side, a total of eight jackets. If one is removed, its absence is most noticeable.
- On counter tops, displayed in patterns so the removal of an item changes or destroys the pattern and is noticeable—e.g., six boxed items can be displayed in a pyramid,

three boxes upon which two more boxes are stacked, upon which a final box caps off the top. Or, if not boxed, presented in patterns of three with space between each pattern, assuming the merchandise lends itself to this approach.

- With hangers reversed (every other hanger with the "hook" in the opposite direction) to discourage grab-and-run thefts.

The preceding limited examples simply suggest aspects or dimensions to the display of open merchandise: space, balance, and patterns. The effective and creative loss prevention practitioner, supervisor, and executive should be sensitive to this and help by being instrumental in bringing about a storewide, if not companywide, understanding of the problem and ways to reduce losses.

Visual Presentations

Those displays which are not "open" pose their own unique loss prevention problems—namely, the potential for theft by employees, although customers will try, and some will successfully access the secured display and remove merchandise. The internal theft potential is exacerbated by the merchant's demanding the removal of goods from one part of the store to be made a part of a display elsewhere in the store.

For example, a female mannequin in a showcase window is dressed in a blue spaghetti strap after-dinner dress, with a gold and blue silk scarf around her neck, wearing a string of pearls, carrying a sequin dinner clutch bag, wearing high-heel shoes, and a faux white fox cape draped over one shoulder. On her left wrist is a white stone bracelet. The display could have her standing by a chair, upon which pillows are casually tossed to create this smart look, to capture the imagination of the customer.

The visual presentation employee, a unique and creative persona, must imagine in his or her mind what merchandise will be needed. The employee will then go to each area of the store and select two, three, or more items in each category (three dresses, four or five scarves, various necklaces, various handbags, several pair of shoes, etc.) to eventually select the one best suited to create this artistic display.

This employee more often than not visits the many departments within the store and takes all these items before the store is open to the public and assembles the bulk of the merchandise in the display area, an area stacked with everything from Christmas decorations to 4th of July banners, and invariably goods for or from various past and present displays. It is not unfair to say that most display departments maintain only a modicum of neatness.

The question which begs to be asked is, for example, does the custom jewelry department manager know a visual presentation employee has 21 items of merchandise from that department? And what are those items? And what is the retail price of those items? And so it is with every department from which the display person pulled merchandise.

Clearly, there must be some control over these activities, and that control is a "loan book," which is maintained in each department (in a department store setting) or a centrally housed "goods on loan" book (for smaller stores). These books are designed to record the quantity, description, price, date placed on display, and employee who removed the goods from the selling department. Similarly, the books record notations and signatures for goods no longer on display that have been returned from floor displays to the selling department. These loan books should be subject to auditing by loss prevention on both a scheduled and random basis.

This accountability is crucial to maintaining control and preventing the loss, intentional or through carelessness, of merchandise. It's simply the nature of the beast.

Distribution Centers/Warehouses

Richard Frank

We will discuss the various security and loss prevention considerations for the distribution center or warehouse operation in the retail environment. Distribution centers that serve both retail stores and direct to customers are considered here. Taking our discussion from the outside in, we will start with considerations of sites and their selection, eventually moving inside to the security operations.

The Distribution Center Site

"Location, location, location" is often spoken of as the determination of real estate value; in the distribution center world, this is true as well. Whether we have a say in the selection of a particular site, whether it is a new build or an existing structure, security professionals must consider elements of the location, such as crime rates, labor force, proximity to transportation hubs, and public safety access. Will the center be located in an area that has predominantly union workforces or nonunion? This factor can mean the difference between devoting significant amounts of time to union-related activities or not. If the center is in an area that has easy access to public transportation, the labor draw there may be significantly different than it is in the areas immediately surrounding the facility. Also consider the employment rate for the counties and state, as low unemployment rates can make it more difficult to recruit quality employees, causing a lowering of pre-employment standards just to attract workers. Another set of risk factors can come into play if the local labor market conditions make it attractive for the company to use temporary worker agencies to fill jobs. Each of these factors deserves investigation in planning appropriate countermeasures to the associated risks they present.

On the physical side of the distribution center, we are still working from the outside inward. It is ideal to have a site that contains some natural boundary delineation—elements that naturally communicate that we have moved from public to private space. This is a basic provision of Crime Prevention Through Environmental Design (CPTED) and it works. Often, this is nothing more than an expanse of open space between the public roadways surrounding the site and where the property is protected with physical barriers such as walls or fences. Use of fences and gated entranceways is a desired feature, especially in cargo trailer areas. It may not be possible to completely fence employee and public parking and access ways, but controlling traffic in and out of the trailer yards should definitely be pursued. The yard should also have a quality form of electronic protection in addition to physical barriers. Only if the distribution center is relatively small, maybe less than 200,000 square feet with the ability to move all trailers with merchandise or supplies offsite at closing, would secured cargo trailer lots be unnecessary. The property should be identified in such a manner that boundaries are clearly marked for trespass enforcement, should that become necessary. If the distribution center receives overseas containers and expects to be Customs Trade Partnership Against Terrorism (CTPAT) certified by the Department of Homeland Security, the containers must be inspected upon arrival to comply with standards for this certification. This means a gated and manned inbound container yard is the best approach.

Still outside the building, we must make some determination about parking areas for employees, contractors, and cargo containers. If at all possible, do not mix any of the aforementioned types of parking in the same areas. Do not allow employee or private vehicles within the areas designated for merchandise (cargo) containers, either inbound or outbound. The same goes for contractors or visitors. These parking areas should not be immediately adjacent to the building as well, leaving at least some open space barrier between. All parking areas must be lit to the degree that night surveillance via closed-circuit cameras or just plain visual observation is easily accomplished. Foot-candle or lumens measurements as standards can be used in order to quantify the level of lighting required and suited to the location. One source for determining the recommended lighting levels is the Illuminating Engineering Society of North America (IESNA). In their guidelines lighting handbook (1993), they recommended from .50fc at the fence lines to as much as 2.0fc for high vehicle activity parking areas.

Interior Space Design

Moving to the interior of the distribution center (DC), certain design characteristics are desirable from both the antitheft and personnel safety aspect. Common to both the DC and corporate office settings are the concept of visitor controls. Unlike the retail store, in the DC we can "hold" visitors until they are accompanied or at least authorized for access. Having said this, a reception or security kiosk is the best method to control and announce visitors and contractors, as well as direct applicants. It is recommended that job applicants be processed in an area ahead of the general offices and merchandise processing locations in the center. In considering employee access controls, an effective approach is, of course, to use ID badges to indicate active employees. Badges are most effective when combined with electronic access control systems that can control days, times, and specific interior points to which an individual can gain entry. If the employee population at a given location is sufficient, a very effective means of entry control is accomplished by combining the electronic ID badge with optical turnstiles. These devices work well in conjunction with the receptionist, allowing only current employees and other authorized persons to enter the facility, yet minimizing the ability to "piggyback" through a doorway undetected. Again this feature goes far in keeping outsiders, terminated employees, or nonscheduled employees from entering undetected and is much more effective than the old method of showing an ID badge at the door to a guard who may not know that an individual is no longer welcome.

Since, in the retail distribution world, we are most often shipping and receiving products that are somewhat portable, wearable, or concealable, it is good security to control what an employee can bring or wear into the DC. Use of an employee locker room where outerwear and parcels not needed in the performance of the job can be stored makes good sense. Consider the issuance of clear plastic bags or purses. This space should be positioned before the DC entry point. Having the workforce enter and exit the merchandise areas without the aforementioned "extra baggage" makes it much easier to view and/or inspect employees as they leave. Exit inspections have proven to be a solid theft deterrent and to have a positive effect on distribution center inventory shrinkage. Be cognizant of items carried within the distribution center that may be commonly worn by the employee population. Examples might be jewelry or portable electronics. Efforts can be made to limit or identify personally owned goods so they can be easily distinguished from company-owned new goods. One company that sold a lot of watches in its merchandise offerings issued all distribution center employees company-branded watches, allowing only those to be brought into the workplace.

Consider enclosing an area or office from which to monitor and control all the security technology that has been installed for the property. In doing so, the general employee population, while aware of the presence, cannot observe specifically what is being monitored or reviewed; additionally, they cannot accurately assess the capabilities of the security technology. Maintenance of this posture fosters a deterrent effect for those considering the risk versus benefits of committing crimes against the company.

Communicate the Rules

Be sure to partner with human resources in order to construct policies that communicate the company's (security) stance on issues such as access control, visitors, lockers, and exit inspections. Security-related policies help map the expectations of the company regarding behaviors in the distribution function and clearly articulate the disciplinary processes for failing to follow the rules. Well-written, well-taught policies will stand the test of both administrative- and labor relations–type challenges.

Transportation Controls

As earlier mentioned, it is recommended to control who goes where in a distribution center. As trucks and their drivers come and go, it is very important to limit the risk of loss through external and internal theft. Keeping drivers separated from the docks is a basic ingredient in risk management. An office or designated area should be provided for drivers to either present or pick up shipping/receiving documents. This area does not give the driver access to the dock and should not allow him or her to come in direct contact with either loaders or merchandise. In the case of what is known as "live unloads" (this is a scenario in which a driver must unload only a portion of the truck and then move on to another location), special dock areas should be designated for this type of activity, usually as close as possible to the office or designated drivers area. Some companies have gone as far as to physically separate even the live unload areas with fencing, creating a buffer space between where the drivers unload and then allowing the company personnel access after the driver has left. These additional controls can be applied in both the live receiving and live shipping routines. All such efforts make it more difficult for collusive theft behavior to take place between company personnel and truck drivers.

No movement of goods should take place on or off the property without the receipt of or creation of proper documentation. Usually, these are referred to as "bills of lading" and/or "manifests." These are the legal documents that give authority to ship or receive a quantity of goods. They are the travel documents that accompany the trailer or container during transit. Careful inspection of these should take place as soon as possible when cargo arrives or as it departs. The best control points for this to happen are commonly referred to as "truck gates." They are the portals into or out of (usually outdoor) areas where trucks and trailers are secured and stored. As previously mentioned, these yards should be fenced and electronically protected.

Trailer Security

Most distribution operations will expect arriving trailers to have been sealed at their point of origin, and an inspection of the seal is completed upon arrival. Seals are numbered, and each number is recorded on the documents that accompany the shipment. The numbers may also have been communicated electronically separate from the shipment to provide an extra layer of security against shipment tampering. Of particular interest is the seal integrity of inbound overseas containers. Careful scrutiny of the seal verification process is required if the facility is part of a CTPAT-certified company. Additionally, it is recommended that all inbound drivers show identification at the inbound inspection point. In general, loaded trailers stored overnight in a secured yard should be sealed and/or locked for general protection. If the yard cannot be secured, additional measures such as (king) pin locks and tail-to-tail parking should be used as a hedge against trailer theft. Also consider random patrols of any unattended facilities. Yard checks should be performed at close and opening to record or verify the presence, condition, and location of all trailers. Anomalies should be investigated immediately, of course. Finally, an assessment should be made as to the local crime rates and experiences of other adjacent properties to help validate the security investment for outdoor protection.

Pre/Post-Employment Offer Screening

This brief discussion offers some recommended screening protocols that should be considered for employees of the distribution center. In many cases, more in-depth screening is possible in the DC than in the stores due to a more centralized and larger human resources function. Also, the employee population is generally larger and somewhat more permanent. The following screening elements are recommended:

- Pre-employment criminal background checks
- Pre-employment drug screens
- Employment history examination and verification
- Post-offer medical questionnaire and review by or with a medical professional
- Verification of truthfulness of other information given in the application process, such as a check of the worker's compensation system to detect undisclosed medical issues that could lead to future workers comp liability
- Social Security number verification, as well as identification document review

Some retail distribution centers have reported as much as a 20% failure rate on the criminal background check process alone, so it is important to do all you can afford to screen in good employees.

Note: When considering the use of contractors for such things as temporary workers, contract drivers, etc., hold these organizations to the same screening standards that are in place for regular distribution center employees.

Receiving

Most distribution operations do not do a count of receipts beyond the carton level. They may, however, employ a system of rating shippers or vendors based on previous experience with accuracy or quality. Such a rating system may flag incoming shipments that require more detailed examination or sampling including down to the individual item level. If any inconsistencies are found during the inbound examination process, such as incorrect seal numbers, evidence of damage, or open cartons, a complete audit of the entire shipment is in order. Any problems suspected even if they are later found not to have resulted in a loss such as "cartons appeared to be crushed or wet" must be noted on the bill of lading. This practice helps the freight claim process if it is determined later that something is wrong with the shipment such as missing or damaged goods.

High-Value/Theft-Prone Goods

Special care is given to products within the DC that are either very high value or very desirable as items to steal. Many times the items are small and easily concealed but carry a relatively high price, sometimes beyond the means of the workforce. For these classes of goods, it is often the practice to have prior notice to their arrival so that special arrangements can be carried out to ensure that they are quickly moved from dock or receiving areas and located in secured storage. Use special security protection in areas designated for secured storage such as electronic access control, CCTV, and special security clearances for those assigned to work there. On the outbound side, "prep" the outer cartons so as not to readily identify them as high value; i.e., make them look like any other carton. Release to shipping under controlled conditions such as onto mechanized conveying systems or manually transferred directly to outbound trailers, minimizing opportunities for internal pilferage. A "best practice" noted for retail store shipments is to pack high-value items within a tamper-evident plastic bag within the carton so as to discourage in transit pilferage as well as pilferage upon arrival at a store.

If the distribution center also handles the returns of high-value products, security arrangements must be made to identify these types of items upon their arrival at the docks so that they can quickly be moved to a secure processing area of the facility. Sometimes this is accomplished via the physical size of the return package (in the case of a direct-type return from a customer). In other cases a special address or code can be used on the return label that would identify the package as one to be routed to the secured returns area. In the case of consolidated returns as they would arrive from a retail store, high-value products will be identified only within the "opener" process, at which time they could be isolated for removal to secured storage.

Shipping

As goods prepare to leave the distribution center for shipment to a customer, store, or back to the vendor, it is commonplace that sealed cartons approach the dock doors and are or have been "electronically scanned" as an outbound event. This scan is generally used to produce part of the shipping documentation, usually the manifest. In some organizations the outbound cartons are scanned numerous times as they move through various processes, including picking and packing. These "system" checkpoints are useful in tracking down inventory losses and/or substantiating freight claims later.

Just a few words about the sealing of cartons: It is helpful to use a proprietary form of sealing tape on the tops and bottoms of cartons. This tape should not be readily available to trucking firms used, nor should it be left at the stores for use in any transfers, if possible. The stores can have a different version or color for store-to-store or returns to the distribution center. Following this practice provides a better means to determine carton tampering at the destination point. Finally, outbound trucks should be inspected at the exit point of the shipping yard to ensure that the "load" is authorized and sealed as notated on the accompanying documents. Again, consider recording a portion of the identification of the exiting driver. Any discrepancies are to be reported/investigated immediately.

Security Functions

As previously mentioned, larger distribution centers should absolutely have a separate dedicated security function that reports to a corporate security/loss prevention organization at least at a dotted-line position. This department is responsible then to monitor the electronic protection systems, provide responses to changing conditions, investigate loss, and plan for emergency actions. Additionally, the local security function can perform certain risk-management–related activities such as fire protection and insurance-related inspections, tests, drills, etc. Several large retail organizations use the security personnel at the DCs to monitor alarm and environmental conditions for their stores, office facilities, and executive residences. Often this is a cost-savings/service-enhancing feature providing value-added measurement to the support nature of security and loss prevention. Certainly, the DC security and loss prevention team can play a role in both safety and inventory shrink-reduction initiatives for the organization. Many of these efforts can and do have cost-reduction metrics that can be measured against the costs of having an active security function within the distribution center function. Best advice: Don't leave security and loss prevention to the receptionist at the distribution center!

Docks (Receiving and Shipping)

CAS, JHC

A store's dock or docks, typically located on the back side of the building facing an alley, a remote part of a parking lot, or in a subterranean area of a shopping center, can be a vulnerable area to theft absent a given set of basic protective measures. A checklist of rules and strategies includes

1. A dock door should be open only when unloading or loading a trailer or truck.
2. If ventilation is required, especially in hot climates, the door may be up, but the opening should be enclosed with fencing locked in place.
3. Employees must never exit or enter the store through a dock door.
4. Customers must never be allowed on the dock.
5. Docks should have a "red-line zone" space of approximately 12 feet back from the edge of the dock, in which merchandise may not be staged. The zone is marked with a painted red line.
6. If a driver's presence is required on the dock, such driver may not leave that zone.
7. If a restroom is required for drivers and it's not possible to have an exterior door to that room, then a red-line walkway should be painted from the dock to the restroom, and drivers may not veer from that walkway.
8. If the store has a pedestrian dock entrance door, it must be locked from the exterior side at all times, and employees may not use this door except for specific duties requiring usage.
9. Dock doors should be on their own separate alarm system to allow early morning receiving while leaving the rest of the exterior of the building under alarm protection.
10. The dock's interior and exterior area should be covered with CCTV.
11. The dock's exterior area should be illuminated during hours of darkness.
12. Employees should be prohibited from parking near the dock doors.
13. Sales associates should be excluded from the dock, unless their presence is specifically required.
14. Temporary lockable security cages may be required for very expensive and highly desirable goods coming into the store (pending their acceptance and removal by the selling department manager).

15. Loaded trailers awaiting removal for inter-store transfer or return to the distribution center, if left over night hours, must be backed up to the dock and must be locked and sealed. For added security, a connection can be provided which ties the trailer into the facility's alarm system. Trailers not connected to a tractor should contain "pin locks," which are designed to prevent the coupling of a tractor to a trailer.

16. If the same dock doors are used for both receiving and shipping, the area used for each should be separated by a cyclone wire fence at least 12 feet high. This fence can be moveable, but incoming goods should always be separated from outgoing goods when they are in the vicinity of dock doors.

17. Trash removal should be supervised.

Retail warehouses and distribution centers are situated in more industrial settings with less activity and traffic and often are shut down at nights and weekends. Those facilities should ideally be surrounded by perimeter fencing, and the dock area should be further enclosed by another fence and gate. This area should have a guard shack and be staffed with a security officer to control incoming and outgoing tractors and trailers, including the logging in and out of each vehicle entering or leaving the facility, identifying the driver and the license number of both the cab and trailer.

The security required for the line of docks and numerous dock doors so common in this environment is similar to that listed previously.

Documentation

CAS, JHC

Of Incidents

In the late 1990s, a Los Angeles law firm produced, periodically, a publication titled "Private Security—A Legal Update." Three of these publications dealt specifically with the issue of report writing and the documentation of security incidents. These three issues were headed: "Documenting Your Way to a Successful Verdict," "Paper Train Your Company," and "Write Those Wrongs!"

These publications, as can be seen from their lead articles, stressed the importance of writing complete, detailed, accurate, and understandable reports of loss prevention incidents. Additionally, they advocated the retention of such reports for at least 3 years. This firm is absolutely convinced that excellent documentation will often mean winning a civil suit before it ever gets to trial or, if tried, the difference between a favorable verdict or losing the suit and suffering a substantial financial penalty.

Good reports will contain the answers to the when, where, who, what, how, and why of an incident developed during its investigation.

An oft-quoted Golden Rule of report writing is this: "If something happened and you didn't report on it, it didn't happen." That's just another way of saying, "If something happened, it damn well better be reported."

What are some qualities of a good report? Reports should

- Be complete, detailed, and accurate, including dates, times, etc.
- Not sacrifice understanding for brevity.
- Be written as soon after the incident as possible.
- Be factual; don't write things which can't be proven.
- Always distinguish between
  - Fact and hearsay.
  - Fact and opinion.
  - Fact and conclusion.
- Avoid ambiguities.
- Quote exculpatory statements as well as inculpatory ones.
- Identify all witnesses.

- Describe all evidence, where found, who found, location found.
- Fully identify subject/suspect of report.
- Avoid slang.
- Be written so a reader 2 years from now with no prior knowledge of the incident will know exactly what happened.
- Avoid spelling and grammatical errors.

Two suggested references for guidance in writing reports are *Report Writing for Security Personnel* by Christopher A. Hertig, CPP, and Gary E. Bittner, Ph.D., published by Butterworth-Heinemann (1991), and *The Process of Investigation*, 2nd edition, by Charles A. Sennewald and John K. Tsukayama, published by Butterworth-Heinemann (2001).

Of Policies and Procedures

Many of the suggestions made with regard to report writing apply as well to the documentation of loss prevention procedures.

As discussed elsewhere in this book, retailers are frequently sued for what the security/ loss prevention department did or didn't do. It is not unusual for discovery or trial in civil cases to occur years after the incident prompting the litigation. It is therefore equally important that the procedures in place at the time of the incident are memorialized, as well as the actions LP personnel should and should not do. Did the company have a policy or procedure outlining the levels of force authorized? How about searches of suspects? Were the six steps in place? Did policy require a female witness whenever a female was apprehended?

How can the company's rules and regulations under which loss prevention operated several years ago be positively established? Testimony is one way, but a written document appropriately dated is hard to challenge. Furthermore, without documentation of policies and procedures, the plaintiff can raise issues of proper training and whether the LP personnel were simply left "to run amok" without any restrictions. The issue of whether a LP manual outlining the company's policies and procedures is a help or hindrance when the company is being sued over LP activities has been the subject of much debate within the industry. It seems fairly well settled that such manuals are discoverable. The debate over their use pits the view that if there are no company rules, then an LP agent can't be found to have violated them against the opposing view that if there are no rules for LP to follow, the company is negligent in not having them. The authors, and most legal authorities, have reached the conclusion that "manuals are a must!"

Drug Store Loss Prevention

J. Patrick Murphy

Introduction

Drug stores have been in existence for centuries; the first American pharmacy opened by a pharmacist was in New Orleans in 1823. In over 150 years, only the look and feel have changed. The mission remains the same. Whether it is a major chain such as Walgreen's or CVS, a large chain of franchised independent pharmacies, or a truly neighborhood drug store, the challenges remain the same, only adjusted for scale. Pharmacies can be part of a grocery store or free standing, in a mall or strip center, even in office buildings that have mostly doctors' offices. As in all other areas of retail, there is no cookie-cutter approach to asset protection and shrinkage.

Business Overview

In 2005 the United States had over a quarter of a million registered pharmacists. They dispensed over 3.4 billion prescriptions that generated $230.3 billion in sales. Most of us are familiar with the free-standing drug stores that are usually located at an intersection. However, they come in all shapes and sizes and are also contained in grocery stores, big box stores like Wal-Mart and Target, and in strip centers. Shrinkage challenges are associated with not only the pharmacy, but throughout the merchandise or front end of the store. While everything is under one roof, there are two distinct businesses (sometimes three including photo labs) that are operating with different types of inventory and accounting practices. For the purposes of this book, I will address the common free-standing store concept.

This book is designed to give broad overview of the loss prevention challenges and efforts within several business sectors of retail. Retail pharmacy is not exclusive when it comes to shrink and its major components of employee theft, external theft, and paperwork errors. The unique problems facing retail drug stores are associated with specialized shoplifting, robbery potential, burglary, and, of course, those confined to the pharmacy itself.

The Retail Store

Operations and Staffing

Within the walls of the common chain drug store, there are three distinct business units: general merchandise, pharmacy, and photo lab. The operational framework under which the store operates varies slightly from chain to chain, but each of those units can have its own reporting structure. The store manager reports through a district operations manager, the pharmacy reports though a district pharmacy manager, and the photo finishing department, too, can have its own district-level reporting structure. The pharmacy will always have what is called the Pharmacist in Charge (PIC), but that is a title that denotes accountability to the State Board of Pharmacy for regulatory compliancy and the inventory. The title means nothing as to supervising the overall business, hiring, training, or other duties related to supervising. Some pharmacies fill large numbers of prescriptions daily and may have a chief pharmacist or pharmacy manager who acts in a managerial capacity. In general, however, the pharmacists are quasi-managers of their department when they are on duty.

The photo department is specialized in its own right and handles a business that in some customers' minds is every bit as critical as medication. Ruining film or losing the entire order of the only pictures of a first birthday or other event is catastrophic to the customer for personal reasons but generally also has a permanent impact on him or her remaining as your customer.

The machines that produce the finished product require maintenance, cleaning, and calibration on a regular basis. The quality of photos depends not only on technology, but on a trained eye as well. The branding of the superior quality of photos is key to all chain drug stores, and therefore it is a critical business unit.

Three departments, with three sets of supervisors and, in most cases, no single person responsible for the total operation. The only common staff would be loss prevention and human resources. This requires a great deal of collaboration both at the store and district levels. The sales makeup is split nearly evenly between pharmacy and front end. The photo department's contribution to store sales is comparatively small, but the gross profit is nearly 70%. Everyone has a focus on sales, shrinkage, and customer service, but it takes a deft hand to bring all of that together in concert.

Drug store management is extremely challenging because this job requires a manager to wear many hats. Payroll management, again, is separated by department, and the front-end payroll is used for everything from ordering and unloading trucks to customer service and cashiering. The management candidates come from many different service industries and obtain training mostly through on-the-job training by a designated training manager. Assistant managers are generally not prepared for the amount of work that is required to run an operation; therefore, turnover can be high. Their supervisory skills are also immature, which opens the door to operational failures that can lead to shrink and internal theft.

The loss prevention facets of store operation lie squarely on the shoulders of the store management and operations. Few stores are of the size and need to have loss prevention agents regularly, and even fewer have off-duty law enforcement on hand. Chains tend to have field loss prevention staffs called by several titles, but all function to oversee loss prevention activities. Field personnel average around 12 to 20 stores depending on their geographic concentration. Their primary roles are:

- Conduct internal theft cases.
- Conduct operational fitness audits regarding shrinkage and compliancy issues.
- Work with operations regarding training and awareness.
- Review regulatory documents that deal with federal DEA requirements in the pharmacy.

The topics covered here are operations related. While they deal with shrinkage reduction, threats, security, and asset protection, they are all under the umbrella of operations. There is extreme importance in recognizing this point not only in this environment, but in all retail organizations.

Front End

The sales floor has a wide variety of merchandise from food to fingernail polish. There are many challenges faced that impact shrinkage from the sales floor. The store manager is his or her own shipping and receiving department, own business office manager, own employee trainer, and virtually his or her own security. All the critical areas in retail are reduced to be managed or accomplished by one or two people, thus leaving a lot of room for error.

Shrink can occur from virtually hundreds of places, and its cumulative effect is erosive to the stores, and ultimately the company's, profitability. While retail in general is a sales-driven operation, focusing on shrink initiatives will yield a faster return on investment than additional sales. Most shrinkage in a drug store environment is controllable or identifiable. Battling it requires attention to detail and a great deal of organization, but not all managers possess those skills. If the store has a poor operational foundation, then attention to shrink falls to the same poor level.

Photo Labs

The one-hour photo finishing department is a high gross profit enterprise. It is nearly 100% automated, and operational problems are few. There are numerous POS systems on the market designed especially for the photo business. The most popular system is bar-code-managed so that the processed film and the register transaction relieve one another. Much like the pharmacy, it allows for an end-to-end inventory process.

By appearance, this department would seem to be fairly simple to operate and would present few problems. On the contrary, it is a very specialized business that has specialized problems.

The film and the processed photos are the proprietary property of the customer. Although processed photos can be clearly seen by the tech and even the public to some degree, there is an expectation of privacy by the customer. This becomes a serious issue when additional copies of the prints are made by employees and then stolen.

For the most part, duplicates are made of events like concerts, car shows, etc., and are stolen because of their uniqueness. Surprisingly, people bring in film that contains nudity or other private subject matter, and those photos become the target of theft. The creation of personal photo albums of stolen photos is not unusual. Photos from insurance investigators, law enforcement, or other such activities are also highly vulnerable to theft. Photos that go beyond nudity and are of sexual conduct are shredded, and the negatives are given to the customer. Photos that portray criminal acts such as child abuse or drugs are referred to the local police. Imagine giving the police a photo taken of three smiling people sitting behind a table with three large bags of marijuana in front of them.

Internal theft of processed photos is rampant. Photographs at parties, graduations, proms, homecoming events, etc., have not changed with the digital age. Reprints, custom poster prints, as well as any other offerings are subject to theft. Another avenue of internal theft in the photo lab is from part-time professional photographers. Naturally, photographers would be interested in working in a photo lab, but photographers who take photos at weddings on the side, for instance, can boost their profit greatly by using the lab as their developer and then stealing the finished product. Lastly, photo paper itself is a marketable commodity. Stealing photo paper to sell to other independent photo labs is infrequent but does occur. As margins are squeezed by major retailers, an independent photo lab would be a good customer for black market paper.

Controlling shrinkage in a photo lab may seem daunting because there are so many ways to commit theft. The key ingredient is the paper. Labs must keep tight control on expenses to maintain their high gross margin. A typical lab may have a profit margin of 68–75%, so when a lab's performance falls below that, measures must be taken to monitor business. If the cost of the paper used to develop photos begins to grow beyond comparable labs, then that variance needs investigation. There are other reasons beyond theft for that variance, but once those are eliminated, there is usually a theft problem. With the offering of Internet transfer of photo files for printing, a new dimension has been added to the theft equation. Now collusion can originate and end anywhere across the country in seconds.

Security and Asset Protection

Shoplifting

Shoplifting takes a heavy toll in a drug store. While drug stores do not carry high-end merchandise, they do carry merchandise that has high street value and high resale value for entities such as flea markets. What was once considered unsophisticated and infrequent has been raised to a new level of interest to both state and federal law enforcement. The growing trend of organized shoplifting has brought together the resources of both law enforcement and retailers.

Drug stores are particularly susceptible to shoplifting of any kind. The height and lay-out of store fixtures, minimal staff, and register placement make the drug store an excellent location for shoplifting. Merchandise security is an extreme challenge in that the self-service nature of the business requires that a customer have ample access to select merchandise. In 2005, the Food Marketing Institute produced a list of the top 50 items stolen by shoplifters involved in organized retail crime (ORC); the top ten of which are shown in Table D-1. FMI is an organization serving the needs of food distribution and related business, including grocery wholesalers and retail supermarkets. These same items are in all drug stores.

Table D-1 Top Ten Items Stolen in Drug Stores in 2005

1: Advil tablet 50 ct
2: Advil tablet 100 ct
3: Aleve caplet 100 ct
4: EPT Pregnancy Test single
5: Gillette Sensor 10 ct
6: Kodak 200 24 exp
7: Similac w/iron powder — case
8: Similac w/iron powder–single can
9: Preparation H 12 ct
10: Primatene tablet 24 ct

ORC: Organized Retail Crime

The items listed in Table D-1 may seem to be an odd assortment of merchandise targeted for theft; however, for those involved in ORC, it is not. "It is estimated that the retail industry loses between $15 to $30 billion annually to such theft," according to University of Florida criminologist Richard Hollinger, Ph.D., who has directed the National Retail Security Survey for the past 16 years. He reports "The average loss per ORC incident is now more than $46,000."

ORC has been plaguing retail for many years, but now these operations have become highly sophisticated and even selective of the items they want. This operation is widely diversified through cells that work in concert to fill "orders" from a "repack" warehouse.

Merchandise delivered to the warehouse is inspected and then repacked into an original cardboard box that was pulled from a dumpster. This merchandise is either sold overseas or redistributed to other retailers. The shoplifters involved in this level of shoplifting are bold and often take every item from the shelf. This type of activity has caused manufacturers to design shelf and peg displays that prevent easy removal of multiple items in one movement.

Shoplifting apprehension and detection are primarily the functions of store management. In drug stores, store detectives and loss prevention agents are relatively few compared to other retail sectors, but they have proven effective even in the small store setting. The primary detection and apprehension method is through electronic article surveillance.

EAS is an important strategic partner in combating external theft. Source tagging by product manufacturers has eliminated much of the store-side labor costs associated with tagging goods. Manufacturers have come to embrace the technology because it increases their sales. Their trade-off by absorbing costs associated with tagging at the manufacturing level has paid huge dividends. R&D has increased to develop better tags in both pick rate (detection) and form factor. Until a common tag format (magnetic versus radio frequency, or RF) is agreed upon across the industry, there will continue to be debate as to which is more effective. EAS also has an impact for deterrent against shoplifting. The tags that are built into the packages are not accessible to be removed by potential thieves.

Theft by Older Customers

The primary business of the business sector is obviously to dispense prescriptions. In many cases the demographics are such that the predominant customer is elderly. In areas of the country where there are large retirement populations, this is especially true. Theft by these adults needs due consideration from a policy standpoint so as not to unnecessarily prosecute those with diminished capacity. This is not to give a certain age group carte blanche, but it is prudent to understand that the risk of negative impact in the community is high should an incident be mishandled. This is an area where simply pursuing civil recovery, if available, is probably the path of least resistance. Having a policy of 100% prosecution in this circumstance can be very counterproductive and produce a negative community perception.

Vendor Theft

Vendors, those companies that provide direct delivery, commonly referred to as direct store delivery (DSD), present a unique variable to shrink. Vendor theft is best described as theft by the delivery person of their own goods. The other aspect is theft of goods from stock rooms or other areas where they deliver to.

Vendors for soft drinks, beer, wine, chips, greeting cards, etc., generally employ the same person for that route day in and day out. There are also delivery people from outside vendors who deliver special-order drugs. Because of their familiarity with people in the store, they form a relationship. This could be simply their personality and is part of excellent customer service. Some, however, have intent beyond customer service to lower the defensive guard of those persons who are responsible for checking in the delivered merchandise.

Checking the invoice of vendors against what they bring in seems to be a simple concept. They count it out; you check it off the invoice. Stop! The cardinal rule of vendor check-in was just broken. The vendor should never just call out the merchandise. The person receiving the goods should put his or her hands on the goods and confirm it to the paperwork. Dishonest vendors will count bags in multiples and easily confuse someone who is not paying attention. This will happen most frequently when a vendor is being checked in by new management. Another seemingly innocent practice that is perceived as great customer service is for vendors to service their products and then bring the invoice to be signed. There is no way to confirm what was actually done.

Why would a vendor steal five bags of chips from a store's order? The answers are many but primarily so he or she can sell that product privately to another retailer. Poor check-in procedures are funding the vendor's black market operation and contributing to the store's shrink.

Robbery

Threat level for robbery is high primarily because the registers are right at the door. The threat potential grows in late hours and 24-hour stores. The primary time of the highest vulnerability is at the time the manager arrives at the store in the morning and as employees are leaving at night. When management arrives, it is usually well before the store opens, and in most cases, managers are by themselves. The cash from the previous night's sales is in the safe and, depending on the whether there is armored car service, the money may be out of the safe for deposit preparation. At the close of business, it is always a good practice for all employees to leave as a group. This reduces the chance for a robbery due to the number of people that need to be controlled.

Armed robberies or strong-armed robberies that take place at a register or in the office can be very fast and, at times, very violent. The cash loss is minimal, but the psychological damage to the victim or victims will be considerable. After the police investigation, the victims should be allowed to go home with pay for the remainder of their shift. Consideration should also be given to additional compensated time off, as well as the offering of psychological counseling. The victim can also be subsequently moved to another store if needed. Homicides during robberies are rare in the chain drug sector but do occur. The most volatile situations are robberies of the pharmacy for narcotics. The suspect is already in an altered state of mind and is extremely dangerous. Both types of robberies require the training of all management personnel to understand and follow the proper response.

Some stores or chains do not used armored car services. This is a difficult decision to make; if such a service is not used, bank deposits become extremely dangerous. Managers must take to the bank the deposits not handled by armored cars. This presents an extreme risk of robbery, injury, or death of an employee and exposes large sums of money to internal theft. This is especially true if a night drop at the bank is used. The use of armored car services should be considered for all stores regardless of volume, as a measure to protect the safety of employees.

Alarms and CCTV play an important role in the event of a robbery. While robbery alarms and panic buttons are widely used in a number of areas, consideration must be given to the possibility of creating a hostage situation if the police arrive quickly. It is always best to allow the suspect to leave before any action is taken to notify police. CCTV is extremely helpful in resolving these cases if the equipment is kept in good repair. With the increasing use of digital recording, it important to remember that the suspect can no longer simply remove a tape from the machine. Instead, he or she will want to take the entire DVR. An effective countermeasure is to maintain a hidden backup DVR that continuously records.

Internal Theft

Drug stores are no different from any other retail organization when it comes to internal theft. The wide range of merchandise presents a lot of appeal to employees, and the opportunity to commit theft is abundant. Items such as cigarettes and beer, for which the sale is governed by age requirements, are typical targets of younger employees. The host of other items could be considered "everyday" merchandise, which has even broader appeal.

The methods employed to commit theft are generally not sophisticated, as the passing merchandise is commonly used. What is unique to this industry is the embedded theft cases in which several employees, including management, are stealing. This problem ranges outward from the store to include friends and family and thus becomes a viral effect. Investigators quickly learn that asking the simple question "Who else is involved?" expands the investigation exponentially. What is most interesting about these cases is that the employees are not working in concert with each other, but rather are simply taking advantage of the known environment. Store management can unwittingly be taken advantage of simply by their work habits. Common examples of this are that they stay in the office, leave the store during their shift, or simply do not have the confrontational skills to effectively deter the activity.

Embedded cases are difficult to detect because they grow slowly over time. The case of individual theft that involves cash register manipulation is much easier to initiate based on exception reports or other factors on the store's profit and loss. The law of averages and comparability are the two factors that drive exception report usage. The drug store is no different, but the difficulty lies in the number of employees that are being reviewed by the software daily. Across the enterprise, tens of thousands of employees have register access, and hundreds of thousands of transactions are rung daily. The amount of data is overwhelming. Those employees who begin to surface on reports are migrating through this myriad of data and should be considered high threat. Unfortunately, this also means that a great deal of theft will be under the radar simply because investigations are working on the worst cases. The training and awareness programs that are implemented in the stores must be powerful enough to deter those employees who are on the fence about stealing.

Deterrent Measures Awareness

The dedicated thief will not be deterred by any means, so, as with any program, the target audience is that group who are opportunists if the circumstances are right and for whom the fear of apprehension is low. That combination must be leveraged to maintain a healthy attitude against theft.

Drug stores have very few people on duty at a given time, so the opportunity to have a storewide meeting, as is common in department stores, is not very effective. At the time the store opens, there may be only four employees in the building. Store management must find alternative methods to combat theft through training and awareness that can be delivered on a wider scale. Here are some simple suggestions that can be quite effective:

- *Bag checks:* This has to be part of company policy and must have strict interpretation as to what it means. Failure to allow a member of management the ability to check a purse, briefcase, backpack, or purchase should be considered a terminable violation of company policy.
- *CCTV:* If the store has CCTV, especially over the registers, employees should be made aware of that fact when first hired. Explain its usage and the fact that video of transactions is frequently reviewed for customer service and training purposes.
- *Break room posters:* Posters may seem to be ineffective but only because there is no way to measure their effect on an individual employee. They are effective, however, because, just like any advertising, they sell by being repeatedly seen. Using one poster all year is ineffective. Posters and like signage should be changed at least quarterly. The store's shrink percent and dollar amount should be part of that process as well. The percent means little to an hourly associate, so the dollars are the important factor. The loss amount must be reduced to a daily average amount so that the figure can be grasped by all employees.
- *Employee hot line:* This call line allows employees to provide tips to the company anonymously. There is debate as to whether rewards for fruitful information are appropriate, so this issue should be thoroughly discussed with the corporate legal department.

These are not new initiatives and, in fact, little has changed in this regard for 20 or more years. It is important, however, that every opportunity be taken to find ways to get the message to all employees in some form. Management must be accountable for ensuring their personal habits reinforce this effort.

Closing

The chain drug environment requires the ability to see potential problems in a single store and project their potential across thousands. While the challenges are the same as in any retail sector, the multiple-store environment, coupled with the specialized knowledge needed for the pharmacy, makes loss prevention a challenge even for the best practitioner.

Drug stores will continue to grow in revenue as the baby boomers age and their need for prescription medication rises. Online sales have grown, but personal interaction with the pharmacist is still as special as it was a century ago. This customer-centric business requires a near flawless operation to stay in compliance with state and federal laws and to protect the health of patients. Loss prevention in this setting plays an important role in assisting to maintain a high standard, which ultimately assists in shrink reduction.

For more information about the retail drug industry, refer to the following resources:

National Association of Chain Drug Stores (NACDS)	www.nacds.org
National Association of Drug Diversion Investigators (NADDI)	www.naddi.org
Pharmacists Recovery Network (PRN)	www.usaprn.org
DEA Drug Diversion Division	www.deadiversion.usdoj.gov
Drug Store News	www.drugstorenews.com
Chain Drug Review	www.chaindrugreview.com

Drug Testing

John J. Fay

Background

In 1986 President Reagan issued Executive Order 12564, which required the head of each executive agency of the federal government to establish a program to test for the illegal use of drugs by employees in sensitive positions. The order reached into the private sector in a very large way because the order incorporated jobs held by employees in companies regulated by the executive agencies. Passage in 1988 of the Drug-Free Workplace Act gave the order greater impetus by adding certain federal contractors and all recipients of federal grants.

Encouraged by the order, private sector organizations of many stripes began their own drug testing programs, and after two decades of challenges in the courts, the practice survived largely intact. Today, a majority of companies that perform safety-sensitive work routinely test for drugs, plus companies in other industries that have their own reasons for testing certain employees in jobs involving money handling, sensitive information, and contact with persons in their homes. Trust and responsibility are now companions with safety in the rationale for drug testing.

The federal program, the model for nearly all programs, has five elements: policy, supervisory training, employee education, employee assistance, and drug testing that is controlled and carefully monitored.

Policy

A policy explains in writing why drug testing is necessary. In the retail sector, the reasons can be prevention of loss, such as by internal theft, prevention of accidents that jeopardize the safety of employees and customers, employee health and welfare, and the public's perception of the company.

A policy defines terms that can be interpreted in more than one way. For example, the terms "drug abuse" and "illegal drugs" can have different meanings depending on context and who is making the interpretation.

A policy describes prohibited drug-related behaviors such as being at work under the influence of an illegal drug or using, possessing, distributing, or selling illegal drugs in the workplace or at any other location while doing the company's business.

Consequences that can result from policy violations are explained. The nature of a violation determines the nature of the consequence. Possessing an illegal drug at work is far less serious than selling drugs. The first may result in a disciplinary action; the second is termination with facts of the matter going to law enforcement.

A policy includes appeal procedures and, depending on the wishes of the employer, can include amnesty provisions and treatment benefits.

Of greatest importance is the nature of the testing program. Persons subject to the policy have a right to know the circumstances that trigger testing, test specimens that are collected, manner of collection, testing methodologies, procedures for challenging test results, consequences for refusing to be tested, and consequences of failing to pass a test.

Supervisory Training

Although most of the efforts in administering a program occur in pre-employment testing, supervisors play an important role in detecting and taking action when they observe on-the-job policy violations. It should come as no surprise that persons seeking employment with a company that tests job applicants will abstain from drug use long enough to pass the pre-employment test. Supervisors are a second line of defense.

Supervisory training includes recognition of drugs and drug paraphernalia, behavior that indicates intoxication, intervention actions, and documentation. Intervention tactics are looking for the remnants of abuse such as an abandoned brown paper bag crumpled in such a way that suggests glue sniffing, a discarded syringe, or the tell-tale odor of burned marijuana.

Supervisors who see symptoms of drug use, such as slurred speech, staggering, and euphoria, are obligated to intervene. When symptoms, and perhaps other factors, lead a supervisor to reasonably believe that an employee is under the influence, the policy might require a test for drugs and alcohol. (Alcohol is not illegal, but possession or use of it in the workplace is a policy violation.) For reasonable belief to exist, the symptoms must be explainable and provable; specific, contemporaneous, and tangible; and be associated with probable drug use. To validate a supervisor's reasonable belief, a Two-Supervisor Rule can be the answer. This rule calls for two supervisors who have knowledge of the facts to jointly make the determination to refer the employee for testing.

Employee Education

The entire workforce is educated as to why drug testing is necessary, the problems it addresses, and the responsibility of each employee to support the drug-free program. A program can be superbly conceived and fully funded, but without the willingness of employees to accept and cooperate, the program will not succeed.

The means for employee education are numerous; for example, classroom, town hall meeting, departmental meeting, bulletin board, email messaging, tutoring, mentoring, and counseling.

Employee Assistance

Treatment benefits can range from nothing or small to the maximum allowable by the company's medical insurance program. A small employee assistance program may consist only of a referral service to a local treatment provider, while a full-blown program will pay rehabilitation and medication costs.

Drug Testing

Testing seeks to identify in a person's body the evidence of illegal drug use. The most common method of testing is the analysis of urine. The person to be tested is asked, not compelled, to provide a urine specimen. Written consent is absolutely essential.

The specimen is collected in a manner that guards against cheating and error. The integrity of the specimen has to be unquestionably reliable. Any indication of switching, contamination, or mislabeling will invalidate test results. A chain of custody form is initiated by the collector, and as the specimen moves from person to person, entries are made on the form that document access to the specimen and why.

Quality assurance protocols at the laboratory include calibrating equipment and minimizing human errors. Calibration and performance of equipment can be verified by insertion of "blind" specimens that contain specific drugs. If the test results of a blind specimen do not agree with what is known about the specimen, the equipment is not working properly. Errors of this type are rare. In fact, errors of any type are rare, and nearly all test result errors are attributable to human failure.

The most common testing methodology is urinalysis. Urine testing follows a two-step process consisting of an initial screen and a second test to confirm a positive finding. If the screen fails to detect a drug, that specimen is not tested further; if the screen shows that the specimen contains a drug, the specimen is examined by a more precise test. The second test is called a confirmation test, and the methodology is usually gas chromatography (GC) or gas chromatography/mass spectrometry (GC/MS). These tests are highly accurate. Because the testing process utilizes two tests that operate by different principles, the margin of error is greatly reduced.

The ability of a screening test to detect low levels of drugs has an inherent limit called the "sensitivity" limit or "cutoff" level. A specimen with a positive finding below the limit is declared negative. The cutoff is set well above true sensitivity, which decreases the possibility of a positive result caused by an outside influence such as ingestion of poppy seeds or passive inhalation of marijuana smoke.

A urine specimen that shows positive for marijuana signifies that the tested person ingested marijuana or a marijuana derivative within the past hour and for as long as 3 weeks depending on frequency of use and strength of the drug. Time of previous drug use, whether for marijuana or other drugs, is immaterial when the employer's only interest is to determine if the tested person's body contained a drug at the time the specimen was collected.

The Role of Security

Security professionals perform four functions in support of a drug-free program: investigating, preventing, educating, and monitoring the collection of specimens.

Offenses that violate policy or law are investigated. Discipline administered for a policy violation is founded on facts, and the fact-gatherers are security investigators. In a violation of law, security investigators interview witnesses, interrogate suspects, and collect evidence. Statements and evidence obtained are turned over to law enforcement. A serious offense, such as trafficking in drugs, can cause an offender to be sent to prison. The magnitude of consequence places a demand on security investigators to be thorough and fair.

Prevention takes two forms: examination of materials entering and moving within the premises. For example, security officers inspect packages at employee entrances, monitor cargo being offloaded at delivery docks, and patrol remote and secluded areas where drugs are likely to be used; security investigators train mailroom employees in how to identify suspicious packages and teach employees how to spot and report coworkers committing drug-related violations.

Prevention is inherent to the company's loss prevention program. It is well understood that drug abusers steal to support their habits or simply steal because the same value system that rationalizes drug use can rationalize theft.

A company's security professionals are ideal for teaching the workforce the criminal aspects of drug-related conduct and for acquiring teaching support from outside agencies such as the Drug Enforcement Administration and the FBI.

Collection of specimens has civil liability implications. Discrimination, sexual harassment, and wrongful termination are matters in the investigative purview of the corporate security department. In that purview also are allegations that specimens were collected in ways that eliminated job applicants from hiring consideration or that caused employees to be disciplined or terminated.

Conclusion

Image, reputation, and customer goodwill are damaged by perceptions that a company has an abuse problem. A company that sells across the counter has to be seriously concerned about what consumers think about the company. A grocery chain or a restaurant chain can be significantly damaged by any suggestion that drug-afflicted employees are contaminating food, and the same holds true when the users of temporary help believe that temps are drug abusers. An airline company will inevitably experience a drop in ticket sales following news reports that one of its pilots showed up for work while under the influence.

No workplace is immune. A company that turns a blind eye to drug abuse in the workplace is one step away from a drug-related loss. A company that believes "it can't happen here" is exactly the type of company that drug abusers flock to when looking for employment.

Drugs in the Workplace

CAS, JHC

It is no longer uncommon to find evidence of workplace drug use. While there are many illegal drugs in use today, the more common ones found in the workplace are listed here. It is suggested that, because violence is often associated with the illegal use of drugs, any suspicions be confidentially reported to the local police and they conduct any required investigation.

This a summary of drugs commonly found in the workplace.

Marijuana (Cannabis)
Visual Description: A dried, green leafy substance mixed with stems and possibly seeds.
Street names: Dope, Pot, Weed, Grass, Smoke, and Mota (Spanish)
Methods of use: Smoked

Amphetamine/Methamphetamine (Stimulant)
Visual Description: Capsules, crystal, pills, double-scored tablets, white or beige powder, solid white crystalline rock
Street Names: Speed, ICE, Crank, Crystal, and Meth
Methods of use: Injected, inhaled, smoked

LSD (Hallucinogen)
Visual Description: Square, perforated, impregnated blotter paper, often with cartoon characters on them
Street Names: Acid, Blotter, Sheets, and Window Pane
Methods of use: Ingested

Opiates (Narcotics)
Heroin: (Black Tar and Mexican Brown)
Visual Description: Black tar-like substance with a vinegar odor; powder that varies in color from white to dark brown
Street Names: Horse, Smack, Stuff, H, and Carga (Spanish)
Methods of use: Ingested, injected, inhaled, and smoked

Ecstasy (MDMA) (Psychedelic)
Visual Description: Brown crystalline powder
Street Names: Adam, Hug, XTC, Beans, Love Drug
Methods of use: Ingested

It is noted that the *common* symptoms of the use of the preceding drugs are elevated pulse and blood pressure.

It must be noted that street drugs are dynamic, and LP practitioners should be alert or sensitive to the appearance of some new exotic drug introduced into our society and also into the workplace.

Electronic Article Surveillance (EAS)

Robert L. DiLonardo

"Electronic article surveillance" (EAS) is the tem used to describe retail antishoplifting protection systems for apparel and packaged consumer products. These systems have been successfully implemented in hundreds of thousands of stores worldwide over the past 40 years. In short, an electronically detectable element (tag/label) is either pinned or affixed via adhesive to the item to be protected. Transmitters and receivers are placed at store exits to detect the presence of the tags as shoppers leave the stores. At the point of purchase, these tags are either removed or rendered inoperative so that the customer may exit the premises without setting off an alarm. If someone were to attempt to leave the store with items containing "live" electronic elements, the detection equipment at the exit would sound an alarm, and store management could take appropriate action.

These systems have proven to be an effective psychological and physical deterrent to shoplifting. In recent years, technological improvements have provided more reliable, smaller, and less expensive products.

The apparel industry was among the first markets for EAS. The primary method of protecting clothing was (and still is) the application of reusable plastic tags at the store or somewhere in the distribution chain. The original tags were large, heavy (27 grams), and costly ($1.40 each), and were pinned to the garments by store personnel as the merchandise was placed out on the sales floor. Even though they were obtrusive and could damage apparel if misapplied, these tags were tolerated because they effectively thwarted shoplifters and reduced inventory losses.

Over the years, the size, shape, and weight of the tags have been steadily reduced. At present, the lightest tag weighs about 7 grams, and the least expensive tag can be purchased in large quantities for about $0.15.

In the past 20 years, thin, label-like electronic circuits have been designed to provide a similar deterrent against the theft of packaged products, such as health and beauty aids, cosmetics, hardware items, toys, electronic media, and other high-volume, high-risk items. The basic principles of use remain the same as with plastic tags, except that the labels are not generally removed at the point of purchase; they are electronically disabled (deactivated) so that they won't activate an alarm as a customer exits the stores. These labels can be mass-produced at high volume for a fraction of the cost of plastic EAS tags. In addition, they can be applied to merchandise packaging using high-speed automated equipment and deactivated with little or no disruption to the checkout process.

Terminology

EAS industry jargon is not necessarily standardized. Following are definitions of major terms:

- *EAS system:* A pair of detection pedestals, or a single transceiver that transmits and receives the basic electronic signals. At certain times, the word "system" may be used to describe all the components of EAS in a store, not just the electronic detection equipment.

- *Tags:* The generic term used for individual EAS circuits of any technology. In some contexts "tag" refers to either a reusable or disposable product. Here, the term is used specifically to describe reusable plastic products, used for protecting apparel, containing an EAS circuit, a pin, and a locking mechanism. It will also be used to describe benefit denial products, such as ink tags.
- *Labels:* The specific term used to describe disposable paper/plastic laminated products, used on packaging, containing an EAS circuit and adhesive.
- *Detacher:* A removal device used for reusable plastic tags and benefit denial devices.
- *Deactivator:* A device used to destroy or distort the EAS circuit in a disposable EAS label.
- *Circuit:* The generic term used to describe the "working" component of an EAS tag or label.
- *Source tagging:* The generic term adopted by the industry to describe the affixation of disposable EAS labels onto merchandise at a convenient point in the manufacturing process, rather than after it reaches the retail store.
- *Tag and label geometry:* The term used to describe the basic shape and dimensions, or footprint, of a disposable label or the circuitry enclosed in a plastic tag.
- *Contact and proximity deactivation:* Contact deactivation is the act of incapacitating a label as it is touched by magnetic material—eliminating the circuit's ability to respond with a recognizable signal. Proximity deactivation is the act of incapacitating a label at a distance—without directly touching the circuit.

Basic Technology Comparison

Worldwide, there are three EAS technologies with a significant share of the market: electro-magnetic (EM), radio frequency (RF), and acousto-magnetic (AM). Each is capable of supporting conventional EAS usage, where tags or labels are affixed at the retail store, or source tagging. Additionally, retailers have chosen to include benefit denial devices, such as ink tags, as an adjunct to EAS programs. Since benefit denial products are an important segment in the North American market, basic information about the technology is included under the heading "Benefit Denial Devices" later in this section.

All types of EAS systems operate from a simple principle: A transmitter sends a signal at a defined frequency to a receiver. This establishes a surveillance field. When an EAS tag or label enters the field, it creates an electronic disturbance that is detected by the receiver. By design, each EAS technology has its own method by which the tag disrupts the signal. Each of the three major technologies occupies a particular space on the frequency spectrum and has its own set of strengths and weaknesses imposed on it by the laws of physics. While they may be similar in appearance and function, and provide the same general benefits, the technologies could hardly be more different.

The *electro-magnetic (EM)* transmitter creates a low-frequency (between 70 Hz and 1 kHz) electro-magnetic field between the two pedestals. Hertz (Hz) is a measurement of wave cycles per second, and 1 kilohertz is 1,000 cycles per second. The field continuously varies in strength and polarity, repeating a cycle from positive to negative and back to positive again. With each half cycle, the alignment of the magnetic field between the pedestals changes. EM EAS "circuits" are made of a strip of wire cut to a specific length. When the circuit enters the magnetic field created by the transmitter, its magnetic characteristics are changed, and the wire generates a momentary signal that is rich in the harmonics of the base frequency. In layman's terms, a harmonic signal is a precise integral multiple of the base signal from the transmitter. The receiver detects the harmonic signal, and an alarm is sounded. Unfortunately, the circuit's signal strength is so weak that the pedestal width restrictions are a maximum of 36 inches. The narrower the pedestal width, the better the receiver can "hear" the harmonic transmission from the tag. A transceiver (combination transmitter and receiver) is available, but effective detection is limited to about 24 inches. Label deactivation is achieved by magnetizing segments of the wire.

For *radio frequency (RF)* systems, the transmitter sends a signal that sweeps back and forth between certain frequency ranges. Currently, the most popular center frequency is 8.2 MHz, with a sweep range of between 7.4 and 8.8 MHz (megahertz = millions of cycles per second). A swept transmit signal is required because tight frequency tolerances cannot be precisely controlled during high-speed manufacturing of disposable EAS labels. The transmit signal energizes the EAS label, which is composed of an etched aluminum circuit containing a capacitor and an inductor, both of which store electrical energy. The EAS circuit in a plastic tag is composed of a tuned coil of wires and a capacitor. When connected together in a loop, the capacitor and etched circuit (or coil) can pass energy back and forth, or resonate. Matching the storage capacity of the two components controls the resonant frequency. The target center frequency, which is at the midpoint of the sweep, is 8.2 MHz. The circuit responds by emitting a signal that is detected by a wideband receiver, meaning a receiver that monitors for signals over a wide frequency range. The wideband receiver is required because of the lack of precision in the mass manufacturing of EAS labels. It is useful to think of this wideband receiver as fishing net carried by a shrimp boat (very large). These nets catch much more than just shrimp. Similarly, a wide band receiver picks up more than just the tag signal. The strength of the RF transmission from the circuit depends on the aperture of the loop (diameter). The larger the loop diameter, the wider apart the pedestal can be mounted. Reusable plastic EAS tags may have a loop diameter of as much as 3 inches—allowing adequate detection at almost 2 meters. The standard label size is about 2 inches square, limiting the practical detection distance to about 4 feet or under. A few of the RF EAS manufacturers have introduced a transceiver that can be mounted either as a pedestal or underneath flooring, but detection is limited to about 3 feet.

To support deactivation in disposable RF EAS labels, a dimple is added to the etched capacitor. The purpose of the dimple is to encourage a short circuit, which is caused by a strong burst of a signal of the same frequency used in detection. This burst causes an arc, which completes the short circuit. Permanent circuits in plastic tags cannot be deactivated. Deactivation can be achieved at a maximum distance of around 12 inches from the circuit.

RF reusable plastic tags are also available with a transponder, instead of the conventional tuned coil. A transponder is made up of a ferrite rod antenna for reception/transmission and a capacitor—forming a resonant circuit. Thin wire is wound around the ferrite. These products can be detected by AM transmitters/receivers, but the performance characteristics differ from those exhibited by acousto-magnetic material.

The *acousto-magnetic (AM)* technology, offered exclusively until 2003 by ADT (trade name is Ultra*Max®), contains a transmitter which sends a signal at a frequency of 58 kHz, but the frequency is sent in pulses. The signal energizes the circuit, and when the transmission ends, the circuit responds, emitting a single frequency signal like a tuning fork. The circuit's transmission is at the same frequency as the system's transmission, not a harmonic like the EM system. While the system's transmitter is "off" between pulses, a narrow band receiver detects the circuit's signal. A narrow band receiver can be used because the AM tag frequency tolerance is just 600 Hz. Compare this with the 1,400,000 Hz tolerance required with swept RF. In the fishing analogy used earlier, a narrow band receiver would be akin to a handheld casting net. Very little other than the target fish will be caught.

AM technology supports both a reusable plastic tag and a disposable, deactivatable label. The "circuit" is a strip of precision-cut amorphous alloy metal called METGLAS®, with exceptional magnetic properties and a noncrystalline structure—like glass. When aligned atop a magnet, the METGLAS® vibrates when it is exposed to the transmit signal. Since the signal is pulsed, when the transmit signal stops, the METGLAS® continues to vibrate. The accurate frequency response of the tags and labels results from the precision cutting of each strip. This "acousto-magnetic" effect, where resonance and magnetism create a unique signal, helps to explain why AM technology is somewhat immune to false alarms from objects that imitate similar electronic characteristics.

AM reusable plastic tags are available with a transponder, instead of acousto-magnetic material. A transponder is made up of a ferrite rod antenna for reception/transmission and a capacitor—forming a resonant circuit. Thin wire is wound around the ferrite. These products can be detected by AM transmitter/receivers, but the performance characteristics differ from those exhibited by acousto-magnetic material.

---

* Reprinted with permission from the June 2006 issue of the HBS *Alumni Bulletin*.

Apart from the physics involved, label geometry plays an important part in the detection and deactivation performance of AM tag/label circuits. A clearly defined cavity is required to guarantee that the resonance can take place when the circuits receive the signal from the transmitter. AM disposable labels *must* contain enough of a height dimension to ensure vibration.

In addition to the METGLAS®, AM disposable labels contain a bias magnet which is made from material similar to razor blades. The AM deactivation process actually increases the intensity of the bias magnet, thereby attracting the METGLAS® and inhibiting it from resonating. This effectively deactivates AM disposable labels. The labels can be deactivated by touch on a pad containing magnetic material (similar to deactivation in EM systems) or by using an electro-magnet intensify the magnetic properties of the metal bias strip inside. The requirement for magnetic field changes creates some issues at the point-of-sale. For example, the deactivators can erase information on bank and credit cards.

EAS Source Tagging

Starting in the late 1980s and early 1990s, Sensormatic/ADT and Checkpoint began working in partnership with retailers, consumer product manufacturers, and packaging experts to develop automated, integrated systems to affix disposable EAS labels somewhere toward the beginning of the product manufacturing process—either by a distributor, packaging provider, or the manufacturer itself. The key perceived benefit to the retailer was to transfer the cost of EAS label procurement and the merchandise tagging itself to a "source" in the manufacturing process where the process could be accomplished most cost effectively. The EAS companies saw source tagging as a "razor and blade" strategy, with the EAS system as the "razor" and the labels as the "blades"—eventually generating endless recurring revenue from label sales. Both companies began marketing source tagging to the largest retail chains in North America, reasoning that once a few nationally recognized retailers adopted the strategy, others could easily follow.

The EAS market is neatly divided into two major subsets according to merchandise type: packaged products (commonly referred to as "hardlines") and apparel. In the developmental stages of source tagging, most of the effort was directed toward hardlines because both EAS manufacturers had developed reasonably inexpensive disposable labels that could be integrated into the packaging process fairly easily. Historically, reusable plastic EAS tags that aren't suitable for source tagging have protected apparel. Efforts to develop security products for apparel that would be suitable for source tagging started in the mid 1990s.

EAS executives had three main objectives in the early marketing of source tagging. First, they had to convince retailers that source tagging was the most effective method of implementing an EAS program. They used a two-pronged approach: the elimination of tagging labor and the prospect of lower shortage and incremental sales as items were preserved from theft and sold instead of stolen. If retailers accepted that logic, then it would be easier for retailers to install EAS detection equipment in all stores (a prerequisite to source tagging). Second, they had to get the retailers to use their influence over merchandise manufacturers to get them to accept the burden of label procurement and placement. This turned out to be a difficult task and gave rise to the Consumer Products Manufacturers Association's efforts to forestall source tagging. Simultaneously, the EAS companies lobbied merchandise manufacturers to embrace source tagging as a customer service. They argued that accepting the task of source tagging would eventually result in more shelf space, or a wider assortment. Third, the EAS companies established in-house organizations whose purpose was to facilitate the actual process of source tagging among the partners. Resources were devoted to establishing standards; assisting in the design, development, and procurement of high-speed tagging equipment; entering into licensing arrangements with packagers and purveyors of specialty security equipment; and providing other necessary assistance to both retailers and manufacturers. In addition to in-house source tagging management, both EAS manufacturers have funded and supported trade association groups that function to promote source tagging and educate retailers, manufacturers, packagers, and other interested parties. The Sensormatic/ADT-sponsored organization is called the Source Tagging Council, and the

Checkpoint-sponsored organization is called the RF Inventory Management Conference. Each of these organizations schedules user group meetings where all pertinent source tagging issues are discussed.

Early Successes

Both Sensormatic/ADT and Checkpoint had early success in convincing a "marquee" retailer to implement a source tagging program. Sensormatic's classic case study is The Home Depot, U.S.A., and Checkpoint's is Eckerd Corporation. Both embarked on source tagging programs at approximately the same time—1993. Home Depot's source tagging program is the model on which most other AM programs have been built. Home Depot probably has more source tagging experience than any retailer in the world. The chain installed EAS for the first time with the proviso that absolutely no tagging would take place inside Home Depot stores. Any and all tagging had to be achieved somewhere in the manufacturing or distribution chain. Home Depot accomplished its goals by establishing a three-phase program. The first phase consisted of the topical application of EAS labels to the outside of packaging. The second phase mandated that the labels be concealed within the packaging. And the third phase suggested (rather than mandated) that EAS labels be incorporated within the merchandise itself, not just the packaging. Currently, Home Depot has converted the vast majority of vendors to phase two tagging, which has become a de facto standard.

At the outset, Home Depot started the program by isolating stock keeping units (SKUs) that incurred high shortages. Targeting SKUs was one of the most practical methods to justify source tagging because isolated shortage statistics could be shown to the manufacturer. Home Depot was saying, "Look at our shortage statistics for your power tool. We're losing money and we want you to help both of us make more money by applying the EAS label for us." As time passed, however, Home Depot realized that focusing on the SKU was an inefficient method of source tagging. In the first place, shoplifters tended to stop stealing the source tagged item, but they began stealing similar products made by vendors that were not yet source tagging. Home Depot management saw this trend reflected in its inventory shortage statistics. Second, Home Depot routinely adds and drops vendors and SKUs, so isolating high-shortage items became more difficult—particularly for seasonal or promotional merchandise.

Recently, Home Depot has broadened its perspective by source tagging by merchandise category. In other words, when management discovers that a particular type of merchandise has become a target for shoplifters, it endeavors to have all like merchandise source tagged—not just the SKUs with high shortage. This shift in philosophy has provided Home Depot with several benefits. First, category source tagging management is easier to administer than SKU or vendor management. Second, broadening the tagging guidelines to include all "at risk" items serves as insurance against high inventory shortage. For example, thieves learn that every power tool is tagged, not just a specific brand. This prevents a low-shortage item from becoming a high-shortage item in the future.

Eckerd Corporation was the drugstore division of J.C. Penney. It was sold to CVS and the Jean Coutu Group in 2004. At the time its source tagging program was started, however, it was an independent public corporation. Under Checkpoint's guidance, Eckerd established most of the same management parameters that were used in Home Depot. There are two concepts for which Eckerd is most noted. It was the first chain to assign a merchandising executive the responsibility of managing the source tagging efforts for the entire chain. This was, and continues to be, a key aspect of a successful program. The manager is able to serve the interests of parties—the Eckerd buyer responsible for the merchandise, the merchandise manufacturer, and the loss prevention department. It has been a vital benefit to the smooth operation of the program. The second concept is called "fractional tagging." In cases where the EAS label is concealed under the product packaging, Eckerd's allows manufacturers to source tag a preset fraction of the merchandise, say 33%. Since the security label is concealed within the packaging, it is logical to infer that shoplifters would not know which items are protected, and the deterrent qualities of the system will remain intact. In practice, fractional tagging has worked well and has helped lower the per-unit cost of the merchandise.

The Economics of Source Tagging

Since the mid-1990s, retailers have been assessing the value of an investment in EAS based on a classical cost versus benefit analysis. Will the reduction in inventory shortage offset the costs? As the EAS industry has matured, improved product offerings have broadened the scope of the asset protection role and changed the basic business model. Originally, a retailer's economic decision with respect to EAS was (a) to invest or not and (b) choose a technology. An EAS program was strictly an internal decision, requiring no outside help from others—except the EAS vendor. Circumstances have now changed. Many retailers are now long-term users of EAS, and technological advancements are forcing conversions from old to new systems.

Additionally, the recent emphasis on source tagging has created an "open system" requirement that was unnecessary in the past. "Open systems," in this context, means the collaboration among EAS provider, retailer, and merchandise manufacturer to work in harmony to ensure the success of the program. Retailers desiring to start a source tagging program must embrace a "wholesale adoption" mindset for the EAS program. EAS should be installed in all stores at the outset. Excess profit contributions from the high-volume, high-theft stores should be used to subsidize the smaller, less-theft-prone units, so the entire chain enjoys the economic benefits of source tagging: the elimination of tagging labor costs, the assimilation of tagging cost out of expense and into the cost of goods, and incremental sales from the role of EAS as a capable guardian of the merchandise assortment.

These developments have altered the risk-to-reward equation and complicated the EAS business model and the cost-justification process. Perhaps the most drastic alteration is that merchandise manufacturers are now, in a sense, EAS users in that they buy tags directly from EAS vendors and apply them to merchandise for retailers. Going forward, a much wider array of business issues must be addressed by groups other than the retailer. The more obvious issues are

- Can a new technology replacement EAS system be cost justified?
- Due to the requirements of source tagging, can EAS be cost justified in *all stores*, regardless of need (as defined by unacceptable shortage levels)?
- What are the economic issues facing merchandise manufacturers? Can they be quantified, and do the benefits outweigh the costs?
- How does the merchandise manufacturer's source tagging business model impact the wholesale cost of the merchandise?

These complexities are forcing all participants to revisit the issues surrounding ROI calculations. The simple arithmetic of "payback" undertaken in years past isn't sophisticated enough to provide the proper economic answer. Several major financial issues must be fully understood to obtain a full understanding of source tagging:

- EAS is difficult to cost justify for all locations at current pricing structures. The vast majority of EAS users apply the technology of their choice to high-theft items in stores exhibiting an inventory shortage crisis. They obtain a return on capital investment on a store-by-store basis. As a rule, they *do not* freely spend the money on EAS if the pro forma ROI calculations in an individual branch store don't justify the expenditure. The Home Depot case in which EAS was installed chainwide at the inception of the program was clearly an exception. Few other North American retailers have been as innovative. For source tagging to be universally recognized as the appropriate platform for EAS, the store-by-store mindset must be changed.
- Individual equipment procurements are depreciated for up to 10 years. New purchases are added regularly, increasing the equipment replacement time horizon. The useful life of EAS equipment generally exceeds its "accounting" life. After the depreciation schedule ends, continued EAS protection is essentially "free." This inhibits technology

conversions. In fact, The May Department Stores Company has successfully slowed its conversion from MW to AM.

- North American retailers generally favor operating a single technology in "user" stores. It is too costly to manage competing systems. Consequently, EAS tag and label procurement and the concomitant tagging labor costs are generally the retailer's highest variable costs associated with an ongoing (non-source-tagged) EAS program. In high tagging volume situations, or in areas with high wage rates, these costs significantly dampen the ROI. From the perspective of the retailer, source tagging provides the opportunity to transfer these costs directly to the merchandise manufacturer. The absorption of source tagging costs creates a new set of inventory management problems for merchandise manufacturers. They must now procure EAS labels, redesign the manufacturing process to absorb the tagging process, and perhaps procure capital equipment for high-speed, automated tagging. The most onerous problem, however, is in the segregation of tagged versus untagged inventory. When a merchandise manufacturer commits to source tagging, three subsets of a single SKU must be managed: untagged, RF tagged, and AM tagged. The magnitude of these costs, and the lack of a clearcut way to recover them, has been the single biggest stumbling block in gaining manufacturers' support for source tagging.

Benefit Denial Devices

In the late 1980s and early 1990s, as the first-generation electronic article surveillance products matured, they began to lose their effectiveness, and losses from shoplifting began to rise precipitously. At the time, retailers were beginning to realize that the existing EAS technologies weren't deterring as many thieves as they had previously. The rewards of successful theft had begun to exceed the risk of detection from the EAS alarm. Retail loss prevention executives began searching for better solutions, and they were willing to try something more radical. Thanks to two enterprising and visionary security equipment manufacturers—Colour Tag of Sweden and Security Tag Systems, Inc., of the United States—the concept of "benefit denial" was born and commercialized.

Thieves routinely steal personal property or retail merchandise either for personal use or to sell the items for cash. The radical idea behind benefit denial is to provide physical protection that would destroy an item instead of allowing thieves to obtain any economic benefit from it. Dr. Read Hayes, the well-known retail security consultant, coined the term "benefit denial" in early 1993, and it has become the universally accepted name for a growing category of security products used in retail and nonretail item-level protection.

There are a few noteworthy examples of benefit denial devices in society at large that explain the concept and that acted as catalysts for the products developed for use in retail.

- Exploding dye packs used by banks to identify stolen currency. Robbers who attempt to spend the currency can be readily identified.
- Clothes hangers in many hotel room closets have closed loops and ball joints that allow separation between the loop and the hanger, so the entire unit cannot be stolen and used in any conventional closet.
- "Breakaway" electronic switch connectors that disable car radio/CD players if they are removed from the dashboard of the vehicle.
- Car security systems that disable a vehicle's electronic fuel pump a few seconds after a theft attempt.

History

The benefit denial phenomenon in retail loss prevention began in the late 1980s when Colour Tag's original system was introduced at a trade show in Europe. Spawned by the bank dye packs, Colour Tag developed a "dye pack" to protect apparel from thieves. The original tags were heavy, large, and expensive (about $6 each). While this design set the current industry standard by using pharmaceutical-grade glass vials, the dye was toxic and the vials were filled under pressure. The tags were rugged and were able to withstand the rigors of repeated use within retail stores. Unfortunately, they were too well engineered and were difficult to break with force, but easy to defeat with common implements, such as a paper clip. When the tags *did* break, however, the garments were indeed ruined, as the vials tended to explode. As with conventional EAS tags, Colour Tags were removed at the point of sale. The "remover" was a portable air compressor that usurped precious space at the checkout stand, required a dedicated electric outlet, and cost $800.

Notwithstanding the safety, liability, and operational issues surrounding the product, and the general lack of understanding of the deterrence concept behind the idea, Color Tag successfully marketed the products in several European countries, and a few visionary American retailers conducted small-scale trials.

Security Tag was a small manufacturer of EAS and access control products. In 1989, its founder returned from a European trade show with samples of the Color Tag and commissioned a more user-friendly design. To succeed, Security Tag management had two tasks. First, the original products were unsuitable for the American retail market place and had to be redesigned. Engineers had to devise a product that was cost effective, easy to affix and remove, would withstand the rigors of apparel retailing without accidental breakage, did not exhibit the safety and liability issues evident in the Color Tag product, and still damaged apparel during tampering. Equally as importantly, Security Tag's marketing organization had to develop a working definition of the deterrent qualities of benefit denial products and full descriptions of the relevant features, functions, and benefits.

Through these efforts, the terms "ink tag," "inkmate," and "benefit denial device" became part of the retail loss prevention lexicon. The first benefit denial product, Inktag I, was introduced in the summer of 1991. Over the next 3 years, Security Tag introduced second- and third-generation ink tags and products designed to mate with EAS tags. The company also applied the benefit denial principles to make products to protect other retail merchandise, such as jewelry, neckties, and leather products. The program became so successful that by the time it was acquired by Sensormatic in 1993, Security Tag had set the industry standards and become the world's largest producer and seller of benefit denial devices.

By the late 1990s, several other companies began to either develop new benefit denial concepts or copy existing ones. These products are made and sold by at least six different security equipment providers, including ADT/Sensormatic, Checkpoint Systems, Inc., EAS SensorSense, Unisen, and Universal Surveillance Systems, among others.

Over time, the ink tag, and its derivatives, has become a popular and effective antishoplifting countermeasure. According to a 2004 study of EAS market penetration conducted regularly by a well-known security equipment manufacturer, among the top 25 department store chains in North America, over 68% of the branch stores use benefit denial devices in some form, but only 48% of the stores use EAS (all technologies). By this measure, benefit denial products have penetrated more department stores locations in 15 years than EAS has penetrated in 40 years.

Ink Tags

The original retail security version of a benefit denial product was designed as a two-piece reusable plastic tag *without* an EAS circuit. One side contains the locking mechanism. The other side contains the pin and one or more glass vials containing a nontoxic, nonflammable dye or stain. The best-designed products also include an internal breakage mechanism that aids in the breakage of the vials and a diffusion pad that disperses the ink onto the fabric after the vials break. This product was originally designed to deter shoplifters in stores without EAS and is known as a "standalone" ink tag. Typically, the tag has a warning label printed on one side.

Combination Ink/EAS Tags

The most popular benefit denial product for apparel is known as an "inkmate." It is a one-piece reusable plastic tag that contains the pin an done or more glass vials containing a nontoxic, nonflammable dye or stain. The more effective products also contain an internal breakage mechanism and a diffusion pad that aids in the dispersal of ink on the fabric. These products are substitutes for EAS pins and are "mated" with reusable EAS tags to form a double deterrent. They are much more popular than conventional standalone ink tags because of their compatibility with EAS systems.

Loss prevention executives soon realized that the combination of EAS and benefit denial forced the thief to "do something" with the tag *inside the store* or run the risk, however insignificant, that the alarm would cause a problem as he left the store. This turned out to be a very powerful deterrent. The inclusion of inkmates added longevity to inferior and first-generation EAS technology. In fact, the success of the inkmate caused at least one major U.S. department store retailer to delay a conversion to second-generation EAS technology—a strategy that is employed to this day.

What began as a case of "field expedience" turned into a lasting legacy of benefit denial for apparel retailers. The combination of an EAS tag mated with ink provided a device that offered the physical security of a clamp, the threat of an EAS alarm, and the certainty that tampering with the tag would ruin the merchandise. The EAS/ink combination remains a "capable guardian" of apparel.

Specialty Tags, Clamps, and Harnesses

Specialty benefit denial tags (not necessarily containing ink vials) have been designed using a variety of methods to protect other categories of merchandise. A small, magnetic release "padlock" was designed to protect jewelry, lingerie, and eyewear. Other lock and clamp arrangements protect accessories and various types of sporting goods.

A stainless steel clip was designed to protect neckwear, lingerie, and scarves. This device, shaped like a man's tie clasp, clamped onto a portion of a necktie and was held in place by a plastic locking mechanism. A similar device shaped like a money clip was made from specially bent stainless steel. A special hand tool, shaped like a pair of pliers, was required to both affix and remove the tag. It protected small leather goods.

At least two manufacturers provide wire harnesses that are wrapped around consumer packaging to prevent thieves from taking the product from the package. These products can be either EAS or non-EAS inclusive. They have gained a measure of popularity in the small electronics merchandise category. At least two manufacturers offer a benefit denial device that clamps CDs, DVDs, game software, and other media products to their primary packaging.

In an effort to emulate the switches employed by the auto industry to deter auto theft, a patent has been issued on an electronic device that disables video game players that were not properly deactivated at the point-of-sale.

References

DiLonardo, R.L. (1993). Fluid tag deterrents. *Retail Business Review*. June.

DiLonardo, R.L. (1997). *Source tagging issues and answers*.

DiLonardo, R.L. (2003). The economics of EAS. *Loss Prevention Magazine*, November-December, 21–26.

DiLonardo, R.L., and R.V. Clarke (1996). Reducing the rewards of shoplifting: An analysis of ink tags. *Security Journal*, 7, 11–14.

Embezzlement: 17 Rules to Prevent Losses

CAS, JHC

1. Never hire an applicant unless his background has been verified.
   - *Small stores:* Obtain a completed application for employment and phone and verify prior employment, particularly the last job.
   - *Chain stores:* Entrust a background investigation to the loss prevention department.

2. Know your employees to the extent that you may be able to detect signs of financial or other personal problems.
   - *Small stores:* Build a rapport so your employees will feel free to discuss such things with you in confidence.
   - *Chain stores:* Supervisory training classes should include the importance of establishing a rapport with subordinates and sensitivity to possible personal problems

3. Avoid "payroll ghosts."
   - *Small stores:* See that no one is placed on the payroll without authorization from you.
   - *Chain stores:* Ensure that the internal audit department does at least an annual audit to validate the payroll.

4. Control incoming checks.
   - *Small stores:* Have checks payable to the company mailed to a post office box rather than your place of business. In any event, personally (or have a key man) open mail and make a record of all payments received. Don't delude yourself that checks can't be converted into cash by an embezzler.
   - Chain stores: Ensure the internal audit department audits procedures to ensure all checks are properly handled.

5. Control cash.
   - *Small stores:* Either personally prepare daily cash deposits or compare deposits made by others with a record of cash and checks received. Get a copy of duplicate deposit slips from the bank. If depositing cash is delegated, make occasional audits and spot checks.
   - *Chain stores:* Cash handling and cash deposit systems must be documented in written policy and procedures and audited.

6. Reconcile bank statements.
   - *Small stores:* Arrange for bank statements and other correspondence from banks to be sent to a post office box; personally reconcile all bank statements.
   - *Chain stores:* Reconciliation of all checks generated, e.g., payroll, accounts payable, miscellaneous expense, etc., must be accomplished, according to procedure, systematically and verified by internal audit, on occasion. Variances or questions must be promptly reported to the controller.

7. Inspect all canceled checks.
   - *Small stores:* Personally examine all canceled checks and endorsements to spot anything unusual. This also applies to payroll checks.
   - *Chain stores:* See #6 above.

8. Bond employees.
   - *Small stores:* Make sure all employees, especially those handling money or company records, are bonded or believe that they are bonded. Have such employees complete a "bonding" form even though the bond may not be processed.
   - *Chain stores:* Bond those finance employees who are deemed to be in sensitive positions.

9. Audit your financial transactions.
   - *Small stores:* Spot check your accounting records and assets to satisfy yourself that all is well and your internal controls are working.
   - *Chain stores:* Ensure your auditing department proceeds with responsibilities as required.

10. Control special and exceptional financial transactions.
    - *Small stores:* Personally approve unusual deposits or disbursements and all bad-debt write-offs. Approve or spot check all credit memos and documentation for sales returns and discounts.
    - *Chain stores:* Ensure all special, exceptional, and unusual transactions are identified as such and proper procedures for their controls are in place and audited.

11. Control all disbursements.
   - *Small stores:* Personally sign all checks and never approve any disbursement without sufficient documentation or prior knowledge of the transaction.
   - *Chain stores:* Ensure an authorized and protected signature indicia is used on checks rather than a signature and use of the indicia requires management's approval
12. Control vendor payments.
   - *Small stores:* Make sure all vendor payments are for goods actually received.
   - *Chain stores:* Ditto.
13. Avoid duplicate payments.
   - *Small stores:* Cancel all invoices when checks are drawn to prevent double payments.
   - *Chain stores:* Implement a software program designed to prevent duplicating payments.
14. Never sign blank checks.
15. Control blank checks and any other negotiable instruments.
   - *Small stores:* Inspect prenumbered checkbooks and other prenumbered forms from time to time to be certain that items from the back of the book have not been removed and used for fraudulent purposes.
16. Periodically "*SALT*" cash registers and cash bags to see whether overages are reported.
17. To check your controls and checks and balances, purposely introduce "errors" into the system to see if, when, and by whom they are reported.

Emergency Planning for Retail Businesses

James H. Ryan

Background

Emergency planning for retail businesses is essentially the same as it is for any other kind of business. To be sure, the retail trade has its own jargon and terminology; however, the basic principles of emergency planning apply regardless of the type of business. Even though there are hundreds of different types of retail businesses from large department stores to kiosks and push carts, the planning principles remain the same.

Why plan for emergencies? This short anecdote will give an answer to the question. The former country director (vice president) of a large international corporation told me this story. War was looming. The country he was in was a target of the forces planning an invasion. The lease for the corporation's main manufacturing facility was up for renewal. The company planned to have a meeting of its governing board to approve the renewal of the lease. In the meantime, the country was invaded. Although no damage was done to the company's facilities, the international borders of the country were closed. Therefore, the outside directors from a variety of countries covered by this international corporation were unable to travel to this country to have a meeting. Thus, the lease was never approved. It soon expired. The result: The large international corporation had to close down its operations in that country until the international borders were reopened 4 years later. What went wrong? The answer is something very simple. There was no plan existing that would have allowed the local country management to approve the renewal of the lease under emergency conditions and for the duration of the closing of the international borders. These same conditions could apply to a retail store chain which had its main storage and distribution center in a country which had to close its international borders because of a belligerent situation; no goods in, no goods out, no one authorized to take action to ameliorate the situation, no governing board to approve or disapprove an action.

Keep It Simple, Stupid

The most important thing I believe I have learned from emergency planning experience is to keep things simple. You cannot imagine the failures I have seen because plans were too complex for retail security managers to carry out and even more complex for line and store managers to carry out. I have seen emergency plans 2 inches thick gather dust on store managers' office shelves because the plans were too complex to be carried out expeditiously. Because of their complexity, emergency plans became obsolete, as the difficulty of keeping them updated and current was just too great to be practicable. When plans are not read or implemented under emergency conditions, things always go wrong. There is a generally-accepted principle in business called KISS, which basically stands for **KEEP IT SIMPLE, STUPID**. There is a saying in the Navy, "Ships are designed and built by geniuses to be operated by idiots." Although that is an exaggeration, the key element is obvious. The other side of the coin tells us if a plan is too complex and impracticable, it is folly to expect it to be carried out efficiently if at all. Therefore, what follows applies the KISS principle throughout. You can take these simple suggestions and apply them to any kind of retail business.

The Basic Emergency Plan

The basic reason for creating emergency plans in retail businesses is to keep enterprises functioning even under extreme emergency conditions. Management has to be able to shift from normal, day-to-day operations to an extraordinarily stressful environment while keeping the enterprise running with reduced resources in communications, transportation, manpower, and funds. If the company is national or international, the emergency conditions create additional burdens in operating on a 24-hour basis across multiple time zones. A basic plan can be created that will be tailored to the size and complexity of the organization. A "mom-and-pop" store will have a very thin plan; an international store chain will have a thicker plan, but everyone must resist the temptation to make the plan more complicated just because it is longer. What follows is the outline of a basic plan that can be used to shift to emergency, sustained operations by any size company.

Outline of a Plan

The following outline can be useful to help publish an emergency plan in the corporation as a General or Special Instruction or their equivalents applying to every element of the enterprise. There should be separate, simple sections covering every principle of emergency operations that can be reasonably anticipated.

Purposes of the Plan. Purposes of an emergency plan are to provide a means of transition from normal to emergency operations efficiently, to delegate emergency authority, to assign emergency responsibilities, to assure continuity of operations, and to provide authorizations for actions contained in the plan.

Execution Instructions. The board of directors or its equivalent delegates authority to execute the plan as an *operations* instruction. Logically, this can be done in the following order: chief executive officer (CEO), officers who report directly to the CEO, local managers, and senior managers of branches of the enterprise. The plan may be executed partially under these conditions: bomb threat, kidnapping or hostage taking, severe weather, or flood. The plan may be executed fully under these conditions: civil disturbance, major riot, insurrection, explosion or major fire in corporate facilities, severe earthquake causing major structural damage to a corporate facility (store, warehouse, distribution center, office building, etc.).

Command and Control. The principal center for command and control is the corporate office. If the enterprise is a group of stores, then the alternate principal center should be the nearest branch office, or, in case there are no branch offices, the nearest store to the emergency condition that is not directly affected by the emergency directly. The controlling person should be the one nearest to the emergency; i.e., a person who can easily travel to the scene of the emergency, take control, and render reports to the corporate office of the conditions observed and actions taken. Corporate board resolutions must be in place at all times to give the person on the spot the authority to implement the plan and carry on actions to benefit the corporation. Only the chief executive officer of the enterprise should be allowed to countermand instructions to persons in the emergency area who are under the command and control of the enterprise's local authority. The chain of command must be absolutely clear: Regardless of his corporate rank, the local person in charge of the emergency area has absolute authority to carry out actions beneficial to the enterprise in accordance with general policies of the enterprise. He is supervised by the chief executive officer (or in some organizations, the chief operating officer), who can countermand orders only when they are clearly not beneficial to the operation of the enterprise in the local emergency area, which could be anything from a single store to many stores, warehouses, and distribution centers. The chief executive officer assures that there is an emergency operations line item in the budget of the enterprise. The line item should take into account security, emergency planning, training, and special funds for operating under emergency conditions. The local person in charge coordinates with local fire, police, and other emergency agencies; informs persons in the emergency area of their various roles according to the plan; and disseminates applicable portions of the plan. Corporate and district managers should have already conducted training, rehearsals, and reviews of insurance against potential loss or obligations resulting from destructive events. Such actions should be started as soon as the corporate office has promulgated the plan. Every person who might be in a managerial or supervisory role in carrying out the emergency plan must have at least one backup person—two are better—trained to be backup(s) and emergency replacement(s).

Continuity of Management. The local manager of the emergency area shall determine which units of the enterprise in the area shall remain functioning. Some criteria for such a decision are availability of local public utilities at the site(s)—e.g., water, sewer, fire suppression, electricity; damage to structures, conditions in streets, availability of emergency medical assistance; morale and welfare of employees; etc.

Coordination and Liaison When the Plan Is Fully Implemented. The local person in charge is responsible for coordinating with local, state, and federal officials. To help with security and around-the-clock operations, it is advisable to keep a list of reliable private security agencies in the areas where the enterprise has facilities. At least one private security agency should be on retainer to help out in emergencies. A private security service can take on the task of coordinating with fire, police, and other emergency services. The person in charge should designate a company employee to be responsible for coordination with adjacent or nearby firms and facilities suppliers. One person only should be authorized to coordinate relations with news media.

Communications. You should expect breakdowns in communication systems for hours, days, or weeks. Alternate communication measures should be arranged before an emergency. If land-line telephone systems go down, you can substitute voice messages and email sent by computer through cell phone towers or satellites. Citizen band or other public band radios can be used locally. It may be necessary to employ messengers, employees, or professional messenger services to travel to the nearest operating communications areas to communicate with corporate offices. One employee per day can be designated to hand-carry important and urgent messages by automobile or airplane.

Personnel. Local and regional managers should maintain an informal list of the secondary skills of employees within their normal areas of responsibility. The secondary skills may become very useful in case of emergencies. For example, a stock clerk may be an emergency response medical specialist off-duty and can apply those skills to help injured fellow employees when necessary and when no other medical support is available. Local and regional managers should conduct periodic training, internally or by contract, to ensure minimum skills are available to operate under emergency conditions. No one knows when, where, or what kind of emergency may occur; therefore, at least rudimentary lists should be kept at the local and regional level of notification procedures, reporting points, and transportation resources. These lists should be kept simple and up-to-date. There should be procedures in place to brief other employees of the daily situation when under emergency conditions. There should be a procedure for notifying employees of evacuation routes in case it is deemed impossible to continue operations in a certain location or area. It should also be expected that when a major natural disaster strikes, most, if not all, employees will feel compelled to give their first priority to the safety of their families and not to the mission of the enterprise.

Utilities. Every corporate facility should have at least one standby generator in expectation of failure of the public electrical power system. Large facilities can use generators powered by natural gas that come on automatically when electrical power fails. Alternatively, there can be a permanent standby diesel-powered generator at large facilities. Small facilities should have small standby generators and an ample supply of fuel for generators to last for several days of operation. Battery-powered lighting such as emergency lights and flashlights should be available for emergencies. Flashlights powered by induction (shaking) can have a long shelf life and are handy in emergencies. Candles should never be used when the water utility has failed. To prepare for failure of the public water supply, 5-gallon containers of water can be kept on hand and be exchanged periodically to keep them fresh. Such emergency water sources can be used also to flush toilets.

Security. As discussed earlier, private commercial security forces that have been retained on a standby basis should be procured on an active contract basis by corporate elements when conditions warrant it. Security forces on a standby, as-needed basis should be invited to participate in all rehearsals of the security plans. Keep in mind that private security forces will be going through almost the same personnel crisis as the employees of the enterprise in the emergency area. If and when security forces are contracted, they should be put under the command and control of the person in charge of the area where the emergency conditions exist. Depending on the nature of the emergency, simple, letter-sized plans can be drawn up in advance to help coordinate the enterprise's employees with the security augmentation. A contract guard agency can assist in the preparation of such plans. In large corporations, there may be a professional security manager who can assist lower elements in preparing such plans. These letter plans become operational directives when an emergency condition is in being. The person in charge of the emergency area may designate a corporate employee to assist him in the following: establishing liaison with local law authorities and reporting to police all actual or suspected acts of espionage, sabotage, or terrorism. Establish alternate record storage sites for all corporate elements. Screen all applicants requesting employment for possible security risks. Brief all new employees on general security procedures and security consciousness.

Fire Prevention. All new employees should be briefed by their supervisors on techniques of and the need for fire prevention. Designate a fire marshal in every enterprise facility no matter how small. The fire marshal should be made responsible for fire detection and suppression. Detectors that recognize the various traits of fires should be installed in all enterprise facilities, especially rooms that are normally not occupied during normal business hours, such as cooking areas, photocopy rooms, conference rooms, visitors' offices, etc. Post fire extinguishers in conspicuous places and have fire extinguishers checked and filled by an outside contractor at least once a year or as often as local ordinances require. Store copies of electronic and paper records critical to operations, large amounts of cash and securities, and insurance policies in fire-resistant containers with the longest fire rating period available. The best place to store such materials is at an off site location.

Here is another anecdote to illustrate the importance of offsite locations. The place is a factory in a foreign country. The security consultant recommended the company make backup copies at least once daily of all computer records. The factory was later expanded and modernized. A contractor accidentally started a fire. The fire destroyed the central computer system and the manager's office. Instead of using an offsite storage facility, the manager had kept the backup copies of the computer records in his office. All records, originals and backups, were destroyed. The company moved its offices to an adjacent site. To restore its records, the company had to depend on records kept by its customers, clients, and suppliers to determine its accounts payable and receivable. Tax records helped to fill in the gaps in data.

Emergency Supplies. In addition to items previously listed, designate persons to be responsible at each enterprise facility for procurement and caring for an industrial-type medical supply and first aid kit and a toolbox with common hand tools for emergency mechanical and electrical repairs.

Testing the Plan. The purpose of tests is to assure completeness of the plan and to correct weaknesses found in carrying out the plan. Tests should not be announced in advance except under extraordinary circumstances. Regional and local managers should have partial tests of the enterprise's emergency plan conducted as they see the need, except that there should be, at a minimum, a full test of the plan every 2 years.

Customizing the Plan. Plans can be supplemented by materials (addenda, enclosures, attachments, annexes, etc.). Each supplement discusses a single topic and usually contains material that changes from time to time. By committing transient information to supplements, you can rewrite materials without having to rewrite the whole emergency plan. Following are examples of some material covered in supplemental documents:

- *Civil Disturbance.* Civil disturbances, riots, and insurrections can occur almost anywhere, even in small towns. Such events can cause severe disruptions of communications and transport, interruptions to the supplying of utilities—water, gas, electricity; shortages of food and like problems that can have serious effects on even the simplest of operations. Normal access routes may be blocked; therefore, employees must plan for alternate routes to reach the corporate facilities where they normally work. Wallet-size emergency identification cards can be issued to assist employees in getting through police lines and to travel to and from the work sites and their homes. Use of such cards should be coordinated in advance with local police authorities by regional managers. Employees should be warned by supervisors not to get involved in discussions or arguments with dissident persons, as this may make employees and the enterprise targets of violence.

- *Bomb Threats.* Bombings and threats of bombings are too frequent to ignore. You might recall the bombing of the Federal Building in Oklahoma City, the bombing of the U.S. Forest Service Office in Carson City, the letter bombings by a crazed serial bomber, the bombing of the World Trade Center in 1993, and the destruction of the World Trade Center by passenger aircraft used as aerial bombs in 2001. The mere threat of bombing can cause consternation and distress. Each time a school gets a bomb threat, the school has to be evacuated and searched. In 1995, the mere threat of a bomb closed down the air mail facility at Lost Angeles International Airport. How would such occurrences affect your enterprise? If a bomb threat is received, the senior person in the facility (store, warehouse, distribution center, office) calls the police. When a special bomb threat number is available, keep it on file; otherwise, use the general police emergency number (normally 911 in the United States). There are basically three methods of attacking with a bomb outside of open warfare: putting a bomb in a motor vehicle or adjacent building, putting a bomb in a letter or package, and suicide bombing. Before calling the police, however, attempt to get the following information: date and time of a threat; any clues which might aid the police in identifying the location of the caller and the telephone number; any mention of the *location, type, or time of detonation*; voice characteristics—male or female. What kinds of background noises are there at the caller's end of the line? Are there machinery noises, traffic, radio, TV? Do you believe the caller is sincere? Call the police and give them the information you have. Follow their advice. Local human resources people, managers, and supervisors should keep records of discharged employees, especially those who may have threatened to "get even." If there is reason to believe the threat is sincere, or if a bomb is discovered, the senior person present should order an *evacuation* of the enterprise's facility, or that part of a facility controlled by the enterprise. The corporate office should have a standard, clear, simple procedure published to managers at all levels well in advance about when an evacuation may be ordered. If an evacuation order is issued without due cause or clumsily, panic may occur. In an evacuation, *use stairs* because elevator shafts are prime locations for explosive devices. Warn other facility occupants. The local manager (store, warehouse, distribution center, office, etc.) should keep track of the results of threats or actual bombings in the local area, including actions involving nonenterprise facilities. Knowing the underlying reasons for threats and bombings of other facilities is important because they may indicate your own facilities could be future targets.

- *Letter Bombs.* Letter bombs are sometimes employed against businesses. If any such bombings are occurring in the local area, the local manager should institute a procedure for screening incoming mail and packages. Get prior advice from local police. Characteristics of letter bombs are origin outside the country; return address, none or fake; addressee is by name; and size, letter size but thicker or simply a large, thick envelope. Trigger devices: envelope—triggered by pressure release activated by cutting open or tearing open an envelope; package—triggered by an electrical circuit breaker activated by opening the package or cutting the tape.

- Countermeasures: awareness, alertness, care; separate mail facilities; X-ray, and similar procedures. Take photographs of the letter or package for identification and follow-up.
- *Recommendations*. Keep in mind that an attacker picks the time and place of a bombing or calling in a bomb threat. It adds an extra protection against revenge bombings if discharged employees or laid-off persons are given the most care possible not to offend their dignity or to treat them disrespectfully. Can you protect against car bombs and suicide bombers? The answer is clear. A retail establishment can build in so much security that it looks like a fortress. People do not like to shop in fortresses. However, in a warehouse, distribution center, or office, especially when the enterprise controls all the space immediately around it, there can be strict security against most kinds of threats. Persons must agree to surveillance, even searches to get into the facility. How open an office, warehouse, or distribution center may be depends on its type and location. Many retail enterprises would not survive unless they foster a welcoming and open image. Preparing in advance to cope with a variety of threats can help control damage and loss, but the amount of security must be balanced against the retail enterprise's image, which is part of its marketing program.
- *Earthquake*. In most of the United States, the prospect of a serious earthquake is remote. In some parts of the country, earthquakes happen fairly often. In many foreign lands, there are regions where earthquakes are common. It is wise to have an earthquake plan just in case. After an earthquake, outside assistance may be cut off. Employees in the earthquake zone may have to "make do" with what is on hand. When serious damage occurs, the damaged enterprise facilities should be shut down so employees can get to their homes and families. However, leaving the facilities and going into the streets may be more hazardous than staying in the building. Bridges and telephone lines will be damaged. There will be fires. Debris will block roads. Because of the enormous physical forces generated, an earthquake can be the most terrifying experience possible. Therefore, cool heads must prevail. Other than the forces of nature, panic is the worst enemy during an earthquake and afterward.
- *Severe Weather and Flood*. After a severe storm (rain, snow, ice, wind) or flood, if employees are still in the enterprise's facilities, they should be released as early as possible to get to their homes before access routes are cut off. When the decision is made to maintain operations, as many employees as possible should be released. If employees are at home, they should be informed through a planned notification procedure whether they should report to work.
- *Explosion or Major Fire*. If an explosion or major fire occurs in one of the enterprise's facilities, operations should be transferred to the nearest enterprise unit. In case of explosion in a store, the whole operation cannot be transferred; however, the "back office" functions can be transferred to another site. Although sales will probably need to be suspended, some store personnel will be necessary for helping in cleanup, restocking, and preparing for reopening. If there is a small fire, it should be fought using available extinguishers. However, small fires have a way of getting out of control. Use common sense. Call the fire department for assistance at the earliest possible time. Even if the fire has been extinguished when fire department elements arrive, the fire experts can determine if the fire is still smoldering and what further needs to be done. No attempt should be made to fight a major fire or operate where there has been an explosion. When ordered to do so by the senior person on duty in the facility, all persons onsite should obey fully a command to evacuate the premises. Do not use elevators as evacuation routes. Practice fire and explosion emergency procedures to keep order in case of evacuation.

- *Kidnapping and Extortion.* This part of the plan sets forth a methodology that can be used to help protect senior executives and their families from kidnapping and extortion. How many of these methods are used and what their composition will be should be determined by the situation existing at any particular time. Some factors determining vulnerability are public exposure; residence; business and social status; finances; political situation; and the type of organization. Kidnapping and extortion are more prevalent in some foreign countries than in the United States, so special precautions need to be taken for executives of the enterprise living in those places. The United States Department of State maintains country profiles that can be used to keep current information on conditions in foreign countries. If management in the enterprise feel executives need special protection, then they should contact professional security consultants and the Department of State. Other countries also publish data on conditions in other countries (e.g., Australia). Many of these publications can be found online. Professional security consultants can provide advice on travel, protection of children, and home security. If a kidnapping occurs, the crisis management team (CMT) is activated to conduct negotiations and to coordinate with police authorities. If a kidnap or extortion call should come into the enterprise at any level, the information should be passed immediately to the head of the CMT.
- *Crisis Management Team.* The crisis management team (CMT) should be activated in case of a long-term emergency situation that can threaten the basic structure of the company. The term "crisis" applies only to situations beyond the scope of ordinary business, e.g., a kidnapping of a key official of the enterprise or a major explosion, flood, or fire at one of the enterprises' facilities. The CMT analyzes threats, develops responses to threats, organizes the responses to the threats, and assigns human resources and material assets to cope with the threats. In situations in which a designated person is in charge of a certain area or facility of the enterprise during an emergency that has risen to a crisis, the role of the CMT is to make human and financial resources available to the person in charge. The CMT does not interfere with the operation in the field but pushes resources down to the emergency area through its relationship with the governing board, its chairman, and the chief executive officer. Members of a CMT must be assigned permanently to it as an extra duty and be trained to minimize losses to the assets of the enterprise. People working on the CMT will be stressed to their utmost because of emotional drain connected with responsibility for human life, dearth of information, time constraints and pressures, strategic implications for the enterprise, and public and employee relations. A decision must be made at the highest corporate level as to the functions of a CMT in a crisis. Some specific functions to be considered are public relations, communication, negotiation, legal matters, control of financial assets, leadership, and health of persons involved in a crisis. The leader of the CMT is responsible for leading, orienting other members on their duties, keeping up on all past and current threats to the enterprise, and training in and simulating crises. There should be created a CMT charter that is then approved by the governing board of the enterprise which specifies the references and authority to delegate and from where it is derived, usually a specific paragraph contained in corporate statutes. Some items to be included in a CMT charter are under what conditions the charter takes effect, which is usually a delegation of authority from the governing board to the CMT; assignment of persons to the CMT from the various functional areas comprising the enterprise, e.g., finance, insurance, store operations, human resources, public relations, security, communications, and legal; the authority to commit company resources; and the primary mission of the CMT, which is normally protection of assets, both human and material. See the addenda to this section for a sample resolution delegating authority to a CMT.
- *Contract Security Services.* Under certain circumstances, it may be necessary to employ contract guard services to assist the enterprise in continuing operations when there are

emergency conditions. Contract guard services may already be employed throughout the enterprise. If so, then it is a relatively simple matter to expand their contract to include the additional emergency services. If there is no contract guard service being used, one should be on permanent retainer in each region of the enterprise to provide services under emergency conditions. Guard services can assist in helping to coordinate with fire and police services; providing after-hours office security and fire checks; identifying and registering visitors; preventing unwanted visitors from entering; keeping a log of events; providing bodyguards; providing backup communications; and providing replacement personnel for around-the-clock operation. Regional managers should keep a list, including contact names and telephone numbers, of local contract guard agencies having the capability of providing the needed services on relatively short notice. A sample letter order to the guard service is contained in the addenda to this section.

Summary

In this section, we have seen the planning process for emergency plans and why we plan for emergencies. We reviewed the KISS principle, which reminds us to keep things simple so that anyone can read, understand, and carry out the plan as an operations document. We put forth an outline of a plan that covered every subject from execution instructions to the use of contract security services. At every step of the process, we have seen the necessity for having one person in charge of all corporate assets and actions to deter damage to the enterprise from natural and manmade disasters. When an emergency becomes a crisis, we have seen how a crisis management team can function to deter losses in the enterprise and to protect not only its physical assets, but its human resources as well. Keeping emergency plans simple and up-to-date helps protect the corporation from losses.

Published Works Consulted

Protection of Assets Manual. (2007). Some elements adapted by permission, copyright American Society for Industrial Security International.
Ryan, J. H. (1995). Before the bomb drops," *Management Review*, August. Some elements adapted by permission, copyright 1995, American Management Association, www.amanet.org.

Recommended Sources for Further Information

ASIS Disaster Preparation Guide. (2003). American Society for Industrial Security International. Call: 703-519-6200.
Sample Emergency Plan. U.S. Department of Homeland Security. Download available at www.ready.gov.
Call-Em-All Voice Broadcasting Service. www.call-em-all.com.
  A. Sample Crisis Management Team Charter
  B. Sample Letter Order for Private Security Agency

ADDENDUM A: SAMPLE CRISIS MANAGEMENT TEAM CHARTER

LIMITED DISTRIBUTION—CLOSE HOLD

Title: Delegation of Authority to the Crisis Management Team

RESOLUTION OF

The Board of Directors, First Ark Corporation

On this _____th day of _____, 200X, the Board of Directors of First Ark Corporation hereby delegates to the Crisis Management Team, organized at the corporate headquarters office in Ararat, Pennsylvania, the following powers in accordance with Article _____ of the Corporation Statutes:

To analyze, develop responses to, organize responses to, and fix responsibility for responses to threats to the Corporation that create long-term emergency conditions. A long-term emergency condition is defined as one that threatens the life of an executive of the Corporation or his or her family, or that threatens the existence or ability to function of the Corporation, or one of its parts, due to the following types of circumstances: war, civil disturbance, riot, insurrection, bomb threat, major natural disaster, explosion, major fire, kidnapping, extortion, or loss of physical contact with a subsidiary.

The Crisis Management Team shall take authority under this resolution to commit Corporate Resources up to $_____.

Signed_____, Chairman of the Meeting

ADDENDUM B: SAMPLE LETTER ORDER

FIRST ARK CORPORATION

ARARAT, PENNSYLVANIA

TITLE: Letter of Instruction: Contract Security Services

This Letter of Instruction is made in accordance with the retaining agreement between First Ark Corporation and Chronos Security Services dated _____.

Chronos Security is authorized immediately to carry out duties for First Ark Corporation in the area of Manhasset, New Jersey, which is now operating under emergency conditions. Your point of contact is our person in charge of the area, Johnny N. Spott, who can be reached at_____ cell phone and at 2120 North Concorde St., Manhassett, NJ.

Chronos Security Services is authorized to provide the following services for Mr. Spott:

- Helping to coordinate with fire and police services and providing after-hours facility security and fire checks.
- Identifying and registering visitors. Preventing unwanted visitors from entering.
- Providing around-the-clock watchman service. Notifying responsible persons when there are unusual occurrences.
- Keeping a daily log of events. "All OK" or its equivalent is not a valid log entry.
- Providing employees with security escorts as requested.
- Assisting in providing backup communications.

Signed_____, Manager, New Jersey Operations, First Ark Corporation

---

Author's note: The following piece about the Oreck vacuum cleaner business's response to the Katrina disaster is not retail LP specific but is deemed of value here in this Emergency Planning "section" of the book. You are directed to the thrust of an important message and that is the value and importance of employees in helping survive a catastrophic event. Remember, employees are our most important asset!

One-on-One with Tom Oreck

Roger Thompson

When Tom Oreck took over the family vacuum cleaner business seven years ago, his biggest challenge was to transform the firm from an entrepreneurial "one man band" founded by his father, David, in 1963 into "a symphony orchestra." Under the elder Oreck's guidance, New Orleans-based Oreck Corporation had steadily grown into a national brand known for its lightweight, powerful vacuums. As it prospered, the company acquired a manufacturing plant eighty miles east in coastal Long Beach, Mississippi.

Tom Oreck took center stage with solid grounding in every aspect of the business. "I like to tell people that I rose up the ranks through the sheer force of nepotism," he deadpans with self-deprecating humor. He made HBS his last training stop before taking over as president and CEO in 1999. Since then, the privately held firm has expanded its home-cleaning product line, opened nearly 500 company stores, and doubled sales (it doesn't disclose figures). The future looked bright—until last August 29.

That's when Hurricane Katrina almost ruined everything. In the storm's aftermath, Oreck, 54, faced a crisis he never imagined possible: Katrina knocked out operations at the New Orleans headquarters and the Long Beach plant, pushing the business to the brink. Advanced planning saved vital data and operations, but Oreck credits employees with actually saving the company. Incredibly, the Long Beach facility, where half of the company's 1,200 employees work, reopened just ten days after Katrina wrought destruction of "biblical proportions" on the Gulf Coast community. Oreck recently talked about that experience and the future.

"Our first responsibility was to our employees—period. The business could wait; the people could not."

Were you prepared for Katrina?

We had always planned on the possibility that either our New Orleans headquarters or our Long Beach facility could be taken out by a hurricane. One of the things we didn't anticipate was a storm that was massive enough to take out both locations simultaneously.

Ahead of the storm, we backed up and shut down our computer systems and transferred all the data to a site in Boulder, Colorado. The building next door to our Long Beach plant is our call center. We shut that down and transferred that function to third-party centers in Phoenix and Denver. We also did a planned shutdown at the plant and moved certain critical components off-site.

From the Houston hotel where you evacuated with your family, how did you learn that the Long Beach plant withstood an almost direct hit?

In a day or so we got a report from one of our employees who had chain-sawed a path through trees on the roads to check on the plant. He found it was damaged but not destroyed. Once we heard that, we knew we were going to be able to put it all together again. We told people, "If you had a job at Oreck before the storm, you still have a job at Oreck." And we continued to pay people even as we were trying to put things together.

What was your reaction when you heard that the levees in New Orleans had been breached?

Our employees had evacuated New Orleans, as they had in advance of previous storms. I left my home with only three changes of clothes. And when I heard that the city was filling with water, I thought, "OK, returning is not a matter of days any longer. This is months. Who knows, maybe never."

Did you ever consider declaring the business a total loss?

As bad as it was, and as great as the uncertainty was, there was never a question about whether we were going to get up and running. No one on the management team ever said, "What's the point? This is a lost cause."

What did you do first?

The first thing we did was try to find our people. And of course, one of the problems was that cell phones didn't work. So we immediately set up an 8 a.m. company-wide conference call on an 800 number. We did that every day, seven days a week, for more than two months until we were back in our New Orleans office. Any employee could dial into the conference call. And we did what you're supposed to do, which is to give people the facts. That communication was vital.

What role did the company play in helping its employees recover?

Our first responsibility was to our employees—period. The business could wait; the people could not. The Long Beach plant's parking lot was turned into what we called Oreckville. We very quickly purchased trailer homes from all over the country and brought them in. We delivered food and water by truck almost immediately. We brought in trauma doctors, and we brought in insurance specialists to help people make insurance and FEMA claims.

When you reopened the Long Beach plant on September 9, did everyone get right back to work?

The first thing we did when the lights went on [powered by hastily purchased generators from Florida] was invite employees and their families to a cookout. The idea was that in the middle of this train wreck people could do something normal that would give them hope.

You clearly put people ahead of the business in the aftermath of the storm. Had that been part of your advance planning?

The people issues involved in this were certainly the one thing we had not been prepared for. It never occurred to us that we would have to deal with such personal devastation. We put people first because it was the right thing to do. As a result, they saved our business. That's the bottom line. We did the right things for our people, and they in turn saved the business. I'm not overstating it. If our employees had not done the heroic things they did here [in Long Beach] and elsewhere, Katrina could easily have put us out of business.

How did you keep the New Orleans headquarters operations functioning?

There was no power in New Orleans, but more importantly, there was no access and no housing. Within five days of the storm, we were operating in an IBM business recovery center in Dallas, where we sent about 120 employees and their families. We had 100 computer terminals there, and they were connected with our backup computer system in Boulder.

What's currently your biggest challenge?

At our Long Beach plant, we are still understaffed. Labor is scarce, and there is tremendous competition for the labor that's available. Even with a dramatically smaller staff than we had before Katrina, December was the biggest shipping month in our history.

In New Orleans, a big issue for us is recruiting. It's very difficult right now to recruit white-collar talent to New Orleans. That may change, but for now that's an issue.

In the aftermath of Katrina, have you considered moving manufacturing inland or onshore?

Because of the way we go to market, there's a real need for significant flexibility and nimbleness. That kind of nimbleness is impossible if you're dealing with an overseas manufacturer.

We now understand the vulnerability we have, and by the next hurricane season we will have a second manufacturing facility away from the coastline. That does not mean we're less committed to this region, or the plant, or the people here. We actually need a second site for growth.

Are you optimistic about the future of New Orleans?

The future of New Orleans and the region depends upon the politicians being redirected by the citizens and the business leadership. If real reform can take place, then this city and this state can flourish. If not, the future will not be pretty.

Did your HBS experience help prepare you for the challenges you have faced since taking charge of the company?

HBS was probably the most significant educational experience I ever had. It really did have a dramatic impact on who I am and who I have developed into as a businessperson. I can't stress how important I think it was in helping me transition into this job

HBS (Harvard Business School) Alumni Bulletin, Soldiers Field, Boston, MA 02163. June 2006

Emergency Exits

CAS, JHC

Every store has emergency exits, including small storefront retailers with only front and rear doors. For the sake of illustration, in the small store, that back door should serve as the "emergency exit" and remain accessible for egress at all times. And so it is with any size store.

The multilevel stores with stairwells which empty down on the street level with emergency exit doors and one-story stores with emergency exit doors should be locked to ingress traffic but must be designed to allow unimpeded egress with only one motion or little effort, e.g., equipped with "panic hardware" or "panic bars."

Because some thieves prefer to exit stores through emergency doors, loss prevention agents or store operations personnel have been known to chain those exits to prevent thefts, but that course of action violates fire codes and subjects the store to fines or exposure to civil suits under certain circumstances.

There is an exception to "unimpeded" egress, and that's the installation, if fire regulations in the area permit, of delayed egress locks on these doors. Typically, the delay time once the exit bar is hit is 15 to 30 seconds, which allows some time for loss prevention/security to respond or allows time for a CCTV camera installed for this purpose to capture the image of the person attempting an unauthorized exit through the door. The culprit may still escape with stolen merchandise, but at least the event is known and some evidence is available for subsequent investigation. And it should be noted that these time-delayed locks, electrically controlled, are designed to immediately unlock in the event of fire.

Clearly, the size, location, and history of crime at the store dictate the decision to employ this strategy. If less sophistication is appropriate, the next level would be such doors wired to a central enunciator reflecting which door was opened but allowing immediate exit, with an audible siren, with or without camera recordation.

Care must be taken to avoid plunger-type switches or exposed screw heads which would allow the signal-transmitting device to be compromised, preventing the sending of an alarm that would normally be sent if and when the door is opened. Such care is best exercised by regular inspection by LP personnel.

Irrespective of the level of security in place at these exits, signage is important. Red or green lettering (or white letters on a red or green background) should inform the reader that the door is an emergency exit only, and depending on the level of security, the sign can indicate the consequences of exiting (unless it's an emergency). The Department of Homeland Security has issued regulations which will eventually require photoluminescent material (non-electrical-powered) for all emergency exit signs.

Emergency exits in stairwells frequently are viewed as available space for excess stock, and consequently, boxes and rolling racks tend to find their way there for storage. Loss prevention personnel should monitor this condition and report to store management if discovered. Fire regulations require that emergency stairwell exit routes be kept free of any obstructions and prohibit their use for storage of any materials.

The inquisitive LP agent, engaged in inspecting the store, will look for any signs the emergency exit is being used. The presence or absence of dust and cobwebs, evidence of tampering, bare metal in otherwise rusty or dark screw heads, etc., could indicate the security system in place is being compromised; i.e., someone is coming and going through that door, and corrective action is required.

Employee Fraud

Daniel Adam Smith

Employee fraud remains a huge problem for retailers. Employee fraud makes up a portion of employee theft, which remains the largest contributor to shrinkage in retail. Rather than simply taking goods, employee fraud requires the employee to manipulate records in the retailer's terminal system. The terminal system will believe that the transaction was legitimate and make adjustments to inventory numbers. During a physical inventory, item numbers used in fraudulent transactions will be short, even though the actual goods were not removed from the store. Rather, the employee benefited by receiving cash, a refund to a credit card, or a merchandise credit.

Like just mentioned, employee fraud will not be noticeable by missing merchandise or cash. Therefore, security checks and balances such as parcel checks will not be effective. Many times, good checks and balances will drive a desperate employee to commit fraud, because of the perceived inability to gain money or merchandise by simply taking it. Creating the perceived inability is good for loss prevention because, while employee fraud requires a more sophisticated approach to theft, it is easy to trace through transaction analysis and exception reporting. Fraud creates a paper trail that, once discovered, is easy to investigate. Direct theft of money or merchandise does not leave a paper trail and, therefore, is more difficult to detect and investigate. Hence, good loss prevention standards will make employee theft more apparent.

Employees are limited to the type of fraud they can enact, due to their limited access to inventory records. As mentioned earlier, it is easy to detect, and there are relatively no innovative approaches for the employee to use. Employees commit fraud because they perceive that they can get away with it. This is mostly due to the fact that the fraud seems sophisticated and innovative to them. Most think that they have developed a method of theft which loss prevention is unaware of. Since no cash will be missing and they won't be walking out with unpaid merchandise, it will appear legitimate. And yes, the transaction will be one that happens regularly through the normal course of business, but employees will always leave signs of dishonesty in the transaction. It is the investigator's job to find the common signs of dishonesty and put together a case.

Investigators will need some tools to conduct their investigations. Gone are the days when the investigator was armed only with receipt journals to put together a case. Today, many sophisticated tools that are available and widely used allow the investigator to analyze, date, and pinpoint fraud quickly. Following are a few tools that aid investigators:

1. *Exception Reporting:* Exception reporting is a valuable tool that can group and sort data based on the user's specified criteria. Most often, reports are generated based on type of transaction, such as refunds without a receipt. Reports can also be generated to narrowly define types of transactions, such as refunds with original receipt from same day. Exception reporting is a must in any large store. The sheer volume of transactions would be overwhelming for an investigator to sift through manually.
2. *Electronic Journal:* An electronic journal allows the investigator to enter in transaction ID numbers and view an exact replication of the receipt in electronic form. The receipt normally contains valuable data that the investigator needs to conduct an investigation. Some exception reporting software has this feature built in.
3. *CCTV:* While it is not absolutely necessary to have CCTV for an investigation, it certainly helps. Video evidence makes the investigator's case much stronger and allows for an absolute confirmation of theft. Digital video recording makes the investigator's job much easier because it allows him to look at archived video of transactions from previous days. When video is paired with exception reports, the investigator has a very powerful set of tools, a set of tools that will allow him to identify a suspicious transaction and verify it with video in a matter of minutes. While DVR technology is being adopted quickly, it may be some time before it becomes a staple for investigators, however.
4. *Terminal Overages and Shortages:* Plotting overages and shortages has been a technique used for many years, but it remains a must-have for an investigator. Identifying overages and shortages will not only point out obvious removals of cash, but will also provide subtle hints of fraud.
5. *Many More:* The investigator will use various different tools for information gathering. These could range from associate files to time-clock records. Different cases will require the investigator to use an array of different resources to develop the case.

These tools are only as good as the investigator using them. No loss prevention tool will identify fraud for you. The investigator will need to use his analytical skills to develop and build a case.

As mentioned previously, dishonest employees leave signs of dishonesty in fraudulent transactions. The investigator will use these common signs to narrow down suspicious transactions and develop the case. Many of these signs are the same in most fraudulent transactions, but some are specific to the type of fraud.

We'll look in detail at several types of employee fraud, what to look for, and how to build the case. We'll start with cash refund fraud, and then look at credit fraud, merchandise credit fraud, and different types of fraud with voids.

Cash Refund Fraud

Cash refund fraud is normally performed by those employees who want cash. Employees could need cash to pay bills, pay debt, or simply satisfy their greed. No matter the need, dishonest employees can put the cash to work immediately. The employee will simply ring a refund transaction for cash, enter an item number for some merchandise, enter original purchase information, and pocket the cash from the refund. This will not create a cash shortage but will create an inventory discrepancy even though no merchandise was taken. The biggest obstacle for the employee is the concealment of the cash. Normally, the employee will make an effort to hide the cash in his palm while concealing it. Sometimes, the employee may take a change bag or deposit bag to a stock area or restroom to conceal cash. The need to disguise his actions makes the employee sloppy when taking the cash, often leaving the most common sign of a cash refund fraud—the small overage or shortage. We'll cover some other indicators of cash refund fraud in addition to how to build the case.

What a cash refund may look like:

XXXXXXXXXXXXXXXXXXXXXXXXXXXXXXXXXXXXXXXX
Store # 4455 Date: 03/04/2006 Time 9:30AM Trans # 4444
Original Receipt: Store 4455 Date 03/01/2006 Term # 1 Trans 3421
Item 00915564   – 26.00 R
Subtotal   –26.00
Tax   – 2.60
Total   –28.60Cash
XXXXXXXXXXXXXXXXXXXXXXXXXXXXXXXXXXXXXXXX

What to Look For

1. *Small overages and shortages:* Rarely will an employee take 27 cents or will a register have $1.37 extra money in the drawer. These small overages and shortages are valuable to the investigator when dealing with cash refunds. As mentioned previously, the employee's effort to make concealment as discreet as possible will often lead to the investigator's biggest clue of cash refund fraud. In the employee's mind, the store won't mind a small shortage and will certainly not be worried with an overage, so he will take an even amount of cash. For example, an employee may ring a refund for an item at $26.00, but the register will add tax, bringing the total refund to $28.60. In an effort to be discreet, the employee may take just $28.00 or even $29.00. In his mind, the store won't mind the 60 cent overage or the 40 cent shortage. The investigator can take the overage or shortage and compare it to refunds for that day to determine if fraud may have occurred. Any cash refund with an overage or shortage correlation should be considered suspicious and investigated further.
2. *Physical signs of employees keeping track of excess cash:* When an associate processes multiple cash refunds, he will often need to keep track of how much cash "belongs" to him through the fraud refunds. Employees can do this by keeping a tally sheet, laying out items to indicate dollar amounts, or by placing "his" cash in a separate area of the register. The investigator may notice any of these when auditing a register. If any of these clues are noticed, the investigator should immediately research cash refund transactions for that day.
3. *No original receipt cash refunds:* Most stores don't allow cash refunds without a receipt, and in those that do, it should not be common. In some cases, managers can override the policy, or associates are empowered to allow it in certain circumstances.

Without the original transaction information, the investigator's job becomes more difficult. The investigator should monitor all no receipt cash refunds closely to identify trends or other indicators in the transaction that would indicate dishonesty.

4. *Same-day cash refunds:* Cash refunds processed the same day as the original purchase should be looked at. Employees may be memorizing, writing down, or printing copies of the original purchase to process a fraud refund later. In some cases, the investigator can observe this behavior by notes at the register of the evidence of duplicate printing of transactions. This may not happen the same day, but it is easier for the employee to keep track of or memorize when he acquires and uses the information in the same business day. By using legitimate original transaction information, the employee can conceal the fraud better. Some same-day refunds are legitimate due to a price adjustment or the customer wanting to use a different form of payment, buy they should be monitored closely. Normally, employees committing cash refund fraud will have more cash refunds than honest employees.

5. *Keyed merchandise item numbers:* When an employee takes original transaction information from a legitimate purchase, he often needs to refund the exact items from the original purchase. Employees may not have or may not want to go through the trouble of locating the same item in order to scan it for the refund, so they hand-key the item number. By hand-keying the item number, they can process the refund without any merchandise present at the register. Dishonest employees tend to think this adds to the discreetness of the transaction because it appears that they are simply using the register to pull sales numbers, etc. There are legitimate reasons to hand-key a refund, such as the barcode won't scan or the tags are missing from the merchandise. However, these instances should be rare. The investigator can use hand-keyed items to build the merits of the case.

6. *Customer names and addresses:* Some register systems require the employee to enter the customer's name and address to complete the refund. When fraud refunds are processed, the employee will normally use one of the following:
   A. Her name or maiden name
   B. A friend or family member's name
   C. A phony name
   D. A name from an unrelated person (i.e., from phone book)

The investigator should monitor the names used for cash refunds and compare them against the associate database to determine if a refund was given to a family member. If an investigator is suspicious, he may validate the address to ensure that it was not fabricated. Another method would be to send postcards to the address used with a message similar to "We are sorry that the merchandise you returned on X date was not to your satisfaction. We hope we may continue to serve you in the future." At the bottom of the postcard, you should include the message "If you did not return merchandise on the date listed above, please call (*phone number to the loss prevention office*)." If the customer calls claiming that she did not process the refund, the investigator will want to examine the refund for possible fraud.

7. *Refunds which don't match original transaction information or the original transaction does not exist:* At times, the dishonest employee will use transaction information that does not match the items returned, or the dishonest employee may use phony original transaction information for the refund. These instances should signal the investigator to look at additional cash refunds from this employee.

8. *Ringing employee was not working:* To cover their tracks, dishonest employees may use other employees' ID numbers to ring fraudulent transactions. In their mind, any suspicion will be placed on the other employee. The investigator can use employee time clock records to determine if the ringing employee was actually working. Just because the ringing employee was working doesn't mean that another employee didn't use his ID number.

Building the Case

The investigator will need to use all the preceding indicators to determine whether a cash refund is fraudulent. Sometimes, there are legitimate explanations to these indicators, but the more dishonest indicators you find, the more likely fraud has occurred. The following can serve as a checklist for investigating cash refunds:

- First, locate the refund receipt by media or electronic journal.
- Is this a no receipt refund?
- Does the original transaction not match the refund?
- Are the item numbers hand-keyed?
- Is this a same-day refund?
- Is there an overage or shortage correlation?
- Does the last name for the customer match the employee's?
- Was the ringing employee not working?

The more times you answered "yes" would indicate how suspicious the refund is. Transactions that meet many or all of these indicators are rarely legitimate.

Many of the indicators mentioned here apply to investigating all fraud refunds, but cash refunds do have a few unique indicators that a investigator will want to use to develop their case.

Fraud Refunds to Third-Party Credit Cards

A third-party credit card is any credit card not issued and controlled by the store it is used in. The most common third-party credit cards are Visa, MasterCard, Discover, and American Express. Nowadays, these cards can be used to pay for just about any good or service. This flexibility makes fraud credits to the cards very attractive for employees because they can use the credit to shop anywhere. Not to mention, with so many employees with large amounts of credit card debt, it is also an easy way for employees to pay the balance on the card.

Employees may ring fraud refunds to credit cards for themselves, family members, or friends. It is processed like any other fraud refund by ringing a refund, entering some items numbers and original purchase information, and then entering the credit card number of the card to be issued the refund.

What a third party refund may look like:

XXXXXXXXXXXXXXXXXXXXXXXXXXXXXXXXXXXXXXXX
Store # 4455 Date: 03/04/2006 Time 9:30AM Trans # 4444
Original Receipt: Store 4455 Date 03/01/2006 Term # 1 Trans 3421

Item 00915564	–26.00 R
Subtotal	–26.00
Tax	– 2.60
Total	–28.60 Visa # k XXXXXXXXXXX4535

XXXXXXXXXXXXXXXXXXXXXXXXXXXXXXXXXXXXXXXX

What to Look For

Indicators may be repeated from previous examples because some indicators remain the same regardless of the type of fraud.

1. *No original receipt third-party refunds:* Most stores don't allow third-party refunds without a receipt, and in those that do, it should not be common. In some cases, managers can override the policy, or associates are empowered to allow it in certain circumstances. Without the original transaction information, the investigator's job becomes more difficult. The investigator should monitor all no receipt third-party refunds closely to identify trends or other indicators in the transaction that would indicate dishonesty.

2. *Same-day third-party refunds:* The investigator should look at third-party refunds processed the same day as the original purchase. The employee could have purchased some merchandise legitimately but refunded it fraudulently later the same day. In addition, the employee could sell merchandise to a friend or family member and allow that person to leave with the merchandise, only to refund it fraudulently later that day. In the case of an employee sale and refund, the investigator should examine the employee parcel log to see if the employee checked the purchase to take home. The employee could easily run the purchase through the parcel check system because he will have a legitimate receipt from the purchase. Some same-day refunds are legitimate due to a price adjustment or the customer wanting to use a different form of payment, but they should be monitored closely. Normally, employees committing third-party refund fraud will have more third-party refunds than honest employees.

3. *Keyed merchandise item numbers:* When an employee takes original transaction information from a legitimate purchase, he often needs to refund the exact items from the original purchase. Employees may not have or may not want to go through the trouble of locating the same item in order to scan it for the refund, so they hand-key the item number. By hand-keying the item number, they can process the refund without any merchandise present at the register. Dishonest employees tend to think this adds to the discreetness of the transaction because it appears that they are simply using the register to pull sales numbers, etc. There are legitimate reasons to hand-key a refund such as the bar code won't scan or the tags are missing from the merchandise. However, these instances should be rare. The investigator can use hand-keyed items to build the merits of the case.

4. *Refunds which don't match original transaction information or the original transaction does not exist:* At times, the dishonest employee will use transaction information that does not match the items returned, or he may use phony original transaction information for the refund. These instances should signal the investigator to look at additional refunds from this employee.

5. *Ringing employee was not working:* To cover their tracks, dishonest employees may use another employee's ID number to ring fraudulent transactions. In their mind, any suspicion will be placed on the other employee. The investigator can use employee time clock records to determine whether the ringing employee was actually working. Just because the ringing employee was working doesn't mean that another employee didn't use his ID number.

6. *Partial or full match of credit card name and employee's name:* As mentioned earlier, employees will normally ring fraud refunds to their own credit card or a family member's credit card. Therefore, the name on the credit card may match their full name or their last name. In the case of a full name match, the investigator should be very suspicious. If it's a last name match, the investigator should determine if this person is related to the employee. Employees with common last names will match customers more frequently, making the investigator's job a bit more difficult.

7. *Keyed credit card numbers:* Much like keying item numbers, the employee may key credit card numbers for a refund in an attempt to be discreet. By doing this, the employee will not have to produce the physical credit card to issue the refund. The employee may do this because he doesn't want to be seen swiping the card, or the card may have left with the friend or family member who took the original purchase. Sometimes, employees key credit card numbers because the card will not swipe, or they simply don't want to bother asking the customer for the card. The investigator should use keyed cards to build on a case, but not build from it.

8. *Cards with more refunds than purchases:* The investigator may run across some credit cards that have been issued more refunds than purchases have been made. An employee may be fraudulently refunding items without a receipt to the card or refunding original transactions multiple times. Some exception reporting software has a built-in report that will alert the investigator of cards with more refunds than purchases. Some customers may purchase merchandise with other forms of payment or different credit cards and later have

a refund issued to one card, creating more refunds than purchases. In this case, the refunds are legitimate. The investigator can determine if other forms of payment were used by checking the original transactions used for the refund.

9. *History of refunds with employee:* If a credit card has several refunds mostly with one employee, this may signal that the employee is fraudulently issuing refunds to that card. This is especially true if the card is used for purchases with various different other employees, but all of the refunds are performed by one employee. This should be very suspicious to the investigator.

Building the Case

The investigator will need to use all the preceding indicators to determine if a third-party refund is fraudulent. Sometimes, there are legitimate explanations to these indicators, but the more dishonest indicators you find, the more likely fraud has occurred. The following can serve as a checklist for investigating third-party refunds:

- First, locate the refund receipt by media or electronic journal.
- Is this a no receipt refund?
- Does the original transaction not match the refund?
- Are the item numbers hand-keyed?
- Is this a same-day refund?
- Is the credit card number keyed?
- Does the last name of the customer match the employee's?
- Was the ringing employee not working?
- Card has more refunds than purchases?
- Is there a history of refunds with this employee?

The more times you answered "yes" would indicate how suspicious the refund is. Transactions that meet many or all of these indicators are rarely legitimate.

Many of the indicators mentioned here apply to investigating all fraud refunds, but third-party refunds do have a few unique indicators that an investigator will want to use to develop his case.

Fraud Refunds to House Credit Cards

House credit cards are those issued by the retailer that can be used only at said retailer. Many department stores issue their own credit cards. Some retailers require that their employees use their house credit card to receive their employee discount. The discount is normally taken off at the credit center rather than at the register.

Investigating house credit card fraud is similar to investigating third-party fraud. The investigator should use all the indicators from the third-party fraud section, but there are some special considerations for house cards.

No receipt refunds to house credit cards are generally acceptable because they are much like store credits. The investigator will have many more legitimate transactions to sift through because there will be many more no receipt refunds to house cards than third-party cards. On a positive note, the investigator will probably have access to all employee accounts and have special access to statements, etc., from those accounts.

Fraud Refunds for Store Credit

At many retail stores, store credits are issued when a customer cannot produce an original receipt for the merchandise that he would like to return. These store credits can be in the form of a paper voucher or an electronic card much like a gift card. The refund amount is placed on the card, and the customer can spend the balance in the store. Most stores require the customer to provide a driver's license so that the employee can enter the name, address, and driver's license number into the register. This personal information can be used to trace refunds or even deny refunds to a particular customer. Most store credits are issued to legitimate customers who misplaced their original sales receipt, but employees may obtain fraudulent store credits to purchase merchandise for themselves or sell the credit for cash.

What a refund for a store credit may look like:

XXXXXXXXXXXXXXXXXXXXXXXXXXXXXXXXXXXXXXXXX
Store # 4455 Date: 03/04/2006 Time 9:30AM Trans # 4444
NO ORIGINAL RECEIPT
Item 00915564   – 26.00 R
Subtotal   –26.00
Tax   – 2.60
Total   –28.60 EMC # 7685342037464535
XXXXXXXXXXXXXXXXXXXXXXXXXXXXXXXXXXXXXXXXX

What to Look For

Indicators may be repeated from previous examples because some indicators remain the same regardless of the type of fraud.

1. *Ringing employee was not working:* To cover their tracks, dishonest employees may use another employee's ID number to ring fraudulent transactions. In their mind, any suspicion will be placed on the other employee. The investigator can use employee time clock records to determine whether the ringing employee was actually working. Just because the ringing employee was working doesn't mean that another employee didn't use his ID number.
2. *History of refunds with employee:* If a customer name has several refunds mostly with one employee, this may signal that the employee is fraudulently issuing refunds to that customer. This is especially true if the card is used for purchases with various different other employees, but all the refunds are performed by one employee. This should be very suspicious to the investigator.
3. *Employee discount card used in connection to the redemption of the store credit:* Even though an employee may have fraudulently received a store credit, he will rarely give up his employee discount. Many times the employee will use the store credit in conjunction with his discount card. When this happens, it should be very suspicious to the investigator, especially if a different name was used to obtain the store credit. This would most likely be the result of the employee using a phony name. The investigator will need to match the store credit used to the originating refund to determine if the employee using it may have issued it or used another employee's ID number to issue it.
4. *Phony information used for store credit:* Occasionally, an employee will fill the name and address fields with obviously made-up information, such as John Smith 222 Main Street. This could be due to laziness or a fraudulent refund.
5. Customer names and addresses: Some register systems require the employee to enter the customer's name and address to complete the refund. When fraud refunds are processed, the employee will normally use one of the following:
   - Her name or maiden name
   - A friend or family member's name
   - A phony name
   - A name from an unrelated person (i.e., from phone book)

The investigator should monitor the names used for refunds and compare them against the associate database to determine if a refund was given to a family member. If an investigator is suspicious, he may validate the address to ensure that it was not fabricated. Another method would be to send postcards to the address used with a message similar to "We are sorry that the merchandise you returned on X date was not to your satisfaction. We hope we may continue to serve you in the future." At the bottom of the postcard, you should include the message "If you did not return merchandise on the date listed above, please call (*phone number to the loss prevention office*)." If the customer calls claiming that he did not process the refund, the investigator will want to examine the refund for possible fraud.

Building the Case

The investigator will need to use all the preceding indicators to determine if a refund is fraudulent. Sometimes, there are legitimate explanations to these indicators, but the more dishonest indicators you find, the more likely fraud has occurred. The following can serve as a checklist for investigating refunds for store credits:

- First, locate the refund receipt by media or electronic journal.
- Does the last name of the customer match the employee's?
- Was the ringing employee not working?
- Is there a history of refunds with this employee?
- Was an employee discount card used in conjunction with the redemption of the store credit?
- Was customer information obviously phony?

The more times you answered "yes" would indicate how suspicious the refund is. Transactions that meet many or all of these indicators are rarely legitimate.

Many of the indicators mentioned here apply to investigating all fraud refunds, but refunds for store credits do have a few unique indicators that an investigator will want to use to develop his case.

Fraud Voids

Voids are common transactions in retail stores. The necessity to void may arise for several different reasons. After the sale is finished, a customer may decide that he does not want the merchandise, he would like to pay for it differently, or the prices were rung up incorrectly for the purchase. Employees may also void a sale before it is finished for the same reasons. Either way, the void cancels the sale as if it had never happened. Inventory records remain the same, and payment taken or refunded is canceled from the register's count.

Employees may also use voids to commit fraud by cash, check, or credit card. By voiding a cash sale that a legitimate customer paid for and left with the merchandise, the employee can take the cash paid for the sale without the register showing the shortage. The reason is that the register assumes the customer did not take the merchandise and the cash was given back to him. If the employee does this fraudulently, the cash will not be short, but the inventory records of the merchandise taken by the legitimate customer will be. Normally, the dishonest employee will keep transaction numbers and amounts of cash sales that he would like to fraudulently void until he perceives is a good time to take the cash. A manager's code or key is normally required for the void. The employee will give the manager a phony reason for voiding the cash sales. At that point, the employee will only need to wait for a good time to conceal the cash.

Employees may also cancel the transaction before it is finished if they notice that the customer is paying cash. This is easier for the employee because a void during the transaction normally doesn't require a manager's approval. The employee will take the cash and make change but without ever finishing the sale. The register assumes that no transaction took place. Therefore, the cash given by the customer is not in the register's records. The associate will normally leave the cash in the register until he thinks he has a good opportunity to conceal the cash without being noticed.

Employees may also void transactions that were purchased by themselves, friends, or family members. The employee will have a legitimate receipt for his purchase, and the friend or family member will have already left the store. These voids can originate from cash, credit card, and check sales. When an employee plans to fraudulently void a friend's or family member's cash or check sale, he typically doesn't take any tender in the first place. Since the employee plans to void the transaction, there is no need to put the cash or check in the register. The employee may also have his own purchase voided. Even though the transaction was voided, the employee will have a legitimate receipt to check the package through the door pass log and leave the building. The investigator should always check non-rerung employee voids against the employee package log.

What a cash void may look like:

XXXXXXXXXXXXXXXXXXXXXXXXXXXXXXXXXXXXXXXX
Store # 4455 Date: 03/04/2006 Time 9:30AM Trans # 4444
Item 00915564   26.00
Subtotal   26.00
Tax   2.60
Total   28.60Cash
Tendered   30.00 Cash
Change   1.40 Cash
XXXXXXXXXXXXXXXXXXXXXXXXXXXXXXXXXXXXXXXX

XXXXXXXXXXXXXXXXXXXXXXXXXXXXXXXXXXXXXXXX
Store # 4455 Date: 03/04/2006 Time 9:30AM Trans # 4464
POST VOID
Original Receipt: Store 4455 Date 03/04/2006 Term # 1 Trans 4444
Item 00915564   26.00 R
Subtotal   26.00
Tax   2.60
Total   28.60Cash
Tendered   30.00 Cash
Change   1.40 Cash
POST VOID
XXXXXXXXXXXXXXXXXXXXXXXXXXXXXXXXXXXXXXXX

What to Look For

Indicators may be repeated from previous examples because some indicators remain the same regardless of the type of fraud.

1. *Small overages and shortages: (Cash voids only)* Rarely will an employee take 27 cents or will a terminal have $1.37 extra money in the register. These small overages and shortages are valuable to the investigator when dealing with cash voids. As mentioned previously, the employee's effort to make concealment as discreet as possible will often lead to the investigator's biggest clue of cash void fraud. In the employee's mind, the store won't mind a small shortage and will certainly not be worried with an overage, so HE will take an even amount of cash. For example, an employee may ring a fraud cash void for an item at $26.00, but the register will add tax, bringing the total refund to $28.60. In an effort to be discreet, the employee may take just $28.00 or even $29.00. In his mind, the store won't mind the 60 cent overage or the 40 cent shortage. The investigator can take the overage or shortage and compare it to cash voids for that day to determine if fraud may have occurred. Any cash void with an overage or shortage correlation should be considered suspicious and investigated further.

2. *Physical signs of employees keeping track of excess cash: (Cash voids only)* When an associate processes multiple fraud cash voids, he will often need to keep track of how much cash "belongs" to him through the fraud voids. Employees can do this by keeping a tally sheet, laying out items to indicate dollar amounts, or by placing "his" cash in a separate area of the register. The investigator may notice any of these when auditing a register. If any of these clues are noticed, the investigator should immediately research cash refund transactions and cash voids for that day.

3. *Partial or full match of the voided credit card name and employee's name: (Credit card or check voids only)* As mentioned earlier, employees will normally ring fraud voids using their own credit card or a family member's credit card. Therefore, the name on the credit card may match their full name or their last name. In the case

of a full name match, the investigator should be very suspicious. If it's a last name match, the investigator should determine if this person is related to the employee. Employees with common last names will match customers more frequently, making the investigator's job a bit more difficult.

4. *Voids in which the original sale was not rerung:* Most voids occur because the customer was not given the correct prices or would like to use a different form of payment. In these cases, the sale will be rerung for the same items at different prices or with a different form of payment. The investigator should look for voids that were never rerung.

5. *Employees that ring more voids as a percent of transactions than other employees:* Employees processing fraudulent voids will naturally process more voids than other employees. The investigator should look at employees that ring more voids as a percent of overall transactions. Exception reporting will generally be used to do this. There will be employees who ring a high percentage of voids by mere coincidence, but they will not be consistently among the top percentage from month to month.

6. *Manager's or another associate's ID used:* If strict controls restricting employees from having access to voiding transactions are not in place, an employee may use a manager's ID or another employee's ID to process the fraud void. The investigator should examine the possibility of an employee having access to voiding transactions with another employee's ID number. If the investigator finds evidence of an employee using another employee's ID number to process a void, it should be very suspicious.

7. *Employees voiding their own sales:* Some retailers allow employees to unilaterally process voids. If this is the case, the investigator should pay close attention to employees processing their own voids. This is especially true if an employee voids a purchase that he made.

Building the Case

The investigator will need to use all the preceding indicators to determine if a void is fraudulent. Sometimes, there are legitimate explanations to these indicators, but the more dishonest indicators you find, the more likely fraud has occurred. The following can serve as a checklist for investigating voids:

- First, locate the void transaction by media or electronic journal.
- Was there any overage or shortage correlation to the amount of the void? (*Cash voids only*)
- Are there physical signs of tally sheets at the register? (*Cash voids only*)
- Was the original sale *not* rerung?
- Was the ringing employee not working?
- Does the employee rank in the top of store by voids as a percent to total transactions?
- Did the original purchase belong to an employee?
- Does the name on the credit card or check match all or part of the employee's name?

The more times you answered "yes" would indicate how suspicious the void is. Transactions that meet many or all of these indicators are rarely legitimate.

Stolen Credit Cards

Credit card theft has become a serious problem for retailers. It is very embarrassing for a retailer to have an employee fraudulently use a customer's credit card. The retailer can spare some humiliation by investigating the employee and referring him for prosecution without the customer's involvement. Credit cards are attractive to employees because they can be used just about anywhere to the extent of the limit on the card. The first act by the employee is to acquire the physical card or card number from the customer. Here are a few examples:

1. The employee may not offer the credit card back to the customer. Since the customer is accustomed to the employee handing back the credit card, she may not notice that it was never given back. The customer will then leave without her credit card. Many times, the customer will have a hard time remembering the last time she had it, and

she will rarely suspect the retail employee of keeping it. Sometimes, the customer may erroneously leave it on the cash wrap. The employee may see it after the customer has left and keep it rather than try to return it to the customer.

2. Employees involved in more sophisticated credit card fraud may use an electronic device to capture the data from the card by simply swiping it. Such devices are widely available and easy to make.

3. Some employees will simply write down the number or make some sort of imprint of the card. Very few retailers print card numbers on receipts and journal tape, but that was once a typical place for employees to acquire card numbers. Employees may also use carbon paper, silly putty, or some other tool to make an imprint of the card. The investigator should look for these items during register audits.

What to Look for If a Stolen Credit Card Has Been Used at Your Store

- Determine from the cardholder the last legitimate purchases that were made.
- Look for keyed purchases. Keyed purchases are typically the fraudulent charges.
- Determine which employee rang the last legitimate purchase transaction. This employee will be the most likely suspect. If several employees rang legitimate purchases on the same day, the investigator should look at all of them as possible suspects.
- Any employee discount card used in conjunction with a stolen card will signal which employee is fraudulently using the card.
- If all the fraudulent purchases were rung up by one employee, it is possible that employee is the one using the card. He could be ringing the fraudulent purchases himself. The employee will assume that the investigator thinks someone else brought the stolen card to him to purchase merchandise.
- Missing media are signs that an employee was involved. If the investigator cannot locate signature slips from the purchase, it is likely that an employee with access to that register destroyed them.

If a credit card was used fraudulently in your store, it is most likely that someone from outside the store obtained the card and used it. On the other hand, keyed credit cards more likely indicate an employee because few retailers allow the use of just a credit card number. Whatever the situation, the investigator should ensure that a store employee is not involved, but if an employee is involved, the investigator should aggressively resolve the case.

Employee Handbook

CAS, JHC

Why do we need an employee handbook? An employee handbook (or a written employee guide or "Rules and Regulations") setting forth the employer's policies regarding employee behavior is essential for several reasons. If employees do not know the rules, they cannot justifiably be disciplined for disobeying them. Can you imagine any game or contest (sports, cards, spelling bee, etc.) being conducted without rules? It would wreak havoc and be unfair to the participants. So it is with employees. They must know the rules by which their employment and behavior will be judged. To assure that all employees know the rules, they should sign a statement indicating they have not only been given a copy of and read the rules, but that they fully *understand* them, and any rules which are unclear they must make an effort to get clarified. Such rules should be written in clear and concise language, leaving no room for more than one interpretation and understanding. Providing each employee a copy of the rules is recommended. Having the rules and policies reviewed by counsel is important to prevent any future claim of discrimination or creating any legal obligations with respect to continued employment under any circumstances.

Considering the documentation of loss prevention policies and procedures is an entirely different question. Obviously, some loss prevention policies should be included in the company's rules and regulations handout, but the procedures outlining methods of investigation of suspected loss prevention violations should be in a document restricted to those whose job requires this sensitive information. (See also "Manuals for Security/LP: Protection of Contents.")

Employee Purchases and Package Control

CAS, JHC

Procedures to control employee purchases and their corresponding employee discount will vary and depend on the mechanics and equipment used to record sales in general.

Stores utilizing computerized POS devices will normally deduct the employee discount "back office," meaning that the sale is rung at the full retail price and the discount deducted by the computer when the employee's statement is calculated. This also requires, of course, that the employee's purchase be charged, since a cash purchase cannot be recognized by the computer as an employee purchase.

Other stores, not relying on computerized sales recordation, can be more flexible in handling employee purchases but should be no less stalwart in their control of these transactions. These stores may allow cash sales to employees and calculate their employee discount at the time of the sale, accepting the discounted price for the purchase in cash.

Why do we suggest that control of employee purchases is important? Because making employee purchases presents an opportunity for theft and/or abuse in a variety of ways. What do we envision as contained in the employee purchase procedure as demanding controls and verification? We suggest that the following elements of employee purchase procedures be subject to scrutiny and verification:

- Accurate current retail price;
- Accurate recording of price;
- Appropriate discount taken;
- Authorized discount recipient;
- Merchandise purchased matches above cited element;
- Employee receives only merchandise purchased;
- Merchandise purchased is secured in a designated location until removed from store.

Once the employee's purchase has been properly made, what should happen then to that package of merchandise? Employees who are not working (day off) may maintain possession of their purchases and leave the store when they've finished shopping. Employees who make purchases in their own store while on duty or at lunch or a break must take their purchases to the designated security site for all parcels and packages and subsequent retrieval. We believe that purchases should be deposited in a secure storage area until employees retrieve them when ready to leave for home. Some companies permit employees with private offices to keep the purchases in their office until leaving for the day. All employees should be required to use the designated employee entrance when coming to or leaving work, and that procedure must also be followed when employees have a package coming into the store. The company rules should require employees to subject that package to inspection by security personnel if requested to do so. No packages should be allowed on the selling floor, register stations, stock rooms, or any workstation. The use of the employee entrance when entering or leaving the store whenever carrying any package of any kind (personal or company property) and having it subject to inspection should be required of all personnel, from the CEO on down.

We believe that the company's rules and regulations should contain the following provisions, violations of which may subject the employees to various levels of discipline, including immediate discharge:

- Concealment or unauthorized storage of merchandise not purchased.
- Refusing a request to inspect personal packages or belongings, lockers, desks, files, or offices which are subject to periodic inspection.
- Marking down or discounting merchandise without proper authorization or selling marked down merchandise to a customer or any associate, including one's self without duly authorized or recorded price changes.

- Failure to use the employee entrance/exit when
  - Arriving and leaving from work at the assigned store or when on business at any company store.
  - When in possession of packages, briefcases, backpacks, handbags, samples, or company property in your assigned store.
- Failure to observe published package checking regulations or regulations for storage of personal belongings.
- Misuse of employee discount.
- Employees may have only one employee charge account.
- Employees may not borrow or wear any merchandise prior to its being properly purchased.

We recognize that the preceding rules and regulations may require modification depending on a given company's situation; in smaller stores lacking dedicated LP, the simple presentation of the purchase to a supervisor should suffice, i.e., to just ensure the purchases made are known to management.

However, the spirit and intention behind our suggestions should not be abrogated. Employees enjoy a distinct benefit by receiving an employee discount, and their employer has every right to regulate the circumstances under which that privilege is exercised.

Employee Theft and Misconduct

CAS, JHC

It has been reliably reported that in 2005 employee theft was responsible for 47% of all retail shrinkage, amounting to over $17 billion annually.[1] In spite of the increased sophistication of loss prevention techniques, including undercover agents, extensive use of CCTV, EAS, and employee screening devices, this amount tends to increase yearly.

To protect profit and shareowners, most companies take action to get dishonest employees off their payroll and out on the street. For years, if a dishonest employee claimed the company was overzealous in its investigation into his dishonesty or violated some of his rights by firing him, that employee would not have gotten very far in pursuing those claims.

Today, the courts are full of cases accepted by willing attorneys based on various theories of what has become known as "wrongful termination," with underlying claims of false imprisonment/arrest, invasion of privacy, assault/battery, defamation, malicious prosecution, tortious interference with employment, and intentional and/or negligent infliction of emotional distress.

How can a company protect itself against the myriad of civil actions which often follow a righteous and justified termination for dishonesty?

In most jurisdictions, an employer may discharge employees "at will" at any time for any reason. However, unless employees are probationary or have otherwise signed a contract establishing their at will status, most employees at some juncture lose their at will status, and thus any termination must be for "just cause."

Any termination for dishonesty must meet the proof "beyond a reasonable doubt" standard, which is best established by a thorough investigation, with documentary, audio, and/or videotape evidence if possible, and a written confession, provided it can be firmly established that it was purely voluntary and not the result of questionable or coercive tactics.

Terminations cannot be discriminatory! If you fire one thief and not the next, you are in trouble! All dishonest employees must be treated equally; all thieves, regardless of the amount of the theft, should be discharged. This same principle applies to misconduct for which the

[1] It is interesting to note that a reliable source (*The Retail Bulletin*) in late 2006 reported that European retailers attributed 30.7% of their shrink to employee theft and 48.8% to shoplifting; these percentages are almost the reverse of those reported for the United States. The shrink percentages resulting from vendor fraud (6.2%) as well as that attributable to administrative errors (14.3%) were approximately the same as those reported in the United States.

penalty is less than termination without prior warning. Consistency is the key: Treat all employees, both staff and executive, equally when it comes to discipline.

Since theft is a "specific intent" crime (i.e., the offender must have intended to steal), it is important that this element be firmly established. An employee who comes into possession of unpaid-for company property by accident or unknowingly cannot be terminated for theft (but may be justifiably terminated for some other policy violation, provided he knew, or should have known, such a violation was a terminable offense).

These situations are not infrequent. Susie Salesclerk inadvertently comes to work without her sweater or perhaps without her makeup. Joe Salesclerk forgets his tie or his belt. Susie is subsequently seen "borrowing" a sweater and Joe a tie. When they leave work at the end of the day, Susie is wearing the sweater and Joe the tie. Both are stopped and challenged regarding the unpaid-for merchandise. Both claim they had no intent to steal the items and intended to return them the next day. Should they be fired for theft? Probably not, lacking further information. Should they be terminated? Yes, for violation of the company policy against borrowing or wearing any company merchandise prior to it having been properly paid for.

Employees suspected of theft will normally, at some point, be questioned by loss prevention or other appropriate company official. Courts have been unanimous in their holding that the Miranda rule does not apply to such questioning *unless* such questioning is in the presence of or has resulted from a joint effort with law enforcement.

Employees who are part of a bargaining unit (i.e., union membership) may, under the terms of the union contract, be entitled to union representation when being questioned, *if they request it*, in any situation which may result in disciplinary action (see 1975 U.S. Supreme Court decision in *NLRB v. J. Weingarten, Inc.*). If the employee requests such union participation, the company has the right not to conduct any interview and base any action on the information available at that point. Interviews scheduled with an employee suspect need not be postponed if no union representative is available, and the union representative is present as a witness only—this representative has no right to counsel the suspect employee during the interview.

Under the rules of the Employee Polygraph Protection Act of 1988 (EPPA), a federal law, no mention of a polygraph may be made to an employee except under the most limited conditions; we recommend that the word "polygraph" be eliminated from loss prevention's vocabulary.

As suggested earlier, we recommend that, at a minimum, employee interviews regarding dishonesty be tape-recorded (with the employee's permission). Better yet, a videotape provides visual and aural evidence of the lack of any coercive techniques and the voluntariness of any confession.

The question of restitution by admitted dishonest employees deserves some discussion. If any employee offers to make restitution for the value of property stolen by him, it can be accepted *provided* the offer was voluntary and not the result of duress or other coercive means. Promissory notes are often used to obtain restitution. The promise, implied or overt, that the payment of restitution will negate any criminal prosecution is improper and, if done, will in all likelihood negate the restitution agreement. Obtaining restitution may, in fact, jeopardize criminal prosecution on the theory that the victim (the company) has been made whole. We suggest that offers of or requests for restitution be made through the courts if the matter is criminally prosecuted. A threat by the employer to prosecute if restitution is not paid is extortion in most jurisdictions and subjects the employer to criminal prosecution.

As stated elsewhere in this work, a witness should always be present during the entire dishonest employee interview process.

While this discussion's thrust is about dishonesty, employers should keep in mind that other forms of misconduct are also legitimate areas of inquiry. Behavior such as insubordination, time card violations, misuse of company property (falling short of theft), and serious policy violations are all topics which may result in investigations, interviews, and ultimate discharge. The same precautions we urge for dishonesty cases also apply to other misconduct situations.

With respect to both dishonesty and other misconduct, it is essential that all employees are fully aware of the company policy respecting these issues and that the policy is in writing, clearly stated, and that the penalties for violation are also clearly annunciated. Employees must know the rules and penalties for violations. If the violation of a rule results in termination without a prior warning, this should be clearly stated. The steps in a progressive discipline procedure must also be made known to all employees and then consistently adhered to. It is desirable to get a written affirmation from all employees that they have both read the company's rules and that they fully understand them.

Once a dishonest employee is off-roll and gone, the less said to others about the circumstances of that employee's termination, the better. While the truth is an absolute defense to a slander or libel action, why provide the potential for such a lawsuit, which will be expensive and time consuming to defend?

Privacy during the investigation and interview phases of a dishonesty investigation is also vital, since a situation in which visual observations by noninvolved personnel leading to the conclusion that the subject was suspected of dishonesty may set the stage for an invasion of privacy suit. While questioning coworkers about their knowledge of information pertinent to the investigation is permissible, inadvertent or casual suggestions that "John" was responsible for a loss and "John's" subsequent disappearance from the workplace should be avoided.

While a good faith, truthful response to an inquiry about a discharged employee from a prospective employer is permissible, blacklisting is not and is a crime in some jurisdictions. Responding to inquiries about former employees is fraught with all sorts of legal pitfalls, and such inquiries are best handled by trained professionals who practice "less is best," and respond with date of hire, date of leaving, position, and rate of pay only.

While on the topic of lawsuits against the employer resulting from a dishonest employee's discharge, we must mention documentation. It is uncontested that the best defense to a civil suit for wrongful discharge or any of its underlying torts is a properly and fully documented record of everything leading up to the discharge. Equally important is the ability to establish that employees know the company rules and penalties for violation of them by having their acknowledgment of that fact in writing.

Finally, unless a company has trained HR and LP personnel on staff, situations which involve dishonesty, investigations, discipline, and terminations may best be discussed with legal counsel for guidance along the way.

Remember the adage: "Better to be safe than sorry."

Entrapment

CAS, JHC

Webster's Dictionary defines "entrapment" as "to lure into a compromising statement or act." From time to time we hear of how a store entrapped a customer into shoplifting. Although enticing and attractive displays of merchandise may be *alluring*, they certainly don't rise to the level of luring a person into stealing the desirable goods.

The essence of the preceding definition lies in the words "to lure." The definition of "lure" is "an inducement to pleasure or gain." "Inducement," then, is the operative word. Entrapment then, in our retail loss prevention setting, would be the dynamics between two persons, wherein one induces the other into doing something wrong, like committing theft. I liken such inducement to the planting of a seed in the garden; i.e., one person plants the seed of the idea to steal in the mind of the second person, and the seed germinates and flowers into an act of theft.

Following are two scenarios involving employee theft. In one there's entrapment. In the other, no entrapment. In which case do you see entrapment?

Scenario #1: The distribution center dock. Two dock employees, Charlie and Ben, are working on a Saturday with the dock supervisor, Mr. Last. Charlie, unbeknownst to anyone, is an undercover agent working for the loss prevention department. Normally, the center is closed on Saturdays, but this is an overtime exception.

At midday, Last decides he's hungry and wants a pizza. He asks the other two if they'd like to share one—he's buying. They're game. Rather than walk through the empty facility, he opts to jump the dock, unlocks the gate which encloses the shipping/receiving area, and leaves the gate open for his return. The two employees stand on the dock and watch their supervisor's car disappear into traffic. Charlie then says to Ben, "Look, Last won't be back for at least 20 minutes. Why don't you pull your van into the yard here, and we'll both get a laptop computer. No one will ever know." Ben likes the idea, jumps the dock, runs through the open gate, drives his van into the yard, and up to the dock, where two computers are loaded. The van is quickly returned to the parking area. Shortly thereafter, Last walks through the open gate, closes and locks it, and the three share lunch.

Scenario #2: Store's Restaurant. Two janitors, Art (an undercover agent working with loss prevention) and Billy, who are regularly assigned to clean up the department store's restaurant kitchen, are among the last employees to leave each night. Final chores include the garbage run using the service elevator down to the basement and dumpsters down there. After that run, all the elevators are turned off. While walking by the refrigerated "walk-in-box," Art notices the manager failed to lock the padlock. He comments on this security breach to Billy. Billy, in the final phase of dry mopping drops his mop and runs to the box, opens the door, looks in, and then whispers to Art to get a couple of large plastic trash bags. Art complies. Billy instructs Art to hold open the bag and in several trips in and out of the refrigerator deposits a half dozen steaks, two hams, and 10 pounds of butter in the bag. While whistling, Billy waves Art away from the door, closes it, locks the padlock, and takes the now-heavy plastic bag and slides it across the tile floor to the push cart containing several other plastic bags of trash and a garbage can. Billy places the bag containing the stolen food into a second bag, places that bag into the garbage can, pushes the cart onto the elevator, and deposits the trash and garbage in the trash area in the basement.

The two clock out and exit through the security door on the main floor. Billy drives down into the tunnel and retrieves the bag. Later, Billy gives Art only a ham, despite the fact Art claims he's entitled to half the food, but Billy does promise to share more later. Art makes his report and turns in the ham to his supervisor as evidence.

Note the clear distinction between the two scenarios. In the first, Ben was the victim of entrapment. Charlie, the undercover agent, planted the seed of the idea to commit a crime in Ben's mind. It wasn't Ben's idea; it was Charlie's.

In the second scenario, there was no entrapment. Art found the door unlocked and told his coworker about his discovery. Even if the door had intentionally been left unlocked with the plan to inform Billy of the breach, there still was no entrapment because no "seed was planted" in terms of suggesting theft. Rather, Billy was given the opportunity to be honest or to be dishonest, according to his own choosing. Had Art said, "Wow, some idiot failed to lock this and we could take anything we want and no one would be the wiser," then Art would have been guilty of entrapment. But Art didn't. The idea to steal—where the light bulb went off—was in Billy's mind. Billy had the choice of saying, "Lock it, and I'll report this to the restaurant manager tomorrow." But Billy chose to steal.

The bottom line, the key question to answer in either scenario is: Whose idea was it to commit theft?

Escort Policy and Procedure

CAS, JHC

Escort or escorting in a retail setting is usually limited to two kinds of tasks:

1. Providing an employee to accompany another employee engaged in some high-theft-risk activity such as drawing down excessive accumulated cash (a.k.a. "first deposits") in POS devices or cash registers and transporting the cash to the cash office or making bank deposits; and
2. Providing an employee to accompany either another employee or a customer from the store to their vehicle in the parking lot, especially at night.

In the former, accompanying cash is as much to protect the cash carrier from any suspicions of some subsequent discovery of missing money and to serve as a second party who could be a deterrent and/or a witness to a robbery or robbery attempt. This "second" party need not be a loss prevention associate. This procedure should be included in the store's cashiering and cash handling manual.

In the latter case, the escorting employee more often than not should be a security or loss prevention employee. If loss prevention is available, gender of the escort is unimportant. What is important is the company's recognition of and response to expressed concerns female employees or customers may have for their safety in walking alone to their vehicle. What should not happen is a situation wherein an employee or customer specifically requests an escort and the request is not granted. If no LP associate or management person is available, a male associate from sales, stock, etc., should be called on to carry out this escort function. This procedure should be included in the loss prevention manual.

Ethical Dilemmas and Conflicts of Interest

Curtis Baillie

Our ethical decision-making process is formed early in life and guided by our parents or people who are influential in our lives. Many of us growing up in the first half of the last century were Gene Autry fans. Gene Autry followed a code worthy of being mentioned in this work. The ethical principles found within that "Cowboy Code" are as applicable today as when first written in the 1940s:

The Cowboy Code—by Gene Autry

1. The Cowboy must never shoot first, hit a smaller man, or take unfair advantage.
2. He must never go back on his word, or a trust confided in him.
3. He must always tell the truth.
4. He must be gentle with children, the elderly, and animals.
5. He must not advocate or possess racially or religiously intolerant ideas.
6. He must help people in distress.
7. He must be a good worker.
8. He must keep himself clean in thought, speech, action, and personal habits.
9. He must respect women, parents, and his nation's laws.
10. The Cowboy is a Patriot.

Deciding Between Right and Wrong: Listening to Our Inner Voice

> *"Conscience is the inner voice that warns us somebody may be looking."*
> —Henry Louis Mencken, *"Sententiae," This and That: A Mencken Chrestomathy,*
> *1948*

We all have it—you know, that inner voice that continuously talks to us. Thomas Magnum, of *Magnum PI* fame, had it. Our inner voice, developed early in life, is the mind's loudspeaker—our moral and ethical subconscious. The inner voice is always right; it's when we try to justify and rationalize that we make poor ethical decisions.

The workplace is full of ethical choices, and we are all aware of someone who has suffered a lapse of ethical judgment. Whether it is the associate obtaining "free items" from the lunchroom snack machine, punching an absent coworker's time card, or the boss falsifying travel expense reports. People rationalize poor ethical decisions by concluding, "It's due me," "I work hard," or "I'm not paid enough." Sometimes a lapse in ethical judgment is a result of wanting to "save face" or not wanting to lose a job.

Many of us in loss prevention have known people who falsified reports to keep from getting into trouble or make themselves look better in the eyes of their boss. One case involved a shoplift agent who reported his supervisor for altering his shoplifter apprehension report. The supervisor, a district investigator who was directly involved in the apprehension, rewrote the report deleting his involvement because not all the requirements to make the apprehension had been met. The supervisor said he had changed the report because he did not want to lose his job.

Three Principles for Deciding Ethical Dilemmas

Not all solutions to ethical issues are addressed by a written company policy. You must think through the process of solving ethical dilemmas. We suggest there are three main guiding principles for deciding ethical dilemmas. Applying these principles aids in deciding not only ethical dilemmas in business life, but also the dilemmas we all face in everyday life. These guiding principles are

1. *Is it legal?* Will this action be against either civil or criminal laws? By taking this action, will you jeopardize yourself or your company in the eyes of the law?
2. *Will I feel good about my decision?* This is where your personal values become vitally important. Think carefully about how you will feel after completing or observing an action. Will it make you proud? Will you feel good if your decisions are published in the newspaper? Will you feel comfortable if your company knows about it? Will you feel good if your family knows about it? Is it morally right?
3. *Is it within the principles of my company's business ethics policy?* Will your actions go against the principles established in your company's business ethics policy? Is it fair to all concerned in the short term as well as the long term?

When deciding ethical dilemmas, take time to think out the problem because this is not the moment to make snap decisions. The courts may review the choice(s) you make for years to come, which could have a negative impact on your career, and deal a financial blow to your company. If your company's ethics policy is unclear regarding a particular scenario, always "take a partner" when making these types of decisions. Seek aid in the decision-making process from a supervisor or a company executive because sharing an ethical dilemma with someone else helps; that person may examine your problem from another perspective.

The Need for Ethics-Based Policies

Regardless of size or the number of employees, every company needs to adopt a written policy regarding the ethical standards expected of its employees. Some of the excuses or rationalizations for not establishing an ethics policy include

- "We're too small."
- "We're just one big family."
- "It's all just common sense."

If you find yourself in court defending yourself against an illegal action, those types of excuses will not bolster your defense. The U.S. Sentencing Commission, in connection with the Sarbanes-Oxley Act *(Sarbanes-Oxley Act 2002)*, has adopted standards that limit liability if a company has implemented an effective compliance program. See *United States Sentencing Commission, Guidelines Manual, §8B2.1 (a)*. However, the standard is high. The Commission wrote, "Establishing an effective compliance and ethics program is essential for an organization seeking to mitigate its punishment (including fines and terms of probation) for a criminal offense." A key factor in determining whether an organization qualifies for a sentence reduction under the guidelines is a finding that the organization had, *at the time of the offense*, an effectual program to prevent and detect violations of law. Simply establishing a compliance program is not sufficient to gain this reduction.

Establishing a Business Ethics Policy

If your company is large and includes several large departments, you may want to consider adopting an overall corporate code and then separate ethical conduct codes for individual departments. Consider the following guidelines when establishing an ethical code of conduct:

1. What key behaviors are needed for adherence to the ethical values found in your code of ethics? Your policies should contain ethical reviews of laws, regulations, and behaviors needed for your specific business needs. A chain of retail pharmacy stores will have a much different ethics policy statement than that of a bookstore.
A pharmacy operates largely on public trust and its ability to accurately fill customer's prescriptions. An incorrectly filled prescription could have a disastrous effect on a customer's health and the business reputation of the drugstore chain.
2. Include a statement that requires employees to conform to your ethical policies. Here's an example: "The Widget Company and its employees shall conduct Widget Company business affairs honestly, fairly, impartially, and in an ethical manner. Conduct that raises questions as to Widget Company's integrity, character, or impartiality, which can damage its reputation, or creates the appearance of illegal, unethical, or improper conduct is prohibited."
3. Tell employees whom they may contact or where they can go to find the answer to their questions. You may want to designate key management staffs who have received specific instruction regarding your company's ethics policies. It is important that the same consistent message be delivered to all who inquire.
4. Make sure your legal counsel and key members of the organization's structure review the proposed policies before publication.

When a company is establishing a business ethics policy, the following are some basic, but not all-comprehensive, commonsense guidelines that include some "real-life" examples.

Use of Company Assets

A business ethics policy of this nature ensures the use of company assets for legal and proper purposes. We in loss prevention have many assets available to us, including company vehicles, computers, and surveillance equipment. From my experience, the misuse of company-owned vehicles is one of the most violated policies.

Consider the employee who uses the company truck to move his family over the weekend or the associate who underreports his monthly mileage to keep from paying extra money for personal use. Examples include a company car turned in by a terminated senior member of management that had 15,000 more miles on it than he had reported on his last monthly mileage statement. He owed the company $1,350 for personal mileage.

Another is the employee who lived and worked in an area bordered, in close proximity, by multiple states. He went home for lunch, driving the company's delivery vehicle in violation of company policy. He decided to take a 2-hour lunch, and later compensate for his time by telling his manager he had been hijacked, driven around, and eventually released by his captors. His "story" included being transported over state boundaries, which not only involved local police authorities, but also now included the Federal Bureau of Investigation. When interviewed by the FBI, he admitted to concocting the story because he was afraid to tell his manager that he had gone home for lunch and spent too much time. He was charged, convicted, and sentenced for filing a false report. Understandably, the company fired him.

Consider the delivery driver who left the store at 7:30 a.m. to start his morning deliveries to customers. His first stop was to pick up his "ride-along," an ex-employee who had been terminated a few weeks earlier. He then returned to his residence and, after waiting an additional 20 minutes, picked up his wife and two children. (If you are counting—there are now five people in a truck cab meant to carry three people.) They then drove to the children's respective schools dropping them off, then on to the grocery store where his wife shopped for 30 minutes.

After returning home, they unloaded the groceries and started for their first delivery... or so I thought. The driver and his "ride-along" drove to a deli, taking a long lunch break. At 11:30 a.m., the two started for the first delivery of the day. Later, when interviewed, the driver related that his wife wanted him to "spend more time with the family." This traveling surveillance took place in New York City. Anyone who has conducted a traveling surveillance in NYC knows this can be difficult at best.

Proprietary Information

The business ethics policy ensures that there is no unauthorized use or disclosure of confidential or proprietary information. Consider the associate who has insider knowledge of a coming acquisition and quickly purchases stock to take advantage of the expected sudden price increase.

Ethical Business Conduct

Business affairs must be conducted in an honest, fair, impartial, and ethical manner. As an example, an employee received money from a customer for creating a second, false receipt showing the customer paid more for his purchases; the employee could then bill the customer for more money. Another employee overheard the conversation and told the employee who was accepting the bribe that he would tell the manager unless he received half of the money. Both employees lost their jobs, and the customer that the contractor wanted to overcharge (a globally recognized retailer) was notified of the illegal transaction. If we had chosen not to notify the retailer, we could have lost any future business with that company.

Accurate Recordkeeping

The business ethics policy ensures that all records and documents accurately reflect transactions. This reminds me of the manager who falsified his store's inventory. He did it for several years in a row until he could no longer keep track of the inflated inventory. His management employees knew of the false inventories and failed to report the violations because they also financially benefited.

Relations with Vendors and Customers

Purchases should be impartial, honest, and fair, based on legitimate business reasons. Purchasing items or materials for your company and accepting payment from a vendor for doing so is a bribe and is illegal. Bribes in some foreign countries are tax deductible and reported as income.

Conflict of Interest

Conflict of interest is any activity that conflicts with an employee's independent exercise of judgment. (A more complete definition of a "conflict of interest" is given later in this section). I have addressed many conflicts of interest regarding misuse of employee discounts, including the manager who purchased products using his liberal employee discount, only to be used on a family member's commercial rental properties.

Then there was the manager who had a competing painting business on the side and hid it from his employer. During our store visit, it was obvious improvements made to the exterior of the building did not comply with company standards. The resulting investigation found that the manager owned a company that contracted for and performed the improvements, charging the building owner. He also stole from the company, using the materials on the project, and covered up the theft by altering his inventory. The case was further aided when the manager's ex-wife called and added critical details to the investigation.

Compliance with Laws

Antitrust laws regulate your company's relationships with its vendors, customers, and competitors. Generally, these laws prohibit agreements and activities that may have the effect of reducing competition. Equal Employment Opportunity laws prohibit discrimination against various groups, and include fair and equal treatment in hiring, compensation, promotion, training, terminations, and disciplinary action.

Trading in Securities with Material Nonpublic Information

The business ethics policy ensures that a person does not buy, sell, or trade while in possession of nonpublic information. Nonpublic information is information about a company that is not yet in general circulation.

Illegal or Improper Payments

The business ethics policy ensures employees are prohibited from giving or accepting personal payment to any person asking to do business with your company. One such example is grocery companies charging vendors for space and product placement within their stores. A store manager was charging vendors for prime space beyond what the contract called for and pocketing the money.

Safety, Health, and Environment Protection

The business ethics policy ensures that business is conducted in such a manner to protect employees, customers, and the public. Ignoring safety issues can be very damaging not only to the company's pocketbook, but also its reputation. As an example, both a store and district manager ignored employee concerns regarding a broken wheel on a piece of power equipment. Both stated that they failed to report or have the equipment fixed due to the costs involved. They had advised store employees to "just be careful." An employee was severely injured using the equipment, and consequently, the government heavily fined the company.

Relations with Government Employees

The business ethics policy ensures no business courtesies are offered to government employees. One such incident involves a company that offered contests to its customers. One particular contest offered a prize of a 2-week all-expenses paid vacation for two in the Bahamas. An official for a state university that did business with the local store filled out an entry blank and dropped it into the entry box. The official's name was picked as the contest winner. It was explained to him that he was not eligible to enter or win the contest. He immediately understood, though I am not sure his wife did. Local, state, and federal governmental entities have enacted many exacting laws governing their employees.

Reporting Potential Unethical Conduct

Employees who become aware of suspected improper activities are responsible for reporting such behavior. The Sarbanes-Oxley Act has mandated companies provide avenues for employees to report wrongdoing. Most programs consist of a telephone hotline and/or computer-based reporting programs. A third-party reporting program is suggested because studies show that employees want to report wrongdoing but prefer to contact a third party.

Political Contributions/Holding Political Office

Employees must be prohibited from contributing to any political election on behalf of the company. Of course, there is no violation when employees contribute on their own behalf. A potential conflict of interest may occur when employees run for and hold local political office. Most companies encourage their associates to be actively involved in their local communities, but there is a fine line between balancing service to the community and employee conduct.

For example, an employee who wanted to run for mayor of his community filed a potential conflict of interest form. The decision was to support the employee and outline the steps or restrictions he needed to follow to avoid a conflict of interest. He ran for public office and, as a restriction, was advised not to campaign during working hours or display any political signage on company property. The employee won the election and held political office for several years. Did this employee receive calls during work regarding municipal business? I know he did but politely told callers he would call them back after he got off work.

Train Employees as to What You Expect

Along with any ethics/conflict of interest policy, there must be a commitment to train all employees as to exactly what conduct the company expects of its associates. A review of many high-profile retailers' polices indicates that they do not include a yearly updated, classroom-style training program to ensure employees understand their ethics policies.

It is not enough to write a policy requiring employees to read and sign an acknowledgment form. It's not uncommon for an ex-employee, during an administrative hearing, to claim, "I just signed a bunch of papers." My own experience includes a manager who told me to "skip" and sign off on the ethics training program because it was just "common sense" and "boring."

To hold employees accountable for their actions, companies need to have documented training conducted by responsible trainers. Security and/or human resource departments normally conduct ethics training programs and certifications because they are the groups responsible for interpreting their company's policy and upholding decisions. The best programs are a collaborative effort between the two departments because deciding potential conflicts can be difficult and directly affect the employment and financial future of the employees. Certification training, covering all aspects of your company's business ethics, and conflict of interest policy training must be documented and placed in each attending employee's training file. During wrongful termination hearings, the ability to produce exact copies of the training program and attendance records leaves little room for speculation as to whether the employee received adequate training.

Identifying and Reporting Potential Conflicts of Interest

A definition of "conflict of interest" is any activity, financial investment, interest, association, or relationship, (including relationships with family members, relatives, friends, and social acquaintances) that conflicts with an employee's independent exercise of judgment concerning employment. Although it is not possible to identify all possible situations, reasonable business judgment should be sufficient to evaluate most situations. Managing a potential conflict of interest starts with the employee notifying an immediate supervisor that the potential for conflict exists. When employees submit a potential conflict of interest, your goal is to help guide them through the process, and come to a conclusion that is fair to all concerned.

Many conflicts can be attributed to the employment of relatives working for the same company. Many businesses place restrictions on relatives working for the same company or, at least, the same business location. A basic rule to follow is a direct relative, including sibling, parent, aunt or uncle, even a first cousin, should not work in the same work location.

At the district or higher level, a manager should never be in the position of supervising a relative either directly or indirectly. Although a manager may not be the immediate supervisor, a potential conflict exists because he or she could be involved in deciding disciplinary action or the evaluation of job performance. At all costs, an appearance of a conflict of interest must be avoided.

At store level, when a direct relative conflict is discovered and employees have already been hired, it may be possible to relocate one of the employees to a nearby store. Where relocation is not feasible, restrictions should be placed on their business conduct. An example is two brothers working in the same business unit. It would be a conflict of interest if they were allowed to ring sales or supervise each other. These restrictions would be effective as long as both relatives worked for the same company.

Another example of a direct employment conflict is a chain of department stores that allows spouses to work in the same business unit. In one such store, the executive manager directly supervises his spouse, who, in turn, directly supervises the rest of the management staff. This employment arrangement has created an air of distrust throughout the store because employees "feel" there is preferential treatment. Whether or not preferential treatment exists, there is an appearance of an impropriety.

Some additional areas of potential conflicts include

- A conflict may exist if your employee acquires ownership of stock in a company that is also a customer of yours. This would not include nominal or noncontrolling interest in holdings of stocks, bonds, or securities. It is generally accepted that a less than 10% ownership is not a conflict of interest.
- Maintaining outside employment with or providing consulting services to any competitor, vendor, or customer. Some companies limit providing consulting services for 1 year after your employment terminates. In a service-related environment, consider the employee who also works for one of your best customers. If your other customers know of this employment relationship, they may think that the contractor is getting a better price on their purchases than they are.
- Soliciting, demanding, or accepting gifts, gratuities, services, or anything of value from or to any person in conjunction with the performance of their duties is a conflict of interest. Some companies place a dollar value limit on receiving gifts ($25–$100–$200). Others allow accepting gifts and gratuities of single bottles of liquor, tickets to professional sporting events, etc.
- Authorizing, or causing another to authorize, a business transaction with a relative or any business organization with which the employee or relative is associated is a conflict. One investigation involved a store associate who called another store, telling the employee to give a customer, a relative, his employee discount. This company restricted employee discount purchases to relatives living in the same household. The product purchased was used for his cousin's commercial business, a further violation of company policy.
- Taking advantage of a business opportunity that belongs to your company, such as diverting a client to another company you work for or have a financial interest in.

Throughout my career in law enforcement and retail security, I have been a part of the resolution of thousands of potential conflicts. Following is just a small sample of some of the conflicts of interest reviewed over the years:

- From an asset protection associate, "I have accepted a position with XYZ Company and I want to know if this is all right." He had already accepted a position in security at another company and wanted to work two jobs.
- From a manager, "I want to borrow a company paint sprayer to paint my house. I'll just use it over the weekend." There were provisions for employees to rent paint sprayers at a discount.
- From a store manager, "I have a moving business on the side and want to use a company box truck this weekend." This would have been a direct violation of company policy.
- From a cash office employee, "I'm short on cash and would like to borrow money from the safe; I'll write an IOU." This employee was later prosecuted for theft.
- From a store manager, "A vendor wants to give me a $300 leather jacket. Can I accept it"? The response was "no"—unless the vendor wants to give everyone in the store a jacket. The vendor declined to spend $30,000 on leather jackets.

Creating a Conflict of Interest Reporting Program

When companies create a potential conflict of interest program, it is important for them to have a formal plan for potential new hire and existing associates to declare potential conflicts. Ideally, in the case of a potential new hire, the potential conflict of interest form is completed *before* a final offer of employment is made. This is important because it is better to identify and deal appropriately with a potential conflict before the associate starts work.

For reasons of confidentiality and continuity, the conflict-reporting program should flow upward from the individual business location directly to the corporate level. A conflict reporting form should include the following (see Figure E-1):

Potential Conflict of Interest Disclosure Form

Explain any existing or potential conflicts with XYZs' Business Ethics Policy:

Have you previously disclosed a Conflict of Interest?   ☐ Yes ☐ No   If yes, date: _____

_____   _____
Employee Signature   Date

PLEASE TYPE OR PRINT THE FOLLOWING INFORMATION:

_____   _____
Name   Position

_____   _____
Department/Store Location   Business Unit

_____   _____
Business Phone Number   Residence Phone Number

SEND THE COMPLETED DISCLOSURE FORM TO YOUR CORPORATE SECURITY DEPARTMENT
Do Not Write Below This Line

Reviewed By _____   ☐ Approved   ☐ With Controls
                          Name/Date   ☐ Without Controls   ☐ Not Approved

Controls:_____
_____
_____
_____

Management Notice _____   Corporate Approval _____
                          Initials/Date   Initials/Date

Approved Copy
To Personnel File _____   Copy To Employee _____
                          Initials/Date   Initials/Date

FIGURE E-1 A sample conflict reporting form used by employees to report potential conflicts.

- An area to explain any existing potential conflicts;
- Whether or not the employee has disclosed a previous conflict;
- The employee's signature;
- Store location, or unit number, and telephone contact numbers;
- Name of the corporate reviewer;
- Whether or not it was approved
- Controls or restrictions (if any) that have been put into place.

This form is then sent to the district manager or unit manager, who writes the actual response in letter form (see Figures E-2 and E-3) and then counsels the affected employee making sure the employee understands the company's position. The corporate response to the manager should include

Business Ethics Disclosure Response

To: (District Manager)   *District:* (#) 8650

Date. 2/15/06

Employee: **John Jones**   *Position:* **Store Manager**   *Location:* 123 Scottsdale, AZ

Conflict: **My Father, Jack Jones, is the Store Manager at 131 location.**

Disposition:

☐ Approved

☒ **Approved with Controls**

☐ Not Approved

Please generate a letter to the employee using the checked criteria:

☐ May not ring sales to the account.

☒ **May not discuss confidential or proprietary information with their relative.**

☐ May not set pricing for the account. Pricing must be set by the District Manager or the Sales Representative.

☒ **May not ring sales to each other.**

☐ May not work for relative/contractor.

☒ **Cannot hold a direct supervisory position over their relative.**

☒ **May not work in the same store as their relative.**

☐ Other:

Have the employee sign and date the letter and return a copy to Corporate Loss Prevention Department. Retain a copy for your Conflict of Interest records.

Additional Notes: (Further clarification of the checked criteria may be added here).

Curtis Baillie
Title
Contact Numbers

FIGURE E-2 The corporate response.

Company Letterhead

February 18, 2007

Mr. John Jones
Store Manager
Store #123

On February 15, 2007, you declared a potential conflict of interest in that your Father, Jack Jones, also works for the XYZ Company as a Store Manager at the 131 location. As a result of that disclosure, the XYZ Company has determined that a potential conflict of interest does exist. As a result of the conflict, the following guidelines or restrictions are to be followed during your employment at XYZ Company:

1. You may not ring sales to each other.

2. You are not to discuss confidential or proprietary information with your Father regarding your respective business units.

3. You, or your Father cannot hold a supervisory position over each other.

4. You cannot work in the same store location as your Father.

You are required to notify XYZ Company if at any time there is a change regarding your declared potential conflict of interest, or if a new potential conflict exists. Please contact me if you have any questions regarding this determination.

Please sign this letter and return to me, no later than February 23, 2007. Please contact me immediately if you have any questions regarding this letter

_____   _____ Date: _____
John Doe   John Jones
District Manager   Store Manager, Location 123
Contact Information

FIGURE E-3 A sample letter, written by the district or unit manager, instructing the employee on the proper conduct he is expected to follow. It is important that both the manager and the employee sign and date the letter. Both retain copies, and the original is forwarded to the corporate head office.

- A description of the conflict;
- Disposition;
- Control or restrictions;
- Any additional notations.

Figure E-4 shows a flow chart of the entire process.

As an instrument of measurement, your conflict of interest reporting program should be placed on your company's internal audit program. Many times, auditors have discovered an

**Conflict of Interest Disclosure
Flow Chart**

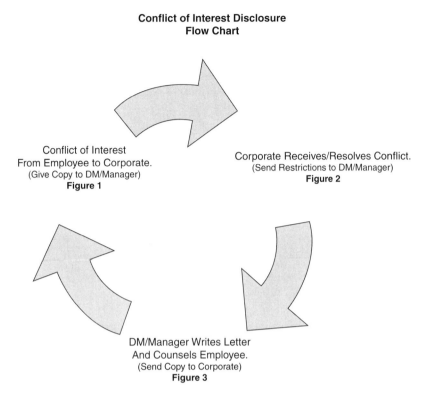

Conflict of Interest
From Employee to Corporate.
(Give Copy to DM/Manager)
Figure 1

Corporate Receives/Resolves Conflict.
(Send Restrictions to DM/Manager)
Figure 2

DM/Manager Writes Letter
And Counsels Employee.
(Send Copy to Corporate)
Figure 3

FIGURE E-4 A flow chart showing the path the reporting of a potential conflict takes. The flow chart shows the disclosure reporting form is sent directly to the corporate entity responsible for responding to conflicts of interest. Potential conflict forms sent to the district level may not be forwarded to corporate in a timely manner. It is important to respond promptly to all potential conflicts because the inquiring associate may consider a lack of response to be permission to continue with the behavior.

old, unresolved conflict reporting form. In many instances, the employee was continuing with the conflicting behavior because there was a lack of response to his declaration of potential conflict. In such cases, it is the responsibility of the auditor to initiate the conflict reporting process. Violations of the company's conflict of interest program are noted on the audit, resulting in points lost. Applying the measurement process at the corporate, district, and store level and tying it directly to bonus potential will find higher compliance to your conflict of interest program. Remember to "Inspect what you expect" or my all-time favorite, "You can expect what you inspect."

> *"Always do right. This will gratify some people and astonish the rest."*
> —Mark Twain

Evidence

CAS, JHC

The proper methods of collecting, preserving, and tracking its possessor and location are essential to assure that any evidence obtained will meet the legal requirements for use in a criminal prosecution and satisfy any standards set in civil and/or administrative hearings.

Let's define "evidence": That which furnishes or tends to furnish proof, including all the means by which any alleged matter of fact, the truth of which is submitted to investigation, is established or disproved. There are many types of evidence, but those which concern loss prevention are primarily (a) circumstantial evidence, (b) documentary evidence, (c) direct evidence, (d) prima facie evidence, and (e) physical evidence. In some cases, one piece of evidence may fit more than one description. For example, circumstantial evidence is that which consists of reasoning from facts which are known or proven to establish such as are conjectured to exist. A bank is robbed of a dye-pack of money, and Tom is found to be covered in dye-pack ink and possess ink-stained currency. These facts would establish circumstantial evidence that Tom robbed the bank, although no one actually saw him do so. Documentary evidence is that established by written documents. Direct evidence directly proves a fact, without an interference or presumption, and which in itself, if true, conclusively proves that fact. Prima facie evidence is evidence which is good and sufficient on its face and sufficient to establish a given fact, which if not rebutted or contradicted, will remain sufficient. Physical evidence is furnished by things, which can be viewed or inspected, as distinguished from a description of an item or event such as furnished by testimonial evidence from a witness.

Let's describe a scenario which further explains these types of evidence. Bill, a cashier at a grocery store, is suspected of stealing money from the till. A shopper presents him with a marked bill, and several hours later, when Bill is interviewed, the marked bill is found in his pocket. While these facts are strong circumstantial evidence (lacking a confession) that Bill took the money, it is possible he obtained the marked bill in a legitimate manner. If the register journal tape shows Bill did not record the sale in question, this is documentary evidence further pointing to his guilt. A CCTV tape showing Bill putting the bill tendered by the shopper in his pocket would be both documentary and direct evidence of his guilt. The marked bill itself would be physical evidence, and the testimony of the shopper and the CCTV operator who personally observed what was portrayed on the tape would constitute direct (testimonial) evidence.

In a shoplifting case where the suspect conceals the merchandise in the store, a state statute that the concealment of unpaid-for goods was prima facie evidence of the intent to steal would establish that intent.

In all cases, the collection of evidence, whether documentary or physical, should be carefully documented and the evidence itself marked (or enclosed in a sealed and marked container) showing the date, time, manner, and name of the person who collected the evidence. Normally, this information will be contained on what is called an "evidence tag."

The proper storage of the evidence, once collected, is also important. Evidence should be stored in a locked cabinet or room with strictly restricted access. Evidence procedures are required to establish the "chain of custody" and eventual admissibility of the evidence. It is essential to maintain this chain of custody that each person handling the evidence after collection be identified and that the evidence is stored in such a manner as to prevent tampering or contamination.

Some jurisdictions allow photographs in lieu of physical evidence. This is of major importance to retail organizations because it does not require that merchandise recovered in an apprehension be taken off the selling floor and stored for long periods of time. It is also most helpful when dealing with evidence subject to spoilage, such a fresh meats. When photographs are submitted with police reports in lieu of the actual evidence, a duplicate set of photographs should be retained in the possession of the store.

The term "inadmissible evidence" is an oxymoron because information or items that are inadmissible are not evidence. Witnesses often make the mistake of attempting to testify to information that is legally not allowed. Inadmissible testimony includes opinions (unless the witness has been accepted as an expert witness), conclusions, and hearsay (what someone other than the defendant said). Witnesses may testify about what they saw, heard, and did, but not about their opinion or conclusion about the admissible evidence. Witnesses may only testify to facts that they know or believe to be true. Hearsay is not allowed as evidence because the court, the jury, and the defendant are entitled to hear testimony directly from the people who said it so that they can evaluate the credibility, subject them to cross-examination, and evaluate the information and its source for themselves.

For purposes of assuring the "chain of custody" is not only properly maintained but adequately documented, we suggest a procedure based on the use of property tags and a log book.

The evidence log should be divided into eleven columns, set up as indicated:

Column #1: Designates the log number and its corresponding page number in the log. Foe example, the first case logged on Page 1 would be shown as 1-1; the second case logged would be 1-2, etc. The individual log numbers should also appear on the property tag.
Column #2: Subject's name, date of birth (DOB), date of arrest (DOA), charge, case #, arresting agent's # or ID.
Column #3: Merchandise department number.
Column #4: Merchandise class number (if applicable).
Column #5: Merchandise season (if applicable).
Column #6: Merchandise style—SKU if applicable.
Column #7: Merchandise color.
Column #8: Description of item (blouse, pants, etc.).
Column #9: Date merchandise placed into evidence—or returned to evidence from court.
Column #10: Date merchandise is removed from evidence for court or other reason, such as returned to stock (RTS) or returned to customer (RTC).
Column #11: Reason the merchandise is removed from evidence, e.g., court, RTS, RTC. In cases involving identical items of merchandise each separate item should be listed.

Another purpose of the evidence log book is to maintain control of merchandise. If the process is correctly done, seasonal inventory can be taken directly from the evidence Log without the necessity to disturb the actual evidence. After inventory, an inventory sticker should be placed on the property tag.

The evidence log should be reconciled on a periodic basis (e.g., monthly, quarterly, etc.) and a record of the date of such reconciliation noted.

After the evidence is either boxed or bagged (in a box or bag appropriate to the evidence to be contained therein), the container should then be sealed in a manner which will provide evidence of any attempt or successful opening of the container. A completed property tag (described later and shown as Figure F-10 under "Forms") should be attached securely to the evidence or the box/bag containing the evidence. The property tag must be filled out completely so the evidence can be easily retrieved from the evidence room, chain of custody identified, and merchandise inventoried accurately:

1. The "property number" on the tag should correspond to the number used in the evidence log book.
2. The "description of the property" need only be a general description, since the specific items are listed in the evidence log book.
3. All movement of the evidence must be indicated on the property tag (e.g., to and from court, returned to stock, returned to customer, etc.)

When the merchandise is returned to stock, the property tag should be signed by the department manager, staff assistant, or an associate. The property tag should be attached to the security/loss prevention/arrest report and filed.

Exception Reporting Software

Robert L. DiLonardo

A retail chain the size of Wal-Mart processes billions of point-of-sale (POS) transactions per year. Although the vast majority of these transactions are correct, complete, and honest, a growing number are dishonest—resulting in either monetary or merchandise losses. POS exception reporting software helps to identify and reduce a wide range of retail fraud perpetrated around the multitude of point-of-sale transactions, such as cash, credit and debit card sales, a "no sale," a merchandise return for a refund, a gift certificate purchase, or a merchandise exchange. Capitalizing on the tremendous power and speed of computers, retail loss prevention executives now use sophisticated database management software to spot transaction patterns that indicate the possibility of theft, collusion, and fraud.

In the retail environment, the components of transaction data can come from several different databases. The point-of sale-system provides the information on items purchased. Credit or debit card numbers are obtained through an interface with the credit card processing network. The human resources department database provides information on employees identified through their employee number entered at the time of a transaction.

All high-quality exception reporting software packages include reporting tools designed to identify and isolate unusual conditions in the mountain of operational data compiled daily. Instead of manually pouring over mounds of computer reports, fraud investigators use the computer to "drill down" into this data by looking at exceptions highlighted through preselected parameters. For example, a drill-down for no sale transactions might include a list of those employees who have exceeded a predetermined number of no sale transactions in a given time period. From there, the investigator can focus on a short list of employees with the most no sales and obtain more details on the specific transactions, as well as the surrounding transactions. Perhaps all the no sale transactions for a specific employee took place before store opening or after store closing? This pattern may be indicative of something dishonest, so the investigator may dig deeper. If enough evidence is obtained, the employee could be interviewed in an effort to obtain an admission of guilt.

These admissions can add up to hundreds of thousands of dollars in identified losses. More importantly, publicizing the active use of the software becomes a powerful deterrent to potentially dishonest employees. As the investigators become more and more proficient with the software, they are able to solve a much higher volume of cases in a shorter time period. Since the exception reports can be accessed the day after a transaction takes place, dishonesty can be discovered much more quickly, reducing the retailers' exposure to losses.

How Exception Reporting Technology Works

Exception reporting systems require three basic components. The heart of the system is complex database management software that scans data directly from the retailer's sales transaction database, compares transactions to predetermined "norms," and highlights and reports the unusual entries (exceptions). The reports can be sorted in a wide range of formats, such as by time and date, by store, by employee number, by transaction type, or by POS terminal. Output can be grouped by district or region. A dedicated server usually absorbs and warehouses the raw data collected from the POS in appropriate databases. Finally, investigators use workstation hardware, like a PC, laptop, or handheld device, to access "canned" or custom-designed reports that focus on predetermined areas of interest.

Depending on its memory capacity, the server archives the data long enough for the investigators to gather sufficient evidence and attempt to "crack" the cases. Then new data replace the old, and the cycle repeats itself. This may sound simple, but the interfacing between the databases is the most complex development task in the system implementation. The exception reporting software must tap into this database at its lowest level (the transaction) without compromising its integrity. This element of the installation can be difficult and most often requires a customized software application and a tremendous amount of cooperation among the computer professionals of both the retailer and the software system integrator.

The Inclusion of Digital Video Surveillance

Recent technological advances in the computer, software, data communication, and video recording industries have given retailers the ability to "re-*view*" what has occurred on the sales floor—good and bad—virtually as soon as it happens. POS exception monitoring techniques, coupled with digital video management systems, allows investigators to find an anomalous circumstance, and then retrieve a video clip with the matching visual. It is now possible for these clips to be transmitted via email to someone who can take immediate action. This convergence of data, video, and instantaneous communications has added a geometric improvement in productivity in all facets of retail transaction analysis.

Reference

DiLonardo, R. L. (1997). 'Drilling down' for dollars. *Security Technology & Design Magazine*. October.

Executive Protection

CAS, JHC

Company loss prevention departments are sometimes called upon to provide executive protection for the company chairman or CEO. These requests often involve conducting a security survey of the executive's residence and making recommendations for alarm systems and other protective strategies, including but not limited to the executive's children's fingerprints, etc. Less frequently, but occasionally, these executive protection requests involve the actual physical protection of the individual from a perceived or actual threat to his life.

The request for a survey of the executive's residence follows the ordinary pattern for such surveys and does not require much discussion here. Obviously, the specifics of the executive's family (spouse, children, pets, etc.) and their lifestyle must be taken into consideration, as well as the location of the home itself (isolated, rural, city, single family, condo, apartment, etc.) as well as "second homes." Alarm specifications must be designed to provide adequate protection yet minimal (if any) interference with normal family activities. Should a given LP department prefer, the actual survey can be outsourced to a security management consultant who has a history of providing this service.

It should be parenthetically noted here we feel that part of LP's responsibilities is also to provide senior company executives with a briefing (or written memo) on some common-sense precautions to take when traveling, particularly overseas. We further suggest that the number of executives traveling on the same plane at the same time be restricted; the number allowed should take into account both the security as well as the business needs of the enterprise.

When the protection of the individual from physical harm is at stake, LP's job becomes more complex and deserving of a considerable amount of planning and coordination.

The first consideration needs to be an analysis of the threat: Is the threat of harm simply a potential one, or has an actual threat been received? What is the source of the threat? What is the specific threat? What is the credibility of the source? What will be the exposure of the target of the threat? What can be done to minimize this exposure? These and many other like questions must be asked and answered before a plan of protection can be established.

Another important question that needs to be answered is whether the police will be notified. If so, what will their role be in protecting the principal? Should the protection be outsourced to a professional agency specializing in "bodyguard" services?

A vital question is that of whether the protective personnel will be armed. If the decision is in the affirmative, how will these personnel be selected? Are they properly and adequately trained? Does their possession of weapons meet all legal requirements? What will the rules of engagement be? In what venue will they be operating? These and many more questions must be considered.

Finally, the principal's wishes regarding his protection must at least be considered and, if possible, without compromising security, complied with.

Of importance is the venue where the protection will be required. A private event or venue is more easily protected than a public one. Pre-event inspection of the venue is essential. Following are some of the items which must be considered:

- Have avenues of ingress and egress been considered?
- What length of time will the principal be at the event?
- How will he arrive there?
- Is the arrival time flexible?
- Can attendees be screened (identified) before entry?
  - ○ Will the principal be highly exposed (e.g., speaking from a podium or from a stage)?
- Does the event location (if indoors) have a balcony?
- What is the length of the principal's stay at the event?
- Where can protective personnel be discreetly, yet strategically, located?
- Are photographs of the individual(s) posing the risk available?

The subject of physical executive protection is a complex one; hence, those with the proper training to accomplish it discreetly but adequately must deal with it so as not to create more of a problem then they are there to solve.

The subject of executive protection is included in this book not to provide a text on how it should be accomplished. Rather, it's to point out the need for a careful analysis of any threat and the depth of the details which must go into the planning for meeting the threat, as well as the suggestion that outsourcing this important function should be considered.

Expert Witnesses

CAS, JHC

An expert witness is a litigation consultant who has a recognized technical expertise on any given activity. There are experts on tires and how and why they fail at high speeds, experts on beer kegs and why they explode, experts on fingerprints and DNA, experts on insects which cause damage to crops, experts on the origin of fires, etc. Some experts teach, consult, write, guide management in corporate direction, and some choose to serve the legal community and courts as a witness.

The expert witness conducts an objective and impartial analysis of the scene, conditions, circumstances, or event; evaluates the merits of each side of a dispute within his area of expertise; and testifies as to his opinion regarding his findings. His expert opinion is unique in our judicial system. Only a court-recognized expert may offer an opinion. All other witnesses, by far the bulk of all testimony, are limited to factual testimony and are denied the privilege of expressing any opinions.

In the retail loss prevention and security industry, expert witnesses are called upon in litigation against retailers involving such areas of expertise as, but not necessarily limited to, the following:

- Use of force by LP agents;
- Adequacy of training of LP agents;
- Adequacy of the background screening of LP applicants;
- Adequacy of supervision and oversight of LP employees;

- Adequacy of organizational policy and procedures;
- Standard of care within the LP industry;
- Custom and practice within the LP industry;
- False arrests and false imprisonment;
- Acceptable standards for interviewing and interrogation and legitimacy of resultant confessions.

Loss prevention contacts with the public and employee population, which result in accusations of dishonesty or some other form of misconduct, have the potential of being litigated, and invariably the store (a.k.a. the defendant) and the "injured party" (customer or former employee; a.k.a. the plaintiff) will, more often than not, obtain the consulting services of an expert witness. Occasionally, the store may choose to designate one of its own loss prevention executives as its witness, but we do not advise this. Remember, the "expert" is expected to conduct an objective assessment of the matter; the question that must arise in the jurors' minds is "How much credence can I place in this expert's opinion when he's part of the organization being sued?" Without doubt, a corporate LP executive could easily qualify as an expert and could be helpful to either side of a dispute, but not in a legal dispute in which one party pays his salary. In the great majority of retail litigation where an expert is utilized, the expert is selected by the attorney (sometimes in conjunction with the insurance carrier) for whom he will testify.

Extortion

CAS, JHC

How would you respond if your store received a letter like the one in Figure E-5?

This letter received by one of your author's stores demanded $25,000 and threatened to blow up the store if the demand was not met.

Such letters are not common, but also are not unheard of, particularly in the case of larger stores. On occasion the threat, coupled with a demand, may be by phone. Irrespective of the means of delivery, threats to do harm unless certain conditions are met, "extortion," should be reported to the police or the Federal Bureau of Investigation, and they should provide the leadership in dealing with this type of crime.

In this instance, both the auto center and the location designated for depositing the $25,000 were placed under surveillance by teams composed of the police and store security personnel. A "bait bag" not containing actual money was left where directed. Fortunately, neither the dynamite-loaded van nor anyone seeking to retrieve the $25,000 ever showed up. After over 48 hours of continuous surveillance, the effort was discontinued; however, periodic checks of the auto center were maintained for the next several days with negative results.

Not all extortion threats arrive by letter. Often the threat is received over the phone. The conversation flows along this line: "Hello. I've got a bomb hidden in your store, and if you don't give me $25,000, I'll set it off. Don't call the police—I can see your store and I'll know if you call them and then I'll set off the bomb. Place $25,000 in small, unmarked bills in a shopping bag and place the bag in the dumpster outside your dock. I'm watching, so I'll know if you call the cops and then BOOM! Place the bag in the dumpster at exactly 6:00 tonight. You won't get another warning."

Although the bulk of such calls are pranks, you cannot afford to take chances, so you should treat them as real.

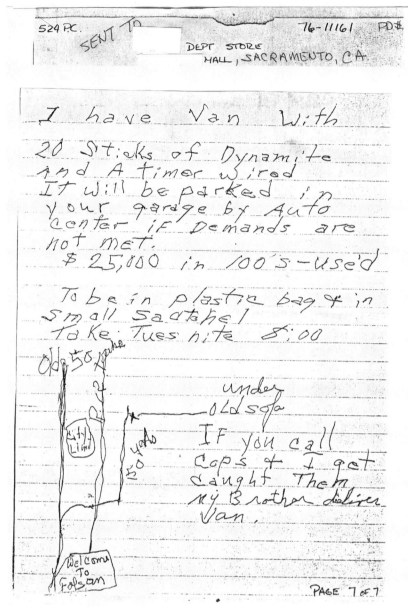

FIGURE E-5 An example of an actual extortion note received at a store in California.

We strongly suggest that, upon the receipt of any communication regarding an extortion attempt, the local police be immediately contacted and their suggestions followed to the letter.

Fences and Fencing

CAS, JHC

The word "fence" or "fencing" usually conjures up the image of the rather typical 7-foot chain-link fence with an angled top extension of barbed wire or razor ribbon, which extends the total height another foot, and that barrier commonly surrounds and defines the perimeter of a given property. Its function is clear and necessary, i.e., to keep unwanted people out or off the property or to keep people inside and on the property.

In the retail industry, this type of fence or various modifications thereof are commonly associated with distribution centers and warehouse complexes. These facilities should be so enclosed, and the security or loss prevention staff should ensure the integrity of the fence is intact. Breaches of integrity include

- Holes or cuts which would allow passage through the barrier
- Trees or other elevated objects or structures which would facilitate scaling the barrier
- Vegetation at the base of the fence which could obscure holes or openings as well as crawl areas, allowing penetration into the property by slipping under the fence

Frequent inspections will reveal these breaches, resulting in the problem's correction or repair.

But there's another kind of "fencing" in retail which isn't widely known or used to advantage, and that's the use of "chicken wire" fencing material, which can be productively used behind the scenes in dock and stock areas within the store itself.

There are three common applications:

1. To prevent "horizontal traveling" behind the selling floor
2. To protect small high-theft/high-shrinkage merchandise in stock areas
3. To discourage entry into areas requiring special protection, including such property or equipment as POS terminals held in reserve

Prevent "Horizontal Traveling" Behind the Selling Floor

Many stores are laid out with the center space of the store dedicated to the public display and sales of merchandise (selling floor), and the stock areas are behind the sales area. Picture if you will a square building with an outer perimeter wall and then a second interior perimeter wall.

That space between the two walls is where the stockrooms are located, as well as restrooms, break rooms, and offices. The large empty square in the center is the selling floor. This imaginary building's exterior perimeter has one door in front (for the public), one door in the back for shipping and receiving, and two side doors for emergency exits.

The inner wall has numerous doors and openings, most of which lead into the stock area for the goods displayed in that area of the building. In a sporting goods store, the stock area for fishing rods and tackle is accessed through a door close to where that kind of merchandise is displayed and sold. Further down the store is the place where archery goods, bows and arrows, and targets are offered for sale, with reserve stock accessible through a door in that area. So-called horizontal travel is the condition in which a thief (employee or customer) can carry an item or goods from the fishing department and then enter the stock area of that department and come out in the archery department a good distance away with no merchandise in sight. The employee in the fishing department lost sight of the customer while his back was turned and that customer reappears elsewhere and no one is the wiser.

Inexpensive pinewood-framed gates of chicken wire erected between given stock areas, secured with padlocks, preclude this kind of behind-the-scenes movement and deny or impede employees from roaming through stock areas in which they have no business.

Prevent "Vertical Traveling"

In a multistory store, traditional behind-the-scene stairwells (often in corners of the store, which also serve as fire exits), up and down (vertical) travel is discouraged by fences (here, more typically chainlink instead of chicken wire because damaged chicken wire doesn't bother the crook quietly fleeing downstairs to hit the street exit) and fence gates alarmed with audible alarms. Since, as mentioned, these stairwells are often fire exits, we must be sure that the fence gates permit emergency exit but not without a short (15-second) delay, permitted by fire codes, and audible notification of the breach. Not only do we want to restrict this kind of travel down to the street exit (unless an emergency, of course), we don't want bad guys disappearing into stairwells and traveling up only to cross the store and descend on the other side. Preferably, doors leading from stairwells into the store cannot be opened from the stairwell side—only from the store's interior, the result of which is that, once in the stairwell, a person can exit only onto the roof or onto the street or outside. If that strategy is adopted, signage on each door explaining this emergency exit and its consequences is required.

Protect Small High-Theft/High-Shrinkage Merchandise in Stock Areas

Inexpensive "cages" constructed of 1-inch pine board and chicken wire can be effectively used to control high-shrink items in stock rooms, merchandise which typically is held in reserve on open shelving. Clearly, this limits access and reduces theft by stockroom prowlers and employees. Chicken wire can easily be defeated or cut, but the protective power in such cages (and barriers) is the evidence of the entry or breach is so apparent that it serves as a good deterrent.

Discourage Entry into Areas Requiring Special Protection, Including Such Property or Equipment as POS Terminals Held in Reserve

Your authors have seen areas within stores which are indeed fenced off with regular cyclone fencing, and appropriately so. In cases in which extremely high value merchandise is caged, the "ceiling" of such a cage may also be covered with cyclone fencing, but typically such internal fencing doesn't go to the ceiling, nor is it topped with barbed wire. And such protective configurations have been breached by employees. With the erection of but a 2-foot chicken wire "fence" on top of the cyclone fence, breaches can be averted because of the predictable tell-tale evidence of crushed or flattened chicken wire.

Scissors Gates

Scissors gates constitute a form of "fence" or barrier which has application in both exterior and interior situations. Small storefront retailers can pull this form of barricade across the front of their front windows and door to prevent entry or looting through windows that have been smashed in. These collapsible gates don't guarantee total security; they are vulnerable to those burglars who use a vehicle to pull the gates off with a heavy chain. Some stores, depending on this configuration, opt to install the gates on the interior side of the windows, which precludes them, normally, from being ripped off by a vehicle. For example, in a fashion department store, a large single window in an alcove containing the men's suit department had a series of window smashes and many expensive suites removed. An exterior scissors gate was considered objectionable in terms of its appearance. Instead, the store opted to install the gate on the inside, and when the store was open to the public, the gates were concealed behind attractive drapes.

Fire and Fire Prevention

CAS, JHC

For those stores fortunate enough to have a security or loss prevention department, their personnel will normally be the first responders to a fire and are usually given the responsibility for fire prevention. For smaller stores, these duties fall to either the owner, manager, or in some cases, whoever happens to be on duty. For these reasons, it is vital that all employees have some understanding and knowledge of fire prevention and the safe and correct response to an actual fire.

It can be reasonably said that a fire, regardless of how small it may be, is perhaps the most devastating event that can occur to a retailer. Why is a fire so devastating? The answer is the cause of all the ancillary things that accompany a fire. The retailer is concerned not only with items that may be destroyed or damaged by the actual blaze, but also the resultant damage to merchandise from water and from smoke, in addition to the damage to the fixtures, displays, carpeting, walls, and structural or physical damage to the property itself. The damages just described do not even address the lost business from having to close the store for renovations and repairs.

For these and other reasons (an increase in insurance premiums, for example), fire *prevention* becomes an essential part of retail loss prevention. Additionally, for those fires that do occur from unpreventable causes, knowledge of ways to minimize fire damage also becomes important.

Since fire prevention is so important, it is helpful to know something about the technology of fire. Just what is fire?

Fire Technology

A. The intent of this section is to provide a basic working knowledge of the technology of fire, which will be required when outside help is not available. It is possible to be in a situation (e.g., in the case of either a major earthquake or riot) in which municipal fire protection would not be available, and it would be entirely up to the store to handle the firefighting either until it was extinguished or it posed no threat to personnel safety.

B. Fire results principally from the combination of combustible materials with oxygen and the presence of heat. In order for a successful fire to develop, it is necessary that the chemical union resulting be the combination of circumstances whereby heat, fuel, and oxygen are united under conditions which produce combustion.

 1. It is not possible to maintain combustion if you remove any one of the three required elements of heat, fuel, or oxygen.

 2. The principal hazard to control is the ignition or energy source due to the fact that fuel and oxygen are present throughout all the store in various forms.

C. Fire-suppression methods commonly employ a combination of removal of oxygen and lowering of ignition temperature. Removal of fuel seldom is practical or even feasible.

 1. The most common method of fire suppression is to lower the ignition temperature of the fuel with large quantities of water. Once the fuel temperature is below an ignition or flash point, there will no longer be an active fire.

 2. The normal atmospheric oxygen content is in the range of 21%. In a fire situation, once the oxygen content in the surrounding atmosphere drops below 15%, the quantity of oxygen available will no longer support combustion.

 3. Under normal extinguishment when large quantities of water are used, the portion which is converted to steam generally displaces a portion of the oxygen in the surrounding atmosphere and, consequently, has a secondary resultant of not only lowering the fuel temperature but also displacing the available oxygen.

    4. The principal means of operation of the carbon dioxide fire extinguisher is to displace the oxygen with carbon dioxide gas and, consequently, the surrounding atmosphere will no longer support combustion. The one principal disadvantage is frequently the fuel continues to be at a temperature above the flash or flame point and will reignite when oxygen becomes available.

D. The control of availability of oxygen is of primary importance as an initial action in fire suppression. Closing all windows and doors and isolating the fire to a confined space are of primary importance. A normal fire can consume the oxygen in a confined space, and oxidation or burning will cease.

    1. When you are extinguishing a flame or fire in a confined area, it is vital to attempt to contain the enclosed area, rather than to open doors and windows during the process of fire suppression.

    2. When windows and doors are opened or left open during a fire situation, large quantities of oxygen are being made available, and necessary ventilation for complete combustion is provided.

    3. It is important to note that the rate of flame spread, intensity of flame buildup, and concentration are directly related to the availability of oxygen.

E. The ignition temperatures of ordinary combustible materials lie between 400 and 1,100 degrees Fahrenheit.

F. Most combustible materials such as wood and textiles are broken down by heat to form combustible gases. The flame is the burning gas, and for the most part, the actual combustion is that of the gases produced rather than the wood or textile items. Gases are often produced in fires, under conditions in which they do not completely burn but accumulate in the building and flash or explode later when there is an additional supply of air with the normal quantity of oxygen supplied to the fire area.

G. Heat is transferred from one material to another by one or more of three methods: (1) conduction, (2) radiation, or (3) convection.

    1. *Conduction* is the transfer of heat from one body to another by actual contact.

        a. A steam pipe passing through wood construction transfers its heat to the wood by actual contact or conduction.

        b. The amount of heat transferred by conduction depends on the conductivity of material through which the heat is passing. Conductivity varies greatly in different materials.

        c. Wood and solid asbestos have about the same heat conductivity. Fibrous material such as cotton, wood, and mineral wood have heat conductivity a quarter to one-third that of solid wood. Concrete and brickwork have a heat conductivity four to six times that of wood. Iron has a conductivity about 300 times greater than wood; and aluminum, about 12,000 times greater.

    2. Heat transfer by *radiation* is transferred from one body to another by heat rays through intervening space, much the same as light is transferred by light rays. The heat from a steam pipe mentioned in the previous example can be transferred to some extent to the wood construction by radiation, even though there is a space between the two.

        a. Radiated heat is not absorbed by the air to any extent. Like light, it travels through a space until it encounters a solid object where it is absorbed and proceeds through the object by conduction.

        b. Like light, radiated heat is reflected from bright surfaces and will in turn pass through glass, but the absorption for a dull surface is relatively a high factor.

    3. *Convection* heat transfer is by a circulating medium—either a gas or a liquid. Thus, heat generated in a stove is distributed throughout a room mostly by heating the air by conduction and, through circulation, heats distant objects in the room by convection.

        a. Heated air expands and rises, and for this reason heat transfer by convection is mostly in an upward direction.

        b. Since heat transfer by convection is most typically in an upward direction, it is of paramount importance to protect vertical openings between floors such as keeping elevator shafts closed as well as enclosed stairways closed from the floor to prevent heat transfer and communication between levels.

    c. Because heat transfer by convection is in an upward direction, all sprinkler heads are located next to the ceiling; they are always actuated by convection heat transfer.

    d. The area immediately below the radiation source is normally heated by radiation only and not by convection or conduction.

Fire Prevention

"An ounce of prevention is worth a pound of cure" is certainly an axiom worth following when it comes to fire prevention.

What are some steps that should be routinely taken to prevent avoidable fires? We strongly suggest that the following items be on a checklist for periodic (at least monthly) inspection:

- Check the overuse or improper use of extension cords, paying particular attention to the gauge of the wire to be certain it is adequate for the load. Inspect for worn insulation. Never place cords on nails or under carpeting. All electrical items should be UL approved.
- Watch for hot (temperature) lights, particularly if near inflammable materials.
- Dispose of all trash on a regular basis; use proper containers.
- Avoid "do it yourself" electrical repairs.
- Inspect all fire extinguishers at least annually for condition and currency (proper charge levels).
- Avoid too many appliances, lights, etc. on a circuit or extension cord.
- Avoid blocking sprinkler heads with stock.
- Clearly mark locations of fire extinguishers and hoses.
- Clearly sign emergency exits.
- Inspect monthly to assure that the sprinkler system control valve is fully open. Some authorities recommend these valves be chained and locked in the open position; if this is done, hang a small sign on the chain reading "OPEN." This is fine as long as a key is quickly available to enable the valve to be closed when necessary.
- Never block exit corridors, fire exits, or fire equipment.
- Paints, solvents, spray adhesives, etc., should be tightly sealed or capped while not in use and stored in proper containers. Almost every type of aerosol dispenser is extremely flammable and should be kept away from heat, sparks, and flames.
- Conduct periodic fire drills.

In the Event of a Fire

Upon detecting a fire or odor of smoke, or receiving a report of the same:

A. IT IS ABSOLUTELY ESSENTIAL THAT ALL FIRES, HOWEVER SMALL, MUST BE IMMEDIATELY REPORTED TO THE FIRE DEPARTMENT. THERE ARE NO EXCEPTIONS TO THIS RULE.

B. Attempt to put out the fire if it can be safely done. Never try to fight electrical fires.

C. When calling the fire department, do the following:

    1. Give your exact location (name of store, street address, and town).

    2. Tell what is burning.

    3. Do not hang up until told to do so.

If store is located in a mall, notify the mall office.

If so equipped, make the following announcement over the public address system: "May I have your attention, please. Because of municipal codes, we are required at this time to conduct a fire drill. Your cooperation is required. Please proceed quickly, but calmly, to the nearest customer exit. The store will resume normal operations in a few minutes at the end of the drill."

If the store has elevators, a paramount priority should be evacuating individuals trapped in elevators.

Classification of Fires and How to Extinguish Them

A. All types of fuels have been classified into four general categories or fire classes to determine the best method of extinguishment.

B. This classification system is the principal guide in selecting the portable fire extinguisher to be used on a fire.

    1. Class "A" fires are those in ordinary combustibles such as paper, wood, and textiles.

       a. Class "A" fires are normally extinguished by cooling.

       b. The normal extinguishing agent is water or an extinguisher which is filled with a water-based mixture.

    2. Class "B" fires are in flammable liquids, greases, and other viscous materials.

       a. For extinguishment, it is necessary to blanket or smother the surface of the liquid.

       b. The principal method of extinguishment must be excluding oxygen from the burning surface.

       c. The use of water in this type of fire is unsatisfactory because it does not blanket the surface, and it further complicates the situation by either floating or spreading the burning liquid.

    3. Class "C" fire is one in "live" electrical equipment. A class "C" fire is commonly referred to as an "electrical fire."

       a. The principal means of extinguishment must be the utilization of a nonconducting extinguishing medium.

       b. The principal objective of extinguishment must be to cool or to remove or displace oxygen from the burning area, or both of these.

       c. De-energizing the subject electrical equipment is paramount for successful suppression of the fire.

       d. When a fire extinguisher is selected for an electrical fire, it must be of the approved type; to utilize an extinguisher with water or other electrically conductive material could prove fatal to the individual attempting to control the fire.

    4. In Class "D," magnesium, potassium, powdered aluminum, zinc, sodium, titanium, and zirconium are all in the combustible metal category and require careful fire attack with special extinguishers; in most cases water will accelerate the oxidizing or combustion process.

Portable and Manual Fire-Suppression Equipment

A. General Information

    1. At their start, most fires are relatively small and can be easily handled. Because of this, it is essential that you be completely familiar with the locations and use of portable fire extinguishers.

    2. Fire is usually a chemical action between fuel and oxygen, producing light and heat. The ignition temperatures of different "fuels" or combustible materials vary, but once ignited, these fuels produce enough heat to keep the fire burning. By eliminating any one of the preceding factors, fire can be extinguished. This can be done as follows: heat, by cooling; oxygen, by smothering; and fuel, by removal.

       a. To cool a fire, some substance must be provided which will absorb heat to bring the burning material to a point below its ignition temperature. Water is the most common method of cooling a fire to the point where it is extinguished because the contents' temperature drops below the point of ignition. Another common method of extinguishing a fire is to exclude enough of the oxygen so that combustion

will stop. This can be done by either foam or by a noncombustible vapor, usually carbon dioxide gas (CO_2) or even water vapor in the form of steam.
  b. To remove the fuel is generally an oversimplification which is not practical except in certain types of fire. In the case of an electrical fire, a circuit may be de-energized. In the case of a deep-seated fire in a mattress or upholstery, the item may be removed from the premises.

B. General Procedure and Use of Extinguishers
1. Fire extinguishers are designed for small fires and therefore are used close to the burning material. The following general guidelines should be observed in utilizing fire extinguishers:
   a. Do not attempt to extinguish a blaze of major involvement because precious time will be lost, and little or no effect of the extinguisher will be realized.
   b. A fire extinguisher should not be expected to take the place of either the automatic sprinklers or a direct hose stream.
   c. In using fire extinguishers, a difficult fire should not be tackled with a single extinguisher; the procedure should be to immediately call for the municipal fire department and then with help use several fire extinguishers to suppress or control the blaze.
   d. The stream of the extinguisher should always be aimed directly at the base of the fire.
   e. When extinguishing a flame, never let the fire come between you and the route of emergency egress. If possible, always keep your back to the exit facilities and the fire *in* front of you.
   f. Never use a pressurized water or soda and acid extinguisher on an electrical fire due to the severe hazard of electrical shock.

C. Choosing the Correct Extinguisher
1. To be effective, the correct extinguisher must be chosen as relating to specific fire conditions depending on the type of combustible involved.
   a. Water solution extinguishers, including plain water, pressurized water, water with pressure carbon *dioxide* cartridges, and pump tanks. In addition, there is soda and acid, which is operated by a chemical reaction of *sodium* bicarbonate solution and sulfuric acid.
   b. Dry chemical extinguishers: specially treated *sodium* bicarbonate, or potassium bicarbonate, expelled by compressed gas, either nitrogen or carbon *dioxide*.
2. The suitability of a particular extinguisher must be judged in the light of the situation under which it may be used. The variety of types and sizes available throughout the store should include seven or eight specific types:
   a. The water solution type extinguisher should be the most frequently utilized and *is* the most frequently installed extinguisher.
   b. Most situations will normally involve use of the water solution extinguisher on ordinary combustibles.
   c. Two exceptions are liquid and electrical fires, where the water type would prove both ineffective and dangerous to the operator. Both the compressed gas, carbon dioxide extinguisher and dry chemical extinguisher are well suited for liquid and electrical fires. Preferably, the dry chemical is best for liquid fires in the kitchen area and in the paint area, and the carbon dioxide unit is best for electrical fires.

D. Method of Operating Extinguishers
1. The method of operating the extinguisher is clearly outlined on the extinguisher label, but the potential extinguisher user should have a thorough knowledge of how to operate the extinguisher prior to any need to do so.

2. The common methods of operation are to invert the soda acid units, or to operate a lever in the case of the pressurized water units and the dry chemical units as well as the carbon dioxide units.
   a. It is important that the units be inspected annually and immediately recharged after use.
   b. The pressurized water tanks have an indicator gauge which should be serviced immediately if it drops below the desired pressure.

Handling Hose from Permanently Installed Fire Installation

1. There may be permanently installed fire hoses in several strategic locations.
2. These hoses consist of either a wall-mounted reel or a hose rack with folded hose. The hose size is 1½ inches in diameter.
3. It is essential that the entire rack or reel be unloaded before the hose is charged or filled with water.
   a. There are several types of nozzles available. One is an open nozzle without a shutoff which requires an operator to stay by the control valve.
   b. In involving yourself with larger fires, it is essential that an exit path be available and that you not become trapped in handling a fire situation. If breathing becomes difficult due to smoke and fumes, you should discontinue the fire-suppression operation immediately and leave the area.

Automatic Sprinkler System

A. Many buildings are equipped with automatic sprinkler systems, which in turn are supervised by automatic fire alarm systems.
B. The activation of a single automatic sprinkler head (or more) will not only provide a water spray over the fire but also will automatically trigger an alarm.
   1. The alarm is transmitted to the central facilities.
   2. They in turn notify the fire department that there is a water flow alarm, and the fire department will always respond with the normal equipment for a major structural fire.
C. Sprinklers generally cover an area between 100 to 130 square feet. The normal discharge is in the vicinity of 30 gallons per minute per sprinkler head activated. With the exception of any penthouse, roof areas, and kitchen areas which are subject to higher temperatures, the normal sprinkler heads will activate at 165 degrees Fahrenheit. The following special conditions are likely to reduce sprinkler effectiveness:
   1. Large single areas which are well ventilated due to open shafts, whether elevators, stairways, or electric stairways.
   2. Storing a quantity of merchandise in service areas which would tend to *exceed* the capacity of the sprinkler systems.
   3. Shielded sprinklers due to merchandise being stacked too high or closer than 18 inches to the ceiling.
D. You should have a thorough knowledge of the distribution of the sprinkler system in your building. This includes both the main risers as well as the system of lateral mains. An enunciator panel, if present, will indicate the area of operation of the sprinkler system. In addition, it is essential that the following supplies be maintained:
   1. An adequate supply of spare sprinkler heads, but under no conditions fewer than 25 units. In addition there should be a minimum of 5 sprinkler wrenches and 15 sprinkler wedges.
   2. An adequate supply of bagged sawdust should be on hand to allow for diking of standing water from sprinkler leakage in order to control water damage.
   3. An adequate supply (minimum of one dozen) of low-cost disposable painter's plastic drop covers should be on hand in the approximate size of 9 × 12 feet. These plastic covers frequently cost less than $1 per unit and can provide considerable protection for merchandise and displays in the event that either smoke or sprinkler operation occurs.

Some Cautions

A. It is essential that designated persons report to the scene where any sprinkler head has been activated either by fire or a malfunction, or a damaged sprinkler system, such as a sprinkler head being knocked off.
B. It is absolutely essential in the event of a fire that the sprinkler system be allowed to function until there is no question of the fire being out. *Only an officer of a responding fire department should have the authority to shut off the sprinkler system.* The valve should be left open until ordered to shut down by the commanding officer of the firefighting force responding from the municipality having jurisdiction. The system should remain shut down only long enough to replace the fused (open) sprinkler head.
C. Service and the water supply must always be restored *immediately*.

Controlling Water and Smoke

A. Personnel should know the location of sprinkler shutoff valves and be familiar with the operation of the store sprinkler system, including procedures for operating floor sectional shutoff valves.
B. If a sprinkler system exists, a supply of emergency sprinkler head stem flow plugs should be maintained for stemming the flow of water in an activated sprinkler head.

Salvage Operations: Recovery

Salvage operations include all measures after a fire or other emergency for the purposes of reducing loss from smoke, fire, or water, plus minimizing business interruption.
A. An important part of salvage is actually in prevention of property damage from water, whether it be from hose streams, automatic sprinklers, broken piping, or flooding from storms or sewer backup.
B. The water damage phase of salvage work involves protecting merchandise from contact with the water and removing the water from the premises with a minimum amount of damage.
C. In addition, salvage operations involve the protection of property from the effects of heat, smoke, and contaminants in the various gases generated as the byproduct of a fire. This is most effectively accomplished by removal of the smoke and gases in an efficient manner through the use of exhaust venting and directional exhausting as accomplished by portable fans. In some cases, air conditioning and exhaust fans may be reversed to clear an area.
D. It is important to use chemical deodorants promptly after the fire to minimize smoke odors.
E. Salvage also includes the protection of records and associated equipment essential in maintaining the business operation.
F. Salvage equipment on hand for use by the fire brigade should include sacks of sawdust for diking standing water and controlling surface water from an automatic sprinkler operation, low-cost disposable plastic covers normally in a size of 9 × 12 feet or larger, and adequate containers for removal of surface water, along with mops and squeegees.
G. There should be a supply of sprinkler wrenches, sprinkler heads, and sprinkler wedges.

Fitting Rooms and Their Control

CAS, JHC

Fitting rooms represent, because of the privacy they are intentionally designed to provide to the customer, a high-risk theft environment with a relatively low probability of theft detection potential. With this fact in mind, how can a merchant minimize fitting room thefts?

We begin by dealing with the fundamentals. Once we establish why customers feel more comfortable stealing from fitting rooms than elsewhere, we can then devise policies and procedures to make stealing from fitting rooms more uncomfortable and thus reduce the amount of theft occurring there.

Customers, quite naturally, feel a sense of privacy and anonymity in fitting rooms because these rooms are designed to provide that very privacy. If we can reduce the feeling of privacy for potential thieves in ways which do not create aversion in honest customers, we should be able to reduce the corresponding theft rate.

What is the most effective shoplifting deterrent? Good customer service, of course! Honest customers appreciate good service, while the potential thief hates it because it limits the opportunity to steal. Remember, in order to commit a theft, three things must coexist: the motive to steal, the means to steal, and the *opportunity* to steal. Good customer service ("that nice sales person is looking in on me again to offer help—how nice of her") removes much of the opportunity to steal. While many means (e.g., CCTV, peek-holes, two-way mirrors) are illegal to use to monitor fitting rooms, the attentive knock on the fitting room door with an offer of assistance by a sales associate is not.

We do not want to tempt honest customers into a theft by almost inviting them to steal. Leaving merchandise from a previous user in a fitting room may tempt the next user to steal it, since that person was not seen taking it into the room and is not associated with those goods. Therefore, the frequent removal of merchandise left in fitting rooms ("clearing" fitting rooms) is a simple but effective way to reduce theft opportunities.

What else can be done to help deny the opportunity to steal from fitting rooms?

A very inexpensive technique is signing the fitting rooms or fitting room banks (see Figure F-1). Attractively designed signs stating that "this area is patrolled by sales and security for your safety" may do the job in a tasteful way. A more forceful sign used by some stores states "Shoplifting is a crime. We prosecute all shoplifters." Every store must determine the bluntness bluntness (or subtleties) of any signs used.

Stores can also limit the number of garments allowed in fitting rooms at any one time. When stores limit the numbered of garments allowed, it is easier from associates to better observe what is being taken into the fitting room and, equally important, what is brought out.

Limiting the number of garments can be on the "honor system" by simply posting signs stating that there is an "x" garment limit on merchandise taken into fitting rooms at any one time. A more sure method of obtaining compliance is to have fitting room checkers (see following description) stationed at the entrance to the fitting room bank who hand the customer a colored and numbered disk indicating the number of garments taken into the fitting room. When this system is utilized, the store may determine to allow any reasonable number of garments into the fitting room. It is important, however, to provide a method for securing these disks when not in use and periodically checking to be certain none are missing. A stolen disk for two garments is literally a license to steal merchandise, if the customer was issued a disk for three or four items.

Fitting room checkers (women who are associated with the loss prevention department) are often utilized by larger stores. These stores maintain "banks" of fitting rooms (i.e., a number of fitting rooms accessed by a common hallway with a single entrance/exit to the hallway). The fitting room checker (FRC) is stationed at the entrance to the bank hallway, thus maintaining control of the use of the fitting room.

For smaller stores that may have only one or two isolated fitting rooms, we suggest some system for determining if the room is occupied. One simple way to accomplish this is to provide a motion detector or an old-fashioned "pressure mat" under the carpeting which, when the room is occupied and a customer is standing on the floor, closes an electrical circuit and either sounds a chime or illuminates a small red light above the fitting room entrance. Another strategy is to have the pressure mat activate the light which illuminates the room; hence, all rooms which are "dark" are unoccupied, and only those rooms in actual use are illuminated. This chime, light, or illuminated room or light not only signals the room is occupied (thus letting the occupier know that someone knows he or she is there), but also permits sales associates to both monitor the room and be in a position to offer customer service, as well as rehang merchandise brought back out and not purchased.

SHOPLIFTING APPREHENSION REPORT

Store	Arrest Date	Day of Week	Arrest Time:	Charge:

Suspect Last Name	First Name	Middle Initial	Sex	Photo Taken:	Was Apprehension Result of Tag Alarm Sounding (Circle) YES NO

Home Address	City	State	Zip	Phone

Age	Date of Birth	Race	Height	Weight	Hair	Eyes	Occupation	Drivers License Number

Handcuffed: On Contact _____ In Office_____ Not Handcuffed _____	Admission Card Signed YES NO	(Circle) Prosecuted Released	Time PD Called: _____ Time PD Arrived: _____ Time PD Left:_____	Police Dept. Responding PD Report #

Quantity	Description	Price	Total
			Total $

DESCRIBE WHAT HAPPENED   (Include Who, What, When, Where & How) [Use reverse side if needed]

-

Print Name of Person Making Arrest If Contract Guard, What Company:	Signature of Person Making Arrest	Witnesses

FIGURE F-1

The design of fitting rooms can also either encourage or deter fitting room theft. While it is obvious that privacy to those using the room prevents viewing inside the room from public areas, that same level of privacy is not necessary if the room is within a fitting room bank whose access is restricted to only one sex. In such situations (i.e., within a fitting room bank), it is permissible in many jurisdictions to utilize so-called reverse louver fitting room doors, which permit FRCs to monitor the inside of the room from the hallway bank. Installing doors which have 12 to 18 inches of space between the bottom of the door and the floor and which extend only to a height of about 5½ to 6 feet above the floor also discourages theft. If hanging curtains or drapes are used to cover the entry, they should be approximately 4 inches short of the width of the fitting room's entrance. This arrangement should never be used if the fitting room is accessed directly from the selling floor.

Finally, it is suggested that all cracks (between the walls and built-in seats, mirror edges, signs and sign holders, etc.) be caulked to prevent hiding torn-off price and manufacturers' tickets in these areas. Seats with cushions should have the cushions permanently attached. There should be no wastebaskets in fitting rooms. Rooms should be periodically inspected for hidden tickets and/or places where such tickets could be hidden or disposed of, including light fixtures, loose edges of carpeting, and the even the narrow top ledge of the room dividers.

There is a widespread but mistaken belief that once a shoplifter enters a fitting room to steal, he or she is immune from detention, arrest, or prosecution. Nothing is further from the truth. While the detention of shoplifting suspects who have stolen while in a fitting room must be handled with care and caution, that does not mean they are "home free" and the store is unable to react. Many companies either prohibit or place stringent restrictions on detaining persons suspected of fitting room theft. We are of the opinion this is a flawed strategy, not well thought through, which only encourages theft.

The genesis of this mistaken belief and fitting room detention restrictions is that the industry's generally acknowledged "six steps," which are required before detaining a shoplifter, prevent detaining fitting room shoplifters. Specifically, Step 4 requires loss prevention to "[m]aintain an uninterrupted surveillance to ensure that the suspect doesn't dispose of the merchandise." The fact is that an uninterrupted surveillance is often broken after a loss prevention agent sees the customer pick up a red sweater and a blue sweater and enter a fitting room with both sweaters. If the fitting room does not have "reverse louvers" permitting a same-sex LP agent to observe, surveillance is lost while the customer is in the fitting room. The agent, however, keeps the fitting room under constant observation and subsequently observes the customer leaving the fitting room carrying only the red sweater. A quick check of the fitting room, while still maintaining surveillance of the customer, discloses the blue sweater is not there, and there is no physical way the customer could have disposed of the blue sweater while in the fitting room. Thus, the only logical conclusion any reasonable person can reach is that the customer (now a suspect) must still be in possession of that blue sweater. The agent then continues an uninterrupted surveillance of the suspect until she is observed leaving the store without having paid for the blue sweater. Can the agent now detain the suspect? We maintain that even though the customer could not be seen while in the fitting room, the room and its door was, and surveillance continued once she came out of the room and continued until she left the store; accordingly a detention is permissible under what we have identified as the "constructive unbroken chain of surveillance." This concept is discussed in depth in *Shoplifting: Managing the Problem*, published by ASIS International, 2006.

Bear in mind the authors are the pioneers of the Six-Step Rule, and the steps were created to reduce the possibility of error. The six steps are not the law of the land, but are industry standards and are recommended as an internal strategy to reduce mistakes. The overriding rule or law is *probable cause*, the law of the land, which would support the notion if a lady enters a small room with no one else in the room, and when she enters she's carrying in full view a blue sweater, and she exits shortly thereafter without the blue sweater, and the sweater is not in the room (and the sweater was not thrown over the partition or under the partition into another room), the sweater did not evaporate into thin air! It's most probable the lady has the sweater hidden on her person or out of sight among her affects. And consequently, the merchant has every right to investigate, and, we maintain, probable cause to detain for that purpose.

Remember, most merchants' detention statutes require "probable cause" to detain; we maintain that under the limited scenario of a missing identifiable item, with no chance of prior disposal, the fitting room situation described provides such probable cause.

While we repeat that fitting room thefts require deft handling and caution, they do not require that common sense be surrendered and such thefts be done with impunity.

Obviously, aside from this or a like kind of exception, the proper course of action would be to start the six-step process all over again.

Forms

CAS, JHC

Set out in Figures F-2 through F-15 are generic forms used frequently in the security/loss prevention discipline.

Note While this work is copyrighted, we urge you to avail yourself of these forms and use them as guides for the development of forms meeting your specific needs.

Fraudulent Outsourcing and Invoicing

CAS, JHC

In the 21st century, outsourcing functions traditionally performed by company employees has become a sign of the times in businesses of all types, retailing being no exception.

Our concern, however, is the *fraudulent* outsourcing of functions and/or the fraudulent invoicing for allegedly outsourced functions or services.

Two actual cases of fraudulent "outsourcing" will serve to demonstrate the vulnerabilities involved.

Case # 1: The display department of a major retailer received, over a period of time, invoices for services rendered, including the delivery of common items used by in-house display departments such as paints, mannequins, paper items, etc., all from a local company submitted on very authentic-looking stationery. The bills were submitted to a first-line supervisor who was the person responsible for authenticating the receipt of the supplies and legitimacy of the invoice. Since the invoices were all for relatively small amounts (nothing over $1,000), they did not attract senior-level scrutiny. At some point, a new employee in the department questioned an invoice and reported his concerns to a senior display executive. This executive reported the matter to the company's security department, which initiated an investigation. The investigation disclosed that the "company" that was invoicing the department did not exist; there was no business license in that name, and the address on the invoices was a residential address. Further investigation disclosed two employees, including the first-line supervisor who had been initially approving the invoices for payment, were submitting invoices for goods and services never received. The loss to the company was in the several thousands of dollars; the employees responsible for the fraudulent billing were terminated and criminally prosecuted.

The lesson learned from this case is that all vendors (except for nationally recognized companies) should be vetted to provide assurances of legitimacy and ownership, including, but not limited to, a legitimate business address, a valid business license, references, and periodic audits verifying the existence of the goods and services being invoiced.

Case # 2: A major national cosmetics vendor required that its selling area be defined by a wooden display which met design specifications. A retailer selling its products assigned an employee to seek out and obtain estimates for the fabrication of this design. Several estimates were submitted, and the contract for fabrication was given to the bidder whose sample work met the acceptance of both the company and the vendor. What was unknown was that the chosen "bidder" was, in fact, a carpenter employed by the store who, by conspiring with a display department employee, won the bid on the wooden displays and then built them in his garage at night and on weekends. Eventually, the cosmetic line became extremely popular and was expanded into many other stores in the chain. The carpenter could not keep up with

BONDING INFORMATION
PLEASE PRINT

OFFICE USE ONLY

STORE _____
(NAME)

FULL NAME _____
(LAST) (FIRST) (MIDDLE)

SOC. SEC. # _____

COMPLETE ADDRESS _____

PHONE NO. _____ HOW LONG AT THIS ADDRESS? _____ HOW LONG IN AREA? _____

PREVIOUS ADDRESS _____ HOW LONG? _____

MARITAL STATUS—
MARRIED ☐ DIVORCED ☐
WIDOW(ER) ☐ SINGLE ☐

PLACE OF BIRTH _____ DATE OF BIRTH _____

DRIVER'S LICENSE NO. _____ OR OTHER I.D. (TYPE & NO.) _____

NAME OF SPOUSE, PARENTS (IF LIVING), OR OTHER NEAREST RELATIVE

NAME	RELATION	ADDRESS	EMPLOYER	POSITION

HAVE YOU EVER USED ANOTHER NAME? _____ IF YES, WHAT NAME AND WHEN? _____

HAVE YOU EVER BEEN BONDED? _____ IF YES, WHERE WERE YOU WORKING? _____

HAVE YOU EVER BEEN REFUSED A BOND? _____ IF YES, EXPLAIN: _____
DATE _____ PLACE _____

HAVE YOU EVER BEEN CONVICTED OF A CRIME? _____ IF YES, ☐ FELONY ☐ MISDEMEANOR
EXPLAIN: _____ DATE _____ PLACE _____

HAVE YOU EVER BEEN DISCHARGED FROM A POSITION? _____ IF YES, EXPLAIN: _____
DATE _____ PLACE _____

PLEASE ACCOUNT FOR ALL TIME SINCE LEAVING SCHOOL, INCLUDING CURRENT EMPLOYMENT, MILITARY SERVICE AND PERIODS OF UNEMPLOYMENT. STATE IF ANY OF THESE EMPLOYERS ARE RELATED TO YOU.

DATES EMPLOYED MONTH AND YEAR	Name/Address, City and State of Previous Employer(s) Show present or last employer first.	SUPERVISOR AND YOUR JOB TITLE	REASON FOR LEAVING
FROM: TO:			
FROM: TO:			
FROM: TO:			

I HAVE VERIFIED THE BIRTH DATE OF THIS EMPLOYEE PERSONALLY WITNESSING THE DOCUMENT SO NOTED.

PRIMARY
☐ Birth Certificate

SECONDARY SOURCE *(Need One)*
☐ Church Record ☐ Passport
☐ Entry in Bible ☐ Life Insurance Policy
☐ Census Certificate (One in force at least 5 years)

SECONDARY SOURCE *(Need Two)*
☐ Relative's Affidavit ☐ School Verification
☐ Marriage Certificate ☐ Will or Testament Entry
☐ Military Record ☐ Naturalization Papers

_____ / _____ / _____
WITNESSED BY   TITLE   DATE

DO NOT WRITE IN THIS SPACE

DEPT. NAME	STAFF NO.
HOURS	CREDIT DEPT.
SECURITY DEPT.	SPA.

I HEREBY CERTIFY THAT ALL ANSWERS TO THE ABOVE QUESTIONS ARE TRUE AND COMPLETE. I FULLY UNDERSTAND THAT ANY FALSE ANSWERS WILL RESULT IN DISMISSAL OR DENIAL OF EMPLOYMENT.

_____ _____
(SIGNATURE OF APPLICANT)   (DATE)

WHITE . . . . PERSONNEL FILE
YELLOW . . . . CREDIT DEPT.
PINK . . . . SECURITY DEPT.

FIGURE F-2 Apprehension form.

EMPLOYMENT APPLICATION

IS AN EQUAL OPPORTUNITY EMPLOYER.

Please Print Clearly And Complete Both Sides Of This Employment Application. Applications Will Remain Active For One Month. Following An Offer Of Employment All Applicants Will Be Required To Supply The Following:

TODAY'S DATE

A - WORKING PAPERS (as nec.)   B - SOCIAL SECURITY CARD   C - PROOF OF CITIZENSHIP OR AUTHORIZATION TO WORK IN U.S.
D - NAME AND ADDRESS OF 3 REFERENCES   E - PROOF OF AGE   F - PERMISSION TO DO A REFERENCE AND CREDIT CHECK.

| NAME (LAST) | (FIRST) | (MIDDLE) | HAVE YOU EVER WORKED OR ATTENDED SCHOOL UNDER ANOTHER NAME THAT WE NEED TO KNOW TO VERIFY OUR RECORDS? IF YES, NAME: ☐ YES ☐ NO |

ADDRESS (NUMBER, STREET, CITY, STATE & ZIP CODE)   ☐ PERMANENT   ☐ TEMPORARY   ☐ MAILING ADDRESS

| HOME PHONE NUMBER ( ) | BUSINESS OR TEMPORARY PHONE ( ) | SOCIAL SECURITY NUMBER | DO YOU HAVE THE LEGAL RIGHT TO REMAIN AND WORK IN THE U.S.? ☐ YES ☐ NO |

PREVIOUS RESIDENCE

CURRENTLY EMPLOYED ☐ FULL TIME ☐ PART TIME ☐ NOT EMPLOYED

HAVE YOU EVER BEEN CONVICTED OF A CRIME (MISDEMEANORS OR FELONIES) BY A CIVILIAN OR MILITARY COURT? ☐ YES ☐ NO
Conviction Of A Crime Will Not Automatically Prohibit Employment.

| POSITION DESIRED | MINIMUM SALARY DESIRED | SCHEDULE PREFERRED ☐ FULL TIME (7 Or More Hours Daily) ☐ PART TIME (3-5 Hours - days) ☐ PART TIME (evenings and weekends) | |

LIST ALL TIMES YOU ARE AVAILABLE TO WORK

HOW WERE YOU REFERRED TO ☐ EMPLOYEE ☐ AD ☐ AGENCY ☐ OTHER (SPECIFY)

SUNDAY	MONDAY	TUESDAY	WEDNESDAY	THURSDAY	FRIDAY	SATURDAY
FROM	FROM	FROM	FROM	FROM	FROM	FROM
TO	TO	TO	TO	TO	TO	TO

HAVE YOU EVER APPLIED FOR EMPLOYMENT WITH   OR ANY SUBSIDIARY OF ?
IF YES, INDICATE DATE AND LOCATIONS.
☐ YES ☐ NO

HAVE YOU EVER BEEN EMPLOYED BY   OR ANY SUBSIDIARY OF ? ☐ YES ☐ NO

IF YOU WERE EMPLOYED, UNDER WHAT NAME WERE YOU EMPLOYED? STORE LOCATION?

RELATIVE IN OUR EMPLOY?   NAME   DEPARTMENT
☐ YES ☐ NO

FOREIGN LANGUAGES SPOKEN FLUENTLY WHICH WOULD BE HELPFUL IN POSITION SOUGHT

LIST YOUR INTERESTS, HOBBIES, OR SPECIAL SKILLS

LIST NAMES OF ALL ORGANIZATIONS OF WHICH YOU ARE A MEMBER (EXCLUDE ANY ORGANIZATION WHICH WOULD INDICATE THE FOLLOWING: RACE, COLOR, CREED, ANCESTRY, NATIONAL ORIGIN, RELIGION, SEX, OR MARITAL STATUS.)

PREVIOUS EMPLOYMENT

LIST IN ORDER OF EMPLOYMENT STARTING WITH YOUR PRESENT EMPLOYMENT. PLEASE ACCOUNT FOR ALL TIME, INCLUDING CURRENT EMPLOYMENT, MILITARY SERVICE, PART TIME JOBS, AND PERIODS OF UNEMPLOYMENT. IF YOU HELD TWO JOBS AT THE SAME TIME, BE SURE TO LIST BOTH JOBS. STATE IF ANY OF THESE EMPLOYERS ARE RELATED TO YOU. USE ADDITIONAL SHEET IF NECESSARY.

DATE FROM MO YR	DATE TO MO YR	NAME OF BUSINESS	ADDRESS/PHONE OF BUSINESS	JOB TITLE OR NATURE OF JOB	SALARY START END	REASON FOR LEAVING

PLEASE COMPLETE REVERSE SIDE - DO NOT WRITE BELOW THIS LINE

COMPLETE THIS SECTION ONLY AFTER AN OFFER OF EMPLOYMENT

| JOB TITLE | SCHEDULE DESCRIPTION (DAYS, HOURS, ETC.) | TOTAL NO. DAYS |

| STORE | GROUP/DEPT.# | PAYROLL NUMBER | HOURLY RATE | COMMISSION RATE | SCHEDULED HOURS | Initial review cycle ☐ 6 MOS./12 MOS. |

| DATE OF EMPLOYMENT YEAR MONTH DAY | TMP. REG. | DATE OF BIRTH YEAR MONTH DAY | EMPLOYED BY | DATE | ☐ 9 MOS./18 MOS. |

FIGURE F-3 Bonding form.

EDUCATION

SCHOOL	NAME & ADDRESS OF SCHOOL	COURSE OF STUDY	DATE FROM MO YR	DATE TO MO YR	CIRCLE LAST YEAR COMPLETED				LIST DIPLOMA/DEGREE
HIGH SCHOOL					1	2	3	4	
COLLEGE					1	2	3	4	
OTHER (SPECIFY)					1	2	3	4	

UNITED STATES MILITARY SERVICE RECORD

BRANCH OF SERVICE	DATE INDUCTED	DATE OF SEPARATION OR DISCHARGE	RANK AT DISCHARGE	SERIAL NUMBER

HAVE YOU RECENTLY RECEIVED NOTICE TO REPORT FOR DUTY IN THE ARMED SERVICES? ☐ YES ☐ NO | DESCRIBE SPECIAL TRAINING OR DUTIES

DO YOU HAVE ANY MENTAL OR PHYSICAL HANDICAPS WHICH WOULD PRECLUDE YOU FROM PERFORMING THE JOB FOR WHICH YOU ARE APPLYING?   ☐ YES   ☐ NO

LIST THE TYPE OF JOBS/PROFESSIONS OF YOUR FRIENDS/RELATIVES (ie: TEACHER, LAWYER, PLUMBER). WHAT WERE THE BEST & WORST FEATURES OF THE JOB?

JOBS OR PROFESSIONS	BEST FEATURES	WORST FEATURES

WHAT ARE THE MOST IMPORTANT THINGS THAT MAKE A COMPANY A GOOD PLACE TO WORK?	WHAT ARE SOME OF THE THINGS YOU DIDN'T LIKE ABOUT JOBS YOU'VE HAD?

IN CASE OF EMERGENCY DURING WORKING HOURS, NOTIFY:

NAME	ADDRESS	TELEPHONE NUMBER

IMPORTANT (PLEASE READ AND SIGN)

The facts set forth in this application are true and correct. I understand that if employed, any false or misleading statements, omissions or failure to fully answer any question will result in my immediate dismissal, regardless of when such information is discovered. I further understand and agree that I may be bonded if employed. I agree to submit myself at any time upon request for medical examination and or testing as permitted by law. I authorize to secure a consumer report from consumer reporting agencies (i.e. Credit Bureau Inc., Stores Protective Association, etc.), to investigate and verify all information submitted in connection with my application for employment and subsequently as deems appropriate. Upon written request from me to I will be informed of the name and address of each consumer reporting agency, if any, from which has obtained a consumer report relating to me.

I understand and agree that nothing contained in any handbook, manual, rules or regulations, practice, policy, etc., shall be deemed to create to create an employment contract between myself and It is further understood and agreed that my employment relationship with may be terminated on any day by myself or for any reason, or no reason, without liability. I represent that I am not relying upon any promises or representations regarding either the nature or duration of my employment in accepting employment if it is offered to me. I understand that no supervisor, manager or other representative of has any authority to enter into any express or implied contract. I further understand and agree that no promise, representation, inducement or agreement contrary to the above is binding unless it is in writing, expressly states that it is a contract, and is signed by the Chairman of

I CERTIFY THAT I HAVE READ THE ABOVE, UNDERSTAND IT AND AGREE TO IT ....

SIGNATURE OF APPLICANT (DO NOT PRINT)

REASON FOR NON-HIRE	☐ MORE QUALIFIED PERSON NECESSARY/HIRED	☐ CANDIDATE NOT INTERESTED IN JOB AVAILABLE GIVE REASON - SALARY, SCHEDULE, ETC.
	☐ NO SUITABLE OPENINGS AT THIS TIME	
	☐ HOLD FOR FURTHER CONSIDERATION (one month)	INTERVIEWER'S INITIALS AND DATE

FIGURE F-4   Employment application–page 1.

EVIDENCE LOG

PROPERTY #	SUBJECT'S NAME, DOB, DOA, CHARGE, CASE #, AGENT	DEPT.	CLASS	SEASON	STYLE/SKU	COLOR	DESCRIPTION	DATE IN	DATE OUT	REASON OUT

10.04

FIGURE F-5   Employment application–page 2.

required production needs, which resulted in the retailers seeking other sources for the display. This resulted in the submission of quotes which were about one-third the cost of what was being paid to the off-duty employee carpenter. An investigation discovered the ruse, and the errant carpenter was fired; attempts to recover the overcharges for the displays were unsuccessful, since the retailer had accepted the bid which formed the basis for a valid contract.

The lesson to be learned from this case is the same as that from case #1: know whom you are dealing with and have all estimates and bids arrive through the mail direct from the originator.

Important note: A P.O. box address is not an acceptable address for a supplier or vendor. Such addresses cannot be verified. An actual street number and name must be required and subject to drive-by validation, should that be deemed necessary. We recommend an annual inspection of the "vendor's wheel" or printout of the electronic list of vendors and suppliers to ensure complete addresses are on file, and an investigation into any which are deemed questionable. Invoices and/or envelopes which are rubber-stamped with the company name and address should receive extra scrutiny.

Fraudulent Refunds

Randy Tennison

When Aaron Montgomery Ward began using the phrase "Satisfaction Guaranteed Or Your Money Back" in 1875, the customer refund was born. Stores allowed customers to return merchandise for any reason or no reason, and receive a full refund of the purchase price. Almost immediately afterward, the fraudulent refund appeared. Retail stores, in their effort to provide customer service, opened a very large door which dishonest individuals were more than happy to enter. Refund fraud has been perpetrated by everyone from housewives to an aide to the President of the United States.

EXCLUSION NOTICE

(Note: Also known as Trespass Notice)

TO: _____
Name

_____
Address

_____

     You are hereby being advised and put on notice that (store name) has determined that you are to be barred from and prohibited entry into any (name of store) store for one year commencing from this date.

     Should you disregard this notice and enter a (name of store) store during this period of time you will be subject to immediate arrest for trespassing under the provisions of (name of State) Penal Code Section xxxxx.

The undersigned employee of (name of store) certifies that

_____
Name

was personally given a copy of this document and its contents and meaning was fully explained to _____ and witnessed by
                                    (him/her)

_____ on _____
(Witnessing employees name)   (date)

at _____
(time)

_____
Employee Signature

FIGURE F-6 Evidence log.

Refund fraud is a very appealing alternative to traditional shoplifting, as there is normally no need to leave the store. The basic concept of the fraudulent refund is this: Merchandise is represented as being purchased, either by the refunder or received as a gift, and is returned in accordance with the store's refund policy for valuable consideration (i.e., money, store credit, etc.). Fraudulent refunds can be committed by one person who returns many items or by large organized crime rings, ultimately costing stores and subsequently consumers millions of dollars through increased prices. The fraudulent refund can be more damaging to a store's finances than other theft methods. If the store's accounting methods book returned items back into the inventory, a fraudulent refund can cause a double loss. First, the store loses the monetary value of the item when it is paid out to the fraudster (since the payment to the refunder effectively has the store purchasing the item at full retail), which adversely affects the store's gross margin, and thus its profits. Second, the store's inventory is now artificially inflated due to an item already in the inventory being booked a second time

INTERVIEW LOG

SUBJECT				DATE	

POSITION		/FT, SH, or PW	STORE		STAFF #

HOME ADDRESS

LENGTH OF EMPLOYMENT	

SUBJECT/PURPOSE OF INTERVIEW

INTERVIEWED BY	WITNESS

	TIME			TIME
Began Interview		Began Written Statement	
Approval To Tape		Finished Statement	
Taping Started		Signed Statement	
Admission/Confession		PD Called	
Taping Concluded		PD Arrived	
DISPOSITION:	Released To PD	☐ YES ☐ NO	
	Suspended	☐ YES ☐ NO	
	Returned To Work	☐ YES ☐ NO	

TOTAL TIME FROM START OF INTERVIEW TO DISPOSITION: (Minutes)

OTHER EVENTS: _____

BATHROOM: REQUESTED ☐ YES ☐ NO   Accompanied By:_____

Time From_____To_____

FOOD/WATER (Specify) :_____Time_____

OTHER PERSONS IN/OUT OF ROOM: 1._____Time In_____Out_____

2._____Time In_____Out_____

LOG FILLED OUT BY:_____(Print Name)

SIGNED: _____

WITNESSED:_____ (ROI # _____)

FIGURE F-7 Exclusion form.

Security Department   **REPORT OF INVESTIGATION**

PADE 1 OF   CASE #

SUBJECT	CHARACTER OF CASE	
	REPORT SUBMITTED BY	
	PERIOD COVERED	
	STATUS/DISPOSITION	
REFERNCE:	CONFESSION	$
	MERCHANDISE RECOVERY	$
	CASH RECOVERY	$
	RESTITUTION PROMISED	$
	RESTITUTION RECEIVED	$

SYNOPSIS

COPIES TO	ENCLOSURES	APPROVED BY:

FIGURE F-8 Interview log.

into the inventory. Thus, when the store takes an inventory, it will show shrinkage in the item that was fraudulent refunded, because the book inventory was artificially increased by the refunded item being booked into inventory.

Refund fraud is a multimillion dollar issue in the United States. It has become so much an issue in retail that few stores today have unqualified "No Questions Asked" return policies, but have begun taking a harder stance to ensure that refunds are legitimate and that policies are not violated. Despite the increase in more restrictive return policies to establish proof of purchase as well as the use of technology, refund fraud continues to grow, mostly due to the advent of the merchandise gift card.

The basic fraudulent refund is a simple activity. A fraudster enters a store, picks up a piece of merchandise, and then takes it to an employee and represents that he has purchased the item but now would like to return it. The employee processes the refund and gives the fraudster cash back for the item. Thus, the fraudster now has cash, and the store has purchased back the merchandise at full retail, creating a loss of gross margin.

(STONE NAME) MMR Missing Merchandise Report	Date Of Report (Turn in same day)	Time Found	0 AM 0 PM
	Submitted By: (Last name, First name)	Payroll No.	Area / Dept Name

#1	#2	#3	#4
PLACE PRICE TICKET HERE CUT OUT SKU/UPC CODE. DO NOT ATTACH PACKAGING.	PLACE PRICE TICKET HERE CUT OUT SKU/UPC CODE. DO NOT ATTACH PACKAGING.	PLACE PRICE TICKET HERE CUT OUT SKU/UPC CODE. DO NOT ATTACH PACKAGING.	PLACE PRICE TICKET HERE CUT OUT SKU/UPC CODE. DO NOT ATTACH PACKAGING.

FILL IN THE FOLLOWING TO IDENTIFY THE MISSING MERCHANDISE

	SKU	DEPT.	Grid Location Displayed	Grid Location Found	Quantity	Unit Retail
#1			–	–		
#2			–	–		
#3			–	–		
#4			–	–		

WAS MERCHANDISE SECURED?	YES	No	WAS MERCHANDISE REQUIRED TO BE SECURED?	YES	No	UNKNOWN	

WHY IS THIS EVIDENCE OF THEFT

FOR OFFICE USE ONLY	**SUBMIT TO STORE LP MANAGER OR**
☐ Entered Into S.I.S.	**STAFF IMMEDIATELY**
Initials Date	

FIGURE F-9   Investigation report.

More elaborate refund schemes can include purchasing an item in order to receive a receipt. Then the refunder selects an identical item to return using the receipt as proof of purchase. If the receipt is not either retained by the store or marked to show the item returned, the original item may also be returned with the original receipt. Even more elaborate refund schemes may involve the copying or computer printing of phony receipts for items to be stolen and returned, and the use of fraudulent refunds to increase open to buy on credit or gift cards. Unless valid original receipts are required or other methods of verifying the original sale price are in place, items purchased on sale may later be returned for full price.

In addition, dishonest employees also commonly use refund fraud, although the methodology is a bit different. Often in employee refund fraud, the employee will process refunds using only SKU information instead of actually selecting items. The employee will ring the refund as cash, as a credit to a personal credit card, or as a credit to a store gift card. No merchandise is present for these transactions, and there is no customer present, so the chances of spotting an employee processing a fraudulent transaction in this fashion are increased.

There are numerous methods in use today to deter fraudulent refunds. One of the biggest misconceptions involving refunds is that a store must issue a refund for merchandise purchased. In fact, a store is under no legal requirement to refund merchandise. Stores have

PROPERTY TAG

Suspect: _____

Charge: _____   Date: _____

Arresting Officer: _____

Description of Property

Property No.

_____

_____

Custody Log

Date:	In/Out	To	By:
_____	_____	_____	_____
_____	_____	_____	_____
_____	_____	_____	_____

FIGURE F-10   Missing Merchandise Report.

FIGURE F-11   Property Tag.

FIGURE F-12   Restricted area sign.

STANDARDS OF CONDUCT FOR ALL SECURITY PERSONNEL

The standard of conduct expected of Security personnel should be such that no person will have cause to question our character, honesty, integrity or discretion. In the performance of our job, we must be highly professional and must meet more exacting standards of behavior and adherence to rules. The nature of our function, authority and responsibility requires this higher standard.
The following type of behavior is not in keeping with (store name) Standards of Conduct:

1. Any misuse of company equipment or property, misuse of position or authority, or agreement to accept "favors" not granted others and available or offered us because of our position is prohibited. Covered under this statement are such things as the following:
   a. Use of company phones for personal calls, whether local or long distance.
   b. Removal of company property for personal use.
   c. Use of parking validation cards, stamps, machines, etc. to avoid personal non-business parking charges.
   d. "Borrowing" company property for use in decorating or furnishing Security Offices without proper documentation and approval.
   e. Taking advantage of your position to secure favored treatment with regard to obtaining merchandise or any other advantage not granted other employees.
   f. Any misuse of the (store nemae) Security ID or badge.
2. Failure to objectively and factually report information required or obtained within the scope of employment. This statement covers not only the willful misstatement of facts but also knowingly omitting pertinent Information from reports or the purposeful "slanting" or "coloring" of reports.
3. The failure to report any information, however obtained, which could conceivably bear on or be pertinent to any security investigation or be of legitimate interest to company management.
4. Failure to submit reports as required by Security policy and procedures.
5. Violation of any of the provisions of (store name) "Use of Force and Weapons" policy.
6. Any misuse, careless or improper handling of funds, evidence, company property or records entrusted to our care.
7. Any activity which reflects adversely on the ethical or professional stature of the Security Department. Covered under this statement are such activities as:
   a. Improper or inappropriate language in dealing with suspects or employees.
   b. Any activity which could be construed as entrapment.
   c. Any investigation or other activity which is designed to "harass" or embarrass an individual and which has no other legitimate purpose.
   d. Discussion or disclosure, by any means, of past, pending or proposed Security investigations or activities with persons without a legitimate "need to know".
   e. Misuse or unauthorized disclosure of company confidential information or Security or Personnel information obtained in the course of employment.
   f. Mistreatment or abuse of persons in custody.
8. Failure to follow Security policy and procedures with regard to stopping, questioning, or apprehension of both employees and the public.
9. The failure to be completely truthful and candid in response to any official request for information.
10. I also understand and agree that due to the nature of my job, I may be required to remain in the building and/or at my work assignment during my meal periods.

The above statements are not intended to cover all situations, rules, policies, regulations, etc., and should not be construed as such. They are, however, indicative of the spirit and intent of (store name) policy and the expectations of your conduct and behavior. These standards are of such importance that any person failing to comply with them will be subject to disciplinary action including discharge without prior warning.

Maintaining the standards outlined above, and the philosophical framework created by them, should be the guideline in your professional approach to your daily activities.

I HAVE READ AND UNDERSTAND (store name) Security Department Standards of Conduct.
I understand these standards are not intended to establish any express or implied contractual rights. I also understand that any violation of these may result in disciplinary action, up to and including termination of my employment without prior warning.

_____   _____
NAME (Print)   Employee Number

_____   _____
SIGNATURE   Date

FIGURE F-13 Shelf edge sign.

(CONFIDENTIAL)

Company Name

LOSS PREVENTION DEPARTMENT
TRANSMITTAL OF INVESTIGATIVE RESULTS

To: _____   Date: _____

Attn:_____

From: _____

Subject of Investigation:_____   Position:_____

Type of Investigation: 0 Full Background   0 Records Check

0 Limited Background   0 Other

During the period of_____ to _____, an investigation, as indicated, was

conducted regarding the Subject with the following areas checked:

Employment - Yes 0   No 0_____

References - Yes 0   No 0_____

Public Records - Yes 0   No 0_____

Education - Yes 0   No 0_____

Credit - Yes 0   No 0_____

SMPA - Yes 0   No 0_____

Company files - Yes 0   No 0_____

Other - Yes 0   No 0 _____

Based upon our investigation, there was:

0 No known derogatory information revealed   0 Derogatory or questionable information revealed showing
    satisfactory results.   Unsatisfactory results.

0 Background investigation can not be satisfactorily completed.
Additional information from Subject is needed. See reverse side for details.

We are returning, herewith, Subject's:

0 Application   0 Bonding Form   0 Resume   0 Other_____

LP Department files contain details of this investigation.

FIGURE F-14   LP Standards of conduct.

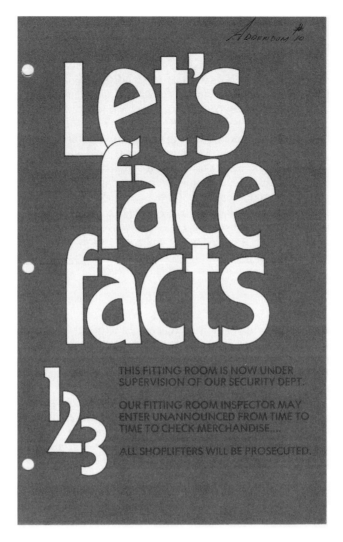

FIGURE F-15 Transmittal of investigative results.

chosen to offer refunds as a form of customer service but have the right to refuse to process refunds. This is one of the keys in combating refund fraud. Stores have begun to take a much stricter approach in dealing with refunds. Instead of offering a "no questions asked" approach, stores are enforcing policies requiring receipts, proper identification, and method of payment (the latter to combat the bad check or credit card which has not yet been cleared or fully processed).

Previous methods to validate the legitimacy of refunds consisted of sending post cards to the name and address shown on the refund document in the guise of a survey on customer service. In actuality, these mailings are used to determine if addresses were correct, or if people responded that they never returned an item, or, more commonly, the letter is returned by the post office marked "address unknown" or similar marking indicating a phony address.

Historical data on returns by employees have also been maintained to help identify employees who have a large percentage of no-receipt refunds, cash refunds, or refunds to the same credit card.

Another method historically used was the issuance of a check instead of cash for non-receipted refunds. In this method, a customer refunding an item without a receipt would not receive a refund at the time of return. Instead, the customer's name and address would be taken, after which the customer was advised a check would be mailed to him or her for the purchase amount within 30 days. This deterred any fraudsters from obtaining immediate cash from their fraudulent refunds, but more importantly, if the refunder provided a fictitious name or address when the form was being completed, the check would be returned to the store as undeliverable. This also provided a means whereby such phony addresses could be tracked.

Stores have also begun using other technology to combat refund fraud. Some examples include several department store chains which attach individual bar code stickers to items that identify that specific item back to a sales transaction. An item returned without the bar code is denied a refund. Other retailers are maintaining records of sales activity in their computerized system and can look up an individual purchase by use of the customer's credit card number, thus enabling that customer to receive instant refunds. Customers who do not have a receipt or whose sale cannot be identified receive either a mailed check or a credit good only for merchandise. Still other retailers are placing bar codes on the customer receipt for transaction history purposes. Thus, an item purchased can be returned only one time.

Stores are maintaining databases of frequent returners. Those people are identified in the system by means of their identification and can be denied a refund if their refund activity meets a predetermined level. The important component of this is to ensure that proper identification is obtained each time a refund occurs.

Lastly, stores have begun giving out merchandise credit cards in lieu of cash on nonreceipted refunds. While this method has had some success, the unanticipated consequence of it has been a large increase in the sale of merchandise credit cards over the Internet, on websites like eBay or Craigslist. Fraudsters will sell the card for a lesser amount of cash and never need to return to the store to use the card.

Refund fraud will continue to be a problem for any retail company that accepts merchandise back. However, proper policies, the enforcement of those policies, and technological advances can help lower the impact that refund fraud has on a business.

Author's Note: If fraudulent refunds are suspected, some areas which may be illuminating and should be examined are

- Associate accounts with large number of No Receipt Returns (NRRs)
- Third-party accounts with large numbers of No Receipt Returns
- Associates making large numbers of No Receipt Returns
- Third-party accounts with high dollar amounts of No Receipt Returns
- Associate accounts with high dollar amounts of No receipt Returns
- Registers with large numbers of No Receipt Returns
- Registers with large dollar amounts of No Receipt Returns

Additionally, whatever policies are created to deal with refunds, they must be universally applied to similar situations so as to avoid charges of discrimination.

 G

Ghost Employees

CAS, JHC

The term "ghost employees" refers to nonexistent people on the payroll; i.e., a check is regularly issued to an alleged employee who doesn't exist. Typically, someone in the human resources department or timekeeper/payroll department creates this "ghost" and creates the necessary paperwork to cause this "ghost" to become part of the organization.

A regular payroll check is automatically issued and is either intercepted in the check distribution system or is automatically mailed to a designated address (or post office box) for subsequent cashing by the culprit employee who is managing this fraud.

A "ghost" may also be a real person who is unaware of this payroll fraud; e.g., when the employee is discharged or otherwise terminates employment, an HR employee, rather than processing the status to "terminated," keeps the now ex-employee on the payroll and intercepts the check.

This risk and problem are usually checked, in a well-managed and sophisticated company, by someone in the finance division, such as internal auditors. Loss prevention investigators may be called in to assist during early stages of the discovery, to verify actual addresses or bank accounts, and depending on corporate policy may be charged with the interrogation of the employee identified as being a principal in the fraud.

Gift Card Fraud

Paul Cogswell

A prerequisite of understanding gift card fraud is understanding both the history of the gift card as well as how it fits into the overall structure of retail business. According to published sources, the domestic gift card market grew from $1 billion in 1995 to roughly $70 billion as of 2006. Gift cards began as a substitute to paper gift certificates. Companies such as Kmart and Blockbuster began testing their use in 1995. They initially were utilized in the retail business to reduce the headcount associated with the accounting of the certificates and ancillary escheatable property records. The industry grew from roughly $1 billion in sales to approximately $70 billion today. The initial reticence to their being given as a gift has long since subsided. It is estimated that stored value cards represented 12% of holiday sales.

Marketing studies have published that 75% of all adults have either given or received gift cards and 93% of all U.S. teens have bought or received a gift card. The reason for such explosive growth and maintained interest in gift cards is not only due to sales, but also due to a concept known within the industry as "lift." Lift has been defined as the amount of funds that a consumer spends above the original gift card amount. It is estimated at anywhere between 40% and 200%. Other factors include "breakage," or the residual amount that is left on gift cards and not redeemed. Accounting for breakage in a more refined manner allows the retailer to recoup these funds rather than escheat them to the state. Publicly traded companies have reported significant amounts of below-the-line income in their annual statements due to breakage. It is estimated that consumers never redeem between 3% and 5% of the value of a gift card. While this estimate may be aggressive, you can plainly see that the combined financial leverage of breakage and lift make the gift card a financially attractive product to the retailer.

Understanding both the financial model and history is essential to understanding the strategic importance of gift cards to retailers and why they will be here to stay.

Gift cards for most retailers operate in a closed loop environment. A closed loop gift card can be redeemed for merchandise only at the same retailer who sold the card. The life cycle of a gift card begins with their manufacture and personalization. Personalization is the process in which a specific account is assigned to the piece of plastic. Gift cards, unlike credit cards, are not limit based. The process of valuation and redemption is similar to that of opening and maintaining a safety deposit box at a bank. Simply put, the bank has a safety deposit box available to any customer. Once a safety deposit box account is opened, you still need both keys (the customer and the bank) to open it, and if there is nothing in it to retrieve, it is due to the fact that the customer has not placed anything in the box. Prepaid cards such as gift cards have no value until the customer places value on them by recording the transaction; when a card is used, the value is subtracted accordingly.

Some cards can be used only once, and some cards can be revalued. Gift cards can also be sold at third-party locations as well. Gift cards are valued using either a magnetic stripe or bar code method. The vast majority of gift cards utilize the magnetic stripe method, but many large retailers use the bar code as well. As mentioned earlier, using the safety deposit box analogy, the gift card's magnetic stripe or bar code represents the key. When the retailer values the card, the "value" is placed in the safety deposit box. This transaction is recorded in the POS system of the retailer, as well as in a gift card processing system. Security features present in the magnetic stripe of the gift card prevent mass counterfeiting of cards. These features are similar to the complex algorithm created by the Card Verification Code (CVC) when a credit card is issued. Similar technology such as two-dimensional bar codes offers protection on bar code gift cards as well. Since the focus of this book is on retail loss prevention efforts, a more detailed discussion of the manufacturing security features is not warranted here.

According to published research, gift cards presently represent between 3% and 5% of tender types at point of sale. This is an important statistic to keep in mind.

In 2005 the highly respected annual National Retail Security Survey undertook to study gift card fraud. Their findings attribute the average loss to retailers from gift card fraud were approximately $72,000. The retailers that responded to the survey attributed 62% of the losses to employee conduct, 13% due to counterfeit or "skimmed" cards, and 13% to stolen cards. This study was the first loss prevention effort to quantify the issue of gift card fraud. Retailers will undoubtedly draw their own conclusions as to the quantity and type of gift card fraud that exist within their own organizations. The study attempted to provide some answers on a broad base as to how much fraud exists specific to gift cards.

As in any discussion of fraud, you must understand that fraud, by its very nature, defies scientific measurement. After all, if fraud is not concealed, it would be easily discoverable, and fraud investigators would probably need to find another line of work. That being said, the experiential nature of individuals in the fraud fighting business would apply that set of skills to the issue of gift card fraud and would be able to deduce intuitively the conclusions of the survey.

One adage that has always been forefront in the mind of this author is that there is only one area of any retailer where one individual controls almost all the assets of a retail institution, and that is at the point of sale. Simply put, it is where the customer, the tender, the inventory, the employee, and most important, the reputation of the retailer meet. Any loss prevention effort that does not consider that as a crucial opportunity for control will undoubtedly be less than effective. This is also true for gift cards as well. Good loss prevention controls at point of valuation and redemption are essential to a successful gift card loss prevention effort.

The types of theft that can occur at point of sale utilizing gift cards are numerous, but all controllable. An example of a simple fraud is when an employee gives the customer a blank card and retains the one that he or she just valued. A sleight of hand is all that is really required. Controls at point of sale would include a regular inspection of the cash wrap area to ensure that gift cards are not hidden or separated from their packaging.

A variation of this type of fraud is when an employee retains a gift card with a residual balance, using that balance for tender in exchange for a cash sale, and then keeping the cash. Good POS controls, including a regular review of multiple tender sales, would be warranted here. Some firms utilize gift cards rather than script or cash for nonreceipted returns. Dishonest employees in these environments are restrained from stealing cash by creating fictitious returns; however, they may attempt to create fraudulent returns and retain the gift cards for sale. Retailers that track returns by employee and utilize separate gift cards for returns (separate bin numbers, signature panels, and nontransferability language) are better protected against this type of fraud as well.

An employee who switches bar codes on gift cards will also utilize these schemes as well, but with a slightly different twist. The dishonest employee will switch the bar code of another item with that of the gift card. When an individual purchases the item, he or she is actually valuing a gift card, one that the dishonest employee retains. Again, with exception reporting, the smart employer can highlight and eliminate this type of fraudulent behavior. With the present state of exception reporting in the retail environment, many retailers can design reports that highlight or model potentially fraudulent behaviors involving gift cards.

Prior to discussing exception reports and their use in fighting employee fraud, we need first to cover another operational aspect of gift cards—that of making balance inquiries through use of an 800 number. This is often referred to as an Interactive Voice Response, or IVR, number. Customers often want to determine the balance of a gift card without going to the store. Most gift cards offer an IVR number to check out balances or check transactions on cards. Some gift card companies utilize an Automatic Name Identification (ANI) platform to capture information about the caller. This information is useful in obtaining information that can assist in investigation and prevention of gift card fraud both externally and internally. Exception reports that utilize information from the ANI platform are often effective. A powerful exception platform that includes IVR information and various aspects of timing is very useful in fighting internal types of gift card fraud. Indicators of gift card fraud are not usually detected at store level. Some of the more common indicators of internal fraud are

- Customers who complain about not having balances on their card at time of first redemption
- Gift cards that are redeemed within hours of valuation
- POS terminal shortages that match or follow gift card sales
- High numbers of manually entered valuations and redemptions and multiple gift cards offered for tender on employee sales

These are just some of the more common indicators of internal fraud that can be highlighted through comprehensive exception reporting.

For purposes of brevity, I have compiled a number of the more useful exception reports that can be utilized when fighting gift card fraud. The list is hardly comprehensive but has been useful in modeling fraudulent behavior patterns with gift cards:

1. Gift cards with the number of balance IVR inquiries greater than X (X is user defined)
2. Phone numbers with multiple IVR inquiries on multiple cards
3. Store phone numbers with multiple IVR balance inquires
4. Sequentially numbered gift cards with the same phone number making the IVR balance inquiry
5. $0 balance gift cards with the number of IVR balance inquiries greater than X (X is user defined)
6. Gift cards with the number of balance inquiries (POS generated) greater than X (X is user defined)

7. Stores with multiple balance inquires (POS generated)
8. $0 balance gift cards with the number of balance inquiries (POS generated) greater than X (X is user defined)
9. Valued gift card transactions immediately followed by balance inquiries (POS generated) in the same day
10. Valued gift card transactions followed by IVR balance inquiries in the same day
11. Mass valuation cards redeemed on employee purchases
12. Mass valuation cards redeemed on employee purchases greater than $X or by frequency
13. Mass valuation cards valued and redeemed on the same day
14. Multiple mass valued cards redeemed within a single store within X number (user-defined) of transactions
15. Gift cards valued at store with insufficient funds (check) transactions
16. Gift cards valued at store with stolen or over-limit credit cards
17. Gift cards valued at store and redeemed online the same day
18. Gift cards valued at store and redeemed online more than X (user-defined) times
19. Mass valuation valued and redeemed online in the same day
20. Cards sold at store and redeemed at same store within 1 day more
21. Cards issued and redeemed in same day by same associate
22. More than X (user-defined) issued by same associate
23. Gift card sales followed by either line item or post transaction voids

While the list is hardly comprehensive, many of the reports are easily compiled with existing POS data and are extremely useful in noting internal fraud trends at point of sale.

An interesting trend of late has also emerged in the area of gift card fraud. That is dishonest employees working with members of organized retail crime groups to obtain receipts. This is usually done so that ORC groups can obtain gift cards for shoplifted items returned to the store. This topic provides a good segue into external gift card fraud. This topic is one of great interest to the media especially around holiday time and is laced often with more rumor than fact; however, as in any good news/bad news story, the good news is that external gift card fraud has not been a major problem facing retailers; the bad news is that most individuals engaged in committing gift card fraud are usually organized at some level.

There are three areas of interest when it comes to external fraud and gift cards:

(a) Skimming or making duplicates of gift cards
(b) Intentionally purchasing gift cards with bad tender (either NSF checks or stolen or skimmed credit cards), and
(c) Utilizing the Internet to sell gift cards of questionable value

"Skimming" is the fraudulent act of reading, storing, and sometimes recopying the encoded information on either a bar code or magnetic stripe of a gift card. Individuals will steal amounts of blank gift cards, utilize a bar code or magnetic stripe reader-writer to read these cards, and transfer them on to other cards, thus making two copies of one card. An individual replaces these cards in stock and waits for a legitimate customer to value "his" card and then immediately uses the card, beating the customer to the funds. As you can imagine, this makes for incredible effort with little reward, so it is not frequently seen. However, when this act is discovered, the number of cards stolen will be significant. Good loss prevention would suggest regular inspections of gift cards to ensure that they are intact.

Additionally, some retailers use a gift card with a scratch-off electronic security code (an algorithm that validates the account number of the gift card). This feature can be used when a gift card is redeemed online or even in stores. Skimming (sometimes referred to as "cloning") requires some knowledge of the account layout of the magnetic stripe as well as equipment. The important point to remember is that good loss prevention controls, protective packaging, and scratch-off electronic codes prevent skimming from happening.

You must also understand that, under the law, there is no distinction between a counterfeit or skimmed gift card and its corollary, credit cards. In other words, cloning gift cards is the same offense as cloning credit cards and is often prosecuted as such. There are also groups of organized retail criminals who, after sending in shoplifting crews, send in return crews to obtain gift cards from retailers, offering them for nonreceipted returns. These cards are usually offered in some alternative venue, as they provide more of a return for the criminal than more classical pawn shops and fences. The gift card industry and retailers have utilized techniques such as the 800 number to capture telephone numbers and, working with law enforcement, have made significant inroads in stopping these individuals as well.

Perhaps one of the more common uses of gift cards for the external fraudster is to try to extend the life of an identity theft or credit card theft by buying and utilizing gift cards with a stolen credit card or manufactured identity. The gift card is then sold in some electronic venue. With real-time accounting of gift cards, they are often devalued quickly after finding out that the tender used to purchase them was bad. As a result, the gift card is often left without value.

Since this text emphasizes loss prevention, I have strived to provide techniques meant to dissuade the ethically challenged from getting away with gift card fraud. Good loss prevention is holistic and often provides ancillary benefits to all assets. This is also true for gift card fraud as well. There are some generic best practices that will greatly stem any gift card fraud from occurring, and that list is included here as well. As this area of the business evolves, each retailer will need to find the correct return on loss prevention effort based on the commodity and opportunity that gift cards offer to the consumer.

Good loss prevention technique and process will need to evolve at a rate commensurate with the business changes in the gift card industry. Collaboration and cooperation will always overcome the challenges presented by the fraudster when it comes to gift cards.

"10" Loss Prevention Practices for Gift Cards

1. Ensure that the POS sequence values the card upon completion of the transaction.
2. Antifraud packaging
   a. Shrinkwrap of card
   b. Antifraud double card with magnetic stripe in the middle to prevent skimming
3. PIN-based cards to be used on all redemptions and online purchases
4. Active review of IVR exception reporting tools on a regular basis:
   a. Multiple inquiries (>10) in a 30-day period from the same phone number
   b. Multiple inquiries (>10) in a 30-day period on $0 balance cards
5. Exception reporting in conjunction with external or internal POS IT resources that address certain gift card transactions (see attached spreadsheet)
6. Placement of gift cards in highly trafficked areas that provide "heat and light" on the offering
7. Periodic in-store counts of prevalued gift cards to account for any possible large shortages
8. Periodic reviews of personalization vendors to review process and physical security issues
9. Active liaison by gift card vendor in industry LP forums such as Food Marketing Institute, Retail Industry Leaders Association, and the National Retail Federation to discuss antifraud trends and developments
10. Active participation with the gift card vendor and in-house loss prevention staff to consolidate active investigations and discuss cross-client issues as well as provide a conduit to the proper government agencies that will investigate issues of suspected gift card fraud

Good Housekeeping as a Shrinkage Prevention Tool

CAS, JHC

While engaged in a survey of a chain of drug stores, I had occasion to inspect a small outbuilding serving as a warehouse for a remote store. It was dusty, dimly lit, poorly ventilated, and jammed full of off-season goods. My focus was on the physical security of the merchandise in this building; i.e., could the building's physical security features be breached and theft occur without management's knowledge? As I moved through one aisle, I found myself walking on Halloween paper goods, i.e., paper pumpkins, black cats, orange and black paper tablecloths, merchandise stored for the fall. Closer examination of just that aisle disclosed some of those goods had been on the floor and walked on for some period of time. Further examination revealed similar conditions in two other areas of this mini-warehouse. Generally, both the store and its warehouse lacked good housekeeping practices, and interestingly, this store led the chain in inventory shrinkage. The company's executive who accompanied me on my visits to various locations was embarrassed by this condition, but a very important message came out of this experience. My reaction and my message as the consultant was: How can you expect employees to relate to the importance of a company-wide shortage prevention program when there's an obvious disrespect for merchandise? If the paper goods on the floor were paper money, would people walk on it? Merchandise is money, not necessarily negotiable money, but a direct representative of the value of money, and deserves respect.

This whole issue of respect for merchandise is reflected in retail stores by well-illuminated, clean, neat displays and presentations of goods in their proper locations.

Merchandise tossed about and ignored in empty fitting rooms is clearly an invitation to theft. There's a relationship between unkempt stores or departments within stores and theft, if not by customers, by employees who sense no one is really concerned about the merchandise. Conversely, clean, orderly, neat, folded merchandise in clean, well-illuminated stores and stockrooms, reflecting good housekeeping, commands increased respect. Similarly, new merchandise or seasonal merchandise being stored for future use must be carefully identified, stored, and preserved and protected.

Grab and Run

CAS, JHC

The "grab & run" theft technique is simple: The thief simply runs into the store, grabs an armload of merchandise from a display or a large bag of preselected goods staged in a specific and agreed-upon location, and runs out the nearest exit, to a waiting car driven by an accomplice. These kinds of sizeable "shoplifting" losses are accomplished in less than a minute.

The grab-and-run technique is the most unsophisticated, brazen, and thug-like shoplifting technique that will be encountered. Of course, there are some variations, such as a confederate can precede the runner and arrange the goods on the designated display stand or rack. If the merchandise, such as leather jackets are on hangers which are reversed, the confederate, in making ready for the "hit" can turn the hangers to all face the same direction to accommodate the quick lifting and removal for the run. Or, if secured with plastic ties, the confederate can cut the ties, defeating that obstacle to prevent the loss of an armload of expensive jackets. Or, as referred to previously, the goods can be already bagged and stashed by a different confederate (or even the guy who eventually runs in and grabs it) waiting for its quick removal from the store.

In those uncommon events, when LP agents may be in the area, and even aware of and waiting for this crime to unfold (based on investigative or intelligence information), it should be anticipated the results would be for the runner to dump or throw down the merchandise or throw it at the pursuing agents and further, if intercepted before reaching the waiting vehicle, use violent force to resist and escape.

The most vulnerable store areas are those near entrances and exits, particularly those with streets or roadways immediately outside. Such vulnerability can be somewhat minimized by placing displays containing expensive goods deeper into the interior of the store, and preferably close to employee workstations.

All available information connected with such losses should be memorialized, shared with other merchants where such sharing is an ongoing protection strategy, and reported to the police.

Grocery Loss Prevention

Curtis Baillie

The purpose of this section is to present and consider some different areas of grocery loss prevention to operators who are looking for ways to add value and dollars to their bottom line. We will cover areas such as combining services to the improper trimming of lettuce. Yes, the small things really do count!

According to the *Progressive Grocer* (1), as of 2005 there were 34,052 supermarkets in the United States. The Food Marketing Institute (FMI) (2) reports that the average super-market consists of 48,058 square feet and has annual sales of over $27 million. According to the 2005 National Retail Security Survey Final Report (NRSS) (3), retailers spent just 0.47% of annual sales on their overall loss prevention budget. The NRSS reported shrink in the supermarket/grocery segment was 2.38% as compared to 1.59% for the overall retail market. When you consider the profit margins in grocery are historically low, that translates to big dollars. Just reducing shrink from 2% to 1% is like adding 35–40% in profits to the bottom line. Industry experts put the per-store loss to shrink at over $400,000.

Combining Services

Combining services under one loss prevention umbrella makes good business sense.

Operations such as internal audit, check and credit/debit card fraud, external/internal investigations, crisis management, facilities security, and food safety are all functions directly related to loss prevention services.

Today's loss prevention personnel are better educated, are more business oriented, and are partners and true assets to their organizations. This can be directly attributed to organizations like the Food Marketing Institute (FMI) and leaders like Charles I. (Chuck) Miller, who held the position of Vice President of Loss Prevention Services at the Food Marketing Institute for 15 years. Grocery operators realize the benefits of seeking out the best-qualified individuals to head their security efforts.

During a recent conversation with a group of supermarket executives, I was asked to describe, in one word, what one quality it took to be successful in grocery loss prevention. My immediate thought was this is impossible but then boldly stated, "A jack-of-all trades." A member of the discussion group quickly pointed out that my answer was more than one word. I told him—not when you hyphenate it. This made for a humorous moment but made me think about the question more in depth. The Loss Prevention Director or Security Director in a grocery operation today is viewed as a true expert in many phases of the operation. Some areas of knowledge include but are certainly not limited to

- External theft (shoplifting)
- Internal theft (employee)
- Organized retail theft (ORT)
- Risk management
- Internal audit, compliance and financial
- Check and credit fraud
- Crisis management operations
- Food safety/product tampering
- Environmental protection
- Physical security measures—corporate, warehousing, and manufacturing.

Some additional areas of proficiency should include

- Business management
- Interpersonal skills-communication
- Budget—preparation and execution
- Public speaking
- Writing skills

As you can see, the Manager or Director of Loss Prevention Services must be well versed in many areas of the entire operation. It makes good business sense to combine numerous service areas under one department.

Paying attention to the bottom line is the focus of any effective asset protection department. The subsequent highlighted topics are just a number of areas that can add value to your business. They are not meant to be all encompassing, just informative.

Electric Article Surveillance (EAS)

One of the most effective ways to reduce shrink in grocery is to use a tag-and-alarm system, also known as "electronic article surveillance" or EAS. In the early stages, the supermarket industry was slower to embrace electric article surveillance systems due to issues with the different climate variations found in the stores. As technology progresses, grocery retailers find EAS to be a real profit saver. My own experience found the monthly return on investment (ROI) from $2,500 to $5,000 per store. Being the first in a geographic location helped.

Systems are used primarily to protect high theft areas around the store like meat, liquor, razor blades, and other high-ticket items or merchandise targeted by professional thieves. One of the real benefits of a tag system is you can choose what products to tag. One grocer tags school supplies at the start of the new school year. He says that it only takes about a week until the message gets out.

A part of any successful EAS campaign is communicating with your customers. A month before installing a system in your store, develop a bag stuffer and signage that explains to your customers you are installing an antishoplifting device. Explain that theft of products causes retailers to raise their prices, thus penalizing honest customers. Communicating this early message to customers has a positive impact on your business. EAS is not for every store location. Careful planning and research of crime statistics will guide you in the proper placement of systems. Don't forget, proper training and effective customer communication are just two of the keys to a successful EAS program.

Employing Biometrics

Biometric readers are used for recording employee work time, ensuring backdoor security, cashing customer checks, and processing payments at the checkouts. Using a biometric payment system at the checkout reduces the transaction costs to the grocer as credit and debit card transaction fees continue to increase. Biometric payment is also considered safer to use when considering increasing concerns regarding identity theft. Using biometrics at the back door makes sense when considering the costs of constantly issuing and replacing lost or stolen keys and reader cards. Although the use of biometrics in the grocery setting is stronger in Europe, the technology is catching on in the United States.

Closed-Circuit Television (CCTV)

Within the grocery industry, CCTV has a wide array of uses including recording (and deterring) employee theft, shoplifter activity (external theft), and one my favorites, observing and recording high-risk areas of the stores, looking for situations that could cause injury to customers. Very early in my grocery loss prevention career while I was observing, with CCTV, a high-theft aisle in a store, a woman entered the aisle pushing a grocery cart. She stopped, pulled a small plastic squeeze bottle from her purse, and sprayed water on the floor. She then ran her foot through the water and sat on the floor, yelling very loudly for someone to come help her. Had we not been using CCTV and been able to prove her false claim of injury, our potential for liability could have severely impacted the company's bottom line. Grocers spend $450 million annually to defend slip and fall claims. It makes good sense to use technology to protect your business.

With concerns mounting about food safety and product tampering, the use of CCTV in the grocery environment is a valuable tool. Many supermarkets have salad bars and public space areas for food preparation. It is important to take all necessary measures to protect your business. In another section of this book, I wrote about a product tampering case, "The Turkey Crisis." This is just one example in which a tampering incident or threat of tampering can have a very devastating, negative impact on your profit margin.

Direct Store Delivery (DSD)

Direct Store Delivery systems are now commonplace in large grocery companies. This electronic, paperless receiving system automatically checks in a vendor delivery by scanning the incoming inventory. DSD removes the chance for potentially inaccurate or fraudulent hand counts. This procedure removes the invoice from the vendor's hands, thus greatly reducing the possibility of fraud or collusion with the receiving employee. Benefits of a DSD system include

- Item management
- Payment management
- Backdoor check-in management
- Cost and price management
- Category management.

Not all grocery operators use a DSD system. If you are a small, independent operator and rely on a "hands-on" receiving system, here are some tips to help you save your bottom line.
   Be cautious of

- A vendor who gives out samples.
- A vendor who unloads his truck on the sidewalk area away from the store.
- A vendor who is constantly "on the move" in and out of your store.
- A vendor who begins servicing his product before signing in.
- A vendor who wants to evenly exchange product without issuing a credit slip.
- A vendor who enters no description-of-merchandise invoice for merchandise delivered.
- A vendor who does not extend the unit costs on the invoices.
- A vendor who extends or adds invoices incorrectly or adds the date or invoice number into sales.
- A vendor who charges the store for merchandise not delivered.
- A vendor who states the missing merchandise was "left on the truck." If, for any reason, you give the invoice back to the vendor after checking it, he may alter it. The vendor can set you up by asking you for the invoice to add on additional product.
- A vendor who wants to deliver merchandise before the store opens.
- A vendor who gives you an invoice pad to sign without separating the blank invoice underneath.

Alarm Systems: Getting More for Your Money

I once worked for a grocery chain that was open 24 hours a day. The stores did not even have front doors, just a continuous curtain of air to keep out the outside environment. A wire gate rolled down when we closed early on Thanksgiving and Christmas Day. We were having trouble with backdoor thefts, and our key system had been compromised. Loss prevention was able to sell the idea of a card access alarm system only because we were able to show added value. In other words, the system would do more than keep track of who was coming and going. One of the big selling points was the system had the ability to monitor the temperatures of all the freezer cases and cold boxes. If a case temperature fell outside the acceptable range, an alarm was activated within the store and at the monitoring station. The system was also able to monitor the produce cases and activate the automated watering system, keeping the produce fresh.
   There was much resistance to installing an alarm system, as we were open 24-7. Some company executives thought it was an unnecessary expense. This is just one example in which the loss prevention demonstrated added benefits in order to move a security program forward.

External Theft (Shoplifting)

According to the 2005 National Retail Security Survey (NRSS), shoplifting, or retail theft, accounted for 31.3% of the shrinkage in the grocery industry. The average percentage rate for the retail industry as a whole was 32.6%. Typically, small grocery operators do not employ security or loss prevention staff to work in individual locations, but hire small, traveling teams to work all their stores, concentrating on larger high-volume units or stores in high crime areas. It is also popular to outsource this function, keeping the investigative staff in-house. Outsourcing the shoplifting functions requires close monitoring of the contractor's activities in your stores. Develop an operating policy and ensure your contractor follows your policies. Using an outside contractor for this function has the potential to add value to your bottom line by reducing your payroll and benefits expense. There is also a potential savings on liability claims. As an example, when I outsourced the shoplifting apprehension efforts at a company, we saved over $200,000 in the first year alone. This included salary, benefits, company vehicles, and reduction in liability insurance premiums. During my overall experience with outsourcing shoplift apprehension activities, a lawsuit was never filed; this was not the case with in-house operations.

Internal Theft (Employee)

The rate of internal theft in the grocery business is historically higher than other segments of the retail industry. According to the NRSS report in 2005, the percentage of employee theft in grocery was 51.3% vs. an average of 47.6% for the rest of retail. I think one of the reasons for this higher rate of internal theft is the high turnover rate within the associate ranks. For example, the turnover rate in the courtesy clerk or bagger positions is typically 200% or higher. These are young people, often starting at the early age of 15, who are experiencing their first job and have yet to develop any loyalty to their employer. The temptation and peer pressures are great, and these young employees find it hard to resist. Even though most companies have policies regarding key control, store managers still give keys indiscriminately to clerks, telling them to "clean up the back room and when you're through, return the keys to me." Consider the manager who fails to inspect the daily bookkeeping process (as per policy), thus enabling a dishonest bookkeeper to walk out of the store with $50,000. When he went to make the deposit, he found the bag contained cutup paper.

   In my experience, I have found that the majority of internal, or employee, theft is due to management, at all levels, not following their own policy and procedures, thus creating opportunity for people to steal.

Organized Retail Theft (ORT)

My first experience with organized retail theft was when I worked for a, then small, retailer in Northeastern Ohio. We had received a memo, from the corporate office, on a "gang" of record album thieves (this tells you how long ago this took place), who were traveling throughout the Northeastern United States in a group of about five individuals, stealing large quantities of record albums. About 3 hours after receiving the memo (no email in those days), I was sitting in an observation tower overlooking the record department when I spotted four individuals sorting and stacking albums on the floor. They were showing all the signs, such as looking around to see if anyone was watching. Little did they know, I was only 15 feet away.

   They proceeded to make their selections and hide the albums in their coats. It was later discovered they had very large pocket areas sewn inside their coats. By that time, I had alerted management who contacted the police. When these individuals exited the building, walking with some difficulty due to the weight of the albums, the police apprehended them, thus ending their criminal spree. I later found that these individuals were linked to an organized crime ring based out of New Jersey. Before they were apprehended, it was estimated this group of criminals had stolen over $15,000 in record albums from our store alone.

   Organized retail theft threatens every grocery company's profitability. Some of the most common items targeted by professional thieves are

- Razor blades
- Baby formula
- Over-the-counter medicines
- Batteries
- DVDs
- Smoking cessation products

ORT activity injures not only the retailer, but also the consumer, who has to pay higher prices at the register. The loss to communities has a real, direct impact to the tax base. "The Retail Alliance, an organization serving retailers in the Virginia Beach, Norfolk, Chesapeake, and Hampton Roads communities in Virginia, estimates that retailers in these communities suffered $200 million of loss to shoplifters in 2001. Tax loss to Virginia amounted to $9 million; $5 million of that loss would have gone into the state budget and $4 million to local cities and schools. Organized retail theft is a crime that has spread to all reaches of the U.S. The tax loss nationally is hundreds of millions of dollars." (4)

Today's large grocery retailers have investigation units within their loss prevention departments that exclusively direct their energies toward organized retail theft activities, working closely with local, state, and federal law enforcement agencies. The small, independent grocery operator has limited resources to devote to this type of retail crime but can help reduce losses by reporting suspected activities to local law enforcement agencies.

Exception Reporting

Exception reporting is, basically, the collection of information that falls outside a predetermined value. Exception reporting is fast becoming a favorite tool in the fight to combat internal theft. As an example, a clerk attaches a $0.98 price tag to the bottom of her wrist and then proceeds to price scan a stack of porterhouse steaks. The exception reporting system, programmed to record such an event, activated the CCTV system, capturing the transaction on video. Such a system can be set up to report the violation at either the store or corporate office. There are many software retailers in the marketplace offering exception-reporting programming, and large retailers often develop their own.

Risk Management

Risk management is exactly what the title implies—managing your risk. Most small grocery operators employ a risk management or insurance company to implement and run their risk programs. At some point, it becomes economically feasible to bring risk management operations in-house. In many grocery companies, this function falls under the auspices of the loss prevention department. Some areas under the risk management umbrella are described next.

General liability includes customer accidents. One of the most common customer accidents in a grocery store is slips and falls. Grocers spend $450 million annually to defend slip-and-fall claims.(5) Constant attention to floor care must be maintained, as this is one area you can effectively reduce your exposure. Use non-slip floor waxes or all-weather carpeting at the store entryways. Put down special matting during grape sales. I once consulted with a grocery company that was bagging its grapes but still experiencing customer accidents due to grapes falling on the sales floor. By using special floor matting, along with increased attention by store staff, the store reduced its risk exposure.

Workmen's compensation—employee accidents. There are many ways for employees to become injured. One of the most common, in grocery stores, is the improper use of box cutters. Make sure your safety program includes the proper use of box cutters. Use box cutters that have a protective covering over the blade and limit the depth of blade, thus not only saving your employees from injury, but also saving product from being damaged.

Strict adherence to laws that restrict minors from using machinery, such as trash compactors or working in the meat preparation room, is mandatory. The Occupational Safety and Health Administration (OSHA) fines and the focused scrutiny of your operations can be devastating to your business. Make sure your managers are training staff about the proper use of power equipment. Full documentation of the training received will help in reducing fines. It is not uncommon for OSHA fines, for allowing minors to operate restricted equipment, to exceed $100,000.

Proactive vs. Reactive Loss Prevention

Ed Van Fleet, CCP of Brookshire Grocery Company, has written an excellent article titled "Why Are You Here? Reflections on the Role and Impact of Loss Prevention in the Retail Supermarket World." On the subject of proactive and productive efforts, Mr. Van Fleet writes:

> With proactive and productive efforts in any of these areas, you can impact the two most important lines of business-the top line (sales) and the bottom line (profits). Combine the two and you have profitable sales. Remember, profitable sales are the lifeline of your company. What can you do to increase sales?

- Help keep your associates on the job and accident free.
- Prevent out-of-stocks by reducing theft.
- Find ways to open merchandise rather than lock it up.
- Improve shelf life and product integrity through proper sanitation.
- Make your stores safe and enticing places to shop through crime prevention.

> *What can you do to increase profits?*

- Reduce costs related to associate or customer accidents.
- Deter theft of assets, not just merchandise.
- Increase recycling income, and/or reduce supply costs.
- Avoid lawsuits, regulatory fines, or other penalties.
- Increase productivity through an improved work environment.

> The grocery business is a simple business. We bring the merchandise in the back and sell it out the front. It is the same as it always has been, yet everything has changed in how we do it. You have to change as well.(6)

The article also appears in FMI's 2006 Supermarket Security and Loss Prevention Survey Report. This report, produced annually, may be obtained through the Food Marketing Institutes website at www.fmi.org.

Paying Attention to the Small Details

Remember earlier where I mentioned that the small things really do count? Consider this: A bunch of leaf lettuce sells for 90 cents per pound. If the company standard is to trim a very thin slice from the butt, and a produce clerk slices too deep into the butt and cuts off just one leaf at an average retail of 9 cents per leaf, the store would lose an average of 85 cents per day, assuming the lettuce is packed 12 bunches to a case. The loss would amount to $8.10 per day for just one store, or $421 dollars a year, by just one clerk in one store. If your grocery chain has 100 stores, and this scenario occurred in every store throughout the chain, the loss could amount to $42,120 annually.

If just one apple per day, at 25 cents each, falls from a display onto the sales floor and becomes bruised, the cost to a single store amounts to $1.75 per week, or $91 a year. The loss to a chain of 100 stores amounts to $9,100. These two examples demonstrate how paying attention to the seemingly little things will protect your bottom line profits.

Suggested Reading

Christman, J., and Sennewald, C. (2006). *Shoplifting–Managing the problem*. ASIS International.
FMI, Supermarket Security and Loss Prevention – 2006, http://www.fmi.org/forms/store/ProductFormPublic/search?action=1&Product_productNumber=2145.

Miller, C. I. *A report on organized retail theft*. Available online in PDF format at http://www.
     fmi.org/loss/ORT/ORT_report.pdf
Sennewald, C. (2000). *Shoplifters vs. retailers—The rights of both*. New Century Press.

References

(1) *Progressive Grocer*. (2006). 73rd Annual Report of the Grocery Industry. (April) 55.
(2) FMI Facts and Figures. www.fmi.org/facts_figs/keyfacts/stores.html.
(3) National Retail Security Survey Final Report. (2005). University of Florida. Supervised by
     Richard C. Hollinger, Ph.D.
(4) Miller, C. I. (2003). *A report on organized retail theft*. Food Marketing Institute.
(5) National Floor Safety Institute (NFSI).
(6) Van Fleet, E. (2006). Why are you here? Reflections on the role and impact of loss preven-
     tion in the retail supermarket world. *Loss Prevention Magazine*. (November–December),
     92–93.

Handcuffs

CAS, JHC

Handcuffs are a restraint and safety device used on uncooperative arrestees to serve as a temporary restraint until the suspects can be incarcerated (see Figure H-1).

Some companies prohibit loss prevention personnel from using handcuffs, while others impose limitations on their use, such as prohibiting their use on juveniles, pregnant women, and senile individuals; some prohibit handcuffing a suspect to a permanent object such as a bench or wall which has been equipped with a ring or other means of securing one of the cuffs to it.

Several factors are important when using handcuffs:

- Handcuffs do not immobilize a person.
- You must maintain constant control over the handcuffs.
- You must maintain a reasonable degree of tightness of application. Tight enough to touch the skin is considered correct. If a person is handcuffed too tightly, nerves can be damaged, blood circulation can be reduced, and the cuffs can be very painful.
- Double locking prevents the cuffs from tightening beyond that intended.
- You must maintain proper position of key outlets (facing out) and double locks (on exterior side).
- You must maintain proper positioning of the suspect's hands–palms facing out.
- You should handcuff a person with hands behind his or her back.

The purpose of restraint devices is to limit the following actions:

- Attack on agent by prisoner
- Escape of prisoner
- Destruction or concealment of evidence
- Self-inflicted injury

Whenever a security/loss prevention agent has a person in custody, the agent is responsible for that person's well-being. If the person in custody attacks someone, destroys evidence, or harms himself or herself, the agent is responsible and may be liable.

The use of handcuffs must be part of the loss prevention policy and procedure manual which spells out their use and any and all limitations and restrictions.

We encourage the proper use of handcuffs for their above-stated reasons; however, some form of certification should be required; i.e., agents must be trained in their use by an authorized trainer or police officer with the local police department. The training material must be part of the LP department's training manual or LP operation manual. Attendance at the training must be memorialized in the agent's file, specifying the date of the training, amount of time spent, and name of the trainer.

Finally, remember that handcuffs can be used as a weapon against an officer if control is not maintained throughout the cuffing process.

FIGURE H-1   Handcuffs.

Highjacking Prevention

CAS, JHC

Preventing highjacking is a worldwide activity of many sorts, but for the sake of some insight into how it might apply to the retail community, the best example, based on our experience, deals with the movement by truck of high-price goods for whatever reason.

For example, when the company would plan, advertise, and conduct a fashion sale of furs, pieces would be transferred from various branch stores throughout the division to the distribution center (DC) in preparation for shipment to the store in which this special event was to be held. We recall a major event in one of our Las Vegas stores. The "collection" of pieces, ranging from full-length sable coats to fox throws, would represent a significant amount of value and, from security's point of view, an attractive target for highjacking.

The strategy employed was as follows: A nondescript box truck designed for movement of hanging goods was rented and backed into a dock at the distribution center. The furs were loaded during the late afternoon prior to the end of the shift. All documents pertaining to the load did not reflect the normally required destination, by design. Once the truck was locked and sealed, and the dock door was closed, a call was made to the dispatcher of the driver's pool that regularly provided drivers for all inter-store transfers (the company did not employ drivers, but rather contracted for that service). An order was made for one driver to report to the DC at midnight for an assignment that would require 20 hours, including a paid rest period. Invariably, the dispatcher would ask where the driver was going and was informed the final decision had not yet been made but the driver would be informed upon arrival at midnight.

When the driver appeared at midnight to the distribution center's security office, he was met by a security department special agent. "Where we going?" the driver would ask.

"Let me check and I'll tell you in a couple of minutes," the agent would reply. The driver had his thermos of coffee and sandwiches for the road, as did the special agent. The agent would escort the driver to the loaded and waiting truck, hand the driver the keys, and the two would drive through the yard gates onto the street. The agent would direct the driver to the appropriate freeway on-ramp and, once underway, the agent would say, "We're on our way to Las Vegas, store #19. Do you know the way to that store?"

"Yes, sir. Wow! What's our load?

"Just a million one-dollar bills, my friend, just a million one-dollar bills," and the agent would laugh.

Today, with the advent of GPS and cellular technology, many trailers are equipped with electronic devices which, when queried, report on their location. These same devices can trigger an alarm, along with their location under specified circumstances, such as road breakdown, excessive speed, or highjacking.

History of Private Security

CAS, JHC

Contrary to popular belief, private security, particularly as a profession, is not a relatively modern development. A study of history from the beginnings of mankind shows that the protection of life and property is one of the oldest tasks both faced and undertaken by man.

Thus, the security and loss prevention industry today is a multifaceted and broad-based business and profession with specialties and subspecialties, employing more people than law enforcement, and financially representing over 1% of the entire gross national product of the United States, with projections of continued growth, particularly in light of the post-9/11 emphasis on security at all levels of the public and private fabric. Private security has experienced an evolutionary growth, with its roots buried deep in history and extending back to antiquity.

Because private security as we know it today has developed as a result of a multitude of ideas, concepts, historical events, and identifiable individuals and personalities, and because private security has become an essential and necessary ingredient of modern business, industry, and society, some knowledge of how it developed is not only interesting, but also helpful in understanding this emerging profession and its future.

Ancient and Biblical Periods

Archaeological digs and historical evidence indicate that the most primitive of man was concerned with security and developed rudimentary security techniques. Cave drawings and other evidence clearly demonstrate that protection and enforcement of social codes were concerns of earliest man. Meeting these needs, from then until now, has resulted in the development of modern day public law enforcement and private security, and the development of those two now distinct and separate disciplines was, in the past, often interwoven and indistinguishable.

In tribal society, needs were basic; security probably did not extend beyond keeping marauding animals from devouring others in the tribe while they slept. While "laws," as such, did not yet exist, we do know that tribal customs were followed and that some means of identifying and bringing violators of those customs before the tribal chief for punishment existed.

Because private security and public law enforcement had common origins, and their development has only really bifurcated in more recent times–and because to understand the development of both, we need first to understand the development of the concept of law (a very complex subject)–let's define the term "law."

According to *Black's Law Dictionary*, law is "that which is laid down, ordained, or established and that which is obeyed and followed by all citizens, subject to sanctions or legal consequences."(1)

Keep in mind that "law" is a general term and can be used in many concepts. For example, we have the law of gravity, "Murphy's Law," natural laws, criminal laws, civil laws, laws of nature, the law of the jungle, etc. Our use of the term "law" relates solely to those laws (codes of conduct) considered necessary for an orderly society.

We must not, however, confuse "law" in this sense (i.e., a code of conduct which carries sanctions) with "morality," even though in many cases laws develop *from* moral codes, or refine or reinforce moral concepts. For example, the moral concept "thou shalt not bear false witness (lie)" is defined and refined by the law in the various penal codes enacted by the appropriate authority, which proscribes such conduct, attaches sanctions, and refines degrees of violations such as petty theft, grand theft, etc. In other areas, moral laws such as "thou shalt not lie" are limited to application only under certain circumstances, such as lying under oath (perjury) and under certain other specified situations; it is only then that lying is "illegal" or "against the law" and that sanctions apply if such behavior is proven to have been undertaken.

It has been said that the establishment of laws and a means of enforcing them is essential to a well-ordered society and is a keystone of democratic forms of government.

The earliest law was probably a combination of tribal custom and the wishes of tribal chiefs. It was passed on by word of mouth (not written or codified as it is today), and its sanctions, the implementation of which were probably overseen by the tribal chief or the entire tribe, were primarily personal, which is to say, designed to satisfy the aggrieved party.

The earliest evidence of any written law does not appear until about 2000 B.C. At that time, Hammurabi, King of Babylon, compiled a legal code which dealt with the behavior of individuals among themselves, as well as their responsibilities to the society as a whole.

The Code of Hammurabi set forth in writing the long-established customs regarding intra-group and interpersonal relationships, defined unacceptable behavior, and spelled out the penalties and punishment for violations. Penalties, for the most part, reflected the ancient "eye for an eye" philosophy; in many cases the offender suffered a penalty similar to the hurt or wrong done the victim.

The Old Testament is replete with laws relating to intra-group and inter-personal relationships. Laws relating to property, inheritance, slaves, and criminal offenses (theft, murder, and prostitution, among others) can be found throughout the Old Testament. In the New Testament, there are references to various crimes, including what we would call "highway robbery" and the placement of "watchtowers" in vineyards to prevent theft of the vines, its fruit, and the wine produced there. And "temple guards" with a "captain" were deployed in the Jewish Temple in Jerusalem way before the time of Jesus Christ.

The next significant development in the chronology of the development of law and the protection of life and property occurred about 600–500 B.C. when the early Greek city-states developed systems for guarding highways and other strategic parts of their cities, including the protection of their ruler, the earliest evidence of executive protection.

The Roman Empire (100 B.C.–500 A.D.)

Significant events relating to the development of law, security, and law enforcement took place with the development of the Roman Empire (see Figure H-2). The "Twelve Tablets," which covered the broad spectrum of the existing body of Roman law, appeared.

Augustus (63 B.C.–14 A.D.), Emperor of Rome, formed a military unit known as a "Cohort" to protect the city. Members of the Cohort were known as "Praetorians" and the now-historically famous "Praetorian Guard" is considered by many historians as the first police force, even though its members were military personnel.

Later in his reign, Augustus formed the "Vigiles of Rome"; its members were civilian *freemen* whose task was to control fires and assist in controlling crime and quelling riots.

The Roman Empire (100 B.C. – 500 A.D.)

- Augustus (63 B.C.–14 A.D.), military unit known as a 'Cohort'
- 'Vigiles of Rome'; private citizens
- Justinian (483-565 A.D.), "Corpas Juris Civilis"

FIGURE H-2

Perhaps the most significant contribution by the Romans came under the Byzantine Emperor Justinian (483–565 A.D.), who summarized Roman law into the world's first law book known as "Corpus Juris Civilis" (Body of Civil Law).

Thus, by the end of the Roman period, tribal customs and trial by ordeal evolved into written laws, standardized punishments, and the beginnings of such concepts as proof of guilt and fair trials.

Anglo-Saxon Period (500–1066 A.D.)

England, from whence came the foundation of the current U.S. law, was a country of instability and confusion from 500 A.D. until the late 800s. The failure of the Roman conquest of England produced several hundred years of turbulence, aimlessness, and general lack of direction and forceful leadership in England.

Not until King Alfred (872–901) do we see the beginnings of legal developments in England which will continue and ultimately change and influence the entire body of legal concepts in the world of that time. The influence of Alfred is significant in two respects: He established the concept of the "King's Peace" (i.e., widespread unlimited private warfare among the various English kingdoms was inconsistent with preserving the peace within the whole of England and would no longer be tolerated), and he established a new code of law which set forth standardized forms of punishment, including specific fines for certain offenses.

The Anglo-Saxon period also saw many customs and practices in the handling of the protection of the citizenry which are recognizable as the forerunners of today's practices. For example, crime prevention and law enforcement were community responsibilities; therefore, whenever an offense occurred, a "hue and cry" went up and all persons were expected to assist in apprehending the offender. The term "hue and cry" is still heard today, and the concepts of citizen arrest and "posse comitatus," which were first evidenced in this period, are very much alive and still in use today.

It was also during this time that the English kingdoms began to be subdivided to meet both agricultural and societal purposes. One of the larger geographical subdivisions was called a "shire" and governed by an appointed person with the title "ealdorman."

A smaller subdivision, the "hundred," was governed by a person known as a "reeve." Eventually, "ealdorman" became an "Earl" (our present-day term "alderman," common in East Coast cities to designate a political leader, emanates from "ealdorman").

The King soon appointed a person to assume primary control of the reeve; that person was known as a "Shirereeve," and our present day "sheriff" derives from the "Shirereeve." Our office of sheriff has similarities to the duties of the Shirereeve, who was responsible for tax collection, law enforcement, and who served as an agent of the king.

Also during this period, we see the first primitive form of a court system. Landowners and royal officials met from time to time to conduct the business of the "shire" or "hundred," which included resolving lawsuits and criminal complaints. While sitting on these matters, the officials became known as "courts," and each had its own jurisdiction depending on the composition and residency of its members.

For persons charged with a criminal offense, guilt or innocence was determined by either "ordeal" or "oath," neither of which placed any reliance on facts, but rather relied on some outward and resultant manifestation of God's indication of guilt.

The ordeal took many forms. An accused might, for example, be required to carry hot coals for a specified distance. If his hands healed from the burns within a specified time, this was a sign from God of his innocence; conversely, if his hands had not healed, he was guilty.

Trial by oath consisted primarily of obtaining the required number of "compurgators" to testify as to the accused's truthfulness or innocence. As might be expected, the higher the rank or position of the "compurgators," the greater the weight given their oath. Compurgators were essentially character witnesses; it was not required that they have any knowledge of the events in question.

While capital punishment was used occasionally, branding, mutilation, and fines were more common forms of punishment. Fines were on a graduating scale: low for petty offenses and/or persons of lower rank and increased in amount for more serious offenses or persons of higher rank or class.

The Anglo-Saxon period can, with respect to law and justice, be characterized as a period when the law of private vengeance prevailed, and where the biblical law of Moses, which regarded a crime primarily as an offense against the individual rather than society as a whole, was totally accepted. Thus, a person who suffered an injury from another could seek his own redress; if a person was slain or disabled, it became the duty (and right) of his clan or village to exact atonement in kind from the transgressor.

The Middle Ages

The Middle Ages period began with William the Conqueror's successful (and last in history) invasion of England and his accession to the throne on Christmas Day of 1066, and ends with the beginnings of the modern era at the end of the reign of Henry VII (1485–1509), the first of the Tudors. It is during this period that we see the development of many of the concepts of law, justice, and legal principles which form the underpinnings of our own cherished Western judicial system.

Norman Period (1066–1199)

One of the principal results of the Norman conquest was the establishment of feudalism in England. Feudalism was, among many things, a reciprocal and contractual relationship between the lord (landlord of the fief or land) and the vassal or tenant. Both parties had rights and responsibilities–one of which was for the vassal to report to the lord's court and assist the lord in the administration of justice.

It must also be pointed out that during this period, there were two distinct legal jurisdictions: the lord's courts and the ecclesiastical (church) courts. The church had an elaborate code of laws (canon law) governing the lives of the clergy and certain aspects of laymen. Lord's courts had jurisdiction over nonchurch matters, although there were frequent disputes as to who had jurisdiction.

The Norman conquest produced three significant developments in England, all of which impacted upon the justice system. These three events were

1. The introduction of feudalism
2. The centralization of government
3. The reorganization of the church

Some of the direct results of William the Conqueror's leadership on the justice system were

1. The formation of the "curia regis," or King's court
2. The institution of itinerant justices

The King's courts had jurisdiction over more major matters and serious offenses such as homicide and robbery. The King's courts were generally in-session, followed their own precedents, developed uniform procedures, and tended to be more impartial than local courts.

The Middle Ages (1066–1500 A.D.)

- **Norman Period (1066–1199)**
- **Post Norman Period (1200–1500)**

FIGURE H-3

As a result of the preceding factors, these courts became quite popular among the citizenry. Because the "curia regis" traveled with the king on his constant journeys, it was difficult for prospective litigants to know the location of the currently sitting court. To solve this problem, the king often sent members of the "curia regis" to various parts of the country to hold court. These justices became known as itinerant justices.

The end of the Norman period saw Henry II (1154–1189) on the throne. Henry II's reign saw the writing of a treatise on the law of England, and the development of the differentiation of the various levels of crime and the first use of the distinction between felonies and misdemeanors. Other significant changes under Henry II included

- Widely extended jurisdiction of the King's court
- Enlarging of the criminal jurisdiction of the King's court
- Extending the writ process to assure that any freeman having business before the King's court would be heard
- Expansion of itinerant justices
- The recording of court decisions and the use of previous decisions as precedent for future holdings, thus establishing a body of common law and the principle of "stare decisis" (to stand by decided cases and uphold precedent)

Finally, and most significant, was the introduction of the forerunner of our jury system as a standard part of the King's court procedures. In fact, in cases involving land ownership, a freeman had an absolute right to trial by jury. Simultaneously, deciding cases by oath was abolished. For these reasons, Henry II is generally credited with laying the foundation of our modern system of trial by jury.

Post Norman Period (1200–1500)

The year 1215 was perhaps the apogee of the Middle Ages in the development of modern legal concepts. In this year

- The Lateran Council abolished trial by ordeal.
- King John issued the Magna Carta, which not only made significant changes in the relationship of the crown (state) to the people in the areas of taxation and the exercise of royal power, but more importantly in the area of the administration of justice. The Magna Carta contained language which is similar to and the foundation of the United States' fifth amendment to the Constitution, which provides that no person shall "be deprived of life, liberty or property, without due process of law."
- Of equal or greater importance, the Magna Carta implied that the king was not above the law and provided means for redressing royal transgressions.

Edward I (1272–1307), a prolific legislator in the areas of law, is remembered in history as the "English Justinian." Among his accomplishments were

- Issuing the Statute of Winchester (also known as Westminster), which made harboring a felon illegal.
- Writing the Second Statute of Westminster, which

Established the practice of having legal issues decided by the courts while questions of fact were left to juries for resolution.

- Began citizen participation in crime prevention by "requiring" that the hue and cry be raised whenever crimes were committed and witnessed by citizens.
- Established the principle that ignorance of the law was no excuse.
- Established the concept of "hot pursuit."
- Forbid strangers from lurking about at night–a forerunner of current vagrancy and loitering laws.
- Established a "watch and ward" system, which required night watchmen or bailiffs selected from the citizenry to maintain order and prevent crime.
- Regulated prostitution in cities.

- Provided for clear areas next to roads to prevent and discourage criminals and highwaymen from hiding there and committing crimes against travelers.
- Required male citizens to arm themselves to the ability their station in life permitted.
- Expanded and formalized the court system and local responsibility for administering justice.
- Ordered free elections; forbid judges from permitting corrupt lawsuits from being pursued in court.

Under Edward II (1327–1377), we see the appointment of justices of the peace and the first use of coroners to inquire into unexplained deaths. Edward III also issued the Statutes of Treason, which made giving aid or comfort to enemies of the land treason; counterfeiting the land's currency was declared treasonous.

The Middle Ages ended with the reign of Richard III (1483–1485) and the ascendancy to the throne of the first of the Tudors, Henry VII (1485–1509). From the foregoing, it is quite reasonable to conclude that the Middle Ages outshone any other era in the number of revolutionary and significant advances made in the development of legal concepts which have survived to modern day.

Modern Period (1500–Present)

The 1500s

The rule of Henry VII (1485–1509) was marked by social turbulence and the emergence of a new merchant or middle class in England which profited at the expense of both the lower (serf) and upper (nobleman) classes. Henry's having been dubbed the "Big Policeman" resulted from his major efforts in restoring law and order to England when it was threatened by social unrest and upheaval.

Henry found that trials had become corrupt and perjury prevailed. He established the Court of Star Chamber, which sat without a jury and was thus less subject to corruption; the court did its job under Henry (although it was later subject to royal abuse under Charles I) and the end of his reign saw England peaceful again; the Crown had consolidated power; the spirit of individualism flowered, and the Renaissance was in full bloom.

The 1600s

Changes in the administration of justice and innovations to the system slowed down for the next couple of centuries. The 1600s saw the development of "private police" to protect the property of merchants. Parochial police were formed to protect parishes or districts within a city. Night patrols were popular to prevent crime and give early warnings of fire.

During the reign of Charles I (1625–1649), his constant feuding with Parliament over their refusal to provide him adequate funds led Charles to subvert the Court of Star Chamber into an instrument of royal abuse synonymous with tyranny.

The Star Chamber became famous for "third degree" methods; to be charged with an offense was tantamount to being condemned. Punishment was often corporal or considered "cruel and unusual." Charles was finally forced by Parliament in 1628 to sign the Petition of Rights, many of the provisions of which were restatements of the Magna Carta.

In 1641, Charles was forced to totally abolish the Star Chamber. His tyrannical rule resulted ultimately in a civil war which saw Charles beheaded in 1649.

Oliver Cromwell (1653–1658) assumed leadership after Charles's execution and was known as Lord Protector rather than King.

Cromwell maintained order by martial rule and was eventually replaced by Charles II (1660–1685). Under Charles II, Parliament, rather than the King, was given the power to make new laws. In 1679, the Habeas Corpus Act was passed, requiring law enforcement officials to bring an accused before a judge to explain why the prisoner was being held. (For a modern-day comparison, refer to Article I, Section 9, and the six amendment to the U.S. Constitution.)

The continued emergence of mercantile establishments resulted for the first time in 1663 in the formation of a force of paid constables to protect business property at night. This force became known as the "shiver and shake" watch.

The late 1600s also saw the proliferation of private police in the form of merchant police, parish police, dock police, warehouse police, etc. This period also saw the first use of "rewards" to entice the public to report known criminals and participate in the control of crime.

The 1600s saw developments in America which paralleled those in England. Sheriffs and constables were appointed as representatives of the English king. Citizen participation in law enforcement took the English form: the night watch system could be found in Boston, Philadelphia, and New York.

The 1700s

The 1700s saw an increase in the concern for individual rights; individuals were no longer "conscripted" into night watch service. Rather, tax revenues were used to pay for night watch personnel. The concept that a criminal offense was an offense against the crown or state (i.e., the whole of society) rather than a personal offense against an individual victim, which had been slowly developing since the 1600s, was by now well established.

In 1748, lawyer and novelist Henry Fielding was appointed magistrate for the second district of London, the Westminster area. In 1750, Fielding published "An Enquiry in the Causes of the Late Increase of Robberies," which was probably the first security survey. Fielding took over the Bow Street police station as chief magistrate and proceeded to make significant improvements in the London police force, including the formation of the first plain clothes detective unit known as the "Bow Street Runners"–since its members ran to the scene of crimes hoping to apprehend the culprit.

1800s & World War II

The 1800s

The year 1829 is generally conceded as the year in which the real beginnings of a modern police system took place. It was in this year that Sir Robert Peel, Home Secretary of England, guided a bill through Parliament titled "An Act for Improving the Police in and Near the Metropolis." This legislation authorized a new uniformed, full-time salaried 1600-member police force.

These features, coupled with other new ideas such as rigorous pre-employment screening, semi-military principles of discipline, and lifetime tenure (provided established standards were maintained) resulted in a growth of the force to over 3200 men within 3 years.

Of historical note is the fact that the headquarters of this new force was on a small London side street called Scotland Yard, and that the term "Bobbie," which is recognized worldwide as the nickname for London police officers, derives out of respect for Sir Robert.

In the United States, such famous lawmen as Wyatt Earp, Bat Masterson, Pat Garrett, "Wild Bill" Hickok, along with the Texas Rangers, all gained fame in the "Old West" for their own methods of bringing law and order to the frontier.

In the East, cities were growing and forming their more formalized police departments. True police agencies, following Peel's example, began to flourish in the 1800s. Police departments were established in New York (1844), Chicago (1850), Cincinnati (1852), Philadelphia (1855), and Detroit (1865).

On a national level, crime was also a problem, and we see the federal government forming investigative agencies. The Post Office Investigative Service was formed in 1828, the law enforcement arm of the Treasury Department was formed in 1864, and the U.S. Justice Department in 1902 began its law enforcement arm, which was the forerunner of the FBI. The Federal Bureau of Investigations, as we know it today, began in 1932 under J. Edgar Hoover.

We have spent a good deal of time reviewing the development of law and policing agencies, not without reason. The development of private security was, by the very nature of its function, closely related to public law enforcement and under the proscriptions of the law. As will be subsequently noted, some aspects of loss prevention have a "law enforcement" correlation and must be conducted within the parameters of established laws and statutes. For these reasons it is helpful for security personnel to understand how their work-related laws developed and essential that they keep up-to-date with changes and court decisions affecting them.

It was in the mid- to late-1890s that modern-day private security had its beginnings. This was the era of the department store's beginnings. Macy's in New York opened in 1858; Marshall Fields in Chicago opened in 1860; Strawbridge & Clothiers opened in Philadelphia in 1866; Wanamakers opened in New Jersey in 1876, and The Broadway in Los Angeles opened its doors in 1897. And with multistory big-city department stores came shoplifting problems, which caused the creation of the early term "floor walkers," private citizen-employees who were responsible for the repression and/or detection of crime inside the stores. One of your authors had the occasion to review turn-of-the-century security department records of San Francisco's Emporium Department Store, reflecting numerous shoplifting arrests made by the staff.

Records as well as oral accounts tell of how some "floor walkers" were conspicuous, wearing a bowler hat, smoking a cigar with thumbs inside suspenders, whereas others worked "undercover" and worked stealthily to observe and detain shoplifters. Books were kept bearing photographs of those caught, utilizing in those days the most current technology, photography. Clearly, the genesis of retail security and "loss prevention" was in the big department stores and their "floor walkers."

Remember, this was during the time when police departments were new and forming to provide "security" services to their respective communities.

Alan Pinkerton, who was born in Scotland, emigrated to the United States after his police officer father died when Alan was a small boy. In 1850, after 4 years as deputy sheriff in Cane County, Illinois, Pinkerton was made a deputy in Cook County (Chicago). Later, he became a special agent of the U.S. Post Office Department, and then Chicago's first and only police detective. He then left the police department to form a private detective agency, specializing in providing investigative and security services for railroads and industrial organizations (see Figure H-4).

Pinkerton's reputation as a "master sleuth" led to his acquiring a national reputation. During the Civil War, Pinkerton's agency and its agents provided the Union with the organization for intelligence and counter-espionage services and also served to provide personal protection for President Lincoln.

Beginning of Modern Private Security

Alan Pinkerton began the first national
investigative agency.

FIGURE H-4

After the Civil War, Pinkerton returned to private clients, and because of the relatively few number of public law enforcement agencies coupled with jurisdictional restrictions, he provided the only investigative agency with truly national capabilities.

In 1885 William G. Baldwin commenced his private detective career at the age of 25 with an agency named the Eureka Detective Agency in Charleston, West Virginia, and with the passage of time created one of the foremost private police agencies in America. His Baldwin-Felts Detective Agency, with strong ties in the railroad industry, often received and exercised governmental powers in handling criminal investigation assignments which public sector police agencies were unable or unwilling to undertake.(2)

In 1889, Brinks Incorporated was formed to protect property and payrolls. In 1909, William J. Burns, Inc., formed a private detective agency and became the investigative arm of the American Banking Association (see Figure H-5). The Pinkerton, Brinks, and Burns companies all continue in business today. Regrettably, there were no "Pinkertons," "Baldwins," or "Burnses" who led the way in the early giant department store security programs.

Simultaneous with the founding and growth of these giant pioneers, the various railroads, which had great political power, got state legislatures to pass Railroad Police Acts authorizing the railroads to establish their own security forces with full police powers. By 1914, over 12,000 railroad police agents were in operation.(3)

World War II

World War II was the real source and stimulus of the modern and complex private security industry. Private security in a sense was born of the war, went through adolescence during the Cold War period, and reached maturity in the 1960s–and continues to grow and prosper, all the while developing more specialization and sophistication.

The military services in WWII trained thousands of men in law enforcement (MPs, SPs, CIDs, etc.) and in the various intelligence services (OSS, ONI, CIC, etc.). At the same time, the FBI and the Immigration and Naturalization Service (INS) and other federal agencies (and their counterparts in the other Allied nations) were expanding to countersabotage and espionage threats.

Additionally, thousands of others were trained as auxiliary police and plant guards to provide physical security at home and in defense plants. By 1945, there were literally thousands of businesses, plants, factories, etc., engaged in "classified" government or war contracts. Each of these facilities required physical security, thus producing a large pool of personnel trained–to some degree at least–in "security." After the war, this large resource of military police, intelligence agents, auxiliary police, and plant security guards entered the civilian workforce with hopes of putting their wartime training to use in the civilian marketplace.

Founders: Pinkerton, Brinks, and Burns

Brinks Armored Car, 1925

William J. Burns

FIGURE H-5

The Cold War produced, among its many ramifications, the continued need for classified defense contracts, thus requiring these now civilian-orientated operations to maintain some degree of security. Additionally, the many employees who worked in these facilities needed security clearances, thus creating the need for a large force of investigators to do background investigations in order to grant security "clearances."

Congressional committees and government agencies of all sorts began investigating both aspects of the "War" and contemporaneous domestic matters requiring more hundreds of investigators. Thus, while the war itself gave birth to the multitudes of personnel trained in security and investigations, it was the post-war period which provided a means for them to use their training in the civilian world.

The trend begun during the Cold War to use investigative and security-trained personnel by both government and civilian agencies and private business in numbers never before visualized not only continued, but increased after the so-called Cold War years—albeit for somewhat different reasons.

As the Cold War thawed, and the need for private security normally would have abated, the concurrent increase in street crime and white collar business crime began escalating, more than taking up the slack in the need for private security and its many related specialties. Department store security programs continued to grow with the use of more "store detectives," many of which were women. Some store's programs were labeled "Protection Departments" and store detectives relied heavily on police officers who worked traffic control at the street and boulevard intersections adjacent to the stores to help apprehend fleeing shoplifters.

By the mid-1970s, the best available statistics indicated that there were over 500,000 persons engaged in private security and that this number exceeded those engaged in public law enforcement. By 1985, estimates place the number of persons in private security jobs at 700,000—exceeding those in the public sector by at least 100,000. Most observers agree that the private security growth will continue to outstrip the public sector.

One has only to peruse one of the numerous trade or professional publications devoted to private security to appreciate the growth of this industry. An examination of the organizations devoted to the private security profession (and it truly has become a profession) reveals both the widespread applications of the profession and its diversity.

Organizations range from those with a very broad membership base (e.g., the American Society for Industrial Security–International) to those with rather specialized interests (e.g., organizations devoted to credit card fraud, hospital security, banking security, multinational corporation executive protection, security consulting, and antiterrorism organizations, etc.).

Naturally, when considering the scope of private security and its economic implications, we must also consider all the supporting functions which accompany the practicing security professional, such as training schools, equipment manufacturers, expositions and seminars, consultants, and yes, even these specialized books and literature devoted to the subject, more of which are being published every year.

The Future

The future of private security is (on balance) bright. The rapid growth of our industry, over the past two or three decades, has seen the leaders of industry recognize the importance of the security (in some businesses known as "Loss Prevention") as evidenced by the elevation of the head of security to the vice president level in many organizations over the past decade or two. The post-9/11 world has seen the dramatic increase in security in both public and private. Terrorist bombings and other threats have led to the demand for tighter and increased security at all levels of everyday life. Consider the use of large numbers of security officers at sporting events, transportation systems, and theatrical and social events, to name just a few. The increased use of CCTV, once used almost exclusively by the private sector, to monitor public streets and gatherings is unprecedented. The recent designation of Chief Security Officer (CSO) on a level with the COO, CFO, and CIO of major corporations attests to the vitality and importance of this function in the 21st century. These advances, however, also give rise to some challenges which our profession must meet and overcome if it is to enjoy both continued growth and the respect and confidence of its employers, clients, the public, and governmental and regulatory agencies.

Some of the challenges facing us are described next.

Professionalism

A profession is defined as a vocation or occupation requiring advanced training and usually involving mental rather than manual work. A professional is one engaged in a skilled profession. The caliber of persons entering private security with a long-term commitment to grow in and with the industry continues to improve. We must encourage this trend by improving pay scales (particularly for entry-level positions and uniformed security personnel) and by offering opportunities for upward mobility for qualified persons. The early 20th century image of the retail "floor walker" or manufacturing plant night watchman is, or should be, history. Those "bottom of the ladder" and generally unskilled and untrained persons have no place in today's security profession. Many states have enacted legislation to require a minimum level of uniformed security officer competence. California began private security regulation for contract uniformed security officers in 1915; other states have followed suit.

A more recent trend in state regulation of private security (e.g., New York and California) is the requirement that not only uniformed contract security officers meet state training minimums and licensing requirements, but that proprietary security and loss prevention personnel also meet these requirements.

Note: Your authors reluctantly support state mandated training minimums for proprietary security personnel since, regrettably, some companies fail to voluntarily adequately train their loss prevention personnel. We also acknowledge that state-required training is rudimentary at best (sometimes a little knowledge is a dangerous thing), and we encourage companies utilizing loss prevention staffs to supplement state curricula with in-house training and supporting loss prevention personnel's attendance at industry-sponsored LP seminars.

Training is the key to this challenge. No longer can we hire someone and put that person on assignment with only a new uniform and a pat on the back. The American Society for Industrial Security–International (ASIS) began its Certified Protection Professional (CPP) professional certification program in 1977, and today it is a "desired" qualification of security applicants by many companies. In 2003 ASIS added two new certifications:: Physical Security Professional (PSP) and Professional Certified Investigator (PCI). The International Information Systems Security Certification Consortium, Inc., or ISC^2, a nonprofit organization, also issues a Certified Information Systems Security Professional (CISSP) certification. The International Foundation for Protection Officers' Certified Protection Officer (CPO) program is directed primarily toward uniformed security officers. The International Association of Professional Security Consultants (IAPSC) began a certification program for security consultants (CSC) in 2006. Finally, the Loss Prevention Foundation, a not-for-profit organization, planned to launch its $LPC_{QUALIFIED}$ certification in early 2007 followed shortly by its higher status $LPC_{CERTIFIED}$ program. All these certifications require study and passing what are described as "rigorous" written examinations. These efforts, and others under study, are designed to upgrade and assure qualified and trained personnel in the various security subsets.

Legal Status and Liability

With few exceptions, private security personnel have no police powers beyond those of their fellow citizens. Their work, however, is often quasi-law enforcement in nature, and thus they interact with and confront their fellow citizens in adversarial situations very much like public police. Effort must be made to keep the distinction clear and to concentrate private security efforts on asset protection and loss prevention programs. When apprehensions and arrests must be made, it is essential that the procedures followed are both legal and ethical. The courts of many jurisdictions are just beginning to realize the full extent of the private security industry and how frequently its practitioners interact with the public.

These court reviews of arrest, privacy, malicious prosecution, assault, and search and seizure issues, to name a few, are producing both constantly changing rules and laws under which private security must operate, as well as large money judgments against both security companies and individual security officers when their behavior violates often-changing and unclear "rules of the game."

Image

The public's perception of private security is rapidly outgrowing the "rent-a-cop" or "floor walker" image, but there is still room for improving both the relationship between and the perception of us by police agencies.

The International Association of Chiefs of Police (IACP) has recently officially recognized our industry and formally noted our contribution to crime prevention and control, and has urged its members to work for a closer degree of cooperation between the public and private sectors." The IACP has formally requested a private security organization to submit material relating to specific loss prevention issues for formal issuance by police departments across the country.

Proprietary Security

Corporations now expect its security personnel, particularly those in middle and upper management positions, to be more than simple "security experts." Businesses today expect their security to come out of its traditional "isolation" from other company functions. Today, security executives are expected to be conversant with overall business operations, and to contribute in a tangible way to the overall profitability and success of the venture.

Certainly, security expertise is still essential, but in addition security executives are expected to be knowledgeable of general business concepts and the goals of their organization and to make a contribution in these areas. Top management is looking for a larger return on their investment of security dollars.

Contract Security

Those businesses which hire contract security officers are demanding more than simply a person with a uniform, badge, and (on rare occasions) a gun. Business is becoming more and more sensitive to its "image" and how it is perceived by the public. The public rarely distinguishes whether a security guard is contract or "in-house"–the guard represents and "is" the company. Therefore, a guard who is slovenly in appearance, rude, unknowledgeable, or who makes a serious legal error in accomplishing his or her duties becomes either unacceptable or a serious liability–or both.

Thus, the contract officer must be well trained not only in the technical aspects of the job, but also in the expectations of the client employer, and must be a knowledgeable and courteous representative of the client. The contract security officer must be sensitive to the unique relationship that exists between him or her and the client.

Summary

Traditionally, society's efforts to prevent and control crime have been the province of public (government) law enforcement, although private "security" efforts have been woven into the fabric of crime control since earliest times.

Beginning in the second half of the 20th century, private security (whether proprietary or contractual) has taken an increasingly larger role in crime control and prevention, so that as of 1985 the resources of money (over $20 billion annually) and personnel (over 700,000) exceed that of public law enforcement. Indeed, the most recent trend is the "privatization" of functions such as running jails and prisons, which were previously the jobs of government exclusively.

Private security is big business and growing in all free-world countries and ranges from the single owner/operator private detective agency or security consultant through national contract security guard companies and investigative agencies, to multinational security firms and alarm companies. The thousands of proprietary security personnel, working only for a single employer and in his or her interests only, must also be included.

The industry, because of its size, has begun to attract the attention of legislatures and of the courts, and in those instances in which self-restraint and legal and ethical considerations are neglected, the legislatures and courts are establishing the standards under which we are required to operate.

In other cases, the courts are also punishing, through monetary awards to injured parties, those private security practitioners who "go too far" and offend public sensibilities.

The industry is also growing in sophistication and professionalism. It is attracting personnel and leaders who would be a credit to any profession. With both continued growth and professionalism, both of which seem assured, the future of private security and that of those in the profession seems bright.

References

(1) Black, H.C. (1951). *Black's law dictionary*, St. Paul, Minnesota: West Publishing Company, 1028.
(2) Velke, J. (2005). *The true story of the Baldwin-Felts Detective Agency*. Velke. *Note:* John Velke is a contributing author to this work.
(3) Green and Farber. (1975). *Introduction to security*. Los Angeles, California: Security World Publishing Co., Inc., 27.
(4) For a thorough discussion and detailed analysis of the relationship between private security and public law enforcement in America, see: Cunningham, W.C., and Taylor, T.H. (1985). *The Hallcrest Report: Private security and police in America*. Chancellor Press.

The History of Retail Security/Loss Prevention

John Velke

Writing a history of retail security/loss prevention can be like trying to say which drop of water hits the ground first when it starts to rain. So many retailers started doing things around the same time that it is often difficult to determine who started something "first." Therefore, this history does not attempt to designate "firsts" but is simply intended to give you an overview of the history of retail loss prevention from the perspective of significant developments that impacted the industry and became commonplace.

1850–1899

Until the mid-1800s retail stores in the United States were typically owner-operated businesses. Merchandise was primarily offered for sale from behind counters, and the selling staff waited on each customer. Shoplifting was primarily accomplished through sleight-of-hand tricks within close proximity of a sales clerk. Retail stores relied on the management staff and sales clerks to detect theft and therefore had no need for full-time dedicated security personnel.

This 1869 account serves as a typical example, "Storekeepers are often victimized by that class of depredators known as shoplifters, who frequently stop in a shop, and, at a glance, ascertain what can most easily be removed without detection. Grocers, especially, frequently find a whole or part of a ham, which has been left on the block for convenience, among the things taken."

During the 1870s things began to change. Retailers in some of the major metropolitan areas began to grow rapidly, adding selling square footage faster than sales clerks. Some stores began to recognize the need for in-store dedicated security personnel. One of the first of these was Frederick Loeser's & Company, a New York City department store, which hired David N. Corwin as a full-time store detective in 1880. Corwin had spent the previous 25 years in the detective bureau of the New York City Police Department, where his specialty was identifying and apprehending shoplifters and pickpockets. The police commissioner described Corwin this way, "There isn't an old hand he doesn't know, and it takes him a mighty short time to find out the new ones. He's made some good arrests in his day, and he's pulled in shoplifters that other officers wouldn't have dared to touch. It's a risky thing, sometimes, a man has to be very shrewd and very sure too, and Dave is just that man. There were a couple of women he brought in one day, and I doubt if anyone else would have risked it. Why, one of them had on a thousand dollar shawl, and the way they kicked against being arrested was a caution. They were respectable people, they said, and if they were arrested they would sue the department and have the officer imprisoned for false arrest. All this sort of talk went in one of Dave's ears and out the other. They were searched, stuff found on them, and sent up (to prison), they proved to be old shoplifters too, a couple of professionals."

In the early 1890s, Corwin left Loeser's & Co. store and went to work handling the store detective duties at Abraham & Strauss, where he stayed until his death in 1901. Corwin's 20-year career in retail security/loss prevention is worth recognizing because most retail stores did not begin hiring dedicated security personnel until after 1900. Up until that time, most stores relied on the local police to handle shoplifting, pickpockets, and other petty crimes. When significant crimes and employee theft occurred, store owners typically engaged the services of a private detective agency.

A great example is the relationship that existed for nearly 100 years between the Jeweler's Security Alliance and the Pinkerton Detective Agency. First created in 1883 by a group of independently owned jewelry stores, the Jeweler's Security Alliance was one of the first to recognize the value of taking a proactive stance against retail criminals by retaining the services of a well-organized and professional group of detectives. With offices located in nearly every major city in the United States, Pinkerton detectives were at the disposal of the Jeweler's Security Alliance members anytime a need arose.

1900–1949

Two major developments at the beginning of the 20th century significantly changed patterns of criminal behavior and made a significant impact on retail security that have been felt to this day. In 1903 Henry Ford and 11 Detroit-area businessmen founded the Ford Motor Company, and 10 years later, by implementing assembly line processes, made automobile ownership affordable for many Americans. A year later, the first commercial airline began operating between St. Petersburg and Tampa, Florida. Suddenly, professional criminals (including shoplifters) had a much wider territory they could work in. No longer were they at the mercy of train schedules and horse-drawn carriages. Criminals could move quickly from one city to another and then move on before being recognized by the local police.

Many more retailers began establishing an in-house security department, drawing largely on the experience of police officers to fill the newly created role of Director of Security. The R.H. Macy Company serves as a good example. Located at Herald Square in New York City, Macy's soon became known as a retail innovator and the "World's Largest Store." In 1907 Macy's hired William H. Wall to lead the security function, then called the "protection department." Wall was a former police officer with the New York, New Haven, and Hartford Railroad and was uniquely qualified to take on the multiple and unusual tasks associated with running the security department at Macy's. In 1901, while still employed by the railroad, William Wall was appointed the Chief of the Special Police for the Pan-American Exposition in Buffalo, New York. In that capacity he handled the planning for the safety and well-being of an estimated eleven million exposition visitors. This experience served him well, as he later became responsible for handling security for the Macy's Thanksgiving Day Parade.

During his 27 years as the Director of the Protection Department at Macy's, William Wall introduced a number of innovative retail security concepts. He instituted the use of guard dogs to supplement the night watchman in the store, he had jail cells built in the store where shoplifters could be held until turned over to the police, and he played an important part in establishing the first Stores Mutual Association, then known as the Stores Mutual Protective League.

The original Stores Mutual Protective League was an organization supported by member retailers that provided store detectives to all members in New York City. Each store detective was a sworn special police officer with the authority to make arrests anywhere in the city. It was not unusual for store detectives to follow a potential shoplifter from Macy's, to Gimbels, and then to Lord & Taylor, until they caught the person in the act of stealing or became satisfied that the person was not a thief. This freedom to work in more than one store on a given day and to follow suspects through the public streets made it much easier to recognize and apprehend professional shoplifters.

This 1918 account serves as an interesting example. On September 25 of that year, store detectives Anna Coschina and Frances Mullin noticed two 30-something women acting suspiciously in the New York City Wanamaker's store. One of the women appeared to be acting as a lookout and shielding for the other as merchandise vanished. The detectives struggled to remain inconspicuous while trying to obtain a clear observation of the theft. The two shoplifting suspects left Wanamaker's and went to Best & Co., then to Saks Fifth Avenue, on to Macy's, and then to Lord & Taylor. Finally, after spending several hours following the women all over town, the detectives watched as the younger of the two women concealed two pairs of ladies gloves in her handbag. Anna and Frances waited until the two women left Lord & Taylor and then apprehended them on the sidewalk.

In addition to the two pairs of gloves, each valued at $2.00, the detectives found two handbags from Lord & Taylor valued at $6.50 each; two veils from Best & Co. valued at $2.25 each; two sets of pins from Saks Fifth Avenue valued at $1.50 each; one waist from Wanamakers valued at $2.85; and nine pairs of ladies gloves, valued at $12.41, from Macy's. The women gave their names as Bessie Clark, age 33, and Mary Leaman, age 39. Both women acknowledged that they supported themselves by shoplifting and that they were currently living at the Hotel Marie Antoinette. They were turned over to the police and each held on $300.00 bail. They remained incarcerated until October 7, when they appeared in court and pleaded guilty. Bessie was fined $50.00 and released. Mary, who had been charged as an accomplice, was fined $25.00 and released.

As the aforementioned account illustrates, another noteworthy aspect of early retail security is that stores recognized that plainclothes store detectives needed to represent the populations they served. Women and minorities were hired in these quasi-law enforcement positions long before opportunities occurred in public law enforcement. In fact, the first recorded example of a woman given full police powers did not occur until 1905, and even then, police departments did not generally embrace the hiring of women until the 1970s. Meanwhile, women like Anna Coschina and Frances Mullin demonstrated that they had the patience, fortitude, and ability to trail criminals and make arrests.

1950–1999

Perhaps the most significant change to ever affect retail security/loss prevention occurred in 1950. That year television ownership leapt from fewer than 5 million to more than 10 million by the end of the year. This 100% plus increase marked the beginning of a decade of explosive growth. By 1960, 80% of homes in the United States had at least one television set. Combined with the post World War II "baby boomer" generation beginning to reach their teenage years, the result was a sharp increase in the number of teenagers with a desire to own things they could not all afford.

Retailers soon realized that catching every shoplifter was impossible. The concept of *preventing* retail crime began to take root. A renewed emphasis on customer service and the introduction of "uniformed" (red blazers) security personnel led many departments to change their name from "Security" to "Loss Prevention."

The "prevention" mantra exploded during the 1970s as retail business organizations began sponsoring antishoplifting public service announcement campaigns; electronic article surveillance technology was introduced in many stores; state legislatures began passing civil recovery statutes so that retailers could recoup some of their losses from shoplifters; and store mutual associations shared apprehension data with member retailers in an increased effort to prevent the hiring of known criminals. The convenience store retailers were now staying open 24 hours per day and began aggressive prevention campaigns to reduce the probability of armed robberies. Their tactics included using drop safes so that a limited amount of funds would be available, installing CCTV equipment with public view monitors, increasing both interior and exterior lighting, and removing obstructions blocking the view of police officers driving by.

Some of these concepts and many others became known as Crime Prevention Through Environmental Design (CPTED) after the 1971 publication of C. Ray Jeffery's book by that name. Jeffery, a criminologist at Florida State University, postulated that environmental design features influenced the probability of certain types of criminal behavior. His theories were refined and updated in the 1977 edition of his book and expanded further in his 1990 book, *Criminology: An Interdisciplinary Approach*. Retail security/loss prevention professionals followed these studies and began working more closely with their construction and planning departments to incorporate crime prevention design features in new store and remodel projects.

Recognition of retail security as a legitimate and distinct profession began to occur in the 1970s as books like *Successful Retail Security: An Anthology* by Mary Margaret Hughes (1974); *Retail Security: A Management Function* by Denis E. Byrne (1977); *Effective Security Management* by Charles A. Sennewald (1978); and *Investigative Technique for the Retail Security Investigator* by Joseph M. Di Domenico (1979) gained widespread attention. The "rent-a-cop" and "door-shaker" stereotypes were being replaced with images of educated professionals serving an important business function.

By 1980 some of the best retail security directors had come to realize they could mold and develop their replacements and provide high-caliber candidates to the retail industry by developing and promoting from within. Prior police, military, or federal law enforcement experience was no longer felt to be a prerequisite for a top-level retail loss prevention position. Succession planning and comprehensive training programs began to become commonplace.

The Commodore 64 "personal computer," first introduced in 1982, and the Apple Macintosh released in 1984 completely revolutionized retail loss prevention. Within a decade, criminals were using home computers to counterfeit everything from fraudulent receipts to United States currency. Progressive loss prevention professionals found hundreds of ways to use computers to mine point of sale data, improve efficiency, and collect and retain information for later use. Time-keeping systems, return authorization systems, advance ship notices, electronic fund transfers, electronic gift cards, and many other computerized programs created new vulnerabilities for retailers. This ever-expanding use of computer technology in all aspects of the retail business soon made computer literacy a requirement among loss prevention personnel.

The conventional role of the vice president or director of security/loss prevention began to change dramatically during the 1980s and 1990s. Whereas previously the position often focused on shoplifting, internal theft, and shortage, by the end of the century it was not unusual to find the vice president not only overseeing security/loss prevention, but also supervising internal audit, safety, and/or risk management.

2000–Present

On September 11, 2001, terrorists flew planes into the World Trade Center, the Pentagon, and a Pennsylvania field, killing over 3,000 innocent victims. The retail loss prevention profession underwent a dramatic change that day. Suddenly, shoplifting, internal theft, and shortage seemed a whole lot less important than safety and disaster recovery. The few retail companies that already had a disaster recovery plan discovered that there were ways to improve on their plan, and those companies that did not have a plan began working to develop one immediately. Retail loss prevention personnel began learning all they could about terrorism, anthrax, hurricanes, bird flu, and many other potential business-interrupting possibilities. The safety of retail employees and the protection of the business was now of paramount importance.

In many companies the responsibilities of the senior loss prevention executive expanded to include human resources, information security, and/or ethics and compliance programs. A few companies began to recognize the talent and importance of multifaceted retail loss prevention executives and began promoting these individuals to senior vice presidents, executive vice presidents, and chief security officers.

The beginning of the 21st century also ushered in an unprecedented increase in the use of technology. Remote video monitoring and digital video recording became much more prevalent, and radio frequency identification (RFID) began to gain momentum. Online auctions became popular and created a new method for the disposal of stolen merchandise. Global positioning satellites were used to enhance tracking of company trucks and other vehicles. Cell phones and Blackberrys became standard equipment among retail executives. The speed of information exchange (both accurate and inaccurate) made it more important than ever that the security/loss prevention personnel communicate quickly, clearly, and accurately. Rumors, Internet bulletin board postings, and blogs having the potential to hurt a company's reputation and thus cause loss became the concern of security/loss prevention.

In many respects the security/loss prevention profession has changed dramatically since David Corwin caught his first shoplifter. Shoplifting has become big business with organized retail theft gangs stealing millions of dollars' worth of merchandise each year. Retailers are working more closely with local and federal law enforcement than ever before, and some retailers have implemented their own organized retail theft squads that actively seek out fences and the groups that keep them supplied. But two things haven't changed. Sometime today a sales clerk will steal cash out of a register, and somebody else will try to walk out of a grocery store without paying for a ham hidden under his or her clothing.

"Holds"/ Hold Procedures

CAS, JHC

"Holds," or holding merchandise for a prospective customer, is that procedure whereby a given item is removed from the selling floor to give that customer a limited period of time to make a decision to either purchase the item or the item will be returned to the selling floor and then available to other customers. Each company makes its own determination as to how long the "hold" will be allowed, but 3 days is the average time. The retailer recognizes each day the item is held off the floor in a given "hold area," potential interest in and sale of that item are lost. Yet, to accommodate customers, the removal of the item is deemed good customer service. This is an old, time-tested practice, and it's a management and merchandising decision of merit.

Procedurally, a "hold form" or "hold slip" is filled out by the sales associate with the customer's name, the date the item is removed from the floor, and the date it's due back on the floor. The sales associate affixes his or her signature, and the form is attached to the goods in question. The company relies on the selling staff to monitor the dates and, if the item is not claimed, to return it to the floor. Clearly, sloppy controls, including holding goods for extended periods of time, result to some degree in the goods going out of season or otherwise losing value due to periodic markdowns.

Loss prevention agents, in the normal course of inspecting stock and other noncustomer areas of the store, will check the dates on the hold slips and inform the manager of past-due holds needing to be returned to the floor. On the surface, this appears to be some task hardly in the purview of security-type employees. Yet, abuses of the hold system, if not monitored, tend to cost the company money. The abuse is in employees who take advantage of the system to place items on "hold" for themselves (sometimes using fictitious customers' names) pending known or suspected upcoming markdowns of the item. This means if the item was on the floor available to the public at its current marked price, the company would realize the planned benefit/profit of its sale, but if sold at a markdown price, less the employee discount, the profit is lost.

Hotlines: The Modern Employee Hotline: Incident Report Management From A to Z

Eugene F. Ferraro and Lindsey M. Lee

Rocked by corporate scandal, the turn of the century brought about significant changes for the modern American workplace and the culture of corporate America, not the least of which was the passage of the Sarbanes-Oxley Act in 2002. Many years earlier, legislators and the courts recognized the need for a manner by which organizational criminals could be held legally accountable for their misconduct in a structured and standardized way. The result was the development of the Federal Sentencing Guidelines in 1991. Both mandates require organizations to implement mechanisms by which to receive reports of employee misconduct. Sarbanes-Oxley took the requirement a step further, however, requiring organizations to put in place an *anonymous* method by which to receive reports of financially related misconduct or concerns. (1) Perhaps the most widely chosen and cost-effective compliance option in any case is the implementation of an anonymous employee hotline.

Traditional employee hotlines presume to offer complete anonymity to the reporting employee; however, many times the hotline is directed to an individual or group of individuals within the organization's human resources department. Under such circumstances, employees are often fearful that they cannot truly remain anonymous (should they wish to do so) due to caller identification technology and the possibility that their voice may be recognized. Hotlines of this nature are further plagued by additional restrictions inherent in the hotline's structure. For example, reports can typically be received in only one language, usually English. Therefore, employees who speak little to no English may be discouraged from reporting misconduct of which they are aware, which is particularly problematic for U.S.-based multinational organizations. Also, internal hotlines are often not available 24 hours per day, 7 days per week. Therefore, employees making reports after regular business hours are required, at best, to leave a voicemail. Organizations are then limited in their ability to continue communications with reporting employees who leave a voicemail, especially if they do not provide their name and contact information. Such limitations make proper incident investigation particularly problematic.

Documentation of reports received through a traditional employee hotline is an extremely manual process and is highly susceptible to error and misrepresentation. There is also no guarantee that reports are stored in a centralized location, potentially compromising the organization's ability to conduct a good faith investigation. Such difficulties often preclude the communication loop from remaining intact, and individuals responsible for responding, investigating, and/or making disciplinary decisions may not be fully informed. In short, traditional internal employee hotlines are inadequate at best and potentially increase an organization's liability exposure.

As a result of the serious pitfalls described here, many third-party vendors have developed sophisticated solutions to the challenges the traditional employee hotline poses. The most comprehensive vendors will provide not just a hotline by which employees can submit reports, but will also provide an Internet-based reporting portal as well. A third-party vendor will also typically house all incident data in a secure, centralized Internet location to which only the designated organizational users have access. The technology that vendors can provide should also include a means by which organizations can maintain ongoing communication with reporting employees, even those who choose to remain completely anonymous. Such technology ensures organizations the ability to conduct thorough investigations into reported matters. Vendors also typically provide 24/7/365 hotline staffing in multiple languages to ensure all employees have equal opportunity and ability to report their knowledge of workplace misconduct. The experienced vendor will also have the ability to provide the organization with instantaneous notification of and access to all reported matters, allowing the organization to respond in a timely and efficient manner, as the law requires.

The implementation of a third-party anonymous incident reporting system provides many additional benefits to the savvy employer. Organizations with an anonymous system in place find that employees are much more likely to report concerns, given that the fear of retaliation or reprisal is often diminished when the possibility of identification decreases. (2) In this way, such systems serve as early detection mechanisms for employers; they are often notified of fraudulent activity and other costly employee misconduct as it is "brewing" rather than after it has escalated beyond a reasonably manageable point. (3) The establishment of a sophisticated hotline solution further communicates to employees that the organization cares about them and their safety, furthering loyalty and decreasing costs associated with employee turnover. Employers who invest in their most valuable asset—their employees—reap the benefits associated with doing so: increased productivity, decreased turnover, and a more stable and profitable organization overall. The cost of a third-party anonymous incident reporting system is minimal in comparison to other annual business expenses (such as toilet paper in many cases!), and the rewards gained often pay for the system itself after only a short time of use.

Next Steps

The employee hotline, functioning as the report receipt mechanism, however, is only part of the overall solution. The legal mandates described previously also require organizations to effectively investigate, document, and retain all records related to the initial employee report. Effective incident report management should not be viewed from a "one size fits all" perspective but rather requires the commitment of multiple organizational decision makers and the development and implementation of a structured management process. Furthermore, the implementation of any employee reporting mechanism must fit into the overall objectives and mission of the organization and be appropriately communicated to employees as part of a comprehensive ethics and compliance program.

Prior to implementation of any hotline solution, the appropriate organizational representatives should conduct an analysis of their present situation. How do employees bring concerns forward? Is there a way to do it anonymously yet maintain ongoing communication for the purpose of proper investigation? Who is responsible for investigating reports of employee misconduct? How is incident report management documented, and where is it stored? Is the existing documentation process efficient, and are records readily located by the appropriate individuals? What are the company policies governing standards of conduct? Are the policies up-to-date? How does an employee hotline solution fit into the organization's overall objectives and corporate governance program? Answering questions like these will help identify the strengths and opportunities in the organization's program and highlight the areas needing improvement. Communications to employees can then be targeted to those specific areas of opportunity.

Perhaps most importantly, all relevant organizational parties must be well informed of the implementation plan and take responsibility for whatever aspects directly impact them or their department. Without whole-organization commitment to the solution and the corporate processes and procedures put in place, a hotline solution, in any form, is destined to fail. At best, the system will fail to live up to its potential in terms of making the workplace safer and more productive—typically one of the foremost objectives in the implementation of such a reporting mechanism. Designating and enlisting the cooperation of all those responsible for reviewing, investigating, and responding to the incidents reported are critical to the organization's ability to limit its liability exposure should employee misconduct, fraudulent activity, or unsafe work conditions be uncovered.

Another critical activity impacting the success of an employee hotline solution relies on the effectiveness of its communication to those on whom it has the greatest impact—the employees. It probably goes without saying that the hotline will only rarely, if ever, be utilized if employees are not made aware that it exists and how to use it. Further, failure to communicate the purpose of the hotline to the employee base will often lead to the organization being inundated with frivolous or routine complaints that are more appropriately resolved through other reporting channels, such as directly through human resources. The poorly communicated hotline will find itself used for purposes of resolving payroll problems, scheduling complaints, and office temperature control—all of which impact employee morale but also are more efficiently handled directly by the responsible department. Anonymous hotlines, typically, should be reserved for more serious and potentially costly and safety-compromising issues such as substance abuse problems, embezzlement schemes, and theft activities.

Communication of the employee hotline is typically most successful when it is rolled out in conjunction with company policy reminders as well as reminders regarding existing communication and reporting channels, such as "open door" policies. An anonymous hotline should never serve to replace existing reporting avenues; rather, it should serve to augment a culture of openness, response, and resolution in which employees have multiple ways to bring workplace concerns forward. Communication, further, should come in multiple forms to ensure the entire employee base is reached. Such methods can include a companywide email announcement, an article in the company newsletter, a company-issued memo or letter, posters placed in high-traffic areas, updates to the employee handbook or policy manual, or an announcement posted to the company intranet.

It will then be the responsibility of those designated within the organization to review each employee incident report generated through the hotline. If the communication campaign was successful, the organization is likely to see an overall increase in incident reports (in comparison to those received prior to the implementation of the hotline), but a good percentage of those reports will be of a relatively serious nature, necessitating the appropriate organizational response. The astute and prudent organization will recognize the benefits of this increase in employee incident reports, namely, that they have an opportunity to uncover potentially costly employee misconduct and avoid the liability exposure resulting when such behavior (e.g., sexual harassment, substance abuse) is allowed to continue. Sophisticated employee hotlines, in conjunction with a robust and targeted employee communication campaign, serve to provide employers with a keyhole view of their organization that may, perhaps, be otherwise unavailable.

Organizations should respond to reported incidents in a manner consistent with their existing company policies and past practices. A complete and thorough investigation is often warranted and requires commitment of the necessary resources to that end. Again, in the interests of minimizing the organization's potential exposure, such an investigation should proceed according to existing protocols. Also, recognizing circumstances and incidents which may be beyond the expertise of those charged with the investigation of particular matters is a critical step in the process of reviewing incidents. Requesting consultative and/or investigative assistance, both internally and externally, may be the best approach if it appears a problem may be widespread or particularly egregious.

If the organization has chosen to contract its employee hotline services with a third-party vendor, the organization will often find that documenting all investigatory measures will be much more streamlined, and all relevant organizational parties can easily be kept up-to-date regarding all developments. Many vendors offer a robust case management system within the software or web-based database they provide. Such a system often has the capability to house all activities related to a particular incident report in a secure, centralized Internet-based location, which all appropriate organizational managers can access when necessary. Furthermore, this type of tool drastically reduces the amount of paperwork associated with any given investigation. As organizations expand both nationally and internationally, having the ability to make records available to all appropriate individuals, no matter their location, is critical to the successful companywide resolution of identified problems.

Final Thoughts

The implementation of an anonymous employee hotline makes good business sense for a variety of reasons, not the least of which is compliance with federal mandates. However, an employee hotline can further provide organizations with insight into the organization which may be otherwise unavailable to those charged with ensuring a safe and productive workplace is provided for all employees. Such insight can prove invaluable to the savvy employer with a desire for and commitment to principled corporate governance. Outsourcing employee hotline services can provide the organization an added layer of benefit, potentially increasing the likelihood that employees will feel a greater sense of comfort and confidence in bringing their concerns forward. The organization can go a long way in engendering employee confidence by responding to reported matters in a timely and efficient manner according to existing company protocols. Premier hotline solutions greatly assist organizations in doing so.

If the hotline is properly communicated to employees, organizations have an opportunity to reinforce existing reporting channels as well as remind employees of key company policies governing workplace conduct and employee responsibilities. Providing employees another method of communication to the organization helps them recognize that the organization does care about them and their well-being in the workplace. The organization committed to resolving problems, especially those posing a safety risk to employees, will reap the benefits of a healthy workplace: increased job satisfaction among employees, increased physical and psychological health of employees, lower levels of stress in the workplace, decreased rates of on-the-job accidents, decreased tardiness and absenteeism, etc. (4) The lists of benefits goes on and on with the end result being the same: increased productivity and profitability for the organization, securing the organization for the long term.

References

(1) Sarbanes-Oxley Act of 2002. Available: http://fl1.findlaw.com/news.findlaw.com/cnn/docs/gwbush/sarbanesoxley072302.pdf.

(2) Near, J. P., and Miceli, M. P. (1996). Whistle-blowing: Myth and reality. *Journal of Management*, 22, 507–527.

(3) The American Institute of Certified Public Accountants. (2003, November). Fraud hotlines: Early warning systems. *The Practicing CPA*. Retrieved December 9, 2005, from www.aicpa.org/pubs/tpcpa/nov2003/fraud.htm.

(4) Kelloway, Ł. K., and Day, A. L. (2005). Building healthy workplaces: What we know so far. *Canadian Journal of Behavioural Science*, 37, 223–235.

Identifying and Recognizing Risks

CAS, JHC

Irrespective of the size of company, from a single retail outlet to a multiunit chain of stores, and irrespective of the goods offered for sale to the public, be it high-end jewelry or a thrift shop, various risks inherent to retail face management and must be addressed. At the risk of oversimplification, let's briefly examine a single store which sells auto parts and review but a handful of the risks that must be considered:

- The number of incoming cartons of oil received from a vendor can be less than the number reflected on the manifest. The missing oil creates a shortage which may result from a simple error or intentional theft by the shipper, or it may have been stolen from the shipper's truck or trailer during its initial loading, an earlier delivery, or even during the current delivery.
- The store can be forcibly entered during the hours it's closed, and goods can be carried out.
- The store's daily receipts must be secured, or they can be taken during a forcible entry, unless secured in a safe.
- The safe itself may be vulnerable to being carried out during a forcible entry.
- The store can be surreptitiously entered when it's closed, without leaving evidence of a forcible entry by unknown means, during which time items are stolen.
- The many items of goods offered for sale can be stealthily stolen by customers (shoplifted).
- Goods can be pocketed by one or more employees and never paid for.
- Employees can sell items to friends or family members at any price lower than the marked price.
- Employees can sell items and not record the sale but rather pocket part or all of the sale proceeds.
- Employees can give away items to people who appear to be legitimate customers but who are in reality friends or associates.

The situations described represent only a small sampling of the types of incidents which can easily drain profits and, in the extreme, threaten the continued life of a business.

Not included in these scenarios are criminal threats involving robbery, arson, credit card fraud, fraudulent and NSF checks, bomb threats, gift cards, returned merchandise fraud, as well as the potential for civil suits (with their concomitant damage awards) should merchants mishandle their response to such situations.

Two questions immediately come to mind: *Who* is going to deal with these problems? And *how* are they going to be dealt with? This section will provide suggested answers to both questions.

Who's going to deal with these risks? Clearly, in a single store, the owner will need to address these issues, or in the owner's absence, the store "manager." But what about the manager? We know of a manager in a ladies' apparel store who "ran" the store, along with two part-time employees on Saturdays. The manager always arrived early in her station wagon and brought her own cash register. Half the sales were duly recorded on the store's register, and the other sales she captured on her own. Needless to say, Saturday sales were never remarkable. One Saturday the owner happened to drop in and discovered what was happening.

How will the problem be dealt with? The answer to this question is equally if not more important, since errors may not only place the owner or manager in physical jeopardy, but also subject him to potential civil liability.

We know of another situation at an auto parts store, wherein the owner admitted he was aware of the fact his long-time employees were stealing, but he allowed the thefts because the employees were judicious in the amount they took each week (the loss was "tolerable," i.e., affordable). The employees were most diligent about protecting the assets of the store from outside pilferage. To terminate the current employees for dishonesty and replace them with "unknowns" was not an acceptable option for this owner. It was a business decision to stay with the status quo. While we would not opt for this option, it remains a business decision for the owner.

Single or even two-store operations can tolerate or survive criminal events if they're not catastrophic; owners may survive a marginal level of theft which they consider "acceptable." After all, hundreds of thousands of sole proprietor or family-owned stores have survived throughout the world with only a rudimentary knowledge of and/or without any particularly sophisticated security or loss prevention program in place. But how many didn't survive? There's no answer, except, perhaps, too many!

Clearly, though, big box single unit retailers and multiunit operations can't achieve financial success unless the assets are protected in a systematic, professional fashion.

Before a retailer, large or small, can implement security and loss prevention strategies and the programs to achieve them, some fundamental questions must be asked and answered. These questions fall under two categories: (1) The impact of retail inventory shrinkage not related to a criminal act and (2) inventory shrinkage is suspected or known to have resulted from criminal victimization.

For clarification purposes, let's define "inventory shrinkage." This is the perfect time to ensure this most important retail term is fully understood, and thereafter, all security and loss prevention *losses* can be held up to and measured against the term. An "inventory shrinkage" or "inventory shrink" or "inventory shortage" is the difference between book inventory (what the records reflect we have) and actual physical inventory as determined by the process of taking one's inventory of goods on hand (what we count and know we actually have). So, if our records reflect we purchased 100 bottles of wine, our sales records reflect we sold 60 bottles, and inventory of actual bottles on the shelf reflects we have 35 bottles, we have 5 bottles unaccounted for, amounting to an inventory shortage of 5 bottles or 5% shrinkage. We don't know what happened to those missing 5 bottles.

If, during the night, someone breaks through the skylight in the ceiling and steals our 40 bottles, we know they were taken. Hence, their absence is not a mysterious or otherwise unexplained disappearance but is considered a known loss. Nevertheless, it is considered shrinkage unless and until it is accounted for financially as something other than shrink.

When the Crime Doesn't Affect Inventory Shrinkage

Our preceding example of the nighttime burglary clearly is one crime which, while initially affecting inventory shrinkage, may eventually be financially accounted for in another category (e.g., known losses replaced by insurance or carried on the books as separate from shrinkage). The store suffers, by virtue of being victimized by a burglar, exactly the same loss, but the loss caused by the burglar is really more easily managed because we know how that loss occurred. Depending on how known losses are carried on the books determines whether they or note are included as shrinkage.

Say the sale of the 60 bottles was recorded on a POS terminal or cash register, and at the end of the night the cash, checks, and credit card receipts were placed in a bag in anticipation of making a bank deposit the next morning. During closing, a man enters, produces a gun, and demands the bag. In this case, the loss is certainly real, but such loss would never be reflected in the year's inventory shortage, since the merchandise can be accounted for and the theft of cash would be reflected in another financial account, but not as inventory shrink.

If the sale of the 60 bottles was handled by an employee who rang the sale but failed to put the money in the register and pocketed the money, the store again has no inventory shortage, only a shortage of cash. Cash shortages have nothing to do with inventory shortages. But if the same sales associate did not record the sale, just pretended he handled the transaction correctly and pocketed the cash, we would have no cash shortage but would have an inventory shortage!

The bottom line is that the retailer is harmed and suffers a reduction of profitability whether the losses are in the form of cash receipts or pure product; the form of the loss, however, dictates that differing strategies of prevention are required.

Other forms of retail crime victimization which need attention include injuries to customers or employees as a consequence of crime, loss of goodwill or customers, business continuity issues if the store is a victim of an arson attack, and so on.

When Losses Affect Inventory Shrink

What is the shrink or shortage in terms of a percent of sale? 1%? 1.4%? 3%? Is it high or low compared to industry averages? Do we know what is causing an above average shrink? What can we do without further assistance to reduce these losses? Do we need professional help?

Before a retailer, large or small, can implement security and loss prevention strategies and the programs to achieve them, some fundamental questions must be asked and answered.

These questions include

How much can my business afford to obtain professional loss prevention assistance?
Where is such help available?
What form need such help take?
How are the alternatives determined?
How is such help selected?
Does the local "merchant's association" offer any solutions?

Assuming the retailer's shrink is average or below, and the owner is comfortable with the level of shrink, perhaps nothing more need be done except to maintain vigilance and monitor the shrink for signs of emerging problems.

If, however, the shrink is excessive and above tolerable levels, action is indicated to both prevent further deterioration and reduce current losses.

For the average single-store operation and smaller multiunit businesses, often the most cost-effective approach is to bring in a security consultant for a one-shot review of the business and shrink reduction suggestions. Such an approach may be, depending on budget and business type, nothing more than a half-day walkthrough and discussion with the owner. Larger operations may require a more extensive review, beginning with the owner/manager (and perhaps others) answering a detailed questionnaire about various aspects of the business, followed by an extensive onsite inspection and interviews with both key executives and staff, and ending with a detailed written report by the consultant detailing his or her observations and recommendations.

For those large regional and national chains with existing security/loss prevention staffs, whose efforts senior management feels are less than effective or produce other unintended adverse consequences (e.g., civil damage suits or unfavorable employee reactions), the use of a security consultant is perhaps the only viable alternative.

In any event, narrowing down the causes of excessive shrink (and there are usually more than one) is the first step toward reducing it. This process will often also dictate the type and degree of response required: Will changes in internal policies be sufficient? Or will full- or part-time loss prevention personnel be required? Or does the solution lie somewhere in between?

Losses of cash or product from known criminal attack will probably require a totally different set of potential prophylactic treatment, generally requiring less investigative effort to determine the source and means of the loss and more directed toward hardening those weaknesses (whether physical or procedural) which permitted the attack. For example, consider a burglary which went unreported during its commission because of a failure of the alarm system to signal an intrusion. This situation is normally easily fixed. Once the system itself is determined to be functioning properly, a formalized and systematic procedure for daily testing can be initiated. This system should prevent future intrusions that go unreported to the central monitoring station, who in turn will request police to be dispatched.

How are the causes of loss identified? Aside from those which are obvious (e.g., robbery or burglary), most causes of shrinkage are more subtle and less obvious. Frequently, they require someone with some expertise in loss prevention to discover them and suggest appropriate means to correct the root causes of the problems identified. Aside from paperwor k errors or other procedural aspects of handling the business's financial accounting, more than likely, the causes involve some element of criminality.

Seeking Appropriate Assistance

At this point, the retailer has various options as to how and where to seek help:

1. He may approach a fellow retailer or members of any local retail group of which he is a member and make inquiry of them. However, he may be reluctant to do this, since he may not want to either disclose his problem and/or any shortage numbers. He might also simply make an inquiry as to whether any fellow members know someone who can help him with a problem described by him only in general terms. How quickly he will find a qualified person to help him using this approach is problematic.
2. He can consult the local yellow pages for a security consultant.
3. He can consult the local yellow pages for a private detective.
4. He can consult with any local police department crime prevention officer.
5. He can search the Web.
6. He can do nothing and hope the problem solves itself, an alternative not recommended since shrinkage from criminality normally increases over time rather than decreases.

Once a decision as to the approach to be taken is made, we suggest that the owner conduct interviews with at least two of the potential sources of help so that the best "match" is made and all the specifics of the owner's expectations are understood and the costs connected with the help are fully disclosed and agreed to. Only after this procedure can an owner best select the person/or organization to which he will turn for help.

Incident Reporting: Electronic

Jason Elwell

In recent years, we have seen an explosive growth in the area of loss prevention technology. Retailers are choosing to implement expensive solutions like digital video systems and exception-based reporting software in hopes that these solutions will help investigators to control shrink more effectively.

Recently loss prevention departments have begun to invest in centralized incident reporting systems. Incident reporting tools can help an organization to collect, process, and analyze incident data in a way that traditional methods cannot offer.

Elements of an Incident Report

Regardless of whether an incident report is completed on paper or electronically in an incident reporting system, it includes several universal elements.

- *Who:* Information about the principle subject and witnesses. This typically includes contact information and a review of that person's involvement in the incident.
- *What:* Details about what happened. Generally, this is in narrative form and is written by the report taker. Often witness statements are included in the incident report.

- *When:* The date and time the initial incident occurred as well as other major milestones (i.e. interview and court dates).
- *Where:* Information about where an incident occurred. This would include street address, physical location within a store, etc.
- *Why:* Information about what caused the incident.

Loss prevention professionals are probably familiar with writing incident reports for the typical shoplifting and internal theft cases. Almost all reports contain *who* stole it, *what* they stole, *when* they stole it, *where* they stole it from, and *why* they stole it.

Interestingly, this same methodology is used by many other departments in the retail organization. For example, the human resources department typically handles reports of violation of company policy. The human resource representative's report will include *who* violated the policy, *what* policy they violated, *when* they violated the policy, *where* they violated the policy, and *why* they violated the policy.

Another example is the risk management department. They are typically tasked with providing a safe work environment but are also responsible for processing customer and employee accident reports when things go wrong. *Who* had the accident, *what* kind of accident occurred, *when* did the accident occur, *where* did the accident occur, and *why* did the accident occur?

Get the idea? Incident reporting systems are not just for loss prevention. The flexibility provided by many solutions allows for the system to be utilized by other parts of the retail organization. Incident reporting systems can help the risk management team to manage accident reports just as easily as they can help the loss prevention group to manage theft investigations.

Benefits of Electronic Incident Reporting

Besides the ability to store incident data for many different groups within the retail organization, an incident reporting system has several other benefits. Most importantly, an incident reporting system has the capability to store the incident data in an electronic format at a central location. This seems obvious, but it actually represents the fundamental difference between centralized incident management and traditional methods of collecting and storing incident data. The data collected by an incident reporting system (database) can be a powerful tool.

Incident reporting systems can be configured to interact with other business systems such as

- *Internal employee databases:* Link to the HR department's employee master file for enhanced statistical reports.
- *Civil collection providers:* Transmit theft incidents electronically to the collection agency.
- *Background screening providers:* Transmit a prospective employee's (or suspect's) information to the vendor and order a background check.
- *POS exception-based reporting tools:* Start an incident from within an exception-based reporting tool.
- *Digital CCTV systems:* Easily attach video clips to an incident report.

The database can be used to generate statistical reports that can help an organization to gauge various metrics. When combined with other data sources, the data in the incident reporting system can be used to identify trends that otherwise would not be visible. For example, when linked with data from an HR system, it would be possible to pull a report to analyze the relationship between store shrink, employee turnover, and theft incidents. Another possibility would be to analyze the department in which a suspect was first observed compared to the time of day in shoplifting cases. These types of reports would require significant resources if compiled by hand, but with the use of an electronic incident reporting system, the data are easily accessible.

Pitfalls of Incident Reporting

The benefits of using a centralized incident reporting system can be numerous but require more than just a financial investment in order to be achieved. The successful implementation of an incident reporting system requires planning, communication, and follow-through. During the implementation process, it is important to maintain partnerships with the departments that will be utilizing the system, the IT department, and the vendor's technical staff. With communication, the vendor can provide a solution that is tailored to the needs of everyone involved.

After a solution is implemented, it is critical that management support the system. It is important that managers train end users on system operations. No matter how easy the system is to use, end users should be taught the proper way to input, retrieve, and report on incident data.

Finally, it is important that the system be kept up-to-date with changes in corporate policies. Invariably, with time, things change. Make sure that the system is reconfigured as needed to accommodate these changes.

Conclusion

Before any system is purchased, research and planning are needed. With a strong commitment from all involved, an electronic incident reporting system can provide a significant contribution to a retail organization.

Insurance

CAS, JHC

It is well recognized that nearly every business needs insurance, often of several varieties, including fire, general liability, worker's compensation, and others. In some cases insurance is legally mandated.

There are several aspects of insurance which are of specific interest to loss prevention. For example, assuming the store has adequate coverage (at least $1 million) for its general liability, it is important that whenever a loss prevention function is contracted to an outside service provider, the store should require the service provider to also carry adequate liability coverage. In addition, the provider should be required to name the store as "an additional insured" to its general liability policy. In no case should that amount of coverage for general liability be less than $1 million.

Retailers should also be aware that while their general liability coverage will cover damages awarded (within policy limits) as the result of a suit for intentional torts or negligence resulting for loss prevention activities, in most venues it is against public policy for insurance to pay awards for punitive damages.

International Foundation for Protection Officers (IFPO)

Sandi Davies

A Training Resource for the Loss Prevention Industry

Organization Background

The International Foundation for Protection Officers (IFPO) was established in 1988 as a nonprofit organization dedicated to serving security industry professionals worldwide.

As a former officer with the Royal Canadian Mounted Police, IFPO founder Ron Minion recognized the importance of training and certification to enhance job performance, increase safety, boost morale, and gain respect for the security profession. Because of Minion's focus on training, the IFPO offers an extensive line of training products and certification programs.

The foundation is governed by a board of directors, with the guidance of a 14-member International Advisory Board. Day-to-day operations are handled by an executive based in Naples, Florida. Over the years, the IFPO's influence has extended to 42 countries, and more than 25,000 officers have completed certification, with thousands more currently enrolled.

The IFPO serves all career stages, from entry level through experienced professional, with training, industry publications, and the latest industry news. It allows new officers to learn from the experienced professionals, and it gives the experienced professionals an opportunity to share their knowledge with newcomers.

Members work in a broad range of settings including retail stores, warehouses, factories, hospitals, campuses, apartment complexes, and many more. For retail LP operatives, belonging to an organization like IFPO that serves so many different industries gives them an opportunity to benchmark with other industries to find the best solutions to common challenges while still having access to retail-specific training and information.

IFPO's Training

The training that is available through the IFPO and its partners is a good resource for individual officers working in the retail sector who want to ensure they are well prepared to handle situations they may face on the job. While the foundation's training is suitable for many environments, loss prevention practitioners can rest assured they're building their careers on a solid foundation with the basic training options before they move on to more detailed, specific training.

The IFPO's training programs are also a valuable resource for smaller retail establishments that may not have an existing training program or as add-ons to existing training for large retail operations that already have their own training programs. Security officers in the retail industry face unique dangers and challenges every day. High-quality training can reduce liability while ensuring the officers, customers, and establishments they protect stay safe and secure. At the time of this writing, three well-known high-profile retailers are using IFPO's specialized retail training.

Training and Certification Options

IFPO's training and certification programs were developed as *distance-delivery style* courses, suitable for self-paced home study. They include

- Entry Level Protection Officer (ELPO)
- Basic Protection Officer (BPO)
- Certified Protection Officer (CPO) program
- Security Supervision and Management (SSMP) program
- Certified in Security Supervision and Management (CSSM) program

The ELPO and the BPO programs are available online as well as on CD-ROM. Many corporations and institutions have adopted these programs and integrated them with their existing staff development process and training goals.

The foundation works regularly with ASIS International and has formed partnerships with two leading training service firms: Advanced Systems Technology, Inc. (AST) and PTSN. Through these partnerships, IFPO members receive a discount on the broad array of training options these organizations offer.

AST developed the High Impact Training Solutions (HITS), which includes web-based and CD-based instruction. The HITS series has basic programs for entry-level officers, as well as specialty topics such as Homeland Security, Retail Loss Prevention, Public Events Specialty, and Physical Security.

AST's Retail Loss Prevention Specialist track covers essential topics geared to keeping officers, customers, and establishments safe and secure. The track includes five areas:

1. First Aid
   - First Responders and Patient Assessments
   - Shock and Substance Abuse
   - Wounds, Bleeding, and Head Injuries
   - Fractures and Heat/Cold Injuries
   - Heart Attacks and CPR

2. Retail Loss Prevention 2—External Theft Protection
   - Types of Shoplifters
   - Shoplifting Methods
   - Apprehension of Shoplifters
   - Anti-Theft Technology
   - Credit Card Fraud
   - Check Fraud
3. Retail Loss Prevention 3—Internal Theft Protection
   - Stopping Internal Losses
   - Types of Fraud
   - Employee Motivation, Education, and Training
   - Background Investigations
   - Legal Review
4. Fire Safety Basics
   - Basic Fire Chemistry
   - Extinguisher Operation
   - Hazardous Materials
   - Fire Hazards
   - Evaluating Situation
5. Interviews & Interrogations
   - Getting the Facts
   - Interviewing Victims, Witnesses, and Suspects
   - Preparing for the Interview
   - Conducting the Interview/Interrogation
   - Interpreters, Kinesics, and Polygraph

The IFPO's other partner, PSTN, offers an extensive library of several hundred video programs. It offers a monthly subscription service consisting of training tapes, tests, and related courseware for continuous professional development. PSTN's *Basic Security Officer Training Series (BSOTS)* is widely used throughout North America.

IFPO Membership

The IFPO offers individual and corporate membership levels. Each type of membership comes with various discounts on training and other industry products; access to several special plans, including dental, prescription and legal; and complimentary publications.

Combined, the IFPO's training opportunities, the networking opportunities, and access to industry news make membership one of the industry's best investments.

Integrity Testing of Sales Associates

CAS, JHC

While many companies rely on mystery shoppers and their reports to assess the quality of their service, they may be unaware of the variety of information and other services so-called mystery shoppers can supply.

The value of mystery shoppers lies in the fact that their reports are generated from on-the-ground, face-to-face dealings with a company's employees and their interaction with the public. Put another way, these "shoppers" are not recognized as representatives of management, and the quality of service, or the lack thereof, could be a fair representation of how tested employees perform.

There are three types of shopping services:

- Comparison shopping
- Customer service shopping
- Honesty or "integrity" shopping

Comparison Shopping

Comparison shopping is typically performed by a member of middle management of a store interested in what the competition is doing. The thrust of the effort is to compare prices of like items. Such shopping invariably includes assessment of visual presentations of goods, mix of goods, and other items of interest to merchants, and designed to answer the question "What is Jones doing at the other end of the mall?"

Customer Service Shopping

Customer service shopping is aimed at assessing the conditions and treatment customers experience, as well as compliance with company policy. For example, one well-known coffee shop has its mystery shoppers weigh and measure the temperature of its hot coffees. Companies which sell regulated distribution products such as tobacco and alcohol utilize mystery shoppers to shop their stores to make certain there are no underage sales. Other companies use shoppers to assure that every store or franchisee provides the proper level of courteous service and that these locations are up to cleanliness and environmental standards.

Integrity Shopping

Integrity shopping is based on the premise that the company has a clear and understood rule that every sale must be recorded at the time of the transaction and the cash or other form of payment must be placed in the cash register at the time of the transaction.

Integrity shopping, also known as "honesty shopping" (or testing), is conducted to observe how employees handle cash transactions and, in some instances, is used to test the honesty of specific employees who may be suspected of dishonesty. The food industry, for example, has estimated that as much as 20% of a bar's revenues can end up in employees' pockets.

Honesty of employees need not be limited to testing for the handling of cash sales, but for other forms of conduct deemed detrimental to the organization. For example, does the employee refer customers to his brother-in-law's store, which is a competitor? Does the employee selling women's shoes make inappropriate or sexually suggestive comments while handling the shopper's foot? Needless to say, if such a complaint were received from a customer and the employee was confronted with that complaint, adamant denial could be expected. But replicate the shopping experience with a professional shopper, and there's a chance of confirming the original complaint.

Aside from these unusual "shopping" challenges, the bulk of integrity shopping deals with the handling of sales and the suspicion of theft of cash. It must be kept in mind that integrity shoppers can also, if so tasked, perform customer service and comparison shopping functions.

Detecting Improper Handling of Cash Sales

Since the focus of this book is loss prevention, we will limit our further discussion of mystery shoppers (hereinafter called "honesty shoppers") to their use in detecting and obtaining proof of the improper handling of cash tendered for cash sales.

Honesty shopping is a style of shopping which has been developed to assist in detecting employee dishonesty. Using various shopping techniques, honesty shoppers act as ordinary customers to create situations which test employees' compliance to policies and procedures, and provide an opportunity to pocket cash if inclined to do so.

It is important that the store have some basic rules regarding the handling of cash at the register. For example, one rule should be that cash must be placed in the register immediately after the sale is rung—never placed on the counter or some other location. Another rule should be that each sale must be rung at the time of purchase and the tendering of money by the customer should never be delayed. Another basic rule is that customers must always be given a receipt for their purchase. Similarly, all cashiers must operate from closed register drawers; i.e., register drawers must be closed after each sale is rung.

The ultimate goal is really not to catch the employee stealing the cash, but rather to document and prove the fact the cash transaction was not handled as required by company rules. Proving theft can be onerous, whereas proving the cash sale wasn't recorded is relatively simple, as will be explained further in this section.

The reasons these rules (and others covering such things as incomplete sales, etc.) are important are two-fold: First, it provides procedures which establish an orderly means for handling sales and cash, and second, it provides a basis for disciplinary action to be taken against employees who fail to follow these rules. When a shopper detects an employee who fails to follow established procedures, it is often easier to simply terminate that employee for a rule violation than to attempt to obtain an admission of theft, if in fact the employee was stealing. Additionally, an employee who violates cash handling rules out of carelessness, if not stealing, is probably creating cash shortages/overages which must be investigated in an effort to reconcile them, a time-consuming and costly process. Thus, either way, you have removed a problem employee, if not a thief.

There are two types of integrity shops:

- Random testing without a specific suspect in mind. The professional shoppers are free to exercise their own judgment and test any employee they feel may be prone to steal. These types of shops are not as productive in terms of a "hit," i.e., detecting a "failure to record" a test made of a suspected dishonest employee.
- Directed testing, i.e., employee Jones in the toy department is suspected of theft and the shops are limited to this employee exclusively. Directed te sts may be coordinated with an LP agent monitoring the scene and who may witness an actual theft or, for whatever reason, the shop may not be witnessed. If not witnessed, the subsequent interview, which could be the next day, would be for policy violation.

Basic Shopper Procedurers

1. The shoppers generally work as a team of two: a shopper and observer, a shopper and a loss prevention agent, or a shopper and a manned camera.
   A. As one shopper makes a purchase, the second shopper observes the transaction, particularly watching the money.
   B. The shopper making the purchase must not be obvious in his surveillance of the sales associate. This shopper must also conduct the shop in a "normal" and consistent manner.
   C. The shopper observing the sale must do so in such a way that other sales associates and customers are unaware of this observation.
   D. Any violation or irregularity must be made the subject of a written report immediately after the conclusion of the shop, and depending on the circumstances, then reported to store management. The observing shopper must pay scrupulous attention to the other shopper and the associate's activities.
2. Shoppers may only use currency which they have initialed and whose serial numbers were previ ously recorded and witnessed.
   The purpose of recording the serial numbers and initialing the bills used by the shoppers is so that, should the need arise, these bills can be identified and used as evidence. For example, suppose that if the employee being tested is observed actually pocketing the unrecorded cash. That employee should then be immediately taken into custody (by store management or loss prevention employees) and interrogated regarding the observed pocketing of the cash. Because they are contract personnel, shoppers should not take any detention, arrest, or interrogation action, unless such action is specifically authorized in advance by contractual agreement. The fact that the bills are initialed and serial numbers recorded may be used to induce an admission to the theft and/or used as evidence of the possession of the company's money by the employee. In those cases where the employee hides the cash, waiting for a more opportune time to actually pocket the money, the fact that the bills can be identified removes any excuse that the cash is other than that which belongs to the store, has not been properly recorded, and that the employee violated acknowledged cash handling procedures.

3. Shoppers should always make the purchases when the sales associate is alone. If this is not possible, the shoppers must be certain that others in the department are busy or their attention is elsewhere.
   A. Shops should be arranged so the schedule of subject of the shop coincides with the shops.
   B. To shop a specific sales associate, the shoppers should make initial contact with the associate and avoid making purchases from other associates who approach them.
   C. Timing is extremely important, and shoppers should quickly utilize any opportunity to shop the associate when they are alone.
4. The shoppers should always approach the register from the front (the side opposite the keys and drawers).
   A. While the sale is being recorded, the shopper who is purchasing should be in view (in front of) but not watching the sales associate.
   B. After tendering the money (usually an even amount), the shopper should walk away from the register.
   C. The shopper who is observing the sale should be out of the sales associate's view, some distance from the register, but positioned so that he can observe the money.

Definitions and Techniques

1. *The Single Buy* is simply one purchase with one register transaction. The one purchase may include any number of items, as long as only one transaction is completed.

   To carry out a single buy, the shopper selects either one item or two different items, mentally adding the price(s) and the tax. The shopper makes the purchase and leaves the register area. If the shopper tenders even money, he may be able to leave the department before the sale is recorded. (If the sales associate asks the shopper to wait, the shopper should do so.) The shopper should not look back when leaving.

   The other shopper will be nearby observing the entire transaction. Should the sales associate fail to give the first shopper a receipt, the second shopper will make an uneven money purchase (a blocking sale) to obtain a receipt. The observer must also note the number of transactions which occur between the shop transaction and the block sale.

2. *The Double Buy* is two separate purchases, each with even money tendered. Two register transactions are made.

   The double buy is similar to the single buy with one exception—the shopper makes two separate purchases with two separate register transactions. The shopper gives the sales associate an even amount of cash for the sale and leaves. A few minutes later, the shopper returns and purchases a second item, offering an excuse if one seems necessary. The shopper gives the sales associate the exact amount and leaves the department. The shopper should place the second item in the bag with the first item, to prevent the sales associate from keeping it until the sale has been recorded.

   One variation of the double buy is for the shopper to return and buy another identical item, indicating that he decided to buy two. This is advantageous because the total price is known, and the sales associate may be less inclined to give the shopper a second identical receipt. If the shopper noticed that the first transaction was handled correctly, he may instantly make the second purchase without leaving the area.

   The second shopper should be observing the transactions and, if necessary, make a block purchase.

3. *The Combination Buy* consists of two separate purchases; uneven money is tendered for one purchase, and even money is tendered for the second purchase.

   There are two different parts to the combination buy. The first part of the shop is usually the block, made with uneven money to obtain a register receipt. After this purchase, the shopper browses around the department and makes a second purchase, tendering even money. The shopper should place the second item in the bag with the first and leave the department. (The shopper should wait for the receipt if the sales associate asks him to wait.) In the combination buy, several things should be considered:

    A. The first purchase should always be more expensive than the second, and the second purchase should be a small, even amount, e.g., $10 or $20, so that the tax is easily known to the shopper and the sales associate.

    B. The two purchases cannot be intermingled in any way. The second part of the buy cannot be made until the first purchase has been recorded, packaged, receipt issued, and given to the customer.

    C. The first purchase should be physically larger than the second purchase so that the second one can be placed into the bag with the first.

4. *The Interrupt Buy* requires the shoppers to enter the department separately. The first shopper makes a purchase from the suspect, tendering uneven money to obtain a receipt. The first shopper then accepts the purchase but alludes to the fact that he may get something else in the department. The first shopper then moves away from the register to consider a second piece of merchandise.

    When the first shopper has chosen something and appears to be ready, the second shopper will approach the suspect at the register. The second shopper will begin to make a purchase and, while it is being recorded, will move away from the register. In the middle of this transaction, the first shopper will approach the suspect at the register and interrupt the buy. The shopper will have the suspect *acknowledge or realize* that he is going to make another purchase by showing the suspect the merchandise and establishing the price and tax. The shopper will state the amount of money he is leaving and then place the even money on the counter. The shopper will state that he will place this purchase in the bag with the previous purchase before leaving the department.

    The second shopper will observe what happens to this money. It is important that the suspect realize that the first shopper is making a second purchase, and the money is being left prior to the shopper exiting the department. (The end product of this buy is generally failure to record the sale and a theft of the cash.)

    Upon completion of the interrupt buy, employees have been found in the past to take one of these actions with the shopper's money:

    A. Continually move the money on the counter or leave it by or on the register.

    B. Hide the money (drawer, displays, etc.).

    C. Put the money in the register when the other shopper is making his purchase but fail to record it. The employee may wait for a more opportune time to take the money, i.e., at closing or when alone.

    D. Place the money on his person almost at once.

    E. Record the sale.

5. *The Pay Away Buy* also requires that the shoppers enter the department *separately*. One shopper is the buyer; the other is the observer. The buyer chooses one item to buy and mentally selects an area of the department, ideally secluded or blocked from the register and away from other customers/employees. The buyer should also choose the second purchase and calculate the tax. All this can be done while waiting for the right opportunity to shop the sales associate. The buyer goes to the register and makes the first purchase. Uneven money should be tendered to get a receipt. While this purchase is being recorded, the buyer should move away from the register area. The observer should be in a position to make sure the transaction is recorded properly. The shopper then takes his purchase from the sales associate and asks the associate to assist him in a preselected area. The shopper asks the sales associate questions about the second piece of merchandise that he is considering. This purchase is smaller than the first purchase so it can go the bag inconspicuously. The shopper attempts to tender money for this second purchase on the selling floor. If the sales associate accepts the money, the shopper tells the associate that he can put the second item into the bag with the first. If the sales associate is honest, he will insist that the shopper return to the register with him. If the employee takes the money, the shopper immediately leaves the department. The observer will then see if the sales associate returns to the register and rings the sale.

    When the buyer is ready to make the second purchase, the observer must concentrate on the shop and observe where the money is placed.

Interviewing for a Shopping Policy Violation

The LP agent who conducts the interview for a shopping policy violation would have on the table or desk the items purchased, their receipts, and the journal tape of the day the test was made. After a courteous introduction, the agent will inform the employee of the company's use of shoppers as a routine LP strategy. The agent will produce the journal tape and will locate on the tape the date, time, transaction number (transaction #200 for the sake of this example), the amount of the sale, and the employee number of the employee being interviewed. This sale should be the sale immediately preceding the test buy. This purchase is made by a regular customer or by one of the shoppers. This purchase marks the start of the integrity shop process and may be referred to as the "identification buy."

The agent then locates and marks transaction #200 on the journal tape and asks the employee if he agrees it's on the tape. The agent then presents the merchandise that was purchased by the shopper (the test buy) for which the exact amount of the purchase ($10.20) was tendered and for which the shopper did not wait for a receipt. The agent then presents the merchandise that was purchased after the test buy (the blocking buy), in which change was required, and the receipt for that purchase reveals it was transaction #201. The employee examines the receipt and then is asked to locate transaction #201 on the journal tape. The agent then asks the employee what he did with the $10.20, for which there is no transaction on the journal tape. *Note:* No accusation of theft; merely the question. If the employee says he doesn't recall but it was rung, as required, the agent asks, "If you recorded the sale, please show me where on the tape it is found."

On occasion an employee may admit to theft but most often will appear to be puzzled over the absence and then may offer, "Well, I may have been in a hurry and put the money in the register." The agent then produces the sales audit for that register/terminal for that date, and the audit reflects it is either balanced or over/short by only pennies. The agent points out that if the money was placed in the drawer without being properly recorded, the register would be $10.20 over, "wouldn't it?"

"Are you accusing me of stealing that $10.00?"

"No. I'm merely asking you what you did with the money."

The bottom line of this exchange is explaining to the employee the company's insistence (and policy requirement) on every sale being recorded at the time of the transaction, and hence, the LP department will recommend termination for failure to follow one of the keystone rules in retailing. If the employee says "Okay, you got me. I took the money," at this point the interview then turns into an interrogation for theft.

Summary

Honesty shoppers serve a variety of needs for retailers. By uncovering poor customer service (which contributes greatly to shoplifting) or by identifying employees whose sloppy cash handling and register procedures lead to cash shortages or whose purposeful mishandling of cash leads to outright theft, these shoppers support loss prevention. Failing to utilize honesty shoppers both as a yardstick of customer service and a proactive investigative tool where cash shortages or low gross margins are a problem may be penny wise and pound foolish.

Integrity Tests

Randy Tennison

An integrity test, also known as a "test shop," is a controlled test used to measure the integrity/honesty of an employee by placing him in a situation in which he has an opportunity to be dishonest. It can also be used to test the effectiveness of procedural controls. Integrity testing can be used when a specific employee has been identified as possibly being involved in dishonest activity or as a blanket "random" test, used to test random employees for dishonesty.

There is argument concerning the ethical nature of an integrity test, where people believe it is or compare it to entrapment. Indeed, a poorly designed and conducted integrity test can border on entrapment. But, when properly planned, conducted, and reviewed, an integrity test is a valuable tool in identifying dishonest employees and investigating losses in a company.

In the retail environment, an integrity test is often conducted on a sales clerk, but can also be on a cash office employee, merchandise delivery employee, service technician, or any other employee. The basic elements of the integrity test involve creating an immediate opportunity for the employee to believe that he could easily, and without fear of discovery, commit a violation of policy, whether it is theft, improper discount, freebagging, etc. The dishonest employee, seeing the opportunity before him, will often avail himself and commit the violation of policy. The honest employee, seeing an unusual circumstance, will follow company policy and complete the transaction as normal.

The primary element that distinguishes a well-designed integrity test from a poorly designed test is that it is "winnable." In other words, the test provides an easily identifiable way for an honest employee to do the right thing. An integrity test cannot be so narrow in scope that it leaves an honest employee no way to follow policy. The test must allow an employee a way to follow company policy easily and without embarrassment.

Another important element is that the test is not set up in such a way as to unduly influence the choice of the individual being tested—for example, putting the individual in a situation in which he can violate policy and then placing pressure upon him that acts on his sense of compassion or caring, or that causes him fear of retaliation or threats. An example might be an integrity tester trying to get an employee to price negotiate the cost of a refrigerator, telling the story that she needs to keep her sick child's medicine cold, or the medicine will be ineffective, and that she cannot afford to spend any more than the negotiated price. In a case like this, a judge, jury, or unemployment hearing officer may decide that the undue influence placed on the employee was so strong as to cause an otherwise honest person to violate policy.

When a person is selected to conduct the integrity test, special consideration should be given to that person's ability and experience. The shopper should be selected to complement the nature of the shop as well as the subject to be shopped. The shopper should dress similarly as a normal customer for that business and must assume the identity of a typical customer. Therefore, the best person for an integrity test is normally someone who is familiar with the business and with loss prevention.

It is not the job of the shopper to "trick" the subject or to exert undue influence. It is merely the shopper's job to conduct the integrity test in a proper and professional manner, staying with the parameters established. It is best to select a shopper who can easily establish a rapport with the integrity test subject, providing the opportunity for wrongdoing, without creating unusual or intimidating situations.

A typical and effective integrity test is called a "double buy." In this integrity test, the integrity of a sales clerk is being tested. The "integrity tester," the person who conducts the test, will make a purchase of a predetermined item. It is often best if that item's value, after adding tax, is close to a whole dollar amount. The integrity tester then creates an excuse to purchase the same item a second time, possibly using the excuse that she is unsure of size, color, etc. The shopper removes the price tag from the item, lays the money on the counter, and places the second item in the bag with the first. She explains that she is in a hurry and needs to leave, but here's the money for the item. She then walks off.

As you can see, in this example, the situation is completely "winnable" for the employee. He has the price tag from the item. He has the cash for the item. It is a simple matter for the employee to ring the item into the cash register and account for the sale. However, the dishonest employee sees an opportunity to steal the cash paid by the customer, as there has been nothing entered into the register. He will normally throw away the price tag, steal the money, and make no mention of the transaction.

Another integrity test used is called "overage the cash office" (this is also called "salting"). In this test, the funds in the cash office are verified, and then extra money is placed in the safe of the cash office. The test is conducted on the next employee to work in the cash office. There is no explanation left for the overage in the cash office funds.

Again, this shop is completely winnable by the employee, in that the honest employee can report that the cash office was "over" on his cash office summary worksheet. However, the dishonest employee may steal the overage amount, believing that it will not be discovered, as no record of it existed. This test is obviously best conducted where there is camera coverage of the cash office so that the actual theft of the funds can be witnessed. It will also require a complete reconciliation of all funds prior to and following the integrity test.

"Negotiation shops" can be used to test commission sales persons, merchandise delivery persons, and repair persons. When this test is set up, it is important that the test is designed so that the shopper does not suggest or request the employee to commit any violation. The test shopper should develop rapport with the employee and then say something to the effect, "I would love to buy that item, but I don't have enough money." The employee can either underring the merchandise or not underring it.

There are many different integrity tests available for different situations. Additionally, new integrity tests can be developed to address specific loss scenarios, as long as those tests follow the basic guidelines. An effective program of integrity testing can assist loss prevention personnel in identifying dishonest employees and measuring the effectiveness of internal procedural controls.

Interactive Video Training

CAS, JHC

A relatively new (mid -980s) arrival on the LP training scene is what has been labeled as "interactive video training." It is the use of a computer which presents to the student a series of LP situations which may or may not include an LP agent responding to the situation.

At the conclusion of each individual scenario, the student is asked a series of questions. Answers indicate what would constitute the correct response to the situation portrayed and/or whether the actions of the LP agent, if included, were correct or incorrect, and if incorrect, what should have been the proper response.

Some programs will, if the agent has given an incorrect answer, go back and review the correct scenario at the end of each individual section of the program; others will hold all reviews until the completion of the entire video.

The computer is programmed to keep score of the student's answer and to categorize them as either correct or incorrect, as well as identify the specific subject matter with which the answer pertained. For example, if the incorrect answer deals with the use of force, that answer, if incorrect, will be identified with the subject. At the conclusion of the video session, the computer analyzes all the answers and provides the trainer with a graded series of scores identifying those areas in which the student needs further training, as well as personality traits which may opt against employment as an LP agent. For example, if the student's answers indicate a proclivity toward the use of excessive force, such will be reflected by the computer's summary report.

The use of a computer which can accurately measure both the student's cognitive understanding of the LP processes and procedures as well as provide an insight into the student's personality traits is obviously a helpful training tool. The fact that it is a consistent measuring tool and not influenced by any factors other the answers provided by the student makes it extremely immune to any charge of discrimination or favoritism. An added benefit is that once the initial capital expense is invested (several thousand dollars), the testing protocol requires minimal involvement of training personnel and further costs.

A number of training companies offer a variety of LP programs covering such topics as listed here. These are actual catalog descriptions of one company's programs, generously provided by Rume Interactive Corporation:

1. *LOSS PREVENTION—COMPREHENSIVE:* This course introduces the student to the world of loss prevention. The course is designed for the retail store associate or new loss prevention agent who may be less familiar with general loss prevention terms and concepts. Subject matter includes a broad overview of both external and internal theft situations illustrated by video example. The student is introduced to common terminology and practices and educated on proper response and approach.
2. *LOSS PREVENTION—ADVANCED:* This course focuses on customer approach techniques in external theft situations. The course is designed for the associate

who has a working knowledge and understanding of the loss prevention process of apprehension and/or recovery.

3. *SENSITIVITY TRAINING FOR LOSS PREVENTION:* In today's multicultural society, a need exists for a heightened awareness and sensitivity to cultural perception and bias. Recognizing the issues increases the ability to adapt one's approach to promote and ensure consistency in professionalism and respect regardless of circumstances. This course is designed to increase loss prevention's self-awareness and skill development in maintaining respect in human relations.

4. *USE OF FORCE:* This program presents industry best practices using video scenarios that assist the loss prevention associate in determining how to apply use of force principles in detainment situations in order to gain and maintain control. The proper application of these principles will have a significant impact in achieving a more favorable perception of the loss prevention professional, and the company, while also ensuring a safe and effective apprehensions.

5. *LOSS PREVENTION ORIENTATION:* This course is designed as an introduction to loss prevention. This course will include the guiding principles as well as standards and expectations for loss prevention personnel. The course is designed for new hires to the loss prevention department.

6. *LOSS PREVENTION FOR MANAGEMENT:* This course is designed for the retail manager who may be less familiar with general loss prevention terms and concepts. Subject matter includes a broad overview of internal theft situations illustrated by video example. The student is introduced to common terminology and principles.

7. *USE OF HANDCUFFS:* This program is directed at the retail loss prevention associate and applies basic handcuffing skills to detainment situations.

8. *SECURITY GUARD EXPECTATIONS AND PATROL PROCEDURES:* The focus of this training is to provide an overview of the basic expectations a company has for the role of a security officer and to review the fundamental guidelines and patrol procedures you will follow as part of your daily routine. This program is designed to deliver a consistent message to ensure that everyone in your position is provided with the same understanding of what is expected.

9. *SHORTAGE AWARENESS TRAINING:* This program is designed to heighten your awareness to the various factors that cause shortage. By making you aware of the problems, you can do your part to become part of the solution and help keep shortage to a minimum.

10. *PHYSICAL SECURITY:* This course is designed to demonstrate the role of loss prevention in general store operation and in regards to emergency procedures. The course focuses on the physical security of the building and the company assets on a daily basis.

11. *EAS PROCEDURES:* This course is designed to explain and demonstrate the proper procedures in responding to and tracking EAS system activation alarms. The course includes an overview of the components of an EAS system, expectations for the proper use and maintenance of both the system and the data generated by the system.

International Association of Professional Security Consultants

CAS, JHC

A Consulting Resource for the Loss Prevention Industry

Organizational Background

In 1983 Charles A. Sennewald, a security consultant specializing in servicing the retail industry, envisioned the need for a security consultant's forum or association. With the support of the then *Security World Magazine* and the International Security Conference (ISC), meetings were scheduled in Los Angeles, Chicago, and New York, inviting consultants to meet together and discuss the possibility of forming a professional society or association. As a consequence of those meetings, Sennewald sent out invitations, and in January 1984, a total of 18 consultants met in El Segundo, California and founded The International Association for Professional Security Consultants (IAPSC). The primary and guiding principle was that membership was restricted to those "pure" consultants who sold no product or service and in no way benefited from their recommendations and advise other than the professional fee they charged for their service.

IAPSC's Growth and Development

Today the organization has a membership of 124 consultants with expertise capable of servicing the entire broad range of interdisciplines found in the greater security industry, from aviation to zoo security. Eighteen members specifically have expertise in retailing.

To further ensure the level of professionalism of security consultants, the organization undertook the task of developing a certification program in 2005, resulting in the first testing a earned Certified Security Consultants (CSC) in 2006. This certification is not restricted to IAPSC membership, and a number of consultants who have chosen not to belong to the organization have earned, through testing, this important certification.

Services Available

A variety of needs surface in the loss prevention industry which can be beyond the normal in-house expertise of even the majority of vice presidents of LP. For example:

- VIP and VIP family protection, including emergency preparedness in the event of the kidnapping of the company's CEO;
- Computer security;
- Electronic eavesdropping countermeasures.

Highly focused consulting assignments are not uncommon. "Highly focused" means there's but a limited and specific need for an outside consultant's review. We've been engaged in such limited "scope of the work" assignments as

- Evaluation of the transfer of merchandise from the distribution center (DC) to individual stores and inter-store transfers;
- Development of an in-house certification training program to qualify LP agents to make detentions;
- Review of the post-detention processing procedures of detainees and the records connected with detentions;
- Revamping of the LP training manual;
- Introduction of and assistance in the implementation of a "prevention" strategy to augment the existing detect-and-apprehend strategy.

Areas of Security Expertise

Membership expertise include

- Access Control
- Alarm Systems
- Antiterrorism
- Bank Security
- Bioterrorism
- Bomb Threats
- Business Intelligence
- Campus Bookstore Loss Prevention
- Campus Crime
- Campus Security
- Campus Violence
- Cargo Security
- CCTV (Closed-Circuit Television)

- Communication/Data Centers
- Computer Security
- Corporate Security
- Counterespionage
- Counterterrorism
- Crime Prevention
- Crisis Management
- Disaster Planning
- Eavesdropping Detection
- Electronic Countermeasures
- Emergency Planning
- Employee Theft
- Engineering
- Executive Protection
- Facility Security
- False Imprisonment/Arrest
- Financial Crimes
- Fire/Life Safety
- Fraud/Embezzlement
- Gang Activities
- Guard Operations
- Guard Performance
- Guards Contract/Proprietary
- Guards/Security Personnel
- High-Rise Security
- Hostage Negotiations
- Information Security
- Intellectual Property
- Kidnapping Prevention
- Law Enforcement
- Loss Prevention
- Malls
- Parking Lots
- Physical Security
- Police Operations/Procedures
- Policies/Procedures
- Pre-Employment Screening
- Project Management
- Proprietary Information
- Research & Development
- Risk/Vulnerability Assessments
- Safety
- School Security
- Security Audits
- Security Design
- Security Management
- Security Misconduct
- Security Programs
- Security Standards
- Security Surveys
- Security Systems
- Security Training
- Shoplifting
- Special Event Security
- System Evaluation/Design

- Terrorism
- Threat Assessment
- Trade Secrets
- Use of Force
- Violent Crime
- Workplace Violence

Clearly, should a loss prevention department require or desire a reassessment of operating costs; need guidance in improving an existing program; or seek an objective and outside evaluation of a problem, policy, facility, or loss prevention operation, the IAPSC is a viable professional resource.

For more information about IAPSC, go to www.IAPSC.org.

Inter-Store and Other Transfers

CAS, JHC

Merchandise, in multistore operations, is often transferred between stores to balance stock. In single-store operations, merchandise is frequently transferred from stock to return to the vendor (RTV), transferred to damaged or salvaged goods, and/or transferred to claims. Whatever may be the reason for transfers, they present the opportunity, if improperly or sloppily handled, for loss and shrinkage.

When goods are transferred between stores, it is essential that proper records be kept so that subsequent financial accounting of transferred merchandise is possible and accurate. The means to accomplish this recordkeeping is an "inter-store transfer" form. This form is essentially an inter-store bill of lading or manifest; it lists the specific description (SKUs are frequently used) and number of goods being transferred on multiple self-carbonizing copies of the form. One copy is kept at the sending store, another at the receiving store, and a third copy sent to the appropriate financial department. Obviously, the receiving store is under the obligation to count and verify that all goods transferred are actually received, since the receiving store will be held financially accountable for these goods and the sending store relieved of financial accountability. In the case of extremely expensive merchandise, the listing of goods transferred may, if appropriate, include serial numbers.

When merchandise is transferred to other accounts (such as RTVs or salvage), there must be an accurate means of transferring the financial accounting for those goods as well. Various companies use various forms or methods to accomplish this accounting. The important point is not *how* it is done but *that* it has been done accurately. The required financial accuracy can best be achieved by a "closed end" system of accounting, which simply means that, at the end of the process, what has been transferred is matched with what is received by the transferee, and a paper record confirming the match is kept on file at each end of the process.

To satisfy yourself that the system in place is achieving its goals, we suggest two possible means of testing the procedure for accuracy. One means of testing is known as an "extraction" process. In this process, some items listed on the transfer form are surreptitiously removed from the transfer. The test is whether this extraction will be discovered on the receiving end and the proper personnel notified.

The second test method avoids actually removing goods from the transfer but accomplishes the same result by surreptitiously altering the count of goods being transferred. Again, it is hoped the arrival of an incorrect number of goods will be noted and reported. It is also suggested that occasionally the test counts be both reduced and raised from actual counts; by overstating the count number, it will become evident if such advantage is not reported when the financial advantage goes to the receiver, as opposed to its always being discovered and reported when the receiver is short-shipped.

Each company can devise its own method of testing whether its systems are performing as designed, not only with respect to movement of inventory, but also for other financial systems (such as cash counts in registers and vaults), where surreptitious overages and shortages should be discovered and reported.

The movement of merchandise in transfer trucks or trailers should be locked and sealed, and the seal numbers must be controlled and validated.

With respect to balancing stocks, seasonal goods can create headaches for buyers and stores; e.g., one store has sold out of Valentine's Day candy and cards on February 13, the day before Valentine's Day, and a sister store has more than it can possibly sell. A system is required to accommodate this "emergency" transfer. Frequently such transfers are accomplished in private vehicles; i.e., the candy buyer or a member of his staff will load the surplus candy in his auto and take it right over to the store awaiting the goods. Clearly, the carrying out of goods from the store in armloads to achieve these kinds of transfers, if not controlled, could be an invitation to theft. The transfer form must be completed as though the goods were being moved in normal company transfer trucks, but in this case store management or loss prevention must oversee the loading and unloading and process the paperwork.

Interviews and Interrogations: The Process of Interviewing and Interrogation

David E. Zulawski and Douglas E. Wicklander

Imagine not being able to question a victim, witness, or suspect during an investigation. How many cases would ever be resolved? It would probably be only those instances in which the individual was caught in the act that would ever be brought to a successful conclusion.

The most productive component of any investigation is the investigator's effective use of interviewing and interrogation. The process of interview and interrogation resolves more cases than any other forensic or laboratory examination of recovered evidence. Unfortunately, interview and interrogation are applicable when the controls of the organization have failed. They can, however, help a company identify the full scope of the fraud or theft when only a small portion has been revealed.

Unfortunately, many new investigators pay little attention to developing their skills and instead rely on techniques seen on television or in the movies. However, once an investigator understands the process of interview and interrogation, it becomes readily apparent that it is an incredibly productive avenue of case resolution.

The difficulty in learning to effectively use interview and interrogation is that almost any technique or attempt to gain information may work at sometime. Simply sitting silently across from a suspect[1] might obtain a confession, but it is not a very effective or consistently reliable way of getting one. As a result, the new investigator may be rewarded with a successful outcome even though the technique employed will not work well when applied against hundreds or thousands of other encounters. For example, one interrogator who was having difficulty obtaining information from suspects was asked to recount her approach to the interrogation. She related she would have the suspect placed alone in a room for a short period of time before she entered. She said when she arrived, she would make strong eye contact with the suspect and slam the door. When asked why, she said it was a replication of her first interrogation where she had obtained a confession. In the preceding example, the techniques employed were counterproductive, but the interrogator

---

1. *In this discussion, the term "subject" refers to someone who is a victim, witness, or suspect, and the "interviewer" is attempting to obtain or confirm information, but not a confession from the individual. The term "suspect" is used when the investigation has focused on an individual who is believed to be responsible for the incident, and the "interrogator" is attempting to obtain an admission or confession from that person. These definitions are the same as those used by the Center for Interviewer Standards and Assessment in its examination to receive the Certified Forensic Interviewer (CFI) designation. The term "investigator" is used to describe the work of either an interviewer or interrogator where the context of gaining information or a confession is not relevant.*

had been rewarded with a confession, which reinforced her continued use of the approach. Skilled interrogators know that the best techniques are the ones that work the most often with the most people.

Demeanor

Generally, people who like others and are comfortable communicating tend to make the best interviewers and interrogators. They have a natural curiosity about people, and their comfortable approach puts others at ease, opening the lines of communication.

Even though television and the movies tend to portray the investigator as abrasive, demanding, and aggressive, this is almost always contrary to the personality of a good investigator. Instead, a good investigator will adjust his demeanor and personality to the individual with whom he is speaking, establishing a comfortable dialogue.

When attempting to obtain information either through an interview or interrogation, the investigator must not appear to value either the information or confession excessively. When it appears to the subject that the information he possesses is of great importance, its value increases and the resistance to sharing the information may increase as well. During any negotiation, the buyer is always at a disadvantage once the seller discovers the importance of the purchase to the buyer. Once discovered, the price always increases, since it is now apparent that the buyer is unwilling to walk away. It is the same with information or a confession. The information possessed by the subject may actually be critical to the resolution of the investigation, but the investigator must use methods of rapport and persuasion to encourage the individual's cooperation without appearing to desperately need the information.

Rapport

Almost every interview and interrogation textbook addresses the necessity of establishing rapport between the investigator and the individual from whom he is seeking information. However, establishing rapport is often easier said than done.

Most people know someone who has the unique ability to walk into an establishment and within a short time talk with strangers like they are old friends. Others just never seem to grasp this skill. This ability to establish rapport is often as simple as finding something in common between yourself and another. It could be a community, interest, person, or even a question that leads to rapport. Most start a conversation with a stranger by commenting on something that is common to both. How often do we make a comment about the weather as a starting point to begin talking? The weather affects all of us and is a common experience which is easy to begin talking about.

The investigator who tries too hard to establish this connection with the subject will appear forced and unnatural. This is like the overly friendly salesman whom we immediately distrust. People often distrust another person's motives when he is overly friendly. This overt friendliness may actually cause the person to become more guarded instead of open. The investigator must be aware of the other person's response to his rapport-building attempt and be flexible in what he says and does. Some people are no nonsense and get to the point, whereas others want to talk and connect before getting down to business. The investigator's observation, flexibility, and interest in people will go a long way in opening the lines of communication.

Once rapport has been established, an interesting phenomenon called "mirroring" can be observed. Mirroring means the participants in the conversation unconsciously begin to posture themselves and pace their speech in similar fashions. People may stand the same way, moving to follow one another's posture change to maintain the comfort of rapport. This mirroring of behavior is the result of rapport. Watch any conversation, and the observer quickly will see by the group's body positioning whether they are in a state of rapport or conflict.

Depending on the individual, establishing rapport can be accomplished quickly or may take some time to achieve. People are much more likely to establish rapport when they do not feel threatened or uncertain about another's motives. If the investigator is perceived as attempting to be unnaturally friendly, this likely will foster suspicion and resistance in the subject. The subject's uncertainty and distrust of the overly friendly investigator will result in less information being obtained.

Interview and Interrogation

It is important that the investigator understand the distinction between the process of interview and interrogation. The dynamics of the two are exactly opposite, and the investigator must clearly establish in his mind what he is attempting to accomplish before talking with a subject.

An interview is a nonaccusatory fact-gathering or behavioral-provoking conversation to determine facts, sequence of events, alibis, or to confirm information with a victim, witness, or suspect. The interviewer allows the subject to do the majority of the talking by asking open-ended questions to encourage a narrative response. In the latter stages of the interview, the investigator may use closed-ended questions to clearly establish or confirm details. Because of the dynamics of interviewing, the investigator should not expect a confession, but only for the subject to confirm or deny information.

An interrogation is conducted when a suspect is believed to be guilty. It is a search for the truth to obtain admissions or confession, which independently confirms the investigative findings. The admissions or confession should support the details of the investigation and establish the individual's participation in the act. In an interrogation, the interrogator seeks information that establishes the suspect's culpability and mental state, which will provide sufficient details to prosecute, discipline, or discharge the individual.

Behavior

The process of interviewing and interrogating is essentially a conversation between two people desiring information. Each is reacting to the other's questions and moods. An important aspect of interview and interrogation is the careful observation of the subject's behavior and then reacting to it. Observing the individual's behavior as he is questioned often provides the investigator clues to concealed information; plus, it can assist in determining the person's candidness.

Carefully listening to the individual's word choice, speed of delivery, tonal qualities, and pauses may provide the astute interviewer with clues where to develop information. In addition, observing the physical behavior, attitudes, and behavioral changes during questioning may also assist the interviewer in knowing where to develop additional information.

For behavioral clues to be relevant in detecting deception, they must be on time and consistent. There is no single behavior, either verbal or physical, that always indicates an individual is being truthful or attempting to deceive. Instead, the interviewer must observe the behavior's timeliness and consistency to determine its usefulness for detecting deception.

For example, a subject may scratch his ear during the interview, which could indicate either his ear itched or he was under stress because of a question being asked. It will be the consistency of a response either to the question asked, topic introduced, or even a word used that will indicate that the behavior is relevant. When the interviewer returns to the word, topic, or question, does another behavioral response occur? This may or may not be the same physical behavior on each occasion but rather a consistent response, or lack thereof, to the stimulus of the topic, word, or question. It might occur that the first indication of stress was the scratching of the ear, next a folding of the arms, and finally the crossing of the legs. Although each of the behaviors is different, what is common is the consistency of some type of behavior occurring after the interviewer returns to a particular area of questioning. The preceding examples of behavior all consisted of movements after the stress, but just as relevant is the subject's lack of movement.

Behavior offers the investigator direction, and although it is observable, its true meaning can be inferred only from the context of the conversation, never absolutely known. The investigator views the behavior of a subject in two ways: comparing the subject to the population as a whole and to the subject's normal everyday actions. First, the subject's behavior is compared to what most people's action would be in a given context. Does the subject's behavior conform to the population's norm, or are the actions or attitudes different? If they appear different, this may be a clue to deception, or it may just be the individual's behavioral norm. The second thing that must be done is for the investigator to establish how the individual responds truthfully under the given set of circumstances of the current conversation.

Establish a Behavioral Norm

In either an interview or interrogation, it is essential for the investigator to establish a behavioral norm for the individual being spoken with. The interviewer is attempting to identify the normal pattern of behavior for the individual when he is responding truthfully to questions under a given set of circumstances.

Being interviewed, even when truthful, may put the individual under some level of stress. Recognizing this, the interviewer asks biographical or non-issue-related questions to which the individual is likely to respond truthfully. The interviewer calibrates the individual's speech pattern and physical behavior during this portion of the conversation and uses it as a tool of comparison when the conversation moves into those areas under investigation.

To establish the individual's behavioral norm, the interviewer might ask questions to which the answer is known or easily checkable. Those questions could be similar to the following:

- What is your current address?
- How old are you?
- How long have you been at your current job?
- What is your supervisor's name?

The interviewer may use questions like these to observe behavior associated with truthful information that readily is used by the subject every day, such as the individual's age or address. The interviewer also asks questions that require the individual to retrieve information from his long-term stored memory or to create responses. For example:

- Who was your immediate supervisor at your first job?
- What did that individual look like?
- Where did you go on your first business trip?

Questions such as these force the individual to have to search his long-term memory for information that is not readily available to him nor often used. The investigator's careful observation of the subject's behavior as he attempts to retrieve information from his memory may be useful during the other portions of the interview to determine whether the individual is recalling or creating this information.

It is also useful for the investigator to observe the subject's pattern of behavior as he creates information. The created responses to the interviewer's questions may be either deceptive or entirely truthful. For example, if an individual was asked to describe a person's voice, a resulting answer is in all probability created but could either be truthful or deceptive. This pattern of behavior is useful for the investigator to know because there will be instances in which the subject should be recalling information from his memory, not creating it. If the subject is creating a response when he should be recalling, the investigator may now infer that the response may be inaccurate.

After carefully observing the individual's responses, the interviewer now has a pattern of behavior to use as a comparison when the subject retrieves short- and long-term information or creates an answer to a question.

Another factor which may influence the interviewer's behavioral observation is his personal bias. If the interviewer is predisposed to believe the subject's answers, it is unlikely he will observe contradictory behavior that may indicate deception. Conversely, if the investigator distrusts the subject, he is more likely to interpret behavior as deceptive, rather than truthful. An interviewer must constantly monitor himself to avoid biases for or against the individual.

One other consideration in the interpretation of behavior is the ability of the individual to conceal his emotional state. When an individual expresses an emotion, there may be a leakage of behavior as the subject attempts to suppress the physiological manifestations of the emotion. When a deceptive subject first becomes aware that he must answer questions regarding the incident under investigation, his body explodes physiologically and psychologically. The deceptive subject must attempt to control his body's autonomic nervous system and his mental state of panic. The individual who attempts to control his body under stress will often leak behavior that is contradictory to the image the subject is attempting to portray.

If the individual has been prepared for the interview or is able to anticipate it, he is much more likely to be able to control the stress he is under from his autonomic nervous system. When he first becomes aware that he is going to have to attempt to deceive, his body reacts, but later when he is actually interviewed regarding the situation, he is in a much more controlled state. This controlled state makes it more difficult for the interviewer to identify possible deception.

As the interviewer moves from the behavioral norm questions into the issue under investigation, he looks for changes in the subject's verbal and physical responses that may indicate the individual is being deceptive or withholding information.

Movement and gestures may indicate stress or simply could be a method the subject uses to help explain the story. It is also common for someone attempting to deceive to lock himself down, limiting any movements or gestures. The investigator concealing what is known from the investigation is in a unique position to evaluate the candidness of the subject and his associated behavior. The subject, if he chooses to, may attempt to lie and conceal derogatory information in a number of ways.

Types of Lies

During an interview or interrogation, the subject may engage in a variety of different attempts at deception. There are five basic types of lies that the individual may use when attempting to deceive his interviewer.

The simple *denial* is the first type of lie, which would seem to be the easiest to carry off by the subject. "I didn't do it." Though its brevity and simplicity on the surface would seem to indicate that it would be chosen often, many guilty individuals avoid denying the incident directly. It seems that a direct denial of involvement creates a significant discomfort internally; psychologists call this "cognitive dissonance." To avoid this internal discomfort, many deceptive individuals will go to great lengths to avoid having to say, "No, I didn't do it."

Instead, they will respond to a question that was not asked or talk off the subject, giving an indirect response to a question that simply could have been responded to with a denial. It is important for the interviewer to evaluate each response to a question in light of what was asked instead of simply accepting what on the surface may seem like a good answer.

For example, an interviewer may ask

Interviewer: "Bob, let me ask you. Did you steal that missing deposit?"

Subject   : "You know, I didn't even know that that deposit was missing. I was off for several days and just heard about the missing deposit when I got to work today."

Notice, in the preceding exchange, the subject never denied stealing the missing deposit, but instead offered a piece of information that was not requested by the interviewer.

The second type of lie, the lie of *omission*, is the most commonly used by deceptive individuals. It is the simplest lie to tell because the subject merely relates the truth while leaving out information that would prove embarrassing or incriminating. The subject relates a sequence of true events, which, because true, can be told repeatedly in a consistent manner. It is only those details that would incriminate him that need to be left out. If the interviewer later offers information that contradicts the subject's story, he can defend himself by telling the interviewer that he "just forgot" to mention those details. A lie of omission can succeed only if the interviewer does not ask the detailed questions to force the subject to commit to a story or to be forced to fabricate one to cover his deception.

The third type of lie is the lie of *fabrication*. This type of lie is the most difficult for an individual to carry off, since it requires inventiveness and good memory to remain consistent. A fabricated lie creates the most stress for the subject, which will result in leakage of deceptive behavior that the interviewer may be able to observe. An interviewer, whenever possible, should ask questions that will result in the deceptive subject manufacturing a story or details. These manufactured details and events will not hold up to inspection during the investigation, since they do not exist outside the subject's mind. If the investigation can disprove the subject's sequence of events or details, it may prove as damning as a confession of wrongdoing. Plus, an interrogator who can use the suspect's own lies to challenge him has a significant advantage should there ever be an interrogation.

Unfortunately for the subject, a lie of fabrication requires third parties, documents, or some other piece of nonexistent evidence to support it. For example, an employee stole $900 dollars from the store safe and was later found to have made a deposit to his checking account in the same amount. Under questioning, he said the deposit was in the form of a check from his mother for exactly the same amount as was stolen, and it was merely a coincidence that the amounts were the same. This lie depended on the nonexistent check from his mother. However, bank records would indicate that it was a cash deposit in the same denominations as those missing from the safe. And unfortunately for the suspect, there was no check from the mother's check account that would match his story. Had he not confessed, his alibi could have been broken factually using bank records.

Even stories agreed upon in advance with coconspirators often will contain glaring contradictions and inconsistencies. If an interviewer suspects that the story has been concocted, he should carefully ask about the details, which is where the contradictions most often will be found. When most stories or alibis are constructed, there will be a discussion about what makes the most sense among the group. The problem then lies in the memories of the participants as they try to recall which variation was finally agreed upon. It is no wonder why there will be variations in the fabricated memories.

The fourth type of lie the interviewer may be faced with is minimization. In using the lie of minimization, a subject offers a small admission in hopes that the interviewer will be satisfied and discontinue any further questioning. A subject under the influence may concede that "he had a beer or two" but continue to deny he was intoxicated. A cashier might minimize the admission of theft by acknowledging he borrowed "some change for a soda" instead of admitting to taking a larger amount of money from the safe. In each of the preceding examples, the individual's strategy was the same—offer a small, less incriminating admission in hopes that the interviewer or interrogator would be satisfied and discontinue the conversation. Generally, when this type of lie is used, it is a strong indication that additional information is being withheld.

The final type of lie is the lie of *exaggeration*. This type of lie often is found on employment applications where the applicant exaggerates his qualifications and salary at previous positions. An interviewer might also find this type of lie with a witness who exaggerates the violence of an encounter or some other aspect of a conversation. This type of lie essentially uses the truth as its foundation, while exaggerating some aspects of the story.

Investigators also find that lies of exaggeration are used by informants who want to increase the value of their information or the interviewer's perception of the informants' importance. Informants often take some peripheral access to a previous case and, through exaggeration, inflate the importance of their role in bringing it to a resolution. Remaining skeptical of the information provided by informants allows the interviewer an opportunity to carefully question each claim, looking for contradictions and places where points may be confirmed through investigation.

Remember that lies told by an individual during an interview, such as the employee's mother's check for $900, can be as powerful as a confession. Subsequent investigation can establish the person's deception and destroy his credibility at trial or in a disciplinary hearing. The investigator must constantly be aware of the possibility the subject is withholding information or intentionally attempting to deceive. Changes in the subject's verbal and physical behavior, along with the evaluation of the information offered, will assist the interviewer in determining its veracity.

A second key factor is withholding what has been learned from the investigation. The evidence should confirm the subject's story, matching the timing and sequence of events. The deceptive subject, unaware of the investigator's knowledge, may fabricate information and circumstances that are easily contradicted by the investigation. Clearly, when the subject's story differs from the investigation, he will likely be lying.

Preparation and Room Setting

Prior to any interview or interrogation, there must be preparation for the encounter, both in terms of reviewing the investigative information and arranging the room setting. Most organizations have a policy or procedure for proceeding with investigative interviews or interrogations that should be strictly followed. Often these policies will lay out the prior notifications required, criteria to interview, and selection of witnesses.

The interviewer should evaluate the subject to identify potential information and the probable level of cooperation that might be expected from the individual. Generally, a cooperative witness is handled easily by an interviewer and usually provides any information requested. However, this is not necessarily the case from all witnesses or suspects in an incident. Depending on a witness's anticipated level of cooperation, the interviewer may select a more or less formal location to conduct the conversation. In instances where the witness's cooperation may be suspect, a more formal interview may be appropriate.

The interviewer should also assess the elements of the crime or policy violation that may be important in proving the case. Questioning and evaluating information become easier when the interviewer has a clear idea of what must be proved. This also identifies what is relevant evidence that should be secured. Knowing what must be proved to obtain a conviction or termination assists the interviewer in developing questions to explore these areas more fully.

The interviewer also should be aware of any special areas of concern from the decision makers that also might indicate areas of inquiry. For example, it is not unusual for some decision makers to be concerned about whether the individual knew what he was doing was wrong. Once they have expressed this concern, the interviewer can now address this area during his questioning and elicit responses that satisfy the decision makers' needs. There may also be less obvious legal aspects that may not be apparent to the interviewer, but may become important in subsequent litigation. Clearly identifying needs and concerns of investigative partners at the onset of the interviews will make each conversation more productive.

Another area of preparation is considering what the end result of the investigation will be. Is the organization interested in prosecution, termination, civil litigation, or some other decision? Knowing the end point of the investigation will allow the interviewer to allocate resources and investigative dollars in the most appropriate fashion. Since there are differing levels of proof in civil and criminal hearings, having an end point in mind helps direct the process.

One question that should always be asked is, "If this person has ever been previously interviewed, interrogated, or disciplined, how did he react?" People tend to fall into patterns of behavior, which either have been successful for them in the past encounters or have become a habit. Being able to anticipate the subject's attitude toward the investigator increases the likelihood of success by selecting appropriate strategies. By recognizing the possible pitfalls, the interviewer can choreograph the conversation in ways most likely to assure its success. If the individual tends to react in a rude and aggressive fashion, the interviewer should attempt to find an approach that would avoid this particular response. This could include the selection of the interviewer, location of the interview, and perhaps even the selection of an appropriate witness.

The investigator should also consider whether a witness should be present during the conversation. Many organizations require a company witness be present during the encounter. The interviewer should preselect an appropriate witness, instructing him on his duties during the interview or interrogation. In general, the witness is told to sit quietly and observe without joining in the conversation unless instructed to do so by the interviewer. In some cases it may be appropriate for the witness to take notes of the encounter, especially noting times of specific admissions and the confession.

Sometimes a witness may be useful because he knows the organization's business practices. It is unlikely the subject will attempt to lie about current procedures with another knowledgeable person in the room. The advantage for the interviewer is that the subject must now describe what he should have done, rather than offer excuses for what he did do. Once he has confirmed what he should have done, the existing contradictory evidence becomes a powerful persuasive tool to get to the truth.

When a telephone interview or interrogation is going to be conducted, the witness may become critical in arranging the room, bringing the employee to the phone, and obtaining a statement. The witness, in this type of case, becomes the eyes and ears of the investigator onsite, handling all those things the investigator would normally do himself.

The investigator should also test any audio/visual recording devices that might be used to document the conversation. There may be background noise that will obscure the conversation, so a test of the system always should be conducted using the anticipated positioning of all parties. The audio/visual recording of an interview or interrogation should be performed only when authorized by an organization's policy and in accordance with state and federal eavesdropping laws.

The investigator also should consider the appropriateness of making an appointment with the subject. Interviewers will often find people much more cooperative when they have set aside time for the conversation; however, interrogators often find that when suspects have time to prepare for the encounter, they become more resistant to a confession and difficult to handle. In the case of employee interviews, many of these problems can be overcome by planning with management for the associate's daily schedule, taking into account breaks, lunch, and dismissal times. To conduct a productive interview or interrogation, there must be adequate time; sometimes this is just a phone call to management away.

Room Setting

The selection of a setting for the interview or interrogation is often a matter of convenience for the subject. In certain situations the interviewer may be talking with the victim, witness, or suspect at his residence or place of business. In these types of interviews, it is difficult for the investigator to control the setting or distractions that may be present. On occasion, these distractions and inappropriate settings can be minimized by prearranging the interview with the individual, but the potential problems must be weighed against this course of action.

Regardless of the location chosen for the interview/interrogation, the overriding concern in preparing the environment should be establishing privacy for the conversation. The individual is being asked to admit to something that he may never have divulged to another. It is always more difficult to tell something confidential to a group than it is to a single interviewer.

Removing distractions also assists in establishing privacy for the conversation. The investigator should attempt to avoid interruptions in the conversation by turning off phones and, when possible, putting a Do Not Disturb sign on the door. Each of these actions may prevent a break in the encounter that could disrupt the flow of information and break rapport.

Distractions in an interview/interrogation can vary widely. They could be loud noises from machinery or ringing phones, or as simple as people walking in and out of the room. When the location for the interview has been prearranged and under the control of the investigator, many of these types of distractions easily are avoided. This is more difficult to do when the investigator has no control over the setting because he is visiting the individual's home or place of business.

When an interview room is selected, generally it should be small and uncluttered. The interviewer should prearrange the seating for the subject, himself, and possibly a witness. Often a small table or desk is useful should a statement need to be taken. A room that comfortably holds three or four people is usually fine for the job. In most cases the room will be occupied by the investigator, subject, and possibly a witness. However, there may be occasions when another party may be asked into the room to witness the subject's final verbal or written statement, and having the extra space can be convenient.

Most interviewers will position the subject with his back to the door and the witness slightly behind and off to one side. The placement of the witness in this fashion avoids the distraction of having an additional person in the room and maximizes the feeling of privacy. By positioning the subject with his back to the door, the interviewer minimizes the accusation that the subject was being held against his will. Were the interviewer or witness to position themselves between the subject and the door, this allegation would appear much more plausible.

The interviewer should position the subject across from himself without the barrier of a table or desk between them. By positioning the subject in this position, the interviewer can observe the subject's demeanor and body language without having a desk interfere with his line of sight. In addition, positioning the interviewer directly across from the subject without a barrier allows the interviewer an opportunity to move closer should the need arise.

If the interview is going to be recorded, the subject's chair should be placed in such a fashion that he can be clearly observed and heard by the camera and microphone. However, there may be circumstances in which this is difficult or impossible. In professional interview rooms, often this is done with concealed equipment that does not influence the subject's statements or cooperation. Before using any audiovisual recording, the interviewer should investigate applicable state and federal laws regarding eavesdropping and adhere to company policy on recording interviews.

Interviewer Appearance and Demeanor

Another step prior to the interview or interrogation is to determine the appearance and demeanor of the investigator. The appearance of the investigator should always be clean and professional. The decision to dress up or down for the encounter should be based on the status of the subject, the clothing he normally wears, and the formality of the organization. If an interviewer were going to talk to a senior-level executive, it would be proper to dress up to the more formal level chosen by that individual; interviewing an hourly associate might lead to a much more casual form of dress.

Contrary to the actions of detectives shown on television, an investigator is much more likely to gain the cooperation of an individual using a calm persuasive demeanor than an aggressive one. Even when the investigator is dealing with hardened criminals, the softer approach will be much more effective than attempting a hard, aggressive tack.

After considering the elements of the crime or policy violation, personality of the individual, arrangement of the room, and briefing of the witness, the interviewer is ready to begin his conversation with the subject.

Conducting the Interview

Understanding and Establishing the Case Facts

Before the interview, the interviewer reviews the available case facts and evaluates the implications of the information uncovered. If procedures or events are not clear from the file, it may be useful to conduct background interviews with people who can help the interviewer understand the information. Knowing in advance the process used by the witness to do his job will help the interviewer ask more specific questions, potentially identifying areas where the individual is being deceptive or omitting relevant information.

The interviewer should also evaluate what is known to determine other possible plausible explanations for the subject's actions. For example, a surveillance video observes a member of management removing merchandise from the company and placing it into his vehicle. This certainly could be a possible theft, or there could be other less sinister reasons why the manager was putting merchandise in his car. The merchandise could be being transferred, returned to a vendor, or used in conjunction with a presentation, any of which would not be a theft. Before the interview, or revealing the evidence, it would be important for the interviewer to determine under what circumstances merchandise might legitimately be removed by employees and who must authorize any removals. If there were legitimate circumstances why an employee might remove merchandise for transfer, the interviewer should know before the interview what authorizations are required and what paperwork is necessary for that to happen. This information would allow the interviewer to investigate whether this was a legitimate action, policy violation, or theft.

In cases where there is specialized knowledge required, the interviewer should conduct sufficient preliminary interviews with subject matter experts so he is familiar with the terminology used, ordinary operating procedures, and documents produced to conclude the task. In certain cases it may be useful to select a person with this knowledge as a witness or at least have him available for consultation during the interview.

Purpose of the Interview

The interviewer should be clear about what information the subject is likely to possess and any potential evidence that may be recovered during the conversation. Clearly identifying what the interview is trying to establish and what is going to be important to the resolution of the case often will point the interviewer to the areas of inquiry.

For example, if the interviewer was going to question the manager of a store about inventory shortages, the interviewer has a number of areas of inquiry. The obvious difficulty is that inventory shortages could be the result of theft of either merchandise or cash.

Some questions that might be useful to the interviewer would be

- What inventory system does he use to keep track of merchandise at the store/
- When merchandise is transferred, what paperwork must be prepared? Are signatures required? Who must authorize the transfer?
- How is receiving handled at the store?
- What cash handling practices are used?
- Who authorizes customer refunds, voids, and check purchases?

These are but a few of the logical questions that might help provide additional areas of inquiry and identify potential evidence that might resolve the case. In addition, the manager's responses to these questions might identify other interviews that should be conducted to fully investigate the circumstances surrounding the case.

Types of Questions

In an interview, the subject is asked a variety of questions to produce information useful to the investigation. During an interview, the subject should do the majority of the talking, with the interviewer asking questions only when necessary to direct the individual's story or expand on details. Silence is an interviewer's best friend, since most people will continue to talk, to fill the void in the conversation. As the subject continues to talk, he often will expand on relevant information or offer new information not yet addressed.

However, the order that the questions are asked must be planned so as not to reveal what the actual target of the questioning is meant to be. If the interviewer immediately approaches the topics of interest, the subject may recognize his exposure and become more difficult to handle.

Interviewers will use a variety of questions to develop information during the interview.

Open-Ended Questions

The interviewer uses open-ended questions to encourage a narrative response from the subject. These questions allow the subject to respond, selecting what he believes is important. An open-ended question such as "Tell me what happened yesterday?" offers the subject an opportunity to tell his story regarding the events without direction from the interviewer. The subject offers his version of events, selecting and omitting details based on what he believes was important. The open-ended question offers the interviewer a framework for his questioning by first allowing the subject an opportunity to highlight what he believes are relevant points.

It is also important to note that this question does not in any way indicate what is known by the investigator. It forces the subject to decide if it is safe to tell the truth or if it is necessary to lie about what went on. Either way, the subject may provide new information, confirm important relevant evidence, or attempt to lie, all of which benefits the investigator. In addition, this question encourages an untainted narrative that can be evaluated as to what was important to the subject uninfluenced by the investigator.

Expansion Questions

The interviewer, now having the framework of the story, can begin to expand it using the subject's own words. By using the subject's own words, the interviewer does not influence the story by either adding or directing the individual's responses. The subject, during his telling of the story, said, "After we had finished dinner, we had a couple of beers and then later on we went to the movies." The expansion question might be, "Now, you said, after we finished dinner, we had a couple of beers—what happened during that time?" The interviewer, recognizing that the subject had left something out between drinking beer and going to the movies, seeks to expand the individual's story into that missing time frame. Note that the question uses the subject's own words, adding nothing to contaminate the story, but encouraging the subject to expand on the details himself.

Closed-Ended Questions

Once the interviewer has had an opportunity to create a framework for the story and expanded it, there may be specific details that must be determined. Closed-ended questions are designed to elicit the specific details. For example, the interviewer might specifically ask for the number of beers consumed. "Exactly how many beers did you drink before leaving for the movies?" Or, "What movie did you see?"

When these questions are used, they should be presented in a neutral manner, not offering information, but rather encouraging the witness to provide specific information. It would be much better to say, "What color was the shirt?" than to ask, "Was the shirt blue?" By asking for confirmation of the color blue, the interviewer inadvertently may taint an individual's recall or encourage him to provide faulty information not actually recalled. The description of the shirt as blue may require additional questions to understand exactly what color blue the witness saw.

Closed-ended questions are best saved until the end of the interview, since they interrupt the flow of the story or sequence of events being recalled by the subject. Once the subject has committed to the overall story, the interviewer now asks the specific questions to which he has an interest with less risk of tainting what the subject is saying. This is where the interviewer should make sure that he clearly understands what the subject means by a specific word. "You said he hurried. What did you mean by that?" The witness can now define what he means to make sure there is clarity in the communication.

When the interviewer uses these questions later in the interview, it is likely the subject has brought up the topic himself, again concealing the interviewer's interest in the topic at hand. Since it is the subject's own words that are being explored, there is less suspicion about the interviewer's inquiry and perhaps more to be revealed.

Leading Questions

In most instances the interviewer should avoid using leading questions with a victim or witness. Many individuals can be extremely suggestible when responding to leading questions. They respond not with an actual memory, but rather with a response encouraged by the interviewer's question. Consider the difference between the words "accident" and "crash." Using the term "crash" implies greater speed and a more violent impact, which could alter the witness's impression of the vehicle's speed and resulting damage. An interviewer should be aware that the younger the victim or witness, the more suggestible he may be to altering his story because of the interviewer's leading questions. The easiest way to avoid contaminating the witness's statement is to use his words exactly when expanding the observation.

It may be useful in the interview to use a leading or assumptive question when the interviewer is certain the subject is lying. For example, if the subject is concealing information about his participation in the situation, the interviewer might ask

Interviewer : "So how many times do you think that he carried product to the manager's car?"

Subject   : "Well … I'm not sure, maybe three or four."

Interviewer : "What would you say would be the most number of times you did that?"

Interviewer : "Ten or fifteen?"

Subject   : "No … just a few."

In this situation the interviewer either knew or strongly suspected that the subject was withholding information. The use of the leading or assumptive question elicited an admission from the subject before he had time to consider his response. If he was asked, "Did you carry merchandise to the manager's car?" the likely response would be a denial.

An interviewer should also attempt to keep his questions simple and to the educational level of the subject. Nothing creates more difficulty than a using a compound question, such as "Did he run through the yard and then jump over the fence?" The potential problem with a compound question is one part of it is accurate, but the second part might not be. The witness simply could agree, accepting the inaccuracy, thus tainting the interviewer's impression of the event. It is much better to let the witness independently confirm the recollections of other witnesses than to taint his recall of the event.

Compound Questions

The interviewer should avoid using compound questions unless absolutely certain that both portions of the question are accurate. The compound question asserts that two things must be true for that question to be answered accurately. For example, "Then Dan ran across the street and jumped the fence, correct?" This requires that Dan had both run across the street and jumped the fence for it to be correct. The problem with this type of question is that the witness may answer yes when only one part of the question is actually correct. Compound questions increase the possibility of incorrect information becoming part of the investigation.

The Final Question

An extremely effective last question in the interview is, "Is there anything else that we should talk about that I might not have specifically asked you about?" This question can also be asked assumptively, "What else is there that we should talk about?"

It is amazing how often people will offer additional information or even make admissions of guilt when faced with this final question in the interview. Attorneys taking depositions often will ask this question to prod additional information from the witness being deposed. Many times attorneys will preface their most significant area of inquiry with the statement, "I am almost done here." This tactic often causes the witness to drop his guard thinking that the process is over, thus becoming more susceptible to giving up critical information to the most important areas of inquiry.

Selling the Interview

In some situations the interviewer must convince the subject to cooperate in the interview, which requires that the interviewer provide a reason. In essence, the subject is asking, "What's in it for me? Why should I cooperate?" Many people will provide information simply because they have done nothing wrong and see no harm in cooperation. However, in our litigious society many people are afraid of being drawn into a lawsuit or criminal proceeding that is not of their making. With the uncooperative witness, the interviewer must work to encourage cooperation.

With a difficult subject, the interviewer faces the hurdle of overcoming the individual's reluctance to cooperate. Most of the time the person has some concern that must be addressed by the interviewer before he can open a dialogue with the individual. These concerns could be losing wages, having to testify, giving up valuable time, fearing retaliation, involving cultural issues, or even potentially involving themselves in a crime. Essentially, the interviewer must offer some benefit to the subject to encourage his cooperation. In most instances, the benefit provided by the interviewer will be some form of an intangible. These intangibles might include encouraging the subject to do the right thing, protecting the individual's self-image, and on occasion, allowing the person to relieve his guilt.

A little honey goes a long way, and an interviewer who is personable and takes the time to develop rapport with the subject is already a long way ahead of the game. People often will go out of their way to help someone that they like or have positive feelings toward. The interviewer who takes the time to expresses interest in the person and establish rapport will gain significant amounts of information when a more aggressive approach would have provided nothing.

Statement Analysis: The Untainted Story

Whenever possible, the interviewer should attempt to obtain an untainted story from the subject. As a story or sequence of events is told over and over, additional information is incorporated as a result of questions asked. The resulting story can have significant differences in content and emphasis from its first telling. The first telling of a story or sequence of events is the untainted version. In the untainted story, the witness is telling the interviewer what he believes is important and omitting those areas he believes are not. This might be done in an attempt to deceive, or it might be done simply as a means of telling the story in an expedient manner.

If a subject was asked to tell an interviewer what happened yesterday, he would most likely respond with the significant details of the day. It would be unlikely for that person to tell every single event incorporating every detail that had occurred. To do so would be to tell a story that was unending:

> I woke up at 6:33 a.m. after my clock radio on the nightstand, which is set to WXJL, went off.

> I listened to one minute of the weather before I rolled onto my right side and pushing up I placed my left foot on the floor before slowly placing my right foot next to it. I felt a small twinge in my lower back that I attributed to the gardening I had done the previous day. I used my right hand. . .

It would be much more likely for someone to tell the story utilizing the highlights of the day:

> I woke up at 6:30 when my alarm went off. Then I went down and had breakfast before I showered and shaved. I got to work about quarter to nine and had a marketing meeting until about 10:30.

In this example the subject is selecting what he considers to be important points relating to what he did yesterday. Notice, however, there are significant gaps of information in this telling. How long was breakfast? How did he get to work? How long did it take to get to work? Did the marketing meeting start immediately upon his arrival or at some point later?

The untainted story does provide some indication for the interviewer whether the subject is being truthful. When evaluating the subject's story, the interviewer compares the level of detail that preceded the incident, the incident itself, and the teller's relating of what followed the incident. In the untainted story, these three components are likely to be comparable in length and detail. However, when the untainted story's components are not equal, it often indicates an attempt at deception. If the subject was attempting to deceive the interviewer using a lie of omission, thus deleting the incriminating components from his story, the resulting description of the incident likely will be shorter and contain less detail. This will contrast to the portions of the story that preceded or followed the event, which will have greater detail and length. However, once the subject has been questioned repeatedly about the incident, it will naturally distort the parts by adding additional detail to the event itself in response to the questions. This does not indicate deception; it is simply a natural progression of a story with the witness incorporating details that were inquired about previously. Because a question was asked, the information requested must be important. Therefore, in the next telling the witness simply includes it so he does not have to answer the same question over again.

A careful examination of the subject's untainted story can assist the interviewer in evaluating its truthfulness and identify areas where omitted information may be sought. Some interviewers will have a subject write the untainted story about the incident in a statement form and conduct an extensive evaluation of the story and language used by the subject. This statement analysis can be effective in eliminating individuals from the incident as well as focusing on the guilty.

Fact Gathering

Fact gathering interviews are generally one of the most easily accomplished since they primarily revolve around confirming facts and establishing information. These types of interviews seek to answer the questions who, what, where, when, how, and why. The interviewer often has an understanding of what information is available from the witness, along with the types of documents or evidence available, so the focus of the interview is very directed.

These types of interviews often are conducted by making an appointment, since the cooperation of the individual will be dependent on his ability to make time for the conversation. Since the interviewer merely is confirming or following up a previous inquiry, this interview is usually relatively focused on a particular piece of information. The location selected for this type of interview is often where the witness's access to the document or information is easily achieved.

Lifestyle Interviews

In certain investigations a lifestyle inquiry might be made into the background of a particular individual. Instead of identifying or confirming specific facts, this interview is designed to develop information about how an individual lives. These types of interviews tend to be much more broadly based and may address likes and dislikes, expenditures, travel, personality, and general demeanor.

The lifestyle interview may be conducted with neighbors, family members, friends, acquaintances, and coworkers. The purpose of the interview is to develop an understanding of how the subject lives his life, makes decisions, and spends his money. This type of information may be useful in the interrogation of the subject should he be proved to be involved. Lifestyle information also might be relevant when doing background investigations for pre-employment selection.

Cognitive Interviewing

Another type of interview is called the cognitive interview. The cognitive interview is designed to assist a cooperative victim or witness in recalling details about a particular incident. Researchers evaluating interviewing techniques determined that although many of the techniques and tactics used during the interview were effective, they were being used in an improper order. Through their research, the cognitive interview was developed to take advantage of how memories are made, stored, and retrieved in the human mind.

When storing a memory, the victim or witness must first make the observation, store the memory, and then at some later point be able to retrieve it. There are a number of obvious difficulties in retrieving a memory. First, was the individual prepared to make the actual observation, or was it, as in many instances, an unexpected event? Second, where was the memory stored by the individual? It could have been associated with a visual observation, smell, sound, taste, or even a feeling. An additional problem that occurs when retrieving a memory is the subject's choice of words to describe what it is that he observed. The interviewer listening to these words must now interpret what the witness actually saw, and the two meanings may differ greatly.

For example, a witness reports an observation of a suspect, "He rushed across the parking lot." What does this actually mean? The interviewer's definition of "rushed" might be entirely different than the meaning intended by the witness. It is important that the interviewer carefully question the individual to clearly understand what was meant by his word choice.

The interviewer can use a number of tactics to assist the witness to expand on the story being told. Already mentioned was silence. In general, people talk when there is silence, thus adding information to what was already said. However, silence by the interrogator during an interrogation is likely to result in the suspect voicing a denial or heading off topic. Another simple tactic to add information is to ask, "What happened then/next?" This encourages the witness to continue his description in the same direction he was telling the story. A simple "um hmm" or "OK" identifies that the interviewer is listening and encourages the witness to continue with his story from that point.

Another technique is to logically explore the memory in order of happening rather than jumping from one part of it to another. Jumping around while attempting to retrieve a memory often causes the witness to omit large amounts of information that otherwise would have been recalled. Additional information also can be recalled when a victim or witness makes repeated attempts to retrieve information on the incident. Much like a jogger warming up, the witness is asked to begin his story at a point before the incident was actually observed. This allows the individual to re-create his mental and physical state at the time of the observation. By using the warmup, the interviewer encourages the witness to re-enter his state of being at the time of the observation, thus increasing the likelihood of retrieving the stored memory.

The cognitive interview consists of a number of distinct phases through which the interviewer leads the subject. Each of the following is used to enhance the recollection of the cooperative victim or witness:

1. *Establish rapport.* As in most interviews, the first step is establishing rapport with the individual. One of the primary findings of the researchers was that most interviewers neglect this important component, failing to adequately establish a relationship with the victim or witness prior to questioning, which then hinders the freedom of exchange.

2. *Provide interview preparation instructions.* The interviewer provides the witness with a set of instructions, which effectively prepares the individual to provide complete answers. The interviewer lets the witness know that it is all right to say that he does not know the answer to a question if he does not recall. The interviewer also lets the witness know that if he does not understand a question, he should ask him to rephrase it or use different words. If appropriate, the interviewer will also discuss with the witness how natural it is to be nervous during an interview. It is during this point as well that the interviewer reminds the witness to be as detailed as possible, providing even minute details when they are recalled.

3. *Reconstruct the circumstances.* The interviewer begins by asking the witness to begin his recollection at some point prior to the incident under investigation. This effectively provides a context for the witness's memory and helps with recall. The interviewer reminds the witness to include as much detail as possible about the people who were present, feelings, or other general observations that may seem irrelevant to him. The interviewer reiterates his previous statement encouraging the witness to be as comprehensive as he can in his recollection.

4. *Change perspective of observation.* Once the interviewer has obtained as much information as possible from the witness's first recitation, he now asks the witness to change the perspective of the observation. This might include asking what he would have seen if he had observed the incident from another position or asking the witness to begin telling the story from a different point. Another effective technique is asking the witness to tell the story in reverse, which often will result in additional details being remembered. The interviewer may also use memory jogging techniques such as asking if the individual observed reminded him of anyone that he knew. The interviewer might also ask the witness to draw a diagram of the incident to clarify certain aspects of his responses.

5. *Close the interview.* Once the interviewer has obtained as much relevant information as possible, he should attempt to extend the interview with the witness through general conversation or gathering additional biographical information. By extending the interview, the witness often will remember additional details regarding the incident. Prior to leaving, the interviewer should give a statement of expectation to the witness. This statement of expectation tells the witness that he will remember additional details regarding the incident because everyone does. The interviewer then asks the witness to commit to reporting these new details. Obtaining the witness's commitment to call often will result in additional information being reported.

Behavioral Interviewing

Another form of investigative interview is the behavioral interview. Unlike the fact-gathering or cognitive interview, the behavioral interview is designed specifically to elicit verbal and physical behavior from individuals to eliminate them from suspicion. In this very structured interview, the interviewer asks questions and observes the subject's verbal and physical behavior along with the content of the answer to make a judgment about the individual's involvement in the incident under investigation.

In many types of criminal activity, such as arson, theft, burglary, or vandalism, there is rarely a witness and only a minimum of evidence available to the investigator. There was one witness, however—the perpetrator of the crime. This interview relies on the guilty party's fear of detection, which alters the body's autonomic nervous system, contributing to a change in the individual's physical behavior. As the body reacts to the possibility of discovery, the guilty subject's body undergoes a series of physical changes. The heart rate, respiratory pattern, and blood flow in the body change to prepare the individual to either fight or flee the threat. These physiological reactions often can be observed and may provide indications for the investigator to assist in eliminating individuals or focusing the investigation on them.

In addition to physical behavioral changes, a guilty individual's verbal behavior may be notably different from that of a truthful person. The interviewer evaluates the content of the individual's answers along with his verbal and physical behavior to determine whether the individual can be eliminated from suspicion. Each question asked in the behavioral interview has a general principle, allowing the interviewer to determine whether the subject is answering like a truthful person or one who is attempting to deceive.

One question an interviewer often asks in the behavioral interview is, "How do you feel about the company conducting an investigation into the missing deposit?" The general principle applied to this question is that an innocent person will be accepting of the investigation and expect that it will be carried out fully. A guilty individual is much more likely to deny the need for an investigation or be somewhat put out by the company's decision to investigate. The evaluation of the response to this question and others assists the interviewer in eliminating individuals from suspicion, leaving a fewer number of subjects to investigate.

Diagrams

An interviewer's use of diagrams can help clarify the witness's frame of reference and recollections. If a victim or witness provides a diagram to assist in the recollection of the incident, it should always be dated, signed by the witness, and retained in the investigative case file.

The use of the diagram helps the interviewer visualize what it is that the witness observed. The diagram also locks the witness into his story or alibi, possibly opening new investigative leads relating to the plausibility of the observation. For example, a witness may indicate that he observed an altercation on the street from his bedroom window. After this witness diagrams the position of the window and his position near it, the investigator can now determine whether that line of sight actually exists. If the line of sight for the observation does not exist, the diagram now provides damning evidence of the person's deception.

Common Interviewer Errors

Numerous common errors are made during interviewing, the most common of which is interrupting the victim or witness in the middle of a response. This interruption disrupts the retrieval of the memory and effectively discourages the victim or witness from offering information to the interviewer.

In addition to interrupting victims or witnesses while they are responding, many interviewers use closed-ended questions much too early during the interview. Interrupting the retrieval process with closed-ended questions hampers the recovery of memories much like a speed bump reduces the vehicle speed on a road.

Another common error is the use of rapid-fire questions. Asking questions rapidly does not provide an individual the opportunity to completely answer one question before proceeding to the next. A more appropriate use of rapid-fire questioning is in the latter stages of an interrogation, where the interrogator is attempting to develop an admission, rather than in an interview setting.

Interviewers may also make the error of revealing the specific target information that they are seeking or revealing evidence to the individual. It is often useful to conceal the target of the information from the subject. Once a subject determines the importance of a piece of information, his resistance to cooperation may increase. Much like supply and demand, the cost of obtaining the information in terms of effort may rise dramatically. In addition, interviewers who reveal what it is that they know lose an important tool in determining whether the individual is cooperating or truthful in his statements. It is much more difficult for the individual to lie successfully when he does not know what evidence the interviewer has discovered.

Finally, another common problem is the failure of the interviewer to adequately establish rapport with the victim or witness. People are much more likely to cooperate or go out of their way for an individual with whom they feel comfortable rather than someone who expects or demands they cooperate.

Interrogation

Once the investigation has been completed and a suspect identified, it is time to consider how to confront the individual involved. The purpose of the interrogation is to obtain the truth from the individual with details that independently corroborate the investigative findings.

In many cases it will be the suspect's own words that will provide the final elements of proof to successfully close the investigation. The confession is the crown jewel of any case and links all the investigative findings together in a definitive manner that proves the individual's guilt.

The interrogation process is much too complicated for a single chapter to deal with. However, be aware that obtaining a confession is, in fact, a learnable process that is customized based on the needs of the suspect. There are a number of ways an interrogator may approach a suspect when attempting to get a confession. Many people learn to interrogate by observing another, who then mentors their performance and helps them develop their skills. This works well if one happens to have a mentor who understands the process.

Unfortunately, many excellent interrogators who excel at obtaining admissions are less skilled at communicating what it is that they do and why to the student. Becoming skilled at interrogation requires practice, patience, and an understanding of the process and human behavior.

Preparation

The preparation to conduct an interrogation of a guilty suspect is much like preparing for an interview. The interrogator must clearly understand the case facts and the implications of evidence discovered during the investigation. It is important for the interrogator to be familiar with the investigative findings so he does not have to review information during the interrogation. The interrogator should also anticipate the individual's response to a confrontation by having looked at the suspect's past actions.

Next, the interrogator considers potential problems that might occur during the interrogation. By anticipating problems, the interrogator either can avoid them entirely or have a plan in place to address them. Although it is impossible to anticipate each and every problem that may arise prior to the interrogation, the interrogator still should consider the more common pitfalls he may encounter:

- What action should be taken if the suspect decides to leave?
- What action should be taken if the suspect asks for an attorney?
- What action should be taken if the suspect demands to see the evidence?
- What action should be taken if the suspect claims that he is ill?
- What action should be taken if the suspect becomes angry or threatening?

The answers to these and other questions will depend on company policy and the evidence available. However, the interrogator is well advised to consider his responses to these pitfalls in advance of encountering them so he has a ready-made plan.

Another aspect to be considered is the company policy regarding confronting an employee. There may be specific notifications to be made prior to the confrontation or policies that control the interrogator's actions. The interrogator also should identify the criteria that will be used to determine whether or not an individual will be terminated or prosecuted. Clearly understanding the decision maker's criteria for action will assist the interrogator in determining what information is relevant to include in the suspect's statement.

Decision to Confess

The interrogator should also understand why an individual might choose to confess or not confess to a crime he committed. It is counterintuitive that an individual would find a benefit in confession, since it may result in his incarceration, termination, and loss of reputation.

As children, we are taught that confession is the right thing to do, but then there is a punishment that is associated with the confession. It does not take children long to discover that by lying they may avoid punishment for their indiscretion. As people grow up to become adults, this learned behavior is acted upon, and they lie to avoid the consequences of their actions as well.

As a result, the interrogator faces a number of hurdles that must be overcome to convince a suspect that there is a benefit to confession. Most suspects are afraid of one or more of the five most common hurdles:

1. Loss of employment
2. Embarrassment
3. Arrest and prosecution
4. Restitution
5. Retribution from others

In general, the interrogator should anticipate that suspects will be more likely to confess, even in light of the hurdles, when a combination of three factors is present. The most common reason individuals confess is that they believe their guilt is known and the interrogator can prove it. The second most common reason for confession is a desire by the suspect to put a spin on the story to make his position more understandable. For example, the suspect might offer that he was merely going along with others when in actuality he was the leader of the group. This statement allows him to save face even while confessing to the incident. Finally, some people will confess because they feel guilty about what they have done. These reasons, either individually or in combination, are why an individual normally will confess to an incident.

The interrogator must be careful with his language, or he may convey to the suspect that the suspect's guilt is uncertain. For the interrogator to say "We're pretty sure what happened here" could indicate to the suspect that his guilt is not really known and a lie might extricate him from the situation. It would not be unusual for the suspect, in response to the interrogator's previous statement, to offer a denial of involvement while waiting to see what develops.

The interrogator must take into account these three primary reasons why people confess when constructing his strategy and approach to the interrogation. Simply offering evidence without a face-saving device may make it difficult for a suspect to confess even in the face of overwhelming evidence.

Rationalization

The backbone of the emotional appeal is the use of rationalization, which offers a face-saving device for the suspect. The interrogator bases his selection of the rationalization on the background of the individual. For example, if the interrogator was aware of financial difficulties in the suspect's background, he might use rationalizations based on financial pressures.

The previous rationalization could be illustrated by stories that portray people making errors in judgment because of financial difficulties. In essence the rationalization is a face-saving device used by the interrogator to make the individual's actions more understandable. The interrogator might suggest through the use of the story that the individual's theft of money was committed because of a need to take care of his family.

The rationalization allows the individual to save face without removing the elements of the crime. The fact that money was stolen to provide for one's family does not change the elements of the crime of theft. Regardless, the suspect has acknowledged permanently depriving the organization of a valuable asset, which establishes an essential element for the crime of theft.

Even when there is significant evidence proving an individual's involvement in the crime, rationalizations will make it easier for the suspect to confess. In essence, he will confirm the evidence while being allowed to offer understandable reasons for having committed the crime.

Denials

One of the most common difficulties in any interrogation is a guilty suspect who denies involvement. The interrogator must be prepared to handle two forms of denials that will be offered by the guilty suspect attempting to derail the interrogation.

Emphatic Denial

The most common form of denial is the emphatic denial. The suspect, in response to the interrogator's accusation or later during rationalization, simply says, "I didn't do it." Less skilled interrogators often revert to presenting evidence of involvement to the suspect instead of handling the denial. Or, just as commonly, the conversation will evolve into a did-too, did-not debate between interrogator and suspect.

The optimum way for the interrogator to handle an emphatic denial is to stop it before it is verbalized. The interrogator, observing the physical behavior associated with an emphatic denial, interrupts the suspect and continues with his rationalization. If the suspect is able to verbalize the denial, the interrogator must re-accuse him and return to the rationalization.

Emphatic denials also can be used as a measure of progress for the interrogator. The interrogator compares the frequency and intensity of the suspect's denial to the one preceding it, thus determining whether the individual is strengthening or weakening his defense. Normally, emphatic denials become less frequent and less intense as the individual moves toward confession.

When emphatic denials do not weaken, the interrogator first should change the rationalization to offer a different face-saving device. If the emphatic denials still do not become less frequent, the interrogator should consider presenting evidence of the individual's guilt or backing out of the interrogation.

Explanatory Denial

Another form of denial is called an explanatory denial. In an explanatory denial, the suspect offers a reason or excuse why he could not or would not be involved in the incident. In most cases the explanatory denial will be a truthful statement or one that will be difficult for the interrogator to disprove. The following illustrates a properly handled explanatory denial. The interrogator stops rationalizing and asks for an explanation from the suspect. This will cause the suspect to provide an explanatory denial, which the interrogator acknowledges, changing rationalizations and offering a new face-saving option.

Interrogator : ". . . and some people just do things on impulse. . ."

Suspect　　　: "That's impossible."

Interrogator : "Why is it impossible?"

Suspect　　　: "I wouldn't want to hurt anyone."

Interrogator : Great, that's what I thought all along. That just tells me that it was someone else's idea. You know I remember a time when. . ."

The following are some additional examples of explanatory denials:

- I wouldn't do that because I wouldn't want to risk my job.
- I wouldn't do that because I don't need the money.
- I wouldn't do that because my reputation is too important to me.

Each of the preceding statements would be difficult for an interrogator to disprove. Attempting to do so merely offers the suspect an opportunity to move the interrogation away from the incident into a nonthreatening immaterial issue. Instead of attempting to disprove the statements, the interrogator accepts them at face value and changes his rationalization to take advantage of the suspect's thought process. For example, if the interrogator was talking about the incident occurring because of a financial need and the suspect said he didn't need the money, the interrogator would agree and change rationalizations.

Interrogator : "Many people have problems because of financial difficulties."

Suspect　　　: "But, I don't need the money."

Interrogator: "Okay, then, what that tells me is that this was done on the spur-of-the-moment without thinking. Anyone can make a decision that they later regret. Especially when it wasn't carefully thought out. . . ."

In the preceding example, the suspect offered an explanatory denial, and the interrogator immediately agreed and offered a new rationalization based on an impulsive behavior. The interrogator also could have blamed peer pressure, opportunity, or used some other rationalization based on the circumstances of the case.

Methods of Interrogation

There are a number of different ways to conduct an interrogation of a suspect. The interrogator's selection of an interrogation method often is based on the background of the suspect, amount of evidence available, and possible response of the suspect to the interrogation. In instances in which a number of people were acting together to commit the crime, it may be useful to have multiple interrogators available to confront all of them at one time. It usually is preferable to conduct the interrogation in a surprise fashion rather than alert the suspects that they are going to be questioned.

Preparing for the interrogation requires that the interrogator have sufficient rooms, interrogators, witnesses, and resources to handle the number of suspects involved in the incident. In larger cases, such as organized theft rings, this may become as much of an administrative problem as an interrogational issue.

Factual

In cases where extensive factual information and evidence are available to the interrogator, he may elect to use a factual approach. However, when considering whether to use a factual attack, the interrogator should evaluate the amount of evidence available and whether it should be revealed to the suspect. In some instances, revealing the evidence may compromise informants or other ongoing investigations.

The most effective use of evidence is to contradict statements or assertions previously made by the suspect. The interrogator should ask the suspect questions to which he will likely lie to conceal his involvement in the incident. Once the suspect has been sufficiently locked into his story or alibi, the interrogator can now begin to dismantle it using the evidence discovered during the investigation.

The evidence is presented in a nonemotional fashion by the interrogator. The interrogator offers a piece of evidence that contradicts a previous statement by the suspect and asks for an explanation from the suspect. The interrogator usually starts with seemingly insignificant pieces of evidence that are at odds with the suspect's earlier statements. The suspect at first usually will attempt to explain away the evidence until it becomes evident to him that he has been caught as the contradictions mount.

An interrogator using a factual attack generally will get an admission only to the incident he already knows about and not other areas of involvement. The use of facts establishes to the suspect what his area(s) of exposure are and also tells him what the interrogator likely does not know. This then limits admissions into other areas of wrongdoing that were unknown to the interrogator. A second consideration is that using a factual approach alone, without rationalization, means that the suspect must admit to the crime and to the fact that he is a bad person. Combining rationalization with a factual approach often makes it easier for the suspect to confess since he is able to save face.

Classic Emotional

The classic emotional approach to an interrogation does not require the presentation of evidence. In this approach it generally begins with the use of a direct accusation, which accuses the suspect of involvement in a specific issue.

Interrogator: "Our investigation clearly indicates that you are involved in the theft of the missing cargo from the trailer."

Suspect : "No, I didn't do that."

Interrogator: "No, there is no question that you did, but what we are here to discuss is the reason why it happened."

In response to the direct accusation, the suspect almost always will deny using an emphatic denial. The suspect often will continue to deny, since he has to protect his initial lie. The interrogator will re-accuse the suspect and then immediately turn to rationalization to offer face-saving reasons why the suspect became involved in the incident. It is not unusual for the suspect to interrupt the interrogator's rationalization to offer another denial. The interrogator must be alert for the behavioral clues associated with a denial so he can interrupt the suspect before he can verbalize one.

If the rationalizations are successful, the suspect's denials will weaken and become less frequent while his physical posture becomes much more open. As the suspect internalizes the rationalizations, he begins to think about confessing. Outwardly, the suspect's physical behavior appears defeated. The head drops, the shoulders round, and the eyes begin to tear as the suspect goes into submission. While the interrogator is observing the suspect's physical behavior, it becomes evident to him that the suspect is ready to confess.

After carefully observing the suspect's physical behavior and recognizing that it is associated with confession, the interrogator offers an assumptive question. The assumptive question is designed to make it easier for the individual to confess. Instead of asking, "You did this didn't you?" the interrogator asks a choice question based on the rationalization. "Did you plan this out, or did you do it on the spur-of-the-moment?" The suspect can make one of three responses to this question. He could select either choice, or he could continue to deny. Selection of either of the choices is an admission of guilt to the incident under investigation and is supported by the interrogator, "Great, that's what I thought."

The interrogator then begins to develop the admission, answering the investigative questions who, where, when, why, and how. The suspect is locked into the details of his crime, and the admission is fully developed into a confession. Once this has been adequately developed, the interrogator then goes on to obtain a statement from the suspect to preserve the confession for later use.

Wicklander-Zulawski Non-Confrontational Method®

The Wicklander-Zulawski Non-Confrontational Method® is a modified emotional appeal. The primary strategy in this approach is to avoid forcing the suspect into a position where he has to deny his involvement, which makes it more difficult for him to confess later. Instead, the Wicklander-Zulawski (WZ) method takes advantage of the three primary reasons why a person confesses and structures the interrogator's approach to move the suspect from resistance to acceptance without denial.

The first part of the WZ method uses an introductory statement that helps the interrogator convince the suspect that his guilt is known. The interrogator also has an opportunity at this time to observe behavior and identify other areas of criminal activity that the suspect may be involved in. The introductory statement consists of three parts:

- A description of the security function and its purpose;
- A discussion of the different methods that could be used to cause losses or crimes;
- How investigations are conducted.

When adequately done, the introductory statement and the supporting process of showing understanding become a powerful tool to convince the individual that his guilt is known. The WZ method also affords the interrogator an opportunity to behaviorally observe the suspect's responses to a number of different methods of theft or crimes. Many suspects will react behaviorally to methods of theft or crimes that they have committed, allowing the interrogator to gather intelligence relating to the scope of the suspect's criminal activity.

The interrogator then moves through a highly structured approach using rationalizations and dealing with internal conflicts in the suspect's mind. This approach concludes with the use of an assumptive question called a "soft accusation." Instead of the choice question, which essentially gives an admission to what was known, the soft accusation asks for an admission that may expand the suspect's involvement into other areas of theft or criminal activity. The following is an example of the soft accusation.

> *Interrogator*: "When would you say was the very first time that you took money from the company?"

The suspect may make an admission to this question or pause to consider his response. If the suspect pauses, the interrogator will use a follow-up question to achieve the first admission:

> *Interrogator*: "Was it your first week on the job?"
>
> *Suspect*   : "No!"
>
> *Interrogator*: "Great, I didn't think that was the case."

The suspect now has admitted stealing money but denied that it was the first week on the job. The interrogator continues to develop the admission with the suspect confirming theft of cash prior to the missing deposit. In this way the interrogator is more likely to get closer to the true scope of the suspect's involvement in theft activity than by focusing on the single missing deposit theft of which he was suspected. In the event that the deposit is the sole theft incident the suspect has been involved in, he will confess to that while strongly denying other activities. The interrogator develops the total admission with the suspect and reduces the confession to some permanent form for later use.

There are a number of additional approaches that an interrogator could use to begin the interrogation. These approaches vary in complexity and difficulty, so the new interrogator is encouraged to use those described previously before attempting new strategies. More information and examples on these approaches are detailed in the textbook *Practical Aspects of Interview and Interrogation*.

Backing Out

There may be instances in which the suspect will not confess to the incident under investigation. The interrogator should be prepared to back out of the interrogation without obtaining an admission.

Prior to backing out, the interrogator should present the evidence discovered during the investigation. On occasion, the individual may be able to explain the evidence or provide proof of his innocence. If the suspect cannot provide an adequate explanation for the evidence, the interrogation could continue using one of the emotional appeals. Sometimes presenting evidence at this point will cause the suspect to confess or to lie when confronted with it, which may prove damning at some later point.

If the suspect still refuses to acknowledge his involvement after presenting the evidence, the interrogation shifts to the suspect's knowledge or suspicion of who was involved. From there, the interrogator either will discuss the individual's suspicion or talk about why he does not believe the others were involved.

Another way of backing out of the interrogation is to use the behavioral interview, which allows the suspect to begin to talk. The interrogator asks the questions included in the interview and then slowly draws the encounter to a close.

Documenting the Confession or the Interview

At the conclusion of the confession, the interrogator should consider obtaining a thoroughly documented statement from the suspect, committing him to the details of his admission. The interrogator should link any evidence by having the suspect identify and incorporate that evidence into his statement. It may also be useful to have the suspect create a diagram to clarify points in the statement. If the suspect creates a diagram, it should be dated, signed, and referenced in the body of the suspect's statement.

There are various forms that a statement may take depending on the type of case and needs of the interrogator. The subject may write his own statement or have the interrogator write this statement for him. In other situations, the suspect's statements may be preserved using audiovisual recordings or a court reporter. Regardless of the form used, the contents and general structure of the statement will be the same.

The opening part of the statement identifies the individual and pertinent biographical information from his background. This portion of the statement also the notes the date and time the statement was obtained. Beginning with this information provides the suspect with a non-threatening opening to begin to tell his story. Since the information regarding his background is also truthful, it sets the stage for the suspect to continue a truthful recounting of the situation.

The second component of the statement summarizes the overall admission made by the suspect. This is often as simple as "During the time I worked for the company, I stole $1,000 in cash and $700 in merchandise." The suspect has now committed in writing to the overall admission that leads to the third section, substantiation.

The third component of the statement is substantiation of the admission. Here, the suspect details how he stole the thousand dollars from the organization. This would include the method, amounts, and timing of the thefts. The suspect would then go on to detail the merchandise he stole that made up the $700 figure. Again, the suspect identifies the merchandise, its cost, and the method used to steal it.

The fourth component of the statement is the suspect's statement of regret or reason for committing the theft. Often referred to as "speaking from the heart," suspects will explain their motivation for the theft, such as paying bills or some form of personal emergency. Many suspects will apologize to the organization in this section of the statement.

The fifth component of the statement contains the suspect's commitment that the statement was written voluntarily without any threats or promises. Many suspects will also include statements relating to their fair treatment during the interview.

The final component of the statement is the signatures of the suspect and witnesses to each of the pages. The pages are then numbered, e.g., page 1 of two and page 2 of two. The suspect initials any scratchouts or changes that he made in the statement. The interrogator should protect the statement as it is being written by removing each page from the subject's control as soon as it is completed.

If there was not a witness in the room, the interrogator now should bring in a witness to listen to the suspect's admission and his commitment to the statement's truthfulness. Once the interrogator has had the suspect repeat his confession in front of the witness, both the interrogator and witness should sign and date each page of the document. If necessary, the witness also should complete a statement relating to any relevant conversations or observations made while in the interrogation room with the suspect.

Conclusion

The process of interview and interrogation is a complex one, which requires patience and practice. The investigator who masters the skills of interview and interrogation will find that his cases are resolved in a much more professional, timely manner. The statements of victims, witnesses, and suspects lie at the heart of any investigation. Preserving the statement or confession in an accurate manner will confirm circumstances, alibis, and the guilt of those involved.

Following are some suggested readings, which will expand on the ideas presented in this chapter.

Suggested Reading

Ekman, P. (1985). Telling lies. Berkley Books.
Ekman, P. (2003). *Emotions revealed*. Henry Holt & Company.
Ekman, P., and Davidson, R. J. (1994). *The nature of emotion/fundamental questions*. Oxford University Press, Inc.
Ekman, P. and Rosenburg, E. (1997). *What the face reveals*. Oxford University Press.
Gudjonsson, G. H. (2003). *The psychology of interrogations and confessions, a handbook*. John Wiley & Sons, Ltd.
Nissman, D. M. and Hagen, E. (2004). *Law of confessions*. Clark, Boardman Callaghan.
Zulawski, D. E. and Wicklander, D. E. (2002). *Practical aspects of interview and interrogation*, 2nd ed. CRC Press.

Investigations

CAS, JHC

While it may not be immediately apparent, retail loss prevention personnel are frequently required to conduct a variety of investigations, including, but not limited to, those involving

- Background investigations
- Bomb Threats
- Employee theft
- Extortion
- Frauds against the company
- Lost children
- Organized retail theft
- Sexual harassment
- Threats and crank letters
- Vendor dishonesty

Crimes against persons are typically under the jurisdiction of the public sector; however, follow-up investigations of such crimes are often conducted by the private sector. Perhaps a good example might be the O.J. Simpson murder case. The police in support of the criminal prosecution of Simpson conducted the criminal investigation. However, the subsequent civil action required investigators in the private sector to gather and pursue information deemed necessary in the prosecution of the civil complaint. This is often the case when retailers are sued civilly. How are such investigations best handled? The answer lies in determining several factors: the capabilities of the in-house LP personnel, the seriousness (is a crime involved?) of the event to be investigated, the availability of outside resources (e.g., private investigators, police, or federal agencies), and the time criticality of investigative results.

Further, many "in-house" investigations, at least the initial investigations, are necessary because of the question of access and knowledge, e.g., a fraud involving pilfering blank accounts payable checks from a controlled bundle and causing the check to be written to a fictitious vendor. That "vendor" may be a family member of the employee working in accounts payable; a special P.O. box has been created to accept payments and an account opened at a local bank to deposit and subsequently cash the check. A public sector investigator would be overwhelmed, if not inhibited, from doing at least the initial investigation.

If a serious crime against property (why exclude serious crimes against persons, e.g., rape, robbery?) is involved, local police or federal agencies may be interested in getting involved. For example, bomb threats or the finding of an incendiary or explosive device may best be handled by local police or the Alcohol, Tobacco & Firearms (ATF) federal agents. Organized retail theft may be of interest to the recently formed ORT section within the FBI. Background investigations, employee theft, and vendor dishonesty may be appropriate for in-house investigative efforts, perhaps assisted by private investigators, depending on the degree of sophistication and depth of experience available with in-house personnel. The important thought to be kept in mind is that all needs for an investigation should be carefully analyzed to determine the best use of available resources to achieve the most professional results possible.

Assuming that an investigation is handled by in-house loss prevention personnel, what are some of the considerations that must be kept in mind to avoid criticism for using techniques which exceed either public acceptability or legal permissibility?

A recent (2006) nationally publicized case involving Hewlett-Packard, a Fortune 500 firm, reported how a company's inept investigation into news leaks from the company's board resulted in the forced resignation of its chairwoman and lawsuits filed against HP by other firms that alleged HP's actions were injurious to them.

The main issue in the HP matter was the use of an unethical and possibly illegal investigative technique known as "pretexting"—in which an investigator masquerades as someone else to obtain that individual's phone records. In the HP case, this technique was allegedly used by an outside investigative firm hired by HP executives. As of this writing, five persons have been criminally indicted; two are former HP executives (their chairwoman and a senior counsel) and three outside investigators.

The HP case is a classic demonstration illustrating where a legitimate reason for conducting an investigation can turn into a publicity nightmare and legal minefield when the investigation is improperly or illegally conducted. Areas which can lead to claims of improper use of investigative techniques include, but are not limited to the following:

- Violations of federal laws, including
  - Violations of National Labor Relations Board (NLRB) provisions;
  - Violation of Fair Credit Reporting Act (FCRA) provisions;
  - Violations of Federal Trade Commission (FTC) provisions;
  - Violation of the Employee Polygraph Protection Act (EPPA) provisions.
- Improper techniques can constitute violations of state laws and/or commission of torts, including
  - Invasion of privacy;
  - False imprisonment;
  - Unreasonable use of force;
  - Defamation;
  - Assault/battery;
  - Tortious interference with employment;
  - Malicious prosecution;
  - Entrapment.

Any investigation is designed to answer six fundamental questions: who, what, when, where, why and how. These questions must be answered with only facts; giving credence to gossip and hearsay can lead to making faulty decisions based on investigative results which lack credibility and potential exposure to legal action based on any faulty personnel action.

An example of an investigative report which answers all six questions might look something like the following:

WHEN: On Tuesday, October 31, 2006, at approximately 1600 hours,

WHO: This investigator overheard John Bigjerk, a grocery stocker,

WHERE: after entering the employee lounge,

WHAT: inquire of Sally Source, a cashier/checker, as she was about to leave the lounge, about buying some "pot." Sally responded by stating, " I've got some weed in my locker, and I could use the money." John said he could afford about $20, took out his wallet, and handed Sally a $20 bill. Sally said to wait a minute and left the lounge. She returned about two minutes later and handed John a small plastic baggie which appeared to contain a green leafy material. After thanking Sally, both John and Sally left the lounge.

HOW: This apparent drug transaction was possible because the lounge was unoccupied and the time (1600 hours) is one during which breaks and shift changes are not scheduled and the lounge is predictably not in use. The investigator was not seen because he was in the restroom whose entrance is in the far corner of the lounge.

WHY: This apparent drug transaction was consummated because John expressed a desire for some marijuana and Sally both had some in her locker and sold it because she needed the money.

Jewelry (Fine)

CAS, JHC

This discussion will relate to *fine* jewelry, not costume jewelry. Fine jewelry can be described as high price point jewelry, such as diamonds, estate jewelry, gold, sterling silver, semi-precious stones, and fine watches.

Fine jewelry (hereinafter jewelry) stores and jewelry departments in larger stores both require special security and operational procedures because of the high value of the merchandise and its attractiveness to thieves and con artists.

This discussion will not attempt to set forth in detail procedures to cover all aspects of a jewelry store/department operation; we will provide the basic areas which require security attention and suggest some aspects of security precautions to be taken.

It goes with saying that a jewelry store needs to be adequately alarmed for protection against both burglary and robbery. Since the nature and extent of such alarms will depend on many factors individual to each location, we recommend that a quality alarm company be contacted and the specifics of the alarm coverage be developed in conjunction with them.

With respect to security procedures, we have listed areas which should be reviewed and have suggested procedures which should be considered.

Receipt and Check In of Goods from Vendors

- Perform 100% piece count check-in off selling floor.
- Immediately secure items after check-in.
- Require signature of associate certifying no discrepancies.
- Immediately notify proper authority of any discrepancy.
- Require signature of associate certifying no discrepancies.

Key Control

- Keys accounted for twice a day.
- Keys locked in safe at night; logged in and out.
- Keys never left on countertops.
- Keys never removed from store/jewelry area.
- Keys never given to nonjewelry associates.
- Keys signed in/out with each set of keys identifiable.

Opening Procedure

- Turn off alarms.
- Perform visual check of area.
- Determine opening diamond/precious gem counts.
- Restock all showcases with goods from the safe.
- Secure all showcases.

Closing procedure

- Count diamonds/precious gems and log into safe.
- If showcases are not alarmed, log gold chains/bracelets and pearl strands into safe.
- Lock/cover remaining showcases.
- Set alarms.

Sales Procedures

- Wait on only one customer at a time.
- Show items only one at a time (except watches).
- Never permit merchandise to leave department.
- Never place jewelry trays on countertops.
- Close display cases when showing merchandise.
- Lock display cases when not showing merchandise.
- Consider using "cord" to show diamond rings. (The securing of the ring to the counter prevents a "palm and switch" theft wherein the genuine ring is palmed and a counterfeit is substituted during its examination.)

Other Considerations

- Consider using tags on diamond rings which, if removed, disqualify the ring for return.
- If merchandise is transferred between locations, fully manifest it and use locked and sealed containers for transfer.
- Count 100% of transferred merchandise off the floor upon receipt.
- Require signatures on all paperwork at each step of any process.
- Retain trash from department in sealed bag and in a secure area for at least 3 days before disposing of it.
- Conduct thorough background investigation on all employees.
- Change safe combination whenever personnel change.
- Conduct (and document) monthly alarm tests.
- Ensure the glass countertops in showcases are cemented in to prevent professionals with suction cups from lifting up the glass to obtain access to inside of case.

Job Descriptions

CAS, JHC

Job descriptions are essential in any work environment. Descriptions inform the employees what's expected of them in terms of performance, their authority, and where they "fit" in the organization. Job descriptions, from management's perspective, guide the supervisor in an objective and consistent evaluation of employees' performance. A job description is literally a compass.

The basic elements of a job description should be as follows:

- It tells what the *objective* of the job is.
- It tells the dimensions of the job.
- It tells the nature and scope of the job, such as
  - Position in the organization
  - Mission and environment
  - Specific function
  - Functions of subordinates
  - Principle challenge of the job
  - Authority of the position
  - The relationship to those "above" and "below" that position
  - Requisites

Example of a Job Description for a loss prevention manager might look like this:

Position: Loss Prevention Manager

Objective of the job: To ensure the store-level loss prevention officers are properly trained in, understand, and comply with company LP policies and procedures, and the totality of the in-store program meets store and company expectations.

Dimension of the position: Directly supervisors five (5) full-time and part-time loss prevention officers.

Nature and scope of the position:

- *Position in the organization:* Reports up to the District Loss Prevention Manager (DLPM) and downwardly supervisors five LPOs.
- *Mission and environment:* Protection of employees, customers, invitees, property, and merchandise in the store of assignment 365 days a year.
- *Specific function:* Trains, schedules, and supervises the LPOs and serves as liaison between LP and store management by doing the following:
  - Reviews and approves or corrects all LP-generated reports including arrest reports
  - Coordinates corrective and/or maintenance follow-up identified or discovered
  - Assists store management in in-store shrinkage awareness programs and new hire orientation programs
- *Function of subordinates:* Monitor CCTV cameras and patrol floor of store to identify and either prevent acts of theft by customers or detect and detain customers engaged in shoplifting. Conduct investigations into suspected internal theft, as assigned. Conduct store inspections, as assigned.
- *Principle challenge of the position:* Ensure that subordinates understand and comply with the extremely important rules, as the "Six Steps" required in detentions and reports are professionally prepared documenting detentions.
- *Authority of the position:* The LPM has the authority to conduct internal interviews when approved by the DLPM and has the authority to discipline subordinates up through the third written final warning. The LPM has the authority to conduct the annual performance evaluation and rate his or her subordinates.
- *Relationships to those above and below the position:* The LPM is the representative and voice of the DLPM, ensuring store-level compliance with company LP policies and procedures. The LPM is the spokesperson for subordinates for problems, suggestions, or questions which arise at the store level. The LPM has essentially the same "middleman" representative role between in-store LPOs and store management.
- *Requisites:* The LPM must have knowledge of
  - Loss prevention policies and procedures, in depth
  - Local and state laws relating to the crimes which commonly occur in the retail environment, including the authority of LPOs to make arrests
  - Causes of inventory shrinkage, and the company's inventory shrinkage history
  - Interviewing and interrogation skills
  - Proven leadership skills developed through formal supervisory training
- *Experience:* A minimum of three (3) years experience as a LPO or two (2) years of proven supervisorial experience in a related LP or security function coupled with one (1) year LPO experience in the company.
- *Education:* High school graduate plus a minimum of thirty (30) college credits (1 year) in security management, criminal justice, or industrial safety (or combination of the above).

Clearly, when every position in the company is thusly spelled out with such clarity, performance from top to bottom invariably improves, and the general welfare of all members of this well-ordered organization is enhanced.

Juveniles

CAS, JHC

Juveniles (persons between the age of 13 and 17) represent a significant shoplifting threat to retailers nationwide. Research by credible authorities indicates juveniles constitute between 25% and 33% of all shoplifting activity in the United States. Hence, their presence in a store deserves attention.

Practical experience tells us juveniles prefer to shop and shoplift while with friends as opposed to being alone. And juveniles share their "secrets" about stealing and boast as to how easy it is and how rewarding shoplifting can be. Hence, successful juvenile shoplifting can proved somewhat endemic in given schools, which consequently impacts on the retail community. The best and most productive strategy in dealing with these young people is to provide the best possible customer service to discourage theft.

Despite the best service and efforts to thwart shoplifting, some will nonetheless steal and be caught. Whenever juveniles are dealt with, they must be handled differently than adults.

When a juvenile is apprehended for shoplifting, for example, the following procedures should be followed:

- Always release to a parent, legal guardian, or the police. Never release a juvenile on his or her own.
- Photograph juveniles only if allowed by local laws and never if under age 10.
- Do not get written or signed confessions from juveniles under age 15.
- Avoid handcuffing juveniles unless you can clearly articulate the necessity to do so.
- Avoid searching juveniles.
- Generally avoid prosecuting juveniles under the age of 17, unless the juvenile is a repeat offender, is combative, commits a felony, has stolen more than one item, or other extenuating circumstances exist.

While the preceding procedures are designed to protect both the store and the juvenile, the agent must always keep mind that, when apprehending an adult or a juvenile, he or she does not know the background of the individual. The fact that a suspect is a juvenile does not remove the potential for violence, and the person making the detention must remain vigilant and aware of his or her surroundings at all times, whether dealing with juveniles or adults.

With respect to "dealing" with juveniles, the professional loss prevention agent, store executive, or store owner should bear in mind these young people are still impressionable, and some positive results can arise from this otherwise negative contact. Juveniles, in most cases, want to be respected and treated as adults. Courtesy can go a long way in making this contact a learning experience which could contribute to the youngster's later decisions on how he or she should steer his or her future conduct.

Key Control

CAS, JHC

Locks—and keys to open them—have been used for hundreds of years as a means of controlling physical access. In the retail environment, keys are used to provide access to the store itself and, in many instances, also to provide working access to cash registers, display cases, stockrooms and secured areas within stockrooms, fitting rooms, management offices, cash boxes, supply cabinets, dock doors, roof hatches, and other spaces and/or devices which require controlled access and security.

It is not unusual for retail facilities to use locking systems which rely on a hierarchy system of keying commonly referred to as a "master-keyed system." Such systems utilize a master key which operates any lock in the system, with subcategories of keys which may operate one or more (but not all) locks or simply one lock in particular in that system. Such systems provide owners or others who have broad access needs a convenient way to gain access without requiring a large number of individual keys. The downside of master-keyed systems is that the loss or compromise of the master key compromises all the locks in that system. If a master-keyed system is employed, strict accountability and control of the master key must be maintained.

We will not attempt to provide the technical aspects of the various types of locks, of which there are many. For example, locks can by classified in broad categories as mechanical, electrical, or a combination of both. Mechanical locks can be classified as warded locks, lever locks, pin tumbler locks, wafer tumbler locks, changeable core locks, or dial combination locks. Each of these lock types varies in its mechanical complexity, from simple, inexpensive warded construction utilized primarily in padlocks to the more complex cylinder pin tumbler found on the average home's front door. Similarly, electrical locks can be classified as electromagnetic, electric deadbolt, electric strikes, and electric latches.

Combination mechanical/electrical may be opened only by use of a mechanical key in combination with an electronic key or electronic biometric device (such as a retinal scan or fingerprint reader).

Locks can be attacked by pure force (use of a hammer or crowbar), by picking (use of tools which, in skilled hands, substitutes for a key), by unauthorized keys (made by wax impression of the original key), by a new phenomenon called "lock bumping" (a relatively simple strategy, once understood, of tapping on the lock while force is applied in the keyway), or by sophisticated devices to simulate electronic keys.

If an electronic locking device is used, it is important that the loss of electrical power does not automatically cause an unlocked condition. Likewise, care must be exercised that all systems controlling building emergency exits, whether mechanical or electronic, provide egress during an emergency, irrespective of any other consideration or condition.

There are numerous methods of key control, the most elementary being simply numbering each key and keeping a paper record identifying the key holder and periodically verifying his or her possession of that key. Electronic systems not only keep lists of key holders assigned electronically numbered keys, but on command will "deactivate" keys, thus making them use-less. The important lesson is that regardless of the system used, key control is a must.

A final note: Many authorities warn that locks are only a delaying device, and given the right circumstances (time, talent, and tools), any lock can be breached.

Kleptomania

CAS, JHC

The dictionary defines kleptomania as "An obsessive impulse to steal in spite of the absence of economic necessity or personal desire." It is deemed a mental disorder. A person suffering from kleptomania is known as a "kleptomaniac." In the retail world, kleptomaniacs are encountered, but very rarely. As the definition states, a kleptomaniac has no economic or personal reason to steal; he or she simply has a psychological abnormality which results in stealing compulsively. Bottom line: So-called kleptomaniacs do not constitute a significant threat to the retail community.

But kleptomaniacs do steal and from time to time are detected shoplifting. How should persons who are legitimate kleptomaniacs be dealt with? While some claim that a kleptomaniac's stealing is a call for help, the definition belies this. Kleptomaniacs are mentally disturbed individuals and should be treated as such. Interestingly, it is legally questionable if kleptomaniacs can form the necessary specific intent required for committing a crime of theft (shoplifting), or, if they can, that they can be held responsible for it.

When a kleptomaniac is apprehended, his or her condition more often than not will surface during the interview in the loss prevention office with an admission of the problem. Verification with that person's mental health provider can confirm the detainee is under care or has been under care and or treatment. The kleptomaniac's family should be notified, and they will normally arrange to be billed and pay for the stolen items. Appropriate records should be kept on kleptomaniacs, including the dates they are in the store, items stolen, which family member was notified, and date payment received. This method of handling kleptomaniacs avoids embarrassing them and their families and also protects the store from losses.

Known Loss Reports

CAS, JHC

Loss reports, most commonly called known loss reports, are those reports which retailers and loss prevention use to document losses from theft which justify the loss being written off financially, thus removing it from being reported as shortage or shrink. "Written-off financially" means removed from the book inventory.

The basis for a known loss report is often a document which is known by various names but most commonly as a "missing merchandise report" or MMR.

Figures K-1 and K-2 show examples of missing merchandise reports.

As part of a loss prevention awareness program, sales associates should be instructed to report situations in which merchandise appears to be missing. For example, a sales asso-ciate puts an expensive leather jacket on display at store opening. At 11:30 a.m. it is gone from the display rack, and no one remembers selling it. Examination of the journal tape (or other media or electronic record) fails to reflect its sale. The evidence indicates the jacket was stolen.

Another example: Ten bubble packs of walkie-talkie radios were displayed when a count was taken at 10 a.m., and at 2:30 p.m. an opened but empty bubble pack that contained a set of walkie-talkie radios identical to those counted at 10:00 a.m. is discovered hidden under a rack of RTW in an adjacent department. A check shows six packs of radios on the shelf, and the POS terminal verifies that three were sold; one empty pack is found, leading to the reasonable conclusion that the actual radios are missing and probably stolen.

A final example: Loss prevention believes a female stole a dress while in the fitting room. The fitting room was thoroughly checked at the start of the day and was clean of merchandise

MISSING MERCHANDISE REPORT

Store: -------------------- Date of Loss: ------------------ Report By: --------------------------------

Department: ---Floor: -------------------------------------

Discovered By: ----------------------------------

MISSING:

Dept   SKU   Description   Qty   Price   Total $

===

Where was the Loss Discovered?

_____

Salesfloor____Empty Box_____Breakroom ____Stockroom _____

Cause:

Unlocked Door_____Unlocked Case_____Other_____

 How:

Alarm _____ Paperwork _____ Count _____

Other _____

++

Corrective Action Taken by Management: --------------------

Correction Verification:

Case Locked _____

Door Locked _____

MDSE. Reloc. _____

Training Given _____

COMMENTS: ---

****

Please circle the appropriate factor:

INTERNAL THEFT   EXTERNAL THEFT   UNKNOWN

****

CC: Shortage Committee

Store LP

FIGURE K-1 Missing merchandise report.

(STONE NAME) MMR Missing Merchandise Report	Date Of Report (Turn in same day)	Time Found	0 AM 0 PM
	Submitted By: (Last name, First name)	Payroll No.	Area / Dept Name

#1	#2	#3	#4
PLACE PRICE TICKET HERE CUT OUT SKU/UPC CODE. DO NOT ATTACH PACKAGING.	PLACE PRICE TICKET HERE CUT OUT SKU/UPC CODE. DO NOT ATTACH PACKAGING.	PLACE PRICE TICKET HERE CUT OUT SKU/UPC CODE. DO NOT ATTACH PACKAGING.	PLACE PRICE TICKET HERE CUT OUT SKU/UPC CODE. DO NOT ATTACH PACKAGING.

FILL IN THE FOLLOWING TO IDENTIFY THE MISSING MERCHANDISE

	SKU	DEPT.	Grid Location Displayed	Found	Quantity	Unit Retail
#1			–	–		
#2			–	–		
#3			–	–		
#4			–	–		

WAS MERCHANDISE SECURED?	YES		NO		WAS MERCHANDISE REQUIRED TO BE SECURED?	YES		NO		UNKNOWN	

WHY IS THIS EVIDENCE OF THEFT
_____
_____
_____
_____

FOR OFFICE USE ONLY	
☐ Entered Into S.I.S.	
Initials	Date

SUBMIT TO STORE LP MANAGER OR STAFF IMMEDIATELY

FIGURE K-2 Another example of a missing merchandise report.

and any price tickets. After the suspected theft, a search of the fitting room reveals a price ticket matching the suspected stolen dress hidden in a crack in the corner of the room.

Each of these examples should be the basis for immediately preparing a missing merchandise report, which will provide the justification for entering the value of the merchandise on those reports into the known loss journal maintained by the Accounting department. Before the report is processed by the financial division for "mark out" purposes, it should be forwarded to and approved by the approved ranking loss prevention employee in the store or the district.

In addition to accounting financially for the merchandise that the evidence points to as having been stolen, the MMR fulfills another important function. When reviewed by loss prevention, all aspects of the circumstances surrounding the display and disappearance of the merchandise reported on should be carefully scrutinized to determine whether any measures can be taken to prevent further similar thefts. Perhaps the merchandise is displayed in an area lacking easy observation by sales associates; perhaps the merchandise should be physically secured by locked case or a metal cable; perhaps all fitting rooms should be checked for places where illegally removed tickets can be hidden and these defects repaired; perhaps loss prevention should patrol the area more frequently. Whatever may be the appropriate solution, the MMRs provide a timely heads-up to theft activity to which all hands can be alerted and preventive measures undertaken.

The procedure itself ensures an ongoing awareness on the part of all store associates that merchandise is important and valuable, and when it's missing, some action is triggered rather than just being shrugged off and forgotten.

Known losses, by department or category, should be tallied, displayed, and compared this year versus last year to indicate possible trends and, therefore, increased alertness to the problem of theft.

Labor Disputes: Managing Them

Kathleen A. Smith

Introduction

Few events tax an organization at the level of a labor dispute. Most critical incidents—natural disasters, bomb threats, workplace violence incidents, and the like—quickly move from the "acute" phase of the crisis situation to the resolution and recovery phases. Not so with labor disputes, which can carry on for days, weeks, or even months with, at times, seemingly no end in sight. Moreover, labor disputes can rapidly alternate from relative calm to, at times, full-scale riotous situations, only to return to a manageable level once again. This constant state of "alert" causes an enormous drain on many branches within an organization, not the least of which is the loss prevention or security department.

A key distinction, however, between the crisis events cited here and a labor dispute is that with the latter there is almost always ample warning. In the security and crisis management world, *ample warning* unequivocally means *preparation time*.

Preparation Is Key

It is important to keep in mind why we prepare for a strike. Our objective is to protect lives, protect property, and maintain business continuity to the extent possible. Therefore, *the preparation phase is the most important phase of a labor dispute*. Many problems can be mitigated or averted altogether with an exhaustive preparation and contingency plan in place.

Given that most strike-related activity centers around company facilities (offices, stores, plants, warehouses), these should be the main areas of focus when preparing for a labor dispute situation. The following are a number of pre-strike preparation areas to consider for company facilities. Note that these are all areas to address *prior* to a strike even beginning (time permitting).

1. *Key control:* Make certain you know the location of all facility keys. Collect those not in use and secure them in a safe.
2. *Lock protection:* The age-old gimmick of squirting glue into keyholes lives on. This problem can generally be mitigated by applying petroleum jelly into keyholes because most glues do not stick to this lubricant.
3. *Sensitive interior rooms:* Most facilities have one or more "high-risk" rooms (e.g., manager's office, cash room, computer room, motor room). For these, make certain that all doors can be locked and are functioning. If you have double louvered doors, make certain that deadbolt locks are installed. Have a locksmith respond if time allows.
4. *Armored safes and lock boxes:* Open only when necessary, namely only to transfer funds to an armored transport. Keep in mind that armored transport personnel generally have a second key. Place important documents inside a safe or lock box.

5. *Personal safety:* Labor disputes are emotional and traumatic events. People involved oftentimes act in a manner quite different from their "normal" behavior. Educate employees not involved in the dispute regarding personal safety and security. Remind them to be on alert and avoid "routines," such as travel routes home.

6. *Receiving dock:* This area is oftentimes more isolated and thus presents a tempting target for acts of arson, vandalism, or attempted break-in. The area should be made clear of extraneous items, such as bales, pallets, and totes. The area should be well lighted, kept secure, and, if at all possible, under video surveillance.

7. *Lighting:* Ensure that all parking lights, signs, and perimeter building lights are in working order. Re-inspect frequently.

8. *CCTV:* If so equipped, ensure that all cameras and recording systems are in working order. If time permits, add cameras as deemed necessary. A minimum camera standard should include all points of ingress/egress, building perimeters, and "high-risk" areas (e.g., parking areas, loading dock).

9. *Alarms:* Ensure that all alarms (intrusion, fire) are in working order. Ensure that fire extinguishers are available and accessible.

10. *Front doors and windows:* Items that obstruct external viewing should be removed from doors and windows. This also allows patrolling law enforcement visibility into the facility.

11. *Facility perimeter:* Ensure that all emergency exits are not accessible from the outside. Make certain that tree branches, fences, etc., do not allow access to the roof. Ensure that external phone lines, if present, are shielded to protect against cutting.

12. *Strike incident forms:* Draft and produce strike incident forms for local management personnel to use in documenting strike-related incidents. Include specific instructions as to what should and should not be documented. Assign incident "levels" to help in minimizing data overload. Online incident forms also assist in quick and uniform data collection.

13. *Strike "kits":* Build a strike kit to include multiple disposable cameras with flash, flashlight and batteries, strike incident forms (discussed later), pens/pencils, petroleum jelly, emergency phone numbers (fire, police, security or loss prevention, management personnel).

14. *24-hour hotline:* Establish, disseminate, and post a 24-hour hotline for reporting of emergency strike incidents. Ensure that this can be manned 24/7.

During a Strike

Once a strike begins, there are additional steps to take. These steps can be broken into two categories: steps to follow immediately after the strike begins and best practices for the duration of the event.

Once the Labor Dispute Begins

- As striking employees leave at the end of their shifts, retrieve and secure keys, access cards, and other company-owned property
- Be mindful that some employees may attempt to sabotage or tamper with equipment, stock replenishment orders, product displays, and security systems on their way out.
- Ensure that all "preparation" steps described previously have been considered and implemented, where possible.
- Make arrangements to have all lights (inside and outside) remain on throughout the night.
- Verify that there are no flammables outside the facility, such as cardboard bales, trays, crates, pallets, or boxes.
- Bring in merchandise or other property as able.
- Secure all perimeter doors, roof hatches, and interior "high-risk" doors (see preceding description).

Best Practices Throughout the Strike

- *Documenting strike incidents:* Begin the strike incident reporting process immediately (see previous comments). It is important to maintain accurate and timely records of all strike-related incidents. Make certain that all assaults, vandalism, and other crimes are reported to local law enforcement and to security or loss prevention. Obtain full names, complete addresses, and all other pertinent information of witnesses and victims (the strike incident form should contain boxes for this information). Document license plate numbers, if applicable, and take photographs when illegal strike activity is witnessed (before ordering the perpetrators to stop). Illegal strike activity may include, but is not limited to, the following:

  1. Blocking free access/movement of a vehicles or persons
  2. Vehicle tampering
  3. Vandalism
  4. Assaults, battery, spitting, throwing objects
  5. Threats of personal harm

- *Physical threats:* In the event that an employee, customer, or vendor/contractor is verbally or physically threatened, the person-in-charge of the incident location should contact local law enforcement.
- *Bomb threats:* Expect an increase in bomb threats. Follow established bomb threat procedures.
- *Property damage:* Expect an increase in vandalism incidents. Remember that employee and customer safety and business continuity have priority, and that minor vandalism incidents can be dealt with when/if time permits.
- *Temporary personnel:* Many labor disputes involve temporary employees. Make every effort to ensure temporary employee safety and security. If the employee parking area cannot be observed from the store, have employees park offsite and carpool to the work facility. Provide a secured area for storage of employees' purses and personal property.

Obtaining and Enforcing Injunctions

At some point during the labor dispute, it may become necessary to seek a restraining order or an injunction. There are certain considerations to keep in mind.

The Right to Strike and Picket

Employees have the right to strike in support of their bargaining demands or to protest alleged unfair labor practices. Employees and unions also have the right to engage in peaceful, nondisruptive picketing to publicize their strike. Companies mush respects these rights and must not do anything that unlawfully interferes with them.

Limits on the Right to Picket and Injunctions Against Unlawful Conduct

The right to engage in picketing and other activities to publicize or support a strike is not absolute. For example, picketers may not engage in violence, make threats, unreasonably interfere with ingress or egress to or from private property, or engage in other unlawful conduct. If a company can prove that picketers or other individuals, acting at the union's direction or with the union's knowledge, engaged in any of these prohibited activities, it may request that a court issue a temporary restraining order (TRO) to stop such activities. (TROs and injunctions do not necessarily prohibit picketing altogether. The union and its supporters may still engage in peaceful, nonthreatening, and nondisruptive activities in support of their strike.) A TRO generally remains in effect for 10 to 30 days, after which time the company may seek a preliminary injunction, and ultimately, a permanent injunction. Violations of such court orders constitute contempt of court.

The Procedure for Obtaining Injunctions

Courts are generally very reluctant to limit anyone's free speech rights, and some states, such as California, have made it even more difficult to secure an injunction limiting the number or conduct of picketers in support of a labor dispute. For example, in many instances an employer must now present live testimony in court to obtain a TRO. This has changed from earlier procedures wherein mere written declarations would suffice. Moreover, law enforcement has generally refrained from becoming involved unless and until a TRO or injunction is in effect.

Preparing to Get an Injunction

The foregoing requirements are very strict, and the evidence that you must present to convince a court to issue a TRO or injunction must be very specific. Whenever possible, you should cite the names of wrongdoers and the union representatives who were present when unlawful conduct occurred. In addition to describing said conduct in as much detail as possible based on eyewitness observations, the employer must also be prepared to present evidence which establishes that the union directed, condoned, or was present when the unlawful conduct occurred and did nothing to stop it. Hearsay, speculation, rumor, and innuendo are *not* sufficient to convince a court to issue a TRO.

Enforcement of Injunctions: Dealing with Law Enforcement

TROs or injunctions normally contain specific limitations on the number of picketers and/or prohibit certain conduct by the picketers and by union representatives and other supporters. The union, its representatives, and its supporters who are served with these court orders are legally obligated to comply with their limits and prohibitions.

Law enforcement agencies' policies and practices regarding the enforcement of TROs and injunctions vary by jurisdiction. Some will actively enforce the TRO, whereas others will refrain from doing so because they do not want to be perceived as taking sides in the dispute. The Vons' experience demonstrated that establishing a good relationship with law enforcement could make all the difference in determining whether they will enforce any TROs and injunctions. There are three steps a company can take to improve such relations with law enforcement:

1. Establish good communications with law enforcement before a labor dispute starts.
2. Provide them with sufficient advance warning if there is an indication that problems are brewing.
3. Avoid making needless calls or unnecessary complaints.

Citizen's Arrests

Some law enforcement agencies will arrest individuals who knowingly violate the limits or prohibitions of a TRO or injunction. Others may require that company personnel make a "citizen's arrest," especially if officers did not observe the unlawful conduct themselves. Employers should become aware of the various practices of the law enforcement agencies in their area.

Conclusion

The keys to surviving a labor dispute are preparation, communication, teamwork, and flexibility. If these four factors co-exist, the affected company—*and* the loss prevention team managing the strike—will successfully see the event through to its end.

Labor Disputes: Some Considerations

CAS, JHC

Having gone through a major labor dispute involving hundreds of retails clerks from a headquarters store of a national chain, I discovered, primarily through trial and error, some techniques that proved most helpful. These "tips" are listed here by subject matter.

Identification of Replacement Workers

During a labor dispute when the regular employees go out on strike, replacement workers, consisting of executives, friends, and relatives, are usually used as replacements for the regular staff. Since a strike rarely occurs without some warning, these replacements can be identified and trained prior to their first day of work.

These replacements should be instructed where to report for work, and after being positively identified, they should be issued some form of identification. In addition to issuing a company "pin-on" name badge, we found that also issuing a distinctive pin, the design and/or color of which changed daily, served as a second security measure to help assure that only legitimate persons were operating cash registers or POS terminals. We found we could obtain from a variety of sources (which should also be changed frequently) small pins which were issued each day after replacements were positively identified. Security/LP personnel were aware of the "pin of the day" and could challenge any worker who was not displaying one. Frankly, this procedure was copied from the Secret Service's routine use of such a procedure.

Employee Entrance

We found maintaining more than one employee entrance helped eliminate the replacement workers having to go through the gauntlet of jeering, shouting, and rarely overly aggressive strikers massed outside the store's regular employee entrance.

Temporary Restraining Orders (TROs)

The company's labor attorneys should, at the first opportunity, seek a temporary restraining order (TRO) limiting the number and location where picketers are permitted. Obviously, every effort should be made to minimize the picketers' ability to interfere with customers attempting to enter the store. We were successful in obtaining a TRO which limited the number and distance from store entrances picketers were permitted. We also found it helpful to use an orange color spray paint to mark the areas denied to picketers, as spelled out by the TROs. This procedure eliminated arguments between labor leaders, picket captains, and store security agents in maintaining the terms of the TRO. In those few cases in which the restrictions were violated, this arrangement also help the police when called to enforce the TRO.

Police Liaison

It is essential that liaison with the local police department be established, since it is the police who are responsible for enforcing TROs. A TRO is a court order and has the full force and effect of law. Violators are subject to arrest for TRO violations, and while this ultimate means of enforcing them is most often not required, we have seen arrests for TRO violations.

Merchandise Delivery to Stores and DCs

Depending on which unions recognize the dispute and choose to honor picket lines, pre-arrangements for delivery of merchandise and supplies by nonunion drivers will assure both adequate replenishment of stock but also minimize the potential for disputes and/or violence. Again, police presence, arranged for in advance, will prove beneficial.

Planning

The follow items were on a pre-event planning checklist; a specified security executive was assigned responsibility for each item:

- Have coordination meeting with key security personnel.
- Review security department personnel availability; review vacation schedule.
- Issue standby order for all or part of security staff.

- Coordinate with outside contracted guard companies for labor dispute locations and offsite or temporary locations.
- Obtain and have on hand sufficient security equipment, such as bullhorns, video, still photography equipment, and portable recorders. Also provide training for personnel who will use equipment.
- Determine number, placement, and dates for contract guard placement.
- Develop and conduct contract guard orientation.
- Develop contract guard post orders.
- Perform total in-store inspection of sensitive areas and emergency equipment; note deficiencies.
- Coordinate armored car money pickup.
- Assign official recorder at all affected sites.
- Secure panel rooms and cabinets.
- Pick up time cards.
- Obtain distinctive identification badges.
- Establish extra employee entrances.
- Place nonstriking security managers and other security personnel from stores on standby.
- Close extra fitting rooms.
- Ensure exterior window covering availability, i.e., precut and sized plywood panels.
- Coordinate possible alarm company schedule changes.
- Check radio for control center.
- Obtain extra beepers for key command center or executive committee members and security executives.
- Rent van or station wagon.
- Provide security orientation for new hires.
- Update emergency phone numbers at guard office.
- Establish data processing center access control and security.
- Install external guard phones at distribution centers.
- Verify physical security of temporary distribution centers.
- Obtain and have on hand special security equipment and supplies for running temporary distribution centers, e.g., cameras, videos, bullhorns, etc.
- Ensure security of staged trucks and sites.
- Establish liaison with police department senior officers and dispatch.

Special Equipment

Arrange for the availability of any special equipment which it is anticipated may be needed, including

1. Extra walkie-talkies.
2. Two portable battery-operated camcorders and replay equipment; these items are required to record any untoward events taking place by pickets, for use both to obtain injunctive relief and for possible later legal action.
3. Pocket cards with emergency phone numbers.
4. Photos of store including
   a. 8×10s of all entrances
   b. Aerial photos of city blocks
5. Topographical map of blocks containing buildings with distances and all entrances shown.
6. Yellow caution tape.
7. Portable battery-operated bullhorns.
8. 35 mm automatic camera, with telephoto lens, and supply of ASA 200 film.
9. Portable battery-operated tape recorders.
10. A direct telephone line between the control center and the divisional security office.
11. An adequate number of outside line and internal line telephones for the control center.
12. A supply of "incident cards."

13. A chalkboard for titling, dating, and showing other ID data for videotapes.
14. Portable cellular phone.
15. Extra pagers for all security executives.

It is important to assure that qualified and properly trained personnel are available to operate the special equipment listed here; any training of such personnel should take place well in advance of the anticipated need for the use of such equipment.

Law Enforcement Officers as LP Agents

CAS, JHC

Some companies hire law enforcement officers (LEOs) to augment their regular LP staff, some hire only off-duty LEOs for the LP staff, while still others have a prohibition against using LEOs as LP agents. If used, should these officers be in uniform or plainclothes? Is there a police department policy regarding working off duty in uniform? What happens if the officers are injured? Who is responsible for medical and disability benefits? What is the correct position to take on these issues?

We believe that with rare exceptions (special events, executive protection, or other unusual situations) the practice of using LEOs as LP agents should be avoided.

Why? It is our experience that the training of LEOs is reactive in nature, whereas LP training is preventive in nature. Additionally, LEOs have a different mindset than LP agents: LEOs tend to obtain their objectives through the authority and power of their peace officer status, whereas LP agents tend to recognize their restricted limitations and hence rely more on persuasion.

In most jurisdictions LEOs are required to be armed at all times—on duty or off. This means armed LP agents—a situation which is not recommended.

Another consideration: LEOs are rarely willing (or able) to put in the hours we suggest are necessary for training in LP procedures and policies and thus are poorly trained for their LP responsibilities. Contrary to common belief, police academy training does not prepare a person for the legal issues and responsibilities in the private sector.

If LEOs are employed to work with proprietary LP agents, we have found this arrangement produces a real potential for a contentious relationship between them. The company agents are upset over the normally higher pay given to LEOs for the same work and, as noted, with less total knowledge of the job.

Finally, law enforcement officers' primary loyalty is to their public sector department, not to the part-time employer and that can create conflict in judgment calls. Also of concern is the fact that in times of a civil emergency, off-duty police officers must report to their department at a time when they are also needed at their secondary employer.

In summary, we believe that, as a rule, the disadvantages significantly outweigh the advantages of utilizing LEOs as loss prevention agents; therefore, we do not recommend this practice.

Law Enforcement Retail Partnership Network

Joseph LaRocca

LERPnet.com: Getting Connected

Within the United States, thousands of public and private sector databases collect information about people, crimes, and retail. Many of these systems draw from publicly available data sources such as credit, court, property, and personal data records maintained by consumer reporting agencies. Others, such as mutual associations, share information about employees dismissed from retailers or shoplifters apprehended, regardless of prosecution. All of these data sources serve as a tool for us to identify repeat offenders or employees who fail to disclose incidents in their background. The Law Enforcement Retail Partnership Network (LERPnet) will serve as a national repository for major retail incidents, linking retailers and law enforcement across the nation to this valuable source.

Drawing on the experience of law enforcement to share information in near real-time, LERPnet was modeled on the National Crime Information Center (NCIC); see http://www.fbi.gov/hq/cjisd/ncic.htm. On January 20, 1967, the Federal Bureau of Investigation (FBI) created the NCIC to provide a computerized database for ready access by a criminal justice agency making an inquiry and for prompt disclosure of information in the system from other criminal justice agencies about crimes and criminals. This information assists authorized agencies in criminal justice objectives, such as apprehending fugitives, locating missing persons, locating and returning stolen property, as well as in the protection of the law enforcement officers encountering the individuals described in the system.

[*Legal background:* The system is established and maintained in accordance with 28 U.S.C. 534; Department of Justice Appropriation Act, 1973, Pub. L. 92–544, 86 Stat. 1115, Securities Acts Amendment of 1975, Pub. L. 94–29, 89 Stat. 97; and 18 U.S.C. Sec. 924 (e). Exec. Order No. 10450, 3 CFR (1974).]

An everyday use of the NCIC data:. Law enforcement agencies enter records into the NCIC, which are, in turn, accessible to law enforcement agencies nationwide. For example, a law enforcement officer can conduct an inquiry of NCIC during a traffic stop to determine if the vehicle in question is stolen or if the driver is a wanted person, and the NCIC system responds instantly. However, a positive response from the NCIC is not probable cause for an officer to take action. NCIC policy requires the inquiring agency to make contact with the entering agency to verify the information is accurate and up-to-date. Once the record is confirmed, the inquiring agency may take action to arrest a fugitive, return a missing person, charge a subject with violation of a protection order, or recover stolen property.

Unfortunately, the losses suffered as a result of burglaries, organized retail crime, robberies, etc., may never be entered into NCIC. If a store is burglarized in one city, the local agency will take a report and, as resources allow, investigate the crime. In larger cities, hundreds of cases may be filed each day, so the retailer suffers a significant financial loss without much hope of recovering any product, or making an arrest.

Smart criminals may commit the same crime over several cities, counties, or states and at a variety of retailers. Without good communication and coordination, they could do so for months or years before anyone would connect the dots.

Over the past decade we have seen a transformation within our industry. The ability and need to share information on a near real-time basis with hundreds or even thousands of users has become a minimum standard of any technology application. To create a system to share crime data within the private sector and between traditional competitors would require precedent-setting work on behalf of the private and public sector, many with competitive corporate philosophies, not to mention the financial support.

Why did we start this effort?

According to the National Retail Security Survey, produced by Dr. Richard Hollinger at the University of Florida, shrinkage in 2005 was $37.4 billion, the largest loss in the history of his report.

When you look at the latest official crime statistics available, in 2004 the FBI Uniform Crime Report claimed losses from auto theft at $7.6 billion, burglary $3.5 billion, larceny $5.1 billion, and cargo theft between $12 and $15 billion. These crime categories combined do not total the annual shrinkage rates suffered by the retail industry. In fact, since crimes like fraud and cargo theft are not included as company shrinkage, the $37.4 billion is much, much higher.

The current efforts to combat retail crime are a collection of disparate and redundant deployments and efforts, with some successes, between various retail segments and individual companies. Unfortunately, the loss prevention and law enforcement community data, systems, and efforts are not coordinated and integrated to address common goals.

Since there is no commonly used standard, schema, taxonomy, or directory for finding, integrating, and linking data elements and content, there are insufficient ways to selectively share or widely disseminate information about retail crime to all parties.

Retail crime intelligence is not widely available or used by law enforcement to fight retail crime. Most data-sharing opportunities do not provide sufficient flexibility as to what is shared and how it is shared to allow corporate managers and legal departments to approve participation.

In January 2006, the Federal Bureau of Investigation announced LERPnet as the single national database to prevent, detect, and investigate major retail crime incidents. LERPnet connects traditional competitors and law enforcement nationwide, using a high-security web interface with links to retail case management systems. The system developed by retailers and law enforcement officials was designed to

- Prevent crime and apprehend criminals;
- Reduce the cost of retailing by reducing crime against retailers and their customers;
- Provide a safe shopping experience and excellent customer service;
- Serve as a data source to educate legislators, the public, and the media about retail crime across the country.

The core platform, designed by members of the retail community, were led and supported by the National Retail Federation loss prevention team, Richard J. Varn, and a group of talented information technology folks at ABC Virtual.

Richard Varn, the former CIO of Iowa and currently the president and CEO of RJV Consulting, was the perfect person to lead the technology aspect of this effort. Mr. Varn has extensive experience serving both government and private sector clients, making him an ideal project manager. He served as a state representative for 4 years and served as a state senator for 8 years. During that time, he was twice elected majority whip; created and chaired the first Communications and Information Policy Committee; and chaired the Education Appropriations, Human Services Appropriations, and Judiciary Committees. In addition, he was the director of Telecommunications and IT Production Services at the University of Northern Iowa. Mr. Varn brought a wealth of technical knowledge and background to this project, given his public sector background and work in the private sector, specifically with retailers.

ABC Virtual (ABCV) was selected based on its experience with the public and private sector. What impressed us was their experience building systems to share information across diverse entities in the financial and local government communities. Al Baker, Adrienn Lanczos, and Jim Howard at ABCV designed LERPnet to support millions of records with a clean front- and back-end interface. In addition, their experience in the financial community gave us the ability to apply top-tier security.

There were many law enforcement advisors during the development stage; however, three played a major role in their feedback and support of the system: FBI Major Theft Unit Chief, Eric Ives; FBI Supervisory Special Agent, Brian Nadeau; and Montgomery County Police Department, Detective David Hill. Without the exceptional effort of these dedicated folks, LERPnet would not have obtained a national presence in the law enforcement community.

LERPnet was launched with high expectations:

- Provide the retail loss prevention and law enforcement communities with information, data, and analysis to prevent, detect, respond to, prosecute, and recover from retail crime;
- Provide a forum and technology platform for the exchange of information and data;
- Enable the retail LP community to work together toward common goals as much as possible in a competitive environment;
- Develop systems and processes for maintaining strict adherence to participants' wishes regarding the ownership, access, privacy, security, and integrity of the information and data provided;
- Maintain a high standard of excellence in the provision of services in their availability, reliability, accuracy, interoperability, and usability.

Three extremely important factors were unanimously voiced during the initial meetings with retailers and law enforcement.

First were system security levels. One of our steering committee members had just been involved with the theft of proprietary data for a contracted company. This raised the concern that retailers would be entering not just proprietary information, but also their ugliest secrets about robberies and other major crimes taking place. In response, we deployed the system with a mandatory third-level authentication schema.

Second was the need to suppress, or hide, data elements by the submitting company. This would allow companies to report large losses without fear of their out-of-stock position being disclosed to a competitor or users of the system inadvertently releasing confidential information (see Figure L-1).

Finally was the need for vendor neutrality. During the discussion about financing the system, several individuals proposed having key vendor partners fund the system on behalf of retailers. As the discussion progressed, it became clear this was a contentious issue. Loss prevention executives are somewhat partial to their existing vendors, and we recognized early on that LERPnet would need to connect to all the various commercial and proprietary case management platforms.

Following the initial meetings we began working on the project in three ways:

- Design and implementation;
- Legislative action to support and potentially fund the system;
- Garnering the support of law enforcement agencies at all levels.

Design and Implementation

Using a comprehensive development model, the programmers coded the system to the specifications our steering committee members provided. Simultaneously, the system was reviewed by retailers and legal experts to validate the process and make recommendations along the way.

We utilized several legal experts during the development and deployment process. The system needed to exceed the standards of security and data privacy and remain unregulated by the Fair Credit Reporting Act. Our ultimate goal was to provide loss prevention executives with every argument for supporting the system with public relations (users can suppress any data about their company), general counsel (most data are already public record with police agencies, and LERPnet secures the data even further), and operations (providing a tool for preventing, detecting, and investigating losses within the company).

Current State

The first version of LERPnet was originally shown to NRF Loss Prevention Conference attendees on June 28, 2005 (then under the name the Retail Loss Prevention Intelligence Network, or RLPIN). The pilot system was not operational; however, the screenshots gave attendees a good feel for the future functionality and the feedback was overwhelmingly positive. We were also able to discuss the system functionality with attendees and gain additional requirements before the public pilot period.

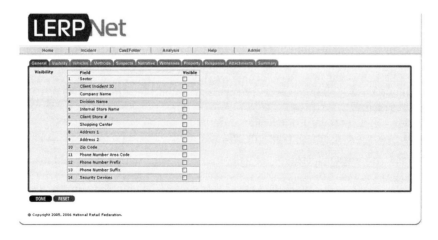

FIGURE L-1

Basic Operating Protocols

Since LERPnet was developed with busy loss prevention and law enforcement professionals in mind, the system is largely made up of check boxes, drop-down menus, and quick entry fields (see Figure L-2). Anyone who works with databases today understands a misspelled word or inconsistent data capture techniques can seriously impact the results of a query or report.

Our steering panel of retailers recommended we focus on major retail crime incidents to start and expand the content over time. Information in LERPnet is classified by sector and incident type, as shown in Table L-1.

Data are fed into the system using three different techniques:

- *Direct entry:* Users can enter data directly into the system using a series of friendly web-based forms.
- *Import:* Knowing a majority of retailers already capture incident information using Excel, Access, or a case management program, LERPnet is set up so that companies can export case information from their system and the technical gurus can upload the data into LERPnet.
- *Automatic feed:* Several companies are developing direct data feeds into LERPnet. For example, one large department store chain is developing a check box on each company incident report that instructs its internal system to automatically send the information to LERPnet.

The benefits of feeding data into LERPnet work both ways. Today, when a company examines incidents by month, it has exposure only to data within its system. With LERPnet data, that company can compare internal statistics to stores within its sector or the industry as a whole. We see this capability as having residual benefits in resource acquisition and deployment nationwide.

Each incident has unique attributes, so it was important to build intuitive screens to guide users throughout the reporting process. When a user enters incident details about an organized retail crime incident, the system requests information about how the crime was completed (distracted associate, booster bag, lookout, removed sensor tags, etc.). If the user changes this incident to a robbery, the attributes change (displayed weapon, took employee

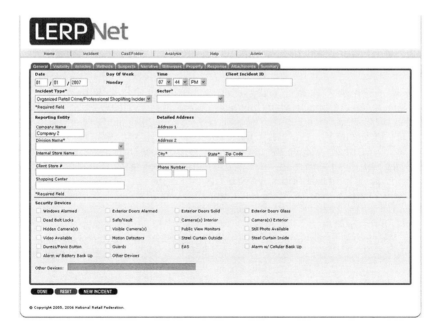

FIGURE L-2

Table L-1

Sectors	Incident Types
• Auto Parts	• Organized Retail Crime
• Jewelry	• Burglary
• Cargo/Logistics	• Robbery
• Mass Market	• Auction Fraud
• Gaming/Video	• Refund/Exchange Fraud
• Grocery	• Cargo Theft
• Department Stores/Large Box	• Gift Card Fraud
• Drug Stores	
• Specialty Stores	
• Restaurant	
• Home Improvement	
• Electronics	

hostage, threatened customers, etc.). The attributes for each type of incident are different, so LERPnet keeps users on track through these structured forms.

The page layout was designed to capture every important detail about an incident and structures the information in a manner easily understood by law enforcement or loss prevention professionals from other retailers.

One of the big benefits of developing LERPnet with public and private sector input was our ability to capture diverse data elements. For example, when capturing information about suspects, you would expect to find information about height, weight, clothing, and weapons used. Law enforcement would want to capture information about tattoos, street names, and any link back to NCIC records (Federal ID #). While some of this information would be useful to retail professionals, they are also interested in items like email address, instant messenger screen name, and auction/seller ID. All these elements are attributes captured in LERPnet.

The core system today allows users to upload photographs into the system. We are working with several technology experts to allow video uploads and have the streams return to users through a common format (such as Windows Media Player). Another module in the development plan is what we call "photo array." Imagine taking a group of incidents with like methods and photos and displaying them side by side to see if the suspects look alike. All of this is possible in LERPnet.

Some other features that users find very useful are custom email alerts, queries, and reports. Each user can develop a library of commonly request data elements:

- *Email alerts:* If you work in specialty retail and are responsible for stores in California, you may want to see only incidents in California occurring in specialty stores. When an incident matches the criteria you specify, an email is sent to your computer, cell phone, or pager.
- *Queries:* Everyone loves to benchmark and LERPnet is the ultimate tool. Based on the data today, California leads the country for ORC cases, followed by New York. With LERPnet, you can identify the best/worst sector, incident type, and with enhanced reporting tools, you can find the worst city and state for each incident type. Whether you are in the public or private sector, imagine using this type of information when presenting a case to your boss about getting more resources.
- *Reports:* From a "top-down" perspective, look at the entire industry or just pick a sector. As the results come back, they are hyperlinked to the data below, so you just have to point and click to see the detailed data you're looking for in LERPnet.

Law Enforcement Access/Support

When the LERPnet system was built, it was decided that law enforcement needed free access to the system. Working with the FBI, approved public sector officials will access LERPnet through Law Enforcement Online (LEO.gov), a secure system the FBI uses to share information between agencies.

Law enforcement officials will simply access LEO.gov and go to the Organized Retail Theft section on the site. From there, each user can request access to LERPnet. Once approved by the FBI Headquarters team, the user will have access from any secure terminal at the station or patrol vehicle with the proper permission to enter the system.

The National Retail Federation is the world's largest retail trade association, with membership that comprises all retail formats and channels of distribution, including department, specialty, discount, catalog, Internet, independent stores, chain restaurants, drug stores, and grocery stores, as well as the industry's key trading partners of retail goods and services. NRF represents an industry with more than 1.6 million U.S. retail establishments, more than 24 million employees (about one in five American workers), and 2006 sales of $4.7 trillion. As the industry umbrella group, NRF also represents more than 100 state, national, and international retail associations. See www.nrf.com for more details.

Legal Cases by Subject Matter (Case Law)

CAS, JHC

Accomplices:
    Cervantez v. JC Penney Co, 156 Cal Rptr 198 (1979)
Detention versus. Arrest:
    See *Cervantez* (supra)
Discrimination:
    Hampton v. Dillard Department Stores, Inc 18 fed Supp 2d 1256 (1998)
Duty:
    Ann M. v. Pacific Plaza Shopping Center, 6 Cal 4th 666 (1993)]
Extortion:
    People v. Beggs (1918) 178 Cal 79
False Imprisonment:
    Fermino v. FEDCO, 30 Cal Rptr 2d 18 (1994)
    Parrott v. Bank of America, 97 C.A. 2d, 14 (1950)
    Ware v. Dunn, 80 C.AS. 2d 936 (1947)
    Scofield v. Critical Air Medicine, Inc, 45 Cal App 4th 990 (1996)
    Moffatt v. Buffums' Inc., 21 Cal App 2d 371
Fitting Room Surveillance:
    Peo v. Randazzo, 220 C.A. 2d 768 (1963)
    Peo v. Deborah C. 117 Cal Rptr 852 (1981)
Joint Police Action:
    Stapleton v. The Superior Court of LA County, 70 Cal 2d 97 (1968)
Miranda:
    See *Deborah C* (supra)
    People v. Jones 393 N.E. 2d 443 (1979)
Negligence:
    Pool v. City of Oakland 42 Cal 3d 1051 (1986)
Off Duty PD:
    Peo v. Corey, 21 Cal 3d 728 (1978)
    Cervantez v. JC Penney CO, 156 Cal Rptr 198
Parking Garages:
    Sharon P. v. Arman Ltd., 55 Cal App 4th 445 (1997) Cal App LEXIS 429
Police Officers:
    See *Cervantez* (supra)
Premises Liability (Causation):
    Miller v. Pacific Plaza Shopping Center, 16 Cal App 4th 1548 (1992)
    Cert granted by CA SC
    Rest 2d Torts, § 431
    Nola M. v. Univ Southern Calif, 16 Cal App 4th 421 (1993)

Privacy:
Peo v. Deborah C, 177 Cal Rptr 852 (1981)
Private Searches:
Peo v. Randazzo, 220 C.A. 2d 768, (1963)
Private Security:
Peo v. Zelinski, 24 Cal 3d 3576 (1979)
Private Strip Search:
Bodewig v. K-Mart, 635 P. 2d 657 (1981)
Punitive Damages:
Cruz v. Home base et al. (Temp LA Sup Ct # YC 019081)
Ratification:
Kelly-Zurian v. Wohl Shoe Co., 22 Cal App 4th, (1994)
Refunding:
Peo v. Davis, 98 C.D.O.S. 8223
School Searches:
Bilbrey v. Brown, 738 F. 2d 1462 (1984)
Searches:
Minnesota V. Dickerson, 61 LW 4545 (1993)
Peo v. Ornelas, 253 Cal Rptr 165 (1988)
Peo v. Taylor, 90 C.D.O.S. 5640 (1990)
Security Manual versus Law:
K-Mart Corp v. Washington, Supreme Court of Nevada (Dec 30, 1993)
Self-Help:
Restatement of Torts, 2nd, § 100 – 106
Similar Incident:
Ann M. v. Pacific Plaza Shopping Center et al. (Supra)
Theft;
Elements of theft: People v. Davis, Cal Supreme Ct, 95 C.D.O.S. 8223

Legal Considerations

CAS, JHC

Our legal system attempts to strike a balance between the rights of persons and private organizations to protect their lives and property and the rights of citizens to be free from the power or intrusion of others. This balancing act is nowhere more evident than in the field of security.

In the security business, many of our "tools of the trade" may easily and unintentionally become the catalyst for a civil lawsuit. How is the injured party redressed or made "whole"? In our system, money is the means of redress; a court or jury decides how much money will adequately compensate the injured party to basically put that person in the position he was in before the injury or damage. Our tort system is really a "redistribution of wealth" system.

Damages awarded in security-related lawsuits have skyrocketed in recent years; 20 years ago, suing for tens of thousands or even thousands of dollars was considered high; today suing for hundreds of thousands and millions of dollars is almost commonplace. Let's examine how these awards reach these levels.

- *Special damages* are awarded to replace actual out-of-pocket expenses of the plaintiff, e.g., medical bills, lost wages, attorney fees, etc.
- *General damages* are awarded to "make the plaintiff whole"; these are the monies awarded to compensate for pain and suffering, emotional distress, mental anguish, loss of consortium, etc. The more the jury is outraged by the defendant's conduct, and the greater the injury or damage to the defendant, the higher these awards will be.
- The combination of special and general damages is commonly referred to as *compensatory damages*; i.e., they compensate the plaintiff for injury.

- *Punitive damages* are awarded when the plaintiff can establish that the defendant was grossly negligent, wanton, or was motivated by malice. For punitive damages to be awarded, there must be clear and convincing evidence that the defendant's conduct was not merely negligent or the result of honest error, but rather that he acted with malice, fraud, gross negligence, or oppression. Punitive damages are designed to punish and/or set an example to others to avoid such conduct.

While compensatory damages can be covered by insurance, in California (and most other states) it is against public policy for insurance to cover the cost of punitive damages.

Now that we've seen the severe damage that can result from successful and even unsuccessful civil lawsuits resulting from the alleged tortious conduct of security personnel, the next question is this: Why is the employer held accountable for the wrongdoing of an employee, particularly if the employee is acting against the instructions or directions of the employer? After all, don't we as employers instruct our security personnel as to how we want them to behave and conduct themselves? Don't we tell them to be polite, not use excessive force, not make "bad stops"? So why are we held accountable?

The reality is that most security employees are not wealthy and don't have the financial resources or assets to provide any significant (or even insignificant) amount of money damages. Therefore, the plaintiff seeks a corporate "deep pocket" (or someone of financial stature) to sue so that the money is available to pay any damages awarded. This quest for big dollar assets usually brings the plaintiff to the employer who has assets or is at least insured for big dollar policy limits. So how do the misdeeds of employees get imputed to their employers? Several legal theories are utilized to impute employee liability to the employer.

Ratification

If an employee commits a tort and the employer, upon learning of it, doesn't take appropriate corrective action, which many will argue means termination, then the employer may be said to have "ratified" or approved of the act. the employer is therefore just as liable as if the employer had directed or committed the tort.

Respondeat Superior

Respondeat superior is a legal doctrine which holds that an employer (principal) is vicariously liable for the acts and omissions of its employee (agent) committed "within the scope of employment" but not generally liable for acts committed outside the scope of employment. The primary questions which determine if the employee was within or without the "scope" are as follows: Did the employer benefit from the act of the employee? Was the employee acting under the authority or direction of the employer?

A relatively new theory in the law, that of negligent hiring, may be used to circumvent the respondeat superior defense that the employer is not liable because the employee acted outside the scope of employment.

Agency

Agency is a relationship wherein one party is empowered to represent or act for the other under the authority of the other. Agency means more than tacit permission; it involves a request, instruction, or command. There are three types of agency relationships: principal and agent, master and servant, and proprietor and independent contractor.

- A principal directs or permits another to act for his benefit; e.g., a real estate or insurance agent acting for the broker or company.
- A master is a principal who employs another and has the right to control the servant's physical conduct.
- A proprietor owns or operates a business; an independent contractor contracts with another to do a job but is not controlled by or subject to the other's right to control the physical conduct in the performance of the job.

Course and Scope of Employment

Is the act of the employee either directed by or for the benefit of the employer? Obviously, liability for an employee who assaults his neighbor on his own time cannot be imputed to the employer. But what about the employee who, on his own time, invades the privacy of another in furtherance of an investigation connected with his employment? Is the employer liable?

These are complicated legal issues. When such questions are raised in lawsuits, they will be answered by the court if the question is a legal issue or the jury if it is a factual issue.

What Is a Tort?

A tort, or civil wrong or injury excluding breach of contract, is a violation of a duty owed to the individual who claims to have been injured or damaged. Tort law governs the civil relationships between people in any given situation. Some of these relationships that may become the focus of tort law arise from

- *The U.S. Constitution:* search, arrest, etc.
- *Federal statutes:* Civil rights violations
- *Agency law:* When an employee acts for his employer.
- *State law:* Criminal statutes, which are also torts, e.g., battery, assault and false imprisonment, invasion of privacy.
- *Other administrative, regulatory, or state and federal statutes which may regulate security activities:* Citizen's arrests, merchant's detention laws, licensing, insurance, use of force, privacy (eavesdropping), etc.
  Let's look at the two types of torts.

Unintentional Tort
The only *unintentional* tort is *negligence*, although there can be many alleged negligent acts.

Negligence
Negligence is an act or omission to act in the absence of ordinary care, carelessness, or oversight.

For one to commit a negligent act, there must be

- A legal duty owed to the plaintiff;
- A breach of this duty or unreasonable conduct;
- A foreseeable proximate cause;
- Injury or damages suffered by the plaintiff.

The California Supreme Court, in a case involving a retailer, instructed the jury as follows regarding negligence:

Negligence is the doing of something which a reasonably prudent person would not do or the failure to do something which a reasonably prudent would do under the circumstances similar to those shown by the evidence.

It is the failure to use ordinary or reasonable care.

Ordinary or reasonable care is that care which persons of ordinary prudence would use in order to avoid damages to themselves or others under circumstances similar to those shown by the evidence.

You will note that the person whose conduct is set up as a standard is not the extraordinarily cautious individual, nor the exceptionally skillful one, but a person of reasonable and ordinary prudence.

A test that is helpful in determining whether or not a person is negligent is to ask and answer whether or not if a person of ordinary prudence had been in the same situation and possessed of the same knowledge, he would have foreseen or anticipated that someone might have been damaged by or as a result of his action or inaction.

If that answer is "yes," and if the action or inaction reasonably could be avoided, then not to avoid it would be negligence. [Pool v. City of Oakland, 42 Cal 3d 1051 (1986)]

Simply put, a store owner has a *duty* to provide customers (legally, business invitees) with a safe shopping environment. If that duty is *breached*, and if it was for *foreseeable* that harm might arise from the breach, and that "but for" that breach the victim would have suffered no *injury* or *damage*, then we have negligence.

For example, is it foreseeable that a shoplifter being chased by a store detective may run into a customer and injure that person? *Yes*. If this happens, is the shopkeeper negligent? *Maybe*. Does this mean that store security should never chase shoplifters? Not necessarily, but it is an element of store security procedures which should be well thought out and perhaps some perimeters established.

It is curious that courts have ruled both ways on this issue; the majority of courts have held the likelihood of customer injury is not so great that stores should refrain from chasing shoplifters. What, however, if the store employee is the one knocking over and injuring the customer? Here, this issue is much clearer.

When the employee acts outside the scope of employment, the employer may be insulated from liability. Since most employees are *not* of adequate financial stature to pay large awards, attorneys have developed a relatively new body of negligence law designed to bring liability to the employer where previously it would not have fallen. These cases are the various *negligent hiring, training, supervision, entrustment and retention* cases.

How do you avoid negligence? By conducting yourself in a reasonable manner and doing those things which a prudent person would do to avoid the foreseeable injury or damage to someone which could arise by failing to do those reasonable and prudent things.

Negligence torts require no *intent*.

Intentional Torts

It is the reasonable subjective view of the victim of intentional torts which is normally determinative of tortious conduct. In other words, it is not what the actor thought or intended, but rather what the victim thought or felt.

False Imprisonment/Arrest

False imprisonment is the intentional, unjustified detention or confinement of a person; false arrest is the unlawful restraint of another's person's liberty or freedom of locomotion. Note: This may also be a criminal offense.

In shoplifting situations, you can avoid false arrest allegations by being certain your cause to believe shoplifting is taking place is based on reasonable observations, not mere suspicion.

Merchant's Privilege

Many states, recognizing the tremendous shoplifting problem, have enacted so-called Merchant's Privilege statutes, which grant merchants and their agents the right, under specified conditions, to detain suspected shoplifters and which grant them protection from certain civil suits, provided that all the provisions of the statutes have been met.

While the exact language of the Merchant's Privilege or Merchant's Detention statutes varies from state to state, in general, such statutes require that

- The detention be based on probable cause that the person to be detained was committing a theft;
- The detention be for the purpose of investigation;
- The detention be for a reasonable period of time;
- The detention be done in a reasonable manner.

Additionally, many such statutes limit the use of force to nondeadly force and prohibit or limit searches of the person.

If the merchant meets all the statutes requirements in making the detention, these statutes then provide that in a civil action resulting from a detention, the merchant has a statutory defense to such action, provided he acted reasonably under all the circumstances and that the detention was based on probable cause to believe the person detained had stolen or attempted to steal merchandise.

All these laws require that the merchant act reasonably and on probable cause in making the detention, so the issue becomes how the merchant can clearly establish probable cause. We believe that the long recognized "Six Steps" to a shoplifting detention, if followed, clearly establish probable cause for the detention.

Six Steps for Shoplifting Detentions
1. You must see the suspect approach the merchandise.
2. You must see the suspect take possession of the merchandise.
3. You must see where the suspect conceals the merchandise.
4. You must maintain an uninterrupted surveillance to ensure that the suspect doesn't dispose of the merchandise.
5. You must see the suspect fail to pay for the merchandise,
6. You should approach the suspect outside the store.

As stated, the merchant must also have acted reasonably. How is this behavior established?

In torts, the element of "reasonableness" is a key factor. Just what is this concept of reasonableness? Essentially, actions which are reasonable are those that a hypothetically prudent, reasonably intelligent person would consider to meet the judgment that society requires of its members for the protection of their own interests and the interests of others. Conversely, actions which outrage, vex, appear malicious or excessive, or tend to make one angry when considering the alternatives available may be considered "unreasonable."

Torts Alleged as a Result of Shoplifting Detention
What are the torts which may be alleged as the result of a shoplifting detention? They are

- *Assault/battery:* Unconsented to or unprivileged physical contact or privileged contact which becomes unreasonable. *Note:* This may also be a criminal offense.
- *Malicious prosecution:* Prosecution (civil or criminal) with malice (evil intent). To succeed, prosecution must have resulted in a verdict for defendant and prosecution initiated without probable cause.
- *Invasion of privacy:* Invading someone's reasonable expectation of privacy.
- *Defamation (libel-slander):* Written or spoken words that tend to damage another's reputation. *Defenses:* Truth, privileges (qualified and absolute).
- *Tortious interference with employment:* Maliciously interfering with the employment of another.
- *Tortious infliction of emotional distress:* Intentionally and maliciously inflicting emotional distress on another.

Since the test of negligence or appropriate behavior when reviewing intentional torts is reasonableness, the ability to avoid unreasonableness is essential. How do you avoid being unreasonable? Since the question of reasonable behavior is one of fact for a jury to decide, no black-and-white answer can be given. However, if you know the concept and limit your behavior to actions that are demonstratively necessary and prudent, and which do not exceed the bounds of propriety, which would not be offensive to the average person under the circumstances, then chances are those actions, if reviewed, will be considered reasonable.

Malice, as mentioned earlier, is something done solely to annoy or vex; something that is done out of ill will with no justification and in wanton and willful disregard of the likelihood that harm will result. Malicious acts can never be reasonable

Why Is All This Important?

In today's litigious society, avoidance of expensive lawsuits (whether won or lost) is important. We are in the business of loss prevention, and creating situations resulting in civil suits results not only in adverse publicity for our companies, but in unnecessary financial expense and losses as well.

Little we do in the retail environment can so easily result in lawsuits as the activities involved in loss prevention. Shoplifting detentions are, by their very nature, adversarial and confrontational. Dealing with employee dishonesty enters domains which may be the subject of federal and state regulations, privacy issues, and labor relations.

Thus, when taking loss prevention actions, it is essential we know *who* should do it, *what* should be done, *when* it should be done, *where* it should be done, and *how* it should be done.

The ultimate object is to convince a jury that we acted reasonably under all the circumstances and our actions were commenced based on probable cause.

Civil Litigation: Avoidance and Cost Control

It goes without saying that the best way to avoid civil litigation is to avoid doing the things that result in injury to others for which they seek remedy through civil lawsuits.

However, as Alexander Pope wrote in the 18th century "To err is human; to forgive divine." We can anticipate that mistakes will be made and that, in many cases, they will not be forgiven; hence, lawsuits are inevitable, and the ability to control their cost becomes important.

The time to start controlling civil suit costs is before the suit is a reality. When an improper or inept loss prevention action insults or injures a customer, one of several things will likely happen:

- The retailer will receive a phone call or letter from the customer.
- The customer's attorney may call or write.
- The store is served a summons and complaint noticing a lawsuit.

How should these actions be dealt with?

In the case of a phone call or letter from the customer complaining of mistreatment during a loss prevention incident, the store should immediately contact the customer and state its concern over the allegations and advise the customer that an immediate inquiry will be made into the complaint and he will be contacted within a short period of time. This contact with the customer should be made by a company executive, and while no specific commitment should be made, the company's sincere concern over the complaint should be stressed.

If, after a thorough investigation into the complaint, it is determined that there is no merit to the complaint, the customer should be contacted an advised that an unbiased inquiry has determined his complaint lacks merit, but that in the interests of maintaining the customer's good will, the store is willing to … here, the store must determine what action it will take. It is noted that in some cases the complaint is totally without merit and the store may simply relay this to the customer. In other cases, where there was a good faith and reasonable basis for the store's action, but nevertheless the action was unjustifiable, the store may offer a letter of apology or some monetary compensation. Obviously, if the action was totally unjustifiable (e.g., store policies were violated), the extent to which the store will go to satisfy the customer will be more generous and extensive.

The secret, however, is to do everything within reason to keep the customer from contacting an attorney. When attorneys get involved, costs automatically escalate, since now both the attorney and customer require compensation, and attorneys recognize that most retailers hate adverse publicity and have "deep pockets"; i.e., they have insurance and the ability pay large monetary awards. Stores should avoid having their own attorney or insurance carrier make the initial contact with the customer because the customer may then feel the need, in self-defense, to seek legal advise.

We note that any written apologies should be relatively general in nature, apologizing for any embarrassment or inconvenience the customer suffered. Such letters should avoid language which could establish legal admissions of tortious or criminal conduct. We suggest that such letters be cleared by company counsel before being mailed.

If a phone call or letter is received from the customer's attorney, the same general strategy as described previously should be followed. It is important that the attorney be assured that the store is sincerely interested in resolving this matter as quickly and fairly as possible and that any resolution will be achieved by dealing with the attorney rather than directly with the customer. This caveat assures the attorney that any monetary settlement will go through him, assuring him he will not be bypassed or uncompensated for his efforts.

If a summons & complaint (or other formal means of advising that you are being sued) is received, the store should contact its insurance carrier at once and let the carrier and its designed lawyer deal with the issue from that point forward.

A final thought: In dealing with the customer, his attorney, or your insurance carrier, it is vital that you are as forthright as possible. Nothing is gained (and there is much to lose) if facts are withheld, distorted, or manipulated. Document everything completely, beginning with the initial report covering the action which caused the complaint, and every subsequent action taken in an effort to resolve it. If a suit is filed, it may take years to reach court, and complete documentation, together with evidence of your sincerity and honest efforts at resolution, constitutes one of the best defenses and damage mitigation in such suits.

Liaison with Law Enforcement

CAS, JHC

The question frequently arises as to the proper relationship between loss prevention and law enforcement (LE). The answer is: It depends on several factors, including

- The size of the city/town and its LE department;
- The attitude of LP toward law enforcement;
- The attitude of law enforcement toward LP;
- The policy of the company toward cooperation with law enforcement.

We have found, throughout our careers in various venues, that an honest effort toward establishing a close relationship with law enforcement had a real benefit to LP efforts. Several examples of these benefits will underscore this point.

Local law enforcement officers (LEOs) recover obvious stolen merchandise during an unrelated investigation. If they know and have confidence in the professionalism of the local head of LP, they are likely to call him and report their find of stolen merchandise, which may alert LP to a serious problem as well as a recovery.

In another venue, LP's relationship with local LE was so close that LP agents were frequently invited to participate in raids on fencing operations known to deal in merchandise carried by that store. In addition, the store often "loaned" fairly significant amounts of merchandise to LE for use in sting operations. I found this close relationship with the local LE's fencing unit to be mutually rewarding and beneficial.

I had a colleague who was formerly employed by a leading federal investigative agency, and this fact resulted in another beneficial relationship with that agency.

Finally, knowing not only working LE officers but also senior LE personnel, from the chief on down, on a first-name basis was found to helpful; when the assistance of LE was needed, it was certainly not a disadvantage to be able to call the chief of police by his first name and make a request for assistance.

We realize that some LP senior executives feel that LE "looks down" on LP and feel that they represent "a bunch of wannabes" who were unsuccessful in their efforts to join the ranks of LE. It is true that some LE personnel, both of senior and lower rank, harbor these views. We also believe, however, that one way to convince LE that these views are misguided is to establish a working relationship with LE and demonstrate that LP personnel can be just as professional as their counterparts in public LE.

While we do not, as a general rule, support hiring LE personnel as security/LP agents, (See "Law Enforcement Officers as LP Agents"), in some situations the hiring of a retired senior law enforcement officer who is otherwise qualified by education and experience for a staff position in the LP department may prove to be a good investment. If such a hiring is considered, it must be done with great care, since my experience has been that very few LEOs at any rank make successful LP agents. Occasionally, however, a young command-level LEO with a college degree who has demonstrated management skills may be a wise hire. Such a person can often help both LP and LE to appreciate the skills and professionalism of both groups to their mutual benefit.

Lighting: Outside

CAS, JHC

The need for adequately illuminated parking areas is discussed in the "Parking Area Crimes" section of this book, and the thrust of that piece deals with lighting while customers and employees use the parking area. However, there's a need for some outside lighting when the store is closed. Some exterior lighting should be provided to the dock or receiving area, to the dock pedestrian door, any emergency exits, and to the employees' entrance. The latter is to accommodate early morning employees, such as housekeeping personnel, who arrive before sunrise.

There are risks at these locations, albeit not high, but they include entry made by cutting an opening in the closed and locked metal dock doors with an acetylene torch, and interception of early morning employees by gunmen intent on a major robbery of the cashier's cage. Additionally, lighting these areas makes it easier for routine police patrols to spot any suspicious activity, and the light itself will act as a deterrent to criminal activity. Failure to light such areas, should a major crime occur, would be a form of security negligence.

Lockers

CAS, JHC

Employee Lockers

Many employers provide lockers for their employees to store personal items while at work. The problem is that such lockers can also be used to stash stolen property and/or items whose possession is prohibited in the workplace, such a drugs, weapons, or pornography.

How can the misuse of employee lockers be minimized? By utilizing the following procedures:

- Do not permit employees to provide their own locks; provide company locks and have the employees sign for them. This should be spelled out as policy, and we suggest the topic be a part of the employee handbook. The policy should state that if private locks are used, employees must remove the lock in the presence of a supervisor or LP and replace it with a company-provided lock. Private locks are subject to being cut and removed.
- Locks provided should be of the type which permits a master key to open them.
- Post signs in the locker area stating: "Employee lockers are subject to inspection at any time with or without prior notice; use grants permission."
- When conducting locker inspections, always have a witness, preferably a nonexecutive staff associate.

Public (Coin Operated) Lockers

We strongly recommend that all coin-operated lockers be removed. We urged this position prior to 9/11, and do so even more adamantly now. The potential for use for illicit or terror-related purposes is too great to overcome any so-called customer convenience or income generated by their use.

The "terror" threat means an explosive or otherwise dangerous device could be placed in the locker and be armed to detonate at any given time.

The "illicit" threat, best exemplified years ago when they were common in large stores, was that lockers would be loaded with unpaid-for merchandise by employees who worked inside the building while the store was closed to the public, such as janitors, and the key to such lockers would be passed to a friend or relative who entered the store when open and removed the goods.

Loss Prevention as a Concept

CAS, JHC

Historically, retail security departments focused primarily on apprehending shoplifters and dishonest employees. Although continuing, and rightly so, to place a major emphasis on deterring and detecting employee theft, studies have been less than convincing that there is any correlation between apprehension statistics and shortage. Therefore, to totally address shortage reduction, which, after all, is the main objective of a protection program, the focus had to be modified. This was accomplished by the concept of "loss prevention"; i.e., the protection efforts should be directed toward shortage reduction, which in turn increases profitability.

Four elements are necessary for a successful loss prevention program:

1. Total support from top management
2. A positive employee attitude
3. Maximum use of all available resources
4. A system which establishes both responsibility and accountability for loss prevention through evaluations that are consistent and progressive

There are many loss prevention programs, but we suggest that to maximize the shortage reduction potential, the program must include several key elements, including

- The program must be ongoing and have an impact on shortage throughout the inventory period.
- The program must have a consistent method of addressing shortage such that any new executive or employee can immediately pick up where the former employee left off.
- A process must be in place which enables total loss prevention efforts and involvement on the part of all employees, from the officers of the company down to the newest hires, as well as individual efforts toward shortage reduction to be evaluated.
- Evaluation can be done at any time, anywhere, by anyone.

The preceding elements can be achieved by a program which targets those areas or merchandise groups which comprise 50–60% of total shortage. These areas are audited frequently on a set schedule, with consistent audit topics, covering all conditions which contribute to shortage. Such conditions include (but are not limited to) neatness, evidence of missing merchandise, missed markdowns, salvage, found EAS tags, fitting room conditions, misrung merchandise, missed price changes, employee awareness, staffing levels, missing price tags, etc.

By frequent auditing of high-shortage areas and responding with appropriate fixes to problems found, shortage cannot help but be reduced.

Loss Prevention Manuals: Content & Preparation

CAS, JHC

Recognizing that loss prevention manuals are obtainable through legal discovery procedures in the event of a civil suit, we suggest that, with the approval of legal counsel, the following subjects be included in a security/LP manual:
Introduction
    LP Mission Statement
    Role of LP Chief Executive
    LP Reporting Chain
    LP Organization Chart
    LP Standards of Conduct or Code of Ethics
Loss Prevention: Theory and Procedures
LP Training Programs

LP Policies and Procedures as They Relate To
    External Theft
        Shoplifting
        Fraud, including
            Refunding
            Bank check
            Credit card
        Internal Theft
Reports
Alarms: How They Work, Response To
Security Equipment
Emergency Procedures
Investigations
Interviewing
CCTV
EAS
Civil Recovery

While we have suggested some subtopics under the Introduction section, we have not endeavored to do so for the other sections, since each company's philosophy and operating procedures will vary, and any such attempt by us would not only be presumptuous, but inapplicable to many readers.

What we do suggest, however, is that a manual be prepared by major categories of operations, with pages numbered by a numerical system that allows for periodic updating and the insertion of new pages, which can be properly indexed. For example, the Introduction section may start with Page 1.00. The first subtopic, the LP Mission, would be numbered 1.1.0, followed by the Role of the LP Chief Executive numbered 1.2.0, etc. The next major section, Loss Prevention: Theory and Procedures, would be numbered 2.00, with subtopics following the numbering system for Section 1. Should an additional page be subsequently required, for example, The Role of the LP Chief Executive in 1.2.0, that page could be easily inserted as page 1.2.1 without necessitating completely renumbering the entire section.

It is also important that a permanent record be kept of revisions or additions to the manual by topics, page number, and date. This information is extremely important should the manual (and its contents) ever be used in court when a particular policy or procedure, and adherence thereto, comes into question.

Every loss prevention employee, from new-hire entry personnel to new employees who come to the company with prior LP experience, should be required to read the LP manual and sign and date a statement they did read and do understand the material contained therein. That statement should be made a part of each employee's training or personnel file.

A copy of the manual should be available in each of the company's facilities for easy reference by LP personnel.

Since manuals are discoverable and contain proprietary information, we strongly suggest making every effort to protect this information from becoming public, and that the procedures outlined in our section on "Proprietary Information" form the basis for this protection.

Lost or Unaccompanied Children

CAS, JHC

Lost children are defined as preteenage boys or girls down to toddlers who clearly are separated from their parents and appear to be without adult supervision in the store.

The merchant has a duty to take reasonable steps to ensure harm does not befall customers or children while in the store, and youngsters wandering in the store pose a risk of harm to themselves, i.e., are vulnerable to abduction or sexual assault while in the confines of the store. There is also the potential risk of injury from using escalators or knocking down mannequins or other items that could injure them or others. Abductions and assaults are not common fare but, on the other hand, are not unknown. Aside from the shear tragedy of any untoward incident victimizing a child, the store would be exposed to the a risk of civil liability.

Policy, then, should require the training of all store associates to approach such children and determine where their parents are. Parents engaged in shopping can and do lose sight of their children, and often the associate can guide the child back to a grateful (and often an abashed) parent.

In the event a parent cannot be immediately located, a member of management or LP must be contacted, and two or more either should search the store with the child in tow or retire to the office and announce over the store's paging system that a little boy named Charlie is looking for his Mom, for example. In the unlikely event no parent can be located, the police should be called.

We strongly recommend these suggestions be covered by written policies and procedures.

Malls and Shopping Centers

CAS, JHC

There is a symbiotic relationship between stores and shopping centers (malls) because one is dependent on the other. If either is considered unsafe or to present a security risk to patrons, there is a transfer of such concerns to their business partners. While malls and shopping centers have traditionally had at least minimal levels of uniformed security personnel, their function has been primarily pedestrian and vehicular traffic control and the prevention of juvenile vandalism and rowdiness. Historically, many malls and stores generally have "soft-pedaled" security in fear of their customers perceiving the environment as unfriendly and unsafe and avoiding shopping there.

Events subsequent to 9/11 have, however, prompted a reevaluation of mall security needs. As of this writing, two men have been charged in separate incidents (the latest in December 2006) with allegedly plotting to attack malls to disrupt shopping. Despite these indictments, and the fact that malls are considered "soft targets" by the Department of Homeland Security, few malls have undertaken any realistic actions to address the threat of a terrorist attack. True, some malls have increased the number of CCTV cameras and perhaps even increased uniformed security officer hours, but it is also fair to say these malls are the exception rather then the rule.

Beginning in 2007, however, the International Council of Shopping Centers (ICSC) in conjunction with the Homeland Security Policy Institute of George Washington University rolled out a program (at a cost of $2 million) providing a standardized antiterrorism training program for mall security officers. The program is reported to focus on awareness and effective response and uses a instructional DVD for the core of the training. The ICSC is funding the initial training, and private security companies providing mall security services have agreed to participate. The long-term viability of this program remains unknown.

This program is not without its critics, however. They claim that the retail industry and shopping malls are simply a small part of other public venues representing potential terrorist targets. It is also reported that mall security suffers from high turnover; most security officers allegedly leave their jobs within 1 year, and thus the effectiveness of antiterrorism training is questioned. Some authorities claim it is not feasible to teach mall guards the skills needed to identify potential terrorists and that, in reality, malls cannot prevent attacks but only respond to one. It is also alleged that mall security officers are poorly trained in terrorism awareness and ways to respond to any such attack. It is suggested that the best approach to dealing with potential terrorist threats at malls is for malls to develop well-thought-out emergency plans and train personnel to respond to any event effectively.

Irrespective of the security/loss prevention aspects of potential acts of terrorism, retailers have a distinct interest in the overall security of the malls and shopping centers in which they operate. More than likely, patrons of individual stores obtain their perception of their safety while shopping not from any individual store, but rather from the mall or shopping center. This is true because the mall generally has more visible security with the presence of uniformed security officers, whereas the stores' security tends to be more invisible. Another factor that tends to translate the level of mall security to the mall's tenants is the fact that incidents in the mall and its parking lot generally receive more publicity than incidents in individual stores within the mall. Consider also that the mall/shopping center has more exposure to untoward incidents when parking lots are taken into consideration.

Tenants' association meetings are routinely held by mall/shopping center management. If the mall's security is weak, it will eventually reflect on and affect the business of the tenants of that mall; it is, therefore, in the interest of the tenants, particularly the anchor stores, to assure that mall security is up to par.

And the tenants' association is not the only vehicle for communication. Your authors have met on numerous occasions with mall management as well as the chief of a shopping center's security department to discuss concerns, review incidents and problems, and coordinate efforts. One occasion comes to mind in which our employees in a major center were complaining about thefts from their vehicles and poor security in the lot. We met with the center's management and security and learned our employees weren't the only victims; other stores were experiencing similar problems. As a consequence, the mall erected a tower in the employees' designated section of the lot and staffed it from time to time. There was a dramatic downturn in attacks in that area.

Manuals for Security/LP: Protection of Contents

CAS, JHC

In many situations, a company can be shown, via its manual, that it was reasonable in its loss prevention program and procedures, even if a particular agent may have veered off-course and broken the rules. It is generally agreed that this is a better position than having no rules at all, the absence of which tends to make the company appear more culpable, thus more vulnerable.

Care should be taken in the preparation of a loss prevention manual; the LP manual should be reviewed by counsel or other qualified persons to assure that no unethical or illegal methods of investigation are authorized or included. Should a company be sued over a security or loss prevention issue, the LP manual will certainly be sought, and usually successfully, by the plaintiff in discovery (the legal process whereby attorneys may obtain proprietary information, including documents, from their adversary).

One issue which frequently arises with respect to LP manuals is their proprietary nature and protection of their contents. As just noted, the LP manual is one of the first items sought by attorneys when they bring a suit against a retailer involving LP issues. Since manuals are discoverable, it behooves the retailer who wants to protect the information in the manual to insist upon confidentiality agreements and protective orders prior to releasing the manual.

In recent cases (2006), disgruntled ex-LP employees have published copies of their ex-company's LP manual on the Web; obviously, this was an unauthorized publication. We have heard of other cases in which persons who received copies of manuals legally but inadvertently have threatened to expose them to widespread publicity. Protecting the confidentiality of LP manuals is, we feel, important.

To accomplish this protection, we suggest that some, or all, of the following steps be taken:

1. Label every page "Company Confidential and Restricted Dissemination."
   If appropriate, also label each page "Duplication Prohibited."
2. Number each copy of the document (e.g., Copy #10 of 50) and document the recipient of each copy.
3. Conduct periodic audits to assure each copy is where it is supposed to be.
4. Prohibit duplication of these documents. If duplication is necessary, treat every duplicated copy identical to original documents.
5. If the content is reduced to electronic form, require password access, and if on disc, make the disc password-protected and subject to the same accountability as a restricted paper document.
6. Have all LP agents and all other recipients sign "nondisclosure" agreements; renew such signing every year.

7. Use copyright procedures if applicable.
8. Take aggressive action if any of the preceding rules are violated, including termination of offending employees and criminal/civil prosecution if available.

Finally, with respect to manuals, we strongly urge that manual pages be dated and/or that revisions be noted as "Rev. Mo/Yr" so that when changes are made, there is a time reference as to the date of the change.

The nondisclosure agreement signed by LP agents could, at the company's discretion, also include LP reports, videos, budgetary matters, etc.

Membership Stores

CAS, JHC

Membership stores are subject to much the same loss prevention problems as nonmembership stores but do have some advantages when it comes to controlling external theft.

To begin with, membership stores are just that: one must be a member to gain entrance. This requirement is waived by federal regulations to customers desiring to obtain medical prescriptions and also waived by many state laws for the purchase of alcohol. Membership card requirements at time of purchase prevent abuse of these waivers.

Based on the fact that membership requires a payment up front (usually $100 or less, depending on the level of membership), the store has some degree of control over who is permitted membership benefits. Members are also issued photo ID membership cards, which provide additional proof of identity.

Additionally, the membership agreement normally provides an agreement between the customer and the store which, in part, requires the customer to agree to merchandise checks, which compare goods being taken out against receipts, when exiting the store. This procedure, which cannot help but deter some shoplifting, does not, however, totally prevent all thefts. Indeed, we've assisted in some shoplifting arrest matters which found their way to litigation.

The store may revoke membership of any member apprehended shoplifting.

Merchandise Inventory

CAS, JHC

Prior Book Value	$ 50,000
Plus: Purchases	50,000
Mark-ups	-0-
Returns from customers	-0-
Book Value of Merchandise	$100,000
Minus: Sales	$ 50,000
Markdowns	-0-
RTVs	1,000
Present Book Value	$ 49,000
PHYSICAL COUNT	$ 48,000
SHORTAGE	**1,000** *
*	As % of a sales: 2%
National Average Shortage for Retail (1)	
As % of:	Retail Sales
2005	1.59
2004	1.54

2003	1.65
2002	1.70
2001	1.80
2000	1.69

(1) Hollinger, R. C. (2005). *2005 National Retail Security Survey, Final Report*. University of Florida.

Miranda Rights

CAS, JHC

In March 1963, Ernesto Miranda was arrested by Phoenix police for the theft of $8. He was questioned for two hours, without the benefit of an attorney by his side. During that interrogative period, he admitted not only to the $8 theft, but also to the kidnap and rape of an 18-year-old girl a few days earlier. On the strength of that confession, Miranda was convicted and sentenced to 20 years.

His attorney's appealed to the Arizona Supreme Court, which upheld the trial court's conviction.

His attorneys then took the matter to the U.S. Supreme Court. That court, on June 13, 1966, reversed the decision of the Arizona Supreme Court in deciding the now famous case of *Miranda v. Arizona*, 384 U.S. 436 (1966), which established the "Miranda" rights of persons accused of crimes.

Those "Miranda" rights are best reflected in the common warning required of the police (or any law enforcement or investigative local, state, or federal agency) as follows:

> *You have the right to remain silent. Anything you say can and will be used against you in a court of law. You have the right to speak to an attorney, and to have an attorney present during any questioning. If you cannot afford a lawyer, one will be provided for you at government expense.*

The basic premise upon which this decision and subsequent requirement is made is that an individual is prone to intimidation by the weight of the sovereignty of government, and every person who becomes suspect must not and cannot be forced by any governmental agency into making incriminating statements against himself or herself without the benefit of counsel of an attorney.

Note the word "sovereignty."

Private persons, such as retail loss prevention agents, bank security investigators, utility company security agents, etc., who are employed by private sector businesses and enterprises *don't represent the sovereignty of the state*. They represent the interests of their employer, private companies or corporations, and hence, unless specifically working with the police (or allied agency), are immune from the requirement to "Mirandize" or provide a suspect with his or her "Miranda" rights.

Indeed, we caution all those in the private sector against "Mirandizing." Some have adopted the policy to Mirandize, which could only lead to the setting of an unwanted and unneeded restriction on our rights to protect such private enterprises. While we are comfortable in stating private security personnel need not Mirandize persons arrested by them, we suggest that local policies be checked, since we have heard of isolated cases in which local courts require that "Miranda" rights be given by private personnel.

Mission Statement

CAS, JHC

What function or role does the loss prevention department play in a retail company? What is its purpose and function? These questions are best answered by a "mission statement."

Every security and loss prevention department must have (or should have) a mission statement. The mission statement is a proclamation of the department's role in the greater organization, and its direction and purpose. Every loss prevention employee should know and understand that statement.

A mission statement could read as follows:

The objective of the department is to professionally engage in the prevention of criminal attacks against the company's employees, customers, vendors, and other invitees, as well as prevent criminal attacks against the company's assets, merchandise, proprietary information and to protect the company's reputation and customer goodwill.

Here's another example of a mission statement:

The Loss Prevention Department mission is to
Develop and implement policies, programs, and procedures which

1. *Prevent loss of company assets due to dishonesty and procedural error;*
2. *Investigate when preventative measures fail or are circumvented;*
3. *Detect dishonesty and procedural error through inspection or investigation;*
4. *Protect all associates, customers, invitees, and facilities from intentional harm or wrongdoing;*
5. *Preserve the good will and reputation of the organization.*

An actual mission statement used by one company is reproduced here:

Security Department Function

The primary function of the (Name of Store) Security Department is to protect the company's assets. The assets include personnel, merchandise, money, property, proprietary information, and reputation.

The goal of the Security Department is to create a "shortage Awareness and Loss Prevention atmosphere" among both our employees and customers. Our efforts must create an atmosphere which will establish a pleasant shopping environment, while protecting the assets of the company.

Inherent in this philosophy is the selection, training and retention of a highly skilled and professional security staff. Establishing the Loss Prevention atmosphere, as well as detecting and apprehending those who commit offenses and violate policies, is essential to our success. We must strive to remain an integral part of the company through daily liaison with departments such as merchandising, Operations, Human Relations and all other areas of the company.

These contacts must be tailored toward promoting the success of the company's business efforts, while maximizing the security and loss prevention efforts that are essential to that success.

Security personnel must deal with all individuals they come into contact with in a fair, courteous, and impartial manner.

We must demonstrate competence, integrity and professionalism in all of our actions. The Security Department should take pride in their role within the company, and complete their responsibilities in a manner that affirms our role as an integral part of (Name of store).

Note the reference to protecting people as well as objects in both examples. The question arises: Is there a duty to protect people who work or visit your property? The answer lies in another question: If you have the resources and commitment to protect goods and material assets, should you not have the same reasonable protective responsibility for people? The answer, in the affirmative, is clear.

Negligence in the Employment of LP Personnel

CAS, JHC

As discussed under "Legal Considerations," several torts are frequently alleged in civil suits against retailers resulting from the activities of store or loss prevention personnel. Aside from intentional torts, the unintentional tort of negligence is often alleged. Negligence torts include allegations of negligent hiring, training, supervision, and retention. Since these torts (civil wrongs) are so prevalent, particularly in suits involving loss prevention activities, they deserve more than a cursory mention.

What is negligence? Simply stated, it is "the failure to use ordinary or reasonable care" in a given situation. This failure then results in someone being injured, either mentally or physically, and that injury forms the basis for a lawsuit.

Why would an employer not use reasonable care in hiring, training, supervising, or retaining an employee? The answer is not that the employer wouldn't do, but rather lies in what a jury may ultimately determine was "reasonable" under the circumstances. For example, an employer may follow his or her ordinary custom and practice when hiring a loss prevention agent. However, should this LP agent cause a customer an injury, the jury may determine that an LP agent's duties are unique when compared to a sales associate. The LP agent will be detaining customers in a predictably adversarial and confrontational atmosphere, unlike the sales associate's normal interaction with customers. Thus, the jury may determine that the employer's ordinary custom and practice in pre-employment screening was too superficial, deficient, or inadequate in the case of an LP agent. The employer's hiring of the agent under these circumstances was, therefore, negligent.

One state's supreme court recently stated: "[A] special relationship exists between 'a possessor of land and members of the public who enter in response to the landowner's invitation'" and that "a business proprietor has a 'duty to take affirmative action to control the wrongful acts of third persons which threaten invitees where the [proprietor] has reasonable cause to anticipate such acts and the probability of injury resulting therefrom.'"

Simply put, a store owner has a *duty* to provide customers (legally called "business invitees") with a safe shopping environment. If that duty is *breached*, and if it was *foreseeable* that harm might arise from the breach, and "but for" that breach the victim would have suffered no *injury* or *damage*, then we have negligence.

Negligent Hiring

In the case of hiring LP personnel, knowing their duties will involve confronting customers reasonably believed to be shoplifting, is it foreseeable that an LP agent with a history of aggressive behavior may injure a customer? The answer must be "yes." Is it then also incumbent upon the employer to determine if the prospective agent has a history of violence or aggressive behavior? Again, the answer must be "yes." If the employer's ordinary and customary pre-employment screening does not address the issue of aggressiveness, has the employer who hires an LP agent without checking this aspect of the applicant's behavior then exercised ordinary care? The answer here must be "no." Hence, the employer is negligent, and if this agent should injure someone by the use of excessive force while within the course and scope of his or her employment, and his or her employer is sued as a result thereof, the employer would be vulnerable to civil damages.

The duty of a store owner (as outlined previously) applies equally to the other torts of training, supervision, and retention, which we will now discuss.

Negligent Training

Is it foreseeable that an untrained LP agent may, out of ignorance, injure a customer by reason of a false detention, an illegal search, or perhaps the improper application of handcuffs? Of course! If the employer fails to provide adequate training, as well as assure the agent understood the training provided, has the employer met his or her obligation with respect to duty to his or her customers? No.

Here's an example. Company A requires LP agents to make detentions and use force if necessary to effect such detentions. The employer's failure to provide adequate training in the use of force would or could be, under the circumstances, unreasonable and negligent, unless the employer assures himself or herself that such training has previously been given to the applicant and the applicant is conversant with it and it comports to the employer's desires, policies, and procedures. Again, if the agent's ignorance of correct procedures resulting from a lack of training results in an injury when engaged in his or her duties, the employer may be in jeopardy.

Negligent Supervision

Let's assume an applicant has been carefully screened, and his background is impeccable. Let's also assume he has received adequate training and demonstrated his understanding and retention of that material. Let's also assume that 1 year after his hire, this agent, while making a shoplifting apprehension, detains an old and valuable customer and, in the process of the apprehension, forces her to the ground and twists her knee in the process. This should never have happened because the employer's policies, which the agent knew, prohibited any physical contact with the shoplifting suspect other than a "holding force." Additionally, the employer required a full report anytime a customer was injured in any way in the process of an apprehension.

We have established that this agent was properly hired and trained, so what went wrong? When the customer's attorney called the store to complain, he asserted that not only was his client injured, but that she did not possess any stolen merchandise when she was apprehended. He wanted to inquire what the store intended to do about this affront and injury to his client. If not satisfied with the store's response, he stated his intention to file a lawsuit. At this point, the store was ignorant of the incident, since a review of the apprehension reports on file by this agent disclosed no report on this incident.

Management immediately began an inquiry into the alleged incident and learned that this agent has not been visited by an LP supervisor within the past 6 months, although he did receive a phone call from his supervisor 2 months ago wondering why his shoplifting apprehensions had been declining.

When contacted about the incident, the agent at first denied any knowledge of it. Upon further investigation, it was apparent the incident occurred as described by the attorney, and the agent finally admitted he made a "bad stop" but denied any physical injury to the suspect. He stated he failed to report the stop because he didn't want a bad stop on his record.

A case of negligent supervision could be made under these circumstances. What was negligent about his supervision, or lack of it?

When an agent's productivity declines, there is always some reason. It may be the result of the agent's "goofing off," improper scheduling to match peak customer hours, the agent's loss of confidence in his or her ability to spot shoplifters, lack of support from sales associates in reporting suspicious customer behavior, etc. The point is there is a reason—or several reasons. The only way to establish those reasons and return the agent to his or her potential effectiveness is through a personal visit and discussion with the supervisor. A phone call asking about a decline in productivity "doesn't cut it." Further, an agent who hasn't seen his or her supervisor in 6 months is bound to feel somewhat abandoned and "left out of the loop." Agents experiencing a decline in any kind of productivity for any period of time many become concerned about their job longevity and start taking "shortcuts" to obtain apprehensions. If the "productivity" happens to be detentions, the shortcuts usually involve skipping one or more of the six steps. Invariably, this practice will result in a bad stop sooner or later, and most likely sooner rather than later.

Long-range supervision is, in our view, not a substitute for personal face-to-face conversations with agents, at which time their concerns, as well as those of their employer, can be discussed and resolved. There's an management adage that states, "Employees don't do what you expect; they do what you inspect." Simply reminding the agent to be more careful and not let the incident be repeated doesn't qualify as sufficient discipline in such a serious matter.

Should the store's actions not satisfy the victim's attorney, it is almost certain one of the allegations in the lawsuit will be negligent supervision, and in our view, the chances of the jury's finding for the plaintiff are quite high.

Negligent Retention

In the scenario just cited, it was noted that there was no apprehension report submitted by the erring agent covering this incident. Such an omission was in direct violation of his employer's rules and at least led to the inference the agent knew his conduct during the apprehension was improper. Indeed, the agent's violation of rules was deliberate and was further compounded by his initial denial (lying) it ever happened. This is egregious misconduct.

Yet the agent was neither given any written warning (such an offense should result in his termination) or other discipline. His supervisor recalls telling the agent to "be more careful and not let this happen again." That rather innocuous remark, however, does not qualify as a warning sufficient to alert the agent to the seriousness of his offense.

Unfortunately, some 15 weeks after the agent was told "to be more careful and not let this happen again," it did. Another customer was stopped and found not to be in possession of any stolen merchandise. In the lawsuit which followed, negligent retention was claimed. Why? The allegation was that the employer was negligent in retaining an agent who not only broke the rules regarding following the six steps, but also opted not to file the required reports on the incident. Was it foreseeable this would happen again? Perhaps. Did the employer sufficiently impress upon the agent the seriousness of the first incident? No! Did the *employer fail* to use ordinary or reasonable care by retaining this agent on the payroll under the totality of the circumstances? Yes, the *employer failed!* Was this employer vulnerable to a jury finding he was negligent. More than likely yes.

When a retailer employs LP personnel, extreme care must be taken when hiring, training, supervising, and making decisions regarding retention after their involvement in an untoward incident. To do otherwise invites adverse verdicts when sued for negligence in connection with LP activities.

Night Depositories

CAS, JHC

"Night depositories" are those financial institution receptacles designed to accept monetary deposits during the hours the bank or institution is closed. A store's cash receipts for the day, placed in a sealed or otherwise locked bag along with a deposit slip can be dropped into the receptacle on the outside of the building. When the depository door is closed, the deposit bag is dropped into a chute that empties into a secure enclosure. The design of the depository exterior door is such that, when open, there is a physical barrier to the chute and secure enclosure below, thus preventing any "fishing" for deposit bags from above in an attempt to remove them and make off with the deposit. The money is safe, and the deposit into the store's account is accomplished the following morning, two functions accomplished by the store in one process.

There is, or was formerly, another type of "night depository" used in the retail industry which may be a relic of the past but noteworthy to include in this book in the event similar systems still exist somewhere in the country. This piece is also included to highlight the value of careful inspections of unexpected ways to bypass the store's night intrusion alarm system.

The Store Night Depository System

Night depositories are cubicles constructed on the inside of a store; one side of the cubical is the exterior wall of the store with a small exterior door. The size of the door would allow a person to enter, remove, or leave chests containing business documents and packages. The exterior of the door has no hardware, only a keyway in which a key is inserted to open the door. On the opposite side of the cubical is another small door which opens into the interior of the store (often in the receiving and shipping area), and that door can only be opened with a key from the inside of the store. The exterior door is not alarmed, but the interior door is alarmed and part of the store's perimeter alarm system.

This physical configuration allows a company van to visit stores at night, and the driver can open the depository door with a key and remove contents that will be transported to the DC or corporate headquarters, as well as deposit (leave) any chest or parcel meant for that store. Clearly, this is a quick and expeditious expansion of the inter-store transfer system, with multicopy paperwork covering both items left in the depository as well as those taken by the driver. That driver cannot continue on through the cubical because it is alarmed, just like any other door.

The Security Inspection

The loss prevention program should include physical security inspections of every store to ensure compliance with required security-related systems and procedures. On one such inspection of a relatively new store, the agent, upon inspecting the night depository, discovered the interior door was alarmed but the switch that would activate the alarm if that door was opened was compromised. This switch was the plunger-type and was compromised with a toothpick; i.e., the plunger was recessed and shimmied shut by the wedging of a toothpick, so when the door was open, the plunger could not pop out and activate the alarm. Clearly, someone who had, legitimately or illegitimately, obtained keys to the outer door could, in collusion with the inside employee, enter and leave the store at night without activating the perimeter alarm system.

Within hours, the plunger switch was replaced with a switch that was tamper-proof, providing integrity to the system. Various employees were present when this discovery was made and corrected, and the risk disappeared.

"No Touch" Policy

CAS, JHC

"No touch" policy refers to that strategy adopted by some retailers who prohibit employees, most specifically their loss prevention agents (at all levels), to have any physical contact with a suspect who has committed theft (shoplifting). That is to say, if an agent observes a young person conceal merchandise and exit the store, that agent may intercept the shoplifter verbally; e.g., "Excuse me. I need to talk to you about that CD under your sweater." However, if the shoplifter continues on or refuses to stop and engage in a conversation, the agent may not physically stop or otherwise touch the customer. Such policy and strategy are contrary to long-established custom and practice in the industry of detaining shoplifters. Indeed, the shoplifter can laugh and even taunt the agent and walk or run away, and the agent can only watch the culprit leave with the stolen store merchandise.

Granted, in this singular restricted policy, the agent is permitted to follow, but not run, and should the agent observe the shoplifter getting into an automobile, the agent can record the license tag and report it to the police. The police may or may not recover the stolen goods or may not take any action against the shoplifter. More likely than not, the store will not be advised as to the identity of the culprit. Your authors liken this strategy to the police department prohibiting its motor officers, in trying to stop a speeder, from using their red light and siren, exceeding 20 miles per hour, and not providing them with a citation book.

Many times, this "no touch" policy is expanded into a further-compounded prohibition policy titled a "no touch—no chase" policy. The functional reality of that policy is if the shoplifter declines to cooperate and walks away, the agent may not follow the offender.

Indeed, the following actual telephone conversation took place the week this particular segment of the book was being written. An attorney representing a retailer who was seeking advice initiated the conversation. Please understand the thrust of the inquiry had to do with the importance of the loss prevention manual and its value to the retailer:

Attorney: "And, in furtherance of our need to be competitive, we recently adopted the 'no touch–no chase' policy."

Author : "Why did you adopt that policy?"

Attorney: "We decided it was too costly to deal with all the injuries and claims of excessive use of force lawsuits caused by our loss prevention people."

Author : "You did not have a 'policy' issue; you had a training issue. And frankly, you're not going to be competitive because once it becomes known you have this no touch—no chase policy, more shoplifters and crooks will come to your store, actually making you less competitive in terms of shrink and profitability."

We've heard loss prevention agents claim they have no trouble "talking" suspects back into the store, but it only stands to reason the noncriminal element of our society who shoplift may be scared when confronted and will comply. But, the bad element such as those involved with organized retail theft, who constitute a much more serious threat to the retailer, will not comply. That suggests the agents who have no problem with people walking away haven't been observing the professionals, only the amateurs.

We have no problem with the "no touch–no chase" policy for those stores that have no professional loss prevention employees. We also have no problem with stores with professional loss prevention employees whose job descriptions prohibit them from making detentions; i.e., their task is solely to discourage, dissuade, *prevent* shoplifting. If it's not preventable, let the shoplifter walk. We do object to charging loss prevention agents with the task of detaining and processing shoplifters with one hand tied behind their back with a policy that leaves them helpless and embarrassed outside the store.

The issue that was of concern to the attorney referred to in the preceding example and that caused the company to change its policy on apprehensions was a concern over the high numbers of claims resulting from apprehensions in which some degree of force was used. In our view, the answer to this problem is training, coupled with an adequate degree of supervision or oversight of field activities. If LP agents are properly trained in the use of reasonable and minimal force (only when necessary to affect an apprehension) and provided with strict regulations and policies with respect thereto, and given an adequate level of supervision, the number of claims filed should be minimal. Of course, when the supervisor finds a violation of the rules regarding the use of force by an agent, then appropriate discipline will reinforce the rule and demonstrate the company's insistence on compliance.

"Oh Shit Syndrome"

CAS, JHC

We knew—in fact, everyone in the security business knew—that the biggest problem on the floor in catching shoplifters was some innocent customer or sales associate coming on the scene and inadvertently "burning" what surely was going to be, if uninterrupted, a theft followed by an arrest. The eye contact was all that was necessary to spoil a shoplifting act in progress. This was the nemesis of the store detective—good work shattered by eye contact.

In the 1970s I labeled this the "Oh Shit Syndrome," i.e., the emotional and personal reaction on the part of a person engaged in an evil deed because of the inevitable sense of guilt (guilt aura) and belief he or she has been detected by virtue of seeing someone looking at him or her. It wasn't a "scientifically" proven phenomenon, but rather recognition of reality.

In view of that "reality," it led to one of your authors taking the lion's share of the store detective staff and outfitting them in red blazers with a gold-embroidered "security" patch on the pocket, and training them to patrol the floor for the purpose of making eye contact with every customer possible. We pursued this experiment with the firm belief we would prevent more possible acts of shoplifting then ever before imagined. It worked! The agents, amazed at what they were witnessing, reported they would go down one aisle, turn to the left, and find themselves facing a woman who could almost be heard saying (sometimes they did hear) "Oh shit!" and the customer would reverse direction and stash an item under other merchandise and proceed out the store. Other customers would promptly produce an item from their purses or bags, an item the agent knew nothing about, and say words to the effect of "I didn't want this anyhow." Numerous "preventions" occurred each day compared to the number of detentions. The "Red Coats," as they became known, found the work rewarding, with visible and quantitative results.

The cream of the store detective staff, those who were predictably effective (those who could sense the aura of guilt), were left to continue with their detection and apprehension work. That meant, if a person wasn't deterred by the presence of the Red Coats and opted to shoplift anyhow, he or she risked arrest by the traditional store detectives. Once the detectives were detained, those shoplifters were invariably baffled by our strategy and expressed resentment over being fooled to think we were only preventing thefts.

On-the-Job Training (OJT)

CAS, JHC

There are two basic strategies to training: on-the-job training (OJT) and formal classroom training. OJT can be a totally unstructured, unplanned, ill-advised teaming up of a new employee with whomever is available, or it can be a meaningful and informative process that adequately prepares the novice to perform satisfactorily in a relatively short period of time. The difference lies in properly structuring the experience and the careful selection of the trainer.(1)

Structured OJT is a powerful and effective tool to train the new employee to perform in keeping with the full expectations of management. "Structure" means and includes the following:

1. The trainer is trained to train and is ranked and compensated for that important function.
2. The numerous tasks to be learned are specifically identified and enumerated, and when each has been taught and understood, that task is signed off by the trainer as having been achieved.
3. The training period required to learn the tasks is identified, and progress through the program is measured accordingly.
4. The program has a conclusion, which includes a final examination or testing to ensure the trainee comprehended the information and instructions.
5. Successful passing of the examination results in some form of recognition, such as a certificate of completion and recognition on the part of the company that the employee is trained and now ready to perform in keeping with expected standards.

Regrettably, more often than not, so-called OJT is unstructured and is but a façade, providing less than a meaningful learning experience, but many retailers see it as an expeditious and inexpensive strategy of transitioning the novice into a "productive" employee. In reality it's shameful for retailing to subject the public to the risk of being detained by a loss prevention officer who doesn't even know or understand the state law addressing the crime that the officer is attempting to enforce. Even sales associates get more structured training in learning how to operate a register or POS terminal than many LP agents receive. New hires can be productive, not necessarily efficiently so, in folding or rehanging clothes or restocking goods or loading or unloading trailers with little training, without serious consequences if mistakes are made. Why, then, do many retailers place LP agents in service without even rudimentary training in their obligations under merchant's detention laws, considering the dire consequences which frequently flow when they exceed their authority or make other errors when detaining shoplifters?

As experienced consultants and expert witnesses involved in many significant lawsuits against retailers, we see that the issue of training, or its absence, tends to be a focal point for plaintiff attorneys representing a "customer" who somehow was injured as a consequence of the LP agents action. The skillful lawyer can chew up and spit out most companies' claims they adequately trained their agents through OJT. Plaintiffs' attorneys will have the jury see the agent was assigned to work alongside another agent who was never properly trained and ill prepared to train a new, inexperienced agent. In a significant case, the plaintiffs will require the "trainer" to appear in court and then expose the "trainer" as inadequately trained, with perhaps a history of the same errors of performance that his or her "trainee" committed and that constitute the issues that drive the case being presently litigated.

Bottom line: The new hire learns what the trainer likes and dislikes about the company, what supervisors and mangers the trainer likes and dislikes, the company's policies and procedures as filtered by the trainer, the "shortcuts" that can be taken, what policies to ignore, where the hot buttons are, whom to avoid, and where to go for lunch. That's the downstream consequence of *unstructured* OJT.

Fortunately, some retailers understand and agree with the preceding diatribe and have instituted professionally structured OJT programs that ensure the new employee understands what the company wants, why the company wants it, and how the company wants it done, as well as the potential consequences to both the agent and the company when errors are made. Based on that learning experience, the employee can go forward and serve the best interests of the company in productive and constructive fashion.

---

(1). Sennewald, C. (2003). *Effective Security Management*, 4th ed. Elsevier Science.

Organized Retail Theft

King Rogers

A young teenage female is in the cosmetics aisle. She is dressed in a hooded sweatshirt that zips all the way up the front, with half pockets on each side of the zipper. She is wearing it half zipped, and the hood drapes in folds down her back. In her jeans she looks just like any other teenage girl from the high school three blocks away. She is looking over the lip gloss display rack and checking out a few different shades. As you observe her on the video monitor to your upper left front in the loss prevention office, you wonder if she is going to go for it or not. So far, no telltale signs like furtively looking around or picking up a tube of lip gloss and walking away from the display rack and checking to see if anyone is following her.

Movement on the video screen alongside to the right catches your eye. Several aisles over in the razor and razor blade aisle, an older male has just walked up the aisle and turned around to walk back. He is carrying a shopping bag by the handles from a grocery store across the street. Probably nothing, you say to yourself as you turn back to watch the adolescent in cosmetics. If she takes the lip gloss and sticks it in her pocket as she walks away from the display, it will be a quick and easy apprehension, a "stat" for your self-kept records.

You glance back to the screen on the right and, just as you do, you observe the gentleman easily and quickly remove razor blade pack after pack from the peg hooks and drop each one into the grocery bag he is carrying. He swiftly moves from peg hook to peg hook, cleaning off each one with sure, deft movements. In only a third or less of the time that the young woman pondered the lip gloss decision, this man had swept almost all the razor blade packages from the peg hooks and was leaving the aisle.

He turns left onto the "racetrack" and walks briskly toward the front of the store. As you try to follow him by "handing him off from one camera to the next," he suddenly turns left again into an aisle where there is no camera coverage. That's the aisle where the bulk paper goods are stocked, and they are not a high-risk category. You momentarily lose sight of him. Some 10 seconds later you spot him again, this time nearing the exit of the store. He is empty handed. There is no grocery bag in sight.

You are working that part of the shift alone. There is no backup to radio for assistance, so you quickly leave the loss prevention office and head for the front exit of the store. As you arrive at the exit, the man has walked out onto the sidewalk in front of the store and headed into the parking lot. Several other customers are also leaving the store: a couple of women pushing shopping carts with bagged merchandise in them and, there she is, the teenager you were watching in cosmetics. Suddenly, the EAS alarm begins to insistently sound, just as the young woman goes through the pedestals. You quickly move into position, identify yourself, and politely and professionally ask her if she has any merchandise that she might have forgotten to pay for. She knows you know. She is very new at this impulsive opportunistic shoplifting, and immediately her eyes well up with tears as she pulls the lip gloss from the right front pocket of her sweatshirt to try to return it to you. Following proper procedures, you direct her to accompany you to the loss prevention office and signal a female store associate to come with you. Once all three of you are in the office, you bring up the case report screen on the desktop and begin to ask her the questions that will provide you with her identity, including her age. As you suspected, she is a sophomore student in the local high school. You call her mother's work number and tell her mom what has happened and ask her to come to the store to pick up her daughter.

An hour later, the teenager and her mother are gone, and all your paperwork is complete. You then remember the older male and go to the paper goods aisle to see if you can find the bag. It is not there. You return to the razor blade aisle and see that it has been cleaned out. A stocking associate standing there says to you, "I can't understand it. I just filled this area this morning." Your heart sinks. While you went after the $6.99 lip gloss and an easy "stat," $832.00 worth of razor blades left the store unpaid for.

What happened to this loss prevention agent is not that unusual. If he had been able to observe what happened in the paper goods aisle, he would have seen a very quick and surreptitious handoff to a female customer who passed the man in the aisle. They made very little eye contact and did not even slow down as the handoff occurred. She placed the shopping bag, which was full of razor blades, into her shopping cart along with store bags containing a few cheap items she had already purchased. She was one of the two women who exited the store when the EAS alarm sounded. The grocery bag from the store across the street was lined with foil and duct tape, and the tagged merchandise inside the bag did not trigger the EAS alarm. In fact, the alarm was triggered by an item in a bag belonging to the other woman who was exiting the store at the same time. This customer had actually purchased the offending item, but the cashier had failed to deactivate the EAS tag contained inside the package. A series of unfortunate circumstances? Perhaps. But scenes like the one just described happen in retail stores all over the world every day.

If a person is a crook, thief, or someone who just wants to make a quick, easy buck, participating in organized retail theft may just be the perfect crime. As a "booster," this person doesn't work too hard or too long, there is relatively minimum risk, the payoffs can be huge (and tax-free), and usually no one gets hurt. Plus, even if this person gets caught, the consequences are little more than a slap on the wrist. But the retailers and the consuming public are the ones who suffer because organized retail theft (ORT) is *not* a victimless crime.

The victims in organized retail theft are many. First, the direct victim is the retailer whose bottom line is negatively affected. Retailers lose millions of dollars in merchandise each year to ORT. Their plundered shelves remain empty until the losses are discovered and are restocked, and their stores become less safe for their employees and their customers as the professional thieves, the "boosters," become more and more brazen. The second victim is the consumer; every person in America is victimized as prices are increased to cover the losses generated by ORT. The consumer is also the victim because, when those stolen goods reenter the marketplace after being tampered with, their safety is possibly compromised. Local, state, and federal governments are victimized, as the tax revenue base is eroded because the sales tax on the stolen merchandise was not realized, and the booster certainly does not claim the proceeds from selling boosted merchandise to the IRS.

ORT has been connected to some of the major issues facing the United States today: terrorism, illegal immigration, drug trafficking, and other homeland security issues. Some tentacles of ORT are connected to funding terrorism and impacting homeland security, but this issue is more of an economic problem for retailers and our communities than it is anything else. There are crimes associated with organized criminal enterprises woven throughout ORT. Money laundering, gangs, illegal immigration, and black marketing are just some of the legal challenges associated with ORT.

In typical shoplifting incidents, the perpetrator is someone who works alone and steals either for thrills or to get something that he or she will use. This person sometimes shoplifts while selecting items for which he or she intends to pay. The typical shoplifter steals one, two, or a few items generally for personal use. The typical shoplifter is very different from a booster, a thief who is involved in organized retail theft. A booster is part of a large, sometimes loosely, sometimes formally arranged network of thieves, "fences" (who buy from the boosters) and dishonest wholesalers and retailers who, in an organized hierarchical structure, steal from retail stores and eventually sell those items back to the public. Boosters often work together with other boosters. They will enter the store separately, and one may take the items and then later give them to the other booster, as in the scenario described earlier. Or one booster may intentionally take an item or two and then walk away from the targeted items, causing assets protection personnel to pursue that decoy booster while one or two others then go in and steal multiple items. In fact, in the earlier scenario, the young woman, if she was involved in the larger theft, could easily have been a decoy if she had "ditched" the lip gloss before leaving the store. The number of items stolen is another way in which boosters differ from the typical shoplifter. Whereas the typical shoplifter steals only a few items, a booster will go in and steal armfuls of targeted merchandise. They know they have an outlet for the merchandise they are stealing. Clearly, these items are not intended for personal use, but rather for reselling to a fence; ultimately, the items find their way back to the public. Stealing is often a booster's full-time job and sole means of income. Some boosters make several hundred thousand dollars per year, tax free, own their homes, pay for their children's educations, and look like a typical suburban family. The booster will hit a number of stores on a typical day of stealing, going from one retailer to another to get all the products he or she intends to steal and then sell. Boosters steal hundreds of dollars of merchandise from one store and then repeat the same activity in four or five more stores that same day. Multiply the $832 in our previous scene by the five or six stores that hit that day, and we are talking about serious money—in this case, almost $5,000 for a day's "work." The booster may only receive 20% of the retail value, but any way you look at this scenario, $1,000 a day, tax free, is a pretty good income.

So, to whom do boosters sell the stolen merchandise? Who buys it from them?

Well, the next person in our illicit supply chain could be a "fence," or it could even be another retailer, usually one that is small and is generally a neighborhood store. The fence is not a retailer, but the person in an organization who buys all the things that the booster steals. The fence typically works with a number of boosters. The fence also works with people higher up in this illegal supply chain. The fence could then unload the merchandise in any of the following ways:

- Flea markets formerly were the ways fences would both sell their stolen goods as well as "market" to other illicit buyers that they were "in the business and had access to stolen product."
- Increasingly, Internet auction sites are more and more popular places for fences to sell their goods. The public shops these sites expecting to get a good deal, often not questioning the legality of the items they are purchasing. These marketplaces also serve as a way for fences to advertise to buyers and middlemen that they have certain illegally obtained items and can get more of them.
- Another way that fences sell their stolen goods is directly to buyers and middlemen. Sometimes, these buyers and middlemen are retailers, but often these criminals act as representatives for organizations that repackage the stolen items to sell them to illicit wholesalers.

Repackaging operations use a number of ways to "clean" the stolen items, making them as untraceable as possible back to their original retailers. These operations usually occupy about a 3,000 square foot space and often employ illegal immigrants to clean the items, removing any sticky security tags or price tickets and adhesive residue with lighter fluid or other solvents. They also alter lot numbers and expiration dates to make it harder to trace the origin and original destination of the items. Obviously, this activity can cause huge safety issues, from product tampering to the inability for a manufacturer to recall products to products losing their potency due to expired shelf life. Employing illegal immigrants is useful to these operations because what they are doing is illegal in every way. The government will have no record of the operation or even who worked there, since there is no documentation for the IRS or ICE. The cleaned merchandise is then often repacked into larger bottles or larger multipacks, and then packed into cardboard shipping boxes which appear legitimate to the untrained eye, as the cartons are even stamped with the legitimate manufacturer's logo. The "cleaner" the items are, the further out the expiration date, the higher the price that will be paid by the illicit purchaser.

The illicit purchaser could be a wholesaler who buys the stolen product and perhaps comingles it with illegally diverted products, counterfeit products, and even products legitimately obtained from the manufacturer. These wholesalers can be described as looking like an iceberg: we can see part of the huge chunk of ice sticking out above the surface of the water (the legal part of these operations), but there is a very large illegitimate business that is not easily seen lurking beneath the surface of the water. The part of the business this wholesaler conducts that is not readily seen is the purchase and sale of stolen products, counterfeit products, and products that have been illegally diverted. Illegal diversion occurs when products are purchased from a manufacturer for less than what they would normally be sold by the manufacturer because they are purchased under the pretense that they are intended to go to another country where they are then retailed for substantially less than they sell for in the United States. The diversion is illegal because a crime has been committed (false pretenses, altered documentation, etc.). Counterfeit products are those that were not made by the manufacturer who owns the rights to make the products, and these counterfeit products might very well contain hazardous ingredients. This unsavory part of the wholesaler's business (the part of the iceberg that lurks beneath the surface of the water) then gets comingled with the legitimate part of the wholesaler's business (the tip of the iceberg we see on top of the water), which is products purchased from the manufacturer in a legitimate business deal. The wholesaler then sells the comingled goods to unsuspecting retailers who can purchase the entire order of goods from the wholesaler for substantially less than they can purchase them for directly from the manufacturer.

Obviously, retailers also have a problematic role in this illegal supply chain. When a retailer knowingly buys products from a questionable source, whether or not they know the products they are getting are legitimate, they are making it possible for this entire illegal chain to remain in business. One of the reasons a retailer might be tempted to do business with a questionable wholesaler is the intense price competition in the retail market. If retailers can get an item at a lower price from a wholesaler than they can get it from the manufacturer, these retailers may choose to do so because they will make more money and be much more competitive even if they sell it at a very low price to the consumer. Retailers may claim that they have no knowledge of a wholesaler's illegal practices, but this isn't always true. When a retailer's purchase order with an illegitimate wholesaler includes contractual language that states that the retailer is not liable for any problems with the product that they get from the wholesaler, we have to suspect that there is knowledge or at least suspicion on behalf of the retailer regarding the legitimacy of the wholesaler's business practices and product safety. Retailers are taking a huge liability risk when they agree to sell questionably obtained products. Who knows how safe or unsafe these products may be? The adage probably holds true: You do get what you pay for. Retailers must hold themselves to a higher standard and refuse to do business with these questionable wholesalers. By doing so, the retailers are doing their part by refusing to again participate in this illegal supply chain.

What makes certain products more attractive to boosters than others? As in traditional retail environments, stores stock more of what sells well and less of what sells slowly. Likewise, boosters steal more of what they can sell faster and for a higher return against the full retail value. Items that are most popular with the public are also those most often stolen. Boosters sell things that are in high demand, things that are easy to resell, commodity-type items that are small and easy to move, as well as items that can be easily stolen in large quantities from a store or the supply chain. During the early part of the 21st century, items that topped the most stolen list included razor blades, film, batteries, infant formula, smoking cessation products, analgesics, and other over-the-counter pharmaceuticals. What made these items more attractive to the thief and not others? They are all relatively small items, which makes them easy to steal. All these items are readily available on store shelves. They are in high demand with consumers. And they are all easy to repackage, which makes them easier to sell back to retailers and to the public.

Today, however, the boosters have grown in both number and acts of thefts. The targeted products they choose to steal have also grown in assortment and diversity. If an item is good enough to be offered for sale to consumers, there is a market demand for it and therefore it is subject to be stolen. In the 1970s, leaders of ethnic organizations would meet at a restaurant in Providence, Rhode Island, every Monday morning. At that meeting, these leaders would agree on which geographical area their organizations would go steal from for the balance of the week. The ethnicity was various Central and South American countries, and the leaders might decide that the Peruvians were to go to Michigan and Ohio, the Ecuadorians to New Jersey and Pennsylvania, the Chileans to Maryland and Virginia, and so forth. They did this every week because they didn't want to "stumble" onto another gang's territory while that group was working it, and they didn't want the same faces in the same stores week after week. These groups targeted brand name apparel from department stores, and they sold the stolen goods through small shops in ethnic neighborhoods in big cities. Often, these shops were not known by the general public, and customers found out about them by word of mouth.

Organizations behind ORT vary in structure from very loose to the more traditional hierarchical structure involved in other types of organized crime. Ethnicity is still sometimes a factor in the organization, but ethnic origin is now as varied as citizens and noncitizens alike in America. There are Asian groups, Middle Eastern groups, Eastern European groups, Russians, South and Central Americans, etc. There also are nonethnic groups that are criminal enterprises engaging in this low-risk, high-reward criminal activity.

So, how did these groups get started, how have they grown, and how do they recruit the boosters to steal for them? Essentially, many of the groups started relatively small in number, and their leadership was simply inclined to criminal behavior. As they enjoyed early success in their stealing and fencing activities, they began to recruit others into their organizations because the rewards were attractive. Illegal immigrants joined the ethnic enterprises, and prisoners serving time for other criminal activity were recruited by organizations with tentacles in prisons during conversations occurring in exercise yards when the topic "what are you going to do when you get out" came up.

In the late 1980s and early 1990s, some of the mass merchant chains with stores around the country began to recognize the growing problem of ORT and began to take proactive steps to attack the issue. Small, very mobile teams of investigators were formed to ferret out this activity. At first, trying to stop it was like the little Dutch boy who put his finger in the dike to stop the flood as it felt like the teams were relatively ineffective in impacting these swarms of boosters and the organizations behind them. But soon a few successful cases occurred, some of the teams began to work together with each other (after all, this was a common enemy these competitive retailers were confronting), and they leveraged their success with state and federal law enforcement agencies. Although there was no formal training program in those early days, many of the leadership in loss prevention hired former law enforcement personnel with experience in conducting investigations, conducting surveillance, and resolving large multistate property crime rings. Those early efforts by retail loss prevention practitioners have evolved to the point where there are now formal training programs for selected ORT investigators, store-based loss prevention teams, and best practices by store operations in detecting, observing, and reporting evidence and incidents of ORT activity in the stores.

In the scenario at the beginning of this section, the loss prevention agent made some wrong choices. When the agent observed the older man with the grocery bag in the aisle merchandising the razor blades, he should have immediately gone to the selling floor to continue the surveillance without the cameras when he realized there were not enough cameras installed throughout the store to provide full video coverage of the selling floor. Had the agent done this, the teenaged girl would probably have been able to successfully steal the lip gloss. But given the loss of the lip gloss value compared to the loss of the razor blades, the agent obviously made the wrong decision.

It is not the intent of this section to be a training manual to teach loss prevention agents how to resolve the issue of ORT. Those training programs exist in many of the more forward-thinking and proactive retail loss prevention departments today, and experienced loss prevention consulting firms have developed some programs that can assist retailers in combating ORT.

However, it is necessary to point out that store loss prevention personnel should deal with persons suspected of engaging in ORT as professional boosters very differently than they would handle typical shoplifters. When dealing with a typical shoplifter, generally the store detective or loss prevention agent observes the shoplifter come in empty handed, look around, and take an item or two and conceal it on his or her person. The shoplifter might then select some other items for purchase but never declare the item that is concealed when he or she is at the point of purchase. This person pays for some items, but not the concealed one, and then leaves the store. The store detective stops the person at the exit (although policy and state statute may require different action to be taken), identifies himself or herself as security personnel, and then asks the shoplifter to come into the office to talk about what wasn't paid for. The security agent asks the shoplifter to come with him or her so that both the stolen products as well as the person can be identified. The security agent makes sure that he or she is following all applicable state laws and company policies and procedures while interviewing the detained suspect. This method is effective in prosecuting shoplifters but is not as effective or relevant to persons suspected of engaging in ORT as boosters.

The loss prevention agent can certainly follow the same procedure with a professional booster, but to what end? When a professional booster is sweeping product from shelves and peg hooks into his or her bags or pockets, it is vital that the loss prevention agent gathers as much evidence as possible so that he or she is not just stopping this incident, but is having an effect on the ORT criminal organization beyond that one thief among many. Some loss prevention agents have been trained to observe but not stop these individuals in order to see where they go when they leave the store. The key is to observe and report. Loss prevention agents should record the description of the individuals involved in the incident, as well as the vehicle make and model and plate number that the suspected thieves get into. Obviously, video recordings of these individuals will become very helpful in later proceedings, provided that the rules of custody for this evidence are understood and in place. This information should then be reported to law enforcement. Often, if reported to law enforcement as the theft unfolds, it may enable law enforcement to take immediate action, such as continued surveillance or even apprehension.

Someone who is trained may then make the decision to stop the thief upon exiting the store or, instead, to keenly observe and report for follow-up action by others. The objective when engaging in ORT investigation is to follow the money, go all the way up the snake to the extent you can. There is an old saying that the only way to kill a snake is to cut off its head. Well-trained investigators may communicate with other well-trained investigators about certain known boosters and their methods of operations. And, if they are trained, they may even follow a professional booster to a fencing location. But at that point their surveillance must stop unless they have been instructed by law enforcement and have the permission of their employer's general counsel. If they do continue their involvement because they have been directed by law enforcement and they have permission for the company's legal counsel, they do so "under color of law." That means that they have the same legal restrictions and obligations as sworn law enforcement has. It is, therefore, usually wiser to let law enforcement do their job while retail loss prevention investigators performs their responsibility representing the private sector and not sworn law enforcement.

Statutorily, there is no provision in any state's retail theft statute to continue the investigation of a retail thief outside the store. It is essential to work cooperatively with law enforcement when dealing with ORT boosters. If a loss prevention agent apprehends a booster, then he or she should ask the right questions but not expect to get the answers he or she is seeking. For example, who are you working for? Where were you intending to take this merchandise? Where was the last stop you made? Is there other stolen product in your car? If the booster says yes to that question, the LP agent cannot search the car. Law enforcement has to conduct the search of the car and only under the following circumstances: (a) with the permission of the owner of the vehicle or (b) if the contraband is in plain view or (c) with a search warrant or (d) incidental to a lawful arrest. All the LP agent's efforts will go down the drain if he or she conducts any part of the investigation illegally, which would include an illegal search and seizure.

It's extremely important for you to know the laws of your state that apply to the location where you are doing your job. It is also important to document any information learned and enter it into the case management system. If you have any store surveillance video that has captured images of the suspects and/or their vehicles, then it should be entered into case management system as well. Law enforcement, from the officer who responds to the call from the store to the prosecutor who tries the case to the judge who hears the case, must all be educated about this problem of ORT in order to treat this offender as the professional thief he or she really is. Otherwise, the offender will likely fall through the cracks in the criminal justice platform and simply be treated as just another shoplifter.

How can we educate the criminal justice system, all retailers, and the public in general about this very real and rapidly growing problem?

- We need new laws to help define and differentiate ORT from state statute addressing retail theft to enable us fight it and prosecute it as ORT—make these crimes have *real* consequences. Prosecutors and law enforcement need to be educated in how to investigate and prosecute the crimes. HR 3402 was signed into law in early 2006. Section 1105 of that bill reads: "*(This Bill)* Requires the Attorney General and the FBI to establish a task force to combat organized retail theft and provide expertise to the retail community for the establishment of a national database or clearinghouse to track and identify where organized retail theft type crimes are being committed." This is a good start inasmuch as it is recognition of a problem, but there is a lot more to be done on the legislative front both federally and within each state.

- Bringing this battle down to the individual store level is a critical step in an effective offense plan. Making an individual store less desirable to steal from (great customer service, good lighting, an educated local criminal justice system, etc.) will help to drive boosters elsewhere, seeking the path of least resistance. Utilizing technology which will assist in tracking stolen products from the store to their destination, in addition to effective video capture of the suspects, their theft acts, and their vehicles, will enable law enforcement to secure search and arrest warrants more easily and efficiently. Remember that we need to "follow the money," and tracking technology enables us to do that. We have to be diligent in analyzing data so that we can recognize patterns and then be quick to change and adapt new ways to counteract new theft methods.

- EAS systems are easy for professional boosters to defeat, but they are the forerunner for the next generation of technology. Some of the features of this emerging technology may include the ability of the detection systems at the store exits to read tags through foil-lined bags and defeat other methods that boosters use to avoid alarming EAS systems. Thieves are always going to get smarter, finding cracks in our systems. The bad guys stay up later at night than we do, figuring out ways to get around the systems that we put in place in the daytime. So technology always has to be evolving.

- We need to increase the presence of law enforcement in and around our stores and parking lots. Increase their knowledge of the issue of ORT so that we can fight this together. Equip them with the knowledge to fight this crime, much in the way they have been equipped to fight other crimes.

- We need to teach store employees, cashiers, and sales associates about ORT, what to look for, and about effective customer service. Train them to look for other seemingly innocent customers who may receive the 'hand off' if and when it occurs. Train them to notify law enforcement and train them to observe the details of the suspects. Train them not to put themselves in harm's way. Boosters can react violently sometimes, and no theft is worth life or limb.

- Although retailing is a competitive business, combating ORT requires that retailers work together. Boosters typically don't target just one retailer. Statistics have proven that if an organized retail theft ring is working a market area, then they will hit as many retailers in that area as they can.

The best defense against ORT is to develop a comprehensive plan. Good comprehensive plans are utilized effectively by some very different types of retailers. Some large store mass merchants, large department stores, regional grocery chains, national drug chains, and fashionable and trendy apparel specialty store chains have very effective comprehensive plans that work well in their stores. Components of the comprehensive plan include a trained loss prevention investigations team.

A well-known specialty chain developed such a team after management began to recognize that the company was being victimized by ORT. The team was trained to gather intelligence from the malls where their stores were located, to work with mall security and law enforcement to identify crews of boosters hitting the stores in the malls, to search for company merchandise being offered for sale on Internet auction sites, to look for their merchandise being sold in noncompany stores, and to understand the limitations of what they can and should do and what law enforcement is capable of doing. This chain provides store associate training and awareness which extends into providing intelligence support to the loss prevention investigations team. Store associates are trained to use an Incident Reporting

Software program that includes a section for ORT. Associates can record detailed information about each incident, including the day; time of day; number of associates on the floor; which manager was working; the size, color, and type of product stolen; area of store; number of customers in the store; as well as any other relevant information. Investigators used this information and began to notice trends such as which days and what time of day incidents were most likely to occur.

And, finally, another key component in a comprehensive program is a legal strategy to support the investigators' efforts in the apprehensions and prosecutions of ORT perpetrators. The legal strategy component is effective in educating prosecutors during the criminal proceedings, but it is even more effective in pursuing civil remedies through lawsuits against the ORT organizations. This strategy of aggressive civil penalties (damages, asset forfeitures, etc.) has driven some ORT organizations away from sending their boosters into the stores in this specialty chain. Chances are very good, however, that those boosters are still stealing somewhere. They will continue to seek retailer victims who are not as diligent in protecting themselves. This criminal displacement simply moves the theft elsewhere to the path of less resistance.

As long as there are stores selling merchandise, there will be some people who will be inclined to take that merchandise without paying the store for it. As long as there are people like that, the likelihood is great that some of them will steal in some type of organized manner. Because of this likelihood for continuing organized retail theft, ongoing diligence by the retail community will be essential to survival.

 P

Parking Area Crimes

Ralph Witherspoon

Parking lots and garages represent a fruitful hunting ground for robbers, rapists, auto thieves, and purse snatchers. While often lucrative, they also represent a huge potential legal liability for operators, plus damaging publicity if pictured on the evening news in connection with a horrible crime.

Because of their layout and construction, there is no "one size fits all" security program for lots and garages. The keys to security are

- Access control where possible
- Visibility (lighting and sightlines)
- Stewardship and control

To the extent that access can be controlled by the operator of the garage or lot, many criminals can be deterred or prevented from entering. This typically requires perimeter barriers such as fencing and/or walls at ground level. If walls and fences cannot be used, lesser demarcation of the lot boundaries with partial fencing, hedges, planters or shrubs, etc., can provide a psychological barrier to criminals and a clear indication of where the "private" property begins.

In many lots and garages, access to the garage can be controlled or closely monitored. A parking attendant can view the occupants of cars entering and leaving, and a closed-circuit television (CCTV) camera can record license numbers and drivers' faces—both major deterrents to criminals.

The threat to persons and property in covered/enclosed parking garages can be very high. To limit access to garages, ground-level doors away from any parking attendant should not be accessible from the exterior of the building. There should not be any openings in the building walls within 15 feet of the ground through which a person could enter.

Isolated garage floors and garage and lot locations often make effective surveillance or monitoring difficult; however, live and recorded CCTV monitoring can reduce the risk (*Note:* If the CCTV cameras are not monitored live—and instead only recorded for later review and prosecution—prominent signage should state this so that customers do not rely on cameras which they think are being monitored and will produce immediate help).

When CCTV is used, good-quality color cameras that can operate in low light, along with high-resolution color monitoring/recording systems, are essential. Black-and-white monitors offer poor detail definition, a critical issue when attempting to identify suspects or potential problems.

Adequate lighting not only helps people recognize and avoid dangers, but also in many cases deters criminals by creating in them the fear of detection, identification, and apprehension.

Interior garage lighting should be a minimum of six foot-candles (measured both vertically and horizontally) throughout the garage, 24 hours per day. Sunlight seldom enters garage interiors and cannot be relied upon for lighting. If the facility has a significant history of crime or a recent history of violent crime, a higher level of illumination may be needed.

Energy-efficient metal-halide lighting provides reasonable color rendition for CCTV and direct viewing. Interior walls and ceilings should be painted with a glossy or semiglossy white paint to increase light reflection. This also increases the ability of parkers to observe movement and potential threats. Pillars and ramp corners should be painted in contrasting colors for driving safety.

Where appropriate, the use of a parking lot attendant can also serve as a powerful deterrent, if the attendant is able to view the lot and be seen. However, if there is no CCTV for remote viewing on large lots, and with the attendant's booth facing out toward the street with his head often stuck in a book or portable TV, some attendants can't see much of anything and don't provide much, if any, security.

A key element of security in many surface parking lots is visibility, for employees, customers, and passers-by. Within the lot, trees and shrubs should not obstruct viewing. Tree branches and leaves should not be lower than 10 feet above the lot surface, and interior shrubs and bushes should not be higher than 18 inches above ground or curb so as not to obstruct vision or provide concealment for a robber or rapist.

A significant part of visibility is lighting. Lighting should enable parkers and employees to note individuals at night at a distance of 75 feet or more, and to identify a human face at about 30 feet, a distance that will allow them, if necessary, to take defensive action or avoidance while still at a safe distance. A minimum maintained illumination throughout open parking lots of not less than three foot-candles (measured vertically and horizontally) is recommended. This will also provide adequate illumination for driving purposes. Lighting at the entry/exit points should be at least 20 to 30 foot-candles for safety and security, and for adequate direct observation by employees or CCTV monitoring. Energy-efficient metal-halide lighting offers good color recognition.

Parking Lot Crimes and Other Problems

CAS, JHC

Use of the term "parking lots" does convey the nature of the problem to be addressed here, but more properly, the topic should be "Parking Environment Crimes and Other Problems" because not all parking is in "lots.." Parking environments are divided into three distinct parking facilities:

- Parking lots, which are outside surface parking areas, typically at grade level with the business or institution they serve, like the parking lots common around shopping centers.
- Parking ramps, which are typically multistory above-ground parking "garages" and may be
  - Free-standing structures, which may be a commercial entity in and of itself and accommodate or service many businesses including retailers and other enterprises, more often than not in a dense urban or downtown setting.
  - Adjacent or an abutment to and part of a shopping or other business complex, used by employees, customers, and other invitees as well as visitors to other commercial facilities in the immediate area.
- Subterranean parking garages, which may or may not be part of an above-grade ramp complex.

Too few loss prevention practitioners, especially those at the store level, have an understanding of or an appreciation for the inherent risks in parking environments and how those risks impact on the retailer's business. The security and LP industry concerns itself with two general areas of risks: crimes and torts which occur in the store's parking areas. The impact of crimes in the parking areas, which really has no direct bearing on the nature of the retail business, is the victim of a crime, who, in our modern times, may commence a legal action against the retailer if the retailer has any control over or responsibility for the parking area. Civil lawsuits as a result of crime victimization in a store's lot are commonly based on such theories as *inadequate security* or *negligence* in not providing sufficient security to prevent crimes, a condition which our society has come to expect when they park and walk in a store's parking area. The second risk is the threat of crime (or other tortious conduct) may scare or drive away customers who will shop at other locations where the general perception is that it's safer there.

Common Parking Lot Crimes

Crimes Against Persons in Parking Environments

1. Murder of a robbery victim
2. Murder connected with spousal abuse
3. Murder connected with violence in the workplace
4. Serious injury to victim caused by an assault by an armed robber
5. Rape in the victim's auto
6. Rape in the shrubbery/landscaping of the parking area or other remote areas of the parking complex
7. Abduction of a customer or employee
8. Armed robbery, no physical injury to the victim
9. "Mugging" (robbery) with injury
10. Purse snatching with injury to victim
11. Purse snatching without injury
12. Assaults
13. Indecent exposure to female customers and employees
14. Assaults on car owners who accidentally come upon a thief entering or inside their auto

Crimes Against Property in Parking Facilities

1. Auto theft
2. Theft of auto parts, such as batteries, wheels, emblems, etc.
3. Theft of auto accessory or after-market equipment inside the vehicle
4. Theft of packages and other personal property from the interior of autos
5. Theft of equipment, supplies, materials, and tools from trucks
6. Vandalism to autos, such as "keying" a car or truck, puncturing/deflating tires, etc.

Victims may, and do, sue stores, and those victims who do not sue tend thereafter to shop elsewhere. And they certainly share the story of their victimization with many other people.

Courts across the land have universally held that parking environments are "inherently dangerous" because of the concentration of wealth in terms of property which is easily sold on the street and the sheer remoteness and isolated areas of such environments, with limited foot traffic. Further, the very nature of the environment is tolerant of lone males wandering among the cars, presumably "looking for" their own vehicle. But some are looking for victims or objects of theft.

Other Problems in Parking Environments

1. Panhandling (begging)
2. Union organizing efforts
3. Solicitations for various causes
4. Unauthorized selling
5. Skateboarding
6. Teenagers or other unique groups who gather for social contact
7. Drag racing after hours

An interesting example of "solicitations" took place in Los Angeles in the 1970s when a Muslim mosque became active in distributing its paper *Mohamed Speaks*, which then was a centerpiece of the Black Muslim community. Their efforts to distribute the newspaper were focused on the Crenshaw Shopping Center. The young men dressed in black suits, white shirts, and ties were universally well groomed and were passionate about their faith. The paper was free, but there was an air of expectation for a donation for the "free" paper, and many customers began to complain to store management that they felt intimidated by these young men and reported they were becoming too aggressive. The customers further informed management they would not return if something wasn't done to shield them from the confrontations; they would shop elsewhere.

The security department was charged with gathering the necessary evidence to prove to the court the solicitors were threatening. Evidence was gathered and presented, and a restraining order was granted which denied these young men access to the parking lots. The problem was solved.

What Can Be Done at the Store Level?

Retail LP/Security practitioners aren't expected to be experts in parking environment security, but there are some basic principles everyone should be aware of. Such basics include

- Parking areas must be well illuminated. Some daily/nightly effort should be taken to check the lights, and if a lamp is burned out, it must be reported and replaced.
- Exterior CCTV cameras, conspicuously mounted, should monitor the parking areas. They need not be monitored at all times, but they should part of a system which records the activity in the lot.
- We recommend signage in the lots which state, essentially, the area is monitored by CCTV for the safety of all.
- Large parking areas require some form of patrol by security personnel, either by foot or motorized. Vehicles used for this purpose should be distinctively and conspicuously marked and be equipped with some form of flashing light and voice communication equipment.
- A policy must exist wherein any "parking lot incident" is memorialized and maintained by LP personnel; i.e., if a sales associate reports her battery was stolen during her shift, that must be reported to LP and a report made and filed. Such incidents are just as important as is the report of a shoplifting detention.
- Monthly LP statistical reports should always reflect the number of parking lot incidents so the frequency of the crime is perpetually monitored (for corrective action if deemed appropriate or necessary).
- Every incident of a criminal nature that occurs in the parking area must be reported to the police.
- The store should have an after-dark "parking area escort service" if requested by a female customer.
- Female employees leaving the store at night, at either the conclusion of their shift or upon store closing, should be escorted to the employee parking area or required/ encouraged to walk to the area in groups for their mutual safety.
- Designated employee parking areas must be illuminated as brightly as all other parking areas or, depending on geographical location, enjoy a greater level of lighting.

What Is the Store's Role If the Parking Areas Are Not Specifically Under the Control of the Retailer/Store?

Let's assume the store is in a mall, and the shopping center management is responsible for the common areas, including parking. Within reason, the store should nonetheless be aware of and concerned that the basic protection of the lots is in line with the points listed previously. We encourage an ongoing and regular meeting between store loss prevention and shopping center management, including the mall's security director, to review and discuss security in the parking areas and known incidents of criminal attacks, as well as any other behavior or conduct of concern. Records of such meetings should be maintained by the store. The store is paying a common area maintenance fee for the overall management of the mall, including security, and is entitled to have a voice in making the parking safe for its employees and customers. To abrogate this responsibility is not only a moral failure, but could be construed as tortious, under certain circumstances.

Case in point: A medium-size retailer was a tenant in a large strip center. Doors to the store were on opposite sides of the selling floor; that is, one set of doors opened onto the interior of the mall, and the second set of doors opened onto the surface parking lot that surrounded the mall. Shopping center management was responsible for the maintenance and security of the parking lots.

One night two teenage girls entered the store through the parking lot doors. After shopping, they exited the store and entered their pickup truck, which was parked approximately 75 feet directly in front of the store. Several other vehicles were clustered in the same area. As the driver attempted to close her door, a man appeared, seized the door, forced his way into the cab of the truck, and drove the girls to a remote location, where he sexually molested them. A lawsuit was filed against the shopping center and the store for maintaining an unsecured and dangerous place to shop and inadequate security.

Upon examination of the lighting at the center, it was determined to be below the Illuminating Engineering Society's minimum recommendations, hence inadequate. However, the store in question, upon recommendations made 5 years earlier by a security management consultant, had mounted extra lights to increase illumination in the immediate parking area outside the doors, shining into the lot. As a consequence, the suit against the store was dropped. The suit against the shopping center succeeded.

Performance and Development Review Process

Lawrence Schuck

When supervisory staff think of doing performance reviews, they often think of a time-consuming process and dislike the confrontations that often arise during the process. Those being evaluated sometimes view the process as one-sided and often see limited or no value in the process. There was a time in the not-too-distant past when it was acceptable for a retail loss prevention supervisor to do an employee's evaluation, call the loss prevention employee into the office, have the employee read the evaluation, and then ask the employee to sign it. The employee had little or no input. It was little wonder the employee felt the process was one-sided. When done correctly, the performance evaluation process can be both positive and productive for both employee and supervisory staff.

The employee is often the most valuable resource in an organization.(1) The performance review process for a retail loss prevention organization should be designed so that it requires the employee and supervisor to work together at formalizing a plan to enhance the performance of the employee. Enhanced performance leads to greater job satisfaction for the employee and improvement in the organization's performance. For that reason, the process should be more appropriately called a "Performance and Development Review Process."

There are five main objectives in any effective performance evaluation process. They are

1. Evaluate performance since the last performance evaluation.
2. Recognize the areas where the employee has demonstrated strong performance.
3. Identify and address those areas where the employee needs to improve.
4. Formulate a plan for improvement that is measurable.
5. Find ways to better utilize the employee's strengths.

If everyone involved follows a step-by-step process, all five objectives can be successfully attained, and the employee, the supervisor, and loss prevention organization will benefit.

Benefits of an Effective Process

To get people, whether management, supervisors, or employees, to buy into any process, they have to see some benefit from it. So let's start with the retail loss prevention employee.

A well-defined performance and development review process revolves around communication between the supervisor and the employee. The process will benefit the employee in two ways. First, it will benefit the employee by providing him with a clear understanding of what is expected and what needs to be done to meet those expectations.(2) During the process, the supervisor will discuss what specific performance factors the retail loss prevention employee will be evaluated on and what rating scale will be used. Second, it will also allow the employee an opportunity to discuss aspirations and get support and/or training needed to fulfill those aspirations.

The supervisor also benefits from the process in three ways. First, the process establishes a means for forming a more productive relationship with the retail loss prevention staff. Second, it provides an opportunity to clarify the expectations the supervisor has of the employee. Third, the process can provide a means to clarify the relationship between effective performance and the potential for promotions or merit increases.

The retail loss prevention organization stands to benefit in two important ways. First, the process will assist in identification of training and development needs to better enable employees to work toward the organization's goals. Second, the process will assist in identification of employee potential so career development plans can be formulated. Many companies keep a list of where employees rank in the organization based on their evaluations. When opportunities for promotion open up, the evaluation results are weighed into the decision-making process. Third, the process can also serve as documentation in cases where employees are ultimately dismissed for poor performance.(3)

What Performance Gets Measured

Every employee position in the retail loss prevention organization should have a job description. The job description should detail the tasks the job holder is expected to undertake and how the job contributes to the overall mission of the organization. The Performance and Development Review form should define performance standards for the tasks associated with each employee's job description. Therefore, the performance review factors will vary depending on the various tasks performed by the different occupations and levels of management.(4) The first line supervisor's performance factors will differ from those of the loss prevention officer, the performance factors for the loss prevention officer will differ from those of the investigator, the investigator's performance factors will differ from those of the secretary, and so on.

The factors used to measure performance should focus on results and be based on observable behavior. Action verbs should be used to describe the desired behavior. Table P-1 illustrates a few performance factors that could be used on a Performance and Development Review worksheet form for the loss prevention officer in a retail establishment.

The Six-Step Performance Review Process

An effective Performance and Development Review process in a retail loss prevention environment is designed around a six-step process. Those steps are shown in a circular diagram (see Table P-2) because the steps must be taken in order, and like any process, it is ongoing. The process should be done every year or more often if needed, as each individual's circumstances require. There will be more discussion on that part of the process later.

Step 1: Prepare Employee for the Review

The process should not be a surprise to the employee being evaluated. Contact the employee and arrange a time and date to meet to start the process. It is very important to make sure the supervisor keeps the appointment. Not keeping the appointment can send a signal that the process is not important.(5)

Give the employee being evaluated a copy of the Performance and Development Review worksheet. The worksheet will list the performance factors he will be evaluated on. If there will be any additional performance factors discussed in addition to the standard factors, they should be listed on the copy provided to the employee. Explain to the employee that he is to perform a self-evaluation on his performance during the period from his last evaluation forward to that date. In most cases, that time frame will be approximately 1 year. It should be

Table P-1 Loss Prevention Officer Performance Factors

FACTOR	TASK	RATING
JOB KNOWLEDGE	Knowledgeable of job expectations	
	Demonstrates knowledge of legal requirements related to position	
	Conducts effective building and facility security checks	
	Demonstrates good knowledge of policies and procedures	
APPEARANCE	Consistently exhibits a professional appearance	
	Demonstrates good personal grooming	
	Consistently conforms to dress code required for assigned duty	
COMMUNICATION SKILLS	Effectively expresses thoughts verbally	
	Effectively interacts with fellow employees	
	Establishes and maintains constructive rapport with citizens	
	Demonstrates being a good listener	
INVESTIGATIVE SKILLS	Consistently recognizes suspected criminal activity	
	Conducts effective investigations	
	Utilizes proper evidence collection and preservation techniques	
	Takes detailed statements from suspects/witnesses	
REPORT WRITING SKILLS	Demonstrates ability in completing proper forms	
	Completes reports in timely manner	
	Completes reports thoroughly and accurately	
	Submits well-written reports and correspondence using proper grammar and spelling	

explained to the employee that he will be rated on how he typically performs in the retail loss prevention environment, not how the employee performs compared to other employees.

Make expectations clear as to what the employee is to do with the forms. Encourage the employee to make notes on the form and write the rating somewhere near each performance factor. If a rating scale will be used, provide the employee with the rating scale. Review the rating scale to make sure the employee understands the definition of each rating. Keep the process simple by making the rating scale easy to understand. Table P-3 and Table P-4 provide examples of rating scales used by several organizations.

Once the process is explained to the employee, agree on a place, date, and time to meet again to go over the self-evaluation part of the Performance and Development Review form, as well as the form you will have completed. Be sure to allow at least 7–10 days for completion of the forms. To allow more time than that can result in procrastination on the part of the employee or supervisor. Sufficient time should be allowed for both the supervisor and the employee to do their evaluations without rushing through it. The key to this step in the process is educating the employee on the process and getting the employee to participate.

Step 2: Complete the Performance and Development Review Forms

Before starting the Performance and Development Review form, the supervisor needs to do three things. First, review the employee's last performance review. Check to see if the employee has taken action to improve in the areas where improvement was needed. Check to see if the short-term goals listed by the employee have been achieved. Has progress been made toward long-term goals?

Table P-2 The Performance and Development Review Process

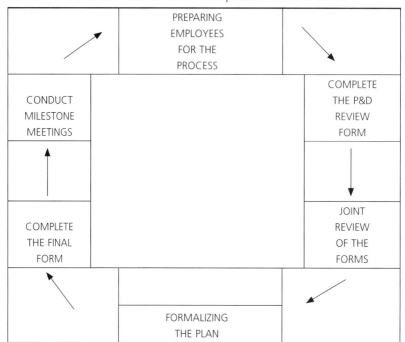

Table P-3 Example of Simple Rating Scale

RATING	DEFINITION
UNSATISFACTORY	CONSISTENTLY FAILS TO MEET EXPECTATIONS REQUIRED OF THE POSITION
NEEDS IMPROVEMENT	OCCASIONALY MEETS EXPECTATIONS BUT NEEDS TO DO SO MORE CONSISTENTLY
MEETS EXPECTATIONS	CONSISTENTLY MEETS EXPECTATIONS OF THE POSITION
EXCEEDS EXPECTATIONS	FREQUENTLY EXCEEDS EXPECTATIONS OF THE POSITION

Table P-4 Example of Rating Scale with Points

POINTS	RATING	DEFINITION
1	UNSATISFACTORY	CONSISTENTLY FAILS TO MEET EXPECTATIONS REQUIRED OF THE POSITION
2	NEEDS IMPROVEMENT	OCCASIONALY MEETS EXPECTATIONS BUT NEEDS TO DO SO MORE CONSISTENTLY
3	MEETS EXPECTATIONS	CONSISTENTLY MEETS EXPECTATIONS OF THE POSITION
4	EXCEEDS EXPECTATIONS	FREQUENTLY EXCEEDS EXPECTATIONS OF THE POSITION

Second, the supervisor should review the incident file kept on the employee. Supervisors should establish an incident file for all retail loss prevention employees.(6) Some supervisors keep an employee journal where they make notations on specific events that involve the employee. The incident file or journal should contain both positive and negative documentation of the employee's performance.

The incident file is very important. It provides the documentation to support the rating. Employees should be encouraged to also keep an incident file or journal. The employee should use it during the self-evaluation process. When they are reviewing information in the incident file, it is important that the supervisor and the employee are reviewing only the performance taking place since the last evaluation.

Third, the supervisor should review some of the most common problems encountered when conducting performance reviews. One common problem is rushing through the process. Do not wait until the day before the scheduled meeting with the employee to start completing the review form. Another common problem is evaluating personalities instead of performance. Be aware of your feelings toward each employee and avoid being biased. Refrain from using the word "weakness" when referring to a performance area where improvement is needed.

Now the supervisor is ready to complete the Performance and Development Review worksheet in preparation for the meeting with the employee. The worksheet will list the performance factors the employee is being rated on as well as the various task associated with that performance factor. The supervisor should rate the employee on each performance factor based on how the employee typically performed since the last review. If a point system is used in conjunction with the rating scale, the point total should be noted after each performance factor. If just the rating is used, note it after the performance factor. The supervisor should feel free to make notes on the form for support of the rating or for discussion with the employee. This form should be considered a worksheet. The final form will be cleaned up and not have all the notes.

If a point system is used, the points should then be totaled up and divided by the number of performance factors to produce an average rating. The overall average will indicate the employee's overall performance rating. Tenths of a point should be rounded off on the scale as follows:

1. 49 and below = UNSATISFACTORY
1. 50 and above = NEEDS IMPROVEMENT
2. 49 and below = NEEDS IMPROVEMENT
2. 50 and above = MEETS EXPECTATIONS
3. 49 and below = MEETS EXPECTATIONS
3. 50 and above = EXCEEDS EXPECTATIONS

A system may be used wherein each factor's rating stands alone and there is not an average used. Many times the size of the retail loss prevention organization dictates the method used. The important point is not to get too hung up on the numbers game. The objective is to evaluate performance and communicate to the employee what he can do to make himself a greater asset to the organization. It is important to remember that the performance review process is about managing and improving performance in the retail loss prevention environment and not about completing forms (7)

The last item to complete prior to meeting with employee is the area where the supervisor will list first areas of strengths and then areas where improvement is needed. There should be two or three areas listed for each. The area where strengths have been demonstrated is listed first so it can be discussed first. You want to reinforce the positive performance before starting a discussion on what areas the employee needs to work on before the next performance review.

After completing the performance and development review form and prior to discussion with the employee, be sure to give consideration to the employee's reaction to those ratings where there may be disagreement. Make sure you have proper documentation to support your rating for those areas that may generate unfavorable reaction by the employee. Disagreement usually results from the employee thinking he is meeting expectations when he is not. The performance and review process is designed to correct that situation.

Step 3: Joint Review of the Evaluation Forms

There are steps the supervisor can take to make the employee feel more at ease when the time comes for the employee and supervisor to meet for review of the Performance and Development Review forms. If possible, schedule the meeting in a conference room or location other than the supervisor's office. It is important to have the meeting on neutral ground. The location should afford privacy and be free from interruptions such as telephone calls and other employees barging in. Cell phones should be put on vibrate and not answered unless there is an emergency. The process is important and should be taken seriously.

The supervisor should state the purpose of the meeting. It should be made clear from the start that only the performance and development review will be discussed during the meeting. There should not be any discussion of salary issues. If the employee has questions or wants to discuss salary issues, arrangements should be made to do so at another time. The focus of this meeting needs to be on the employee's performance.

Start the process by reviewing the last Performance and Development Review with the employee. If the organization's Performance and Development Review includes a place for goals, review them as well. Did the employee accomplish the short-term (1-year) goals? Was significant process made toward long-term (5-year) goals? Did the employee take the steps planned for improvement in the last review?

The supervisor should also explain to the employee that both will review each performance factor one at a time. Do not exchange the performance factor worksheets. That can be done later. *Let the employee go first* by asking what rating he assigned to the first performance factor. The supervisor should encourage the employee to explain how the rating was decided on. This is an excellent opportunity to let the employee talk about himself. The supervisor then explains what rating he gave for the same factor and why. The supervisor should avoid using the term "weakness" when pointing out an area where improvement is needed. Documentation should be used by both to support the rating in cases where a disagreement arises. As both parties work their way through the performance factors, they can make notes on their worksheets. The supervisor should let the employee do most of the talking. A lot can be learned by being a good listener in this setting. The supervisor will be responsible for keeping the focus on the task at hand.

When a performance factor is reached where the rating is UNSATISFACTORY or NEEDS IMPROVEMENT, there should be discussion by both the employee and the supervisor as to why that situation exists and what can be done to help the employee improve. This process is designed to open up communication between the employee and the supervisor. It is an excellent opportunity for both to clarify expectations each has of the other.

It is not all that unusual for the employee's self-rating to be lower than the evaluator's. When ratings are not close, there should be discussion to point out why that might be. Documentation kept in the employee's incident file or journal should be referred to in an effort to support the rating. Once all the performance factors have been reviewed and the ratings on each discussed, the overall rating should be agreed on.

The supervisor and the employee should then review the two or three areas where each feels there has been strong performance demonstrated and where improvement is needed. Once again, let the employee go first. The employee should review the areas where he feels he demonstrated an area of strength. An example might be a loss prevention officer who feels investigative skills is an area of strength. The supervisor would encourage the employee to explain why he feels that way. The supervisor then reviews the areas he feels is an area of strength. It would not be unusual for the supervisor to have the same areas listed. The same process is followed with the two or three areas where each feels improvement is needed. These same areas should already have been discussed while working through each performance factor. Doing it again at this point sets the stage to formulate a plan for development of the employee. The important part of the exercise is for quality communication between the employee and the supervisor that will clarify expectations each has of the other.

Step 4: Formalizing a Plan

Now that the employee and the supervisor have identified two or three performance factors where the employee needs improvement, they can both put together a plan with a goal of raising the employee's performance from NEEDS IMPROVEMENT to MEETS EXPECTATIONS. If the employee's performance is rated at MEETS EXPECTATIONS or better in all performance factors, two or three areas can still be picked where the employee can strengthen the MEETS EXPECTATIONS performance or elevate it to the EXCEEDS EXPECTATIONS level of performance.

The plan developed by the employee and supervisor should include actions that can be implemented by both and designed to improve the employee's performance in each of the specified factors. Those actions should be measurable so that each can review the plan during the course of the year to make sure a sincere effort is being made and the employee's progress is on track for improvement. An example of development actions that can be implemented are as follows.

The Loss Prevention Officer is rated NEEDS IMPROVEMENT in the area of Job Knowledge. The plan could require the employee to take training related to increase job knowledge in retail loss prevention, either in-house or through an outside agency (college or career training institution). The supervisor's commitment to the plan would be to locate retail loss prevention training that is available, secure funding for it, and/or arrange time in the work schedule for the employee to attend the training. The expected actions of each are measurable and easy to monitor for progress.

If the performance and development review process in place has a section for short-term and long-term goals, they should be discussed at this time as well. Both the short-term (1-year) and long-term (5-year) goals should be career-related goals that the employee hopes to accomplish. Examples of short-term goals would be to attend some specialized loss prevention training of personal interest to the employee or complete the last couple of classes needed for degree work at a college. Examples of long-term goals might be to get promoted to a supervisory position or complete work on a master's degree. The supervisor can play an important part in assisting the employee with both short-term and long-term goals. This area is also important for the development of the employee.

Once this portion of the process is completed, the supervisor should explain to the employee that he will be transferring the results of their review, with their plan for improvement, onto a final Performance and Development Review form. It is that final form that goes into the employee's Personnel File and gets forwarded to the human resources department. A date should be agreed on for the supervisor to meet back with the employee for the employee's review of the finalized form. The supervisor should allow sufficient time prior to the next planned meeting date for completion of the final form. This is also an excellent opportunity to seek comments from the employee on his thoughts about the performance review process.

Step 5: Complete the Final Form

Now that the meat of the performance review process has been completed, the plan agreed upon by both should now be transferred from the worksheet to the final form that will be filed with the human resources department. A copy of the completed form will also be placed in the employee's personnel file. The final form can take whatever design the organization chooses to use. It should be typed or computer-generated so it is neat and legible. The supervisor should meet with the employee again and allow him to review the final form.

The final form should contain the following information:

- All the performance factors reviewed should be listed. There should be a space next to each factor for the employee's rating and a space for supporting comments for that rating. (See Table P-5 for an example)
- The form may have a place for the employee to list short-term and long-term goals.
- There should be a section of the form reserved for the employee to add his plan for improvement in those factors agreed on, as well as a section for the supervisor to add what actions will be taken to assist the employee in his improvement efforts.
- The form should have a section that will allow the employee to write in his comments about the performance review process. This area will also be where the employee can add comments if he disagrees with any ratings and why.
- There should be a place for the employee and the supervisor to sign and date each page of the form.

Table P-5 Example of Performance Factor Section on Final form

PERFORMANCE FACTOR	RATING	SUPPORTING COMMENTS
DECISION MAKING	MEETS EXPECTATIONS	Makes sound decisions based on utilization of all information available at the time. Will seek advice of others before making decisions.
CARE OF EQUIPMENT	EXCEEDS EXPECTATIONS	Keeps equipment in excellent condition. Orders equipment when needed. Updates inventory in timely manner.
COMMUNICATION SKILLS	MEETS EXPECTATIONS	Communicates effectively with public and other loss prevention officers. Utilizes correct grammar in oral communication

The employee should be given a copy of the completed, signed form. The supervisor should attach his worksheet used to his copy of the final form and place it in the employee's incident file. It will be used as a reference during the course of the next review period and when training opportunities arise.

Step 6: Conduct Milestone Meetings

"Milestone meetings" should be arranged periodically throughout the year to review the retail loss prevention employee's progress at reaching goals and taking steps agreed upon to improve performance. Ideally, the milestone meetings should take place quarterly or at a minimum of twice a year. The meetings do not need to be of a formal nature but should be documented by the supervisor. The meeting can be done over a cup of coffee or during a visit with the employee in the supervisor's office. The important aspect of conducting the milestone meetings is to let the employee know you take his development serious enough to check on his progress. It also affords an excellent opportunity to monitor training agreed upon or for the employee to discuss any new concerns or problems he might have.

Summary

Conducting performance appraisals can be productive for both the employee and management in any retail loss prevention organization if they are thought of as a developmental tool. The time the employee and supervisor spend together to review the employee's performance should provide an excellent opportunity for both to communicate and clarify expectations each has of the other. This is especially important in the retail environment where performance directly affects the organization's bottom line.

Performance appraisals or evaluations should be done as often as needed and at least once a year. They should be a review of the employee's performance since the last appraisal or evaluation. Some keys to the process would be for the supervisor to explain it to the employee; encourage participation from the employee; review and evaluate performance, not personality; and document positive performance as well as negative performance. Effective performance and development reviews are part of a continuing process all retail loss prevention organizations should be using to increase the value of the most important asset—their employees.

References

(1) Sachs, R.T. (1992). *The productive appraisal*. New York: American Management Association.
(2) Fisher, M. (1996). *Performance appraisals*. London: Kogan Page Limited.
(3) Sachs, R.T. (1992). *The productive appraisal*. New York: American Management Association.
(4) Fisher, M. (1996). *Performance appraisals*. London: Kogan Page Limited.
(5) Ibid.
(6) Ibid.
(7) Ibid.

Pharmacy LP Investigations

J. Patrick Murphy

Introduction

The operation of a pharmacy is one of the most complex businesses in retail. The pharmacy provides critical patient care that requires a special level of customer service. Customers visiting a pharmacy are comforted by seeing the same pharmacists and drug technicians because this is truly a relationship business. While the customer's interaction is brief, the operation, as a whole, is a complex machine that is full of opportunity for shrinkage and theft.

For the loss prevention practitioner, the pharmacy can be an intimidating and even unfriendly place to work. My observations over the years is that knowledge of the operation, and therefore knowledge of the causes of shrink, can be gained only by being immersed in the pharmacy itself. Some loss prevention department staff are required to become certified pharmacy technicians in an effort to familiarize them with everything from the filling process to potential drug interactions. It is a highly technical business that is closely regulated by the Drug Enforcement Administration (DEA). It is a business of trust that a customer builds with the pharmacy staff. Most importantly, it is a business that cannot afford mistakes in the prescription filling process. Misfilling a prescription can be extremely harmful to the patient and could ultimately cause death.

What is important to understand about pharmacy shrinkage is that the traditional areas for loss are comparable to other retail sectors, but there are many more additional opportunities for shrink through insurance accounting issues, returning expired drugs for credit, acquisition costs of pharmaceuticals, LIFO inventories, and an endless list of other, more subtle areas. With the pharmacy of a typical drug store generating about half the sales of the entire store, shrinkage is critical from a financial standpoint. The twist that makes shrink wholly different in this case is that the shortage could be medication.

The true depth of internal thefts is unknown but pharmacy shrink is comparatively low to the rest of the store. Beneath the surface of that shrink, though, lies an unfathomable thirst for pharmaceutical narcotics bought on the street. In 2005 a Reuters report cited the National Center on Addiction and Substance Abuse at Columbia University survey that showed that more Americans were abusing controlled substances than cocaine, hallucinogens, inhalants, and heroin combined. According to that same Reuters article, the number of prescription drug abusers doubled from 1992 to 2003 to nearly 15 million.

A 100-count bottle of OxyContin 80 mg (street named Oxy's, OC's, Killers, Poor Man's Heroin, and Hillbilly Heroin), the brand name of a powerful prescription pain medication, has an average street value of about $8,000, or $80 per tablet. A 500-count bottle of hydrocodone/acetaminophen 5/500, the generic name of another prescription pain medication with multiple brand names, the most common being Vicodin, has a value of ab out $2,500, or $5 per tablet.

Auburn University's Harrison School of Pharmacy conducted a study in July 2004 that reported approximately 10% of pharmacists become chemically impaired at some point in their professional career. The University of Georgia in 2002 reported that 40% of the pharmacists they surveyed voluntarily admitted to taking a regulated prescription substance without a prescription, and 20% admitted to repeated use.(1)

Loss prevention's role in the investigation of drug loss due to theft is a highly specialized combination of art and science. Shrink causation as a whole is deeply rooted in accounting and may not be ascertainable only at the store level. Shrink reduction in the pharmacy must be attacked from a corporation standpoint and not left to the imagination of only those at store level.

The Growing Addiction Problem

It is estimated that 8–12% of healthcare workers have substance abuse problems. Furthermore, 11–15% of pharmacists, at some time in their career, are confronted with alcohol and/or drug dependency problems, and the median age of recovering pharmacists is 43 years.(2)

Drug abuse has become a national health epidemic among young people. Diverted pain medications are widely sold across the United States and are second only to marijuana in illicit sales. The quantity of pharmaceuticals diverted through theft from legitimate sources, particularly pharmacies, is approximately 6.8 million dosage units (excluding liquids and powders) each year.(3)

According to the 2004 National Survey on Drug Use and Health, approximately 3 million persons aged 12 or older had used OxyContin nonmedically at least once in their lifetime. This is a statistically significant increase from the 2.8 million lifetime users in 2003.(4)

A questionnaire about OxyContin was included in the 2006 Monitoring the Future Study for the first time. During 2005, 1.8% of 8th graders, 3.2% of 10th graders, and 5.5% of 12th graders reported using OxyContin within the past year. During 2004, 1.7% of 8th graders, 3.5% of 10th graders, and 5.0% of 12th graders reported using OxyContin within the past year.(5)

During 2004, 2.5% of college students and 3.1% of young adults (ages 19–28) reported using OxyContin at least once during the past year. This is up from 2.2% and 2.6%, respectively, during 2003.(6)

Primer on Controlled Drugs

A *controlled* (*scheduled*) drug is one whose use and distribution is tightly controlled because of its abuse potential or risk. *Controlled* drugs are rated in the order of their abuse risk and placed in *Schedules* by the Federal Drug Enforcement Administration (DEA).

- *Schedule I:* Drugs with a high abuse risk. These drugs have *no* safe, accepted medical use in the United States.
- *Schedule II:* Drugs with a high abuse risk, but also have safe and accepted medical uses in the United States. These drugs can cause severe psychological or physical dependence. Schedule II drugs include certain narcotic, stimulant, and depressant drugs.
- *Schedule III, IV, or V:* Drugs with an abuse risk less than Schedule II. These drugs also have safe and accepted medical uses in the United States. Schedule III, IV, or V drugs include those containing smaller amounts of certain narcotic and non-narcotic drugs, antianxiety drugs, tranquilizers, sedatives, stimulants, and non-narcotic analgesics.(7)

There is not a state or federal requirement that a pill-to-pill perpetual inventory be kept of all narcotics. Narcotics are grouped by class of 2 through 5 and are represented as here: CII, CIII, CIV, CV (see Table P-6). CII drugs are the most addictive and are generally pain medication. All drugs are regulated by the DEA, but CII is the only drug class that the DEA closely regulates and monitors as far as ordering and dispensing. OxyContin, as mentioned previously, is a CII.

Theft of Controlled Drugs

Basic Pharmacy Inventory

Drugs, just like clothes on a rack, are simply merchandise items as far as inventory accounting is concerned. Pills come from the manufacturer in bottles of 100 or 500 or even 1000, and liquids are usually shipped in bottles containing 480 milliliters (1 pint) or 960 ml (2 pints).

Table P-6

C I	C II	C III	C IV
Marijuana	oxycodone (Percodan®),	Tylenol #3	alprazolam (Xanax®),
Heroin	methylphenidate (Ritalin®),	hydrocodone with acetaminophen (Vicodin®),	Chlordiazepoxide (Librium®)
LSD	dextroamphetamine (Dexedrine®).	diazepam (Valium®),	
Ecstasy	Morphine	Benzphetamine (Didrex®)	

Controlled drugs are on the shelves with the other drugs and are in alphabetical order. There is not a federal or state requirement to keep the CII drugs under lock and key; therefore, they can be dispersed (kept on the shelves). Retail chains will generally maintain the CIIs under lock and key, but that is a company requirement and not a mandate by administrative order. Dispersing the CII drugs has a distinct advantage when considering loss mitigation against burglary or robbery. If kept in a locked drawer, all the most theft-prone drugs are simply in one place. There are specially made drug safes, but they are normally used in hospitals and require dual control. These are simply impractical for a pharmacy due to its size and the staffing requirements needed to manage its use.

The inventory replenishment/ordering is fairly basic: Each drug has a specified quantity on the shelf that is based on the volume of sales for that item. As prescriptions are filled, the physical and book inventory are decremented. When that quantity meets a specified threshold, more is ordered (automatically or manually) to replenish the stock. It is the common min/max concept. In a perfect world, it would be a perfect system.

Most drugs have a "name brand" product and a generic equivalent. As an example, Ritalin© is also sold under the generic as methylphenidate. While both are chemically the same, generic brands are manufactured by various companies and are generally less expensive than the name-brand product. Some insurance plans will not allow dispensing name-brand products if a generic is available, so doctors must designate that the prescription be "dispensed as written" or DAW.

The significance of this basic environment (brand versus generic) is that it allows for the appearance of shortages when in actuality one was probably substituted for another. These false variances would only cause investigative time to be spent needlessly. There are times when pharmacists change the prescribed medication to generic because the name brand is out or the customer's insurance plan will pay only for generic and the doctor wrote for name brand. This is a common practice, but once the prescription is entered into the computer for generic, the inventory will be adjusted accordingly. If the record is not changed in the pharmacy system to properly reflect the correct medication dispensed, it will create "paper" variances. These factors and others make the detection of theft extremely challenging. Without an internal or commercially available inventory variance software, identifying theft is nearly impossible. As with any enterprisewide system, it would be impossible to investigate all shortages that are detected by a variance software. This truly creates an investigative process that deals with only "high" variances that surpass a certain threshold. Defining "high variance" is different for nearly every store.

Once Filled

Once the prescription is entered into the computer, the medication is removed from the shelf and staged for the pharmacy tech or pharmacist to fill. The prescription is filled, bagged, and placed in a "will call" bin. This process can be repeated as many a 1,000 times a day or more, and in the 24-hour stores, it's repeated at all hours.

From an inventory accounting standpoint, the filled prescriptions are still considered to be in the physical inventory and are not relieved from inventory until they are rung through a register. Ideally, this would be accomplished through a bar-coding system of the bag's label that was created by the pharmacy system. When the register transaction is completed, the inventory is relieved. This creates an end-to-end transaction process. This, too, depending on the system, assists in maintaining a proper stock amount so that the pharmacy does not run out of that particular drug.

Point of Sale

The final step of the sales process is at the register. This point provides the means to use subterfuge to pass stolen drugs and, more frequently, presents the opportunity to fail to properly record a transaction and steal cash. The cash register is an enormous point of theft of cash because the sales are predominantly insurance co-pays that are even dollar amounts such as $10, $20, etc. Prescription bags have large labels attached to them which include literature for the drugs. Customers would not be suspicious of not receiving a register receipt and, as such, the cashier would not need higher level math skills to manipulate a register. The No-Sale function on a pharmacy register can prove to be disastrous if not properly managed.

Register manipulations through voids of any kind and refunds are equal opportunity offenders. Refunding a prescription is rare, but the highest dollar merchandise in the store can be found near the pharmacy. Cash register exception reporting must be fine-tuned for the pharmacy. The number of transactions is much lower than the front end, but they are, by average, much higher average transactions. A successful search for theft tracks can be accomplished only if the pharmacy sales transactions are separated from the rest of the store. Their transactions are unique and would skew any reporting system if included within the store as a whole.

Many POS systems are tied to the pharmacy dispensing system to maintain an accurate perpetual inventory. Rigorous enforcement of policy and procedure will always act as a deterrent. However, work flow in a pharmacy tends to break down those standards during peak pickup times. This is especially true in high-volume pharmacies.

Return to Stock

The desired final destination for all filled prescriptions is in the customer's hands. Surprisingly, many prescriptions are never picked up, and the medication must be returned to the shelves. This process is accomplished through the pharmacy management system to correct the inventory accuracy. The actual bottle or vial is placed back in the location from which it was filled and can be used again to fill later prescriptions. It is a violation of law to combine the contents of a returned prescription with the contents of what is on the shelf. The shelf contents may have a different manufacturer or a different lot number, and therefore the vial or bottle is placed on the shelf. This practice allows for easy monitoring of how return-to-stock procedures are being handled. If there are no containers on the shelves from previously filled prescriptions, then the contents are being mixed.

The shrinkage and theft opportunity here is that a person can indicate that the prescription was returned to the shelves and then actually steal it. Again, this will create a variance in the system but does little to point an investigation in the right direction. Additionally, as with all theft, detection is severely limited if the subject steals small amounts of drugs at a time.

Drug Diversion Investigation

Stealing drugs is just a variation of a old theme. Whether with narcotics or some other medication, the pharmacy business is no different from any other retail sector as far as theft is concerned. The primary concerns are as follows:

1. Theft can be of a filled customer's prescription, either partially or in total.
2. Fictitious or forged prescriptions can be created, and the drug is then either passed or actually paid for at the register.
3. The automated or manual ordering system can be overridden to bring in more drugs than the order should be.
4. Large quantities of drugs are purchased through a licensed pharmacy and sold on the street. Part of the proceeds are used to purchase more drugs, and the rest of the money must be laundered through shell companies or other cooperating pharmacies. This is a multimillion dollar enterprise.

Diversion as described in point 4 is large-scale fraud. It is as pervasive as the trafficking in illicit drugs, and there is no centralized database that can be tapped into either on the state or federal level that would assist investigators to be proactive. Investigations begin through normal law enforcement activity and audits conducted by the DEA and State Boards of Pharmacy. Retail pharmacy chains have a great deal of exposure if diversion occurs within their stores. For that reason, operations and loss prevention must work hand in glove to properly monitor and investigate unusual drug movement. That is not to say that large pharmacy cases do not exist, but they are the exception and not the rule. Diversion of "small" quantities for sale will be the primary topic here.

It should be stated that diversion can occur with any drug and it does not necessarily have to be sold on the street. Drugs can be diverted to a privately owned independent pharmacy to be sold to defraud Medicare. A pharmacist who normally works at a hospital and is diverting drugs there can use the retailer's pharmacy as a method of replacing those stolen.

Second, there is theft of narcotics for personal use due to addiction, also known as "impairment." A percentage of healthcare workers are addicted to narcotics to which they have access. In the sense that theft is theft, there are some extenuating circumstances that should be discussed.

The scenarios are endless, but the major areas of vulnerability are fairly common. How could there be so much vulnerability in an area of such confined space? The truth is that the confined space adds to the opportunity for theft. A pharmacy, during high traffic times, is a beehive of activity with little time to notice the behavior of those around you.

Discovery Phase

Identification of potential drug loss is really simple inventory math. In its most basic description, the suspect must order more drugs than is being used to fill prescriptions. Diversion on a large scale is rare in a chain drug store because of the monitoring that takes place. Unusual ordering activity, P&L book inventory values spiking, and other areas might also give some insight to operations. Being able to detect a problem across numerous stores or across an entire chain would be impossible without software monitoring.

Following is the typical scenario that initiates an investigation. This is a generalization as every company has different methods to order drugs: A pharmacy orders two bottles of Drug A. The bottles contain 100 tablets each. The order can be entered manually through a handheld device, or it can be ordered through an automated replenishment system. Its source can be a company distribution center or an outside vendor. Two bottles of 100 tablets are sent to the store, where it is received and placed on the shelf. Over a period of time, the pharmacy fills prescriptions that equal 100 tablets. In a perfect scenario, there would be one bottle of 100 left (see Figure P-1). Either through auto replenishment or through manual orders, more bottles are ordered. To successfully steal drugs, the normal order quantity must be overridden in the system. Over time the number of bottles (or number of dosage units, in this case tablets) ordered begins to exceed the amount needed for filled prescriptions. A data mining program would begin to alert the investigator that the pharmacy was experiencing ordering activity that was not justified for the number for actual prescriptions. According to a report, over the period of time reviewed, the pharmacy had ordered 13 bottles (1300 dosage units) and had dispensed only 2 bottles (200 dosage units). Again, in our sample case, there should be 11 bottles of tablets on the shelf. A visual inspection of that specific drug reveals there are only 2 bottles. The next phase of the investigation begins.

Investigative Phase

Pharmacy drug loss investigations are initially highly confidential because the number of potential suspects includes anyone who has access to the pharmacy or who can potentially gain access to the pharmacy. The one saving grace of these types of investigations is that if the suspect is a pharmacy employee, the thief is usually going to be the person who is overriding the internal systems replenishment process. However, even with that group narrowed, it is unknown as to how the drugs are leaving the pharmacy. This could involve accomplices, multiple suspects, or outside vendors. Carrying out one bottle of pills is fairly easy to do on your person, especially if the pills are no longer in the bottle. Diverting large quantities may present a challenge but may be overcome by simply using the mail or commercial carrier to ship them home.

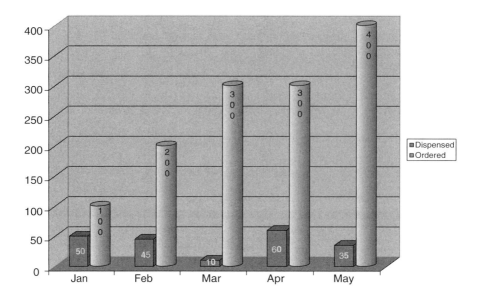

FIGURE P-1 The dark bars represent the number of tablets dispensed through prescriptions. The lighter bars represent the number of tablets (100 per bottle) ordered.

Once a loss has been determined, the DEA must be notified in writing within 1 business day. This can be accomplished by faxing a simple memo to the local DEA office regarding the initial reporting of a loss. Further investigation would be needed to confirm the actual loss. The DEA has very stringent administrative policies regarding loss reporting, but unless it is a special circumstance, the agency will not become actively involved. Every state also has a State Board of Pharmacy that regulates the licensing of the pharmacists and the pharmacy itself. The reporting requirements vary for each state, but, in general, there is no requirement to inform them of any investigation. However, it is a good practice to do so.

Narrowing the scope of the investigation to an individual takes a thorough review of store-level paperwork, schedules, or through any technological means. Again, the sensitive nature of the investigation generally prohibits the usual hands-on investigative techniques at the outset. Unless a trusted individual is cooperating with loss prevention, a great deal of work must be done before store opening or after store closing. To reinforce the sensitive nature of the investigation, a confidentiality agreement can be requested of any assisting employee. Breaking the confidentiality agreement would result in termination.

CCTV is almost paramount, and it may require multiple cameras. The layout of the pharmacy makes camera placement difficult, as an overhead view of the target drug severely limits view. Theft of one bottle of pills from shelf to pocket takes 2 seconds, but there is no need to review video unless there is a known shortage. This will required frequent, if not daily, reconciliations of that drug to determine if there is a shortage.

Investigative Scenario

Whether detected by automated means, audit, or tip, the investigative process can be very long. However, with proper preparation, these cases are likely to last no more than a few weeks.

When surveillance is begun, there is a period of time when it requires total confidentiality. Operations staff should be notified, however, because they may have to escort you in to the pharmacy during nonoperating hours. A licensed pharmacist must be present if you are entering the pharmacy. Entering the pharmacy is key obviously to physically recording the on-hand count of any targeted drugs. Using an automated system allows decisions to be made as to where to position a camera(s) to get the most likely theft.

The difficulty of these investigations is confirming a loss. An actual pill/liquid count is generally not necessary, as the theft usually involves full bottles. Nonetheless, it requires surveillance to determine where suspicious activity is occurring. In the multistore environment of retail drug establishments, there is not always the luxury of having stores closely clustered together. Pharmacies at great distances from the investigator's home may require a revised approach to complete the investigation. Retrieval of video may be an issue if a DVR is used. Using time-lapse VCR may be of more benefit if the investigation is being assisted by a member of store management.

If the amount of stolen drugs is high, it is very likely that that local authorities or the DEA will be involved. There may be requests to allow the thefts to continue to occur while their criminal investigation proceeds. This should obviously be reviewed by a corporate legal department.

Apprehension Stage

Closing out an investigation can occur with or without an apprehension. In both instances, several administrative items must be concluded.

If a company employee is apprehended, the usual internal steps should be taken regarding evidence and statements. Prosecution has several variations that are of interest. Drugs are generally inventoried at cost and may be converted to retail for physical inventory purposes. This sometimes presents a challenge to local authorities as to how to assess value. This is important because most jurisdictions will charge the individual with theft because there is no statue that provides for illegally taking of controlled drugs. This truly points out the value of having the DEA or State Board of Pharmacy involved even if just as an advisor. Those agencies can assist in the proper framing of criminal charges if necessary. In the case of a pharmacist and in some states a drug tech, the State Board of Pharmacy will hold an administrative hearing to determine the fate of the offender's license. More importantly, the state can sanction the license of the store's pharmacy too and levy a fine against the company. While the pharmacy's license could be revoked, it would be extremely rare in a chain drug store.

If a good relationship exists between the investigator and law enforcement, loss prevention should be allowed to complete the internal investigation. This allows the company to fulfill all obligations to protect company assets and at the same time still provides law enforcement with a prosecutable case. Collaboration is the key to successfully investigate any drug loss.

Drug Testing and Polygraph as an Investigative Tool

Because narcotics are involved, there are two additional investigative avenues afforded: drug testing and polygraph. Despite common belief, the use of the polygraph is still viable. The Employee Polygraph Protection Act of 1989 allows pre-employment and investigative use of polygraph. This is a thorny subject. Policy and procedure for its use should be well planned and distributed to all employees. There should be a formal review process in place that includes the legal department and loss prevention senior management for requesting the use of polygraph. It is recommended that the polygraph request is presented to the employee in writing. That request should outline why the examination is being requested and should outline both company policy and the Employee Polygraph Protection Act of 1988 (EPPA) for the employee's review. The employee should be allowed to keep a copy of this document as well. If considering the use of polygraph, keep in mind that neither refusal to take the polygraph nor the results of the polygraph can be used solely as justification for termination. The polygraph is simply a tool within the totality of the investigation. It has been my experience that it is rare when an employee actually appears for the process.

Note: While we believe the polygraph is a valuable investigative tool, as noted in the preceding text, the nuances of the EPPA are many and complicated, and the penalties for violation of its provisions can be severe. Therefore, before any mention of the use of the polygraph is made during an investigation, we strongly suggest competent legal counsel be consulted. *CAS/JHC.*

Employee Polygraph Protection Act(7)

Prohibitions

Employers are generally prohibited from requiring or requesting any employee or job applicant to take a lie detector test, and from discharging, disciplining, or discriminating against an employee or prospective employee for refusing to take a test or for exercising other rights under the act.

Examinee Rights

The act permits polygraph (a kind of lie detector) tests to be administered in the private sector subject to restrictions, to certain prospective employees of security service firms (armored car, alarm, and guard), and of pharmaceutical manufacturers, distributors, and dispensers.

The act also permits polygraph testing of certain employees of private firms who are reasonably suspected of involvement in a workplace incident (theft, embezzlement, etc.) that resulted in economic loss to the employer.

Drug Testing

Drug testing can also be employed, but it must comply with the Federal Workplace Drug Testing Guidelines. If a drug test is conducted for a pharmacy investigation involving personal use or addiction, it is recommended that the test be administered after the investigation target has been on duty for a few hours. Most companies have very clear drug testing policies, and retail drug chains have fundamental policies and procedures firmly in place. Those policies will generally state that failure to submit to a drug test is basis for termination. Due to the nature of the test, it will be unannounced, and proper relief of staff is critical to maintain the operation of the pharmacy. If an employee refuses to submit to a drug test, there should be sufficient policy in place to seek termination.

Confirming the Loss and Conducting an Audit

Regardless of the end result of the investigation, an inventory is recommended for all controlled drugs at the conclusion of the internal investigation. This should be done for two reasons:

1. The physical inventory is evidence to corroborate the computerized analysis.
2. This ensures that there are no undiscovered losses.

There are variables as to how the inventory is performed to ensure that the pharmacy's record keeping is in compliance. There is somewhat of a Catch-22 with this process, however. By law, the initial loss was reported to the DEA and possibly the State Board of Pharmacy. They can accept your internal inventory results or conduct independent audits of their own. The State Boards of Pharmacy have the power to adjudicate any violations of record keeping found during an audit. Even though their audits were initiated by the company itself, penalties such as fines can be assessed. Obviously, if a pharmacist is involved, the board will take action against his license.

This is truly an end-to-end investigation that provides a paper trail and a reconcilable inventory to determine exact loss. These cases require extreme patience that may even dictate that thefts are allowed to occur to expand the investigation as needed.

Forged Prescriptions(8)

Signs to aid in the detection of fraudulent prescriptions: Forged prescriptions are a significant problem for today's pharmacies. Pharmacists should be aware of the various kinds of fraudulent prescriptions which may be presented for dispensing:

- Legitimate prescription pads are stolen from physicians' offices, and prescriptions are written for fictitious patients.
- Some patients, in an effort to obtain additional amounts of legitimately prescribed drugs, alter the physician's prescription.

- Some drug abusers will have prescription pads from a legitimate doctor printed with a different call-back number that is answered by an accomplice to verify the prescription.
- Some drug abusers will call in their own prescriptions and give their own telephone number as a call-back confirmation.
- Computers are often used to create prescriptions for nonexistent doctors or to copy legitimate doctors' prescriptions.

Characteristics of Forged Prescriptions

1. The prescription looks "too good"; the prescriber's handwriting is too legible.
2. Quantities, directions, or dosages differ from usual medical usage.
3. The prescription does not comply with the acceptable standard abbreviations or appears to be textbook presentations.
4. The prescription appears to be photocopied.
5. Directions are written in full with no abbreviations.
6. The prescription is written in different color inks or written in different handwriting.

Theft and the Impaired Pharmacist

Impaired pharmacists are no different from any other person with an addictive disease. The addiction may start with taking pills to take the edge off the day or to help with backache from standing all day. Taking the drugs may initially be circumstance driven, but then the drugs may be taken in anticipation of the original problem. As the body increases its tolerance, larger doses or more powerful drugs are needed to obtain the same effect. The early stages are difficult to detect unless it involves CII drugs, as there is a requirement of perpetual inventory on these.

These types of thefts are long term, however, and the loss begins to accumulate. The pharmacist or drug tech knows that continued abuse of one specific drug will eventually be detected, so he begins stealing a variety of drugs that deliver the same effect. A unique factor to the investigation of impairment thefts is that some pharmacists "float." They are not assigned to a specific store, or they act as part-time pharmacists who are called in for staffing reasons. These are absolute moving targets who take advantage of the variety of stores they work. Now the situation is complicated by a person stealing multiple drugs and multiple locations. However, once a possible suspect is identified, that person can be moved to one store for surveillance purposes.

Narcotics, specifically pain medication, are the most abused type of drug. Whether liquid cough syrups with codeine or heavy pain management pills such as Vicodin or OxyContin, the theft methodology is fairly consistent. Drugs must be brought into the pharmacy by any means available and then be hidden or must be removed from the pharmacy as quickly as possible. Liquids are often drunk directly from a bottle and then placed back on the shelf. The consumed liquid is then replaced by adding distilled water to the container. This practice creates an obvious health risk for patients.

The impaired pharmacist has a disease that cannot be addressed through awareness meetings or poster campaigns. These individuals need professional help and, like most addicts, are reluctant to come forward to get the help they need. Their biggest fear is that their license to practice pharmacy may be in jeopardy. Pharmacies should have available the phone numbers of the state's impaired pharmacist hotline so they can get immediate help. One of the primary organizations that deal with pharmacist rehabilitation is the Pharmacy Recovery Network (www.usaprn.org). The success rate for many of the PRN programs is as high as 85%.

Understanding addiction as a disease will help the loss prevention professional a great deal in this industry. This is somewhat of a learning curve for those coming from other types of retail. The interplay between the theft of narcotics and the need to satisfy an addiction is important to understand. An impaired pharmacist may seek medical treatment on his own, and it may be through that process he will divulge the amount of drugs stolen. Even though the pharmacist stole from the company for his own use, restitution may be the final outcome. In short, a pharmacist may be allowed to enter into a rehabilitation program, make restitution for the drugs stolen, and be returned to work upon successful completion of treatment.

This situation is not to be confused with a theft investigation whereby the offending pharmacist is identified and apprehended. There is no "get out of jail free" card for the pharmacist by announcing that he wants to go into a rehabilitation program after he has been caught. Theft cases are handled just as any other.

Reinstating an impaired pharmacist is not as problematic as you might think. Every state has special programs legislated for health professionals with addictions, where the treatment is rigorous and the penalty for relapse is the possibility of permanent loss of license to practice. While the risks are high, the rewards are substantial, as these highly successful state-sponsored programs allow professionals to regain their health and their careers.

These voluntary programs, paid for through health professional license renewal fees, operate on the same basic requirements in each state. The health professional undergoes detoxification before signing a contract agreeing to 3 years of monitoring and random drug tests between 3 and 10 times each month. Weekly group therapy meetings, regular sessions with an addiction physician, at least three 12-step meetings per week are also required. The patient also identifies a sponsor and a work-site monitor.

Approximately 95% of participants in state health professional recovery programs remain sober for at least 5 years, which is a remarkable success rate, especially when compared to other treatment programs that display relapse rates of 66% or higher.(9)

Additionally, reinstatement is a sound business decision because, quite simply, there is a shortage of pharmacists. If the retailer did not reinstate the pharmacist, the pharmacist would certainly work for another company. It is an issue of supply and demand.

Conclusion

The pharmacy is a valuable resource for the community and, when properly managed, can build sales and profit for the retailer. However, this business sector demands great internal care regarding theft, shrinkage, and compliancy. It is an attractant for criminal activity on many levels that requires special investigative strategies and techniques. It requires detailed knowledge of systems and procedures unlike any other retail sector. The challenges for loss prevention staff are enormous because of the complexity of just the business aspects that need to be understood.

Investigations must be concluded quickly and with precision so that the public's interests are not harmed. At the same time, however, there must be insight into addiction as a disease to allow the practitioner to be somewhat proactive while in the stores. It is a novel business sector that will continue to demand skills and technology that are outside the scope of traditional loss prevention.

References

(1) Muha, J. (2006, September 1). Drug diversion—Preventing retail pharmacy theft. *Loss Prevention Magazine* and LossPreventionMagazine.com.

(2) Terrie, Y.C. (2006, November). Pharmacy times lean on me: Help for the impaired pharmacist. http://www.pharmacytimes.com/Article.cfm?Menu=1&ID=4115

(3) Drug Enforcement Administration. *National drug threat assessment, DEA, Pharmaceutical Drugs.* http://www.dea.gov/concern/18862/pharm.htm

(4) Substance Abuse and Mental Health Services Administration. (2005, September). Results from the 2004 National Survey on Drug Use and Health: National Findings.

(5) National Institute on Drug Abuse. (2006, April). Monitoring the future national results on adolescent drug use: Overview of key findings, 2005.

(6) National Institute on Drug Abuse. (2005, October). Monitoring the future national survey results on drug use, 1975–2004. Volume II: College students and adults ages 19–45.

(7) Texas State Board of Pharmacy. Controlled drugs. http://www.tsbp.state.tx.us/consumer/broch2.htm

(8) WH Publication 1462. (2003, June). www.dol.gov/esa/regs/compliance/posters/pdf/eppac.pdf

(9) Drug Enforcement Administration, Office of Diversion Control. (2000, February) A pharmacist's guide to prescription control. *1*(1), www.deadiversion.usdoj.gov/pubs/brochures/pharmguide.htm

(10) Programs for Addicted Professionals National Institute on Chemical Dependency. www.nicd.us/addictedprofessionals.html

Photographing Shoplifting Suspects

CAS, JHC

We recommend that photographs be taken of apprehended shoplifters, together with the merchandise taken by them, when they are in the LP office being processed. The photograph should also contain on a piece of paper (taped to the wall behind it) or on a chalkboard similarly located the name, date, time, and dollar amount of merchandise stolen, together with the name(s) of the apprehending LP agents, written in felt-tip pen or chalk letters large enough to be easily read. It is not unknown for shoplifters to use false names, and a photograph will remove any question at trial as to who was actually arrested. Either a Polaroid or digital camera can be used for this purpose, and if the apprehension report is computerized, the digital photo can be "pasted" onto the report.

Note: State laws should be checked regarding photographing suspects; some states prohibit such photos.

The time is important because "savvy" shoplifters will often, immediately after their release, return to the store and purchase an item identical to the one stolen, giving them a receipt for that item. When appearing in court, they will then claim a "mistake" and produce the receipt alleging the item was purchased. If the time is in the photo and on the arrest report, combined with the fact that modern POS terminals show the time of purchase, their subterfuge will be readily apparent.

Photographs of the stolen merchandise are also allowed as evidence in lieu of the actual merchandise in many jurisdictions. If permitted, this permits recovered and undamaged merchandise to be returned to stock immediately, thus minimizing any loss of sales because of the incident.

In any investigation (excluding shoplifting as noted previously), photographs of the crime scene and any recovered evidence, together with both still and video footage of surveillances and scenes of pertinent activities captured by CCTV, should be obtained and retained as part of the investigative file, and all photographs and video footage should meet the chain of evidence requirements.

Polygraph

CAS, JHC

The polygraph (frequently called a "lie detector") is an instrument which measures and records, via a paper graph and/or computer, psychological phenomena that may be used by trained persons as a reliable technique for diagnosing truth or deception. The instrument records the test subject's breathing, blood pressure and pulse, and electrodermal conductivity (GSR—galvanic skin reflex). There are several techniques (the most common known as the "control question technique") for the development of questions to be answered by the subject and for the diagnosis of deception.

The Employee Polygraph Protection Act of 1988 (EPPA) generally prevents employers from using the polygraphs, either for pre-employment screening or during the course of employment, with certain exceptions. Employers generally may not request or require any employer or job applicant to take a polygraph test, or discipline or discharge or take any employment action against an applicant or employee for refusing to take a polygraph test. Additionally, employers are required to display the EPPA poster (explaining workers' rights) in the workplace.

Since the exceptions to the act are complicated, we suggest that, before any mention of the polygraph is made in the work environment, competent legal advice be sought.

Post Orders

CAS, JHC

The issuance of "post orders" (what to do and how to do it) by security guard providers is an industry standard. Security officers are not expected to remember everything about their duties. Thus, post orders are essential. The individual guard can refer to these orders (instructions) for guidance whenever he is unclear as to what should be done or how it should be done. Post orders should have been prepared by the security provider, after consultation with the client, then approved by the client, and maintained at and available to all security personnel assigned to the client.

A redacted copy of a good example of post orders follows:

2055 GOODVIEW BLVD
SAN DIEGO, CA
POST ORDERS
......
DATE: June 1, 200x
POST: 187
PREMISES: 2055 GOODVIEW BLVD
SAN DIEGO, CA. 92125
Number of Security Officers: (1) PER SHIFT
Equipment Required: KEYS, PAGER
PRIMARY DUTIES

    A. This security post is a foot patrol post. The primary function is to provide a random security patrol of the entire complex, continuously while on duty, noting all violations and reporting all incidents and observations to the management in writing on your post logs.

    B. Officer on duty shall *be* responsible for ticketing all vehicles illegally parked in compliance with customer regulations.

    C. See attached sheets for specific site instructions. Should you have any questions while on duty, contact your field supervisor through the Dispatch Center at 555–1234.

PURPOSE

To provide security for the client in a manner that will make our presence highly visible and deter those who might consider committing theft or vandalism and provide direction to visitors or the general public. Security, in this context, shall be defined as providing a contact point for employees or tenants experiencing problems within the boundaries of the complex, to investigate such problems, to initiate corrective action for such problems, to report to the civil authorities such matters properly within their jurisdiction, and to properly and completely document such actions. Security services shall not include personal services to the employees or tenant, nor shall you honor any request that will distract you from your duties outlined herein. Any difference of opinion in this matter shall immediately be reported to your field supervisor. A written report shall be forwarded to the management representative the following business day.

CONDUCT AND APPEARANCE

At all times you are to conduct yourself in a professional manner. All contact with employees, management, or the public are to be carried out in a business-like manner. You are to avoid all familiarity even if specifically invited. Verbal contacts are to be carried out in a polite but firm manner. ARGUMENTS ARE TO BE AVOIDED AT ALL TIMES. In the event that someone refuses to comply with your requests, or questions your authority, you are directed to immediately report the matter to your field supervisor or to the proper civil authorities.

While on duty you are to be in complete and proper uniform. Uniform shall be neat, clean, well pressed, and in good repair. Your uniform is the visual representation of your authority. You are a professional; wear your uniform with pride.

STARTING OF POST

Immediately upon arrival, begin your log and receive a briefing from the retiring officer. Upon reporting for duty you shall notify the dispatch center stating your name and the post number. Check for any specific instructions left by the management for the night's shift. Commence your initial security inspection of the premises.

REPORT WRITING

All reports will be written in a clear and legible hand, and shall be concise, informative, and restricted to the facts. Facts shall be labeled as facts; hearsay and supposition shall be labeled as such.

Reporting is one of the most important aspects of any security post. A security officer might view the log sheet as an invoice as well as an information pas down. It is an invoice to each client because it shows the client what he has received in return for his investment in security services. It is also a means by which the client can judge the quality of our service.

PERFORMING YOUR PATROL

During your patrol rounds, you are to observe and report any items found in the building or on the grounds that may constitute a potential hazard. Potential hazards include, but are not limited to, the following: damaged gates or fences, broken windows or doors, fire equipment blocked, stairways or fire escapes obstructed, lights burned out or broken, or fixtures on the common areas that are not functioning properly. It is your duty to inform the management of any repair or maintenance problems in writing on your log sheet.

CLOSING YOUR POST

Before closing the post for your shift, be sure that you have completed your security log sheet for the shift and any incident reports necessary. Brief *your* relieving officer on all items of interest, and call the dispatch center to inform them that your have completed your shift. Leave a copy of your log on site in the designated area. Check in any equipment issued to the officer assuming duty or to the center office.

EMERGENCY OPERATION PROCEDURE

When an emergency occurs which requires the police department, fire department, or paramedics to respond, immediately contact the dispatch center either by radio or phone (1–800-*xxx-xxxx*) When the dispatcher comes on the line, give him/her the name of the complex and the complete address, including the unit and the nearest street access. State the nature of the emergency, speak slowly and distinctly. DO NOT HANG UP THE PHONE UNTIL THE DISPATCH OPERATOR STATES THAT YOU CAN. Then proceed to the appropriate access area to assist the emergency service.

When the emergency service arrives, assist if requested. When the emergency is over, advise the dispatch of your status and resume normal operation as soon as possible.

Emergency Phone Numbers:

Police Department	911
Fire Department	911
Paramedics	911
Harbor Police	223–1133
ProtectAll Security	
Dispatch	555–1234
800 Line	800-555-1239
Sales and Service	555–2345

SEE ATTACHMENT HERE TO FOR THIS POST
POST ORDER ATTACHMENT FOR 2055 Goodview Blvd, San Diego
DATE: June 1, 200x

*NEED TO PICK UP KEYS PRIOR TO SHIFT AND RETURN AFTER LAST SHIFT WITH LOGS. DO NOT LEAVE KEYS IN OFFICE AT ANY TIME.

ASSUME POST—CALL 10–41 TO DISPATCH OFFICE.

MAKE CONTINUOUS PATROLS OF THE SHOPPING CENTER. CHECK THE REAR OF THE CENTER FOR LOITERING, UNAUTHORIZED WASTE REMOVAL, KIDS/YOUNG ADULTS, UNAUTHORIZED VEHICLES LEFT OVER NIGHT (ONLY VEHICLES FROM AUTO IMPORTS ARE ALLOWED TO PARK OVERNIGHT). MOVE KIDS OFF PROPERTY, CANNOT BE PLAYING ANYWHERE OR RIDING SKATE BOARDS. BE SURE NO LOITERING AND SKATEBOARDING SIGNS ARE UP.

MAKE VISIBLE PATROLS OF THE FRONT OF SHOPPING CENTER, INCLUDING JOE'S GRILL AND MAX 8 THEATER. THE FAST FOOD PLACE IN THIS CENTER DOES NOT PAY FOR SECURITY SERVICES; DO NOT FOLLOW ANY INSTRUCTIONS FROM THEIR MANAGEMENT. NO LOITERING IS ALLOWED AT ANY TIME ON PROPERTY.

YOGI'S ALSO DOES NOT PAY FOR SECURITY, BUT MONITOR THEIR LOT IN CASE PROBLEMS START THERE AND MOVE INTO OUR RESPONSIBILITIES.

GAS STATIONS ARE NOT PART OF OUR RESPONSIBILITY; PROVIDE NO COVERAGE IN THESE AREAS....

IF FRESH GRAFFITI IS DISCOVERED, ADVISE DISPATCH TO CALL CLIENT AT DAY CONTACT NUMBER SO THEY CAN ARRANGE TO HAVE IT PAINTED OVER.

THERE HAVE BEEN A LOT OF PROBLEMS AROUND PIZZA PLUS AND THE ARCADE AREAS. SPEND A LOT OF TIME NEAR THERE.

IF VEHICLE ACCIDENT OR ANY INJURY OR DAMAGES TO PATRONS, TENANTS OR BLDGS ON SITE, CLIENT MUST BE ADVISED ALONG WITH A SUPERVISOR. DETAILED INCIDENT REPORT MUST BE TURNED INTO OFFICE AT E.O.S. THAT DAY REPORT MUST INCLUDE NAMES OF PARTIES, DESCRIPTION OF WHAT HAPPENED, DAMAGE OR INJURY DESCRIPTION, IF POLICE OR AMBULANCE CAME AND THE NAMES AND IDS OF THESE EMERG PERSONNEL AND TIMES OF ALL.

POST COMPLETED—CALL 10–42 TO DISPATCH OFFICE.

LOG SHEET TO BE LEFT: AT OFFICE, INCIDENTS/PROBLEMS WILL BE SENT TO MGT. COMPANY.

TOWING OF ILLEGALLY PARKED CARS ALLOWED: YES

Pre-Employment Screening

CAS, JHC

Is pre-employment screening necessary? If so, of what should it consist of, and how should it be accomplished?

We believe pre-employment screening is a business necessity today for the following reasons:

- The acknowledged rising levels of theft, drug abuse, and other counterproductive behavior in the workplace.
- The growing legal responsibility of employers for actions of their employees. Although the courts have laid down no hard-and-fast rules as to the required thoroughness of pre-employment investigations required to mitigate such liability, they have held employers liable for not conducting adequate pre-employment investigations.
- The scarcity of qualified workers and the extremely high cost of turnover, estimated at 38% of annual salary.
- The increasing trend of job applicants to falsify their educational, employment, and other job-related background information.

While statistics vary, companies have reported the following for blue-collar applicants: 39% of walk-in applicants left when told that background investigations would be conducted; 15% left when given the background forms to fill out; and 5% never returned after filling out the forms. Many applicants, when they see notices that drug screening is a part of the application process, simply turn around and leave.

The 2005 National Retail Security Final Report indicates that nearly $15 billion is lost to U.S. businesses each year from employee theft. Intangible theft (late arrivals, bogus sick days, deliberate unproductive time, etc.) and drug abuse add significantly to this amount.

It is apparent that the penalties for guessing wrong when it comes to making an employment decision can be extremely costly; therefore, it is essential that some method be utilized to screen job applicants to minimize losses which result from poor employee selection.

The next question is: What should pre-employment screening be designed to accomplish?

Because employees are complex human beings, a multidimensional approach to selection is demanded. Simply put, we should screen for success and effectiveness. How can this be accomplished? The answer is to utilize proven and validated techniques which can assess both the strengths and weaknesses of applicants, thereby providing the decision maker with all the information which will enable an intelligent decision and permit matching the applicant to existing jobs and the personality of the employer and its work environment.

Pre-employment screening should be designed to "pass" as many applicants as possible and yet reject those whose employment will result in counterproductive or dishonest behavior or who will fail because they cannot meet the performance standards of the job. The bottom line is that short-tenured or unproductive employees are extremely costly and a drain on profitability.

The goal of pre-employment screening should be to identify those applicants who possess those factors of personality (stability, stress and frustration tolerance, learning ability, and self-reliance) together with a work ethic which stresses high work quality and quantity; who will have low tolerance of absenteeism, theft, and antiorganizational attitudes; and who will tend to stay with the company.

What are some of the techniques which have been traditionally utilized to accomplish pre-employment screening?

- *Polygraph:* Legislated unlawful by the Employee Polygraph Protection Act of 1989.
- *Interviews:* The courts are now saying that interviews must be limited to purposes such as verifying background data, assessing skills, developing employment history information, reviewing educational background, etc.

Interviews, while they may develop employment history, cannot really be predictive of honesty or integrity on the job. There is also an inherent danger that interviews may be discriminatory in that we tend to hire in our own self-image. There is no question that interviews, properly structured and conducted by a skilled interviewer, can be most helpful in determining skill levels and some personality factors and may develop information with respect to falsified credentials or background data.

- *Records (DMV and Credit) Checks:* Such checks must be relevant to the job. For example, a DMV driving records check for a sales associate that was used to deny employment would probably be impermissible. There are also restrictions on using credit checks for other than certain few selected job categories. Credit checks are subject to the federal rules under the Fair Credit Reporting Act (FCRA).
- *Arrest Records:* Use for granting/denying employment is illegal.
- *Conviction Records:* Allowable but can be used to deny employment only if the crime for which the applicant was convicted can reasonably be expected to occur on the job in a way harmful to the employer. It is also worthy to note that nationally it is estimated that only one in six criminals is ever caught or arrested; therefore, there is only a 1 in 6 chance of a record existing. Conducting such records checks can be a good defense to wrongful hiring or retention suits, particularly in the case of loss prevention personnel.

- *Reference Checks:* Obtaining written information from references or former employers is very difficult; employers are afraid of defamation suits. However, a skilled investigator, armed with properly executed releases, can develop reliable information in many instances. Reference and employment checks are singularly important because they tend to disclose recent prior performance, which psychologists universally agree is a highly reliable predictor of future performance.

Typical of what is allowed in checking references is outlined in the Arkansas Department of Labor's Code § 11-3-204:

Providing references to prospective employers.

(a)(1) *A current or former employer may disclose the following information about a current or former employee's employment history to a prospective employer of the current or former employee upon receipt of written consent from the current or former employee:*

    (A) Date and duration of employment;
    (B) Current pay rate and wage history;
    (C) Job description and duties;
    (D) The last written performance evaluation prepared prior to the date of the request;
    (E) Attendance information;
    (F) Results of drug or alcohol tests administered within one (1) year prior to the request;
    (G) Threats of violence, harassing acts, or threatening behavior related to the workplace or directed at another employee;
    (H) Whether the employee was voluntarily or involuntarily separated from employment and the reasons for the separation; and
    (I) Whether the employee is eligible for rehire.

  (2) *The current or former employer disclosing such information shall be presumed to be acting in good faith and shall be immune from civil liability for the disclosure or any consequences of such disclosure unless the presumption of good faith is rebutted upon a showing by a preponderance of the evidence that the information disclosed by the current or former employer was false, and the current or former employer had knowledge of its falsity or acted with malice or reckless disregard for the truth.*

(b)(1) *The consent required in subsection (a) of this section must be on a separate form from the application form or, if included in the application form, must be in bold letters and in larger typeface than the largest typeface in the text of the application form. The consent form must state, at a minimum, language similar to the following:*

    "I, (applicant), hereby give consent to any and all prior employers of mine to provide information with regard to my employment with prior employers to (prospective employer)."

  (2) *The consent must be signed and dated by the applicant.*
  (3) *The consent will be valid only for the length of time that the application is considered active by the prospective employer but in no event longer than six (6) months.*
(c)   *The provisions of this section shall also apply to any current or former employee, agent, or other representative of the current or former employer who is authorized to provide and who provides information in accordance with the provisions of this section.*
(d)(1) *This section does not require any prospective employer to request employment history on a prospective employee and does not require any current or former employer to disclose employment history to any prospective employer.*
  (2) *Except as specifically amended herein, the common law of this state remains unchanged as it relates to providing employment information on present and former employees.*
  (3) *This section shall apply only to causes of action accruing on and after July 30, 1999.*
(e)   *The immunity conferred by this section shall not apply when an employer or prospective employer discriminates or retaliates against an employee because the employee or the prospective employee has exercised or is believed to have exercised any federal or state statutory right or undertaken any action encouraged by the public policy of this state.*

- *Handwriting (Graphology):* No scientific validity; however, I experienced some startling and accurate assessments made by one graphologist. Based on that experience, she was recommended to the ASIS program chair for the annual national program. She appeared and received high ratings by attendees in her session.
- *Full Background Investigations:* Can be very thorough when properly done. Expensive. Should be used for the most sensitive or high-level positions.
- *Drug Testing:* Becoming more popular; some legal restrictions or prohibitions. Programs must be well thought out and implemented only after careful study and legal advise. Tend to be expensive and slow. Can be invasive.

The U.S. Navy found a policy of random testing reduced positive results by 66%. Should be considered for certain classes of employees (e.g., those involved with industrial equipment or vehicles or in very sensitive or high-theft exposure areas).

- *Store's Mutual Associations:* Inexpensive and worthwhile; names filed limited to those caught and therefore not very extensive.
- *Public (for Fee) Pre-Employment Screening Firms:* These firms offer services such as criminal background checks, education and professional license verification, motor vehicle reports, reference checks, and more.

Services can be purchased individually or in a package. Concerns include accuracy of data and currency.

- *Resume and Application Form Review:* Inexpensive but relatively unreliable; 30% contain material misrepresentations. Should be done by trained personnel. Reliance on this alone takes little time but can result in a lot of trouble.
- *Psychological Tests:* Also known as "Honesty Tests" and/or "Pencil-Paper Polygraph Tests." Those which are validated are legally permissible. There is predictive validity for several tests. Under legislative (both federal and state) scrutiny. While there may be some legal risks attached to the use of psychological tests and particularly "honesty tests," many have found them to be useful to either predict or deter dishonesty. Other types of tests have also come under fire; a former security employee at a Target store in Oakland, California, sued that company for race discrimination because he was denied employment after taking the Minnesota Multi-Phasic Inventory (a long-used and well-validated psychological test), and the court ruled in his favor.

What should a test publisher be able to prove?

- The publisher must demonstrate research on validity and peer review in accepted professional publications and journals.
- The publisher must have full-time professional staff.
- The publisher must have history and validity performance and national clients.
- The publisher must have research staff.
- The test must be easy to use, time efficient, and results must be available when needed.
- Test results must be clear and unambiguous.
- The test publisher must have long record of either a lack of claims or successful defense of adverse impact claims/suits.
- There should be evidence that applicants do not feel the test is intrusive.

A model pre-employment screening program will

- Be cost effective;
- Raise the quality of the workforce;
- Reduce turnover and improve morale;
- Reduce theft and counterproductive employee behavior;
- Be easy to administer and produce no adverse reaction or resentful result on the part of the applicant.

Finally, most studies conclude that measures of integrity correlate with other types of coun-terproductive behavior, and that to discover any flaw in an applicant, whether it be honesty or some other defect, will probably be predictive of other problems as well.

Recommendations

Companies should adopt an escalating protocol for pre-employment screening and testing of applicants/new hires which will begin with the least expensive procedure and work its way up to the more costly techniques, consistent with the level of risk and exposure for a given position. Such a protocol should meet the objectives of a model screening program as noted previously. We suggest this can be accomplished by a pre-employment screening program which follows the steps outlined here, consistent with the sensitivity and risk level of the position applied for.

Thus, under these recommendations, for some positions (to be determined in conjunc-tion with human resources), the process might eliminate steps 4 and/or 6; the length, detail, and depth of step 5, the Interview, would be keyed to job level.

Hence, the recommended steps would be as follows:

1. The applicant appears personally and fills out an employment application and is preliminarily qualified by employment desk personnel.
2. A careful application/resume review is performed by a trained reviewer.
3. For applicants whose applications are accepted, a proven integrity test is administered for all applicants. To be of value, this test should be used consistently, and agreed-upon cutoff or disqualifying scores should not be modified.
4. A background investigation is performed which may include any or all of the following items: credit check, conviction checks, reference checks, education verification, DMV check, SSN check, etc.
5. A structured behavioral interview is performed by trained personnel. This step would be mandatory for all applicants as the final step before placement.
6. Drug testing is performed.

Premises and Personal Injury Liability

CAS, JHC

It is a legal reality that a store owner owes a duty to his customers (legally called "business invitees") to provide them with a safe shopping environment.

Premises liability is the civil liability of a property owner which arises when the property owner fails to provide a reasonably safe environment, and as a result, someone is injured. The owner was negligent and thus liable.

Negligence is an "unintentional tort" (civil wrong). Negligence is established if

- There is a legal duty owed to a person.
- There is unreasonable conduct or a breach of that duty.
- There was a foreseeable proximate cause that a person might be injured.
- There was injury or damage to that person.

Let's look at an example of the concept of negligence: This morning, one of your maintenance people decides to wash and wax the entry hallway. The hallway's surface is very slippery when wet. Your worker has wet-mopped the floor but failed to put out a caution sign warning of the slippery conditions. A guest enters the hallway, slips, and falls, breaking a hip.

Now we all agree that you have a duty to provide a safe environment for your residents and their guests. A wet and slippery floor is not a safe environment—right. So your conduct in not warning of this unsafe condition was unreasonable; in other words, you have breached your duty. Is it foreseeable that a person may slip and fall on a slippery floor? Of course.

That event has now happened—someone (soon to be called a "plaintiff") has slipped, fallen, and is injured. There is now an injury or damage resulting from that breach. The slippery floor coupled with the failure to warn was the direct or proximate cause of the injury. "But for" the slippery floor and failure to warn, the injury would not have happened. You, because of the foreseeability of such an event, and your unreasonable conduct in not warning, were negligent.

Remember, too, negligence can be either an act or a failure to act when a reasonable person would have acted or avoided an action.

Simply stated, a duty is a legally sanctioned obligation the breach of which results in liability.

Recent years have seen the development of another type of negligence claim against retailers and property owners, which is more directly related to our concerns.

This development is the ever more popular premises security liability, which is the civil liability of property owners for the foreseeable criminal acts of third persons. It arises when property owners or their agent manager fails to provide adequate security to reasonably respond to the foreseeable harm which could injure persons invited onto the property. As a rapidly developing area of tort law, premises security liability is also often referred to as "negligent" or "inadequate" security cases.

Courts have recognized that landowners, despite their best efforts, cannot render their properties immune from crime. Therefore, where a duty is found to exist, businesses are required to provide "reasonable security" measures. These measures may depend on whether the injury causing incident was "foreseeable."

What is the basic issue in all security negligence or inadequate security cases? It is whether the defendant (premise's owner, manager, or operator) took notice of the signs of risk, responded with adequate security measures, and whether deficiency in security was a causal factor of the plaintiff's injury.

The judgment of "adequacy" is made by a jury based on its understanding of the nature of the risk.

There are always three interconnected issues in connection with premises liability: duty, breach of duty, and foreseeable causation or proximate cause, with resulting injury to someone.

Foreseeability is simply answering this question: Did the owner know, or should he have known, that an event similar to the one which caused the injury or harm was likely to happen, and did he take reasonable steps to minimize the risk? If the answer is "yes," then it is likely foreseeability exists.

Causation, or proximate cause, is simply defined as that which produces an event without which the injury would not have occurred. In California, for there to be causation the event must be a substantial factor in bringing about the injury.

Additionally, if enhanced security would not have deterred the incident, there may not be causation.

Remember the "But For" rule: "But for" the lack of proper lighting, this criminal attack and subsequent injury would not have occurred.

These types of security cases frequently result from injuries suffered in parking lots by patrons of big box stores and malls of all sizes and by patrons of bars, sporting events, and any other venue where there a crowds.

Retailers, however, face a third type of civil liability related to their dealing with shoplifters. This liability stems not from our failure to act or acting negligently, but rather actions of a more positive nature. The acts, or "intentional torts," include false arrest/imprisonment, assault, malicious prosecution, defamation (libel-slander), invasion of privacy, tortious interference with employment, and tortious infliction of emotional distress.

If an allegation of inadequate security is made, and the retailer is sued, one of the issues will be how that retailer compares with other similar businesses. If you fall short in meeting the "standard"—if your security standards fall below those of your competitors in like situations—you will probably be held negligent and liable. The typical areas of comparison are

Fencing—lack of, inadequate, broken or in disrepair
Lighting—inadequate, broken, low power
Locks—key control; door peep viewers
Alarms
Security policies—written, publicized, followed
CCTV—real, dummy, monitored, taped
Guards—post orders, training, screening, contract/proprietary, use of watch clocks
Notices and warnings—how publicized
Knowledge of crime in area and reports kept; documentation and responses
Parking lots—a subject unto themselves.

When a person is injured and sues, the object of that person's lawsuit is to, as the courts say, "make them whole again." How is this done? In our system, money is the means of redress; a court or jury decides how much money will adequately compensate the injured party to basically put that person in the position he was in before the injury or damage. Our tort system is really a "redistribution of wealth" system.

Damages awarded in security-related lawsuits have skyrocketed in recent years. A jury awarded a plaintiff over $7 million in 2006 when it found he had been unfairly treated by loss prevention and the company.

Awards in these cases can be made up of three parts:

- *Special damages:* To replace out-of-pocket expenses (e.g., lost wages).
- *General damages:* Awarded to make the plaintiff "whole." This money is to compensate for pain and suffering, mental anguish, and emotional distress. If the jury is outraged by the retailer's conduct, the higher these awards will be.
- Compensatory damages: The combination of special and general damages; they compensate the plaintiff for his injury.
- *Punitive damages:* Awarded when the plaintiff can establish the retailer was grossly negligent, wanton, or motivated by malice. For punitive damages to be awarded, it must be clearly shown the retailer was not merely negligent or the injury was the result of an honest error, but rather that he acted with malice, fraud, gross negligence, or oppression. Punitive damages are designed to punish and generally cannot be covered by insurance.

It should be clear by now that the retailer is vulnerable to a variety of tort claims by customers who claim injury by some act or failure to act on the part of the retailer. For this reason, it behooves the retailer to

- Avoid those acts or failures to act which, foreseeably, may lead to a person's injury.
- When dealing with shoplifters, be sure that industry standards (such as the six steps required for a shoplifting stop) are meticulously followed.
- Have well-developed and reasonable security policies which are (a) written, (b) publicized, (c) followed, and (d) enforced.

Remember, a retailer has a duty to provide a safe shopping environment.

Preteen and Teenage Shoplifting

CAS, JHC

Experts agree that minors (juveniles and preteens) are responsible for about one-third of the shoplifting problem. If this is so, and it is, what percent of this problem is caused by the age group of 8–12 or preteen? The dilemma is no one knows for certain, but you can bet the answer is plenty! No one knows because statistics aren't kept in any universal fashion, nor is there any central repository for such information in the country. Indeed, the last people to be made aware of this social problem are the police. Retailers are reluctant to call the police when they have a youngster in custody for stealing a candy bar or a bracelet from the fashion jewelry display. Many police jurisdictions, overworked and underfunded, have suggested their presence in such a small matter takes their attention away from more serious crimes. Stores understand this and develop policies that takes the police out of the shoplifting loop when the offender is a child.

With a youngster in tow for a small theft, the store has the option of scolding the child and sending him away or holding the child for a parent or other relative to come and take the child home. The first option is a great disservice to the parents, as well as the child. No lesson is learned when admonished by a stranger and released for a bad deed. And the parent is denied critical information about the conduct of the child. The second option often ends with at least one employee sitting with the child, sometimes for up to an hour or more until an adult comes. Or, a parent comes and is critical of the store for making a big fuss of the event. In the latter scenario, the lesson learned, for the child, is that it's "no big deal" to get caught stealing. I am aware of times when the child claims innocence and the parent believes the child over the word of the store's employee. Again, what lessons are learned here?

Of equal concern to our society is the not uncommon problem of adults using children to actually assist in their shoplifting efforts—from concealing goods in baby strollers, having toddlers innocently carry stolen items, to older children actively being engaged in the conceal-ment of goods, fully knowledgeable of what's occurring. Without question, some of these little people will grow into a life of crime, by design.

But what about children who aren't coached or driven to learn antisocial behavior, who come from good homes, but have "sticky little fingers"? Most readers will probably agree that stealing small things, successfully, more likely than not will continue over time, and the next thing we know is the child is a young adult and still stealing. Grownup crooks typically don't start being outlaws when they become adults.

Our hope, then, is to nip the problem in the bud. How do we do that, you ask? Following are some suggestions which we hope will effectively deal with the dilemma of youngsters who become involved in shoplifting:

- Set an example for your children about *your* respect for others' property. This can be done in many ways, from little comments in a store such as "put it back on the shelf now; it's not ours" to "Oh, my! This is Mr. Miller's pen. I need to take it to the post office and send it to him."
- Instill in your children a respect for others' property. That begins with playmates' toys and siblings' possessions. Children must be taught about others' property and their rights to property.
- Children must be corrected in a positive manner when caught taking others' property, and the offender must return it in person. This "correction" or discipline goes something like this: "You're okay, but what you did is not okay." No berating. If the child has been discovered with merchandise, including candy, from a store, the child must be taken back to the store and must return the item with an apology. Merchants are accustomed to this and typically thank the child and instruct him not to do this again. This is good medicine.
- Ensure you know the source of everything your children possess. It's necessary to say, "Mary, that's a pretty necklace; where did you get it?" If she answers that her friend gave it to her, privately call her friend's mother and inquire. The child will soon understand that any new items which show up in the room will be challenged.
- Know when your children are out "shopping," where the shopping is taking place, and with whom. When the children return, express interest and curiosity about any package brought in and check the contents. Ask questions if there's any doubt whatsoever.

People in their "tween" years are in a learning mode. Everyone needs to be taught the dif-ference between right and wrong, and the parents who understand that can and will make a wonderful contribution to the children's development. "Sticky little fingers" only need to be discovered early and washed clean—a wonderful opportunity for Mom and Dad, and such a wonderful lesson learned!

Preventing Theft of Merchandise by "Customers"

CAS, JHC

Minimizing the theft of merchandise by the public requires the implementation of various physical and procedural steps and an awareness by employees of the important role they play in preventing customer theft. This "awareness" by employees doesn't come naturally. It must be taught.

What are the policies and practices which, if adopted, may significantly reduce theft? The following list identifies some of these relatively simple and inexpensive procedures:

- Acknowledge all customers as promptly as possible.
- If busy with a customer, acknowledge other customers either verbally ("I'll be with you in a moment") or visually (by a wave of the hand or a nod of the head).
- Try not to turn your back on customers.
- Try not to leave your service area unattended.
- If, as a nonsales associate, you are on the selling floor performing stocking, marking, or other functions, do not be oblivious to customers' presence but rather acknowledge them with eye contact, smile, and ask if they are in need of assistance.
- Develop a warning system so that all employees can be alerted when the presence of potential thieves is suspected.
- Lock up expensive merchandise.
- Avoid stacking merchandise so high on counters or displays that it blocks a view of nearby areas.
- When merchandise is made up of pairs, display only one of the pair.
- Display countertop items in patterns or pyramids.
- Display hanging goods in such a manner as to make the removal of one item conspicuous. On a "T" stand, for example, hang three items on each side.
- Alternate hangers on racks containing expensive goods, like suits or expensive jackets.
- Keep counters and displays neat and orderly.
- Place telephones so sales associates can view their selling area when on the phone.
- Destroy discarded sales receipts.
- Pay special attention to known high shortage merchandise.

In addition to the preceding procedures, additional suggestions for merchandise protection can be grouped into four categories.

1. *Protective Design:* Protective design involves store layout and observation booths. A store's layout, including the height of displays and width of aisles, can discourage or encourage shoplifters. Lighting should be designed so that there are no dark or shadowy corners. Restrooms and public telephones should be located away or separate from merchandise areas. In existing stores with restrooms immediately adjacent to displayed merchandise, those rooms should kept locked, requiring customers to obtain a key from a salesperson. In general, store layout should allow for eye coverage of most, if not all, of the selling area.

   Observation booths can easily be designed into any store layout. These are booths high above the selling floor, manned by an employee often behind a two-way mirror, who has a good view of the entire store. Invisible observation booths have been an effective method of detecting theft activity.

2. *Protective Devices:* Protective devices include such things as two-way and convex mirrors, cameras, and electronic article surveillance tags. Some stores have found that stapling shut bags containing purchased merchandise has thwarted theft. Closed-circuit television cameras both deter some theft as well as assist in spotting theft activity. Electronic article surveillance (EAS) tags placed on expensive and easily stolen merchandise not only act as a deterrent to theft, but, if not defeated by a thief, also alert store personnel to the theft when the

alarm sounds as the tagged merchandise is removed from the store. Even if tags are removed by a thief, their presence alerts to the fact that merchandise has probably been stolen. Care must be taken, however, to assure that EAS tags are either "deactivated" or removed from legitimately purchased goods. If not, honest customers will be unnecessarily detained, annoyed, and potentially create more harm than good.

3. *Human Deterrents:* Human deterrents involve uniformed guards or visible security officers and/or loss prevention agents, award programs, and employee education. The sight of a uniformed guard or visible security officer (VSO) often discourages both the professional and amateur shoplifter.

Award programs which reward employees who alert loss prevention to shoplifting activity can be very effective. Award programs are discussed elsewhere in this book.

Employee education programs, such as shortage awareness seminars and contests, films and videos, and reading material or posters available in break rooms, are designed to make your employees more knowledgeable and conscious of the theft problem. Remember, employees are the first and most important line of defense against external theft.

4. *Psychological Deterrents:* The use and type of psychological deterrents will depend on the size of the store, customer base, and the attitude of management toward these types of deterrents. For example, while shelf-edge signs displaying the message "Shoplifting is a crime and will be prosecuted" may be appropriate for a grocery or liquor store, such signs would most likely be unacceptable for a high-end specialty store. Similarly, PA announcements stating "Security is needed in area 4" may be useful in a drug store, but not in a jewelry store. Some stores have encouraged local police to park in front of the store, which arguably could discourage potential lifters from entering. Psychological deterrents may be useful and should not be discarded out of hand.

Product Tampering:—An Historical Perspective

CAS, JHC

The generally accepted definition of "product tampering" is the intentional adulteration or corruption of goods post manufacturing. It can be done to cause panic or hurt consumers, or faked to extort money from the manufacturer through product liability lawsuits. In rare cases, the merchant may become part of the lawsuit as a defendant under an allegation of negligence.

The first acknowledged case of product tampering occurred in 1978 when health officials in 18 countries were alerted that "oppressed Palestinian workers" had injected Israeli oranges at the source with liquid mercury, as part of an effort to damage the Israeli economy, of which orange exports amounted to about 10% of their economy.

Beginning in the 1980s and throughout that decade, there were numerous product tampering incidents, including one (1982) of the most remembered, which involved the death of seven persons in Chicago as the result of ingesting cyanide-poisoned Tylenol. Other incidents included

- Girl Scout cookies with needles (April 1984)
- *Salmonella typhimurium* bacteria in restaurant salad bars in The Dalles, Oregon, area by the Rajneesh cult (1984)
- Glico-Morinaga candy cyanide poisoning incidents in Japan (1984)
- Excedrin cyanide deaths in upstate New York (1986)
- Lipton Cup-a-Soup cyanide (1986)
- Glass in baby food (1986)
- Tylenol cyanide (another case) (1986)

- Chicken fruit scandal (1989)
- Goody's Headache Powder cyanide (1992)
- Sudafed deaths in Washington state (1993)

Based on the Tylenol case, the federal government passed the Federal Anti-Tampering Act (FATA) making it (in laymen's terms) a federal crime to tamper with a consumer product or its labeling, conspiring to, threatening to, or claiming to have tampered or tainted consumer products for the purpose of causing illness or death or harm to the business.

Food and Drug Administration (FDA) agency regulations proscribed tamper-resistant packaging for many over-the-counter (OTC) drug products destined for retail sales. Various techniques for meeting FDA regulations covering antitampering packaging have evolved.

A recent case (2005) which received nationwide publicity that falls under the general "tampering" blanket was the "Chili-Finger" case at a San Jose, California, Wendy's restaurant. A woman claimed to have found and bitten into a human finger in her chili while eating at Wendy's. Subsequent investigation disclosed the woman, with her husband's knowledge, planted the finger to file a false insurance claim. They were subsequently arrested, and the woman was sentenced to more than 12 years in prison. Wendy's claimed to have lost $2.5 million in sales because of the adverse publicity.

While most retailers will not be named in the average product tampering civil law suit, the Wendy's case shows the potential vulnerability to this type of case. Should such a complaint or claim of this type ever be made against a retailer, every effort should be made to preserve all possible evidence, retain the names of all witnesses and employees who could possibly have any knowledge of the incident, notify the police at once, and, if indicated, quickly involve any corporate structure that can work to control the public relations and adverse publicity aspects of the case, as well as employ professional forensic and investigative personnel.

Product Tampering and Contamination

Curtis Baillie

The Turkey Crisis

I will never forget my first couple of weeks as the newly hired Director of Loss Prevention of a grocery chain. Early one morning, a week before the Thanksgiving holiday, the president of the company summoned me to his office. When I arrived, I immediately knew he wanted to discuss a matter of a serious nature. As two other senior company executives joined us, he announced we had been contacted by a local television affiliate in Tucson, Arizona. The network representative said they received a telephone call from a male caller who informed them that he had put cyanide in turkeys at our company's supermarkets throughout the Tucson area. All eyes turned in my direction as the president asked me, "What are your recommendations?" The first thought that came to my head was to call the Federal Bureau of Investigation. I soon discovered the company did not have a written policy for handling product tampering cases or a crisis management team (CMT).

Most threats involving tampering have been shown to be hoaxes, but when a threat is received, it must be handled in a manner that assumes it to be real unless and/or until proven otherwise. Although the "turkey crisis" proved to be a hoax, the damage to the company, financially, was in the millions. The loss of public trust and lost sales dollars could not be quantified. Since the caller did not identify which stores contained contaminated products, all turkeys were removed from every store. We were aided by the news media in this product recall because they blanketed the airwaves informing the public to return any turkeys they had purchased. On the other side of the coin, it also created panic with our customers because our stores and corporate offices were undulated with calls. We paid for doctors' visits as people thought they were sick (no contaminated turkeys were ever found), gave double refunds, and spent untold dollars in advertising to regain public confidence in our products, not to mention secured storage and eventual destruction of over 30,000 turkeys once the FBI and the Food and Drug Administration completed their investigations. The Environmental Protection Agency (EPA) was involved in the disposal of the turkeys, as it was not possible to test all the birds.

Famous Product Tampering Cases

The first reported product tampering case in the United States occurred in 1982 when seven people died after taking Tylenol capsules containing cyanide. An individual whose intent was random killings placed the tainted capsules on six different stores' shelves in the Chicago area. This case remains unsolved, and the reward offered by Johnson & Johnson still stands today. The 1982 Tylenol case spawned further copycat cyanide tampering cases:

- In 1986, Louis Denber died from drinking cyanide-laced Lipton Chicken Noodle Cup-a-Soup.
- Excedrin tampering cases in 1986 resulted in several deaths. In June of that year, a 40-year-old Washington state woman woke at 6:00 a.m., with a headache and took two Excedrin capsules. Later, a family member found her lying on the bathroom floor, unconscious. She was rushed to the hospital, but she later died as a result of taking cyanide-laced capsules. Three days following a highly publicized recall, due to the previous death, police received a call from a woman, Stella Nickell, who suspected her husband had died from taking four Extra-Strength Excedrin capsules. His death had previously been listed as "complications from emphysema." Subsequent testing revealed he had died of cyanide poisoning. Over a period of a few months, two more bottles of tainted Excedrin capsules were found on grocery shelves in Washington. The resulting investigation found Stella Nickell had murdered her husband and placed bottles of tainted Excedrin on store shelves to make it look like a copycat serial killer. She was convicted and sentenced to 90 years in prison, being the first person to be tried and convicted of product tampering.
- In 1991, Joseph Meling attempted to murder his wife by filling Sudafed capsules with cyanide. He also placed boxes of tainted capsules on store shelves; those capsules did kill two other people. Meling's motive was to collect $700,000 in insurance money.

As I stated with my own product tampering example, the financial cost to a company can be devastating. In 1993 PepsiCo conducted a contest in which you were a winner if you found the words "Be young, have fun, drink Pepsi" in the bottom of a Diet Pepsi can. A retired meat salesman and his wife reportedly found a syringe in the bottom of a can when looking for the winning slogan. They gave the materials to their attorney, who then contacted the Pierce (Washington) County Health Department. After news stories aired on television, many more reports of finding objects including needles, pins, screws, a crack cocaine vial, and a bullet in Diet Pepsi cans surfaced. None of the tampering incidents were ever proven to be real; however, they cost PepsiCo over $35 million to repair the damaged caused by the tampering scare.

As I write this section, a series of food-related product tampering cases is occurring in the Northeast. In Pennsylvania, several grocery companies are experiencing issues ranging from a pin found in an onion, metal pellets found in ground beef, and a needle found in a sealed can of soup. In Maryland, a manager found two pins in a loaf of bread on the store shelf. A number of these tampering cases involve the same grocery chain.

Product Tampering:—The Public and Media Threat

Product tampering cases are a real threat, not only to the public, but also to your company's profits and reputation. In most cases, unlike the "turkey crisis," the news media are not notified until you make them aware. With food product tampering cases, the FBI or the Food and Drug Administration will be involved in the decision-making process when determining whether a public warning is necessary. When your store is deciding to go public, make a determination of whether the threat is real or a hoax. When the decision is made to inform the public, the possibility of encouraging copycat crimes is very high. In 1982, the FDA counted 270-suspected incidents of product tampering, of which 36 were listed as "hard core, true tamperings." These copycat tampering threats were a direct result of the Tylenol tampering murders.

If the threat is determined to be a hoax, all agencies involved will back off, except for law enforcement agencies. You're left with a very costly public relations nightmare. In the Pepsi product tampering crisis (described earlier), the original complaint was made on Wednesday, June 9, 1993. Seattle area television stations aired the story on Thursday, June 10. The *Seattle Times* reported the story that Friday morning, and another claim was made that evening. On Sunday, June 13, another claim was made by a Cleveland woman. At the end of the day on Monday, June 14, eight more claims of finding contaminated items in Diet Pepsi cans had been made. By Monday evening, the story was the number-two story on the Associated Press headlines. The number-one story was the nomination of Ruth Bader Ginsburg to the Supreme Court.

PepsiCo decided to fight the media crisis with media. The company produced video news releases that were estimated to be aired on 403 television stations and seen by 187 million viewers. The words "copycat" and "hoax" appeared in their news releases. On Thursday, June 17, Pepsi executives had a supermarket video surveillance tape of a Colorado woman putting objects into a Diet Pepsi can. Pepsi pressured the FDA to issue a statement calling the incidents a series of hoaxes. PepsiCo Inc. declared that its "needle-in-the-can scare was over." Ads were prepared: "As America knows, those stories about Diet Pepsi were a hoax. Plain and simple, not true." Pepsi took out full-page newspaper ads which read, "Pepsi is pleased to announce...nothing." Several weeks later, over the July 4 holiday, Pepsi took out more ads celebrating its freedom and gave out coupons with the slogan, "Thanks, America." As a result of PepsiCo's aggressive handling of the media crisis, the scare ended in less 8 eight days. A very large crisis for the company was diverted by adhering to the plan developed and being upfront about the situation.

Reacting to the Product Tampering Threat at the Store

Threats can be received by mail (snail/electronic) or by telephone. Telephone threats, in my own experience, have been the most popular vehicle for delivering a product tampering scare. The following steps are recommended in the event your store receives a product tampering threat of *noncompany-manufactured product*:

1. Upon receiving a threat of product tampering *at the store,* the person receiving the call or letter must immediately inform the store manager. Do not contact any law enforcement agency. The crisis management team coordinator should contact the appropriate law enforcement agency. In most tampering cases, the Federal Bureau of Investigation is called.
2. If the threat was received over the telephone, immediately complete your company's Bomb Threat Checklist with the associate who took the call.
3. If the threat is received in the form of a letter or note, handle the document, using gloves, at the corners only. Do not allow anyone to handle the note, except when placing it into a large envelope.
4. Instruct the associate *not* to discuss the matter with anyone other than the store manager or the CMT.
5. For threats received over the telephone, do not hang up before the caller is finished talking. Do not make any disparaging remarks to the caller. Do make sure you have the message properly recorded in writing, repeat it to the caller, and ask when he or she will call again.
6. If the caller states the location of a tampered product, complete the following steps:
   a. Take photographs of the products. Then use gloves and remove all units from the shelves in the order they appear on the shelves, left to right.
   b. Place items in cardboard boxes.
   c. Close and seal the tops of the cases.

    d. Record the identity of each item in the case, date, and time removed the name of the company, store number, and address.

    e. Write "DO NOT OPEN" on the cases.

    f. Check each item removed. Look for loose caps, lids, or box tops. If an item has been opened, has been defaced in any way, or has a particular odor, place it in a paper bag and label for the CMT.

    g. Store management personnel should conduct the packaging operation.

    h. Remove and quarantine the threatened items in a secure, predetermined location. Make sure the consignment is properly labeled and secure from restocking.

    i. The store manager should instruct cashiers not to sell any of the products until further notice. Cashiers simply explain to customers that the product is being recalled.

The In-House Contaminated Manufactured Product Recovery Program

Although the contaminated product recovery program I have outlined here is directed toward the retail grocery industry, and its company-owned manufacturing plants in mind, I have found that this program may be modified to fit any retail operation. Large grocery operations maintain their own processing plants, such as bakery and dairy processing. Consumer health and satisfaction are primary concerns of any grocery company, and companies are dedicated to investigating complaints of in-house manufactured products when the possibility exists that the manufactured product may be contaminated.

The company's crisis management team coordinator (CMTC) should direct all investigations involving alleged contaminated product. Along with the CMT, other members should include, but not be limited to, the loss prevention department, the manufacturing general manager, and an independent laboratory for the evaluation and analysis of the product in question. The following guidelines should be considered when a customer returns *company-manufactured products* to the store due to alleged contamination:

1. Responsibilities of the store manager or the person in charge include
   a. The store manager completes a customer complaint form and advises the customer that an independent laboratory will analyze the product. If the customer wants feedback, advise the customer that a company official will contact her.
   b. Do not suggest the customer seek medical attention; that is the customer's decision.
   c. If a customer has sought medical attention, obtain the name and address of the doctor or medical facility. Include this information on the customer complaint form.
   d. Give a full refund.
   e. Secure the product and any associated foreign substance in the store office or lock it in a secure room. Do not pull the product apart or tamper with any evidence.
   f. Visually inspect any like product still on the shelf or in the stockroom areas for possible contamination. If additional product is found, remove the product and store in a secure place.
   g. Call a member of the crisis management team and then your district or regional supervisor.
   h. Give the product and the customer complaint form to the responding loss prevention investigator.
   i. If the CMTC orders a product withdrawal, follow the directions outlined in the product tampering section earlier.
2. The crisis management team coordinator's responsibilities include
   a. Contact the loss prevention department to pick the contaminated product.
   b. Communicate with the investigator evaluating the situation. Contact and inform the other members of the CMT and appropriate merchandiser.
   c. Communicate with the manufacturing general manager in an attempt to determine the cause of contamination.
   d. Determine if the product should be removed from the stores.
   e. Contact the company president to advise and keep him informed regarding the investigation.

    f. Contact the food laboratory representative for the product involved.

    g. Follow up with the customer, authorities, store manager, and other company person-nel as needed.

3. Loss prevention investigator responsibilities include

    a. Pick up the contaminated product and any other material associated with the product, along with the customer complaint form. If the pickup is at the customer's residence, complete the customer complaint form and advise the customer that an independent laboratory will analyze the product. Advise the customer she can receive a full refund at the store. If the customer wants feedback, advise her that a company official will contact her.

    b. Do not suggest the customer seek medical attention. If the customer has sought medi-cal attention, obtain the name and address of the doctor and/or medical facility.

    c. Transport the contaminated product to the corporate offices and report to the crisis management team coordinator.

    d. Package all evidence according to laboratory instructions.

    e. Complete overnight express forms and deliver to the mailroom along with the packaged evidence. If after business hours, deliver to the appropriate package pickup location.

    f. Complete the report, documenting the details of the investigation.

Examining Returned or Refunded Medicines

Retailers commonly allow customers to return previously purchased over-the-counter (OTC) medicines. It is important to have a program in place to ensure all returned medicines are inspected prior to being returned to the shelves for resale. The *Consumer Healthcare Products Association* has recommended the following important safety tips for inspecting returned OTC medicines and dietary supplement products:

- Check for dirt or discoloration on the package. This could be a sign of improper storage.
- Check for tape on the package. This may indicate that the product has been removed and replaced with something else.
- Check for ink spots on the package. Some individuals who replace the contents of a package with another product or even foreign material mark the tampered-with carton so they do not accidentally repurchase it themselves.
- Check for excess glue on the package. If applied by the actual supplier, the glue should be virtually unnoticeable.
- Check for loose flaps, cuts, or tears on the packaging.
- Check for stickers or strange tags.
- If the package makes a strange sound when shaken, this could be a sign that something other than the intended product is in the container.

Makeup of the Crisis Management Team (CMT)

As I stated in "The Turkey Crisis" section, the company did not have a crisis management team in place. If there had been one, certainly the process of handling the tampering threat would have gone smoother. It is crucial to have a written policy manual outlining the responses to be taken when a crisis strikes. The crisis management policy manual must be kept in each business location, in a secure location, easily retrievable by store management, and placed on your operational audit program. Every member of the CMT should have copies of the policy manual in their

- Office
- Home(s)
- Car

Members of a crisis management team may include

- Senior Vice President of Administration
- Vice President of Operations
- Chief Financial Officer

- President and CEO
- Senior Vice President of Finance
- Senior Vice President of Marketing
- Vice President (Director) of Loss Prevention.

A senior member of the CMT should be designated as the team coordinator. There can be only one captain of the ship, and this principle applies here. One problem we experienced was that senior members of management were accepting calls from the news media, and we were not communicating a consistent message. All communications with the news media, initial contacts with law enforcement, and crisis communication updates are the responsibility of crisis management team coordinator.

Summary

Product tampering cases, whether real or a hoax, are very demanding on a company's resources. It is imperative that you take a proactive approach and have written procedures and actionable contingency plans in place. Have a prepared list of industry professionals to contact when a crisis strikes. Contract with a nationally recognized laboratory to analyze company-manufactured products when needed. In other words, BE PREPARED. The next "turkey crisis" is just around the corner.

References

Progressive Grocer, February 14, 2006; March 17, 2006
Time, October, 11, 1982; November 1, 1982; November 8, 1982; June 28, 1993
Chicago Tribune, October 1, 1982; October 3, 1983
New York Times, October 3, 1982; February 14, 1983
Consumer Healthcare Products Association (CHPA)

Proprietary Information

CAS, JHC

Every retailer should have a written policy reflecting the rules and regulations necessary to safeguard company proprietary information. For the sake of this section, we view all company internal records and documents not specifically designed or designated for public consumption as confidential.

The risk, which must be addressed, has to do with the unauthorized disclosure of company information, and such disclosures can be in the form of the spoken word, written documents, computer or video images, or recordings.

An example of a common rule throughout business and industry as it relates to company information is "No employee may speak to a representative of the media without authorization." That sets the tone for the need to ensure that everyone understands the WWII caution, "What you see here, what is said here, what you do here, stays here."

Such rules and regulations are intended to apply to everyone in the general employee population. For those employees in LP, however, we feel the need for further and more detailed or specific restrictions with regard to proprietary and/or confidential information.

Suggestions for the company to assist in protecting the loss prevention manual are contained in the section "Documentation" in this book.

We now make some recommendations with respect to policies which apply singularly to LP employees, whether they are clerical personnel, agents, investigators, or executives. We suggest that a "nondisclosure agreement" be signed by all LP employees, the violation of which could subject them to immediate termination and, if appropriate, civil action. This signed agreement would prohibit the unauthorized discussion, disclosure, release, duplication, or publication of confidential, proprietary, restricted or sensitive LP information or documents, including, but not necessarily limited to

- The LP manual
- Investigations, past or current
- Names of persons arrested for or suspected of criminal offenses
- Shrinkage (shortage) figures
- Number of LP employees
- LP budgetary information, including salary information
- Proposed or planned reorganizational structure
- Proposed or pending promotions within the LP department
- Names of witnesses in current investigations
- Disciplinary action taken with regard to any LP or company employee
- Any proposed LP operations designated as "sensitive" by proper authority
- Disclosure of any confidential informants, including names or locations
- Disclosure of any undercover personnel or assignments

While the preceding list may seem imposing, the nature of security/LP operations is such that any unauthorized disclosure of information, the sensitivity of which may or may not be known by the discloser, can adversely impact the company and/or personnel, and must be prevented. (See also "Code of Ethics for LP Personnel.")

Prosecution vs. Release

CAS, JHC

The decision, and any conditions thereto, as to whether to prosecute, release, or conditionally release persons apprehended shoplifting is a senior management responsibility. What are some of the factors that should be considered in reaching this decision?

To begin with, any prosecution will become a matter of public record, which, if the case involves a celebrity or public figure, will also receive publicity. Additionally, unless the suspect pleads guilty, there will be the requirement for the arresting persons and perhaps other store witnesses to spend time testifying in court. In the case of a small store, such required absence of employees may create a major interruption to normal business activities and become the deciding factor in reaching a decision to prosecute.

Local prosecutorial policies of the prosecuting authority (normally the district attorney) and police resources and response time may well be appropriate for calculating into the decision process.

Some retailers are repelled by the idea of letting a thief get off without consequence, and their decision to prosecute is emotional rather than a more reasoned one.

The use of a conditional release should not be overlooked; it is considered by some as a compromise between a simple release and prosecution. (See "Conditional (Controlled) Release" in this book.)

Whatever decision is made, and any conditions connected with that decision, such as what we consider the infamous rule adopted by a major retailer mandating release if the theft is a first-time offense involving merchandise valued under $25 (and then published in 2006), it is essential that it must be applied consistently. Any selective release or prosecution outside company-stated policy opens up the company to charges of discrimination.

Note: The less publicity given to apprehension and prosecution policies, the better. Public awareness, for example, that first-time offenders who shoplift under a specified dollar amount will be automatically released can, in my opinion, do nothing but increase theft activity.

Public Restrooms

CAS, JHC

Public restrooms in stores can present a number of potential problems, including unauthorized entry, illicit sexual activity, and the potential for child molestation.

I contacted as this section was being written about a case in which a male store janitorial employee entered an occupied ladies restroom and violated the customer's privacy and allegedly committed a sexual assault. The issues in this case were whether the store had adequate security, and/or if it had employed more loss prevention personnel and/or CCTVs outside the restroom entrances, would this incident have occurred? Since this book may be published while this case is still in litigation, we will not comment further on the merits of either the plaintiff's or defendant's case.

Public restrooms are known as places for engaging in illicit sexual activities, and restrooms in stores are no exception. This activity has the potential for creating several problems, among which are

- The offense taken by customers encountering this activity.
- The potential that a customer will be approached for illicit activity in error.
- The potential for the exposure of children to this activity.
- The store getting a reputation as a place known for this illegal activity and thus being avoided by customers.
- The potential for serious crimes such as rape or murder occurring in restrooms; I once testified in a case involving the murder of a young girl who was taken by a man into a restroom to commit the crime.

Stores, particularly the larger ones, must be alert to the potential for crime in their restrooms and develop a policy on how persons caught engaging in such activity will be dealt with. Signs indicating that restrooms are routinely patrolled by security personnel and law violations will be prosecuted are perfectly proper and may discourage those with improper reasons for entry.

Additionally, stores should establish policies and procedures to cover how janitorial and other maintenance will be performed in restrooms to avoid opposite sex personnel entering restrooms and creating embarrassment and privacy invasion of those legitimately occupying the restroom.

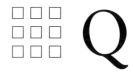

Q

Quick Change Artists

Better Business Bureau

Quick change con artists usually travel in groups of two or more and are criminals well versed in the art of fast-talking. Typically, the con artist or artists will bring a small purchase to a cashier and offer to pay with a large denomination bill. As the cashier hands over the proper change, the con artist "discovers" that he or she has a smaller denomination bill and withdraws the large denomination bill. With their hands already on the change, they attempt, through rapid exchange of money, to confuse the cashier into believing that the correct amount of money has changed hands. In reality, the con artist ends up walking away with all the change from the small bill plus all or part of the change issued on the larger denomination.

Your defense: The best defense against quick change cons is an alert, cautious cashier who understands the importance of taking time and not becoming rattled when money is being transacted. The cash register should be well out of the reach of customers so a con artist is prevented from "assisting" the cashier in making change. When the cashier rings up the sale, he or she should take the bill from the customer and place it on a safe but open spot away from the open cash drawer. The customer's money should not be immediately placed in the cash drawer.

The cashier should count out the change at least twice, once to himself or herself and a second time to the customer. If the customer attempts to exchange a smaller bill for the original large bill, the cashier should retrieve the change he or she was about to give to the customer, return it to the cash register, and start over with the new bill. Until the sale has been completed, the customer's money and the money in the cash register should not be mingled.

If the cashier becomes confused, he or she should close the cash drawer immediately and call for the store manager or supervisor to assist in the transaction. Speed and confusion are the quick change con artists' allies: When complications develop, or their scam is slowed down, they will usually abandon the scam.

Quick change con artists take advantage of a retailer's customer traffic (they proliferate during holiday seasons) and rely on an inexperienced or busy cashier who may not have the time to realize that scam is occurring. Often, it's not until the cashier's cash drawer comes up short that the business realizes that it has been victimized by a quick change con artist.

Reproduced with permission from the BBB News Release, December 13, 2001, by Better Business Bureau of South Alabama, PO Box 2008, Mobile, AL 36652.

Quotas and Goals

CAS, JHC

A "quota" in the loss prevention industry refers to a specific number of detentions each LP agent is expected to make in a given week or month or, in a more sophisticated setting, the number of detections per hours worked.

This has long since been deemed not only a poor management practice, but an invitation to severe criticism if unveiled in the court room during a civil trial for "false arrest." The court and/or jury understand the argument that employees under pressure to produce can and do make poor decisions, and ill-advised decisions in making arrests can prove injurious to innocent customers and a threat to the shopping public. Despite this archaic and flawed practice, it still exists in some stores today.

Some retailers, recognizing the word "quotas" is no longer professionally acceptable, have switched to the word "goals," which is no more and no less than a camouflage for the term and the practice of quotas. The authors have seen cases of companies that "skirt the line" by comments in performance reviews suggesting that the agent's arrest production "falls below the average" or "needs improvement," and the agent is given a goal to either improve or to reach the company's average arrest production. Whether these goals are, in reality, quotas can be argued, but if the agent *thinks* they are quotas, and he or she believes tenure is dependent on achieving the assigned goal, the agent invariably tends to take "shortcuts" in making detention decisions, thus increasing the potential for errors and resulting civil suits.

When measuring or accessing the performance of loss prevention agents charged with detentions, such evaluation should be on the quality of detentions, i.e., the sophistication of the theft, the level of professionalism of the shoplifter, the amount recovered, and the level of professionalism manifest in the written report of the detention, and the processing and ultimate disposition of the offender. Which is the detention of highest quality: a teenager caught stealing $4.99 necklace or the adult who filled a black trash bag with several hundred dollars worth of goods, hides it in the center of a sales rack and then a colleague returns, retrieves the sack, and leaves the store? Each one counts as one arrest!

Radio Frequency Identification (RFID)

Robert L. DiLonardo

"Automatic identification" (Auto ID) is the broad term given to a host of technologies used to identify objects. A number of technologies are considered subsets of Auto ID, including bar codes, smart cards, voice recognition, biometric scanning technologies, optical character recognition (OCR), and radio frequency identification (RFID).

RFID Overview

RFID is a method by which data is transferred via an electronic signal. In very basic terms, an RFID system includes a transponder tag (carrier of the information), an interrogator or reader, and a computer. The tag enters a radio frequency (RF) field transmitted by the reader. The signal received from this field powers the tag and enables it to transmit its unique identification number along with the application data. The interrogator identifies the signal as valid, captures the data, and sends it to a computer. The computer and its relevant application software determine whatever action is to be taken. In the most sophisticated versions of RFID, the computer can transmit additional data to the tag via the reader, changing the contents of the stored information. The use of RFID is widely viewed as the mechanism that will induce a quantum leap in productivity in the area of wholesale and retail logistics management, and other work processes. For the past few years, some of the world's leading retailers, consumer products manufacturers, academic institutions, and technology companies have been attempting to create a unified product identification and tracking system that could revolutionize the process behind ordering, manufacturing, shipping, tracking, stocking, selling, and reordering merchandise.

It is estimated that by 2010, RFID will become cost effective enough to be utilized on individual pieces of merchandise (items). One of the large markets for these products is retail, but many other nonretail applications are possible. In addition to the operational and logistical applications, there are a number of security-oriented applications, including antitheft and fraud protection and anticounterfeiting.

Tags

The most common RFID tags consist of an integrated circuit with memory and an antenna. Active tags have a transmitter and their own power source (typically a battery), used to run the microchip's circuitry and to broadcast a signal to a reader—the way a cell phone transmits signals to a base station. Passive tags have no battery. Instead, they draw power from the reader, which sends out electromagnetic waves that induce a current in the tag's antenna. Semipassive tags use a battery to run the chip's circuitry but communicate by drawing power from the reader. Active and semipassive tags are useful for tracking high-value items requiring long read ranges, such as railway cars or sea containers. They are costly and too cumbersome to use on smaller items.

Memory Capacity

Within limits, memory capacity varies by tag vendor and is often dictated by the requirements of the application. Typically, a tag carries no more than 2 kilobits (Kb) of data—enough to store some basic information about the item to which it is attached. The current trend is toward tags with less memory capacity. A simple "license plate" tag contains only a 96-bit serial number. These tags are cheaper to manufacture and are more useful for applications where the tag will be disposable.

Frequencies

RFID systems use many different frequencies, but the most common are low-frequency (125 kHz), high-frequency (13.56 MHz), and ultra-high-frequency or UHF (860–960 MHz). Microwave (2.45 GHz) is also used in some applications. Since radio waves exhibit different characteristics at different frequencies, the proper frequency must be chosen for each application type. Lower frequencies (under 10 MHz) are less sensitive to substances such as moisture or metal that inhibits the reception of the signal. However, these low frequencies are incapable of being identified at long range and require a long time within the field to transmit data. Higher frequencies are capable of longer read ranges and advanced functionality, such as the ability to read multiple tags in the field at the same time. Long-range (over 2 meters) reading requirements are prevalent in the "back end" of the retail logistics chain, where merchandise is packaged in cartons and loaded on pallets within trucks or sea containers. However, the higher the frequency, the more susceptible the signals are to blockage by moisture and metals.

Frequency Standardization

The RFID industry is attempting to follow the bar code industry by establishing worldwide frequency standards. All bar codes printed on retail merchandise in the United States contain the same convention. In essence, the bar code on a package of batteries can be scanned by virtually any retail establishment in the United States. The same approach for RFID frequency standardization will allow the industry to optimize the effectiveness of the technology and provide a stimulus to growth.

Individual countries have jurisdiction over the assignation of radio frequencies. Most countries have assigned the 125 MHz and 134 MHz areas for low frequency RFID applications. The 13.56 MHz area is used universally for high-frequency systems. Ultra-high-frequency (UHF) RFID systems have existed only since the mid-1990s, and all countries have not yet agreed on a single area of the UHF spectrum for RFID. Europe has adopted 868 MHz, and the United States uses 915 MHz. Until recently, Japan did not allow any use of the UHF spectrum for RFID but is considering 960 MHz for RFID. Many other devices utilize the UHF spectrum, so it may take years, if ever, for all governments to agree on a single frequency.

System power output is also government regulated to limit interference with other devices. Some umbrella groups, such as the Global Commerce Initiative, are encouraging governments to agree on frequencies and power output levels. RFID tag and reader manufacturers are developing systems that can work at multiple frequencies to limit the impact of a lack of uniform global standards.

Where Do Current EAS Frequencies Fit?

EAS technology is the forerunner of RFID. An EAS "system" contains every element of an RFID system. The major limitation of EAS is in the amount of "intelligence" (the amount of information that can be stored and retrieved) built into the tag. EAS systems simply interrogate the tag, determine that it is a valid component, and activate an alarm. Some EAS systems utilize this activation to activate another component, such as CCTV, via a simple electronic switch closure.

Neither acousto-magnetic EAS (58 kHz) nor Radio Frequency EAS (8.2 MHz) will be adopted as standard RFID frequencies. The acousto-magnetic EAS frequency is incapable of transmitting a sufficient quantity of data at an appropriate speed. While the RF EAS frequency may be "borderline" appropriate for item-level applications, the choice of a higher frequency allows for the creation of a much smaller tag because the antenna size can be reduced.

Assuming that the RFID industry standardizes around 13.56 MHz for item-level activities, both of the current EAS frequencies will remain antitheft tools, and not RFID tools.

References

Bhuptani, M., and Moradpour, S. (2005). *RFID field guide*. Prentice Hall.

DiLonardo, R. L. (1998). RFID emerges as technology of choice. *Security Technology & Design Magazine*. July.

IBM Business Consulting Services. (2002). *Applying Auto-ID to reduce losses associated with product obsolescence*, IBM-AUTOID-BC-004.

RFID Journal. Frequently Asked Questions. *RFID Journal* [Electronic Version]. Retrieved April 20, 2006, from http://www.rfidjournal.com/faq.

Security Technology & Design Magazine. (1998). Protecting consumer products with RFID. August.

Reference Materials: Suggested Sources

CAS, JHC

Books

General

Confidential Information Sources, 2nd ed., John M. Carroll, Butterworth-Heinemann, 1991.

Critical Incident Management, Rod Paschall, OICJ, University of Illinois, 992.

How to Protect Yourself from Crime, Ira A. Lipman, Contemporary Books, 1997.

Industrial Security, David L. Berger, Butterworth-Heinemann, 1979.

Introduction to Security, Glen Green and Raymond Farber, Security World Publishing Co., 1975.

Never Be Lied to Again, David J. Lieberman, PhD, St. Martins Press, 1998.

Principles of Security, 2nd ed., Truett A. Ricks, CPP, Bill G. Tillett, CPP, and Clifford W. VanMeter, PhD, Anderson Publishing Co., 1988.

Protection Officer Training Manual, Compilation, 6th ed., International Foundation For Protection Officers, Butterworth-Heinemann, 1998

Retail Security & Loss Prevention, by Read Hayes, CPP, Butterworth-Heinemann, 1991.

Retail Security Policy Manual, Kenneth R. Grover, PhD, Butterworth-Heinemann, 1992.

Risk Analysis and The Security Survey, James F. Broder, CPP, Butterworths, 1984.

The Security Officer's Field Training Guide, Lt. Phillip M. Satterfield, MPA, Cypress, CA, 1988.

Truth and Deception, John E. Reid and Fred E. Inbau, The Williams & Wilkins Co., 1966.

Violence in the Workplace, S. Anthony Baron, PhD, Pathfinder Publishing of CA, 2003.

Legal

Avoiding Liability in Retail Security 1986; *Avoiding Liability in Premises Security 1989*; R. Keegan Federal, Jr., Stafford Publications Inc.

Barron's Dictionary of Legal Terms, 2nd ed., Steven H. Gifis, Barron's, 1993.

Legal Aspects of Private Security, Arthur J. Bilek, John C. Klotter and R. Federal Keegan, Anderson Publishing Co., 1981.

Legal Guidelines for Covert Surveillance Operations in the Private Sector, John Dale Hartman, Butterworth-Heinemann, 1993.

The Legal Side of Private Security, Leo F. Hannon, JD, Quorum Books, 1992.

Private Security and the Law, 2nd ed. Charles P. Nemeth, JD, LLM, Anderson Publishing Co., 1995.

Private Security in America, Clifford E. Simonsen, PhD, CPP Prentice-Hall, 1998.

Private Security Law—Case Studies, David A. Maxwell, JD, CPP, Butterworth-Heinemann, 1993.

The Privatization of Police in America, James F. Pastor, McFarland, 2002.

The Right to Privacy, Ellen Alderman and Caroline Kennedy, Vintage Books (Random House), 1997.

Safe Places? Security Planning and Litigation, Richard S. Kuhlman, Esq., The Michie Company, 1989.

Use of Force, Brian A. Kinnaird, Looseleaf Law Publishers, 1973.

Investigations

A Guide to Internal Loss Prevention, Roy L. Wesley and John A. Wanat, Butterworth-Heinemann, 1986.

Are Your Employees Stealing You Blind, Edwin C. Bliss and Isamu S. Aoki, Pfeiffer & Co., Butterworth-Heinemann, 2001.

Employee Theft Investigation, J. Kirk Barefoot, Butterworth-Heinemann, 1980.

Employee Theft Investigation, 2nd ed., J. Kirk Barefoot, Butterworth-Heinemann, 1990.

How to Keep Your Employees Honest, Bob Curtis, Lebhar-Friedman Books, 1979.

Investigations in the Workplace, Eugene F. Ferraro, CPP, and Norman M. Spain, JD. Auerbach Publications, 2006.

Practical Aspects of Interview and Interrogation, David E. Zulawski and Douglas Wicklander, Elsevier Science Publishing Co., 1992.

The Process of Investigation, 3rd ed., Charles A. Sennewald and John K. Tsukayama, Butterworth-Heinemann, 2006.

The Process of Investigation, 2nd ed., Charles A. Sennewald and John K. Tsukayama, Butterworth-Heinemann, 2001.

Risk Analysis and the Security Survey, James F. Broder, CPP, Butterworth-Heinemann, 2006.

The Safe Hiring Manual, Lester S. Rosen, Esq., Facts on Demand Press, 2004.

Thieves at Work, Ira Michael Shepard and Robert Duston, Bureau of National Affairs, 1988.

Training Seminars on Interviewing & Interrogations, John E. Reid and Associates, Inc. Chicago, IL.

Management

Corporate Security Administration & Management, J. Kirk Barefoot, CPP, and David A. Maxwell, Butterworth-Heinemann, 1987.

Effective Security Management, 4th ed., Charles A. Sennewald, CPP, Butterworth-Heinemann, 2003.

Encyclopedia of Security Management, John J. Fay, Butterworth-Heinemann, 1993.

Industrial Security Management, Richard J. Healy and Timothy J. Walsh, American Management Association, 1971.

Protection Management & Crime, Richard B. Cole, W. H. Anderson Co., 1974.

Security Administration, 2nd ed., Richard S. Post and Arthur A. Kingsbury, Charles C. Thomas, 1973.

Security Operations Management, Robert D. McCrie, Butterworth-Heinemann, 2001.

Shoplifting

Shoplifters vs. Retailers, Charles A. Sennewald, CPP, New Century Press, 2000.

Shoplifting Control, Read Hayes, CPP, Prevention Press, 1993.

Shoplifting: Managing the Problem, John H. Christman, CPP, and Charles A. Sennewald, CPP, ASIS-International, 2006.

Shoplifting: What You Need to Know About the Law, Stanley L. Sklar, Fairchild Publications, 1982.

The books listed above are on your our bookshelves and can be referenced without reservation. For a more comprehensive list of security/loss prevention reference sources, obtain a copy of the *ASIS Bookstore* (from ASIS-International, online at asis@asisonline.org, or by phone at 703-519-6200), listing hundreds of books relating to loss prevention.

Newsletters:

Security Letter (twice monthly), 166 East 96th Street, New York, NY 10128, $217 Yrly.

Corporate Security (bi-weekly), Strafford Publications, 590 Dutch Valley Road, PO Drawer 13729, Atlanta, GA 30324, $348.95 Yrly.

Premises Liability Report (monthly), Strafford Publications (*Supra*), $301.95 Yrly.

Private Security Case Law Reporter (monthly), Strafford Publications (*Supra*), $361.95 Yrly.

Security Director News (monthly), United Publications, Inc., P.O. Box 996, Yarmouth, ME 04098, FREE.

Security Director's Report (monthly), Institute of Management & Administration, 3 Park Ave., 30th Floor, New York, NY 10016, $279.00 Yrly.

Security Law Newsletter (monthly*)*, Strafford Publications (*Supra*), 30324, $311.95 Yrly.

Note: Prices current as of January 1, 2007.

Magazines

LOSSPrevention Magazine, 8037 Corporate Center Dr., Suite 400, Charlotte, NC 28226, FREE.

Security Management, ASIS-International, 1625 Prince St., Alexandria, VA 22314, $48 yr for nonmembers.

Security Design & Technology, 100 Colony Park Dr., Suite 203 Cumming, GA 30040, FREE.

Security, 600 Willowbrook Lane, Westchester, PA 19382, FREE.

Vendor Sources:

The Security Industry Buyers Guide by ASIS—International

The annual January/February issue of *LOSSPrevention Magazine Resource Guide*

The preceding lists are not meant to be, nor are they, complete. Other publications and sources of information and training are available, and we apologize for any omissions.

Report Writing

CAS, JHC

The importance of a good written report of a security or loss prevention incident—whether an apprehension, fire, bomb threat, employee dishonesty case, or anything else—cannot be overstated. A written report memorializes the event, one hopes in a manner which permits the reader, at any later date, to fully understand the *who, what, when, where, why,* and *how* of the incident. The effectiveness of an investigator is judged, in large measure, by the quality of his reports. A well-conducted investigation, poorly reported, negates the degree of skill utilized in conducting the investigation.

1. The purpose of an Investigative report is to achieve the following objectives:
   Record: Provide a permanent record of all significant information.
   Leads: Provide information necessary to advance the investigation.
   Action: Provide a factual basis for determining appropriate action.
2. The nature of the report is an objective narrative of findings.
3. The qualities of an investigative report are as follows:
   Accuracy
   Completeness
   Clarity
4. The sequence of reports is Generally, chronologically
5. The parts of a report are as follows:
   Administrative Data
       Date
       File Number
       Subject
       Classification
       Complaint
       Reporting Investigator
       Origin of Investigation
       Status
       Distribution of report
   Synopsis
   Details
   Conclusions and Recommendations (clearly identified as such)
   Undeveloped Leads
   Enclosures

All reports should answer these basic questions: who, what, when, where, how, and why.

Careful attention should be paid to grammar and syntax; avoid errors such as the following: "Me and him"; "Him and I"; "They run away"; "We was going to"; "We come back"; "He say that"; "He rung up the sale"; "We done everything possible."

Reports must be careful that any quotes are exactly as stated. Opinions and conclusions must be clearly identified as such, and reports should be signed by the writer.

As stated elsewhere in this book, a clear, concise, accurate, and well-written incident report is frequently the best tool a company has in defending itself in a loss-prevention-driven lawsuit.

Considering the preceding required qualities of a well-written report, read the following report and see how many obvious errors you can identify.

REPORT OF INVESTIGATION
Name of User: Iam N. Investigator
Date: 07/19/2007
Case #: RWA-01 07 -00353-C-00006
Details of Investigation:

An investigation was initiated at this location on 7-15-07, based on information received from an informant, Joe Goodman, DOB 3/12/66 (phone 555–5555). When reporting, Goodman stated that he had witnessed Very Tuff and Security Guard I. M. Trouble stealing merchandise. Goodman stated that Trouble was allowing Very to exit the facility with stolen merchandise concealed in bags and under clothing.

Based on the above information, a surveillance was conducted on 7-16-07. with no results. It was then decided to interview both Tuff and Trouble on 7-17-07.

Based on this information, I. Gotchya interviewed Tuff 7-17-07, who in a signed statement acknowledged to stealing $5,000.00 to $6,000.00 of unpaid Cheap Brothers merchandise. Tuff would conceal the items under his clothing or in a bag and Trouble would allow him to exit the facility. Tuff signed a indebtness and promise to pay document for the amount of $5,000.00

Subsequently, on this same date, I interviewed I. M. Trouble on 7-17-07 who in a signed statement acknowledged to allowing Very Tuff, and B. A Filcher to exit the facility with unpaid for Cheap Brothers merchandise. Trouble admitted that the total dollar value of the merchandise is $7,000.00. Trouble further explained that both of the above associates would conceal merchandise on there person or in various bags. Trouble signed a indebtedness and promise to pay document for $6.183.55.

In addition on this date, I interviewed B. A Filcher who in a signed statement acknowledged to stealing $3.350.00 of Cheap Brothers merchandise. Filcher stole merchandise by concealing it on his person or in some type of bag and exit the guard shack while Trouble was working. Filcher' signed a indebtness and promise to pay document for $3,350.00.

The facts surrounding this case were reviewed with M. Y. Boss and Big Boss and it was decided that Tuff, Filcher and Trouble employment be terminated.

Note: The significant errors are underlined and explained in the report reprinted here. Note the reference numbers which refer to errors.

REPORT OF INVESTIGATION
Name of User: Iam N. Investigator
Date: 07/19/2001
Case #: RWA-01 07 -00353-C-00006
Errors in Report Heading:
1 No Subject; 2 No Classification 3 No Complaint
4 No Reporting investigator 5 No Status of investigation
6 No Distribution 7 No Synopsis
Details of Investigation:

An investigation was initiated at <u>this location</u>[8] on 7-15-07, based on information received from an informant, Joe Goodman, DOB 3/12/66 (phone 555–5555). When reporting, Goodman stated that he had witnessed <u>Very Tuff</u>[9] and <u>Security Guard I. M. Trouble</u>[10] stealing merchandise. Goodman stated that Trouble was allowing Very to exit the facility with stolen merchandise concealed in bags and under clothing.

Based on the above information, a surveillance was conducted on 7-16-07 <u>with no results</u>[11]. It was then decided to interview both Tuff and Trouble on 7-17-07.

Based on this information, I. Gotchya <u>interviewed</u>[12] Tuff 7-17-07, who in a signed statement acknowledged to <u>stealing $5,000.00 to $6,000.00</u>[13] of unpaid Cheap Brothers merchandise. Tuff would conceal the items under his clothing or in a bag and Trouble would allow him to exit the facility. Tuff signed a <u>indebtness</u>[14] and <u>promise to pay document</u>[15] for[16] the amount of $5,000.00

Subsequently, on this same date, I <u>interviewed I. M. Trouble</u>[17] on 7-17-07 who in a signed statement <u>acknowledged to allowing</u>[18] Very Tuff, and <u>B. A Filcher</u>[19] to exit the facility with <u>unpaid for Cheap Brothers merchandise.</u>[20] Trouble admitted that the total dollar value of <u>the merchandise is $ 7,000.00.</u>[21] Trouble further explained that both of the above associates would conceal merchandise on <u>there</u>[22] person or in various bags. Trouble signed a indebtedness and <u>promise to pay document</u>[23] for <u>$6.183.55.</u>[24]

In addition <u>on this date,</u>[25] I <u>interviewed B. A Filcher</u>[26] who in a signed statement acknowledged <u>to stealing $3,350.00</u>[27] of Cheap Brothers merchandise. Filcher stole merchandise by concealing it on his person or in some type of bag and <u>exit</u>[28] the guard shack <u>while Trouble was working.</u>[29] Filcher' signed a <u>indebtness</u>[30] and <u>promise to pay document</u>[31] for $3,350.00.

The facts surrounding this case were reviewed with M. Y. Boss and Big Boss and it was decided that Tuff, Filcher and Trouble employment be terminated.

Errors in Body of Report:

8. Name location 9. Job or Employer 10. Employer 11. There were results; should have been stated "with negative results." 12. Where, times 13. thefts over what period of time 14. Misspelled and improper use of word 15. More correctly, a Promissory Note 16. Should be "in", not "for" 17. Where, times 18. improper language; eliminate "to" 19. Identify Filcher in detail 20. What merchandise? Over what period of time? 21. How much attributable to each thief? 22. Misspelled word 23. More properly, a promissory note 24. This amount requires an explanation 25. Show date 26. Where interviewed, times; Further identification of Filcher needed 27. How does he know this exact amount 28. Tense; "exited" 29. Statement that Trouble knew he was stealing 30. Misspelled word 31. Properly "Promissory Note

Errors/Omissions at End of Report:

32. Should mention whether prosecuted and reason for decision

33. Report not signed

34. No distribution shown

35. Copies of statements and promissory notes should be included as enclosures Did you find any others?

Other Concerns/Comments:

1. I have reservations about mentioning Joe Goodman as the informant and source of the information about these thefts. We suggest that, rather than Joe's name and phone number being shown, he be referred to as "Confidential Informant 25." Without using this comment as a tutorial on documenting and handling confidential informants, Joe's name and identifying data should be kept in a highly restricted and secure file, and he should be identified in any reports which will receive distribution and possible use in open court as a confidential informant, thus protecting his identity as well as, perhaps, his physical well-being.

2. We suggest that obtaining a promissory note from Trouble in the amount of $6,183.55 was improper. Nowhere in this report does it state, nor did Trouble admit, that Trouble stole any merchandise. While he obviously facilitated and permitted Tuff and Filcher to steal, which certainly justifies his termination and possible criminal prosecution as a coconspirator with Tuff and Filcher, Trouble himself did not benefit from their thefts, and *therefore owes the company no restitution. According to the statements of all concerned, the maximum amount of stolen merchandise amounted to $9,350 (the total of Tuff's and Filcher's admissions). The total of all the Promissory Notes obtained is $14,533.55, or $5,183.55 more than the maximum total dollar value of the admitted thefts and loss to the company. The company cannot profit from the illegal acts of its employees.*

A Well-Written Report

Company Name
REPORT OF INVESTIGATION
Date: July 19, 2007   File#: RWA-01 07 -00353-C-00006
Subject: Midtown Warehouse Thefts ($9000)   Class: Theft
Origin: Confidential Informant #25   Charge: 487PC
Report by: Iam N. Investigator   Status: Closed
Undeveloped Leads: None

Synopsis: An investigation, based on information from a Confidential Informant, led to two (2) employees of the Midtown Warehouse admitting the theft of merchandise valued at approximately $9,000.00 over a period of the past 10 months. The theft was facilitated by a company security guard who knew of the thefts but allowed them to occur. Those responsible for the thefts have agreed to make restitution. All three (3) employees were terminated and criminal prosecution will be pursued. This case is closed.

Details of Investigation: An investigation was initiated at the Midtown Warehouse on July 15, 2007, based on information received from Confidential Informant (CI) #25. The informant reported that he had witnessed stockman Very Tuff and Security Guard I. M. Trouble stealing merchandise. Informant further stated that Trouble was allowing Tuff to exit the facility with stolen merchandise concealed in trash bags and under his clothing.

Based on the above information, a surveillance was conducted on July 16, 2007, with negative results.

It was then decided to interview both Tuff and Trouble on 7-17-07.

On July 17, 2007, I interviewed Tuff at Midtown Warehouse from 9:30 a.m. until 10:23 a.m.; Ms. Irma Jones, HR Manager, witnessed the interview. Tuff is a stockman in the Midtown Warehouse and has been employed there for the past twelve (12) months. He admitted, in a signed statement, that he has, over the past ten (10) months, stolen approximately $5,000.00 to $6,000.00 of merchandise from Midtown Warehouse. He stated he accomplished these thefts by concealing these items under his clothing or in a trash bag and then taking them out to his car. He further stated that Security Officer I. M. Trouble was aware of his thefts for many months but did nothing to prevent them. Tuff voluntarily signed a promissory note in the amount of $5,000.00. Tuff was then suspended, his company ID retrieved, and he was told to report to Human Relations on July 20 at 9 a.m.

On July 17 I also interviewed Security Officer I. M. Trouble at Midtown. The interview was witnessed by Ms. Irma Jones, HR Manager, and was conducted from 10:45 a.m. until 11:30 a.m. Trouble admitted in a signed statement that he had allowed Tuff and also stockman B. A. Filcher to remove company property from Midtown without paying for it. He said he allowed both Tuff and Filcher to remove this merchandise by concealing it under their clothes or in trash bags that ostensibly were going into the dumpster. This theft activity started about ten (10) months ago and has continued since then. Trouble estimated that the total dollar value of the merchandise taken by Tuff and Trouble amounted to $7,000.00. Trouble said he did not personally gain from these thefts and was unable to explain why he permitted them to occur. Trouble was suspended from his employment, his security badge and ID taken from him, and he was told to report to Human Relations on July 20 at 11 a.m.

At 1:00 p.m. on July 17 I interviewed B. A Filcher, a stockman at Midtown Warehouse, who has been employed for eleven (11) months. The interview was witnessed by Ms. Irma Jones, HR Manager, and ended at 1:42 p.m. Filcher admitted to seeing Tuff steal merchandise from Midtown about five (5) months ago; he confronted Tuff, and they then agreed that Filcher would also begin taking unpaid-for merchandise. Filcher, in a signed statement, acknowledged that he had stolen about $3,350.00 of Cheap Brothers' merchandise. Filcher utilized the same method of stealing as did Tuff. Filcher said they were careful to steal only when Trouble was in the guard shack. Filcher voluntarily signed a promissory note in the amount of $3,350.00. Filcher was suspended from employment, his company ID recovered, and he was told to report to Human Relations on July 20 at 1 p.m.

All three (3) employees indicated the great bulk of the stolen merchandise consisted of ready-to-wear items, with a relatively few items of costume jewelry and men's fragrances.

The facts surrounding this case were reviewed with M. Y. Boss and Big Boss, and it was decided that the employment of Tuff, Filcher, and Trouble would be terminated on July 20; the investigation will be reviewed with the district attorney for possible prosecution of Tuff and Filcher for theft and Trouble for conspiracy to commit theft.

Signed: ——————-

Encl(s): Copy of Tuff's signed statement and promissory note.

Copy of Filcher's signed statement and promissory note.

Copy of Trouble's signed statement.

Dist: (1) File, (2) Corp LP, (3) District Attorney

Because we consider report writing such an important subject for LP, we have added some additional thoughts and suggestions on report writing. LP reports may be reviewed by senior management, police departments, and/or the district attorney's office, and not infrequently worker's compensation boards and/or hearing officers. In addition, these reports, while confidential, are available under discovery to attorneys, both plaintiff and defense. As stated earlier, the efficiency and professionalism of the LP department is reflected and judged by the quality of these reports.

Confidentiality

Security reports often contain sensitive information; it is therefore absolutely necessary that they be safeguarded against unauthorized disclosure. The reports must be stored in a secure file cabinet when not needed, and disclosure of the contents can be made only to people with the right and need to know. Every effort must be made to maintain the confidentiality of reports.

Elements of Effective Report Writing

A well-written report should provide a complete understanding of an incident to a person with no prior knowledge of the incident.

Reports should include *all* important details, written in a clear, concise manner. Common words are most effective, since they cannot be misunderstood. Professional jargon and police terms should be avoided.

Accuracy in spelling, punctuation, capitalization, and sentence structure *is* vital. If errors are made, they could change the meaning of a report.

The following elements are fundamental to good report writing:

1. *Spelling:* Correct spelling is essential to a professional report. If in doubt, do *not* guess. Refer to a dictionary or spell-check where applicable.
2. *Abbreviations:* Abbreviations can lack clarity. The use of abbreviations should be limited to standard dictionary or department-approved abbreviations. All abbreviations should be in parenthesis, preceded by the complete term; for example, Downtown Distribution Center (DDC).

3. *Brief:* Information in the reports should be stated directly. Every effort should be made to use short, concise sentences for easy reading.
4. *Objective:* Reports must include facts, not opinions or conclusions. Impartiality is mandatory.
5. *Complete:* Every report should contain all relevant facts of the incident. All the basic questions—who, what, where, when, why, and how—should be answered.
   A. *Who:* Often more than one person needs to be identified in a report: the subject, victim, witness(es), etc. For example:
      Who was apprehended?
      Who performed the search?
      Who witnessed the incident?
   B. *What:* This question is multifaceted, for example:
      What offense was committed?
      What type of property was stolen?
      What did the subject say?
   C. *Where:* This question concerns the location. For example:
      Where did the incident occur?
      Where was the subject apprehended?
      Where was the property recovered?
   D. *When:* Chronological order in a report is essential. The reader should be able to understand and follow the events easily, even if they transpired over a long period of time. Reports should be as specific as possible regarding actual dates and times of events.
   E. *Why:* Documenting the subject's motivation for committing the offense is very important. When a subject tells why he committed the offense, his guilt is implied. If a subject is not willing to tell, do not speculate.
   F. *How:* The subject's method of operation is vital to an accurate report. Explaining how an incident occurred allows the company an opportunity to revise policies and procedures, and to determine if standards are adequate or if revisions are necessary.

Identification of Persons

1. Each time a subject is referred to in a security report, his last name must be capitalized. Within the context of the report, the subject may be identified by his last name, or the word "SUBJECT."
2. The names of other persons identified within the report should be typed using normal capitalization rules. Once fully identified, the person should be referred to by his last name.
3. If the proper spelling of a person's name is not known and not obtainable, the name should be spelled phonetically with the word "phonetic" in parentheses immediately following the name.
4. If the security form requests the race of the individual, one of the following must be used:
   - *MW*—Majority, White
   - *NB*—Non-majority, Black
   - *NA*—Non-majority, Asian
   - *NS*—Non-Majority, Hispanic
   - *NO*—Non-majority, Other

General Information

1. LP personnel must write their own reports.
2. *Proofread* all reports. It is recommended that, if practical, another agent read the completed report prior to its submission.

3. Reports may be written in either first or third person. Whichever is used, it must be consistent throughout the entire report.
4. Opinions and/or conclusions of security personnel are not generally included in official security reports. If it is necessary to include such information, it is reported in a separate paragraph, with the heading "Agent's Notes."
5. A "Confidential Source of Information" (CSI) or "Confidential Informant" (CI) is an individual who furnishes information on a specific case with the desire to have his identity protected. Under no circumstances are CSIs or CIs identified by name in any report, and they are not to be named in any official company document. All requests to identify a CSI must be forwarded to the most senior LP executive for approval.
   A. Ideally, each CI is given an individual code used for internal reference purposes. The code is a numerical identification number, consisting on the following:
      1. CI's name
      2. Store number and name of store concerned
      3. A source number
      For example: CI 1701. CI is the Confidential Source of Information, from store #17, Pittsburgh; and 01 identifies the specific individual.
   B. The name of the CI must be placed in a sealed envelope with the coded number on the outside of the envelope. The envelope must be retained in a secured area at all times.
   C. Code numbers are used in a report only when initially referring to a CI. If more than one CSI is mentioned in a report, the complete identification number is required for clarity.
6. The original copy of all reports should be retained in the store's LP or security department files.

Requests by Shoplifting Detainees

CAS, JHC

A particularly sensitive area in shoplifting detentions has to do with requests or demands made by the person in custody of the loss prevention department, pending arrival of the police (or pending the decision whether the police should be summoned). "Particularly sensitive" means subsequent repercussions might stem from the company's response to such requests or demands. For example, a woman is detained for shoplifting at 2:00 p.m. and is brought to the office for processing. At the outset of the processing, she informs the loss prevention personnel she has a child in elementary school a mile away and that child will be waiting in front of the school for her at 2:30 p.m. and therefore needs to be released quickly or needs to call her husband at his place of work to pick up that child. In this case, her request requires immediate attention. The LP agent should either allow her to call whoever is necessary to pick up that child, or the Agent should make the call for her. Ignoring or not believing the woman could have catastrophic consequences. Too many times have we seen detainees' requests ignored or arbitrarily refused, and such insensitivity to the request has the potential of adverse downstream consequences.

Following is a sampling of detainees' requests and the recommended appropriate course of action:

- If a person asks for a drink of water, provide it.
- If a person claims he needs to take medication and has the medication, allow him to take it, but also, if possible, prevent him from overdosing.
- If a person claims he needs to take medication and has the medication and must take it with some food, provide him with the food he requests.
- If a person asks to use the restroom, accompany the person to the restroom and monitor him to ensure he doesn't dispose of merchandise, drugs, or any other item which may be of interest to the police.

- If a person claims he is cold, take reasonable steps to make him comfortable.
- If a person claims he is too hot, again, take reasonable steps to cool him down.
- If a person claims he is sick, injured, or in pain, call the paramedics.
- If a person claims he has a friend or relative with him and that person will be alarmed and panicky over his "disappearance," make every effort to locate that person, page her if necessary, and inform her as to the detainee's status, if the detainee wants that done.
- If a person claims he has children or friends waiting in the car parked in the lot, attempt to locate and confirm.
- If a person claims he has the receipt for the merchandise in question in his vehicle, obtain a full description of the vehicle and its location in the parking lot and inform him the police will be so informed and will make the decision as to searching the vehicle.
- If a person requests or demands to use a phone, including his own cell phone, to call a relative, friend, or attorney, inform him that he may not make the call until the police arrive or may make the call after he is processed and released.
- If a person requests or demands to speak to the store manager, follow company policy as to a store manager's role or responsibility in shoplifting matters.
- If the person offers an exculpatory explanation, such as prior conversation with store personnel of service desk associates, make every attempt to verify the story.

These recommendations are but guidelines for what courts have held to be reasonable responses to customers temporarily held in temporary custody in keeping with laws pertaining to the merchant's privilege and state laws relating to arrests by private persons.

Restaurants in Stores

CAS, JHC

The trend to have restaurants or at least some minimal food service available in retail stores seems to be increasing. The food service may be either proprietary or leased out as a concession, with the store owner realizing an agreed-upon fee. This trend poses some potential security risks of interest to loss prevention.

While not strictly a loss prevention issue, the potential for spills of food and drink products increases the possibility of slip-and-fall accidents, which will undoubtedly lead to claims, lawsuits, and higher insurance costs.

Also not primarily a loss prevention issue but one that can cause losses, both financial as well as to reputation, is that of food contamination which causes illness to patrons. Maintaining sanitary food preparation and serving areas, as well as food servers who are free from disease, is essential to both reputation and business success.

Of more immediate concern to loss prevention professionals are issues connected with food service establishments or operations which can lead to theft or embezzlement.

If the establishment serves alcoholic beverages, not only is serving to underage patrons of concern, but also serving drinks which are either under or over standard alcohol content. Because most bars use a standard number of drinks per bottle of alcohol to calculate profitability, a bartender preparing drinks which are under strength can accumulate alcohol, which can then be used to prepare drinks that he will not ring up on the register and pocket the cash paid. By preparing over strength drinks (generally for friends or regular customers), profitability is adversely affected. Bar operations require "mystery shoppers" for random sampling and testing.

The operation of a restaurant, whether a simple coffee shop or a full-blown restaurant, requires considerable skill to be profitable. Whereas the economic "health" of a retailer has a direct relationship to inventory shortage, food service operations focus on *food costs;* i.e., when a retailer receives 90 pairs of shoes but is invoiced and pays for 100 pairs, that results in increased shrinkage. When a restaurant receives 90 pounds of hamburger but is invoiced and pays for 100 pounds, that drives up food costs. Loss prevention seldom gets involved in food costs except when specifically charged to investigate.

When food spoilage is considered, ordering supplies becomes critical to prevent excessive loss of product through spoilage. Additionally, planning menus to minimize waste is almost a science. Remember that we encounter the same potential for vendor fraud in the food supply business as in any other, but perhaps with less tolerance for losses from this source because of the other critical aspects of this business affecting profitability.

Proprietary restaurants within the confines of a major store, from time to time, will arrange for private parties and banquets which may extend beyond the normal store hours. Special arrangements must be made to accommodate these events, which typically requires loss prevention involvement. "Special arrangements" might include providing security personnel (either plainclothes or uniformed), extending the alarm times with the central station, and gating off or otherwise ensuring a barrier exists between the restaurant and the balance of the store.

Finally, we must consider the increased danger of fire from kitchen operations and the additional fire prevention (CO_2 systems over stoves) devices required.

Retail Fraud

Dave Niemeyer

What marvels the technological revolution has brought us! On any given day at any given time, we can stand in virtually any area of our choice and peruse email, call a friend in a foreign land, check our location to within a few feet using GPS, and perform a variety of other tasks, all with devices that either slip into a pocket or clip on a belt. Inasmuch as the proliferation of technology has been a boon to most of our daily existences, it has also shown itself to be a bane to the retail industry. We utilize a wide array of electronic technology in the retail world. We have come to be very dependent on it in our day-to-day retail operation. From maintaining our supply chains to transacting our sales, electronic technology is integral to the retail world of the 21st century. Where technology has shown itself to be a bane is where it is used to perpetrate fraudulent activity against the world of retail. Whereas criminal minds have employed a wide assortment of technology to advance their ability to move above and beyond the simple techniques of days past, such as simple shoplifting, we in loss prevention must also advance and adapt our ways of doing business in order to develop and maintain programs that prevent and detect fraudulent activity. Development and implementation of fraud prevention and detection programs are as rapidly growing as traditional loss prevention programs and equally as important. Integral to fraud prevention and detection is having a plan in place which can only be referred to as "all inclusive." By "all inclusive," I mean that retailers must be prepared to follow through with legal action, up to and including prosecution, when fraud prevention measures are circumvented and defeated. With simple shoplifting as an analogy, most any fraud prevention and detection program you enact will be tested by the best effort today's well-equipped criminal mind can come up with. Unfortunately, in most cases, even the best programs will suffer the occasional defeat.

Foremost in any adversarial situation is understanding the tricks of the trade of your adversary. Your adversary is the fraud perpetrator, a criminal with a wide array of tools and techniques at his disposal. Using such simple techniques as altering account numbers on checks or complex bar code printing or identity theft schemes, the criminal's abilities are only seemingly limited by his imagination. But by knowing your adversary and knowing what to look for, today's retail loss prevention staffers can prevent and detect fraud. What follows is a random sampling of the fraud schemes that I've seen or researched. In most cases I've effected successful prosecution of the cases. In some cases, others have effected prosecution. Your weapons in this battle: a well-written fraud prevention/detection plan, tenacity, and the drive to put a stop to a rapidly growing source of loss that is significantly affecting your bottom line on a daily basis.

Not unlike any other criminal enterprise, retail fraud has undergone an evolutionary process. It wasn't all that long ago that fraud techniques comprised relatively simple schemes and techniques. Drawing on a bit of an archeology analogy, let's look at specific examples of retail fraud. We'll start with some of the earliest, refund and receipt fraud, and we'll progress to techniques employed by the present day fraud purveyors. You will see that the archeology analogy works quite well. The techniques of old pale in comparison to what the present-day retail fraud perpetrators are capable of.

For years retailers saw refund/return fraud on a regular basis. The methodology of this from the perpetrator's standpoint was relatively simple: Make a legitimate cash purchase of a number of expensive items usually along with one or two inexpensive items. Then either the purchaser or cohorts enlisted to help would make another visit to that store or another store of the same chain in the area. Upon making the subsequent visits, the expensive items matching the original purchase were shoplifted. Once that was accomplished, then yet another person was enlisted, usually to perform a return transaction of the original expensive items on the receipt. The inexpensive items were not returned so that the refunder was ensured that the purchase receipt was returned to them due to the fact that not all the items were returned. Then, either in the same store or by another person, a subsequent theft/return transaction was accomplished using the same receipt. Again and again the receipt would be returned to the refunder due to the fact that not all the items on that receipt were returned.

The proliferation of this eventually drew attention to the activity. Retailers began making notations of "Returned" and the date written on the receipt over the portion that pertained to the returned item. This is when the perpetrators of this activity had to adapt. Their adaptations followed a classic evolutionary path. First, all they would do is simply erase the return notation. This eventually wore out the receipt and was noticeable to alert retail clerks. The second adaptation was coating the receipt with a thin sheen of hairspray. When the transaction was complete, all the refunder had to do was use an ink eraser, and the returned/date notation was easily erased with little or no wear and tear to the receipt. Another variation of this was to give the receipt an acetone bath prior to the return attempts. This served the same purpose as the hairspray coating but was usually a bit more long-lasting than the hairspray technique.

In recent years the with-receipt refunders have evolved their techniques. They've obtained rolls of authentic receipt paper from major retailers and reproduced their own receipts. Using sophisticated printers and laptop computers, they have successfully reproduced authentic-appearing receipts on authentic receipt paper from any given retailer. This approach worked for quite a while until retailers either adapted a bar-coded receipt system or loss prevention professionals investigated this and tracked the activity, which effectively brought receipt fraud to an end. It was primarily through effective inter-store communication and intense examination of the bogus receipts that succeeded in convincing retailers at the corporate level that the scope of this problem, and the losses attributed to it, required sweeping change. One of the convincing pieces of evidence was when I discovered that there was a distinct difference between an authentic receipt and a copied/printed receipt. All the registers in my company used a dot-matrix printer. The dot-matrix printers used a blue ribbon. I discovered that the bogus receipts printed on a computer printer had a distinct difference. Bogus receipts had a barely noticeable blue/red shading around the edges of the printing. Barely visible except upon very close examination, this discovery brought about the slow but sure downfall of the copied receipt scam and led to numerous apprehensions. Depending on the amount and whether the criminals signed their own names, most times they didn't, the majority of these apprehensions were for at least one felony. If your state allows for retail fraud to be non-dollar-dependent, or if the criminals do not sign their own name, then in most cases the crime is felony forgery and/or retail fraud.

During the heyday of receipt/return scams, gift cards came into being. At first, the corporate heads were seemingly under the impression that gift cards would be a fix to years of problematic endeavors. Instead of cash back for a no-receipt return, it was now a gift card. Instead of handwritten paper gift certificates, it was now gift cards. Loss prevention professionals suspected it would only be a matter of time before gift cards were also exploited by the retail fraud element. The wait was not long.

Most major retailers have used gift cards for quite some time in lieu of the age-old store credit slip when a customer presents merchandise for return without a receipt. One of the first manifestations of fraudulent activity we saw was individuals transacting a number of no-receipt returns and either amassing a significant balance on a single card or a number of cards with balances. Then the gift cards would be utilized in a plethora of techniques: sold person to person for a percentage of the card's value, used in a large purchase, used for merchandise that was desired in lieu of the returned merchandise. Since the inception of gift cards, we've seen a noticeable increase in in-store pickup and return shoplifting apprehensions. The shoplifter comes into the store, picks an item off the shelf or rack, and then returns it without a receipt for a gift card. Once this scenario is accomplished undetected, then the choice of what to do with the gift card is only limited by the shoplifter's resources. The shoplifters may use it for what they really want in the store or may trade it off for drugs to their local pusher.

Organization has also entered into retail fraud regarding gift cards. We've seen individuals recruit others to shoplift and refund for gift cards, turn over the gift cards, and then the individuals amass cards and make major purchases. The organizers stay isolated wherein, if the shoplifting refunders are apprehended, it remains just a simple shoplift arrest and/or conviction. We have successfully prosecuted the organizers and participants of this kind of activity, but it requires intense inter-store communication and equally intense investigative tenacity to effectuate a successful conclusion to cases such as these.

Gift cards have also been an employee enticement. Whether for themselves or their friends, employee generation of bogus gift card balances continues to be an ongoing retail problem. For the most part, employee gift card fraud cases have remained at a constant level from year to year. Retailers maintain intense scrutiny of employee gift card activity, but despite this, employees' fraudulent gift card activity has not been significantly curtailed through the years.

Rarely seen but still occurring relative to gift cards is gift card "phishing." Enter any major retailer today, and it's hard not to see a large gift card display or two or more! The gift card "phisher" will swipe a number of gift cards from the displays and then record the numbers. Write them down, digitally photograph, use a camera phone—the techniques vary, but the gift card numbers are obtained nonetheless. The cards are then put back on the display where they came from. Then "phisher" just performs regular balance inquiries using the cards' 800 numbers. When a balance is discovered, the "phisher" uses the card number on an Internet order, store purchase, or simple transfer to another gift card. All the "phisher" has to do is represent himself as one who "lost" the original card. The perpetrator uses numbers to his advantage.

The most number-dependent form of payment, other than a credit card that a retailer accepts as tender for a purchase, is a bank check. We'll simply call it a "check." The fact that a check is so number dependent is an advantage: The routing number points to a specific institution; the account number points to a specific account; the check number indicates to a retailer the "age" of the account. A low check number is indicative of a new account and vice versa concerning a high number. This number dependence regarding checks can be exploited by the retail fraud perpetrator with sometimes devastating results. Check fraud schemes perpetrated against retailers have run the gamut of variable creativity. From as simple as altering the routing and account numbers to using sophisticated computer printing to create entirely fictitious checks, most major retailers have seen them all. Some alter or obliterate digits in the numbers so as to pass the check at a store as one that the system has not seen before. Therefore, provided the check amount falls within the guidelines that pass close scrutiny, the check is approved. Most times, the checks are imprinted with the passer's real name and address, and he has identification to match. Although the check and identification match, the passer has most likely moved or opened the account years prior and since closed, or any of a myriad of reasons the amateur bad check writer uses. It's all a means to an end: pass a worthless check for the purchase.

Whereas the amateur bad check writer is most likely one who is from the local area and is going to stay in the local area, the professional bad check passer is a model of a traveling criminal enterprise. The dawn of the digital age made the traveling check passer a prime example of illicit sophistication. The traveler has a mobile print shop for making checks. Using digital imaging and copying, the mobile check passer has the ability to produce his own checks, driver's licenses, and any supporting documentation deemed necessary to pull off this type of fraud against the retail world. In many cases, there are even bogus verification processes, such as contact phone numbers, already set up by the perpetrator. The purpose of this is that most large purchases using a check require a verification procedure. By having a bogus verification contact or contacts, the professional bad check passer has a chance at circumventing even the best acceptance policy and procedure set in place by most any retail establishment. In most cases if the pro is thwarted, he just moves on to another location and tries again. If one identity doesn't work, maybe another will.

Identity, whether authentic or manufactured, is still identity. In the past few years, authentic versus manufactured identity has grown. Identity theft is perhaps the single most growing nemesis affecting the retail world aside from "regular" theft and error. Far too many major retailers are driven on a daily basis towards the "ICAP," or instant credit application, performed in just minutes at register terminals thousands of times a day at any major nationwide retailer. All it takes is a driver license and a Social Security number. Once the application is approved, there's instant buying power. Once something is bought, there's instant possession. Once the buyer is out the door, there's instant successful perpetration.

Although identity theft and credit fraud in the retail world are seldom correlated, there are significant parallels between the two in today's retail environment. Once an identity is stolen, often the first places to go are major retailers to open up charge accounts and charge to the maximum in a very short time. The favorites are items with a high resale value, with gift cards topping the list. Quite a few identity theft cases have been apprehended on the spot by retailers that have an effective awareness program geared toward watching for just this type of scenario. For example, the perpetrator comes into a nationwide home improvement store and applies for an instant credit with a stolen identity. He gets approved for $10,000 limit. Then, it can go one of two ways: The perpetrator buys five $500 gift cards and two or three major appliances and then leaves, or immediately after the gift card purchase, which should raise a bit of a red flag, an aware employee notifies loss prevention staff who have access to the verification process and they confirm the identity theft. Then LP either effects the apprehension themselves or call in law enforcement. The difference between being the victim and being the end of the line for the perpetrator can be tantamount to slowing what has become perhaps the fastest growing criminal enterprise of modern time. Inasmuch as identity theft and credit fraud seemingly go hand in hand in the retail world, there are techniques that can be employed to detect and prevent loss from this activity. Most retailers simply choose to attempt to prevent and detect fraud of this type and leave it at that. Very few actively pursue remedy through the legal system, although this philosophy is undergoing a bit of an evolutionary change of its own as losses attributed to identity theft/credit fraud are adding up substantially. Some major retail chains outsource their credit departments but are now working with their retail partners more closely as credit fraud losses mount.

Credit fraud techniques in and of their themselves have also evolved as the criminal element has discovered technology. It used to be that the perpetrator simply stole a credit card and proceeded to the nearest place to use up as much of it in as short of an amount of time as possible. The thieves would steal a credit card or cards from a source like an unoccupied purse in an office or a wallet in a locker room and then either pass it off to a fellow criminal or use it themselves as quickly as possible. Speed was of the essence because they wanted to use the card before it was reported missing and cancelled. This particular form of credit fraud is still seen quite often and rarely detected at the point of sale due to one simple device: the electronic self-swiper/signature pad. In the past, the retail associate had possession of the credit card for a moment or two at the point of sale. The associate had the opportunity to check the back of the card for a signature and then compare the customer's signature on the credit slip to the card. If there was not a match, then there was a request for a form of identification. Such is not the case anymore. At the point of sale, the customer swipes his own card and signs the electronic pad. In these times of good customer service comprising how fast we can get customers through the checkout process, we have surrendered the opportunity to be able to scrutinize any given transaction while it's in progress. The vast majority of customers are legitimate, but in the interest of customer service, we have adapted to the criminals' favor. Get them through the point of sale as quickly as possible. Do sales increase if we get customers through fast? Obviously, yes. Is this another angle the credit card fraud perpetrators can exploit? Again, obviously, yes. Self-service checkouts facilitate this all that much more for the criminal element due to the removal of the sales associate.

Even before swipe-your-own devices and self-checkouts, credit fraud still was a relatively technologically based crime if the perpetrator was not the steal-it-and-use-it-fast type. There has been the past and continued use of what's referred to as "skimmer" devices. A skimmer device reads and retains the information off the magnetic strip on the back of a credit/debit card. The usual placement of a skimmer is by a dishonest associate who is employed at a location such as a gas station or convenience store. Skimmers have even been used by dishonest employees at fast-food establishments. The dishonest employee has the skimmer either in-line or adjacent to the real card reader and swipes the customer's credit card through both devices. Once off-duty, the dishonest employee uses the skimmer as a two-way device. First, the gathered information is downloaded onto a computer. Then the skimmer is used to reprogram the magnetic strip on the card of his choice to the skimmed number. The beauty of this technique is twofold: The skimmer can reprogram his own credit/debit card with the purloined information; therefore, if his identification is checked when he uses the card, he has a match to the embossed name on the card. Although this technique does require a modicum of sophistication, it is still on the relatively amateurish side of this endeavor. The professional side has the resources available to obtain blank cards and embossing machines. Coupled with the skimmer, this credit fraud scheme is complete. Aside from hacking into a database and stealing credit card information, skimming still retains a bit of popularity with both amateur and professional credit fraud perpetrators. The arrests and prosecutions of professional credit fraud activity of this nature have made national headlines. One particular case of a semi-pro was a husband and wife team. She was a waitress; he was a computer programmer. She copied down the credit card numbers of the same type of card as an expired debit card of theirs. She would bring the numbers home, and he would reprogram the strip on the expired debit card over and over again. The couple did it a few too many times and established a pattern that was used to aid in their apprehension and successful prosecution.

Note the two big words: "apprehension" and "prosecution." In the retail loss prevention scheme of things, "prevention" is the keyword. Retail fraud is not at all similar to anything else that leads to loss for a retailer. Preventative measures can be quite effectively used against shoplifting, employee theft, errors, and the like. Conventional loss prevention philosophy does not lend itself effective against retail fraud. While there may be some dissention as to the impact of retail fraud, all we have to do is come to the realization the sweeping changes law enforcement is putting into effect to combat this burgeoning problem. The Social Security Administration, Federal Bureau of Investigation, U.S. Postal Service, and Federal Trade Commission have all created or enhanced departments in their organizations that have fraud as a prime focus. All the while, most major retailers have not changed their loss prevention philosophy regarding retail fraud. Inasmuch as federal law enforcement and some state and local agencies have recognized fraud as a growing source of criminal activity, retailers are relatively slow to realize the same.

To combat retail fraud, there must be comprehensive awareness programs enacted as the first step. They must be followed with policy and procedure programs adaptive to eliminating retail fraud. As in all the traditional loss prevention programs already in use throughout the retail world, retailers are starting to adapt to the ever-changing battle against retail fraud. There are finite ways to steal and finite ways to commit error, but retail fraud is limited only by the perpetrators' imagination and resources. Retail fraud has a seemingly infinite variable of perpetration. Retail fraud maintains a growing rate of proliferation. The evolution of loss prevention has been matched and in some cases exceeded by the evolution of retail fraud.

Retail Merchandising in Casinos

D. Anthony Nichter

Depending how you reckon the beginning of gaming, the genesis of this industry stretches as far back as the beginnings of civilization, and possibly even prior to that. Throughout their history, gaming and wagering have evolved over time and across all cultures. Games of chance and games of skill have come and gone in various designs, configurations, and complexities. First evolving as a form of divination, gaming and wagering today are still routed in various mythical notions and urban legends—depending on which country you are placing the wager. Whatever you may think about the merits of gaming and wagering in the United States, the industry is now firmly routed in American culture, psyche, and business. Spanning the great divide of Wall Street to Main Street, from the simple charity Bingo and state-run lottery, to elaborate card parlors, riverboats, and mega-resort casinos, gaming is now a multibillion dollar industry.

Along its evolutionary journey, gaming and wagering have merged with numerous other industries to form an entirely new breed of super-gaming resort. Today, in addition to the standard casino, tourists are likely to find a wide array of nongaming amenities that are designed to add value to their vacation as well as ensure that they do not leave the property and therefore spend every disposable dollar on the premises. Beginning with the hotel, today's gaming mega-resort will have some version of a full-service spa, workout center, business center, vehicle rental center, day care, wedding chapel, movie theater, bowling alley, arcade, showroom, theme park, art museum, antique auto collection, dolphin or shark tank, pools with sandy beaches and manmade waves, and the ever-expanding retail area.

Once upon a time, the retail outlet of a gaming resort or hotel was nothing more than a simple gift shop. Though this may still be the case in some rural or tribal casinos, the ma-and-pa gift shop has evolved into super malls rivaling most freestanding malls or plazas not connected to a casino resort. In some Las Vegas casinos, revenue generated from dining, drinking, dancing, and merchandising is at least equal to or surpasses the income generated from the wagering games in the casino. The modern retail malls built in conjunction with casino mega-resorts have become entertainment centers in their own right. Containing some of the more expensive stores found in the most ritzy retail centers of Los Angeles, Beverly Hills, and New York City, these hospitality-based mega-resort malls can challenge the wallets and credit limits of even international high-rollers.

Along with the revenue generated from these gaming-resort retail plazas and malls has come a range of challenges in the implementation and administration of security and loss prevention. The convergence of gaming and retailing has resulted in the collision of gaming, innkeeping, and merchants' laws. This hybrid business entity and the attendant statutes regulating its operation have created confusion, misunderstanding, and misapplication of the various criminal laws by security personnel. Even among members of the legal community, there can be a raging debate regarding the application of the various statutes, some of which are not only confusing, but are also conflicting.

Notwithstanding the administrative confusion and conflict that sometimes occurs, hospitality-based retail merchandising will continue to grow as gaming expands into other jurisdictions both in size and scope. As this sector of retail grows, it will provide employment opportunities for security and loss prevention professionals who wish to develop and cultivate long-term careers.

From Myth and Magic to Gaming and Wagering

All stories have a beginning, a middle, and an end. The story of gambling and wagering is no different, though the end is probably nowhere in sight as of this writing. A quick journey back into very ancient history, back into Biblical lore, may begin with the story of Adam and Eve, of whom, it is said, made the first recorded wager in the human race. According to one version, to eat or not eat the fruit of the forbidden Tree of Life in the Garden of Eden was a wager as to whether the heretofore-unknown sacred knowledge would be bestowed upon the consumer of the fruit. Another version relates that the actual bet between Eve and the serpent was regarding the number of seeds the apple contained. When Eve apparently swallowed a seed, she lost the bet and, as the saying goes, "you know the rest of the story."

Primitive man was inclined to make any natural phenomenon into some sort of fetish (a superstitious belief that objects contained certain magical powers). Some of the first fetishes were pebbles that had peculiar natural markings and gave rise to "sacred stones"; these were much sought after. Necklaces and bracelets of beads and stones strung together formed a collection of sacred stones, a veritable phalanx of potent charms. Ancient tribes accumulated sacred stones that supposedly possessed many powers—to ward off evil, to attract good fortune, and to divine the future. And as for divination, various references are made in the Old Testament of the Bible regarding lots being drawn, not as an appeal to chance for entertainment purposes, but rather to determine God's will.

Over time as number and counting systems came into being and evolved, certain numbers were regarded as unlucky, such as the number 13. Numbers 3 and 7 were seen as bestowing luck. When early man recognized the four directions of the compass headings, the number 4 was consequently seen as being lucky. And so from such simple induction, primitive man would confer implied good and bad luck.

Overtime, superstitious beliefs became more refined and evolved into ceremonial magic—the method of supposedly manipulating the spirit world so as to explain the inexplicable. The goal of magic and sorcery involving fetishes was to obtain insight into the future and favorably influence nature.

Primitive man concocted magical charms from a wide variety of objects—animal claws, teeth, bones, venom, hair, and plants. As far back as 3500 B.C.E. bones were particularly viewed as being magical, and it was from such material that the first dice were fashioned. The astragal was the earliest form of die. It was a small, four-sided bone obtained from the ankle of a goat, sheep, or other domesticated animal and has been located in vast quantities on prehistoric sites.

The modern six-sided dice have been dated as far back as 3000 B.C.E. in Iraq and India. The configuration of the current die whereby the opposite sides adds up to seven was introduced around 1400 B.C.E. It was at the foot of the Cross for the robe of Christ that Roman Centurions wagered with some form of die or marked stones.

Gaming in America

The Early Days

Centuries before the arrival of the first White Man, Native American Indians wagered on anything where the outcome was apparently uncertain—the weather, harvests, races, animal combat, you name it. Inter- and intra-tribal gambling on contests of skill and chance were very popular. Wagering became such a part of the Indians' sacred ceremonial rituals and so integrated into their culture, there was little hope that future missionary or White Man laws could alter that reality. Archeological sites indicate that many tribes engaged in various forms of wagering. Burial sites of the Zuni, Chippewa, and Crow have revealed artifacts that appear to be ancient gaming devices.

In the early days of the colonies, the Puritan and other religious colonists did not permit gambling and lotteries. Gambling was viewed as an unacceptable occupation that did not contribute anything useful to society. Gamblers it was believed, particularly if they were successful at their trade, only victimized the less fortunate in society. Many of the colonies maintained laws prohibiting gambling on moral grounds; however, throughout the 1700s lotteries were still used to finance many public-works projects. When the American Revolution came along, lotteries were vital in raising revenue to purchase weapons and supplies for the fledging Revolutionary Army.

After the years of the American Revolution, private and public gambling underwent many changes. From the Northeast states to the former states of the Confederacy and extending out to the Frontier Territories of the west, laws came and went that, at first, prohibited gambling and then sought to regulate it and then tax it for revenue.

Throughout the 1830s and 1840s the country experienced a vast movement against moral corruption and "sin and vice." Lotteries were falling in disfavor as part of a growing national movement that was fueled by several widespread lottery scandals. Many states began passing legislation to ban all unauthorized lotteries—in other words, those that were not operated by the state itself. The result of this momentum was that many state constitutions were drafted or amended to prohibit the operation of lotteries altogether or to sanction only state-run lotteries. After the Civil War, many cities witnessed the spawning of criminal gambling syndicates within both the shanty parts of town and the social elite sections. As the American West opened and expanded, frontiersman gambling halls were common while back east state legislators enacted restrictions against the perceived "vice."

The Modern Era

In the early 1900s gambling syndicates were fairly well entrenched throughout the country. In 1919 the United Sates passed the 18th Amendment prohibiting the sale and distribution of alcohol and thus began 3 years of the Prohibition and its byproduct, bootlegging. Immigrants of Jewish, Irish, and Italian descent entered into the lucrative, if not risky, enterprises of operating speakeasies—private gambling salons where the alcohol flowed freely. Parts of the country experienced a "clustering effect" where local illegal gambling became prominent. Such regional gambling centers rose from the east to the west coasts, most notably in Hot Springs, Arkansas; Miami, Florida; and in both Reno and Las Vegas, Nevada. Nevada had already outlawed gambling in 1910, but the illegal activity continued discreetly and less publicly in the backrooms of saloons and hotels.

With the collapse of the stock market and the ensuing Great Depression, the need for finding creative ways to generate revenue became paramount. States began to take a second look at wagering, horse racing, and lotteries as a source for that vital revenue. In 1927 Illinois legalized pari-mutuel on-track betting; both Ohio and Michigan passed the same laws in 1933.

The Volstead Act took effect as a result of the 18th Amendment in 1920, but by 1930 common citizens had lost their zeal and support for Prohibition. In 1931 Nevada passed the "Wide Open Gambling Bill," which legalized gambling throughout all of its 17 counties. Legislators saw the passage of this bill as a way to tap into the revenue already being generated by the illegal games copiously found in the backrooms of Wild West saloons in every town. Half of the tax revenue was retained by the county where the gambling occurred, and the other half went to the State of Nevada.

In 1955 Nevada created the Gaming Control Board, and in 1959 the state passed the Nevada Gaming Control Act. Both of these events were instrumental in bringing gaming and wagering into the modern era. Rules and regulations were established by the board, along with numerous statutes passed by the legislators. Examples of some of the gaming statutes in Nevada are as follows:

> *NRS 463.0169 "Licensed gaming establishment" defined. "Licensed gaming establishment" means any premises licensed pursuant to the provisions of this chapter wherein or whereon gaming is done.*
>
> *NRS 463.0152 "Game" and "gambling game" defined. "Game" or "gambling game" means any game played with cards, dice, equipment or any mechanical, electromechanical or electronic device or machine for money, property, checks, credit or any representative of value, including, without limiting the generality of the foregoing, faro, monte, roulette, keno, bingo, fan-tan, twenty-one, blackjack, seven-and-a-half, big injun, klondike, craps, poker, chuck-a-luck, Chinese chuck-a-luck (dai shu), wheel of fortune, chemin de fer, baccarat, pai gow, beat the banker, panguingui, slot machine, any banking or percentage game or any other game or device approved by the Commission, but does not include games played with cards in private homes or residences in which no person makes money for operating the game, except as a player, or games operated by charitable or educational organizations which are approved by the Board pursuant to the provisions of NRS 463.409.*
>
> *NRS 463.0153 "Gaming" and "gambling" defined. "Gaming" or "gambling" means to deal, operate, carry on, conduct, maintain or expose for play any game as defined in NRS 463.0152, or to operate an inter-casino linked system.*

Today's hotel-retail-gaming resorts have been compared to mini-cities in that they are a self-contained living, working, shopping, dining, drinking, entertaining, and banking mini-metropolis, a veritable "casinopolis." Some of the grandest larger-than-life mega-resorts span many city blocks with thousands of hotels rooms, employing several hundred or more employees per shift and catering to hundreds of thousands of guests and patrons over any given busy weekend. The evolution of gaming and wagering is a complex and historical study in and of itself. Such a journey would span the post-Depression era gambling halls operated by Wild West personalities to the casinos of the mid-20th century run by organized crime syndicates and ending with the contemporary super mega-resorts owned and managed by corporate America trading its stock on the Big Board. Such a comprehensive treatment would also examine gaming as it migrated from state-run lotteries, private horse racing, and Las Vegas casinos and formally entered Native American territory on land and riverboats coursing the waters of the Mississippi.

Retailing in the Hospitality Industry

Gift Shops Within Hotels

Retailing both as a business practice and as a serious source of cash flow to the hotel or motel evolved from humble beginnings. Post World War II America witnessed the rapid expansion of the interstate highway system across the United States. This phenomenon accelerated the explosion of hotels and motels, restaurants and cafes, theme parks and campgrounds, and the ubiquitous gasoline service stations. Prior to this explosion of the modern hospitality industry, hotels simply provided lodging and perhaps an internal eating venue strictly for its guests. If guests required accessories common for travelers, they had to leave the hotel and find an appropriate store in that locale. Higher-end hotels would have such items purchased and retrieved by their staff from nearby stores as a value-added service for their guests. Such amenities were found mainly in larger metropolitan hotels catering to wealthier clientele. Other than a few isolated instances and locations, the concept of merging innkeeping with shopkeeping had not really caught hold at this point.

During the years spanning the mid-1940s through the late 1950s, retailing within a hotel was an unsophisticated practice. Small gift shops stocked with items targeted to travelers and guests were common in larger hotels within metropolitan areas. Not too unlike contemporary gift shops, these early venues provided the typical shaving, cleaning, and other hygiene products, coupled with items for those who smoked, had a sweet tooth, or simply needed the local newspaper. Beyond the outskirts of these city-oriented hotels, suburban and rural motels were even less sophisticated in the art of retailing, though they did not miss the opportunity to address the needs of their guests. Gift shop items were readily provided by vending machines that are still popular within many city and inter-state motel franchise chains.

As highways expanded linking metropolitan freeways with back-country rural byways, larger numbers of Americans loaded up the family station wagon and hit the road in search of adventure and Kodak memories. More travelers, both sophisticated and less-seasoned, translated into an aggregate increase in demand for more inns, lodges, motels, and hotels, along with the attendant amenities they could provide. This demand was also reflected in the hotel gift shop and even within the humble vending machine. By the early 1970s, some hotel gift shops began to resemble mini-grocery stores complete with snack foods, premade sandwiches, beverages, alcohol, and laundry supplies. It is interesting to note that around this time a similar change was occurring within traditional pharmacies and drug stores. Once reserved for filling prescriptions and providing over-the-counter medicines, first aid supplies, and various hygiene items, pharmacies began a radical shift into department store retailing. As with their modern pharmacy counterparts, today's hotel gift shops look more like a synthesis of grocery and department stores. In most cases, they provide a vast assortment of actual trinkets and "gifts"—memorabilia to commemorate yet another vacation or items to address the critical needs of the harried last-minute shopper in need of something for birthdays, holidays, and other celebratory events.

Many state statutes provide some formal definition for hotel premises. In Nevada a hotel premises has been clearly defined in NRS Chapter 651 as follows:

NRS 651.005 "Premises" includes, but is not limited to, all buildings, improvements, equipment and facilities, including any parking lot, recreational facility or other land, used or maintained in connection with a hotel, inn, motel, motor court, boardinghouse or lodging house.

Hotel Gift Shops Emerge as Mini-Department Stores

By the late 1970s hotel establishments had evolved into far more than merely lodging accommodations. Enter now into super-hotels and resorts hosting thousands of rooms with adjoining convention centers and exhibition halls. No longer content with the standard hotel restaurant or cafe, these new resorts provided multiple eating establishments, each catering to a different menu and budget. A new era of the all-inclusive hotel-resort emerged whereby management made every attempt to keep guests on the property as long as possible and, consequently, retain every dollar that the guests could not spend elsewhere shopping or getting groomed. Put simply, if guests did not have to wonder off in search of services that the hotel could already provide, each value-added amenity would constitute yet another revenue stream merging with that of the front desk.

Added to the amenity list were elaborate pools, spas, exercise gyms, hair salons, and onsite auto rental outlets. And as the conventional hotel evolved into modern multiamenity resort, the small town and charming gift shop took on new dimensions. Enter now the super-gift shop, a veritable grocery and department store merged into one single retail unit. Still retaining its core inventory of sundries and hygiene items, these new hotel-retail outlets now offer a wide array of merchandise ranging from prepacked foods and beverages up to small electronics and resort-logo branded clothing. Hospitality retailing has emerged into a precise discipline and business practice no different from that conducted in shopping malls and plazas. Employment has gone from the role of a typically lone elderly cashier to that of employing staff having college degrees in merchandising and/or past experience working in a retail setting. Both the business of merchandising and the psychology of displaying merchandise have evolved to a level where it is not uncommon to find a member of senior management possessing the title of Director (or higher) of Retail Merchandising or some other similar designation.

The amount of cubic feet allocated to any amenity in a resort is usually the function of the rate-of-return that activity is likely to bring to the enterprise. If the increase of square footage is any indication, hospitality retail is adding—and is expected to continue—substantially to the bottom line of most hotel operators.

Specialized Malls as an adjunct Amenity Within Hotels and Casinos

As hotels continued to evolve into full-fledged resorts during the late 1970s and early 1980s, they increasingly became more diverse in their areas of specialization. Though no particular classification scheme is used to categorize hotel-resorts, they generally can fall into one or more of the following market specialties.

1. *Tourist Resorts:* Hotels with lavish facilities and amenities catering to out-of-the-area guests who are seeking rest, relaxation, and entertainment. These facilities are typically situated near some sort of spectacular setting or landscape, such as a coastline (such as Florida or California), a mountain (such as Aspen or Vail), or the desert (such as Las Vegas or Phoenix).
2. *Convention and Conference Resorts:* Hotels with comprehensive facilities capable of hosting large conventions with an attendee base numbering in the tens of thousands.
3. *Business-Oriented Hotels:* Hotels that are typically located in close proximity to concentrations of business venues, usually in heavily populated metropolitan areas. The rooms are designed to accommodate business travelers with high-speed computer connections and 24-hour business-support services.
4. *Gaming-Oriented Resorts:* Hotels that are built in, on, around, or adjacent to a gaming facility, whether that be small-scale European wagering salon or a full-scale Vegas-style casino. These facilities usually provide lavish shows, high-end dining establishments, exotic nightclubs, and eclectic retail venues.
5. *Mix-Use Resorts:* Hotel facilities that represent a combination of one, two, or all the above operating profiles. These unique venues arrived on the scene in the early 1990s

with the opening of the mega-resort hotel-gaming resorts found in Las Vegas, Nevada. Since then, such mix-use facilities have migrated from Las Vegas and catapulted north to Detroit, south to the Gulf, and east to a newly revitalized Atlantic City, New Jersey.

Concomitant with the emergence of these specialized venues came the development of a new concept in hotel-gaming resorts, namely the separate-though-attached shopping mall experience. In all the aforementioned markets, as well as the dozens not referenced, special-ized shopping arenas built in, on, around, or adjacent to the hotel-resort are quite common. Ranging from boutique stores and expanding up to full-scale diversified plazas, these retail portions of hotel-gaming resorts have become self-contained, autonomous malls offering gam-blers, hotel guests, and nonhotel patrons a complete shopping experience.

In Nevada, state statutes provide a clear definition of a "resort hotel" in NRS 463 as follows:

> NRS 463.01865 "Resort hotel" defined. "Resort hotel" means any building or group of buildings that is maintained as and held out to the public to be a hotel where sleeping accommodations are furnished to the transient public and that has:
>
> 1. More than 200 rooms available for sleeping accommodations;
> 2. At least one bar with permanent seating capacity for more than 30 patrons that serves alcoholic beverages sold by the drink for consumption on the premises;
> 3. At least one restaurant with permanent seating capacity for more than 60 patrons that is open to the public 24 hours each day and 7 days each week; and
> 4. A gaming area within the building or group of buildings.

The distinction between hotel premises previously defined and a "resort hotel" under the gaming statutes is that the gaming laws specifically assign lodging, eating, and drinking amenities with a minimum number of rooms or seats that need to be provided. Moreover, a gaming area is also a component that is required in the hotel-resort complex.

Shopkeeper Statutes in the Retail Industry

Shopkeeper Statutes in Non-Gaming Retail Establishments

Practically every state has a set of statutes specifically focused on crimes that may occur in a retail establishment. Known variously as "shopkeeper statutes" or "merchant laws," these statutes address a range of issues, including but not limited to shoplifting by custom-ers, embezzlement by employees, burglary by outsiders, and fraudulent use of credit cards and other financial instruments. For operators of retail outlets, their employees, and loss prevention personnel, the statutes dealing with crimes indigenous to shopping outlets are generally well known, though not necessarily applied correctly. A comparison of merchant law and other areas of specialized law quickly reveals some common similarities—and some interesting distinctions.

As for similarities, private citizens acting as sales associates or security personnel have no greater legal power or authority as that of any other citizen in any other industry. When a situation comes down to the application of law or the utilization of force, store personnel must conduct themselves in a manner that is consistent with the principles of common and case law and the mandates of statutory law.

As for distinctions, most shopkeeper statutes have certain allowances for retail per-sonnel not commonly found in other industries. Generally speaking, shopkeeper statutes accord greater latitude to store personnel in so far as areas of arrest and detention are concerned. This broader latitude is generally referred to as merchant's privilege. Without getting bogged down in specific statutes from any particular state, the general principle at the core of most merchant law is straightforward. Stated simply, if a sales or security associ-ate witnesses a customer concealing merchandise while in the store, the employee can order the suspect to uncover the merchandise and keep it plain view, purchase it, or leave it and exit the store.

If the store personnel did not directly observe any concealment or theft as a percipient witness but were told of the "alleged" theft by another party, whether an employee or not, store personnel may still take appropriate action. The legal basis for the action is founded in the store personnel having, at a minimum, reasonable suspicion that a crime occurred, that such notification the crime was received from a believable source, and that a particular suspect committed the alleged act. Some jurisdictions draw a distinction between "reasonable suspicion" and "probable cause," with the latter having a higher degree of belief than the former. Some jurisdictions do not. In any event, it is on this point that merchant privilege expands its latitude more than nonshopping theft laws.

In the event of a shoplifting incident, store personnel can, with reasonable suspicion, detain the suspect even for a misdemeanor not committed in their presence. This privilege does not extend to other categories of misdemeanor crimes not committed in the presence of store personnel.

Many statutes regarding shoplifting have wording that is similar because certain statutory models are shared and promulgated by legislative bodies across the country. In Nevada the chapter that addresses merchant and shoplifting law is Nevada Revised Statutes (NRS) 597. The NRS, which defines shoplifting and clearly stipulates the legally permissible actions that can be taken by the merchant or its agents, is fully reproduced here as NRS 597.850. The civil liabilities for shoplifting by either adults or minors are enumerated as NRS 597.860 and 597.870, respectively.

NRS 597.850 Shoplifting: Merchant may request person on premises to keep merchandise in full view; detention of suspect; immunity of merchant from liability; display of notice.

1. *As used in this section and in NRS 597.860 and 597.870:*
   (a) *"Merchandise" means any personal property, capable of manual delivery, displayed, held or offered for sale by a merchant.*
   (b) *"Merchant" means an owner or operator, and the agent, consignee, employee, lessee, or officer of an owner or operator, of any merchant's premises.*
   (c) *"Premises" means any establishment or part thereof wherein merchandise is displayed, held or offered for sale.*
2. *Any merchant may request any person on his premises to place or keep in full view any merchandise the person may have removed, or which the merchant has reason to believe he may have removed, from its place of display or elsewhere, whether for examination, purchase or for any other purpose. No merchant is criminally or civilly liable on account of having made such a request.*
3. *Any merchant who has reason to believe that merchandise has been wrongfully taken by a person and that he can recover the merchandise by taking the person into custody and detaining him may, for the purpose of attempting to effect such recovery or for the purpose of informing a peace officer of the circumstances of such detention, take the person into custody and detain him, on the premises, in a reasonable manner and for a reasonable length of time. A merchant is presumed to have reason to believe that merchandise has been wrongfully taken by a person and that he can recover the merchandise by taking the person into custody and detaining him if the merchant observed the person concealing merchandise while on the premises. Such taking into custody and detention by a merchant does not render the merchant criminally or civilly liable for false arrest, false imprisonment, slander or unlawful detention unless the taking into custody and detention are unreasonable under all the circumstances.*
4. *No merchant is entitled to the immunity from liability provided for in this section unless there is displayed in a conspicuous place on his premises a notice in boldface type clearly legible and in substantially the following form:*

   Any merchant or his agent who has reason to believe that merchandise has been wrongfully taken by a person may detain such person on the premises of the merchant for the purpose of recovering the property or notifying a peace officer. An adult or the parents or legal guardian of a minor, who steals merchandise, is civilly liable for its value and additional damages.

NRS 597.860 Shoplifting: Civil liability of adult who steals merchandise from or damages property on merchant's premises.

1. *An adult who steals merchandise from, or damages property on, a merchant's premises is civilly liable for the retail value of the merchandise or the fair market value of the other property, plus damages of not less than $100 nor more than $250, costs of suit and reasonable attorney's fees. An action may be brought even if there has been no criminal conviction for the theft or damage.*

2. *An action under this section may be brought as a small claim in a Justice Court if the total amount sought does not exceed the statutory limit for such a claim.*

NRS 597.870 Shoplifting: Civil liability of parent or guardian of minor who steals merchandise from or damages property on merchant's premises.

1. *The parent or legal guardian, as the case may be, of a minor who steals merchandise from, or damages property on, a merchant's premises is civilly liable for:*
   (a) The retail value of the merchandise; and (b) The fair market value of the damaged property, plus damages of not less than $100 nor more than $250, costs of suit and reasonable attorney's fees. An action may be brought even if there has been no criminal conviction for the theft or damage. Recovery under this section may be had in addition to, and is not limited by, any other provision of law, which limits the liability of a parent or legal guardian for the tortious conduct of a minor.

2. *An action under this section may be brought as a small claim in a Justice Court if the total amount sought does not exceed the statutory limit for such a claim.*

The implication of this Nevada statute, as well as those like it from other states, will be made more apparent in a following section—"Misinterpretation and Misapplication of the Statutes."

Shopkeeper Statutes in Gaming Environments

As previously written, retail establishments can take many forms in, on, around, or adjacent to gaming casinos and as a component to the overall property configuration. Though these retailers are a part of the gaming premises, the shoplifting statutes are just as applicable as they are in nongaming establishments. In other words, there are no separate sets of statutes that apply to retailers who happen to operate stores on gaming premises.

In jurisdictions where gaming is prevalent, there are typically dedicated sections or chapters in the statutes addressing the specialized areas of arrest and detention for the commission of gaming crimes. In Nevada, that chapter is NRS 465. Other gaming jurisdictions have used the Nevada statute as a model to craft their own gaming detention statutes. NRS 465.101 provides clear instructions to gaming personnel regarding the detention of persons on a gaming premise; see the following:

NRS 465.101 Detention and questioning of person suspected of violating chapter; limitations on liability; posting of notice.

1. *Any licensee, or his officers, employees or agents may question any person in his establishment suspected of violating any of the provisions of this chapter. No licensee or any of his officers, employees or agents is criminally or civilly liable:*
   (a) On account of any such questioning; or
   (b) For reporting to the State Gaming Control Board or law enforcement authorities the person suspected of the violation.

2. *Any licensee or any of his officers, employees or agents who has probable cause for believing that there has been a violation of this chapter in his establishment by any person may take that person into custody and detain him in the establishment in a reasonable manner and for a reasonable length of time. Such a taking into custody and detention does not render the licensee or his officers, employees or agents criminally or civilly liable unless it is established by clear and convincing evidence that the taking into custody and detention are unreasonable under all the circumstances.*

3. *No licensee or his officers, employees or agents are entitled to the immunity from liability provided for in subsection 2 unless there is displayed in a conspicuous place in his establishment a notice in boldface type clearly legible and in substantially this form:*

Any gaming licensee, or any of his officers, employees or agents who has probable cause for believing that any person has violated any provision of chapter 465 of NRS prohibiting cheating in gaming may detain that person in the establishment.

In Nevada, as in some other jurisdictions, the issue is not so much of retailing coming to gaming, but just the opposite. Within many retail establishments, it is not uncommon to find a separate area set aside for gaming devices, usually slot machines. In such settings, gaming and wagering laws apply within those small, partitioned sections of the retail stores. In Nevada, retailers are permitted no more than 15 slot machines at any one location. Other states have set a varying number of wagering devices in such locations.

When two different industries such as retailing and gaming merge in a singular business setting, the laws of more regulated of the two, typically gaming, will prevail within the gaming area of the premises. In such circumstances, such as in Nevada, the Gaming Control Board (the enforcement arm of the Gaming Commission) will clearly provide definitions of what constitutes specific retail environments where gaming will be permitted. Regulation One (Reg.1) stipulates, among other things, the definitions of retailers where gaming may be allowed:

> *REGULATION 1*
> *ISSUANCE OF REGULATIONS: CONSTRUCTION; DEFINITIONS*
> *"Convenience store" defined. "Convenience store" means a business selling groceries at retail such as, but not limited to, food for human consumption, articles used in the preparation of food, household supplies, dairy products, meat, and produce, and normally having at least 1,000 square feet and no more than 10,000 square feet of floor space available to the public. (Adopted: 7/99. Effective: 2/1/2000.)*
>
> *1.130 "Grocery store" defined. "Grocery store" means a business selling at retail groceries, such as, but not limited to, food for human consumption, articles used in the preparation of food, household supplies, dairy products, meat, and produce, and having more than 10,000 square feet of floor space available to the public. (Adopted: 7/99. Effective: 2/1/2000.)*
>
> *1.141 "Liquor store" defined. "Liquor store" means specialty retail store which deals exclusively in alcoholic liquors for off-premises consumption, and the incidental sale of related items including magazines, newspapers and snack foods. For purposes of this section, "alcoholic liquors" means the four varieties of liquor, namely, alcohol, spirits, wine and beer, and every liquid or solid, patented or not, containing alcohol and intended for consumption by human beings as a beverage. (Adopted: 7/05.)*
>
> *1.145 "Premises" defined. "Premises" means land together with all buildings, improvements and personal property located thereon. (Amended: 9/82.)*

Application of the Statutes: Theory Versus Reality

The Convergence of Merchant Law, Innkeeper Law, and Gaming Law

Up to this point we have visited key points within the domains of merchant and gaming law but have not done so with innkeeper law (sometimes referred to "hotel/ motel law"). Put simply, innkeeper law is a combination of state statutes and case law addressing the operators of hotels, motels, inns, and boarding establishments that provide lodging, accommodation. and entertainment. When compared to the number of gaming facilities across the United States, there are exponentially far more lodging establishments. Hotels began to be incorporated in and onto gaming premises for the last three-quarters of a century. This integration has progressed in waves commencing in 1931 in Nevada, 1977 in New Jersey, 1988 for approved Native American Indian tribes, and continuing from 1990 to the present for all other nongaming jurisdictions, both land-based and maritime.

In those settings where a casino, retail store, and hotel converge under one roof, understanding the statutes germane to each of these areas is vital to operating and behaving within the law. Misinterpretation and misapplication of the statutes inevitably will open a "Pandora's Box" of legal problems, both criminal and civil.

The following four scenarios illustrate a "best practices" approach where all the statutes from the aforementioned domains converge in a workplace settings.

Scenario One: A Gift Shop Operating Within a Hotel Located in Nevada

In this case a gift shop located in the main lobby is owned and operated by a hotel company, and there is no gambling component to the premises.

The gift shop cashier witnesses a teenage male remove some items from the shelf and conceal them on his person. The cashier telephones a front desk supervisor for assistance. The college-educated 32-year-old manager arrives and is directed to the suspect. The manager is told that the value of the items is around $50, which is well below the $250 statutory limit for a misdemeanor crime. So what can the manager do?

Even though the incident occurred on the premises of a hotel, the alleged crime happened within the gift shop, involving its inventory. Shopkeeper laws extend discretionary latitude to the manager to investigate and challenge the suspect, up to and including detaining the person if that is the only way to recover the merchandise. This latitude is referred to as "merchant's privilege." Since the manager has no reason to disbelieve the cashier, he therefore has sufficient reasonable suspicion or probable cause to take some degree of assertive action to determine what exactly has occurred.

The manager approaches the subject and identifies himself as a front desk manager who has received a report that the teenager may have taken merchandise from its display and concealed it. The next move is up to the subject.

Option # 1: The teenager denies the allegation and commences to quickly exit past the manager. What can the manager do? He blocks the teenager from exiting and informs the young subject that the manager is now exercising merchant's privilege to make a detention and then call the police for an apprehension. The manager takes the subject into custody, recovers the merchandise, and then calls the police to file charges. Even though most citizen's arrest or detention statutes require the person making the detention to have actually witnessed the crime if the violation is a misdemeanor, such is not the case for retail theft. An agent of the store may detain a shoplifter for a misdemeanor theft not committed in the presence of the detaining party. Such is the nature of merchant's privilege. This privilege is extended to agents of the hotel/store, provided that retail outlet is owned and operated by the landlord/hotel itself.

Option # 2: The teenager affirms that he has the concealed items and reveals them to the manager. What can the manager do? Since the subject has not yet exited the store, the manager can (1) advise the youth to purchase the items immediately or (2) remove the items and order the subject to exit the store. Such an order may or may not involve a trespass notice.

In the preceding scenario, no innkeeper law would be applicable because the incident occurred specifically within a retail environment involving merchandise from the store. Let's say (as sometimes happens) the theft of gift shop merchandise occurs by a guest who returns to her room with the stolen items. Has anything changed? No and yes.

No, nothing has changed—from the standpoint that the merchant's privilege would still permit recovery of the stolen items and detention of the guest, since the hotel constitutes the "premises" of the gift shop.

Yes, something else has been added to the equation, since the guest has committed a theft on the premises and therefore breached her common law duty not to harm the innkeeper when residing at the "inn." At this point, the guest can be evicted and her residency privileges terminated.

Scenario Two: A Gift Shop Operating Within a Hotel Located in Nevada

In this case a gift shop located in the main lobby is operated by an outside specialty company under contract to the hotel company, and there is no gambling component to the premises. The space is leased to the retail contractor by the hotel. Typical of such contracts, the hotel earns revenue from the lease and a percentage of the gross sales from the gift shop.

The gift shop cashier witnesses a teenage female remove some items from the shelf and conceal them on her person. The cashier telephones a front desk supervisor for assistance. The college-educated 32-year-old manager arrives and is directed to the suspect. The manager is told that the value of the items is around $50, which is well below the $250 statutory limit for a misdemeanor crime. So what can the manager do?

Option # 1: The manager knows that the gift shop is neither owed nor operated by the hotel; therefore, there is little in the way of direct action that he can take against the alleged thief. The manager cannot act on behalf of another company's interest as a nonemployee. The manager advises the store cashier that she can either (1) make a citizen's detention herself while the manager ensures her safety or (2) call the police and ask for assistance.

Option # 2: While the suspect is leaving the store, the cashier attempts to make a shoplifting detention resulting in her being shoved aside by the would-be thief while this action is observed by the manager. At this point the manager has witnessed a misdemeanor committed in his presence and can intervene with a citizen's arrest with reasonable force upon the thief/assailant.

Option # 3: While the suspect is leaving the store, the cashier attempts to make a shoplifting detention resulting in her being shoved aside by the would-be thief, but this action is not observed by the manager. At this point the manager has not witnessed any crime committed in his presence but is, instead, told of the details of the incident by another employee in the lobby. Since force was being used to take and retain personal (the stolen) property, the simple misdemeanor would escalate into a felony robbery, and the manager can intervene with a citizen's arrest with reasonable force upon the thief/assailant. This would be permitted because, in a significant majority of states, private citizens can take direct action for the commission of a felony not committed in their presence, provided the detaining party has probable cause to believe that a felony has occurred and that the suspect committed the crime.

Scenario Three: A Gift Shop Operating Within a Hotel Located in Nevada

In this case a gift shop located in the main lobby is owned and operated by a hotel company, and there is no gambling component to the premises.

The gift shop cashier witnesses a teenage male remove some items from the shelf and conceal them on his person. The cashier telephones a front desk supervisor for assistance. The college-educated 32-year-old manager arrives and is directed to the suspect. The manager is told that the value of the items is around $255, which is at or above the $250 statutory limit for a felony crime of grand larceny. By the time the manager arrives to the gift shop, the shoplifter has left the store and exited the hotel lobby to the public sidewalk outside. So what can the manager do?

Option # 1: Upon learning of that the shoplifter has left the building, the manager proceeds to catch up with the thief and does so several feet outside the main exit. Can the manager take direct action? Yes, because the theft was a felony, and as stated previously, private citizens can take direct action for the commission of a felony not committed in their presence, provided the detaining party has probable cause to believe that a felony has occurred and that the suspect committed the crime. In this option, the manager takes the shoplifter into custody and returns the thief back to the store to await the arrival of the police.

Scenario Four: A Gift Shop Operating Within a Nevada Hotel-Casino

In this case a gift shop located in the main lobby is owned and operated by a hotel company, and there is a gambling component to the premises.

The gift shop cashier witnesses a teenage male remove some items from the shelf and conceal them on his person. The cashier telephones a front desk supervisor for assistance. The college-educated 32-year-old manager arrives and is directed to the suspect. The manager is told that the value of the items is around $50, which is well below the $250 statutory limit for a misdemeanor crime. So what can the manager do?

Option # 1: The manager arrives and is told of the details of the theft by the cashier while the thief is still in the store. As with Scenario One, the manager can assert direct action and detain the thief either for recovering the merchandise or summoning the police to make an arrest.

Option # 2: The manager arrives and is told of the details of the theft by the cashier while the thief has exited the store. The manager calls the surveillance unit of the casino to assist in locating the suspect, resulting in the thief being spotted halfway across the gambling floor. The surveillance unit calls two nearby security officers and informs them of the location of the shoplifting suspect. They proceed to the designated location, and the question now is: Can the guards take direct action even though they did not witness the shoplifting crime directly? Put simply, yes, and for the same reason given in Scenario One with the hotel manager. Since the gift shop is (1) owned and operated by the hotel-casino and (2) the store is located on the premises, the casino security personnel may therefore detain for a shoplifting misdemeanor crime though not committed in their presence.

The preceding four scenarios and each of their optional outcomes represent only a handful of the numerous permutations of what could, and actually does, take place in the real world. These scenarios represent the correct application and interpretation of the underlying legal principles dealing with the convergence of gaming, innkeeping, and shopkeeping laws. Unless security personnel possess the correct interpretation of the statutes and know the appropriate application, problems can easily occur that will give rise to inevitable legal repercussions.

Misinterpretation and Misapplication of the Statutes

The preceding section examined several scenarios that expressed the legal principles at work when there is a convergence of different bodies of law operating within a hybrid environment, such a retail outlet within a hotel-casino establishment. As you may now appreciate, misinterpretation of the relative statutes could probably result in misapplication of the law in day-to-day business reality.

An environment such as a hotel-retail-casino resort provides some interesting challenges for security and surveillance personnel. States where gambling is authorized usually have a statute that defines and may even describe each category of employee constituting a "gaming employee." This statutory declaration is required when such employees are expected to go undergo more intensive background checks and/or obtain special licenses to be employed on gambling premises. In Nevada the statute listing gaming employees is NRS 463.0157 and it is as follows:

> NRS 463.0157 "Gaming employee" defined.
> 1. "Gaming employee" means any person connected directly with an operator of a slot route, the operator of a pari-mutuel system, the operator of an inter-casino linked system or a manufacturer, distributor or disseminator, or with the operation of a gaming establishment licensed to conduct any game, 16 or more slot machines, a race book, sports pool or pari-mutuel wagering, including:
>   (a) Accounting or internal auditing personnel who are directly involved in any recordkeeping or the examination of records associated with revenue from gaming;
>   (b) Boxmen;
>   (c) Cashiers;
>   (d) Change personnel;
>   (e) Counting room personnel;
>   (f) Dealers;
>   (g) Employees of a person licensed to operate an off-track pari-mutuel system;
>   (h) Employees of a person licensed to disseminate information concerning racing;
>   (i) Employees of manufacturers or distributors of gaming equipment within this State whose duties are directly involved with the manufacture, repair or distribution of gaming devices, cashless wagering systems, mobile gaming systems, equipment associated with mobile gaming systems, interactive gaming systems or equipment associated with interactive gaming;
>   (j) Employees of operators of slot routes who have keys for slot machines or who accept and transport revenue from the slot drop;
>   (k) Employees of operators of inter-casino linked systems, mobile gaming systems or interactive gaming systems;
>   (l) Floormen;
>   (m) Hosts or other persons empowered to extend credit or complimentary services;
>   (n) Keno runners;
>   (o) Keno writers;
>   (p) Machine mechanics;

     (q) Odds makers and line setters;
     (r) Security personnel;
     (s) Shift or pit bosses;
     (t) Shills;
     (u) Supervisors or managers;
     (v) Ticket writers; and
     (w) Employees of a person licensed to operate an information service.
  2. *"Gaming employee" does not include bartenders, cocktail waitresses or other persons engaged exclusively in preparing or serving food or beverages.*

A close examination of the list of gaming employees will reveal that each is involved in some fashion with the administration, application, implementation, and/or enforcement of wagering games, rules, regulations, revenue, credit, and supervision. Considering the number of categories, you can appreciate the fact that large numbers of employees are mobilized on any given day just to make a medium-size casino (50,000—75,000 square feet) operate smoothly, efficiently, and legally. For the moment, our attention will focus on category (r) of this list, security personnel.

A gaming premise is defined as all the buildings constituting the establishment sitting on all the land owned by the gaming licensee. This all-inclusive definition encompasses the entire property and its business operations including, but not limited to, the hotel, conference center, concert halls, restaurants, condos, time-share units, sports arenas, retail outlets, shopping malls, boutique plazas, wedding chapels, and maybe even a specialty theme park. The acreage which this city-like enterprise occupies can range from a dozen acres up to and over 100 acres, especially if the property has an onsite golf course, skeet range, or private lake. Patrolling these buildings and the surrounding acreage is a small army of security officers who are typically directed from a central dispatch and/or surveillance unit. This means that there are very few locations where the security officers are not either present or do not visit at some point on any given shift.

Gaming security officers usually patrol the retail outlets that are owned and operated by the gaming licensee and whose employees work for the gaming operator. This typically includes the gift shop, but also may encompass specialty shops such as boutiques, liquor and cigar stores, pool-side cabanas, and small clothing stores with items bearing the brand and logo of the casino. Since these outlets are owned and operated by the licensee's retail division, security personnel have full authority to respond to incidents of alleged shoplifting and act in accordance with that state's particular shopkeeper statutes. In such cases, merchant's privilege is extended to the casino-resort security personnel.

Where the hotel-retail-casino property has an adjoining shopping mall, the extent of authority for the casino security officers may change. Such adjoining malls or plazas are typically leased and managed to a professional retail management company, which, in most cases involving large shopping outlets, has its own proprietary or contract security force for the common areas of the mall. The individual stores within such malls decide for themselves whether in-store loss prevention personnel are going to be used—or not.

Where the adjoining retail mall is separately leased and has its own security force, the hotel-casino security personnel typically do not venture onto that portion of the property, though there is nothing that would prohibit such visitations. Remember that the entire property is considered part of the gaming premises. However, in such a bifurcated management and security arrangement, there is no merchant's privilege extended to the hotel-casino security officers. The usual scenario whereby hotel-casino security personnel will cross over into the retail mall area is if the mall security force asked for assistance. Such situations usually involve incidents when there is a structural fire, a broken water pipe, a medical emergency, or some sort of business disruption such as when gangs or juveniles congregate or engage in fighting in the common mall area.

Under the typical contractual arrangement between the casino operator and the retail management, the shopping mall's security force is totally and exclusively responsible for the security and safety of the common mall areas, nonpublic areas, and adjoining parking garages. This is important to remember in the event of a lawsuit where the plaintiff is trying to determine who is responsible for what areas of the overall hotel-retail-casino property.

Attempting to keep clear and comprehensible all the complex issues of overlapping ordinances and laws, rules and regulations, contractual obligations, and restrictions, as well as legal and operational boundaries can prove to be quite challenging. Sometimes in the "fog" of protecting and administrating security programs, errors will occur, some of which will give rise to litigation. Experience has shown that these errors originate from one of two general sources.

The first source is simple individual human error; humans make mistakes because of flawed decision making. The only way to remedy this source of error is to learn from the mistakes and share the lessons learned with the entire department or organization. Additional training in both formal classroom settings and on-the-job (OJT) will reinforce the correct way of doings things and, one hopes, alter the erroneous behavior.

The second source is institutional error. This occurs when flawed doctrine regarding policy and procedure is embedded within the department ranging administratively from the top to the bottom. In other words, from the office of the Director of Security down to each supervisor and security officer out on the floor, each has incorporated some fatally flawed practice into daily operations. With nobody really knowing any better, doctrinal error has been inculcated to such a degree that the only real wakeup call occurs after a significant incident has happened and severe litigation results.

Whether individual or institutional in nature, the error in practice, if sustained over a sufficient length of time, will result in the "perfect storm" of problems and litigation. Here are some of the typical misinterpretations and misapplications of overlapping laws.

Scenario One: A female patron in the casino has reported to a male security officer that she believes a particular suspect has unlawfully taken something of value from a nearby customer. The security officer makes an inquiry with the customer and learns that the missing item is a $100 camera. A description is given and a search begins, resulting in the "suspect" being detained in another part of the casino. The security officer has done this sort of thing many times before in the gift shop, so he is familiar with the procedures. The suspect is taken to the security office and questioned, at which time he is also searched to locate the camera allegedly taken. No camera is found. The female witness is asked to personally identify the suspect, and she now reports that, though he looks like the person she saw, she is not certain. The young suspect is told that he is free to go, at which time upon exiting he yells back to the security supervisor that his dad is an attorney and that *"You haven't heard the last from us…I'm going to sue you S.O.B.s!"* Is there a problem here? Yes.

Everything was going fine up to the point where the security officer took custody of the alleged suspect and detained him. The laws are clear—a private citizen must have witnessed the misdemeanor crime before any arrest can occur. The value of the camera clearly renders the crime a petit larceny and one that was not witnessed by the security officer. A mistake in identity is no excuse or exemption to the citizen's arrest statutes, yet it occurs everyday, arising from both individual and institutional errors. The result is that the security officer has committed a false imprisonment (kidnapping in some states), and in Nevada, this is a gross misdemeanor (the level of crime just below a felony.)

Scenario Two: The female cashier of a hotel-casino gift shop waves her arm signaling to get the attention of a passing casino security officer in the lobby. As the guard enters the gift shop, the cashier reports that some merchandise is missing from a nearby display and that a particular middle-aged woman probably took it. As she is relating the story to the security officer, the cashier points to the woman exiting the hotel lobby into the taxi stand area. Without hesitating, the security officer immediately runs out the door and intercepts the woman at the valet curb. He tells her about the situation in the store, and she responds that she did not take any items. The security officer does not believe her story and, while taking the woman's arm, forcibly leads her back into the hotel as she is complaining loudly. The police are called, investigate the matter, and determine that there is insufficient cause to charge or arrest the woman. They inform the security supervisor accordingly. While leaving the store, one police officer sarcastically tells the supervisor that the hotel "*should make sure they have a good lawyer.*" So what went wrong?

Merchant's privilege allows detention of a suspect for shoplifting in the event there is reasonable suspicion or probable cause. The security officer possessed neither in the preceding case. The mere coincidence of a patron in the vicinity of merchandise that might be missing from a display does not probable cause nor reasonable suspicion make. It only amounts to coincidence, nothing more. No items were actually seen being taken or concealed. As with the previous scenario, this one also constitutes battery (taking the woman by the arm) and false imprisonment (taking her forcibly back to the store).

Scenario Three: The supervisor from a shopping mall adjoining a casino-resort calls over to the casino dispatch and informs them that a suspect has exited the common mall area and entered the casino. The dispatcher asks for details and is told that the fleeing suspect allegedly was involved in a juvenile fight by punching another teenager in the food court. Meanwhile, contract security guards from the mall enter the casino, searching for the juvenile suspect. Upon locating the alleged youthful offender, the mall guards give chase as the suspect is merely walking away. When they catch up to him, one of the guards executes a football-like tackle, taking the youth crashing to the ground. The violent fall results in a broken arm for the suspect. The casino then calls the police and requests an ambulance. So did anything go wrong? Yes, and on multiple levels.

The youthful suspect did indeed punch another in the mall, but the guards had no jurisdiction in the casino; their contractual authority extended only to the mall. Even if an argument could be made that the mall guards could pursue their suspect into the casino, they never witnessed the commission of the misdemeanor battery and therefore had no statutory privilege to make an arrest. And even if an argument could be made that there was some sort of statutory privilege, the amount of force used to take the suspect into custody was arguably excessive under the circumstances. As with the previous scenarios, a combination of individual and institutional errors combined to make a "perfect storm" of misapplication of the overlapping laws. Arising from such storms are the probable and inevitable civil lawsuits or even criminal charges against employees who thought they were merely doing their jobs.

Liability Repercussions Arising from Erroneous Application of the Statutes

The aforementioned scenarios are but a handful of illustrations of what could go wrong when the many overlapping statutes involving retailing and gaming are misinterpreted and thus misapplied.

When any employee of the hotel-retail-gaming resort uses unlawful force upon another to make an arrest or seemingly overcome resistance to such an arrest, that employee has, in effect, committed a crime. The victim of such unlawful behavior may, if he so chooses, charge the perpetrator and seek to have him prosecuted under state statutes. This has occurred throughout the industry with sufficient regularity that it is still no less than amazing that such egregious behavior continues as part of some workplace cultures. This is the result of institutional behavior that is implicitly advocated by management and explicitly implemented by staff.

In addition to facing criminal charges by the state, each crime reflects its mirror counterpart, the civil tort. Not only will the errant employees be named as defendants in a lawsuit, but potentially so will their supervisor, shift manager, departmental director, and possibly right up the corporate hierarchy to the general manager. This hierarchy of defendants will be named especially if the plaintiff is advocating that the egregious behavior was rooted in institutional dysfunction and negligence.

Under the general caveat of negligence, the specific allegations will encompass claims of negligent hiring, training, and supervision; negligent procedures and practices; negligently inadequate security; negligently excessive use of force; and negligent retention, just to name a few.

Most states have created statutes that are modeled after the wording found in various federal civil rights legislation. Far too many hospitality-gaming establishments claim in writing (employee handbooks, promotional literature, etc.) to believe in such laws, but in practice, the reality can be very different. This is particularly true for some employees whose personal prejudices are not restricted and abated by management at the earliest manifestations of aberrant behavior.

Nevada, like other states, has declared its intent that places of public accommodation are open to equal enjoyment by all persons. Moreover, specific penalties are stipulated for any person who deprives another of his rights as provided in these public accommodation statutes. An examination of Nevada's NRS 651.050 reveals all the places that the legislators consider to be "public accommodation." The two statutes that follow declare that all persons are entitled to equal access to this place and then provide for penalties for depriving persons of their rights under these statutes (see NRS 651.070 and 651.080, respectively):

EQUAL ENJOYMENT OF PLACES OF PUBLIC ACCOMMODATION

NRS 651.050 Definitions. As used in NRS 651.050 to 651.110, inclusive, unless the context otherwise requires:

1. *"Disability" means, with respect to a person:*
   (a) *A physical or mental impairment that substantially limits one or more of the major life activities of the person;*
   (b) *A record of such an impairment; or*
   (c) *Being regarded as having such an impairment.*
2. *"Place of public accommodation" means:*
   (a) *Any inn, hotel, motel or other establishment which provides lodging to transient guests, except an establishment located within a building which contains not more than five rooms for rent or hire and which is actually occupied by the proprietor of the establishment as his residence;*
   (b) *Any restaurant, bar, cafeteria, lunchroom, lunch counter, soda fountain, casino or any other facility where food or spirituous or malt liquors are sold, including any such facility located on the premises of any retail establishment;*
   (c) *Any gasoline station;*
   (d) *Any motion picture house, theater, concert hall, sports arena or other place of exhibition or entertainment;*
   (e) *Any auditorium, convention center, lecture hall, stadium or other place of public gathering;*
   (f) *Any bakery, grocery store, clothing store, hardware store, shopping center or other sales or rental establishment;*
   (g) *Any laundromat, dry cleaner, bank, barber shop, beauty shop, travel service, shoe repair service, funeral parlor, office of an accountant or lawyer, pharmacy, insurance office, office of a provider of health care, hospital or other service establishment;*
   (h) *Any terminal, depot or other station used for specified public transportation;*
   (i) *Any museum, library, gallery or other place of public display or collection;*
   (j) *Any park, zoo, amusement park or other place of recreation;*
   (k) *Any nursery, private school or university or other place of education;*
   (l) *Any day care center, senior citizen center, homeless shelter, food bank, adoption agency or other social service establishment;*
   (m) *Any gymnasium, health spa, bowling alley, golf course or other place of exercise or recreation;*
   (n) *Any other establishment or place to which the public is invited or which is intended for public use; and*
   (o) *Any establishment physically containing or contained within any of the establishments described in paragraphs (a) to (n), inclusive, which holds itself out as serving patrons of the described establishment.*

NRS 651.070 All persons entitled to equal enjoyment of places of public accommodation. All persons are entitled to the full and equal enjoyment of the goods, services, facilities, privileges, advantages and accommodations of any place of public accommodation, without discrimination or segregation on the ground of race, color, religion, national origin or disability.
NRS 651.080 Deprivation of, interference with and punishment for exercising rights and privileges unlawful; penalty.

1. *Any person is guilty of a misdemeanor who:*
    (a) *Withholds, denies, deprives or attempts to withhold, deny or deprive any other person of any right or privilege secured by NRS 651.070 or 651.075;*
    (b) *Intimidates, threatens, coerces or attempts to threaten, intimidate or coerce any other person for the purpose of interfering with any right or privilege secured by NRS 651.070 or 651.075; or*
    (c) *Punishes or attempts to punish any other person for exercising or attempting to exercise any right or privilege secured by NRS 651.070 or 651.075.*

Summary

The contemporary colloquialism "You've come a long way, Baby!" could be applied to any industry that has evolved and emerged over a 100-year period. This is no less true than of the convergence of retailing within the hotel-gaming environment, except that this merger is still a work-in-progress. In many cases the laws written 50 or more years ago for each industry have not kept pace with the new super-hybrid environments in which these industries jointly flourish. In some states and in some cases, the laws actually contradict one another, and it is for this reason that today's security director must be as informed and educated on these overlapping and seemingly contradictory laws, rules, and regulations. Seeking the advice of in-house legal counsel or from the law firm that has been retained by the company is the ideal way to achieve the level of understanding needed by today's security management professional. Sadly for the employer and gladly for plaintiff attorneys, this readily accessible advice is not sought as often as it should.

As long as the worlds of retailing and gaming continue to grow and operate within the hotel environment, a new constellation of business hybrids will emerge across the country in varying markets toward the mid-21st century. Most of those markets will be ill equipped to address the statutory and regulatory challenges facing such enterprises. The best response to such a forecast is for today's protection and loss prevention professionals to expand their backgrounds to encompass legal training and education. Indeed, a friendly classroom is a far better place than a hostile courtroom to learn such lessons.

RFID—Informed Consent: Ethical Considerations of RFID*

Sally Bacchetta

He who mounts a wild elephant goes where the wild elephant goes.
Randolph Bourne

Radio Frequency Identification (RFID) has incubated in relative obscurity for over 60 years, quietly changing our lives with scant attention outside the technology community. First used to identify Allied aircraft in World War II, RFID is now well integrated in building security, transportation, fast food, health care and livestock management.

Proponents hail RFID as the next natural step in our technological evolution. Opponents forewarn of unprecedented privacy invasion and social control. Which is it? That's a bit like

---

*Originally published in *The America.n Chronicle*, June 1, 2006, and reprinted with the author's permission.

asking if Christopher Columbus was an intrepid visionary or a ruthless imperialist. It depends on your perspective. One thing is clear: As RFID extends its roots into common culture we each bear responsibility for tending its growth.

For Your Eyes Only

RFID functions as a network of microchip transponders and readers that enables the mainstream exchange of more—and more specific—data than ever before. Every RFID transponder, or "smart tag," is encrypted with a unique electronic product code (EPe) that distinguishes the tagged item from any other in the world. "Smart tags" are provocatively designed with both read and write capabilities, which means that each time a reader retrieves an EPC from a tag, that retrieval becomes part of the EPC's dynamic history. This constant imprinting provides real-time tracking of a tagged item at any point in its lifespan.

Recognizing the potential commercial benefits of the technology, scientists at the Massachusetts Institute of Technology (MIT) began developing retail applications of RFID in 1999. Install a reader in a display shelf and it becomes a "smart shelf." Network that with other readers throughout the store and you've got an impeccable record of customers interacting with products—from the shelf to the shopper; from the shopper to the cart; from the cart to the cashier, etc.

Proctor & Gamble, The Gillette Company and Wal-Mart were among the first to provide financial and empirical support to the project. Less than five years later RFID has eclipsed UPC bar coding as the next generation standard of inventory control and supply chain management. RFID offers unparalleled inventory control at reduced labor costs; naturally the retail industry is excited.

Katherine Albrecht founded the consumer advocacy group CASPIAN (Consumers Against Supermarket Privacy Invasion and Numbering) to educate consumers about the potential dangers of automatic-identification technology. She warns that "smart tags"—dubbed "spy chips"—increase retailer profits at the expense of consumer privacy.

RFID provides a continuous feed of our activities as we peek, poke, squeeze and shake tagged items throughout the store. Advocacy groups consider this electronic play-by-play a treasure for corporate marketing and a tragedy for consumer privacy.

Albrecht's apprehension is understandable. However, shopping in any public venue is not private. It's public. The decision to be in a public space includes a tacit acknowledgement that one can be seen by others. That's the difference between the public world and the private world.

What if those worlds collide? CASPIAN and other consumer groups are concerned about retailers using RFID to connect public activities with private information. Because each EPC leaves a singular electronic footprint, linking each item of each transaction of each customer with personally identifying information, anyone with access to the system can simply follow the footprints to a dossier of the customer and their purchases.

Again, we must be clear. RFID does enable retailers to surveil consumers and link them with their purchasing histories. As disconcerting as that may be, it is neither new nor unique to RFID. Anyone who uses credit cards agrees to forfeit some degree of privacy for the privilege of buying now and paying later. Credit card companies collect and retain your name, address, telephone and Social Security numbers. This personal information is used to track the date, time, location, items and price of every purchase made with the card.

Don't use credit cards? Unless you pay with cash, someone is monitoring you too. The now familiar UPC bar codes on nearly all consumer goods neatly catalogue the intimate details of all check and bank card purchases. Cash remains the last outpost for the would-be anonymous consumer. Of course, all things are subject to change. RFID inks may be coming soon to a currency near you, but that's a discussion for another day.

If RFID is no more intrusive than a curious fellow shopper or a ceiling mounted security camera, what is the downside for consumer groups? If RFID is no more revealing than a bank or credit card transaction, what is the upside for the corporate suits? There must be more.

Indeed, there is. Bear in mind that "smart tags" are uniquely designed to pinpoint tagged items anytime, anywhere from point of origin through point of sale. And, theoretically, beyond.

Ah, the great beyond. RFID's potential is limited only by our imaginations. And not just our imaginations; the imagination of anyone who has a reader and a transponder. Wal-Mart. Your employer. The government. Anyone.

Everything Costs Something

Members of German privacy group FOEBUD see shadowy strangers lurking in the imagination playground. Their February 2004 demonstration in front of Metro's RFID-rigged Future Store was intended to raise public awareness of the implications of RFID.

"Because the spy chips are not destroyed at the shop exit, they continue to be readable to any interested party, such as other supermarkets, authorities, or anyone in possession of a reading device (available to the general public).… The antennas used for reading are still visible in the Future Store, but soon they will be hidden in walls, doorways, railings, at petrol pumps anywhere. And we won't know anymore who is when or why spying on us, watching us, following each of our steps."

Freedom Is Slavery

Dan Mullen would call that an overreaction. Mullen is the President of auto-identification consortium AIM Global. He cautions that unrealistic fear can obscure the very real benefits of RFID: "Many of the concerns expressed by some of the advocacy groups are frankly, inflated. The technology can be set up so that identifying information is associated with the item, not with the people interacting with the item. Tracking individuals? That's not how the technology is used."

When asked, "Could it be used that way?" Mullen was doubtful. "I don't think so. Not at this point. And I don't see a benefit to anyone." We'd like to think he's right, but someone obviously sees a benefit. RFID has been used exactly that way.

Wal-Mart is one of the retailers who have tested photographic "smart shelves" in some of their U.S. stores. The technology did what it was supposed to do—photograph customers who removed tagged items from a display. Unfortunately, Wal-Mart didn't do what they were supposed to do. Goliath didn't tell David about the camera.

The most disturbing aspect of the project was Wal-Mart's emphatic denial that they had secretly photographed their customers. They weren't confused. They didn't make a mistake. They chose to lie. It was only after Albrecht exposed the evidence that Wal-Mart finally admitted conducting the pilot tests in an effort to combat shoplifting and employee theft. After all, the argument goes, this type of inventory shrinkage costs U.S. retailers as much as $32 billion each year. Don't feel too sorry for our friends in blue. The bill for this hefty loss is passed on to you and me.

The public was unmoved by Wal-Mart's defense, and the project has been aborted. At least for now. Wal-Mart's smiley face logo belies the arrogance wrought by its success, and we will likely see the photographic "smart shelf" again. Or it will see us, anyway.

Wal-Mart is somewhat like a spoiled child, a casualty of indulgence, who is accustomed to doing quite what he wants when he wants to and rarely anything that he doesn't. It hardly seems fair to expect the child to accept "no" when he only vaguely recognizes the word, and even less so, it's finality.

Bear in mind that RFID does not create opportunities for consumer profiling. We do. Every time we enter a store we expose ourselves to scrutiny. Every time we purchase goods or utilize a service we are assimilated, Borg-like, into the collective revenue stream. Everything costs something.

Worldwide spending on RFID is expected to top $3 billion by 2008, almost triple the market of a year ago. Wal-Mart's decree that its top 100 suppliers must be RFID compliant by 2005 told the rest of the world to either get on the train or get off the track. The U.S. Department of Defense has since issued a similar mandate, and falling technology prices coupled with the establishment of uniform RFID communication standards are making it easier for other industries to do the same.

The War on Drugs

It's no longer enough to just say no to the schoolyard crack jockeys. We have new enemies in the war on drugs. Our increasing reliance on chemical relief—born of a pervasive spiritual poverty as much as our aging demographic—has made us attractive to drug counterfeiters.

Counterfeit drugs are sub-potent or inert imposter pills that are channeled into the prescription drug pipeline and sold as legitimate medication. The World Health Organization estimates that in less-developed countries as many as half of all prescription drugs dispensed are counterfeit. The economic cost to defrauded and dying consumers is staggering. And it is almost meaningless compared to the emotional cost.

In February 2004 the U.S. Food and Drug Administration's Counterfeit Drug Task Force released its report "Combating Counterfeit Drugs." FDA Commissioner Mark McClellan directed the group's six month review of America's prescription drug channels.

Its conclusion? The supply of prescription drugs in the United States is overwhelmingly safe. The FDA's complex system of regulatory oversight insures that with rare exception, the pills we pop have been manufactured to the highest standards of purity and potency, distributed safely and dispensed as the doctor ordered.

However, later in the same report McClellan warns that drug counterfeiters are better organized and more technologically sophisticated than ever before. According to McClellan, the FDA's current system can not meet the evolving challenges of the new century, and he recommends full-scale implementation of RFID technology by 2006.

Without question, RFID is a more formidable guardian than our present paper-based drug audit system. The savviest saboteur will find RFID tags extremely difficult to counterfeit and almost impossible to do so at a profit. EPCs afford flawless accountability, which is a distinct impediment to illegal diversions and substitutions. And no doubt every overworked, carpal tunnel-strained pharmacist would welcome RFID's promise of tighter inventory and simplified service.

Does this justify the enormous expense of a complete system overhaul? Do the benefits outweigh the privacy concerns? Are you comfortable enlisting RFID in the battle against drug terrorism?

Before you decide, consider this: The FDA may incorporate "at least two types of anti-counterfeiting technologies into the packaging and labeling of all drugs, at the point of manufacture, with at least one of those technologies being covert (i.e., not made public, and requiring special equipment or knowledge for detection)...."

"Not made public, and requiring special equipment or knowledge for detection." Hmm ... so, RFID tags can be hidden in our prescriptions without our knowledge or consent ... and we will be unable to detect or remove them.

Consider, too, that companies in the U.S., Canada, Sweden and Denmark have developed electronic blister packs that monitor pill removal and automatically notify the physician's computer when a patient has dispensed (or neglected to dispense) the medication as scheduled.

Here's a better idea. The FDA should explain how concealing information from me about my prescriptions makes the world a safer place. And then they can explain how spying on your medicine cabinet—and tattling to your doctor—thwarts drug counterfeiting.

The FDA's prime directive is to protect and advance the public health. They have done this remarkably well for over 140 years at an annual cost to taxpayers of only about $3 per person. When evaluating any policy change the FDA must always preserve that which is most fundamental to its success—indeed, its very existence—the public trust. RFID may prove vital for the continued integrity of our prescription drug pipeline, but never more vital than the continued integrity of the FDA.

RFID is in its spring. These tiny chips, sown by science and nourished richly by corporate support, will burgeon beyond imagination, penetrating our lives like the roots of a willow. This is the time for discourse. This is the time to shore our boundaries. If we cede the opportunity to deliberate, we accept surveillance as a norm. Our indifference will do nothing to stem its growth.

Riots

CAS, JHC

A riot may be considered the ultimate extension of "civil unrest," which can get physical and extend into violence, whereas a "riot" is pure violence accompanied by the intentional and wanton destruction of property by a large number of people and more often than not results in personal injuries and the loss of life.

We were both previously employed by companies with stores in the Los Angeles area and had occasion to observe the destruction caused by rioters, as well as attempt to take pre-emptive measures to minimize such damage. In the section "Civil Disturbances," we discussed some general approaches to this problem. More specific guidance is perhaps best left to cor-porate attorneys and policy makers, with respect to determining to what extent the company will go to defend its property against damage. Part of the determination of this question is to what degree the company wants to place personnel in harm's way while defending property. These questions require careful and deliberate thought, since the answers are fraught with all sorts of both intended and unintended consequences.

Suffice it to say, based on our personal experiences, once a riot develops, it takes on a life of its own, and little, short of deadly force, which itself may not be sufficient, can prevent damage to property if that property is in the riot area.

Historically, some merchants have retained the service of local security companies to provide armed uniform officers. Many shop owners have purchased weapons and have taken a stand in their own stores, prepared to shoot to protect themselves and their businesses, if necessary.

During the infamous Watts Riots in Los Angeles in 1965, I purchased shotguns and armed approximately 20 of my security agents to protect the Broadway Department Store in the area near the rioting. Nonsecurity personnel were not allowed to remain or be in the store. All the store lights were kept on each night, and would-be attackers could see the armed force inside. No attacks were made.

Based on historical evidence from the Watts riots (during which I worked 12-on/12-off shifts for 5 days as a Reserve LA County Deputy Sheriff), other riots (such as those resulting from Vietnam demonstrations), and policy decisions, the Macy's/Bullock's/Magnin companies determined their policy would be to close stores potentially exposed to riotous conditions. In the case of the April 1992 Rodney King riots, it became evident that rioting would be extensive throughout Los Angeles. Stores in the affected areas were closed at noon on the day rioting began, and all personnel were sent home while public transportation was still function-ing. Windows in stores potentially exposed to rioters were boarded up with plywood.

Figure R-1 shows the back of a caseline in the I.. Magnin Wilshire Boulevard store after the Rodney King riots in Los Angeles in April 1992. The entire first floor of the store was trashed, and only one piece of merchandise remained—only because it got caught in a fixture and couldn't be pulled free. The glass in every showcase was broken or cracked, every POS terminal was destroyed, and carpets showed evidence that someone attempted to set fires. Other floors (the basement, second, and third floors) were also damaged and looted, but less extensively.

Other retailers and businesses in the area suffered similar fates. Witnesses who lived nearby reported seeing cars and trucks being driven up to the store doors and merchandise carried out by the armfull and hauled away. The theft of the merchandise is perversely under-standable, but the senseless and wanton destruction of terminals, showcases, fixtures, and furniture only attests to the "mob psychology" riots produce.

The day following the riot we contracted with professional photographers and vid-eographers to record all the damage for insurance purposes. We also had LP personnel care-fully walk the floors and verbally record on tape recorders all their observations regarding damage.

Based on our observations of the King riots, we formulated the opinion that any attempt to have tried to "defend" that store against damage and looting would have resulted in the death of either the defenders or the looters, or most likely both. Property can be replaced—lives cannot.

Civil unrest and the possibility of rioting ignited by racial or religious reasons is a real-istic threat in modern society, as evidenced not only in the United States, but internationally as well. And the once localized, single-city disturbances have grown to national events, as best demonstrated in France in the recent past; i.e., each night, city by city across the French landscape was illuminated by the fires of rioting.

Do you have a plan to deal with this problem?

FIGURE R-1

Robbery: Prevention Checklists and Questionnaire

CAS, JHC

Store owners and managers of small retail businesses should look at the store as a total environment.

Put yourself in the place of a potential robber. Stand away, detached from your business, and try to determine its attractiveness to a robbery. Are your exterior, access, and parking lot areas adequately lighted? What about the interior of your business? Is your interior lighting sufficient so that major points of vulnerability are clearly visible from the outside? Do any and all window surfaces in your storefront provide unobstructed visibility into the store?

Consider this example: I flew to Las Vegas, Nevada, to meet with lawyers and a private investigator to inspect the crime scene of a violent robbery of a Texaco gas station. From the airport, they drove to the intersection where the station was located, and upon arrival, the occupants of the auto noted there were two Texaco stations, on opposite sides of the intersection. The lead attorney had never been to the scene and was confused as to which station was the one in question, so he commenced dialing his office with his cell phone for the correct address. I calmly pointed to the correct station, saying, in effect, "This is the station that was robbed." Moments later that fact was confirmed. "How did you know?" asked the attorney. "Well, if I was a robber I wouldn't rob the other one; it's too open, widows are too big, and the interior is too visible from the street and customers pumping gas. There's no shrubbery obstructing visibility around the building."

Following is a sample of a Robbery Advisory and Reporting Form that should be available in your business and reviewed with employees periodically. The instructions on this form should be followed in case of a robbery, and observations made during the robbery should be recorded as soon as possible after the robber leaves the premises.

1. STAY CALM! DO NOT ATTEMPT HEROICS! Serious injury or death of employees or customers may result.
2. BE ALERT! Concentrate on getting a detailed description.
   Height
   Weight
   Color eyes
   Age
   Clothing worn
   Jewelry
   Shape of hairline
   Rough or manicured hands
   Color of hair
   Right or left handed
   Scars or tattoos
3. SPEECH CHARACTERISTICS! Listen when the robbers talk.
   Accent
   Impediment
   Rapid or slow
   High or low pitch
4. GUN! Observe the weapon used.
   Long or short barrel
   Color
   Revolver—Automatic–Shotgun
   Make
   Caliber
5. WHAT IS ROBBER CARRYING! Observe bag, briefcase, or other container robber may use.
6. GETAWAY CAR! Observe the getaway car if possible to do so without endangering yourself.
   License Number
   Make
   Year
   Color
   Model (2 or 4 door)
   Whitewall tires
   Other persons in car
   Direction of car when lost seen
7. CALL YOUR NEAREST LAW ENFORCEMENT AGENCY AS SOON AS IT IS SAFE TO DO SO AND GIVE THE FOLLOWING INFORMATION:
   A. "I want to report an armed robbery" or "Two men with guns just held us up." It is of great importance that the police know that firearms were used.
   B. State as accurately as possible the amount of time that has elapsed since the robbery (e.g., one minute ago or five minutes ago).
   C. State your name and address.
   D. Give number, race, and sex of suspects (e.g., two white males).
   E. Direction and mode of travel (e.g., south on Broadway in a black 1963 Ford—California license OXXXOOO).
   F. Brief physical description (e.g., one short wearing dark trousers and blue shirt. One tall wearing dark trousers and white shirt). An investigating officer will take more details later.
   G. Weapon used (e.g., short barreled revolver).
8. SECURITY DEPARTMENT! Call your security department as soon as you have called the police.
9. IMMEDIATELY WRITE AN ACCOUNT OF WHAT HAPPENED! Include time, date, day of week, and every detail you can recall.

10. WITNESS! Have all other employees who were involved or who observed the robbery write their own independent account of what they saw. Do not discuss your observations with other employees; it is important each person report only what he personally observed and not be influenced by others.
11. COMPANY POLICY. Stay informed of company policy regarding what is expected of you.

As stated earlier, when the business is examined in an effort to determine robbery vulnerabilities, it must be viewed in totality. To assist in making such an examination as meaningful as possible, a Robbery Security Checklist follows. A careful and detailed use of this form, coupled with corrections of noted deficiencies, should help minimize the business's vulnerability to robbery.

Robbery Security Checklist

1. Are your exterior, access, and parking lot areas adequately lit?
2. What about the interior of your business?
3. Is your interior lighting sufficient so that major points of vulnerability are clearly visible from the outside?
4. Do any and all window surfaces in your storefront provide unobstructed visibility?
5. Do you have signs placed toward the lower portion of your door which say: "No cash is kept inside" or "Exact change only after 8:00 p.m."?
6. Is your cash register clearly visible from the outside?
7. Using the security checklist that follows, identify your business's points of high vulnerability to the crime of robbery.
8. Do you have an operable recording CCTV system?

A Security Checklist for the Crime of Robbery

1. Is your business a likely target for robbers?
   YES   NO
2. Is your business isolated from other businesses?
   YES   NO
3. Does the business operate late at night?
   YES   NO
4. Does the business make change after dark?
   YES   NO
5. Is the business known to keep substantial cash on hand?
   YES   NO
6. Is cash transferred according to a set routine?
   YES   NO
7. Is the business obviously operated by a single cashier?
   YES   NO
8. Does the business have little exterior lighting?
   YES   NO
9. Is there normally only one employee working at a time?
   YES   NO
10. Can a robber easily case your business?
    YES   NO
11. Is your cash register hidden from other employees?
    YES   NO
12. Is the cash register within reach of customers?
    YES   NO
13. Is there only a single courier for cash transfer?
    YES   NO
14. Do you have a set routine for cash transfer?
    YES   NO

15. Does the business lack a telephone?
    YES   NO
16. Is the light level in your store much higher or lower than outside your store?
    YES   NO
17. Do posters and displays block the view of the cash register from outside?
    YES   NO

If your answer to any of the preceding questions is "Yes," try to improve visibility, money-handling routines, lighting (exterior), employee coverage, use of CCTV, and any other action that turns the answer to any question from "Yes" to "No." Consider, for example, placing a height marker on the exit doorjamb; this will help employees accurately estimate the height of an escaping robber. Also consider the use of a floor safe and make frequent "drops" of cash into the floor safe when it can be done safely and discreetly.

Roof Security

CAS, JHC

Building construction may or may not require approval of the security/loss prevention department. We hope such approval is part of the planning and construction process. It is, however, more likely the risks inherent in unsecured roofs, in stores, distribution centers, and warehouse facilities are a present problem that requires security inspection and possible remedial action. The problem, as discussed in this section, may serve as a guide for future construction planning.

What's the risk? It's a given that any and every commercial building represented by a "box" is secured by various kinds of lock hardware on all four sides, and typically, the various possible points of unwanted entry—i.e., windows and doors—are protected by some type of alarm system. But what about the roof? It's no secret that many criminal penetrations have been negotiated through roofs during the middle of the night, and such entries could have been prevented had a knowledgeable security executive inspected that roof prior to the discovery of the crime.

Here's an example: After I was transferred to a division of stores, local management expressed suspicion of the long-time uniformed security officer who patrolled the interior of the multistory store during the hours at night when the store was closed. They suspected he was engaged in theft but had no idea as to how the officer was removing merchandise. Forearmed with that information, and in the normal course of familiarizing myself with the physical attributes of the store in question in downtown San Francisco, I conducted an inspection of the "warehouse," which was the top floor of the building. During that inspection, I noted a very high vertical latter accessing the roof. At the head of the ladder was roof hatch, secured by a padlock and hasp. The door was also equipped with a mercury switch alarm designed to signal an alarm if the trap door was lifted (the mercury would flow from its regular "level" mode to one end, making contact and sending the electric impulse activating the alarm). I noted, during this daytime inspection, the switch had been tampered with, allowing the opening and the flow of mercury was not sufficient to reach the contact end; hence, the switch was essentially disarmed. Continued inspection of the roof disclosed a long, coiled rope and a few weathered price tags and merchandise tickets.

Further investigation revealed the guard, who had the key to the hatch padlock, compromised the alarm switch and used that roof hatch to access the roof. He would drop the end of the rope back down into the warehouse, bundle merchandise of his choice, pull up the bundle through the hatch, and then lower the bundle on the rear exterior side of the store to an awaiting confederate in the alley below.

Maintenance personnel, who occasionally went to the roof, felt the hatch was secured by lock and key and paid no attention to or never saw the rope, which was stashed in a remote corner, or the weathered tickets. This theft activity lasted for years undetected!

Inspection of the Roof

The "inspector" should answer these questions:

1. How can someone gain access to the roof from inside the building?
   - Is that door or hatch secured by lock?
   - Is that door alarmed?
   - Is that door's alarmed tested (swung) during the hours the alarms are turned on, and if swung, is a signal received by the alarm central station?
2. How can someone gain access to the roof from outside the building?
   - By a tree?
   - By a fire escape?
   - Are the appropriate steps alarmed?
   - By an adjacent building?
   - By a ladder?
   - By standing on the roof of a car or truck and gaining a foothold on or grasping some part of the building?
   - By throwing a grappling hook, which would catch on the roof's coaming? (Slanted sheet metal braced in a slant on the inside would cause any hook to slide back over the coaming and fall to the ground.)
3. Once on the roof, how can someone access the interior of the building without forcing a door or hatch, which may be alarmed?
   - By forcibly opening skylights?
   - By breaking the glass of skylights?
   - By cutting through a wooden door panel or hatch without "swinging" the door (and not activating an alarm)?
   - By cutting through a patched roof which formerly was the location of an old air-conditioning unit?
   - By entering via ductwork?

Bear in mind, once a burglar is on the roof, he's more often than not out of public view and has time to take advantage of any weakness in the structure and penetrate the building. It's the duty and responsibility of the security/loss prevention department to "harden" this part of the store, warehouse, and distribution center. This includes "temporary warehouse" facilities, many times rented during the holiday season.

S

Security and Emergency Communications

CAS, JHC

Perhaps nothing is as important to a security/LP department than the ability of staff to communicate among themselves. This is particularly true because portions of LP's responsibilities involve actions which may be adversarial and confrontational, as well as involve emergencies, and the ability to contact assistance or relay time-sensitive information is essential. For these reasons, a quick, reliable, and secure method of communication is vital.

Years ago, when security staff (or even earlier, when it was known as the "Protection Department") were needed on the selling floor, the "bell" system was used to page them. The procedure was as follows: The person needing LP called the store telephone operator and verbally requested LP in a given area of the store. The telephone operator would then cause chime-like "bells" to sound throughout the store. When LP staff heard their designated bell call, they would call the store operator, who would direct them to the area where their services were required. This bell system was also used to contact store managers and other executives, each of which had a distinctive bell call, which was generally a series of sounds in groups of five or fewer bells. For example, LP may have been assigned 5-1 bells, sounding in several distinct series of xxxxx x, xxxxx x, xxxxx x.

In the 1970s, most LP departments converted to portable radios for in-store communications. These battery-operated radios permitted LP agents to be called by the store telephone operator and/or by any other portable radio on the same frequency. Thus, not only were LP agents able to be paged to a given area of the store, but they could also communicate among themselves. "Privacy" channels (frequencies) enabled them to restrict some communications to specific radios so that "outsiders" like telephone operators could not hear their conversations. Each portable radio had at least two rechargeable batteries so that while one was in use, the other could be charging. Most LP agents choose to use the standard "Ten Code" for their transmissions because it saves time and is easily understood.

Later on, security/LP executives who traveled between stores were issued pagers so that they could be contacted at any time their pager was turned on, which by tradition was almost every waking hour (and when emergency conditions existed, any waking or nonwaking hour). Larger stores eventually installed systems whereby a sales associate or other store personnel could call LP agents over their radios simply by dialing a special number on the store phone system.

The advent of so-called trunked radio systems permitted the use of relay towers scattered throughout the state to permit long-distance radio communication with radios of relatively low power. By utilizing additional equipment, retailers were also able to broadcast through this system from telephones by dialing the correct connection code.

Whatever radio system is selected, it is important to provide for powering it and recharging its batteries from both 110VAC power as well as 12VDC power. In emergencies, local power often goes out, and if radios can be powered/recharged only by 110VAC (house current), their life will be limited to available battery life. If, however, there is a converter or other means of plugging into and powering/recharging from 12VDC (automobile cigarette lighter sockets), then the radio can realistically be used as long as there is a vehicle available.

The latest communication devices utilized by security personnel are cell phones and cell phones capable of "walkie-talkie" operation. These phones can almost communicate instantaneously and privately from one coast to the other.

Modern communications prove indispensable during major emergencies. We can attest to the fact that, during the Loma Prieta earthquake in 1989, the security radio system, which enabled long-distance communications, proved a godsend. Because both local landline and cellular phone systems, as well as local power, were interrupted, the security department's radios, with their ability to be powered by vehicle batteries, were the only method of communication available between affected stores.

Security Mirrors

CAS, JHC

The use of convex mirrors as a security tool is perhaps one of the oldest such tools still in use today. Convex mirrors are utilized to permit viewing specific areas of the store or aisles from a distant location without, one hopes, disclosing the fact that such viewing is occurring. In most situations, however, anyone who is knowledgeable about the use of convex mirrors can easily determine if he is under observation. For this reason, these mirrors present a double-edged sword for the store owner: Not only can the owner see a potential shoplifter, but the potential thief can also see that he is under observation.

It has been our experience that while such mirrors are not particularly useful as operational antishoplifting devices, their existence in a store does send the message to potential thieves that the store has at least some degree of security awareness and in this way may serve as a deterrent to shoplifting.

Another mirror used in retailing is the so-called two-way mirror, which allows representatives of the store, i.e., management or a loss prevention professional, to view the selling floor from such areas as stockrooms or a "Trojan horse," while the opposite or public side of that mirror appears to be no more or less than an actual functional mirror.

A cautionary word about two-way mirrors: During the long history of retail security and loss prevention, there have been instances in which these devices were used in areas with high expectations for privacy, such as fitting rooms and restrooms. Those days have long passed, and two-way mirrors should never be used in those areas today. In most jurisdictions, such use is actually illegal.

Security Surveys

CAS, JHC

Introduction to Security Surveys: A University Bookstore Security Survey

While the trend appears to be for colleges and universities to outsource the operation of their bookstores to companies such as Barnes & Noble, many schools still continue to operate their campus stores. Some universities have ancillary services whose operations fall under the bookstore management. Examples of such ancillary services are Technical Books (e.g., Medical, Legal), Fax and Sales Services, Office Products, Computer Repair Facilities, Vending Operations, Copy Centers, Laundromats, Retail Operations (Clothing, Gifts, and Insignia merchandise), and Food Vending Services. The loss prevention aspects of a college bookstore are generally much like those of any other retail operation, with some aspects which are unique to the college campus environment. We feel the best way to present both a broad picture of the loss prevention aspects of college/university bookstores as well as provide an introduction to security surveys is to reproduce an actual security/loss prevention survey done at a major university (whose name and personnel identities have been disguised). By reviewing the survey, you will gather not only the LP concerns of this venue, but also the format, scope, and details of an actual security survey, which can be adapted and applied to any venue.

☐ ☐ ☐ ▰▰▰▰▰▰▰▰▰▰▰▰▰▰▰▰▰▰▰▰▰▰▰▰▰

CONFIDENTIAL SECURITY SURVEY AND RECOMMENDATIONS
FOR THE STORE
UNIVERSAL UNIVERSITY
MIDDLETON, NY
by
xxxx x. xxxxxxxxx, CPP
Security Consultant
July 2007

CONFIDENTIAL
    Copy 1 of 5
CONSULTANT'S REPORT
SECURITY SURVEY FOR THE UNIVERSAL STORE
UNIVERSAL UNIVERSITY

SCOPE
This report is the documentation of my survey of the existing security/loss prevention policies, procedures, organization and operations at The Universal Store [hereinafter referred to as THE STORE] and its ancillary stores and Warehouse as authorized by Mr. Thomas Martin, CEO and Director. The objective of the survey was to assess existing physical and functional security and to recommend changes or improvements where appropriate to ensure

  a. That efforts to provide a safe working and shopping environment are adequate and reasonable, and that appropriate emergency plans are in place.
  b. That security policies, procedures, and operations comply with all applicable laws and are legally justifiable.
  c. That appropriate checks and balances exist to both deter and detect internal dishonesty.
  d. That adequate programs are in place to minimize losses from shoplifting and customer fraud, and to effectively and reasonably deal with offenders.

    The survey identified twelve (12) Areas of Focus, which are

  1. Overall Security Posture
  2. Security Organization
  3. Security-Related Written Policies and Procedures
  4. Loss Prevention Awareness and Training
  5. Merchandise Handling Procedures
  6. Asset and Property Controls
  7. Shoplifting Controls and Procedures
  8. Internal Theft Controls and Procedures
  9. Physical Security
  10. Inventory Results
  11. Emergency Planning
  12. Miscellaneous

    The 12 areas are not necessarily distinctly separate one from the other, but each does tend to blend with and/or augment another so the totality of the security strategies achieves the desired effect. For ease in presentation and comprehension, they are hereinafter referred to as Areas of Focus, some of which may have subareas. Under each Area of Focus is a listing of Findings, most of which are immediately followed by a Recommendation. Recommendations are consecutively numbered by Area of Focus for ease in referencing. The Areas of Focus are preceded by an Executive Summary.

METHODOLOGY

The Findings in this report resulted from my inspections of the facilities concerned; personal interviews with THE STORE employees; and review of documents, records, and statistics relating to security operations and personnel, inventory shortage, organizational policy, procedures and structure, receipt and distribution of merchandise, and control of cash. We have purposely not included in this report maps, organization charts, statistical summaries, etc., obtained from and readily available to bookstore management unless such documents are integral to this report.

While every recommendation contained herein is a practical enhancement of existing security, some are optional in nature and not absolutely essential to meet the objectives of the Survey; they are presented to provide the reader with a range of solutions and options available.

In all cases the optimal recommendation, in my opinion, is presented first, followed, in some cases, by less than optimal but still useful alternatives which may be temporarily utilized.

It must also be noted that my Survey was conducted shortly after the end of Fall Rush and while THE STORE was still in the process of "getting back to normal." Admittedly, some deficiencies noted herein may well automatically be corrected when THE STORE returns to "normal" operations; however, loss prevention vulnerabilities are the greatest during Rush, so in this sense this survey may actually be more meaningful than if conducted in mid-semester.

Finally, we recognize that there may be inherent conflict between the establishment of some appropriate security procedures for a retail business of the size and type of THE STORE and the requirements, real or perceived, of operating on the campus of a prestigious and world-renowned research university in the somewhat cloistered environment of academia. In these instances, management must be the final arbiter.

The cooperation and assistance of the following persons who were interviewed is noted:

- Mr. Rich Jones, Vice President, Universal University
- Mr. T, Martin, CSP, Director
- Ms. S. Xxxxxxx, Operations General Manager
- Ms. D. Xxxxxx, Human Relations Manager
- Mr. J. Xxxxxx, Warehouse and MIS Manager
- Mr. K. Xxxxxx, Head, Computer Sales and Technology
- Mr. B. Xxxxxx, Security and Retail Supervisor
- Mr. S. Xxxxxx, Buyer—All Text and Trade books
- Mr. B. Xxxxx, Print Shop Manager
- Ms. R. Xxxxxxxxx, Warehouse Supervisor
- Ms. D. Xxxxxxxxxxxxx, Account Representative
- Ms. D. Xxxxxxx, Head Cashier, Sales Audit and Payroll Clerk
- Mr. S. Xxxxxxxxxxxxxxx, Retail Manager (Clothing and Memorabilia)
- Mr. P. Xxxxxxxxx, Retail Manager (Supplies, Electronics, and Gifts)
- Mr. L. Xxxxxx, Sales Associate

    Non-Bookstore personnel:

- Ms. M. Xxxxx, Esq., Judicial Administrator, Universal University
- Mr. G. Xxxxxx, Business Solutions, Program Consulting Manager
- Mr. R. Xxxxxxx, Investigator, Universal Police Department (Crime Prevention
- Mr. G. Xxxxxxx, Investigator, Universal Police Department (Crime Prevention)
- Mr. C. Xxxxxxxxxxx, Xxxxxxxx Alarm Company

Special Thanks to Jane Sxxxxx, Secretary to the Director, for her courtesies and help.

Executive Summary

Universal University is situated in Middleton, New York, a city with a population of approximately 30,000 people. The Universal community, during the school year, consists of 20,000 students and 10,000 faculty and staff.

THE STORE, with $30+ million of annual sales, operates under the overall supervision of Mr. Rich Jones, who, before being appointed a University Vice President several years ago, was THE STORE CEO and Director for many years. While part of the University system, THE STORE is financially self-supporting and pays 5% of its gross sales (with some minor exceptions) as a "royalty" to the University. It is housed in a two- story facility located near the center of the University campus. Its design is unique; University esthetics' requirements [preserving a view] preclude any design changes to the building. This prohibition effectively precludes any expansion, both outward and upward, which is desperately needed.

THE STORE comprises 43,000 square feet of primarily selling space with minimal nonselling support and office space. THE STORE is open 5 days [closed Sundays] for 50 hours a week. THE STORE also operates three remote retail locations: a very small outlet at the Veterinary School, a small outlet in the Xxxxx Hotel lobby, and a brand new retail section added to the Best Copy Center. Additionally, THE STORE operates a Print Shop and a 12,000 square foot Warehouse, which houses the Universal Business Center [Travel Service, Sales Audit, and Accounting Departments] in a 3,800 square foot second floor area. In all, THE STORE has 72 career and from 10–60 part-time student employees and, as needed, from 5 to 65 temporary agency personnel.

The store is open Monday through Friday from 8:30 a.m. to 5:30 p.m. and Saturdays from noon until 5:00 p.m.; a total of 50 hours per week.

The existing security and loss prevention policies, procedures, organization, and operations are inadequate to meet the stated shortage objectives of management.

The security organization is essentially nonexistent. Mr. Ben Johnson, a Retail Manager, was tasked early this year with the responsibility for security/loss prevention. To his credit, Mr. Johnson, with no background in loss prevention, began to acquire some of the fundamental precepts of loss prevention, primarily by using the Web and reading a security magazine. While these efforts are laudatory, this approach is doomed to failure, particularly when his retail operations responsibilities have not diminished and demand his full-time attention. Mr. Johnson's status as a nonmember of senior management coupled with his lack of any formal security/loss prevention training assures not only a mediocre loss prevention effort at best, but a real danger of inadvertently creating civil liability resulting from well-intentioned but legally erroneous procedures.

Shoplifting detection and apprehension had been accomplished by a part-time employee who monitored THE STORE's closed-circuit television (CCTV) cameras. This person is no longer employed and his employment violated New York state law; he has not been replaced. Consequently, the sole shoplifting detection relies on sales associate's response to alarms of the electronic article surveillance (EAS) system at the store exits, a procedure which currently is essentially ineffective.

There is no Security/Loss Prevention Operations Manual. Mr. Johnson, again to his credit, has written a document titled "Security and Operations: Responsibility and Policy Manual." Unfortunately, as a result of Mr. Johnson's lack of training, this document contains numerous procedural and legal errors, which places THE STORE in legal jeopardy. Additionally, this document is totally silent on retail loss prevention techniques, fraud prevention, and internal theft.

Most employees felt THE STORE was "wide open" to shoplifting; nearly all suggested that THE STORE's CCTVs should be monitored and that backpacks/book bags not be allowed in the store. Merchandise handling and distribution procedures seem adequate, but there are no procedures in place to either deter or evidence theft.

Some buyers felt that the computerized inventory control system had glitches resulting in reporting nonexistent missing inventory and exaggerating shrinkage. An examination of THE STORE's back office equipment [laptops, printers, copiers, etc.] disclosed that many had no serialized property tags affixed. It is doubtful that an exact inventory of THE STORE's equipment exists or that losses could, if noticed, be substantiated. Shoplifting controls need improvement; the antishoplifting closed-circuit television (CCTV) system, while in the process of being upgraded, remains below par. The EAS system needs maintenance; portals operate erratically, alarms are not loud enough, and the red alarm lights do not all work. It appeared that even tagged items could pass through the system undetected. Cashiers at registers cannot adequately respond to alarms when they do occur. Successful shoplifting creates the opportunity for fraudulent returns, primarily of textbooks, and there is no procedure currently in place to detect this activity.

Internal theft is a subject which apparently has received little attention. There have been few employees apprehended for stealing and, at least one that was, was reportedly allowed to continue working. Suspicions of internal theft are not referred to Mr. Johnson but rather "investigated" by the Operations Manager. CCTV surveillance of cash register checkout areas is lacking. This is an area which requires a significant increase in emphasis, the adoption of techniques to identify and surface any problems, and the acquisition of personnel trained to investigate and resolve these issues.

Physical security requires considerable attention. Physical protection of reserve stock merchandise and offices containing merchandise all create loss vulnerabilities. The continued upgrading of CCTV will improve both internal and external theft detection and provide management with a valuable tool for improved customer service and staffing evaluation. The fire sprinkler head in the ceiling of the POS computer room should be capped off; an accidental or intentional discharge of the water sprinkler would ruin the computers and put those systems out of business until replacement equipment could be installed. The door to this space should be locked when the room is unoccupied; backup tapes should be stored in a fireproof container. Alarm systems, while adequate, contain capabilities which are being underutilized. Management, therefore, does not gain the advantage of available, but unused, features providing additional safeguards and controls. Testing of alarm systems is not done; there is no exception reporting. Key controls and issuance and deletion of access control codes require written documentation; all keys should be stamped "Do Not Duplicate." Employee package checks are rarely performed, and there have never been any real-time janitor surveillances or checks, even though they are in the store after hours and have keys and alarm codes.

Inventory figures reflect generally increasing shortages over the past several years. In FY 02 [excluding computer sales and shrink], textbooks and educational supplies represented approximately 90% of the shrinkage dollars while responsible for only 55% of sales. It is the consensus that the bulk of these losses occur during Fall and Spring Rush, where space needs and limitations result in the virtual inability to deter and detect shoplifting. Textbook shortages at nearly 6% is triple the industry average.

Dock security in THE STORE is unacceptable and offers opportunities for increased security and minimizing potential loss situations. The lack of security controls and disciplines on the dock present serious vulnerabilities; there is often unrestricted access to the dock, mechanical equipment room, and employee-only areas. The location and accessibility of the employee badges to nonemployees should be eliminated. The University has a comprehensive Emergency Preparedness Plan, and the Universal Business Services (THE STORE) plan has been integrated into it. It was indicated the Emergency Plan is available on campus computer terminals; this policy should be reviewed as to whether having the plan universally available (without password) on terminals for legitimate reference outweighs its general availability to a potential miscreant, particularly since the printed document is marked *Confidential*.

University Police resources, such as their crime prevention officers, are underutilized.

Housekeeping and neatness in general needs significant improvement.

The entire issue of security, loss prevention, and the protection of assets appears, until recently, to have been largely ignored. Efforts to establish better controls for protecting assets must be undertaken. Interestingly, no employees suggested that the community at Universal is, unlike the general population, not subject to human frailties and temptations, which include acts of dishonesty. It is, therefore, management's responsibility to insist that procedures be in place *and* that they be followed to adequately protect the assets of THE STORE.

It is noted that existing policies, procedures, controls and disciplines within the various areas of focus not mentioned herein have been found to be adequate to meet currently recognized minimum security standards and practices.

The recommendations and suggestions contained in this report should help position THE STORE's management in addressing the security needs of this vital facility to assure that THE STORE can continue not only to meet its mission. but to do so at increased profitability.

TABLE OF CONTENTS FOR FINDINGS AND RECOMMENDATIONS
Area of Focus Page

AREA OF FOCUS #1
Overall Security Posture

FINDING:

It is the consensus of those interviewed and the observation of this consultant that security at THE STORE is less than adequate. This situation is a matter of concern to nearly every employee interviewed, but most seemed unwilling or unable to grant the solutions and disciplines required for correction a high priority. This inaction appears to stem from two basic factors: (1) lack of time and other pressing priorities, and (2) the absence of the expertise required to develop and implement loss prevention training, procedures and programs

RECOMMENDATION 1.1:

Loss prevention training, programs, and awareness must become an integral part of THE STORE environment. This will require the employment of a security/loss prevention professional whose basic duties and responsibilities are limited to his area of expertise.

FINDING:

Responses to written questionnaires and personal interviews make it apparent that there are numerous misconceptions and misunderstandings regarding some of the University's and THE STORE's policies, procedures, and operating standards with respect to security issues among store management.

RECOMMENDATION 1.2:

Management must assure that security standards, after adoption by senior management, are adequately promulgated, understood, and followed by all employees.

FINDING:

Senior merchants and department managers must be an integral part of the process toward shortage reduction, and should be intimately aware of the shortage percentages and dollars down to the classification level. Any lack of knowledge about shortage detail does not permit managers to design and then implement the necessary shortage reduction strategies specific to merchandise classifications.

RECOMMENDATION 1.3:

Each department manager should be given all available data regarding his department's shortage. After each inventory, this data should be discussed with the appropriate senior member of management, and shortage reduction strategies and goals for the coming inventory period should be agreed upon in writing. Periodic follow-up should be made to assure implementation of agreed-upon action.

FINDING:

The entire thrust of THE STORE's security program is the apprehension of shoplifters.

The broad concept of loss prevention is totally absent. Basic loss prevention activities as employee security orientations, return/refund analysis, inventory shortage review, merchandise movement control, developing minimum security standards for merchandise presentation, audits of security-sensitive areas, employee package checks, and the development and implementation of security/loss prevention policies and procedures are either completely lacking or barely adequate.

RECOMMENDATION 1.4:   The thrust of THE STORE's shortage control and security activities must be prevention. It is essential the program be redesigned to make prevention of loss a priority with apprehension by security considered a necessary activity only after the prevention efforts fail or are ignored. This effort should (a) start at the top and permeate through all employee levels, (b) establish defined shortage reduction goals, and (c) require that managers and supervisors be held accountable for results. A culture of discipline and controls must be established. While designated security personnel will play a key role in prevention efforts, all employees must be involved for the effort to succeed.

FINDING: THE STORE has assigned the security function as one of the responsibilities of a Retail Manager, which is not a senior management level position. This organizational position of the security/loss prevention function, coupled with the Retail Manager's lack of any formal security training, has, perhaps inadvertently, relegated the perception of the importance of security to a rather subordinate and unimportant role.

RECOMMENDATION 1.5:   THE STORE should recruit and hire an experienced professional security manager who will function at a senior management level. The proper candidate can assume responsibility for new employee security/safety training covering external theft, internal theft, and fraud; supervise and train the security staff; assist in inventory preparation; conduct audits; establish a meaningful shortage control and loss prevention program which functions throughout the year; and be a fully contributing member of senior management.

FINDING: There is no Loss Prevention Manual.

RECOMMENDATION 1.6:   A comprehensive compilation of all policies and procedures designed for loss prevention and shortage control should be prepared as "the Bible" for security/loss prevention personnel as well as guidance to store management.

FINDING:	THE STORE currently has no one dedicated to the loss prevention function.
RECOMMENDATION 1.7:	A qualified Security Manager [see Recommendation 1.5 *supra*] will possess advanced investigative skills and can effectively train, schedule, and supervise subordinates to monitor CCTVs and assist in other security/loss prevention activities. The goal of a close working relationship between security agents and other store personnel is essential to effective loss prevention and shortage control.
FINDING:	THE STORE does not have in place procedures which both deter and provide for early detection of internal dishonesty
RECOMMENDATION 1.8:	That procedures and techniques, such as register "salting," introduced errors, extraction programs in the distribution system, and random surprise audits and inspections be implemented.
FINDING:	THE STORE has no in-house capability to properly and successfully detect and investigate any but the most obvious, basic, and straightforward indicia of employee dishonesty or fraud.
RECOMMENDATION 1.9:	This finding further mandates the hiring of a security professional.

AREA OF FOCUS #2
Security Organization

2.1 Personnel

FINDING:	THE STORE has essentially no security/loss prevention personnel.
RECOMMENDATION 2.1:	Recruit and hire a security professional and adequate subordinate personnel.
RECOMMENDATION 2.2:	Loss prevention personnel below the Manager should be referred to as Security Agents or Loss Prevention Agents.
RECOMMENDATION 2.3:	Devote at least 106 hours a week to dedicated nonstudent loss prevention personnel; typically a 40-hour Manager and 66 hours of Agent's time.

Note: The importance of implementing RECOMMENDATIONS 1.5, 1.7, 2.1 and 2.2 will become evident as the balance of the findings under this and Area of Focus #4 are studied.

2.2   Training

Note: This section will be also referenced in Section 2.7, "Liability Issues."

| FINDING: | The lack of a professional security manager subjects THE STORE to civil liability as well as potential criminal liability. |
| RECOMMENDATION 2.4: | THE STORE must employ a security professional. |

RECOMMENDATION 2.5: A written test should be required to establish comprehension of the training materials given security personnel, and follow-up training should be required at least yearly to update them regarding any new legal issues, shoplifting techniques, etc.

RECOMMENDATION 2.6: A security professional should be responsible for training security personnel who will be making detentions/apprehensions.

RECOMMENDATION 2.7: Anyone hired to monitor CCTVs should also be fully trained to make detentions and perform essentially other loss prevention functions, such as audits, loss analysis, surveillances etc.

2.3 Deployment and Productivity

FINDING: There are no dedicated loss prevention personnel.

RECOMMENDATION 2.8: By utilizing properly trained full-time security agents, performing under the supervision of a qualified security manager, their role could be proactive with all the concomitant benefits deriving therefrom.

RECOMMENDATION 2.9: Security personnel should be scheduled 15 minutes before store opening and until all personnel have left THE STORE at closing.

2.4 Supervision

FINDING: Mr. Johnson is supervised by the Operations Manager, who is questionable with respect to his loss prevention duties.

RECOMMENDATION 2.10: When a security professional is hired, they should report to the Store Director.

RECOMMENDATION 2.11: Agent personnel should report only to the Security Manager.

2.5 Report Writing and Record Retention

FINDING: At present, THE STORE's apprehension reports are prepared on Mr. Johnson's computer terminal. There should be a written report of all detentions, not just apprehensions. It is the detention where no stolen merchandise is found which are the troublesome ones. These must be documented and given thorough review to minimize this liability exposure and to determine if retraining is needed.

RECOMMENDATION 2.12: Detention reports should be reviewed periodically by someone in the University legal office to assure compliance with all codes and statutes.

RECOMMENDATION 2.13: Mr. Johnson's computer should require a password to access Apprehension Reports; this information should not be available to unauthorized persons.

RECOMMENDATION 2.14:	A copy of the security access password should be placed in a sealed envelope and kept in a secure location for use in emergencies.
RECOMMENDATION 2.15:	Arrest report information should be retained for seven (7) years and then destroyed.

2.6 Liability Issues

FINDING:	Existing Security Policies contain inaccuracies. (See FINDING and RECOMMENDATION 2.5 *supra*.)
RECOMMENDATION 2.16:	A security professional should prepare the Security Manual; it should be reviewed by University legal counsel.
FINDING:	Christopher Extra, who monitored THE STORE's CCTV [no longer employed or replaced] violated New York General Business Law Article 7-A [Security Guard Act] § 89-e *et seq.* by not having the required training and registration required by this act.
RECOMMENDATION 2.17:	Conduct all security activities in compliance with state law. A security professional would have known of this law and prevented its violation by THE STORE.
FINDING:	As noted in several sections above, various of my findings point out potential liability exposure for THE STORE/University. These exposures are inherent in the activities of any security department, but by careful and proper selection of personnel, coupled with adequate training and supervision, these risks can be minimized.
RECOMMENDATION 2.18:	The entire security function, when its structure is ultimately determined, should be reviewed with the University's legal counsel.
FINDING:	Mr. Johnson does not have a lockable office or a locked file cabinet.
RECOMMENDATION 2.19:	Mr. Johnson [or any subsequent Security Manager] requires an office which is private and a file cabinet which locks. This protects THE STORE from civil suits for invasion of privacy or defamation.
	For example: If the Security Manager interviews an employee about any issue in an area which is not private, others observing this conversation may draw erroneous conclusions as to the reasons for the interview. Further, sensitive documents, which may be on his desk, are less open to compromise.
	Similarly, arrest reports, investigative reports, and other security information must be securely stored to prevent unauthorized access.

Area of Focus #3
Security-Related Written Policies and Procedures

FINDING:	The use of the current "Security and Operations: Responsibility and Policy Manual" prepared by Mr. Johnson contains various errors, omissions, and inappropriate instructions.
	For example: Under the section "Job Description" A and B state the security employee is responsible for "the maintenance of daily store activities," including such things as "Store errands, clearing rooms, washing vans and doing odd jobs." If loss prevention is to be effective, its personnel cannot also be janitors. There is no mention that, if a suspect is female, *the industry standard is always have a female witness present.*
	The policy states there is a duty to apprehend customers when they conceal merchandise and leave the sales floor without purchasing it. This statement should provide that the employee must *know that the concealed merchandise belongs to THE STORE and was not previously purchased.*
	The policy provides for an apprehension when another employee states he witnessed a shoplift and is willing to provide a written statement. The industry rule is *"If you didn't see it, it didn't happen."* Additionally, New York Criminal Procedure Law § 140.30 provides that for a misdemeanor arrest (under $1000) the crime must be committed in the presence of the arresting person. There is no mention in the Policy of the Industry standard of meeting the "six steps" prior to an apprehension. SEE ATTACHMENT I.
RECOMMENDATION 3.1:	That use of the current Security Manual be discontinued immediately until it is revised to meet acceptable standards.
RECOMMENDATION 3.2:	That all training materials utilized in training store security personnel be thoroughly examined for content and approved by University legal counsel.
FINDING:	There is no document such as "WELCOME TO THE STORE" which contains the work rules, policies, and procedures expected to be followed by employees.
	A draft document, intended for student employees, titled "Policy Manual," which covers some work rules, dress code, use of time clock, breaks, absenteeism, name badges, and other similar topics, awaits final publication approval. This draft document has, in my view, several deficiencies, namely:

(1) "When the store is closed for business, do not leave guests/friends unattended."

(2) There is no mention of the consequences of violating the rules against ringing up your own sale or making your own change.

(3) The stated policy regarding use of store equipment is vague. "Use for other than legitimate store business is discouraged." What does this mean?

(4) There is no stated prohibition against theft of merchandise, money, or time.

(5) There is no specific procedure regarding ringing all sales.

RECOMMENDATION 3.3:

(a) Friends/guests should never be in the store after closing.

(b) A specific statement about theft should be included.

RECOMMENDATION 3.4:

Develop a written set of Rules and Regulations governing employee behavior. State with specificity that any act of theft or fraud against THE STORE will result in immediate dismissal and possible criminal prosecution. (This is covered in the University's "Policy Notebook for Universal Community" given to all students.) However, it does not reach temporary agency personnel employed by THE STORE).

A thorough review of all employee rules and regulations is suggested, since employer liability for employee actions is expanding as a result of statutory law and court decisions. Employee rules must be both comprehensive and clear with regard to the penalty for violations. With regard to register procedures, specific rules regarding:

(a) always giving receipt,

(b) immediate ringing of sales,

(c) all sales must be recorded, and

(d) "open drawer" selling is prohibited [except in Munch] should be published.

FINDING:
I found no specific regulations covering Buyers.

RECOMMENDATION 3.5:
Prepare a "Buyers Guide" which should contain, *inter alia*, the following:

(a) *Cash compensation is NEVER to be accepted by a buyer under any circumstances.*

(b) *Compensation of any kind in any form from publishers, manufacturers or sales representatives must be disclosed to immediate supervisor or THE STORE Director.*

(c) *Any incident that seems unethical must be brought to the attention of THE STORE Director.*

FINDING:
I found no document covering "CUSTOMER SERVICE."

RECOMMENDATION 3.6:

It is well established that the best defense
to shoplifting is good customer service.
While it is not always possible to service
each customer immediately, it is possible
to immediately establish eye contact, and
by words ["I'll be right with you"] or body
language let the customer know that her
presence is known. These actions provide
an effective shoplifting deterrent; the sales
associate should never wait until approached
by the customer to initiate these actions.
Establish a rule or statement (and perhaps
signs in back office areas) to the effect that
employees are expected to: *Recognize each
customer immediately; Establish eye contact;
Smile and be pleasant; Give each customer
excellent service.*

FINDING:

The Emergency Preparedness Plan for
Universal Business Services on page 18 refers
to the appropriate actions to take in case of
criminal activity or bomb threats. While the
information contained in these sections is
accurate, it is unlikely an employee would
have the time to refer to these pages should
such an event occur.

RECOMMENDATION 3.7:

Have available, at appropriate locations,
a Robbery Checklist.
SEE ATTACHMENT II.

RECOMMENDATION 3.8:

Have available, at appropriate locations,
a Bomb Threat Checklist.
SEE ATTACHMENT III.

FINDING:

The Draft document titled "The Universal
Store Employee Policy Handbook" corrects
many of the deficiencies noted above in the
draft "Policy Manual." This Handbook
document is quite detailed and should be
published and distributed to all employees.
My comments for suggested changes are
minor, but include
(a) The statement regarding the keeping of
personal belongings at the cash register
should be stronger; it should state *is prohibited.*
(b) The term "immediate family" in the
employee purchases section needs definition; what constitutes "immediate family"
should be clearly defined.
Under the section on Holding of
Merchandise, the term "any length of
time" should be stated more specifically
in terms of hours or days.
(c) Include comments in Recommendation
3.5 *supra.*
(d) Under the sections on Telephones,
Computers, and Fax Machines, the terms

"discouraged" and "greatly discouraged" are used. If THE STORE wants to
allow employee use for store nonbusiness
[which I don't recommend], then some
approval by a senior management person
should be required.

(e) See Area of Focus # 8 regarding "Hot
Line" recommendation.

(f) see Recommendations 3.7 and 3.8 *supra*.

RECOMMENDATION 3.9: Make changes suggested in (a) through (f)
supra.

FINDING: Neither the draft "Policy Manual" nor the
draft "Policy Handbook" makes provision
for the employees to certify they have read,
understand, and agree to its provisions.

RECOMMENDATION 3.10: Have only one "Policy Manual." Whatever
document is finally approved and issued, it
should contain a tear-off portion at the end
which contains language similar to: "I certify
that I have read the above, fully understand it,
and agree to it. I further understand that any
violations may result in disciplinary action,
up to and including termination without
prior warning." This statement should then
be signed by the employee, removed from the
main document (which should be retained
by the employee), and filed in the employee's
personnel file.

RECOMMENDATION 3.11: Establish a "tickler" system to assure the
return and proper filing in the employee's
personnel file of this signed form from every
new employee.

Area of Focus #4
Loss Prevention Awareness and Training

4.1 Awareness

FINDING: My interviews and observations failed to
disclose any systematic and comprehensive
loss prevention awareness training.

RECOMMENDATION 4.1: Management must give a high priority to
developing and implementing programs
designed to increase loss prevention
awareness among all levels of employees.
This should include a new employee security
orientation [where the CCTV monitoring
room is shown to them].

RECOMMENDATION 4.2: After a professional Security Manager is
onboard, encourage the campus newspaper
to write an article, with photos, about loss
prevention in THE STORE.

FINDING: A relatively high rate of turnover among
student staff and temporary employees
exacerbates the ability to maintain a high
level of loss prevention awareness.

RECOMMENDATION 4.3:

Loss prevention awareness must be generated and maintained by constant attention and emphasis, in varied formats, so interest and participation will be maintained.

4.2 Programs and Training

FINDING:

There are currently no programs directed toward loss prevention as a concept; the emphasis on shoplifting is not considered loss prevention, since it is purely reactive to a problem. Shoplifting apprehensions, in the main, represent the failure of effective loss prevention.

RECOMMENDATION 4.4:

A formalized loss analysis matrix must be designed and implemented so that evidence of loss can be dealt with by prevention strategies throughout the year. A committee, consisting of HR, Security, and Operations representatives should be formed to devise an ongoing loss prevention program. Some suggestions for methods to achieve this recommendation are

(a) Develop and utilize a program called Minimum Security Standards for Merchandise Presentation (MSSMP). Include in the security standards merchandise which it has been determined must be under glass, in locked cases, cabled, EAS tagged, displayed behind registers, under CCTV observation, inventoried daily/weekly/monthly, stored in locked stockrooms, etc. Then audit to these standards on a periodic but random basis. This technique helps develop loss prevention awareness.

(b) Develop and utilize a Security Violation/Discrepancy Notice. This form is a short notification of observed security or MSSMP violations, requiring the violator to respond within 48 hours stating the actions to be taken to prevent future similar violations.

SEE ATTACHMENT IV.

(c) Ensure full use of the currently available "Product Recovery Log." Utilize this form for loss analysis; i.e., determine whether it is the product itself or the location where the product is displayed that is responsible for its theft.

(d) Create a Shortage Prevention or Loss Prevention corner on the employee's bulletin board by the time clock at the employee entrance. Include loss prevention tips, creative solutions to shortage problems, LP tips, etc. Commercial programs can be purchased which provide constantly updated and attractive LP materials, posters, handouts, etc.

(e) Include, periodically, a LP handout as a paycheck stuffer.

(f) Every 6 months have a Shortage Awareness Week. Utilize THE STORE's PA system for before-store-opening announcements related to shortage. Have contests related to shortage; have a catchy theme, e.g., "Get caught with your shortage down." Give out "Shortage Dollars" to contest winners redeemable for small prizes—cokes, candy, donuts, pens, etc. Make the event fun and encourage wide participation. The LP message will get through (even subliminally) and, more importantly, will be remembered.

4.3 Rewards

FINDING: THE STORE has no Reward Program. Awards are not given to employees who are responsible for detecting shoplifting, reporting internal theft, or making other noteworthy contributions to shortage reduction.

RECOMMENDATION 4.5:   The introduction of a Reward Program can provide an opportunity for hyping up LP, if done with enough fanfare and enthusiasm. A formalized, well-publicized program for rewarding employees who contribute to shortage reduction is needed.
SEE ATTACHMENT V.

Area of Focus #5
Merchandise Handling Procedures
5.1 Receipt of Goods

FINDING: Receipt of goods at the warehouse appears to meet required security standards.

RECOMMENDATION 5.1:   None.

FINDING: While opinions differ, it is evident that there is less than a tight control over and accounting for individual units of merchandise received from the warehouse by THE STORE. The best evidence indicates store receivings are not matched against transfer manifests.

RECOMMENDATION 5.2:   This deficiency should be corrected.

FINDING: There is no physical separation between incoming and outgoing shipments at the warehouse or THE STORE.

RECOMMENDATION 5.3:   The physical design of the warehouse dock makes physical separation of receivings from outgoing merchandise extremely difficult. To the extent possible, goods should be staged away from the dock areas as soon as possible to minimize theft potential and inadvertent intermixing.

5.2 Transfer Records and Controls

FINDING:	As noted above, little, if any, attention is paid to manifests relating to shipments from the warehouse to THE STORE.
RECOMMENDATION 5.4:	All merchandise received at THE STORE should be checked against receiving documents.
FINDING:	There is no "extraction" program in use at the warehouse. An extraction program periodically and surreptitiously either adds or removes goods from shipments [assuming the paperwork cannot be easily manipulated to accomplish the same results]. The objective of these manipulations is to see how accurately the receiving personnel check in manifested merchandise and report discrepancies.
RECOMMENDATION 5.5:	Consider an extraction program.
FINDING:	The physical handling of warehouse receivings and the documentation and ticketing functions appear to be in order. Some additions to the physical security aspects of the warehouse will be noted under Area of Focus # 9.
FINDING:	University trucks (vans) are used to move merchandise from the warehouse to THE STORE, but there is no way to determine if merchandise has been removed between the warehouse and THE STORE.
RECOMMENDATION 5.6:	At least during Rush, seal the cages so that, if they are opened before arriving at THE STORE, it will be evident. The extraction program would also be useful in this regard. See Recommendation 5.5 *supra*.

Area of Focus # 6
Asset And Property Controls

6.1 Cash Handling Procedures

FINDING:	No visitor log is maintained in the vault.
RECOMMENDATION 6.1:	Such a log should be in place.
FINDING:	Register drawers are never "salted" to determine if overages are properly reported.
RECOMMENDATION 6.2:	This technique should be adopted and utilized periodically. Doing so is both a check against internal dishonesty as well as a check on whether sales associates are counting their setup (float) funds accurately.
FINDING:	There is no stated limit of the amount of cash allowed to be built up during the day in cash registers and no requirement that when a given amount is reached the register be "bled" by making an interim deposit.
RECOMMENDATION 6.3:	Registers should not be permitted to exceed a predetermined amount of cash as a robbery loss minimization practice. A procedure for

early or interim deposits should be in place to permit this security precaution. Cashiers should be required to telephone the vault when cash exceeds set limits.

FINDING: There are no surprise audits of cash registers.

RECOMMENDATION 6.4: Surprise audits should be done periodically.

FINDING: At store closing, some employees close and count their registers while customers remain in THE STORE.

RECOMMENDATION 6.5: If possible, cash counting should not be done in public areas or when customers are about. Cash should not be transported throughout THE STORE in an obvious way, but rather done as discreetly as possible.

FINDING: No record is kept of the dates when vault combinations are changed.

RECOMMENDATION 6.6: Such a record should be kept.

FINDING: When registers are bled (i.e., excessive cash removed), currency is simply taken out uncounted, placed in an envelope with the appropriate register number, sealed, and taken to the vault to be accounted for when the register is reconciled.

RECOMMENDATION 6.7: Currency removed from a register should be counted by denomination and verified by the cashier. A self-carbonizing "Cash Withdrawal Slip" is then prepared showing the amounts withdrawn and initialed by the cashier and transporting person. The original copy of the Cash Withdrawal Slip should be placed inside the sealed envelope with the currency and taken to the vault. The copy of the Cash Withdrawal Slip is left behind in the register.

FINDING: Both the Photo Shop and the Munch area have locked drawers containing funds for making change when the registers require it. Change is made on a strictly exchange basis [e.g., four 5-dollar bills for 20]. No documentation is kept. The Munch fund is not audited by the vault cashier. [It was reported this fund was a "deal" made between the Munch area and the Business Office.]

RECOMMENDATION 6.8: Funds should never be exchanged without documentation.

RECOMMENDATION 6.9: These funds should be audited on a regular and frequent basis.

FINDING: With regard to the vault, good security practices require additional vault controls:

RECOMMENDATION 6.10: Take the following actions:

(a) Distress (panic) alarms should be tested at least quarterly and a log kept of such tests.

(b) A code should be used between the security person testing the panic alarms with the Police Department to assure the "test," which will not produce a police response, is not being done under duress.

(c) A safe, rather than a wooden cabinet, should be used to store cash.

(d) A log should be kept of all nonvault persons entering the vault.

(e) Too many MOD (Managers of the Day) have both access and vault alarm codes. Access to the vault should be limited to the fewest number of people possible.

(f) Float funds in the Business Office are audited daily; this practice should be continued after the move of the Sales Audit function to THE STORE. Written documentation of such audits should be kept.

6.2 Fraud Controls

FINDING:	There is no review or verification of returns with receipts.
RECOMMENDATION 6.11:	Random phone calls should be made to customers who returned merchandise. The thrust of these calls should be customer service [e.g., what was wrong with the merchandise?]. Such calls serve not only as a fraud detection technique but also a customer service tool.
FINDING:	Registers generate plain paper throw-out receipts headed with the "THE UNIVERSAL STORE."
RECOMMENDATION 6.12:	Register tapes should have a running preprinted or watermarked THE STORE identifiable legend. Such a precaution makes fraud by unauthorized personal computer-generated receipts, used for fraudulent returns of stolen merchandise, more difficult.
FINDING:	I could not ascertain that routine audits of Vendor credits were done.
RECOMMENDATION 6.13:	Routine audits of Buyers' write-offs and vendor credits should be performed.
FINDING:	It is highly likely that, after purchasing textbooks, students return to the textbook area, shoplift one or more books identical to those previously purchased, and then use their original receipt to return the books for credit. Currently, no procedures are in effect to detect and prevent this practice.
RECOMMENDATION 6.14:	Consider stamping the inside cover of the purchased texts with a date stamp using invisible ultraviolet ink. When stolen texts are returned for credit, a quick check with an ultraviolet "blue" light will determine if the book contains a date stamp. An alternative to the date stamp is a unique-designed stamp which would be difficult, if not impossible, for students to duplicate in the time frame required.

Area of Focus #7
Shoplifting Controls and Procedures

FINDING:	The CCTV monitors are not attended; there is no monitoring. [See also Area of Focus 9.2.]
RECOMMENDATION 7.1:	To have an effective antishoplifting program, as well as to get a return on your investment, CCTV must be monitored on a full-time basis.
FINDING:	Civil Remedy is not utilized.
RECOMMENDATION 7.2:	Management should review the use of Civil Remedy. New York State Law provides for merchants to recover damages from shoplifters; see New York General Obligation Law, § 11–105. The University Judicial Administrator, starting in Fall 2002, has begun utilizing " monetary fines" in limited cases of shoplift offenders; however, the fines accrue to the University. Management should consider negotiating with the University to either split, in some fashion, fines collected by the JA or, in the alternative, permit THE STORE to utilize Civil Remedy directly and simply report the matter to the JA for administrative recordkeeping. SEE ATTACHMENT VI.
FINDING:	Backpacks and book bags are allowed in THE STORE.
RECOMMENDATION 7.3:	This policy should be revisited. The prohibition for backpacks is considered essential to reduce shrinkage. Discussions while at THE STORE indicated there is no space for holding backpacks while their owners are shopping. Consideration should be given to whether sufficient space for cubicles to hold backpacks could be created at the two entrances to THE STORE just inside the outer doors. Even universities which normally allow backpacks in their bookstores prohibit them during Rush (e.g., Stanford and UCSD).
FINDING:	The use of a Product Recovery Log should be encouraged.
RECOMMENDATION 7.4:	I suggest this form be renamed "Missing Merchandise Report." It is really not "recovered merchandise" that is reported and it not a "log." A Missing Merchandise Report is used to report merchandise which is known to be missing, or evidence of missing merchandise such as found empty packaging. All sales associates should be provided with a supply of Missing Merchandise Reports [MMR] and instructed on their use. A MMR is a simple form on which a sales associate can report a known or suspected known loss, with specific information about where it was

FINDING:

As noted previously, THE STORE's loss prevention efforts center around reactive shoplifting detection and apprehension. We have also indicated that this approach is not exactly cost effective. There is no proactive loss prevention effort at present.

displayed, when it was noticed missing, etc. These forms are then accumulated daily, collated, and analyzed to determine shortage trends and enable intelligent steps to be taken to tighten security and stop the losses.

RECOMMENDATION 7.5:

That store management should consider a dual program of both visible and undercover security personnel. The visible security, dressed in non-police-type uniforms [e.g., a red blazer with "Loss Prevention" or "Security" on the pocket] would patrol high or known theft areas to discourage shoplifting. They can simultaneously render customer service by answering questions, directing customers to the proper locations, etc. For those customers who are not deterred by the Visible Security Officer [VSO], the undercover security agents will be present and make apprehensions. The use of VSOs and plainclothes personnel can be reserved for peak periods, Rush weeks, etc.

FINDING:

THE STORE's highest shrink (both percentage and dollar wise) is in the textbook world. There is consensus that the bulk of textbook shrinkage occurs during Rush, when traffic is not only very heavy, but lack of space requires merchandising the books in such a way as to deny virtually all CCTV surveillance as well as visual observation of students perusing the books.

SEE ATTACHMENT VII The policy of allowing backpacks in the selling areas only exacerbates the theft problem.

As an aside, the space required to make available in THE STORE all the texts during Rush requires that large segments of Insignia merchandise be relocated to another floor of THE STORE as well as to a temporary text installed outside the west doors.

RECOMMENDATION 7.6:

In this Consultant's opinion, the best solution to this problem is to acquire a venue for textbook sales outside THE STORE. Such a move would accomplish several things:

(a) Prevent this relocation of Insignia merchandise which is disruptive, labor intensive, and exposes the merchandise to damage and loss.

(b) Provide a selling environment which accommodates for a "one way in—one way out" arrangement. With this arrangement, backpacks could be accommodated, since they would have to be emptied at the exit registers, at which time *all* merchandise leaving the exit would have to be paid for.

(c) See also comments in § 6.2, " Fraud Controls" (*supra)* and Recommendation 6.13.

Objections to this solution have mentioned the availability of suitable space, the loss of ancillary purchases of supplies and Insignia goods, and the problem of students getting to and from the offsite [from THE STORE] venue. These objections can be overcome by the following:

RECOMMENDATION 7.7:

(a) Rent a school-type bus to transport students on a fixed ½ hour schedule to and from THE STORE's employee entrance parking area to the warehouse venue.

(b) Place a quantity of school supplies and Insignia items in this venue. Since all items will be paid for, there is little risk.

(c) Consider the warehouse as a Venue. It appeared at first impression that sufficient space could be created in the current area occupied by the "rolling cabinets" used to transport textbooks. Any additional space required could be created and separated from other merchandise stored in the warehouse by plastic netting such as used on construction sites. By forming a large "U" traffic flow pattern from the front of the warehouse to the rear and back to the opposite side front, with netting used as traffic flow barriers, this appears to be a feasible solution. Backpacks could be allowed, since all books and backpacks would be subject to inspection at the checkout registers; this would assure that all textbooks were paid for. It would also eliminate the labor-intensive moves in THE STORE which the present arrangement requires.

FINDING:

When the dollars of loss in textbooks during Rush are considered, an investment of the dollars required to make the suggested changes presents a highly attractive cost/benefit ratio.

RECOMMENDATION 7.8:

If Recommendation 7.7 cannot be accepted, and textbook sales must remain in THE STORE as configured for Rush Fall 2002, consider the following:

(a) Hire a sufficient number of personnel in Red Security jackets to provide full surveillance of all rows of textbook cages.

(b) Prohibit backpacks.

(c) Install very obvious CCTV (some of which may be dummy).

(d) Make frequent PA announcements "Security to area——."

	This practice can also be employed during non-Rush times as well.
FINDING:	The EAS system requires attention and maintenance. The sound level of alarms is too low; the system frequently will not alarm when tagged items pass through the portals. Several of the red alarm lights do not function properly.
RECOMMENDATION 7.9:	Perform required maintenance to bring EAS system up to peak performance.
FINDING:	"Used" textbook stickers do not self-destruct when removed, permitting illicit switching of them to new books.
RECOMMENDATION 7.10:	Use self-destructing "Used" stickers.
FINDING:	There is no form for shoplifters to admit guilt.
RECOMMENDATION 7.11: SEE ATTACHMENT VIII.	Utilize an "Admission Form."
FINDING:	The current store Apprehension/Arrest report form is confusing.
RECOMMENDATION 7.12:	Consider using a revised Detention Report form.
SEE ATTACHMENT IX.	
FINDING:	EAS portal alarms are frequently not responded to.
RECOMMENDATION 7.13:	More intensive training of cashiers specifying not only when to respond, but how to respond.
FINDING:	There is no "advertisement" of the existence of CCTVs, which can serve as a deterrent to shoplifting.
RECOMMENDATION 7.14:	Install one or two fixed CCTV cameras with monitors on the selling floor so students can see that there is a CCTV system and that it works.
FINDING:	It was reported that a large number of empty computer printer ink cartridge boxes are found throughout the store.
RECOMMENDATION 7.15:	Consider corralling the computer area in which ink cartridges, cables, and peripherals are sold. This should be done in such a way as to provide an in-turnstile on one side of the area and an exit by the POS terminal on the opposite side of the area.
FINDING:	There is currently no method whereby selling employees can discreetly call security.
RECOMMENDATION 7.16:	Utilize a "Code 5" or "Mr. Sam" code which, when called over the telephone to Security, will alert them to report to the area (or person) from which the call emanates.
FINDING:	Currently, small electronics (cassette recorders, MP3s, Walkmans) are secured by double-backed tape and plastic ties to a pad which is secured to the display by a cable. No immediate alert occurs if the item is

	removed from the display. There is evidence of attempted and accomplished theft of these relatively high-priced items.
RECOMMENDATION 7.17:	Utilize electronic cables for securing these items; any attempt to remove them will sound an immediate alert.

AREA OF FOCUS #8

Internal Theft Cont rols and Procedures

FINDING:	Employee package checks are rarely, if ever, done.
RECOMMENDATION 8.1:	Routine but surprise package checks are a proven deterrent to internal theft and should be conducted. THE STORE's draft policies provide for such checks by "management or operations/security." We suggest such checks should be done exclusively by management or security; it is not a good practice to have peers doing such inspections.
FINDING:	There is no auditing of employee purchases made under the generous employee discount program.
RECOMMENDATION 8.2:	Employee purchase records should be audited for both the absence of purchasing as well as an extremely heavy volume of purchases; such anomalies should be investigated, since they may indicate either a theft problem or an abuse of the discount program.
FINDING:	There exists no honesty shopping program.
RECOMMENDATION 8.3:	Honesty shoppers should be employed periodically. Such a program not only may provide indications of dishonesty, but also serve to provide an assessment of the level of customer service being given.
FINDING:	There have been very few identified dishonest employee cases in the past 3 years.
RECOMMENDATION 8.4:	Institute those loss prevention/security measures and procedures [recommended throughout this report]. Employ a professional security manager who possesses the knowledge and skills to legally and effectively investigate and resolve internal dishonesty problems.
FINDING:	Bonding forms are not used.
RECOMMENDATION 8.5:	A bonding form should be used for all nonstudent employees. Answers to bonding form questions, *executed after employment*, provide an easy means of comparison with answers to similar background questions contained on employment applications. The use of a bonding form does not require actual bonding of employees. The form itself has been shown to produce more truthful or accurate answers than those submitted on employment applications.

Note: A "bonding form" should contain many of the same basic questions as the employment application, but in a different order. The theory behind this technique is that most persons who lie on an employment application cannot remember the exact nature of their untruths, and thus these will show up as discrepancies. The new employee should be questioned regarding these discrepancies, and if the application was falsified in any material way, it is well established that such falsification is grounds for immediate dismissal.

FINDING: Senior management and "sensitive" positions within THE STORE should received some type of background investigation by the Universal Police Department, consistent with New York and federal law.

RECOMMENDATION 8.6: Consideration should be given to a more thorough vetting of new career personnel and particularly those in cash handling or other sensitive positions. Thought should be given to utilizing additional screening tools for these applicants. The judiciousness of more thorough screening would appear to be more than justified as statutory demands for workplace security increase.

Note: Any use of additional pre-employment screening techniques should be cleared with the University Human Relations office and with legal counsel.

RECOMMENDATION 8.7: Vetting should include

(a) Records checks to include

    [1] A criminal history check covering the past 7 years.

    [2] A DMV driving records check.

    [3] A Social Security number check [did applicant work under any other names?].

    [4] Credit checks of vault employees.

(b) Job offers to applicants can be made under two scenarios:

    [1] A job offer is not made until favorable background check results are obtained, or [2] the job offer is made contingent on a favorable background check.

(c) For all applicants subject to a background investigation, the University will obtain the necessary releases.

[Currently covered with University Employment Application].

RECOMMENDATION 8.8: Anyone driving Bookstore vehicles should be subject to annual DMV checks.

FINDING: No surprise audits are conducted of any of THE STORE's operations.

RECOMMENDATION 8.9:	A program of surprise audits of THE STORE, remote facilities, and the warehouse should be scheduled. These audits should not be confrontational or adversarial in nature, but more of a "Hi, how ya doin'?" approach, during which appropriate auditing can be accomplished in a casual but thorough way.
FINDING:	THE STORE has no covert CCTV, "Trojan horses" (covert observation areas), or two-way mirrors for investigating either shoplifting or suspected internal theft.
RECOMMENDATION 8.10:	Adequate equipment and facilities should be acquired to permit appropriate investigations to be conducted effectively. (See comments in § 9.2 below.)
FINDING:	There is no reported mention of internal dishonesty as part of new employee indoctrination.
RECOMMENDATION 8.11:	The security portion of the new employee orientation should include the topic of internal dishonesty. It is suggested this orientation include the video The Best Defense (covering shoplifting) and its companion, Choices (covering employee dishonesty.) The security aspects of the orientation can be made into a positive event by including some information on personal security issues such as buddy systems, personal security awareness, etc. Note: These videos can be obtained by contacting ETC (Excellence in Training Corporation), 11358 Aurora Avenue, Des Moines, IA 50322-7979, 1-800-747-6569.
FINDING:	There is no procedure for the intentional introduction of errors into control systems.
RECOMMENDATION 8.12:	A procedure for the introduction of errors into control systems is desirable. Such a procedure tests whether such systems are in fact working as designed, and if so, by whom, when, and how the error surfaced.
FINDING:	There is no "hard and fast" prohibition against employee purses and packages on the selling floor.
RECOMMENDATION 8.13:	Implement such a policy and require strict and consistent enforcement. See Recommendation 3.8.
FINDING:	Custodial personnel work essentially unsupervised.
RECOMMENDATION 8.14:	A program of periodic surveillance of custodians is needed.
RECOMMENDATION 8.15:	Occasional package/equipment checks should be made when janitorial personnel leave THE STORE at night.
FINDING:	THE STORE uses common register drawers.

RECOMMENDATION 8.16:   If registers are ever replaced, individual drawers are always preferable to common drawers. Individual drawers significantly increase personal responsibility for cash accountability.

FINDING: THE STORE has no Reward Program.

RECOMMENDATION 8.17:   Consider instituting a Reward Program. See Recommendation 4.5.

SEE ATTACHMENT V.

FINDING: THE STORE has no "Hot Line."

RECOMMENDATION 8.18:   Consider either a commercially available service which provides a confidential means for employees to telephone information to management or an in-house program which accomplished this objective by a post office box. Investigation should be conducted toward perhaps utilizing the University's "Silent Witness" program through www.cupolice.Universal.edu/witness.

SEE ATTACHMENT V.

AREA OF FOCUS #9
Physical Security
9.1   Alarms

FINDING: The is no procedure to assure that the batteries in the emergency flashlights are operating.

RECOMMENDATION 9.1:   A log, similar to those used on fire extinguishers, should be kept in the security office and batteries tested on a monthly basis. Then after each test a notation is made on the log with the date and the initials of the person who made the test. This procedure assures at a glance that the batteries were tested, working, and the date of the test and who did it.

FINDING: There is no written procedure for testing intrusion alarms.

RECOMMENDATION 9.2:   Alarm tests should be conducted every 3 months (after hours). Contact the police department and advise a test will be conducted. Advise them you will break a zone, and have them tell you what zone has been tested. Occasionally, after advising you will break a zone, don't, and see what response you get when you inquire which zone was tested. Document all tests.

FINDING: The Universal Police Department currently receives and responds to alarms. This procedure does not allow for exception reporting. The alarm control panel/server is capable of storing up to 200 prior events (e.g., setting and disarming system) but this information is rarely requested.

RECOMMENDATION 9.3:   A printer should be installed in THE STORE's security office which prints out in real-time all alarm activity. This report should be reviewed daily by the Security Manager for unusual or suspicious events.

FINDING: When alarm access codes are canceled (e.g., when an employee with the code is terminated), the cancellation is done by telephone with Omega (the alarm supplier), but no written record is kept.

RECOMMENDATION 9.4:   Log all such cancellations.

9.2   CCTV

FINDING: Staffing levels, combined with store layout and customer velocity, suggest that new and/or improved CCTV is required in various locations. There are presently five (5) color and twelve (12) black-and-white cameras. Such CCTV will not only deter/detect shoplifting, but also provide the ability to give better customer service when customers are in blind areas of THE STORE(s). Cameras should be in domes and positioned to enable both antishoplifting and internal dishonesty investigation coverage.

RECOMMENDATION 9.5:   THE STORE: Replacement of old cameras with new color cameras is required in several areas. SEE ATTACHMENTS X and XI for location and types of cameras recommended. BEST COPY CENTER: Blind back area needs a small fixed camera with an 8-inch monitor by the cash register. SEE ATTACHMENT XII for details. HOTEL STORE: Install a convex mirror in the southwest corner of the store to enable the sales associate to see the greeting card area from the register. WAREHOUSE: SEE ATTACHMENT XIII for camera location.

FINDING: Some Sensormatic equipment (a camera and controller keyboard) need repair.

RECOMMENDATION 9.6:   Ensure that Sensormatic is responsive in quickly repairing/replacing broken equipment.

FINDING: CCTV camera in vault provides poor image for recognizing currency denominations.

RECOMMENDATION 9.7:   Upgrade vault CCTV.

9.3   Access and Key Controls

FINDING: Keys are issued by key number, and a written record is made, by the Operations Manager, but keys from terminated employees are recovered by the HR Manager.

RECOMMENDATION 9.8:   All keys retrieved by the HR Manager should be turned over to and a notation of its return

	made by the Operations Manager in the key log.
FINDING:	Not all keys are marked "Do Not Duplicate."
RECOMMENDATION 9.9:	ALL keys should be marked DO NOT DUPLICATE.
FINDING:	The Access Control system should be upgraded.
RECOMMENDATION 9.10:	Replace the access control system to operate from University-issued magnetic student or employee cards.
FINDING:	There is no routinely scheduled key inventory to compare issued keys to key issuance log.
RECOMMENDATION 9.11:	Conduct such an inventory at least annually.

9.4 Docks and Stock Areas

FINDING:	THE STORE's dock door is often open and unattended, both during store hours and before THE STORE is open to the public, providing access to employee-only areas and merchandise. Vendors use the open dock for access, thereby bypassing the required sign-in procedure. SEE ATTACHMENT XIV.
RECOMMENDATION 9.12:	Develop a discipline that assures the dock door is only open when attended by a responsible person..
FINDING:	The dock door operates from open/close/stop switches located both inside and outside the dock. These switches are activated/deactivated by a simple on-off switch inside the dock door.
RECOMMENDATION 9.13:	Even though the dock rolldown door is alarmed at night, the on-off switch could easily be left in the on position inadvertently. A mechanical timer should be added to the on-off switch circuit, which will automatically turn off this switch during night hours after the dock door no longer needs to be opened. A red light should also be located by the Director's secretary (and in the CCTV monitoring room) which turns on when the dock door is open. Such an arrangement will alert someone to the fact that the door is open and he can assure that the dock is attended.
FINDING:	There does not appear to be any locked stockrooms; even the small electronic, but expensive, items are stored in a metal filing cabinet in an employee-only area essentially adjacent to the Photo Department. This cabinet was not locked and was usually open.
RECOMMENDATION 9.14:	Effort must be expended to assure stock is secure.
FINDING:	Much stock is intermingled with store supplies in back office areas.

SEE ATTACHMENT XV.

RECOMMENDATION 9.15:   This condition must be corrected. It is easy to miss stock items at inventory when intermingled with nonretail supplies. Insist upon neat and organized stockroom/office areas. In addition to creating difficulty in finding specific merchandise, stockrooms in disarray tend to create safety hazards and lend themselves to theft.

FINDING: There is unrestricted access by customers to back areas via the openings in the computer and backpack sales areas.

SEE ATTACHMENT XVI

RECOMMENDATION 9.16:   Install barriers (e.g., swinging doors) which will deter unauthorized access. Place signs, facing the selling floor, stating: "RESTRICTED AREA – EMPLOYEES ONLY – Trespassers Will Be Prosecuted."

9.5   Warehouse

FINDING: Business office personnel and visitors have unrestricted access to the warehouse.

RECOMMENDATION 9.17:   Complete the wiring of the access control pad outside the door leading up the stairs to the business office. Deny unauthorized access from the stairway to the warehouse.

SEE ATTACHMENT XVII.

RECOMMENDATION 9.18:   Upon completion of Recommendation 9.15, install an access key pad outside the door leading from the bottom of the business office stairway into the warehouse. In this way, access to the warehouse can be gained only by possessing the proper access code. Note: Warehouse personnel must have access to the restroom facilities in the business office.

FINDING: The dock doors at the warehouse are open at times when there is no receiving or shipping for ventilation purposes.

RECOMMENDATION 9.19:   Keep the dock doors closed unless actual shipping/receiving is in progress (an accepted security standard). If the doors must be open for ventilation, then install and secure the openings with rolldown mesh doors.

9.6   POS Computer Room

FINDING: Access to the computer room, a sensitive area, is too easy.

RECOMMENDATION 9.20:   Maintain tighter access to the computer room; keep the door locked.

FINDING: The computer room is protected against fire by a sprinkler head in the ceiling of the room. SEE ATTACHMENT XVIII.

RECOMMENDATION 9.21:   Replace the sprinkler head with a halon (or acceptable substitute) fire suppression system. Water is the biggest enemy of computers. A discharge of the sprinkler head, either intentional or accidental, would essentially ruin the computers, shut down all computer-controlled operations, and probably necessitate the purchase of new equipment.

AREA OF FOCUS #10
Inventory Results

FINDING:	Shortage over the past few years shows a disturbing upward trend, with the bulk of the shortage in textbooks and writing instruments.
FINDING:	Reduction of shrinkage does not seem to be a high-priority item with some merchants and managers.
RECOMMENDATION 10.1:	Inventory results should be disseminated and discussed in detail with individual department managers. Departmental shortage reduction goals should be set and progress toward achievement monitored throughout the inventory period.
RECOMMENDATION 10.2:	Assure that all merchants and managers fully understand the effect of shortage on THE STORE's bottom line and their performance reviews.
FINDING:	There is concern among merchants that missed markdowns and RTVs have resulted in artificially high shortage.
RECOMMENDATION 10.3:	Do what is required to not only assure merchants that all markdowns and RTVs are captured, but also audit to guarantee that they, in fact, are captured.
FINDING:	There is a concern among some merchants that the price lookup (PLU) system contains pricing errors.
RECOMMENDATION 10.4:	Take necessary actions to assure accuracy of the PLU system, and assure merchants of its accuracy. In reviewing the system, if possible, assure that (a) If the PLU amount is overridden at the register, an audit trail and exception report is generated. (b) All markdowns are automatically captured.
FINDING:	It was reported that known losses are written off as markdowns.
RECOMMENDATION 10.5:	If true, this should be considered when reviewing shrinkage figures.
FINDING:	As noted elsewhere in this report, retail merchandise is stored in back office areas, and housekeeping is less than desirable.
RECOMMENDATION 10.6:	Assure that all merchandise is counted at inventory.

FINDING:	Two managers suggested that the inventory system shows more items on hand than physical counts indicate when merchandise is first received.
RECOMMENDATION 10.7:	It is essential that everything be done to ensure that merchants have faith in the accuracy of the inventory control system.
FINDING:	It was reported that changes can be made to the inventory control system by merchants without any audit trail as to who made the adjustment or when it was done.
RECOMMENDATION 10.8:	If such adjustments are permitted, there should be an audit trail identifying not only who did it, when it was done, but also the justification for doing it.
FINDING:	It was reported that outdated merchandise which remains unsold is given to employees.
RECOMMENDATION 10.9:	Discontinue this practice; give it to charity.

AREA OF FOCUS #11
Emergency Planning

FINDING:	Refresher training sessions on dealing with emergencies and other important topics should be discussed with all employees.
RECOMMENDATION 11.1:	Discuss emergency procedures at orientation sessions and once a year thereafter.
FINDING:	THE STORE has no Safety Committee. The Operations Manager functions as the Safety Director.
RECOMMENDATION 11.2:	A Safety and Loss Prevention Committee composed of both management and staff from THE STORE and the warehouse should be formed. The Committee's mission should be as follows: The Safety and Loss Prevention Committee will coordinate and facilitate all aspects of promoting security and safety at all THE STORE's facilities. Purpose: To review all security, emergency, and safety procedures and processes; to develop security and safety programs; to identify risks and hazards; to conduct inspections; to review accidents and recommend corrective action; and to promote enforcement of THE STORE's policies and procedures.
RECOMMENDATION 11.3:	Consider involving members of the Safety and Loss Prevention Committee in appropriate aspects of this consultant's report; this will bring about a feeling of ownership in decisions to adopt recommendations. Names of committee members should be publicized and their photographs displayed on employee bulletin boards, giving recognition to those who serve, underscoring the importance

	of the Committee and making future membership, on a rotating basis, coveted. Note: Recommendations 11.2 and 11.3 will also have a beneficial effect in management's efforts to enhance loss prevention awareness.
FINDING:	Neither THE STORE's receptionist/telephone operator or any of the remote facilities have bomb threat or Robbery Checklists.
RECOMMENDATION 11.4:	Supply all appropriate personnel with a supply of Robbery and Bomb Threat Checklists. SEE ATTACHMENTS II and III.
FINDING:	There were no fire alarm pull stations except at each main entrance to the store.
RECOMMENDATION 11.5:	Check with Engineering and Health Safety to determine if this aspect is up to code.
FINDING:	There were no signs pointing out the location of fire extinguishers which would be hard to find if one did not know where they were located.
SEE ATTACHMENT XIX. RECOMMENDATION 11.6:	Place large red arrows pointing toward and containing the words "Fire Extinguisher" high up on the walls or columns where the extinguishers are located.

AREA OF FOCUS #12
Miscellaneous

FINDING:	The crime prevention officers of the Universal Police Department have not been fully utilized by THE STORE.
RECOMMENDATION 12.1:	This is a resource that should be used from time to time for their input into THE STORE's loss prevention efforts. For example, request the crime prevention officers to review your loss prevention efforts and procedures, alarm systems, etc.
FINDING:	Housekeeping was well below acceptable standards, both on the floor and in back office areas.
SEE ATTACHMENT XX. RECOMMENDATION 12.2:	More attention must be paid to neatness in back areas and stocking the floor before opening. Unkempt areas are safety hazards and create theft vulnerability.
SEE ATTACHMENT. FINDING:	Access to electric and equipment rooms was blocked by storage of miscellaneous items in violation of signs posted to not block access.
RECOMMENDATION 12.3:	Remove obstructions.
FINDING:	Many of the "management" employees felt overworked, understaffed, and frustrated. They complained of severe staffing cuts and an inability to give proper consideration to all aspects of their responsibilities. It was my

	impression that ensuring that proper controls were followed gives way to expediency.
RECOMMENDATION 12.4:	None specifically, except that this is an issue which must be dealt with. It is recognized that there is an inverse relationship between morale and shrinkage: the lower the morale, the higher the shrinkage.
FINDING:	It was my impression that there is a lack of discipline among management and supervisors. It appeared that good procedures are in place, but often not implemented. I am not confident that management accepts their responsibility for the nonperformance of their subordinates.
RECOMMENDATION 12.5:	No specific recommendation; if true, this is a problem which must be corrected.
FINDING:	There are currently no employee recognition programs or suggestion boxes.
RECOMMENDATION 12.6:	Consider the implementation of an employee recognition program and/or suggestion boxes.
FINDING:	Managers are not routinely given cash over/short information for their areas.
RECOMMENDATION 12.7:	Managers should be given this information.
FINDING:	The one fitting room has no controls.
RECOMMENDATION 12.8:	Place a sign on the fitting room reading "Limit 3 items." Employees should be encouraged to check the fitting room frequently for left items; if practical, establish an assigned schedule.
FINDING:	Employee badges are openly displayed by the employee entrance; they are accessible to anyone who is in the area.
RECOMMENDATION 12.9:	They should be in a cabinet with, at least, a self-closing door.

Index of Attachments

□ □ □

Security Technology and the Retail Industry: A Glimpse into the Future of Loss Prevention

Jeffrey A. Dussich

We need not look much further than the latest crime drama on television to see the direction of security technology in the near future. Whether the episode involves DNA evidence from a piece of chewing gum or the analysis of gunshot residue on a suspect's hand, the primetime network line-up is a perfect place for amateur detectives to learn about the latest advances in investigative technology. Whether or not each of the tests is possible, one category of futuristic technology is very real and has already started to work its way into mainstream society.

This technology is called "biometrics," or automated methods of identifying an individual using unique physical or behavioral characteristics. The most familiar example of biometrics, fingerprint identification, is used in law enforcement practices to identify a potential suspect. Though the technology has been limited to the government arena since its inception, modern improvements and decreasing prices have resulted in the appearance of biometrics in everyday life. This section looks at biometrics and its potential relevance in the loss prevention industry.

First, an introduction. "Biometrics" is the general term given to the science of utilizing unique human characteristics to identify an individual or verify his identity. Biometrics are categorized into different modalities, or types, depending on the physical characteristic used for the identification process. Biometrics are based on the presumption that as humans, our physical traits (such as our fingerprints) are unique only to us and that they can be analyzed, measured, and compared to another set of physical traits with a reliable level of accuracy. The most popular modalities include fingerprint recognition, iris scan, hand geometry, and our focus later on in this piece, facial recognition. Fingerprint technology has been widely accepted by law enforcement agencies as a reliable tool when identifying a suspect. Many times you will hear your favorite crime scene investigator talk about "running a fingerprint through AFIS," or Automated Fingerprint Identification System. AFIS is a common methodology of automatically scanning a database of fingerprints in search of a match, or a "hit" as they call it.

Biometric matching is broken down into two general categories: 1-to-1 matching, or "verification," and 1-to-many matching, or "identification." In 1-to-1 matching, a single biometric, for instance, your fingerprint, is used to verify your identity. This type of matching requires you to first present a "token," such as an ID card, pin code, or password, which informs the system that you, or someone claiming to be you, is trying to gain access. The system then waits for you to present your fingerprint to verify "you are who you say you are."

In today's security environment, 1-to-1 matching is most often seen in a physical access control system, for instance, as an enhancement over standard electronic entry systems for an office, home, or any other protected space. In these instances, biometrics are used for reasons of superior protection as well as convenience. A simple pin code and biometric combination means that the user will never again have to suffer the frustration of forgetting his keys.

The second type of matching, 1-to-many, uses largely the same hardware and software as 1-to-1 matching though the purpose is quite different. In 1-to-many matching, a single biometric, again a fingerprint, is used to identify an individual against a database of previously enrolled fingerprints. (*Note:* In the world of biometrics, "enrollment" refers to the actual process of inserting an individual's biometric template into a database or associating an individual's biometric with their identity.) This type of matching is most frequently associated with the AFIS matching referenced above: A single fingerprint is used to figure out the identity of a criminal suspect).

Biometrics have been "almost here," meaning commercially deployable, for quite some time. Few other technologies have been so eagerly anticipated. The reason is simple. Biometrics solve security gaps that have existed since the advent of the modern security era. Now that the price of the technology has decreased to a commercially affordable level, we have finally reached the true launch point for this exciting technology.

An example of a relatively large-scale biometric deployment is a company known as "Pay By Touch." At the time of this writing, Pay By Touch is one of the most publicized usages of biometrics in the world. Pay By Touch is considered a leader in engineering the biometrics crossover from the government sector into our everyday lives. Pay By Touch utilizes fingerprint verification for secure transactions in a retail environment. An alternative to cash or credit cards, Pay By Touch capitalizes on our society's growing desire to become more efficient and, for a lack of better term, more "high tech." Because you need only a unique pin number (likely your home phone number) and your fingerprint, Pay By Touch allows you to leave your cash and cards at home.

Aside from the conveniences offered by such a program, Pay By Touch is also a great example of how biometrics can be used to prevent identity theft. Because your fingerprint must be verified to process the transaction, the risk of credit card fraud is virtually eliminated. As time goes on, we can expect many other companies to leverage the unique benefits of biometrics to achieve a business purpose.(1)

Facial Recognition Technology

Facial recognition technology is one of the most intriguing yet widely used technologies in the field of biometrics, if not security as a whole. Facial recognition technology involves the measuring of facial features to identify an individual or verify his identity. Similar to other biometric modalities, facial recognition algorithms encode a subject's facial image from a standard headshot photograph into a biometric template, based on the dimensions of his face. The template is then used to match against a specific template (1-to-1 matching) or database of templates (1-to-many matching). One of the main reasons facial recognition technology has received so much attention is the potential of widescale deployment with little or no subject authorization. Unlike most other biometric modalities, facial recognition does not require participation and/or cooperation. In certain environments facial recognition software can be integrated with standard CCTV cameras, which look no different from the cameras in your parking garage, the lobby of your office, or a sports arena.

Perhaps the most widely publicized usage of facial recognition in recent history was the 2001 Super Bowl in Tampa, Florida. The administrators of the program compiled a database of facial images of known criminal suspects. The facial recognition software was incorporated into the surveillance cameras that were fixed on the incoming traffic of Super Bowl goers. Presumably, the facial image of each attendee was matched against the watch list database. The system turned up a handful of accurate matches though many more false matches.

After the tragic events of September 11, 2001, the facial recognition community received a tremendous amount of attention. Was there a possibility that this technology could have identified the hijackers as known terrorists prior to their boarding the planes? While this still remains a question, the need for accurate facial recognition technology was spawned.

---

(1) Information about Pay By Touch taken from Pay By Touch official website (www.paybytouch.com).

The Achilles heel of facial recognition technology, more than any other biometric technology, is the occurrence of false matches. False matches are quite simply the facial recognition software mistaking one person for another. The problem arises, however, when too many false matches result in a "boy who cried wolf" situation.

If you think about it, the concept of false matches is quite familiar to us. Many people look alike. How many times have you thought, "Boy, doesn't she look like…?" A false match is the software's way of telling you that it thinks it found someone who looks very much like a particular person. Now, to our human eye, the people may not look anything alike, but to the facial recognition matching algorithm, they are very similar.

The question arises, then, in the balance of false matches to positive matches. How many false matches are you willing to view and dismiss as a trade-off to finding one accurate match of a potentially dangerous person? At what point do you ignore the alerts and disregard the system?

While the government sector will continue to evaluate facial recognition technologies for use in the War on Terror, these same technologies have applications for everyday usage. At the time this piece was written, quite a few companies are beginning to evaluate facial recognition technology in the private sector as a way to combat problems that have plagued them for years. One such application is the retail security market and the fight against shoplifting.

Current loss prevention measures vary from retailer to retailer, from industry to industry. Some of the most common security tactics include electronic article surveillance (EAS) tags, CCTV camera networks, and human security guards. For most shoppers, these measures are enough of a deterrent to steer clear of any temptation. But for experienced thieves, there are always methods of circumventing the system and more sophisticated deterrents are needed to truly make an impact. Enter facial recognition technology.

Many retailers have different procedures when dealing with shoplifters. Certain retailers are interested only in getting the merchandise back. Other retailers prosecute to the fullest extent of the law. Regardless of protocol, the goal is to prevent the shoplifter from ever coming back into the store.

Whether you manage a small retail shop or are a loss prevention professional in a large department store, it is unrealistic to expect your staff to study the facial characteristics of each customer and compare them to a printed list of headshot images. While you would expect them to stop someone in the act, a preemptive measure of this sort is not feasible. In essence, facial recognition technology is handling this job for you.

Because there is no known widescale usage of facial recognition within the retail market at the time of this writing, the following is a theoretical description of usage. A typical facial recognition identification system would include a standard CCTV camera fixed on the incoming flow of human traffic into your store. Each frame captured by the camera would be automatically searched for the presence of any facial images. If any images are found, the images would be converted into a biometric template and matched against a database of previously apprehended shoplifters. If the system finds a match, your staff is notified and, in most cases, given the opportunity to visually compare the match.

How is this database compiled in the first place? The answer to this question depends on the procedures in place for each retailer. In an ideal environment, the shoplifter is apprehended and formally processed. This gives store management the opportunity to capture multiple images of the individual for the enrollment process. If this is not possible, certain facial recognition systems allow you to search through video feeds obtained that day and isolate the facial image of the individual. This is helpful for the scenarios when it is not practical to detain the subject, or, during post-event analysis.

The potential for facial recognition within the retail industry is tremendous. By identifying known shoplifters as they enter the store, management is given the opportunity to trail the person, follow him on camera, or even refuse service. As with any security technology, however, facial recognition deployments must be coupled with human participation to be able to realize the full benefits.

Privacy Concerns

No discussion of facial recognition would be complete without acknowledging the privacy implications of the technology. The word "biometrics" raises eyebrows for many people because there is a growing concern that the move toward a biometrically enabled society will ultimately result in our personal information—financial data, medical history—being connected to our fingerprint, iris pattern, or our facial features. In addition, the increase in surveillance cameras has led people to believe that we are being tracked everywhere we go and that we are one small step from an Orwellian society.

It is important to remember, however, that biometrics are not inherently privacy invasive. As with many other security technologies, the privacy danger lies in the purpose for which they are used and the manner in which they are deployed. For the purpose of tracking citizens from street to street, location to location, facial recognition biometrics poses a serious threat to privacy. For the purposes described previously, namely the identification of shoplifters within a retail environment, the usage of facial recognition is less concerning. But it still does not necessarily mean that customers will be agreeable to their favorite retail store's usage of facial recognition.

Even though the system is not operated or monitored by some sort of centralized tracking agency, the fear of the technology lies in the fear of the unknown. Are the facial images gathered from the entrance cameras linked with other cameras around the city? Are these images being shared with public agencies to help track citizens?

The best method of addressing these questions is by proactively informing your customers as they walk through the door and offering additional information if necessary. There is no risk in being transparent. Shoplifting affects everyone, and to keep prices competitive, the store must try to reduce shoplifting as much as possible. Facial recognition is simply the means to do this.

Summary

As the search continues for effective loss prevention measures, security technology will maintain its major role in the battle against shoplifting. Facial recognition presents a unique advantage in that it is the only practical method of identifying a potential thief as he walks in the door. By deploying such a system, retail stores of all types and sizes will be armed with preemptive knowledge that has never before been offered.

Regardless of performance enhancements, the major barriers to entry will remain largely political. Fears of a surveillance society are very real. We must remember though that facial recognition technology, when used appropriately, is no different from an enhancement to the CCTV cameras that are already in place. It is not the technology that threatens privacy; it is the usage. An active dialogue between privacy advocates and the biometrics community will be a necessary component of introducing the technology into the retail environment.

Selected Security-Related Organizations

CAS, JHC

- *American Polygraph Association:* Organization dedicated to providing a valid and reliable means to verify the truth and establish the highest standards of moral, ethical, and professional conduct in the polygraph field. www.polygraph.org
- *American Society for Industrial Security, International (ASIS):* The world's largest security organization, which is dedicated to increasing the effectiveness and productivity of security practices via educational programs and materials. www.asisonline.org
- *Association of Certified Fraud Examiners:* Organization dedicated to combating fraud and white-collar crime. www.cfenet.com

- *Association of Christian Investigators:* Organization whose mission is to integrate the private security investigative profession with Christian values. www.a-c-i.org
- *Canadian Society for Industrial Security:* A professional association for persons engaged in security in Canada. www.csis-scsi.org
- *High Technology Crime Investigation Association:* Association of high-technology criminal investigators. www.htcia.org
- *International Association for Healthcare Security and Safety:* Professional security management association. www.iahss.org
- *International Association of Auto Theft Investigators:* Organization formed to improve communication and coordination among professional auto theft investigators. www.iaati.org
- *International Association of Campus Law Enforcement Administrators:* Informational website regarding university and college security. www.iaclea.org
- *International Association of Personal Protection Agents:* Informational site for international bodyguards www.iappa.org
- *International Association of Professional Security Consultants:* Members are independent, non-product-affiliated consultants pledged to meet client needs with professional consulting services. www.iapsc.org
- *International CPTED Association (ICA):* Crime prevention through environmental design practitioners. www.cpted.net
- *International Foundation for Protection Officers:* Training and certification of line protection security officers. www.ifpo.org
- *International Process Servers Association:* An online resource designed to assist process servers, private investigators, skip tracers, attorneys, and paralegals. www.serveprocess.org
- *International Professional Security Association:* Organization that promotes security professionalism in the United Kingdom. www.ipsa.org.uk
- *International Security Management Association:* Organization of senior security executives. www.ismanet.com
- *International Society of Crime Prevention Practitioners, Inc.:* Crime prevention organization. www.crimeprevent.com
- *Investigating Associated Locksmiths of America:* Professionals engaged in locksmithing business. www.aloa.org
- *Jewelers' Security Alliance:* A nonprofit trade association that has been providing crime prevention information and assistance to the jewelry industry and law enforcement since 1883. www.jewelerssecurity.org
- *National Alliance for Safe Schools:* Organization promotes safe environments for students. www.safeschools.org
- *National Association of Professional Process Servers:* A worldwide organization that provides a newsletter as well as conferences and training. www.napps.com
- *National Australian Security Providers Association:* Australian industry association. www.naspa.com.au
- *National Burglar and Fire Alarm Association:* Organization that represents the electronic security and life safety industry. www.alarm.org
- *National Classification Management Society:* Classification management and information security organization. www.classmgmt.com
- *National Council of Investigation and Security Services:* Organization for the investigation and guard industry. www.nciss.com
- *National Fire Protection Association:* National Life Safety codes. www.nfpa.org
- *National Society of Professional Insurance Investigators:* Membership, education, and recognition information. www.nspii.com
- *Security Industry Online:* Organization that represents manufacturers of security products and services. www.siaonline.org
- *Security on Campus, Inc.:* Resource for college and university campus crime safety and security issues. www.campussafefy.org

- *Society of Competitive Intelligence Professionals:* The premier online community for knowledge professionals all around the world. www.scip.org
- *Society of Former Special Agents of the Federal Bureau of Investigation:* Publications and member information. www.socxfbi.org
- *South African Security Industry Associations:* Directory listing of South African security associations. www.security.co.za
- *Spanish Association of Private Detectives:* Spanish organization for private investigators and process servers. www.detectives-spain.org/english
- *Women Investigators Association:* An association geared to the special needs of women investigators. www.w-i-a.org
- *World Association of Professional Investigators:* New investigation organization in London. www.wapi.com

Selecting and Hiring Loss Prevention Personnel

Robert M. Denny

Having concise policies and procedures is important, but if you don't select loss prevention people with care, those policies alone won't protect you. Particularly those who are entrusted with the mission of detecting shoplifting and other crimes, and possibly apprehending those responsible, must be carefully chosen and trained before they are cleared to make apprehensions.

The ideal loss prevention agent is a person of good moral character, excellent communication skills, both verbal and written, and with good judgment. The list of desirable attributes we want this person to possess is lengthy, and who wouldn't want *all* employees to live up to these standards? There is no formula for completely ensuring the candidate you select will work out successfully, but by following a consistent, well-conceived process, you greatly increase the odds of developing a good agent. Close evaluation and regular, ongoing training are a must. A candidate who interviews quite well may prove, over a short time, not to possess the acumen, drive, or instincts to detect suspicious activity on the sales floor or in the back rooms. In that case, deal with the issue by providing additional coaching or, if that is not effective, by removing the agent from the position. A probationary period of 3 months or longer is recommended, if consistent with what your HR department and the laws of your state allow.

Recognizing we must recruit from the human race, it may not be possible to recruit a sufficient number of candidates who fully meet your criteria. The liability for selecting the wrong person in a loss prevention agent capacity is so damaging that, only when a candidate meets your high standards should he be hired.

One way to address a shortage of cleared LP agents is to assign the majority of your loss prevention people involved as a visible deterrent. They might be in a uniform or other easily recognized outfit.

They might be called inventory control specialists. These specialists, whether employees or contract workers, deter crime by acknowledging and greeting customers as they enter and exit high theft areas.

They can be trained to "burn out" a suspect by making their presence and observation obvious, but the risks of civil litigation are greatly reduced by not allowing detention or apprehension, unless specifically instructed to assist by a "cleared" loss prevention agent.

Both covert and overt loss prevention staff should receive regular training in the civil and criminal laws pertaining to arrest and detention, as well as store policies and procedures regarding all aspects of behavior that violate either store policy or criminal codes. A good loss prevention agent is assertive but not aggressive. Finding the right person or persons requires careful scrutiny and a clear understanding of the skills and traits desirable for the position.

If you already have a good loss prevention team of professionals, it is worthwhile to have members of the team individually interview the candidate and provide their input on the candidate. Often, they can get a sense of whether the prospect will be a good fit with the team. Ultimately, it is the others on the loss prevention team who must be able to fully rely on observations, judgment, and signals of each cleared agent in making a detention. Such trust comes only from actually working together as a team and through regular training together.

Having a series of interviewers independently asking the same question "So, tell me about yourself" is not that revealing. Instead, give each interviewer a specific objective to explore. For example, one person might concentrate on the person's temperament. "When was the last time you lost your temper?" "What happened?" "When was the last time you were in a fight?" "What irritates you the most in life?" Another person could ask questions about training and experience, and so forth. Taking the time to delve into each candidate's background in a well-planned process not only helps you make the right choice, but also sends a loud and clear message to the candidate that this position is important.

Good candidates want to be challenged. This process changes the candidate's focus from, "Is this position good enough for me?" to "Am I good enough to make the team?" That's what you want to happen. All too often, even in good companies, the people who first interview candidates appear to be unprepared, short on time, and disorganized, asking shallow or nonrevealing questions, or they spend most of the "interview" talking about themselves instead of learning about the candidate. A good interview establishes a balance between listening and giving information. It should be a casual, two-way conversation, but with a clear objective to reveal as much as possible about the way the candidate thinks and acts.

From the ranks of the uniformed LP specialists, some may demonstrate the kind of alertness, judgment, and skill to be considered for promotion to the LP agent team that is cleared to make detentions when appropriate.

Many loss prevention professionals insist on drug testing all candidates for loss prevention positions and subjecting them to random testing on a periodic basis during the course of their service. Likewise, background checks should be updated periodically, at least every 3 years. Each candidate should sign a release authorizing such background checks, to include criminal background, civil records, driving records, and credit reports. This is very important because an employee with a clean record can, over time, change due to traumatic life changes or other reasons not known. In other words, a seemingly "good" person can go "bad" over time. A person facing heavy financial pressures or other emotional trauma may be tempted to violate his position of trust and use the position for personal gain. Theft by a loss prevention person may involve a greater dollar loss than the average loss amount simply because of the unique knowledge and access to back areas, security systems, and programs used to deter and detect crime. Proper hiring of a loss prevention agent requires a detailed job description and a clear understanding of the skills, experience, and background of the successful applicant. The process, if done properly, takes time.

It is unfortunate that, historically, some loss prevention agents have been hired without thorough vetting. This may, and often has, come back to haunt the department and the company later.

Following is a list of items to consider when hiring or selecting a loss prevention agent. Whether you perform all these steps is a choice. Frankly, not enough companies perform all these steps but use some combination in their process.

- Initial review of resume for skill and experience evaluation;
- Series of interviews by LP manager, HR, LP team members, others;
- Criminal records check, to include all counties where lived and worked in past 7 years;
- Credit check;
- Driving record check;
- Reference check and verification of education and training;
- Testing of writing skills by requiring a sample report be typed or written using a standard scenario you supply;
- Written cognitive test to evaluate basic math and language skills and ability to follow instructions;
- Paper "honesty" test and follow-up interview by skilled psychologist.

Drug Test

If you are looking to hire or promote an entry-level person, that person must overcome the lack of experience through regular, documented training on company policies, law, and all elements of required skills needed to perform to the job description. All new hires, regardless of their level of past experience, should be assigned to work with another seasoned LP agent or manager. Only after the new hire repeatedly demonstrates proper judgment, abilities, and tactics should he be cleared to make solo apprehensions or detentions. While it may seem obvious, don't overlook the environment where the successful candidate will be working. For example, you may find a male candidate with excellent background and skills, but if you are hiring for a covert loss prevention position in a store that primarily sells women's shoes or accessories, that person will find it very difficult to blend in with the customers over long periods of time.

Most companies use the services of a third party to perform criminal records checks. Make sure the company you use actually follows up on adverse information by physically reviewing court documents. It may be tempting from an economic standpoint to rely on some of the inexpensive database checks or to purchase the DVD check systems. With cutbacks in public services throughout the country, many records are not entered for several months, if ever. Simply performing a county or state records check where the applicant has lived for the past 4 months is hardly adequate. Unfortunately, this often passes as a "records check" for many companies eager to quickly fill a much-needed position. Some employers ask only about felony convictions.

Limiting the check to only felonies is a mistake. The candidate should be asked about being convicted of any crime. There are some exceptions. For example, in California, you are not supposed to ask about a misdemeanor marijuana conviction over 1 year old. In reality, many felony crimes are ultimately reduced to misdemeanors in a plea bargain. Even grand theft can be reduced to "misdemeanor grand theft." The candidate should be informed in writing that a previous conviction might not automatically eliminate him from hire, but that failure to disclose such conviction will. Primarily, you are looking for violations involving "moral turpitude" or a propensity toward violence. Both should be "show-stoppers" in the hiring of a loss prevention officer. There is room for a judgment call. For example, a 25-year-old candidate who has a conviction for "joy riding" or a minor shoplifting conviction as a teenager might have learned something from his past mistake.

Personally, I recall hiring a candidate who admitted stealing two candy bars when he was 15 (one for his sister and one for himself). There was no criminal record found, but the candidate revealed the offense on his application, as instructed. His sense of honesty and otherwise clean record was taken into consideration. This candidate became one of the finest loss prevention agents I have known and eventually became a security director. I'm glad I gave him the chance.

A welcome new process allows you to submit security candidates to FBI scrutiny. To comply with recent new legislation, consistent with improved homeland security, the FBI will run prospective security candidates through their files to determine whether there is any criminal history known to them. Check with your local FBI office to obtain more specifics on the requirements to take advantage of this service.

A credit check is important. If the check reveals a bankruptcy or the person's seemingly living beyond stated income level, there may be a strong temptation to misuse the position for personal gain. The credit check is also a good means of comparing the listed employers and residences on the job application to those shown in the credit report. Gaps in history or major discrepancies deserve careful follow-up with candidate. Information that leads to other geographical residences or work sites should be followed up with proper criminal background checks in those jurisdictions.

Why is a motor vehicle records check important, particularly if the candidate will not be driving a company vehicle? Often, indicators might appear that may or may not be discovered in the criminal background check. For example, a history of Failure to Appear (FTA) may show a disregard for obeying the law and may even mean there is an outstanding bench warrant. Also, DUI(s) indicate the possibility of an alcohol or other drug addiction.

With current technologies, such as scanners, color printers, and use of the Internet, it is very easy for applicants to produce phony diplomas, training certificates, certifications, etc. It is critical to verify credentials directly with the educational institution or ask the applicant to have the institution send copies directly to your attention. Your HR management has information on the high percentage of applicants who lie or exaggerate on their resume. This is a serious matter when done by any applicant but cannot be tolerated at any level with loss prevention personnel.

Paper testing for honesty, cognitive abilities, and other traits is offered by a number of service providers. It is important to use a standard test that has been documented to be an accurate indicator without being prejudicial to race, sex, or other protected classes. Again, your HR department may be able to assist you in this area.

As for evaluation by a psychologist, if used, it should be performed by one who specializes in high-stress occupational evaluations. Often those involved in vetting law enforcement candidates are a good choice, or they may be able to recommend a psychologist who will be right for your company. The cost in time and money for such testing may seem a small price in comparison with hiring the wrong person.

A number of companies are offering inexpensive drug tests that you administer quickly on the spot. The low cost may seem tempting, but unless you are prepared to administer in a manner that guarantees not intermixing tests or the candidate substituting another's fluids for his own, then you should use a local lab that is experienced in conducting drug tests. All too often candidates for positions at every level try to beat drug tests. Don't this let happen to you. The consequences can be devastating.

One day, in a trial or deposition, you may have to answer how you go about selecting your loss prevention officers. If you follow selected high standards and guidelines consistently, you won't be embarrassed to give your answer.

Sell More, Lose Less: Understanding the Behavior of Shoppers and Thieves

David Donnan

> *"We've stopped the thief from stealing it. Unfortunately, we also stopped the consumer from buying it!" —Typical store manager frustration*

Finding the right balance between loss prevention and shopability is a constant dilemma for store managers. Open merchandise, while attractive and easy to access, tends to let products disappear too easily. At the other extreme, the sales volume of products locked in cabinets or behind counters can suffer. How can product be displayed to entice the shopper and thwart the thief?

Understanding the behavior of both shopper and thief has been a subject of intense research over many years. Various approaches from consumer panels, shopper intercepts, and psychographics have been used by product marketers and retailers to try to unlock the secret psyche of the shopper. Similarly, criminologists have tried to explain shoplifting behavior to determine the underlying causes of theft.

In a recent article, Indiana University professor Raymond Burke contends that consumer research has been transformed as technology has improved. The first wave of consumer marketing research involved the use of POS data coupled with UPC bar codes. Effectively, it measured what we buy. The second wave of consumer research tied the POS/UPC data to individual shoppers using loyalty cards, creating shopping profiles based on purchase history and trends. These approaches measured how we buy. The third wave is just beginning to emerge. It revolves around real-time tracking of consumers in the store and understanding shopping behavior and decisions. Utilizing shopper intercepts, "shop-along," and people-counting technologies, the third wave of analytics hopes to uncover the "why" of shopping behavior.

Knowledge of Thief Behavior

Until now, most in-store sales performance and link-it systems were oblivious to the behavior of consumers. Merchandising displays were placed with little measure of effectiveness or consumer draw. Shrink-management systems tended to catch the thief after the fact and not prevent the activity from occurring.

Understanding the behavior of the shopper and the thief will be the focal point of retailers over the next decade. With the movement toward urban locations, coupled with the increase in organized professional theft, the need for better loss prevention strategies is evident. More sophisticated shrink-management strategies will be needed that can work in higher risk stores, while also providing merchandising support for the store.

For many retailers, the use of real time in-store analysis can help to redirect merchandising and asset-protection measures based on consumer traffic and the interaction consumers have with promotions, displays, and shelf systems. Video-based data can translate in-store consumer movement and relay real-time information to the store personnel to improve customer service, as well as manage professional theft situations. RFID tied to promotional displays can help track sales performance and link it to out-of-stock situations. Sensor-based shelf management systems can help determine the frequency and duration of product handling.

We are witnessing a rapid convergence of technologies that can provide retailers with new insights into the behavior of their customers. Sensor devices that measure traffic flow, temperature variations, motion detection, and entrance activity are now installed in most stores. With sophisticated CCTV software, the movement of consumers through the store can also be monitored.

Islands of Automation

Most of these systems are still "islands of automation" with no easy means to connect their outputs, but a convergence of in-store communications and network architecture is helping to merge the various technologies.

The evolving role of the LP organization in retail will depend on its ability to effectively combine expertise in store operations, merchandising, and IT systems. LP organizations that understand how to use these emerging technologies will contribute significantly to profit optimization of their companies. These real-time, decision-support tools must focus on profit optimization (selling more while losing less), as well as consumer satisfaction.

Measurement will focus on sales, margins, total supply chain shrink, profitability, and internal/external customer satisfaction surveys. For the LP managers, it is no longer sufficient to be an effective manager of loss. Today, they must help their retail organization sell more.

Sex Crimes in the Retail Environment

CAS, JHC

The various types of sex offenses which are known to occur in and/or on retail store property, including distribution centers, and should be considered a security risk include, but are not limited to, the following:

- Abduction from the property followed by a sexual assault off-premises;
- Rape of adult women;
- Detainees threatened with arrest if they don't submit to sexual advances;
- Sexual assault and/or sexual solicitation of young children;
- Exhibitionism in the parking area;
- Exhibitionism inside the store;
- Sexual contact between men in the store's men's restroom;
- "Peeping Tom" (voyeurism) activity into the women's restroom;

- "Peeping Tom" (voyeurism) activity into women's fitting rooms;
- Obscene phone calls allegedly from the store;
- Obscene phone calls into the store;
- Obscene letters, notes, or photos sent to employees;
- Aberrant sexual contact with mannequins;
- Other miscellaneous aberrant sexual activity.
- Consensual illicit sexual conduct inside store or distribution center.

Awareness of and sensitivity to this myriad of bizarre, disgusting, or tragic events may prevent what otherwise could be a serious incident. If a little girl is seen wandering alone among displays of merchandise, the alert loss prevention agent can bring the child and her mother together. A LP associate who notices and acts on the burned-out bulb in the light stanchion which illuminates the employees' parking area could inadvertently prevent a serious attack in the dark. Understanding the potential significance of holes in the ceiling or walls of public restrooms and correcting that condition could discourage unwanted traffic and conduct on the store's premises. Let's explore the above-listed scenarios and benefit from this heightened level of awareness.

Abduction from the Property Followed by a Sexual Assault Off-Premises

Most commonly, female employees and customers are accosted as they near their vehicle in the parking area which serves the store, or are forced into their vehicle once the door is unlocked and opened and are driven to some remote location and sexually assaulted. We have served as consultants and experts in numerous attacks. In some cases, the victim's little children witnessed the assault on their mother.

In those cases in which the victim was an employee, the general employee population is affected and demoralized, and prior efforts to build a climate of mutual respect between the company's associates and the loss prevention department plunge. Basic prevention strategies could include

1. Insuring the parking areas are well illuminated;
2. Adopting an escort policy wherein a sole female associate may ask for and receive an escort to her car;
3. Adopting a policy in which employees are required to proceed to the parking area in groups only;
4. Deploying an LP agent or outside contracted security officer in the parking area at closing time;
5. Monitoring the parking area with CCTV.

Rape or Attempted Rape of Adult Women

With respect to the problem cited in the preceding section, in many cases the actual sexual assault occurs in the vehicle in the parking area itself (rather than removing the victim to another location). The same preventative strategies/measures apply here.

Rape of employees inside the store, especially when the employee works alone at night, is a known operating risk. Some have been savagely brutal. I recall a case in which the customer entered the ladies' restroom and entered an enclosed stall. She noted the adjacent stall was occupied by someone wearing "feminine-appearing" boots. That party exited the stall and moments later the lights were switched off, leaving the restroom in total darkness. An intruder forced open her door and commenced to disrobe and assault the customer. In retrospect, the light switch should have been key operated, rather than the typical home toggle switch which anyone can operate.

In another matter, an attractive young shoplifter was told to submit sexually or she'd go to jail. She opted for jail rather than sex. The LP agent took her to the display storage area of the store and raped her in the privacy of the props and display materials and then released her. She went to the police. Company policy should prohibit a male agent processing a female suspect without at least one witness, preferably a female witness if possible.

Detainees Threatened with Arrest or Submit to Sexual Advances

It's not possible to quantify the number of times a member of management or a representative of the loss prevention department has offered to release a suspected dishonest employee or shoplifter in return for sexual favors or, on the other hand, has threatened to call the police unless the detainee submitted. It is reasonable, however, to speculate that a percentage of such "consensual arrangements" have adversely backfired against the store, causing substantial financial loss. As stated in the preceding category, witnesses are the best preventive strategy. Another deterrent is a careful review of detention/arrest reports to assure full compliance with company policy.

Sexual Assault and/or Sexual Solicitation of Young Children

The most recent case in this category occurred while this section was being written. A 9-year-old boy went into the men's restroom in the store while his mother waited outside the restroom. While the boy was inside the restroom, a customer offered him a dollar if the boy would unzip his pants and allow the man to touch his private parts. The boy declined and exited. His mother sensed something was wrong and asked, but the boy said nothing was wrong. They went home, where the father then inquired, and the boy admitted what had transpired. The store was called.

The store received two calls that day on that same problem. It's unknown how many other similar solicitations (rejected or accepted) occurred that day in that store or how many other children were sexually traumatized or disturbed that week in that community. The assistant store manager called the police, but LP was never advised, nor did anyone go down to the restroom and investigate. A lawsuit was filed.

How many times have children been "lost" in big stores. I recall one incident in which the mother frantically searched in the expansive area dedicated to ladies' lingerie, swimwear, and sportswear, assisted by a number of employees, only to finally find the child outside a fitting room bank, whimpering, with semen dripping from her face. She said there was a "bad man" in there, but no male customers were sighted in that area.

Children are vulnerable in public places, and their presence should always be noted by the professional LP practitioner.

Exhibitionism in the Parking Area

Most "flashers" (exhibitionists) engage in their bizarre behavior of exhibiting their genitals to persons of the opposite sex in parking areas. Why parking areas? The collection and assemblage of vehicles provides avenues for movement to get into the desired location to confront the "victim," and yet the flasher can shield his conduct from those he doesn't want to know what's happening. Further, the place where cars are parked is often some distance from where people are assembled, so help is not close by. Unless the woman is armed with a cell phone, she must reach someone to report the incident to, allowing the bad guy time to casually move on. It takes a pretty aggressive woman with a cell phone to call and stay with the culprit, and it take good luck that any police officer would be close by and respond. Even if a police officer comes immediately to the scene and the customer points him out, there's little, if anything, he can do because the offense is a misdemeanor (a petty crime). Police officers, as a rule, cannot make an arrest for a misdemeanor offense not committed in their presence.

Why does the retailer see this as a problem? Most customers find this conduct disgusting and upsetting. If the police don't show or do show but take no action, the customer is frustrated. Her other recourse is to complain to management of the store. If the store isn't sympathetic, or fails to take some form of corrective action or perceived correction action and the conduct is repeated, the store risks losing a customer.

Customers who report "flashers" should be interviewed for as much information as they are willing to share, and such reports must be memorialized. If the problem persists, LP resources should be committed to identify the culprit and turn the matter over to the local authorities.

Exhibitionism Inside the Store

Whereas most "flashing" occurs outside a store, there are those brave souls who opt to operate inside stores, and they tend to select busy retailers with lots of customer traffic. This way, after the "flash" (exposure), they can turn and disappear into the crowd. Should a customer inform an LP agent "that man just exposed himself to me," pointing to some gentleman, the LP agent, like the police officer cited previously, cannot detain the suspect but rather can covertly follow in hopes of gathering information, such as his auto's tag, or "burning" the culprit. The former is preferable, if possible. Local police detectives, not patrol officers, can be contacted with information obtained for intelligence purposes, not necessarily for the filing of a criminal complaint.

In the event the culprit is seen again in the store, LP has a choice, depending on company LP policy, to maintain a close surveillance in hopes of observing a criminal act of indecent exposure and making an arrest on that observation, or in "burning" the subject so he'll leave the store.

Sexual Contact Between Men in the Store's Men's Restroom

Men's public restrooms (often referred to as "tea rooms" by those who use them for illicit purposes), irrespective of the location, are notorious for accommodating sexual activity between men, i.e., fellatio, mutual masturbation, and anal sex. A store's restroom is no exception. Some time back, a two-way mirror viewed the interior of a big store's restroom located in the basement, and for relief from prowling the selling floor, LP agents watched for and detained men engaged in sexual conduct. Despite the arrests made in that room, the activity continued for all the years it remained open to the public. It was a well-known spot.

This activity is perpetuated by messages printed in the grout lines or on the partitions between stools, in very small print, seeking one another. Big scrawling dirty words or obscene drawings are the work of juveniles, as a rule, but the informed LP agent can monitor for the little messages and understand, if they're found, the likelihood of sex-related traffic in and out of that room. Another indicator of activity is the presence of "glory holes" and peep holes in the partitions. "Glory holes" accommodate oral copulation, where the man in stall #1 stands facing the partition, and the man in #2 puts his mouth to the hole to commit fellatio. Peep holes about the size of marbles allow a stall occupant to look into the adjacent stall and allows the occupant of that second stall to see the first man's eye (and its movement) at that small hole, which clearly indicates intentions.

All writings, when they appear, should be cleaned off or painted over. All holes should be patched. If traffic continues, some stores have gone so far as to remove the stall doors (to preclude privacy) and to place signage on the restroom's entrance door that the room is frequently checked by patrolling security.

In this day and age, LP personnel shouldn't attempt to make arrests, but rather concentrate on discouraging traffic and preventing sexual encounters.

This problem became serious enough for me to write the following procedure in the late 1980s:

> When illicit activity is observed, the offending individual(s) should be told that they are engaged in offending and disruptive behavior not allowed by the store and told to leave the store. They will be escorted out of the store; they are not to be detained for interrogation or taken to the security office. In the process of escorting them from the store, the escorting Security Agent should:

a. Ask for their name(s)
b. Advise them they are not welcome in the store and if they return will be subject to arrest for trespassing
c. Obtain a detailed description of the individual(s) involved.

After the offending individual(s) have left the store, a detailed security information report should be written detailing the observations which led to the eviction, the name(s) and/or descriptions of the person(s) evicted, and comments made by them, any other witnesses, etc.

"Peeping Tom" (Voyeurism) Activity into Women's Restroom

Grates, grills, and vent covers are common camouflage over openings which allow interior viewing of the ladies' restroom from vertical and horizontal surfaces (walls and ceilings). The problem exists in both public and employee-only restrooms. There are men who have this aberrant compulsion to watch women using such facilities. It's incumbent upon the loss prevention department to regularly and carefully inspect such rooms.

"Peeping Tom" (Voyeurism) Activity into Women's Fitting Rooms

Although the fitting room/dressing room areas are definitively different from restrooms, in every conceivable environment, from major theme parks to gas stations, the voyeur's attraction to fitting rooms is obviously restricted to retailers. The following examples should be helpful in understanding the scope and diversity of the problem:

Example 1: A routine security inspection of a closed-off and no-longer-used stairwell disclosed an extension ladder propped against the wall at one of the landings. The ladder led to a fan which apparently pulled air from the stairwell for the interior of the store. Out of curiosity, the agent climbed the ladder and, as he neared the top, noticed layers of a dried substance on the rungs and, higher, relatively fresh deposits of semen. The opening for the fan looked down on a fitting room used for swimwear customers. Clearly, someone was using the ladder as a perch to watch into the room and masturbate.

It was important to determine who the culprit was. It seemed most likely an employee was involved, and it was necessary to identify such a person and remove him from the workplace. A surveillance revealed the voyeur was a customer who would surreptitiously enter the closed-off stairwell. For fire safety regulations, it was impossible to seal the stairwell; only "Closed. Do Not Enter" signs discouraged its use. Evidence clearly indicated this voyeur had been using this ladder-perch for over a year, and past security inspections had overlooked the ladder's location as nothing more than a convenient place to store the ladder.

Example 2: Two teenage girls were in a fitting room trying on swimsuits when a man's leg crashed through the ceiling tiles. The girls screamed. The leg withdrew back into the space above the tiles. The girls and other customers marched to the store manager's office to complain. Later, a lawsuit was filed against the store.

Investigation disclosed two male agents had entered an elevated surveillance post constructed next to a column. Entry into the post was a "secret" door known only to and accessible by LP agents in that store. Agents, in the legitimate use of the surveillance post (which allowed viewing of the selling from through a two-way mirror), became aware that not far away was a bank of fitting rooms which serviced the swimwear department. And one of the agents discovered that, by carefully lifting certain ceiling tiles, he could view the interior of one of the rooms. He shared this knowledge with another agent, and on this occasion while "enjoying" the view, one inadvertently stepped off the braces and placed his weight on the tiles, which immediately gave way.

Example 3: A store detective with keen sense of smell, while walking through a stock area hallway, detected the odor of sawdust. Such an odor was uncommon and caused her to follow her nose, out of curiosity. She sniffed her way into a narrow stockroom and, on one of the many shelves, moved goods aside to find the fresh wood debris created by a brace and bit drill. By standing on the bottom shelf and resting her arms on an upper shelf, she could peer through the round hole that had been made. The hole provided a view into a fitting room.

A scenario was created in which the most likely suspect, a young and new member of the engineering staff, would be asked to change florescent lights above the door of the human resource director's office. As this young man stood on a ladder changing the bulb, the manager of the selling department came to the door, informed the HR director her new swimsuit had just arrived and asked whether she could come down and try it on. "I'll be down in 10 minutes," replied the director. The engineer almost fell off the ladder. Then minutes later the engineer was caught with his eye to the hole.

In one Texas case I handled, an LP agent entered a dead space behind a women's fitting room and made a hole in the plasterboard wall to which the full-length mirror was attached inside the fitting room. He then scratched away a small area of the silvering on the back of the mirror, creating a clear view into the fitting room.

The loss prevention department, or in its absence, store management, has the responsibility to ensure the integrity of every fitting room in the store, with particular emphasis on those rooms in which women are obliged to remove any underclothing. Periodic inspections of fitting rooms for evidence of illicit means of surreptitious viewing, together with keeping a written record of such inspections and the results thereof will help meet this responsibility.

Obscene Phone Calls, Allegedly from the Store

Telephone "surveys" have been used to engage female customers into conversations which are designed to become obscene. For example, "Mrs. Miller, my name is Charles Glotz with the American Department Stores, and we're contacting select customers with a survey about our lingerie department and its assortment, quality, and pricing. Those customers gracious enough to answer fewer than 25 questions will receive a $25 gift certificate that can be used in any of our stores. Can you spare 7 or 8 minutes to respond to this survey?"

Mrs. Miller graciously accepts. Charles then starts with questions which are innocuous and reasonable, such as whether she has personally visited the store's lingerie department and made purchases. If not, which store does she prefer? Why that store? Then he asks questions about color preferences, and from there, the size of her bra, size of her panties, whether she likes roomy sizes or real tight. From there, depending on how long the customer will tolerate the increasingly intimate questions, the "survey" turns obscene. The customer hangs up and calls the store to complain to the manager and complain about Mr. Glotz.

We're not suggesting this an ongoing and common problem. Suffice it to say, it does occur, and you are so advised.

Obscene Phone Calls into the Store

Depending on the store's phone system, incoming calls may be specific to an employee or may be random. The caller may start a string of questions similar to the previous scenario about the items in the department or may directly launch into questions about the employee's sexual preferences. There are two important points in this arena: (1) Employees should be informed that infrequently they may receive bizarre calls; however, they shouldn't be unduly alarmed, but rather report them immediately to management or loss prevention. And (2) such calls should be documented with as much information as possible, similar to a bomb threat call. Depending on what the caller says, it may behoove the store to refer the incident to the police.

Obscene Letters, Notes, or Photos Sent to Employees

Although employees receiving obscene messages isn't an everyday problem, when it does occur, the recipient is often very alarmed. Therefore, the incident must not or cannot be easily dismissed. Loss prevention resources must be committed to identifying. The message can range from a note under the windshield wiper of the recipient's car to a note or photo enclosed in a sealed envelope. The message may be a proposition for a sexual encounter or a self-taken photograph of a person's genitals. Whatever the case, it's a demand on the investigative resources and skills of the loss prevention department. Although it wasn't in a retail setting, I did track down a particularly obscene letter sent to a student about his fiancée and by careful comparison of typewriter samplings, I discovered the student's mother proved to be the culprit. She didn't want her son to marry the girl.

Aberrant Sexual Contact with Mannequins

The precursor to plastic blow-up dolls used for sexual activity was (and still is) the common store mannequin. Indeed, at the time of this writing, I noted in the local newspaper a brief article which reads as follows (the name has been changed):

> *MANNEQUIN FETISH CITED IN BREAK-IN*
> *Ferndale, Mich.(AP)*
> *A Detroit man with a history of smashing store windows to grab female manne-quins has been accused of indulging his fetish again.*
> *Charles Glotz, 39, was arrested and jailed Oct. 9 after breaking a window at a cleaning-supply company to get at a mannequin in a black and white French maid's uniform, police said.*

Now here's a gentleman who is so desperate to possess a new mannequin that he's will-ing to engage in the crime of burglary, with all its consequences. But in the retail industry, many stores have mannequins, some on display and in use for their designed purpose, and some stuck away in reserve. Who really is responsible for the mannequins, and who oversees their disposal, let alone use on premises?

Not all abuse of these objects is of a copulative nature; i.e., some are abused in other ways. One store had a rash of damaged goods while on display. Investigation disclosed all the damaged merchandise was women's apparel limited to blouses, sweaters, coats, and bras. Further investigation and surveillance resulted in the discovery of an employee who had a fetish for large breasts and the compulsion to stab large busts with a knife. Hence, those man-nequins which seemed to emphasize the size of the breasts were stabbed during early morning hours, and the goods used to dress them were damaged.

Other Miscellaneous Aberrant Sexual Activity

Be alert for "crawlers," i.e., those men who crawl on their hands and knees to look up ladies' skirts. If detected, they pretend to be looking for their dropped money or keys.

Less conspicuous was a gentleman who carried a shopping bag which contained only a mirror, facing up when lying flat on the bottom of the bag. His method of operation was to ride the up escalators and place an open shopping bag on the step immediately behind a lady so he could view down into the bag and catch the reflection of her underside. After this man was detained a number of times, the police didn't want to be bothered by him anymore, and LP agents were known to break his mirror and eject him from the store. But he would reap-pear with a new, clean mirror some weeks later.

Of more alarm to early morning employees was the sudden and then daily appearance of a plate containing fresh human feces. The location of this disgusting event varied, and the loss prevention department was hard-pressed to catch the employee responsible. When he was finally apprehended, it was clear the man had a sexual quirk and fetish with respect to feces. When the police were summoned at the close of the LP investigation, they transported him to a local mental institution rather than to the local jail.

Consensual Illicit Sexual Conduct Inside Store or Distribution Center

Although conduct falling in this category more often than not fails to rise to the level of a "crime," it does, or at least should, violate company policy. There are various reasons why policy should prohibit affairs on premises, but that's not the objective of this material. Our objective is to enlighten the loss prevention professional to the wide spectrum of criminal, disruptive, tortious, and otherwise unacceptable activity that exists in the retail environment which does or may require loss prevention intervention. And in this section of the book, the conduct in question focuses on sex-related activities.

Here's a classic example: The marking area of the distribution center, with over three dozen employees, became suspicious of one new female employee who loafed on the job, was often tardy without consequences, and failed to carry her weight in the demands of marking and ticketing literally thousands of pieces of goods that required processing every day. Morale plummeted when it became obvious that the supervisor and this employee were having an affair. Complaints were funneled to human resources and passed on to the security department for investigation. The investigation established where and when sexual relations were being engaged in, and at the appropriate time and place, the two were caught in a compromising position. Both were terminated. Confidence in the professional proficiency of the security department was confirmed, everyone was treated equally, morale rose, and productivity returned to expected and necessary levels.

Summary

The diversity of "sex crimes" which are foreseeable and do occur in the retail environment, as evidenced here, put the professional loss prevention/security practitioner, from line to executive, on notice that there's a lot more to this career path than catching shoplifters and inventory shrink. As a reminder, the loss prevention department has a mission to protect the company, its assets, property, merchandise, employees, customers, proprietary information, and reputation. In meeting these responsibilities, the LP department needs to make every incident of illicit sexual activity the subject of a detailed written report, which should include any recommendations for or remedial actions taken.

Shoplifter Diversion: Don't Just Stop Shoplifters—Get Them to Stop Shoplifting

Peter Berlin

The Future of Shoplifting Prevention: Introduction

The 1992 edition of the book *Shoplifting* by Charles Sennewald and John Christman has all the who, what, when, where, how, and why about shoplifting, and I recommend it as the source for all retail executives and loss prevention personnel. These same experts and authors have now asked me to write a section for this book about shoplifting prevention based on my research and experience with shoplifters since 1968. This section will explain the real problem behind shoplifting, why millions of people (from all walks of life) engage in it, how to realistically address the root cause of the problem (both before or after an incident occurs), and how to become proactive in prevention in a way which will sustain itself over time. This section is not about how to eliminate shoplifting; it's about how to permanently reduce shoplifting to perhaps one-third of its current level.

While the shoplifting problem is typically discussed in terms of lower profits for stores, higher prices for consumers, an increasing crime rate, and the character of our people, it will be discussed here not in theoretical or moral terms, but rather in practical terms.

[*A word of caution*: Reading this section can arouse a variety of emotions because some readers will be the victims of shoplifting, whereas others will have had personal experiences with shoplifters. Hardly anyone is indifferent on the subject. To gain real value from this section, you will find it beneficial to keep an open mind and temporarily put aside any preconceived notions about shoplifting or the people who shoplift and replace them with your own common sense.]

So that you don't have to wait for the end of this section to figure out what it is I am trying to say, the future level of shoplifting will depend on our understanding of the people who shoplift rather than only the devices to try to stop them.

Three key facts identify the future direction of shoplifting prevention:

- Retailers can stop a shoplifter, but they can't stop him from shoplifting. Only he can stop himself.
- People will stop shoplifting when they finally discard the "illusion" that "getting something for nothing" is somehow going to improve their life or is a way to substitute for or compensate for the pressures in their life.

- People won't start shoplifting when the level of education, participation, and cooperation between community resources consistently demonstrate that the "risk is not worth the reward."

The Shoplifting Problem in Our Nation

If we briefly look at the 20-year period from the end of World War II in 1945 to 1965, the losses in department stores remained at about 1% of retail sales. By 1968, the average losses in department stores had risen to 3.5% of sales because of a cultural revolution among our youth and others which sought nonconformity and lessened traditional values. It's been some 40 years, and we have not yet returned to the 1% level. Shoplifting in our nation has become a more serious problem which affects not only kids, parents, families, retailers, consumers, police, courts, state and local government, and the community as a whole, but also negatively affects the lives of an estimated 25–30 million Americans (1 in 11 people) who shoplift from stores each year.

Key Facts You Should Know

There are an estimated 200 million shoplifting incidents in our nation each year, or approximately 550,000 incidents per day.

Retailers estimate they lose about $11 billion per year to shoplifters, or approximately $30 million per day.

Shoplifters rarely get caught. Surveys reveal that shoplifters get caught an average of only once every 35–48 times they steal, and 20% of habitual offenders say they have never been caught.

There are two primary groups of shoplifters: professionals and nonprofessionals. Any approach to shoplifting prevention must recognize these important distinctions:

- *Professional Shoplifters:* These are individuals or organized retail theft groups who steal for resale or profit as a business. The estimated shrinkage losses caused by shoplifting from professional shoplifters is $1 billion per year. There are also professional thieves who steal a substantial amount of merchandise in the cargo, distribution, and retail supply chain, but the bulk of these losses are not recorded as a part of the inventory shrinkage in stores.
- *Nonprofessional Shoplifters:* This category includes everyone else. The estimated shrinkage losses caused by shoplifting from nonprofessional shoplifters is $10 billion per year. Within this group of people, about 1 in 4 say they shoplift on a daily or weekly basis. They have become known as "habitual repeat offenders," and they cause the bulk of the dollar losses simply because of the frequency of their thefts.

When we combine professional and nonprofessional shoplifting, we see that a *small* percentage of the people are responsible for a *large* percentage of the dollar losses.

When we combine both professional and nonprofessional:

Habitual nonprofessional	27% of the people responsible for 85% of the losses
Professional	3% of the people responsible for 10% of the losses
Casual nonprofessional	70% of the people responsible for 5% of the losses

With this current information at hand, the challenge is to focus on both preventing and apprehending the nonprofessional "habitual repeat offender."

In seeking ways to prevent shoplifting, we must first look at the root cause of this problem which drives so many different people who are not career criminals to become "habitual repeat offenders" in stores.

The Shoplifter: Why Do Shoplifters Steal?

Shoplifting—Is it need or is it greed? Or is it something else that tempts approximately 25–30 million people to steal from retail stores each year? Except for the drug addicts and hardened professionals who steal for resale and profit as a business, most shoplifters are otherwise law-abiding citizens. The vast majority of adult offenders have no idea about how or why they become thieves, or why they continue to shoplift, even after getting caught.

Retailers, police, prosecutors, and judges see hundreds of thousands of apprehended shoplifters, of all ages, who don't fit the profile of typical criminals. For example, they don't use shoplifting paraphernalia, they don't use drugs, they carry proper identification, they have no prior criminal record (except perhaps for shoplifting), they don't associate with known criminals, they don't steal for resale, they usually have the money to pay for the item(s) they stole, they frequently have a job and a family, they steal things they don't really need and often don't use, and they know what they did was wrong and frequently feel ashamed and remorseful. Their overall lifestyle is not that of typical thieves or criminals.

Retailers, law enforcement, and the courts process these people through the criminal justice system, as they should, but with little understanding of why they committed the offense and what kind of action would be effective to help prevent such thefts (before an incident occurs) or reduce recidivism (after an incident occurs). Thousands of survey responses and interviews conducted with nonprofessional shoplifters have made it clear that shoplifting behavior among nonprofessionals is rarely related to criminal intent but is rather the result of a person's internal personal struggle with social and psychological issues. People who shoplift are not doing this to hurt the store or cause consumers to pay higher prices or put themselves in jeopardy. Their objective is rarely to hurt anyone.

Of course, whatever their motive, it does not make shoplifting okay for any reason. But, we must ask, if their motive is not criminal intent for profit, why do people shoplift? In simple and concise terms, "TO GET SOMETHING FOR NOTHING."

Let me explain! While we all like to get things for free, like receiving birthday presents or winning the lottery, and while retail stores constantly promote and place merchandise on "sale" to generate excitement about getting a bargain, you and I never cross over the line and steal the item, whereas other people do. Why? The answer is: To most people who shoplift, getting something for nothing is like giving themselves a "reward" or a "gift" or a "lift" at

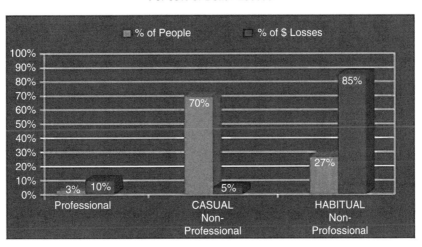

FIGURE S-1

a point in time when they feel they need or deserve it. A study by MasterCard International found that "shopping" was second only to dining out as the primary way that people reward themselves. Take it one step further and you can see how "shoplifting" the merchandise could increase the reward.

People who shoplift have given the idea of "getting something for nothing" a special meaning which (unknowingly) represents something more to them than the value of the merchandise. This is important for us to understand. For different people, it can mean different things, but it all serves the same purpose in the end. For example: For some, shoplifting acts as a "substitute for loss" because they were unfairly deprived in some way (the loss of a parent or partner from a divorce situation, the loss of health because of a serious illness, the death of a loved one, a bad work-related situation, loss of income from a job or investments, or an increase in expense for a car repair, etc.) which often causes people to feel needy. To others, shoplifting represents "justified payback" for all they believe that they give to others and how little they get back in return. It is often described as a feeling of "entitlement" or a way to help make their world fair. For some, it's a "relief mechanism" for anxiety, frustration, boredom or depression. The excitement of "getting away with it" provides temporary relief from these type of uncomfortable feelings.

While most people know right from wrong, when people feel needy in some way (i.e., lonely, fearful, depressed), the need for them to do something to relieve their discomfort creates an impulse to act. After impulsively taking their first item and getting away with it, they often experience what they describe as an incredible "high" or "rush," which gives them temporary relief from their emotional discomfort or need.

Several studies have found diagnosed depression to exist in approximately one-third of the shoplifters studied. Depression was the most frequently found psychological problem and is the result of anger turned inward. The "high" or "rush" helps to temporarily relieve depression. This helps to explain why so many people steal from stores on their birthday and around holiday times.

In truth, to the eye of a trained therapist, shoplifting behavior is no more than simply a "symptom" and a "signal" to the individual (and to others) that a person is in trouble primarily because of his inability to effectively cope with personal issues in his life. Any way you look at it, shoplifters unknowingly pursue shoplifting as a form of compensation or self-nourishment as a way to relieve fear or pain in their life. In truth, shoplifting is self-destructive, not self-nourishing, but shoplifters often can't see the paradox.

While it is the responsibility of the offender to deal with and correct his thinking and behavior, to be able to make needed changes, people often need to be pointed in the right direction because they may have already developed a habit or addiction to shoplifting.

Of course, some people don't want to see shoplifting as a functional or psychological problem. They say, "What do you mean that a person can't stop shoplifting? Of course, they can; they're just greedy." The idea that shoplifting is habit forming or addictive (except for a few "kleptomaniacs") is ridiculous, they say. People who shoplift should go to jail and not be coddled or told they have an addiction. This is like telling them it's okay to steal because they really can't help it.

A person's addiction to shoplifting can develop quickly when the excitement generated from "getting away with it" produces a chemical reaction (i.e., adrenalin, etc.) resulting in that "rush" or "high" feeling, which many shoplifters will tell you is the "true reward," rather than the merchandise itself. Realizing how easy it is to get that "high" feeling, they are pulled toward doing it again … "just one more time" … and their addiction begins to develop. Even though most nonprofessional shoplifters feel guilty, ashamed, or remorseful about what they did and are fearful of getting caught, the pull is too strong for many to resist.

Juveniles

Shoplifting, among juveniles, is remarkably similar to adult shoplifting in many ways. However, the primary issues which are related to shoplifting among youth revolve around family pressure, school pressure, and peer pressure.

If you were to ask juveniles caught shoplifting, "Why did you do it?" the most frequent reply would be "I don't know." As with adults, the reasons teens shoplifted will vary, but most commonly they wanted nice things or felt pressured by friends and wanted to see if they could get away with it, or were angry, depressed, confused, or bored. Sometimes they are just mad at the world and want to strike back.

While teens, like adults, usually know the difference between right and wrong, when their life becomes too stressful, they become more vulnerable to temptation, peer pressure, and other issues that can lead them to shoplift. This is especially true when they feel unworthy, angry, depressed, unattractive, or not accepted.

In summary, shoplifting, for millions of our citizens, is simply another maladaptive way of coping with stressful life circumstances, ways similar to overeating, drinking, taking drugs, gambling, or becoming withdrawn. It is not an issue of good versus bad people, rich versus poor people, young versus old people, or education versus illiteracy. All nonprofessional shoplifters will tell you that, going back as early as they can remember, not a single person had ever decided that they wanted to be a shoplifter when they grew up. It just happened! At any time, or even many times in a person's life, the temptation to "get something for nothing" and to reward oneself can easily be present. Realistically, the many personal issues which all people face in their lives are their own responsibility to correct. There can be no excuse, rationalization, acceptance, or justification for criminal behavior. No question, there must be consequences for people's actions, but there must also be a realistic understanding of the overall problem and a way to point people in the right direction to make needed changes.

You may ask, "So what do we do with this information?" The answer is: To prevent future shoplifting, we need to continue to pursue prosecution, but also find another way to get people to stop themselves from shoplifting.

Getting Shoplifters to Stop Themselves

"This is prevention at its best."

Of course, you might wonder why people would want to stop shoplifting when they get free stuff, they save money, they get a "rush" when they get away with it, they can be more generous to others, they rarely get caught, and the penalties may be no big deal unless they have a record of multiple offenses. The answer is … because they just don't like themselves anymore or find that they like themselves even less than they ever did before. The three primary reasons why nonprofessional shoplifters say they want to stop stealing is (in their own words):

- "To regain my self-respect."
- "To stop hurting myself."
- "It's just not worth it."

Imagine a time in the not-too-distant future when kids and adults who are tempted to shoplift for the first time say to themselves, "I don't want to do it," and those who have shoplifted say, "I don't want to do it anymore." This is clearly a realistic expectation because we have learned that nobody wants to be a shoplifter. This is the "hook" that motivates the willingness to change.

If people really didn't care, there is little anyone could do to stop them. However, when people learn the truth about how self-destructive shoplifting behavior can be for them, they do begin to care (about themselves) and are suddenly willing to discard their current illusions about shoplifting and replace them with current reality. Part of the current reality is that whether a shoplifter is caught or not on a particular day, he is faced with added pressure in his daily life as the result of just being a shoplifter. For example:

When Not Apprehended
- Added anxiety about just going into stores and what might happen
- Fear that eventually they will get caught
- Guilt about their unlawful behavior and acts against "God"

- Pain about having this dark secret about themselves
- Blame and anger that they were driven to this by others
- Guilt about "throwing out the milk" just to have an excuse to go the store
- Loss of self-respect and self-worth every time they take something
- Shame about what they have become
- Loss of friends because they don't want to go "shopping" with them
- Loss of control over themselves when they begin to feel addicted
- Depression about living their life as a shoplifter

When Apprehended (in their own words)
- "Humiliation, embarrassment"
- "The guilt and shame of having to face the court"
- "Being treated as a criminal"
- "Paying legal fees"
- "Facing the judge"
- "Fear of going to jail"
- "Having a criminal record"
- "Paying fines and court costs"
- "Fear that others will find out"
- "Loss of trust by parents, family, and friends"
- "Guilt about hurting others"
- "Loss of self-respect"
- "Loss of time from work"
- "Loss of job"
- "Difficulty in getting another job"
- "Depression"
- "Sleepless nights"
- "Worry about what the judge will do if they get caught again"

While these are all motivating factors toward preventing future thefts, the facts must be presented in a prevention format (which connects the dots for people) to drive the message home. So, how can we get people to stop themselves from shoplifting? Provide them with the information they need to make the right decision for themselves.

People care most about what is best for them, not what is best for society, what their parents want, what the school wants, what the criminal justice system wants, or anyone else. They act in ways that they perceive or feel will benefit them the most (at any point in time), and if it is contradictory to the law or what others want, they will either refrain from doing it or try to hide their act.

Shoplifting is a bad choice for people who care about themselves. The facts which support this statement need to be widely communicated to youth and adults through education in all communities throughout our nation.

The simple fact is that *education* is a powerful way to prevent shoplifters from attempting to steal or to stop stealing. The education must be comprehensive enough, must be "offense-specific," and must be backed up by the ongoing supportive actions of retailers and the juvenile and criminal justice systems. Education is recognized globally as the "treatment of choice" for almost all social behavioral problems, and shoplifting is no exception. However, any type of formal education has rarely been used as a way to prevent shoplifting.

At this point, you might be saying to yourself: "Educate shoplifters … about what? They already know it's wrong to steal. What could you tell them that would make a difference?"

Although you know people shoplift for many reasons, one common denominator is that shoplifters lack an understanding of the problem as it relates to society and themselves. For example:

- They don't know why they do it.
- They don't think anyone really gets hurt.
- They think the stores can afford the losses.

- They don't understand the consequences to themselves and their future.
- They don't know how to handle temptation when they want nice things or feel pressured by friends or are mad at the world and want to strike back.
- They don't know how to resolve feelings of anger, frustration, depression, or feeling unattractive or not accepted.
- They think they won't get caught.
- They don't understand that when life gets too stressful they become more vulnerable to temptation, peer pressure, and other issues that can lead to a shoplifting incident.

Once people hear the truth about shoplifting and themselves, the education "process" begins to take hold on both an intellectual and emotional level. They commonly experience a range of emotions: from initial resistance and denial to concern about what they might become to gratitude that someone really cares to resolve to take greater responsibility for their behavior. They finally choose not to make their life any harder than it is already … by shoplifting.

The value of education to apprehended shoplifters is well documented for tens of thousands of shoplifters in the files of the National Association for Shoplifting Prevention (NASP), a nonprofit organization which provides public awareness, prevention and education programs, and services. However, until a person is apprehended by a store, there is no way to know that a person is a shoplifter.

When and How to Deliver Education (For Prevention)

There are two types of education (for prevention) which are administered at different times:

- Primary prevention: *Before* an incident occurs
- Secondary prevention: *After* an incident occurs

Both forms of prevention must exist because, when primary prevention fails to deter an individual before the fact, secondary prevention must seal the issue after the fact.

Primary Prevention

Primary prevention refers to preventing the primary or first offense. This is the most desirable form of prevention for everyone concerned. People become convinced before an incident occurs that shoplifting is never an option for them. This is accomplished largely with education-for-prevention programs from kindergarten through high school, along with reinforcement from family and community.

It can be a challenge to reach people with a prevention message because many people haven't shoplifted yet and honestly believe they would "never do such a thing." This belief is found to exist within most people who are later caught shoplifting.

Primary prevention involves the ongoing delivery of a consistent message about shoplifting, throughout the community, using various communication channels. These include parents, schools, retailers, police, community youth groups, and agencies that will use shoplifting as their platform to build honesty, integrity, and character within youth and the community.

Secondary Prevention

Secondary prevention refers to preventing a second or future offense. This is for people who didn't get the prevention message or slipped through the cracks. They either recently started shoplifting or have been doing it for years.

Secondary prevention starts with calling the police and pursuing prosecution. While the apprehension of a shoplifter involves cost and potential liability to the retailer, shoplifters still rate prosecution as the most effective action in deterring future thefts, regardless of some of the perceived shortcomings of the criminal and juvenile justice systems. Apprehended shoplifters rate their completion of a comprehensive education program as the second most effective method in deterring future thefts. Of course, the threat of future prosecution always has a positive influence on the value of education.

Where We Are … and … Where We Need to Be

Our nation's response to the shoplifting problem is almost nonexistent on a national level and varies widely on a community level. The reason is that shoplifting is viewed as a state or county problem, and not as a national problem.

In spite of its current magnitude, shoplifting is rarely considered a serious crime and therefore is rarely given serious attention. While it is not murder, it affects many different victims and crime in our society. Various segments of the community which are directly affected by shoplifting address the problem in different ways, largely based on their personal level of interest. Because the message about shoplifting from parents, schools, retailers, police, courts, mental health professionals, and communities at large has been inconsistent or unclear, shoplifting continues to thrive. The lack of a clear message serves to (unintentionally) perpetuate the problem.

Where We Need to Be …

We need to embrace shoplifting as an important social issue in the community.

Parents need to talk to their children about shoplifting. A recent survey by the National Association for Shoplifting Prevention (NASP) revealed that today, 50% more juveniles (31% versus 46%) fail to receive guidance from their parents about why shoplifting is wrong.

- *The Message:* "If my parents didn't talk to me about shoplifting, it can't be so bad." Parents frequently resent the store's apprehension of their child, deny their child's involvement, threaten not to shop in the store again, or excuse their child's behavior by saying, "He's a good boy, gets good grades, and he'll never do it again."
- *The Message:* "My parents will take care of it, if I get caught." Schools need to educate kids about shoplifting. Schools rarely include shoplifting prevention as a part of their curriculum as they do with alcohol or tobacco. They frequently (and naively) deny that their students shoplift.
- *The Message:* "Since the schools don't teach us anything about shoplifting, it can't be that important." Retailers need to pursue prevention, apprehension, and prosecution. Retailers often shy away from apprehending shoplifters as a cost-saving measure or for fear of a confrontation or lawsuit. When they do apprehend, less than 50% of shoplifters get turned over to the police and are simply released.
- *The Message:* "Because the store let me go, I guess the store thinks it's 'No big deal.'" Police need to actively respond to shoplifting incidents. Police need to support retailers by not delaying their arrival to a store, by not discouraging the retailer from filing a complaint, or by not being willing to take the offender into custody. Retailers, too, need to cooperate and encourage police involvement.

Courts need to provide rehabilitation along with punitive sanctions. The courts, which have a "warn and release" policy or provide other minimal sanctions for offenders can cause retailers to question whether their cost and efforts to pursue prosecution have been worthwhile. Courts which provide only punitive sanctions are requiring the offender to pay back his debt to society but are not giving him the education he may need to help ensure he will not repeat the offense.

Mental Health Professionals need to embrace shoplifting as a treatable disorder. Mental health professionals have little knowledge or training about people who shoplift. The mental health community needs to embrace shoplifting as a treatable disorder so that people who shoplift will finally have somewhere to turn, rather than remain uncertain, fearful, and ashamed to seek the help they desperately need.

Who will make it happen? Who else, but you and others in your community.

Whom to Contact for Assistance

- National Association for Shoplifting Prevention (NASP), 1-800-848-9595
  380 North Broadway, Suite 306, Jericho, New York 11753
  nasp@shopliftingprevention.org - www.shopliftingprevention.org
- National Crime Prevention Council (NCPC), 202-466-6272
  1000 Connecticut Avenue NW, 13th Floor, Washington, DC 20036
  www.ncpc.org
- Local Chamber of Commerce or County Government

In Conclusion

This message of this section is about recognizing that anyone can stop a shoplifter, but no one can stop him from shoplifting; only he can stop himself.

- It's about recognizing that while there are professional thieves who steal for resale and profit as a business, the vast majority of people who shoplift in stores are not career criminals but otherwise law-abiding citizens who represent all types of people of all ages, races, religions, education levels, careers, and social classes.
- It's recognizing self-service shopping is here to stay and that security measures in stores are not capable of reducing shoplifting beyond the current high level.
- It's about recognizing that there is no profile of a person who shoplifts because the human causative characteristics exist in all of us. A shoplifter can be anyone.
- It's about our need to acquire an understanding of the people who shoplift rather than only the devices to try to stop them.
- It's about recognizing that the majority of shoplifting is less related to criminal intent and more the result of a personal struggle with social or psychological issues.
- It's about recognizing that shoplifting is rarely about greed, poverty, or values.
- It's about people struggling with their personal conflicts and needs.
- It's recognizing that shoplifting is not about the item stolen; it's about the act of "getting something for nothing."
- It's about recognizing the fact that approximately one-third of nonprofessional shoplifters have diagnosed depression, followed by anxiety disorder, impulse control disorder, addictive disorder, and conduct disorder.
- It's about recognizing and acknowledging that shoplifting can become a habit or addiction which shoplifters say can be as strong as heroin or cocaine. (However, this does not give anyone a license to steal.)
- It's recognizing that with approximately 27% of the shoplifters responsible for 85% of the shoplifting losses, future strategies have to be directed toward the "habitual repeat offender."
- It's about recognizing that when people feel an urge to satisfy a need, they develop an impulse to act.
- It's about people allowing their emotions to override their intellect.
- It's about recognizing that shoplifting is a "symptom and a signal" that a person is in trouble.
- It's about requiring people who shoplift to take full responsibility for their actions, socially and financially, including responsibility for their own rehabilitation.
- It's about looking at preventing shoplifting, not only as a retail security problem, but as a problem with *people* in the community and their ability (or inability) to cope with themselves and their surroundings.
- It's about the community as a whole, setting the tone and the example which supports honesty and condemns dishonesty, at all theft levels including shoplifting.
- It's about remembering that the "carrot" and the "stick" both have shown value in the corrective process and, according to apprehended shoplifters, education can be of equal or greater value than prosecution in preventing repeat offences.

- It's recognizing that without prosecution (being a real threat), there is less value to education.
- It's about the fact that society has not acknowledged shoplifting as a problem like alcohol, drugs, gambling, overeating, anorexia, bulimia, workaholism, or other disorders related to the way people have learned to respond to their life situations.
- It's about recognizing that shoplifting is a dysfunctional, psychological problem for the vast majority of nonprofessional habitual offenders … because nobody wants to be a shoplifter.
- It's about recognizing that shoplifting is a fearful and shameful act to shoplifters, which keeps shoplifting their most protected secret and prevents them from seeking help in controlling their impulses.
- It's about shoplifting, when not effectively addressed by the community, sending a message to the public that "crime pays" and can act as a "gateway crime" which fails to discourage future dishonesty, embezzlement, and fraud.
- It's about addressing shoplifting in a prevention format, to help foster and build honesty, integrity, and character in our youth and our future.

When shoplifting is embraced as an important social issue in a community, we will see a community where parents talk to their children about it; schools address it; kids say "no" to it; consumers resist the temptation to do it; retailers actively pursue it; law enforcement willingly responds to it; courts effectively sentence it; mental health professionals understand it; and people engaged in it seek help to stop.

[Portions of this article were excerpted from an article by Peter Berlin published in the *National Report On Shoplifting*, 1996.]

Shoplifter Profiling: A Retail Loss Prevention Tool

Chris E. McGoey

Does Shoplifter Profiling Exist?

Do retail store loss prevention personnel use profiling tactics as a means of determining which customers are most likely to shoplift? The answer is, undeniably, yes. Shoplifter profiling is a loss prevention technique that many retailers are practicing silently in an effort to reduce inventory losses. Does that seem shocking? It shouldn't. Large marketing firms and national advertising media use profiling every day as a means to improve their efficiency of being able to predict future behavior of consumers.

Can You Judge a Book by Its Cover?

If you think about it, the art of profiling people is part of our daily lives. It is how we judge who is friendly, who is dangerous, who is honest, and who is compatible with our values. The personal attributes of appearance and personality are definitely intertwined in our decision-making process for how we first perceive the image of people we meet. Usually, our initial impression of people changes once we get more information about them. It's easy to be fooled by first impressions. People know how to dress for success and present a positive image when necessary. Similarly, most people have experience being treated differently when dressed up in nice clothes compared to when they looked unkempt. The critics of shoplifter profiling complain that first impressions gained by appearance alone may be incorrect or blinded by a biased stereotype.

Profiling as a Matter of Policy

Most corporate legal and human resource departments fear any mention of the words "shoplifter profiling," let alone the practice of it. They are more likely to issue a policy prohibiting the use of customer profiling and forbid discussion of its benefits in training materials. To many in those protective professions, "shoplifter profiling" is synonymous with the words "bias" and "discrimination." Although this fear is largely baseless, it is not totally unfounded. There have been some high-profile cases where misguided store security officers used poor judgment by harassing shoppers seemingly because of their race. In the past decade alone, several national retailers were embarrassed in the media after accusations of racial profiling were alleged by those wrongfully detained for shoplifting. These retailers further suffered from a series of multimillion dollar lawsuits alleging civil rights violations, false arrest, and negligence claims. After all this negative exposure, you would think that shoplifter profiling is dead … it isn't.

Profiling Is a Naturally Occurring Act

All of us naturally profile the people we meet every day. We constantly make subliminal judgments about people based on their appearance, personality, and conduct. Refusing to talk about it or forbidding the practice in a corporate policy is a futile attempt to mask the exercise of human nature. There is no harm caused from the silent opinions that we all form or the judgments that we make about people we meet. The concept of customer profiling sounds like a valuable tool that every retail loss prevention professional should learn to hone. After all, profiling is a proven tactic used everyday by law enforcement as an efficient method for quickly identifying persons or places likely to be involved in crime. Virtually all investigative agencies use criminal profiling to narrow the field of possible suspects. Why shouldn't retail loss prevention professionals be able to do the same?

Profiling by Another Name

Store inventory control is a common retail store practice used to capture data to track merchandise movement from receiving to sales. This includes a computer-aided system of monitoring physical inventory with point-of-sale and purchasing cross-checks that will keep a progressive store manager ahead of the shrinkage curve. We call this "inventory" and "sales analysis" rather than "inventory loss profiling." These data, when analyzed, provide both a quantitative and qualitative basis for determining where, when, and how inventory shrinkage has occurred and provide a clue where to focus preventive efforts to curb future losses. So what's wrong with loss prevention professionals applying a similar business profiling strategy to prevent shoplifting?

Shoplifter Profiling as a Strategy

Retail loss prevention professionals should be thoroughly familiar with store inventory loss data, as well as knowledge of shoplifter demographic data. Upon request, the best loss prevention professionals can tell you, with a good degree of accuracy, where the high-theft areas are located, what product lines are targeted, on what days of the week, the most active times of day, and who is committing the crime. In addition to objective data, experienced loss prevention agents have developed shoplifter profiles. This includes a list of shoplifters' favorite theft tools of the trade, theft locations, and methods of operation. Profiling shoplifters in a business-like manner makes perfect sense. Without an organized plan, store security personnel will wander the store hoping to randomly spot a shoplifter in the act. This approach is not only highly inefficient, but it also puts pressure on the security officer to be productive. Undue pressure to make arrest quotas is what contributes to bad judgment and bad stops. As you can imagine, profiling shoplifters based on an objective business model using actual incident loss data is preferable to relying on unschooled officer instinct and emotional prejudgment.

For shoplifter profiling to be used as a business model, store security officers should be trained to look beyond shopper appearance alone and focus on shoplifter behavior. Shoplifter profiles can be effective when compared to the behavior of other shoplifters observed in the past in similar circumstances. Obviously, the life experiences of the observer have an effect on his perception of the conduct of people with different backgrounds. Growing up or working in a prejudiced environment can color one's perception of reality. An observer with more training and experience coupled with a more diverse background is more likely to categorize people broadly based on conduct rather than narrowly based on a single characteristic such as race.

You Can't Manage What You Don't Measure

Like anything else, the practice of shoplifter profiling can be abused by biased store security personnel, especially when exercising their power and authority to detain customers based merely on suspicion. For example, it should be considered a red flag if the store shoplifter photo gallery consists only of people of color or only of one sex or only of one age group. A prejudiced security officer might focus surveillance habitually on the race of a customer as an indicator of suspicion. When this occurs, there is a probability of having unreported bad stops as well. In the eyes of the law, racial profiling is considered disparate treatment of the public and can be the basis for a civil rights lawsuit alleging racial discrimination.

Racial profiling is the illegitimate practice that demands justification by store loss prevention agents who focus on ethnic appearance rather than conduct. During litigation or corporate investigation, a retail store might be required to justify a pattern of ethnic shoplifter detentions. This is usually done by studying prior incident reports, videotapes, and customer demographic data in an effort to prove or disprove that irregularities occurred. During this process, some retail store chains have been surprised to learn that their incident records and video surveillance tapes were either incomplete or corroborated the alleged discriminatory acts. In either case, the finding will prove that supervisors are not reviewing incident reports with a trained or unbiased eye. Mark Twain once said, "It ain't what you don't know that hurts you, it's the things you think you know that really ain't true." Since store loss prevention departments are not considered profit centers, security departments may not be required to produce detailed incident reports and statistics for management scrutiny. It is a business reality that you can't manage what you don't measure. It is a litigation reality that you can't defend what you are unable to prove.

Exclude Out as Well as Include In

Shoplifter profiling can further be enhanced and solidified by studying store apprehension demographics and inventory loss data. Armed with this knowledge, a loss prevention specialist can scan the store more efficiently by excluding possible theft suspects, certain store locations, under certain conditions, and behavior patterns. For example, one shoplifter profile suggests that people rarely shoplift while in the presence of their spouse, significant other, or parents. After these persons and their environment are scanned, their conduct might suggest that they have no intention of being dishonest.

Shoplifting is a crime of opportunity and desire. Trained loss prevention staff will spend most of their time observing those customers who demonstrate conduct where they ignore perfectly good opportunities to be dishonest. These customers would be excluded from consideration for the time being. However, a customer standing alone in a remote aisle, carrying a large shopping bag, and looking from side to side would be immediately suspicious until his conduct proves otherwise. Some areas of the store may never yield a theft due to high visibility, high traffic, or undesirable product lines. On the other hand, remote areas of the store may be very active theft locations as items are transported from other areas of the store. A customer walking in this area with a small concealable item may fit the profile of a potential shoplifter regardless of other traits.

A customer wearing tattered shoes might appear suspicious in a self-service shoe department until his conduct disproves a lack of desire to steal. A customer walking across a store carrying a small electronic item partially concealed in the palm of his hand might seem suspicious until several opportunities pass to conceal the product. In contrast, a customer wearing tailored shorts and a t-shirt may demonstrate the desire to steal but has no opportunity to conceal a large item under those clothes. Based on profiling and shopper conduct, the professional plainclothes security officer will scan thousands of customers a day and determine that 99% of them are legitimate shoppers. During this silent surveillance and profiling process, no customers are injured or wrongfully accused.

Surveillance Cannot Be Done Crudely

If trained loss prevention professionals perform shoplifter surveillance properly, most customers will never realize that they were being watched. Merchants don't like monitoring their customers to prevent theft, but it is a matter of economic survival. The retail industry loses over $12 billion a year to shoplifters, and sometimes customer surveillance measures must be employed. No one likes being watched or made to feel untrustworthy. Knowing that you are under surveillance is an uneasy feeling and exacerbates customer relations. A problem arises when untrained store security staff undertake the task of customer surveillance and do so crudely. Common customer complaints about retail store security have to do with the perception of being stalked throughout the store in an effort to intimidate them.

Racial Profiling

Racial profiling is an improper and illegal practice based on the mistaken belief that certain ethnic minority groups are more likely to shoplift than others. Because of this misguided belief, store employees will focus their surveillance on the color of a customer rather than their conduct. Racial bias can blind store personnel and cause them to monitor only the ethic minorities and ignore the real source of inventory losses. Racial profiling eventually leads to a pattern of false theft accusations, wrongful detentions, and harassment when no real probable cause exists. The result is that a particular ethnic group will be made to feel as though they can't be trusted and are unwelcome in the store. African Americans and Latinos have called it "shopping while black or brown." Unless management corrects the wrongful conduct, civil rights violations will occur, and false arrest lawsuits will follow, along with the damaged reputation of the retailer.

Most retail inventory loss statistics have shown that the majority of shoplifters are of the Caucasian race. To concentrate surveillance on minority customers is not only improper, but also is an ineffective method of controlling shoplifting losses at most locations. The thought of racial profiling is distasteful. A 1999 Gallup poll confirmed that 81% of Americans disapprove of the practice. Despite this belief, the same poll indicated that &5% of African-American men said they had been victims of racial profiling while shopping. These polls and other media reports are what give the term "profiling" such a negative connotation. In some circles, any mention of the term "profiling" is tainted from the onset with distrust.

Written Policy May Not Be Enough

Most major retailers have published broad policies against discriminatory acts, but few have specifically addressed shoplifter racial profiling by its security personnel. Not surprisingly, incidents are occurring, which begs the question of how much racial profiling exists in retail stores? For example, in one major department store the security staff used radio codes (code-3) as an alert any time a Black shopper came into a sales area. In another store, 90% of the shoplifting apprehensions were of ethnic customers where the store demographic reports showed only a 15% minority customer base. And in still another store, security officers told sales associates to call them any time a minority shopper entered the sales area. Antidiscrimination policy needs to be put into practice and enforced at the security officer level for it to be effective.

Hiring, Training, and Supervision Are Critical

The only way to eliminate the illegal practice of racial profiling is to prohibit it from the top level of management. Retail stores need to have clearly defined and articulated policies to guide security staffers away from practicing racial profiling and must have a zero tolerance for abuse. The hiring process is a good time to screen out poor candidates who seem predisposed to prejudice. Comprehensive retail security training is absolutely necessary to assure that employees know how to perform the job objectively, lawfully, and with due care. Off-duty police officers working as store security need training too. You can't assume that they understand the mechanics of shoplifting or that they will act appropriately and fairly toward all customers in the retail setting. Off-duty police officers must follow store rules when on the clock and not resort to conflicting street tactics when dealing with retail customer transactions. During the training phase, new loss prevention personnel should be taught how to observe customer conduct, use store loss data, and not base surveillance decisions solely on the race of the customer. Supervisors should always be on the lookout for signs of prejudice in day-to-day conversation and in written reports. Misconduct should be addressed swiftly. If racial profiling becomes routine in shoplifter surveillance and detentions, then it is because store management didn't care enough to correct the problem or instead chose to ratify the behavior.

Conclusion

The concept of shoplifter profiling is a valuable tool that every retail loss prevention professional should learn to hone. Profiling shoplifters is not an evil undertaking in the hands of trained professionals. Shoplifter profiling can be an efficient way to focus on the sources of inventory shrinkage using a store business model that is supported by actual loss data, incident reports, and based on the behavior of other shoplifters observed in similar circumstances. Maintaining accurate business records will allow supervisors to monitor success. These same records will provide an adequate basis to investigate or defend claims of alleged misconduct.

Shoplifting

CAS, JHC

The subject of retail crime cannot be broached without mentioning shoplifting, which is generally recognized as responsible for over $10 billion in annual losses to retailers, which represents about one-third of all inventory shrinkage in this country. Shoplifting has been the subject of a number of books, the most current of which is *Shoplifting: Managing the Problem*, published by ASIS International in 2006. The book you're presently reading, by its very nature, encompasses the broader topic of retail crime in general and must necessarily treat shoplifting with less depth. Those students, researchers, trainers, and practitioners who need to focus on the subject with more specificity should go to a book which devotes its full attention to the subject. Yet much information is nonetheless contained in this work, so let your fingers walk through the index. Whereas a single book has all the information packaged together, much of the same information may be found in this book. The term "shoplifting" itself tends to mean different things to different people; hence, a definition is in order.

> *Shoplifting is the theft of merchandise from displays, presentations, or otherwise available to the public, in a retail store, committed by a person who is or appears to be a customer, during the hours the store is open to the public.*

A store employee who steals merchandise on the job is not a "shoplifter." Nor is a vendor's representative who steals merchandise while alone in the privacy of a stockroom while replenishing stock, or a person who breaks an exterior display window and takes merchandise, or a person who hides in the store at closing time and when the store is empty and void of people goes about and gathers up goods and then breaks out of the store. All these acts are forms of theft, but the perpetrator is not a shoplifter. Shoplifting, however, "steals the show" (no pun intended) because of the magnitude of the problem it causes. Retailers are beleaguered by an almost unending and creative mix of ways people engage in to steal. Commonly accepted and often repeated "statistics' about this pernicious problem include

- One in every 10 customers may shoplift.
- 60% of all juveniles have shoplifted or know someone who has.
- Approximately 5,400 people are arrested for shoplifting each day of the year.

- For every act of shoplifting, 35 to 50 probably go undetected.
- It's estimated 69,000,000 acts of shoplifting occur each year.
- Annual shoplifting losses amount to over $10 billion.

The axiom "the best defense against shoplifting is good customer service" is as true today as when first enunciated. Recent research by a University of Florida master's candidate has opined that a store's design and merchandising standards can influence customer theft activity. "Wide, clear aisles, a clean, well maintained interior...with the cashier's view unblocked by high shelves..." all contribute to minimizing shoplifting according to this research. These views have also been preached by loss prevention personnel for years but are now supported by recognized research.

Most store owners recognize that all sorts of people shoplift, and if steps are not taken to minimize the loss of profit from these thefts, they can jeopardize the very existence of the business. Thus, it is essential for profit protection that careful attention be paid not only to preventive steps but also to an analysis of where losses are occurring so that remedial action can be taken. Since shoplifting occurs on selling floors, from unsecured stockrooms, and from fitting rooms, employee awareness of the potential for loss and those steps which will minimize the temptation for customers to steal should become a major management objective.

Retailers should familiarize themselves with the various strategies and tactics for combating shoplifting. We mention various of these strategies here and suggest further interest in specifics should be directed toward any of the available resources, including books, security/loss prevention periodicals, national and local retail associations, and local loss prevention organizations. Areas which may impact shoplifting losses either positively or negatively are

- Customer service levels;
- Merchandise presentation;
- Employee awareness;
- Signage;
- Display design;
- Register locations;
- Fitting room controls;
- Stockroom controls;
- Lock and key controls;
- Use of CCTV;
- Use of electronic article surveillance tags;
- Use of other article benefit denial tags and/or techniques;
- Use of uniformed and/or nonuniformed loss prevention personnel.

Management Attitudes Toward Shrinkage

We support the prevention-over-apprehension philosophy but recognize that some on-going level of shoplifting is inevitable, despite all preventative efforts. In those instances, the staff must be aware of company policy on how to deal with persons seen shoplifting. Company policy can follow one of a number of options:

1. Obtain a description of the shoplifter, write a report, and notify police.
2. Attempt to prevent the theft by making your presence known, causing the "shoplifter" to "dump" (discard) the merchandise.
3. Allow for legally detaining the shoplifter

Option 3 carries with it the necessity to make the detention legal to avoid potential civil liability and also presents a variety and/or combination of possible actions after the detention, including

- Retrieve the merchandise, identify the offender, carefully document the incident, obtain a signed admission, caution the offender, and turn him loose; this procedure is known as "Warn and Release."

- Release the suspect under the condition that if he repeats the offense within 1 year, he will be prosecuted for both offenses.
- Detain the suspect and after his arrest initiate criminal prosecution.
- Ban the person from the store (or all company stores) for a period up to 1 year.
- Initiate action to recover civil damages.
- Negotiate the suspect's enrollment in a rehabilitation/educational program designed to change the suspect's behavior and prevent recidivism.

The necessity to make a legal detention cannot be overstated! Significant potential legal liability inures if a shoplifter suspect is wrongfully or improperly detained. The guidelines for meeting the legal requirements are contained in state criminal laws commonly known as "Merchants Detention Statutes." These statutes, which vary from state to state, generally provide civil liability protection to the merchant if the merchant has what is legally known as "probable cause" for believing the person detained has, or has attempted to, illegally take the merchant's property. These statutes also set other requirements and/or restrictions on the merchant's behavior.

What Is Probable (Reasonable) Cause?

Probable cause is best defined as existing when the facts and circumstances (known to the arresting person) are sufficient in themselves to warrant a reasonable person to believe that an offense has been committed or is being committed by the person to be arrested. How can the merchant or his loss prevention operative establish probable cause? Does any degree of suspicion rise to the probable cause level? Is second-hand information sufficient to establish probable cause?

In an effort to make establishing probable cause uniform within the retail industry and remove individual interpretations and/or definitions of a complex legal concept, the industry has generally accepted the "six steps" as the standard for assuring that, to the extent humanly possible, the probable cause requirement has been met when the six steps have all been met. While the steps are not a legal requirement for establishing probable cause, they do provide an understandable, objective, and easily articulated standard easily understood by LP personnel, leaving no room for creativity in determining if probable cause exists and minimizing situations which may put the retailer at civil risk.

The "six steps" are

1. You must maintain an uninterrupted surveillance to ensure that the suspect doesn't dispose of the merchandise.
2. You must see the suspect approach the merchandise.
3. You must see the suspect fail to pay for the merchandise
4. You must see the suspect take possession of the merchandise.
5. You must see where the suspect conceals the merchandise.
6. You should approach the suspect outside the store.

The establishment of probable cause does not mean the retailer is now out of the woods when detaining shoplifters. Merchant detention statutes, while permitting detention on probable cause of shoplifting, also set requirements for the conduct of the retailer after the detention is made. A breach of these requirements, or other conduct which is injurious to the suspect, also makes the retailer vulnerable to a civil suit for damages. What are these restrictions on the retailer's conduct?

Merchant detention statutes generally permit detention for the purpose of conducting an investigation into the ownership of the merchandise in question, and such investigation must be conducted in a reasonable manner and for a reasonable time. The merchant's ability to search the suspect for stolen property is either prohibited or limited by these statutes, as may be the retailer's ability to photograph and/or positively identify the suspect.

With regard to the arrest of the suspect, once it has been positively established a shoplift has occurred, we suggest you consult the appropriate state law and/or an attorney. Some states permit a "citizen's arrest" under these circumstances, whereas others permit only detaining the shoplifter until the arrival of the police, who actually make the arrest.

There are still more areas of potential grief for the retailer when detaining shoplifters, including committing (either intentionally or unintentionally) the following torts (civil wrongs):

- *False Imprisonment/Arrest:* The intentional, unjustified detention or confinement of a person (imprisonment); unlawful restraint of another's person's liberty or freedom of locomotion (arrest). *Note:* This may also be a criminal offense.
- *Assault/Battery*: Unconsented to or unprivileged physical contact or privileged contact which become unreasonable. *Note:* This may also be a criminal offense.
- *Malicious Prosecution*: Prosecution (civil or criminal) with malice (evil intent). To succeed, prosecution must have resulted in verdict for defendant and prosecution initiated without probable cause.
- *Invasion of Privacy*: Invading someone's reasonable expectation of privacy.
- *Defamation (Libel-Slander):* Written or spoken words that tend to damage another's reputation. *Defenses:* Truth, privileges (qualified and absolute)
- *Tortious Infliction of Emotional Distress*: Intentionally and maliciously inflicting emotional distress on another.

In torts, the element of "reasonableness" is a key factor. Just what is this concept of reasonableness? Essentially, actions which are reasonable are those which a hypothetically prudent, reasonably intelligent person would consider to meet the judgment that society requires of its members for the protection of their own interests and the interests of others. Conversely, actions which outrage, vex, appear malicious or excessive, or tend to make a person angry when considering the alternatives available may be considered "unreasonable."

Since the test of negligence or appropriate behavior when reviewing intentional torts is reasonableness, the ability to avoid unreasonableness is essential. How does someone avoid being unreasonable? Since the question of reasonable behavior is one of fact for a jury to decide, no black-and-white answer can be given. However, if a person knows the concept and limits his behavior to actions that are demonstratively necessary and prudent, and which do not exceed the bounds of propriety, and which would not be offensive to the average person under the circumstances, then chances are those actions, if reviewed, will be considered reasonable.

Malice, as mentioned earlier, is something done solely to annoy or vex; something that is done out of ill will with no justification and in wanton and willful disregard of the likelihood that harm will result. Malicious acts can never be reasonable.

May we suggest that, for a fuller understanding of the implications of these legal aspects of a shoplifting detention, you review the section "Legal Considerations" for more details.

As stated elsewhere, what may appear to be a simple process (catching a shoplifter) is really quite legally complex. After probable cause for the detention is established and all the requirements (or prohibitions) of investigating the incident are met, properly executing other actions not specified in statutes is also essential to a subsequent successful prosecution. For example, the collection, documentation, and preservation of any evidence (e.g., the stolen merchandise) is extremely important. If the collection or preservation of evidence does not meet accepted legal standards, it may be excluded from admission into evidence at the criminal trial, resulting in the dismissal of the charges against the suspect, opening the door to a possible civil suit for false arrest or malicious prosecution. Careless publication of a suspect's arrest may violate his privacy rights; the use of excessive force may negate an otherwise totally justified arrest and result in being sued.

Because the process of dealing with a shoplifter is fraught with so many dangers unless adroitly handled, documenting the details of how it was handled takes on a vital role. An unbiased, accurate, and detailed written report of all phases of a reasonably conducted detention/arrest is the retailer's best friend if challenged as to the propriety of his actions. A well-written, complete report is a best friend to the defense of a civil suit.

Anything else which requires mention regarding shoplifting? You bet; we're not quite finished yet.

Consider "questionable" stops (sometimes referred to as "bad stops" or a variety of euphemisms such as NPD or nonproductive detention). However they are referred to, they are shoplift detentions where no stolen merchandise is found. Such situations are invitations for civil suits for false arrest/imprisonment unless properly and adroitly handled. Questionable detentions may result from an agent's carelessness in simply ignoring the six-step requirement or from a "customer" who intentionally sets up a situation to appear like a shoplift, hoping the store will make a detention and set the stage for a civil suit. In either event, how such situations are handled will go a long way toward determining the eventual outcome.

We suggest that. in questionable detention situations, the following rules be followed:

1. Avoid accusatory confrontations.
2. Avoid any further physical contact with the "shoplifter."
3. Courteously admit your mistake.
4. Disengage quickly.

The store will normally know shortly after the event whether it will result in further action by the offended customer. We suggest that the store take the initiative after such an event and contact the customer, apologize again, and see what action the store might take to set the matter right. Perhaps sending a dozen red roses or offering to send a gift certificate (in an amount which is not overly large but which will also not offend by its meagerness). Letters of apology for the inconvenience caused the customer, if sincerely and properly written, are also often helpful. Remember, the objective is to avoid getting attorneys involved and to forestall the filing of a lawsuit.

A final note on the subject of potential lawsuits: Whenever a complaint is made against loss prevention personnel or the handling by them of a specific incident, it is incumbent on store management to thoroughly investigate that complaint. One would hope that by reviewing written reports and interviewing percipient witnesses, the complaint will be shown to be unfounded. Occasionally, however, a complaint will be determined to have merit. When this is the case, it is vital that not only is appropriate disciplinary action taken against offending personnel, but that every effort be made, within reason, to satisfy the aggrieved party.

See the index for "Litigation Control"; covered elsewhere herein is the use of civil remedy or civil demand.

Shoplifting, Definition

CAS, JHC

Shoplifting is the act of committing theft from a retailer by a person who is or purports to be a customer, during the hours the store is open for business. The seriousness or gravity of the act depends on the value of the goods stolen and the method used to commit the theft; e.g., if a person enters a store with certain "tools" or devices to be used in the theft, that may constitute a felonious crime, such as burglary (as opposed to simple theft or larceny). The value of the merchandise stolen is also used to determine if theft is a felony or a misdemeanor. Employees who steal merchandise are not engaged in "shoplifting" (unless off duty and engaging in shopping, which is rare, or are in a sister store, unknown to the employees and appearing to be a customer and while therein commit theft).

Burglars who hide in a store at closing time for purposes of committing theft are not "shoplifters," nor are those criminals who break into a store while it's closed and remove merchandise.

Shoplifting and Organized Retail Theft

Karl Langhorst

All retailers, large and small, regardless of the type of merchandise they sell, are faced with the same problem: shoplifting. This is the theft of product by customers or supposed customers who either don't want to pay for it or in some cases cannot afford to pay for the items they are stealing.

Shoplifting has most likely been around since about one minute after the first retail store opened. The temptation to steal is too great for some people, and the reasons they give are many. But at the end of the day, shoplifters, like employees, steal for one of three reasons: need/greed, justification, or opportunity.

Everyone has need for food, shelter, and clothing. Sometimes shoplifters steal because they simply cannot meet the needs for themselves or their family. Many times, though, people think they need something when, in fact, they just "greed" something. Maybe it is a new pair of designer sunglasses or the latest video that they can't afford or simply just don't want to pay for. Shoplifters will sometimes try to justify their actions to themselves and others by saying that the store can afford to take the loss. "After all, retailers make a lot of money right? What's one less leather jacket going to hurt?" Or "Besides, last time I was in here they overcharged me on something I bought." A very popular line from shoplifters who are trying to justify their actions when caught is "I was in a hurry and they did not have enough check stands open."

Retailers' best defense against controlling shoplifting is by not giving shoplifters the opportunity to steal something from them in the first place. That does not mean that all the merchandise in a store can or should be locked up. After all, customers in many cases want to see and touch what they are buying. For customers to do this, the majority of merchandise cannot be locked up in display cases or merchandised behind a sales counter.

Most shoplifters will tell you that if they are denied privacy in a store, they cannot have the opportunity to steal. One of the best defenses retailers have to combat shoplifters is attentive sales associates. Deterring shoplifters is a much more productive and cost-effective methodology in preventing shoplifting in a retail establishment than simply relying on apprehending them. Well-trained sales associates can deter shoplifters through direct eye contact and by way of positive verbal communication skills. Simply approaching shoplifters and asking them if they need assistance and letting them know that you will be in the area if they need anything can go a long way in helping to prevent theft from occurring in the first place. The simple fact is that shoplifters hate to be noticed and customers do. Through the implementation of a strong customer service program, retailers can increase their customer satisfaction ratings while at the same time reduce the amount of their losses due to shoplifting. It can be a win/win situation.

Much research has been conducted on trying to develop a stereotypical profile of the type of person who shoplifts. And for the most part, the research has reflected that anyone can be a potential shoplifter regardless of socioeconomic status, gender, age, race, or cultural background. For a retailer to develop a profile of a stereotypical shoplifter is to do a disservice to not only their patrons, but to their shareholders as well. This philosophy not only could be deemed prejudicial and result in unwanted civil litigation, but could also improperly direct the apprehension or deterrence efforts of a retailer toward the wrong group or groups of people, thereby increasing the risk of losses.

Retailers should also have in place a very well-defined set of guidelines on how to address situations in which shoplifters become physically confrontational. As the likelihood of civil litigation and physical harm to employees increases, it is becoming even more important to make sure that associates are well educated and trained on how to deal with physical altercations with shoplifters. Over the years many retailers have transitioned away from the traditional approach of detaining shoplifters "at any cost" and replaced it with a more nonconfrontational, verbal-force-only approach. The likelihood of physical assaults at the hands of shoplifters seems to be a growing trend. Many would argue that this is as a result of the evolving of shoplifters from what has been perceived as the stereotypical person who has fallen on bad times and is just trying to support his family to a much more modern and realistic portrayal of shoplifters who are known criminals, drug users, and in some cases are actually members of organized retail theft rings. Regardless of the reason why a nonphysical confrontational methodology is being adopted by many retailers, the positive outcome is that the industry is starting to realize that these types of situations have an increased propensity for violence, and that at the end of the day there is absolutely nothing inside any retail establishment that is worth someone's life.

However, retailers cannot afford to avoid taking an aggressive stance toward shoplifters. A relatively new and growing trend in shoplifting is the emergence of organized theft rings. For years, most shoplifters have worked independently of each other or in loosely knit groups. This is no longer the case. Organized retail theft today is becoming an increasingly growing problem that is starting to unite the retail industry. Estimates vary on the losses to the industry, but most sources indicate that it is at least $30 billion annually. Whatever the amount, most retailers have determined that the traditional communication barriers that have been in place in the past between retailers have allowed theft of this type to continually grow to the extent that those barriers are now being slowly dismantled. Professional shoplifters or "boosters" have grown increasingly organized in their efforts to shoplift merchandise from retailers. Much like a retailer's regular customers, boosters enter into stores with a shopping list of goods to steal. They obtain these lists from the individual or individuals called "fences" who buy the stolen property from them. Fences understand what commodities are most desired by the consumer market and as such will give detailed instructions to boosters on what they will buy from them and how much they will give them for the product. Once the fence receives the product, he will dispose of it in several different manners. Flea markets and Internet websites are two popular locations to dispose of stolen merchandise.

Additionally, some fences are sophisticated enough that they have developed a distribution network to repackage the stolen product so that it appears to have come from the original manufacturer. Then they resell it on what is called a "diverter" market. This market is a legitimate means in which retailers buy product from other retailers who have overstocked on a particular item. However, it also provides an easy avenue to dispose of stolen product as well, and sometimes unsuspecting merchants buy product from an illegitimate diverter that was stolen from their own stores. Boosters typically work in a team when they target a retail establishment. Usually, there is a driver waiting in the parking lot for the team that goes inside. This driver is in constant communication via cell phone with the team "lookout" whose job is to spot the product in the store to be stolen and look for any security devices and store personnel who might prove to be a hindrance to the theft. Once the lookout determines that it is safe for the booster or boosters to steal the product, he will signal them as well as signal a "blocker." The blocker acts as a legitimate customer and will usually position himself between the booster and any detected obstacles to the theft such as a CCTV camera or store personnel so that they act as a visual screen. The booster will then load the product to be stolen into his clothing, purse, backpack, or even a legitimate store bag he brought in with him.

Sometimes boosters will even utilize aluminum foil to line a purse or backpack because it prevents electronic article surveillance systems that many retailers use from detecting the radio frequency tags that are typically placed on high-theft products. These tags are deactivated at the register when the product is purchased and, when not deactivated, cause an audible alarm to go off at the store exit, alerting management that merchandise that still has an active tag on it is being removed from the store.

If boosters believe they have been detected by store personnel they will typically abandon the stolen product and leave the store. However, some boosters, because of gang affiliations, drug use, and/or lengthy criminal histories, are becoming increasingly violent in their response when approached by store personnel. This is another reason why retailers should have trained staff who understand the risks that are inherent in dealing with shoplifters and this type of criminal activity.

Because of the increase of shoplifting and the damage that it can cause to the profitability of a company, many retailers have sought out assistance from law enforcement agencies to help in combating this problem. By continuing to educate and communicate with law enforcement about the problems of shoplifting, retailers increase the likelihood that a cooperative partnership can be formed that will help to reduce the occurrence of this crime in their businesses.

Shortage Awareness Programs

CAS, JHC

Employee awareness of shortage (shrinkage)—its causes and what can be done to minimize it—is generally agreed to be an essential part of shortage reduction efforts. Indeed, without employee awareness and involvement, an effective effort to reduce inventory shrinkage would be impotent.

Shortage awareness programs exist to increase and heighten employee shortage awareness and encourage their active participation in store shortage reduction. The best shortage reduction programs should be entertaining and informative, encourage participation, and offer "rewards" to participating employees. We believe the thrust of any program should be grounded on the answer to the employees' unspoken but ever present question, "What's in it for me?" Put another way, the store leaders who create and lead shortage awareness programs must address the issue of why store associates should care about inventory shrinkage. Too many retail employees have no understanding or clue as to profitability and have a distorted understanding as to the profit margin of their employer.

There is no "best" or "recommended" shortage reduction program as long as it includes answers to "What's in it for me?" and a clear understanding of profit and what mistakes and thefts mean in relationship to profit.

For example, with respect to "what's in it for me?" the message or theme can be "Profit builds more stores and more stores means more supervisors and managers."

Here's an example with respect to understanding the significance of thefts: If a $100 item of merchandise is stolen and the store works on a 5% profit margin, the employee must be educated to understand the store must sell 20 more of the $100 items to recover the loss. There are different ways that can be done. What is done will be depend on the extent of the problem, size of the store, history of prior programs, age and tenure of employees, and ability of the program leader to establish enthusiasm.

It's a fact that successful shortage reduction starts at the top of the management ladder with participation in and enthusiastic endorsement of reduction programs. Senior management must become active participants in such programs and demonstrate their commitment to these efforts.

The format of shortage reduction programs can be as varied as the imagination is creative. Among those ideas which have proven successful are

- Shortage trivia questions;
- Shortage clue games;
- Shortage crossword puzzles, which may be included in a specific program or in a monthly "Shrinkage Alert" newsletter;
- Morning PA announcements regarding shortage reduction;
- Periodic storewide shortage meetings which should recognize specific employees who prevented a theft or discovered a serious oversight or shortage in an interstore transfer;
- Formation of a shortage committee, with photos of employees on the committee posted in the break room;
- Use of shortage-control-related posters (e.g., new stores are built on profits, not losses) in employee break/lunch room;
- Inventory "message of the day,", which can be posted at the employee's entrance or announced over the store's PA system before opening. During the day, the manager randomly asks any associate what that message is. If the employee remembers the message, he receives a $5 gift card.

The specific program or idea used is not the most important aspect of shortage reduction; rather, the program is the vehicle to generate interest, resulting in broad participation and increased awareness. While a store may have a shortage awareness week or month, the real secret to shortage reduction is a consistent emphasis on monitoring and immediately correcting those things which create shortage, such as failure to

- Recognize and acknowledge customers in their areas;
- Reticket mispriced items;
- Account for and properly record markdowns;
- Record breakage and RTV merchandise;
- Record all merchandise during inventory counts;
- Keep a neat and organized selling floor;
- Immediately acknowledge all customers;
- Control access to stockrooms;
- Note and record found tickets or other indicia of theft;
- Properly monitor fitting rooms;
- Keep price lookup systems up-to-date;
- Control markdown pens;
- Properly account for interstore transfers;
- Properly train new hires regarding shortage;
- Control access to small, expensive, high-pilferage merchandise;
- Exercise proper key control.

The ultimate goal is to achieve a storewide interest in and concern about inventory and how the collective effort of everyone will benefit the company and, in return, their role and future in the company.

Shrinkage Reduction: A Plan that Actually Reduces Shrink

David Gorman

Senior Management Sets the Tone

The tools that have generally been accepted by retailers to reduce shrinkage losses, such as EAS and CCTV, are widely available and extensively deployed. Likewise, the formation of a loss prevention or assets protection division charged with the establishment and execution of shrinkage reduction initiatives is a very common aspect of any retailer's organizational chart. If you accept these statements as accurate, then a question is necessarily raised regarding how the wide variances in shrinkage losses between one retailer and another can be explained. If the same solutions are applied, how can the results achieved be so dissimilar? As is true with any particular aspect of a successful business enterprise, the level of involvement and support that senior management gives to the control of shrinkage is critical to the success of those efforts. Losses attributable to shrinkage, if not closely monitored and controlled, will have a significantly negative impact on the profitability and sustainability of any company in much the same way as declining revenues or escalating expenses will. Each element must be continuously evaluated with appropriate actions taken whenever results do not match expectations.

You would be hard pressed to find any member of senior management who would not respond in the affirmative if asked whether the control of shrinkage losses was critical to their business. Likewise, most would feel that their level of involvement in these efforts was adequate to establish the priority level needed to achieve the expected results. Unfortunately, this many times is simply not the case.

The key role of senior management, as relates to shrinkage, is threefold. First of all, they must be well versed in the current shrinkage trends, as well as understand the overall elements and objectives of the shrinkage reduction program. Second, they must be seen as advocates of the process. This can be accomplished by their regularly taking the opportunity to discuss specific aspects of the program which may or may not be receiving the required attention or execution level, and offering their assistance if needed. Last, they must acknowledge the results of newly completed store inventories, both positive and negative, and provide the leadership required to reestablish the commitment to necessary programs and goals.

This personal involvement by senior management in the process will place the control of shrinkage losses in its proper place along with the other challenges facing the business and clearly demonstrate that it is a priority for the management group as a whole.

Communicate Results: Both Successes and Failures

Retailers generally perform store inventories on a cycle basis between the months of January through October. This process provides the best opportunity to communicate the results of those during each of the weeks in which inventories are taken. Exactly how this communication takes place depends on each individual company.

Many companies have regularly scheduled weekly meetings which are attended by operations, merchandising, and other headquarters personnel. While the main purpose of these meetings will generally be sales and sales-related topics, they also offer the best opportunity to review both weekly and year-to-date shrinkage results, as well as analyze specific shrinkage issues and solutions. Properly formatted, each week's inventory results can be summarized to provide a clear understanding of overall loss trends as compared to previous years. Depending on the level of detail provided by the physical inventory process itself, similar trends could possibly also be reviewed for key merchandise departments or even specific items (SKUs).

Presentations of the type described will inevitably generate comments and discussions among those present and provide an excellent opportunity for senior management and others to weigh in on the progress being made in the shrinkage effort, or the lack of it. While this type of discussion will certainly generate some level of discomfort during the meetings, it will also squarely establish shrinkage reduction as an important goal which everyone is expected to be attentive to. Where the meeting process described here is not available, the information should be provided in a report format and distributed at the end of each week. In this circumstance, consideration must be given to providing a summary (2 pages maximum) which is both informative and actionable. The first page of the summary might include bullet points of specific highlights from that week's results. Copies of the report should be forwarded to executive management and all department heads. Executives wishing more information on specific inventories shown in this summary can then refer to the more detailed reports available. Again, this provides senior management with an opportunity to acknowledge positive results or raise questions regarding results which did not meet goals.

While the benefits of regularly communicating inventory results are fairly obvious, there is another major benefit that is not. A weekly analysis of shrinkage results, against last year, provides a continuous measurement of the effectiveness of current shrinkage initiatives. As a result, the opportunity exists for adjustments to be made where specific parts of the program are not having the desired impact, or where areas of shrinkage are identified which are not addressed by the current program. It will generally fall to the loss prevention/assets protection group to identify these opportunities and appropriate solutions. Along with this will come the need for LP/AP to coordinate with other areas of the company (such as operations or ISD) and secure their support and participation in the new initiatives.

Shrinkage—Controllable Versus Noncontrollable

Shrinkage losses for any retail organization will ultimately become a line item on the company's Profit and Loss (P&L) statement. While these losses clearly represent an expense, they are unlike most other expense categories which can usually be tracked and monitored on a daily basis. There would be little disagreement that some shrinkage loss occurs each day during the normal course of business. However, the exact amount of that loss can only be known, and properly expensed, following a physical inventory.

Additionally, it is important to recognize that regular and detailed information for other expense items such as payroll allow store management to make appropriate adjustments in the level of spending, and thereby avoid an over-budget result. The reality is that very little can be done to avoid a shrinkage loss which has already occurred by the time it is identified. This circumstance can easily create a sense that shrinkage losses represent an expense which is really noncontrollable. Nothing could be further from the truth.

In a very broad sense, the whole discussion of shrinkage, and a programmed response to it, really starts with a company culture that believes that such losses are completely controllable; furthermore, that the progression of losses must be monitored and dealt with like any other controllable expense on the P&L. If that attitude is part of the belief system within a company, then all the things that would normally be done to keep that expense under control become clearer. If that attitude exists, management at all levels will understand the importance of their daily involvement and their personal accountability for failing to do so. If it is not, then there can be little expectation that any shrinkage reduction program will actually affect the results.

It is here that senior management plays a critical role in establishing the correct thought process.

Know Your Company's Shrinkage Tolerance Level

It is very unlikely that a member of senior management within any retail organization would state that the company does not have a very low tolerance level for shrinkage losses. This would seem to be especially logical if you consider that losses due to shrinkage represent one of the few P&L line items for which a company receives absolutely no benefit.

At this point, however, if senior management is not setting the tone relative to shrinkage response, if inventory results are not widely communicated, and if it is not made clear whether these losses are considered controllable or noncontrollable, then it will not really matter what is *said* about the tolerance level. In this situation, what is really communicated is that a low shrinkage is hoped for, but a higher result is understood and tolerated.

To determine what a company's true level of shrinkage tolerance is, you must merely observe what amount of shrinkage is required before a concern or sense of urgency is expressed. Put another way, what happens when a specific shrinkage goal is not achieved by a store, a district, or a region? In practice, if the stated goal is 1.00%, but specific concerns are voiced only in those instances in which results reach 1.70% or higher, then the true tolerance level is something just under 1.70%. This tolerance level will also more closely represent the actual shrinkage result achieved by the company than either past history or stated goals.

Changing a tolerance level within a company which has previously provided somewhat conflicting messages will require a serious commitment to do so. It is human nature to resist change. To implement a new thought process about something as potentially involved as shrinkage prevention will require an aggressive and determined effort.

Poor Performance Should Require Heightened Effort

Any effective shrinkage reduction program contains a number of elements that generally apply to all operating locations, as well as other key aspects of the business enterprise. These elements represent the basic parts of the program that are proven to reduce shrinkage, and that members of management throughout the company are expected to execute.

However, if you adhere to the business philosophy that 80% of the problems impacting the business are caused by 20% of the operation, then it would follow that those problem aspects should receive more attention than the group as a whole. Another motivation for taking this additional step is that a focus on your biggest opportunities should also provide the largest return on investment (ROI) for your efforts. As sound as this logic appears, the development of specific program elements to address high shrinkage locations and functions is not necessarily a common practice within the retail industry. In fact, it is not at all uncommon to find companies that will continue to approach solving their shrinkage problems in the same way as they always have, but somehow expect different results to occur.

Carrying on with this thought process, it is important to structure a High Shrinkage Response Plan that can be implemented whenever inventory results do not meet goal. While the construction of this plan will depend somewhat on the culture of each company and how things are best accomplished within that environment, an effective plan would normally contain the following elements. While these particular elements relate to a store location, the same thought processes could be used in a distribution center or other operation.

Executive Shrinkage Committee

One of the most effective processes any company can put in place to bring attention and change to shrinkage losses is to establish an Executive Shrinkage Committee. Members should include the CEO, COO, CFO, Head of Merchandising, and the Heads of Distribution, Internal Audit, and Loss Prevention/Asset Protection. The purpose of this committee would be to evaluate the results of, and provide support and leadership for, all aspects of the shrinkage reduction program.

This committee generally meets on a monthly schedule and reviews updated shrinkage information as presented by internal audit and LP/AP, as well as make decisions as needed to strengthen the overall effort.

Thorough Audit of the Location

The best approach to this audit would be for it to involve a combined effort between the internal audit and loss prevention/assets protection departments. The purpose of this exercise is to conduct a detailed review of all store procedures and systems which could possibly have contributed to the loss that occurred. The results must be widely communicated and used as a roadmap in the development of specific action plans for the store during the coming inventory period.

Another important aspect would be holding informal discussions with small groups of store personnel throughout the location. The exercise of asking their views of specific issues which they feel contributed to the loss will not only uncover valuable information, but will also ensure that these individuals understand their critical role in the correction going forward. In circumstances in which it is felt that personnel might be uncomfortable in sharing their views openly, a confidential survey can be administered and summarized to achieve the feedback needed.

The internal audit and loss prevention departments should also maintain a list of the common shrinkage-causing factors identified during the course of these audits. These shrinkage commonalities can then be communicated to all operating locations in an effort to correct those issues prior to future inventories and also to identify enterprisewide solutions which can easily be implemented.

An example of an enterprisewide solution would include a processing error which is commonly found as occurring during the checkin of received merchandise. Can the identified process be altered or systemized to eliminate or dramatically reduce the error's occurrence? If so, the correction will continue to pay dividends year after year.

Action Plans Developed for Store Personnel

It is important that key personnel throughout the store understand the overall store shrinkage results as well as those specific to their area of responsibility. For example, a department manager should know the shrinkage result for his department and have specific plans to address those issues which contributed to the losses within his area. These plans are developed in conjunction with store management and are intended to keep each department focused on the specific actions needed during the coming year to improve the shrinkage performance.

Store management not only must ensure the existence of these plans, but must follow up during the course of the year to verify that the agreed-upon actions are taking place. Issues and solutions which are common to all departments should be raised on a regular basis during store meetings. These discussions serve to reinforce the importance of shrinkage reduction to the profitability of the store.

Specific Shrinkage Training for Store Management

It should not be assumed that all members of store management understand the potential areas for shrinkage within their store or how to identify and correct those issues. To provide them with the tools they will need to reduce the losses in the coming year, management should give serious consideration to providing shrinkage-related training to all management personnel who suffered losses above a specified level.

It must always be remembered that the most critical objective of any shrinkage meeting is to leave the management in attendance with an overall sense of responsibility for fixing the problem. They must also leave with a level of confidence that the things that have been covered with them during the course of the meeting will, if properly executed, improve their losses dramatically.

The manager's sense of responsibility will come only if he perceives that his leadership agrees that he should have it. This is easily accomplished by having several senior members of management help start the meeting and address its purpose as well as the benefits that can come from the training. It is also a good idea to test the attendees on the material to be covered, both at the beginning and at the end of the training. This will provide some data as to management's overall level of understanding of basic processes when they arrived, as well as following the training.

Time should be allotted to provide for a review of the managers' High Shrinkage Response Plan that was developed after the inventory was completed but prior to arrival for training. This will place an additional emphasis on the seriousness of the circumstance and provide the management staff an opportunity to address any concerns they have relative to having the tools they will need to carry out their plan. It must also be understood that these meetings must be conducted in a positive and constructive manner. While it is good business practice to deal with shrinkage problems in a straightforward manner, there will certainly be managers present who arrived at the store in question either just prior to or just after the inventory. Having them feel that their abilities are being questioned over a problem that they did not create is not appropriate. They must see their responsibility as taking a problem that exists and fixing it.

Have Broad Accountability

Like many other aspects of the business, real success in shrinkage reduction is dependent on the concerted effort of a number of different areas of the company—not the least of which is the loss prevention/assets protection division, which plays a critical role that is clearly understood. For the purpose of our discussion here, however, we are going to concentrate on three other key areas: operations, merchandising, and distribution. Senior management must understand the critical role each of these areas plays and ensure that the control of shrinkage is a fundamental part of the thought process employed by each in the daily performance of responsibilities.

Operations

The operations group has the main responsibility for the overall management, control of expenses, and profitability of the stores. As has been discussed previously, a store's shrinkage performance will directly impact profitability and, as a result, must be of paramount concern.

Operations, then, must take the leadership role in the execution of any shrinkage reduction program, including the day-to-day communication relative to this issue with all involved store personnel. While it must certainly be handled with care, the discussion of employee theft should occasionally be part of this communication. If you assume that the majority of the store's workforce is made up of honest people, then it follows that those individuals would want to work with others who were also honest. If the management staff make it clear that they are interested in knowing about issues of employee theft and that they will protect the confidence of all individuals who provide information, then it is very likely that information will be revealed as incidents occur. Equally as important, store management must also provide constant guidance on areas of observed shrinkage that are not being addressed by the company as a whole. To accomplish this latter responsibility, store managers must feel that they are not only empowered, but also duty bound to bring these issues to the surface. Likewise, senior management must actively encourage the analysis of any issue that could potentially be contributing to loss, irrespective of departmental boundaries.

This being said, it cannot be assumed that operations should be in any way solely responsible for the success of company shrinkage initiatives.

Merchandising

While the role that operations and loss prevention play in controlling shrinkage losses cannot be overstated, there are clearly other areas that can significantly contribute to the achievement of corporate shrinkage goals. For example, an involved and supportive merchandising division can substantially enhance shrinkage performance at both the store and distribution center level. However, this can be achieved only if the senior management staff set the expectation that a portion of a buyer's overall performance criteria will be the shortage losses within his department.

What is important to understand in this whole discussion is not that each buyer somehow must develop his own shrinkage initiatives, but that the efforts which he makes contribute to the overall shrinkage reduction plan of the corporation. In other words, the solutions which the buyer assists with should provide answers to issues which are creating loss at the store and distribution center level. The biggest opportunity for merchandising to assist in this way really centers on packaging improvements, source tagging initiatives, and display design for the specific products within the departments which are highly theft prone.

To achieve this objective, it is important that loss prevention have a close working relationship with the buyers involved in high-shrinkage departments, for them to be able to provide assistance in the identification of high-loss products and in coordinating with product suppliers to enhance packaging or to implement source tagging. The buyers, in turn, must fully support the shrinkage initiatives and serve as the company's representative with the appropriate suppliers to ensure the initiatives are implemented.

Distribution

As has been discussed, it is critical to the success of any shrinkage reduction program that store management personnel recognize and accepts their responsibility for their inventory result completely and without reservation. They must believe that it is totally within their power to effect a positive result, which would include the identification and correction of any issues which could create shrinkage.

With many retailers, a large percentage of store shipments arrive through the company's own distribution center network. As a result, this process must be seen as accurate to the extent that there can be no measurable impact of errors on store inventory results. To support this, there should be a process for correcting significant errors or incorrect shipments once found and verified. Only in this way can the issue be identified and dealt with at its source and provide the confidence that stores must have in the process.

Distribution management personnel must accept their responsibility to provide accurate deliveries and take ownership for errors which occur that should not be charged to the store. Even though the correction of these errors will not affect the total losses for the corporation, it will place the loss on the appropriate P&L.

Set Higher Expectations Every Year

Just as sales and profits are expected to improve each year, shrinkage losses must also consistently improve. In an environment where this is not the case, it tends to become somewhat of a self-fulfilling prophecy. Following a year of acceptable shrinkage, where the history of a roller-coaster performance exists, it will generally increase the following year. Everyone expects it to happen, so no one is surprised when it does. This, of course, has less to do with bad luck and more to do with a lack of effort and focus. It is widely accepted that shrinkage results will follow effort by as much as 12 months. Therefore, a company which allows its focus and attention on shrinkage to wane following an acceptable year will very likely experience an increase in shrinkage the following year that will not be acceptable. As a result, it is critical to set challenging, yet obtainable, shrinkage goals every year. Senior management staff must remind everyone at the outset of each inventory period what the goal is and what their expectations are for its achievement. A truly effective shrinkage reduction program is one that produces positive results year after year.

Considerations for Cultural Change

In a perfect environment where the culture of your company will embrace the shrinkage reduction ideas described here, the only thing left to do is implement and execute. Where this is not the case, then, more work will need to be done. Where senior management staff are hesitant or unwilling to implement the admittedly aggressive elements of the shrinkage reduction program outlined in this section, then it falls to the loss prevention/asset protection executive to carefully address the concerns and secure the support of those individuals.

The best process to follow to achieve the desired end will vary somewhat depending on what specific concerns have been voiced by senior management. LP/AP must carefully listen to these concerns and establish an overall strategy to address them. Part of that strategy will certainly involve providing detailed information which clearly shows the shrinkage problems that the program is intended to resolve. Management must understand the size of the problem to clearly put into prospective the return on investment that will come from the effort being recommended.

In circumstances such as this, it is generally always appropriate to demonstrate the effectiveness of your program through a test in a specific area prior to requesting its implementation everywhere. Establish criteria that will show the success (i.e., heightened awareness of shrinkage problems and solutions, reduced losses in the test area, etc.) and ensure that these can be assessed during the course of the test. Make certain to keep the decision makers informed relative to preliminary results as the test is progressing and listen carefully for any suggestions as to how the test can be altered or improved. Quickly implement those changes that are right to do. Be prepared to demonstrate an achievable return on investment and be flexible as to how many capital resources are required to perform the test. One consideration should be to identify a member of operations (district manager or regional vice president) who would be willing to support the test within his respective area. It will be important to the success of this test to have the involvement of someone who can help describe the benefits he experienced as a result of his participation. Of special interest will be comments from affected store managers as to the impact of the program on their store employees. Again, did the increased training and awareness relative to shrinkage opportunities have a positive effect on both the overall operation of the store and the reduction of losses?

Always remember to prioritize the things you need in order to accomplish your goals. Effectively demonstrate how those things will add profit and value to the company. Build partnerships based on respect and trust, which can help you in your efforts to implement new processes within the corporation. Work to ensure that you and your group are viewed as students of the entire business, not just of your specific area of responsibility. Above all, enjoy what you do!

Small Claims Court

CAS, JHC

Small claims courts exist to provide citizens (and noncitizens) with a means of settling minor business and financial disputes without the necessity of hiring attorneys and filing full-blown lawsuits. In most instances, attorneys are barred from representing small claims litigants; the litigant appears personally to face his opposite number before a judge, who will normally render an immediate decision after listening to both sides and examining any documentary evidence or witnesses. In some venues there is an appeal process if the losing party feels particularly strongly that the case was improperly decided.

The small claims court is the venue for filing to collect civil remedy claims which are not paid (see "Civil Recovery" elsewhere in this book). Although the small claims court is recognized as the proper venue for suits involving shoplifting matters, the court can also be a vehicle for the collection of unpaid and ignored promissory notes signed by employees who admit to internal theft or other financial crimes committed against their employer. The caveat here is the amount owing must not exceed the small claims court's limit, e.g., $5,000. We are of the opinion the industry has generally ignored or is unaware of the full potential of this court.

Bear in mind the civil courts (small claims is a division of the civil court system) address civil issues only; however, theft is not only a crime, but is also a tort (civil wrong). Perhaps the best example might be the fact that the criminal prosecution of O.J. Simpson for the crime of murder failed, whereas the civil prosecution of Simpson for the "wrongful death of his victim," a tort, succeeded.

Special Police Powers for Security Officers: Issues for Consideration

Norman D. Bates

Thousands of security officers across the country exercise full police powers granted to them by a state agency or local community. A security officer who has been licensed as a special police officer can, in most locations, exercise authority equivalent to that of a regular police officer in the same jurisdiction. However, the security officer's authority is limited to the geographical boundaries of his location, whereas public police officers are able to assert their authority throughout the community. Since the licensed security officer and the public police officer possess similar authority, both the private company and the municipality gain. However, a number of potential problems may be created when private citizens act like police officers.

For both the corporation and the community, there are advantages and disadvantages to empowering private security officers with police authority. Each entity should carefully weigh both sides of the issues before the authority, its inherent responsibilities, and the associated risks are assumed.

A private company gains several potential advantages when its security force has full police authority. The decision to license a private staff will depend on the company's business, location, amount of crime experienced, corporate philosophy, and other factors. The arguments in favor of police powers include the following:

Increased Authority

With full police powers, the security staff becomes more than a guard force. Specially licensed security officers may make arrests that ordinary citizens are generally not allowed to make. The difference between the inherent authority of a private or citizen's arrest and that of the licensed officer usually depends on whether the offense was a felony or misdemeanor.

In many states, citizens may arrest someone whom they have witnessed committing a felony. In some areas, this authority includes arrests based on probable cause if, in fact, the felony was committed.

Generally, a private citizen may not arrest someone who has committed a misdemeanor except where local legislatures have passed special provisions allowing such arrests. The most common example of this law is found in the merchant's statutes which state that retail merchants or their employees may arrest for shoplifting, generally a misdemeanor offense.

With full police powers, security officers may arrest for felonies committed in their presence, felonies based on probable cause, and certain misdemeanors as provided by statute. In brief, their authority is enhanced considerably to include a wider range of criminal activity.

Authors' Note: In some states (California, for example), a private person may arrest another for a public offense committed or attempted in their presence. *CAS, JHC*

Reduced Risk of Liability

Tort liability caused by arrests that are later ruled illegal because the officer did not possess the requisite authority can be reduced. A misdemeanor arrest made consistent with the officer's special powers would be valid. The same arrest made by an unlicensed private security officer would be invalid and, hence, illegal.

Security Employee Morale

Security personnel who are entrusted with police powers may perceive themselves as being more professional. Although this factor is subjective, security officers who have positive attitudes about their work and employers are more likely to perform better and stay longer with a company. In an industry known for high employee turnover, any corporate action that reduces turnover and improves performance should be considered.

Quality of Staff

When prospective applicants are investigating employment opportunities as a security officer within a private company, they may favor a position that offers the greater level of authority. Further, since increased authority should be synonymous with greater responsibility, the position will, one hopes, pay more.

Relationship with Law Enforcement

If local law enforcement officers do not have to make arrests, conduct investigations, and testify in court for a private company, better relationships may develop between the two. Police officials often complain that their limited resources are burdened by having to handle the crime-related problems of private businesses.

Relations can be further strained when a company decides not to prosecute and instead pursues its own system of justice. Arrests made by police officers that result in dismissals because the company no longer wants to prosecute can cause unnecessary friction. Businesses may be able to operate without police support much of the time, but they will be unlikely to survive a major crime wave, labor dispute, or terrorist attack without police help.

Deterrence to Crime

The reputation of a security department, inside or outside an organization, will affect the level of crime it experiences. If shoplifters know they may be arrested in front of their peers, they may be less inclined to commit the act. If a private company has the reputation of arresting and prosecuting offenders, potential offenders will more likely be deterred.

Conversely, a private company faces a number of potential disadvantages by having a security staff with full police authority. Some of the arguments against private citizens having police powers include the following:

- Negative image. Security officers may become too police-like if they have full arrest authority. In most businesses, the role of security is primarily prevention. Many security professionals take pride in the fact that they are able to control losses within their companies without having to resort to arrest and prosecution.
- Further, many businesses would prefer to project a positive public relations image with their customers, guests, employees, and the community. The high frequency of arrests may not be the best means of accomplishing that goal.

Stockrooms and Other Back-of-the-Store Areas

CAS, JHC

An employee, absorbed in finding an item, comes out between rows of shelving to find a customer back in the stockroom. "Excuse me, sir. can I help you? I mean, what are you looking for back here?" "Oh, I'm looking for the restrooms." That's the common response by those thieves who prowl stock areas.

Stock areas are off-limits to customers, and the company has a duty to inform the public of that fact. Doors leading into stockrooms should be clearly marked "Restricted Area. Employees Only." If the door faces the selling floor and such signage is deemed aesthetically unacceptable, the sign can be posted so it's the first thing you see upon entering the area. The chronic prowler may be detained for trespassing only if the area is properly posted. That same prowler knows he is immune from arrest for trespassing if the area is not posted.

Note the difference between being "detained" and "challenged." Anyone can "challenge" a stranger in a posted restricted area. A detention (read arrest) may be in order, depending on local and state laws, if the person in question has been observed prowling in the past, has been warned, and the area is posted.

If a prowler is detected more than once in a restricted area, loss prevention may warn the party that it's a restricted area, and if he's found again, he will be detained for trespassing and the police will be summoned. That warning must be made a matter of record.

If the opening into a stock area does not have a door, a simple chain draped across the opening on which a "restricted" sign is displayed will suffice. That's a sufficient deterrent to discourage entering areas that do not contain small expensive items of merchandise. Some stockrooms simply don't lend themselves to a door or any restriction of access because of constant traffic, such as a shoe department where every customer must be serviced by a sales associate coming and going repeatedly to and from the stock area. It's the nature of the merchandise. Designing departments such that placing stockroom entrances adjacent or close to register stations, permitting entry to be easily seen, helps in maximizing, to the extent possible, security in shoe department stockrooms. We have also seen such entrances covered with a hanging curtain or hanging beads, which creates a more noticeable and visible and/or audible indication of entry.

In those stock areas which do contain expensive and easily portable items, the doors should be kept locked, despite the objections of the department manager who may opt more for convenience than security. Special procedures may be required for jewelry stockrooms.

Stock areas should be well illuminated and maintained in a clean and orderly manner. Dark and cluttered stockrooms tend to facilitate the hiding of goods which are being staged for possible theft by an employee, or are being held pending anticipated markdowns so the employee can purchase the goods at a bargain price.

High-security stock areas may be constructed within stockrooms (see "Fences and Fencing" in this book), and they should be kept locked at all times. "Other back-of-the-store areas" which require signage include, but are not limited to, the receiving and shipping dock, marking room, offices, display area, sign shop, carpenter shop, employee locker area, and break lounge.

Subliminal Messaging

CAS, JHC

One definition of the word "subliminal" is "existing or functioning outside the area of conscious awareness," meaning, if it's a "message," it's below the threshold of consciousness; i.e. you can't consciously see or hear the message.

This phenomenon surfaced in the 1950s when a movie theater experimented with two messages: one "drink more Coke" and the other "I want popcorn." Allegedly Coca-Cola sales increased over 18% and popcorn sales increased over 50%. Those messages were flashed on the screen at the speed of 1/3000th of a second every 5 seconds (with the use of an instrument called a tachistoscope), and no one could consciously "see" or remember seeing the message.

Some rock musicians were accused of introducing subliminal messages in their music by "back-masking," i.e., recording messages promoting sex and drugs and flipping the messages backward and imbedding those messages in the music. If true, then clearly, this was an effective way to convey their message, whatever that message may have been.

After this messaging concept became known, interest surfaced in the retail industry regarding the possibility of imbedding positive messages in their "Muzak" music-playing PA systems, such as "Don't steal" or "Use your credit card," but there was a strong moral backlash at the prospect of this "mind-altering" technique, which had the potential of more dangerous and negative messages and influences. One expressed fear was that retailers would flash messages such as "Spend more money" or "Buy jewelry," which would increase sales but could cause customers to spend more money than they could comfortably afford to.

Today, the Federal Communication Commission (FCC) will revoke a company's broadcasting license if the use of subliminal messages can be proven. Needless to say, subliminal messaging will never see the light of day in our industry, nor should it.

Subpoenas

CAS, JHC

A subpoena is a *writ* by a court or other judicial or political tribunal commanding a person to appear as a witness in a trial or other adversarial proceeding. The person subpoenaed is compelled by law to appear. Failure to appear may result in a contempt of court charge. Fines and/or imprisonment may be the consequence of not appearing, as commanded by the subpoena. When loss prevent agents refer a detainee to the criminal justice system—i.e., arrest, police involvement, issuance of a criminal complaint, and judicial proceedings—the agent and other witnesses are required to appear in court for trial (or preliminary hearing if a felony) should the defendant plead "Not Guilty" and request a trial.

The subpoena specifies the location where the person must appear (the name of the court, room, department, or division in which the matter is being held), the street address and city in which the court is located, and the date and time of appearance.

Invariably, ample lead time is factored into the delivery or presentation of the subpoena to the witness and the time appearance is required. In the language of the industry, subpoenas are "served" (delivered or presented to the witness), and the date of "service" is noted by the person who serves the document, i.e., a law enforcement officer, officer or representative of the court, a professional "process server," a member of the prosecutor's office or, indeed, anyone so appointed to deliver the instrument.

Some subpoenas are specifically designated as "personal service required" or words to that effect, and the "server" must present the writ to that designee only. Typically personal service is not required in the kinds of cases involving loss prevention people. Hence, a police officer, for example, can arrive at the store with a subpoena for the agent who made the detention and is the key witness, and that agent may not be present. The officer may leave the subpoena with some other employee with the understanding it will be passed to the named party when he returns to work. This has inherent problems because, from time to time, the agent subpoenaed doesn't receive the document and, thus, doesn't appear as required. This can and does prove catastrophic because more often than not, if the store's witness isn't present at time of trial, the court dismisses the criminal complaint, and the store is subject to a civil action because the matter was dismissed by the criminal court.

To preclude this problem, the store should maintain a "subpoena log" in which each subpoena, received in person or by someone other than the named party, is duly recorded in terms of (1) date, (2) time, (3) name of person serving the subpoena, (4) name of person for whom the subpoena was issued, (5) signature of person accepting the subpoena,(6) signature of person for whom the subpoena was intended, with date, as evidence the subpoena is in the hands of the proper person, and, lastl (7) a disposition column with date.

Other complications tend to arise. One is the turnover of loss prevention personnel with matters still pending in the criminal justice system. Should an agent leave the employ of the store, every effort should be made to obtain and secure his next position and new address in the event a subpoena arrives for his presence in your behalf. Sometimes this might be a delicate matter and must be addressed by the ranking LP personnel.

Another problem has to do with the difficulty in tracking court cases; e.g., a subpoena is issued for the appearance of LP Agent John Doe who properly responds. Upon arrival at the court, Agent Doe learns the matter is being continued. Continuances and repeated issuances of subpoenas sometimes get lost in the bureaucracy of it all and no subpoena appears; consequently, unless store tracking is in place, no witness appears and the matter is dismissed. Hence, some tracking or ongoing follow-up by the loss prevention department must occur in a well-managed organization. Every shoplifter whose case is logged in the criminal justice system must be followed on a regularly scheduled basis until the matter is adjudicated.

Should a person receive a subpoena requiring his appearance on a date that conflicts with travel or important personal plans, the only recourse would be for the prosecutor to request the court to reschedule the trial. More often than not, a change won't occur, and the wheels of justice will slowly grind on without regard to anyone's private affairs.

In civil cases, subpoenas may be issued for depositions, a discovery process in which a witness's testimony, under oath, is taken and recorded by a court reporter. In those civil cases where a witness dies or for other acceptable reasons cannot be in court for trial, the transcript of his deposition *may* be read and used in lieu of his court testimony.

Some subpoenas are issued to parties to an action or witnesses with specific instructions (in addition to simply requiring the presence of the person subpoenaed). A *subpoena duces tecum* (Latin meaning "bring with you") means you are required to produce specified items. The subpoenaed person having under his control documents or other things specified in the subpoena and relevant to the controversy is enjoined to bring such items to court during the trial or to his deposition. For example, an LP agent may be required to produce all his reports; an expert witness may be required to produce copies of his writings or a list of all the cases in which he has testified during a specific period of time.

Sudden in Custody Death

Patrick M. Patton

"Sudden in custody death" is a term rarely heard and almost never heard in the loss prevention community. The term refers to any time a subject dies suddenly during an apprehension or shortly after apprehension. "In custody" refers to the point at which a subject feels that he is not free to leave. The term covers a broad list of causes, whether it be a subject who has heart disease which causes a severe heart attack when initially confronted about a crime to what the primary topic of this section is—agitated delirium (AD).

If you think that this occurs only in the sworn law enforcement field, then you need to think again. Wal-Mart has fallen victim to cases filed against it in which agents were even charged with homicide for their part in what appears to be a case of death due to agitated delirium.

Agitated delirium is not a new phenomenon; it was, in fact, first thoroughly noted and researched in the 1840s. More current and up-to-date research began in the 1980s and still continues today. Agitated delirium, in short, occurs when a subject begins bizarre behavior in combination with extremely violent struggle while attempts are made to restrain the subject.

Anyone who has worked in loss prevention can remember a time at which initial contact was made with a subject exiting a store with unpaid-for merchandise and the subject could be described as "flipping out." Perhaps the subject fought for what seemed like forever, or the subject had what could be described as super-human strength. Or possibly, you, along with four other agents, went out to stop the subject, and the subject didn't care how many people he was up against and still fought. This is what is generally coined as agitated delirium.

Generally, agitated delirium occurs following the use of illicit drugs such as cocaine, methamphetamine, Ecstasy, or LSD. It is often seen in subjects who have a past history of mental illness. And in the majority of cases in which AD has proved to be fatal, the subject had been suffering from a combination of mental illness, drug usage, along with alcohol usage prior to the incident.

Four steps take place during AD, and if not treated immediately by medical professionals by the fourth step, imminent death will occur, and the subject cannot be brought back by CPR.

- *Step 1:* Hyperthermia: The body overheats, causing radiating body temperature and profuse sweating.
- *Step 2:* Delirium with agitation: The subject will show symptoms described with a sudden onset. Many times body limbs will become rigid.
- *Step 3:* Respiratory Distress/Arrest: The subject may or may not complain of not being able to breathe, followed by the subject's breathing stopping.
- *Step 4:* Cardiac Arrest: Following respiratory arrest, the heart will stop, which will cause the subject's death.

If a subject is being detained and shows any signs or symptoms such as this, police should be notified immediately, and police dispatch should be told that a medical emergency might be taking place as well.

One other important point to remember to prevent "sudden in custody death" is to pay attention that positional asphyxia is not occurring. Positional asphyxia occurs when a subject is in a position which restricts his ability to breathe. To understand this, try lying on your stomach sometime with your arms pulled behind your back where handcuffs place them. Then imagine attempting to breathe like this if you just had a 5-minute foot pursuit. Then try to imagine this if you are also under the influence of drugs.

The majority of "sudden in custody deaths" which have occurred across the United States have been due to positional asphyxia. Subjects placed in handcuffs in the prone position should immediately be stood up or, at the very least, placed in a sitting position. If the subject needs to be kept lying down, place him in the recovery position, which is on his side. If the subject states he is having trouble breathing, this should be taken seriously. And no matter what, if a subject is in the prone position and LP personnel had to place weight on his back to get him into handcuffs, the second that the cuffs are on, the LP personnel need to get off his back. Applying pressure in this way places weight onto the subject's diaphragm, and if the subject has a large stomach, it adds even more pressure, making it harder to breathe.

The best policy is to follow your instincts, and if you feel that the situation could take a turn for the worse, call for medical assistance before it is too late. It is better to have made the call and have it not be a medical emergency than to not make the call and end up with a "sudden in custody death."

Supply Chain Security Overview for Retailing

David A. Jones

Introduction to the "Supply Chain"

The supply chain...what is it, and how does it affect the retail loss prevention professional? Many in our profession have little or no experience in supply chain security. For many years it has not been a focus of attention. For most retail loss prevention executives, the emphasis has always been on store-line shortage control. The question has always been, "How do we reduce store shrink by implementing physical security controls, procedural controls, and investigative follow-up?" To varying degrees, companies placed some emphasis on distribution center controls, but for the most part these controls paled in comparison to those implemented store-line.

This section will try to bring the retail supply chain to life by showing you how it works, where losses occur, why those losses are important to your company, and last, steps you can take to address those losses and thereby enhance your overall loss prevention program.

Before we can discuss supply chain loss control issues, we must first take a look at the base definition of a supply chain. The International Cargo Security Council defines "supply chain" as follows:

> *The network created amongst different companies producing, handling, and/or distributing a specific product. Supply chains include every company that comes into contact with a particular product. For example, the supply chain for most products will encompass all the companies manufacturing parts for the product, assembling it, delivering it and selling it.*

The one thing you must remember is that your supply chain is your company's lifeline to the products you sell.

As a loss prevention professional, you must remember that addressing the security needs of your supply chain will greatly enhance your overall corporate loss reduction efforts.

Individual companies' supply chains differ depending on the products they offer for sale. For companies with "private label" merchandise, the supply chain starts at the supplier and manufacturing points. These manufacturing points can be anywhere in the world. A typical supply chain diagram would look like this:

Supplier → Manufacturer → Distribution/Consolidation point → Intermodal Shipping (Marine/Air/Truck/Rail) → Your Distribution Center → Retail Store

Retail companies that exclusively sell third-party goods have a supply chain that is much reduced in scope. For these companies, the control of the goods starts when the merchandise hits the loading docks in their own distribution centers. Their supply chain can be as simple as this:

Intermodal Shipping → Your Distribution Center → Your Retail Stores

The Start of the Supply Chain

The supply chains for companies that produce "private label" or "proprietary products" are more elaborate in that more steps are taken to bring a product to market. The process starts with the design and prototype sample being developed. Once the design is accepted, the product is passed onto the "production" area. The name may vary from company to company, but the function is the same: This department is charged with bringing the product to market. The first step in bringing the product to market is for the production area to source material suppliers. Once they are sourced, factories need to be located that can manufacture the product. Factories are selected based on their production capability, area of specialization, manufacturing cost proposal, and ability to address "social compliance" issues such as pay scale, good work environment, and nonexploitation of children. All companies that utilize overseas manufacturers have some level of "social compliance" regulations and use auditing firms to ensure adherence to those regulations.

Since 9/11, the U.S. government has tightened import controls and added cooperative government/private industry security programs such as Customs Trade Partnership Against Terrorism (C-TPAT). The inception of these types of programs has added an additional security requirement layer on top of the normal "social compliance" regulations standards that overseas factories must maintain. We will talk more about this issue later in this section.

Once a factory is selected and production begins on the "private label" item, the physical supply chain has started and so too has the possibility for losses to occur. When the product is ready for shipping, one of two events will happen, depending on how much product is produced. The ideal situation, from a loss control perspective, is to have enough product manufactured to fill an entire container. This would allow the container to be sealed and locked until the product reaches the United States and (unless it is opened and inspected by Customs) the safety of your own distribution center. If the container is "LTL" (Less than a full load), the container would be brought either to another manufacturer, where it will be opened and more product added; or to a consolidation/distribution point, where the container will be offloaded, temporarily stored, and reloaded with other merchandise to make a full container. Conversely, once an LTL container arrives in the United States, it will again be offloaded and repacked at a third-party consolidation facility for final delivery to your distribution center.

The fewer times merchandise is touched, the less likely it is for loss to occur.

Supply Chain Loss Vulnerabilities

Once the goods leave the point of manufacture, where are the major areas of vulnerability or "choke points" that loss can occur? There are many of them, all of them when the cargo is not in motion. As a general rule, remember this adage "Cargo at Rest is Cargo at Risk." When merchandise is sitting, whether in a container, truck trailer, or a warehouse, that's when loss is most likely to occur.

In general, the major supply chain "choke points" of concern for loss prevention professionals are as follows:

Import Flow (vendor to port, port to consolidation center, consolidation center to DC):

- Vendor to DC;
- DC to Store;
- Vendor to Store;
- DC to DC;
- Store to DC;
- Store to Store;
- Store to Return Goods Center;
- Return Goods Center to Vendor;
- Return Goods Center to Third-Party Salvage;
- Third-Party Salvage to Customer;
- Store to Vendor;

Export Flow (DC to Port, Port to Stores)

- E-commerce (DC to Fulfillment House, Fulfillment House to Customer, Customer to Store, Store to Return Goods Center)
- Vendor to Third Party (Overruns, Cancelled POs)

The Cost of Supply Chain Loss: Insurance and Beyond

The FBI has stated, "The theft of cargo has become so widespread that it constitutes a serious threat to the flow of commerce in the U.S." These are powerful words; however, we need to dissect them to be able to put them into proper perspective. What is the cost of supply chain theft to the U.S. economy?

Insurance to Cover Supply Chain Losses?

The cost of losses that occur within the supply chain is enormous. Many of the costs are hidden and are not accounted for in your store "shrink" statistics. One of the main reasons they are often overlooked or not counted by companies stems from the term "risk transfer." In most cases, companies transfer the risk to an insurance classification. Under this scenario, the loss is not viewed as a "real" loss because it is covered by an insurance policy.

In many cases, this thought process is akin to an ostrich sticking his head in the sand. The losses are still very real; your company just chooses not to notice them. What do we mean by this statement? The answer is simple: Insurance is a moving target at best. Insurance coverage varies greatly from company to company, and it is important that loss prevention executives be aware of the extent of your company's insurance coverage. Many companies maintain high deductibles to keep insurance costs down, and others are "self-insured" for the same reason.

When you really drill down for your actual level of coverage, you will likely find that insurance claims are paid at the "cost value" of the product. So, that means no loss, right? Wrong. The loss is realized in several different ways:

1. The deductible becomes part of the loss.
2. The company loses the profit margin value of the product.
3. The company more than likely loses full value on any "deductible" amounts.
4. Most importantly, the company loses the availability of offering the product for sale.

This translates into disappointed customers. On a wholesale side, the loss means you cannot fulfill an order that has already been placed. On the retail side, your product is not on the shelf generating sales. Customers may then purchase another company's goods, switching loyalties and causing residual negative sales impact.

Business Impact of Supply Chain Losses

Where do the stolen goods go after a crime is perpetrated, and how does the loss affect your company? The answer to this question is similar to how you would respond to the same question in the arena of organized retail crime.

Stolen bulk merchandise is generally disposed of in two main ways: (1) It is fenced, showing up in local shops, bodegas, flea markets, and cyber markets such as eBay, or (2) it is shipped out of the country, with Central or South America as primary destinations. When it is shipped out, there is a high probability that Miami and Houston are the two ports from which the merchandise will leave. Many times, the merchandise will be shipped in the same cartons and on the same pallets that they were on when stolen.

Whatever the method of disposition, the impact is the same—loss of business revenue. The victimized company essentially ends up trying to compete in a "no win" market. The stolen merchandise is sold at a much reduced price, while the victim has less merchandise to sell at a much higher price. Margin is hurt and profits are impacted.

The Iceberg Effect: The True Cost of Supply Chain Crime

If you view supply chain loss as an iceberg, the visible part above the waterline is the physical cost of the actual merchandise lost. Utilizing statistics from the FBI and the International Cargo Security Council, that U.S. dollar loss of supply chain crime is estimated at between $15 and 20 billion annually. That's a large number; however, that number jumps to $75–80 billion annually when you factor in the submerged costs to U.S. companies of dealing with supply chain losses. Those factors include

- Lost sales;
- Lost reputation;
- Fraudulent refunds;
- Insurance costs;
- Investigative costs;
- Re-order costs;
- Paying claims;
- Administrative costs;
- Product diversion.

These figures do not include the significant added costs associated with security controls or law enforcement!

Container and Trailer Security

Any supply chain loss control program has to begin with container and trailer security. This is where your cargo spends much of its time while in transit. This is also where your cargo is most vulnerable.

According to statistics from the U.S. Merchant Marine Academy's Cargo Security School, 60% of all cargo thefts are the result of carton pilferage, 25% from pallet/quantity theft, 10% from hijackings, and 5% from burglary.

Other interesting factoids involving cargo crime highlight why supply chain theft has become such a problem:

- The average value of a single cargo theft is $500,000.
- Trucking companies and their facilities (warehouses, etc.) experience the majority of all reported losses (85%), followed by maritime, rail, and air.
- Approximately 80% of cargo thefts are perpetrated by internal employees or involve some level of internal collusion.
- Pilferage is the most common form of cargo theft.
- The FBI estimates that most stolen cargo remains in the possession of those who stole it for less than 24 hours.
- Cargo theft is not in the public spotlight; it is regarded as a victimless crime and therefore it does not carry severe sentencing.
- A kilo of heroin is worth the same as a kilo of Pentium chips. Organized crime is going after the chips and other cargo because the criminal penalties are less severe.
- Today, you can knock off a truck with $1 million worth of cargo, and the courts can treat it as a misdemeanor, but if you rob a bank for $10, it's a major felony.
- New York/New Jersey; Southern California; Atlanta, Georgia; and Miami, Florida, are the four regions where 75% of the nation's cargo theft occurs.
- "When the freight is moving, no problem; when it stops, that is when the problems start."
- "Cargo at Rest is a Cargo at Risk."

The question becomes, "What steps can we take, as retail loss prevention professionals, to prevent and otherwise minimize our losses when our cargo is in route?" The answer is that there any many steps we can take to address this issue. See the following descriptions.

Container/Trailer Inspections

One of the first steps to minimizing your risks is to set up a program to inspect any trailer and/or container that will be used to move your goods. These inspections can provide valuable information about the integrity of the container that will be housing your merchandise and allow you to take steps to counter any noted deficiencies.

Inbound Overseas Shipments

For incoming cargo, if your company owns its own container/trailer fleet, corporate loss prevention or logistics personnel can perform inspections. If you do not own your own fleet or do not possess the personnel resources needed, overseas agents or brokers can perform these inspections.

Outbound Shipments

Checks of outbound containers/trailers leaving your distribution center should be incorporated as part of your security inspection program. These inspections should be documented and maintained on file for quick reference should the consignee report any problems with the load.

How to Inspect

To maximize the effectiveness of any container inspection program, the container/trailer should be inspected prior to "stuffing" (loading). Both the outside and inside of the trailer should be inspected. The following points need to be part of the inspection process:

- Check all sides of the container for holes or other openings. Remember, water damage to goods being transported can also be a loss for the company.

- Check for false walls and/or flooring/ceiling. Containers used to move contraband will often use false walls to conceal unmanifested (smuggled) items. This will be discussed in more detail later in this section. In a sense, the container is used as a giant "booster box."
- Check for signs that the container was modified or altered in any way. Signs of alteration can be fresh paint, new welds, or new locking systems. Remember, if any of these conditions are found, they may be due to normal repairs and not for any vicarious reason.
- Check the rear doors and locking bars. The welds on the lock hasps and any bolted lock plates should be secure to the body.

How Break-Ins Occur

Just how do the bad guys do it? How can it be so easy to break into a locked and sealed container or trailer? The answer is simple. As with any other type of crime, professionals study the dynamics of moving cargo, experiment with finding unique ways to defeat the system, and then practice until it becomes a sort of art form.

The professional cargo thief most likely began his career as a professional shoplifter and graduated to cargo crime because it is more lucrative with a lower risk of being caught. Additionally, teams that perpetrate cargo crime may actually still be active in organized retail crime (ORC). It is not uncommon for these professional groups to move their "resources" from one area to another. If a particular group or individual is identified in ORC circles, gang leaders will move that group or individual into the cargo crime sector and vice versa. Although they are polished and adept at the more sophisticated methods of breaking into a container, cargo thieves are no different from other types of criminals in that they always like to go first for "low-hanging fruit." They will generally opt for an easy score with moderate gains and low risk of detection over the more sophisticated break-in methods. All too often we make it very easy for them to be successful.

1. *Cut the Seal:* The mistake many companies make is believing that simply sealing a container or trailer will protect their goods. Additionally, many of those same companies use the least expensive seal they can find. Many times, these are plain plastic lock seals or thin metal strip seals. The bad guys know this, and they target these trailers. There are no barriers or obstacles to overcome. Of course, cargo thieves generally like to cover their tracks and not advertise the fact that they just broke into a truck. In this method, they will cut the strip seal with a razor so the cut is neat and clean. They then use a couple of drops of "crazy glue" to reconnect the seal. Unless the seal is closely inspected, the defeat will not be detected, and the shipper is charged with the loss. The net outcome is that the thieves took several dozen cartons and nobody is looking for them.
2. *Defeating a Lock:* When trailers are locked, the lock of choice is generally a padlock. The padlocks are of varying quality. Although they are not much more difficult to cut off than a simple seal, they are much more difficult to put back together if the perpetrator plans to hide the theft. The solution: Don't cut the lock; rather, disassemble the lock mechanism. With this method, the perpetrator would take a hammer and chisel to shear off the bolt securing the lock hasp. This action will release the door handle, and the perpetrator is free to help himself to the contents of the trailer. He then replaces the sheared bolt by gluing it back in place or by using a replacement pin. Either way, the entry will go undetected.
3. *Wall Cutting:* In this technique, the perpetrator will actually cut through one of the sides of a container. This method is hard to cover up, so it is usually done after hours when the perpetrator has more time. It is usually accomplished by cutting into the container from the top, where it is less likely to be noticed until the next day. Particularly vulnerable to this type of break-ins are trailers equipped with fiberglass tops.

4. *Slash and Grab:* This method is similar to the "smash and grab" shoplifter. This method utilizes three or more people to commit the theft. One is the driver and the rest grab the goods. Thieves look for distribution centers or truck stops lacking any entry controls, such as fences or gatehouses. They will study the particular receiving habits of the building they are attacking so they can plan where and how long they have to make a hit. Once a driver leaves his cab, usually to enter a building and get a dock assignment, the thieves will back a vehicle up to the back of the trailer, slash (cut) off any lock or seal, and remove cartons from the load. They will then speed away, often not even taking the time to close the rear trailer doors. The success of this method lies in the speed. Thieves can cut the lock and load a small van in under 45 seconds.

Hijackings

Truck hijackings occur everyday in America and around the world. An accurate reporting of hijack statistics within the United States is difficult because statistics on cargo crime have never been kept as a specific UCR code but rather lumped in with all personal property thefts. Additionally, many hijackings go unreported because private companies and cargo haulers do not want this type of negative stigma attached to their companies. Insurance has always been looked upon as the main insulator for the victimized company, but as previously mentioned, that is no longer a given. High-loss deductible thresholds and self-insurance can make many a hijacking a total loss. Where insurance is paid, the company can still be hit with higher premiums.

How Do Hijackings Occur?

1. *Insider Complicity:* An interesting tidbit dealing with hijack situations is that most law enforcement personnel who deal with hijackings on a regular basis will tell you that the vast majority of the hijackings involve driver complicity. The percentage they give you will vary, but 70–80% seems to be an average statistic. Additionally, they will also tell you that in many cases involving high-value merchandise, complicity is also found with internal employees. Generally, this would involve a logistics operation person or dock supervisor who is aware of the specific items and value of a particular container/trailer. This information is passed along to outside accomplices who actually commit the crime.

2. *Yard Break-Ins:* Hauler storage/consolidation points and company distribution centers/warehouses are other likely targets for hijackers, especially those facilities that have little or no perimeter protection. It will take the average professional thief 5 minutes or less to steal a load from an unprotected yard. This includes cutting through perimeter fencing, opening a locked cab, jump-starting the cab, backing up the cab to a container, defeating any trailer collar lock, hooking up truck cables, and driving away with the load. Of course, these types of thieves bring all the proper equipment that makes committing the crime much easier.

3. *Street Jacks:* Street hijackings tend to be the most violent form of hijacking. They generally involve two or more thieves and also likely involve firearms or other weapons. This method is utilized when storage yard controls are tightly controlled and not conducive to a "yard break-in." Street hijacking may or may not involve internal or driver complicity, although this factor should always be investigated as a possibility. Street jacks can occur in many ways: for example, a truck is jumped when stopped at a traffic light, a truck is jumped at a truck stop just as the driver starts to pull out, a truck is jumped at highway rest areas, or a truck is actually pulled over or run off the road. This last example is actually the method of choice for gangs in the United States. In many foreign countries, it is not unusual for the thieves to steal police cars and police uniforms to pull over unsuspecting drivers.

4. *Truck Stops:* Truck stops provide ideal covers for hijackings. As a general rule, drivers will pull into a stop and immediately refuel. They then leave their truck to eat and/or

clean up. Many modern stops are equipped with showers, gyms, game rooms, and bunkhouses that the drivers can use. Thieves know the average time a truck will be left and will wait for their opportunity. All too often, drivers make it easy for the hijackers by leaving their keys in the truck and, in some cases, even leave the truck running.

5. *Fraudulent Paperwork:* In this method, a thief uses fraudulent documentation to enter a gatehouse controlled yard and steal a trailer. This method generally involves some level of complicity between the thief and either someone in corporate operations or yard security. Once in the yard, the driver is free to hook up and drive away.

If you are the victim of a hijacking, don't rely on law enforcement to make a recovery. More often than not, empty trailers are found rather than cargo. Thieves are smart and, chances are, have already made plans to offload the trailer in short order. The common rule of thumb is, if your cargo has not been recovered within 24 hours, your chances of effecting any level of recovery are extremely poor.

How to Prevent Hijackings

As with much in loss prevention, there is no "silver bullet" action you can take that will guarantee you will never be the victim of a hijacking. There are, however, many actions you can take that will help you reduce your company's chances of being victimized by a hijacking event. Let's look at a couple of these actions.

Ensure that you conduct pre-employment background checks on all employees hired into logistics operations and warehouse/distribution center operation departments. Every company's culture is different, but you should strive to perform the most comprehensive check possible. Checks should include criminal and credit checks, as well as prior employment references. These checks will help weed out those who may be inclined to be complicit in passing along information that can aid hijackers.

Ensure all perimeter protection controls are functional and part of a daily audit. Walk fence lines and check gates and CCTV systems to make sure they have not been compromised. Make sure that any full containers/trailers in your yards are kept under constant surveillance. A key best practice is to have a policy that no loaded containers/trailers are left at a bay door location overnight.

If your company has its own truck fleet, make sure background checks are performed on all drivers and that you have an established set of driver protocols and policies detailing how they drive their routes; when, where, and for how long they are permitted to stop; driving with windows up and doors locked. Supply drivers with cell phones and trucks with GPS. Whenever possible, any GPS system should be covertly installed to reduce chances of its being detected and disabled by the hijackers.

If your company contracts out delivery functions, make sure that all the preceding items are included as part of the contractual obligations for doing business.

Seals

Seals…perhaps one of the more boring topics of discussion in the arena of supply chain security. Boring, maybe, but absolutely essential. Understanding the different types of seals and the best application for utilization of each is critical in the development of a well-rounded supply chain security program.

How good are seals at preventing theft from the supply chain? U.S. government tests showed an average defeat time of typically used seals to be 4.3 minutes using tools readily concealed in a pocket or hand. Some were defeated in seconds. This gives cause for concern, but it is important to note that seals are generally not intended to "prevent" theft, but rather to record that an event took place. It is really not a question of whether or not a seal can be defeated, given time and tools, all seals and locks are vulnerable. The real question is "Can it be defeated and tampered with in such a way that it can avoid detection?"

Here, we will discuss some of the major types of seals, the proper application for each type, and how to develop a sound working program for your company.

Types of Seals

No two types of seals are alike. Each type is developed with a specific target use in mind. The effectiveness of any seal is compromised when someone tries to use the wrong product for a specific application. All too often this is done simply because of cost. "Why use a $5 bolt seal to secure a trailer door when I can just as easily spend only a couple of cents and use a band or light wire seal?" To understand why that's a bad idea, you first have to understand the ins and outs of each type of seal.

The International Cargo Security Council defines a "seal: as "a product designed to leave non-erasable, unambiguous evidence of entry." Unlike locks, seals may offer little or no resistance to unauthorized access. Unlike intrusion alarms, seals report entry after the fact. They must be inspected, either manually or electronically, to determine if unauthorized access has taken place. All seals have some kind of unique identifier or "fingerprint," such as a serial number or random pattern."

This definition needs to be narrowed in order to fully discuss the proper applications for each type of seal. As a general rule, seals are classified under two main headings: indicative and barrier. Indicative seals provide no resistance or hindrance against intrusion. Their sole purpose is to tell the end user if the container being protected has been violated. Barrier seals are security devices that function both as a lock and seal, providing all the aspects of the indicative seal, plus some element of physical deterrence against unauthorized entry.

Let's discuss a few of the more common types of seals used for the protection of the supply chain.

Indicative Seals

- *Metal Ribbon Seal:* A light-duty seal made from sheet metal. One end of the ribbon snaps irreversibly into a head at the other end. It is generally stronger than a plastic strap seal but still not considered a barrier seal. Also know as a "car-box" or "car-ball" seal.
- *Padlock Seal:* A "self-locking" seal that looks like a padlock. The seal-locking body is often made of plastic, with the shackle being made of metal. The head usually has a serial number and sometimes a logo or company name. Despite the term, padlock seals are usually not intended to function as locks. Padlock seals are often used on commercial and residential utility meters and are one-time-use seals.
- *Plastic Strap Seal:* A one-piece plastic-molded strap with one end that snaps irreversibly into a head or housing on the other end; it is also known as a plastic ribbon seal. These seals come in a variety of sizes and types, depending on the manufacturer. They are very popular for use on containers/trailers because they are typically very inexpensive. A major weakness of this type of seal is the ease with which it can be cut by a straight-edge razor or knife and glued back together, often without detection.
- *Wire Loop Seal:* A seal consisting of one wire twisted around one or more other wires with a metal or plastic head or housing that crimps, traps, or holds the ends of the wires. This light-duty seal is used for hampers and small bins.

Barrier Seals

- *Bar Lock:* A barrier lock that secures the door bars in place on a container or trailer. These locks are produced in both a reusable and one-time-use variety. Some have an integrated cable seal that serves as both a bar lock and integrity seal. This type of integrated locking/sealing system is typically a one-time-use item. Bar locks arguably provide the highest level of antipilferage protection. Being a "key" operated devise, they are by no means immune from the possibility of tampering or being defeated. Proper key control is essential to maximizing their effectiveness.
- *Bolt Seal:* Possibly the most popular of all barrier seals, it consists of a strong bolt with one end larger than the hasp and the other end designed to snap irreversibly into a cylindrical head or housing. Bolt seals come in both one-time-use and reusable

designs. Reusable seals are removed with the aid of a seal remover devise, similar to EAS removers. Bolt seals are used mainly on truck and container doors. As with all seals, the designs, effectiveness, and unique applications vary depending on the manufacturer, so understand both before making any commitment with a particular manufacturer.

Since 9/11, new government regulation makes the use of bolt seals a requirement on containers being imported into the United States. The International Organization for Standardization (ISO) has developed standards for bolt seals that U.S. Customs has adapted. Therefore, it is important that any bolt seal you decide on meets or exceeds PAS ISO 17712 standards. Ensure the manufacturer provides details of compliancy testing.

Despite being viewed as "acceptable" theft-deterrent seals, bolt seals can and have been defeated. Common defeating techniques include the following:

Bolt seals come in two parts: the shank/bolt and the locking head/locking mechanism. This characteristic makes any bolt seal vulnerable to manipulation. All the parts are interchangeable, which means there are countless ways the seal can be manipulated or defeated. All you need to do is retain the locking head with the seal number. The shank can be cut and replaced easily. Makers like to push double numbering (numbering on the shank and the locking mechanism) as a means for making the seal more secure. This solution is good in theory perhaps but not in practice. The B/L has no area in which to detail that the bolt is double numbered, and few people will look for it or note it. They check that the seal is okay and that the number is correct. They never know that the seal has been tampered with.

Spinning usually happens with inside employee collusion, but it is not required because spinning has also been done in the field. In as much as shanks are ubiquitous, all it takes is an employee to take a few home or an employee to purchase them in the market. The shank is then "prepared" for spinning in any machine shop. The bolt/shank is cut in half below the bolt head, and the two pieces are then prepared to have a male end with threads and a female end to accept them. The two ends are then screwed back together tightly so as not to show the preparation. The bolt/shank is then married with a numbered locking head and put to use on a container of choice. This method is also used by distribution center shipping personnel who have access to genuine seals. Seals are removed from the premises, modified, and returned. Accomplices then follow the truck, and when it is left unattended, they strike. Spinning is also used as a method of collusion with truck drivers.

Once the container is in the field, the prepared shank can be unscrewed and the seal removed. After the cargo is stolen or contraband is inserted, the seal is screwed back together. Upon inspection, the seal number is correct and the seal appears to be fine. The prepared part of the shank is nothing more than a fine line which usually lies unseen within the door hasp. After you have signed off on the seal, you have bought a big problem.

Bolt seals applied only to the door-rod handles can be circumvented and the doors opened and reclosed. The bolt seal remains intact with no apparent evidence of tampering. This is the same method as used in defeating a lock.

- *Cable Seal:* A barrier seal made from aircraft cable with each end crimped or irreversibly clamped onto the head, housing or "locking" body. The cable is both heavy duty and adjustable. The cable portion of the seal imitates the bar lock by securing the doors in a similar manner. Cable locks can be an effective alternative to bolt seals and also meet PAS ISO 17712 standards.

All cable seals are not created equal, however, and care should be taken when selecting the proper product. Cheaper generally never means better. Three common methods of defeating cable seals are as follows:

Twisting the cable out (ratcheting). If the cable is twisted and pulled at the same time in opposite directions, the ball and cable together create a pull strength, which can remove the cable. The only tool needed is a pair of pliers. The seal remains fully functional and is then used to reseal the trailer after intrusion.

Picking the lock to release the mechanism. In this method, a pin is inserted into the aperture holding the cable. The pin releases the pressure of the holding ball inside the seal, allowing the cable to be backed out. Once the cable is released, the trailer door can be opened, and the same seal can then be used to resecure the door. The intrusion goes totally undetected.

Freezing the seal. Seals with empty interior space can be filled with water by using a syringe and frozen with a fire extinguisher. When the water freezes, it forces the internal ball mechanism to retract, releasing pressure on the cable, thereby allowing the cable to be pulled out. In the winter, no extinguisher is needed. Just fill the seal with water and wait 10–15 minutes.

- *Electronic Seal:* A seal that contains electronics and is electrically powered by batteries. Electronic seals typically check continuously for signs of tampering, and some report back to the end user in "real time." Electronic seals can utilize RF and GPS technology that allows the end user to track cargo. Encrypted electronic seals are permanently attached to the rear door of a trailer or truck. These seals automatically generate a new seal number when reset. This type of seal is generally used by companies that own and operate their own fleet of trucks.

Developing Seal Control Protocols

Whatever type of seal you choose to control your supply chain, you must develop a procedural protocol to control the purchase, distribution, and storage of the seals. This would include a methodology for attaching the seal, removing the seal, filing the seal after use, and auditing compliance. Without such controls, the effectiveness of any seal is compromised.

Components of the program should include

- Types of seals you need for all applications.
- Who will purchase the seal, because one-source purchasing is a best practice. This source ensures proper order sequencing of seal numbers.
- How seals will be inventoried and stored once they are delivered. Seals should always be maintained under lock and key.
- Who will be responsible for control of the seals. Seal logs should be maintained by the caretaker detailing when seals were received, number sequencing, and distribution of seals.
- How seals are to be applied to outgoing vehicles and how seals are to be removed from incoming vehicles. This procedure must include checking of all seals for evidence of defects and/or tampering, as well as what to do with those defective seals or seals suspected of tampering.
- The setup of a filing system that requires used seals to be maintained on file for a defined period of time.
- Development of a monthly auditing program to ensure adherence to your seal control procedures.

Distribution Centers

Any review of supply chain security must include a discussion of distribution center security protocols. A company could have extremely tight controls on its supply chain and still have high losses if it ignores its own backyard, the distribution center.

In this section we will examine the distribution center. We will look at some of the many ways losses occur in this environment and the steps we can take to minimize the risk of loss by utilizing physical security controls and auditing protocols.

How Losses Occur

It would take a book dedicated to this subject alone to truly discuss the variety of ways that theft and losses can occur in a distribution center/warehouse environment. Space does not permit such a discussion, so we will look at a few of the more common ways that losses can occur.

As in all sectors of the retail business, internal dishonesty poses a huge challenge for the loss prevention professional. These risks can be even more pronounced than those encountered on a store-line level due to a different set of circumstances. Distribution centers and warehouses are large facilities with many unsecured locations where theft can take place in relative seclusion. Cameras can't be placed everywhere, and security officer resources are generally limited, which leaves plenty of secluded areas where loss can occur.

One of the biggest differences that separates store-line and distribution center theft is the growing trend by many companies to outsource their warehouse operations. "Outsourcing" is when a company hires a third party to run its day-to-day warehouse operations. The workers are employees of the third-party company, not the retail company. Outsourcing may be beneficial to the company in that often it reduces operating expenses, but it also reduces an important mitigating factor that can help reduce a company's vulnerability to loss: That factor is company loyalty.

All companies want "quality" personnel to work in their facility. The quality of the workers goes a long way toward determining productivity and how efficiently the warehouse operates. When a company hires its own workers, it controls the quality issue. When the company outsources, it loses that control. When a company decides to outsource, generally the reason is that it wants to reduce expenses. As a normal course of events, the final selection of a service provider comes through a bidding process. All too often, the low bidder is awarded the contract. To be profitable, the third-party provider needs to keep its expenses as low as possible. Because its main expense is in worker salaries, these tend to be lower paying jobs. Even in union environments, the salary structure and benefits of the contract workers are generally well below what the company that contracted for the services would have paid to its own proprietary staff. To keep costs down, the company does not perform any type of background check on employee candidates. Companies could add that as a contractual requirement before awarding a bid to a third-party provider but seldom do because that would drive up the cost of service and reduce the realized operating expense savings. All this helps drive down the common denominator of "worker quality." When the quality goes down, exposure and risk of loss goes up.

Most outsource companies do not utilize the same hiring practices as the companies that hired them. Screening processes are brief, with an "any warm body will do" mentality. The workforce fluctuates in size depending on the workload, so layoffs are frequent and sudden. Workers know this and act accordingly. The combination of low wages, poor benefits, and uncertain term of employment can add up to trouble for loss prevention personnel. Combine this with the temptation of the merchandise itself and the opportunities for theft afforded by a large distribution center, and you have a formula for real shortage issues.

Understanding how thefts occur means you also need to understand the makeup of your workforce. Just as gangs can "attack" a retail store, they also can attack a distribution center. The difference is the gangs that attack a retail store usually come from the outside, as opposed to the distribution center, where the gangs are part of the actual workforce. It is not unusual for multiple gangs to be working in a single location. The "gangs" that operate in a warehouse, however, differ somewhat from the usual image that the term "gang" normally brings to mind. We are not talking about violent street gangs such as the Bloods and Crips, but rather groupings of individuals who work together in a planned manner to steal merchandise. Often these groups are ethnically or racially bound. These "gangs" know of the existence of the other gangs, but they do not generally operate in a cooperative effort, but rather divide up the distribution center by "turf." Traditionally, they recognize each other's turf and will steal merchandise only from their own areas. Each gang will have a leader who is generally a longer term employee who "knows the ropes." The leader will direct his operatives, collect the stolen items, and arrange compensation for the other gang members.

"Muling" is a term associated with theft of small amounts of merchandise, from the warehouse, on a continual basis over a long period of time. In this method, an individual gang member (the "mule") would hide one or two items of merchandise on his person every time he physically leaves the facility. Body straps are used around the midriff or upper leg, which is a common area where merchandise can be hidden. Restrooms or hidden corners are the prime areas where merchandise is taken, and just as in a retail store, a "lookout" is almost always utilized. These items are then brought to a central collection area manned by a gang leader. The gang leaders are responsible for disposing of the merchandise, either through fencing operations or operation of their own store. The leaders will compensate the "mules" by the piece. Compensation can take the form of either money or goods.

"Short-ship" is a term denoting a shipment from the warehouse that arrives at a destination location missing pieces. All too often, short-ships are not merely mistakes. More and more retailers are reducing store-line staff, leaving fewer people to do the same amount of work. One of the areas that companies look at when they want to reduce in-store work requirements is in the receiving of goods. Reducing or even eliminating the need to detail receiving has given warehouse gangs the freedom to steal almost at will. On a wholesale level, warehouse gangs have become very adept at knowing which clients do and do not perform detail receiving checks of all incoming goods. Likewise, on an in-house warehouse operation, employees know what the corporate rules are for checking in merchandise. When these checks are reduced or eliminated, warehouse gangs can "short-ship" cartons being prepared for shipping. If an order calls for 12 items, they make pack only 10 or 11. The shortage can go undetected because the paperwork piece count is correct leaving the distribution center, and unless the shortage is noted upon arrival at the destination store, it is the store that will be stuck with the shortage.

In "pallet stuffing" or "carton stuffing" an extra pallet or carton is placed on an outbound trailer. Here, collusion is usually in play. The truck driver, dock supervisor, and possibly security personnel may be working together. The truck pulls away from the warehouse and is followed by another vehicle. The truck diver makes an unauthorized stop, where the "extra merchandise" is then divided up.

Delivery "miscounts" most often occur when the delivering driver has become "friendly" with the dock supervisor who is in charge of accounting for incoming deliveries. Oddly enough, this scenario does not usually involve internal collusion. A delivery driver who frequents specific warehouses can become a "trusted" figure with the dock supervisor. When a rush occurs and the dock becomes a hectic place, this "trusted" figure may "help out" by unloading his own truck. The driver takes advantage of the situation by leaving one or two cartons in the truck. The driver then asks the supervisor to sign the bill of lading. If the supervisor does not double count the cartons, he just bought a shortage. If he does double count and finds the discrepancy, the driver then "double-checks" the truck and conveniently finds the missing cartons. The dock supervisor does not detect any foul play.

Preventing Warehouse Theft

The best way to defeat any the methods previously discussed is to have a plan. As with any preventative plan, the extent of your preventative measures is almost always tied into and controlled by budgetary concerns. This is especially true with physical security control methods. A good plan, however, will be a combination of physical security controls, auditing functions, collusion, and internal theft deterrents. Most of elements require little or no funding. Let's look at some best practices for each of these areas.

Physical Security Controls
- Use of CCTV: A monitored system utilizing both PTZ and fixed-location technology:
  - Fixed cameras should be used on those areas that require constant monitoring.
  - Multiple monitoring stations are needed to maximize efficiency.
  - Multiplexed or digitally recorded: A 31-day library should be maintained for investigative follow-up.
  - A video image printer and/or CD burner should be used for event documentation.
  - An Auto-Tour option on all PTZ locations ensures cameras are always directed at critical areas.
- Use of uniformed security personnel either "contract" or "proprietary."
- Guard tour controls—both inside and outside the building.
- Use of perimeter fencing.
- Proper exterior yard lighting: 1 to 3 candlepower is generally sufficient.

- Parking controls: Private vehicles should never be allowed to park in or around truck bay door areas.
- Use of yard gates or gate houses.
- Access control: Use of proximity or other card access control system to limit movement liability:
  o Use of delayed egress/audible crash bars to control fire exits.
  o Truck driver entry cages to control warehouse access; truck drivers should not be able to walk directly into a warehouse proper.
  o Barrier lines taped or painted on the loading dock to psychologically limit a driver's access to the building.
  o Use of day/screen gates on bay doors for use in warm weather.
  o Locking of bay doors when not in active use.

Auditing and Inspection Program
- Provide random escorts of containers from entry ports or depots to your warehouse.
- Perform random audits of goods shipped and received:
  o Have weekly minimum requirements of shipments to be audited.
  o Use in-house and independent outside auditors.
  o Document all audits.
- Ensure opening and closing controls for warehouse access; should be a minimum of two people, one a member of security and the other management.
- Set up security inspections to address the following areas:
  o Key and lock maintenance.
  o Fire door alarms.
  o Parking lot/perimeter checks.
  o Burglar alarms.
  o CCTV maintenance.
- Maintain cargo container lock/seal program:
  o Establishment of container/truck locking standards.
  o Establishment of container seal standards.
  o Locking of "in transit" trailers/containers.
  o Use of "king pin" locks on trailers parked in yard.
  o Logging controls for all incoming and outgoing seals and locks.
  o Storage and distribution controls for all seals and locks.
- Establish auditing and follow-up controls of all noted discrepancies.

Collusion Deterrents
- Ensure random guard post rotation: Never leave a security guard in a permanent assigned post; it reduces your flexibility and invites collusion.
- Rotate dock assignments for shipping/receiving teams.
- Rotate assigned bay/dock locations for regular drivers.

Internal Theft Deterrents
- Establish a single point of access and egress for all employees. This facilitates inspection controls.
- Establish a "dress code." The wearing of jackets, coats, baggy clothes, and "own" brand merchandise while in the warehouse proper should be prohibited.
- Establish exiting security inspection of all parcels, packages, briefcases, etc.
- Establish random inspection of exiting personnel.
- Establish an employee "hotline" for the reporting of dishonest activity along with a reward program.
- Use pre-employment background screening for all warehouse employees.

A Post 9/11 World

Like it or not, 9/11 changed the way we will conduct our business for many years to come. Prior to 9/11, security expenditures for securing the supply chain were predicated mainly on financial ROI versus actual cost of losses due to theft. Post 9/11, government regulations and liability concerns were added in as an additional component in determining supply chain security costs. Several available forums enable security professionals to reach out and make connections with their counterparts in the international supply chain community. A global economy and the need for security in the international supply chain creates the need for such forums. Why? Since 9/11, corporate security executives now have

- More visibility, authority, and often more responsibility within their corporations. It might be said that in many companies, supply chain security has moved up from the basement to the boardroom.
- Increased responsibility for the international supply chain and increased interaction with new areas within their companies, their trading partners, and government agencies.
- The need for reviewing the correct balance of corporate security, cargo security, and homeland security (which itself is a moving target at best) impacted by the latest intelligence or terrorist event.

The impact of the *9/11 Commission Report* was to create a renewed sense of urgency in the U.S. Congress to adopt many of the Commission's recommendations:

> *Private-sector preparedness is not a luxury; it is a cost of doing business in the post-9/11 world. It is ignored at a tremendous potential cost in lives, money and national security. (Quote from the 9/11 Commission Report)*

Over 80 congressional committees have jurisdiction over some aspect of homeland security. This creates funding and turf battles among those committees and among federal agencies. All are trying to do the right thing, but opinions vary. This creates problems for private industry because this segment is never quite certain of what new requirements or regulations may be coming down the pike.

All this poses a real challenge for the retail loss prevention professional. That challenge is how best to balance the cost for loss prevention, security, and safety against the need to conduct day to day business. Most private companies would agree that this is best achieved through voluntary, cooperative efforts between private industry and government rather than mandated regulation. Congress has already authorized several voluntary programs to foster cooperation between private industry and the government. Programs that currently impact U.S. and international cargo security professionals include

- Customs Trade Partnership Against Terrorism (C-TPAT)
- U.S. Customs and Border Protection's Container Security Initiative (CSI)
- Custom's prenotification requirements for shipments to the United States
- Electronic advanced manifest requirements
- Operation Safe Commerce (OSC)

The impact of these government initiatives is that importers and transportation carriers are enhancing their security posture and obligating source manufacturers, freight forwarders, and carriers to do likewise. The result has been that many importers have found that the benefits of making the expenditures needed to participate in these programs outweigh the costs because they have enjoyed large reductions in supply chain losses, and at the same time, the government now has thousands of additional soldiers in the war against terrorism.

For retail loss professional executives, all these provide new challenges for the retail community. Many of these challenges come from trying to plan for the unknown:

- What new rules will come from the U.S. government (100% screening, new recordkeeping requirements, new background inspection requirements for employees handling cargo, ANSI standards, etc.)?

- Will business continuity plans address heightened threat levels or a terrorist event?
- How will other governments respond to these U.S. trade initiatives?
- Will other countries impose harsher, retaliatory regulations in response to U.S. requirements?
- Which rules will take precedence, and will there be multiple sets of rules with which our companies need to comply?

The United States and other governments recognize these pitfalls and are attempting to reach international security standards that are both reasonable and effective.

The balancing of sometimes-conflicting security requirements of our companies and those of government bodies will always be a challenge. The need to stay involved in supply chain issues is imperative if we are to see the big picture and make informed decisions. The importance of being able to represent our companies' positions and concerns and making our expertise available without being seen as a threat to other stakeholders cannot be understated if the loss prevention community is to work together to help shape these debates in a way that assures security measures are both appropriate and effective.

We need to be aware of all this if we are to successfully navigate the growing tendency to blend logistics operation, security, cargo theft, loss prevention, and antiterror measures. If we are not careful, we run the risk of misallocating limited resources and ignoring the traditional responsibilities and role of retail loss prevention professionals. Neither serves our companies or our profession well.

International Cargo Security Council

Based in Washington DC, the International Cargo Security Council was commissioned by the Johnson administration to be an advisory council to the Department of Transportation. It was spun off as a private council during the Reagan administration. The ICSC is dedicated to combating cargo crime and, since 9/11, terrorism. ICSC is the only association that reaches across all layers of supply chain security and includes security professionals in transportation and from the entire spectrum of the supply chain; that includes manufacturers, air, truck, maritime, rail, intermodal, law enforcement (local, state, federal, international), and government.

ICSC has but one single agenda: the safe and secure movement of the world's commerce. Membership is open to anyone who deals with the secure movement of cargo, anywhere in the world.

ICSC's objective is to improve cargo transportation security through voluntary government/industry efforts and act as a central clearinghouse for information relating to trends, techniques, and efforts to prevent cargo-related crimes and terrorism. In addition, the association provides a platform to educate the transportation industry, law enforcement, and private industry on matters relating to security of cargo and support government and transportation center initiatives that lead to the development of more effective programs to combat cargo loss and defend against terrorism.

You can learn more about the International Cargo Security Council and how to become involved in securing the retail communities supply chain by visiting its website at www. CargoSecurity.com.

Surveillance

CAS, JHC

A surveillance is an investigative technique involving the surreptitious observation of a person or place. There are two types of surveillance: fixed and moving.

A fixed surveillance, also known as a "stakeout," is the surreptitious observation of a fixed location conducted for the purpose of gathering evidence of a crime or to apprehend persons who have or are committing a crime. For example, a fixed surveillance of a house may be conducted when information is received that a person on whom an arrest warrant has been issued will visit that location during the surveillance, thus providing an opportunity to perform an arrest. Another example of a fixed surveillance is the stakeout of a distribution center or store in the belief that merchandise is being illegally removed through an emergency exit or over the dock, and a surveillance will establish this fact and the perpetrators can be identified and arrested. Fixed surveillances can be conducted from other fixed locations (such a nearby houses) but most commonly are conducted from automobiles and/or minivans or panel trucks, containing observation positions frequently behind tinted windows. Such vehicles are often disguised as commercial vehicles (painting companies, for example) so their static presence on the street will not attract undue attention.

A moving surveillance can either be a foot or vehicle surveillance, and often is a mixture of both. Such surveillances are normally conducted to follow the movements of suspects for the purpose of identifying other persons contacted or places visited.

In both the fixed and moving surveillances, portable radios are used to maintain contact and communication between the surveilling agents and surveillance vehicles. Photographic equipment, including cameras with telephoto lenses and camcorders similarly equipped, are used to obtain documentary evidence of the suspect's activities. Under specific circumstances as allowed by law, tracking devices may be surreptitiously attached to the suspect's vehicle to assist in keeping its location known, thus permitting a more discreet surveillance.

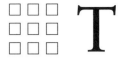

Taking Over a Loss Prevention Department

Mike Keenan

You have just started in your new position as a director of loss prevention. It doesn't matter whether you were hired from the outside or promoted internally: You face the same challenges. The first several months will determine your success or failure. So what do you do?

Start by identifying how you will focus your efforts. What are the company's expectations for you? In most situations you recently went through an interview process with the senior management of your company. What were their expectations for an LP director? They usually have a high-level view of the role of loss prevention; however, their perspectives will help you understand what they would like to see from you. For example, is their focus on shortage reduction/control, apprehensions, investigations, auditing, physical security, or a combination of some or all of them? You can also identify loss prevention challengers and supporters during this process. This can help you better prepare for interactions with senior management in the future.

The next step, which is critical to your success, is to determine what your direct supervisor expects of you. Once you are in place, try to set up a meeting with your supervisor as soon as possible. The quicker you understand his expectations, the quicker you can start developing your action plans. Initially, the best way to do this is simply to ask. Because you're new to the organization, people expect you to ask a lot of questions. Take advantage of that. Usually, your new supervisor will have a list of things that are a priority for him. What are they? The hope is that, by asking, you will start a dialogue that will clearly define these expectations. If not, schedule additional meetings until you fully understand what your supervisor expects from you. Obviously, these priorities should be high on your list of action items.

An important factor for you to consider is the company's reporting structure. Whom do you report to? The CEO, president, COO, store operations, finance? Each of these reporting structures will impact how you approach your job. The executive level that the LP director reports to will dictate how the company perceives LP. The higher the executive level, the more cooperation LP will get throughout the company. Ideally, you want to report to the highest ranking executive in the company. However, this is not always the case. Here are two examples of challenges you may face if you report to either store operations or finance. If you report to store operations, you will be able to effectively impact stores but may be less involved in corporate processes that impact shortage like buying, merchandising, allocation, information technology (IT), etc. If you report to finance, you may be viewed more as an auditor than a partner with store operations. You can be effective in any reporting structure, but make sure you incorporate an understanding of your reporting structure into your planning.

Another part of the company's reporting structure that is important is who your coworkers are? Who are your peers? To be most effective, you need the support from directors in all other areas of the company. Set up "meet-and-greets" with as many department heads as possible to introduce yourself and understand their expectations of LP. Identify their opinions on strengths and areas of opportunity for the LP department. You should also specifically identify whom you need to partner with to achieve maximum results. For example, directors of store operations are critical to running effective LP programs in the stores, human resources people are important to investigations, etc. Make sure you cultivate these relationships.

Now it's time to look at your own department. The first thing to evaluate is the structure. How many direct reports do you have? What are their functions? How many field people do you have? What are their functions? Whom do they report to? For example, some report to LP management, whereas others report to store/distribution center management. Where are they located? The answers to these questions will give you a good idea of the resources you have available to you from a personnel standpoint. Keep in mind that if you have limited LP people or even if you don't have any, your company employees are a great resource to help support and drive your programs.

Meet with your direct reports as quickly as possible. A good approach is to meet them first as a group. This helps to understand the synergy in the group and identify common issues. Then meet with each one individually. This will enable you to understand the specific issues each one is facing. A helpful insight into your direct reports can come from past performance reviews. Take the time to read each one and understand what past supervisors thought of their performance and capabilities.

Schedule visits to your stores, distribution centers, and any other facilities your company maintains. You must observe firsthand how the business looks and works. If your company has a large number of stores, visit a representative sample—for example, different geographical areas, high sales volume stores, low sales volume stores, high-shortage stores, low-shortage stores, unique stores that do not fit the company's standard setup, etc. You do not need to visit every store in the chain during the first few months in your new job; it is more important to understand how stores are physically laid out and operate. However, if you have a small number of distribution centers and ancillary facilities, visit all of them. Since distribution centers and ancillary facilities are usually unique, it is important to understand, similar to the stores, how they are laid out and operate.

Mix up the people you travel with. Visit stores with your LP people, senior management, district managers, regional vice presidents, human resources, etc. Visit your DCs with your LP people and distribution center management. You learn a lot about people when you travel together. Take advantage of the travel time to ask questions and get their perspectives on all areas of the company. You will gain valuable information because they are all great resources.

Many times directors will go into a new company and quickly assess the LP department. Based on their assessment, they quickly roll out new programs. Often these programs fail because the new director has not taken the time to understand the culture and the history of the company. Existing programs are in place for a reason. Existing employees will resent being treated as if what they did before was ineffective. LP people operate the way they do because they were trained and directed by previous LP management to operate that way. Spend the time to understand why current programs are in place. What is the best way to do this? Ask questions and *listen*. Listening is becoming a lost art. You will roll out more effective programs with less resistance if you take the time to understand the culture and history. Knowing the history of your company will help you to avoid mistakes made by previous management. Even though you are looking forward, learn from the past. You may want to change the culture you find, but it is usually more of an evolutionary process than a revolutionary process. Changing the thought processes of your department and the company takes time and effort, but it can be done. Just take it one step at a time.

During this initial time in your new position, you will be exposed to a tremendous amount of information. It is important to take notes from every one of your meetings. Unless you write it down, you will forget a lot of what you have learned. Write down what you see as opportunities. This list will enable you to develop action plans based on prioritizing the input from company management. Refer to this list every month and add new opportunities that you identify.

It's time to start developing your action plans. You've heard what your supervisor's, senior management's and your direct reports' perspectives are on LP; now how are you going to focus the LP department? Internal investigations? External investigations? Shortage reduction/control? Auditing? Asset protection? An effective loss prevention program is best achieved through a balanced approach.

Your two primary objectives should be to protect the assets of the company and reduce shortage. The assets of the company include people, property, merchandise, money (cash, credit, checks, etc.), information, and the company's reputation.

Reducing shortage will add profitability to your company. The three major areas that contribute to shortage are internal theft, external theft (vendor theft can be categorized as external theft), and operational execution. These three areas cover almost everything you will deal with in your role as an LP director. Numerous categories fall into these three areas, and it is difficult to control everything. However, if you focus on only one or two of these major areas, the one(s) you don't focus on will increase and could cancel out the success you've gained in the other areas.

Your vision and strategy should incorporate protecting the assets of the company and the three major areas that can cause shortage. Within your vision and strategy, you must identify your focus areas. Loss prevention can be a very reactionary business. It is important to develop an organization that can react accordingly to the incidents that occur in a retail environment; however, you must also ensure that you are working toward your vision. Sometimes you can spend weeks doing nothing but reacting to the needs of the business, but you must always bring yourself back to your vision. LP directors who do nothing but react may keep their supervisor and business partners happy in the short term, but they won't improve the overall operations of the LP department.

Almost everything you work on should fall into your vision and strategy. Once you define your vision and strategy, you should review it with your supervisor to ensure that you are both in agreement.

You are now ready to get into the details. The first thing to look at is the LP department metrics. What statistics do they measure and hold themselves accountable to? Measurements can include shortage, internal cases, external cases, cash over/shorts, merchandise recovery, credit card fraud, bad checks, counterfeits, etc. Determine how the statistics are trending for the year in each category. Look at the past 3–5 years to understand the history. This will enable you to gauge the productivity of your department and identify areas of opportunity where you can focus your efforts.

How does your LP department track its statistics? Is there daily, weekly, monthly, quarterly, or annual reporting? It is important to have LP statistical measurement reports at least once a month. Does your department track statistics manually or using a case management system? If these reports are not system generated, it is worth the time and energy to develop them. This can be done within your own department if you have the expertise, or you may have to work with your IT people. If you have a case management system, these reports can be easily created. Either way, make it happen. It will definitely enable you to better manage your department.

Does your LP Department look at productivity by individual? One of the most effective tools to monitor and increase productivity is ranking reports. By ranking each person against his peers in every measurable category, you can identify top performers and poor performers. It is not unusual to discover that a small portion of your staff is producing the majority of your statistics. This is especially true with internal and external cases. By improving or replacing poor performers, you can raise the bar for everyone and increase overall productivity. Specifically, these reports will enable you to recognize good performance. A recognition program directly tied into individual productivity is generally well received by investigative personnel. It creates competition, which most LP people thrive on, without creating quotas. Quotas have resulted in numerous civil litigations and should be avoided.

Ranking reports also help you identify areas that might need additional training. For example, if all your investigators have low internal case productivity, what training is needed to improve their performance?

Recognition should be an ongoing component of your department. People are your most important asset. They need to be cultivated on a frequent basis. Do you appreciate being recognized for your performance? Of course, you do. Well, your people do too! If they don't already exist, develop multiple ways to recognize good performance. This can be for statistical performance, effectively handling a specific incident, leadership, or any type of metrics. Just be sure to make this recognition meaningful. Too much recognition can take away the value to the employee. This is a good area to partner with HR. The HR staff usually have a number of programs that they can share with you. A good recognition program encourages people to strive for better performance. The better your people's performance, the better your results.

It is critical that you manage your LP data effectively. All incident reports (internal and external apprehensions, investigations, recoveries, robberies, burglaries, unusual incidents, etc.) must be maintained and accessible. When you are taking over an LP department, it would be unusual to find that it does not already have an existing methodology for documenting and tracking its activities. Understand how it works to make sure you are comfortable that it does what you need it to do. For example, how do you request and receive an investigative report for an outlying store or location?

If you do not have IT capabilities for your LP people, you must have paper reports that capture all relevant information surrounding your areas of responsibility. If you use a systems-based case management program, evaluate its capabilities. Ensure that it provides you with the data analysis tools that you need. If you don't have a systems-based case management system, you should make the effort to get one. Many case management systems are available. By working in partnership with your IT department, you should select the software and system that are compatible with your company's existing IT platform. If you purchase a systems-based LP case management program, make sure it is able to feed external systems, e.g., civil recovery/demand.

If you have a staff that catches shoplifters, most states have statutes that allow merchants to civilly recover damages from adults or the parents/legal guardians of juveniles who shoplift from that merchant. It is usually called "civil recovery" or "civil demand." The collection of restitution and civil recovery/demand should be pursued in all applicable internal and external cases. The amount that can be collected varies by state and statute. You should make sure you have your legal counsel approve the requested amount of damages in each state.

In situations in which employees steal from the company, a promissory note or restitution procedure should be in place. If an employee admits to causing a specific amount of loss to the company and is willing to pay it back, he should be asked to sign a promissory note. This form creates a legal agreement with the employee that enables you to pursue him civilly if he does not pay you back in accordance with the terms and conditions of the promissory note. Again, you should make sure your legal counsel has reviewed and approved this form.

Many companies use external vendors to handle the collection efforts for them. Some companies have their own internal collection departments. Again, in most companies, one of these processes should already be in place. Either way, review the process to make sure that you are maximizing the collection of civil remedy/demand and restitution dollars. The collected funds can be used to purchase LP equipment and services that will deter future losses. By utilizing the collected dollars in LP deterrent programs, you can more easily justify outside legal challenges that you are using civil demand/remedy as a profit center for your company.

Another important area to review is the LP budget. First, understand what your annual budget is and how it was developed. How is the department trending for the year? Is it on budget? Is it over budget? Is it under budget? Are expenses being managed properly? Poor expense management will usually put you under an unwelcome spotlight, so make sure you understand the finance methodology of your company. It is critical that you have mechanisms in place that will alert you to over-budget and under-budget situations before you receive summary reports from the finance department.

The next step is for you to understand how the LP department in your new company operates. The best way to do this is by reviewing the department's existing policies and procedures. Is there an LP department operations manual or just a collection of memos and directives which define the operating platform for the department? Having a comprehensive and detailed operations manual is critical to the success of an LP department. An operations manual should define the expectations for the LP department. It should also contain all the policies and procedures necessary to execute the expectations for the department. The content should include internal investigative procedures, e.g., evidence collection and retention, case development, interview techniques, prosecution guidelines, etc. It should include external theft procedures, e.g., the steps necessary to make an apprehension for shoplifting, use of force, evidence collection and retention, prosecution guidelines, etc. It should also include operational procedures, e.g., audits, checklists, etc. The LP operations manual should be the foundation for the daily operations of the department. It will ensure consistency throughout your LP organization. All training should be developed from the policies and procedures contained in the operations manual.

If there is no LP operations manual, create one. If one already exists, you should revise it in accordance with your philosophy and approach. The LP operations manual should always be a "work in progress." As you grow in the job, you should constantly revise it as you develop your department. Once created or revised, the manual should be made available to all levels of your department.

When creating or revising LP policies and procedures, involve members of the LP department in the process. An effective methodology is to create task forces composed of members of the LP department. Assign these groups to write new or revise existing polices and procedures. This enables you to take advantage of their experience within the department and the company, as well as have them be part of the process. This leads to ownership and makes it easier to facilitate change. This concept works very well if you decide to create or rewrite the LP operations manual.

Are there LP personnel training programs in place? If a training program doesn't exist, develop one. This should become a top priority for you. An effective training program is absolutely essential. Well-trained people enable you to execute your operations effectively and consistently.

If there is an existing LP training program in place, review the content. Is it comprehensive? Does it cover all the areas that are covered in the LP operations manual? Will it keep the company protected from legal challenges of inadequate training? Are the training programs managed by the LP department or the company's training department? Either way, the high risk that goes along with conducting internal and external investigations can be mitigated with thorough training. Multiple methods for training should be utilized—for example, written, video, e-learning, on-the-job, classroom, etc. All training should be documented, and individual training records should be maintained on each LP person. Training should be updated along with new policies and procedures.

The best way to ensure compliance to your policies and procedures by LP personnel is to have a disciplinary action process. If LP people violate the policies and procedures you put into place, there should be accountability. This will allow you to remove nonconforming employees who can put the company at risk by their actions. Effectively managing a disciplinary process will result in better consistency in your operations.

Effective communication is extremely critical to the success of an LP department. You must have some method of communicating timely information to the LP organization. This information can include new LP and/or company policies and procedures, investigative alerts, open jobs, etc. Some type of "communication binder" should be maintained in all field locations. This communication binder can be an actual binder or an electronic folder. An electronic folder that serves this purpose will depend on your company's IT infrastructure.

One concept that helps to develop a team is to create an identity for the LP department. This can include an LP department logo, tag line, and mission statement or any combination of the three. Many companies have a mission statement, but it is not specific to LP. Use the basic concepts from the company mission statement but tailor it to the LP department. Here is an example of an LP department mission statement:

> *Company XYZ Loss Prevention is committed to consistently driving processes that will improve profitability by reducing losses through investigations and operational compliance while providing a safe environment for our Employees and Customers.*

A fun way to create an LP logo or tagline is to hold a contest within the LP department. Your own people can come up with some great concepts that you can turn into the LP department identifiers. The fact that they created the logo and/or tagline themselves will cause them to take ownership. If your LP people can't come up with anything that fits your vision, work with your marketing department or, if you don't have a marketing department, use an outside vendor.

Another concept that helps develop a team and holds your people to a higher level of accountability is a "standards of conduct." A standards of conduct should clearly define your expectations for your LP people. It is an add-on to the company's employee handbook. By spelling out your expectations, you can raise the performance level of your people. Because it sets a higher standard for LP people above that of the regular employees, you must work with human resources staff to gain their support. That way, if an LP person violates the standards of conduct, he can be disciplined in accordance with the standards of conduct, not the employee handbook. It will enable you to foster a higher level of ethics and integrity in your LP team. Here is an example of a loss prevention standards of conduct.

Standards of Conduct

A Company XYZ Loss Prevention employee's conduct must be above reproach at all times. Their conduct must comply both with applicable state and federal laws which define the legal limits of their conduct and with Company XYZ policies and procedures which, at times, are more restrictive than state and federal law.

All Company XYZ Loss Prevention personnel are required to read and sign the "Standards of Conduct" form.

These standards are not intended to cover all situations, rules, policies, regulations, etc., and should not be construed as such. They are, however, indicative of the spirit and intent of Company XYZ policy and the expectation of your conduct and behavior. These standards are of such importance that any person failing to comply with them will be subject to disciplinary actions, up to and including termination without prior warning.

Maintaining the standards outlined on the following pages and the philosophical spirit reflected by them, should be the guideline in each loss prevention employee's professional approach to their daily activities.

These standards are in addition to the policies and procedures defined in the Employee Handbook.

The original, signed "Standards of Conduct" form must be maintained in the loss prevention employee's personnel file. (Copy Attached)

Standards of Conduct

These Standards of Conduct are expected of all Loss Prevention personnel so that no person will have cause to question our professionalism, integrity, credibility, and objectivity. In the performance of our job, we must be highly professional and must meet more exacting standards of behavior and adherence to rules. The nature of our function, authority, and responsibility requires this higher standard.

The following type of behavior is not in keeping with Company XYZ Loss Prevention Standards of Conduct:

1. Any activity, which reflects adversely on the ethical or professional stature of Company XYZ Loss Prevention Department. Covered under this statement are such activities as
   a. Mistreatment or abuse of persons in custody.
   b. Improper or inappropriate language in dealing with suspects or Employees.
   c. Any activity that could be construed as entrapment.
   d. Any activity that could be construed as discrimination.
   e. Any investigation or other activity which is designed to "harass" or embarrass any individual.
   f. Discussion or disclosure, by any means, of past, pending or proposed Loss Prevention investigations or activities with persons without a legitimate "need to know."

g. Misuse or unauthorized disclosure of company confidential information or Loss Prevention or Human Resources information obtained in the course of employment.

h. Personal relationships that interfere with perception of trust, credibility, discretion, and fairness.

2. Failure to objectively and factually report information required or obtained within the scope of employment. This statement covers not only the willful misstatement of facts, but also knowingly omitting pertinent information from reports and/or the purposeful "slanting" or "coloring" of reports.

3. The failure to report any information, however obtained, which could conceivably bear on or be pertinent to any Loss Prevention investigation or be of legitimate interest to company management. For example, any customer or Employee detention must be reported to your Supervisor in accordance with established time frames.

4. Failure to submit reports as required by Company XYZ Loss Prevention policies and procedures.

5. Violation of any of the provisions of Company XYZ "Use of Force and Weapons" policy.

6. Any misuse, careless or improper handling of funds, evidence, or records entrusted to our care.

7. Any misuse of company equipment or property, misuse of position or authority, or agreement to accept "favors" not granted others and available or offered us because of our position is prohibited. Covered under this statement are such things as the following:

a. Inappropriate use of company phones.

b. Removal of company merchandise or property for personal use.

c. "Borrowing" company merchandise for use in decorating or furnishing Loss Prevention offices.

d. Taking advantage of your position to secure favored treatment with regard to obtaining merchandise or any other advantage not granted other Employees.

e. Any misuse of the Company XYZ Loss Prevention Photo ID card and/or badge.

8. Failure to follow Company XYZ Loss Prevention policies and procedures with regard to stopping, questioning, and/or apprehending both Employees and the customers.

9. The failure to be completely truthful and candid in response to any official request for information.

10. Inappropriate use of CCTV cameras and equipment. CCTV cameras and equipment must be used for work-related purposes only.

11. Failure to follow policies and procedures outlined in the Loss Prevention Department Operations Manual or directed by the Director of Loss Prevention in the form of a memo.

The above statements are not intended to cover all situations, rules, policies, regulations, etc., and should not be construed as such. They are, however, indicative of the spirit and intent of Company XYZ Loss Prevention policy and the expectations of your conduct and behavior. These standards are of such importance that any person failing to comply with them will be subject to disciplinary action up to and including termination of employment without prior warning.

Maintaining the standards above and the philosophical framework created by them should be the guideline in your professional approach to your daily activities.

I HAVE READ AND UNDERSTAND Company XYZ Loss Prevention Standards of Conduct. I understand these standards are not intended to establish any expressed or implied contractual rights. I also understand that any violation of these standards may result in disciplinary action, up to and including termination of my employment without prior warning. These standards are in addition to the policies and procedures defined in the Employee Handbook.

NAME (PRINT) Employee NO.

SIGNATURE DATE

Technology should not determine your LP strategies. Technology should help you achieve your LP strategies. As part of your assessment process, you need to evaluate the technology currently available to your department. Do you have CCTV? If so, how is it utilized? Are there fixed cameras; Pan, Tilt, and Zoom (PTZ) cameras; or both? Is it overt, covert, or both? Do you have digital video recording (DVR) technology or analog video recording technology (VHS)? Are there remote monitoring capabilities? Do your people have desktop computers or laptops with docking stations? Do they have access to LP/company systems for investigative purposes?

Physical security is a responsibility that most likely falls directly onto your shoulders: burglar and fire alarm systems, lock strategies for doors, access control (if applicable), cabling of high-value apparel, locking caselines, locking fixtures, safes, securing of high-value products (pharmacy, fine jewelry), protecting of merchandise trailers, etc. There is information available on these topics in this book. You should learn about each category so that you can incorporate your physical security strategies into your overall vision for your LP department. When it comes to physical security, the simpler, the better. The easier a physical security system is to use, the better compliance you will get from the users. This is important because, even if you have a great physical security system, if no one uses it, it has little value.

Now ask yourself, does your current equipment and technology enable you to accomplish your vision for the LP department? If not, determine what you need. How do you know what's available? Simple, talk to the LP vendor community. There are hundreds of vendors who sell and service LP equipment and technology. All of them would be interested in educating you on their product(s). Once you have learned about and are ready to choose a type of equipment or technology, reach out to fellow LP directors that use the particular product(s) and ask them for feedback. Most will be happy to give it to you. Or, reach out to your fellow directors first and then talk to the vendors. Whichever approach you take, other LP directors are a great resource.

Now you've done your homework on the equipment and/or technology you want to buy, and you're ready to start the process to purchase it. The first step is to learn what your finance department requires to justify an expenditure. All companies have different methodologies for this process, but all require that you demonstrate a return on investment (ROI). Learn the formula for your company and incorporate it into all your proposals.

Exception reporting is an essential LP tool. Strategically using exception reporting will improve your efficiency because you can focus on problem (exception) resolution. You don't need to know when things are working as expected, only if there is a problem. Of course, the most common exception reporting systems for LP are POS based; however, exception reports on almost any company process that impacts shortage are valuable. Knowing which stores have high or low results in comparison to the entire store population enables you to focus on areas and locations that are exceptions. For example, for Mark Out of Stock (MOS) percentages, a high number could mean that the store is not handling MOS merchandise properly or there is some other issue. By investigating that high number, you can identify, address, and correct the issue which will reduce the MOS. Reduced MOS improves profitability. If a store has a low MOS number, it could mean that it is not processing MOS properly or possibly even throwing it away. This would cause shortage, and the store would not be replenished for the damaged merchandise. Use exception reporting to identify anomalies and investigate the anomalies. You will be able to spend less time and get better results because you are addressing exceptions only.

To stop return fraud, a refund control program is absolutely necessary. Without an effective refund control program, your company is at risk. Poor refund control can lead to internal theft (fraudulent returns by employees) and external theft (shoplifting for the specific intent to return.) It can also allow duplicate receipts, counterfeit receipts, and the reuse of the same receipt multiple times.

Thieves find ways to circumvent polices at individual stores. The best defense is a corporatewide system to track returns. The main focus should be on nonreceipted returns. If your POS system allows a way for cash to be obtained without a receipt, the thieves will find it. A refund control system that stops nonreceipted returns works by requesting IDs from individuals returning merchandise without receipts. You set the parameters for how many returns you will allow before you shut them down. This is called "velocity." The system should also identify counterfeit receipts and previously used receipts and stop them as well.

Refund control systems can be developed internally or purchased from an outside vendor. Either way, refund control is a must have.

One of the issues that you will face when it comes to the implementation of new company systems is where and when the LP requirements are included in the process. For example, a new POS system needs your involvement to make sure the proper controls are included to prevent losses at the registers and in the cash office. Many times, the LP requirements are scheduled to be implemented at a future date. This future date is often called "Phase 2." Be aggressive in having the LP requirements included in "Phase 1." "Phase 2" may be delayed or even canceled, and you will have lost your opportunity to get the LP components you need. Developing an effective partnership with the IT department will enable you to always be part of "Phase 1."

Organized retail crime (ORC) is a significant part of external theft losses in most retail environments. Evaluate the extent to which your company is a target of ORC. Based on this analysis, determine how to use your LP and store resources to minimize this threat. Do you lock up your targeted product? Do you place it behind counters? Do you work with law enforcement to apprehend the thieves? Do you allocate some of your LP personnel to focus only on ORC? Whatever plan of action you develop, be sure to include ORC in your strategies to control losses.

Shortage programs are an integral part of any LP program. Controlling shortage is a process. You must have all areas of the company working together to control shortage. There must be daily attention to all shortage control procedures. For this to happen, there must be support for reducing shortage that comes from the senior management of the company; otherwise, it will not be a priority.

The first step in creating a shortage program or enhancing an existing one is an Executive Shortage Committee. This committee should include senior management and director-level people. The higher the management levels in these meetings, the better. Representation should include LP, finance, operations, distribution, buying line, IT, internal audit, inventory management, human resources, etc. You want people on the committee who can go back to their departments and make things happen. This committee should focus on all areas of the business that can impact shortage. It should develop action plans that the people on the committee can go out and execute. Examples include store/DC LP standards, focus on high-shortage stores, focus on high-shortage merchandise, EAS tagging standards, etc.

A shortage program should include monthly shortage meetings in all stores and DCs. These meetings should include the facility manager and key people in the location. The monthly topics should focus on high-shortage areas and processes. All facility employees should be made aware of the focus topic each month. This can be done through separate meetings held at different times throughout the day. Retail schedules rarely allow for storewide meetings, so the individual meetings should be scheduled so that all employees are given the necessary information.

Another effective method is the development and implementation of individual store shortage "action plans." These action plans should be based on the shortage results from the most recent inventory. Focus areas can be companywide, store specific, or a combination of both. The plans should define what each store is going to do to address the high-shortage areas. District/regional store operations and LP managers should be required to approve the action plans. The action plans should be inspected throughout the year, and stores must be held accountable for not executing their plans.

Some companies focus their efforts on high-shortage or "target" stores. These "target store" programs are based on the concept that reducing shortage in the highest shortage stores will be the best return on the investment of resources. This approach is usually very successful in those stores. The challenge with this approach is that "nontarget" stores can experience increased shortage because there is not a focus on them. Those stores can then become the new "target" stores.

An effective shortage program must include employee awareness training. Employee awareness starts with educating employees on their role in controlling losses in the company. What can they do every day to positively impact shortage? You must define the expectations for every employee. They need to take ownership for controlling losses. If they have "ownership" for controlling losses, they will be more likely to help than if they don't feel they have any responsibility. This can be done by communicating your message(s) in new hire orientations, company newsletters, posters, etc. Developing a shortage logo and tagline will "brand" your program. As with an LP department logo and tagline, create a companywide contest to get ideas. Your company employees can often come up with some great concepts. If your company employees can't come up with anything that fits your vision, work with your marketing department or, if you don't have a marketing department, use an outside vendor.

Since shortage control requires daily attention, your goal should be to create a culture of loss prevention. You want all employees doing the right things every day. Doing the right things means not stealing, reporting those that do steal, and following established procedures to prevent loss. A loss prevention culture takes time to develop, but it will pay off every year in low shortage if it is maintained throughout the company.

A quote that has been around for a while is "a well run store equals low shortage." This makes perfect sense, but how do you ensure that a store is running well? How about another quote? "You get what you inspect." An LP audit program enables you to monitor store compliance to shortage control policies and procedures on a periodic basis. By monitoring store performance and correcting identified deficiencies throughout the year, you can prevent a poor shortage result.

If your company does not have an LP audit program, you should consider putting one in place. If your company does have an existing audit program, you should evaluate its effectiveness. Often you will find the existing audit program does not have a true impact on controlling shortage.

The two keys to a successful LP audit program are objectivity and accountability. The first key is objectivity. The audits must give an accurate picture of what is actually happening in a store. If they don't, they have limited value. To be able to correct issues, you must know what they are. Auditors must be able to objectively report their findings. Of course, that makes sense, but it doesn't always happen. Here is something to consider. If the person who conducts the audits reports directly to the district manager or regional manager who is responsible for running the stores, can he truly audit objectively? Will this "partnership" be jeopardized if the LP person fails them in an audit? Will performance evaluations be negatively impacted? Review audits for the past year. Are all stores passing? If they are, it is an indicator that the audits may not be objective. It would be a very well run company indeed if every store passed every audit. Try to set up your LP auditors so that they report independently from the people who run the facilities they are auditing.

The second key is accountability. If a store fails an audit, are there consequences? Are the consequences serious enough to get the attention of the person being audited? For example, if a store fails an audit, does it result in disciplinary action? Does it impact its performance evaluation or bonus? If the consequences aren't meaningful, store management will not focus the appropriate attention on taking the actions necessary to pass the audits. You must elicit senior management's support in developing the appropriate consequences so that store management knows that it is a company priority.

If you don't have an effective store audit program or don't have one at all, how do you get started? Create a task force that includes loss prevention executives and store line senior management. If store management is included in this process, there will be more of a sense of ownership, and the audit will have more credibility. Develop an audit that addresses shortage control in all areas of store operations. This does not normally include creating new polices and procedures, but just selecting those that will make a difference in reducing shortage. The contents of an LP audit should include cash office, receiving, point of sale (POS), physical security, EAS tagging compliance (if applicable), and anything else that impacts shortage. As a side benefit, this process can result in strengthening controls in almost all existing store procedures, because when the task force reviews all procedures, they will usually find ways to improve them.

To ensure that the new audit works effectively, make sure you "field test" it. This enables you to identify problem questions and correct them before you roll out the entire program.

Once finalized, the revised procedures and new audit forms should be provided to all stores. Stores should be given some time to "ramp up" before the new audits are scheduled to begin.

One way to ensure auditing consistency is to create a loss prevention auditor's manual which contains detailed explanations of what the auditor should be reviewing for every question on the audit. This manual will ensure that all auditors review the same areas in exactly the same way. The completed manual should also be provided to every store so that they also know every question and the audit instructions. Communicating this information to the stores will eliminate many of the challenges when points are not awarded.

To help stores pass their audits, which is, of course, the goal of the program, stores should be required to complete daily or weekly checklists. These checklists are tools to ensure daily attention to the policies and procedures that are reviewed on the audit. Checklists can be created directly from the audit. Many times stores will break the audit into sections and use them as checklists.

Another component of an audit program that gets results is a random and unannounced audit schedule. The only way to get a true picture of what is really happening in a store is to show up when the store doesn't expect you. Another benefit of a random and unannounced audit schedule is that all stores will operate more consistently on a daily basis in expectation of receiving an audit.

Audits must be conducted often enough to allow "course correction" during the year. Many companies take once-a-year inventories. It is the consistent execution of shortage control policies and procedures that provides the positive end-of-year results. One formula that works well is a quarterly audit in all stores and a monthly audit in high-shortage stores. Of course, your program must fit your company's structure and budget. Timely reporting of audits is also important. As soon as an audit is completed, the results should be communicated to the store and the district manager. After that, audit scores should be tracked along with all the other company performance measurements and be included in annual performance evaluations.

Cash control is an important part of any LP program. Review the existing procedures: "Follow the money." What are the controls in the cash office? Are all cash office personnel background-screened? Is the physical security of the cash office (locks, safe, camera coverage, etc.) adequate? How are the basic funds for each register drawer set up? How are they transported to the sales floor? What are the controls at the registers? How is change handled? How are cash pickups done? Who counts the daily sales and creates the deposits? Who verifies the deposits? Are the deposits taken to the bank by sales personnel, or are they picked up by an armored carrier service? Are there controls in place to make sure that the deposits arrive at the bank? If a deposit does not make it to the bank or there are discrepancies with the deposits that are identified by the bank, how is it communicated and to whom? The answers to these questions will enable you to identify the effectiveness of your company's cash control procedures.

Timely notification of cash register overages and/or shorts to LP is essential. Determine how stores communicate register shortages to LP for investigation. Make sure that LP is notified as quickly as possible. Once notified, how do the LP personnel keep track of the shortages by store? Cash shortage investigations should always be a high priority for your LP personnel. Employees who steal cash are usually stealing in other ways, too.

Credit card fraud, fraudulent and/or bad checks, fraudulent traveler's checks, and counterfeit currency are other concerns that should not be ignored. Each of these areas has available controls that can be utilized by retailers. Meet with your finance department to learn about the controls that are currently in place. Ask the finance staff to provide you with regular reports on fraud losses. Review how employees are trained to accept checks. Is there a check guarantee program? Are ultraviolet lights used to check for counterfeit currency, traveler's checks, and credit cards? Do employees check for identification? Are imprinters used for credit cards that won't scan? The best way to prevent fraud is by having well-trained and alert employees. Train employees to follow all the required steps when accepting credit cards, checks, traveler's checks, and currency.

One of the most effective ways to get information regarding people or issues that are causing theft or shortage is an employee hotline. Implementing a confidential way that employees can communicate information will increase your chances of identifying where and how losses are occurring in your organization. In addition, by paying out cash awards for information that leads to correcting the cause(s) of the loss, you will increase the information flow. Although most people don't call specifically to get the money, they appreciate getting the award.

Employee hotlines can be managed internally or by an outside vendor. As long as the information can be provided and managed confidentially, either way will work. However, make sure it is an 800 number so that employees can call from anywhere. Many companies use an outside vendor because they believe it makes the employees more comfortable in making the call knowing it is not going to a person inside the company.

Once you have established an employee hotline, publicize it through all available methods—employee training and orientations, newsletters, the company website, paychecks, wallet cards, posters, employee handbook, etc. One effective way to ensure that all employees always have access to the number is to print it on their discount cards. In addition to the LP hotline, make sure that you get all your LP messages out using the same methods.

When rolling out LP programs, always use the company's current communication protocol. For example, if you roll out a new procedure on controlling credit card fraud to the stores, use the existing company communication vehicles. If the stores get a weekly operational hardcopy communication, include your LP procedures. If the stores get a weekly email communication, include your LP messages. This way, the stores receive the LP information as part of the other information that is rolled out that week. Incorporating LP information into the communication vehicles of the business is the best way to get your messages out to your audience.

Background screening is the best way to prevent hiring dishonest employees before they even walk onto the selling floor. Review your company's existing background screening program. Do you have one? If you do, is there drug screening? Are there criminal checks? Credit checks? Employment verification? Education verification?

Because of the high turnover in retailing, background screening is expensive, so implement a strategy that is cost effective. Determine the risk levels of your employees. Management and cash office personnel should be at the top of your list in terms of risk level. People in these positions have the most access to cash, merchandise, and company property. Evaluate all the positions in your company and develop a background screening strategy that fits. HR is an excellent partner in this evaluation process.

Participation in a national retail database is an absolute. National retail databases include dishonest employees and shoplifters from fellow retailers. This information is the most specific to the retail industry. They are relatively low cost and usually have a higher "hit" rate than the other checks and verifications. However, these databases are only as good as the information that is submitted to them. Talk to other LP directors and find the national database that includes the most retailers that you are likely to hire your employees from. If your company does not participate in one of these databases, you should definitely consider joining one.

Threat Assessment and Management: An Integrative Approach

John K. Tsukayama and Gary M. Farkas

Introduction

Prevention of crime in the workplace typically is the sole province of the security professional. In the retail sector, internal dishonesty and shoplifting offenses are the primary loss prevention concerns of in-house or contracted security agencies. Aside from those occasions when advanced technology needs to be adopted or mystery shoppers employed, external consultants are rarely used in the typical retail establishment's loss prevention efforts.

Workplace violence is a unique concern in the retail environment. While industrial facilities and many service businesses can establish basic perimeter defenses against suspected threats, the retail establishment's need for open access creates vulnerabilities not seen in other industries. The unrestricted environment of the retail sector allows both the general public as well as former and current employees (some of whom may have hostile intent) to closely approach intended targets.

Because of the unique demands of workplace violence prevention efforts, the retail security professional needs to be aware of the specialized and generally accepted principles of Threat Assessment and Management (TAM). This approach blends the expertise of the security professional with those of other consultants. In this section, we discuss how psychological and security professionals, working closely together, can add value to a retail organization's efforts to reduce the risk of workplace violence due to disgruntled employees or known outsiders.

A Special Loss Prevention Problem

Traditionally, loss prevention investigators have had the task of gathering evidence relating to a known crime that has already occurred, or one that is believed to be already occurring. In those cases, either normal reconstructive or constructive methods will be applied. The *who*, *what*, *where*, *when*, *why*, and *how* aspects of the process of investigation will guide the investigator to collect and present evidence that can be used to justify appropriate action. In the private sector, the goals of loss prevention, economic recovery, and employment termination are typical, whereas in the public sector, the goal is normally the bringing of criminal charges.

There is, however, one kind of investigative problem that differs significantly from these norms. This type of investigation centers on the problem of targeted violence and has received increasing attention in the past 20 years. The relevant questions are not merely "What happened?" or "What is happening?" Rather, they are "What is likely to happen in the future?" and "What can be done to prevent it?"

The approach that has developed since the early 1990s is known as Threat Assessment and Management, or TAM. For our purposes, we will concentrate on the application of TAM to workplace violence prevention because this is an area of frequent occurrence in which loss prevention professionals can make important contributions. Therefore, knowledge of workplace violence is essential.

Types of Workplace Violence

There are generally considered to be four categories of workplace violence.(1) They are

- *Type I:* Violence by criminals with no other connection to the workplace. Entry is solely for the purpose of committing a crime such as robbery.
- *Type II:* Violence by customers, patients, students, clients, inmates, or others receiving goods or services from the organization.
- *Type III:* Violence by present or former employees against supervisors, employees, or managers.
- *Type IV:* Violence by persons who have a personal relationship with an employee but who do not themselves work in the organization.

The first two types of violence will tend to be addressed through normal crime prevention strategies and are typically investigated in a post-incident or reactive context. These violent incidents tend not to involve perpetrators who are targeting specific individuals for violence. One example is the convenience store or gas station robbery, an act whose criminal motive is not violence, but monetary gain. Another example is the outburst of anger that a drunken patron may direct at a bartender. This type of outburst is known as *affective violence* and is typically an immediate emotional reaction to a stressor, devoid of criminal motive.

In the last two categories, there is much more likely to be a specific individual who is being selected for violent victimization by the perpetrator. This is known as "targeted violence" and is the kind of violence that frequently exhibits a number of warning signs. If those warning signs are properly detected and assessed, they can give the organization the opportunity to steer the situation away from a violent outcome.

This kind of violence will tend to be what is known as *predatory violence*, which is violence that is planned, purposeful, and emotionless. The perpetrator will engage in behavior that is akin to hunting the intended victim(s) and may provide clues to intentions, methods, and targets prior to an actual attack. It is in these situations that TAM is intended to be used. Our focus will be on predatory violence relating to type II, III, and IV workplace violence.

Threats

The topic of threats is an area in targeted violence prevention that carries great potential for misunderstanding that leads to ineffective action or overreaction. In many organizations there exist workplace violence policies that prohibit employees from making verbal threats against others. The statement "I'm going to kill you" will generally be understood as a threat, and action will be taken. Consider, too, the statement "Unless something around here changes, people are going to get hurt." Is that a threat or not?

The ambiguity involved in these situations requires refinement. The term "threat" tends to be used in two ways:

- *Threats Made:* The purest form of threat is an unconditional statement of intent to do harm. It is characterized as a communication.
- *Threats Posed:* A person, situation, or act that is regarded as a menace. It is characterized as a danger.

Another term we will use here is "instigator," by which is meant a person who has either made a threat or poses a threat to the targeted victim(s).

Threats Made

There has been some significant research completed regarding threats to do harm that indicates the need to take a more thoughtful approach to threats made. For many years, it was believed that the persons most likely to carry out attacks are those who make direct threats. In the 1990s the U.S. Secret Service, the national Institute of Justice, and the Federal Bureau of Prisons studied the behavior of 83 persons who carried out actual attacks, or came close to attacks, on prominent public figures. As a result of that research, it was concluded that "persons who pose an actual threat often do not make threats, especially direct threats."(2) It was further concluded that, "although some threateners may pose a real threat, usually they do not."(3)

This is not to imply that because a direct threat has been made that you can discount it as an indicator of future violence. In the areas of school violence, domestic violence, and workplace violence, it is not uncommon for direct threats to precede violence. Loss prevention professionals need to heed all threats, both made and posed.

Threat management experts Frederick S. Calhoun and Stephen W. Weston provide a means of sorting the confusion regarding threats. In their book *Contemporary Threat Management*, they introduce the concept of what they term the "Intimacy Effect."(4) Essentially, it is believed that greater intimacy between the instigator and the target will make direct threats more reliable as pre-incident behavior. Therefore, where there has been some degree of intimacy, such as between coworkers or spouses, a verbalized threat should be taken more seriously than one spoken about a public figure not personally known to the instigator.

Threats Posed

While many who make direct threats never attempt an attack, the lack of any threats made cannot lead the investigator to necessarily conclude that there is no threat posed. The central concept of a threat assessment investigation is to attempt to determine whether, at the present time, it appears that the instigator poses a threat to the target.

Persons known to possess all f the following should be considered threats posed to the target(s):

1. A grievance
2. Violent ideation
3. Capability to mount an attack
4. Pre-attack planning and preparation
5. Movement toward target proximity

Lacking one or more of these factors probably lessens the threat posed, although movement toward target proximity would not necessarily be relevant if the means exist to create and deploy a mail bomb (or other similar device) delivered by a third party.

Red Flags

It should be clearly understood that there are no reliable profiles that can be of meaningful use to TAM practitioners. No set of attributes will be present in all those who perpetrate lethal targeted violence. Likewise, the absence of those attributes should not be taken as a signal that the instigator does not pose a danger to a particular target. For these reasons, "profiling" is not a responsible approach to take when considering potential targeted violence.

Some factors have been identified in cases involving targeted violence that do bear attention. Organizations should train supervisors and employees to be aware of these red flag items.

If they are present, the red flags should not be used to conclude that a danger is actually posed. In fact, in the majority of instances, individuals who exhibit one or more of these items never will carry out, or even desire to carry out, targeted violence.

The presence of the red flags should signal to the organization that some level of assessment should be performed to determine whether further concern is justified. Only after an adequate TAM process is completed is it wise to specify appropriate action by the organization. In many cases, TAM investigation will determine that the person of concern lacks the grievance, violent ideation, inclination, means, or preparation necessary to carry out an attack.

Employees should be encouraged to report the red flags (or any other reasons that cause them concern) to the TAM team with the understanding that no negative action will be taken against the person of concern solely on the basis of their report. To do otherwise may make employees hesitant to share information at an early stage when there still exists ample opportunity to address the situation while the instigator is still capable of being diverted.

Red Flags

Following is a list of red flags employees should be aware of:

1. Bringing weapons to work.
2. Excessive alcohol use.
3. Illicit drug abuse.
4. Recently acquiring weapons, especially in conjunction with dispute events.
5. Fascination with weapons.
6. Hypersensitivity to normal criticism.
7. Harboring grudges in conjunction with imagined or actual grievances.
8. Preoccupation with themes of violence.
9. Outbursts of anger.
10. Interest in highly publicized incidents of violence.
11. Loss of significant relationships, including marriage or other intimate relationship.
12. Legal or financial problems.
13. Ominous, specific threats.

14. Suicidal/homicidal thoughts or speech.
15. Stalking or placing employees under observation.
16. Verbalizing a strongly held belief that others mean him harm.
17. Being frequently sad, angry, or depressed.
18. Extreme disorganization.
19. Marked changes in behavior or deteriorating hygiene.
20. Actual or expected job loss or job-related discipline.
21. Those surrounding the instigator fear violence.

No list of red flags or warning signs can be exhaustive, and the fact that something of concern to employees does not appear on this list should not prevent the TAM team from considering it when deciding to proceed with a formal assessment.

TAM Teams

TAM is a complex undertaking that has the twin objectives of determining whether the current situation is apparently moving toward a violent act and specifying a set of measures the organization can undertake to divert the instigator away from violence.

The practice of creating specially trained teams has arisen to provide the talents of a multidisciplinary group to both sort out the complexities and handle the numerous tasks associated with quality assessment and planning in the high-stakes endeavor of targeted violence prevention.

These teams are known by a variety of names. They may be called threat management teams, incident management teams, threat assessment teams, crisis management teams or go by any number of "committee" names. In any case, the teams will often include TAM-trained representatives from the following parts of the organization:

- Human Resources department;
- Legal department;
- Security department;
- Facility Management or Building Management.

In addition, someone in the management chain above the affected employees will often be included so that the team has sufficient information regarding the day-to-day operations of the relevant department.

Certain outside consultants will often be contacted to assist the team in its assessment and planning duties. Some such consultants may include

- Outside legal counsel;
- Psychiatrists or psychologists experienced in violence risk assessments;
- Investigators who specialize in TAM work;
- Employee assistance program counselors;
- Background research firms.

Finally, the TAM team should be headed by a manager with the authority to fully commit the organization's resources to the effort and expense necessary to take meaningful protective measures immediately upon determining that they are essential. This TAM team leader should make the final decision on the organization's response if the team cannot reach consensus. If either the authority to proceed or sufficient decisiveness is lacking in this key person on the team, undue delay, inaction, and very possibly physical harm may ensue.

TAM Principles

While it is common to react to news of a mass workplace murder by assuming that the act was entirely unpredictable and thereby unpreventable, the process of threat assessment investigations relies on a number of major principles that represent an absolutely opposite view:

1. Targeted violence results from a process of thinking and behavior that can be understood and often detected in advance. To be able to carry out an act of targeted

violence, the perpetrator must pass through a series of steps along the way. He must develop a sense of grievance or injustice that motivates him. He must hit upon violence as the only or best option available to him to redress his grievance. He must select the individual or organization to target. He must choose the method of attack as well as the date and time for an attack. To do so, he may conduct research on the target, including stalking the targeted individual or placing the target site under surveillance. He may need to acquire the means to approach the target, breach any security measures in place protecting the target, and carry out the intended attack to the desired conclusion. The instigator's dispute with the target and subsequent planned violence may take center stage in his life and rise to the level of an overriding obsession that the instigator readily and compulsively talks about to those around him.

2. Targeted violence takes place in the interplay between the instigator, past stressful events, the target, and the current situation. It is considered useful to determine how the instigator has reacted to prior instances of unbearable stress. If, in earlier situations involving significant losses (home, family, job, position, etc.), the instigator attempted acts of violence (including directed at himself), this information may be crucial to an understanding of how he may perceive his present situation. Likewise, other information regarding the instigator's background may be critical to the assessment process. Where he lives; his vehicles; his access to or familiarity with weapons; his educational, medical, and employment histories are all among the information about the instigator that the TAM team may require. Information regarding the target will also be critical. The TAM team should seek answers to the following questions. Is the target known to the instigator? Can the target be easily approached at work, home, or other obvious locations? Does the target take the threat posed seriously? Can the target's normal locations be "hardened" (receive additional security measures)? Will the target accept and follow security advice? Finally, the current situation, both in terms of any event likely to trigger untoward acts and the overall atmosphere, environment, and influences acting on the instigator must be examined. Whether the instigator is surrounded by a culture, family, group of associates, or counselors that encourage or discourage violence as a means of conflict resolution is also important to determine.

3. Addressing targeted violence requires determining the "attack-related" actions of the instigator. As noted previously, the instigator will normally travel a path leading to an eventual attack. At each stage of this journey, he may communicate information or be observed in behavior that signals his thinking, planning, and preparation. Searching for information regarding these factors is key to the proper assessment of a situation, to determining whether the instigator poses a present danger to the target(s). If, for instance, the instigator is known to dislike a coworker with whom she has exchanged angry words, is this sufficient reason to consider her to pose a threat to the target? An assessment investigation that determines that the instigator recently has acquired a firearm and was seen sitting outside the targeted employee's home in her car would clearly support an assessment that the situation should be of serious concern.

The Role of the Loss Prevention Professional in Threat Assessment and Management

The conduct of TAM assessment investigations relies on the same skills, techniques, and aptitudes of any other kind of investigation. The loss prevention professional should take steps to prevent the investigation itself from becoming a factor that contributes to an attack. Therefore, much of the work of the TAM team should be kept from becoming obvious to the instigator.

The following should all be considered in TAM assessment investigations by the loss prevention professional:

- Reviewing records. If the instigator is an employee, all available files must be reviewed, including employment application; background reference checks that were completed at the time of hire; all evaluations by supervisors, coworkers, or subordinates; records of counseling or discipline; any complaints, grievances, or even lawsuits against the employer, coworkers, and others; attendance and leave records; training records; and any prior safety or misconduct investigations involving the instigator. Examining the context in which the instigator first became of interest to the TAM team. Care should be taken to understand the reasons for the initial report concerning the instigator and determining the credibility of the complainant. The first notice to the TAM team that the instigator concerns a coworker, supervisor, or other company-related person may contain information that will help the TAM team understand the nature of the dispute or injustice that may be at the heart of any motivation to commit violence.
- Researching in the public record any history of court actions (civil or criminal) involving the instigator. If the instigator is involved in a years-long dispute with an individual supervisor or store, the record may be rich in information that describes the degree of anger that the instigator may harbor against the target(s). Similarly, if the instigator has elevated the grievance to a "cause" or "crusade" against perceived perpetrators of great injustice, the TAM team should carefully consider how committed the instigator may be to punishing the target, regardless of the cost, to himself or others.
- Interviewing persons with historical or current information on the instigator's thinking, capabilities, motives, and plans. Care should be taken that anyone interviewed by the TAM team can be relied on not to disclose to the instigator that the assessment investigation is being conducted.
- Examining the instigator's workspace. In the case of instigators who are employed by the retailer, and if consistent with established company policy, examining the instigator's immediate work areas may be of immense value to the assessment. If the examination can include a review of the company computer files accessed by the instigator, it may be possible to uncover information relating to the underlying grievance held by the instigator, pre-attack planning and actions, ritual settlement of his affairs and disposing of his property, and the identity of intended targets. Also if permitted, the TAM team should try to view the instigator's email traffic on the organization's computer system.
- Making direct contact with the instigator. At some point, the TAM team may decide that the benefits of speaking directly with the instigator outweigh any risks of initiating such contact. Contact with the instigator may allow him to vent his frustrations and reduce his sense that only violence can give voice to his grievance. The instigator may provide a clear view of his intentions to actually cause violence and accept the attendant consequences. An instigator may reveal the amount of research, surveillance, and other attack preparation he has completed. The instigator may convince the TAM team that he lacks the organization, means, or capability to launch an attack during direct contact.

The focus of the TAM investigation should always be on seeking answers to the question of whether the instigator is progressing toward violence and, if so, how far advanced that progress may be. The answers to those questions are the heart of the actual threat assessment.

All the information that the loss prevention investigator is able to develop should be provided to the team and especially to the consulting psychologist. It is critical for the security professional to understand the ways in which the psychologist can contribute to the accuracy of the TAM team assessment and the active management of the instigator.

The security profession can provide the target hardening, investigation, and research capabilities to the overall TAM effort while the psychological profession offers insight into pathology and the likely effectiveness of treatments and health and social service diversions.

Unless the professions see themselves as allied in the TAM process, they are likely to work independently, possibly to cross-purposes. This can lead at best to uncoordinated actions of limited effect, and at worst to a string of actions that create a sequence of frustration, distrust, and hostility in the instigator that together can trigger actions that the instigator might not have otherwise felt compelled to undertake.

Without the TAM team approach, a security investigator could undertake a standard investigation interviewing coworkers, searching the instigator's locker, and admonishing the instigator without knowing that the company human resources department had referred the instigator to a fitness for duty evaluation with a local psychologist. In such a case, the organization may be sending two messages to the instigator. On the one hand, he is likely to believe that he is being viewed as a criminal, while on the other, he is being told that the fitness for duty is intended to assess his suitability for return to work. One message may be perceived as confrontational and threatening, whereas the other may be viewed as collaborative and nonthreatening.

The instigator will likely consider the company to be double-dealing, insincere, and the psychologist to be simply trying to make a case for termination. With such a viewpoint, the instigator will be far less likely to be open to cooperative or therapeutic initiatives proposed by the company. He may also receive reinforcement for paranoid ideas that everyone at the company is "out to get him" and begin to add names to an internal list of people who deserve his retribution.

A key figure in the prevention of targeted violence is the psychologist who may be an active part of the TAM team or may assume other roles. Those roles and important considerations regarding those roles are discussed next.

The Role of the Psychologist in Threat Assessment and Management

Many experts in the field of workplace violence risk management suggest that mental health professionals, particularly psychologists, should be available as consultants to TAM teams.(5) Inclusion in this process acknowledges the necessity of having a better understanding of the mental status of the instigator, and the critical role that psychologists serve in acquiring and using this knowledge.

Psychologists are typically used by TAM teams in one of three capacities: background consultants, co-interviewers, and referral resources. In each capacity, the right psychologist can add value to the TAM effort by sharing their knowledge of mental illnesses, risk assessment, diversion techniques, and community treatment resources.

Background Consultant

As background consultants, psychologists are provided with investigative information. The TAM decision makers may benefit from insights drawn by the psychologist related to the likely mental status, possible future behavior of the instigator, and potential approaches that could be used to divert the instigator. Psychologists acting in this role are drawing on secondary sources of information, as they have no direct contact with the instigator. They are basing their advice on training and experience, combined with intelligence developed about the instigator. Their informed speculation can help guide the deliberations of the TAM decision makers.

Co-Interviewer

As a co-interviewer, the psychologist becomes a TAM investigator, typically partnering with a security professional to more directly assess the needs, motives, and capabilities of the instigator (for an excellent description of risks and benefits of interviewing instigators, see Calhoun & Weston [6]). Clearly, when employed as a co-investigator, the psychologist's direct access to the instigator allows for a more comprehensive consideration of the instigator's mental status. When practical, some interviewers (7, 8) may do this through telephonic interviews with the instigator, although face-to-face interviews must be considered a preferred—if riskier—methodology.

Referral Resource

TAM teams often find mental health professionals as useful referral resources. Psychologists, psychiatrists, and social workers may provide psychotherapy for instigators, helping them to learn socially appropriate ways of directing and managing their hostilities. Professionals used in this capacity are acting as part of a diversion effort. Selecting the right doctor for this job is critical because TAM investigators will want to have a continuous dialogue with the professional. While all mental health doctors will release information with their patients' consent, there is a considerable difference in the information flow obtained by a professional who has a comprehensive understanding of TAM needs, compared to the doctor who rigidly guards what he believes is in the best interests of the instigator/client. The TAM effort can be impeded by a mental health professional randomly chosen or selected just because an opening in the schedule exists.

Having referral resources responsive to TAM needs requires knowing the community and developing a list of cooperating professionals. It is essential to create incentives so that the professional will give priority to your request. In some communities, it can be weeks or months before professionals have openings in their calendars. We have managed to have professionals create space in their busy schedules by having the organization pay them directly their full rate, bypassing insurance programs. This makes payment easier for the professional, and billing at the full rate provides a supplement to the contracted and lower rate typically paid by an insurer.

Another tactic we have used is to initiate payment to a provider to keep a therapy slot available. For example, if TAM considerations suggest that there is a likelihood of needing a referral resource in the near future, we contact the professional and ask that they start scheduling a block of time for our needs. This may be a specific time or just access to some unidentified time in their work week. We have had prescheduling of such therapy times for as long as eight sessions. Whether or not the instigator is actually referred, the professional will be reimbursed for his time. Of course, medical insurance will not reimburse for unused therapy time, and this method requires that the organization directly pay the service provider.

The Fitness for Duty Evaluation as an Investigatory and Diversion Method

The primary goal of TAM processes is to acquire sufficient information to increase the probability that instigators might be diverted into nonviolent courses of action. For those instigators who are employees of organizations, the fitness-for-duty (FFD) evaluation provides a method for not only data acquisition, but also for diversion.

The Standard Fitness for Duty Model

The FFD evaluation typically is used to determine if a mental health condition exists that interferes with an employee's capacity to meet the demands of his job description.(9) The psychologist typically examines the personality and intellectual functioning of the employee to assess whether there are any barriers to continued employment and, if so, what corrective actions might be used to return an employee to work.

The typical FFD evaluation consists of an examination of employer records, followed by psychological testing and an interview. In many professionals' offices, the psychologist or psychiatrist does not communicate with the employee until such time that the interview begins. Appointments and psychological testing are handled by administrative staff or student assistants. The psychologist's or psychiatrist's role typically ends upon submission of a report to the organization.

The Threat Assessment and Management Fitness for Duty Model

When endorsed by the employer, the model (TAM-FFD) used by the second author in TAM situations differs markedly from the typical FFD scenario. While the goals of the standard FFD apply, the TAM-FFD model extends the paradigm. The TAM-FFD process consists of first acquiring all possible available information on an employee and then establishing a relationship that we hope is conducive to enlisting the employee's cooperation in the formal psychological evaluation as well as in future diversion efforts.

The TAM-FFD uses any and all available information about the employee. The organization's human resources (HR) file is first reviewed. It is important to use all files contained in HR offices because general information, investigation reports, medical information, and personnel evaluations are sometimes kept in distinct files or even at several offices. HR files are a rich source of information about past history, beneficiaries, and changes of beneficiaries. These files can also provide information for use in related efforts to investigate the employee.

The TAM-FFD may include interviews with appropriate informants employed by the organization. Great sensitivity is necessary in selecting the informants for interviews because a guiding principle of the TAM process is to protect the dignity of the instigator. For this reason, substantial caution is used to identify discreet informants, and these are typically in a supervisory position. Occasionally, coworkers may be interviewed. In either case, considerable effort is made to alert the subjects of the interview that it is in their best interest to hold confidential the fact that the interview has taken place.

Mining public and nonpublic information databases is an essential part of the TAM-FFD. Public information sources such as web search engines (e.g., Google.com) and meeting places (Myspace.com) can provide a rich insight into the actual lifestyle and aspirations of the employee/instigator. Through initial use of search engines, along with the employee name and email address, we have found extensive and useful leads. For example, on the MySpace.com site, one employee extensively wrote about his real and desired lifestyle, as well as his suicidal ideation.

Any information that can be developed regarding the instigator's access to weapons can be helpful in the later portions of the TAM-FFD or by the threat management decision makers. Knowing how many weapons an instigator possesses allows his own admissions regarding this subject to be an insight into his cooperativeness.

Enlisting the employee's cooperation is a multistep process that begins with how the employer presents the concept of the FFD to the employee. It is always encouraged to have the employer describe the FFD as a process that will assist the employer and employee/instigator to "move forward." It is suggested that the employer describe himself as nonprofessional, who, because of the unique circumstances (reports of threats, unusual behavior, etc.) causes him to need to get the insight of a psychologist specializing in workplace situations. Furthermore, the employer is encouraged to depersonalize the situation, referring to workplace policies or legal advice that tie the employer's hands. This method is generally successful in enabling the organization and employee to keep their focus on "moving forward," which requires some degree of trust in each party.

The next step in the process involves the organization providing the employee/instigator with the appointment times and the psychologist's contact information. It is important that the employee be directed to telephone the psychologist before the initial appointment. While it is described as a call to confirm the appointment and answer any questions that the employee might have, the initial contact, we hope, helps set the stage for a cooperative engagement. During this initial telephone call, accurate information about the assessment process is conveyed to the employee. At this stage, the employee is informed about how the evaluation will be conducted and the limited role of the evaluator. For example, the employee is informed that the evaluator does not make decisions related to termination actions. Alleviating the employee's normal evaluation apprehension allows the employee the opportunity to be less guarded, as he too comes to see the process as a way of "moving forward."

In the TAM-FFD model, the next contact with the employee/instigator is the psychological testing appointment. Our model involves having the psychologist continue to work on relationship building with the employee by having the psychologist fully engaged during the testing process. The TAM-FFD model has the psychologist administering all the tests, sometimes over a period of more than 5 hours. During this process, the psychologist is answering all questions and providing beverages typically found in an office setting.

The intense involvement of the psychologist allows direct observation of the instigator over a prolonged time, leading to a wealth of data that would not otherwise be evident. Furthermore, such a prolonged exposure to the psychologist maximizes the likelihood that the employee might actually share truthful and important information during the clinical interview. Imagine, for instance, the difference between being asked sensitive questions about your own idiosyncrasies, failings, grievances, aspirations, and plans by someone you met 5 minutes ago. Might you be less willing to truthfully share compared to a situation in which you had 5 hours of previous and relatively benign experience with the interviewer? Finally, building this relationship allows for the possible later use of the psychologist as a conduit between the employee and employer, as will be discussed later in this chapter.

The psychological interview enables a continuing check on the employee's mental status (earlier observations of such taking place in the telephone call and testing process). The interview is an excellent forum for determining the presence of paranoid delusions and the possibility of auditory command hallucinations, both of which are critical risk factors in violence. (10, 11) Furthermore, the interview provides a venue for ascertaining the instigator's interest, planning, ability, and value placed in violence. (12) The possible contributing influence of substance abuse also can be determined.

The TAM-FFD interview is focused toward the eventual goal of determining the employee's interest in violence and whether he is willing to take affirmative steps to demonstrate that there is no inclination toward targeted violence. Toward the end of the TAM-FFD interview, the instigator is asked about whether, as a condition of return to work, he would be willing to signify that he has no interest in firearms. This is what is known as the "Test." Of course, the hoped-for answer is that the employee desires to return to work in the worst possible way and would gladly relinquish rights to firearms ownership to accomplish this goal. In our experience, the vast majority of employees eagerly accept this as a condition of continued employment, thus passing the Test.

The passing of the Test allows the employer to confidently set return-to-work conditions that include relinquishing possession of currently owned firearms and disclaiming any intention of future firearms acquisition. While such efforts cannot completely obviate the possibility of the employee accessing firearms, it can be an important step securing a commitment not to injure others and removing already-acquired arms from the instigator. We have successfully used this method to frame not only the return-to-duty process, but also the termination process as part of a benefit package. We have the employee turn their weapons over to police authorities and provide supporting documentation to the employer. In stark contrast, in a case in which we were not a party, an instance of a workplace mass murder using firearms occurred after a return-to-work evaluation that did not address relinquishing firearms.(13)

One of the final aspects of the TAM-FFD is interviewing one or more family members. While this is not always needed or possible, bringing a spouse into the evaluation process provides for additional information to gauge the threat value placed by the instigator. The spousal interview is predicated on the assumption that the spouse does not want her husband to act out violently, hurt anyone, or be subject to incarceration. So long as the psychologist can convince the spouse that their goals are identical, the spouse may provide useful information about planned violence and the lifestyle of the employee. The spouse may share information about violence history, such as incidents of road rage or domestic violence, and confirm a history of substance abuse and weapons possession. Furthermore, a spousal interview allows for assessing whether the spouse might serve a function to de-escalate the situation. By building rapport early on, the spouse may later serve a role in "moving forward." Unfortunately, it is our experience that spouses are only sometimes effectively used in this manner, as they often take the world-view of the instigator, believing that the instigator is being abused by his coworkers and organization.

After the Employer Decides: Monitoring the Status of the Instigator

After receiving the fitness for duty evaluation and also reviewing other consultant reports (e.g., legal and security), the employer ultimately determines whether to retain or terminate the employee. It is our view that this is only a decision that can be made by the employer, and we offer no direction to the employer on this issue. What we do provide, however, is a range of management options that are individually tailored to the needs of each situation and dependent on whether the employee/instigator is ultimately discharged or retained.

In a retention situation, the instigator typically requires a range of treatment options that may include one or more of the following: hospitalization, anger management, psychotherapy, medication, assertiveness and communication skills, or substance abuse treatment. The results of the TAM-FFD can be used by the employer to justify conditions of continued employment including referrals to various programs. While treatment providers can be invited to examine the TAM-FFD report, we urge caution about releasing a copy of the report to the provider if the employer has concerns about the contents of the report being seen by the employee. Once released, the report will become a permanent part of the instigator's treatment file, subject to his review and permanent possession. It is our experience that instigators are unlikely to view their own TAM-FFD with objective detachment.

Some employers may ask, "Why not just make the treatment referral ourselves and save the money on the evaluation?" It is our experience that a comprehensive assessment allows for better case management. For example, a quick and simple organizational referral to, say, an anger management program may miss the complex treatment needs of the instigator. Furthermore, merely sending the instigator to a psychotherapist will not lead to a complete identification of the treatment needs. Rarely will the instigator self-identify all the factors leading to a referral and his own failings that need psychotherapeutic attention. An examination of the TAM-FFD will allow the therapist to better understand the client's situation.

Monitoring compliance with TAM-FFD recommendations is a role frequently performed by the Employee Assistance Program (EAP), the employer's counseling and referral resource. The EAP consultant can review the TAM-FFD and meet with the employee to review conditions of continued employment. The EAP can then monitor the instigator's compliance with the programs and ultimately communicate with the employer about return-to-work readiness. On particularly complex cases (e.g., involving methamphetamine-induced persisting psychosis), the second author has suggested a second, return-to-work FFD, following completion of all treatment. Some employers may feel reassured when their TAM-FFD psychologist makes a final assessment of the employee's readiness to return to duty.

In a discharge situation, the employer may consider the advantages of providing financial security and other benefits to the employee who will be terminated. We typically consider approaching the instigator with a package that includes incentives for him to "move forward" and disengage from his employer. Severance agreements typically include several months of continued salary, medical insurance (considered important so that the instigator can access treatment), and outplacement counseling.

Meeting the goal of disengagement requires that the ex-employee minimize or refrain from contacting the company. Sometimes the discharge agreement specifies that only one person in the organization (typically in HR) is designated as a contact point, either for the instigator or sometimes limited to only the instigator's spouse. Alternatively, we have employed the services of the TAM-FFD psychologist as the contact person. Having previously developed a relationship, the ex-employee may see the psychologist as a comfortable conduit to the former employer. Using the psychologist as the only liaison also helps to sever the perceived bond between the employee and organization, thereby facilitating the separation process.

An additional role that can be employed by the TAM-FFD psychologist is to monitor the progress of the ex-employee. Regular telephonic contacts can assess the instigator's perception of the helpfulness of the outplacement counseling, any problems in finding a new job, and whether the instigator appears to be coping and disengaging from the former employer.

In functioning in this monitoring role, it is important that the psychologist clarify that he is acting as a consultant to and liaison with the employer. The instigator must know that there is no confidential communication and that the consultant's job is to assess "how things are going."

Functioning in this role, the second author has had occasion to suggest modifications of the termination package, such as a longer period for outplacement counseling. Maintaining contact with the instigator also allows for feedback to other providers about the effectiveness of their interventions. For example, after one instigator had difficulty in finding a new job, it became evident that his interview skills needed polishing. A telephone call to the outplacement counselor served to alert the counselor to this need.

TAM Countermeasure Planning

If the TAM investigation substantiates a concern that a legitimate threat is posed by the instigator, certain countermeasures or other actions must be planned.

The key question for the TAM team process is simply, "What can we do to promote safety for the target and others in this situation?"

Unfortunately, the retail environment poses certain security problems not encountered in most office or industrial environments. In a law office, for example, all the working staff can be placed within secure space, and each visitor can be individually screened before being admitted. In insurance companies, all claimant meetings can be placed in a common set of rooms or booths situated outside the secure office space. In a factory, high perimeter fencing, gated driveways controlled by a security access booth, and rolling gates can substantially impede instigator access to targeted individuals. Retail store space is specifically designed to be inviting to the public and must allow visitors unimpeded access to the entire sales floor, other customers, and the majority of employees. In addition, the employee parking areas for retailers tend to be openly accessible to the public, so attacks in these areas are relatively simple to accomplish.

Retailers also have the added burden of loss of public confidence if a worst-case attack is accomplished in one of its retail stores. If a mass murder occurs in the factory where autos are manufactured, the public does not automatically relate it to any personal danger. If a similar attack is successful at a retail location, the resulting television coverage can have wide-ranging negative impact on the store's branding efforts.

The TAM team cannot plan only short-term, immediate safety steps. While some factors, such as improving access control to the workplace, may be of immediate priority, the team should understand that the instigator may be a lasting problem for the target and entire workplace.

In light of the fact that physical separation of the targets from the instigator may not be achievable by barriers, locks, and traditional access control measures, the retail TAM team must consider relocation of the targeted employee to another store. In some cases that relocation may require that the employee agree not to tell friends, family, or associates where the new store is located. In extreme cases, the employee may even have to be relocated to another city or state. Depending on the severity of the threat situation, the employer may wish to negotiate a relocation and employment termination agreement with the targeted employee.

Certain long-term, and expensive, measures may be necessary. For instance, a short-term solution may be to have an armed security officer in the parking lot of a convenience store or at the entrance to a mall store. At the same time the retailer's loss prevention department can ask the mall security department to be on the alert for the instigator. The store staff should be given particular instructions on what to do if the instigator is observed near the store, in the parking lot, or mall security advises that he is nearby. A long-term solution may be the transfer of the targeted staff to other stores. Some retailers, due to the size of their operations, may have the ability to transfer the targeted individual to stores located in other cities or states, effectively hiding the target from the instigator. Even after the period of immediate threat has passed, these security enhancements can continue to provide benefit by making workers feel safer in the workplace.

The TAM team must look at all major components of the problem in addressing possible solutions. The TAM team should ask itself, "What can be done to affect the situation in which the instigator operates to reduce the likelihood of an attack?" Likewise, the question "What can be done to alter the expected event to reduce the likelihood of violence?" should also be answered. Finally, the team should address the question, "What can be done with the target (person or site) to reduce the likelihood of an attack?"

The TAM team should not be afraid to be creative in its approaches to the problem. While it must be cautious, it can often determine solutions that fit the complexities of the situation well if it is willing to think "outside the box."

Examples of this kind of thinking might include using the services of an FFD professional. Based on the results of the assessment, the organization may consider referring the instigator to anger management training, psychological counseling, and psychiatric treatment. If the instigator is willing but not able to afford the training and other services, the organization may consider funding these programs. Further, if the instigator is going to be terminated, and it is known that he is concerned for the long-term treatment of his child's chronic disease, should the TAM team recommend a separation package that includes continuation of medical plan benefits for a certain period paid for by the organization? Also, if the target's current workplace is well known to the instigator, should the organization consider a transfer for the target to another branch or even another city?

In addition, the TAM team should realize that most organizations cannot afford to "go to war" with the instigator. If an organization is pushed, it may fire the instigator or threaten a lawsuit. If an instigator is pushed, he may commit mass murder. He possesses offensive options that organizations simply cannot use.

Provocative, punitive, prosecution-based solutions will rarely net the enhancement in safety that the organization requires. It is often difficult for organizations to put aside an adversarial posture when dealing with instigators. Such actions tend to increase the intensity of the conflict with the instigator, not reduce it.

The TAM team should seek disengagement from the instigator, not further entanglement in lawsuits or criminal actions. While doing otherwise may satisfy an organization's desire to somehow obtain "justice," such pursuits will rarely provide a lessening of the safety problem. The instigator may not initially commit a serious criminal act that will lead to long-term incarceration. Making misdemeanor prosecution a centerpiece of countermeasure planning may only increase the likely danger. Courts will only be able to impose moderate sanctions at an early stage, which are unlikely to reduce the threat posed in a meaningful way. A series of arrests for minor offenses or being dragged through prolonged litigation initiated by the organization may simply add to the instigator's reasons for viewing himself as the victim of injustice. He may then feel warranted in escalating his responses to this perceived provocation.

Having the instigator escalate to a stage where serious criminal justice sanctions can be employed is precisely what the TAM team should be working to avoid.

The Restraining Order

Many employers, police officers, investigators, and human resources managers believe that the best response to a threat situation is for targeted persons to obtain a restraining order (sometimes known as a "protective order"). This is a civil court order requiring the instigator to stay away from the targeted persons and premises and not harass or harm them. The police can arrest the instigator if he approaches or contacts the target(s).

While such an order can sometimes be useful, many people place too much confidence in its true protective power. The following are cautions to consider regarding such restraining or protective orders:

1. The act of being served a court order, typically by police officers, can convince the instigator that the target is escalating the conflict and is not interested in any peaceful settlement to the dispute. Some instigators justify moving to violence in their own minds because they believe the targets have decided to "go to war."
2. The temporary restraining order will be followed by a court hearing at which the instigator and the targets are brought together in a courtroom. In some cases this is exactly what the instigator wants (physical closeness to and interaction with the target) and it results in increased engagement between the parties, rather than the preferred *disengagement*.

3. The court hearing allows the instigator to know the exact time and place where the target will be. If the instigator is bent on violence, especially after losing the hearing, he is afforded a perfect attack opportunity as the target leaves the secured area of the court complex. Parking lots, and even the courthouse steps, have been the scenes of fatal attacks.

4. In many jurisdictions, the court action must be initiated by individuals, as opposed to organizations, thereby requiring a degree of personalization between the individuals and instigator. This may focus the instigator's anger at individual targeted persons, rather than a faceless corporation. This is seldom good for the individuals.

5. In most jurisdictions, the arrest of a person violating the restraining order will result in a low bail and a sense of humiliation and anger in the instigator toward the targets. Penalties tend to be very minimal fines or brief incarcerations. As such, an arrest has the potential of creating an angrier instigator who may have little regard for the restraining order.

Fundamentally, we must consider the wisdom of relying on a person whom we fear is willing to commit murder to conform to rational behavior simply because a court has ordered him to do so. Should we really expect that a person capable of homicide will be deterred because he may commit a misdemeanor contempt of court?

Too often, especially in domestic violence incidents, the victims are shot to death after obtaining the restraining or protective order. Simply put, papers do not stop bullets. TAM investigators and targeted individuals should not think otherwise.

TAM Reports

The TAM team should attempt to express, preferably in writing, its combined opinion on the state of the situation as it relates to whether the instigator appears to intend violence, is capable of carrying out that violence, and has engaged in pre-attack behaviors. The assessment should detail the methods used in obtaining the information and reaching the opinion, including any input received from outside consultants, researchers, and investigators. The assessment should also provide details of the information that persuades the TAM team that the situation is moving toward or away from violence.

The TAM report must also lay out the recommended steps the organization should take to prevent a violent outcome.

It is important to note that the TAM report and the assessment upon which it is based are both valid only as long as the underlying situation remains unchanged. As such, it is a "snapshot" in time which documents conditions as they were at a particular moment. Threat situations are extremely dynamic, constantly changing as new events occur. Therefore, new assessments and management plans also may need to be evaluated in light of these new events or when previously unknown information comes to light.

For example, if the instigator brandishes a firearm on day one, threatening to shoot his estranged wife, the assessment may be that the situation is one of high risk. If the instigator is taken into police custody on the morning of day two, the assessment may be downgraded only to shoot up again in a few hours when the instigator is released on bail. In a similar vein, if the target leaves town for a week to vacation at a location unknown to the instigator, the assessment of danger will probably lower, while it may rise upon the target's return home.

Any TAM report must inform the reader that the assessment is subject to immediate change upon new developments or information. It should also identify any information limitations and assumptions included in the assessment.

Law Enforcement Assistance

If there is a truly imminent danger of serious physical attack, or if the instigator is present and is persistently unwilling to leave or desist from unlawful behavior, *the police should be immediately called for an emergency response.*

In less imminent circumstances, a TAM team may decide at some point to obtain help from the local police. If prepared to properly approach the police, the TAM team can maximize the assistance it can expect. Otherwise, such contact can be an exercise in frustration at best and make the situation much more dangerous at worst.

It is clear that the police in most jurisdictions are inundated with cases. As such, the police concentrate on matters that are judged to be especially serious, such as drug trafficking, organized crime, gangs, and homicides. In most cases, police patrol officers are responding to reports of completed crimes, documenting the available information. Where there is easily obtainable evidence and identified suspects, they will effect an arrest. In cases where a serious crime has not yet been committed, or the evidence is less than perfectly clear, it is rare for the police to go beyond the filing of an initial report. In the more serious crimes, investigations are referred to police detectives to pursue the case. This is not poor police practice, simply a logical allocation of police resources.

Very few police officers or detectives have been trained to see threat situations as matters to be approached with careful assessment and management. Traditional police emphasis has been on enforcement after crimes occur.

TAM teams wanting to obtain law enforcement assistance must therefore make full use of the assessment aspects of TAM in order to inform and educate the police on both the gravity of the threat situation and the ways law enforcement can best help.

The following are considerations to review prior to making law enforcement contact:

1. The TAM team should conduct a full investigation and assessment before calling the police.
2. The TAM team should be willing and able to lay out each and every factor leading to a conclusion that the situation appears to be potentially violent.
3. If the TAM team believes that the instigator represents a serious lethal threat and can point to specific statements and actions by the instigator that would convince police to be involved, the team should seek police assistance in managing the situation.
4. The TAM team should never overstate the credibility or reliability of information that forms the basis of its assessment. The TAM team should carefully review all evidence it is considering and remove all supposition or unsupported conclusions from its assessment. The police will not appreciate later learning that they have been "oversold" on the seriousness of the situation.
5. The TAM team should attempt to contact the police at the highest possible level, preferably through the chief, sheriff, district commander, or precinct commander. Senior police officials, provided with the specifics of a grave situation likely to represent a lethal threat to multiple targets, are much less likely to shrug off the report than the patrol officers. They are also able to command sufficient resources in terms of detectives, officers, and others to effectively help.
6. The TAM team should understand that contacting the police can lead to unintended consequences if the police choose to take aggressive action toward the instigator, such as a confrontation in which he is "warned" by the police on his doorstep. The TAM team should be able to address with the police what the assessment investigation may indicate will happen if such a provocative act occurs.

Law enforcement assistance can be crucial to a good outcome in many threat situations; however, as with restraining orders, TAM teams must properly plan how to approach and use police assistance. To do otherwise is unwise and may worsen the situation.

Case Study: A Threat in the Warehouse

The regional human resources manager of a multinational corporation phoned the first author on Monday afternoon saying that a warehouseman fearfully reported to her a threat by a delivery driver to shoot a supervisor who rescheduled the driver to start his day two hours later than before. They worked at a small branch operation 300 miles away.

The HR manager was authorized by the corporation to engage our TAM services. A temporary TAM team was formed that included two individuals from out of state: a corporate security manager and a psychologist retained for TAM services by the corporation's national headquarters. The regional HR manager and the authors rounded out the team.

While the corporate officials traveled across the country, the first author discretely interviewed two workers who provided information about the instigator, "Tom":

1. Tom had been fired elsewhere, boasting he had entered the office of a supervisor who had "messed with him," pointed a gun at his head, threatening to kill him if not left alone. A friend hid the gun before police were called. There being no witnesses, Tom was never arrested.
2. Tom reportedly fired a rifle at drunken troublemakers menacing his family at a picnic. Police were not called.
3. Tom became violent when drunk, often brawling with little provocation.
4. Tom's wife, a heart patient, cared for her aged father at their home and also babysat for their two grand-daughters. Tom's employment provided the sole family income and health insurance. He was the only one who could pick up another grandchild after school because his old schedule ended so early.
5. Tom said that, if fired for refusing the new schedule, he would punch the supervisor, leave, return armed, and shoot everyone at the warehouse. He claimed his family would be better off if he went to jail.
6. Both informants, who knew Tom well, were convinced he would carry out the threat.

The team, including the corporate officials, met on Tuesday evening. The HR manager confirmed from company records that Tom's health insurance covered his wife and that it was widely known that she could not work due to illness. Several members of Tom's family had died at young ages, and he was afraid to die and leave his family destitute. Early contact with low-ranking police officials netted a directive to call "if something bad really happens."

It was decided to directly contact the chief of police that night. The corporate security manager placed the call, informing the chief that there was a grave situation which had called him and the corporate psychologist to town, but that he was hesitant to discuss it on the phone. The chief agreed to meet the following afternoon.

Early the next morning the TAM team flew to the small town and secretly met with the local branch manager at a local hotel. He was shocked by the information the team had developed, but believed Tom was capable of carrying out the threat. Later that day the team briefed the police chief and his senior commanders. They pledged their cooperation, and one commander was assigned as liaison. The police believed Tom could have access to guns.

It was decided that Tom needed to be quickly removed from the workplace and armed security officers placed at the warehouse as soon as he knew he was being suspended. The TAM team wanted to get possession of his guns and allow the two psychologists to interview him at length. Obviously, the physical security of the psychologists during any meeting was paramount.

Flying home that night, the team discussed how to ensure Tom was not armed during the intervention meeting. Passing through the airport security checkpoints produced an idea. On Wednesday morning, the team had the HR manager telephone Tom at work and tell him that he was to fly to the regional headquarters to participate in an employee focus group over the next 2 days. He would stay at a hotel paid for by the company. He agreed.

On Thursday, the HR manager picked up Tom at the airport. Tom carried a small bag, which he had carried aboard the plane. Having passed through airport security, we were certain that he was not armed.

Meanwhile, we arranged for a provider of armed security guards to have two officers posted at the warehouse each day from 5:30 a.m. until 7:30 p.m., covering all hours that staff was at the site.

The psychologists and corporate security manager waited at the interview site, which included a conference room outfitted with covert audio and video monitored by two armed security officers in a nearby room. The first author's investigators coordinated all the diverse parts of the plan.

Upon Tom's arrival, the HR manager introduced him to the security manager and the psychologists. During the course of the next 4 hours, the psychologists spoke with Tom, assessing his attitudes, willingness to follow direction, and introducing him to the idea of his suspension. He was persuaded to allow the police to search his residence and vehicle for weapons. The first author coordinated with the liaison police commander, who dispatched a team of detectives to Tom's house. They met with his wife and, after conducting the search, took away a number of weapons. Tom agreed to meet with a psychologist in his town who had previously been contacted by the second author. When he flew home Friday, he was calm, had explained the situation to his wife, and understood that the company was going to continue its inquiry into his actions and complaints. He accepted the fact of his suspension (with pay and benefits).

The armed security presence remained in place for a few more days, until it became clear that Tom was continuing his sessions with the psychologist, and a determination was made that he no longer posed a significant threat. The second author kept in phone contact with him on a regular basis, monitoring his progress and attitudes toward the company. He also conferred with the treating psychologist to confirm Tom's compliance with his treatment plan. A few weeks later, Tom agreed to separate from the company and accepted a settlement package that provided a small amount of severance pay, extended family health coverage, and provided for the services of an outplacement firm. At last report, Tom had embarked on a new career, with different attitudes about work and coworkers.

This case study illustrates perfectly how a well-ordered response to a frightening initial informant report, using a multidisciplinary team and the threat assessment and management process, can move a potentially violent situation to a safe outcome. The investigative professional can fulfill a crucial role in that team, but only if he understands the proper methods and goals of TAM.

Conclusion

TAM investigations are becoming increasingly important for loss prevention professionals to master. The opportunities for coworker dispute, employee terminations, or even domestic violence to create real danger for the workplace through targeted violence are incalculable. The stakes can be extremely high, and the complexity of each situation must be carefully considered.

The retail loss prevention profession must take seriously its duty to protect employees from targeted violence. TAM is the set of actions, if learned and carefully employed using all the resources available to the employer, which minimize the likelihood of a catastrophic event occurring in the retail workplace.

As the specialized approaches used in workplace violence threat scenarios have become more widely adopted, the loss prevention practitioner is provided with the chance to divert, delay, redirect, or disrupt situations that might otherwise escalate to lethal violence.

While the threat may be forestalled today, the instigator may someday return. As such, these cases are rarely considered fully closed. They may become dormant for a while, but as long as the instigator can focus on the target and is at liberty to mount an attack, the situation will probably bear long-term monitoring.

We have found that, when an integrated approach is used and security professionals and psychologists work together, better outcomes can be achieved than when the professions work separately. Simply put, using such an approach creates a safer and more promising future for both the instigator as well as the rest of the workforce.[14]

References

(1) U.S. Department of Justice, Federal Bureau of Investigation. (2003). *Workplace violence issues in response*, 13.

(2) U.S. Department of Justice, Office of Justice Programs. (1998) *Protective intelligence & threat assessment investigations* 14.

(3) Ibid.

(4) Calhoun, F.S. and Weston, S.W. (2003). *Contemporary threat management*. San Diego, CA: Specialized Training Services 48.

(5) McElhaney, M. (2004) *Aggression in the workplace: Preventing and managing high-risk behavior*, AuthorHouse.

(6) Calhoun, F.S., and Weston, S.W. (2003). *Contemporary threat management*. San Diego, CA: Specialized Training Services, 145–181.

(7) Marc McElhaney, personal communication, 2004.

(8) Corcoran, M.H., and Cawood, J.S. (2003). *Violence assessment and intervention: The practitioner's handbook*, 57.

(9) Stone, A.V. (2000). *Fitness for duty: Principles, methods, and legal issues*. Boca Raton: CRC Press.

(10) Junginger, J. (1995). Command hallucinations and the prediction of dangerousness. *Psychiatric Services*, 46, 911–914.

(11) Junginger, J., Parks-Levy, J., and McGuire, L. (1998). Delusions and symptom-consistent violence. *Psychiatric Services*, 49, 218–220.

(12) DeBecker, G. (1997). *The gift of fear*. Boston: Little Brown, 156.

(13) We are fully aware that some hold a very strong belief in the right to bear arms. Some may consider the Test as a provocative intrusion into this right. We are of the belief that the potential gain outweighs any potential risk, and in practice, we have had no problems in using this method.

(14) We thank Dr. Marc McElhaney for his kind review and comments of an earlier portion of this chapter.

Resources

Association of Threat Assessment Professionals

www.atapworldwide.org/index.htm

Premier professional association for those engaged in high-stakes threat management. The purpose of ATAP is to afford its members a professional and educational environment to exchange ideas and strategies to address such issues as stalking, threats, and homeland security.

Documents:

Threat Assessment: An Approach to Prevent Targeted Violence (1995)

www.ncjrs.gov/pdffiles/threat.pdf

In-depth introduction to the concepts of threat assessment and management prepared by the U.S. National Institute of Justice.

Recommendations for Workplace Violence Prevention Programs in Late-Night Retail Establishments (1998)

www.osha.gov/Publications/osha3153.pdf

Information prepared by the U.S. Occupational Safety and Health Administration which primarily addresses the issue of robbery.

Dealing with Workplace Violence: A Guide for Agency Planners (1998)

www.opm.gov/Employment_and_Benefits/WorkLife/OfficialDocuments/handbooksguides/WorkplaceViolence/

Prepared by the U.S. Office of Personnel Management as a guide to federal government agency planners in creating workplace violence prevention programs.

Workplace Violence: Prevention, Intervention, Recovery (2001)

http://hawaii.gov/ag/cpja/quicklinks/workplace_violence/

Comprehensive guide for private employers for establishing effective violence prevention programs, TAM interventions, and post-incident responses. Prepared by the Crime Prevention and Justice Assistance office of the State of Hawaii Department of the Attorney General.

Workplace Violence: Issues in Response (2004)
www.fbi.gov/publications/violence.pdf
This is the Federal Bureau of Investigation's publication examining the issue of workplace violence and the role of law enforcement in its prevention.

ASIS International: Workplace Violence Prevention and Response Guideline (2005)
www.asisonline.org/guidelines/guidelineswpvfinal.pdf
Prepared by the American Society for Industrial Security International, this is a comprehensive guideline for private sector employers; it incorporates prevention and incident management information.

Examples of the Workplace-Related Situations Typically Encountered

Love Obsessed Kidnapper Begs to be Killed
Concord, California 1996
Jociel G. Bulawin entered the store from where he was fired and confronted owner Mary McIntyre with two pistols. McIntyre had previously obtained a restraining order against Bulawin, who was romantically obsessed with her. When McIntyre and others in the store attempted to flee from him, Bulawin grabbed her by the hair and pulled her back into the store. Bulawin pointed a pistol at her, handed McIntyre a pistol, and begged her to kill him or he would kill her. The standoff lasted for 5 hours before McIntyre shot and killed Bulawin.

Domestic Attacker Killed In Store
Albuquerque, New Mexico 2005
Carrying a knife, Felix Vigil entered the large discount store where Joyce Cordova, his ex-wife, worked. Cordova had a restraining order against Vigil, but he repeatedly stabbed her. Albuquerque Police credit an armed customer, Due Moore, with saving Cordova's wife when he shot and killed Vigil using a pistol which he was licensed to carry concealed.

Attacker Lays in Wait
Taylorsville, North Carolina 2006
Jerald Chapman waited in his car at the garden center of the store where his former girlfriend Rebecca Grogan worked. When she arrived shortly before 8:00 a.m., Chapman approached her car and shot her twice. He then shot himself, dying 6 days later. Grogan had recently moved out of the home shared with Chapman. Police credit the domestic dispute as the cause of the attack.

Delayed Attack
Las Vegas, Nevada 2001
Paul Cook and his wife divorced in 1996. Five years later, Paul walked into the grocery store where she worked and pushed a grocery cart through the aisles for 10 minutes. He then approached an employee and asked for his ex-wife. After he was told that she was in a back room, Cook handed an employee a note that he was intending to kill her. Despite being told not to go into the back room, Cook found his ex-wife, exchanged words with her, and shot her. When confronted by arriving police, Paul shot and killed himself.

Employee Intervenes and Is Shot
Canal Winchester, Ohio 2004
Sharma Rochester confided to friends that she was concerned about her stepson Christopher Rochester wanting to do her harm. She obtained a restraining order to keep him away from her at both her home and the grocery store where she worked. John Brining, a 19-year-old bagger at the store was one of the people Sharma told. He made it a practice to check

the parking lot before Sharma left to make sure that Christopher was not around. In March 2004, Christopher entered the store and put a gun to Sharma's head while she stood at her checkstand. Sharma ducked behind the counter and John Brining intervened. Brining was shot once in the abdomen but survived. Christopher fled and later turned himself in to police.

"I'm Not Sorry for What I Did"
Fairlawn, Virginia 2006

During a struggle at the store where she worked, Donna Jean Angelo was heard yelling "Let me go." Her former boyfriend, Rodney Gene Startz, allegedly shot her in the head, leaving her to die. He fled to his home, eventually surrendering to responding police officers after a 7-hour standoff. Testimony indicated that Startz telephoned the victim's brother to brag about the shooting. Angelo's family said that Startz harassed her for months prior to her murder. Press accounts note that Startz had been arrested one month earlier for making harassing or obscene phone calls to Angelo. An arresting sheriff's deputy testified that Startz told him, "I am not sorry for what I did. A man has to do what a man has to do."

Returned Weapon Fired at Responders
Chesterfield, Virginia 2005

After arriving at work, Elwood Lewis argued with coworkers and his boss, eventually firing a pistol at the boss. He was wrestled to the ground and coworkers unloaded the weapon, returning it to him when he promised to leave. When the police arrived, they found Lewis in the parking lot, having reloaded the weapon. He fired several shots at police, hitting no one. He was persuaded to surrender and subsequently charged with, among other things, attempted capital murder of a police officer, firearms charges, and attempted murder.

Fired Worker Kills Boss
Waikoloa, Hawaii 2004

The day after Yasushi Kato was terminated, he returned to the closed restaurant where he had worked. He confronted restaurant owner Yukichi Ito, and an argument ensued. Kato stabbed Ito multiple times with a sushi knife. At trial, Kato blamed stress from being an undocumented foreign worker, having no money, and feeling isolated. He claimed that he was afraid of Ito. Under cross-examination, Kato admitted that he had told a psychiatrist that he wanted to kill Ito. Convicted of manslaughter, Kato received a 20-year sentence.

Threat Assessment in the Retail Environment

Karim H. Vellani

Risk assessments are the first step in creating an effective security program and are made up of a number of smaller components, including asset identification, security measure inventory, threat assessment, vulnerability assessment (security survey), and finally the overall risk assessment. Figure T-1 outlines these steps as a flowchart. This chapter focuses on the threat assessment step as it relates to retail security.

A threat is anything that can exploit vulnerabilities, intentionally or accidentally, and obtain, damage, or destroy an asset. Threats are classified as either human or natural. Threat can also be defined as an adversary's intent, motivation, and capability to attack assets. A threat assessment, then, is an evaluation of human actions or natural events that can adversely affect business operations and specific assets. Historical information is a primary source for threat assessments, including past criminal and terrorist events. Crime analysis is a quantitative example of a threat assessment, whereas terrorism threat analysis is normally qualitative. In the retail environment, there are a number of common threats, inherent threats so to speak, that are common to all retailers. These inherent threats include internal theft and external theft. If retail security personnel know that theft is an inherent threat, why should they perform a threat assessment? We know that theft is a central issue for a retailer's bottom line, but what about other crimes that affect profits in a less obvious way. Violent crime, for example, is a rare crime, but the impact is high. Customers victimized by third parties at a retail store are

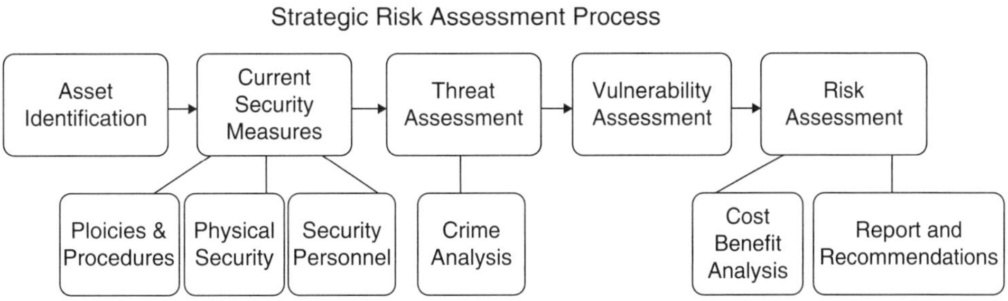

Strategic Risk Assessment Process

FIGURE T-1 Strategic Risk Assessment Process, Copyright ©2007 by Threat Analysis Group, LLC. Used by permission. Additional information available from Threat Analysis Group, LLC via www.threatanalysis.com.

not likely to return. If a number of customers are victimized, a reputation for poor security can develop and impact sales. Liability exposure for third-party crimes is also a threat.

On the other end of the spectrum is the retail security professional who engages in *security overkill*, whereby security measures are overdeployed given the threat level, or *security otherkill*, where security resources are directed at a nonexistent problem. For example, a retail store experiencing a high level of robberies in a short time span decides to deploy security personnel. The security officers are charged with patrolling the store four times per hour, making frequent stops in the cash office. Despite the increase in security, the robberies persist. What happened? After a thorough analysis of the crime data, the retail security personnel might be shocked to find out that the robberies were mostly of customers in the parking lot. *Otherkill*.

What about the retail security professional who deploys security based on retail store managers who scream loudest. Often, this leads to security overkill, where stores with a low threat level are afforded a high level of security and stores with high threat levels are provided with minimum security. A threat assessment of all company stores, at least annually, will afford the retail security professional the ability to understand the threat at each store. Unfortunately, retail security professionals perform threat assessments only for stores they *think* are high crime. All too often, retailers have security personnel at a store where they don't need the coverage, but at other stores where they don't have security personnel, they need them. Threat assessments cure this problem.

Data-Driven Security

It has been argued that security is more of an art than a science. While that belief is generally true, the business of security is not an art. The security department is a business unit, not unlike other business units within a company that must justify their existence. The higher security moves up the corporate ladder, the more challenges the security director will face and the more business acumen will be required. A commonly accepted business paradigm is *what cannot be measured cannot be managed*. With the exception of shrink rates, the acceptance of this paradigm within retail security is not far reaching. No longer can retail security professionals rely solely on gut instincts. Data-driven security refers to using measurable factors to drive a retail security program, and one of the tools for allowing data to drive a security program is a threat assessment. Too often recommendations from the security department are presented with little or no thought as to why certain procedures or security equipment should be used. Often, the reason for deploying a security measure is that other companies are doing it. It is all too common in the security industry for there to be a propensity for using certain security measures without complete understanding of the problem or a thorough analysis of the security measure's ability to be effective given the specific situation. Threat assessments can help retail security directors overcome this problem by identifying key concerns. How can security professionals justify to senior executives a sizable and usually growing annual security budget? By now, most security directors are keenly aware that a security program's success depends on the commitment and support, or "buy-in" as it is commonly known today, of senior executives. Using anecdotal evidence to justify spending on physical security measures and costly protection personnel no longer suffices. A data-driven security program helps management understand that security is more than a must-have expense; it justifies costs to management by showing the proof of success that, when presented effectively, can garner the necessary buy-in from upper management and demonstrate a convincing return on investment. Security expenditures, just like other departmental budgets, need to be justified with empirical data and supplemented with cost-benefit analyses and comparisons.

Security Metrics

Threat assessments are also helpful in developing security metrics, which communicate vital information about threats to the retail stores and drive decision making. Metrics for various security components, such as the protection force or access control system, can be an effective tool for security professionals to understand the effectiveness of the overall security program. Metrics, as previously discussed, may also identify risk based on failures or successes of security components and can provide solutions to security problems. Security metrics focus on the results of security decisions such as reduction in thefts after implementation of a closed-circuit television (CCTV) or an electronic article surveillance (EAS) system. Security metrics help define how secure we are. They assist retail security professionals in answering basic questions posed by management, such as

- Are company assets protected?
- Which assets need more protection?
- Can the asset protection program be improved?
- What resources should be allocated to security?
- How does our company compare to others?
- Are we reducing our liability exposure?

Baseline measurements are often difficult to obtain, especially in the business of security where companies are, out of necessity, secretive about their protection systems. In recent years, security industry associations such as ASIS-International, the National Fire Protection Association (NFPA), and the International Association for Professional Security Consultants (IAPSC) have promulgated standards, guidelines, and best practices. In addition to published and accepted industry standards, the courts have outlined baselines of measurement for the security industry. An example of this is a Texas Supreme Court case, *Timberwalk v. Cain*, which outlines the specific factors necessary for establishing foreseeability of crime in premises liability lawsuits. In Timberwalk, the court set forth five criteria for measuring the risk of crime including recency, proximity, publicity, frequency, and similarity of past crimes. The professional security practitioner will stay abreast of industry standards and the law. While laws must normally be reasonably followed, security professionals may fine-tune published industry standards to meet the needs of their company.

Asset Identification and Existing Security Measures

All security programs, regardless of their complexity or industry application, are designed to protect assets, and generally speaking, assets are anything of value. Generally, assets consist of people, property, and information. A retail company's assets include customers, employees, products sold by the retailer, and the supply chains and support services for getting the product to store shelves.

Asset attractiveness should also be considered in the threat assessment. Certain assets and businesses have a higher inherent threat level because of their inherent attractiveness to the criminal element. One example is electronics stores. Despite no previous crimes at a particular electronics store, the threat level for thefts of MP3 players is still high. The threat exposure is there, but the vulnerability need not be.

Existing security measures may include security personnel, physical measures, and policies and procedures. Security personnel include people specifically designated or indirectly working toward the protection of assets. Uniformed security officers would be the most visible and recognizable example of security personnel. Others may be involved in the protection as well who are not as easily identified, including undercover shoplifting agents, security managers dressed in business attire, and clerks trained in crime prevention. Physical security measures may include a range of low technology items such as barriers and curbing to high-tech measures such as closed-circuit television (CCTV) cameras, biometrics, and fencing. Physical security measures may also include items not visible to the naked or untrained eye, such as pressure mats and alarm sensors. Policies and procedures are written documents which relate directly to asset protection and guide the security program. Security manuals and security post orders are examples of policies and procedures.

Asset + Threat + Vulnerability = Risk

"Risk" is a commonly misused term, often used interchangeably with "threat." Risk is basically a function of threats and vulnerabilities. In essence, risk is the possibility of asset loss, damage, or destruction as a result of a threat exploiting a specific vulnerability. Since threats are the focal point of this section, it is important to understand how threats impact a retailer's assets. As you can see Figure T-2, reducing one of the factors that cause risk can reduce losses. A comprehensive security program attempts to limit all three in an effort to reduce risk to an acceptable level. Vulnerabilities are reduced through the application of security measures; assets are reduced to a level needed for business operations, with excess product stores in offsite warehouses; and threats are reduced through prosecution of shoplifters, proactive policing, and other methods.

The retail security professional's strategic goal of countermeasure deployment is to reduce the opportunity for security breaches to occur by reducing vulnerabilities. Opportunities relate to targets in that removing or hardening an asset will lead to a reduction or an elimination of vulnerabilities. Asset protection programs integrate a combination of policies and procedures, physical countermeasures, and security personnel to protect assets against a design-basis threat. The characteristics of asset protection programs include deterrence, detection, delay, and defeat.

Controlling the capability and motivation of adversaries is a difficult proposition for retail security professionals. Motivation is created by the actual crime target and is considered the reason for security breaches. Since businesses usually require assets to operate, the removal of motivation is not always possible. Most retailers must instead turn their attention to blocking the opportunity of crime.

FIGURE T-2

Threat Assessments

As discussed previously, threat assessments are evaluations of human actions or natural events that can adversely affect business operations and specific assets. Historical information is a primary source for threat assessments, including past criminal events, while real-time information is also being used with increasing frequency due to its availability in some arenas. Threat assessments are used to evaluate the likelihood of adverse events, such as robberies and assaults, against a given asset. Threat assessments can be quantitative or qualitative. Crime analysis is a quantitative example of a threat assessment. Retail security professionals use threat assessments as a decision-making tool that helps to establish and prioritize safety and security program requirements, planning, and resource allocation. The process of threat assessment includes

- *Threat identification:* Identify potential adversaries and their characteristics.
- *Asset classification:* Identify targets and determine their criticality.
- *Consequence/criticality analysis:* Assess the effect of an asset's compromise.

Threat Information Sources

Retail security professionals should endeavor to seek out all possible sources of threat information. Threat information should come from multiple and redundant sources. Depending on the nature of the assets in need of protection, the sources of threat information may include internal information, security breach investigative reports, law enforcement data, security consultants, media news reports, and industry associations, such as the Food Marketing Institute (FMI), National Retail Federation (NRF), and Retail Industry Leaders Association (RILA). Among the basic questions that retail security professionals ask are

- What assets have been targeted in the past?
- When were assets attacked?
- Who targeted the assets?
- Why is that asset(s) targeted?
- How was the asset attacked?
- Were any remedial security measures implemented in response to the attack?
- If so, were they effective?

Many retailers also maintain internal records of security incidents, breaches, and crimes. This information should be reviewed by retail security professionals on a regular basis while looking for trends and patterns that might indicate existing threats or point to a vulnerability that can be solved with remedial measures. External threat information should also be reviewed. This includes crime data from the local law enforcement where the facility is located. This is known as crime analysis and will be discussed in depth later in this section. Other external sources include private threat specialists.

Assessing Threats

After collecting, reviewing, and summarizing threat information from all available resources, retail security professionals must apply the threat to specific assets. Critical assets are the primary concern during the assessment; however, other assets may also be considered during the assessment phase. The goal of the assessment then is to estimate, quantitatively or qualitatively, the likelihood of occurrence that a threat will attack an asset.

Because of a lack of quantitative data, scenario-driven, qualitative assessments are appropriate for high-value assets that have suffered no prior attacks. A qualitative threat assessment is defined as a type of assessment which is driven primarily by the threat's characteristics and are highly dependent on the assessment team's skills. The threat assessment team or individual, using a qualitative approach, considers each asset in light of the given threat information for that asset and develops scenarios that may be used by adversaries to estimate the likelihood of attack. Using a qualitative rating system, the threat assessment team assigns a linguistic value to each scenario.

Accurate threat assessments are critical for retail security professionals; however, not even the best threat assessment can anticipate every possible scenario, including the addition of more assets. Criminals always adapt to and overcome updated countermeasures. In today's world of technology, state-of-the-art countermeasures are outdated at an increasing pace, and criminals usually move at a similar pace. Retail security professionals should keep abreast of the latest threat information using the best available sources of information. Using the threat information sources discussed previously and adding to them where possible will assist in keeping the security professional abreast of the latest threats and the assessment report up-to-date.

Threat Dynamics

Everyday crimes, rather than terrorism or natural disasters, are the most common threat facing retail security professionals in protecting their assets, and a thorough assessment of the specific nature of crime and security breaches can reveal possible weaknesses in the store's current security posture and provide a guide to effective solutions. A full understanding of everyday crime's dynamic nature allows retail security professionals to select and implement appropriate countermeasures to reduce the opportunity for these incidents to occur in the future. Thus, the following section focuses on the dynamics of everyday threats, identifying their key elements, and how to analyze these elements to block specific threats. The retail security professionals should be well versed in a number of threat dimensions before selecting countermeasures. As conceptually outlined previously, these dimensions include

- The facility's situational elements;
- Target/asset characteristics;
- Criminal motivation and capability;
- The criminal's target selection factors;
- Opportunity reduction strategies.

Situational elements are those characteristics of the retail store that create an environment which is more or less conducive to certain types of crimes or security violations. For example, a shopping mall may suffer more from auto thefts in the parking lot than the average number in the community due to the number of targets (customer cars) in a small area. Another example of situational elements affecting crime may be the proximity of the facility to escape routes such as dense fields or wooded areas that can be used to conceal the offender on foot or quick escapes via highways used by the criminal in a motor vehicle. Situational elements also include the nature of the activities that occur on the property. Businesses face different problems than residential areas. The type of business that is conducted on a property may attract more crime. Jewelry stores, for example, maintain two types of attractive assets: large amounts of money and small, easily concealed property. While retail stores' primary concern is usually shoplifting, an analysis of past crime data may reveal other threats that may not be evident. For example, a retail store that has a history of car-jacking robberies and assaults of customers may only be fully known by reviewing internal security reports or police crime information. Stores with high levels of auto thefts can narrow the field of targets by using threat assessments and crime analysis to determine which cars are more prone to theft.

Criminal motivation and capability are key to understanding the nature of crime on the property. Criminals, more often than not, are rational decision makers capable of being deterred or enticed to commit their acts. In modern criminal justice, it is widely accepted that certain people can be generally deterred from committing crimes given swift and severe punishment. Specific deterrence measures can be taken at the property level by introducing countermeasures that increase the risk of detection. For example, the presence of an EAS system or closed-circuit camera systems (CCTV) may deter many criminals. By the same token, people may also be encouraged to commit crime by providing them with ample opportunity and a low risk of detection. The criminal's capability must also be considered by the retail security professional, whose goal is to reduce encouraging elements and increase the risk.

A criminal's ability to select specific targets is a process by which the rational criminal will select the easiest target that provides the highest reward. Criminals also select targets where the rewards are high. Malls, for example, provide ample auto theft opportunities for the perpetrator who specializes in stealing cars. Target selection can be thought of primarily as a force of opportunity. The goal, then, for retail security professionals is to reduce the available crime opportunities at the facility.

Opportunity reduction strategies address the characteristics of the store that either encourage or deter crime. Each store will be different in terms of the solutions that are effective because each property has its own unique characteristics and unique threats. Unfortunately, what works at one store may not work at a similar store in a different geographic area. Opportunity reduction strategies may take the form of enhanced policies and procedures, physical security measures, or security personnel. Though the focus of this section is on cost-effective solutions to everyday crime concerns, you should not feel limited to using what is discussed herein, but rather are encouraged to be creative in your search for appropriate solutions for your particular concerns. While this section is not intended to be comprehensive in addressing every possible threat, it will endeavor to cover the more common crimes that affect many facilities. Retail security professionals are encouraged to study in depth the particular crimes that have historically occurred at their facilities.

Robbery

Robberies are a big concern for most retail security professionals and adversely affect business in a number of ways, including injuries, loss of property, negative reputation, and liability. There are two primary types of robberies: robberies of people and robberies of business. Shoplifting escalation (shoplifting incidents which legally escalate into robbery with the introduction of violence or force) and retail holdups are business-related robberies, and personal robberies include carjacking, purse snatching, and mugging.

A store's situational characteristics which contribute to a robbery-prone environment are easily identified by experienced retail security professionals once they understand the precise type of robbery impacting the property. Poor lighting, hiding places, and unprotected assets provide ample opportunity for personal robberies. Poor employee training, unfettered access, and easy escape routes can create an environment prone to business robberies. Among the better security concepts developed in recent years is improved parking lot designs at retail stores and shopping malls. Additional curbing has been used to control the flow, direction, and speed of traffic, all of which create a deterrence to robbery and other crimes by creating obstacles to a robber's escape from the property.

Robbery target characteristics depend on the nature of the robbery. Purse snatchings obviously require an unaware female holding a purse, while carjackings are limited to areas where cars can travel or park. Why does a convenience store experience more business robberies than another convenience store located across the street? Perhaps poor lighting and store windows cluttered with signs at the robbery-prone location are factors.

A robber's motivation is typically a rational balancing of risk and reward. If an asset is valuable (high reward) and unprotected (low risk), the probability of attack increases. Jewelry stores are susceptible to robbery because of the high reward for perpetrators. As such, jewelry security professionals institute various strategies for protecting assets. Capability is dependent on the type of robbery executed. Jewelry store robberies take more skill than purse snatchings.

What does a robber look for in an attractive target? Regardless of the type of robbery, targets are rarely selected randomly. Obviously, the balancing test of risk and reward is a factor. Purse-snatch robbers seek out unaware women to target, with the reward being higher in higher socioeconomic areas.

Robbery opportunity reduction strategies vary with the type of robbery occurring on the property, but generally increased physical security measures, enhanced natural and artificial surveillance, and security personnel provide protection. Retailers may implement silent alarms or install bulletproof glass to protect against robbery. Convenience store owners may remove obstructive signs from windows to increase surveillance both into and out of the store. Often, simple and inexpensive changes in policies and procedures can have a positive impact on robbery reductions.

Theft and Auto Theft

Similar to robbery, there are many types of thefts. Situational elements at a facility are a primary determinant to the types of theft which occur. Retail stores are prone to shoplifting, while large parking structures experience auto thefts and burglaries of motor vehicles. Each year the automobile insurance industry releases data on the nation's most frequently stolen cars and trucks. While it might surprise some readers that BMWs and Mercedes don't make the top-10 list, it won't surprise most security professionals. Other cars, such as Hondas, Toyotas, and Chevrolets, are easier to hide among the masses, are more easily fenced, or are more easily parted out for use in other cars. These characteristics lend certain cars to auto theft more than BMWs and Mercedes. What characteristics of your assets make a target more attractive? Cigarettes are a good target for young men, hence their location behind the counter in convenience stores.

The motivation and capability of thieves are subject to the risk-and-reward balancing test. Grocery stores, for example, often suffer from high levels of baby formula and over-the-counter drug thefts because of the high value of both items. These items are often turned over to a fence, or middle man, who will pay decent amounts to the thief and then sell the items back to the retailers. The capability of a thief is limited only by his skills and creativity. Some thieves work alone committing petty thefts, stealthy thieves may be pickpockets, and organized thieves may band together to commit larger thefts.

Normally, what a property owner finds valuable about an asset is also the same characteristic that a thief finds attractive. Jewelry is a good example, since it is valuable and easy to conceal because of its size. Financially motivated thieves will seek assets which they can later sell for a profit. Personally motivated thieves will steal assets which they can personally use, like drugs or expensive basketball shoes.

Opportunity reduction strategies for theft range from simple to the most complex, from moving an asset out of sight to installing vaults, alarms, and camera systems. Auto theft reduction may take the form of simple alarm systems to monitored tracking systems. Some grocery stores have taken to storing baby formula and over-the-counter drugs in locked cabinets. Clothing retailers have used electronic security tags (EAS) to prevent their clothes from being shoplifted. Here again, it is incumbent upon the retail security professional to fully understand the type of theft experienced at the facility to implement appropriate countermeasures.

Regardless of the retail crime experience, the threat assessment will help identify the problem qualitatively or quantitatively. While most retailers use a quantitative approach, a quantitative approach is much better for their needs given the vast amount of crime data available in the retail environment. It should be noted that the biggest failing in threat assessments is a lack of specificity. This is the key shortcoming of demographic social disorder models, which is a qualitative approach. Crime analysis, on the other hand, is a quantitative threat assessment approach and is as simple to implement as the qualitative approach.

Crime Analysis

The use of information regarding crimes and other security incidents helps the retail security professional plan, select, and implement appropriate security measures that address the actual risks of the store. Retail security professionals, after assessing the crime problem, can select the most effective countermeasures that eliminate risk or reduce it to an acceptable level. Budget justification is also accomplished through the use of statistics, since effective security measures will reduce the risk, and returns on security investments can be calculated and considered in the bottom line.

A common application of statistics in the security arena is the use security reports and crime data to determine the risks to a facility, including its assets and personnel. The use of statistics extends beyond planning security at an existing facility. Statistical data may also be used to select and plan security at new facilities. For example, the real estate department of a retail company may provide the retail security professional with a list of potential new sites, one of which will be selected based on, among other things, the threats at the location. In this role, the retail security professional serves as an advisor to the real estate department by conducting crime analysis of the proposed sites, as well as performs security surveys of each site to identify vulnerabilities in an effort to select the location that poses the least or a tolerable level of risk. In this scenario, the retail security professional will gather and analyze crime data for similar stores in the area surrounding each site to determine the security problems. The sites that have the fewest crimes can be evaluated further by means of a security survey which identifies potential or existing vulnerabilities. After the sites have been narrowed down by threat and surveys completed, the retail security professional has the necessary information to advise the real estate department.

Crime Triangle

Reducing the opportunity for crime to occur is a strategic goal of retail security professionals. The reason for this is the concept of a crime triangle, whereby three elements must exist for a crime to occur:

- Motive;
- Capability;
- Opportunity.

With little or no control over a determined offender's desire, retail security professionals focus their attention on the remaining elements of the crime triangle by attempting to block opportunities and remove motivation, both of which can be controlled to a large extent by an effective security program. Motivation is created by the actual crime target. In the private sector, a criminal's motive is the asset(s) that the security program is created to protect. Here again, assets include people, property, and information. Since organizations usually require assets to operate, the removal of motivation is a difficult task, if it is possible at all. Most businesses must instead turn their attention to blocking the opportunity of crime. The crime triangle is a simple yet effective method for illustrating how a crime can be prevented. As you can see in Figures T-3 and T-4, blocking opportunities for crime leads to a reduction in crime.

FIGURE T-3

FIGURE T-4

Purpose of Crime Analysis

Sir Arthur Conan Doyle, in his Sherlock Holmes mystery *A Study in Scarlet*, wrote, "There is a strong family resemblance about misdeeds, and if you have all the details of a thousand at your finger ends, it is odd if you can't unravel the thousand and first." It is on that basic premise that crime analysis is based. Whether a security professional is working proactively to address security concerns or reactively in litigation or during the investigation of a crime, crime analysis is an effective tool. From a security perspective, crime analysis is the identification of risk and vulnerability, and from a liability prevention perspective, crime analysis is the determination of foreseeability. Broadly speaking, crime analysis is the logical examination of crimes which have penetrated preventive measures, including the frequency of specific crimes, each incident's temporal details (time and day), and the risk posed to a property's inhabitants, as well as the application of revised security standards and preventive measures that, if adhered to and monitored, can be the panacea for a given crime dilemma (see Vellani and Nahoun).

While the preceding definition of crime analysis is holistic, it can be dissected into three basic elements:

- The logical examination of crimes which have penetrated preventive measures;
- The frequency of specific crimes, each incident's temporal details (time and day), and the risk posed to a property's inhabitants;
- The application of revised security standards and preventive measures.

Examining crimes perpetrated at company facilities is commonplace in today's business environment. In larger retail companies, there may be a person or group of people who are solely dedicated to the function of crime analysis usually working under the risk management or security departments. In smaller retail companies, the crime analysis function is carried out by someone who also has other security management duties. Crime analysis may also be an outsourced function, whereby company personnel simply utilize crime data that a contractor has collected, entered into a database, and possibly provided some analytical workup or the tools to do so.

The second element is the analytical component. Crimes are analyzed in different ways depending on what security professional is trying to accomplish. Most commonly, facilities are ranked based on the crime level or rate. Generally, facilities with more crime or a higher crime rate are given a larger piece of the security budget, whereas less crime-prone sites are given less security money. Crimes are also analyzed on a store-by-store basis, allowing retail security professionals to select appropriate countermeasures. The various types of crime analysis methods are discussed in depth later in this section.

Finally, crime analysis is used to assess and select appropriate countermeasures. Crimes that are perpetrated on a property can usually be prevented using security devices or personnel; however, it should be noted that not all measures are cost effective nor reasonable. Certainly, a criminal perpetrator would be hard-pressed to steal an automobile from a small parking lot patrolled by 20 security officers, though that type of security extreme is not reasonable nor inexpensive. Crime analysis guides security professionals in the right direction by highlighting the types of crimes perpetrated (crime-specific analysis), problem areas on the property (spatial analysis), and times they occur (temporal analysis), among others. Using this information, security professionals can more easily select countermeasures aimed directly at the problem.

In summary, crime analysis seeks to

- Evaluate actual risk at a company facilities and rank facilities by risk level;
- Reduce crime on the property by aiding in the proper allocation of asset protection resources;
- Justify security budgets;
- Continually monitor effectiveness of the security program;
- Provide evidence of due diligence and reduce liability exposure.

Why would a retail security professional need to know how crime occurs? Understanding the factors that lead to crime, coupled with a comprehensive study of crime on the property, assists retail security professionals in creating effective security programs to block opportunities for crime. Crime analysis seeks to answer these questions:

- What?
- Where?
- When?
- Who?
- How?
- Why?

Answers to these questions helps retail security professionals better understand the particular nature of crime on a given property and formulate specific responses. The *What* question tells us what specifically occurred. For example, was the crime against a person or property, violent or not, completed or attempted? *What* also distinguishes between types of crimes that require different solutions, such as whether a reported robbery was actually a burglary.

Where answers the location-specific question. Did the crime occur inside the walls of the location, in the parking lot, in the alleyway behind the site? If the incident occurred inside, did it occur in a public area or a controlled area? Determining the precise location assists retail security professionals in creating additional lines of defense around targeted assets. For example, if the crime analysis indicates that a vast majority of loss at a small grocery store is occurring at the point of sale, then little will be accomplished by installing a lock on the back office where the safe is located. In this example, the crime analysis will rule out certain measures, but by the same token, crime analysis will also spotlight certain solutions, such as increased employee training or updated accounting systems at the point of sale.

The *When* question gives the temporal details of each incident. Knowing when crimes are most frequent helps in the deployment of resources, especially costly security measures such as personnel. Temporal details include the date, time of day, day of week, and season that a crime occurred.

Who answers several important questions that help a retail security professional create an effective security program. Who is the victim(s), and who is the perpetrator? Knowledge of the types of criminals who operate on or near a given property assists retail security professionals in selecting the best measures to reduce crime opportunities.

How is the most consequential question to be answered by the crime analysis. How a crime is committed often directly answers this question: *How* can the crime be prevented in the future? More specific *How* questions may also be asked. How did the criminal access the property? If we know that a criminal has accessed the property via a hole in the back fence of the property, efforts can be taken to immediately repair the fence. Other specific questions reveal the method of operation (MO). How did a criminal enter the employee entrance of an electronics store to steal a television? How did a burglar open the safe without using force? Obviously, the list of examples is unlimited and retail security professionals need to ask as many questions about the criminal's actions as possible to learn the most effective solutions. It is true that often the *How* will be the most difficult question to answer. This leads into a problematical area, as crime sources can be divided into two categories: internal and external. Internal sources of crime can be employees and other legitimate users of the space. They are called "legitimate users" of the space because they have a perfectly valid reason for attending the location, but in the course of their regular activities, they also carry out criminal activities.

External sources of crime are illegitimate users of the space whose prime motivation for coming to the site is to conduct some type of criminal activity. Security strategies may be vastly different between legitimate versus illegitimate users of space. For example, there can be several barriers between the outside public access and a specific target. If the property or retail security professional is concerned only with someone breaking into an area, then he will be ignoring the legitimate user who may have an access control card, personal identification number, password, biometric feature, or any number of other avenues of entry.

With these answers, security professionals are better armed to attack the crime problem.

Data Sources

Security Reports

A valuable and highly encouraged source of data is in-house security reports (SRs). As the name implies, these are reports of criminal activity and other incidents (parking, loitering, and security breaches) which may be of concern to retail security professionals. These reports may be generated by management directly or through contracted security companies. The validity of SR data is only as good as the policy which outlines the reporting and recording procedures, the quality of supervision over security personnel, and the verification process used to eliminate subjectivity. Regardless of the quality of their SRs, management should be cautious not to exclude other sources of data and rely solely on in-house security reports. In requiring the collection of security reports, management can stipulate precisely what information is beneficial for their purposes and is contained within each report. Having said that, management should strive to include the following minimum elements:

1. Incident reported;
2. Date of incident;
3. Time of incident;
4. Precise location where the incident occurred on property;
5. Victim(s), if any;
6. Witness(es), if any;
7. Modus operandi (MO), or method of operation used by perpetrator, if any;
8. Follow-up investigation(s);
9. Remedy.

Law Enforcement Data

Police data are the most widely used source data for crime analysis because they present an accurate crime history for a property and are from an objective source. Since police departments don't have a stake in a company or any associated liability exposure, their crime data are considered reliable and unbiased. Though some instances of crime statistics manipulation have occurred historically, rarely, if ever, are the statistics for specific facilities skewed. Most crime data manipulation occurs to overall city crime levels to serve various political goals. At the facility level, there is little reason for law enforcement agencies to skew the statistics.

Another advantage of police crime data is the vast availability due to extensive reporting, capturing, and maintenance of the crime statistics across most jurisdictions in the United States. While costs for the data vary from jurisdiction to jurisdiction, most fees are reasonable. The only downside to police data is the time required to obtain it from police agencies, with the necessary time ranging from hours to weeks.

Various crime data and analysis methodologies have been published and used by many cutting-edge companies in the protection of assets. Crime analysis methodologies have been published and subjected to peer-review in various security and police text books, the definitive security book being *Applied Crime Analysis*.

Law enforcement data are almost always accepted by the courts, and in fact are sometimes required by the courts in determining foreseeability of crime. Though a particular methodology may be subjected to scrutiny, the data are normally admissible. The security professional tasked with testifying on behalf of his employer is safe to rely on crime data from police departments as long as the methodology used is sound.

Law enforcement data sources include Calls for Service (CFS), Offense Reports, and Uniform Crime Reports (UCR). These data sets are typically easy to obtain, and in the case of UCR for large geographic areas are online at the Federal Bureau of Investigation website (www.fbi.gov). Local law enforcement data are normally accessible via Freedom of Information requests or under individual state laws regarding public information. For state laws and detailed instructions, contact the state's Office of the Attorney General.

Uniform Crime Report

According to the Federal Bureau of Investigation, "the Uniform Crime Reporting Program was conceived in 1929 by the International Association of Chiefs of Police to meet a need for reliable, uniform crime statistics for the nation. In 1930, the FBI was tasked with collecting, publishing, and archiving those statistics. Today, several annual statistical publications, such as the comprehensive *Crime in the United States*, are produced from data provided by nearly 17,000 law enforcement agencies across the United States. *Crime in the United States* (CIUS) is an annual publication in which the FBI compiles volume and rate of crime offenses for the nation, the states, and individual agencies. This report also includes arrest, clearance, and law enforcement employee data."

The Uniform Crime Report, or UCR as it is commonly known, is the nation's crime measure. The UCR employs constant crime definitions across the country's many law enforcement jurisdictions and measures the following crimes:

Part I Offenses:

1. Murder
2. Rape
3. Robbery
4. Aggravated Assault
5. Burglary
6. Theft
7. Motor Vehicle Theft
8. Arson

Part II Offenses:

9. Other Assaults
10. Forgery and Counterfeiting
11. Fraud
12. Embezzlement
13. Stolen Property—Buying, Receiving, Possessing
14. Vandalism
15. Weapons—Carrying, Possessing, etc.
16. Prostitution and Commercialized Vice
17. Sex Offenses
18. Drug Abuse Violations
19. Gambling
20. Offenses Against the Family and Children
21. Driving Under the Influence
22. Liquor Laws
23. Drunkenness
24. Disorderly Conduct

These crimes were selected because they are serious by nature, they occur frequently, they are likely to be reported to law enforcement, they can be confirmed by means of investigation, and they occur across all jurisdictions in the country. Developed by the FBI, the UCR includes crime data for most geographic areas in the United States ranging from counties and cities to the nation as a whole. Intermediate areas such as state and metropolitan statistical area (MSA) crime data are also available. Though these areas are too large to be included as the primary focus of crime analysis, the methodology and classification system is what security professionals should understand and use at the property level.

When the UCR is used, it is best to examine violent and property crimes separately because they pose different concerns to retail security professionals and may require the application of different security measures. To be certain, crimes should be evaluated individually and as specifically as possible. For example, the crime of robbery can be further divided into robbery of a business and robbery of an individual. Often, the security measures used to counteract these two robbery types are different.

Calls for Service (CFS)

Though internal security reports and police crime data may overlap, it is incumbent upon the retail security professional to consider both in determining a store's true risk. Thus, the next step is to contact the local police department and determine what types of data are available by address. Though it is rare, UCR data, or actual crime information, can be obtained by address; it should be requested and analyzed. If UCR data by address are not available, Calls for Service (or "911 dispatch logs" as they are referred to in some departments) should be requested from the law enforcement agency.

The primary data set is Calls for Service (CFS), which serves as the basis for crime analysis and provides for the most accurate portrayal of criminal and other activity at a property. Calls for Service can be thought of as the complete array of fragments that, when joined, form the most strikingly grounded survey of criminal activity for a specific property. Calls for Service consist of every report of crime, suspected crime, and activity called in to the police from a property. No other crime information source is as focused on a specific address for such a vast time span as Calls for Service, with the possible exception of in-house security reports generated by personnel operating on property 24 hours a day, 7 days a week. These inclusions, by definition, omit the imprecise factor of unreported crime. Research has concluded that unreported crime accounts for a 10% higher crime index, though this is highly dependent on the type of crime under observation. Despite the exclusion of unreported crime, Calls for Service still provide representative illustrations of criminal activity on a property.

Calls for Service are those crimes or other activities reported by a victim, witness, or other person to a local law enforcement agency via 911 emergency system and other channels. These reports may consist of actual crimes, from murder to theft, or suspicious activity, and other incidents such as missing children, motor vehicle accidents, and parking complaints. Whatever the concern, if it is reported by a person, it is noted by the law enforcement agency. The synopsis of the given incidents is included on the record, along with the location, date, and time the event was reported. In addition to the more obvious crimes, Calls for Service add elements that may be of interest to retail management, such as the previously mentioned suspicious activity, accidents, and parking violations which could be realized to be important in the holistic concept of crime prevention.

Being hyperinclusive, no single set of data exists that rivals Calls for Service for its accuracy. As with any set of statistics, many more desirable possibilities can be derived by performing additional correlations such as sorting crimes by precise location on the property and by times at which they occurred. When more raw data are available in a database, more meaningful cross-references and correlations are possible. You can consider that some of the fundamental ways people learn about various disciplines is through comparison, trial-and-error, or cause-and-effect methods; CFS allows trends or patterns in crime activity to come to light, which aids in the selection of appropriate crime countermeasures and provides for more enlightened comparisons between properties.

Among other considerations which users of Calls for Service should remember, Calls for Service data reflect information from the location where a complaint was made, which may or may not be the site of the incident. However, the location and precise nature of the calls can be verified and reliability enhanced when CFS are used in conjunction with the local law enforcement agency's offense or incident reports, which will be discussed in depth later in this section.

Some newer Calls for Service systems encode data using the Federal Bureau of Investigation's Uniform Crime Report codification system; thus, crimes can be easily differentiated from false reports and easily compared to city, state, and national crime levels. Older systems, though, must be converted to UCR through verification with offense reports.

Calls for Service are generally available from the local police department at a reasonable cost. In light of the availability and aforementioned considerations, CFS data can be used effectively to produce a fairly accurate crime history of a property, distinguish any crime trends or patterns, and compare properties.

Offense Reports

Offense reports are the written narrative of a crime investigation and are used to verify Calls for Service. This verification process is necessary because Calls for Service data reflect the location from where a complaint was made, not necessarily the incident location. Offense reports also confirm the type of crime committed, as well as the date and time of the offense. In many jurisdictions, only select portions of the offense report are available; however, there is usually enough information contained in the public information section to accurately build a database of crime incidents. Generally speaking, crime analysis seeks to build the most accurate database possible using only public information. During the course of a lawsuit, complete offense reports including arrest records and final case dispositions become available by subpoena, but the goal here is to proactively address the crime situation to prevent injuries and lawsuits.

More of an expansion of Calls for Service than an independent data source, offense reports, or "incident reports" as they are sometimes known, should clear up ambiguities and possible inaccuracies through verification of Calls for Service. Sometimes, however, an offense report is generated when police officers discover a crime independent from a call into the 911 emergency system. More precisely, offense reports are the written narrative of a call for service that resulted in an actual crime and includes the individual reports of all law enforcement agents, including officers, detectives, and supervisors who worked the case.

Although availability of offense reports may be limited by law because of inclusion of personal information, victim names, criminal methods, or ongoing investigation, retail security professionals should attempt to obtain them from the local law enforcement agency while in the process of conducting crime analysis. Often, however, most states allow the report or a portion of the narrative to be released to the general public upon request. As with all information, retail security professionals should seek access to as much relevant crime information as possible to help make knowledgeable management decisions. By no means should retail security professionals feel that they are in error for not including offense reports when they are not available, and on the contrary, they can only do what is reasonable and possible.

Methodology

The best method for learning the true threat at a retail store is to analyze internal security reports and verified police data using a computer spreadsheet application or database software program, such as Microsoft Excel or Access. Once this information is in a usable format, a number of basic and advanced statistical analyses can be performed. The retail security professional will adapt the analysis to best meet the needs of his organization. While some security professionals prefer highly detailed charting and graphing functions, others prefer to view the raw numbers. Either way is fine as long as the security professional is comfortable and able to disseminate the information to those who need the data. Among the statistical tools available to the retail security professional are crime specific analysis, modus operandi analysis, crime rate ranking, forecasting, temporal analysis, spatial analysis, and pattern analysis.

The crime analysis methodology outlined in this section has been tested in the courts and in private organizations, is based on a logical foundation, and provides useful information for a retail security professional. By no means is the methodology limited to what is described, as to a large extent, retail security professionals may find that the information requires customization to meet company needs. Whatever the case, this methodology provides the cornerstone from which to build a more comprehensive analysis when necessary.

Whatever methodology is utilized in crime analysis, it should at minimum coincide with case law on issues of foreseeability so that claims of negligent security can be negated. Most states use crime data to determine if crime was foreseeable (predictable) and if management is on notice of crime. If management is found to be on notice of crime in the area or on the property, they normally have a duty to protect their invitees (customers, employees, etc.) against it. Though a foreseeability analysis is a good place to start the process of crime analysis, it certainly need not be the end. To be proactive, retail security professionals require more data analysis to efficiently track security deficiencies and deploy more effective security measures.

Courts have typically accepted 2–5 years of historical crime data in premises liability lawsuits, while for security purposes, 3 years of crime data is recommended. At this point, the Calls for Service and corresponding offense reports should have been requested and received from the law enforcement agencies, and in-house security reports will have been incorporated into the database or spreadsheet application. Though crime analysis can be conducted using paper and pen, software applications are recommended because they allow for quicker data entry, sorting, and analysis of the data. Software applications also allow users to easily create graphs, charts, and maps. A typical spreadsheet will start with keying in basic elements from the CFS and offense reports, including

- *Site* (address and/or site number).
- *Reported crime:* This information is located on the CFS sheets and may also be listed in the offense report.
- *UCR code:* Since most police departments do not include this code, this may be inserted later.
- *UCR description/actual crime committed:* The first page of the offense report will normally have the final crime classification.
- *Date:* This is the date on which the crime occurred, not the date reported.
- *Time:* This is the time at which the crime occurred, not the time reported.
- *Day of week:* This may be inserted manually if not listed on the offense report.
- *Offense report (or incident) number:* This is the number listed on the offense report.
- *Crime location:* This is a description for advanced analysis and may not be known or gleaned from the offense reports. As mentioned earlier, when a security professional reviews a crime scene location, it is often important to determine whether the crime is internally or externally generated.

Since most law enforcement agencies use different offense report forms, at first it may be difficult to ascertain each of the elements which are to be included in the database; however, given some practice with each law enforcement agency's forms, the process is rather routine. Once all the information from the offense reports has been entered, security report information can be entered, taking caution not to duplicate entries from the offense reports. Additional codes may be created for incidents of concern to management that are not included in the UCR coding system. The crime analysis format should be versatile and expandable so that, when new data become available or when management needs change, different types of analysis may be added.

Once the data, including calls for service, offense reports, and in-house security reports for the property, have been assembled, they need to be translated into a standardized set of codes that denote actual crimes. To ease comparisons, the UCR codification system should be used because it is simplistic and other data sets already use it. If anything other than UCR codes are provided, then the crimes must be transferred to UCR codes. This is required because police reports may differ in how they are worded or coded from the norm or from one another. To simplify matters, the UCR coding system is recommended because it includes a fairly complete listing of possible crimes, which will make analysis that much more complete.

Using this main database, retail security professionals can sort information by store; by type of crime; or by date, time, or day of week. The database will also allow retail security professionals to begin performing basic calculations such as totals for specific types of crime at each site and the average crimes per site. They may also be able to discern any patterns or trends in crime types or temporally (date, time, day).

Another piece of data that should be entered on the spreadsheet is the store's annual traffic level, which is generated from internal records. The traffic level will be used as the store's population to calculate crime rates and trends. Traffic levels may also be calculated using transaction counts or other data which reflect the number of persons at a property. Most retail security professionals would add other people who are frequently on premises, including employees such as store clerks.

Several different types of analysis make up a crime analysis as a whole. They include temporal analysis, crime-specific analysis, crime rate analysis, spatial analysis, modus operandi analysis, and forecasting. Each of these modes of analysis examines an aspect of crime's impact at a facility, identifies crime patterns and trends, and indirectly identifies security measures that are appropriate to counter the known risks.

Return on Security Investment

In today's business environment, it is important for all departments to show bang for the buck, and this philosophy applies to the security organization all too much because often its budget is among the first to be cut. Showing a return on investment simply means that security measures are either paying for themselves or better, adding to the bottom line. Return on security investment is important because it helps the retail security professional justify costs and obtain future budget monies. Some security programs will not pay for themselves, whereas others actually become a profit center.

For example, crime analysis almost always pays for itself because it helps the retail security professional select the most appropriate security solutions for specific problems and efficiently deploy the resources. Without it, the effective retail security professional has little to guide him toward effective, adequate, and reasonable solutions. More expensive countermeasures such as CCTV systems and personnel are harder to show return on investment; however, over the long run, these measures become relatively inexpensive when compared to the financial turmoil that can occur from even just one indefensible claim of negligent security.

A recent case study published by the American Society for Industrial Security International in Volume 6 of its *Security Business Practices Reference* discussed a retail company that was able to generate a 7% savings on its projected security budget using crime analysis. To select and deploy appropriate security measures, the retailer outsourced its crime analysis needs to my security consulting firm. Using the crime data generated for each of its stores, the retailer expanded its risk model from internal security reports only to include the police crime information in assessing the threat level at each of the company's retail stores.

Since the company's retail stores cater to a diverse group of people and are normally the anchor stores in strip centers, a lot of the crimes reported from each store did not actually occur at the facility. Offense reports were used to verify all violent crimes to ensure that only those that actually occurred at the property and occurred as reported were included in the database.

The security department utilized a crime analysis software application to analyze the databases of crime data for each of its stores. The database includes the time and date of each crime and the specific nature of the crime that occurred. The software allows the department to quickly determine where the violent crimes occurred on the property and identify the victim. With this information, the security personnel are able to determine not only whether a store is high, medium, or low risk, but also who is being targeted—customers or the store itself. With this specific information, the security department can deploy appropriate security measures to reduce the risk at each store specifically.

By the end of their first year with this new program, the security department was able to realize a sizable return on investment. Based on the company's 300 stores, an annual savings, or cost avoidance, of $9.2 million was gained in the first year after implementation. This savings reflects a number of changes to the retailer's security program but primarily constitutes the redeployment of security personnel during higher risk times. Prior to this new program, security personnel were used haphazardly with no regard for actual risk levels.

Though the preceding example is tangible, most savings in the business of security are intangible and not as easy to assess quantitatively. One of these categories is the savings generated by reducing crime and thus the avoidance of security-related litigation. Regardless of a security measure's ability to be quantitatively assessed, retail security professionals should strive to calculate a return on security investment.

Sources

Sennewald, C.A. (2003). *Effective security management,* 4th ed. Woburn: Butterworth-Heinemann.

Vellani, K.H. (2004). Achieving return on investment from crime analysis. *Security Business Practices Reference*, vol. 6. ASIS Council on Business Practices, ASIS International.

Vellani, K.H. (2006). *Strategic security management: A risk assessment guide for decision makers.* Woburn: Butterworth-Heinemann.

Vellani, K.H., and Nahoun, J. (2001). *Applied crime analysis.* Woburn: Butterworth-Heinemann

Ticket Switching

CAS, JHC

Ticket switching (also called "price switching") is a form of theft that, in some jurisdictions, may be considered as shoplifting. In this situation, the price ticket from an inexpensive or lower priced item is removed from the merchandise and placed on an item which is higher priced, with the hope that the cashier will not notice the price is incorrect and the higher priced item will be purchased for the lower price.

Some ticket switchers may choose to keep the merchandise purchased for their own use, whereas others will try to return the merchandise and obtain a cash refund. Those returning the merchandise will claim it was a gift because their receipt will obviously show the incorrect (lower) price.

A variation on ticket switching is container "substitution." In this situation, goods from a higher priced item are placed in a container originally containing and marked for a lower priced item. Such attempts at fraud often occur in shoe departments, since shoe boxes are all the same size but contain merchandise varying dramatically in price.

It is also not unheard of that employees misticket goods. So care must be exercised when dealing with ticket switchers, to ensure that the switch is actually observed and that the suspect is seen discarding the higher priced ticket.

The advent of computers and their ability to read and reproduce universal product codes (UPCs) and/or bar-coded labels has seen the traditional ticket switcher turn to making his own bar-coded labels reflecting a low price and affixing them to merchandise cartons containing expensive items. Electronic items and components thereto are frequently targets of this fraud. A second person, working in conjunction with the person who affixed the fraudulent price label, is often utilized to make the actual purchase. Since this scam is relatively new, local laws should be checked to ascertain the correct charge for arrests made for this fraud.

Retailers with policies which permit loss prevention agents from detaining the customer who successfully completes a purchase of a switched-ticket item should require the agent not only to follow the "six steps," but further, to recover, as evidence, both the ticket or tag representing the higher price as well as the lower price or both containers, depending on the nature of the theft.

One further caution is important when dealing with ticket switchers: If a switch is observed, the cashier handling the sale should not be alerted. If the cashier catches the fact the item is mispriced and corrects the price, fine—a fraud has been prevented. If the cashier is alerted and told to permit the fraudulent sale to be completed, many jurisdictions may take the position you facilitated the fraud and refuse criminal prosecution.

Till Taps

Karl Langhorst

A "till tap" is the theft of money from a cashier's till by an individual who reaches in the till, usually when it has been opened for a transaction, and grabs whatever bills are easily available to remove. Till taps are unlike a robbery in that the suspect will not make a demand for the money in the register but will simply reach in the opened till and take whatever bill is readily available and run, often without any use of physical force and even utterance of a word to the cashier.

The likelihood of till taps occurring can be greatly reduced in several ways. Subjects who are interested in committing till taps generally will watch a cashier's actions prior to committing their crime. If the cashier is aware of who is standing near them and makes eye contact and acknowledges those individuals, this action in itself can sometimes help to prevent the offense from occurring. Most criminals do not like to be noticed or engaged in a conversation prior to committing their act.

An alert cashier can be a great deterrent to this and other types of criminal activity. Cashiers should also be trained to make sure large currency bills are not kept in the till. Till tap suspects are generally aware of where the cashier places large bills. If these bills are being placed underneath the till, in a secured drop box at the check stand, or being pulled by management on a regular basis, these actions alone, if observed by the suspect, may be enough for him to decide that the risk of apprehension is not worth the amount of money that is readily available for him to take. Secured drop boxes are available from several manufacturers and are relatively inexpensive; they can be mounted unobtrusively at the check stand so that a cashier can quickly slip large bills in them.

Typically, store management controls the keys to the drop boxes and makes regular pulls from the boxes to collect the excess funds and transport them to a secure counting area.

Another deterrent to till taps is for the register drawer to remain open a minimum amount of time during a transaction. Cashiers' training should dictate that the till drawer be opened only during transactions and that they should not enter into a conversation with customers while leaving the drawer open. Obviously, the threat of a till tap is only during the period when a till is open and thus eliminated if the cashiers are diligent about minimizing the time it is left open. Cashiers should be instructed not to count down their tills at the checkstand and should be afforded a secure location to do this that is not in public view. Bills inside the till should be continually kept in a neat and orderly manner so that cashiers are not required to open the drawer for a long period of time to organize it.

Although the use of physical force by a suspect is rarely involved in a till tap situation, cashiers should use the same protocol as that of dealing with robbery suspects in that they should never try to restrain the individuals or chase them. Just because suspects did not display a weapon or make verbal demands does not mean that they are not dangerous and cannot cause physical harm to the cashiers or other store personnel who might decide to intervene in the situation to recover the money or apprehend the suspects. Employees should be trained to understand that no amount of money or store property is worth their risking their life.

Store design can also serve as another deterrent to till taps, as it does to other types of criminal activity. Whenever possible, registers should be located so that customers cannot stand out of the line of sight of the cashiers. Counters should be designed to be high enough so that register till is not easily accessible to the customer view or reach, keeping in mind that compliance with the American with Disabilities Act (ADA) must be maintained during this design process. Additionally, retail establishments must always be concerned with the flow and ease of customer traffic during the checkout process, and loss prevention practitioners need to understand this concern and try to propose reasonable compromises to achieve some degree of preventive deterrence.

While a till tap may not be the greatest loss prevention opportunity that a retail establishment faces, it certainly is one that is relatively easy to either deter or reduce the amount of loss if proper training is given to the cashiers and if procedures are put in place and consistently followed at the operational level.

Time Card Violations and Time Falsification

CAS, JHC

Falsifying an individual's time is commonly achieved by the mechanical or electronic process of "timing in" and "timing out," requiring the presence of the employee or another person representing the employee in a physical act to record the time. Hereafter, we'll refer to this act as a "time-clock violation."

The second common method of recording the hours an employee works is the sign-in and sign-out log, which memorializes the hours of work of a given employee but is hand recorded. Again, it does require someone to note the times with pen or pencil.

The last method of recording hours worked is the individual time sheet, which the employee keeps in his possession and completes day by day and submits to the human resources department or the timekeeper's office on a weekly basis.

- Time-clock violations:
    1. The employee presents himself for work, times in, and subsequently leaves the premises, although the time records reflect he is on the job.
    2. That employee returns at this end of the work shift and times out, and the imprints of time in and time out reflect the hours the employee was presumably on the job.
    3. The employee punches in but does not return at the end of the shift, but rather a coworker clocks him out at the end of the shift (called "buddy-punching").
    4. The employee doesn't appear at the job site at all, but a coworker "buddy-punches" him in and out.
- "Sign-in" logs or sheets:
    1. The employee presents himself to work, signs in, and subsequently leaves, per example 1 above.
    2. The employee arrives late for work and intentionally fails to sign in. At the end of the shift when signing out, the employee signs himself in at the required and expected start time, thus hiding his tardiness and yet expecting compensation for a full day's work.
    3. That employee returns at the end of the shift and signs out, per example 2 above.
    4. Same as example 3 above, except a "buddy" signs in instead of punches in.
    5. Same as example 4 above, except a "buddy" signs his friend in and out.
- Individual "time sheet"
    1. This time-keeping method is typically reserved for those classifications of employees who travel among stores in a given region or district, supervisors, and managers. Clearly, such employees who enjoy a position of trust have the relative freedom to falsify their time, and some do.

Any employee who falsifies the time he works should be terminated. And any employee who assists or facilitates such falsification of time for others should also be terminated.

Training

CAS, JHC

"Training" means different things to different people and, hence, is widely misunderstood. In 1978, in the first edition of *Effective Security Management*, I defined security training as follows:

> *Training is an educational, informative, skill development process that brings about anticipated performance through a change in comprehension and behavior.*

Training, in our industry, must result in employees fully understanding three things:

1. What management wants them to do;
2. Why management wants them to do it; and
3. How management wants it done.

No one other function can reap greater rewards than the training effort aimed at achieving these three absolutely critical steps!

	COMPANY PROGRAM	EMPLOYEE FUNCTION
POLICY (What Management Wants Done)	Arrest and prosecute every shoplifter.	Has been hired by the company to specifically detect and apprehend shoplifters.
OBJECTIVE (Why Management Wants It done)	Reduce shoplifting losses. Deter others by example of arrests. Punish or discourage offenders.	• Helps to reduce losses caused by shoplifting. • Deters others from shoplifting. • Helps to punish offenders through the criminal justice system.
PROCEDURE (How Management Wants It Done)	Lawful gathering of the necessary evidence to justify arrest and support prosecution of shoplifters.	• Sees customer approach merchandise. • Sees customer select merchandise. • Sees secretion of merchandise. • Sees that no payment is made. • Sees removal of merchandise from store. • Approaches customer and says, "Excuse me, etc." • Carries out arrest with justification. • Makes written report of incident, etc.

FIGURE T-5 The POP formula for effective shoplifting detective training. [*Source:* Sennewald, C.A. (1985). *Effective security management.* Stoneham, MA: Butterworths.]

Those steps are interrelated to a company's policies, objectives, and procedures. Figure T-5 shows the relationship between the enumerated three factors and policies, objectives, and procedures.

We recommend a structured 3-week training program leading to in-company "certification." Those 3 weeks would unfold as follows:

Week 1
Day 1 Orientation (company, store, department) — 8 hours
Day 2 Department operating manual and laws — 8 hours
Day 3 Shoplifting detention/prevention guidelines — 8 hours
Day 4 The processing of a detainee — 8 hours
Day 5 Litigation avoidance — 3 hours
Local procedures and courtroom demeanor — 4 hours
Written Exam #1 — 1 hour

Week 2
Day 1 Loss prevention awareness and concepts — 5 hours
Safety and fire prevention — 3 hours
Day 2 Customer and employee accidents — 3 hours
Store physical security and store inspection — 5 hours
Day 3 Internal theft, Part I — 6 hours
Written documentation — 2 hours
Day 4 Internal theft, Part II — 6 hours
Review/discuss Exam #1 — 1 hour
Written Exam #2 — 1 hour
Day 5 On-the-job training (OJT) on the floor with training officer — 7 hours
Report by trainee of experience on the floor — 1 hour

Week 3
Days 1–3 OJT on the floor with training officer — 24 hours
Day 4 Unsupervised detection/prevention — 8 hours
Day 5 Unsupervised detection/prevention — 4 hours
Written report by trainee of experiences — 1 hour
Review/discuss Exam #2 — 1 hour
Course review, Q&A, certification — 2 hours

The new loss prevention agent, upon successful completion of this program to the satisfaction of LP management, then becomes "certified" to function as an independent agent with the authority to make detention decisions. No agent may make such decisions until certified; i.e., certification is a professional "must" in the enlightened and modern loss prevention department. We encourage the actual awarding of a certificate which the agent can proudly display in his own home.

A note about the "training officer": Historically, OJT means novices or new hires are scheduled to work side-by-side with an established member of the LP team. This should not occur, as is explained in the "On-the-Job Training (OJT)" section elsewhere in this volume. Depending on the size of the department and size of the LP staff by store, district, region, etc., specific and trained agents should hold a "rank" of training officer (TO) and be compensated for that level of responsibility, a position midway between LPO and LPM and only these officers may work in OJT teams.

On through the totality of the structured program, under the guidance of training officers (and members of LP supervision and management), can a retail company discharge its moral and legal duty to ensure

1. The new loss prevention agent understands what management wants (requires) him to do;
2. The new loss prevention agent understands why management wants (requires) it be done that way; and
3. The new loss prevention agent understands how management wants (requires) him to do it.

Trash

CAS, JHC

One operational necessity in retailing is the disposal of trash. "Trash disposal" is a multifaceted need and deals with a wide range of waste such as hazardous waste, unsaleable food items or items which have passed their "sell by" date, recyclable waste items, general housekeeping trash, and employee canteen or cafeteria garbage, etc. Depending on the size and nature of a given store, trash disposal is a cost and yet can be a source of income. Many larger businesses employee cardboard balers and have enough volume to receive money back from their baled cardboard.

Irrespective of the kinds of trash generated at a given retailer's site, trash—where and how it's stored and its disposition (removal from the site)—should create some level of interest in and concern by the loss prevention professional.

The hiding of store merchandise in trash for the purpose of recovering the goods once outside the store is an age-old problem. Typically, employees or their confederates return to the property at night, for the purpose of recovering merchandise stashed in the trash or garbage. One common theft strategy is sealing expensive merchandise in waterproof plastic bags and placing them in larger bags filled with garbage. Soft goods are sometimes placed in between layers of cardboard and baled. Such bales are then marked and the goods recovered after the bales are removed to a recycling facility. Small items, such as jewelry, are secreted inside used vacuum cleaner bags and recovered once outside the store and in the trash. Merchandise is submerged in mop water or window washing water and wheeled out of the store in the morning past any security controls.

Maintaining some level of control over trash isn't the most pleasant task. After all, who wants to crawl into a dumpster? But control is a must. Various theft prevention measures can be employed which could reduce theft in this area. They include but aren't limited to the following:

• Ensure that all loss prevention personnel are aware of this risk.

- Ensure all employees who have any involvement in handling trash are aware that loss prevention is aware of the risk.
- At night, illuminate the area where all trash and trash containers is staged outside the store.
- Lock trash containers at night.
- Have an LP agent conduct periodic inspection of trash containers. One common method is to move the trash around with a long stick or rod looking for any containers or packages which could hold merchandise.
- Inspect bales for any unusual markings which set one bale apart from all the others.
- From time to time, monitor housekeeping personnel who exit the store during early morning hours for outside chores.

Trespass

John Dahlberg

The diplomatic and practical skills of store managers are often tested by the wide spectrum of human problems related to "trespass." In this section we will briefly review what trespass is, the widely different scenarios that involve trespass, and the remedies available to the merchant, which are often far from being satisfactory. All these potential problems should be reviewed well before they arise with counsel and the local police.

Criminal trespass laws vary from state to state, and often differentiate between misdemeanor and felony trespass. Broadly put, and for our purposes, trespass occurs when a person is on the premises of another without permission. Depending on the jurisdiction, the premises manager may need to post "no trespassing" signs on its property for trespass laws to be enforced.

We review here several different "trespasser" scenarios, along with the practical problems each presents.

The Homeless Trespasser

Some trespassers come on to business premises looking for a place to sleep. This may sound harmless enough to the public, as homeless people often want only to use deserted parking lots and similar spaces quietly to spend the night. However, homeless people may also engage in loud and disturbing behavior, may consume alcoholic beverages or controlled substances, may squabble or fight among themselves, may be a nuisance to neighbors, or may engage in violent crime. Quiet or not, they may also leave garbage and human waste behind.

No business wants to have such trespassers use business property in these ways. If a business premises has the appearance or reputation of being a place where homeless people camp, many customers, especially the elderly and the infirm, will shop elsewhere.

Store managers, or security personnel, should document and photograph the conditions created by homeless occupiers whenever it is possible to do so safely, in case their behavior needs to be described later to the police or in court. When homeless people are present, whether they are quiet trespassers or are engaged in disturbing or criminal behavior, it is advised that store managers or security personnel contact local law enforcement to help. Police can contact the trespassers, identify them, determine if they are arrestable for warrants or public intoxication, and often simply persuade them to move along.

But arresting trespassers is another matter. The laws of the states vary concerning who may actually arrest for trespass. In California and other states, a responding peace officer will usually tell store personnel that he cannot make an arrest for misdemeanor trespass, but that rather the arrest must be made, if at all, by a representative of the store, through the process commonly called "private" or "citizen's arrest." Store managers will often feel that they therefore should arrest for trespass to solve the problem. In reality, arrest for trespass is rarely satisfactory for several reasons. Caution is required.

It is very important that store personnel fully discuss what this type of arrest really means, and can accomplish, not only with the responding peace officer, but also with the store's lawyers, because these arrests may create many traps for the unwary and usually do not solve the store's problem anyway. First, the arrest itself will usually change nothing because the officer will commonly cite and release the trespasser at the store where the trespass has taken place or perhaps only a few blocks away. Second, trespassers are almost never brought to trial. And, in some instances, the trespasser will hire counsel and sue the store, claiming that he was arrested on account of his homelessness or for some other improper reason, not for trespass.

Another option, but a far more expensive one for dealing with chronic trespass, is for the store to seek an injunction against the individual who is using its property as a camp. If a judge enters an injunction, a peace officer, rather than by an employee, can arrest trespassers for its violation, for the trespass itself. But this approach has the same problems mentioned previously because the trespasser may not be convicted of anything at the end of the process.

In many instances, the legal approach to dealing with trespass is expensive and ineffective: store management may conclude therefore that making premises physically unavailable or inhospitable to the homeless will work better than arrests or lawsuits.

The Irate Customer

Another common scenario involves the "irate customer" who has entered a business's premises with permission, express or implied, but who becomes angry, loud, and abusive toward store personnel. Typically, store personnel will approach irate customers and try to calm them so that store business and customers are not disturbed. When these efforts fail, store personnel can do one of two things: First, they can seek to use minimal reasonable force physically to eject the trespasser. Second, they can call the police for help. Both of these approaches are risky.

The law allows a business owner or manager to tell the irate customer to leave the premises, without providing reasons. Should the customer refuse a clear command, he is a trespasser. At this point, store personnel are allowed to use reasonable minimal force necessary only to eject the trespasser from the premises. While this course of conduct is generally not considered to be an assault or battery, it can often lead to litigation anyway. The irate customer may claim, rightly or wrongly, that he was defamed, belittled, or was the victim of intentional infliction of emotional distress. Or, the trespasser may claim to have been injured by assault or battery. Also, onlooking customers will usually be disturbed by any use of force, no matter how loud or irate the customer may have been. If force is to be used, it should be performed only by employees with training.

Although a loud and obnoxious customer may distract or disturb other shoppers, the risk arising from touching such a person is rarely justifiable in the absence of a threat to safety. All in all, the use of physical force should be reserved for situations in which ejection of the irate customer is both safe to the employees, the customer, and onlookers and is reasonably necessary to protect against the threat of violence or other crime.

The other option for dealing with the irate customer is to call the police. If there is any threat of violence, or of harm to anyone, the police should, of course, be called without regard to the threat of civil liability or the embarrassment of the customer or others. The police often will seek to mediate disputes, and the presence of uniformed officers can have a calming effect. However, store personnel should resist the temptation to arrest irate customers for trespass, or for anything else, without the advice of company attorneys and higher management, for the reasons stated previously with regard to homeless trespassers.

Usually, genuinely irate customers want to be heard and will calm down after they fail to get their way or feel that they have expressed themselves fully. Although a loud and angry irate customer may offend and distract onlooking customers, these same onlookers can sympathize quickly with the irate customer if they feel that the store used a heavy-handed or overly physical response. In short, store personnel seeking to protect the tranquility of onlookers may end up disturbing them more by poor responses to the situation.

One caveat: Sometimes people will pretend to be irate customers as a diversionary tactic, while their confederates shoplift or commit other crimes.

Signature Gatherers

Some states, like California, have case law that recognizes the right of persons under limited circumstances to express their political views or, more commonly, to collect signatures for ballot initiatives and petitions at malls and in front of large stores. Many malls, property management companies, and retailers have policies disallowing this conduct altogether or regulating it. As is the case with the homeless and irate shopper scenarios, it is important for store management to contact company lawyers for guidance when these problems arise. In California, professional signature gatherers tend to be very aggressive and often intentionally dare mall and store personnel into arresting them for trespass, hoping they can bring a false arrest claim and turn a quick buck.

When signature gatherers arrive in front of a store or at a mall common area, responsible personnel should provide them with a copy of the written policies and guidelines governing the use of the premises. It is often helpful to identify the initiative, petition, or candidate for whom signatures are being gathered so that company lawyers or others can contact the political organization for which the signature gatherers are working in an effort to win compliance. Often, signature gatherers will not listen to reason, but the candidates and initiatives for whom they are working will.

"Trespassing" a Violator

Many merchants will document and inform shoplifters and others who violate the law at their stores that they will be arrested for trespass in the future anytime they return to the store where the incident took place or to any other store the merchant operates. If such warnings are given, they need to be thoroughly documented.

In theory, a merchant may indeed arrest a known shoplifter, troublemaker, or lawbreaker, etc. for trespass, as long as the decision is based on the trespasser's documented crimes, and not his status, e.g., race, ethnicity, religion, gender, etc. Caution is required in these cases for several reasons: First, in the normal trespass situation, the merchant will typically tell the trespasser to leave and may even seek to escort the trespasser out if this can be done safely. Making a private arrest for trespass based on an earlier warning is something else again: Store personnel may need to detain and restrain the trespasser until police arrive, and they may therefore open up the merchant to a lawsuit for false arrest, excessive force, and related claims.

The laws of the different states may also vary as to whether an initial warning not to trespass will remain valid over time and space. The safer course is therefore to treat the returning trespasser as if no earlier warning had been given and to ask him or her to leave. We recommend that store retail and security personnel review these policies with management, and that managers be aware of the potential risks and high costs of litigation before authorizing such arrests.

Labor Picketing and Handbilling

Merchants may occasionally be faced with persons wishing to picket or handbill about labor issues directly outside a store. Such activities may have a legally protected status, and therefore, merchants should immediately call on knowledgeable labor counsel for guidance before taking action. Picketers are not allowed to use violence, to make threats, or to block the doors of retail premises. In most cases, local police will not get involved, unless violence or other crimes (such as vandalism) are involved. However, courts may set reasonable limits upon what picketers may and may not do.

Making Decisions Based on Behavior, Not Status

In any situation involving trespassers, store personnel must never take action against anyone based on race, ethnicity, color, sexual orientation, gender, religion, or other "protected" characteristics. Instead, just as police officers must articulate specific facts to a judge to obtain search and arrest warrants, so too must store personnel be prepared to identify specific facts concerning what trespassers have said and done, to obtain assistance from the police and the courts.

When stores deny full service and accommodations to people in whole or in part because of their status, it is a sure thing that sooner or later the stores will be sued on a theory of discrimination. For that reason, we strongly recommend that when trespassers create problems, store personnel closely document their behavior.

Uniform Crime Reporting System

Karim H. Vellani

The vast majority of law enforcement agencies across the country contribute their crime statistics to the Federal Bureau of Investigation for use in a national crime statistics database known as the Uniform Crime Report (UCR). For retailers, the UCR helps determine the level of specific crime threats that exist in different cities. More importantly, the UCR provides per capita crime rates for eight crimes known as Part 1 offenses. Part 1 offenses include murder, rape, robbery, aggravated assault, burglary, theft, motor vehicle theft, and arson. Since legal crime definitions vary by state, the UCR uses standardized offense definitions by which law enforcement agencies submit crime data without regard for local and state crime definitions. These uniform definitions allow accurate comparisons across the many jurisdictions in the nation. The eight crimes were selected because they are serious by nature, occur frequently, are likely to be reported to law enforcement, can be confirmed by means of investigation, and occur across all jurisdictions in the country.

The Federal Bureau of Investigation's annual publication *Crime in the United States* is the result of the approximately 17,000 law enforcement agencies that provide their crime data to the UCR program. *Crime in the United States* supplies retailers with summary crime information for most cities and counties in the country. The book compiles crime volume and crime rate for the nation, each state, and individual agencies along with arrest and clearance information. Ten years' worth of *Crime in the United States* books can be downloaded from the Federal Bureau of Investigation's website, www.fbi.gov. Another source of crime data is the *Sourcebook of Criminal Justice Statistics,* which provides raw crime data available for download in portable document format (PDF) and in spreadsheet format. The Sourcebook may be accessed via www.albany.edu/sourcebook/. A guide to the use of the Uniform Crime Report data by retail security professionals can be found in the chapter titled "Threat Assessments in the Retail Environment."

While the Uniform Crime Report system has been in use since the late 1920s, the need for an even more robust national crime reporting system has increased in recent years. This need has prompted the development of the National Incident-Based Reporting System (NIBRS). While the new program is not yet fully operational, the National Incident-Based Reporting System will eventually provide a wealth of information to law enforcement agencies, policy makers, researchers, students, and security professionals. According to the FBI, "Although participation grows steadily, data is still not pervasive enough to make broad generalizations about crime in the United States."

The National Incident-Based Reporting System collects data on each incident and arrest within 22 offense categories made up of 46 specific crimes called "Group A offenses." For each incident known to police within these categories, law enforcement collects administrative, offense, victim, property, offender, and arrestee information. In addition to the Group A offenses, there are 11 "Group B offenses" for which only arrest data are collected. The goal of NIBRS is to make better use of the detailed and comprehensive crime data collected and maintained by law enforcement agencies.

Sources

Federal Bureau of Investigation (2004). *Uniform crime reporting handbook*, U.S. Department of Justice.

Vellani, K. H. (2006). *Strategic security management: A risk assessment guide for decision makers*. Woburn: Butterworth-Heinemann.

Use of Force: A Primer

Paul Mains

If you're going to make policy, it helps to know the language. As a guide, it is good to know the private sector generally adopts the law enforcement model when creating force policy.

That does not mean things are the same in healthcare as they were 20 or 30 years ago. At that time many security directors came directly from the police experience into their position. The resulting "hard-core" enforcement style scared administrators who supported a more benign and socially oriented method. What evolved in many cases, and is still the norm in some locations, is the "Observe and Report" and the "Don't get involved; you're not a police officer" response, which let that mentality take over. This idea, coupled with other limitations, low pay, and lack of respect given some officers, had generally bad results. Security was not effective in times of extreme need.

As the security director has become more professional, the need to provide a more effective response became more important. Even the most conservative administrator can be convinced in time to support the need to physically intervene in cases of imminent threat to employees, visitors, or patients. This does not mean throwing the security officer under the knife of the attacker, and this is not meant to be a debate about carrying weapons. What it does mean is to have a policy and training that will support the first responding officer so that the officer knows what his or her options are and that he or she can take control of the situation and limit the damage until the police can arrive on the scene.

The goal here is to provide for an effective security policy that will let the officers carry out their duties in a controlled, supervised, and responsible manner.

There is no national standard for private security use of force. Many local, state, and federal law enforcement agencies have developed and written a use-of-force policy. Many use a matrix or relationship model as a guide for the officers in use-of-force incidents. Paralleling local law enforcement policy can be beneficial, assuming similar or same criteria are used. The difficulty is that many security directors don't have or see the need in most cases for a SWAT-type unit that routinely engages in high-risk operations. What to do until the SWAT team gets there is more the norm.

That brings us back to "Observe and Report." The news is replete with violent incidents involving patients, visitors, and employees being accosted, victimized, and in some cases, being the ones doing the assaulting. The question is: Do you want security officers intervening in emergency situations in which a physical assault is imminent or happening? If the answer is "yes," there should be a written policy for the officer's response to the subject's actions. That response is at the heart of the use-of-force policy. What follows may be considered an introduction on how to develop such a policy.

Knowing what you want and what the administration will support is an obvious first concern. You can't have the vice president calling about the SWAT truck with the hospital logo parked in the back lot unless he or she agreed you need it. Directors do ongoing audits to determine risk, probability of occurrence, and so on. Having the support and budget to implement a basic plan has to be in place before the policy is written.

Things to know beforehand include whether you want the officer getting involved in property crimes. Do you want the officer, assuming he or she has the authority in your state, to detain someone who has just committed an aggravated assault (a felony in most jurisdictions) but who is on his or her way out? If we are shooting for a middle of the road policy here, we might say no to the property crime detention, no to detaining the subject who just committed the aggravated assault, but definitely doing what he can to keep the crime from getting worse. This would include the officer getting involved physically up to and including using force to defend himself or herself or a third party.

Determining whether the officers will carry weapons is something that has to be known upfront. Most supporting organizations recommend leaving that decision to the individual facility. To carry or not and what to carry often depend on location, crime rate, administration philosophy, etc. If weapons, including aerosols and/or batons, are carried, ongoing training and certification must be documented.

Know the legalities of the power of the officer. There is a big difference in the authority of a sworn officer versus a nonsworn officer. Check the applicable state laws and regional court precedents for references to "citizen's arrest." I did a Basic Hospital Security class years ago and had an 8-year veteran tell me at the end, "Now I know what I can do." Imagine the officer wandering and wondering for 8 years unsure of what his authority was. He had been told, "Do what you have to do." That advice would not have gone over well in court.

Security officers can be an integral part of the administration's conforming to the OSHA General Duty clause. Since we are going to mimic law enforcement, the *Graham v. Conner* case is very important. The Supreme Court's ruling in *Graham v. Conner 490 U.S. 386 104 L. Ed. 2d 443, 190 S. Ct. 1865 (1989)* established the phrase "objectively reasonable" in the minds of all use-of-force trainers and should be kept in mind when developing policy.

The policy could have a disclaimer stating the administration supports the proper implementation of the policy. The idea of using force as a last resort and the need to communicate and practice effective "customer service" skills should be endorsed. The policy definitely should not have any wording that demands "minimum force" be used prior to the escalation to the next step. There are too many examples of when a higher level of force is justified right away to trap the officer with this policy. The phrase "use only the force that reasonably appears necessary to effectively bring an incident under control..." appears in several high-level organizational policies and is recommended.

Don't confuse the policy with training. The policy document should not have all the "how are we going to get there?" information. The policy is an outline, speaking to the overall objective of the institution. It is not a step-by-step process of how the goal is to be accomplished. That being said, the policy has to be specific enough to protect from generalities. "Doing what has to be done" is not what we are looking for. Generating specifics that can be identified and trained to is the goal. Knowing the language is a basic step.

The use-of-force model can be a matrix, circle, steps, or a 90-degree angle diagram with a diagonal line indicating escalation. Models come in shades, colors, and lots of "X's." The common element is the relationship between what the subject does and what the officer does.

How things are described can make a difference in their being accepted by the population. Some call the "Use-of-Force Matrix" a "Response Matrix." Many are shying away from terms that use the word "force." "Level of Resistance" would be preferred to "Level of Force." I once had a nurse tell me she wouldn't use a "pain compliance technique" because "We don't cause pain." That same nurse had no problem doing the same technique but calling it a "sensory discouragement adjustment." Today's use-of-force guidelines generally include a "Level of Resistance" describing what the subject does and a "Level of Response" describing what the officer does.

Common descriptions of well-known behaviors include the following:

Levels of Resistance

1. *Presence:* A subject is present. Many times an officer can come onto the scene and recognize who he was called about just by seeing this person. The subject may be agitated, upset, pacing, or physically clasping and unclasping her hands. She may react when she sees the uniformed officer. If the officer had a description, he would key in on this person. It is important to realize the officer may not have complete information at this point. The person may be upset and causing a problem for a variety of reasons, not all of them criminal or with disorder in mind.

2. *Verbal Resistance:* A subject verbally refuses to do what the officer asked him to do. This may be in word only, refusing to leave, for example, or even refusing to speak with the officer. The speech may or may not be obscene, and the tone and volume might vary. This may be attended by aggressive body language, raised voice, and belligerent manner.

3. *Passive Physical Resistance:* At this point the subject is physically nonresponsive. In the case of a protester, she could be dead weight blocking a doorway. She physically refuses to obey but does not offer further resistance. Here, a police response might be called for if the officer's communication skills are not effective.

4. *Active Physical Resistance:* A subject tries to get away from the officer's attempts to control him. This could include "bracing or tensing" flailing the arms and running to elude capture. At this point the subject is not attacking the officer but is actively trying to get away. He might knock the officer down, but this act is clearly in an attempt to escape. At this point, many law enforcement officers are allowed to escalate to aerosol use.

5. *Aggressive Physical Resistance:* A subject attacks the officer. The subject is trying to do more than just get away at this point. The officer is clearly targeted and, from a legal standpoint, becomes a victim. The actions of the subject may cause injury but are not likely to cause death or great bodily harm. Verbal threats are common at this stage.

6. *Aggravated Physical Resistance:* A subject attacks the officer with or without a weapon with the intent and apparent ability to cause great bodily harm or death. This could be evidenced by great rage with threats and wild erratic body movements actively seeking to engage the officer.

Levels of Response

1. *Presence:* The officer is there in uniform and easily identifiable. Many times, this alone is sufficient to de-escalate the situation. A nonuniformed officer has the burden of establishing his authority and has to jump to dialogue immediately

2. *Interview Stance:* The officer stands in a bladed position, strong side away with his hands in front of him. He stands outside the reach of the subject.

3. *Dialogue:* This response is a nonemotional two-way conversation with the subject and is considered investigatory. The officer is trying to find out what is going on, and the subject is expressing himself.

4. *Verbal Direction:* The officer tells a subject or gives a command to the subject to do or not do a specific action.

5. *Touch:* The officer guides with a gentle social touching or uses a firmer grip prior to escalating to a higher level of force. The officer must exercise good judgment at this stage because "social touching—the guiding on the arm or shoulder" might be offensive and counterproductive to some. Other guidelines eliminate this step altogether and go right to "custodial touching," such as a transporter.

6. *Transporters:* The officer uses a control technique to guide the subject from point A to point B with minimal effort. Transporters include a "straight-arm escort" and a "bent-wrist" technique.

7. *Pain Compliance:* The officer uses pressure-point techniques to encourage the subject to comply with the officer's wishes. The "lateral thigh" technique and the "center ear control point" are two of these techniques.

8. *Take Down:* The officer directs the subject to the ground in a controlled manner. Takedowns include the "straight-arm technique" and the "bent-elbow push."

9. *Restraint Device:* The officer uses restraint devices to temporarily restrain a resistive or potentially resistive subject to protect the citizens, the officer, and the subject. Restraint devices include handcuffs, leather restraints, flex cuffs, and Velcro restraints. Checking that restraints are properly applied and double-locking are critically important in this phase.

10. *Counter Moves:* An officer uses counter moves to impede a subject's movement toward the officer. Counter moves include blocking, striking, kicking, and redirecting. Counter moves are followed up by controlling techniques such as a takedown.
11. *Intermediate Weapons:* Historically, intermediate weapons have been classified as batons and electrical and chemical weapons. Here, batons are used to control rather than strike the individual. Some put the taser in this category. The chemical weapons (aerosols) are often broken down into OC (pepper) sprays and all the other sprays. OC historically can be used at a much lower level than CS or CN sprays.
12. *Incapacitation:* In this phase the officer stuns or renders the subject unable to resist with nonlethal strikes. Batons are commonly used at this level. Tasers could be placed here also.
13. *Deadly Force:* Any force which is likely to cause death, great bodily harm, or in some cases, permanent disfigurement could be classified as deadly force. Strikes to the head, groin, or spine may be deadly force, and firearms are generally considered deadly force.

Many times the Levels of Response are grouped together under one number. For example, presence and interview stance are number 1. Dialogue, verbal direction, and touch are Number 2, etc. This allows for six Levels of Resistance and six Levels of Response.

Now that we have identified the Levels of Resistance and Levels of Response, we need to know how to coordinate the two. This is where the matrix comes in (see Figures U-1 and U-2).

Training will address how the officers are going to respond with appropriate demeanor and defensive tactics as noted on the Levels of Response. The training should be regular, ongoing, and documented. If the training is not documented, then it did not happen. The training should be done by certified trainers with a documentable expertise in this particular

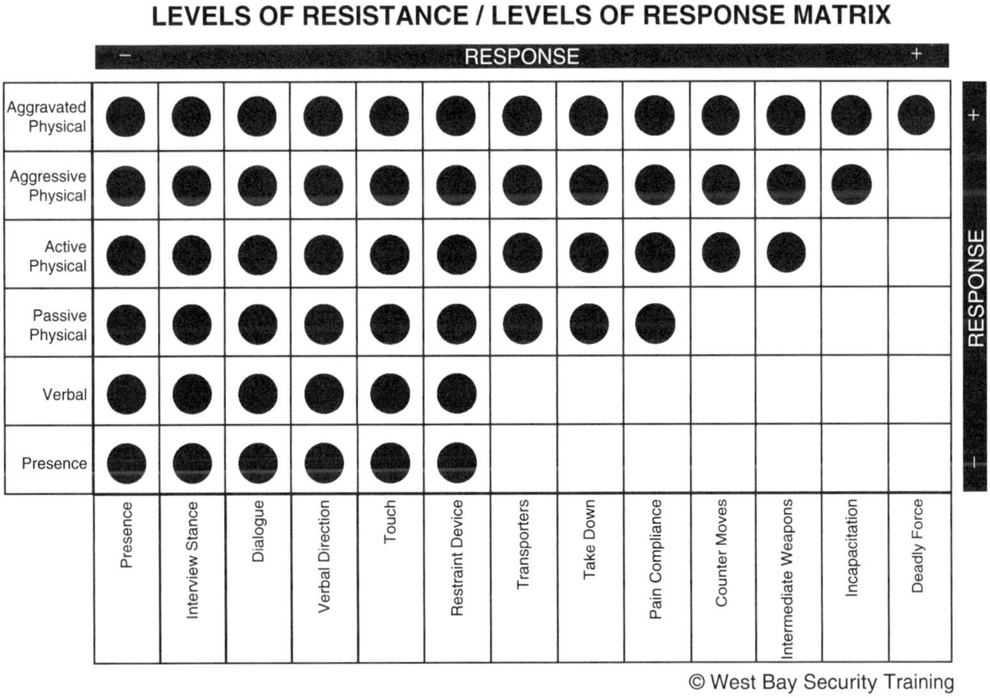

LEVELS OF RESISTANCE / LEVELS OF RESPONSE MATRIX

© West Bay Security Training

FIGURE U-1 A basic law enforcement matrix. Note which boxes are checked.

LEVELS OF RESISTANCE / LEVELS OF RESPONSE MATRIX

© West Bay Security Training

FIGURE U-2 A private security matrix. Fewer boxes are checked due to a more restrained response. For example, I have several clients who carry aerosol sprays and want them used only as a last resort when someone is being attacked. That changes which boxes are checked. Another example is that if you don't use restraints at all, that category would not be on the matrix.

field. This could be done by in-house staff that have attended "Train the Trainer" seminars or by bringing in outside subject matter experts. All documentation should be prepared and maintained as if it is subject to the "discovery" process of the legal community. Timed certifications are highly endorsed. State and federal guidelines, including but not limited to CMS and other regulatory agencies, must be obeyed. The legal units of the administration will have signed off on the policy.

Use-of-force training routinely involves helping the officer decide what type of response is justified. "Officer and Subject Variables" need to be considered when the officer is deciding how to respond. Some common factors include

1. *Age:* If the subject is old and the officer is young, the Level of Response might be appropriately less. If the officer is old and the subject is young, the age difference might justify a different response. The goal is to control.
2. *Gender:* The general public harbors the idea that females are weaker and therefore must be treated with less of a response than a man.
3. *Size:* Big subject, little officer could dictate a justified strong response.
4. *Influence of drugs or alcohol:* We know that 70% of the subjects arrested by police are under the influence of drugs or alcohol. The subject might not be comprehending the lower levels of communication attempted by the officer.
5. *Previous history or known subject:* This could determine the involvement and the Level of Response due to being able to get with the subject later. This could be a patient with a known history of aggressive behavior.

6. *Injury or exhaustion of the officer or the subject:* The average 35-year-old police officer has 45 seconds of full-blown fight in him. This might justify an escalation by the officer to apprehend or even being able to disengage.

7. *Multiple offenders or multiple officers:* It is not good to have the officer outnumbered. Multiple officers with a single subject would minimize the Level of Response.

This is the basic material used to construct a responsible use of force (Level of Response) to perceived threats. Think of it as a puzzle. Some parts you will use, others not. Cut and paste if you will, but remember the entire process must be blessed both by the administration and legal counsel. With such a policy in place, the facility can demonstrate a proactive posture toward maintaining a safe and secure campus.

References

Florida Department of Law Enforcement Criminal Justice Standards and Training Commission Basic Law Enforcement Defensive Tactics Curriculum
St. Petersburg College Criminal Justice Institute
Personal Protections Consultants, Inc.
IACP National Law Enforcement Policy Center Use of Force Model Policy
The Federal Law Enforcement Training Center Use-of-Force Model

Use of Off-Duty Police Officers in Loss Prevention

CAS, JHC

For several decades there's been the on-going debate on the issue of using armed off-duty police officers to supplement the Loss Prevention staff in protecting a store. We refer to "armed" versus "unarmed" because, typically a police officer will not work unless he has his weapon. This issue of being "armed" is but one factor to consider when using police personnel. Your authors have had an off-duty officer shoot and kill a shoplifter and on another occasion an officer had his gun taken from him during a struggle and was shot with his own gun. Another situation saw a shoplifter take both the officer and LP agents hostage in the security office after taking the officer's weapon. These are but three of many similar serious if not fatal events involving the use of off-duty police officers. If for no other reason, we are of the opinion the presence of firearms in a retail setting poses an unacceptable and unnecessary risk.

Historically, sworn officers are hired by various entities in the private sector specifically because their training is in keeping with special tasks, such controlling traffic for a film production, labor disputes, crowd control, temporary protection of high-profile dignitaries, etc. We urge their use be restricted to those type situations unless their use is clearly demanded and security cannot be achieved by traditional means.

But their use in mainstream loss prevention duties, such as detecting dishonest employees and shoplifters, often conflicts with the officer's training and they tend to act on "suspicion", quite appropriately in the general public, but not acceptable in the retail environment. One major big box retailer who has chosen to use off duty officers exclusively for LP functions has encountered national adverse publicity and numerous law suits resulting from the alleged use of excessive force (frequently resulting in death) by officer's apprehending shoplifters. Following are other factors which mitigate against the use of off-duty officers:

- Police officers are not trained to consider "customer service"
- Police officers are trained to be reactive, not proactive.
- Police officers' pay is generally much higher than that of LP personnel, tending to create some animosity when both are doing the same job.
- Police officers tend to follow police procedures and not the LP procedures of the retailer employer.

- Police officers have their primary loyalty to their city or county employer, and in times of emergency will be unavailable to the retailer.
- Police officer's utilized as LP agents create a variety of complicated legal issues when engaged in making any but basic and "routine " shoplifter or dishonest employee apprehensions, including such issues as the officer's obligation to "Mirandize" detainees whereas the "civilian" LP agent has no such requirement.
- The time required and wholehearted acceptance of store LP training of off duty officers is often missing.

The following is an excerpt from a posting made on a Loss Prevention website forum. It's not to be construed as a universal attitude, but does subtly underscore a not uncommon mind-set of public sector officer's commitment to what the retailer's needs are:

"I once caught an off duty police officer sitting in the food court, reading a book, instead of patrolling the mall area I had hired him for. He told me, "You don't pay me for what I do, you pay me for what I might have to do"."

As security/loss prevention consultants, we advise caution in the use of off-duty police officers in the Loss Prevention setting.

However, all that said, it should be noted that our concerns are directed toward the use of police officers as line level store agents. Many police officers have made a career transition to middle and senior management in the retail LP industry, bringing with them the expertise gleaned from their public sector training, experience and responsibilities.

Use of Private Investigators by Retailers

Michael S. Gach

Most but not all states have specific statutes for licensing private investigators (PIs) and private patrol operators (PPOs). Licensees must meet minimum experience levels designated by their respective states. PIs must pass a test administered by the state licensing authority. Licensees must pass a background investigation conducted by the licensing authority or other government agency statutorily authorized to do so. Most states require companies that provide investigative or security services to have a minimum amount of liability insurance, and some states require licensed companies to possess Errors and Omissions insurance.

It is wise for prospective clients to check with the licensing authority in their state to ensure that the licensee that they are planning to contract with is properly licensed and insured in the state that they are working in. Some clients take an additional step and require investigative and security companies to have their insurance carriers name the client as an additional insured.

Retailers' use of private investigators (PIs) depends largely on a company's size and culture and structure. Small business owners including retailers often contract with PIs to perform due diligence investigations when they plan on purchasing an existing business. PIs conduct background investigations on the business owners and their businesses to help determine if the information presented by the seller is true and if the prospective business is viable.

Small retailers use licensed investigators as loss prevention consultants when designing their security systems and policies. PIs conduct background investigations on prospective and existing employees and perform honesty and courtesy shops. Investigators often are hired to investigate internal dishonesty and various types of external frauds.

Mid-sized and large retailers generally employ security directors whose job it is to design security programs based on the company's culture and needs. Security directors generally report to upper management and often to the company president or CEO.

Security directors are responsible for directing the company's loss prevention efforts and developing and directing programs that are dedicated to identifying potential and actual shortage causing issues and responding appropriately to decrease retail shortage, often called "shrinkage," and protecting the company's assets and reputation. Security directors who are employed by companies with a proactive loss prevention culture usually control a substantial loss prevention budget. Private investigators are often part of the security director's arsenal to supplement proprietary retail security department staffs.

PIs have years of investigative experience and provide specialized services like honesty shopping, interviewing suspected dishonest employees, and providing undercover operatives. Many PIs also provide loss prevention consulting, background investigations, certified fraud examiners, paleographers, security consulting, and a host of other specialties.

Private investigators have special skills sets, contacts, training, experience, and equipment that make them ideal for this task. By utilizing outside investigators, retailers take advantage of the expertise of PIs only when they require their services and don't have to pay the high cost of salaries and benefits that would be required if the investigators were part of the retailers' permanent staff.

PIs are often used for internal investigations because they may be viewed as more objective when investigating internal theft or other sensitive cases like threats of workplace violence, sexual harassment, hostile work environments, and executive misconduct.

I have worked a variety of internal cases for mid-sized retailers and reported directly to the CEO or the company president. In these instances, the companies did not have a security director on staff or the security director was a fairly low-level position more akin to a security supervisor, and the company did not feel confident that the security director had the experience or the ability to deal confidentially with sensitive internal investigations.

Small retailers use private investigators to investigate specific problems, or they may use them as security consultants or as liaisons with law enforcement. Some companies, large and small, outsource their entire security operation and investigative duties to licensed PIs and PPOs.

In most states private patrol operators are licensed to protect property and people. Private investigator licenses permit investigators to conduct investigations to identify a potential or existing problem so that the company's management team can take the appropriate action to resolve the problem. Many private investigators have dual licenses and perform both investigative and preventative tasks.

Security directors who use PIs or PPOs often set aside a portion of their budget to employ PIs and PPOs to assist them in accomplishing their objective. By hiring outside professionals, they get a fresh set of eyes and skill sets that allows them to identify issues from a different frame of reference. They also reduce civil exposure because generally PIs and PPOs carry liability insurance that a retailer can subrogate against if the PI or PPO made an error and the retailer suffered damages.

Employment Background Investigation

Private investigators are often called upon to conduct background investigations on potential or current employees. PIs are considered credit reporting agencies (CRAs) when conducting most employment-related investigations. CRAs must follow the Fair Credit and Reporting Act (FCRA) and other applicable state and federal laws when conducting employment background investigations. Employers and their proprietary employees are not considered CRAs, and they do not fall under the FCRA when conducting employment background investigations unless they obtain information from a CRA.

The FCRA was written to protect the rights of consumers, which includes employees and potential employees. It was amended in 2003. FCRA rules prohibit CRAs from furnishing "consumer reports" for employment purposes unless the "consumer" is notified and consents in writing to the disclosure of the report. The signed release must be on a separate sheet of paper and cannot be mixed with any other forms, including an employment application.

At the time of this writing, if an employer has a properly worded and signed background investigation release, it is valid for the entire period that the employee works for the company. Employers and investigators should not utilize release forms that require prospective or current employees to waive their rights against an employer or CRA because these waivers have been ruled unlawful when challenged in the courts.

If adverse information is discovered as a result of the CRA's investigation, and the employer intends to use the information for a personnel action including not hiring, terminating, demoting, or transferring the employee, or performing some other type of discipline, then the employer is required to provide a pre-adverse action letter to the employee, and the employee must be provided with a copy of the credit report. The applicant/employee is then given a reasonable amount of time to refute the information in the credit report prior to the employer taking adverse action. The applicant/employee may request that the CRA reinvestigate the matter and correct the credit report if the information that the CRA reported was incorrect. If adverse action is taken against the employee, an "adverse action letter" and a copy of the credit report must be provided to the employee who received the adverse action. There are additional requirements of the FCRA, and employers should familiarize themselves with the FCRA.

Two types of reports relative to background investigations may be requested from a CRA: consumer reports and investigative consumer reports.

Consumer Reports

Consumer reports are reports that a CRA gathers from public records like Department of Motor Vehicle records, court records, and credit reports that bear on a consumer's creditworthiness, credit standing, credit capacity, character, personal characteristics, or mode of living. These reports are to be used or are expected to be used for employment purposes.

Investigative Consumer Reports

Investigative consumer reports contain information on a consumer's creditworthiness, credit standing, credit capacity, character, personal characteristics, or mode of living, which will be used or is expected to be used for employment purposes. An investigative consumer report is produced from information gathered from interviews with friends, relatives, coworkers, former employers' neighbors, and a host of other sources that might have information on the consumer/applicant/employee relative to the preceding criteria. Investigative consumer reports are generally more subjective than consumer reports.

It is legal for an employer who has obtained a valid release from the consumer to order both a consumer report and an investigative consumer report; however, the two reports must be separate and may not be blended together as one report. The Federal Trade Commission has been designated as the lead federal agency in enforcing the FCRA in employment matters. The Federal Fair Credit Reporting Act can be obtained online from the Federal Trade Commission's website at http://www.ftc.gov/os/statutes/fcra.htm.

The FCRA has severe civil and criminal penalties if an employer or a CRA violates the FCRA. The FCRA has been changed several times in recent years. CRAs and employers must always be aware of the changes and apply the rules set forth in the current version of the FCRA. If a retailer does not have an active human resources department, it is recommended that the retailer become a member of an employers' association or contract with a law firm that specializes in labor law to stay abreast of current labor laws.

Employers must ensure that the investigator that they are going to hire has a working knowledge of the FCRA before they hire him or her to proceed with an employment investigation. An employer's representative must certify in writing to the CRA/investigator that the company will follow the FCRA before the CRA/investigator can proceed with the investigation. I have discovered that many employers and many attorneys who are advising employers are not familiar with the obligations and responsibilities of employers and CRAs under the FCRA.

Some states, including California, have their own version of the FCRA that has specific procedures written into the law that must be followed when dealing with employee cases. State versions of the FCRA are generally more strict than the federal FCRA. They sometimes have restrictions on the time periods for reporting information, and some states dictate what types of items can and cannot be reported on.

Undercover Operations/UCs

Retailers often hire private investigators to conduct temporary "undercover operations" when they suspect drug use, theft, or breaches of confidentially. There are advantages and disadvantages to using private investigators to work undercover.

The primary advantage of hiring a private investigator for UC services is that the retailer can place a fresh face in the business who can observe and report on activities of employees when company management does not inhibit the employees. UCs provide an accurate picture of employees' activities and loyalties. The retailer can then take action as needed to resolve any problem that was discovered during the UC operation.

Licensed investigators meet with the employee, the UC, frequently to guide and direct his or her activity. The investigator must provide a method for the UC to make contact on short notice for guidance. A competent UC should be able to establish good enough rapport with the retailer's employees that he or she is viewed as a confidant and may even take a passive role in the employees' improper activities to obtain their confidence. The UC must do this without compromising the case or exposing the retailer or licensee to legal exposure. Retailers are able to change UCs or have the services of the UC terminated without fear of unemployment claims.

Disadvantages are that hiring a private investigative company to perform UC services is an expense. The retailer is paying the investigative company, and it pays the investigator performing the UC service. The retailer also pays the UC the going rate for the retail job being performed. The private investigator supervises the UC investigative activities, and the retailer supervises the retail activities.

Private investigators often hire investigators to perform UC investigations from locations that are a distance away from the retailer's location, so there is little chance of the UC being recognized by one or more of the retailer's employees. This adds to the expense for the retailer because the retailer is charged travel and housing expenses for the UC during the period he or she is working for the retailer. The retailer's representative responsible for hiring the private investigator should interview the UC the investigators intends to place in the retailer's business to make sure that he or she is compatible with the culture of the retailer's business and properly understands the purpose for the undercover investigation.

The private investigator should perform a thorough background investigation on the UC and ensure that he or she is properly trained prior to being placed in the client's business. The UC must take care not to report on union organizing activities or invade the privacy of coworkers, as these are violations of state and federal law. Retailers that have collective bargaining agreements with their employees must review their contracts to ensure that conducting undercover operations does not violate the collective bargaining agreement.

We have conducted a number of successful undercover operations for retailers. In one case, in his second week on the job our UC identified six associates that were stealing merchandise from their employer and violating numerous policies and procedures, including leaving early and having others punch them out on a time clock.

In another case, our UC worked at a large retail establishment for 5 months. During that time, he socialized with associates and was invited into their homes. He developed substantial information about associates who were violating numerous company policies and stealing and selling the merchant's product on eBay. We concluded the case by interviewing the associates and obtaining written and tape-recorded confessions. Two of the associates were prosecuted, and several were terminated, along with our UC, for violating company policies.

Frauds

Private investigators are sometimes hired by retailers to investigate frauds that have been perpetrated against their retail businesses. Criminals who defraud retailers can be employees, outside people, or a combination of both.

Video surveillance systems are widely used in retail stores and shopping centers and have been successful in identifying many perpetrators of fraud. Private investigators can sometimes obtain valuable leads and even identify people who have committed a fraud by reviewing video of the area where the fraud occurred. Accepting proper identification when a customer passes a check and requiring customers to place their index fingerprint on checks are also means of deterring and identifying people who commit retail fraud.

The typical fraud that retailers suffer involves passing nonsufficient funds (NSF), account closed, or counterfeit checks. Perpetrators of fraud often pass a series of checks or a high-value check. Because law enforcement is reluctant to pursue these cases unless they meet the law enforcement's minimum value threshold, PIs are sometimes hired to combine a serious of bad checks from one passer so that they cumulatively meet the agency's cases. Even after an arrest warrant has been issued for bad checks, the perpetrators are sometimes arrested only if they are stopped by law enforcement for traffic or other violation of law.

Most areas of the United States have a team of law enforcement officers from city, county, and federal agencies. The teams are called a "fugitive task force" and led by a Deputy U.S. Marshal. They are charged with locating and arresting suspects who have outstanding felony arrest warrants. I have an agreement with the Supervising U.S. Marshal in my community that if I locate a person with a felony warrant and the marshal is able to confirm the warrant, the task force will arrest the suspect.

Many states have adopted Bad Check Diversion Programs for NSF checks. If a retailer accepts a check within the guidelines set by the local prosecutor's office, and the retailer has notified the check passer that his or her check did not clear, the prosecutor's office will send a letter to the check passer advising that person that if he or she does not make the check good within a limited amount of time, he or she will be prosecuted.

Generally, Bad Check Diversion Programs also require the check passer to pay the merchant for the check plus protest fees and involve paying a fee to the prosecutor's office for processing and the case. In addition, check passers are required to pay an additional fee and attend a class to learn how to manage their checking account.

Check Diversion Programs usually limit the number of times that the check passer can go through a check diversion program to one time. If the person persists in passing bad checks, the prosecutor's office may file charges against the check passer.

Unless check cases involve a significant loss, most metropolitan law enforcement agencies are hesitant to investigate these frauds unless the perpetrator is being detained or there are significant solvability factors to indicate that there is likelihood that the perpetrator will be identified. In recent years, law enforcement agencies has been inundated with violent crimes, and they generally do not have the personal assets or the time to investigate minor check frauds.

Law enforcement agencies and prosecutors' offices often set a minimum limit on the amount of the check before they will investigate; sometimes in metropolitan communities the threshold is as high as $25,000. PIs sometimes fill in the gaps of the justice system and investigate fraud cases and identify the perpetrators. As a result of their investigation, PIs can often convince a criminal justice agency to pursue the case even though it is below the agency's threshold.

Counterfeit Checks

PIs are sometimes hired to investigate counterfeit check cases in which a retailer has accepted the check. All that is needed to counterfeit a check is some basic knowledge of the banking system, a computer, a color copier, and check paper. These tools can be obtained at most office supply stores. Because these tools are easy to obtain, check counterfeiting has become popular. PIs are sometimes hired by retailers to conduct interviews, run down leads, and network with other investigators and law enforcement agencies in an attempt to develop a case against a counterfeiter. Counterfeiting of checks is often perpetrated by drug users and organized criminal gangs. People caught for counterfeiting checks usually are discovered because they pass numerous checks in a small geographical area in a short period of time or are arrested for some other crime.

Requiring the people writing checks to place their fingerprint on the check is a good means of deterring people from passing counterfeit checks and identifying them if they do. *Note:* A common trick of the criminal passing a counterfeit check is to place clear super glue on his or her index finger prior to entering a business to fill in all or part of the fingerprint and make it difficult or impossible for law enforcement to make a positive identification from the fingerprint.

Check Forgeries

Dishonest people who know the true account holder or have gained access to the account holder's check supply often perpetrate check forgeries. They are frequently family members, friends, coworkers, or people who have access to the account holder's business or residence. A common technique of the check forger is to steal checks from the center of the account holder's check pad so that the account holder does not realize that checks are missing.

Retail employees should ensure that when taking checks for payment, they accept only official current government-issued identification. They must also make sure that the check passer is the person whose name and photograph appear on the identification.

These procedures will not protect a retailer against a person who has obtained the true account holder's identity and has obtained valid government-issued ID in the victim's name, but it will protect the merchant against the novice criminal who stole and passed the checks because he or she took advantage of the access opportunity and a relationship with the account holder.

Fraudulent Credit Card Investigations

Federal law says that in most instances a credit card holder is responsible for a maximum of $50 per credit card if the card is used fraudulently and the card holder follows established guidelines. Most credit card issuers waive the $50 fee as a customer service if the customer reported the loss of the card when he or she became aware of it.

Credit card companies have strict guidelines that merchants must follow; otherwise, they will not be paid if a perpetrator fraudulently purchases products or services with a credit card. Because storeowners, managers, and sales associates are customer oriented, they often waive one or more of the credit card company's dictates. Because they can charge back the merchant for the fraudulent purchases, credit card issuers have little incentive to investigate the fraud. Private investigators are sometimes hired by retailers to investigate these cases. Investigators examine documents, interview witnesses, review video, and attempt to determine who actually committed the crime. If a suspect is identified, a case is put together and referred to the local police.

I investigated one credit card case in which a merchant transposed a number when inputting the customer's credit card number into a point of sale cash register and a different person was charged for the purchase. This was due to an employee error and not theft.

When the account holder received his bill and was charged for items that he did not purchase, he filed an affidavit of fraud. We were able to identify the person who actually made the purchase with the assistance of the credit card company through the customer's name and signature. The purchase was then charged to the correct cardholder.

In another case, a former employee of a mid-sized retailer obtained his roommate's newly issued credit card from the U.S. mail while his roommate was traveling on business. The criminal used the card to make a large purchase from his former employer and was not recognized because he had not worked for the retailer in recent years. The perpetrator had been in the navy for the past 4 years. The roommate who had not opened an account eventually received a letter from the retailer and a gift certificate thanking him for his purchase. The roommate called the retailer and discovered that someone had obtained his identity, opened an account, and charged several thousand dollars' worth of merchandise to him. The perpetrator had ordered the merchandise by telephone and came into the retail business and picked up the merchandise.

When the local police were contacted by the retailer, the police showed little interest in the case, which is fairly common in fraud cases. We were retained to investigate the case and discovered that the retailer has a sophisticated telephone system that logs incoming telephone numbers. We traced the cellular telephone number used to order the merchandise, and we identified and located the owner of the telephone who was not the perpetrator.

This retailer also had a video surveillance system in the store that photographed the perpetrator when he entered the store, picked up the merchandise, and when he left the store.

We made photos from the video and interviewed the owner of the telephone, who reluctantly led us to the perpetrator. We brought the case to U.S. postal inspectors, who are now perusing this case because the credit card had been sent by U.S. mail. Postal inspectors are also perusing charges against the same person for identity theft because he opened numerous charge accounts using his roommate's name and information. The perpetrator and several of his associates made numerous purchases in northern Nevada and California using several fraudulently obtained credit cards in the roommate's name.

Civil Cases

I have investigated a variety of cases for retailers and their insurance carriers. The most common retail civil cases have been for false arrest, slips and falls, worker's compensation, and sexual harassment.

False Arrest/Unlawful Detention

Most states have laws that permit merchants to reasonably detain people that they suspect of shoplifting to determine whether the items that the suspect have in their possession have been shoplifted. When I have investigated these cases, the main issue has been whether the merchant saw the person remove the product from the shelf, conceal it, and exit without paying for the product. Taking a product without the intent to steal it is not a crime.

If a retailer cannot show intent by the suspect's actions, like looking around, removing price tags, concealing product under clothing, leaving his or her own shoes in the new shoe box, and a host of other actions that tend to show intent, then it is probably unwise to attempt to prosecute someone or detain that person for a significant period of time. The merchant can detain the person to recover the product, but once the product is recovered, the clock starts ticking.

The false arrest cases that I have been involved in usually occurred because the person detained felt that he or she was treated unreasonably. Often the person placed the merchant's product on another shelf and did not take it out of the store and the merchant's agent placed him or her in handcuffs or embarrassed him or her in front of customers and employees.

I have investigated a couple of cases in which a security officer was apparently mistaken and did not see what he thought he saw. This sometimes happens to people who have years of experience in surveillance techniques. Light and shadows, distance, and obstructions sometimes create an optical illusion whereby a person thinks that he or she saw something, and the facts don't confirm the vision. In one case a security officer caused minor injury to a person while trying to physically restrain and handcuff the suspect. The suspect, a juvenile, had not resisted and had not attempted to flee. There was no video in the area where the suspicious activity occurred or where the suspect was stopped.

When investigating these cases, I generally look at the scene and any evidence. I examine the company policy for detaining shoplifters. Was the policy reasonable? Did the agent follow the policy? Was the agent properly trained? Were witnesses present, and are their observations positive or negative for the retailer? Were the alleged suspicious activity and the arrest captured on video? I look at the agent's training, experience, and work history. Had the agent made mistakes in the past, and were they similar in nature?

In this case, the suspect was a 13-year-old boy who was being accused of stealing a pair of sunglasses that retailed for under $10. He was detained for about 15 minutes until his parents were located. His parents and careful examination of the sunglasses confirmed that the glasses were not the merchant's product, and they belonged to the juvenile.

The plain clothes security officer (agent) was a 19-year-old criminal justice major in his freshman year of college.

The company that employed the security officer rented retail booth space to small merchants at a weekend flea market. The business structure was a sole proprietorship. The agent had no security experience or training. There was no video, and the suspect's 14-year-old friend was the only witness who had been identified.

I checked the civil history of the suspect's immediate family and could not locate any prior lawsuits. In this case the suspect came from working class law-abiding family. According to his family, he had never been in serious trouble—only minor mischief. I spoke with a school police officer who described the juvenile as a good kid. The suspect was not seriously injured when he was detained, and he suffered only a sore wrist and some minor scratches, but he and his family were embarrassed.

The company did not have written policies but told the agent to detain anyone that he saw shoplifting and hold the suspect for the police. The security officer involved in the case had not been trained, and he purchased and was using his own handcuffs.

In this case the company was able to settle the case out of court a week after the detention for what the retailer and his attorney considered a token amount. The flea market owner was satisfied with the outcome, and he hired a licensed guard service for future events.

Slips and Falls

Slips and falls are common in retail stores and parking areas. Generally, if a person falls and is injured on a retailer's premises solely due to the customer wearing inappropriate footwear or not paying attention, the retailer is not responsible for damages. Unfortunately, customers sometimes erroneously feel if they were injured on a retailer's property, the retailer is responsible and they make a demand for damages. I have investigated numerous slip-and-fall cases. In some instances, the retailer created a hazard with poor lighting, lack of maintenance, or not cleaning up displays after customers have rummaged through the retailer's merchandise.

In other cases, the floor was slippery and caused a customer to fall because the janitorial crew used a product on the floor that was not compatible with the flooring, and use of the product created a coefficient of friction of less then .05. In some cases, the floor was wet due to mopping and the retailer failed to properly identify and notify customers of the hazard and to block off the area until the floor dried, or the janitorial crew had left an electrical cord pulled across the floor and the customer tripped over it.

If a retailer created the hazard or failed to correct a problem that had occurred in the past when it should have been able to foresee the danger, the retailer will generally be held responsible in a court of law for the injured person's damages.

I had one case that showed that the product was not compatible with the flooring that had been installed and it should not have been applied to the that type of flooring material.

In another case, the retailer, a franchise restaurant, had different levels of flooring and steps going to the various platforms. The stairs did not meet the uniform building code standard for steps. A customer who was wearing footwear that was slippery tripped and fell, severely injuring her arm. A paramedic who responded to the accident also stumbled on the steps where the customer fell. When I interviewed the paramedic at a later date, she told me that approximately 3 months prior to the customer being injured, she was patronizing the restaurant with her husband. At that time the off-duty paramedic tripped and fell on the same steps where the customer had fallen. In this case, there were uniform building code violations and a prior history of falls at the same location. As a result, the restaurant paid a significant settlement to the injured customer.

Worker's Compensation Cases

In most if not all states in the United States, if a worker is injured on the job, his or her medical costs are paid for by the business's worker's compensation insurance policy, or if it is a large business, it may be self-insured. The company's experience rating influences the employer's cost because the insurance rates increase. If a company has few claims, then its rates are fairly low. If a company has an inordinate number of accidents or serious accidents with high medical cost or continuing medical treatment, its rates will be high.

Employers, including retailers, try to get their injured employees back to work as soon as possible even if they have to place the employees temporarily in a light-duty job so that they can be productive. This way, the employers or the worker's compensation insurance carrier do not have to pay the employees when they are not contributing to the company's success.

Some employees are malingerers, and they take advantage of their employers by embellishing their injuries and obtaining medical restrictions that they don't really need or extending the amount of time that it takes to recover from their injuries when they have already healed.

I recently completed a job for a retailer whose employee suffered an on-the-job shoulder injury. The retailer brought the employee back to work in a light-duty job created just for him. He was in the light-duty job 16 months. The injured worker constantly complained that he was in pain and had to take frequent breaks; he called in sick many times due to the pain that he said he had from his injury. The injured worker's employer knew that the injured worker had been a drummer in a local band prior to his injury. The employer requested that we perform a "Subrosa" investigation on the injured worker in an attempt to determine if he was physically performing beyond his medical restrictions when he was not working. "Subrosa" is a Latin term that means "Under the rose" or "undercover." The injured worker had medical restrictions that prohibited him from lifting more than 15 pounds or raising his right arm above his shoulder.

I conducted Internet research on the injured worker's band and located a photograph of the injured worker. The band's web page contained a schedule of dates, times, and locations where the band was scheduled to play. I set up a mobile video surveillance outside the injured worker's residence 2 hours prior to the next scheduled band appearance and observed him carrying and loading a complete drum set into his vehicle.

I followed the injured worker to the nightclub where the band was scheduled to play and videotaped him unloading his drum set and carrying it into the club. I paid the fee to enter the club and videotaped the injured worker setting up his equipment and assisting other band members with unloading, carrying, and setting up their equipment. When the band was performing, I videotaped the injured worker playing his drums for almost an hour and then breaking down his equipment and carrying it to his car.

Two days later I provided two copies of the video to the injured worker's employer. The employer provided a copy of the video to the injured worker's physician who had established his medical restrictions. The physician was embarrassed that the injured worker had duped him and immediately removed the medical restrictions. When the employee showed up to work Monday morning, his employer played the video of his band performance for him and then terminated his employment.

Worker's Compensation/Subrogation Case

A 25-year-old female who was married and had four small children was working at a rural Nevada convenience store that had a gas and propane station. The oldest of the woman's children was 5 years old.

A man brought in an empty 5-gallon propane tank to the store and requested that it be filled. The tank was within code and looked like it was new. It was early evening and beginning to get dark. The customer accompanied the clerk to the propane pump, and she began filling the customer's propane tank. The clerk and the customer apparently heard propane escaping, so the customer backed off. The clerk turned the 5-gallon propane tank over, and the tank exploded. The bottom portion of the tank was propelled upward, and it blew the clerk's face off. The clerk expired at the scene almost immediately.

Investigation by the local sheriff's department, Nevada State Fire Marshal, and the Nevada Propane Board disclosed that the bottom of the 5-gallon propane tank had been cut and caulked in place and painted over to hide the caulking.

When law enforcement officers interviewed the customer, he said that his propane tank was out of date, so he went to his neighbor's residence and asked if he could borrow a propane tank. His neighbor located a tank in her garage and gave it to the customer.

Propane tanks that are caulked on the bottom are sometimes used to smuggle drugs into the country. An interview by law enforcement officers confirmed that the woman had given the propane tank to the customer. The woman's husband was serving a term in Nevada State Prison for possession of drugs for sale and selling drugs. When the husband was interviewed at the prison, he said that he had purchased the propane tank at a flea market and was not aware that it had been modified.

Investigators from the worker's compensation insurance carrier, a state agency, conducted a subrogation investigation. Their investigation determined that the customer and the woman who lent the customer the tank did not have sufficient assets for the state to subrogate against. I received the case one and a half years later with a request to re-investigate and attempt to determine where there was an opportunity for subrogation. I discovered that the customer had died of a heart attack and left only a small trailer to his elderly parents. The woman who lent the propane tank to the customer was a renter, and she had few assets and a husband in prison.

I interviewed the retailers and discovered that there was a contract with the propane company. I read the contract and discovered that the propane vendor, a large corporation, was responsible for training the managers and owners of the store in proper procedures for filling propane tanks. This training is necessary because propane is a hazardous product.

The contract spelled out exactly how the vendor was to train the owners and management of the convenience store and that the training must be documented on the propane vending company's forms and kept on file by the propane vending company.

The contract also required that the owners and managers of the store train their subordinates in the proper procedures for safely filling propane tanks. The training was to be recorded on the propane company's forms, and a copy was supposed to be sent to the propane company to be reviewed and filed.

I examined copies of the training records and interviewed the station owners and their employees. The interviews disclosed that the propane company had not properly trained the owners and managers who were training their employees. The propane company's policies and forms required that the people being trained demonstrate proficiency by checking and properly filling a certain number of propane tanks in the presence of the instructor. In this case the instructor cut the number of training cycles from 7 to 3, and the instructor scratched off 7 from the form and wrote in 3 and initialed the forms.

This accident could have been prevented if the deceased employee had properly inspected the propane tank. As a result of training deficiencies on the part of the propane company, it settled with the state and the family of the deceased worker for $1,000,000.

Had the case not been subrogated, the insurance carrier—in this case, the State of Nevada—would have been responsible for all damages and support of the deceased's four small children until they were 18 years old. The retailer's workman's compensation insurance cost had been raised significantly because of the death claim. After the settlement, the insurance company reduced the retailer's insurance rate to the former amount and repaid the retailer the additional monies that had already been paid as a result of the claim.

Sexual Harassment Investigations

Private investigators are often hired to perform sexual harassment investigations when an employee makes a complaint that his or her employer, manager, or supervisor has made unwanted sexual comments, touched him or her inappropriately, or sexually harassed him or her in some other way as defined by state and federal laws.

Private investigators are often retained to conduct an unbiased investigation to determine if the allegation is true. Investigators review the complaint and interview any witnesses and in some cases other employees who are subordinate to the accused.

I conducted one investigation for a restaurant where the manager was accused of constantly touching, making lewd comments, propositioning female employees for sexual favors, and telling sexual jokes. All these things were against company policy.

One of the accusers was terminated prior to her complaint for excessive cash register shortages. After her termination, she filed a sexual harassment complaint with the State Equal Rights Commission. She said that she had verbally notified her employer of prior instances of sexual harassment and requested that they speak with the manager.

The restaurant group's CEO and the female human resource manager visited the restaurant weekly and always spoke to all the employees. They said that they had not received any complaints of sexual harassment until after the employee was terminated for cash register shortages. The former female employee returned to the restaurant several times after she no longer worked there, and she talked to female employees, encouraging them to join her in a lawsuit against the company for sexual harassment. No one else joined her. About a month later, another female employee told the restaurant manager that her family circumstances required her to request a schedule change. The manager was not able to grant her request, and the employee resigned. Soon after, she complained to the company that her manager had sexually harassed her, and she filed a case with the Equal Opportunity Commission.

I interviewed all the restaurant's employees individually at an off-premises location. I provided them with the definition of sexual harassment and asked if they had ever been victims or witnessed anyone sexual harassing anyone at the restaurant. A few of the female employees said that customers had harassed them, but they dealt with the problem without telling management. They said that they would sometimes hear and tell sexually oriented jokes among themselves, but these jokes were not usually told in the presence of their manager. None of the employees heard or saw their manager do or say anything that could be considered sexual harassment.

After the initial accuser was terminated, she told several of the employees that she had been sexually harassed. She told them this when she tried to get them to join her lawsuit. She also said that if they joined her lawsuit, they could get a bundle of money. The employees said that they did not believe her and said that she often told lies.

I interviewed the manager. He denied the complaint and said that the complaints were made in retaliation for terminating the initial accuser and for not granting a schedule change to the second accuser. I conducted background investigations on the manager and his accusers. The manager did not have a criminal record. A female employee at a former job had accused him of sexual harassment; however, the complaint was never substantiated, and it did not go beyond his former employer.

Investigation disclosed that both of the accusers were currently admitted drug users who were in a court-supervised drug program at the time of their complaints. The initial accuser had an active felony arrest warrant for failure to comply with a drug court order.

I interviewed the accuser's former employers and found that neither of them had made complaints of sexual harassment; however, both had been terminated for company policy violations. I located and interviewed the initial accuser's ex-husband; he described the accuser as being extremely promiscuous and constantly lying. He said that he had married her because she was pregnant with his child. He introduced me to several friends of his who have known the accuser for many years. They also described her as extremely promiscuous and constantly lying.

This case was eventually tried in U.S. District Court, and the court found in favor of the employer.

 V

Vandalism

CAS, JHC

Vandalism is best defined as the willful and malicious destruction, infliction of damage, or defacement of public or private property. The various acts of vandalism are frequently referred to or known as acts of "malicious mischief." We know of no empirical data about what institution or enterprise is victimized more often than another, but we suspect retailers probably head the list.

The loss prevention professional is ultimately responsible for the prevention of such acts against company property and merchandise as well as employee and customer property when on company premises. It only stands to reason that if employee vehicles are vandalized, especially if parked in specified areas (it is a common practice in big store environments to designated employee parking areas) and the vandalism continues despite reports made to the police, something must be done to halt the problem. It also only stands to reason, if customers' cars are broken into or otherwise damaged by vandals, something must be done. Reporting such crimes to the police is necessary but doesn't necessarily guarantee relief from an ongoing problem.

How do loss prevention professionals discharge that "responsibility" to protect property and merchandise, inside as well as outside the store? They bring to the problem the same expertise and tools used to deal with shoplifting and other forms of theft, i.e., surveillance and detention of persons engaged in criminal acts.

The range and diversity of acts of vandalism in the retail environment almost defy imagination. We've prepared lists based on our own professional experience, but surely other experienced loss prevention practitioners and executives could add to our list. We've divided the acts into those which have commonly occurred inside the store and then outside the store. The purpose and challenge of the lists is to inform and challenge you to consider your strategy if faced with a series of any of the acts listed.

Inside the Store

- Randomly slashing merchandise with a razor-sharp instrument
- Slashing merchandise methodically, e.g., an entire rack of men's suits
- Spraying an acid solution on merchandise
- Spraying paint on merchandise
- Placing paper bags containing rats or mice among merchandise, and when knocked over, the pests disperse, terrorizing customers (and employees)
- Placing small uncapped bottles of butyl mercaptan among goods, and when knocked over, the chemical emits a strong odor similar to vomit
- Stabbing mannequins
- Writing or scratching obscene words and images in public restrooms
- Defacing/scratching mirrors in public restrooms
- Intentionally plugging up sinks and toilets, causing them to flood

- Defacing/scratching interiors of elevators and elevator doors
- Igniting smoke bombs
- Setting off fireworks
- Draping toilet paper over sprinkler heads, igniting the paper, and activating the sprinkler
- Writing or scratching obscene words and images in fitting rooms
- Urinating or defecating in fitting rooms or trash containers
- Demonstrators in conga-chain weaving through the store, knocking over displays and trampling or breaking goods
- Activating manual fire alarms

Outside the Store

- Random intentional breaking of glass windows
- Systematic breaking of glass windows with slingshots or air guns
- Throwing or spraying of paint on buildings
- Writing obscenities in paint on buildings
- Applying graffiti to buildings
- Destroying the landscape in flower beds and flower boxes
- Applying paint or graffiti to parking light stanchions
- Shooting out stanchion lamps
- Breaking auto windows
- "Keying" autos
- Deflating auto tires
- Pulling out or breaking trees in the lot
- Putting epoxy or crazy glue in door-lock cylinders

Vendor Fraud, Badging, and Control

CAS, JHC

Vendors (and vendors' representatives) play an important role in many retail operations. They may stock or restock goods, fulfill some inventory-taking functions, rotate or exchange goods or products, and/or otherwise provide retailers with an extra pair of hands in the daily operations of a store.

Many vendors are seen and accepted as part of the store team and, as such, are accepted without question as they come and go pushing or carrying in merchandise and leaving with "merchandise."

According to the annual National Retail Security Survey, so-called vendor frauds amount to over a billion dollars in inventory shrinkage in the industry each year. Part of those vendor frauds include vendor reps engaged in the theft of their own line, which the store has purchased and which the rep will resell, or carrying out other unpaid-for merchandise which the rep has opportunistically picked up while engaged in otherwise legitimate access to goods in the store or store's stockrooms.

One example of vendor fraud which is not uncommon to grocery stores is the vendor who delivers his or her merchandise in bulk cartons, such as dairy products and baked goods, and leaves a void in the center of the stacked goods, thus delivering less than the apparent quantity. Prevention of these thefts requires that, when checking in goods susceptible to this theft technique, all cartons be broken down and a piece count be made of all receivings.

A store doesn't know who the vendor representative really is, nor is that rep's background and work history known. And the very nature of the vendor's in-store tasks precludes serious loss prevention or manager oversight. Clearly, then, some reasonable controls must be in place. The following suggested "controls" may not be applicable to the bread delivery man or similar daily reps who access the store through the receiving area, but where otherwise applicable, they should be in place:

- Vendor reps and any assistants are required to "sign in" in the store's vendor log, which should be maintained in the store manager's office.
  That log requires the following information:
  1. Rep's name and company
  2. Date
  3. Time in
  4. Time out
  5. Vendor badge number
- Vendors will be issued a vendor's badge, which must be worn at all times in the store.
- If employees are prohibited from taking their purses into merchandise areas, the same rule should apply to vendor reps. Lockers should be provided for vendors' briefcases, large handbags, or other personal containers.
- When vendors are through with their in-store tasks, they should present themselves at the manager's office to sign out and turn in their badge.
- If the store has a designed employee entrance, vendor reps should be required to enter and leave the store through that door unless the logic of their tasks dictate the use of the dock. However, the need to access the store through the dock does not preclude following the specified badging procedure.
- Vendors and/or their representatives must understand that any and all containers are subject to inspection, just like all store employees, upon exiting the store.

Vendor Relations

Stanley Kirsch

Communication Is Your Bottom Line

On May 10, 1869, the nation was connected by rail at Promontory Summit, Utah. The Golden Spike marked the completion of rail service from Sacramento, California, to Omaha, Nebraska. These 2000 miles of track laid in the 1800s were, by far, the greatest physical and engineering undertaking in this country's history. Just picture the logistical nightmare to be in touch with your vendors without even the use of a telephone, which was only patented in 1876.

The one tool available besides the written or printed letter was the telegraph. Samuel Morse's first message, sent from Washington to Baltimore, was "what hath God wrought." This was the communication means to order supplies, labor, and capital to pursue this project. "Telegraph," from the Greek words *tele* = *far* and *graphein* = *write,* is the transmission of written messages with physical transport of letters. How far has the transportation of letters, numbers, and words come since the telegraph, and how can we best utilize it for communications?

What made this railroad project successful without all the tools we have available in this day and age? The simple answer is clear and concise communications with vendors. Sitting on both sides of desk has given me a fairly concise insight into how important spoken words and the transmission of words are needed to reach your purchasing goals.

A checklist is very important. By using one, your vendor can give you the answers you need for presentations or budgets. Being precise in the direction you want to take your company is key to having a successful program. The motivational speaker Anthony Robbins said "successful people ask better questions and as a result they get better answers." Vendors have their own list of product priorities they would like to follow, which are directed by their management. Having a clear information path to your desk will help you make the right decision. This is accomplished by having various vendors with similar products visit or spending adequate time at their offices or convention platforms. Having the knowledge to integrate similar products, from different vendors, helps you realize your goals. In this day of changing technologies, it's important to be updated constantly to make sure you are deciding on the best products available.

There are a number of points which should always be followed when deciding on a product or service.

- Poll your peers.
- Always get at least three company references.
- Clearly state your needs.
- Determine if the sales rep is avoiding your needs just to put you in another product or service.
- Ask for new concepts and request real R&D information.
- Ensure contracts are clear and concise to determine cost responsibility of installation and removal, if necessary, of products being tested at a facility.
- Work within a critical path for timely goals. They should lead to realistic timelines that tie into penalties if goods and services are not realized.
- Work with your vendors to furnish a way out of contracts that is fair to both parties. The customer should have a termination clause in a contract, since it gives the customer more clout in contract renewals and the vendor understands that contracts are not forever.
- Ensure warranties and maintenance policies are in writing versus verbal assurances.

The bottom line is not always the bottom line. Just as your company runs on making a profit, your vendors are no different. Calling on your peers is important to make sure that you are working and communicating with vendors who are honest with their pricing and the quality of their products or services. When you want to trigger their response, you want be in the position to give the vendors a true picture of the product you will be purchasing. Find out were you have to be, in dollars, to maximize the budget you have or will be requesting. When you work with your staff or persons you know in the industry, channels will open which give you knowledge of how products or services are priced.

Never hold back on asking questions such as "Where is my product being manufactured and shipped?" Simple questions can save you the agonizing feeling of waiting for a product that is sitting in customs, delaying your store openings or renovations.

Sometimes your vendors do not have all the answers. Service questions usually are easier to resolve than products. Services are a true interpersonal resource, and you should look to their efficiencies. Whether you're dealing with a product or service, the answer you receive should always be an honest answer. Working with your vendors' logistics, warranties, shipping schedules, pricing, and installation times is based on their honesty in replying back with concise answers. Vendors who will call you with a disruption of a time line, instead of letting it lie dormant, are your partners, and you should thank them in replying to their honesty.

You should always keep an open communication portal, be it email, letters, telephone, or any transmissions from vendors you might not be doing business with at the present time.

Choice is key in addressing the best interests for your company. New relationships should be continually built, even if you are not doing business with a particular vendor.

We all have time constraints, but time should be spent for new vendor presentations, so you always maintain the best knowledge base possible. It really does not matter if you have a single- or multiple-person operation. The flow of information that is now available should be utilized to maximize benefits. When you communicate with knowledge, it will make your vendors react with the vigor that you expect.

Communication will give you the foundation for success.

Video Surveillance: From CCTV to IP and Beyond

Tom Yuhas

The use of video surveillance has been evolving since the mid-1970s and escalated in the 1980s with the development of Charge Couples Device (CCD) image technology. CCD technology has led to an evolution in the use of video cameras in security surveillance applications such as government, banking and finance, manufacturing and industry, transportation, retail, and education.

The traditional video surveillance infrastructure, commonly known as closed-circuit television (CCTV) systems, has become commonplace over the past two decades and accepted technology for most video security surveillance applications.

CCTV systems in the mid-1970s started with a simple hardwired environment of analog security cameras to image multiplexers that would combine several cameras into one analog image to a video cassette recorder (VCR) for storage and playback (see Figure V-1).

As the acceptance of a hardware video camera system in surveillance became more commonplace, products such as the VCR with a built-in multiplexer were developed (see Figure V-2).

These CCTV systems allowed the capture and storage of video events that provided security personnel with the capability of viewing an event after the occurrence but did not provide for immediate access and assessment of events unless viewed and monitored by security personnel at the time of the occurrence. Once an event occurred, in order to review the event, security personnel would need to take the recorder offline to view the video. This created an instance in which no video surveillance would occur. This period of time would leave the system user vulnerable with no video surveillance.

Continued CCTV system evolution, along with the acceptance of IT network infrastructure, saw the creation of the digital video recorder (DVR). It provided the same recorder capabilities of recording the cameras, but also provided a network interface that allowed for the simultaneous recording of events and viewing and monitoring of events by an individual and/or a group of individuals who had access to the back-end surveillance network (see Figure V-3).

These CCTV environments provided for expandability to multiple cameras and allowed for the development of larger enterprise security camera systems with multiple DVRs and

Traditional Analog CCTV 1970's

FIGURE V-1

FIGURE V-2

Current CCTV (Backend Digital) 1990's

FIGURE V-3

multiple analog CCTV cameras tied to a local area network (LAN) and a large-scale monitoring environment that was utilized by security teams with larger facility deployments of security cameras, such as large corporations and government (see Figure V-4).

Although this system architecture was accepted and implemented in many security system environments, there continued to be several drawbacks to the architectures that precluded the end user from utilizing the information being captured.

For one, CCTV systems rely on single-purpose cameras, cabling, recorders, and monitoring, which provides a complex point-to-point infrastructure in which expansion of the system can increase cost for installation, expansion, and maintenance of the system.

Monitoring of the system has been made available with the development of the DVR. The system design is limited to lack of information control, which needs to flow into the DVR and then convert the image into a digital signal that can be monitored over an IP network. The DVR becomes the limiting technology point of the CCTV system as the end user has limited access to the camera control, limited scalability due to the DVR input capabilities, limited remote access, limited system mobility as the system is hardwired back to the DVR, and as the typical DVR uses time-division multiplexing, the record/refresh capabilities are limited to the global refresh capability of the overall system.

The CCTV to IP Surveillance System Evolution

With the IT revolution of 2000, continuous growth and acceptance of network technologies and high-speed IP networks fueled the movement of businesses and institutions to add new applications which benefited the network capabilities of the emerging IP network infrastructure.

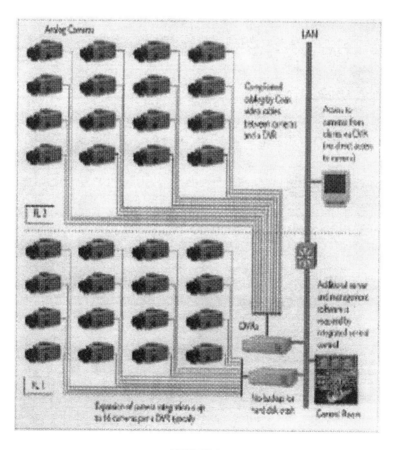

FIGURE V-4

The addition of IP video surveillance applications leveraged the same IP network system infrastructure which already was in existence to move data. In addition, the acceptance of compression standards for digital video applications over IT networks helped to increase the use of video as an acceptable IT application.

The first step of IP surveillance into the IP network system was analog CCTV camera technology attached to a network server, which converted the camera image to a compressed image that could be moved around on an IP network without compromising network traffic and without decreasing the available network bandwidth that businesses and institutions used to move data.

This approach provided a link between the traditional CCTV system and the networked IT systems. These network server products provided for the video to be changed into an IP stream and feed out over the network. Further advancements in server technology allowed for the loop-though of the analog video to allow for the continued use of the DVR (see Figure V-5).

Further camera development created IP cameras with built-in web servers and Ethernet connectivity, which can feed an IP network, provided system flexibility is beyond the traditional CCTV system technology.

IP surveillance systems can generate the same high-quality images as analog cameras but provide simplicity when increasing the cameras connected to the network by leveraging the LAN already in place. When the existing LAN is leveraged, the addition of new IP cameras provides for easy scalability without the addition of new hardware cabling. This provides for easy and faster additions to the IP surveillance system.

By using this distributed network architecture, the system user can configure control of the system to be centralized or distributed to various users, and with a single server, with a software application, can record and run the entire system. The server environment can also store the recorder IP surveillance video and have network-attached storage such as tape backup or reside on a storage area network (SAN) system for increased capabilities. In addition, the use of server technology provides for future upgrades with faster processing power, larger storage disk drives, and new software application.

As the use of IP surveillance systems has grown, increased development of software applications has also grown to accommodate the expanding need for instant access to IP video surveillance to be used in rapid deployment and collaborative communications of events as they are occurring. The user can configure the system to provide permission levels which allow remote access to authorized clients who have received permission for monitoring the IP camera video.

Lastly, IP networking allows for the addition of bidirectional audio, which allows for two-way communication from the camera to the security control station if a microphone and speaker are added. These developments deliver high-quality images over an IP network. Going beyond the IP network is also possible.

Additional advancements to the IP system such as Power over Ethernet (POE) provide for easy, rapid deployment of cameras in various environments (see Figure V-6).

POE use of CAT5E or CAT6 cables delivers data and power to IP cameras via a mid span unit, which injects the power into the CAT5E or CAT6 cable to IP cameras that are enabled to accept such. In addition, cameras that cannot accept the POE directly to the camera can be powered using a splitter adapter. The POE is limited, though, by the CAT5/6 cabling to a distance of 100 meters from the mid span unit. However, the benefit of POE—such as no

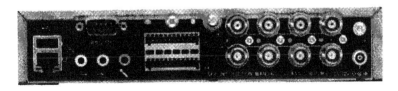

FIGURE V-5 IP output: analog video in and out

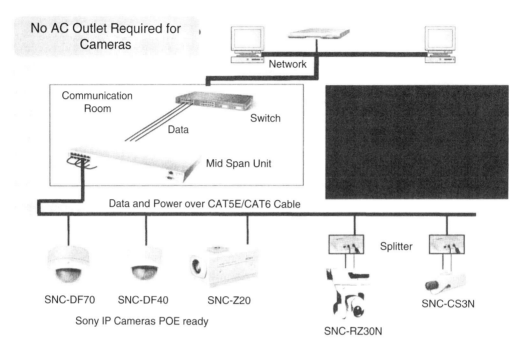

FIGURE V-6

AC outlet required for each IP camera, reduced installation cost, and flexibility to reposition cameras by moving the CAT5/6 cable—has increased the use of such systems in schools and small business facilities, for example.

Wireless system capabilities have also allowed for the use of IP cameras without the need for cabling installation for video and control, which saves both time and money. From a simple 802.11 wireless transmission from a light pole in a parking lot to the guard station, to mesh networks that provide multiple cameras to link together wirelessly feeding video to hotspots in a given area or a facility network, wireless systems have been used in many different applications.

Video analytics are also becoming a large part of IP surveillance system technologies that end users can obtain great benefits from. Analytics will continue to grow within the security industry over the foreseeable future as new software and hardware products come to serve the expanding IP surveillance market. IP surveillance system video analytics will allow end users to overcome the limitations found in traditional "back-end heavy" CCTV video analytics systems, such as the high cost of the system, and the limitations to post-recording search and processing performance of the analytic system. Whether such video analytics will become accepted in the market will depend on the ease of use and affordability of such technology.

IP camera products are available today and can provide preprocessing to the video image, such as intelligent motion or nonmotion detection, that creates the necessary metadata to feed the back-end video analytic processing systems. This preprocessing of the video image by the IP camera, as an intelligent edge device, can be found in products in the market today. This camera edge device intelligence can help conserve infrastructure bandwidth and save the processing power of the video analytic system back-end processing, which in a traditional CCTV systems requires full-time video streaming in order to obtain the same results. The preprocessing information combined with the post-processing use of the generated metadata can greatly improve the accuracy and performance of the video analytic system. This infrastructure provides the user a distributed and enhanced processing architecture that can greatly benefit him or her.

A wide range of these applications products is coming to market today. These products range from highly specific deep data analysis packages to general-purpose security suites. These products will enable the growth in the IP surveillance market that will allow intelligent video-based analytics to be deployed in a variety of settings by a large number of security operations.

However, the creation of an infrastructure for broad-based, economical deployment of these advanced video analytic capabilities is necessary to support the use of the expanding IP surveillance systems. Security system professionals need to review and determine if their existing security system strategy can support the expanding requirement of such video analytic applications that are becoming available and to begin planning for the migration of existing CCTV system architecture to an IP-based surveillance architecture that can take advantage of these applications.

In conclusion, continued utilization of the traditional CCTV systems will benefit from advancements in camera technologies that will enhance the use of the existing systems. Network server bridge products will allow CCTV system users to migrate and integrate their existing CCTV system to become a part of the expanding IP surveillance system architectures that are being implemented today and into the future. The increase in the quality and functionality of IP-based security systems will quickly establish a new standard for the use of video surveillance systems. In the post 9/11 world, heightened expectations for rapid response to events with increased use and quick access to the event video information that can be made available by an IP surveillance infrastructure will drive the increased use and demand for IP systems across many industries, schools, transportation hubs, and municipalities.

Visitor Badging and Control

CAS, JHC

Visitors to a retail facility such as a store, corporate headquarters, buying offices, or distribution center should be required to sign a "visitor log" and be issued a "visitor badge." The issuer need not be a security or loss prevention employee; any receptionist or representative of management may undertake this task. The purpose of the visitor badge program is to maintain a historical record of nonemployees who access the facility in question in terms of

- Their identity
- Whom they represent
- The purpose of the visit
- The employee or executive they are visiting
- The date of the visit
- The time they enter
- The time they leave the property

Visitors must be escorted at all times by their host and must not be allowed to wander through merchandise areas or office complexes at will. Vendors may be an exception to this rule. Please refer to "Vendor Fraud, Badging, and Control."

The badge itself may be fabricated in a hard material, prenumbered format, to be returned and retained for subsequent reuse. Such numbering serves as an inventory control. Visitor badges may also be of a temporary paper or fabric material, on which is printed (in ink) the name of the visitor and the date and time the badge was issued; these badges are intended for one-time use and are to be disposed of at the end of the visit. There is also a temporary badge which "self-destructs" by turning black after a predetermined period of time.

Any person observed in nonpublic areas of the facility, such as store stockrooms, who isn't known or identified as an employee should be challenged regarding presence. If it's determined the individual is a bona fide visitor but somehow bypassed the signing-in process, such visitor must be escorted to the reception desk, manager's office, or other appropriate area (depending on the nature of the facility) and issued a badge. An effort should also be made to determine what enabled the visitor to bypass the visitor control procedures, and the deficiency corrected.

VSOs vs. Plainclothes

CAS, JHC

Which strategy is most effective: deploying a visible security officer in some form of uniform or utilize agents in plainclothes? Clearly, the logic behind the visible agent is the hoped-for benefit of deterring shoplifting because of the presence of a representative of management dedicated to security of the store and its contents. The visible officer is a reminder of security just like the sudden appearance of a black-and-white state patrol car causes motorists to check their speed and thereafter be mindful of their speed, at least for a while.

The logic behind the plainclothes agent is to surreptitiously blend the protection staff in with the customers in hopes they *won't* be identified as representatives of management and enable them to observe and subsequently detain those customers who choose to steal merchandise.

The use of the former is unquestionably a loss prevention technique. The latter is more of a security technique, albeit there are advocates whose stance is that detection and apprehension are just two of many forms of "loss prevention."

To put the issue in the proper prospective, we need to go back and look at the historical background of protection strategies in retailing.

Up through the 1960s, major retailers staffed "Protection Departments" (which evolved into "Security Departments") with "floor walkers," "store detectives," "operatives," and "agents." The emphasis of such departments was *solely* the detection and apprehension of shoplifters and dishonest employees, and this was achieved through a covert strategy (plainclothes). Plainclothes staffs were augmented from time to time, principally during major sales or holiday periods, with off-duty police officers in uniform or uniform contract guards, but such use was more for crowd control and assistance in arrest cases.

The measure of success and the justification for security budgets was directly related to "production," i.e., the number of shoplifters apprehended, the number of dishonest employees caught and terminated, the number of credit card forgers jailed, and, in some cases, the level of inventory shortage. And store security departments at multistore companies unofficially competed for the most arrests each year.

The year that proved to be pivotal for one retailer was 1969. The company, a leading fashion department store chain headquartered in Los Angeles, California, had a remarkably successful production record of shoplifter and employee detections; however, amazingly, the company experienced the worst inventory shrinkage performance in its history—3.2% of sales! We use the word "amazingly" because there was then a belief, which still exists today, that there's a relationship between theft and shrinkage; i.e., the less theft, the less shrinkage. And there was also the belief, which still exists today, that the more thieves a store identifies and removes, there will be less theft and hence less shrinkage.

However, the reality was just the opposite. Management didn't care how many crooks its security department caught, but it did care about the loss of profits reflected in the high inventory shortage. So, for the first time, the presumptive value of the security department's contribution to the benefit of the enterprise (the department store company) was challenged. Security management had to come up with a better plan. What to do?

In casting about for some answers, some insight into a new strategy, one thought occurred over and over. We knew, and everyone in the security business knew, that one problem on the floor which impeded catching shoplifters was some innocent customer or sales associate coming on the scene and inadvertently "burning" what surely was going to be an arrest. The eye contact was all that was necessary to spoil a shoplifting act in progress.

In the 1970s, this was labeled the "Oh Shit Syndrome", i.e., the emotional and personal reaction on the part of a person engaged in an evil deed who rightly or wrongly believes he or she has been detected in that act by virtue of seeing someone looking at him or her. It wasn't a "scientifically" proven phenomenon, but rather, the recognition of reality.

Senior management of the Broadway was concerned about the language but acquiesced to the production of an internal video production explaining the syndrome for use in training.

We also knew many man-hours were consumed when a detention was made by the processing and waiting for the police to respond to the store and dispose of the detainee, be it by citation or transportation to the station. And all the while the store detective was in this processing mode, many acts of shoplifting could be ongoing, uninterrupted. With this knowledge, we determined that for the time required to process one detection (and the processing), we could intentionally burn approximately 30 would-be acts of theft (depending on the size, volume, and location of a given store), giving us a ratio of up to 1:30.

This was the genesis of a whole new strategy, which we titled "Loss Prevention"; i.e., what can we do to *prevent* the acts of theft, rather than try to catch them all, because it was apparent that we couldn't stop or even slow down the thefts through a detection program. Indeed, we knew that when we "blitzed" a store (assigned an entire team of store detectives to saturate one store), we could increase the number of arrests, and we never reached a saturation level. Put another way, the more store detectives we assigned to a store, the more arrests were made. So if 5 store detectives in a one million square foot store could generate 12 shoplifting arrests in 1 day, could 1 or 2 "loss prevention" agents potentially deter over 300 would-be thefts? And this was right after a nationally published survey which suggested that 1 in every 10 customers shoplifted. With literally thousands of customers coming into the store, was 300 an unrealistic possibility?

This strategy led to the first and often-copied "Red Coat" program, wherein about 80% of the store detective staff was retrained to prevent shoplifting by being highly visible (wearing a tailored red sport coat with a gold cloth pocket badge reading "Security") and constantly moving about the store with a pleasant expression on their face, making eye contact with as many customers as possible. The retraining included how to deal with or respond to "Are you watching me?" "Are you following me?" to "Here, I didn't want this anyhow "(as the customer pulled an item out of her purse and handed it to the loss prevention agent). "Loss prevention," which meant "burning" the would-be thief, worked in most cases. The balance of the staff (20%) continued in plainclothes and continued in their detection and apprehension mode. Those who couldn't or wouldn't be deterred, and felt confident they could succeed in a theft because they knew where the Red Coats were, wound up being arrested. It was a balancing act that worked.

At the end of the first full year, this radical program and departure from the universal retail security practice across the industry and across the country resulted in less than half the detentions of the infamous 1969 figures, but the inventory shrinkage dropped from 3.2% to 1.7% of sales, representing many millions of dollars. Year after year for the next 10 years, with the Red Coat program in use, orchestrated with a variety of other "shortage awareness" activities and programs, the shrinkage continued to decline.

The program was introduced in annual national meetings, and many in the industry replaced the title "Security Departments" for the then-modern and apparently successful "Loss Prevention Department" program. The name given the function is really immaterial; it's how the department operates which is important.

With the passage of time and personnel, the philosophy of deterrence over detection lost momentum and the majority of programs in existence today are "loss prevention" in name only.

Back to the original question: Which strategy is most effective: deploying a visible security officer in some form of uniform or placing agents in plainclothes? The first answer is: In these times, a balance of the two could be effective. The second answer is: It depends on whom you ask.

Weapons

CAS, JHC

The possession and use of weapons, both lethal and less-than-lethal, in retail loss prevention is a subject which has been long debated. The majority opinion is that only rarely is there a need for weapons, and we agree with this position.

We emphatically state that any weapons possessed or used must be properly licensed and the user properly trained and licensed. Training in the use of weapons should be repeated semiannually and qualifying in the use of the weapon documented. Weapons, if kept on company property, must always be stored securely. Any use of weapons must be approved by the highest loss prevention authority.

Rarely, an executive protection assignment will best be performed if the protecting agent is armed. In these situations, care must be exercised to assure that all laws are followed with respect to the carrying of concealed weapons.

Another possible situation in which weapons may be desirable is when staking out a location when there is credible information indicating it will be the target of a robbery or burglary. Normally, such surveillances will be the primary responsibility of the police, with security personnel serving in a support role. Even so, if the police have no objections (or suggest it), qualified security personnel participating in the surveillance may be better served by being armed.

When either contract or proprietary security officers are required to patrol the exterior of building at night, particularly if these are locations are known as high crime areas, we feel it is permissible for them to be armed with pepper spray (also known as OC spray, from *Oleoresin Capsicum*), which is a *lachrymatory agent* (a chemical compound that irritates the eyes to cause tears, pain, and even temporary blindness) that is used in personal *self-defense*. Pepper-type spray was formerly often called "mace," which is no longer in general use. These security officers may also carry a baton (provided they meet local and state law requirements).

While we see no objections to the use of taser or so-called stun guns as a self-defense nonlethal weapon by properly trained personnel, our experience has shown such devices are not popular with loss prevention personnel. The taser weapon, which shoots small darts on thin wires into an aggressor to disable him or her by an electric shock, has proved very effective with law enforcement personnel; however, this weapon has not yet been universally available to non-LEOs. Stun guns operate on the same principle as tasers but require direct contact with the aggressor. An electrical high voltage (50,000 volts) but low amperage current disturbs the subject's central nervous system, causing disablement. While available to civilians and generally unregulated, they are not seen in wide use by loss prevention.

In summary, deadly weapons should be used only by properly trained personnel and only when there is a clear and present danger to their lives or the lives of others. Nonlethal (control) weapons may be used, if authorized and legal, when their use is reasonable and can be fully justified.

Why Do Our Employees Steal?

Richard C. Hollinger, Ph.D.

Based upon almost 30 years of personal research experience, I can testify that explaining why employees steal from their employers is an extremely difficult task. What makes identifying the cause of employee dishonesty so difficult is that there is no single factor or theory that can explain each and every occurrence. Instead, social scientists have concluded that a variety of factors contribute to the occurrence of theft behavior. Three logically required conditions have to be present before a theft can occur. This is sometimes called the "theft triangle." First, the deviant act must be **motivated** by one or more precipitating factors. Second, there must be ample **opportunity** present for the theft to occur. Third, there must be a perceived **absence of deterrence**. In the following, I will discuss each of these three necessary conditions.

I. Motivations for Dishonesty

Most people employed in business organizations are conventionally socialized individuals. Generally speaking, the vast majority of our employees are law-abiding citizens who know the difference between right and wrong. After all, to be hired they have survived a pretty extensive interview and screening process. For a theft to occur, then, it is necessary for these persons to rationalize their law-breaking activity as completely justified under the circumstances. These motivating circumstances can originate either from within the work organization or can be the result of personal problems external to the work setting.

External Economic Pressures

There is extensive debate among both scholars and security experts regarding the extent to which external (or non-work) economic pressures provide the principal motivation for employee dishonesty. Despite extensive anecdotal supporting evidence, John Clark and I concluded in our 1983 book, *Theft By Employees*, that most incidents of employee pilferage were unrelated to an employee's particular economic situation. That is, highly paid employees reported taking property from the company just as often as did poorly paid employees. Our data suggested that the adequacy of one's compensation is extremely relative. Employee satisfaction with pay seemed to be independent of the absolute amount of money received. Moreover, employees who reported having personal economic problems were no more theft-prone than those who did not. This research study conducted two decades ago concluded that most employees do not steal from the company as a way of resolving their personal debts and other external economic pressures. This may not be the case today. In fact, as personal debt piles up, contemporary employees may be feeling a much stronger economic pinch than they did 20 years ago when I first started researching employee dishonesty.

Some employees do seem to be strongly motivated by what criminologist Donald Cressey called "non-sharable problems." The best examples of this situation are the rare persons who steal relatively large amounts of money from their employers. In his now-classic study of convicted embezzlers published in 1953, Cressey found that most became involved in "trust violations" as a result of some personal financial problem that they could not share with anyone else. Perhaps they had incurred a sizable gambling debt, were involved in an expensive love affair, were secretly addicted to drugs, or made a bad financial mistake with the company's assets. All the above are examples of "non-sharable problems" which precipitated the taking of a large amount of their employer's money to solve these personal problems. While large-scale embezzlements do occur—often crippling the business victimized—we must remember that these large-dollar thefts are quite rare. The typical employee thief is not a cash embezzler but rather a person who pilfers much smaller amounts of company property and money on a more regular basis. It is this more prevalent "nickel and dime" theft activity that over time costs companies far more in lost assets than all the embezzlers combined. It is for this reason that we need to look beyond purely economic motivations for an explanation of employee theft. The negative effects of employee dishonesty cannot be measured in economic costs alone. Quite obviously there are also social, psychological, and ethical impacts to consider. Supervisors can easily appreciate how dishonesty affects the social relationships among every employee in the work milieu—both those who are and who are not involved.

Job Dissatisfaction

A principal negative effect of pervasive employee dishonesty is a deterioration of workplace morale. Where theft is widespread, employees tend not to trust one another. The secretive nature of deviant activity tends to constrain on-the-job interaction and after-work socializing. The *esprit de corps* that characterizes successful businesses is often not present in the company filled with deviant workers. (The only exception to this may include groups of deviant employees who get together after work for the specific purpose of conspiring to steal from their employers.) As a result of inadequate communications, we often observe a lack of helpfulness to fellow workers, customers and clients. With limited peer cooperation, the employee's personal identification with the company may begin to erode. With this may come inattentiveness to job responsibilities.

Research has shown, for example, that deviant employees are less likely to report shoplifting incidents and are more likely to engage in sloppy workmanship. The deviant employee is significantly more likely to also engage in a wide range of counterproductive activities, such as absenteeism, sick leave abuse, on-the-job drug use and alcohol intoxication, workplace accidents and, eventually, turnover. We will also see that employee deviance is often the result of job dissatisfaction. However, it is also true that job satisfaction can sometimes be adversely affected by a prevailing atmosphere of worker deviance. In theft-filled companies, employees often grumble and complain and are generally a fairly unhappy group of people. This general feeling of malaise eventually affects those who are not stealing from the company. For example, the physical devices and security countermeasures that management often installs to deter high theft levels sometimes make honest employees feel as if they are not trusted. Sometimes this "we don't trust anyone" attitude can aggravate an existing adversarial relationship between management and labor. In short, as a consequence of employee dishonesty, the entire social atmosphere of the workplace may seriously deteriorate.

A commonly expressed dishonesty theory assumes that employee theft is caused by job dissatisfaction. This explanation is based on the assumption that unhappy employees will steal from their employers in order to resolve feelings of inequity. Theft is viewed as the employee's way of "getting back" at an employer who does not provide a satisfactory work experience. In other words, employees "rip-off" their companies when their employer is perceived as "ripping" them off (Altheide et al., 1978).

One of the most commonly observed dishonesty explanations is based upon the assumption that disgruntled employees will steal from their employers in order to resolve feelings of perceived inequity in the way in which they have been treated. Theft is viewed as the employee's way of "getting back" at an employer who does not provide a satisfactory work experience. In other words, employees "rip off" the company when their employer is perceived as "ripping" them off (Altheide et al., 1978).

Although the job dissatisfaction explanation makes plenty of intuitive sense, until recently there was surprisingly little empirical evidence to confirm its accuracy. The relationship between job dissatisfaction and workplace deviance was first tested by Mangione and Quinn (1975), who found only mild support among males 30 and older. Later in 1982, John Clark and I examined the job dissatisfaction hypothesis with a much larger data set, discovering a more consistent pattern of support. Among employees in three different industries studied, those dissatisfied with their present jobs and looking for another job were more involved in employee theft. Retail employee thieves were most unhappy with the inadequate "task challenges" of their work and the fact that their employers seemed not to care about them. In the hospital, employees who take property were most unhappy about their employer's lack of caring, in addition to poor treatment by immediate supervisors and limited job responsibility. Although slightly less influential in the manufacturing plant, deviant employees were again more likely to express dissatisfaction both with their employers and with limited span of authority. In all three industries studied, employees who felt that their employers were dishonest, unfair, and uncaring about their workers were significantly more involved in theft and other forms of workplace deviance. Immediate supervisors were often viewed as the source of the workplace inequity, since employees usually view their supervisors as the personification of their employers.

There is substantial documentation for the job dissatisfaction explanation. For example, Jason Ditton (1977), maintains that from the earliest days of the industrial revolution both employees and their employers have assumed that a certain portion of one's wages were represented by non-monetary perks. Other researchers studying a variety of work and occupational experiences have verified the existence of these "wages in kind" that over the years have become an institutionalized part of many work experiences (Henry, 1978).

In recent years, more and more scholars have found empirical support for the relationship between job dissatisfaction and employee dishonesty. Generally speaking, if the prevailing worker attitudes toward the organization, management, and supervisors are positive, one finds lower levels of all types of deviant behavior in the workplace, including theft and dishonesty. However, if the employees: 1) feel exploited by the work organization, 2) believe that supervisors are not interested in them as persons, and 3) are generally unhappy with their work situation—we find higher than average levels of theft and deviance. High levels of turnover in the retail industry can be viewed as a barometer of this pervasive worker dissatisfaction problem.

In summary, one of the most commonly observed dishonesty explanations is based upon the assumption that disgruntled employees will steal from their employers in order to resolve feelings of perceived inequity in the way in which they have been treated. Theft is viewed as the employee's way of "getting back" at an employer who does not provide a satisfactory work experience. In other words, employees "rip off" the company when their employer is perceived as "ripping" them off (Altheide et al., 1978).

II. The Opportunity Factor

In this section, I will examine the "opportunity" component of the theft triangle. The amount, the frequency, and the prevalence of theft are each determined by the possible range of theft opportunities. Some jobs permit more opportunities for stealing as compared to other occupations, professions, or positions. If the product is without much value or no cash handling occurs, we would expect correspondingly less theft. Alternatively, if there are many things of value that can be taken from the workplace, we should not be surprised to discover higher prevalence levels of theft.

Unfortunately, almost everywhere one looks in retailing, we can find desirable merchandise of significant value, as well as plentiful amounts of cash. Given the high levels of opportunity for theft, it not surprising that employee dishonesty abounds in retailing. In fact, perhaps we should ask the question in the opposite direction, namely, "why isn't there even more theft given the numerous opportunities for taking things in the retail store?"

Most readers would probably agree that employee theft is already bad enough. In the most recently conducted 2002 National Retail Security Survey, for example, we discovered that senior retail loss prevention executives reported that nearly one-half of their inventory shrinkage (48%) was attributable to employee dishonesty.

Reduce the levels of opportunity, and theft rates should decline. The solution to the problem seems so obvious. Lowering levels of sales associate dishonesty should be the direct result of strictly limiting an employee's access both to money and merchandise. However, as we eventually discovered with shoplifting, simply constraining access can backfire, since physical controls can seriously interfere with the ability of the retail employee to do their job. Just as the shopper must be able to touch the merchandise to facilitate sales, the sales associate must also have unrestricted access to both merchandise and cash to serve the customer and to complete their purchase transactions. In other words, locking things up, putting items under the counter, or physically chaining things down may not be the ideal answer to this problem.

When I first began researching this topic 30 years ago, I remember reading a variety of articles on the subject. At the time it seemed like they all focused on the opportunity factor.

Then it seemed that most security experts believed that unlimited opportunity was the predominant cause of dishonesty in the workplace. Virtually all argued that if items are not properly secured, eventually your merchandise will be taken. At the time it was very common to believe that all employees are vulnerable to temptation. While most experts feel that this is an overly pessimistic image of the typical employee, it is undeniable that opportunity can facilitate theft and dishonesty in the workplace. Given its obvious importance, I find it interesting that there has been so little systematic research on the role that opportunity plays in the employee theft equation.

In our book, *Theft by Employees*, published in 1983, John Clark and I compared theft levels among the various occupations in three different industries, namely, retailing, healthcare, and manufacturing. Generally speaking, employees working in those jobs possessing the greatest uncontrolled access to money and property did report slightly higher levels of theft. It is also important to note, however, that the majority of employees with high opportunity to steal were *not* involved in dishonest activity. In other words, from my own research and other scholarly studies, it has become clear that just having access to things of value does not necessarily produce theft. Opportunity also has an important subjective dimension. Three factors that can affect the subjective value of merchandise include social desirability, concealability, and proximity.

Social Desirability

Obviously, money has objective (or extrinsic) value. However, the same cannot always be said for merchandise, which has both objective (extrinsic) and subjective (intrinsic) value. Some merchandise in our stores is highly priced, but could not be given away. Other less expensive merchandise cannot even be kept on the shelves. Most internal theft (and shoplifting) is focused on those items that are at present highly desirable. This is especially true for younger employees with minimal tenure with the firm. Opportunity then is not just access to merchandise, it is also directly dependent on how "hot" the merchandise is. In other words is the item currently in vogue? Or, as my generation said, "Is it cool?" We should not just ask ourselves whether stolen items can be fenced or sold to strangers. Of greater importance might be: Does the merchandise in our stores have subjective value to the person who takes it, either for their personal use or to give to a close friend or family member? In other words, we need to continually re-evaluate the social desirability of the merchandise in the store.

Concealability

Can the item easily be hidden on one's person to be taken from the store? Americans are afraid to violate a person's private social space. This is why we have so much objection to current airport security screening policies. It occurs to me that many things that are socially desirable are getting physically smaller and as a result, easier to conceal on our persons. Just think of how much easier it is to conceal a CD when compared to a vinyl record of an earlier generation, or a DVD when compared to a VHS tape in its box.

Proximity

The old saying goes, "familiarity breeds contempt." Perhaps in the retail store the saying should be re-stated "proximity breeds devaluation." Merchandise that is handled continuously every day can allow the employee to eventually view these items as just "things" without great value to the company. When I worked for the Air Force one summer, we often threw out equipment worth thousands, largely because everyone had forgotten its real value. POS terminals automatically price items which allows associates to lose appreciation for the real value and price of store merchandise. Eventually it just all becomes "stuff" with little or unknown value, making it much easier to steal and not worth protecting.

Neutralizing the Guilt

One of the most complicated behaviors that social scientists attempt to explain is the person who takes the property of another without feeling any guilt or remorse. I continue to be amazed by how many dishonest employees fail to appreciate the wrongfulness of what they have just been caught doing. Apparently, many people believe that stealing is perfectly acceptable, especially if you do not get caught. This belief is most commonly observed when the victim of the theft is a large, faceless bureaucracy, such as the government or a business corporation.

Paradoxically we continue to observe increases in employee dishonesty while our country's official and self-reported larceny rates are both in decline. National Retail Security Surveys over the past 10 years indicate that that the increasing problem of employee dishonesty is not the result of a sudden breakdown in hiring practices. In fact, the NRSS has shown in each of the past 10 years that more numerous and sophisticated screening tools are being used routinely by employers. This enhanced level of applicant screening often involves multiple interviews, drug testing, criminal background checks, credit evaluations, and honesty testing. These countermeasures have successfully eliminated many risky and marginal persons from the applicant pool. Nevertheless, despite our best efforts to screen out known or potentially dishonest job candidates, employee theft not only persists but also seems to be increasing in prevalence. The question is "why?"

I believe that the reason for the continuing growth in the prevalence of dishonest employees is attributable to the fact that many conventionally socialized people have discovered a way to overcome guilt for doing something that they know is wrong. In other words, normally honest and ethical employees are stealing without feeling remorse for their behavior. This process is not based on simple rationalizations in which one excuses or justifies unethical behavior "after the fact. " No doubt many of us have engaged in these ex post facto rationalizations for our dishonesty after we have been caught doing something wrong or illegal. For example, the driver who receives a speeding ticket blames the police officer. The person who underreports their income blames the overly zealous IRS auditor. The student who cheats on a test blames the instructor for preparing an extremely difficult exam.

These examples of "after the fact" rationalizations are not causal explanations of behavior because they do not occur prior to the deviant act. To prove causation, the factors that contribute to the behavior must be present before, not after, the offending behavior.

One of the most useful theories to explain why associates who have passed the rigorous interview and screening process will eventually steal is what criminologists, Gresham Sykes and David Matza, call "techniques of neutralization." In other words, we need to understand how conventionally socialized persons negate the guilt or remorse that one should be expected to feel for their deviant behaviors. These techniques allow for the traditional ethical bonds of society to be temporarily broken or suspended. Prior to the introduction of this theory, crime was presumed to be a product of lower-class life. Alternatively, this theory helped to explain why middle- and upper-class adolescents, after growing up in a morally and financially sound social background also engaged in delinquent behavior.

Sykes and Matza identified a number of specific types of neutralization techniques that were later expanded upon by other criminologists. I have listed the major types below, along with a definition for each in words that a retail store employee might use to express the concept.

1. Denial of Responsibility

"My store doesn't make any sincere attempt to protect its merchandise. We have no working cameras or EAS tag alarms like other retailers do, so it's not my fault when merchandise is missing. It's obvious the company doesn't care."

2. Denial of Injury

"My employer sells so much merchandise that nobody will miss the few items I take. They can afford it."

3. Denial of the Victim

"This company makes so much profit that they have no right to claim that they are hurt by a few petty thefts. I consider pilferage my "fringe benefit package."

4. Condemnation of the Condemner

"The store has no right to condemn me for stealing small amounts of money and merchandise. My manager shouldn't be surprised when we take things. In fact, if there is any victim around here it is me, given the pitifully low wages that we are paid. The company should not be surprised when their hard working employees steal. The more appropriate question they should be asking is, 'why is everybody not stealing?'"

5. Defense of Necessity

"I really need the money to buy food and pay my rent." Or, "If the company expects me to dress well at work then I am going to have to take money or merchandise to look presentable."

6. Appeal to Higher Loyalties

"My friends and family are far more important to me than this company that I have been working at for just a few short weeks. So, I let friends have free or reduced price items when I ring them up at the cash register." Or, "I need money to pay for my child's doctor bills, since my kids and family comes before my temporary allegiance to this company."

7. Metaphor of the Ledger

"We all work really hard around here, especially during the holiday season I keep track of what the company owes me in my head. If I steal, it is only fair compensation for unpaid extra hard work."

There is substantial research support for this theory. In a paper published in 1991 (i.e., *Deviant Behavior 12*: 169–201), I found that many of the above-listed guilt neutralizing techniques were statistically more likely to be utilized by employees to excuse their dishonest behavior. Moreover, I discovered that techniques of neutralization were slightly more likely to be used by older, than the very youngest employees. Apparently, older associates, who better understand right from wrong, are more likely to need sophisticated guilt-neutralizing vocabularies to excuse their own crimes.

In summary, employees' perceptions of how they are treated by management have a great deal to do with creating and perpetuating a "climate of dishonesty" in the workplace. Research shows that the most productive explanations are based on variables directly related to perceived workplace conditions or the attitudes held by workers. Managers must be more attentive to the extent to which these neutralizing techniques are present within the culture of their organizations. If neutralizing language and expressions are commonly expressed by workers, managers should not be surprised to discover that rates of employee dishonesty are above an acceptable level.

III. Deterrence

Lastly, perhaps the single most important factor influencing employees' decisions to steal involves whether or not they believe that they will get caught. This is known in criminology as the question of deterrence. The third and final side of the theft triangle is the lack of an effective "deterrent."

Assuming that an employee wants to steal and has the prerequisite opportunity, he or she will be affected by the two primary dimensions of deterrence. The first dimension of deterrence is the offender's perceived certainty of detection. In other words, in their own minds, what is the chance of getting caught? The second dimension of deterrence is known as the perceived severity of punishment. In other words, if the offender does get caught, what bad things do they believe will happen to him or her as a result? Notice that I have phrased this in terms of perceived deterrence. The actual (or objective) certainty of detection and severity of punishment are not really important. All that really matters is the perceived reality on the part of the offender.

Both the perceived certainty of detection and the perceived severity of punishment work together in combination to provide the optimal deterrent effect. Put in the context of highway speeding, the perceived certainty of detection consists of "what are the odds that I might get pulled over by the police if I exceed the speed limit?" In addition, the severity of punishment amounts to "how many dollars will I be fined if given a ticket?" For deterrence to work effectively, the law violator must believe two things. First, that there is a high probability of getting caught, and second, if caught, that the punishment will be severe or costly.

Research has shown that most new employees believe (albeit inaccurately) that they will be caught if they attempt to steal from their employers. Fortunately for most businesses, the vast majority of these easily deterred employees will never attempt to steal. Most troubling, however, is that further research suggests that there is a small but significant number of employees who believe that there is little or no chance that they will ever be caught. Unfortunately, as we all secretly know, these employees are factually correct in their assessment that the risks of detection are quite low.

Moreover, even if detected, many employees correctly assume that they will not be punished very severely. In fact, the more times that they successfully steal without detection increases their assessment that they are invincible to the efforts of loss prevention. This is especially true for young males. In fact, many long-time thieves actually believe that they will never get caught and are quite surprised when they eventually do.

Given the virtually impossible task of detecting employee theft, the unspoken truth remains—most dishonest workers will never be caught. And, even if they are detected, they know that realistically the worst consequence which can happen to them is that they will be fired. Most employees who are actively engaged in theft believe that they will not be criminally prosecuted. Unless the offense is particularly costly or notable, these offenders are, more often than not, correct.

If your company is known not to aggressively prosecute employee dishonesty cases in criminal court, this situation provides very little deterrence, especially to younger employees who report the very highest levels of theft even when the chances of detection are significant. So, if the employees at the bottom of the bureaucratic hierarchy believe that they won't be prosecuted, and know that they can get another job the very next day, how can the employer ever hope to prevent theft? The answer is that in most companies there is very little perceived certainty of detection and even lower perceived severity of punishment. It would appear that for the very experienced and confident employee thief, whatever loss prevention is doing to deter theft simply does not work very well. The obvious question is, "what can we do to change the current state of affairs?"

Here are some essential questions that each company must continually review to determine their current state of deterrence:

- What is the chance of a manager or a loss prevention investigator detecting an employee involved in theft?
- What is the chance of one's co-workers turning in a fellow employee for theft?
- What is the chance that an employee thief will be fired if detected?
- What is the chance that an employee thief will be criminally prosecuted if detected?
- Do all employees, regardless of rank, have an equal chance of being caught and punished for theft?
- Are some employees immune from detection and prosecution given their position or rank?
- Do your employees think that the loss prevention department is a "joke"?

How did your company do in this quick assessment? If your employees are not deterred, you are not alone and have plenty of company. In my experience, most retail chains do not present much of a convincing or credible deterrent to the highly motivated offender with abundant opportunities for theft. Given this situation, perhaps we should not be asking the question, "why do my employees steal?" Instead, the more accurate question should be, "why don't all of our employees steal, given the rather obvious fact that most could probably get away with it?" An even more scary thought is the possibility that the astronomically high levels of turnover in retail may inadvertently be working in the favor of loss prevention, given that so few employees have been working long enough to fully understand how miserably low the chances of getting caught really are!

Window Smashing

CAS, JHC

Just 50 years ago, stores big and small had windowed "store fronts," and huge glass windows featured interesting displays of fashion goods and from time to time automated scenes, like electric toy trains winding their way through villages and over rivers and through the mountains, to everyone's delight. Children were taken to big stores to gaze at the wonder of Christmas depicted or featured through those windows and to visit Santa Claus inside the store. The wonderful fantasies of yesteryear's window displays have been replaced with the likes of Macy's Christmas Parade.

With the passage of time (relatively speaking, recent times), windows became targets not only for growing criminal activity in modern society, but for acts of civil disobedience, commencing with so-called civil unrest and magnified by the Vietnam war. Large masses of marching protesters against any number of social and racial issues found smashing windows punctuated their expression of disobedience. And large windows that were smashed facilitated looting. As an indirect consequence, store windows have shrunk in size. It's been an evolutionary process to the point today where stores which still have sizeable windows are relatively limited to secure environments, such as enclosed shopping malls, where window smashing is discouraged by the nature of the shopping center and its ever-present security force.

All that said, store windows of any size represent a vulnerability and potential access to the interior of the store, the theft and looting of all goods on display, and they must be alarmed and plans laid for temporary repairs in the event of smashing or breakage, by either man or nature.

The following simple policies and procedures should be considered:

- Do not display high price-point merchandise in window display presentations.
- Do not display alcoholic beverages in window displays.
- Number every window for emergency reference.
- Cut and store plywood panels sized by window for prompt but temporary installation (with each panel painted with the number of the window it is designed to fit).
- Arrange for whatever perimeter alarming is appropriate for that opening; e.g., if the intrusion sensing system is hard-wired, arrange for temporary lacing.
- If penetration of a window is made, especially large windows, attempt to harden the interior barrier which separates the interior of the store from that access point.

Is your store ready for the next episode of street demonstrations and the potential for window smashing?

Winning the Battle Through Pre-Employment Screening for Loss Prevention Professionals: Ten Critical Things You Need to Know

By Lester S. Rosen, Attorney at Law, Employments Screening Resources (ESR)

For Loss Prevention professionals, it is a well-established fact that internal theft accounts for a large percentage of inventory shrinking. According to industry sources, losses from employee theft can account for about 47% of total shrinkage, amounting to some $17.6 billion dollars.

Unfortunately there is no magic formula to alert loss prevention professionals in advance as to which employee is likely to steal. However, there are three general guiding principles that can substantially help loss prevention professionals manage the risks involved in employee theft.

First, there is a strong likelihood that someone who had been dishonest in the past may more likely be dishonest in the future. This proposition is borne out not only by common sense and experience, but is demonstrated by recidivism statistics showing a high rate of offenders re-offending.

Second, if a person is dishonest in the manner in which they obtained employment, such as by use of false past employment and education credentials, then it is arguably more likely that the applicant may be dishonest on the job. According to research cited in the May 1, 2006 issue of *Time Magazine*, there is "a lot of evidence that those who cheat on job applications also cheat in school and in life." That was the opinion of Dr. Richard Griffith, director of the industrial and organizational psychology program at the Florida Institute of Technology, and an expert on job applicant faking. According to the article, he is concerned that if applicants fake a degree, it is likely they cannot be trusted to tell the truth when it comes to financial statements.

Third, internal theft and fraud can occur if there is the right combination of motive, opportunity, and means. Motive to steal is something that a loss prevention professional may be able to ascertain prior to the commencement of employment. For example, an employer can utilize pre-employment tools such as an employment credit report to determine if an applicant is under such extreme financial stress that there may be motivations to engage in illegal acts.

To address these concerns, Loss Prevention professionals should carefully review their current pre-employment screening practices for hiring new employees. These processes are important not only for the loss prevention staff but also for all employees with access to cash or assets. The fundamental thrust of a pre-employment screening program is to prevent employee theft by not hiring a risky employee in the first place.

Pre-employment background screening works in four critical ways:

1. Just having background screening can discourage applicants with something to hide. If an employer makes it clear that they perform background checks, then a person with a criminal record or false resume will simply apply to a company that does not pre-screen.
2. Having a screening program encourages applicants to be especially forthcoming in their interviews.
3. It limits uncertainty in the hiring process. Although using personal judgment in the hiring process can be important, basing a decision on hard information is even better. This is especially important due to recent research that suggests that human beings are often not able to detect who is lying just by observing them.
4. A screening program demonstrates that an employer has exercised due diligence, providing a great deal of legal protection in the event of a lawsuit. Every employer has a legal duty to exercise an appropriate degree of care so that they do not hire someone who is dangerous, unfit, or unqualified for the job, and it is foreseeable that harm could occur. Failure to exercise a duty of care can result in an employer being sued for negligent hiring.

It is important to keep in mind that pre-employment screening is not a guarantee that all problematic applicants will be spotted. Rather, it is intended as a cost-effective and large-scale due diligence process designed to minimize the risks of a bad hire by utilizing tools that have proven effective at weeding out bad applicants. There are four typical tools used for pre-employment screening. The first is a check of governmental records. An example can be checking public courthouse records for criminal records. Driving records are another type of record that employers may obtain from governmental agencies. Driving records are of course needed for drivers. However, anyone who does any driving for an employer during working hours, even if it's just driving between employer locations, can create liability for an employer. The second tool is a check of private records, such as credit reports or a social security trace reports. A third tool is a factual verification of credentials by checking past employment, education, and licenses. A fourth tool is reference interviews with past employers.

In implementing or evaluating a pre-employment screening program, here are ten things that every loss prevention professional should consider when hiring employees:

1. **What can happen if an employer does not screen employees**
    There is a near-statistical certainty that a failure to screen employees, including loss prevention team members, will result in hiring someone with an unsuitable criminal record. Screening industry studies show that up to 10% of job applicants had some sort of criminal record. Various studies have also established that one-third, or even more, resumes contain material misstatements or omissions, such as mistating the nature or length of past

employment or exaggeration of educational accomplishments. The problem is that the past can be prologue and that dishonest behavior that an applicant lied about in the application process can come back to haunt an employer in the form of dishonest behavior on the job.

The same exposure can happen if employers fail to screen essential non-employees as well, such as vendors, independent contractors, and temporary workers. All these workers have access to company premises and assets. Vendors, for example, may enter an employer's premises day or night to fix machines or bring supplies. Temporary workers may have access to client lists, cash drawers, or computer programmers. An employer should require that all vendors as well as any temporary worker should be screened, and exercise a degree of control over the process, such as the type and extent of the screening, who does the screening, and the criteria for passing the screening.

2. **Do not use databases as a substitute for real background screening**

Another mistake employees can make is taking shortcuts in screening by relying on databases as a substitute for real background checks. The most accurate source of information on criminal records is to obtain it directly from each courthouse. The courthouses that are searched are typically selected from a tool known as a Social Security trace report, which matches name and address to Social Security number based upon records from credit bureaus and other sources. Since there are over 8,000 courthouses in the United States, a count level search is limited geographically to just the counties searched.

Employers also have access to a number of so-called "National" multi-jurisdictional databases covering millions of criminal records and sex offenders across all 50 states. Because of their low price, large geographic coverage and instant results, loss prevention directors can be lulled into a false sense of security that using such databases shows due diligence and is a better alternative then a courthouse search.

Unfortunately, even though such databases can be a valuable part of a screening program, in reality they are only a secondary or supplemental tool and by themselves probably do not represent due diligence. Such databases are NOT taken from the national FBI criminal database, but instead are a patchwork of records available for sale or downloading from various correctional or law enforcement authorities, state court repositories or some individual count courts. As a result, there can be issues as to completeness, accuracy, and timeliness. The problem is that these database can produce both "false positives" and "false negatives." A "false positive" is where there were insufficient identifiers so that a person is falsely accused of being a criminal or information as to a pardon or expungement was not updated. A "false negative" is where a person really is a criminal but the database missed them, either due to lack of converge, name variation, or some other issue. In the case of a possible match, the best practice is to pull the actual record from the court to verify identity and to ensure that the information is complete and up-to-date.

The bottom-line: the multi-jurisdictional databases are excellent supplemental tools in a screening program to help employers cover a broader area and suggest additional counties to search for records, but may not constitute due diligence as a stand-alone tool.

3. **An employer must understand and comply with the federal Fair Credit Reporting Act (FCRA) and state laws**

Background checks are typically performed by professional third-party background firms who have the specialized knowledge, resources, and software to accomplish the task. Third-party background checks are governed by a federal law called the Fair Credit Reporting Act (FCRA). Although the law refers to credit reports, that is a misnomer, because it covers any type of background checks performed by a Consumer Reporting Agency, not just credit reports. A background firm is defined under that act as a Consumer Reporting Agency, and includes not only background firms, but private investigator who performs checks.

The important points to know about the FCRA are:

a. Before obtaining background checks, the employer must certify to the background firm that they will follow the FCRA and not use the information to discriminate in violation of any state or federal law.

b. Each applicant must provide a written authorization and received a standalone disclosure about the background report. It is important to ensure that the background firm understands the FCRA and state law or that a local labor attorney is contacted, since the content of the forms are legally regulated and the requirements can be complicated.

c. If an employer finds information, such as a criminal record or an employment discrepancy, that causes them to reconsider employment opportunities, the employer must first send out a notice to the job applicant, as well as a copy of the report and a statement of rights prepared by the Federal Trade Commission before any adverse action is taken. This gives the applicants an opportunity to review the background report and to notify the employer if there is anything that is incorrect or incomplete. If the decision is to be made final, then a second letter must be sent that contains certain required language. An employer should resist a temptation to not follow the adverse action procedures and instead claim there was some other reason to not hire the candidate. The law places a clear obligation on employers, and any attempt to circumvent the rules can create unnecessary liability.

d. Employers need to be aware of the impact of state laws, since at least 20 states have their own version of the FCRA. California for example, has numerous requirements that are different and in addition to federal rules, and the potential civil damages for each violation can be $10,000 or more. That is another reason why an employer should review the legal aspects of their screening program with their attorney. Many states also have their own rules on which criminal records may be used for employment and laws that limit the use of arrests that did not result in a criminal conviction. A number of states have laws that in some way limit the reporting of criminal records by a background firm to seven years, although most states have exceptions based upon the anticipated salary of the job. California, however, is a state with a flat seven-year rule. In the seven-year states, the way the seven years is calculated can be complex as well. A criminal conviction can be older than seven years but can be reportable if the person was given a sentence of incarceration that came into the seven-year period. There are other limitations that various states have imposed as well, such as limits on using deferred adjudications or first offenses. Some of the states regulate what a screening firm can report and other limits on what an employer can utilize regardless of their source.

Another trap for the unwary is performing background checks in-house. Although the FCRA only apples to third-party agencies, employers with an internal security department can trip the FCRA by utilizing third party resources to assist in a screening, such as hiring investigators who are out of town to check remote court records, or accessing private databases for information assembled by third parties. Unless employers do everything themselve with in-house resources, an internal investigation can end up violating the FCRA. In addition, one state, California, has enacted rules that apply FCRA-like responsibilities on private employers who obtain public records. See California Civil Code section 1786.53.

4. **Understand how discrimination laws affect the use of criminal records**
Employment applications typically contain language that a criminal record does not automatically disqualify an applicant. Why? Because the Equal Employment Opportunities Commission has found that the automatic disqualification of applicants with a criminal record can have the effect of creating a disparated impact among certain groups, and therefore may be discriminatory. That does not mean that an employer is obligated to hire a criminal. It does mean, however, that an employer should not automatically reject an applicant without considering if there is a business justification.

It is critical for employers to understand that the background screening is conducted to determine whether a person is fit for a particular job. Society has a vested interest in ex-offenders re-entering society in order to become taxpaying and law-abiding citizens, and that typically means getting ex-offenders back into the workforce. However, an employer is also under a due diligence obligation to make efforts to determine if a person is reasonably fit for a particular position. For example, a person just out of custody for a theft crime may not be a good candidate for a loss prevention position, but may perform very well on a supervised work crew. If a criminal record is found, an employer must determine if there is a business reason not to hire the person, based upon the nature and gravity of the offense, the nature of the job, and when the crime occurred.

A possible trap for the unwary is the use of an automated decision making system. Some background firms provide security directors with a grading system based upon search results. For example, a "traffic light" may be used, and if it shows green, it means the applicant did not have a disqualifying criminal record. If a disqualifying criminal record is found, then the light will be red, which means "do not hire." If the screening firm comes across a criminal record that has not been addressed by the employer's work rules, then the applicant is given a yellow flag which means "caution." The problem is that this could violate Equal Employment Opportunity law. Federal EEOC rules and many state laws prohibit the automatic elimination of a person with a criminal conviction unless the employer can show a business justification. This means each potential negative decision should be reviewed individually.

The EEOC also cautions against the use of an arrest that did not result in a conviction, since the arrest itself is essentially just the police officer's opinion. However, if the employer is able to determine the underlying facts, then the behavior may be something an employer can potentially consider.

5. **Understand the issues associated with the use of contributory Merchant Databases**

Some background firms offer a product commonly referred to as a merchant database, typically used by large retailers who hire a large sales staff. They are databases in which retail stores contribute information about employees who have admitted to theft, whether or not a criminal case occurred. The database may also contain other information, such as records from various state criminal databases and Social Security Number information. These searches are relatively inexpensive, which is an advantage for employers. Since retail positions are often filled by lower-paid employees with high turnover rates, there is pressure on retailers to keep background screening as low-cost as possible.

The difficulty with using these databases is the underlying reliability of the data. The database includes information on individuals who were never prosecuted. The information is often based upon a report from a store loss prevention professional concerning an interrogation where a person admitted they committed the theft in exchange for not being prosecuted. Since the matter did not go to court, there would not be a court file, police report, or any sort of adjudication in any factual matter.

Given the nature of these databases, there are two obvious problems with their use. First, use of such a database may run contrary to the EEOC rules. An applicant may be the victim of a negative decision without any underlying factual determination. Considering the EEOC is concerned about the use of arrest records on the basis that an arrest is not a factual determination, unsubstantiated reports of a confession to store personnel are potentially troublesome.

The second issue is whether these databases are in fact FCRA compliant. Under the FCRA, a Consumer Reporting Agency (CRA) must take reasonable procedures to ensure accuracy. If information from a merchant database is a reported confession with no judicial findings, a CRA may have difficulty justifying the negative information unless it independently contacts the person performing the interview to confirm the facts. Otherwise, a person denied a job on the basis of a merchant database could claim a lack of reasonable procedures.

The bottom line is an employer should carefully balance the potential benefits versus any risks before utilizing such a database.

6. **Credit reports: uses and limitations**

Employers seek credit reports on job applicants for a variety of reasons. However, employers should approach the use of credit reports with caution. There is currently no mathematical model that attempts to "score" a credit report for employment purposes.

Employment credit reports in fact do not contain "FICO" credit scores. Such a scoring would face substantial challenges to prove it is a valid and non-discriminatory predictor of job performance. As a result, the use of credit reports tend to be "judgment calls," where the credit report is utilized in conjunction with all other available information.

Some employers take the position that a credit report shows whether an applicant is responsible and reliable by looking at the way that applicant handles his or her personal affairs. The logic is that a person who cannot pay his or her own bills on time, or make responsible personal financial decisions, may not be the best fit for a job that requires handling the company's funds or making meaningful decisions. Employers may also request credit reports to alert them to applicants whose monthly debt payments are too high for the salary involved. The concern is if a person is under financial stress due to a monthly debt that is beyond their salary, then that can be a "red flag." One of the common denominators in cases of embezzlement is a perpetrator in debt beyond his or her means may form a motive to steal.

However, employers should approach the use of credit reports with caution. A credit report can contain information that is incorrect or not applicable to employment. In addition, there have been changes recently that credit reports can be discriminatory if their use produces a disparate impact.

Before utilizing negative information found in a credit report, the employer should consider:

- Is the negative information a valid predictor of job performance?
- Is the information current and correct?
- Is there negative information reported outside the applicant's control and therefore having no relationship to employment. For example, is a negative entry in the report a result of a disputed bill, medical bills, dissolution of marriage, or some other problem? Many Americans, for example, are forced to use credit cards to pay for medical bills.
- Is there any reason not to consider the negative information? (For example, an employer generally should not consider a bankruptcy.)
- Is the employer consistent in the use of negative information? For example, have other applicants been hired with the same type of negative information and, if so, is there a rational reason why it was overlooked for others? Is there a company hiring policy or some documentation put in the file to demonstrate that the employer is consistent?
- Has the employer followed the FCRA and obtained consent and provided a stand-alone disclosure before obtaining a credit report, and if the credit report forms the basis of an adverse action, followed the pre-adverse and post-adverse action notification rules?

7. **Use employment applications effectively to limit problematic hires in the first place**
The application process is one of the most effective screening tools and it costs an employer nothing. Here are some key points.

First, make sure the application form contains all necessary language. Use the broadest possible language for felony and misdemeanor convictions and pending cases. One of the biggest mistakes employers make is to only ask about felonies on an application form, since misdemeanors can be very serious. Employers should inquire about misdemeanors to the extent allowed in their state. In addition, application forms that contain statements that lack of truthfulness or material omissions are grounds to terminate the hiring process or employment no matter when they are discovered. This is particularly important if a criminal record is found. Although a criminal record may not be used automatically to disqualify an applicant, the fact an applicant has lied about a criminal matter can be the basis for an adverse decision.

Second, it is critical to require a release for a background check in the application process. Have each job applicant sign a consent form for a background check, including a check for criminal records, past employment, and education. Announcing that your firm checks backgrounds may discourage applicants with something to hide, and encourage applicants to be truthful and honest about mistakes they have made in the past. If a firm outsources to a third-party vendor, then under the federal Fair Credit Reporting Act there must be a disclosure on a separate stand-alone document.

Third, employers should review the application carefully. Often when there is an employee problem or lawsuit, a careful review of the application would have alerted the employer in advance that they were hiring a lawsuit waiting to happen. Look for the following red flags:

- Applicant does not sign application.
- Applicant does not sign consent or background screening.
- Applicant leaves criminal question blank.
- Applicant self-reports a criminal violation. (Applicants can self-report matters incorrectly.)
- Applicant fails to explain why he or she left past jobs.
- Applicant fails to explain gaps in employment history.
- Applicant gives an explanation for an employment gap or the reason leaving previous job that does not make sense.
- Excessive cross-outs and changes (as though making it up as they go along).

Fourth, in reviewing applications, look for unexplained employment gaps. It is critical to verify past employment to determine where a person has been for the last 5 to 10 years, even if you only get dates and job titles. Not everyone has a continuous job history, but generally, if you can verify that a person was gainfully employed for the last 5 to 10 years, or their whereabouts can be verified, it is less likely the person spent time in custody for a serious offense, although this does not eliminate the possibility of a lesser offense.

8. **Effective interviews are also a critical part of the screening process**
   Another extremely effective tool that also costs nothing is the use of the interview process. It is recommended to always ask the following questions at an appropriate stage of an interview. These questions are designed to encourage applicants to be honest and forthcoming about employment-related issues. Since they have signed a consent, and believe you are doing background checks, applicants have a powerful incentive to be truthful. Good applicants will shrug it off and applicants with something to hide may reveal vital information.

   a. We do background checks on everyone we make an offer to. Do you have any concerns about that you would like to discuss? (Good applicants will shrug off.)
   b. We also check for criminal convictions for all finalists. Any concerns about that? (Make sure the wording of the question reflects what an employer may legally ask in that state.)
   c. We contact all past employers. What do think they will say?
   d. Will past employer tell us that you were tardy, did not perform well, etc.?
   e. ALSO, use interview to ask questions about any unexplained employment gap.

These questions are particularly important for the loss prevention staff. In addition, other questions can be asked pertaining to the integrity of loss prevention employees, such as:

- Are there any false statements on your application?
- Did you leave any jobs off?
- Have you ever been suspended, terminated, or asked to resign?
- Have you ever had knowledge of a co-worker stealing and if so, what did you do?
- Has the use of alcohol ever interfered with your work?
- Is gambling a problem for you?

9. **Conduct past employment checks and look for unexplained employment gaps**

Verifying past employment is one of the single most important tools for an employer. It can be as important as doing criminal checks. Past job performance can also be an important predictor of future success. Some employers make a costly mistake by not checking past employment because they believe past employers may not give detailed information. However, even verification of dates of employment and job titles are critical.

First, calling past employers verifies the truth and accuracy of the employment application.

Second, contacting past employers can eliminate any unexplained gaps in employment or can uncover an attempt to hide past gaps or jobs the applicant does not want to reveal. Although there can be many reasons for a gap in employment, if an applicant cannot account for the past 7 to 10 years, that can be a red flag,

Third, documenting the fact that an effort was made to contact past employers will demonstrate due diligence.

Finally, it is also critical to know where a person has been because of the way criminal records are maintained in the United States. Contrary to popular belief, there is not a national criminal database available to most private employers. Searches must be conducted at each relevant courthouse, and there are over 8,000 courthouses in America. However, if an employer knows where an applicant has been as a result of past employment checks, it increases the accuracy of a criminal search, and decreases the possibility that an applicant has served time for a serious offense.

10. **Audit your current practices to see how they would stand up in court**

Finally, it is critical for employers to audit their program to determine how they would stand up in court. Employers can be sued both by victims of a bad hiring decision as well as applicants who can claim they were treated unfairly. A sample audit can be fond at: http://www.esrcheck.com/articles/Safehiringaudit.php

For additional resources on pre-employment screening, see:

1. ASIS Guidelines on background screening: http://www.asisonline.org/guidelines/guidelinespreemploy.pdf
2. "The Safe Hiring Manual," by Lester S. Rosen (Facts on Demand Press/512 pages)
3. www.ESRheck.com for more articles and resources
4. The National Association of Professional Background Screeners (www.napbs.com) for information on the background screening industry

Witnesses and Their Reports

CAS, JHC

For our purposes in this encyclopedic reference, there are three types of witnesses:

1. Loss prevention practitioners appearing and testifying in a criminal court proceeding or some form of administrative hearing
2. A witness to an event from whom the LP employee or LP investigator wishes to obtain a written or oral statement
3. A security or loss prevention expert witness engaged for or against a retailer for alleged tortious conduct

Let's examine them individually.

Loss Prevention Practitioner

We've discussed courtroom testimony in some depth elsewhere in this book. Other venues such as state employment/unemployment or labor arbitration hearings would require the same or similar appearance and testimonial standards as in the criminal courts. The "report" or "reports," as such, would be the work product of the loss prevention agent, i.e., investigation report or report of arrest, originally generated by that agent.

A Non-LP Witness

The non-LP category of witness more often than not does not testify, but rather is solicited (or volunteers) to share what he or she observed or heard. For example, an LP agent approaches a suspected shoplifter outside the store, and upon learning the agent's true identity, the shoplifter bolts in an effort to escape. In that sudden motion, a customer is knocked to the ground and is injured. It would behoove the store to obtain the identity of any witness to the incident and memorialize what that witness observed. In some circumstances the witness is invited to write down his or her observations. In others, the LP agent may listen to the witness's version and write it down for the witness to read, approve, and sign.

Sometimes the police will take witness statements and share those statements with the store for the LP department's records. In other circumstances the LP agent may simply identify, quote, or paraphrase what the witness or witnesses have to say within the body of the report memorializing the entire event.

Witnesses may be subject to criminal court subpoena, and if so, they will be directed by an officer of the court, such as the prosecutor. Witnesses may also be subject to civil court subpoena, initially for purposes of deposition testimony, and if so, they will be directed by the attorney who initiated the service of the subpoena.

The complete identification of any witness, regardless of how his or her memorialization of observed events is recorded, is essential.

An Expert Witness

An "expert witness" is an industry-recognized "expert" claiming an expertise in a given area of specific knowledge beyond that known or understood by the general public. When testifying in a civil or criminal matter, this witness is recognized by the court as "an expert" and permitted to testify as such. The area of expertise might be in shoplifting, interrogation in the private sector, the retail industry's "custom and practice," the "use of force," or other specialized or focused areas. Such experts have the unusual freedom to testify under oath as to their opinions on matters being litigated, whereas all other witnesses, referred to as "percipient witnesses," are not allowed to opine, but rather must testify only as to what they know through their own observations (what they saw, touched, heard, smelled).

Expert witnesses normally are required to prepare, as part of their retention in lawsuits, a report reflecting their findings in their review of events and their opinions as to such issues as "Was the force used in this detention excessive and unreasonable, or was the force used reasonable and within industry standards?" Such reports must contain not only the expert's opinion, but his or her basis for that opinion. Lawsuits are frequently settled based on such expert witness reports.

The report is the source and basis of the expert's deposition as well as trial testimony.

Women and Minorities in Retail Security Today

Liz Martínez

The latter half of the first decade of the new millennium is an optimal time to assess the state of retail security. There are many ways to measure the progress and effectiveness of the field. This section focuses on the opportunities that female and minority workers have in today's retail security arena.

Are there opportunities for women and minorities in retail security today? The answer is "yes." And "no."

There are several reasons why there is not one clear answer regarding this issue. Part of the answer has to do with word definitions. It is pretty clear what the meaning of the word "woman" is. But how exactly are "minorities" defined? And what is meant by "opportunity"?

In business, minorities are generally defined as non-White persons or persons with a disability. Ethnic minorities, such as African Americans, Asians, Hispanics, and Native Americans come to mind. Because of historically limited opportunities in the business world, females as well as those with disabilities are often included when encouraging "diversity" in a company.

In the new millennium, it would be rare to find a hiring manager who flatly refuses to hire someone because the person is ... (fill in the blank). However, giving lip service to diversity or mouthing platitudes such as "We don't discriminate here; everyone is welcome to apply"—even if the manager believes what he or she is saying—is *not* the same thing as putting out the welcome mat for workers from diverse backgrounds.

Think about it: If you lived in a world in which the people around you were a different race and/or gender, would you feel perfectly welcome everywhere? Or would you need a special kind of welcome in order to feel as though you belonged?

The security industry is still top-heavy with White males—frequently White male former police officers. Given the fact that many of these top managers began their careers in the 1970s or 1980s, it is not surprising that their idea of "competent personnel" runs to people like themselves—other White males. They are used to working in a heavily male, Caucasian-dominated world, and they bring that mindset with them to their security careers.

We are all products of our environment and experience, so it often requires a tremendous effort on the part of these managers to make the leap to the belief that other kinds of people can be valuable workers. And it may require a Herculean effort for them to roll out the red carpet to recruit people different from themselves.

Add to these factors the reality that many of the top managers spent their police careers arresting minorities for various crimes (just take a look at the inside of any prison or jail, or a peek at the national arrest statistics, and it becomes clear that the majority of incarcerated persons are overwhelmingly members of minority ethnic groups). So it is understandable that, regardless of how much diversity training a company provides managers like these, they are going to stick with what their experience tells them is the appropriate candidate to recruit: someone like themselves.

However, the security world is changing. Many people are becoming security professionals without first having a career in law enforcement. These people, once they make their way into management, will be more accustomed to working side-by-side with women and ethnic minorities. They will know from their own experience that diversity in the workforce is valuable and will look to recruit people who are not necessarily their own mirror images.

The fact is that at the upper levels, there is a growing number of females in security management—although they are still well in the minority. There is also an increase in the number of ethnic minorities claiming their seats at the head tables, but that number is climbing even more slowly.

Opportunities for females and minorities in retail security abound at the lower levels. Quite a number of women and minorities do work in entry-level loss prevention jobs, but they are not making the trip from the ground floor to the executive suite.

As an illustration of this top-heavy representation of Caucasian men, it is interesting to note that as of 2007, ASIS International's leadership remains overwhelmingly White-male-dominated. (The organization's Retail Loss Prevention Council is about 12% female and 1% ethnic minority, with nary an African American or other dark-skinned person in sight.)

A lack of upward mobility for women and minority workers is attributable to several factors. Many executives fear having a frank discussion about these issues because they're afraid of sounding prejudiced; nevertheless, certain topics do impact their hiring decisions and judgments regarding who gets promoted.

To put these issues into perspective, it is important to recognize that at the entry level, retail security workers earn only slightly more than minimum wage. Therefore, the type of person who will be drawn to such a low-paying job is often someone without prospects for a better job. That means that employees who have a limited amount of education, a lack of cultural capital, and possibly difficulties with written and spoken English will be the ones filling out the loss prevention job applications.

"Cultural capital" is a term that has come to include academic credentials or qualifications, intangibles such as behavior and attitudes, as well as "linguistic capital," or the manner in which one speaks. People in management tend to be from the middle class or the upwardly striving (if not upwardly mobile) working class. Workers who were not raised to conform with middle-class behavior or who do not speak or write standard American English are not able to be competitive in the workplace when they are being evaluated on their levels of education, experience, and cultural capital.

Because many ethnic minorities in this country do not bring the same amount of cultural capital with them to the job, they are often passed over for promotion. Their lack of suitable communication skills or the "soft skills," such as appropriate attitudes and workplace behaviors, may hold them back some of the time. Other times, their lack of upward mobility may be due to acknowledged or unacknowledged prejudices on the part of upper management, as is the case for many females.

In addition, when bright, talented members of ethnic minorities with excellent communication skills do enter the loss prevention field, they are often courted away by other, more lucrative industries, where it is desirable to employ a more diverse workforce. And who wouldn't want to trade in long hours and an often thankless, never-ending task for better pay, greater prestige, and more money?

Very often, the members of ethnic minorities who do move up the ranks are first- or second-generation immigrants to the United States. Foreign-born workers, or those with parents or other close ties to the "old country," tend to be more articulate and better educated and possess a greater amount of cultural capital. This fact is borne out by the 2007 study, "Black Immigrants and Black Natives Attending Selective Colleges and Universities in the United States," in which researchers from Princeton University and the University of Pennsylvania found that first- or second-generation immigrants comprise a disproportionately high percentage of the Black student population at U.S. universities. According to the study, Black immigrant fathers were far more likely to have graduated from college than American fathers, reflecting the fact that Africans and Afro-Caribbeans are the most educated immigrant groups, with many originally coming to the Unites States to pursue a degree.

This idea is also demonstrated on a grand scale, such as with presidential hopeful U.S. Senator Barack Obama of Illinois, who is lauded as the first serious African-American candidate for president. But he is actually biracial, with a Caucasian mother and a father from the African country of Kenya. Likewise, the wildly popular former Secretary of State Colin Powell, a four-star army general who also served as the Chairman of the Joint Chiefs of Staff, is the son of Jamaican-born parents. These icons of Black America, like so many African Americans in positions of high power and prestige, are not from families with roots in the United States. Instead, they bring with them the manners and skills from cultures that value education and proper deportment.

Women face different challenges in the retail security workplace. The number of single mothers with children under 18 has more than tripled since 1970, going from 3 million to the present number of 10 million. And even when females have a partner, they are often the primary caregiver for their children. So women—especially those who work at lower-paying jobs—wind up taking more time off from work in order to care for their children than men do. Excessive absences, regardless of the reason, make employees less desirable candidates for jobs and promotions. For this reason—legal or not—some managers prefer not to hire women, or to hire females whom they know are free of family responsibilities.

Complicating the issue for women is the fact that they are often competing against males for security positions, which have traditionally been seen as "men's jobs." Security jobs are perceived to be "dirty" jobs, and, as with ethnic minorities, women with college degrees are often heavily courted by other industries that offer more attractive work atmospheres and compensation packages.

Low-paying loss prevention jobs have tremendous turnover, regardless of an employee's gender or background. But once a worker manages to climb above the entry level and into management—or if the worker has the credentials to start his or her career in a supervisory-level job—the prospects for advancement are brighter.

The upper levels of management are still not populated by as many women as men or as many minorities as Caucasians, but females and minority members do have an opportunity to advance if they are willing to put in the time and the effort. While other, oftentimes more desirable, career paths beckon to these talented employees, once they decide to stay in loss prevention, the chances to move up do exist and promotions can be attained.

Women and minorities may, as the adage has it, have to work twice as hard to be recognized as half as good as their White male counterparts, but the opportunities are there for these workers to prove themselves to be valuable members of a loss prevention team and make it to the top.

Women in Loss Prevention

Joan Manson

Women in the field of retail loss prevention today are afforded many rewarding opportunities. From entry-level store positions, field investigations, and management to women now operating and leading progressive and productive organizations designed to meet the challenging needs of their business, women as leaders in this industry are enthusiastically embracing this ever-changing retail segment with great success.

We have seen tremendous growth over the past 25 years in the number of women in retail loss prevention leadership positions. As we all know, diversity is critical to the success of our businesses, and having women succeed will help ensure a diverse future for our industry.

The Journey

In speaking with many of my peers, I have discovered that we have all shared personal experiences we believe have created a foundation to help women be even more successful in the future of this profession. By firsthand knowledge, I can attest to the difficulties many of us have faced over the past quarter of a century. Women as leaders in this profession were unheard of years ago. Women were viewed and classified as best suited as store detectives, floor walkers, fitting room checkers and secretaries. Men were the dominant leaders and managers, and were considered the absolute best investigators and interrogators, dominating these well-respected positions.

Today, women in loss prevention are making significant progress to move beyond these past stereotypes. Women still occupy many of the mid-management positions, but we are seeing more and more women taking on the top loss prevention positions in retail. In many companies, even today, women have to work twice as hard to prove themselves to be taken seriously to attain more responsibility in this profession. Thus, it is most important for women to understand the roadmap to ensure our success in this field. We need to focus on building our personal influence to make a powerful contribution to this profession. Women also need to understand that hesitancy or reluctance to move ahead is really the only barrier that will hold them back.

During my first job interview, I recall the over 50-year-old White male district manager, providing me with his sound career advice. He informed me that I would not be eligible for the security and safety manager training program; however, I might be able to work in a store as an entry-level store investigator tasked with detecting shoplifters. Or better yet, I should look into pursuing store merchandising. Fortunately for me, my next interview was with a store manager, previously involved in the Store Management Training Program, who saw some potential in this recent college graduate. He hired me on the spot without involving the security and safety manager of the department. It wasn't long until I was a natural. Yes, I was hesitant in the beginning. My peers and supervisors were all male, and most were ex-police officers with years of experience. My initial training and experience was obtained by working the sales floor, assisting with internal investigations, and proving myself with good cases. I was offered some very sound advice: *Work twice as hard as my male counterparts to be able to move ahead*. As I look back, I know a few of the men I worked with saw me more as a "necessary statistic," rather than a peer. I was working for

Montgomery Ward, and hiring women was required on everyone's performance appraisals. After I obtained some proven experience and gained my confidence, I was on the road to a great and rewarding career.

Yes, there were obstacles when I started out. A few of the men in similar positions became envious and made accusations about how I worked my way up. This seemed to be the best response a peer could invent as I was promoted, due to my proven performance. However, being a bit naïve and, fortunately, obstinate enough to never consider my gender as a problem, I persevered. A close male coworker also provided me with a piece of sound advice; it was simply to ignore the demeaning comments and jealousy by maintaining my focus on doing the best I could. Another very important lesson I learned was to be true to myself. Your performance and integrity will earn all the respect you will ever need. In time, my male peers began to see me for my contribution to the organization.

Let's face it, women have challenges our male counterparts have never had to confront. At the 2006 National Retail Federation Loss Prevention Conference, there was a roundtable discussion for women in loss prevention. An attractive young female bravely brought up a problem a few of us sitting around the table had faced many years before. She asked the group, "How do you get the male police officers to take you seriously, or to stop flirting and asking you out for a date?" We reflected back to the not-so-distant past, looked at each other, laughed, and all offered up advice we had used in our careers when faced with similar circumstances. It seems like a few of the challenges 25 years ago still hold true today. With this in mind, women in loss prevention need to support one another. We all know as we become more experienced in dealing with situations like this, we become stronger, more assertive, and firm in our aspirations to excel and succeed. A strong mentoring program, partnering with other women to help them succeed, will help build the foundation to ensure the success of women in this profession. In my case, I find it very rewarding to be able to give back to the community of women who pursue a loss prevention career. I also know the importance of our long-term contribution to our businesses. Diversity is an important component that will ensure our businesses succeed for many years to come.

Survey Regarding Women in Loss Prevention

Cheryl Blake has been involved with the retail loss prevention industry for more than 25 years, holding positions ranging from store detective to director for companies such as Kids R Us, Funcoland, and GameStop. As Vice President of Loss Prevention Services for the exception-based reporting company, Aspect Loss Prevention, she was involved in conducting a survey in 2006, regarding the differing perceptions and experiences of male and female loss prevention professionals. While the survey was unscientific, Cheryl stated, "… the responses were extremely telling and should serve as a guide to companies that are looking to increase the diversity of their Loss Prevention departments. Women and men are both well suited to this industry, but it is obvious that there are significant differences, actual and perceptional, that must be acknowledged if change is to be accelerated."

Of the more than 200 survey respondents, 22% were women. Of the 58 senior loss prevention executives (director or above), 13% were women. Interestingly, 75% of the female senior leaders had more than 20 years of experience while this was true for less than 15% of the men. This may imply that women must prove themselves for a longer period of time before attaining a senior-level position. It is also plausible that some very qualified females choose to leave the industry due to their lesser chances of reaching the top position. The majority of men entered this field from government service, law enforcement, or as an entry-level store detective, while only four women had a law enforcement background, and none had started as a store detective. More than twice as many men came from the operations side of retail than women, suggesting that loss prevention is not seen as a career path for women in retail. Clearly, there are differences between the sexes in recruiting paths and retention strategies.

There were notable differences in how men and women perceived gender characteristics as an advantage or disadvantage. Over 60% of the women said that a woman's empathy, strong communication skills, nurturing nature, and approachability were major advantages in several aspects of the job. Cheryl stated, "As a woman, I believe I am a much better interviewer since I can naturally relate to the subject on more levels than a man." Conversely, only 25% of the men named these attributes as an advantage. Similarly, many women named business skills, analytical ability, and the ability to multitask as advantages for women. Less than 10% of the men reported the same. Almost one-half of the men said that women had no unique advantage in the field, but less than one-quarter of the women made a similar statement.

Both men and women stated the most significant disadvantage to women in this field was the fact that loss prevention is a "Man's World," with the existence of the proverbial "glass ceiling." Just under 25% of the men acknowledged this disadvantage compared to almost 50% of the women. The more limited opportunity to network with other industry leaders and vendors was mentioned numerous times by women. More women than men cited a negative perception of strong women, or women in business. Many commented that while a forceful male was considered a strong leader, the same characteristics in a woman gave her a negative reputation. Significantly more men stated that family responsibilities were a disadvantage to women. One male commented, "Men are believed to be more willing to move their families for a new opportunity than are women." A surprising 50% of the men saw no disadvantages to women compared to only 10% of the women who felt that way.

The results were reversed when examining the advantages that men had in the field. Here, only a quarter of the men stated that men benefited because loss prevention is a male-dominated environment, but almost 50% of the women saw this as true The same statistics were seen regarding the statement that there is an inherent respect for men in business and loss prevention. Forty-six percent of all responding men stated that men had no advantage, while only 12% of the women believed this to be true.

The survey asked men to state the biggest disadvantage they faced in this career field. The results revealed there was no disadvantage for men. Men stated this significantly more than women, 59% to 35%. Women were more likely to report that men were at a disadvantage due to their weaker interpersonal skills and lack of empathy, 30% to 15%. It was also very interesting to note that over 15% of the respondents from both sexes identified reverse discrimination as a disadvantage to men.

Finally, the survey asked contributors to identify the things that made them successful. Men were much more likely to comment on their personal drive to succeed, hard work, passion, and work ethic. Women most often mentioned flexibility and willingness to learn. However, the biggest difference between the sexes was the number of times that "having a great mentor" was mentioned. Women remarked on this three times as often as men. This leads to the possible conclusion that, in this male-dominated industry, having a mentor is one way for women to overcome the perceived disadvantages.

The Road to Success

The road to success for women does has its road blocks, speed bumps, and a few deep chuck holes, but there are no mountains in the road we can't drive around. Some of the obstacles can be heart breakers, while we glide over other hurdles with ease. These obstacles must be faced straight on with a plan to forge ahead. The women who have succeeded have possessed the tenacity to push ahead with a willingness to accept change, or be an agent of change, to increase their personal influence to attain their goals. Utilizing your resources, partnering with others, and finding a mentor or coach to provide the encouragement, counsel, and support to persevere are key in this pursuit of your goals. It has been proven time and time again that support and guidance are critical to accomplish your professional goals. We need to exemplify decisiveness and be determined to attain our goals. We all need to understand that it is all right for us to be focused on ourselves. Women tend to be less egotistical than men, yet we need to demonstrate the self-confidence men exude with the determination and persistence to persevere. The woman who is aware of the hurdles in this business has a much better chance of overcoming them with fewer bumps and bruises along the way.

We see successful women in loss prevention excel due to their ability to effectively communicate, along with their desire to exceed the expectations of their responsibilities. This results in the development of beneficial business relationships. A compassionate management and communication style which demonstrates the genuine desire to be a business partner is advantageous to our success. Building relationships outside your own department in other areas of your company, and even outside with other retailers, merchant associations, vendors and educators, is helpful to succeed in this profession.

The essential elements for success include

- Develop a written plan with action steps for everything you want to achieve.
- Find a mentor to help you along the way. Every successful woman in loss prevention can name at least one mentor who helped her attain success. A mentor is the most effective resource you can have to ensure you meet your objectives. Mentors provide an independent source of objective feedback, support, and aren't judging you or your performance. Mentors will share their life experiences with you to help you learn from their challenges, successes, and the wisdom they gained along the way.
- Be true to your personal values and principles.
- Understand your personal priorities; balance work and home.
- Utilize your self-motivating principles to maintain the focus on your goals.
- Be well organized and utilize every available resource.
- Be responsible for your own education and development.
- Develop a keen awareness of your work environment. Truly understand the "big picture" of your business and be future oriented.
- Gain expertise in your field.
- Know and support your company's goals.
- Know the business operations inside and out.
- Volunteer in areas outside loss prevention to gain exposure to others within the organization.
- Engage men and the masculine dynamics that operate in loss prevention, but don't forfeit your feminine skills and innate nature as a woman. The industry needs it, and it keeps you sustainably engaged in this field.
- Build and nurture relationships. Build a strong support system inside and outside work; then use it. It can get lonely out there if there aren't many like you around.
- Network! Be involved in professional organizations and women's groups focused on career growth; volunteer in your community.
- Maximize your innate sense to communicate with clarity.
- Develop your skills to effectively handle difficult conversations and managing conflict. This can be what makes or breaks your personal success in loss prevention.
- Leaders (male or female) need to model both masculine (action, directness, problem solving) and feminine (intuition, synthesis, collaboration) traits.
- Be consistent.
- Maintain high expectations for yourself and your team.
- Deliver with excellence. Your work product represents you.
- Make well-informed decisions and provide sound recommendations based on what is best for the company overall.
- Be prepared and have your facts straight.
- Demonstrate your conviction with the bravery to take risks.
- Exude confidence in all interactions and presentations.
- Understand the differences of power and influence. Be willing to use either at the appropriate time.
- Don't take yourself too seriously; humor is still the universal equalizer and sanity saver.
- Develop your own personal brand and market yourself.

And, if you believe there are no impossible barriers, the opportunities are boundless!

The Women in Loss Prevention Caucus

In 2004, the National Retail Federation (NRF) sponsored the first platform for *all* women in the field of retail loss prevention. The NRF understood the need to support women in this profession and knew the value this forum could provide to retailers. Company membership with the National Retail Federation organization is not required for a female in loss prevention to participate.

The mission statement of the Caucus reads,

> *The Women in Loss Prevention Caucus is a forum that encourages women to network and learn from each other. Our purpose is to provide opportunity for empowerment through shared learning and mentoring, to support women in reaching their career goals.*

The Women in Loss Prevention Caucus was created and initially chaired by Laurie Sorenson, Vice President of Loss Prevention for Bon-Macy's. The first annual breakfast at the NRF Loss Prevention conference in June 2004 had more than 100 participants. The Caucus membership has flourished over the past few years to more than 350 members.

Rosa Maria Sostillio, the Senior Vice President of Asset Protection for Saks Fifth Avenue, launched the Women in Loss Prevention Caucus Mentoring Program. This mentoring program was immediately embraced. Women with great depths of experience are eagerly willing to extend their life experiences and field expertise to the protégés. In turn, the protégés are eager to learn from their mentors' infinite wisdom and know the extreme importance mentors offer to their long-term growth and success. Any women wishing to secure support in their career should reach out to this mentoring program. This invaluable resource available to women in loss prevention is an outstanding opportunity to ensure a successful career path in our profession.

Quarterly conference calls are held to provide a networking opportunity and a formalized professional development presentation by experts on the topic of interest. These topics are determined by the Caucus members via an annual survey. A few of the professional development topics presented by recognized business experts have included "The Power of Women," "Helping Women Find a Voice and Place in Corporate America," "Building and Maintaining Your Personal Brand," and "Goal Setting and Tools for Success."

This networking resource is invaluable to women in loss prevention. The women participating in this Caucus are pleased to assist one another. There is a genuine understanding and willingness to give back to the community of women, and this is the most rewarding gift to all our peers.

I have had the honor to represent the Women in Loss Prevention Caucus for the past year. I am truly amazed at the growth and expansion of the Caucus, the willingness to actively participate, and most of all the selfless commitment my peers have shown not only to me, but to women just entering this profession. There are so many opportunities in loss prevention and retail. This is a rewarding profession that has afforded me, and many others, great career success personally, and for our employers. We all have so many wonderful stories and life experiences to share. Now, with the Women in Loss Prevention Caucus we have a forum to pass along our wit and wisdom.

Successful Women Leaders in Loss Prevention

Today we see the retail industry promoting gender diversity resulting in women filling higher level positions in all areas of the organization. There are several companies where women competently hold the top loss prevention roles. These women fill positions of director and vice president roles within their organizations. Many of these women have worked their way up the corporate ladder through their strong convictions and steadfast commitment to the loss prevention profession.

Loss prevention leaders today also have the opportunity to transition into other business disciplines such as store management, operations, human resources, finance, risk management, legal, or to create their own special niche.

Best wishes for your success!

Helpful Resources

Books:

Becoming a Woman of Influence: Making a Lasting Impact on Others by Carol Kent
The Woman's Workplace Survival Guide by Sarah Kiap
Talking 9 to 5 by Deborah Tannen, a professor of linguistics at Georgetown University. She also has other articles of interest regarding gender communication.
Fierce Conversations Achieving Success at Work & in Life, One Conversation at a Time by Susan Scott.

Websites:

www.weatherhead.case.edu/seminars/certificate_women.cfm offers courses such as "Communication in the Workplace: Closing the Gender Gap" and "Women & Organizational Politics: Developing Power and Influence."
www.wmwgroup.com Personal & Professional Development Specialists
www.workforceexcellence.com
www.networkofexecutivewomen.com
A very helpful resource for diversity, loss prevention and the retail industry: Mimi Welch, Transition Dynamics, www.TransitionDynamics.NET

Working to Stop Robbery—A Grocery Store Perspective

Carol A. Martinson

Robberies can occur in any of the following locations within a grocery store:

- At the register in a checkout lane
- Express lane
- Customer Service Desk
- Cash Office
- Bank located within a grocery store
- ATM located within the store
- Armored car courier or vehicle

The target of the robberies may also include media other than cash, e.g., lottery tickets at the customer service desk. Hence the need to ensure that all processes look at the negotiability of what is being handled or processed at each point of customer contact.

The occurrence of a robbery, however, can be minimized by following sound cash-handling procedures, providing good physical security (alarms, cameras, restricted access), and providing training to all employees.

Cash-Handling Procedures:

Minimize exposure by keeping cash-on-hand as low as possible in all registers.

- Minimal starting cash in each register drawer
- Frequent pick ups or skims
- Restrict use of no sale function
- Ensure supervisor override in place for "risky" functions

Supervision of express lane (not staffed by a full-time cashier)

- Drawer open alarm/warning to supervisor
- CCTV oversight of area

Customer Service Desk

- Account for all non-cash, but negotiable items, e.g., lottery tickets, postage stamps, money order stock

- Keep cash-on-hand at minimal levels
- CCTV oversight of area

Cash Office

- Restrict access to only those who work in the office
- Maintain a photo list of armored car couriers, and allow no other armored car couriers into the office unless they are on the list
- Have a peep hole or CCTV capability to see who is on the other side of the door prior to opening the door
- Open and close the office with two individuals
- Maintain a written log of all who come in to the office (sign in and out)
- Provide a secure area for counting down of drawers, if done by cashiers, that is out of the public, but NOT in the cash office itself

Physical Security:

Store should have a burglary alarm system that is capable of separate partitions. The goal is to alarm areas when not in use, e.g., loading dock alarmed when receiving done; fire exits always alarmed.

Cash Office should be a separate partition on the burglary alarm system, so that it can be set when closed, even though the store may still be open, or there is an overnight crew working in the building.

Bank and ATM alarms should NOT be on the store's burglary system, they should have their own alarm system provided by the bank and/or provider of the ATM.

Cash Office should be for cash handling only. It should not be the front end supervisor's office.

CCTV system should cover the inside of the cash office, key overnight registers if a 24-hour location, and entry and exit points from the building. It is critical to get a good facial picture of the person(s) in the facility.

Customer Service Desk should have restricted access, be covered by CCTV system, and be in a line of sight to rest of the check out area.

Training for Employees:

Robbery training should be formatted and/or presented to address before, during, and after segments of dealing with a robbery.

- Before—how to prevent a robbery from occurring
- During—what do I do when the person is in front of me?
- After—how to deal with notifying law enforcement, management, media, and helping the involved employees deal with the stress of a robbery.

Robberies of In-Store Banks, ATMs, and Armored Car Couriers or Vehicles

Talk to the bank's security manager to understand what they have in place for security and robbery procedures.

Will they have their own security guard? Armed, unarmed? What is that person's role? What will they expect the store to do in the event of a robbery at the bank?

- Provide video if store's video covers the exits?
- Close the store if the FBI or police department wants restricted access until they have talked to all witnesses? If so, what does that do to your customers, sales, etc.?
- Provide a quiet location (conference room, office) for the victims or witnesses?

ATMs—make sure that with any ATM placed in your store there is a clear understanding of the following issues:

- Service is to be provided by the ATM Company, NOT the store
- Funds in the ATM do not belong to the store

- There is no expectation that you will store extra cash canisters for the ATM
- Customer disputes are to be resolved by the ATM Company, not the store
- In the event of a robbery of the ATM service team or a customer who has just used the ATM, make sure your role is clear, i.e., call police, assist if any medical issues, and notify the ATM owner.

Armored Car Courier or Vehicle Robbery

- Ensure that the armored vehicle can park as close as possible to the entrance to the store so the distance they have to carry the cash is as short as possible.
- Ensure that there is proper company/courier identification and signing for the pick-up, so that ownership of the deposit is always clear.
- Ensure that the courier signs in and out of the cash office (name, date, and time).
- In the event of a robbery, notify police, assist if medical issues, and notify the armored vehicle company.

Note: If the in-store bank is the depository bank for your store, consider making daily check deposits at the in-store bank so you can reduce the number of armored vehicle pick-ups per week. There are also automated cash systems being put into grocery stores now that greatly reduce cash exposure. The two systems that are in use at some of our retail divisions are AT Systems and Brinks.

World's Largest Retail Trade Association: The National Retail Federation's Role in Retail Loss Prevention

Angelica Rodriguez

The National Retail Federation (NRF) is one of the world's largest retail trade associations. Membership comprises all retail formats and channels of distribution, including department, specialty, discount, catalog, Internet, independent stores, chain restaurants, drug stores and grocery stores, as well as the industry's key trading partners of retail goods and services. NRF represents an industry with more than 1.6 million U.S. retail establishments, more than 24 million employees—about one in five American workers—and 2006 sales of $4.7 trillion. As the industry umbrella group, NRF also represents more than 100 state, national, and international retail associations.

In the U.S., retailing is more than just a business—it is a way of life that influences so much of what we do. If you ever doubted the power of retailing, just reflect on the immense impact our industry has on the economy:

- Watch the economists who hunger for the monthly Commerce Department report on retail sales
- Listen to the market analysts or the industry gurus whose very future may hang on their prediction of holiday sales, or
- Pay attention to how our industry's performance can alter the direction of the stock market.

Retailers turn to NRF to give them a voice, whether it's in the media or on Capitol Hill. That voice can take several forms: from serving as retail's advocate before Congress, to representing the industry's point of view with the media, coordinating interaction between and among retailers from around the world, and providing research or information that helps the industry move forward.

Through the years, NRF has played all these roles and more. In 2006, the Federation gathered its members in Washington, DC, to express their concerns in face-to-face meetings with some of the nation's most influential lawmakers. Additionally, NRF was an aggressive advocate on the most difficult issues retailers face: bringing the issue of credit card interchange fees to the attention of Congress, fighting restrictions on international trade, testifying before Congress against hackers/botnet creators, and working to hold down soaring health care costs.

NRF's four divisions have continued to break new ground across the retail landscape.

- The National Council of Chain Restaurants (NCCR) led the business community on the difficult issue of immigration reform.
- The Retail Advertising and Marketing Association (RAMA) continued to inspire retailing's most creative minds through its annual Retail Advertising Conference, and honored retail advertising geniuses through the creation of its RACie Award.
- The Association for Retail Technology Standards (ARTS) continued to bring standards education to its members both at home and across the globe.
- Shop.org, NRF's multi-channel division, experienced soaring success with its Cyber Monday promotion and creation of the Ray M. Greenly Scholarship Fund, which provides financial support to students pursuing careers in the e-commerce industry. In its first month, Shop.org's Cyber Monday website raised an astonishing $100,000 for the scholarship fund, and the number just keeps growing.

The retail discipline topics that NRF services include: Diversity, Finance, Government Relations/Public Policy, Human Resources, Independent Retailers, Information Technology, Loss Prevention, Marketing, Merchandising, Online and Multichannel Retail, Store Operation, Supply Chain, and more. Lobbying support, committee activity, media coverage, networking opportunities, webinars, conference calls, grassroots efforts, conference/events and C-level summits are the components that NRF offers retailers.

The NRF Loss Prevention community has burgeoned over the last five years. The community is composed of 15 committees and the Investigator's Network.

LP Advisory Council
LP Brand Protection Committee
Conference/Event Planning Committees
Education Committee
Food Industry Loss Prevention Committee
Gift Card Working Group, LP Subcommittee
Homeland Security Information Network
Investigator's Network
Joint Organized Retail Crime Task Force (JORCTF)
Latin Loss Prevention Caucus
Loss Prevention Awards and Recognition Committee
Loss Prevention Legislative Committee
Loss Prevention—NCCR Food Safety Task Force
Mall and Retail Loss Prevention Partnership Committee
Women in Loss Prevention Caucus

Astounding Steps with the Committee Structure

The NRF LP Advisory Council is composed of senior loss prevention executives from diverse retail sectors, and provides direction on conference content and develops subcommittees to better serve the industry. In response to the burgeoning LP community (and the formalization of the profession), the Advisory Council created new committees in 2006: Brand Protection Committee, Education Committee, Food Industry Loss Prevention Committee, and they restructured the Awards and Recognition Committee.

The Brand Protection Committee will initially work on benchmarking and case studies for retailers to share information on how they have approached counterfeiters and fraudsters. The Conference/Event Planning Committee oversees the content of the annual LP Conference, which is growing year-over-year. The newly formed Education Committee was assembled to work with universities and certification programs to assist current LP professionals on continuing education for professional development, and to attract college students to the industry by creating university courses and baccalaureate programs in Loss Prevention. The Food Industry Loss Prevention Committee focuses on loss prevention and security issues that are unique to food retailers.

The Loss Prevention Awards and Recognition Committee was recently restructured, as three new awards were created to honor loss prevention, law enforcement, and security professionals. The longstanding Law Enforcement Retail Partnership Award will continue to honor law enforcement professionals/agencies who have gone above and beyond the call of duty, and the National Retail Federation will now honor the industry with three additional awards. The awards present at the Annual NRF Loss Prevention Conference will now include:

- **Law Enforcement Retail Partnership Award**

  To acknowledge law enforcement professionals or agencies who have gone above and beyond the call of duty to support the retail industry in combatitng fraud and other types of losses.

- **Loss Prevention Case of the Year**

  This award is the premier recognition program for Loss Prevention professionals. The award will recognize an LP Investigator whose investigation has made a positive impact on his company, community, and industry.

- **LP Volunteers in Action**

  This recognizes Loss Prevention professionals making significant and measurable contributions to charitable organizations. These contributions include fundraising, outreach, volunteering, and activities that have made a positive impact in their community.

- **Ring of Excellence Award**

  The Ring of Excellence Award is a recognition program for loss prevention professionals whose achievements and outstanding leadership have shaped the industry. The award will recognize pioneers in the loss prevention community whose honor, integrity, and character serve as an example for the LP industry. Inductees to the Ring of Excellence can be honored in person or posthumously.

The LP Subcommittee of the Gift Card Working Group is a very active group, especially during the holiday season. This subcommittee is composed of retail loss prevention and gift card fraud specialists. The group was established to address fraud and other vulnerabilities identified in the gift card life cycle. In 2006, the NRF Gift Card Survey, conducted by BIGresearch, found that gift card sales would total $24.81 billion during the holiday season, an impressive $6 billion increase over 2005, when gift card sales hit $18.48 billion. The average consumer spent $116.51 vs. $88.03 on gift cards in 2005. Congruently, gift card fraud has also risen. According to the National Retail Security Survey conducted by the University of Florida, gift card fraud amounts to $72,000 per company. Thus, the activity of this committee continues to increase.

Over the past year, the NRF Investigator's Network has seen astounding growth with nearly 700 loss prevention professionals nationwide participating. The Network was formed to provide retail loss prevention executives, shopping center security, and law enforcement officials a forum to network and discuss critical issues at a local, regional, and national level. Currently there are five regions that meet: Northeast Region (NY, NJ, CT, PA), Central Region (Midwestern states), Atlantic Region (DC, VA, MD), Southwest Region (TX, NM, LA, OK, AR), and Western Region (CA, NV, OR, WA, AZ).

NRF launched the Women's Resource Center website, www.nrf.com/wrc, in cooperation with the NRF Women's Retail Council and the NRF Women in LP Caucus (WLPC). The interactive website allows visitors to access conference call recaps and other resources generated by NRF's Women's Retail Council and the WLPC. The WLPC experienced phenomenal growth. Launched in 2004, the committee grew from 25 members, representing 21 different retailers, to over 340 members two years later. The mission of the Caucus is to provide a forum that encourages women to network and learn from each other. Their purpose is to provide opportunity for empowerment through shared learning and mentoring, to support women in reaching their career goals.

Continuing to support diversity in the industry, NRF launched the Latin Loss Prevention Caucus, which, similar to the Women in LP Caucus serves as an avenue for professional development. The Latin LP Caucus meets annually at the NRF Loss Prevention Conference each June and was developed to build relationships and enhance the resources for participating members, and to provide a forum to improve communication within the Latin LP community and the NRF.

The NRF LP Community also consists of the Mall and Retail Loss Prevention Partnership Committee. This committee is composed of members of the LP Advisory Council and International Council of Shopping Center Security Advisory Council. The group meets annually to determine strategies for retailers and mall developers to collectively address issues such as terrorism, organized retail crime, and physical security.

Orc Database Is Nationally Recognized

In response to the growing threat of organized crime against retailers, NRF developed a leading, secure, web-based computer database that allows retailers to share information with each other and with law enforcement. The Law Enforcement Retail Partnership Network (LERPnet) was created by the NRF in partnership with other industry associations and endorsed by the Federal Bureau of Investigation. LERPnet has been nationally recognized as the standard for sharing information in a secure and confidential manner, giving retailers and law enforcement the ability to collaborate like never before.

NRF also created the Joint Organized Retail Crime Task Force (JORCTF) with a primary focus of investigating and intelligence-sharing as it relates to organized retail crime activity, and fencing of illegal and counterfeit goods. This invitation-only group shares investigative methods and tactics, as well as develops and maintains law enforcement relationships across the nation.

NRF Continues to Work with the Public Sector to Combat Crime

Continuing to work in cooperation with the public sector to battle crimes that affect retailers, NRF serves on several key councils and committees, including the Food & Agriculture Sector Coordinating Council, Commercial Facilities Coordinating Council and Homeland Security Intelligence Network Governance Board with the Department of Homeland Security, and works with the Federal Bureau of Investigation on a regular basis. The 2007 NRF's vice president of loss prevention, Joseph LaRocca, testified before the United States Congress in favor of a bill that would give the Justice Department new criminal tools with which to prosecute hackers and botnet creators. He also submitted testimony to the Vermont State Senate on the topics of organized retail crime, counterfeit receipts, and theft detection technology. In 2006, NRF's efforts were recognized by FBI Director Robert Mueller for playing a supporting role in a major organized retail crime case.

Select retailers are invited to participate on the NRF Legislative Committee, which was developed to set the legislative agenda of the industry, educate the loss prevention community and company executives on the legislative process, and to educate the legislative bodies and their members about loss prevention issues. Through efforts such as those above, the committee has heightened the awareness of impacting legislation at the local, state, and federal levels and continues to forge new ground on combating crime.

Through the NRF's LPInformation.com web portal, loss prevention executives can sign up for access to the Homeland Security Information Network (HSIN). Through partnership with governmental boards and task forces, NRF serves as a liaison between the public and private sector and helps to get retailers attending business continuity/crisis management meetings that would affect their business in the event of a catastrophic event.

2006 Loss Prevention Conference Sees Outstanding Growth

NRF's 2006 Loss Prevention Conference and Exhibition shed new light on leading industry trends, when more than 2,600 loss prevention executives gathered in Minneapolis to explore new ideas, research, and strategies. Growing along with the conference, this year's EXPO Hall increased from 32,800 square feet in 2005 to more than 39,000 square feet in 2006.

The three-day event included more than forty educational sessions and forums, featuring loss prevention experts from Limited Brands, Gap, Inc., Best Buy Co., and the U.S. Department of State, exploring topics such as curbing shrink, enhancing global security programs, business continuity and recovery, and combating organized retail crime.

2006 keynote highlighted speakers included:

—Mike McCurry, veteran communications strategist and former press secretary to President Bill Clinton
—Harold Lloyd, a business person, owner of family-style restaurants and author, who identified qualities of effective leaders.

Also during the conference, the NRF Law Enforcement Retail Partnership Award was presented to Federal Bureau of Investigation special agent Chris Frazier of the Portland, Oregon Field Division, who assisted Safeway, Inc. in shutting down a complex organized retail crime ring.

In the fall of 2006, NRF held the second annual Loss Prevention Senior Executives Summit in Dallas, Texas. Led by Dan Doyle, vice president of loss prevention, human resources and administration for Beall's, and chairman of the NRF LP Advisory Council, a diverse group of 90 professionals came together and clearly articulated the current vulnerabilities and opportunities in the areas of organized retail crime, personnel development, homeland security, and loss prevention equipment. A white paper unveiling these findings was presented at the NRF Loss Prevention Conference in June 2007.

Bio

In 2007 Angélica Rodríguez was named as the National Retail Federation's Director, Loss Prevention. Prior to this position, Rodríguez worked in the NRF membership department as a Manager, Member Relations.

Rodríguez will join Vice President of Loss Prevention Joseph LaRocca in serving as a liaison for loss prevention committees, members and governing boards. She will also act as an NRF spokesperson on loss prevention topics.

Previously, Rodríguez worked with an international destination management company based in Washington, DC where she was their Manager of Marketing and Communications. Before she arrived in DC, Rodríguez worked for a security design and installation company in Austin, Texas as their Manager of Business Development and Communications.

Rodríguez holds a Bachelor of Arts degree from Rice University in Political Science with a focus on International Relations.

The National Retail Federation is the world's largest retail trade association, with membership that comprises all retail formats and channels of distribution, including department, specialty, discount, catalog, Internet, independent stores, chain restaurants, drug stores, and grocery stores as well as the industry's key trading partners of retail goods and services. NRF represents an industry with more than 1.6 million U.S. retail establishments, more than 24 million employees—about one in five American workers—and 2006 sales of $4.7 trillion. As the industry umbrella group, NRF also represents more than 100 state, national, and international retail associations.

Workplace Violence: Zero Tolerance is Not Enough

W. Barry Nixon

Some wise person once said, "Success in life is not as dependent on the talent that you possess as much as it is based on the quality of the decisions that you make." I believe this to be absolutely true in the business world as well and with regards to workplace violence. Every company's management is faced with making decisions and choices that may very well impact the future profitability, lives of employees, and perhaps even the fate of the firm.

Boiled down to the simplest denominator, there are only three choices that a firm has to deal with concerning the risk of workplace violence occurring:

- *To ignore the risk (in other words, you can throw the dice and believe that it won't happen in your organization).*

This approach is the most frequent one taken to deal with the risk of workplace violence. This belief, better known as the "ostrich approach," is the number-one obstacle to managers taking a proactive, preventative approach to dealing with workplace violence. Generally, this approach is characterized by either a formal or intuitive assessment of the statistical risk of violence occurring in the workplace, and because the odds are very small of being victimized, not much is put into addressing the issue.

- *To transfer a portion of the risk via insurance.*

This approach is one in which the organization does what it is legally required to do to address issues to minimize any legal liability and purchases Employment Practices Liability Insurance. This approach fundamentally trades the cost of taking preventative efforts for getting payment in the event that an incident does occur. Management can rest easier knowing that the financial impact of a violent incident on the continuity of business has been mitigated. Unfortunately, this approach does not mitigate the actual impact on people who are actually injured or whose lives are lost or damaged forever.

- *To eliminate a substantial amount of the risk by reducing "at risk" behaviors (individual and organizational behaviors that tend to increase risk of workplace).*

This approach is the one taken by progressive organizations that actually operationalize their mission statement that people are their most important resource and genuinely focus on providing a safe workplace free of known hazards. These organizations focus on implementing a comprehensive strategy designed to prevent injuries before they occur and recognize the importance of assessing both individual and organization risk factors. Some organizations get defocused and put the sole focus on individual behaviors.(1)

This third approach—focusing on reducing risk—is the focus of this section. In particular, retail businesses need to simultaneously address reducing risks that come from within the workplace, as well as the more formidable risks that come from outside. It should be noted that while we will reference some "internal" strategies, the intent of this section is primarily to address external risk. For an extensive coverage of how to deal with internal threats, go the website of the National Institute for the Prevention of Workplace Violence, Inc., located at www.workplaceviolence911.com/.

An effective approach for dealing with "at risk" behaviors is to classify them and then develop appropriate actions that need to be taken at each of the commensurate levels of risk. One model, which borrows from the threat levels used for Homeland Security, can be used to guide your actions (see Figure W-1).(2)

It should be noted that, to successfully implement the actions necessary at each level, an infrastructure for dealing with workplace violence must already exist. Typically, this would include

- A Workplace Violence Prevention or Threat Management Committee
- A workplace violence prevention policy
- A No Weapon policy
- A Crisis Response plan
- Integrated and synchronized human resources, security, safety, and risk management policies
- Law enforcement protocol
- Robbery prevention strategies
- Training for supervisors and employees

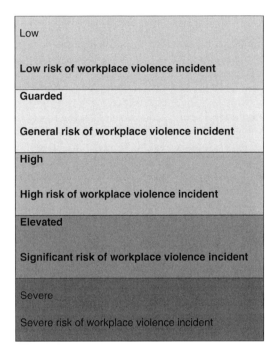

FIGURE W-1

Each of the preceding infrastructure items will be covered in more depth later in this section.

Actions that can be taken based on identified level of risk are described next.

Low

- Identify the risks of violence that your specific organization, industry, or geographic location may be exposed to and develop a plan to mitigate any potential exposure. For example, if you operate a warehouse in an area where several robberies or rapes have occurred in other company parking lots, you should increase your lighting, provide security escorts for employees, etc., in your parking lot.
- Train your supervisors and employees on your workplace violence prevention policy, how to recognize the "early warning signs," as well as how to avoid being a victim of robbery and how to survive a robbery.
- Conduct a facility risk assessment to ascertain vulnerabilities and take actions to address identified problems and improve perimeter security.
- Establish a protocol with local law enforcement to expedite response to an incident. This includes familiarizing police personnel with your facility and its physical layout.

Guarded

- Conduct a desktop review or rehearsal of your workplace violence crisis response plan to test how the components work and learn where improvements are necessary (remember plans rarely work exactly as they are supposed to).
- Conduct an organizational assessment in the departments, stores, etc., that have a heightened pattern of risky behaviors, events, etc., and work with management to develop a positive employee relations plan to address the problems identified.

Elevated

- Review factors common to organizations that have a higher propensity for incidents of workplace violence and identify the departments stores, etc., that have multiple factors.
- Conduct an individual threat assessment of persons who are identified as being "at risk." This may include having security conduct a background check, having a Workplace Violence Prevention professional conduct a threat assessment, or conducting a "fitness for duty" evaluation and taking specific actions based on the information learned.
- Using the input of your labor attorney, law enforcement, security management, and workplace violence prevention professional, determine appropriateness of obtaining a "workplace restraining order." Note that this should not be an automatic decision and should be well thought out because in many cases a restraining order can exacerbate or contribute to the situation escalating.

High

- Involve law enforcement to take preventative actions.
- Enlist private security professionals to conduct surveillance of "at risk" employees and monitor their movements.
- If specific individuals have been identified as being potential targets, relocate their work location and/or provide security protection.

Severe

- Cooperate with and follow the directions of law enforcement, who should be handing the situation at this point.
- Close the facility.

It should be noted that the "low risk" level is the point where you should put the most prevention efforts. You should focus on "doing the right things" upfront that will reduce the likelihood of situations escalating to higher risk level.

Note that the specific steps presented in the preceding action orientation example are intended to illustrate the stepping stone nature of actions that can be implemented. In reality these steps must be developed specifically to meet the unique requirements of a specific organization based on their culture, stage of business maturity, etc. It would be unwise to plug in the risk levels as stated into an organization without customizing them to fit the organization's needs.

Before we switch the dialogue to a discussion of the infrastructure that is necessary to reduce violence in the workplace, it is important to address the transition of philosophies occurring about violence. "Zero tolerance" (a policy stating that certain behaviors are not acceptable and any deviations or violations of the policy will not be tolerated) is the philosophy that dominated the thinking in how to address violence in the workplace from the late 1980s through the late 1990s. It is my strong belief that zero tolerance is a modern day example of the adage, "the road to hell is paved with good intentions."(1)

To some extent, zero tolerance policies in the workplace describe the American backlash to violence, unwanted behavior, and actions in schools and professional sports leagues. In the early 1990s, politicians began to hear the public outrage and discontent with violence, crime, drugs, and other antisocial problems. Fueled by media hype, in the aftermath of a number of high-profile, extremely violent incidents at public schools, fear of the unthinkable, and perhaps even a bit of guilt, more parents started demanding that school boards implement strict policies to deal with kids who step out of line. As a result, zero tolerance had its beginnings from the larger societal discontent and subsequent Congressional response to students with guns. It was proclaimed as a policy to provide safe school environments and took on the mantra of a harsh, mandatory, "take-no-prisoners," overzealous approach to discipline that has been increasingly used in this country's criminal justice system.(3) Thus, we have seen the implementation of a draconian one-size-fits-all approach to deal with school disciplinary issues sweep the American landscape.

Having been born of this well-intentioned focus on keeping our kids safe, zero tolerance initially was defined as consistently enforced suspension and expulsion policies in response to weapons, drugs, and violent acts in the school setting. Over time, however, zero tolerance has come to refer to school or district-wide policies that mandate predetermined, typically harsh consequences or punishments (such as suspension and expulsion) for a *wide degree* of rule violations. Most frequently, zero tolerance policies address drug, weapons, violence, smoking, and school disruption in efforts to protect all students' safety and maintain a school environment that is conducive to learning. Many administrators perceive zero tolerance policies as fast-acting interventions that send a clear, consistent message that certain behaviors are not acceptable in the school.(4)

Corporations reacted to the public outcry by following suit and started to implement zero tolerance policies as well. Faced with this historical perspective, let's examine the journey that zero tolerance has taken in corporate America.

Viva La Difference

Although corporations started implementing zero tolerance policies, they quickly recognized some significant differences in implementing a policy for a business versus one for a school. First and foremost, it was quickly recognized that the one-size-fits-all approach would not work, since most firms have some form of progressive discipline which is built on the premise of "just cause" and "due process." In addition, employers had to be diligent about paying attention to the myriad of discrimination laws that require consistent treatment of employees.

"Just cause" refers to the principle that "the punishment should match the severity of the crime"; thus, an employee who physically assaults another employee should be more severely disciplined than an employee who makes a threat to "throw another employee's radio out the window if he doesn't turn it down."

"Due process" refers to the concept of applying progressive discipline, which promotes that an employee should be advised of inappropriate behavior and given an opportunity to correct it based on receiving coaching, feedback, and/or a series of warnings.

Both of these principles pose severe problems for a one-size-fits-all approach. This incongruence led to one of the major problems with zero tolerance: Employees perceived that it was a one-size-fits-all approach because this is what exists in the schools where their children attend; this is the reason they first learned about zero tolerance, and this is also what the media focused on. The reality is that, in the business world, it was really an incident-based approach in which each situation would be judged based on the circumstances involved, the nature of the situation, the employee's record, current policies, etc. Consequently, if an employee made a low-level threat like the "radio incident" mentioned earlier, employee perception was that with a zero tolerance policy, the employee should be terminated. Since the employer is obligated to follow company human resource policies and apply the principles of "just cause, due process, and nondiscrimination," employees believed the company was not serious about addressing violence because warning the person did not fit their image of zero tolerance. Their translation is that the company was willing to tolerate violence unless an employee was seriously injured or killed, which to them was ridiculous and did not mean zero tolerance. This perception leads to a serious case of cognitive dissonance, which leads to mistrust of management and the belief that the company does not have the best interests of employees in mind. Once again, best intentions gone awry.

Stephen Hirschfeld, senior partner at the San Francisco law firm, Curiale Dellaverson Hirschfeld Kelly & Kramer, LLP, said it best, " It's easy to state that you have a zero tolerance policy: it's another thing to really think through what it means." Does it mean "one strike and you're out"? Does it mean that if you slam your fist on a desk in frustration, you're guilty of workplace violence and will be terminated? Too often policies backfire because they're not properly crafted or haven't been thought through all the way." Or as Dave Ulrich, who is widely recognized as one of the top gurus in human resources, states, "It's one thing to state that the organization will not tolerate any form of undesirable or illegal activity, but it's impossible to apply a standard punishment or solution for every incident. A policy needs teeth, but it also needs to be fair."

A second problem with the zero tolerance approach is that it is reactive in nature. It, in essence, states "if you violate our workplace violence policy or act in an inappropriate manner, this behavior will not be tolerated and you will be punished." While that approach is fine, it ignores the fundamental principle of providing a safe work environment, which is to prevent people from being injured in the first place. No safety program worth its salt would dare focus on passively waiting for injuries to occur and putting a focus on "how to" react after the fact.

The zero tolerance approach is characterized by the creation of a human resources or security policy that focuses on the organization having no tolerance for threats, threatening behavior, or violent acts. Primary focus is put on how the organization will react once inappropriate behavior has occurred. For example, one firm's policy states, "The intent of this policy is to increase employee awareness of the procedures to be followed in the event of workplace violence." In my opinion, this is a bit late in the process, since once violence has occurred, it is likely that someone has already been injured or worse.

Despite these issues, corporations persist with implementing zero tolerance policies because such policies make them appear to be "getting tough on violence" and they make management feel good that they are taking a stance. The sad reality is that this overzealous and politically driven approach, in many cases, undermines truly addressing potential violent situations in the workplace and, in addition, leads to discord between management and employees.(5)

As Samuel Greengard stated in his article, "Zero Tolerance: Making It Work," "zero tolerance has become the rage. But dealing with workplace problems requires more than rhetoric. It's about crafting an effective policy and putting all the pieces in place to make it work. Zero tolerance is a concept that sounds straightforward and simple, but is inherently complex."(6)

In contrast to zero tolerance, we advocate a "zero incident" approach, which focuses on reducing "at risk" behaviors and organizational practices to attack the root causes of injuries so that we can intervene before incidents happen. An example of a workplace violence policy written following the zero incident approach is as follows: "It is our intent to create a work environment where all employees are safe and secure from hazards. To ensure this happens, we are placing a high priority on implementing *practices and procedures that prevent work violence*, and strongly encourage the support of all employees in helping us to create an accident- and hazard-free environment."

Can you image going to an award banquet for Best in Class Human Resources Practices and a firm getting an award for having the "Best Response Plan for Reacting to Workplace Violence Incidents" (despite the reality that it had numerous incidents of employees getting injured or killed) and another firm getting an award for having the "Best Prevention Plan for Identifying At Risk Behaviors and Avoiding Workplace Violence Incidents" (and it has a very low incident rate of violence)? Think about it. Which firm would you vote for?

The Goal Is Zero Incidents, Not Zero Tolerance

To further illustrate the difference in the two approaches, see the comparison in Table W-1.

The difference in the two approaches is that one focuses on prevention, whereas the other focuses on reaction.

The primary focus of the zero incident approach is to prevent incidents from occurring by identifying possible problematic or "at risk" behaviors, situations, or practices and intervening to deal with them before conflict actually erupts or escalates to violence. Second, the intent is to focus on reducing the number of "close calls" and situations in which conflicts erupt by discovering the root causes of issues and taking mitigating actions or eliminating them. And, the third phase of this approach is to resolve conflicts once they have developed in a manner that all parties feel respected and valued.

Table W-1

Zero Tolerance	Zero Incidents
If you make a threat, you will be reported.	People know how to influence others without needing to make threats.
If you get in a fight, you will be terminated.	People know how to resolve conflict in positive ways to avoid escalation.
Abusive or intimidating behavior is not allowed.	Treating each other in a respectful manner is valued and rewarded.
Focus is on policy controlling behavior (rules driven).	Focus is on culture controlling behaviors (values driven).

Excerpted from "Zero Tolerance Is Not Enough: Making Workplace Violence Prevention Really Work."

The essence of the zero incident approach is to

- *Prevent:* Anticipate and deal with possible problematic situations before violence actually erupts.
- *Reduce:* Lessen the number, intensity, and duration of incidents within an organization.
- *Resolve:* Pre-prepare and develop workable solutions to violence once an incident occurs.

In 1998 the Supreme Court determined in *Faragher v City of Boca Raton* that companies must prevent—not simply react to—a hostile workplace. Thus, the concept of having zero tolerance for workplace violence, which focuses on "how the firm will react once violence has occurred," becomes an insufficient approach; it needs to evolve to the more progressive approach of zero incidents, which focuses on elimination of "at risk" behaviors before an incident occurs.

Implementation of a zero incident approach involves the following steps. As mentioned earlier, the number-one obstacle to developing a proactive preventative approach to reducing violence in the workplace is to face the reality that most executives and managers in organizations are in denial and believe that "it couldn't happen here." Results from a Gallup survey indicated that many American businesses are turning a blind eye toward warning signs of workplace violence. "The warning signs are well known, but too many companies are burying their heads in the sand," said Frank Kenna III, president of The Marlin Company who commissioned a recent Gallup study. A lot of people rationalize the fact that they're not confronting the issue. They say they don't want to overreact and figure any fears are unfounded, so they ignore the signs, hoping they'll go away. The survey reported that only 25% of respondents indicated they received any training in how to identify warning signs and what to do about them. Overcoming this mindset is the starting point to implementing a strong and effective effort to prevent workplace violence.

The Nix Model for Managing Violence Prevention is a comprehensive approach to preventing workplace violence (see Figure W-2).

Establishing a Workplace Violence Prevention Committee

Management must demonstrate a commitment by taking workplace violence seriously and appoint an influential manager to be responsible for the workplace violence prevention effort. This manager should establish a Workplace Violence Prevention Committee (frequently referred to as a Threat Management Committee). Participants on the committee should include

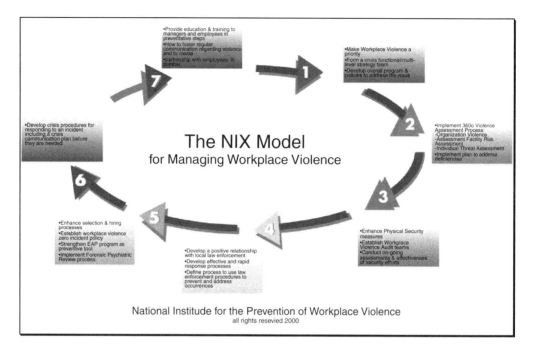

FIGURE W-2

representatives from security, human resources, occupational health and safety, legal, finance, risk management, public relations, operational management, and a union representative, if applicable. Their role is to shepherd the overall implementation of the workplace violence prevention program, to provide guidance on how to address emerging workplace violence situations, and to continuously improve the overall program. Annually, the committee should be required to produce a report on the state of the workplace violence prevention program for the organization's senior management team.

An exemplary example of the success of a committed focus on workplace violence prevention and employee safety is 7-Eleven Corporation, which has reduced its robbery rate by 71% since implementing its program in 1976.

As a convenience store, open for long hours with items such as lottery tickets and cigarettes that can be resold quickly for cash, 7-Eleven is vulnerable to shoplifting and robberies. However, the company's philosophy is that employee safety always comes first. According to its occupational health and safety department, "Employees are trained that there is nothing in the store more valuable than them."

7-Eleven puts this policy into practice through training that outlines specific response procedures in the event of a shoplifting incident or robbery. "We instruct our employees to ask politely if the customer would like to pay. If the customer refuses or becomes aggressive, employees are not to chase the robber. ... Try to treat it like any other transaction." The procedures are also posted in the back of each store in a helpful list of do's and don'ts (e.g., keep it short and smooth). All employees are equipped with a personal safety device and instructed to use it if they feel they are about to be physically hurt. When a clerk is working alone, a buzzer activates every 2 hours; the clerk must push a button to disarm it. If the alarm isn't cancelled, a system is in place to check on the clerk.

Another key to 7-Eleven's successful violence prevention program is continual evaluation. All incidents are reported to a hotline and immediate action is taken where necessary. "It's not a risk assessment that's done once a year. It is done immediately after a store is robbed." (7)

Focusing on Eliminating "At Risk" Behaviors

The Workplace Violence Prevention Committee should focus on creating a violence-free work environment by eliminating "at risk" behaviors on both an individual (internal and external) and organization level. One of the key responsibilities of the committee should also be to establish a workplace violence prevention policy which focuses on zero incidents as the goal. In a retail environment, the committee must be sure to address not only internal workplace violence, but also the more probable external threat as well, given that robbery and other crimes were the motive for 80% of workplace homicides. Bureau of Labor Statistics (BLR) Research indicates that the greatest risk of work-related homicide comes from violence inflicted by third parties such as robbers and muggers. On average, one in 100 gun robberies results in a homicide (8), and annually over 300,000 retail workers become the victims of workplace violence, according to the U.S. Department of Justice. In addition, a large proportion of the homicides occurring in the retail sector are associated with robberies and attempted robberies.

The bottom line message is that the most effective way to deal with the risk of workplace violence is to recognize the risk that it poses, identify what those risks are, develop mitigating strategies to reduce or eliminate the risks, and have a comprehensive strategy that is focused on early identification and averting issues. With the value of hindsight, after an incident of workplace violence has occurred, we are generally able to identify how the incident could have been prevented. So the simple trick is to anticipate incidents by conducting "what if" planning and then implement those preventative actions in real-time, which will save real lives or prevent real injuries.

For example, a man charged with five murders at two Nashville fast-food restaurants was arrested in connection with 10 similar slayings, including the massacre of seven workers at a Palatine, Illinois, chicken restaurant in 1993. This same person was paroled in 1990 after serving about 8 years of a 20-year sentence for aggravated armed robbery at a steak house in suburban Houston. If any of the restaurants that hired him had done a background check, it is likely that he would never have been hired, and these murders could have been avoided.

The cold truth about workplace violence is that, with serious "what if" planning and diligent application of proactive measures, we have the capability of preventing most incidents.

"At risk" behaviors and organizational practices refer to individual- (internal and external) or organization-based variables or contributing factors that, when present, create a heightened possibility of workplace violence occurring.

Let's first look at internal "at risk" behaviors (see Figure W-3):

1. The occurrence of a stressful event
2. An emotionally charged individual
3. An insensitive, uncaring, inflammatory, reactionary, toxic work environment

It is important to note that the first variable, a stressful event, is a wild card because what one person views as stressful, another takes in stride. At the same time, we can clearly predict that some events are likely to induce stress in most people, e.g., a termination, a bad performance review, criticizing someone in front of other people, addressing a person in a disrespectful or demeaning manner, etc.

The second of the three variables, an emotionally charged individual, has to do with the mental and emotional state of a person, and this is something that, if we are observant and knowledgeable regarding what to look for, we can often recognize these early warning signs. Once supervisors recognize the warning signs, if they are properly trained to intervene, they can generally interrupt escalation up the aggression scale.

The third variable, interestingly enough, focuses on the setting or environment that the person is subjected to. Within a company context, this means that an organizational culture, management style, ways of treating employees, perceived fairness of problem

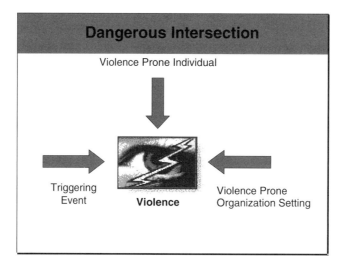

FIGURE W-3

resolution processes, etc., can have a great bearing on either escalating or de-escalating potential hostile situations. This reality is generally overlooked by firms which tend to find it convenient to focus all the attention and responsibility regarding violence on an individual.

Research has indicated that a number of organizational variables make an organization more prone to having a violent outburst. The fact that organizational practices may be a contributing factor to a violent incident is a "dirty little secret" that businesses do not want to admit.(9)

When the three variables illustrated in Figure W-3 collide, you have a very real and present possibility for violence to occur. A fundamental belief that we subscribe to is that, if you can predict or anticipate an event, you can plan for how to deal with it.

Since this belief is not a revolutionary concept, you may be wondering why more businesses don't take action to prevent violence in the workplace. The answer is a simple but perplexing one: Most firm's managers are in denial that a violent incident could occur where they work. This belief subsequently freezes them and prevents any action being taken to address the problem.

Defining the Nature of External Threats/Risks to the Company

The Workplace Violence Prevention committee should research the nature of risk to retail operations based on the geographic area in which the firm operates its stores. Where there is evidence of known hazards that exist within this type business, industry, or area, specific actions should be taken to mitigate and address the problems. This is essential because these are the signs which indicate the greatest potential for violence to occur and, commensurately, represent the highest potential liability.

To illustrate the point, if you have located a retail outlet in a low-cost area, and crime data for the area indicate several robberies have occurred at other retail facilities near your location, it would be prudent to take precautionary steps to enhance security in and about your facility. This could include making sure you have sufficient lighting in the parking lot areas, providing escort service for employees leaving the building at night, asking for increased police patrols, etc. To ignore the crime data and not anticipate a potential problem puts you in a defensive position. If one of your employees is victimized while on your property or injured during a robbery, you will have to defend why you chose not to take any preventative actions.

Charles LeGrand said it best: "Failure to assess risks and take the necessary protective actions must be regarded as negligence."

Facility Risk Assessments

Conduct periodic facility risk assessments to identify vulnerabilities that exist in your stores and/or operations facilities. Be sure to identify hazards, conditions, operations, and situations that could lead to violence. The risk assessment includes a walkthrough survey to provide the data for risk identification and the development of a comprehensive workplace violence prevention program.

Possible sources to help conduct a walkthrough survey include insurance carriers, crime prevention units of local police departments, and security or workplace violence prevention consultants.

The assessment process should include the following:

- Analyze incidents, including the characteristics of assailants and victims. Give an account of what happened before and during the incident, and note the relevant details of the situation and its outcome.
- Identify any apparent trends in injuries or incidents relating to a particular worksite, job title, activity, or time of day or week, including specific tasks that may be associated with increased risk.
- Identify factors that may make the risk of violence more likely, such as physical features of the building and environment, lighting deficiencies, lack of telephones and other communication devices, areas of unsecured access, and areas with known security problems.
- Evaluate the effectiveness of existing security measures. Assess whether those control measures are being properly used and whether employees have been adequately trained in their use.

With the continued advancement of biometric technology and their use in security, consider how these tools might be used to combat crime. For example:

- Link facial or automatic gait recognition (AGR) tools to a criminal database to identify potential robbers immediately (this has obvious limitations given that many robbers will not be in the database because they have not been convicted). Gait is technology that recognizes those distinct characteristics or unique "signature" we all create by the way we move our limbs as we walk.
- Use smart cameras that are programmed to set off a silent alarm to a police department if someone enters the premises with a mask on or shows a gun (a major limitation of this approach is that in places that have very cold weather during the winter, a lot of false positives will happen due to people having a scarf around their face).
- Use smart cameras to take a picture of each adult's face before he or she enters the store (similar to ATM machines) between the hours of 9:00 p.m. and 7:00 a.m. and have it control the entry door. Post signs conspicuously at the entrance advising people that their picture must be taken to enter the store. A challenge with this approach will be managing multiple people who are at the door at the same time and having them enter in the appropriate manner.

Note that the preceding suggestions are only ideas intended to stimulate your thinking about possible biometric solutions which may provide new ways to fight crime in retail operations, since new tools and applications are being created every day.

Trade associations and other organizations also have materials that can help employers assess the risk of violent incidents in their business. In some areas, local law enforcement agencies provide free advice to business owners on ways to reduce exposure to crime. Security management consultants, workplace violence prevention consultants, insurance safety auditors, and loss prevention specialists also can help employers analyze workplace risks and offer advice for solutions. Independent experts such as these can provide fresh perspectives on implementing and improving a violence prevention program.(10)

Facility risk assessments should be an ongoing process. An effective violence prevention program will institute a system of periodic risk assessments or safety audits to review workplace hazards and the effectiveness of the control measures that have been implemented. These audits also can evaluate the impact of other operational changes (such as new store hours or changes in store layout) that were adopted for other reasons but may affect the risk of workplace violence. A safety audit is important in the aftermath of a violent incident or other serious event for reassessing the effectiveness of the violence prevention program.

According to the National Institute for Occupational Safety and Health (NIOSH), the leading risk factor that exposes workers to the potential of violence while working is direct interaction with the public. This reality is one of the contributing factors to retail workers being highly exposed to violence, since handling money transactions and selling merchandise including alcohol or drugs are commonplace.

In addition, the following risk factors deal with the nature of the work environment:

- Store located in high crime areas
- Employee working alone
- Workplace layout
- Lighting and security provisions
- Hours of operations, e.g., working late night or early morning hours

In addition, delivery of passengers, goods, or services can create a risk as well, since thieves target these as well as brick-and-mortar stores.

Assessing the *store location* deals with understanding and being knowledgeable about criminal activity and security issues that exist within a reasonable proximity to your retail operations. In many jurisdictions, this information is available from local law enforcement, and additionally, there are several firms that provide crime watch data.

The *number of employees on duty* is of particular relevance, since working alone or in isolation is one of the working conditions that can potentially increase the likelihood of exposure to violence. Consequently, when you have employees working alone, some special precautions need to be taken:

- Enhance the lighting inside and around the business.
- Ensure workers have a panic or emergency alarm placed in an inconspicuous place that is easy to access.
- Design store so that workers have a clear line of sight to all parts of the business.
- Set up a regular communications process to check on workers or have them check in to ensure they are safe.
- Install security cameras to capture all activities.
- Post signs that state there is no cash on premises or that it is locked in a safe that the clerk does not have a key to access.
- Keep your doors and windows free of posters to ensure a clear line of sight.
- Use overhead mirrors so employees can see all parts of the store from the cash register area.
- Train your staff not to resist or engage the assailant if there is a robbery.

The *workplace layout* is important because you want to ensure that an employee on duty has clear visibility of what is going on in the store. This means that you should carefully consider the placement of signs or posters on windows as well as shelving or merchandise displays that might obscure the view.

Lighting should be appropriate both inside and outside your establishment. A well-lit parking lot and entrance area makes your store a less attractive target than one where the lights are dim.

Hours of operations are important because research has shown that with late night and early morning hour operations, risk of robbery increases.

Delivery of passengers, goods, or services creates and additional set of risks beyond those of the brick-and-mortar stores. Whether it is delivering food for consumption, e.g., pizza, or to warehouses, stores, etc., delivering goods is wrought with dangers. Robbery in the trucking industry is a major issue and is a significant enough problem that it warrants a section of its own within this book to adequately address it. Short-term deliveries can also be robbery targets but are also impacted by nonpayment, assaults, rape, etc. Training drivers in how to avoid potential issues and how to react is a critical step in addressing this problem.

Employees in some retail establishments may be exposed to multiple risk factors. The presence of a single risk factor does not necessarily indicate that the risk of violence is a problem in a workplace. The presence, however, of multiple risk factors or a history of workplace violence should alert an employer that the potential for workplace violence has increased.

Organizational Violence Assessments

Part of a second level of analysis the employer should undertake is to review the experience of the business over the previous 2 or 3 years. This involves collecting and examining any existing records that may shed light on the magnitude and prevalence of the risk of workplace violence. For example, injury and illness records, workers' compensation claims, and police department robbery reports can help identify specific incidents related to workplace violence. Finding few documented cases of workplace violence does not necessarily mean that violence is not a problem in a workplace because incidents may be unreported or inconsistently documented. In some cases management may not be aware of incidents of low-intensity conflict or threats of violence to which employees have been exposed. To learn of such incidents, an employer could canvass employees about their experience while working for the business. The following questions from OSHA Recommendations may be helpful in compiling information about past incidents:

- Has your business been robbed during the past 2–3 years? Were robberies attempted? Did injuries occur due to robberies or attempts?
- Have employees been assaulted in altercations with customers?
- Have employees been victimized by other criminal acts at work (including shoplifting that became assaultive)? What kind?
- Have employees been threatened or harassed while on duty? What was the context of those incidents?
- In each of the cases with injuries, how serious were the injuries?
- In each case, was a firearm involved? Was a firearm discharged? Was the threat of a firearm used? Were other weapons used?
- What part of the business was the target of the robbery or other violent incident'?
- At what time of day did the robbery or other incident occur?
- How many employees were on duty?
- Were the police called to your establishment in response to the incident? When possible, obtain reports of the police investigation.
- What tasks were the employees performing at the time of the robbery or other incident? What processes and procedures may have put employees at risk of assault? Similarly, were there factors that may have facilitated an outcome without injury or harm?
- Were preventive measures already in place and used correctly?
- What were the actions of the victim during the incident? Did these actions affect the outcome of the incident in any way?

These types of data can be key in identifying "at risk" factors on the organization level. Employers with more than one store or business location should review the history of violence at each operation. Different experiences in those stores can provide insights into factors that can make workplace violence more or less likely. Contacting similar local businesses, community and civic groups, and local police departments is another way to learn about workplace violence incidents in the area. In addition, trade associations and industry groups often provide useful information about conditions and trends in the industry as a whole.(11)

Establishing a Workplace Violence Prevention Policy

A cornerstone of your program is to establish a clear workplace violence prevention policy that will set the framework and provide guidance to managers, supervisors, and employees.

(See model policies at www.workplaceviolence911.com/ModelPolicies.) The focus should be on violence prevention, with the ultimate goal being zero incidents. In addition, the policy should make the concept of treating people in a respectful manner and maintaining their dignity a central theme that is integrated into the policy and its communication.

Illustrative of a good workplace violence policy statement is the U.S. Department of Transportation's Workplace Violence Policy:

> *A safe working environment for all employees, free from violence or any threat of violence, is one goal of the U.S. Department of Transportation. Violence and threatening behaviors in any form are unacceptable and will not be tolerated. ... The cooperation of supervisors, managers, and employees is necessary to implement this policy and maintain a safe working environment. ... Supervisors and managers are expected to take immediate action to investigate reported threats or violence and any suspicious items or activities, and with the assistance of appropriate officials, reduce or eliminate the risk of workplace violence.*

Note that from an internal perspective, many organizations are also starting to incorporate directly into their workplace violence prevention policy statements that make it clear that bullying behaviors are not acceptable. Make it clear that bullying is considered threatening behavior because it can cause emotional abuse, can lead to situations which create a hostile work environment, and also can create hostile feelings between employees, which can lead to violence.

In addition, firms need to address domestic violence in their policy to ensure that a supportive work environment is created for victims of domestic violence and that also takes a stance against employees that are abusers. Businesses are playing an important role in helping to address domestic violence (see the website for the Corporate Alliance to End Partner Violence at www.CAEPV.org for more information on the employer's role). Note that encouraging employees to report domestic violence situations and restraining orders is important too so that you can appropriately react and plan to prevent for potential violent intrusions from significant others.

Establish a process for record keeping to be able to track actual threats, incidents, close calls, escalating conflicts, etc., for trends or patterns. Also evaluate interventions and programmatic efforts to evaluate their success and to maintain continuous improvement.

Assess the organization's conflict resolution process and bolster it to ensure it is an effective tool for fairly addressing employee concerns and conflicts and resolving problems. Usage should be tracked (keep in mind that high usage is not necessarily a bad indicator and many times indicates people trust your process) and periodically assess how employees are feeling about the process.

Translate your workplace violence policy and training into multiple languages based on the predominant languages spoken in your workplace.

When employees are represented by a union, you should consider introducing a workplace violence prevention initiative to be jointly developed as a part of the next contract. You should work with the union to predetermine how cases, complaints, and situations will be handled; define processes to be used; and consider including mediation to provide an objective third party to negotiate outcomes.

No Weapons in the Workplace Policy

Incorporate a "No Weapons in the Workplace" provision into your workplace violence prevention policy or establish a separate policy that clearly establishes that no weapons are allowed on the premises and employees are prohibited from possessing a weapon while on duty.

There is a lot of noise right now about the right to bear arms and that right extending into the workplace; however, as an employer, you have to ask yourself whether you really want a bunch of employees walking around with or having easy access to a firearm given the drama of human behavior that occurs in organizations. It is a formula destined for disaster.

On the other hand, small convenience stores have a challenging situation when they have employees working alone. In this situation, I advocate several options that could help provide a more secure store:

- If possible, have an armed guard on duty in the store. This could be on a full-time or rotational basis. Note that if a rotational basis is chosen, it should be structured so that it is not a predicable schedule that can easily be identified. Recognizing the potential cost for hiring an armed guard, one option would be to see if other retailers in the area are interested in sharing the expense to have the guard patrol their stores as well. If guard service is chosen, I suggest you conspicuously post signs stating "Armed Guard on Duty."
- Another option that should be considered is to build relationships with police officers by offering incentives to frequent your store. This could be in the form of free coffee and donuts if you are a food retailer or other merchandise discounts to attract them to frequently visit your store. Some police departments prohibit this process; however, an easy way to address this is to offer police officers a significant discount, e.g., for $1 they can have unlimited coffee and donuts for the week.

Enhancing Physical Security Using Crime Prevention Through Environmental Design (CPTED)

Use CPTED engineering/architectural control processes to remove the hazards identified from the workplace or create a barrier between employees and the hazard (see www.cpted.net/home.html for more information). The following physical changes in the workplace can help reduce violence-related risks or hazards in retail establishments:(12)

- Improve *visibility*, as visibility is important in preventing robbery in two respects: First, employees should be able see their surroundings; and second, persons outside the store, including police on patrol, should be able to see into the store. Employees in the store should have an unobstructed view of the street, clear of shrubbery, trees, or any form of clutter that a criminal could use to hide. Signs located in windows should be either low or high to allow good visibility into the store. The customer service and cash register areas should be visible from outside the establishment. Shelves should be low enough to assure good visibility throughout the store. Convex mirrors, two-way mirrors, and an elevated vantage point can give employees a more complete view of their surroundings.
- Maintain *adequate lighting* within and outside the establishment to make the store less appealing to a potential robber by making detection more likely. The parking area and the approach to the retail establishment should be well lit *(during* nighttime hours of operation.) Exterior illumination may need upgrading in order to allow employees to see what is occurring outside the store.
- *Use fences* and other structures to direct the flow of customer traffic to areas of greater visibility.
- *Use drop safes* to limit the availability of cash to robbers. Employers using drop safes can post signs stating that the amount of cash on hand is limited.
- *Install video surveillance equipment* and closed-circuit television (CCTV) to deter robberies by increasing the risk of identification. This may include interactive video equipment. The video recorder for the CCTV should be secure and out of sight. Posting signs that surveillance equipment is in use and placing the equipment near the cash register may increase the effectiveness of the deterrence.
- *Put height markers on exit doors* to help witnesses provide more complete descriptions of assailants.
- *Use door detectors* to alert employees when persons enter the store.
- *Control access* to the store with door buzzers.
- *Use silent and personal alarms* to notify police or management in the event of a problem. It is a good idea to have them in multiple places in the store.

652   RETAIL CRIME, SECURITY, AND LOSS PREVENTION

- Make sure that your staff understands that the rule in using silent or panic alarms is that they have to be able to press the alarm button without endangering their life. For this reason, many holdup systems are designed such that the act of removing a certain bill in the register activates the alarm, which means there are not additional movements to alert the robber to your actions.
- In some cases to avoid angering a robber, however, an employee may need to wait until the assailant has left before triggering an alarm.
- *Install physical barriers* such as bullet-resistant enclosures with passthrough windows between customers and employees to protect employees from assaults and weapons in locations with a history of robberies or assaults and located in high-crime areas.

Also note that when you are building or retrofitting facilities, it is a good time to maximize crime prevention by using CPTED. For example, wiring a building for closed circuit security when it is being built is much more economical than retrofitting it later.

Also provide store personnel with handheld alarms or noise devices and/or communication devices to be able to get help, e.g., cellular phones, pagers, etc., to use while on duty alone.

Prevention Strategies to Avoid Being a Target of Robbery

After you assess violence hazards, the next step is to develop measures to protect employees from the identified risks of injury and violent acts. (13) Workplace violence prevention and control programs include specific engineering and work practice controls to address identified hazards. The tools listed in this section are not intended to be a one-size-fits-all prescription. No single control will protect employees. To provide effective deterrents to violence, the employer may wish to use a combination of controls in relation to the hazards identified through the hazard analysis.

Since the major risk of death or serious injury to retail employees is from robbery-related violence, an effective program would include, but not be limited to, steps to reduce the risk of robbery. In general, a business may reduce the risk of robbery by *increasing the effort* that the perpetrator must expend (target hardening, controlling access, and deterring offenders); *increasing the risks* to the perpetrator (entry/exit screening, formal surveillance by employees and others); and *reducing the rewards* to the perpetrator (removing the target, identifying properly, and *removing inducements*)(14)

Physical and behavioral changes at a site can substantially reduce the frequency of robberies. A test group of 7-Eleven stores that eliminated or reduced several risk factors experienced a 30% drop in robberies compared to a control group. Target-hardening efforts, including a basic robbery deterrence package, were implemented in 7-Eleven stores nationwide in 1976. The 7-Eleven program tried to make the store a less attractive target by reducing the cash on hand, maximizing the take/risk ratio, and training employees. After implementing the program throughout the company, the robbery rate at 7-Eleven stores decreased by 64% over 20 years.(15)

The National Association of Convenience Stores (NACS) developed a robbery and violence deterrence program based on these elements and has made it available to its members and others since 1987. NACS also has supported research in this area. NACS has available on CD-ROM a training program that is available to address this issue: "Robbery Deterrence & Personal Safety Training Program."

Other deterrents that may reduce the potential for robbery include making sure that there are security cameras, time-release safes, other 24-hour businesses at the location, no easy escape routes or hiding places, and that the store is closed during late-night hours.

OSHA has some very good suggestions in its "Recommendations to Prevent Workplace Violence in Late-Night Retail Industry:"

Avoiding Being a Target of Robbery

(a) Safer Working Practices

- Be alert—keep an eye on people in the shop.
- Make sure you have safety, security, and emergency procedures.

- Train your staff and make sure they know and follow safety procedures.
- Minimize cash—keep only a small amount of money in the cash register.
- Bank regularly—keep a minimum amount of money on the premises.
- Restrict access to cash-handling areas.
- Keep the back door locked (but make sure you have an emergency exit).
- Keep safes and drop boxes locked; don't leave the keys in sight.
- Have your cash collected or do your banking at different times of the day.
- Keep doors locked before and after business hours and, if possible, when counting cash.
- Don't tell people how much cash you keep on the premises.

(b) Physical Options
- Position the cash-handling areas away from entries and exits.
- Separate the cash-handling area from the general workplace.
- Make sure staff can see in and out of the store (remove posters from windows).
- Mirrors can be used to help staff see the whole shop; however, make sure that the mirrors do not allow potential offenders to see the cash area.
- Lighting can make the target highly visible and increase the chances of offender identification.
- Remove signs that may block your vision of the store.
- Install counters with an elevated place for the cash register.
- Have antijump barriers fitted in front of cash-handling devices.
- Have a mini safe/drop box, strong room, or other safety box fitted and make sure it's out of public sight.
- Bullet-resistant barriers or ascending ballistic screens can be fitted to the cash-handling areas.
- Block all alternative accesses to building (without blocking off a fire exit).
- Have time-delay locks fitted to all compartments and counter safes.
- Use security guards or other security guarding devices.
- Display emergency numbers in a prominent position for staff.
- Make sure you have a first aid kit available to all staff.
- Place a colored height chart next to the entrance of the store.

(c) Electronic Security
- Closed-circuit television (CCTV)
- Digital camera surveillance and recording
- Still 35 mm cameras mounted in predominant positions
- Holdup alarms fitted in all workplaces, centrally monitored and silent in operation
- 24-hour perimeter alarm system
- Camera and alarm activation points in frequently used positions
- Note clip activators
- Roof cavity protection
- Mobile and fixed duress alarms
- Cash dye bombs
- Door alarms—to alert staff that someone is entering the premises

Synchronizing Your Personnel, Security, and Safety Policies

Synchronize your personnel, security, and safety policies to ensure they create an integrated workplace violence prevention effort. It is not unusual that we see conflicting policies developed in their respective "silos" that have conflicting or incongruent information. This can really hurt you in court.

Developing Crisis Response Procedures

Establish a crisis response team (specially trained to deal with crisis) and develop crisis response procedures to deal with an incident. Retail operations should have a robbery response team, since the possibility of an occurrence in this area is high. Select members based on pre-established criteria, which should include their ability to remain calm during a crisis or pressure situations, special skills related to handling crises or emergencies as well as technical competency related to health care, mental health, knowledge of facilities, public relations, security, etc. The team should put a crisis communication and public relations plan in place before a crisis occurs, and the overall plan should be rehearsed.

Myths of Disaster Planning

One of the cruelest myths in crisis and workplace violence prevention planning is the belief that plans adopted, but not tested, will actually work as planned.

Another costly fallacy is for organizations to focus solely on protecting their hard assets—e.g., facilities, technology, information, and networks—and to forget their people. It is one thing to test your alarm systems, system recovery processes, backing up information protections, and another to have your people improperly trained or not trained in what they need to do. Even worse is when the actions they have been told to do cause confusion because they have never been tested to see that the procedures actually function as intended. You need to prepare your people for crisis because they will make the difference in how quickly and effectively you are able to return to normal business operations.

The third myth regarding crisis planning is the belief that you can effectively insure losses in a disaster. It is highly likely that "settling claims after a disaster is not a pretty picture" and that insurers trying to mitigate casualty losses often will not make it easy for executives trying to recover quickly.

Note that while the responsibility for addressing prevention of workplace violence typically is assigned to either human resources or security, remember that the controller has a critical role and responsibility with regards to business continuity and protecting the organization's assets. Consequently, make sure they are included in the process.(16)

Additionally, pre-establish a critical incident debriefing process and skilled counselors to be able to assist victims after an incident. Your employee assistance program or an external community psychological network will be able to provide these types of support services.

Keep in mind that the speed at which you are able to address the needs of employees who have experienced a traumatic event will dictate how fast you are able to return work levels to normal operations. It is not unusual that within a few days following an incident reactions such as fear, anxiety, and exhaustion, as well as anger may surface. In the long run, lack of confidence, depression, and the development of post-traumatic stress disorder (PTSD) are possible outcomes.

Emergency Protocol with Police

Create an emergency protocol with police. This should include identifying who is the contact person when an incident needs to be reported. It is also important to identify a backup contact and also to pre-inform the contacts regarding who is responsible to contact them from your firm. You should also have the contacts visit your site and learn your facility layout, if possible. In addition, you should make your address and building numbers clearly visible.

While it is prudent management to have established a protocol with law enforcement, the stark reality is that in most serious workplace violence situations involving a homicide, the incident is over in 3–5 minutes. According to Department of Justice statistics, for 65% of police departments, the time to respond to life-threatening situations is more than 6 minutes, and the best response times hover around 5 minutes, 20 seconds. This means that if your plan is built on the premise that the police will "save the day," it may be wishful thinking. Thus, your workplace violence prevention team has to think about how to develop a plan that presumes you are on your own.

Note: My statements should not be construed to mean that you should not call the police, because they have a critical role to play and should be contacted immediately.

However, practically speaking from a logistical response viewpoint, even the most responsive police force will be challenged to reach you in time to prevent many incidents, so you have to plan for this reality.

Enhancing Hiring Procedures

Enhance hiring procedures to include background screening processes focused on screening out dishonest or low-integrity applicants before they are hired. This step is essential because it is estimated that a significant amount of theft is committed by employees, and a significant number of robberies are assisted by an "insider." Taking every step you can to try to weed out these problematic individuals before you hire them is very important to your business.

There are several other tools available to help you screen applicants. Use critical behavior traits to identify behavior-based interview questions to recognize potential problems during your interviews. (See "Complete Hiring Guide to Screen for Violence Prone Individuals" for detailed coverage of enhanced hiring procedures, available at www.Workplaceviolence911.com.)

There are also numerous psychological tests and assessments on the market that purport to be able to identify dishonesty and low integrity traits. The Conover Company provides "The Violence Prevention Map," which is a tool to gauge how an individual views himself or herself in relationship to violence. The total score is a predictor of how individuals view their own ability to control their behavior and get along with other people, especially in potentially stressful, hostile, or threatening situations. The higher the score, the greater the risk of violence the organization may expect.

Firms should closely evaluate the potential effectiveness of these tools. However, when a validated tool is used as a part of an overall set of screening tools, they will likely provide additional information that can help make a better informed hiring decision.

In addition, it is critical that firms conduct background screening. Following are some of the types of background checks that you should consider:

- Reference checking from previous employers
- Criminal background checks (counties, state, nationwide, international)
- Education and credential verification
- Verification of identify
- Driving record
- Credit history
- Drug testing
- Terrorist check

You will need to decide whether you want to conduct these background screenings internally or outsource them to a firm that specializes in this area. An excellent source to identify potential background screening firms is www.PreemploymentDirectory.com, which is a comprehensive online listing that features background screening firms. Also be sure to review the site's "Guide to Selecting a Background Screening Firm."

Accurate Background, Inc. (www.accuratebackground.com), a background screening firm in Lake Forest, California, has created "Risk Reduction Technology," a patent-pending rules-engine application which reduces liability within the retail industry, as well as the workload for their human resources and recruitment sectors by streamlining the review process of a candidate's background report. Retailers with multiple locations benefit from Risk Reduction Technology because it was created to eliminate human error and personal bias across the board. It stores the retailer's hiring threshold criteria and allows the retailer to define and refine adjudication needs as necessary.

Training Managers, Supervisors, and Employees

Provide ongoing workplace violence prevention training for managers, supervisors, and employees. Training your employees how to respond during a robbery can lower the risk of their being killed on the job. Some organizations are reluctant to be associated with such training because they fear it sends the message that their stores are dangerous places to work or shop.

Such companies may face not only increased risks from robberies, but also greater liability in court. For example, the California Court of Appeals recently ruled that every business has a legal duty to tell employees how to handle robberies. It appears that the company named in the suit was held liable because it had not trained its employees on what to do during a robbery.(17)

Training should be provided in the following areas:

- Implementation of workplace violence prevention policy
- How to identify early warning signs and how to appropriately intervene
- Robbery prevention and survival

What should be included in a training program?

- How to be alert and identify possible suspicious behavior
- Cash-handling procedures
- Emergency procedures
- How to make sure staff vision is not blocked
- What to do during an incident

Some key points for training include the following:

- One of the most important points to teach employees is to give up the cash willingly. Explain to them that their life is not worth whatever is in the register and to cooperate with the bad guy. Resistance is futile and may get the employee killed.
- Also, teach employees to announce their actions to the robber by saying something like, "I'm going to reach in the cash register and get the money now." They should keep their hands in plain view and not make any sudden movements.
- 7-Eleven, Inc,. of Dallas also "tells employees not to try to stop a shoplifter from fleeing the store. ... The merchandise is not worth the risk of injury."
- In contrast to a robbery, if a criminal attempts to abduct employees or take them to a back room or sexually assault them, employees should be taught to get away using any means possible.

Following are tips on what to do after an incident, including whom to contact:

- Train employees to lock the store and avoid touching anything the robber may have touched. If the store has a video camera, remove the tape as soon as possible so that it will not be copied over.
- Train employees how to use security devices.
- Ensure confidentiality. Make sure employees do not tell anybody about how much money is kept on the premises, etc.
- Ensure safe work practices; e.g., don't leave the rear door open late at night because it's hot, or don't haul the trash out late at night without looking to see if someone is there, or even better, avoid putting trash out until later.

Survival is the number one priority during a robbery or violent incident.

WorkCover (www.workcover.nsw.gov.au/Publications/Industry/RetailandWholesale/default.htm) provides an excellent overview that everyone in the retail industry should follow. It includes a number of simple rules to reduce the likelihood of injury if an incident occurs.

Surviving a Robbery or Violent Incident

1. Follow instructions; do exactly what the offender says.
2. Stay calm and quiet.
3. Avoid eye contact.
4. Do not make a sudden movement.
5. Remain inside the workplace; do not chase the offender.
6. Show your hands: If you have to move, keep your hands where the offender can see them and tell them what you are going to do.
7. Do not attack the offender.

Mental notes: Note as much information about the offender as possible, if it is safe to do so. Look at things like height, hair color, eyes, physical condition and tattoos/special marks.

- Importance of reporting and responding to threats, incidents, etc.
- How to de-escalate potentially hostile situations including during a robbery
- Effective ways to deal with domestic violence

Focus on developing *core competencies* in effective conflict resolution, hostility/anger management, emotional intelligence, and respectful communications.

WorkCover's Survival Rules for a Robbery or Violent Incident

What to Do After a Robbery or Violent Incident
After a robbery or a violent incident, employers and the person in charge at the time of the incident should follow a number of steps to help them deal with the situation.

Person in Charge at the Time of the Incident

- Make sure that victims receive *prompt medical attention* if injured.
- Notify the police.
- Notify your employer, if he or she is not onsite.
- Prepare an incident report.

Employer

- Notify the police.
- Arrange counseling for the victims because they may suffer from post-traumatic stress. The symptoms of post-traumatic stress disorder include increased heart rate, insomnia, muscle tension, hypersensitivity, fear of returning to work, depression, grief, guilt, and anxiety

New staff should be trained prior to commencing duty. Existing staff should be given training as soon as possible if they have not yet received it. Refresher training should be provided regularly, at least twice a year or when there are changes to procedures.

Involving Employees in the Prevention Effort

Make sure all employees know that workplace violence prevention is everybody's business and help them understand the important role they can play in reducing violence. A truly effective prevention effort must maximize the participation of employees and their support. By encouraging the following practices, employers can enlist employee support, and they will contribute substantially to a successful effort to prevent violence at work.

Employee involvement is important for several reasons. First, front-line employees are an important source of information about the operations of the business and the environment in which the business operates. This may be particularly true for employees working at night in retail establishments when higher level managers may not routinely be on duty. Second, inclusion of a broad range of employees in the violence prevention program has the advantage of harnessing a wider range of experience and insight than that of management alone. Third, front-line workers can be valuable problem solvers because their personal experience often enables them to identify practical solutions to problems and to perceive hidden impediments to proposed changes. Finally, employees who have a role in developing prevention programs are more likely to support and carry out those programs.(17)

Additional interventions that employers can use to focus on preventing workplace violence internally include

- Collect utilization data from the employee assistance program and analyze the results to identify potentially problematic issues and areas.
- Conduct a "respect" audit of your human resource and security policies to ensure "treating people in a respectful manner" is built into your processes. This is particularly

important in designing termination, layoff, and discipline procedures, which need to sensitive to ensuring fair, respectful, and dignified treatment of employees. Special precautions should be taken when "at risk" behaviors are present. Heed the words of Dick Ault, PhD, a former FBI agent specializing in profiling: "You have to approach the firing of anyone with the utmost of dignity, even people who really don't deserve it."

- Publish a list identifying whom to call and resources available to assist with issues.
- Use external expert resources as appropriate.

For large retailers, an emerging direction for internal incidents of workplace violence you should be aware of is that covert sabotage of work processes often occurs when employees feel angry toward their employer. Studies reveal a direct correlation between prevalence of employee conflict and the amount of damage and theft of inventory and equipment. Much of the cost incurred by this factor is hidden from management's view, often excused as "accidental" or "inadvertent" errors. This cost is almost certainly greater than you realize.

A Time Bomb

A former computer network administrator was found guilty in May 2000 of intentionally causing irreparable damage to his company's computer system. He created a "time bomb" program that permanently deleted all the high-tech manufacturing company's sophisticated manufacturing programs. The damage, lost contracts, and lost productivity totaled more than $10 million.

Why did he do it? He was demoted after working for the company for about 10 years. He soon began developing the bomb, which he set off 2 weeks after he was terminated the following year.(18)

According to an article published in the August 2005 edition of *COMPUTERWORLD*), in today's era of increased outsourcing, corporate downsizing, salary reductions, and failed pension-plan promises, company networks are increasingly being attacked by disgruntled employees. In this hostile environment, searching for the source of sabotage should start inside.

A recent study sponsored by Risk Control Strategies, a threat management and risk assessment firm, found that an overwhelming majority of 223 security and human resources executives who manage between 500 and 900 employees said workplace violence is a bigger problem now than it was 2 years ago. As a result, 23% said employees have intentionally and maliciously downloaded viruses over the past 12 months. The study found that hitting employees in the pocketbook is prompting the burgeoning retaliation.

A recent study of IT outsourcing trends sponsored by DiamondCluster International Inc., a business and technology consulting firm, supports this conclusion, stating that 88% of outsourcers cited employee backlash as their primary concern. Cognizant of buyers' unease, outsourcing providers limit their onsite presence to keep the "face of outsourcing" out of sight from employees, according to the study.

Using viruses as a weapon against senior management is a people problem that can't be solved solely through technological means. For IT security managers, internal investigations will require a whole new set of workplace violence-prevention skills and unprecedented coordination with HR executives.

Summary

To summarize, many managers view workplace violence as random acts of violence that are unpredictable, and therefore nothing can be done to address them. While we can't eliminate robberies, we can harden our facilities or make them less attractive to criminals, which has been shown to reduce robbery rates. Remember, if we can anticipate it, we can plan for it.

Despite our best attempts to place the blame on the individual's behavior, the organization is not blameless. Individual violence is the tragic aberration of an organization's culture—the culmination of personal frustration that has built to a crescendo because of perceived injustice, humiliation, loss of dignity, shame, perceived loss of value and/or control, which ultimately explodes into a desperate act.(19) External violence is likewise an aberration of our society's culture, which, for numerous sociological reasons, has led a person to a life of crime. Nevertheless that person's behavior patterns are oftentimes predictable and follow a pattern, which means we have an opportunity to combat them.

Consequently, acts of workplace violence can be reduced and many costs can be avoided with forethought, strategic planning, and progressive action. Anticipating being a target is not wishful thinking, but instead is prudent and good business decision making.

In the final analysis, Suzanne Milton, manager of the workplace environment improvement program for the U.S. Postal Service is right in stating, "There is absolutely no way to eliminate all workplace violence. But it is possible to take a stand on the issue and back it up with training and assistance programs that really work."

Workplace violence prevention is no simple proposition; however, we have presented a comprehensive framework that can be used to intervene in the cycle and address many of the known factors that lead to violence in the workplace. The intent has been to provide retail store managers, human resource professionals, and security professionals with an increased understanding of the crucial role that firms can play in implementing an effort to address workplace violence prevention and to mitigate the avoidable cost impact.

In an era when tough talk and catchy rhetoric too often eclipse any real action, some organizations are beginning to understand that an effective workplace violence prevention policy is more than a battle cry engineered to satisfy customers, shareholders, and the media. It's just plain smart. Saving lives and preventing violence don't happen in a vacuum. They require careful thought, action, and leadership. Companies that are serious about workplace violence prevention and understand the importance of implementing a comprehensive approach to addressing this life-threatening phenomenon will in the long run come out ahead.

References

1. Dealing with the Risk of Workplace Violence,' Security Magazine, April 2005.
2. Ditto
3. Pistol, Erik, A Road To Hell Paved with Good Intentions, September 19, 2002, NewsWithViews.com.
4. Zero Tolerance and Alternative Strategies: A Fact Sheet for Educators and Policymakers, The National Association of School Psychologists, http://www.naspcenter.org/factsheet/zt_fs.html.
5. Zero Tolerance is Not Enough: Making Workplace Violence Prevention Really Work, National Institute for the Prevention of Workplace Violence, Inc., March 2003.
6. Greengard, Samuel, Zero Tolerance: Making It Work, Workforce Magazine, May 1999, Vol. 78, No. 5.
7. "Preventing Violence in the Workplace," WorkSafe Magazine, April 2005, Common Factors to Violence Prone Organizations, National Institute for the Prevention of Workplace Violence, Inc., September 2004.
8. Recommendations for Workplace Violence Prevention Programs in Late-Night Retail Establishments, U.S. Department of Labor Occupational Safety and Health Administration, OSHA 3153, 1998.
9. Common Factors to violence prone organizations (2004, September) National Institute for the Prevention of Workplace Violence, Inc.
10. The theoretical concepts for this approach include "situational crime prevention;" Clarke, 1983, and "crime prevention through environmental design" (CPTED), Hunter and Jeffery, 1991.
11. Recommendations for Workplace Violence Prevention Programs in Late-Night Retail Establishments, U.S. Department of Labor Occupational Safety and Health Administration, OSHA 3153, 1998.
12. Ibid.
13. Comments submitted to OSHA by the Southland Corporation, 1996. bid.

14. The Financial Impact of Workplace Violence, National Institute for the Prevention of Workplace Violence, Inc., March 2004.
15. "Targets behind the counter – workplace safety and security," HR Magazine, August 1999.
16. Recommendations for Workplace Violence Prevention Programs in Late-Night Retail Establishments, U.S. Department of Labor Occupational Safety and Health Administration, OSHA 3153, 1998.
17. The Financial Impact of Workplace Violence, National Institute for the Prevention of Workplace Violence, Inc., March 2004.
18. Dan Dana, Ph.D., Dana Mediation Institute, Inc., The Dana Measure of the Financial Cost of Organizational Conflict: An Interpretive Guide, 2001, www.mediationworks.com.
19. Ibid.
20. Dana, D. (2001). The Dana measure of the financial cost of organizational conflict: An interpretive guide. www.mediationworks.com.
21. Ibid.

Other Resources

1. Greengard, Samuel, Zero Tolerance: Making It Work, Workforce Magazine, May 1999, Vol. 78, No. 5.
2. National Association of Convenience Stores (NACS): www.Nacsonline.com
3. www.Workplaceviolence911.com
4. WorkCover, http://www.workcover.nsw.gov.au/Publications/Industry/RetailandWholesale/default.htm
5. "Preventing violence in the workplace," WorkSafe Magazine, April 2005, http://www.worksafebc.com/

Definitions

CAS, JHC

Agency: A relationship wherein one party is empowered to represent or act for the other under the authority of the other. Agency means more than tacit permission; it involves a request, instruction, or command. There are three types of agency relationships: principal and agent; master and servant; and proprietor and independent contractor. See the section titled "Legal Considerations."

Alpha negative file: A file consisting of either 3 × 5-inch cards or a computerized listing of the names of known "bad guys," such as known shoplifters, dishonest employees, fraud artists, bad check passers, etc.

AP: Asset Protection.

APO: Asset Protection Officer.

APM: Asset Protection Manager.

APS: Asset Protection Specialist (same as APO).

Assault/battery: Unconsented to or unprivileged physical contact or privileged contact which becomes unreasonable. *Note:* Assault and Battery may also be a crime.

Auras (guilt auras): There is a belief, especially among long-time loss prevention professionals, that some agent practitioners can "see" or "sense" a guilt "aura" radiating around someone in the store who is in the process of shoplifting (or employee about to or is engaged in theft). It's that aura which attracts the attention of the LP agent. Consider this: How does a floor agent pick through hundreds or thousands of customers who shop or appear to shop in the store each day and pick out that one person who ends up stealing? One answer: Auras. And consider this: Why do some agents excel in detecting shoplifters while coworkers struggle to make a detention? One answer: The former can sense auras and the latter can't.

Persons engaged in the crime (or for that matter, any evil deed) often fear their state of guilt is detectable and that makes them uneasy. That uneasiness is what makes them so "goosey" or hyper, and they dump so quickly, hence the "Oh Shit Syndrome."

Bad stop: A detention of a suspected shoplifter wherein no stolen merchandise is found to be in the possession of the suspect. See also *NPD*.

Bait: The piece of currency or other item which has been secretly marked (usually with an ultraviolet pen) and made available when similar items have disappeared through theft and theft is suspected. If possible, a covert CCTV camera should be aimed at the bait so that, if taken, a recording is made and the bait can be identified by the ultraviolet markings.

Battery: The unconsented to or unprivileged contact or privileged contact which becomes excessive or unreasonable. *Note:* This may also be a criminal offense.

Book/booking: The police process of removing the shoplifter or detainee from the store, transporting such person to the police station, and subjecting the party to the formal process of being admitted to temporary custody, pending bail or release.

Booster: A slang term used to describe shoplifters. Some LP professionals limit this term to refer only to shoplifters who are involved with organized theft rings or ORT; others use the term more generically.

Boosted: A slang term to used to describe merchandise which has been stolen.

Booster equipment: Implements or gadgets used by shoplifters to assist them in concealing shoplifted merchandise. Following are examples:

- *Booster Bags:* Normally shopping bags lined with duct tape or aluminum foil to defeat EAS tags.
- *Bloomers:* Women's bloomers, tied off at the knees, with a flexible elastic waistband. Shoplifted goods can be dropped into the bloomers, and the women's skirts conceal the presence of the merchandise.
- *Boxes:* Medium to large cardboard boxes tied with string or wrapped in brown paper or gift wrapping. The box has a spring-loaded side (trap door) which permits the entry of stolen merchandise, after which the trap door closes, giving the appearance of a wrapped package.
- *Cages:* Hollow cages which can be worn by women to give the appearance they are pregnant. Stolen merchandise is then concealed in the hollow cage.
- *Coats:* Loosely fitting top or trench-like coats with hidden pockets sewn inside the coats for the concealment of shoplifted merchandise.
- *Girdles:* These items work much in the same way as booster girdles.
- *Purses:* Women's purses that have been modified much like booster boxes. Use of a booster purse permits surreptitious placement of merchandise into the purse by placing the purse over the item to be stolen. By appearing to be looking for an item in the purse, the shoplifter secures the stolen item in her purse and makes sure the bottom of the purse is back in place. Theft with this device is virtually impossible to detect.

Note: The use of any of these "booster devices" will normally raise the level of the theft to that of a felony.

Breakage: Merchandise that has been broken beyond either repair or salvage and is segregated for disposal and financial write-off. Breakage occurs most frequently in glassware, china, and crystal departments.

Burglary: Any entry into or remaining in a building or vehicle with the intent to commit a crime. Hence, a person who enters the store (building) with some form of booster equipment and uses such equipment or device to conceal or steal merchandise is viewed as a burglar. Burglary is a felony in most jurisdictions.

Burn: A term used by loss prevention personnel to describe their making their presence known to shoplifters with the hoped-for result that they will "dump" the stolen merchandise.

Burned: This term is also used by police and investigators when conducting surveillance to indicate that the subject of the surveillance has discovered their presence. The term used in this way has the same meaning as saying, "We've been made," meaning our presence is known.

Bust: A slang term meaning to make an arrest.

Busted: A slang term meaning arrested.

Chain of custody: See the section titled "Evidence."

Cite/citation: The process in which a police officer responds to a store with a shoplifter or other offender in custody and such officer issues a citation requiring the offender to appear in court at a specified time, similar to a traffic citation. This action is taken in lieu of transporting the detainee to the police station and undergoing the formal booking procedure.

Claims: Merchandise scheduled to be returned for credit to the vendor because it was damaged and/or made unsaleable prior to receipt by the retailer. Claims are generally placed in a different financial category than RTVs for stock balancing purposes. See also *Salvage* for more information about claimed goods.

Cloning cards: See the section titled "Gift Card Fraud."

Collar pin lock: A lock for use on fifth-wheel tractors to prevent the unauthorized "hooking up" and theft of trailers.

Collusion: The making of a secret agreement with another person to commit a crime or some other illegal act.

Conspiracy: When two or more persons agree to commit a crime or an illegal act and do some overt act in furtherance thereof.

Compensatory damages: The combination of special and general damages; they compensate the plaintiff for his or her injury.

"Cooperative unbroken chain of surveillance": See *Uninterrupted surveillance.*

Coops: A term used (mostly on the East Coast) meaning a hidden observation post for the surreptitious surveillance of shoplifters.

"Constructive unbroken chain of surveillance": See *Uninterrupted surveillance.*

Course and scope of employment: See the section titled "Legal Considerations."

CRA: Consumer Reporting Agency. See the section titled "Pre-employment Screening."

Crotching: The act of female shoplifters wherein they place merchandise between their thighs, concealed by a flowing skirt, and have the ability to walk out of the store with the merchandise between their legs.

Daisy chain: A procedure under which, by prearrangement, one person (normally by phone) warns two others of a given circumstance, those two persons each call two others, and so forth until all persons in the "chain" have been contacted.

Databases (investigative): Sources of data (such as arrest/conviction records, addresses, employment history, etc.) available on the Internet and used for background investigations. See the section titled "Pre-employment Screening" for cautions on use.

Damages: Money awarded by a court to redress or make whole an injured party to basically put him or her in the position he or she was in before the injury or damage. See *Compensatory damages*, *General damages*, *Punitive damages*, and *Special damages*.

Decoy: An accomplice of a shoplifter who is sent into the store to attract attention and/or distract employees and draw them away from the area where the shoplifter intends to commit the theft.

Defamation (libel/slander): Written or spoken words that tend to damage another's reputation. Defenses: Truth, Privileges (Qualified and Absolute).

Demands to produce documents: Demands, made in discovery, to produce documents are written requests to a party to produce documents so they can be examined by the other side. The documents are due on the date stated in the demand.

Deposition: A method of pretrial discovery that consists of a stenographically transcribed statement, taken under oath, of a witness in response to an attorney's questions with opportunity to be cross-examined by opposing attorneys.

Discovery: A pretrial procedure by which one party gains or is given pertinent information held by the opposing party. There are different methods of gathering information in a case to prepare the case for trial. These methods, which include depositions, interrogatories, demands to produce documents, requests for admission, and site inspections, are collectively referred to as "discovery."

Discovery motions: If the parties disagree on what constitutes proper discovery, or if a party fails to respond to a proper discovery request, a motion may be brought to compel responses or further responses. If a party is abusing the discovery process to harass the other side, or is demanding information which is privileged or otherwise protected *from* disclosure by law, the responding party may bring a motion *for* a protective order. Sanctions can be imposed for discovery abuse.

Ditch: A slang term meaning when something (normally stolen goods) is surreptitiously thrown away or disposed of.

DAPM: District Asset Protection Manager.

DLPM: District Loss Prevention Manager.

DSD: Direct Store Delivery.

Dump: The act of a shoplifter who, before leaving the store, believes the theft has been detected and secretly or overtly discards or abandons the stolen property somewhere in the store.

EAS: Electronic Article Surveillance (EAS) systems or tags. Detachers used to remove EAS tags from protected merchandise should be kept in a secure manner to prevent their theft and subsequent illicit use in assisting shoplifters to remove EAS tags.

EEOC: Equal Employment Opportunities Commission. See the section titled "Pre-employment Screening."

Eighty-six (86): To trespass, eject, and/or deny access to a given establishment, such as a store or casino. For example, "86 him/her" means to eject or deny access.

Enjoin: A court's authority to command, instruct, or restrain.

Entrapment: The act of inducing a person to commit a crime not contemplated by him or her, for the purpose of instituting a criminal prosecution against that person. Put another way, it is suggesting to or enticing a person to commit a crime which he or she initially had no intention to commit for the purpose of then arresting and prosecuting that person for that crime. It is *not* entrapment merely to provide an opportunity for a person to commit a crime which he or she then independently takes advantage of to commit a crime.

False Imprisonment/Arrest: The intentional, unjustified detention or confinement of a person (imprisonment); unlawful restraint of another person's liberty or freedom of locomotion (arrest). *Note:* This may also be a criminal offense.

FCRA: Fair Credit Reporting Act; a federal law. See the section titled "Pre-employment Screening."

Felony: A generic term employed to distinguish certain high crimes from minor offenses known as misdemeanors; felony crimes are punished by imprisonment in a state prison for more than 1 year or by death.

Fences: Persons who deal in stolen merchandise. Fences generally buy stolen merchandise from the original thief for 20–25% of its original value and then sell the goods to another fence or, in some cases, to wholesalers who repackage/remark the goods and then sell them to unsuspecting (or perhaps suspecting) retailers at bargain prices.

FIFO: First In, First Out, referring to how inventory is distributed.

Fitting room (dressing room): A room (or a room within a bank of rooms), usually immediately adjacent to the selling floor, designed to provide privacy for customers wishing to try on merchandise prior to purchasing it. Because of the privacy fitting room provides, it is a popular place for shoplifters to use to conceal and steal merchandise.

FRC: Fitting Room Checker. An individual stationed at the entrance to a bank of fitting rooms whose purpose is to control access to the rooms. Frequently, this function includes counting the garments going in with individual customers and limiting that number to one specified by management. In some cases, the FRC will issue a colored disk containing a number which represents the number of garments taken into the fitting room; this number is then compared with the number of garments brought out by the customer, assuring that no garments are unaccounted for. FRCs may also be assigned the job of checking the fitting rooms periodically to be sure they are empty and that any garments found in them are returned to the selling floor.

FTR: Failure to Record. See the section titled "Cash Register Manipulations."

FTR: Failure to Remove (an EAS tag).

General damages: Compensation awarded to "make the Plaintiff whole"; these are the monies awarded to compensate for pain and suffering, emotional distress, mental anguish, loss of consortium, etc. See the section titled "Legal Considerations."

Ghost employees: People who do not exist but are paid through a fraudulent manipulation of payroll records.

Grab and run: A theft wherein the thief runs in the store and grabs a quantity of merchandise (often preselected and positioned) and immediately runs out of the store, usually to a waiting vehicle driven by an accomplice.

Graphology: The study of handwriting with the purpose of analysis to determine character traits and honesty.

Grazing: Consuming of foods items while customers are shopping; thus, when they reach the checkout counter, they have less than they originally had. Since they pay for the lesser amount, they not only create a shortage for the merchant, but in effect have stolen the quantity they consumed.

Gross margin: The amount, generally reported as a percentage, of the difference between the cost of an item and its selling price. Gross margin influences but does not represent profit, since others items, such as taxes, overhead, etc., must be deducted before profit is determined.

Guiding force: The degree of force, described in many LP manuals, permitted when apprehending shoplifters. The term "guiding force" means the agent is restricted to simply using his or her hand on the suspect's elbow or upper arm to "guide" the suspect into the store and to the LP office.

Heist: A slang term meaning to steal (lift).

Holding force: That level of force which is minimally required to return a shoplifting suspect to the store.

Hook 'em (up): A slang term meaning to handcuff someone.

Ink tags: A benefit denial tag. See the section titled "Electronic Article Surveillance."

Interrogatory/interrogatories: Written questions posed in discovery to a party which require a written response. There are form interrogatories for use in civil cases; however, parties can draft supplemental interrogatories, generally called "special interrogatories."

In a civil action, a pretrial discovery tool in which one party addresses written questions to the opposing party, who must reply in writing under oath.

Invasion of privacy: Invading someone's reasonable expectation of privacy. Invasion of privacy is a tort for which a violation may subject the violator to a civil suit and, under certain conditions, a criminal charge.

Inventory shortage: The difference between the dollar value of merchandise a retailer shows on book stock and that actually on hand as shown by a physical inventory. Shortage is usually expressed as a percentage of sales. Stated differently, "inventory shrinkage" (or "inventory shrink" or "inventory shortage") is the difference between book inventory (what the records reflect the retailer has) and actual physical inventory as determined by the process of taking an inventory of goods on hand (what the retailer counts and knows he or she actually has).

For example, if our records reflect we purchased 100 bottles of wine, if our sales records reflect we sold 60 bottles, and if our inventory of actual bottles on the shelf reflects we have 35 bottles, we have 5 bottles unaccounted for, amounting to an inventory shortage of 5 bottles or 5% shrinkage in wine, usually reported as a percentage of dollars of shrink at retail as a percentage of total sales. We don't know what happened to those missing 5 bottles.

If, during the night, someone breaks through the skylight in the ceiling and steals 40 bottles, we know they were taken, and hence their absence is not a mysterious or otherwise unexplained disappearance but is considered a known loss. Nevertheless, it is considered shrinkage unless and until it is accounted for financially as something other than shrink.

When the Crime Doesn't Affect Inventory Shrinkage

Our example of the nighttime burglary clearly is one crime which, while initially affecting inventory shrinkage, may eventually be financially accounted for in another category (e.g., known losses replaced by insurance or carried on the books as separate from shrinkage). The store suffers, by virtue of being victimized by a burglar, exactly the same loss, but the loss caused by the burglar is really more easily managed because we know how that loss occurred. Depending on how known losses are carried on the books determines whether they are included in inventory shortage.

Say the sale of the 60 bottles was recorded on a POS terminal or cash register, and at the end of the night the cash, checks, and credit card receipts were placed in a bag in anticipation of making a bank deposit the next morning. During closing, a man enters, produces a gun, and demands the bag. In this case, the loss is certainly real, but such loss would never be reflected in the year's inventory shortage, since the merchandise can be accounted for, and the theft of cash would be reflected in another financial account, but not as inventory shrink.

If the sale of the 60 bottles was handled by an employee who rang the sale but failed to put the money in the register and pocketed the money, the store again has no inventory shortage, only a shortage of cash. Cash shortages have nothing to do with inventory shortages. But if the same sales associate did not record the sale, but just pretended he handled the transaction correctly and pocketed the cash, we would have no cash shortage but would have an inventory shortage!

King pin lock: A lock for use on fifth-wheel tractors to prevent the unauthorized "hooking up" and theft of trailers.

LEO: Law Enforcement Officer.

LIFO: Last In, First Out, referring to how inventory is distributed.

Libel: Written words that tend to damage another's reputation. See the section titled "Legal Considerations."

Loan books: Books kept in departments (or, in smaller stores, at a central location) into which are recorded merchandise removed (signed out) from the department for display, photography, or other purposes and which are "signed in" when the merchandise is returned. Loan books are a merchandise and inventory control device.

Loss reports: Reports prepared in stores by LP or other approved persons to account for known losses (theft, breakage, spoilage, etc.). Such reports are the basis for removing the dollar amount of such losses from the financial inventory records so they do not reflect such amounts as shortage.

LP: Loss Prevention.

LPO: Loss Prevention Officer.

LPM: Loss Prevention Manager.

Malicious prosecution: Prosecution (civil or criminal) with malice (evil intent). To succeed, prosecution must have resulted in verdict for defendant and prosecution initiated without probable cause.

Merchant's privilege: Laws on the books in all 50 states plus the District of Columbia relating to shoplifting and the merchant's right to detain suspected shoplifters when certain preconditions have been met. Many of these statutes provide varying degrees of legal protection from civil suits by persons detained if the merchant acted legally and reasonably under the circumstances prevailing.

Mid (transaction) void: A voided sale or portion of a sale voided during the sales process and before the transaction has been totaled and fully recorded in the register or terminal. Such midtransaction voids are often explained by "customer changed mind."

"Mirandize"/Miranda Warning: The legal requirement for public sector law enforcement personnel to advise a suspect of his or her rights. Private sector agents (security or loss prevention employees) are not bound by this requirement unless acting as "agents" of the police.

Misdemeanor: A criminal offense less serious than a felony and sanctioned by less severe penalties including imprisonment in a jail for 1 year or less, or a fine.

MO: *Modus operandi* (Latin), meaning the method of operation. The means by which a criminal accomplished a crime.

Negligence: -See the section titled "Legal Considerations."

NPD: Non-Productive Detention; a detention in which the person detained is found not to have any stolen merchandise. See also *bad stop*.

ORT: Organized Retail Theft.

Observation post/platform: A place for the surreptitious observation of the selling floor and/or shoplifters. Two-way mirrors and heating and air-conditioning vents are used for viewing of the selling floor.

Palm: To surreptitiously conceal a small item of merchandise in one's hand with the intent to shoplift or steal such item.

Pass Off: The passing of stolen merchandise from one person to another; normally done thinking the pass-off will not be seen and the original thief will no longer have possession of the stolen merchandise when detained.

POS: Point of Sale, referring to a physical location, but more generally an electronic or computerized piece of equipment to record sales and which is the modern equivalent of the cash register.

Post (transaction) void: A void made after the entire transaction is completed and recorded; the sales associate at a later time voids the sale and offers an explanation such as "customer lacked enough money."

Probable cause: The reasons considered sufficient in themselves to warrant a reasonable person to believe that an offense has been committed or is being committed by the person to be arrested when the facts and circumstances are known to the arresting person.

PTZ: Pan, Tilt & Zoom, referring to the actions possible from CCTV camera lenses with this capability.

Punitive damages: Compensation awarded when the plaintiff can establish that the defendant was grossly negligent, wanton, or was motivated by malice. Punitive damages are designed to punish and/or set an example to others to avoid such conduct. –See the section titled "Legal Considerations."

Ratification: If an employee commits a tort and the employer, upon learning of it, doesn't take appropriate corrective action, which many will argue means termination, then the employer may be said to have "ratified" or approved of the act, and the employer is therefore just as liable as if the employer had directed or committed the tort. See the section titled "Legal Considerations."

Requests for admissions: Such requests, made during discovery, can ask that a party admit certain facts or admit to the authenticity of certain documents. If the party who receives the request for admissions fails to respond on time, the party who sent the requests can bring a motion to have the requests deemed admitted.

Respondeat Superior: A legal doctrine which holds that an employer (principal) is vicariously liable for the acts and omissions of its employee (agent) committed "within the scope of employment," but not generally liable for acts committed outside the scope of employment. The primary questions which determine if the employee was within or without the "scope" are as follows: Did the employer benefit from the act of the employee, and/or was the employee acting under the authority or direction of the employer? See the section titled "Legal Considerations."

RAPM: Regional Asset Protection Manager.

RDAP: Regional Director of Asset Protection.

RDLP: Regional Director of Loss Prevention.

Red coats: The nation's initial pure "loss prevention" program in which the majority of security employees were outfitted in red blazers (bearing a gold cloth "security" patch). They patrolled the selling floor, highly visible, making eye contact with as many customers as possible, creating awareness of security's presence, hence discouraging or "burning" would-be thefts.

RLPM: Regional Loss Prevention Manager.

Robbery: The felonious taking of property from the person of another by violence or by putting him or her in fear.

RTV: Return To Vendor.

Salt/Salting: An investigative/audit technique wherein the surreptitious addition of cash or merchandise is performed to determine if, when, and by whom the overage of cash or goods is reported.

Surreptitiously adding cash to a cash register or POS terminal, or a bundle of bills or a cash drawer in a cash vault, is a means of testing how well procedures are being followed, and if, when, and by whom the additional cash (an overage) is reported.

No report coupled with a balanced cash condition indicates that the added cash has probably been stolen.

The same technique can be used with merchandise by surreptitiously adding one or more garments or other merchandise to a shipment, without adjusting the count on the paperwork, to determine if extra goods are discovered and reported. The same test can be conducted by lowering the count of goods shown on a manifest or transfer document (thus creating an overage of merchandise vis à vis the documented count) to see if the overage is reported.

Such techniques are great for occasionally testing the system and/or for use as an investigative tool when theft is suspected.

Salvage: Merchandise which has been broken, damaged, or otherwise made unsaleable and is scheduled to be discarded and written off the books. It is important that a careful inventory is made of salvage goods and that their value be removed from the book stock inventory to prevent such goods from creating a shortage. Salvage goods are viewed as junk, and there are "junk" or "salvage" dealers who come in and truck this "junk" away. Care must be taken to ensure it is, in fact, junk. We're aware of an interesting case in which expensive leather purses from Spain were damaged by rain while in transit to the distribution center. Some of the purses were kept, but the majority appeared damaged. A claim was processed, but the vendor in Spain paid it but did not want the goods shipped back there. The bulk of the shipment, now removed from book inventory, was sent from Claims to Salvage. The salvage dealer discovered that many of the purses had not been damaged and were as good as new. He sold the purses to a "salvage store" where "distressed goods" were offered to the public. In this kind of store, the public may purchase grocery items, like canned food at bargain prices because the cans are dented or otherwise unattractive in a first-line store. Suddenly, the original department store found itself "buying" back the purses from customers who claimed they received the purses as gifts or refunding their purchase because they changed their mind, etc. Clearly, customers saw an opportunity to purchase the undamaged purses at $10 and return them to the department store for $100.

One way to avoid this problem or at least reduce its frequency is to inspect "salvage" goods and, if deemed possibly saleable, make their status obvious. One technique is to cut out the labels in garments. We are aware of another case in which store-branded merchandise was being sold in a "distressed merchandise" store, which triggered an investigation only to discover the sales were legitimate but the labels had not been removed.

Shield: A person or the act of a person who deliberately blocks the view of any person who could observe an act of shoplifting being committed by a confederate. This blocking or "shielding" may be achieved by the positioning of one's body or by holding up and/or positioning merchandise, e.g., holding up a coat as though examining its size, behind which the accomplice slips merchandise into a shopping bag.

Shrink: Slang and abbreviation for the word "shrinkage," such as "inventory shrinkage." See *Inventory shortage.*

"Simple uninterrupted surveillance": See *Uninterrupted surveillance.*

Site inspections and physical examinations: A party can demand that another party make a property available for inspection when the property or some par" of it is the subject matter of a case. A party can also require a person to undergo a physical or mental examination if the person is claiming injuries of a physical or mental nature. These requests are made during discovery.

Six Steps:
1. You must maintain an uninterrupted surveillance to ensure that the suspect doesn't dispose of the merchandise.
2. You must see the suspect approach the merchandise.
3. You must see the suspect fail to pay for the merchandise
4. You must see the suspect take possession of the merchandise.
5. You must see where the suspect conceals the merchandise.
6. You should approach the suspect outside the store.

Skimming: See the section titled "Gift Card Fraud."

SKU: Stock Keeping Unit; a unique number applied to a specific piece or style of merchandise for both inventory and financial accounting purposes. For example, the SKU would differ between Motorola and Panasonic headphones of similar electronic characteristics, as well as between Motorola headphones of different electronic specifications.

Slander: Spoken words that tend to damage another's reputation. See the section titled "Legal Considerations."

Slide (sliding): The act wherein the cashier moves some merchandise past the register without the recording of the price as a sweethearting strategy.

SO: Security Officer.

Source tagging: The process of affixing Inventory control tags (EAS tags) to merchandise at the point of manufacture rather than relying on the retailer to tag such merchandise.

Many hard-good items which are packaged in hard plastic are sourced tagged; for example, men's razors and blades, photo products (film), electronic items, and costume jewelry items such as watches. Generally, the EAS tag is concealed within the packaging.

RTW items are not yet the target of source tagging because of the variety of places different retailers prefer the tag to be located and the potential for damage to the goods during transit. Various EAS manufacturers are working on developing an EAS "trigger" that can be incorporated into a garment label and that would require no removal (only deactivation and desirably reactivation if goods are returned and resaleable) at the point of sale. We predict such tags will be available before the end of the decade.

Special damages: Compensation awarded to replace actual out-of-pocket expenses of the plaintiff; e.g., medical bills, lost wages, attorney fees, etc.

SSN: Social Security number. By using the following chart, you can identify the state in which a SSN was issued. This information can be useful when reviewing applications for employment since an SSN issued from a state in which the applicant shows no residence or employment can indicate potential fraudulent information and provide a point of further investigation.

Social Security numbers by area: The following chart includes the complete listing of assigned numbers for the Social Security Administration by state. By checking the first three numbers of Social Security number, you can determine the issuing state. This information is useful in verifying applications.

Social Security Number by Area

New Hampshire	001–003	Mississippi	425–428
Maine	004–007	Arkansas	429–432
Vermont	008–009	Louisiana	433–439
Massachusetts	010–034	Oklahoma	440–448
Rhode Island	035–039	Texas	449–467
Connecticut	040–049	Minnesota	468–477
New York	050–134	Iowa	478–485
New Jersey	135–158	Missouri	486–500
Pennsylvania	159–211	North Dakota	501–502
Maryland	212–220	South Dakota	503–504
Delaware	221–222	Nebraska	505–508
Virginia	223–231	Kansas	509–515
West Virginia	232–236	Montana	516–517
North Carolina	237–246	Idaho	518 519
South Carolina	247–251	Wyoming	520
Georgia	252–260	Colorado	521–524
Florida	261–267	New Mexico	525
Ohio	268–302	Arizona	526–527
Indiana	303–3l7	Utah	528–529
Illinois	318–361	Nevada	530
Michigan	362–386	Washington	531–539
Wisconsin	387–399	Oregon	540–544
Kentucky	400–407	California	545–573
Tennessee	408–415	Alaska	574
Alabama	416–424	Hawaii	575–576
Washington, D.C.	577–579		

Stake-out: Surveillance.

Stick-up: Armed robbery.

Subpoena: A writ commanding a person to appear under penalty. It is used to compel the testimony of witnesses in a trial or other adversarial proceeding.

Summary Judgment: A decision made on the basis of statements and evidence presented for the record without a trial. It is used when there is no dispute as to the facts of the case, and one party is entitled to judgment as a matter of law.

Subliminal messages: The technique of broadcasting messages which are not discernable as such but which are buried in the background and are (some claim) absorbed by the mind. In the visual realm, photos are shown in very brief flashes which prevents them from being seen by the eye, but (some claim) the image is absorbed by the mind.

The use of subliminal messages broadcast over the store's public address or "music" system is highly controversial, and its effectiveness has not been proved. Its controversial aspects rise from its perception by many people as a mind-altering technology that can be used for purposes other than to prevent shoplifting. For example, *if* subliminal messages are effective at deterring shoplifting, then why not use it to encourage shoppers to make more purchases? Because subliminal technology cannot consciously be perceived by those exposed to it, the potential or abuse is always present.

Aside from little data on its effectiveness, the most troubling aspect of subliminal technology for the retailer is perhaps the adverse publicity that might result should the public become aware of its use. Subliminal messages are mentioned here in the interest of thoroughness. It is an available technology, but we make no recommendation or claim for its effectiveness or appropriateness.

Sweethearting: The failure of a cashier to ring up or charge for items presented by friends or relatives when presented for payment.

Testers: Samples, usually of cosmetic items (perfumes, scents, fragrances, etc.), provided by the vendor or manufacturer to enable customers to "sample" the product. Testers are usually displayed on counter tops. Should someone shoplift a tester, we suggest they should not be arrested or referred for prosecution. While testers have an intrinsic value which validates the initial detention, they do not have a retail value in terms of actual shortage. The same rules suggested for testers would also apply to the theft or total consumption of candy or other food items available for customer sampling, an act often engaged in by homeless or other indigent persons.

Testimony: A statement made under oath by a witness or oral evidence given by a witness under oath in a trial or legislative proceeding.

Tort, intentional: See the section titled "Legal Considerations."

Tort, unintentional: Negligence. See the section titled "Legal Considerations."

Tortious infliction of emotional distress: Intentionally and maliciously inflicting emotional distress on another. See the section titled "Legal Considerations."

Tortious interference with employment: Maliciously interfering with the employment of another. See the section titled "Legal Considerations."

Trojan horse: A term used to describe an observation post. See also *Observation post/ platform.*

Under-ring: The intentional misringing of an item or total sale, typically by an even amount such as $10 or $20 but nonetheless charging the customer the correct or full price and keeping (stealing) the amount not rung or recorded. That cash theft is not reflected as a cash shortage in the audit process but would reflect an inventory shortage. The best means of preventing under-ringing is to require that every customer receive a receipt for his or her purchase.

Uninterrupted Surveillance:
1. **"Simple uninterrupted surveillance":** The most common surveillance in which one person observes the taking and eventual removal of merchandise out of the store without paying for it.
2. **"Cooperative unbroken chain of surveillance":** The coordinated effort of two or more agents using CCTV and radio communication in which all "six steps" required for a detention are satisfied.
3. **"Constructive unbroken chain of surveillance":** This type of surveillance typically involves thefts which occur in private locations such as fitting rooms. In this case, the agent observes the person enter and exit, but an item taken in is not present when the person exits, and the item is not left behind in the room or otherwise disposed of; The only logical conclusion any reasonable person can draw is the subject must have possession of the item hidden on his or her person.

VIP: Very Important Person.

Void: Removal of the amount received from a sale from inclusion in the gross sales total for a cash register sale (either mid-transaction or post-transaction). See the section titled "Cash Register Manipulations."

VSO: Visible Security Officer.

Wardrobing: The purchase of merchandise for the purpose of wearing or using it for one occasion and then returning it for a refund. Normally, this type of fraud involves high fashion garments or expensive jewelry purchased for one-occasion social events.

Zoom: The ability of a photographic or CCTV camera lens to (bring in closer, thus magnifying, the image being photographed.

Index

Note: Page numbers followed by *f* for figures and *t* for tables.

Litigation avoidance & cost control. *See* Legal
    considerations
Local area network (LAN), 600
Lockers, 301
Locking systems, 275
Locks
    delaying device, 276
    lock bumping, 275
    type of, 275
Lord's court, 206
Loss prevention (LP), 29, 302–303
    agent
        negligence in hiring of, 311–312
        retention, 313
        in training and supervision, 312–313
    aspects of potential acts, 305
    assets protection, 493
    certification program of, 213
    as concept, 302
    content and preparation, 302–303
    contents protection of, 306
    department
        challenges faced by, 519
        personnel training programs for, 523
    foundation, 213
    identification cards, 15
    industry organizations, 230–231,
        240–241
    magazine for, 1
    manuals for, 306–307
    membership stores, 307
    mission statement, 308–309
    personnel, selection and hiring procedure
        for, 458–459
    publications (*See* Reading list)
    software programs, 522
    as strategy, 237
Loss reports, 276, 647
Lost children, 267, 303–304
LPC_QUALIFIED certification program, 213

M
Magna Carta Act, 207
"Malicious mischief." *See* Vandalism
Malls, 305, 325, 390, 394–395, 402
Management of LP personnel,
    240, 282
Managing labor disputes, 281
Man trap, 33
Manuals LP, 94, 201, 302–303, 306, 645
Manufacturing plant night watchman, 213
Mark Out of Stock (MOS), 526
Master-keyed system, 275
Membership stores, 307
Mentally disturbed persons, 8

Merchandise
    delivery
        pre-event planning, 285–286
        special equipment, 286–287
        to stores and DCs, 285
    handling procedures, 419
    inventory, 307–308
    physical security of, 192
    theft, prevention of, 360–361
Merchant's guide for dealing with shoplifting,
    297–298
Merchant's privilege. *See* Legal considerations
Metropolitan statistical area (MSA), 562
Military unit, 204
Minorities in loss prevention, 610
Miranda rights, 308
Mirrors. *See* Security mirrors
Misdemeanors. *See* Definitions
Missing merchandise report, 182, 276. *See
    also* Loss reports
    prevention measurement for, 279
    proformas for, 277, 278
Mission statements, 308, 309
MMR. *See* Missing merchandise report
Motion detection alarms, 3, 4, 7
Mystery shoppers. *See* Integrity testing

N
National Crime Information Center
    (NCIC), 288
National Fire Protection Association
    (NFPA), 552
National Incident-Based Reporting System
    (NIBRS), 577
National Labor Relations Board, 268
National Retail Federation, 290, 293, 554,
    615–616. *See also* Retail Trade
    Associations
National Retail Security Survey (NRSS), 98,
    193, 196, 288, 308, 596
Neatness. *See* Good housekeeping
Negligence in LP personnel employment
    hiring, 311–312
    retention, 313
    in training and supervision, 312–313
Negligent hiring. *See* Legal considerations
Neighborhood checks. *See* Pre-employment
    screening
Night depositories, 313, 314
NLRB. *See* National Labor Relations Board
Nonproductive detention
    (NPD), 486
Nonsufficient funds, 190, 225, 588
No touch-no chase policy. *See* No-touch
    policy